Concepts of Physics

①

Concepts of Physics

CONCEPTS OF PHYSICS

[VOLUME 1]

H C VERMA, PhD
Retired Professor
Department of Physics
IIT, Kanpur

Bharati Bhawan
PUBLISHERS & DISTRIBUTORS

Published by

BHARATI BHAWAN (Publishers & Distributors)

www.bharatibhawan.in   email: editorial@bbpd.in

4271/3 Ansari Road, Daryaganj, NEW DELHI 110 002, Phone: 23286557
A-61 B/2 Sector 63, NOIDA 201 307, Phone: 4757400
Thakurbari Road, PATNA 800 003, Phone: 2670325
10 Raja Subodh Mallick Square, KOLKATA 700 013, Phone: 22250651
No. 98 Sirsi Circle, Mysore Road, BENGALURU 560 018, Phone: 26740560

First edition 1992
Revised print 2017
2022 print

Concepts of Physics 1
Printed at Manipal Technologies Limited, Manipal

FOREWORD

A few years ago I had an occasion to go through the book *Calculus* by L V Terasov. It unravels intricacies of the subject through a dialogue between Teacher and Student. I thoroughly enjoyed reading it. For me this seemed to be one of the few books which teach a difficult subject through inquisition, and using programmed concept for learning. After that book, Dr Harish Chandra Verma's book on physics, *CONCEPTS OF PHYSICS* is another such attempt, even though it is not directly in the dialogue form. I have thoroughly appreciated it. It is clear that Dr Verma has spent considerable time in formulating the structure of the book, besides its contents. I think he has been successful in this attempt. Dr Verma's book has been divided into two parts because of the size of the total manuscript. There have been several books on this subject, each one having its own flavour. However, the present book is a totally different attempt to teach physics, and I am sure it will be extremely useful to the undergraduate students. The exposition of each concept is extremely lucid. In carefully formatted chapters, besides problems and short questions, a number of objective questions have also been included. This book can certainly be extremely useful not only as a textbook, but also for preparation of various competitive examinations.

Those who have followed Dr Verma's scientific work always enjoyed the outstanding contributions he has made in various research areas. He was an outstanding student of Physics Department of IIT Kanpur during his academic career. An extremely methodical, sincere person as a student, he has devoted himself to the task of educating young minds and inculcating scientific temper amongst them. The present venture in the form of these two volumes is another attempt in that direction. I am sure that young minds who would like to *learn physics in an appropriate manner* will find these volumes extremely useful.

I must heartily congratulate Dr Harish Chandra Verma for the magnificent job he has done.

Y R Waghmare
Professor of Physics
IIT Kanpur.

PREFACE

Why a new book?

Excellent books exist on physics at an introductory college level so why a new one? Why so many books exist at the same level, in the first place, and why each of them is highly appreciated? It is because each of these books has the privilege of having an author or authors who have *experienced* physics and have their own method of communicating with the students. During my years as a physics teacher, I have developed a somewhat different methodology of presenting physics to the students. *Concepts of Physics* is a translation of this methodology into a textbook.

Prerequisites

The book presents a calculus-based physics course which makes free use of algebra, trigonometry and co-ordinate geometry. The level of the latter three topics is quite simple and high school mathematics is sufficient. Calculus is generally done at the introductory college level and I have assumed that the student is enrolled in a concurrent first calculus course. The relevant portions of calculus have been discussed in Chapter 2 so that the student may start using it from the beginning.

Almost no knowledge of physics is a prerequisite. I have attempted to start each topic from the zero level. A receptive mind is all that is needed to use this book.

Basic philosophy of the book

The motto underlying the book is *physics is enjoyable.*

Being a description of the nature around us, physics is our best friend from the day of our existence. I have extensively used this aspect of physics to introduce the physical principles starting with common day occurrences and examples. The subject then appears to be friendly and enjoyable. I have taken care that numerical values of different quantities used in problems correspond to real situations to further strengthen this approach.

Teaching and training

The basic aim of physics teaching has been to let the student know and understand the principles and equations of physics and their applications in real life.

However, to be able to use these principles and equations correctly in a given physical situation, one needs further training. A large number of *questions and solved and unsolved problems* are given for this purpose. Each question or problem has a specific purpose. It may be there to bring out a subtle point which might have passed unnoticed while doing the text portion. It may be a further elaboration of a concept developed in the text. It may be there to make the student react when several concepts introduced in different chapters combine and show up as a physical situation and so on. Such tools have been used to develop a culture: *analyse the situation, make a strategy to invoke correct principles and work it out.*

Conventions

I have tried to use symbols, names, etc., which are popular nowadays. SI units have been consistently used throughout the book. SI prefixes such as *micro, milli, mega,* etc., are used whenever they make the presentation more readable. Thus, $20\,\mu F$ is preferred over 20×10^{-6} F. Co-ordinate sign convention is used in geometrical optics. Special emphasis has been given to dimensions of physical quantities. Numerical values of physical quantities have been mentioned with the units even in equations to maintain dimensional consistency.

I have tried my best to keep errors out of this book. I shall be grateful to the readers who point out any errors and/or make other constructive suggestions.

H C Verma

ACKNOWLEDGEMENTS

The work on this book started in 1984. Since then, a large number of teachers, students and physics lovers have made valuable suggestions which I have incorporated in this work. It is not possible for me to acknowledge all of them individually. I take this opportunity to express my gratitude to them. However, to Dr S B Mathur, who took great pains in going through the entire manuscript and made valuable comments, I am specially indebted. I am also beholden to my colleagues Dr A Yadav, Dr Deb Mukherjee, Mr M M R Akhtar, Dr Arjun Prasad, Dr S K Sinha and others who gave me valuable advice and were good enough to find time for fruitful discussions. To Dr T K Dutta of B E College, Sibpur I am grateful for having taken time to go through portions of the book and making valuable comments.

I thank my student Mr Shailendra Kumar who helped me in checking the answers. I am grateful to Dr B C Rai, Mr Sunil Khijwania & Mr Tejaswi Khijwania for helping me in the preparation of rough sketches for the book.

Finally, I thank the members of my family for their support and encouragement.

H C Verma

TO THE STUDENTS

Here is a brief discussion on the organisation of the book which will help you in using the book most effectively. The book contains 47 chapters divided in two volumes. Though I strongly believe in the underlying unity of physics, a broad division may be made in the book as follows:

Chapters 1–14: Mechanics

15–17: Waves including wave optics

18–22: Optics

23–28: Heat and thermodynamics

29–40: Electric and magnetic phenomena

41–47: Modern physics

Each chapter contains a description of the physical principles related to that chapter. It is well supported by mathematical derivations of equations, descriptions of laboratory experiments, historical background, etc. There are "in-text" solved examples. These examples explain the equation just derived or the concept just discussed. These will help you in fixing the ideas firmly in your mind. Your teachers may use these in-text examples in the classroom to encourage students to participate in discussions.

After the theory section, there is a section on *Worked Out Examples*. These numerical examples correspond to various thinking levels and often use several concepts introduced in that chapter or even in previous chapters. You should read the statement of a problem and try to solve it yourself. In case of difficulty, look at the solution given in the book. Even if you solve the problem successfully, you should look into the solution to compare it with your method of solution. You might have thought of a better method, but knowing more than one method is always beneficial.

Then comes the part which tests your understanding as well as develops it further. *Questions for Short Answer* generally touch very minute points of your understanding. It is not necessary that you answer these questions in a single sitting. They have great potential to initiate very fruitful dicussions. So, freely discuss these questions with your friends and see if they agree with your answer. Answers to these questions are not given for the simple reason that the answers could have cut down the span of such discussions and that would have sharply reduced the utility of these questions.

There are two sections on multiple-choice questions, namely OBJECTIVE I and OBJECTIVE II. There are four options following each of these questions. Only one option is correct for OBJECTIVE I questions. Any number of options, zero to four, may be correct for OBJECTIVE II questions. Answers to all these questions are provided.

Finally, a set of numerical problems are given for your practice. Answers to these problems are also provided. The problems are generally arranged according to the sequence of the concepts developed in the chapter but they are not grouped under section-headings. I don't want to bias your ideas beforehand by telling you that this problem belongs to that section and hence use that particular equation. You should yourself look into the problem and decide which equations or which methods should be used to solve it. Many of the problems use several concepts developed in different sections of the chapter. Many of them even use the concepts from the previous chapters. Hence, you have to plan out the strategy after understanding the problem.

Remember, no problem is difficult. Once you understand the theory, each problem will become easy. So, don't jump to exercise problems before you have gone through the theory, the worked-out problems and the objectives. Once you feel confident in theory, do the exercise problems. The exercise problems are so arranged that they gradually require more thinking.

I hope you will enjoy *Concepts of Physics*.

H C Verma

Table of Contents

□

CHAPTER 1

INTRODUCTION TO PHYSICS

1.1 WHAT IS PHYSICS ?

The nature around us is colourful and diverse. It contains phenomena of large varieties. The winds, the sands, the waters, the planets, the rainbow, heating of objects on rubbing, the function of a human body, the energy coming from the sun and the nucleus ...... there are a large number of objects and events taking place around us.

Physics is the study of nature and its laws. We expect that all these different events in nature take place according to some basic laws and *revealing these laws of nature from the observed events* is physics. For example, the orbiting of the moon around the earth, falling of an apple from a tree and tides in a sea on a full moon night can all be explained if we know the Newton's law of gravitation and Newton's laws of motion. Physics is concerned with the basic rules which are applicable to all domains of life. Understanding of physics, therefore, leads to applications in many fields including bio and medical sciences.

The great physicist Dr R. P. Feynman has given a wonderful description of what is "understanding the nature". Suppose we do not know the rules of chess but are allowed to watch the moves of the players. If we watch the game for a long time, we may make out some of the rules. With the knowledge of these rules we may try to understand why a player played a particular move. However, this may be a very difficult task. Even if we know all the rules of chess, it is not so simple to understand all the complications of a game in a given situation and predict the correct move. Knowing the basic rules is, however, the minimum requirement if any progress is to be made.

One may guess at a wrong rule by partially watching the game. The experienced player may make use of a rule for the first time and the observer of the game may get surprised. Because of the new move some of the rules guessed at may prove to be wrong and the observer will frame new rules.

Physics goes the same way. The nature around us is like a big chess game played by Nature. The events in the nature are like the moves of the great game. We are allowed to watch the events of nature and guess at the basic rules according to which the events take place. We may come across new events which do not follow the rules guessed earlier and we may have to declare the old rules inapplicable or wrong and discover new rules.

Since physics is the study of nature, it is real. No one has been given the authority to frame the rules of physics. We only *discover* the rules that are operating in nature. Aryabhat, Newton, Einstein or Feynman are great physicists because from the observations available at that time, they could guess and frame the laws of physics which explained these observations in a convincing way. But there can be a new phenomenon any day and if the rules discovered by the great scientists are not able to explain this phenomenon, no one will hesitate to change these rules.

1.2 PHYSICS AND MATHEMATICS

The description of nature becomes easy if we have the freedom to use mathematics. To say that the gravitational force between two masses is proportional to the product of the masses and is inversely proportional to the square of the distance apart, is more difficult than to write

$$F \propto \frac{m_1 m_2}{r^2} \qquad \qquad \ldots \ (1.1)$$

Further, the techniques of mathematics such as algebra, trigonometry and calculus can be used to make predictions from the basic equations. Thus, if we know the basic rule (1.1) about the force between two particles, we can use the technique of integral calculus to find what will be the force exerted by a uniform rod on a particle placed on its perpendicular bisector.

Thus, mathematics is the language of physics. Without knowledge of mathematics it would be much more difficult to discover, understand and explain the laws of nature. The importance of mathematics in today's world cannot be disputed. However, mathematics itself is not physics. We use a language to express our ideas. But the idea that we want to express has the main attention. If we are poor at grammar and vocabulary, it would be difficult for us to communicate our feelings but while doing so our basic interest is in the feeling that we want to express. It is nice to board a deluxe coach to go from Delhi to Agra, but the sweet memories of the deluxe coach and the video film shown on way are next to the prime goal of reaching Agra. "To understand nature" is physics, and mathematics is the deluxe coach to take us there comfortably. This relationship of physics and mathematics must be clearly understood and kept in mind while doing a physics course.

1.3 UNITS

Physics describes the laws of nature. This description is quantitative and involves measurement and comparison of physical quantities. To measure a physical quantity we need some standard unit of that quantity. An elephant is heavier than a goat but exactly how many times ? This question can be easily answered if we have chosen a standard mass calling it a *unit mass*. If the elephant is 200 times the unit mass and the goat is 20 times we know that the elephant is 10 times heavier than the goat. If I have the knowledge of the unit length and some one says that Gandhi Maidan is 5 times the unit length from here, I will have the idea whether I should walk down to Gandhi Maidan or I should ride a rickshaw or I should go by a bus. Thus, the physical quantities are quantitatively expressed in terms of a unit of that quantity. The measurement of the quantity is mentioned in two parts, the first part gives how many times of the standard unit and the second part gives the name of the unit. Thus, suppose I have to study for 2 hours. The numeric part 2 says that it is 2 *times* of the unit of time and the second part *hour* says that the unit chosen here is an hour.

Who Decides the Units ?

How is a standard unit chosen for a physical quantity ? The first thing is that it should have international acceptance. Otherwise, everyone will choose his or her own unit for the quantity and it will be difficult to communicate freely among the persons distributed over the world. A body named *Conférence Générale des Poids et Mesures* or CGPM also known as *General Conference on Weight and Measures* in English has been given the authority to decide the units by international agreement. It holds its meetings

and any changes in standard units are communicated through the publications of the Conference.

Fundamental and Derived Quantities

There are a large number of physical quantities which are measured and every quantity needs a definition of unit. However, not all the quantities are independent of each other. As a simple example, if a unit of length is defined, a unit of area is automatically obtained. If we make a square with its length equal to its breadth equal to the unit length, its area can be called the unit area. All areas can then be compared to this standard unit of area. Similarly, if a unit of length and a unit of time interval are defined, a unit of speed is automatically obtained. If a particle covers a unit length in unit time interval, we say that it has a unit speed. We can define a set of *fundamental quantities* as follows :

(a) the fundamental quantities should be independent of each other, and

(b) all other quantities may be expressed in terms of the fundamental quantities.

It turns out that the number of fundamental quantities is only seven. All the rest may be derived from these quantities by multiplication and division. Many different choices can be made for the fundamental quantities. For example, one can take speed and time as fundamental quantities. Length is then a derived quantity. If something travels at unit speed, the distance it covers in unit time interval will be called a unit distance. One may also take length and time interval as the fundamental quantities and then speed will be a derived quantity. Several systems are in use over the world and in each system the fundamental quantities are selected in a particular way. The units defined for the fundamental quantities are called *fundamental units* and those obtained for the derived quantities are called the *derived units*.

Fundamental quantities are also called base quantities.

SI Units

In 1971 CGPM held its meeting and decided a system of units which is known as the *International System of Units*. It is abbreviated as SI from the French name *Le Systéme International d'Unités*. This system is widely used throughout the world.

Table (1.1) gives the fundamental quantities and their units in SI.

Table 1.1 : *Fundamental or Base Quantities*

Quantity	Name of the Unit	Symbol
Length	metre	m
Mass	kilogram	kg
Time	second	s
Electric Current	ampere	A
Thermodynamic Temperature	kelvin	K
Amount of Substance	mole	mol
Luminous Intensity	candela	cd

Besides the seven fundamental units two supplementary units are defined. They are for plane angle and solid angle. The unit for plane angle is *radian* with the symbol *rad* and the unit for the solid angle is *steradian* with the symbol *sr.*

SI Prefixes

The magnitudes of physical quantities vary over a wide range. We talk of separation between two protons inside a nucleus which is about 10^{-15} m and the distance of a quasar from the earth which is about 10^{26} m. The mass of an electron is 9.1×10^{-31} kg and that of our galaxy is about 2.2×10^{41} kg. The CGPM recommended standard prefixes for certain powers of 10. Table (1.2) shows these prefixes.

Table 1.2 : *SI prefixes*

Power of 10	Prefix	Symbol
18	exa	E
15	peta	P
12	tera	T
9	giga	G
6	mega	M
3	kilo	k
2	hecto	h
1	deka	da
− 1	deci	d
− 2	centi	c
− 3	milli	m
− 6	micro	μ
− 9	nano	n
− 12	pico	p
− 15	femto	f
− 18	atto	a

1.4 DEFINITIONS OF BASE UNITS

Any standard unit should have the following two properties :

(a) *Invariability* : The standard unit must be invariable. Thus, defining distance between the tip of the middle finger and the elbow as a unit of length is not invariable.

(b) *Availability* : The standard unit should be easily made available for comparing with other quantities.

CGPM decided in its 2018 meeting that all the SI base quantities will be defined in terms of certain universal constants and these constants will be assigned fixed numerical values by definition. In this case both the criteria of invariability and availability are automatically satisfied. The new definitions became operative since 20th May 2019. We give below the definitions of the these quantities. The fixed values given to the universal constants will appear in the definitions only. The definitions carry certain physical quantities and concepts that are beyond the scope of this book but you need not worry about it.

Second

1 second is the time that makes the unperturbed ground state hyperfine transition frequency $\Delta \nu_{Cs}$ to be 9192631770 when expressed in the unit Hz which is equal to s^{-1}.

Metre

1 metre is the length that makes the speed of light in vacuum to be 299792458 when expressed in the unit $m \cdot s^{-1}$, where the second is defined in terms of the caesium frequency $\Delta \nu_{Cs}$.

Kilogram

1 kilogram is the mass that makes the Planck's constant h to be $6.62607015 \times 10^{-34}$ when expressed in the unit J·s which is equal to $kg \cdot m^2 \, s^{-1}$, where the metre and the second are defined in terms of c and $\Delta \nu_{Cs}$.

Ampere

1 ampere is the current which makes the elementary charge e to be $1.602176634 \times 10^{-19}$ when expressed in the unit C which is equal to A·s, where the second is defined in terms of $\Delta \nu_{Cs}$.

Kelvin

1 kelvin is the temperature that makes the Boltzmann constant to be 1.380649×10^{-23} when expressed in the unit $J \cdot K^{-1}$ which is equal to $kg \cdot m^2 \cdot s^2 \cdot K^{-1}$, where kilogram, metre and second are defined in terms of h, c and $\Delta \nu_{Cs}$.

Mole

1 mole of a substance is defined to contain exactly $6.02214076 \times 10^{23}$ elementary entities. This number is the fixed numerical value of the Avogadro constant N_A when expressed in the unit mol^{-1} and is called Avogadro number.

Candela

The candela is the SI unit of luminous intensity. 1 candela is the luminous intensity that makes the luminous efficacy of monochromatic radiation of frequency 540×10^{12} Hz, K_{cd} to be 683 when expressed in the unit $lm \cdot W^{-1}$ which is equal to $cd \cdot sr \cdot kg^{-1} m^2 s^3$, where kilogram, metre and second are defined in terms of h, c and Δv_{Cs}.

1.5 DIMENSION

All the physical quantities of interest can be derived from the base quantities. When a quantity is expressed in terms of the base quantities, it is written as a product of different powers of the base quantities. The exponent of a base quantity that enters into the expression, is called the *dimension of the quantity in that base.* To make it clear, consider the physical quantity force. As we shall learn later, force is equal to mass times acceleration. Acceleration is change in velocity divided by time interval. Velocity is length divided by time interval. Thus,

$$force = mass \times acceleration$$
$$= mass \times \frac{velocity}{time}$$
$$= mass \times \frac{length/time}{time}$$
$$= mass \times length \times (time)^{-2}. \qquad \dots (1.2)$$

Thus, the dimensions of force are 1 in mass, 1 in length and −2 in time. The dimensions in all other base quantities are zero. Note that in this type of calculation the magnitudes are not considered. It is equality of the type of quantity that enters. Thus, change in velocity, initial velocity, average velocity, final velocity all are equivalent in this discussion, each one is length/time.

For convenience the base quantities are represented by one letter symbols. Generally, mass is denoted by M, length by L, time by T and electric current by I. The thermodynamic temperature, the amount of substance and the luminous intensity are denoted by the symbols of their units K, mol and cd respectively. The physical quantity that is expressed in terms of the base quantities is enclosed in square brackets to remind that the equation is among the dimensions and not among the magnitudes. Thus equation (1.2) may be written as $[force] = MLT^{-2}$.

Such an expression for a physical quantity in terms of the base quantities is called the *dimensional formula.* Thus, the dimensional formula of force is MLT^{-2}. The two versions given below are equivalent and are used interchangeably.

(a) The dimensional formula of force is MLT^{-2}.

(b) The dimensions of force are 1 in mass, 1 in length and −2 in time.

Example 1.1

Calculate the dimensional formula of energy from the equation $E = \frac{1}{2} mv^2$.

Solution : Dimensionally, $E = mass \times (velocity)^2$, since $\frac{1}{2}$ is a number and has no dimension.

$$\therefore \quad [E] = M \times \left(\frac{L}{T}\right)^2 = ML^2 T^{-2}.$$

1.6 USES OF DIMENSION

A. Homogeneity of Dimensions in an Equation

An equation contains several terms which are separated from each other by the symbols of equality, plus or minus. The dimensions of all the terms in an equation must be identical. This is another way of saying that one can add or subtract similar physical quantities. Thus, a velocity cannot be added to a force or an electric current cannot be subtracted from the thermodynamic temperature. This simple principle is called the *principle of homogeneity of dimensions* in an equation and is an extremely useful method to check whether an equation may be correct or not. If the dimensions of all the terms are not same, the equation must be wrong. Let us check the equation

$$x = ut + \frac{1}{2} at^2$$

for the dimensional homogeneity. Here x is the distance travelled by a particle in time t which starts at a speed u and has an acceleration a along the direction of motion.

$$[x] = L$$

$$[ut] = velocity \times time = \frac{length}{time} \times time = L$$

$$\left[\frac{1}{2} at^2\right] = [at^2] = acceleration \times (time)^2$$

$$= \frac{velocity}{time} \times (time)^2 = \frac{length/time}{time} \times (time)^2 = L$$

Thus, the equation is correct as far as the dimensions are concerned.

Limitation of the Method

Note that the dimension of $\frac{1}{2}at^2$ is same as that of at^2. Pure numbers are dimensionless. Dimension does not depend on the magnitude. Due to this reason the equation $x = ut + at^2$ is also dimensionally correct. Thus, a dimensionally correct equation need not be actually correct but a dimensionally wrong equation must be wrong.

Example 1.2

Test dimensionally if the formula $t = 2\pi\sqrt{\dfrac{m}{F/x}}$ may be correct, where t is time period, m is mass, F is force and x is distance.

Solution : The dimension of force is MLT^{-2}. Thus, the dimension of the right-hand side is

$$\sqrt{\frac{M}{MLT^{-2}/L}} = \sqrt{\frac{1}{T^{-2}}} = T.$$

The left-hand side is time period and hence the dimension is T. The dimensions of both sides are equal and hence the formula may be correct.

B. Conversion of Units

When we choose to work with a different set of units for the base quantities, the units of all the derived quantities must be changed. Dimensions can be useful in finding the conversion factor for the unit of a derived physical quantity from one system to other. Consider an example. When SI units are used, the unit of pressure is 1 pascal. Suppose we choose 1 cm as the unit of length, 1 g as the unit of mass and 1 s as the unit of time (this system is still in wide use and is called CGS system). The unit of pressure will be different in this system. Let us call it for the time-being 1 CGS pressure. Now, how many CGS pressure is equal to 1 pascal ?

Let us first write the dimensional formula of pressure.

We have $\qquad P = \dfrac{F}{A}.$

Thus, $\qquad [P] = \dfrac{[F]}{[A]} = \dfrac{MLT^{-2}}{L^2} = ML^{-1}T^{-2}$

so, $\qquad$ 1 pascal $= (1\text{ kg})(1\text{ m})^{-1}(1\text{ s})^{-2}$

and $\qquad$ 1 CGS pressure $= (1\text{ g})(1\text{ cm})^{-1}(1\text{ s})^{-2}$

Thus, $\dfrac{1 \text{ pascal}}{1 \text{ CGS pressure}} = \left(\dfrac{1\text{ kg}}{1\text{ g}}\right)\left(\dfrac{1\text{ m}}{1\text{ cm}}\right)^{-1}\left(\dfrac{1\text{ s}}{1\text{ s}}\right)^{-2}$

$$= (10^3)(10^2)^{-1} = 10$$

or, $\qquad$ 1 pascal $= 10$ CGS pressure.

Thus, knowing the conversion factors for the base quantities, one can work out the conversion factor for any derived quantity if the dimensional formula of the derived quantity is known.

C. Deducing Relation among the Physical Quantities

Sometimes dimensions can be used to deduce a relation between the physical quantities. If one knows the quantities on which a particular physical quantity depends and if one guesses that this dependence is of product type, method of dimension may be helpful in the derivation of the relation. Taking an example, suppose we have to derive the expression for the time period of a simple pendulum. The simple pendulum has a bob, attached to a string, which oscillates under the action of the force of gravity. Thus, the time period may depend on the length of the string, the mass of the bob and the acceleration due to gravity. We assume that the dependence of time period on these quantities is of product type, that is,

$$t = k\, l^a\, m^b\, g^c \qquad\qquad \dots (1.3)$$

where k is a dimensionless constant and a, b and c are exponents which we want to evaluate. Taking the dimensions of both sides,

$$T = L^a M^b (LT^{-2})^c = L^{a+c} M^b T^{-2c}.$$

Since the dimensions on both sides must be identical, we have

$$a + c = 0$$
$$b = 0$$

and $\qquad -2c = 1$

giving $\quad a = \dfrac{1}{2}, \ b = 0 \ \text{and} \ c = -\dfrac{1}{2}.$

Putting these values in equation (1.3)

$$t = k\sqrt{\frac{l}{g}}. \qquad\qquad \dots (1.4)$$

Thus, by dimensional analysis we can deduce that the time period of a simple pendulum is independent of its mass, is proportional to the square root of the length of the pendulum and is inversely proportional to the square root of the acceleration due to gravity at the place of observation.

Limitations of the Dimensional Method

Although dimensional analysis is very useful in deducing certain relations, it cannot lead us too far. First of all we have to know the quantities on which a particular physical quantity depends. Even then the method works only if the dependence is of the product type. For example, the distance travelled by a uniformly accelerated particle depends on the initial velocity u, the acceleration a and the time t. But the method of dimensions cannot lead us to the correct expression for x because the expression is not of product type. It is equal to the sum of two terms as

$$x = ut + \frac{1}{2} at^2.$$

Secondly, the numerical constants having no dimensions cannot be deduced by the method of dimensions. In the example of time period of a simple pendulum, an unknown constant k remains in equation (1.4). One has to know from somewhere else that this constant is 2π.

Thirdly, the method works only if there are as many equations available as there are unknowns. In mechanical quantities, only three base quantities length, mass and time enter. So, dimensions of these three may be equated in the guessed relation giving at most three equations in the exponents. If a particular quantity (in mechanics) depends on more than three quantities we shall have more unknowns and less equations. The exponents cannot be determined uniquely in such a case. Similar constraints are present for electrical or other nonmechanical quantities.

1.7 ORDER OF MAGNITUDE

In physics, we come across quantities which vary over a wide range. We talk of the size of a mountain and the size of the tip of a pin. We talk of the mass of our galaxy and the mass of a hydrogen atom. We talk of the age of the universe and the time taken by an electron to complete a circle around the proton in a hydrogen atom. It becomes quite difficult to get a feel of largeness or smallness of such quantities. To express such widely varying numbers, one uses the *powers of ten* method.

In this method, each number is expressed as $a \times 10^b$ where $1 \le a < 10$ and b is a positive or negative integer. Thus the diameter of the sun is expressed as $1 \cdot 39 \times 10^9$ m and the diameter of a hydrogen atom as $1 \cdot 06 \times 10^{-10}$ m. To get an approximate idea of the number, one may round the number a to 1 if it is less than or equal to 5 and to 10 if it is greater than 5. The number can then be expressed approximately as 10^b. We then get the *order of magnitude* of that number. Thus, the diameter of the sun is *of the order of* 10^9 m and that of a hydrogen atom is *of the order of* 10^{-10} m. More precisely, the exponent of 10 in such a representation is called the order of magnitude of that quantity. Thus, the diameter of the sun is 19 *orders of magnitude larger* than the diameter of a hydrogen atom. This is because the order of magnitude of 10^9 is 9 and of 10^{-10} is -10. The difference is $9 - (-10) = 19$.

To quickly get an approximate value of a quantity in a given physical situation, one can make an *order*

of magnitude calculation. In this all numbers are approximated to 10^b form and the calculation is made.

Let us estimate the number of persons that may sit in a circular field of radius 800 m. The area of the field is

$$A = \pi r^2 = 3 \cdot 14 \times (800 \text{ m})^2 \approx 10^6 \text{ m}^2.$$

The average area one person occupies in sitting $\approx 50 \text{ cm} \times 50 \text{ cm} = 0 \cdot 25 \text{ m}^2 = 2 \cdot 5 \times 10^{-1} \text{ m}^2 \approx 10^{-1} \text{ m}^2$. The number of persons who can sit in the field is

$$N \approx \frac{10^6 \text{ m}^2}{10^{-1} \text{ m}^2} = 10^7.$$

Thus of the order of 10^7 persons may sit in the field.

1.8 THE STRUCTURE OF WORLD

Man has always been interested to find how the world is structured. Long long ago scientists suggested that the world is made up of certain indivisible small particles. The number of particles in the world is large but the varieties of particles are not many. Old Indian philosopher Kanadi derives his name from this proposition (In Sanskrit or Hindi *Kana* means a small particle). After extensive experimental work people arrived at the conclusion that the world is made up of just three types of ultimate particles, the proton, the neutron and the electron. All objects which we have around us, are aggregation of atoms and molecules. The molecules are composed of atoms and the atoms have at their heart a nucleus containing protons and neutrons. Electrons move around this nucleus in special arrangements. It is the number of protons, neutrons and electrons in an atom that decides all the properties and behaviour of a material. Large number of atoms combine to form an object of moderate or large size. However, the laws that we generally deduce for these macroscopic objects are not always applicable to atoms, molecules, nuclei or the elementary particles. These laws known as *classical physics* deal with large size objects only. When we say a particle in classical physics we mean an object which is small as compared to other moderate or large size objects and for which the classical physics is valid. It may still contain millions and millions of atoms in it. Thus, a particle of dust dealt in classical physics may contain about 10^{18} atoms.

Twentieth century experiments have revealed another aspect of the construction of world. There are perhaps no ultimate indivisible particles. Hundreds of elementary particles have been discovered and there are free transformations from one such particle to the other. Nature is seen to be a well-connected entity.

Worked Out Examples

1. Find the dimensional formulae of the following quantities :
   (a) the universal constant of gravitation G,
   (b) the surface tension S,
   (c) the thermal conductivity k and
   (d) the coefficient of viscosity η.
   Some equations involving these quantities are

$$F = \frac{G m_1 m_2}{r^2}, \qquad S = \frac{\rho g r h}{2},$$

$$Q = k \frac{A(\theta_2 - \theta_1) t}{d} \quad \text{and} \quad F = -\eta A \frac{v_2 - v_1}{x_2 - x_1}$$

where the symbols have their usual meanings.

Solution : (a) $\quad F = G \dfrac{m_1 m_2}{r^2}$

or, $\qquad G = \dfrac{F r^2}{m_1 m_2}$

or, $\qquad [G] = \dfrac{[F] L^2}{M^2} = \dfrac{MLT^{-2} \cdot L^2}{M^2} = M^{-1} L^3 T^{-2}.$

(b) $\qquad S = \dfrac{\rho g r h}{2}$

or, $\qquad [S] = [\rho][g] L^2 = \dfrac{M}{L^3} \cdot \dfrac{L}{T^2} \cdot L^2 = MT^{-2}.$

(c) $\qquad Q = k \dfrac{A(\theta_2 - \theta_1) t}{d}$

or, $\qquad k = \dfrac{Q d}{A(\theta_2 - \theta_1) t}$

Here, Q is the heat energy having dimension $ML^2 T^{-2}$, $\theta_2 - \theta_1$ is temperature, A is area, d is thickness and t is time. Thus,

$$[k] = \frac{ML^2 T^{-2} L}{L^2 KT} = MLT^{-3} K^{-1}.$$

(d) $\qquad F = -\eta A \dfrac{v_2 - v_1}{x_2 - x_1}$

or, $\quad MLT^{-2} = [\eta] L^2 \dfrac{L/T}{L} = [\eta] \dfrac{L^2}{T}$

or, $\qquad [\eta] = ML^{-1} T^{-1}.$

2. Find the dimensional formulae of
   (a) the charge Q,
   (b) the potential V,
   (c) the capacitance C, and
   (d) the resistance R.
   Some of the equations containing these quantities are
   $\qquad Q = It, \; U = VIt, \; Q = CV \text{ and } V = RI;$
   where I denotes the electric current, t is time and U is energy.

Solution : (a) $Q = It$. $\qquad$ Hence, $[Q] = IT$.

(b) $\qquad U = VIt$

or, $ML^2 T^{-2} = [V] IT \qquad$ or, $\quad [V] = ML^2 I^{-1} T^{-3}.$

(c) $\quad Q = CV$

or, $IT = [C] ML^2 I^{-1} T^{-3} \qquad$ or, $[C] = M^{-1} L^{-2} I^2 T^4.$

(d) $V = RI$

or, $R = \dfrac{V}{I} \qquad$ or, $\quad [R] = \dfrac{ML^2 I^{-1} T^{-3}}{I} = ML^2 I^{-2} T^{-3}.$

3. The SI and CGS units of energy are joule and erg respectively. How many ergs are equal to one joule ?

Solution : Dimensionally, $\text{Energy} = mass \times (velocity)^2$

$$= mass \times \left(\frac{length}{time}\right)^2 = ML^2 T^{-2}.$$

Thus, 1 joule $= (1 \text{ kg})(1 \text{ m})^2 (1 \text{ s})^{-2}$

and $\quad$ 1 erg $= (1 \text{ g})(1 \text{ cm})^2 (1 \text{ s})^{-2}$

$$\frac{1 \text{ joule}}{1 \text{ erg}} = \left(\frac{1 \text{ kg}}{1 \text{ g}}\right)\left(\frac{1 \text{ m}}{1 \text{ cm}}\right)^2 \left(\frac{1 \text{ s}}{1 \text{ s}}\right)^{-2}$$

$$= \left(\frac{1000 \text{ g}}{1 \text{ g}}\right)\left(\frac{100 \text{ cm}}{1 \text{ cm}}\right)^2 = 1000 \times 10000 = 10^7.$$

So, $\quad$ 1 joule $= 10^7$ erg.

4. Young's modulus of steel is $19 \times 10^{10} \text{ N/m}^2$. Express it in $dyne/cm^2$. Here dyne is the CGS unit of force.

Solution : The unit of Young's modulus is N/m^2.

This suggests that it has dimensions of $\dfrac{Force}{(distance)^2}$.

Thus, $\qquad [Y] = \dfrac{[F]}{L^2} = \dfrac{MLT^{-2}}{L^2} = ML^{-1} T^{-2}.$

N/m^2 is in SI units.

So, $\qquad 1 \text{ N/m}^2 = (1 \text{ kg})(1 \text{ m})^{-1} (1 \text{ s})^{-2}$

and $\qquad 1 \text{ dyne/cm}^2 = (1 \text{ g})(1 \text{ cm})^{-1} (1 \text{ s})^{-2}$

so, $\quad \dfrac{1 \text{ N/m}^2}{1 \text{ dyne/cm}^2} = \left(\dfrac{1 \text{ kg}}{1 \text{ g}}\right)\left(\dfrac{1 \text{ m}}{1 \text{ cm}}\right)^{-1} \left(\dfrac{1 \text{ s}}{1 \text{ s}}\right)^{-2}$

$$= 1000 \times \frac{1}{100} \times 1 = 10$$

or, $\qquad 1 \text{ N/m}^2 = 10 \text{ dyne/cm}^2$

or, $\quad 19 \times 10^{10} \text{ N/m}^2 = 19 \times 10^{11} \text{ dyne/cm}^2.$

5. If velocity, time and force were chosen as basic quantities, find the dimensions of mass.

Solution : Dimensionally, $Force = mass \times acceleration$

$$= mass \times \frac{velocity}{time}$$

or, $\qquad mass = \dfrac{force \times time}{velocity}$

or, $\qquad [mass] = FTV^{-1}.$

6. *Test dimensionally if the equation $v^2 = u^2 + 2ax$ may be correct.*

Solution : There are three terms in this equation v^2, u^2 and $2ax$. The equation may be correct if the dimensions of these three terms are equal.

$$[v^2] = \left(\frac{L}{T}\right)^2 = L^2\, T^{-2};$$

$$[u^2] = \left(\frac{L}{T}\right)^2 = L^2\, T^{-2};$$

and $$[2ax] = [a]\,[x] = \left(\frac{L}{T^2}\right) L = L^2\, T^{-2}.$$

Thus, the equation may be correct.

7. *The distance covered by a particle in time t is given by $x = a + bt + ct^2 + dt^3$; find the dimensions of a, b, c and d.*

Solution : The equation contains five terms. All of them should have the same dimensions. Since $[x]$ = *length*, each of the remaining four must have the dimension of length.

Thus, $[a]$ = *length* = L

$$[bt] = L, \qquad \text{or,} \ \ [b] = LT^{-1}$$
$$[ct^2] = L, \qquad \text{or,} \ \ [c] = LT^{-2}$$
and $$[dt^3] = L, \qquad \text{or,} \ \ [d] = LT^{-3}.$$

8. *If the centripetal force is of the form $m^a v^b r^c$, find the values of a, b and c.*

Solution : Dimensionally,

$$Force = (Mass)^a \times (velocity)^b \times (length)^c$$
or, $$MLT^{-2} = M^a (L^b\, T^{-b})\, L^c = M^a\, L^{b+c}\, T^{-b}$$

Equating the exponents of similar quantities,
$$a = 1, \ b + c = 1, \ -b = -2$$
or, $$a = 1, \ b = 2, \ c = -1 \qquad \text{or,} \ \ F = \frac{mv^2}{r}.$$

9. *When a solid sphere moves through a liquid, the liquid opposes the motion with a force F. The magnitude of F depends on the coefficient of viscosity η of the liquid, the radius r of the sphere and the speed v of the sphere.*

Assuming that F is proportional to different powers of these quantities, guess a formula for F using the method of dimensions.

Solution : Suppose the formula is $F = k\, \eta^a r^b v^c$.

Then, $$MLT^{-2} = [ML^{-1}T^{-1}]^a\, L^b \left(\frac{L}{T}\right)^c$$
$$= M^a\, L^{-a+b+c}\, T^{-a-c}.$$

Equating the exponents of M, L and T from both sides,
$$a = 1$$
$$-a + b + c = 1$$
$$-a - c = -2$$

Solving these, $a = 1$, $b = 1$, and $c = 1$.
Thus, the formula for F is $F = k\eta r v$.

10. *The heat produced in a wire carrying an electric current depends on the current, the resistance and the time. Assuming that the dependence is of the product of powers type, guess an equation between these quantities using dimensional analysis. The dimensional formula of resistance is $ML^2 I^{-2} T^{-3}$ and heat is a form of energy.*

Solution : Let the heat produced be H, the current through the wire be I, the resistance be R and the time be t. Since heat is a form of energy, its dimensional formula is $ML^2\, T^{-2}$.

Let us assume that the required equation is
$$H = kI^a\, R^b\, t^c,$$
where k is a dimensionless constant.
Writing dimensions of both sides,
$$ML^2 T^{-2} = I^a (ML^2 I^{-2} T^{-3})^b\, T^c$$
$$= M^b\, L^{2b}\, T^{-3b+c}\, I^{a-2b}$$

Equating the exponents,
$$b = 1$$
$$2b = 2$$
$$-3b + c = -2$$
$$a - 2b = 0$$

Solving these, we get, $a = 2$, $b = 1$ and $c = 1$.

Thus, the required equation is $H = kI^2\, Rt$.

□

QUESTIONS FOR SHORT ANSWER

1. The metre is defined as the distance travelled by light in $\dfrac{1}{299,792,458}$ second. Why didn't people choose some easier number such as $\dfrac{1}{300,000,000}$ second ? Why not 1 second ?

2. What are the dimensions of :
 (a) volume of a cube of edge a,
 (b) volume of a sphere of radius a,
 (c) the ratio of the volume of a cube of edge a to the volume of a sphere of radius a ?

3. Suppose you are told that the linear size of everything in the universe has been doubled overnight. Can you test this statement by measuring sizes with a metre stick ? Can you test it by using the fact that the speed of light is a universal constant and has not changed ? What will happen if all the clocks in the universe also start running at half the speed ?

4. If all the terms in an equation have same units, is it necessary that they have same dimensions ? If all the terms in an equation have same dimensions, is it necessary that they have same units ?

5. If two quantities have same dimensions, do they represent same physical content ?

6. It is desirable that the standards of units be easily available, invariable, indestructible and easily reproducible. If we use foot of a person as a standard unit of length, which of the above features are present and which are not ?

7. Suggest a way to measure :
   (a) the thickness of a sheet of paper,
   (b) the distance between the sun and the moon.

OBJECTIVE I

1. Which of the following sets cannot enter into the list of fundamental quantities in any system of units ?
   (a) length, mass and velocity,
   (b) length, time and velocity,
   (c) mass, time and velocity,
   (d) length, time and mass.

2. A physical quantity is measured and the result is expressed as nu where u is the unit used and n is the numerical value. If the result is expressed in various units then
   (a) $n \propto$ size of u (b) $n \propto u^2$
   (c) $n \propto \sqrt{u}$ (d) $n \propto \dfrac{1}{u}$.

3. Suppose a quantity x can be dimensionally represented in terms of M, L and T, that is, $[x] = M^a L^b T^c$. The quantity mass
   (a) can always be dimensionally represented in terms of L, T and x,
   (b) can never be dimensoinally represented in terms of

L, T and x,
   (c) may be represented in terms of L, T and x if $a = 0$,
   (d) may be represented in terms of L, T and x if $a \neq 0$.

4. A dimensionless quantity
   (a) never has a unit, (b) always has a unit,
   (c) may have a unit, (d) does not exist.

5. A unitless quantity
   (a) never has a nonzero dimension,
   (b) always has a nonzero dimension,
   (c) may have a nonzero dimension,
   (d) does not exist.

6. $\int \dfrac{dx}{\sqrt{2ax - x^2}} = a^n \sin^{-1}\left[\dfrac{x}{a} - 1\right]$.
   The value of n is
   (a) 0 (b) −1
   (c) 1 (d) none of these.
   You may use dimensional analysis to solve the problem.

OBJECTIVE II

1. The dimensions $ML^{-1}T^{-2}$ may correspond to
   (a) work done by a force
   (b) linear momentum
   (c) pressure
   (d) energy per unit volume.

2. Choose the correct statement(s) :
   (a) A dimensionally correct equation may be correct.
   (b) A dimensionally correct equation may be incorrect.
   (c) A dimensionally incorrect equation may be correct.
   (d) A dimensionally incorrect equation may be incorrect.

3. Choose the correct statement(s) :
   (a) All quantities may be represented dimensionally in terms of the base quantities.
   (b) A base quantity cannot be represented dimensionally in terms of the rest of the base quantities.
   (c) The dimension of a base quantity in other base quantities is always zero.
   (d) The dimension of a derived quantity is never zero in any base quantity.

EXERCISES

1. Find the dimensions of
   (a) linear momentum,
   (b) frequency and
   (c) pressure.

2. Find the dimensions of
   (a) angular speed ω, (b) angular acceleration α,
   (c) torque Γ and (d) moment of interia I.
   Some of the equations involving these quantities are

$\omega = \dfrac{\theta_2 - \theta_1}{t_2 - t_1}$, $\quad \alpha = \dfrac{\omega_2 - \omega_1}{t_2 - t_1}$, $\quad \Gamma = F.r$ and $I = mr^2$.

The symbols have standard meanings.

3. Find the dimensions of
   (a) electric field E,   (b) magnetic field B and
   (c) magnetic permeability μ_0.
   The relevant equations are
   $$F = qE, \ F = qvB, \text{ and } B = \frac{\mu_0 I}{2\pi a};$$
   where F is force, q is charge, v is speed, I is current, and a is distance.

4. Find the dimensions of
   (a) electric dipole moment p and
   (b) magnetic dipole moment M.
   The defining equations are $p = q.d$ and $M = IA$;
   where d is distance, A is area, q is charge and I is current.

5. Find the dimensions of Planck's constant h from the equation $E = h\nu$ where E is the energy and ν is the frequency.

6. Find the dimensions of
   (a) the specific heat capacity c,
   (b) the coefficient of linear expansion α and
   (c) the gas constant R.
   Some of the equations involving these quantities are
   $Q = mc(T_2 - T_1)$, $l_t = l_0[1 + \alpha(T_2 - T_1)]$ and $PV = nRT$.

7. Taking force, length and time to be the fundamental quantities find the dimensions of
   (a) density,   (b) pressure,
   (c) momentum and   (d) energy.

8. Suppose the acceleration due to gravity at a place is 10 m/s^2. Find its value in cm/(minute)^2.

9. The average speed of a snail is 0.020 miles/hour and that of a leopard is 70 miles/hour. Convert these speeds in SI units.

10. The height of mercury column in a barometer in a Calcutta laboratory was recorded to be 75 cm. Calculate this pressure in SI and CGS units using the following data : Specific gravity of mercury $= 13.6$, Density of water $= 10^3 \text{ kg/m}^3$, $g = 9.8 \text{ m/s}^2$ at Calcutta. Pressure $= h\rho g$ in usual symbols.

11. Express the power of a 100 watt bulb in CGS unit.

12. The normal duration of I.Sc. Physics practical period in Indian colleges is 100 minutes. Express this period in microcenturies. 1 microcentury $= 10^{-6} \times 100$ years. How many microcenturies did you sleep yesterday ?

13. The surface tension of water is 72 dyne/cm. Convert it in SI unit.

14. The kinetic energy K of a rotating body depends on its moment of inertia I and its angular speed ω. Assuming the relation to be $K = kI^a\omega^b$ where k is a dimensionless constant, find a and b. Moment of inertia of a sphere about its diameter is $\frac{2}{5}Mr^2$.

15. Theory of relativity reveals that mass can be converted into energy. The energy E so obtained is proportional to certain powers of mass m and the speed c of light. Guess a relation among the quantities using the method of dimensions.

16. Let I = current through a conductor, R = its resistance and V = potential difference across its ends. According to Ohm's law, product of two of these quantities equals the third. Obtain Ohm's law from dimensional analysis. Dimensional formulae for R and V are $ML^2I^{-2}T^{-3}$ and $ML^2T^{-3}I^{-1}$ respectively.

17. The frequency of vibration of a string depends on the length L between the nodes, the tension F in the string and its mass per unit length m. Guess the expression for its frequency from dimensional analysis.

18. Test if the following equations are dimensionally correct :

    (a) $h = \dfrac{2S\cos\theta}{\rho rg}$,   (b) $v = \sqrt{\dfrac{P}{\rho}}$,

    (c) $V = \dfrac{\pi P r^4 t}{8\eta l}$,   (d) $\nu = \dfrac{1}{2\pi}\sqrt{\dfrac{mgl}{I}}$;

    where h = height, S = surface tension, ρ = density, P = pressure, V = volume, η = coefficient of viscosity, ν = frequency and I = moment of inertia.

19. Let x and a stand for distance. Is $\displaystyle\int \dfrac{dx}{\sqrt{a^2 - x^2}}$
    $= \dfrac{1}{a}\sin^{-1}\dfrac{a}{x}$ dimensionally correct ?

□

ANSWERS

OBJECTIVE I

1. (b)   2. (d)   3. (d)   4. (c)   5. (a)   6. (a)

OBJECTIVE II

1. (c), (d)   2. (a), (b), (d)   3. (a), (b), (c)

EXERCISES

1. (a) MLT^{-1} (b) T^{-1} (c) $ML^{-1}T^{-2}$
2. (a) T^{-1} (b) T^{-2} (c) ML^2T^{-2} (d) ML^2
3. (a) $MLT^{-3}I^{-1}$ (b) $MT^{-2}I^{-1}$ (c) $MLT^{-2}I^{-2}$
4. (a) LTI (b) $L^2 I$
5. ML^2T^{-1}
6. (a) $L^2T^{-2}K^{-1}$ (b) K^{-1} (c) $ML^2T^{-2}K^{-1}(\text{mol})^{-1}$

7. (a) $FL^{-4}T^2$ (b) FL^{-2} (c) FT (d) FL

8. 36×10^5 cm/(minute)^2

9. 0.0089 m/s, 31 m/s

10. 10×10^4 N/m^2, 10×10^5 dyne/cm^2

11. 10^9 erg/s

12. 1.9 microcenturies

13. 0.072 N/m

14. $a = 1,\ b = 2$

15. $E = kmc^2$

16. $V = IR$

17. $\dfrac{k}{L}\sqrt{\dfrac{F}{m}}$

18. all are dimensionally correct

19. no

□

CHAPTER 2

PHYSICS AND MATHEMATICS

Mathematics is the language of physics. It becomes easier to describe, understand and apply the physical principles, if one has a good knowledge of mathematics. In the present course we shall constantly be using the techniques of algebra, trigonometry and geometry as well as vector algebra, differential calculus and integral calculus. In this chapter we shall discuss the latter three topics. Errors in measurement and the concept of significant digits are also introduced.

2.1 VECTORS AND SCALARS

Certain physical quantities are completely described by a numerical value alone (with units specified) and are added according to the ordinary rules of algebra. As an example the mass of a system is described by saying that it is 5 kg. If two bodies one having a mass of 5 kg and the other having a mass of 2 kg are added together to make a composite system, the total mass of the system becomes 5 kg + 2 kg = 7 kg. Such quantities are called *scalars*.

The complete description of certain physical quantities requires a numerical value (with units specified) as well as a direction in space. Velocity of a particle is an example of this kind. The magnitude of velocity is represented by a number such as 5 m/s and tells us how fast a particle is moving. But the description of velocity becomes complete only when the direction of velocity is also specified. We can represent this velocity by drawing a line parallel to the velocity and putting an arrow showing the direction of velocity. We can decide beforehand a particular length to represent 1 m/s and the length of the line representing

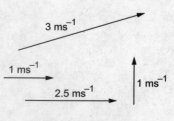

Figure 2.1

a velocity of 5 m/s may be taken as 5 times this unit length. Figure (2.1) shows representations of several velocities in this scheme. The front end (carrying the arrow) is called the head and the rear end is called the tail.

Further, if a particle is given two velocities simultaneously its resultant velocity is different from the two velocities and is obtained by using a special rule. Suppose a small ball is moving inside a long tube at a speed 3 m/s and the tube itself is moving in the room at a speed 4 m/s along a direction perpendicular to its length. In which direction and how fast is the ball moving as seen from the room ?

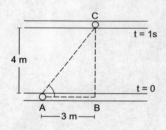

Figure 2.2

Figure (2.2) shows the positions of the tube and the ball at $t = 0$ and $t = 1$ s. Simple geometry shows that the ball has moved 5 m in a direction $\theta = 53°$ from the tube. So the resultant velocity of the ball is 5 m/s along this direction. The general rule for finding the resultant of two velocities may be stated as follows.

Draw a line AB representing the first velocity with B as the head. Draw another line BC representing the second velocity with its tail B coinciding with the head of the first line. The line AC with A as the tail and C as the head represents the resultant velocity. Figure (2.3) shows the construction.

The resultant is also called the sum of the two velocities. We have added the two velocities AB and BC and have obtained the sum AC. This rule of addition is called the "triangle rule of addition".

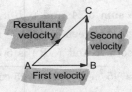

Figure 2.3

The physical quantities which have magnitude and direction and which can be added according to the triangle rule, are called *vector quantities*. Other examples of vector quantities are force, linear momentum, electric field, magnetic field etc.

The vectors are denoted by putting an arrow over the symbols representing them. Thus, we write $\overrightarrow{AB}$, $\overrightarrow{BC}$ etc. Sometimes a vector is represented by a single letter such as $\vec{v}$, $\vec{F}$ etc. Quite often in printed books the vectors are represented by bold face letters like **AB**, **BC**, **v**, **f** etc.

If a physical quantity has magnitude as well as direction but does not add up according to the triangle rule, it will not be called a vector quantity. Electric current in a wire has both magnitude and direction but there is no meaning of triangle rule there. Thus, electric current is not a vector quantity.

2.2 EQUALITY OF VECTORS

Two vectors (representing two values of the same physical quantity) are called equal if their magnitudes and directions are same. Thus, a parallel translation of a vector does not bring about any change in it.

2.3 ADDITION OF VECTORS

The triangle rule of vector addition is already described above. If $\vec{a}$ and $\vec{b}$ are the two vectors to be added, a diagram is drawn in which the tail of $\vec{b}$ coincides with the head of $\vec{a}$. The vector joining the tail of $\vec{a}$ with the head of $\vec{b}$ is the vector sum of $\vec{a}$ and $\vec{b}$. Figure (2.4a) shows the construction. The same rule

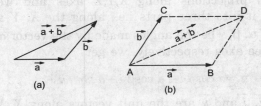

Figure 2.4

may be stated in a slightly different way. We draw the vectors $\vec{a}$ and $\vec{b}$ with both the tails coinciding (figure 2.4b). Taking these two as the adjacent sides

we complete the parallelogram. The diagonal through the common tails gives the sum of the two vectors. Thus, in figure, (2.4b) $\overrightarrow{AB} + \overrightarrow{AC} = \overrightarrow{AD}$.

Suppose the magnitude of $\vec{a} = a$ and that of $\vec{b} = b$. What is the magnitude of $\vec{a} + \vec{b}$ and what is its direction ? Suppose the angle between $\vec{a}$ and $\vec{b}$ is θ. It is easy to see from figure (2.5) that

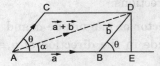

Figure 2.5

$$AD^2 = (AB + BE)^2 + (DE)^2$$

$$= (a + b\cos\theta)^2 + (b\sin\theta)^2$$

$$= a^2 + 2ab\cos\theta + b^2.$$

Thus, the magnitude of $\vec{a} + \vec{b}$ is

$$\sqrt{a^2 + b^2 + 2ab\cos\theta}. \qquad \text{... (2.1)}$$

Its angle with $\vec{a}$ is α where

$$\tan\alpha = \frac{DE}{AE} = \frac{b\sin\theta}{a + b\cos\theta}. \qquad \text{... (2.2)}$$

Example 2.1

Two vectors having equal magnitudes A make an angle θ with each other. Find the magnitude and direction of the resultant.

Solution : The magnitude of the resultant will be

$$B = \sqrt{A^2 + A^2 + 2AA\cos\theta}$$

$$= \sqrt{2A^2(1 + \cos\theta)} = \sqrt{4A^2\cos^2\frac{\theta}{2}}$$

$$= 2A\cos\frac{\theta}{2}.$$

The resultant will make an angle α with the first vector where

$$\tan\alpha = \frac{A\sin\theta}{A + A\cos\theta} = \frac{2A\sin\frac{\theta}{2}\cos\frac{\theta}{2}}{2A\cos^2\frac{\theta}{2}} = \tan\frac{\theta}{2}$$

or, $\alpha = \dfrac{\theta}{2}$

Thus, the resultant of two equal vectors bisects the angle between them.

2.4 MULTIPLICATION OF A VECTOR BY A NUMBER

Suppose $\vec{a}$ is a vector of magnitude a and k is a number. We define the vector $\vec{b} = k\vec{a}$ as a vector of magnitude $|ka|$. If k is positive the direction of the vector $\vec{b} = k\vec{a}$ is same as that of $\vec{a}$. If k is negative, the direction of $\vec{b}$ is opposite to $\vec{a}$. In particular, multiplication by (–1) just inverts the direction of the vector. The vectors $\vec{a}$ and $-\vec{a}$ have equal magnitudes but opposite directions.

If $\vec{a}$ is a vector of magnitude a and $\vec{u}$ is a vector of unit magnitude in the direction of $\vec{a}$, we can write

$$\vec{a} = a\vec{u}.$$

2.5 SUBTRACTION OF VECTORS

Let $\vec{a}$ and $\vec{b}$ be two vectors. We define $\vec{a} - \vec{b}$ as the sum of the vector $\vec{a}$ and the vector $(-\vec{b})$. To subtract $\vec{b}$ from $\vec{a}$, invert the direction of $\vec{b}$ and add to $\vec{a}$. Figure (2.6) shows the process.

Figure 2.6

Example 2.2

Two vectors of equal magnitude 5 unit have an angle 60° between them. Find the magnitude of (a) the sum of the vectors and (b) the difference of the vectors.

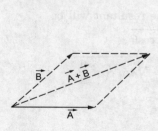 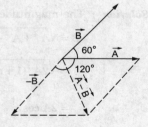

Figure 2.7

Solution : Figure (2.7) shows the construction of the sum $\vec{A} + \vec{B}$ and the difference $\vec{A} - \vec{B}$.

(a) $\vec{A} + \vec{B}$ is the sum of $\vec{A}$ and $\vec{B}$. Both have a magnitude of 5 unit and the angle between them is 60°. Thus, the magnitude of the sum is

$$|\vec{A} + \vec{B}| = \sqrt{5^2 + 5^2 + 2 \times 5 \times 5 \cos 60°}$$
$$= 2 \times 5 \cos 30° = 5\sqrt{3} \text{ unit.}$$

(b) $\vec{A} - \vec{B}$ is the sum of $\vec{A}$ and $(-\vec{B})$. As shown in the figure, the angle between $\vec{A}$ and $(-\vec{B})$ is 120°. The magnitudes of both $\vec{A}$ and $(-\vec{B})$ is 5 unit. So,

$$|\vec{A} - \vec{B}| = \sqrt{5^2 + 5^2 + 2 \times 5 \times 5 \cos 120°}$$
$$= 2 \times 5 \cos 60° = 5 \text{ unit.}$$

2.6 RESOLUTION OF VECTORS

Figure (2.8) shows a vector $\vec{a} = \vec{OA}$ in the X-Y plane drawn from the origin O. The vector makes an angle α with the X-axis and β with the Y-axis. Draw perpendiculars AB and AC from A to the X and Y axes respectively. The length OB is called the projection of $\vec{OA}$ on X-axis. Similarly OC is the projection of $\vec{OA}$ on Y-axis. According to the rules of vector addition

$$\vec{a} = \vec{OA} = \vec{OB} + \vec{OC}.$$

Thus, we have resolved the vector $\vec{a}$ into two parts, one along OX and the other along OY. The magnitude of the part along OX is $OB = a \cos\alpha$ and the magnitude of the part along OY is $OC = a \cos\beta$. If $\vec{i}$ and $\vec{j}$ denote vectors of unit magnitude along OX and OY respectively, we get

$$\vec{OB} = a \cos\alpha\, \vec{i} \text{ and } \vec{OC} = a \cos\beta\, \vec{j}$$

so that $\vec{a} = a \cos\alpha\, \vec{i} + a \cos\beta\, \vec{j}.$

Figure 2.8

If the vector $\vec{a}$ is not in the X-Y plane, it may have nonzero projections along X,Y,Z axes and we can resolve it into three parts i.e., along the X, Y and Z axes. If α, β, γ be the angles made by the vector $\vec{a}$ with the three axes respectively, we get

$$\vec{a} = a \cos\alpha\, \vec{i} + a \cos\beta\, \vec{j} + a \cos\gamma\, \vec{k} \quad \dots (2.3)$$

where $\vec{i}$, $\vec{j}$ and $\vec{k}$ are the unit vectors along X, Y and Z axes respectively. The magnitude $(a \cos\alpha)$ is called the component of $\vec{a}$ along X-axis, $(a \cos\beta)$ is called the component along Y-axis and $(a \cos\gamma)$ is called the component along Z-axis. In general, the component of a vector $\vec{a}$ along a direction making an angle θ with it is $a \cos\theta$ (figure 2.9) which is the projection of $\vec{a}$ along the given direction.

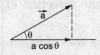

Figure 2.9

Equation (2.3) shows that any vector can be expressed as a linear combination of the three unit vectors $\vec{i}, \vec{j}$ and $\vec{k}$.

Example 2.3

A force of 10·5 N acts on a particle along a direction making an angle of 37° with the vertical. Find the component of the force in the vertical direction.

Solution : The component of the force in the vertical direction will be

$$F_\perp = F \cos\theta = (10·5 \text{ N})(\cos 37°)$$

$$= (10·5 \text{ N})\frac{4}{5} = 8·40 \text{ N}.$$

We can easily add two or more vectors if we know their components along the rectangular coordinate axes. Let us have

$$\vec{a} = a_x \vec{i} + a_y \vec{j} + a_z \vec{k}$$

$$\vec{b} = b_x \vec{i} + b_y \vec{j} + b_z \vec{k}$$

and $\qquad \vec{c} = c_x \vec{i} + c_y \vec{j} + c_z \vec{k}$

then

$$\vec{a} + \vec{b} + \vec{c} = (a_x + b_x + c_x)\vec{i} + (a_y + b_y + c_y)\vec{j} + (a_z + b_z + c_z)\vec{k}.$$

If all the vectors are in the X-Y plane then all the z components are zero and the resultant is simply

$$\vec{a} + \vec{b} + \vec{c} = (a_x + b_x + c_x)\vec{i} + (a_y + b_y + c_y)\vec{j}.$$

This is the sum of two mutually perpendicular vectors of magnitude $(a_x + b_x + c_x)$ and $(a_y + b_y + c_y)$. The resultant can easily be found to have a magnitude

$$\sqrt{(a_x + b_x + c_x)^2 + (a_y + b_y + c_y)^2}$$

making an angle α with the X-axis where

$$\tan\alpha = \frac{a_y + b_y + c_y}{a_x + b_x + c_x}.$$

2.7 DOT PRODUCT OR SCALAR PRODUCT OF TWO VECTORS

The dot product (also called scalar product) of two vectors $\vec{a}$ and $\vec{b}$ is defined as

$$\vec{a} \cdot \vec{b} = ab \cos\theta \qquad \dots (2.4)$$

where a and b are the magnitudes of $\vec{a}$ and $\vec{b}$ respectively and θ is the angle between them. The dot product between two mutually perpendicular vectors is zero as $\cos 90° = 0$.

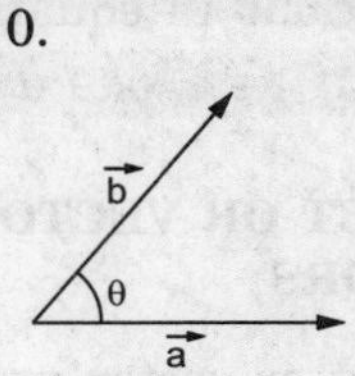

Figure 2.10

The dot product is commutative and distributive.

$$\vec{a} \cdot \vec{b} = \vec{b} \cdot \vec{a}$$

$$\vec{a} \cdot (\vec{b} + \vec{c}) = \vec{a} \cdot \vec{b} + \vec{a} \cdot \vec{c}.$$

Example 2.4

The work done by a force $\vec{F}$ during a displacement $\vec{r}$ is given by $\vec{F} \cdot \vec{r}$. Suppose a force of 12 N acts on a particle in vertically upward direction and the particle is displaced through 2·0 m in vertically downward direction. Find the work done by the force during this displacement.

Solution : The angle between the force $\vec{F}$ and the displacement $\vec{r}$ is 180°. Thus, the work done is

$$W = \vec{F} \cdot \vec{r}$$

$$= Fr \cos\theta$$

$$= (12 \text{ N})(2·0 \text{ m})(\cos 180°)$$

$$= -24 \text{ N-m} = -24 \text{ J}.$$

Dot Product of Two Vectors in terms of the Components along the Coordinate Axes

Consider two vectors $\vec{a}$ and $\vec{b}$ represented in terms of the unit vectors $\vec{i}, \vec{j}, \vec{k}$ along the coordinate axes as

$$\vec{a} = a_x \vec{i} + a_y \vec{j} + a_z \vec{k}$$

and $\qquad \vec{b} = b_x \vec{i} + b_y \vec{j} + b_z \vec{k}.$

Then

$$\vec{a} \cdot \vec{b} = (a_x \vec{i} + a_y \vec{j} + a_z \vec{k}) \cdot (b_x \vec{i} + b_y \vec{j} + b_z \vec{k})$$

$$= a_x b_x \vec{i} \cdot \vec{i} + a_x b_y \vec{i} \cdot \vec{j} + a_x b_z \vec{i} \cdot \vec{k}$$

$$+ a_y b_x \vec{j} \cdot \vec{i} + a_y b_y \vec{j} \cdot \vec{j} + a_y b_z \vec{j} \cdot \vec{k}$$

$$+ a_z b_x \vec{k} \cdot \vec{i} + a_z b_y \vec{k} \cdot \vec{j} + a_z b_z \vec{k} \cdot \vec{k} \qquad \dots (i)$$

Since, $\vec{i}, \vec{j}$ and $\vec{k}$ are mutually orthogonal, we have $\vec{i} \cdot \vec{j} = \vec{i} \cdot \vec{k} = \vec{j} \cdot \vec{i} = \vec{j} \cdot \vec{k} = \vec{k} \cdot \vec{i} = \vec{k} \cdot \vec{j} = 0$.

Also, $\vec{i} \cdot \vec{i} = 1 \times 1 \cos 0 = 1$.

Similarly, $\vec{j} \cdot \vec{j} = \vec{k} \cdot \vec{k} = 1$.

Using these relations in equation (i) we get

$$\vec{a} \cdot \vec{b} = a_x b_x + a_y b_y + a_z b_z.$$

2.8 CROSS PRODUCT OR VECTOR PRODUCT OF TWO VECTORS

The cross product or vector product of two vectors $\vec{a}$ and $\vec{b}$, denoted by $\vec{a} \times \vec{b}$ is itself a vector. The magnitude of this vector is

$$|\vec{a} \times \vec{b}| = ab \sin\theta \qquad \dots \ (2.5)$$

where a and b are the magnitudes of $\vec{a}$ and $\vec{b}$ respectively and θ is the smaller angle between the two. When two vectors are drawn with both the tails coinciding, two angles are formed between them (figure 2.11). One of the angles is smaller than 180°

Figure 2.11

and the other is greater than 180° unless both are equal to 180°. The angle θ used in equation (2.5) is the smaller one. If both the angles are equal to 180°, $\sin \theta = \sin 180° = 0$ and hence $|\vec{a} \times \vec{b}| = 0$. Similarly if $\theta = 0$, $\sin \theta = 0$ and $|\vec{a} \times \vec{b}| = 0$. The cross product of two parallel vectors is zero.

The direction of $\vec{a} \times \vec{b}$ is perpendicular to both $\vec{a}$ and $\vec{b}$. Thus, it is perpendicular to the plane formed by $\vec{a}$ and $\vec{b}$. To determine the direction of arrow on this perpendicular several rules are in use. In order to avoid confusion we here describe just one rule.

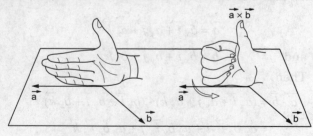

Figure 2.12

Draw the two vectors $\vec{a}$ and $\vec{b}$ with both the tails coinciding (figure 2.12). Now place your stretched right palm perpendicular to the plane of $\vec{a}$ and $\vec{b}$ in such a way that the fingers are along the vector $\vec{a}$ and when the fingers are closed they go towards $\vec{b}$. The direction of the thumb gives the direction of arrow to be put on the vector $\vec{a} \times \vec{b}$.

This is known as the *right hand thumb rule*. The left handers should be more careful in using this rule as it must be practiced with right hand only.

Note that this rule makes the cross product noncommutative. In fact

$$\vec{a} \times \vec{b} = -\vec{b} \times \vec{a}.$$

The cross product follows the distributive law

$$\vec{a} \times (\vec{b} + \vec{c}) = \vec{a} \times \vec{b} + \vec{a} \times \vec{c}.$$

It does not follow the associative law

$$\vec{a} \times (\vec{b} \times \vec{c}) \neq (\vec{a} \times \vec{b}) \times \vec{c}.$$

When we choose a coordinate system any two perpendicular lines may be chosen as X and Y axes. However, once X and Y axes are chosen, there are two possible choices of Z-axis. The Z-axis must be perpendicular to the X-Y plane. But the positive direction of Z-axis may be defined in two ways. We choose the positive direction of Z-axis in such a way that

$$\vec{i} \times \vec{j} = \vec{k}.$$

Such a coordinate system is called a *right handed system*. In such a system

$$\vec{j} \times \vec{k} = \vec{i} \qquad \text{and} \qquad \vec{k} \times \vec{i} = \vec{j}.$$

Of course $\vec{i} \times \vec{i} = \vec{j} \times \vec{j} = \vec{k} \times \vec{k} = 0$.

Example 2.5

The vector $\vec{A}$ has a magnitude of 5 unit, $\vec{B}$ has a magnitude of 6 unit and the cross product of $\vec{A}$ and $\vec{B}$ has a magnitude of 15 unit. Find the angle between $\vec{A}$ and $\vec{B}$.

Solution : If the angle between $\vec{A}$ and $\vec{B}$ is θ, the cross product will have a magnitude

$$|\vec{A} \times \vec{B}| = AB \sin\theta$$

or, $15 = 5 \times 6 \sin\theta$

or, $\sin\theta = \dfrac{1}{2}$.

Thus, $\theta = 30° \text{ or, } 150°$.

Cross Product of Two Vectors in terms of the Components along the Coordinate Axes

Let $\vec{a} = a_x \vec{i} + a_y \vec{j} + a_z \vec{k}$

and $\vec{b} = b_x \vec{i} + b_y \vec{j} + b_z \vec{k}$.

Then $\vec{a} \times \vec{b} = (a_x \vec{i} + a_y \vec{j} + a_z \vec{k}) \times (b_x \vec{i} + b_y \vec{j} + b_z \vec{k})$

$= a_x b_x \vec{i} \times \vec{i} + a_x b_y \vec{i} \times \vec{j} + a_x b_z \vec{i} \times \vec{k}$

$\quad + a_y b_x \vec{j} \times \vec{i} + a_y b_y \vec{j} \times \vec{j} + a_y b_z \vec{j} \times \vec{k}$

$\quad + a_z b_x \vec{k} \times \vec{i} + a_z b_y \vec{k} \times \vec{j} + a_z b_z \vec{k} \times \vec{k}$

$= a_x b_y \vec{k} + a_x b_z (-\vec{j}) + a_y b_x (-\vec{k}) + a_y b_z (\vec{i})$

$\quad + a_z b_x (\vec{j}) + a_z b_y (-\vec{i})$

$= (a_y b_z - a_z b_y) \vec{i} + (a_z b_x - a_x b_z) \vec{j}$

$\quad + (a_x b_y - a_y b_x) \vec{k}.$

Zero Vector

If we add two vectors $\vec{A}$ and $\vec{B}$, we get a vector. Suppose the vectors $\vec{A}$ and $\vec{B}$ have equal magnitudes but opposite directions. What is the vector $\vec{A} + \vec{B}$? The magnitude of this vector will be zero. For mathematical consistency it is convenient to have a vector of zero magnitude although it has little significance in physics. This vector is called zero vector. The direction of a zero vector is indeterminate. We can write this vector as $\vec{0}$. The concept of zero vector is also helpful when we consider vector product of parallel vectors. If $\vec{A} \parallel \vec{B}$, the vector $\vec{A} \times \vec{B}$ is zero vector. For any vector $\vec{A}$,

$$\vec{A} + \vec{0} = \vec{A}$$

$$\vec{A} \times \vec{0} = \vec{0}$$

and for any number λ,

$$\lambda \vec{0} = \vec{0}.$$

2.9 DIFFERENTIAL CALCULUS : $\frac{dy}{dx}$ AS

RATE MEASURER

Consider two quantities y and x interrelated in such a way that for each value of x there is one and only one value of y. Figure (2.13) represents the graph

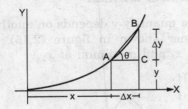

Figure 2.13

of y versus x. The value of y at a particular x is obtained by the height of the ordinate at that x. Let x be changed by a small amount Δx, and the corresponding change in y be Δy. We can define the "rate of change" of y with respect to x in the following

way. When x changes by Δx, y changes by Δy so that the rate of change seems to be equal to $\frac{\Delta y}{\Delta x}$. If A be the point (x, y) and B be the point $(x + \Delta x, y + \Delta y)$, the rate $\frac{\Delta y}{\Delta x}$ equals the slope of the line AB. We have

$$\frac{\Delta y}{\Delta x} = \frac{BC}{AC} = \tan\theta.$$

However, this cannot be the precise definition of the rate. Because the rate also varies between the points A and B. The curve is steeper at B than at A. Thus, to know the rate of change of y at a particular value of x, say at A, we have to take Δx very small. However small we take Δx, as long as it is not zero the rate may vary within that small part of the curve. However, if we go on drawing the point B closer to A and everytime calculate $\frac{\Delta y}{\Delta x} = \tan\theta$, we shall see that as Δx is made smaller and smaller the slope $\tan\theta$ of the line AB approaches the slope of the tangent at A. This slope of the tangent at A thus gives the rate of change of y with respect to x at A. This rate is denoted by $\frac{dy}{dx}$. Thus,

$$\frac{dy}{dx} = \lim_{\Delta x \to 0} \frac{\Delta y}{\Delta x}.$$

For small changes Δx we can approximately write

$$\Delta y = \frac{dy}{dx} \Delta x.$$

Note that if the function y increases with an increase in x at a point, $\frac{dy}{dx}$ is positive there, because both Δy and Δx are positive. If the function y decreases with an increase in x, Δy is negative when Δx is positive. Then $\frac{\Delta y}{\Delta x}$ and hence $\frac{dy}{dx}$ is negative.

Example 2.6

From the curve given in figure (2.14) find $\frac{dy}{dx}$ at $x = 2$, 6 and 10.

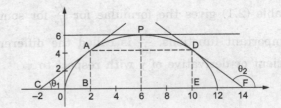

Figure 2.14

Solution : The tangent to the curve at $x = 2$ is AC. Its slope is $\tan\theta_1 = \dfrac{AB}{BC} = \dfrac{5}{4}$.

Thus, $\dfrac{dy}{dx} = \dfrac{5}{4}$ at $x = 2$.

The tangent to the curve at $x = 6$ is parallel to the X-axis.

Thus, $\dfrac{dy}{dx} = \tan\theta = 0$ at $x = 6$.

The tangent to the curve at $x = 10$ is DF. Its slope is

$$\tan\theta_2 = \dfrac{DE}{EF} = -\dfrac{5}{4}.$$

Thus, $\dfrac{dy}{dx} = -\dfrac{5}{4}$ at $x = 10$.

If we are given the graph of y versus x, we can find $\dfrac{dy}{dx}$ at any point of the curve by drawing the tangent at that point and finding its slope. Even if the graph is not drawn and the algebraic relation between y and x is given in the form of an equation, we can find $\dfrac{dy}{dx}$ algebraically. Let us take an example.

The area A of a square of length L is $A = L^2$.

If we change L to $L + \Delta L$, the area will change from A to $A + \Delta A$ (figure 2.15).

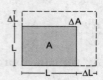

Figure 2.15

$$A + \Delta A = (L + \Delta L)^2$$
$$= L^2 + 2L\,\Delta L + (\Delta L)^2$$

or, $$\Delta A = 2L(\Delta L) + (\Delta L)^2$$

or, $$\dfrac{\Delta A}{\Delta L} = 2L + \Delta L.$$

Now if ΔL is made smaller and smaller, $2L + \Delta L$ will approach $2L$.

Thus, $$\dfrac{dA}{dL} = \lim_{\Delta L \to 0} \dfrac{\Delta A}{\Delta L} = 2L.$$

Table (2.1) gives the formulae for $\dfrac{dy}{dx}$ for some of the important functions. $\dfrac{dy}{dx}$ is called the differential coefficient or derivative of y with respect to x.

Table 2.1 : $\dfrac{dy}{dx}$ for some common functions

y	$\dfrac{dy}{dx}$	y	$\dfrac{dy}{dx}$
x^n	nx^{n-1}	$\sec x$	$\sec x \tan x$
$\sin x$	$\cos x$	$\operatorname{cosec} x$	$-\operatorname{cosec} x \cot x$
$\cos x$	$-\sin x$	$\ln x$	$\dfrac{1}{x}$
$\tan x$	$\sec^2 x$	e^x	e^x
$\cot x$	$-\operatorname{cosec}^2 x$		

Besides, there are certain rules for finding the derivatives of composite functions.

(a) $\dfrac{d}{dx}(cy) = c\,\dfrac{dy}{dx}$ (c is a constant)

(b) $\dfrac{d}{dx}(u + v) = \dfrac{du}{dx} + \dfrac{dv}{dx}$

(c) $\dfrac{d}{dx}(uv) = u\,\dfrac{dv}{dx} + v\,\dfrac{du}{dx}$

(d) $\dfrac{d}{dx}\left(\dfrac{u}{v}\right) = \dfrac{v\,\dfrac{du}{dx} - u\,\dfrac{dv}{dx}}{v^2}$

(e) $\dfrac{dy}{dx} = \dfrac{dy}{du} \cdot \dfrac{du}{dx}$

With these rules and table 2.1 derivatives of almost all the functions of practical interest may be evaluated.

Example 2.7

Find $\dfrac{dy}{dx}$ *if* $y = e^x \sin x$.

Solution : $y = e^x \sin x$.

So $\dfrac{dy}{dx} = \dfrac{d}{dx}(e^x \sin x) = e^x \dfrac{d}{dx}(\sin x) + \sin x\,\dfrac{d}{dx}(e^x)$

$= e^x \cos x + e^x \sin x = e^x(\cos x + \sin x).$

2.10 MAXIMA AND MINIMA

Suppose a quantity y depends on another quantity x in a manner shown in figure (2.16). It becomes maximum at x_1 and minimum at x_2.

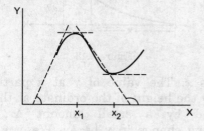

Figure 2.16

At these points the tangent to the curve is parallel to the X-axis and hence its slope is $\tan \theta = 0$. But the slope of the curve y-x equals the rate of change $\dfrac{dy}{dx}$. Thus, at a maximum or a minimum,

$$\frac{dy}{dx} = 0.$$

Just before the maximum the slope is positive, at the maximum it is zero and just after the maximum it is negative. Thus, $\dfrac{dy}{dx}$ decreases at a maximum and hence the rate of change of $\dfrac{dy}{dx}$ is negative at a maximum i.e.

$$\frac{d}{dx}\left(\frac{dy}{dx}\right) < 0 \text{ at a maximum.}$$

The quantity $\dfrac{d}{dx}\left(\dfrac{dy}{dx}\right)$ is the rate of change of the slope. It is written as $\dfrac{d^2y}{dx^2}$. Thus, the condition of a maximum is

$$\left.\begin{aligned} \frac{dy}{dx} &= 0 \\ \frac{d^2y}{dx^2} &< 0 \end{aligned}\right\} \text{— maximum.} \qquad \ldots (2.6)$$

Similarly, at a minimum the slope changes from negative to positive. The slope increases at such a point and hence $\dfrac{d}{dx}\left(\dfrac{dy}{dx}\right) > 0$. The condition of a minimum is

$$\left.\begin{aligned} \frac{dy}{dx} &= 0 \\ \frac{d^2y}{dx^2} &> 0 \end{aligned}\right\} \text{— minimum.} \qquad \ldots (2.7)$$

Quite often it is known from the physical situation whether the quantity is a maximum or a minimum. The test on $\dfrac{d^2y}{dx^2}$ may then be omitted.

Example 2.8

The height reached in time t by a particle thrown upward with a speed u is given by

$$h = ut - \frac{1}{2}gt^2$$

where $g = 9{\cdot}8 \text{ m/s}^2$ is a constant. Find the time taken in reaching the maximum height.

Solution : The height h is a function of time. Thus, h will be maximum when $\dfrac{dh}{dt} = 0$. We have,

$$h = ut - \frac{1}{2}gt^2$$

or,

$$\frac{dh}{dt} = \frac{d}{dt}(ut) - \frac{d}{dt}\left(\frac{1}{2}gt^2\right)$$

$$= u\frac{dt}{dt} - \frac{1}{2}g\frac{d}{dt}(t^2)$$

$$= u - \frac{1}{2}g(2t) = u - gt.$$

For maximum h,

$$\frac{dh}{dt} = 0$$

or, $\qquad u - gt = 0 \quad$ or, $\quad t = \dfrac{u}{g}.$

2.11 INTEGRAL CALCULUS

Let PQ be a curve representing the relation between two quantities x and y (figure 2.17). The point P corresponds to $x = a$ and Q corresponds to $x = b$. Draw perpendiculars from P and Q on the X-axis so as to cut it at A and B respectively. We are interested in finding the area $PABQ$. Let us denote the value of y at x by the symbol $y = f(x)$.

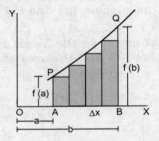

Figure 2.17

Let us divide the length AB in N equal elements each of length $\Delta x = \dfrac{b-a}{N}$. From the ends of each small length we draw lines parallel to the Y-axis. From the points where these lines cut the given curve, we draw short lines parallel to the X-axis. This constructs the rectangular bars shown shaded in the figure. The sum of the areas of these N rectangular bars is

$$I' = f(a)\,\Delta x + f(a + \Delta x)\,\Delta x + f(a + 2\Delta x)\,\Delta x + \ldots$$

$$\ldots + f[a + (N-1)\,\Delta x]\,\Delta x .$$

This may be written as

$$I' = \sum_{i=1}^{N} f(x_i)\Delta x \qquad \ldots (2.8)$$

where x_i takes the values $a, a + \Delta x, a + 2\Delta x, .., b - \Delta x$.

This area differs slightly from the area $PABQ$. This difference is the sum of the small triangles formed just under the curve. Now the important point is the following. As we increase the number of intervals N, the vertices of the bars touch the curve PQ at more points and the total area of the small triangles decreases. As N tends to infinity (Δx tends to zero because $\Delta x = \dfrac{b-a}{N}$) the vertices of the bars touch the curve at infinite number of points and the total area of the triangles tends to zero. In such a limit the sum (2.8) becomes the area I of $PABQ$. Thus, we may write,

$$I = \lim_{\Delta x \to 0} \sum_{i=1}^{N} f(x_i)\Delta x.$$

The limit is taken as Δx tends to zero or as N tends to infinity. In mathematics this quantity is denoted as

$$I = \int_{a}^{b} f(x)\, dx$$

and is read as the integral of $f(x)$ with respect to x within the limits $x = a$ to $x = b$. Here a is called the lower limit and b the upper limit of integration. The integral is the sum of a large number of terms of the type $f(x)\,\Delta x$ with x continuously varying from a to b and the number of terms tending to infinity.

Let us use the above method to find the area of a trapezium. Let us suppose the line PQ is represented by the equation $y = x$.

The points A and B on the X-axis represent $x = a$ and $x = b$. We have to find the area of the trapezium $PABQ$.

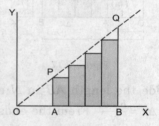

Figure 2.18

Let us divide the length AB in N equal intervals. The length of each interval is $\Delta x = \dfrac{b-a}{N}$. The height of the first shaded bar is $y = x = a$, of the second bar is $y = x = a + \Delta x$, that of the third bar is $y = x = a + 2\,\Delta x$ etc. The height of the Nth bar is $y = x = a + (N-1)\Delta x$. The width of each bar is Δx, so that the total area of all the bars is

$$I' = a\Delta x + (a + \Delta x)\,\Delta x + (a + 2\Delta x)\,\Delta x + \ldots$$
$$\ldots + [a + (N-1)\Delta x]\Delta x$$
$$= \big[a + (a + \Delta x) + (a + 2\Delta x) + \ldots$$
$$\ldots + \{a + (N-1)\Delta x\}\big]\Delta x \qquad \ldots (2.9)$$

This sum can be written as

$$I' = \sum_{i=1}^{N} x_i\,\Delta x$$

where $\Delta x = \dfrac{b-a}{N}$ and $x_i = a,\ a + \Delta x,\ \ldots b - \Delta x$.

As $\Delta x \to 0$ the total area of the bars becomes the area of the shaded part $PABQ$.

Thus, the required area is

$$I = \lim_{\Delta x \to 0} \sum_{i=1}^{N} x_i\,\Delta x$$
$$= \int_{a}^{b} x\, dx. \qquad \ldots (i)$$

Now the terms making the series in the square bracket in equation (2.9) are in arithmetic progression so that this series may be summed up using the formula $S = \dfrac{n}{2}(a + l)$. Equation (2.9) thus becomes

$$I' = \frac{N}{2}[a + \{a + (N-1)\Delta x\}]\Delta x$$
$$= \frac{N\Delta x}{2}[2a + N\Delta x - \Delta x]$$
$$= \frac{b-a}{2}[2a + b - a - \Delta x]$$
$$= \frac{b-a}{2}[a + b - \Delta x].$$

Thus, the area $PABQ$ is

$$I = \lim_{\Delta x \to 0} \left[\frac{b-a}{2}\right][a + b - \Delta x]$$
$$= \frac{b-a}{2}(a + b)$$
$$= \frac{1}{2}(b^2 - a^2). \qquad \ldots (ii)$$

Thus, from (i) and (ii)

$$\int_{a}^{b} x\, dx = \frac{1}{2}(b^2 - a^2).$$

In mathematics, special methods have been developed to find the integration of various functions $f(x)$. A very useful method is as follows. Suppose we wish to find

$$\int_{a}^{b} f(x)\, dx = \lim_{\Delta x \to 0} \sum_{i=1}^{N} f(x_i)\,\Delta x$$

where $\Delta x = \dfrac{b-a}{N}$; $x_i = a,\ a + \Delta x,\ \ldots b - \Delta x$.

Now look for a function $F(x)$ such that the derivative of $F(x)$ is $f(x)$ that is, $\dfrac{dF(x)}{dx} = f(x)$. If you can find such a function $F(x)$, then

$$\int_{a}^{b} f(x)\, dx = F(b) - F(a)\,;$$

$F(b) - F(a)$ is also written as $[F(x)]_{a}^{b}$.

$F(x)$ is called the indefinite integration or the antiderivative of $f(x)$. We also write $\int f(x)\,dx = F(x)$. This may be treated as another way of writing $\dfrac{dF(x)}{dx} = f(x)$.

For example, $\dfrac{d}{dx}\left(\dfrac{1}{2}x^2\right) = \dfrac{1}{2}\dfrac{d}{dx}(x^2) = \dfrac{1}{2}\cdot 2x = x$.

Thus, $\displaystyle\int_a^b x\,dx = \left[\dfrac{1}{2}x^2\right]_a^b$

$= \left(\dfrac{1}{2}b^2\right) - \left(\dfrac{1}{2}a^2\right)$

$= \dfrac{1}{2}(b^2 - a^2)$

as deduced above.

Table (2.2) lists some important integration formulae. Many of them are essentially same as those given in table (2.1).

Table 2.2 : Integration Formulae

$f(x)$	$F(x) = \int f(x)\,dx$	$f(x)$	$F(x) = \int f(x)\,dx$
$\sin x$	$-\cos x$	$x^n\,(n \neq -1)$	$\dfrac{x^{n+1}}{n+1}$
$\cos x$	$\sin x$	$\dfrac{1}{x}$	$\ln x$
$\sec^2 x$	$\tan x$	$\dfrac{1}{x^2 + a^2}$	$\dfrac{1}{a}\tan^{-1}\dfrac{x}{a}$
$\csc^2 x$	$-\cot x$	$\dfrac{1}{\sqrt{a^2 - x^2}}$	$\sin^{-1}\dfrac{x}{a}$
$\sec x \tan x$	$\sec x$		
$\csc x \cot x$	$-\csc x$		

Some useful rules for integration are as follows:

(a) $\int c\,f(x)\,dx = c\int f(x)\,dx$ where c is a constant

(b) Let $\int f(x)\,dx = F(x)$

then $\int f(cx)\,dx = \dfrac{1}{c}F(cx)$.

(c) $\int [\,f(x) + g(x)\,]\,dx = \int f(x)\,dx + \int g(x)\,dx$.

Example 2.9

Evaluate $\displaystyle\int_3^6 (2x^2 + 3x + 5)\,dx$.

Solution : $\int (2x^2 + 3x + 5)\,dx$

$= \int 2x^2\,dx + \int 3x\,dx + \int 5\,dx$

$= 2\int x^2\,dx + 3\int x\,dx + 5\int x^0\,dx$

$= 2\dfrac{x^3}{3} + 3\dfrac{x^2}{2} + 5\dfrac{x^1}{1}$

$= \dfrac{2}{3}x^3 + \dfrac{3}{2}x^2 + 5x$.

Thus, $\displaystyle\int_3^6 (2x^2 + 3x + 5)\,dx = \left[\dfrac{2}{3}x^3 + \dfrac{3}{2}x^2 + 5x\right]_3^6$

$= \dfrac{2}{3}(216 - 27) + \dfrac{3}{2}(36 - 9) + 5(6 - 3)$

$= 126 + 40\cdot 5 + 15 = 181\cdot 5$.

2.12 SIGNIFICANT DIGITS

When a measurement is made, a numerical value is read generally from some calibrated scale. To measure the length of a body we can place a metre scale in contact with the body. One end of the body may be made to coincide with the zero of the metre scale and the reading just in front of the other end is noted from the scale. When an electric current is measured with an ammeter the reading of the pointer on the graduation of the ammeter is noted. The value noted down includes all the digits that can be directly read from the scale and one doubtful digit at the end. The doubtful digit corresponds to the eye estimation within the smallest subdivision of the scale. This smallest subdivision is known as the *least count* of the instrument. In a metre scale, the major graduations are at an interval of one centimetre and ten subdivisions are made between two consecutive major graduations. Thus, the smallest subdivision measures a millimetre. If one end of the object coincides with the zero of the metre scale, the other end may fall between 10·4 cm and 10·5 cm mark of the scale (figure 2.19). We can estimate the distance between the 10·4 cm mark and the edge of the body as follows.

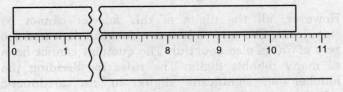

Figure 2.19

We mentally divide the 1 mm division in 10 equal parts and guess on which part is the edge falling. We may note down the reading as 10·46 cm. The digits 1, 0 and 4 are certain but 6 is doubtful. All these digits are called *significant digits*. We say that the length is measured up to four significant digits. The rightmost or the doubtful digit is called the *least significant digit* and the leftmost digit is called the *most significant digit*.

There may be some confusion if there are zeroes at the right end of the number. For example, if a measurement is quoted as 600 mm and we know nothing about the least count of the scale we cannot be sure whether the last zeros are significant or not. If the scale had marking only at each metre then the edge must be between the marks 0 m and 1 m and the digit 6 is obtained only through the eye estimation. Thus, 6 is the doubtful digit and the zeros after that are insignificant. But if the scale had markings at centimetres, the number read is 60 and these two digits are significant, the last zero is insignificant. If the scale used had markings at millimetres, all the three digits 6, 0, 0 are significant. To avoid confusion one may report only the significant digits and the magnitude may be correctly described by proper powers of 10. For example, if only 6 is significant in 600 mm we may write it as 6×10^2 mm. If 6 and the first zero are significant we may write it as $6 \cdot 0 \times 10^2$ mm and if all the three digits are significant we may write it as $6 \cdot 00 \times 10^2$ mm.

If the integer part is zero, any number of continuous zeros just after the decimal part is insignificant. Thus, the number of significant digits in 0·0023 is two and in 1·0023 is five.

2.13 SIGNIFICANT DIGITS IN CALCULATIONS

When two or more numbers are added, subtracted, multiplied or divided, how to decide about the number of significant digits in the answer ? For example, suppose the mass of a body A is measured to be 12·0 kg and of another body B to be 7·0 kg. What is the ratio of the mass of A to the mass of B ? Arithmetic will give this ratio as

$$\frac{12 \cdot 0}{7 \cdot 0} = 1 \cdot 714285\ldots$$

However, all the digits of this answer cannot be significant. The zero of 12·0 is a doubtful digit and the zero of 7·0 is also doubtful. The quotient cannot have so many reliable digits. The rules for deciding the number of significant digits in an arithmetic calculation are listed below.

1. In a multiplication or division of two or more quantities, the number of significant digits in the answer is equal to the number of significant digits in the quantity which has the minimum number of significant digits. Thus, $\frac{12 \cdot 0}{7 \cdot 0}$ will have two significant digits only.

The insignificant digits are dropped from the result if they appear after the decimal point. They are replaced by zeros if they appear to the left of the decimal point. The least significant digit is rounded according to the rules given below.

If the digit next to the one rounded is more than 5, the digit to be rounded is increased by 1. If the digit next to the one rounded is less than 5, the digit to be rounded is left unchanged. If the digit next to the one rounded is 5, then the digit to be rounded is increased by 1 if it is odd and is left unchanged if it is even.

2. For addition or subtraction write the numbers one below the other with all the decimal points in one line. Now locate the first column from left that has a doubtful digit. All digits right to this column are dropped from all the numbers and rounding is done to this column. The addition or subtraction is now performed to get the answer.

Example 2.10

Round off the following numbers to three significant digits (a) 15462, (b) 14·745, (c) 14·750 and (d) 14·650 $\times 10^{12}$.

Solution : (a) The third significant digit is 4. This digit is to be rounded. The digit next to it is 6 which is greater than 5. The third digit should, therefore, be increased by 1. The digits to be dropped should be replaced by zeros because they appear to the left of the decimal. Thus, 15462 becomes 15500 on rounding to three significant digits.

(b) The third significant digit in 14·745 is 7. The number next to it is less than 5. So 14·745 becomes 14·7 on rounding to three significant digits.

(c) 14·750 will become 14·8 because the digit to be rounded is odd and the digit next to it is 5.

(d) 14·650 $\times 10^{12}$ will become 14·6 $\times 10^{12}$ because the digit to be rounded is even and the digit next to it is 5.

Example 2.11

Evaluate $\frac{25 \cdot 2 \times 1374}{33 \cdot 3}$. All the digits in this expression are significant.

Solution : We have $\frac{25 \cdot 2 \times 1374}{33 \cdot 3} = 1039 \cdot 7838\ldots$

Out of the three numbers given in the expression 25·2 and 33·3 have 3 significant digits and 1374 has four. The answer should have three significant digits. Rounding 1039·7838... to three significant digits, it becomes 1040. Thus, we write

$$\frac{25 \cdot 2 \times 1374}{33 \cdot 3} = 1040.$$

Example 2.12

Evaluate $24·36 + 0·0623 + 256·2.$

Solution :

$$24·36$$
$$0·0623$$
$$256·2$$

Now the first column where a doubtful digit occurs is the one just next to the decimal point (256·2). All digits right to this column must be dropped after proper rounding. The table is rewritten and added below

$$24·4$$
$$0·1$$
$$256·2$$
$$280·7$$

The sum is 280·7.

2.14 ERRORS IN MEASUREMENT

While doing an experiment several errors can enter into the results. Errors may be due to faulty equipment, carelessness of the experimenter or random causes. The first two types of errors can be removed after detecting their cause but the random errors still remain. No specific cause can be assigned to such errors.

When an experiment is repeated many times, the random errors are sometimes positive and sometimes negative. Thus, the average of a large number of the results of repeated experiments is close to the true value. However, there is still some uncertainty about the truth of this average. The uncertainty is estimated by calculating the standard deviation described below.

Let $x_1, x_2, x_3, ..., x_N$ are the results of an experiment repeated N times. The standard deviation σ is defined as

$$\sigma = \sqrt{\frac{1}{N} \sum_{i=1}^{N} (x_i - \bar{x})^2}$$

where $\bar{x} = \frac{1}{N} \sum_i x_i$ is the average of all the values of x.

The best value of x derived from these experiments is $\bar{x}$ and the uncertainty is of the order of $\pm \sigma$. In fact $\bar{x} \pm 1·96\,\sigma$ is quite often taken as the interval in which the true value should lie. It can be shown that there is a 95% chance that the true value lies within $\bar{x} \pm 1·96\,\sigma$.

If one wishes to be more sure, one can use the interval $\bar{x} \pm 3\,\sigma$ as the interval which will contain the true value. The chances that the true value will be within $\bar{x} \pm 3\,\sigma$ is more that 99%.

All this is true if the number of observations N is large. In practice if N is greater than 8, the results are reasonably correct.

Example 2.13

The focal length of a concave mirror obtained by a student in repeated experiments are given below. Find the average focal length with uncertainty in $\pm \sigma$ limit.

No. of observation	focal length in cm
1	25·4
2	25·2
3	25·6
4	25·1
5	25·3
6	25·2
7	25·5
8	25·4
9	25·3
10	25·7

Solution : The average focal length $\bar{f} = \frac{1}{10} \sum_{i=1}^{10} f_i$

$$= 25·37 \approx 25·4.$$

The calculation of σ is shown in the table below:

i	f_i cm	$f_i - \bar{f}$ cm	$(f_i - \bar{f})^2$ cm^2	$\Sigma (f_i - \bar{f})^2$ cm^2
1	25·4	0·0	0·00	
2	25·2	− 0·2	0·04	
3	25·6	0·2	0·04	
4	25·1	− 0·3	0·09	
5	25·3	− 0·1	0·01	0·33
6	25·2	− 0·2	0·04	
7	25·5	0·1	0·01	
8	25·4	0·0	0·00	
9	25·3	− 0·1	0·01	
10	25·7	0·3	0·09	

$$\sigma = \sqrt{\frac{1}{10} \sum_i (f_i - \bar{f})^2} = \sqrt{0·033 \text{ cm}^2} = 0·18 \text{ cm}$$

$$\cong 0·2 \text{ cm}.$$

Thus, the focal length is likely to be within (25·4 ± 0·2 cm) and we write

$$f = (25·4 \pm 0·2) \text{ cm}.$$

Worked Out Examples

1. *A vector has component along the X-axis equal to 25 unit and along the Y-axis equal to 60 unit. Find the magnitude and direction of the vector.*

Solution : The given vector is the resultant of two perpendicular vectors, one along the X-axis of magnitude 25 unit and the other along the Y-axis of magnitude 60 units. The resultant has a magnitude A given by

$$A = \sqrt{(25)^2 + (60)^2 + 2 \times 25 \times 60 \cos 90°}$$

$$= \sqrt{(25)^2 + (60)^2} = 65.$$

The angle α between this vector and the X-axis is given by

$$\tan\alpha = \frac{60}{25}.$$

2. *Find the resultant of the three vectors shown in figure (2-W1).*

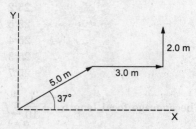

Figure 2-W1

Solution : Take the axes as shown in the figure.

The x-component of the 5·0 m vector = 5·0 m cos37°
$$= 4·0 \text{ m,}$$

the x-component of the 3·0 m vector = 3·0 m

and the x-component of the 2·0 m vector = 2·0 m cos90°
$$= 0.$$

Hence, the x-component of the resultant
$$= 4·0 \text{ m} + 3·0 \text{ m} + 0 = 7·0 \text{ m.}$$

The y-component of the 5·0 m vector = 5·0 m sin37°
$$= 3·0 \text{ m,}$$

the y-component of the 3·0 m vector = 0

and the y-component of the 2·0 m vector = 2·0 m.

Hence, the y-component of the resultant
$$= 3·0 \text{ m} + 0 + 2·0 \text{ m} = 5·0 \text{ m.}$$

The magnitude of the resultant vector

$$= \sqrt{(7·0 \text{ m})^2 + (5·0 \text{ m})^2}$$

$$= 8·6 \text{ m.}$$

If the angle made by the resultant with the X-axis is θ, then

$$\tan\theta = \frac{y\text{-component}}{x\text{-component}} = \frac{5·0}{7·0} \text{ or, } \theta = 35·5°.$$

3. *The sum of the three vectors shown in figure (2-W2) is zero. Find the magnitudes of the vectors $\overrightarrow{OB}$ and $\overrightarrow{OC}$.*

Solution : Take the axes as shown in the figure

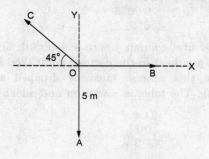

Figure 2-W2

The x-component of $\overrightarrow{OA} = (OA)\cos 90° = 0$.

The x-component of $\overrightarrow{OB} = (OB)\cos 0° = OB$.

The x-component of $\overrightarrow{OC} = (OC)\cos 135° = -\frac{1}{\sqrt{2}} OC$.

Hence, the x-component of the resultant

$$= OB - \frac{1}{\sqrt{2}} OC. \qquad \text{... (i)}$$

It is given that the resultant is zero and hence its x-component is also zero. From (i),

$$OB = \frac{1}{\sqrt{2}} OC. \qquad \text{... (ii)}$$

The y-component of $\overrightarrow{OA} = OA \cos 180° = -OA$.

The y-component of $\overrightarrow{OB} = OB \cos 90° = 0$.

The y-component of $\overrightarrow{OC} = OC \cos 45° = \frac{1}{\sqrt{2}} OC$.

Hence, the y-component of the resultant

$$= \frac{1}{\sqrt{2}} OC - OA \qquad \text{... (iii)}$$

As the resultant is zero, so is its y-component. From (iii),

$$\frac{1}{\sqrt{2}} OC = OA, \text{ or, } OC = \sqrt{2} \, OA = 5\sqrt{2} \text{ m.}$$

From (ii), $OB = \frac{1}{\sqrt{2}} OC = 5$ m.

4. *The magnitudes of vectors $\overrightarrow{OA}$, $\overrightarrow{OB}$ and $\overrightarrow{OC}$ in figure (2-W3) are equal. Find the direction of $\overrightarrow{OA} + \overrightarrow{OB} - \overrightarrow{OC}$.*

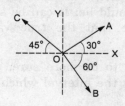

Figure 2-W3

Solution : Let $OA = OB = OC = F$.

x-component of $\overrightarrow{OA} = F \cos 30° = F\dfrac{\sqrt{3}}{2}$.

x-component of $\overrightarrow{OB} = F \cos 60° = \dfrac{F}{2}$.

x-component of $\overrightarrow{OC} = F \cos 135° = -\dfrac{F}{\sqrt{2}}$.

x-component of $\overrightarrow{OA} + \overrightarrow{OB} - \overrightarrow{OC}$

$$= \left(\dfrac{F\sqrt{3}}{2}\right) + \left(\dfrac{F}{2}\right) - \left(-\dfrac{F}{\sqrt{2}}\right)$$

$$= \dfrac{F}{2}(\sqrt{3} + 1 + \sqrt{2}).$$

y-component of $\overrightarrow{OA} = F \cos 60° = \dfrac{F}{2}$.

y-component of $\overrightarrow{OB} = F \cos 150° = -\dfrac{F\sqrt{3}}{2}$.

y-component of $\overrightarrow{OC} = F \cos 45° = \dfrac{F}{\sqrt{2}}$.

y-component of $\overrightarrow{OA} + \overrightarrow{OB} - \overrightarrow{OC}$

$$= \left(\dfrac{F}{2}\right) + \left(-\dfrac{F\sqrt{3}}{2}\right) - \left(\dfrac{F}{\sqrt{2}}\right)$$

$$= \dfrac{F}{2}(1 - \sqrt{3} - \sqrt{2}).$$

Angle of $\overrightarrow{OA} + \overrightarrow{OB} - \overrightarrow{OC}$ with the X-axis

$$= \tan^{-1} \dfrac{\dfrac{F}{2}(1 - \sqrt{3} - \sqrt{2})}{\dfrac{F}{2}(1 + \sqrt{3} + \sqrt{2})} = \tan^{-1}\dfrac{(1 - \sqrt{3} - \sqrt{2})}{(1 + \sqrt{3} + \sqrt{2})}.$$

5. *Find the resultant of the three vectors $\overrightarrow{OA}$, $\overrightarrow{OB}$ and $\overrightarrow{OC}$ shown in figure (2-W4). Radius of the circle is R.*

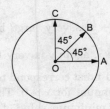

Figure 2-W4

Solution : $OA = OC$.

$\overrightarrow{OA} + \overrightarrow{OC}$ is along $\overrightarrow{OB}$ (bisector) and its magnitude is
$$2R \cos 45° = R\sqrt{2}.$$

$(\overrightarrow{OA} + \overrightarrow{OC}) + \overrightarrow{OB}$ is along $\overrightarrow{OB}$ and its magnitude is
$$R\sqrt{2} + R = R(1 + \sqrt{2}).$$

6. *The resultant of vectors $\overrightarrow{OA}$ and $\overrightarrow{OB}$ is perpendicular to $\overrightarrow{OA}$ (figure 2-W5). Find the angle AOB.*

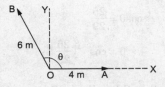

Figure 2-W5

Solution : Take the dotted lines as X, Y axes.

x-component of $\overrightarrow{OA} = 4$ m, x-component of $\overrightarrow{OB} = 6$ m $\cos\theta$.

x-component of the resultant $= (4 + 6\cos\theta)$ m.

But it is given that the resultant is along Y-axis. Thus, the x-component of the resultant $= 0$

$$4 + 6\cos\theta = 0 \quad \text{or,} \quad \cos\theta = -2/3.$$

7. *Write the unit vector in the direction of $\vec{A} = 5\,\vec{i} + \vec{j} - 2\,\vec{k}$.*

Solution : $|\vec{A}| = \sqrt{5^2 + 1^2 + (-2)^2} = \sqrt{30}$.

The required unit vector is $\dfrac{\vec{A}}{|\vec{A}|}$

$$= \dfrac{5}{\sqrt{30}}\vec{i} + \dfrac{1}{\sqrt{30}}\vec{j} - \dfrac{2}{\sqrt{30}}\vec{k}.$$

8. *If $|\vec{a} + \vec{b}| = |\vec{a} - \vec{b}|$ show that $\vec{a} \perp \vec{b}$.*

Solution : We have $|\vec{a} + \vec{b}|^2 = (\vec{a} + \vec{b}) \cdot (\vec{a} + \vec{b})$

$$= \vec{a} \cdot \vec{a} + \vec{a} \cdot \vec{b} + \vec{b} \cdot \vec{a} + \vec{b} \cdot \vec{b}$$

$$= a^2 + b^2 + 2\,\vec{a} \cdot \vec{b}.$$

Similarly,

$$|\vec{a} - \vec{b}|^2 = (\vec{a} - \vec{b}) \cdot (\vec{a} - \vec{b})$$

$$= a^2 + b^2 - 2\,\vec{a} \cdot \vec{b}.$$

If $|\vec{a} + \vec{b}| = |\vec{a} - \vec{b}|$,

$$a^2 + b^2 + 2\,\vec{a} \cdot \vec{b} = a^2 + b^2 - 2\,\vec{a} \cdot \vec{b}$$

or, $\vec{a} \cdot \vec{b} = 0$

or, $\vec{a} \perp \vec{b}$.

9. *If $\vec{a} = 2\,\vec{i} + 3\,\vec{j} + 4\,\vec{k}$ and $\vec{b} = 4\,\vec{i} + 3\,\vec{j} + 2\,\vec{k}$, find the angle between $\vec{a}$ and $\vec{b}$.*

Solution : We have $\vec{a} \cdot \vec{b} = ab \cos\theta$

or, $\cos\theta = \dfrac{\vec{a} \cdot \vec{b}}{ab}$

where θ is the angle between $\vec{a}$ and $\vec{b}$.

Now $\vec{a} \cdot \vec{b} = a_x b_x + a_y b_y + a_z b_z$

$$= 2 \times 4 + 3 \times 3 + 4 \times 2 = 25.$$

Also $a = \sqrt{a_x^2 + a_y^2 + a_z^2}$

$$= \sqrt{4 + 9 + 16} = \sqrt{29}$$

and $b = \sqrt{b_x^2 + b_y^2 + b_z^2} = \sqrt{16 + 9 + 4} = \sqrt{29}$.

Thus, $\cos\theta = \dfrac{25}{29}$

or, $\theta = \cos^{-1}\left(\dfrac{25}{29}\right).$

10. *If* $\vec{A} = 2\,\vec{i} - 3\,\vec{j} + 7\,\vec{k},\;\; \vec{B} = \vec{i} + 2\,\vec{k}\;\; and\;\; \vec{C} = \vec{j} - \vec{k}\;\; find$ $\vec{A} \cdot (\vec{B} \times \vec{C}).$

Solution : $\vec{B} \times \vec{C} = (\vec{i} + 2\,\vec{k}) \times (\vec{j} - \vec{k})$

$$= \vec{i} \times (\vec{j} - \vec{k}) + 2\,\vec{k} \times (\vec{j} - \vec{k})$$

$$= \vec{i} \times \vec{j} - \vec{i} \times \vec{k} + 2\,\vec{k} \times \vec{j} - 2\,\vec{k} \times \vec{k}$$

$$= \vec{k} + \vec{j} - 2\,\vec{i} - 0 = -2\,\vec{i} + \vec{j} + \vec{k}.$$

$$\vec{A} \cdot (\vec{B} \times \vec{C}) = (2\,\vec{i} - 3\,\vec{j} + 7\,\vec{k}) \cdot (-2\,\vec{i} + \vec{j} + \vec{k})$$

$$= (2)\,(-2) + (-3)\,(1) + (7)\,(1)$$

$$= 0.$$

11. *The volume of a sphere is given by*

$$V = \dfrac{4}{3}\,\pi\,R^{3}$$

where R is the radius of the sphere. (a) Find the rate of change of volume with respect to R. (b) Find the change in volume of the sphere as the radius is increased from 20·0 *cm to* 20·1 *cm. Assume that the rate does not appreciably change between R =* 20·0 *cm to R =* 20·1 *cm.*

Solution : (a) $V = \dfrac{4}{3}\,\pi\,R^{3}$

or, $\dfrac{dV}{dR} = \dfrac{4}{3}\,\pi\,\dfrac{d}{dR}\,(R)^{3} = \dfrac{4}{3}\,\pi \cdot 3R^{2} = 4\,\pi\,R^{2}.$

(b) At $R = 20$ cm, the rate of change of volume with the radius is

$$\dfrac{dV}{dR} = 4\,\pi\,R^{2} = 4\,\pi\,(400\ \text{cm}^{2})$$

$$= 1600\,\pi\ \text{cm}^{2}.$$

The change in volume as the radius changes from 20·0 cm to 20·1 cm is

$$\Delta V = \dfrac{dV}{dR}\,\Delta R$$

$$= (1600\,\pi\ \text{cm}^{2})\,(0·1\ \text{cm})$$

$$= 160\,\pi\ \text{cm}^{3}.$$

12. *Find the derivative of the following functions with respect to x. (a)* $y = x^{2}\sin x,$ *(b)* $y = \dfrac{\sin x}{x}$ *and (c)* $y = \sin(x^{2}).$

Solution :

(a) $y = x^{2}\sin x$

$$\dfrac{dy}{dx} = x^{2}\,\dfrac{d}{dx}\,(\sin x) + (\sin x)\,\dfrac{d}{dx}\,(x^{2})$$

$$= x^{2}\cos x + (\sin x)\,(2x)$$

$$= x(2\sin x + x\cos x).$$

(b) $y = \dfrac{\sin x}{x}$

$$\dfrac{dy}{dx} = \dfrac{x\,\dfrac{d}{dx}\,(\sin x) - \sin x\left(\dfrac{dx}{dx}\right)}{x^{2}}$$

$$= \dfrac{x\cos x - \sin x}{x^{2}}.$$

(c) $\dfrac{dy}{dx} = \dfrac{d}{dx^{2}}\,(\sin x^{2}) \cdot \dfrac{d(x^{2})}{dx}$

$$= \cos x^{2}\,(2x)$$

$$= 2x\cos x^{2}.$$

13. *Find the maximum or minimum values of the function* $y = x + \dfrac{1}{x}$ *for* $x > 0.$

Solution : $y = x + \dfrac{1}{x}$

$$\dfrac{dy}{dx} = \dfrac{d}{dx}\,(x) + \dfrac{d}{dx}\,(x^{-1})$$

$$= 1 + (-x^{-2})$$

$$= 1 - \dfrac{1}{x^{2}}.$$

For y to be maximum or minimum,

$$\dfrac{dy}{dx} = 0$$

or, $1 - \dfrac{1}{x^{2}} = 0$

Thus, $x = 1\;\; \text{or}\;\; -1.$

For $x > 0$ the only possible maximum or minimum is at $x = 1$. At $x = 1$, $y = x + \dfrac{1}{x} = 2.$

Near $x = 0$, $y = x + \dfrac{1}{x}$ is very large because of the term $\dfrac{1}{x}$. For very large x, again y is very large because of the term x. Thus $x = 1$ must correspond to a minimum. Thus, y has only a minimum for $x > 0$. This minimum occurs at $x = 1$ and the minimum value of y is $y = 2.$

14. *Figure (2-W6) shows the curve* $y = x^{2}.$ *Find the area of the shaded part between* $x = 0$ *and* $x = 6.$

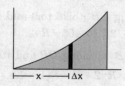

Figure 2-W6

Solution : The area can be divided into strips by drawing ordinates between $x = 0$ and $x = 6$ at a regular interval of dx. Consider the strip between the ordinates at x and $x + dx$. The height of this strip is $y = x^2$. The area of this strip is $dA = y\, dx = x^2 dx$.

The total area of the shaded part is obtained by summing up these strip-areas with x varying from 0 to 6. Thus

$$A = \int_0^6 x^2\, dx$$

$$= \left[\frac{x^3}{3}\right]_0^6 = \frac{216 - 0}{3} = 72.$$

15. Evaluate $\int_0^t A \sin \omega t\, dt$ where A and ω are constants.

Solution : $\quad \int_0^t A \sin \omega t\, dt$

$$= A\left[\frac{-\cos \omega t}{\omega}\right]_0^t = \frac{A}{\omega}(1 - \cos \omega t).$$

16. The velocity v and displacement x of a particle executing simple harmonic motion are related as

$$v\frac{dv}{dx} = -\omega^2 x.$$

At $x = 0$, $v = v_0$. Find the velocity v when the displacement becomes x.

Solution : We have

$$v\frac{dv}{dx} = -\omega^2 x$$

or, $\qquad v\, dv = -\omega^2 x\, dx$

or, $\qquad \int_{v_0}^v v\, dv = \int_0^x -\omega^2 x\, dx \qquad \ldots \text{(i)}$

When summation is made on $-\omega^2 x\, dx$ the quantity to be varied is x. When summation is made on $v\, dv$ the quantity to be varied is v. As x varies from 0 to x the velocity varies from v_0 to v. Therefore, on the left the limits of integration are from v_0 to v and on the right they are from 0 to x. Simplifying (i),

$$\left[\frac{1}{2}v^2\right]_{v_0}^v = -\omega^2\left[\frac{x^2}{2}\right]_0^x$$

or, $\qquad \frac{1}{2}(v^2 - v_0^2) = -\omega^2 \frac{x^2}{2}$

or, $\qquad v^2 = v_0^2 - \omega^2 x^2$

or, $\qquad v = \sqrt{v_0^2 - \omega^2 x^2}.$

17. The charge flown through a circuit in the time interval between t and $t + dt$ is given by $dq = e^{-t/\tau}\, dt$, where τ is a constant. Find the total charge flown through the circuit between $t = 0$ to $t = \tau$.

Solution : The total charge flown is the sum of all the dq's for t varying from $t = 0$ to $t = \tau$. Thus, the total charge flown is

$$Q = \int_0^\tau e^{-t/\tau}\, dt$$

$$= \left[\frac{e^{-t/\tau}}{-\frac{1}{\tau}}\right]_0^\tau = \tau\left(1 - \frac{1}{e}\right).$$

18. Evaluate $(21\cdot6002 + 234 + 2732\cdot10) \times 13$.

Solution :

21.6002	22
234	$\Rightarrow$ 234
2732.10	2732
	2988

The three numbers are arranged with their decimal points aligned (shown on the left part above). The column just left to the decimals has 4 as the doubtful digit. Thus, all the numbers are rounded to this column. The rounded numbers are shown on the right part above. The required expression is $2988 \times 13 = 38844$. As 13 has only two significant digits the product should be rounded off after two significant digits. Thus the result is 39000.

□

QUESTIONS FOR SHORT ANSWER

1. Is a vector necessarily changed if it is rotated through an angle ?

2. Is it possible to add two vectors of unequal magnitudes and get zero ? Is it possible to add three vectors of equal magnitudes and get zero ?

3. Does the phrase "direction of zero vector" have physical significance ? Discuss in terms of velocity, force etc.

4. Can you add three unit vectors to get a unit vector ? Does your answer change if two unit vectors are along the coordinate axes ?

5. Can we have physical quantities having magnitude and direction which are not vectors ?

6. Which of the following two statements is more appropriate ?

   (a) Two forces are added using triangle rule because force is a vector quantity.
   (b) Force is a vector quantity because two forces are added using triangle rule.

7. Can you add two vectors representing physical quantities having different dimensions ? Can you multiply two vectors representing physical quantities having different dimensions ?

8. Can a vector have zero component along a line and still have nonzero magnitude ?

9. Let ε_1 and ε_2 be the angles made by $\vec{A}$ and $-\vec{A}$ with the positive X-axis. Show that $\tan\varepsilon_1 = \tan\varepsilon_2$. Thus, giving $\tan\varepsilon$ does not uniquely determine the direction of $\vec{A}$.

10. Is the vector sum of the unit vectors $\vec{i}$ and $\vec{j}$ a unit vector ? If no, can you multiply this sum by a scalar number to get a unit vector ?

11. Let $\vec{A} = 3\,\vec{i} + 4\,\vec{j}$. Write four vector $\vec{B}$ such that $\vec{A} \neq \vec{B}$ but $A = B$.

12. Can you have $\vec{A} \times \vec{B} = \vec{A} \cdot \vec{B}$ with $A \neq 0$ and $B \neq 0$? What if one of the two vectors is zero ?

13. If $\vec{A} \times \vec{B} = 0$, can you say that (a) $\vec{A} = \vec{B}$, (b) $\vec{A} \neq \vec{B}$?

14. Let $\vec{A} = 5\,\vec{i} - 4\,\vec{j}$ and $\vec{B} = -7{\cdot}5\,\vec{i} + 6\,\vec{j}$. Do we have $\vec{B} = k\,\vec{A}$? Can we say $\dfrac{\vec{B}}{\vec{A}} = k$?

OBJECTIVE I

1. A vector is not changed if
   (a) it is rotated through an arbitrary angle
   (b) it is multiplied by an arbitrary scalar
   (c) it is cross multiplied by a unit vector
   (d) it is slid parallel to itself.

2. Which of the sets given below may represent the magnitudes of three vectors adding to zero ?
   (a) 2, 4, 8   (b) 4, 8, 16   (c) 1, 2, 1   (d) 0·5, 1, 2.

3. The resultant of $\vec{A}$ and $\vec{B}$ makes an angle α with $\vec{A}$ and β with $\vec{B}$,
   (a) $\alpha < \beta$
   (b) $\alpha < \beta$ if $A < B$
   (c) $\alpha < \beta$ if $A > B$
   (d) $\alpha < \beta$ if $A = B$.

4. The component of a vector is
   (a) always less than its magnitude
   (b) always greater than its magnitude
   (c) always equal to its magnitude
   (d) none of these.

5. A vector $\vec{A}$ points vertically upward and $\vec{B}$ points towards north. The vector product $\vec{A} \times \vec{B}$ is
   (a) along west   (b) along east
   (c) zero   (d) vertically downward.

6. The radius of a circle is stated as 2·12 cm. Its area should be written as
   (a) 14 cm^2 (b) 14·1 cm^2 (c) 14·11 cm^2 (d) 14·1124 cm^2.

OBJECTIVE II

1. A situation may be described by using different sets of coordinate axes having different orientations. Which of the following do not depend on the orientation of the axes ?
   (a) the value of a scalar   (b) component of a vector
   (c) a vector   (d) the magnitude of a vector.

2. Let $\vec{C} = \vec{A} + \vec{B}$.
   (a) $|\vec{C}|$ is always greater than $|\vec{A}|$
   (b) It is possible to have $|\vec{C}| < |\vec{A}|$ and $|\vec{C}| < |\vec{B}|$
   (c) C is always equal to $A + B$
   (d) C is never equal to $A + B$.

3. Let the angle between two nonzero vectors $\vec{A}$ and $\vec{B}$ be 120° and its resultant be $\vec{C}$.

   (a) C must be equal to $|A - B|$
   (b) C must be less than $|A - B|$
   (c) C must be greater than $|A - B|$
   (d) C may be equal to $|A - B|$.

4. The x-component of the resultant of several vectors
   (a) is equal to the sum of the x-components of the vectors
   (b) may be smaller than the sum of the magnitudes of the vectors
   (c) may be greater than the sum of the magnitudes of the vectors
   (d) may be equal to the sum of the magnitudes of the vectors.

5. The magnitude of the vector product of two vectors $|\vec{A}|$ and $|\vec{B}|$ may be
   (a) greater than AB (b) equal to AB
   (c) less than AB (d) equal to zero.

EXERCISES

1. A vector $\vec{A}$ makes an angle of 20° and $\vec{B}$ makes an angle of 110° with the X-axis. The magnitudes of these vectors are 3 m and 4 m respectively. Find the resultant.

2. Let $\vec{A}$ and $\vec{B}$ be the two vectors of magnitude 10 unit each. If they are inclined to the X-axis at angles 30° and 60° respectively, find the resultant.

3. Add vectors $\vec{A}$, $\vec{B}$ and $\vec{C}$ each having magnitude of 100 unit and inclined to the X-axis at angles 45°, 135° and 315° respectively.

4. Let $\vec{a} = 4\,\vec{i} + 3\,\vec{j}$ and $\vec{b} = 3\,\vec{i} + 4\,\vec{j}$. (a) Find the magnitudes of (a) $\vec{a}$, (b) $\vec{b}$, (c) $\vec{a} + \vec{b}$ and (d) $\vec{a} - \vec{b}$.

5. Refer to figure (2-E1). Find (a) the magnitude, (b) x and y components and (c) the angle with the X-axis of the resultant of $\overrightarrow{OA}$, $\overrightarrow{BC}$ and $\overrightarrow{DE}$.

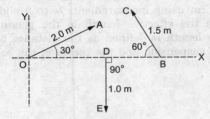

Figure 2-E1

6. Two vectors have magnitudes 3 unit and 4 unit respectively. What should be the angle between them if the magnitude of the resultant is (a) 1 unit, (b) 5 unit and (c) 7 unit.

7. A spy report about a suspected car reads as follows. "The car moved 2·00 km towards east, made a perpendicular left turn, ran for 500 m, made a perpendicular right turn, ran for 4·00 km and stopped". Find the displacement of the car.

8. A carrom board (4 ft × 4 ft square) has the queen at the centre. The queen, hit by the striker moves to the front edge, rebounds and goes in the hole behind the striking line. Find the magnitude of displacement of the queen (a) from the centre to the front edge, (b) from the front edge to the hole and (c) from the centre to the hole.

9. A mosquito net over a 7 ft × 4 ft bed is 3 ft high. The net has a hole at one corner of the bed through which a mosquito enters the net. It flies and sits at the diagonally opposite upper corner of the net. (a) Find the magnitude of the displacement of the mosquito. (b) Taking the hole as the origin, the length of the bed as the X-axis, its width as the Y-axis, and vertically up as the Z-axis, write the components of the displacement vector.

10. Suppose $\vec{a}$ is a vector of magnitude 4·5 unit due north. What is the vector (a) $3\,\vec{a}$, (b) $-4\,\vec{a}$?

11. Two vectors have magnitudes 2 m and 3 m. The angle between them is 60°. Find (a) the scalar product of the two vectors, (b) the magnitude of their vector product.

12. Let $A_1 A_2 A_3 A_4 A_5 A_6 A_1$ be a regular hexagon. Write the x-components of the vectors represented by the six sides taken in order. Use the fact that the resultant of these six vectors is zero, to prove that
$\cos 0 + \cos \pi/3 + \cos 2\pi/3 + \cos 3\pi/3 + \cos 4\pi/3 + \cos 5\pi/3 = 0$.
Use the known cosine values to verify the result.

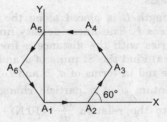

Figure 2-E2

13. Let $\vec{a} = 2\,\vec{i} + 3\,\vec{j} + 4\,\vec{k}$ and $\vec{b} = 3\,\vec{i} + 4\,\vec{j} + 5\,\vec{k}$. Find the angle between them.

14. Prove that $\vec{A} \cdot (\vec{A} \times \vec{B}) = 0$.

15. If $\vec{A} = 2\,\vec{i} + 3\,\vec{j} + 4\,\vec{k}$ and $\vec{B} = 4\,\vec{i} + 3\,\vec{j} + 2\,\vec{k}$, find $\vec{A} \times \vec{B}$.

16. If $\vec{A}$, $\vec{B}$, $\vec{C}$ are mutually perpendicular, show that $\vec{C} \times (\vec{A} \times \vec{B}) = 0$. Is the converse true?

17. A particle moves on a given straight line with a constant speed v. At a certain time it is at a point P on its straight line path. O is a fixed point. Show that $\overrightarrow{OP} \times \vec{v}$ is independent of the position P.

18. The force on a charged particle due to electric and magnetic fields is given by $\vec{F} = q\,\vec{E} + q\,\vec{v} \times \vec{B}$. Suppose $\vec{E}$ is along the X-axis and $\vec{B}$ along the Y-axis. In what direction and with what minimum speed v should a positively charged particle be sent so that the net force on it is zero?

19. Give an example for which $\vec{A} \cdot \vec{B} = \vec{C} \cdot \vec{B}$ but $\vec{A} \neq \vec{C}$.

20. Draw a graph from the following data. Draw tangents at $x = 2, 4, 6$ and 8. Find the slopes of these tangents. Verify that the curve drawn is $y = 2x^2$ and the slope of tangent is $\tan \theta = \dfrac{dy}{dx} = 4x$.

x	1	2	3	4	5	6	7	8	9	10
y	2	8	18	32	50	72	98	128	162	200

21. A curve is represented by $y = \sin x$. If x is changed from $\dfrac{\pi}{3}$ to $\dfrac{\pi}{3} + \dfrac{\pi}{100}$, find approximately the change in y.

22. The electric current in a charging R–C circuit is given by $i = i_0\, e^{-t/RC}$ where i_0, R and C are constant parameters of the circuit and t is time. Find the rate of change of current at (a) $t = 0$, (b) $t = RC$, (c) $t = 10\,RC$.

23. The electric current in a discharging R–C circuit is given by $i = i_0\, e^{-t/RC}$ where i_0, R and C are constant parameters and t is time. Let $i_0 = 2·00$ A, $R = 6·00 \times 10^5\,\Omega$

and $C = 0.500 \ \mu F$. (a) Find the current at $t = 0.3$ s. (b) Find the rate of change of current at $t = 0.3$ s. (c) Find approximately the current at $t = 0.31$ s.

24. Find the area bounded under the curve $y = 3x^2 + 6x + 7$ and the X-axis with the ordinates at $x = 5$ and $x = 10$.

25. Find the area enclosed by the curve $y = \sin x$ and the X-axis between $x = 0$ and $x = \pi$.

26. Find the area bounded by the curve $y = e^{-x}$, the X-axis and the Y-axis.

27. A rod of length L is placed along the X-axis between $x = 0$ and $x = L$. The linear density (mass/length) ρ of the rod varies with the distance x from the origin as $\rho = a + bx$. (a) Find the SI units of a and b. (b) Find the mass of the rod in terms of a, b and L.

28. The momentum p of a particle changes with time t according to the relation $\frac{dp}{dt} = (10 \ \text{N}) + (2 \ \text{N/s})t$. If the momentum is zero at $t = 0$, what will the momentum be at $t = 10$ s ?

29. The changes in a function y and the independent variable x are related as $\frac{dy}{dx} = x^2$. Find y as a function of x.

30. Write the number of significant digits in (a) 1001, (b) 100.1, (c) 100.10, (d) 0.001001.

31. A metre scale is graduated at every millimetre. How many significant digits will be there in a length measurement with this scale ?

32. Round the following numbers to 2 significant digits. (a) 3472, (b) 84.16, (c) 2.55 and (d) 28.5.

33. The length and the radius of a cylinder measured with a slide callipers are found to be 4.54 cm and 1.75 cm respectively. Calculate the volume of the cylinder.

34. The thickness of a glass plate is measured to be 2.17 mm, 2.17 mm and 2.18 mm at three different places. Find the average thickness of the plate from this data.

35. The length of the string of a simple pendulum is measured with a metre scale to be 90.0 cm. The radius of the bob plus the length of the hook is calculated to be 2.13 cm using measurements with a slide callipers. What is the effective length of the pendulum ? (The effective length is defined as the distance between the point of suspension and the centre of the bob.)

□

ANSWERS

OBJECTIVE I

1. (d)	2. (c)	3. (c)	4. (d)	5. (a)	6. (b)

OBJECTIVE II

1. (a), (c), (d)   2. (b)   3. (b)   4. (a), (b), (d)
5. (b), (c), (d)

EXERCISES

1. 5 m at 73° with X-axis
2. 20 cos15° unit at 45° with X-axis
3. 100 unit at 45° with X-axis
4. (a) 5   (b) 5   (c) $7\sqrt{2}$ (d) $\sqrt{2}$
5. (a) 1.6 m   (b) 0.98 m and 1.3 m respectively
   (c) $\tan^{-1}(1.32)$
6. (a) 180°   (b) 90°   (c) 0
7. 6.02 km, $\tan^{-1} \frac{1}{12}$.
8. (a) $\frac{2}{3} \sqrt{10}$ ft   (b) $\frac{4}{3} \sqrt{10}$ ft   (c) $2\sqrt{2}$ ft
9. (a) $\sqrt{74}$ ft   (b) 7 ft, 4 ft, 3 ft
10. (a) 13.5 unit due north   (b) 18 unit due south

11. (a) 3 m^2 (b) $3\sqrt{3}$ m^2
13. $\cos^{-1}(38/\sqrt{1450})$
15. $-6\vec{i} + 12\vec{j} - 6\vec{k}$
16. no
18. along Z-axis with speed E/B
21. 0.0157
22. (a) $\frac{-i_0}{RC}$ (b) $\frac{-i_0}{RCe}$ (c) $\frac{-i_0}{RCe^{10}}$
23. (a) $\frac{2.00}{e}$ A   (b) $\frac{-20}{3e}$ A/s   (c) $\frac{5.8}{3e}$ A
24. 1135
25. 2
26. 1
27. (a) kg/m, kg/m^2 (b) $aL + bL^2/2$
28. 200 kg–m/s
29. $y = \frac{x^3}{3} + C$
30. (a) 4   (b) 4   (c) 5   (d) 4
31. 1, 2, 3 or 4
32. (a) 3500   (b) 84   (c) 2.6   (d) 28
33. 43.7 cm^3
34. 2.17 mm
35. 92.1 cm

□

CHAPTER 3

REST AND MOTION : KINEMATICS

3.1 REST AND MOTION

When do we say that a body is at rest and when do we say that it is in motion ? You may say that if a body does not change its position as time passes it is at rest. If a body changes its position with time, it is said to be moving. But when do we say that it is not changing its position ? A book placed on the table remains on the table and we say that the book is at rest. However, if we station ourselves on the moon (the Appollo missions have made it possible), the whole earth is found to be changing its position and so the room, the table and the book are all continuously changing their positions. The book is at rest if it is viewed from the room, it is moving if it is viewed from the moon.

Motion is a combined property of the object under study and the observer. There is no meaning of rest or motion without the viewer. Nothing is in absolute rest or in absolute motion. The moon is moving with respect to the book and the book moves with respect to the moon. Take another example. A robber enters a train moving at great speed with respect to the ground, brings out his pistol and says "Don't move, stand still". The passengers stand still. The passengers are at rest with respect to the robber but are moving with respect to the rail track.

Figure 3.1

To locate the position of a particle we need a *frame of reference*. A convenient way to fix up the frame of reference is to choose three mutually perpendicular axes and name them *X-Y-Z* axes. The coordinates, (*x, y, z*) of the particle then specify the position of the

particle with respect to that frame. Add a clock into the frame of reference to measure the time. If all the three coordinates *x, y* and *z* of the particle remain unchanged as time passes, we say that the particle is at rest with respect to this frame. If any one or more coordinates change with time, we say that the body is moving with respect to this frame.

There is no rule or restriction on the choice of a frame. We can choose a frame of reference according to our convenience to describe the situation under study. Thus, when we are in a train it is convenient to choose a frame attached to our compartment. The coordinates of a suitcase placed on the upper berth do not change with time (unless the train gives a jerk) and we say that the suitcase is at rest in the train-frame. The different stations, electric poles, trees etc. change their coordinates and we say that they are moving in the train-frame. Thus, we say that "Bombay is coming" and "Pune has already passed".

In the following sections we shall assume that the frame of reference is already chosen and we are describing the motion of the objects in the chosen frame. Sometimes the choice of the frame is clear from the context and we do not mention it. Thus, when one says the car is travelling and the rickshaw is not, it is clear that all positions are measured from a frame attached to the road.

3.2 DISTANCE AND DISPLACEMENT

Suppose a particle is at *A* at time t_1 and at *B* at time t_2 with respect to a given frame (figure 3.2).

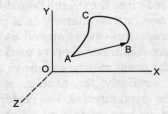

Figure 3.2

During the time interval t_1 to t_2 the particle moves along the path ACB. The length of the path ACB is called the *distance* travelled during the time interval t_1 to t_2. If we connect the initial position A with the final position B by a straight line, we get the *displacement* of the particle. The magnitude of the displacement is the length of the straight line joining the initial and the final position. The direction is from the initial to the final position. The displacement has both the magnitude as well as the direction. Further the displacements add according to the triangle rule of vector addition. Suppose a particle kept on a table is displaced on the table and at the same time the table is also displaced in the room. The net displacement of the particle in the room is obtained by the vector sum of the two displacements. Thus, displacement is a vector quantity. In contrast the distance covered has only a magnitude and is thus, a scalar quantity.

Example 3.1

An old person moves on a semi-circular track of radius 40·0 m during a morning walk. If he starts at one end of the track and reaches at the other end, find the distance covered and the displacement of the person.

Solution : The distance covered by the person equals the length of the track. It is equal to $\pi R = \pi \times 40·0$ m = 126 m.

The displacement is equal to the diameter of the semi-circular track joining the two ends. It is $2R = 2 \times 40·0$ m = 80 m. The direction of this displacement is from the initial point to the final point.

3.3 AVERAGE SPEED AND INSTANTANEOUS SPEED

The average speed of a particle in a time interval is defined as the distance travelled by the particle divided by the time interval. If the particle travels a distance s in time t_1 to t_2, the *average speed* is defined as

$$v_{av} = \frac{s}{t_2 - t_1}. \qquad \ldots (3.1)$$

The average speed gives the overall "rapidity" with which the particle moves in this interval. In a one-day cricket match, the average run rate is quoted as the total runs divided by the total number of overs used to make these runs. Some of the overs may be expensive and some may be economical. Similarly, the average speed gives the total effect in the given interval. The rapidity or slowness may vary from instant to instant. When an athelete starts running, he or she runs slowly and gradually

INDIA 210/4
Overs 42
Average Run rate 5.00
Runs in prev. over:16

Figure 3.3

increases the rate. We define the *instantaneous speed* at a time t as follows.

Let Δs be the distance travelled in the time interval t to $t + \Delta t$. The average speed in this time interval is

$$v_{av} = \frac{\Delta s}{\Delta t}.$$

Now make Δt vanishingly small and look for the value of $\frac{\Delta s}{\Delta t}$. Remember Δs is the distance travelled in the chosen time interval Δt. As Δt approaches 0, the distance Δs also approaches zero but the ratio $\frac{\Delta s}{\Delta t}$ has a finite limit.

The instantaneous speed at a time t is defined as

$$v = \lim_{\Delta t \to 0} \frac{\Delta s}{\Delta t} = \frac{ds}{dt} \qquad \ldots (3.2)$$

where s is the distance travelled in time t. The average speed is defined for a time interval and the instantaneous speed is defined at a particular instant. Instantaneous speed is also called "speed".

Example 3.2

The distance travelled by a particle in time t is given by $s = (2·5 \text{ m/s}^2)\, t^2$. Find (a) the average speed of the particle during the time 0 to 5·0 s, and (b) the instantaneous speed at $t = 5·0$ s.

Solution : (a) The distance travelled during time 0 to 5·0 s is

$$s = (2·5 \text{ m/s}^2)(5·0 \text{ s})^2 = 62·5 \text{ m}.$$

The average speed during this time is

$$v_{av} = \frac{62·5 \text{ m}}{5 \text{ s}} = 12·5 \text{ m/s}.$$

(b) $s = (2·5 \text{ m/s}^2)\, t^2$

or, $\frac{ds}{dt} = (2·5 \text{ m/s}^2)(2\,t) = (5·0 \text{ m/s}^2)\, t.$

At $t = 5·0$ s the speed is

$$v = \frac{ds}{dt} = (5·0 \text{ m/s}^2)(5·0 \text{ s}) = 25 \text{ m/s}.$$

If we plot the distance s as a function of time (figure 3.4), the speed at a time t equals the slope of the tangent to the curve at the time t. The average speed in a time interval t to $t + \Delta t$ equals the slope of the chord AB where A and B are the points on the

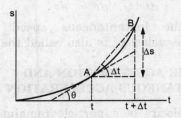

Figure 3.4

curve corresponding to the time t and $t + \Delta t$. As Δt approaches zero, the chord AB becomes the tangent at A and the average speed $\frac{\Delta s}{\Delta t}$ becomes the slope of the tangent which is $\frac{ds}{dt}$.

If the speed of the particle at time t is v, the distance ds travelled by it in the short time interval t to $t + dt$ is $v\,dt$. Thus, $ds = v\,dt$. The total distance travelled by the particle in a finite time interval t_1 to t_2 can be obtained by summing over these small distances ds as time changes from t_1 to t_2. Thus, the distance travelled by a particle in the time interval

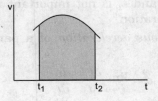

Figure 3.5

t_1 to t_2 is

$$s = \int_{t_1}^{t_2} v\,dt. \qquad \ldots (3.3)$$

If we plot a graph of the speed v versus time t, the distance travelled by the particle can be obtained by finding the area under the curve. Figure (3.5) shows such a speed-time graph. To find the distance travelled in the time interval t_1 to t_2 we draw ordinates from $t = t_1$ and $t = t_2$. The area bounded by the curve $v - t$, the X-axis and the two ordinates at $t = t_1$ and $t = t_2$ (shown shaded in the figure) gives the total distance covered.

The dimension of speed is LT^{-1} and its SI unit is metre/second abbreviated as m/s.

Example 3.3

Figure (3.6) shows the speed versus time graph for a particle. Find the distance travelled by the particle during the time $t = 0$ to $t = 3$ s.

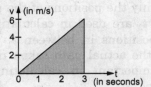

Figure 3.6

Solution : The distance travelled by the particle in the time 0 to 3 s is equal to the area shaded in the figure. This is a right angled triangle with height = 6 m/s and the base = 3 s. The area is $\frac{1}{2}$ (base) (height) $= \frac{1}{2} \times$ (3 s) (6 m/s) = 9 m. Thus, the particle covered a distance of 9 m during the time 0 to 3 s.

3.4 AVERAGE VELOCITY AND INSTANTANEOUS VELOCITY

The *average velocity* of a particle in a time interval t_1 to t_2 is defined as its displacement divided by the time interval. If the particle is at a point A (figure 3.7) at time $t = t_1$ and at B at time $t = t_2$, the displacement in this time interval is the vector $\overrightarrow{AB}$. The average velocity in this time interval is then,

$$\vec{v}_{av} = \frac{\overrightarrow{AB}}{t_2 - t_1}.$$

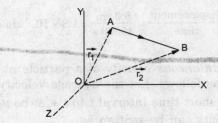

Figure 3.7

Like displacement, it is a vector quantity.

Position vector : If we join the origin to the position of the particle by a straight line and put an arrow towards the position of the particle, we get the *position vector* of the particle. Thus, the position vector of the particle shown in figure (3.7) at time $t = t_1$ is $\overrightarrow{OA}$ and that at $t = t_2$ is $\overrightarrow{OB}$. The displacement of the particle in the time interval t_1 to t_2 is

$$\overrightarrow{AB} = \overrightarrow{AO} + \overrightarrow{OB} = \overrightarrow{OB} - \overrightarrow{OA} = \vec{r}_2 - \vec{r}_1.$$

The average velocity of a particle in the time interval t_1 to t_2 can be written as

$$\vec{v}_{av} = \frac{\vec{r}_2 - \vec{r}_1}{t_2 - t_1} . \qquad \qquad \dots (3.4)$$

Note that only the positions of the particle at time $t = t_1$ and $t = t_2$ are used in calculating the average velocity. The positions in between t_1 and t_2 are not needed, hence the actual path taken in going from A to B is not important in calculating the average velocity.

Example 3.4

A table clock has its minute hand 4·0 cm long. Find the average velocity of the tip of the minute hand (a) between 6·00 a.m. to 6·30 a.m. and (b) between 6·00 a.m. to 6·30 p.m.

Solution : At 6·00 a.m. the tip of the minute hand is at 12 mark and at 6·30 a.m. or 6·30 p.m. it is 180° away. Thus, the straight line distance between the initial and final position of the tip is equal to the diameter of the clock.

Displacement = $2 R = 2 \times 4·0$ cm = 8·0 cm.

The displacement is from the 12 mark to the 6 mark on the clock panel. This is also the direction of the average velocity in both cases.

(a) The time taken from 6·00 a.m. to 6·30 a.m. is 30 minutes = 1800 s. The average velocity is

$$v_{av} = \frac{\text{Displacement}}{\text{time}} = \frac{8·0 \text{ cm}}{1800 \text{ s}} = 4·4 \times 10^{-3} \text{ cm/s}.$$

(b) The time taken from 6·00 a.m. to 6·30 p.m. is 12 hours and 30 minutes = 45000 s. The average velocity is

$$v_{av} = \frac{\text{Displacement}}{\text{time}} = \frac{8·0 \text{ cm}}{45000 \text{ s}} = 1·8 \times 10^{-4} \text{ cm/s}.$$

The *instantaneous velocity* of a particle at a time t is defined as follows. Let the average velocity of the particle in a short time interval t to $t + \Delta t$ be $\vec{v}_{av}$. This average velocity can be written as

$$\vec{v}_{av} = \frac{\vec{\Delta r}}{\Delta t}$$

where $\vec{\Delta r}$ is the displacement in the time interval Δt. We now make Δt vanishingly small and find the limiting value of $\frac{\vec{\Delta r}}{\Delta t}$. This value is instantaneous velocity $\vec{v}$ of the particle at time t.

$$\vec{v} = \lim_{\Delta t \to 0} \frac{\vec{\Delta r}}{\Delta t} = \frac{d\vec{r}}{dt} . \qquad \dots (3.5)$$

For very small intervals the displacement $\vec{\Delta r}$ is along the line of motion of the particle. Thus, the length

Δr equals the distance Δs travelled in that interval. So the magnitude of the velocity is

$$v = \left| \frac{\vec{dr}}{dt} \right| = \frac{|\vec{dr}|}{dt} = \frac{ds}{dt} \qquad \dots (3.6)$$

which is the instantaneous speed at time t. Instantaneous velocity is also called the "velocity".

3.5 AVERAGE ACCELERATION AND INSTANTANEOUS ACCELERATION

If the velocity of a particle remains constant as time passes, we say that it is moving with uniform velocity. If the velocity changes with time, it is said to be accelerated. The acceleration is the rate of change of velocity. Velocity is a vector quantity hence a change in its magnitude or direction or both will change the velocity.

Suppose the velocity of a particle at time t_1 is $\vec{v}_1$ and at time t_2 it is $\vec{v}_2$. The change produced in time interval t_1 to t_2 is $\vec{v}_2 - \vec{v}_1$. We define the *average acceleration* $\vec{a}_{av}$ as the change in velocity divided by the time interval. Thus,

$$\vec{a}_{av} = \frac{\vec{v}_2 - \vec{v}_1}{t_2 - t_1} . \qquad \dots (3.7)$$

Again the average acceleration depends only on the velocities at time t_1 and t_2. How the velocity changed in between t_1 and t_2 is not important in defining the average acceleration.

Instantaneous acceleration of a particle at time t is defined as

$$\vec{a} = \lim_{\Delta t \to 0} \frac{\vec{\Delta v}}{\Delta t} = \frac{d\vec{v}}{dt} \qquad \dots (3.8)$$

where $\vec{\Delta v}$ is the change in velocity between the time t and $t + \Delta t$. At time t the velocity is $\vec{v}$ and at time $t + \Delta t$ it becomes $\vec{v} + \vec{\Delta v}$. $\frac{\vec{\Delta v}}{\Delta t}$ is the average acceleration of the particle in the interval Δt. As Δt approaches zero, this average acceleration becomes the instantaneous acceleration. Instantaneous acceleration is also called "*acceleration*".

The dimension of acceleration is LT^{-2} and its SI unit is metre/second^2 abbreviated as m/s^2.

3.6 MOTION IN A STRAIGHT LINE

When a particle is constrained to move on a straight line, the description becomes fairly simple. We choose the line as the X-axis and a suitable time instant as $t = 0$. Generally the origin is taken at the point where the particle is situated at $t = 0$. The position of the particle at time t is given by its coordinate x at that time. The velocity is

$$v = \frac{dx}{dt} \qquad \ldots (3.9)$$

and the acceleration is $a = \frac{dv}{dt} \qquad \ldots (3.10)$

$$= \frac{d}{dt}\left(\frac{dx}{dt}\right) = \frac{d^2x}{dt^2}. \qquad \ldots (3.11)$$

If $\frac{dx}{dt}$ is positive, the direction of the velocity is along the positive X-axis and if $\frac{dx}{dt}$ is negative, the direction, is along the negative X-axis. Similarly if $\frac{dv}{dt}$ is positive, the acceleration is along the positive X-axis and if $\frac{dv}{dt}$ is negative, the acceleration is along the negative X-axis. The magnitude of v is speed. If the velocity and the acceleration are both positive, the speed increases. If both of them are negative then also the speed increases but if they have opposite signs, the speed decreases. When the speed decreases, we say that the particle is decelerating. Deceleration is equivalent to negative acceleration. An acceleration of $2 \cdot 0$ m/s^2 towards east is same as a deceleration of $2 \cdot 0$ m/s^2 towards west.

Motion with Constant Acceleration

Suppose the acceleration of a particle is a and remains constant. Let the velocity at time 0 be u and the velocity at time t be v. Thus,

$$\frac{dv}{dt} = a, \quad \text{or,} \quad dv = a\,dt$$

or, $$\int_u^v dv = \int_0^t a\,dt.$$

As time changes from 0 to t the velocity changes from u to v. So on the left hand side the summation is made over v from u to v whereas on the right hand side the summation is made on time from 0 to t. Evaluating the integrals we get,

$$[v]_u^v = a[t]_0^t$$

or, $$v - u = at$$

or, $$v = u + at. \qquad \ldots (3.12)$$

Equation (3.12) may be written as

$$\frac{dx}{dt} = u + at$$

or, $$dx = (u + at)dt$$

or, $$\int_0^x dx = \int_0^t (u + at)dt.$$

At $t = 0$ the particle is at $x = 0$. As time changes from 0 to t the position changes from 0 to x. So on the left hand side the summation is made on position from

0 to x whereas on the right hand side the summation is made on time from 0 to t. Evaluating the integrals, the above equation becomes

$$[x]_0^x = \int_0^t u\,dt + \int_0^t at\,dt$$

or, $$x = u\int_0^t dt + a\int_0^t t\,dt$$

$$= u[t]_0^t + a\left[\frac{t^2}{2}\right]_0^t$$

or, $$x = ut + \frac{1}{2}at^2. \qquad \ldots (3.13)$$

From equation (3.12),

$$v^2 = (u + at)^2$$

or, $$= u^2 + 2\,uat + a^2t^2$$

or, $$= u^2 + 2a\left(ut + \frac{1}{2}at^2\right)$$

or, $$= u^2 + 2ax. \qquad \ldots (3.14)$$

The three equations (3.12) to (3.14) are collected below in table 3.1. They are very useful in solving the problems of motion in a straight line with constant acceleration.

Table 3.1

$$v = u + at$$
$$x = ut + \frac{1}{2}at^2$$
$$v^2 = u^2 + 2ax$$

Remember that x represents the position of the particle at time t and not (in general) the distance travelled by it in time 0 to t. For example, if the particle starts from the origin and goes upto $x = 4$ m, then turns and is at $x = 2$ m at time t, the distance travelled is 6 m but the position is still given by $x = 2$ m.

The quantities u, v and a may take positive or negative values depending on whether they are directed along the positive or negative direction. Similarly x may be positive or negative.

Example 3.5

A particle starts with an initial velocity $2 \cdot 5$ m/s along the positive x direction and it accelerates uniformly at the rate $0 \cdot 50$ m/s^2. (a) Find the distance travelled by it in the first two seconds. (b) How much time does it take to reach the velocity $7 \cdot 5$ m/s ? (c) How much distance will it cover in reaching the velocity $7 \cdot 5$ m/s ?

Solution : (a) We have,

$$x = ut + \frac{1}{2} at^2$$

$$= (2 \cdot 5 \text{ m/s}) (2 \text{ s}) + \frac{1}{2} (0 \cdot 50 \text{ m/s}^2) (2 \text{ s})^2$$

$$= 5 \cdot 0 \text{ m} + 1 \cdot 0 \text{ m} = 6 \cdot 0 \text{ m}.$$

Since the particle does not turn back it is also the distance travelled.

(b) We have,

$$v = u + at$$

or, $7 \cdot 5 \text{ m/s} = 2 \cdot 5 \text{ m/s} + (0 \cdot 50 \text{ m/s}^2) t$

or, $$t = \frac{7 \cdot 5 \text{ m/s} - 2 \cdot 5 \text{ m/s}}{0 \cdot 50 \text{ m/s}^2} = 10 \text{ s}$$

(c) We have,

$$v^2 = u^2 + 2ax$$

or, $(7 \cdot 5 \text{ m/s})^2 = (2 \cdot 5 \text{ m/s})^2 + 2(0 \cdot 50 \text{ m/s}^2)x$

or, $$x = \frac{(7 \cdot 5 \text{ m/s})^2 - (2 \cdot 5 \text{ m/s})^2}{2 \times 0 \cdot 50 \text{ m/s}^2} = 50 \text{ m}.$$

Example 3.6

A particle having initial velocity u moves with a constant acceleration a for a time t. (a) Find the displacement of the particle in the last 1 second. (b) Evaluate it for u = 5 m/s, a = 2 m/s² and t = 10 s.

Solution : (a) The position at time t is

$$s = ut + \frac{1}{2} at^2$$

The position at time $(t - 1 \text{ s})$ is

$$s' = u(t - 1 \text{ s}) + \frac{1}{2} a(t - 1 \text{ s})^2$$

$$= ut - u(1 \text{ s}) + \frac{1}{2} at^2 - at(1 \text{ s}) + \frac{1}{2} a(1 \text{ s})^2$$

Thus, the displacement in the last 1 s is

$$s_t = s - s'$$

$$= u(1 \text{ s}) + at(1 \text{ s}) - \frac{1}{2} a (1 \text{ s})^2$$

or, $s_t = u(1 \text{ s}) + \dfrac{a}{2} (2t - 1 \text{ s}) (1 \text{ s}).$ ... (i)

(b) Putting the given values in (i)

$$s_t = \left(5 \frac{\text{m}}{\text{s}}\right)(1 \text{ s}) + \frac{1}{2}\left(2 \frac{\text{m}}{\text{s}^2}\right)(2 \times 10 \text{ s} - 1 \text{ s}) (1 \text{ s})$$

$$= 5 \text{ m} + \left(1 \frac{\text{m}}{\text{s}^2}\right)(19 \text{ s}) (1 \text{ s})$$

$$= 5 \text{ m} + 19 \text{ m} = 24 \text{ m}.$$

Sometimes, we are not careful in writing the units appearing with the numerical values of physical quantities. If we forget to write the unit of second in equation (i), we get,

$$s_t = u + \frac{a}{2} (2t - 1).$$

This equation is often used to calculate the displacement in the "tth second". However, as you can verify, different terms in this equation have different dimensions and hence the above equation is dimensionally incorrect. Equation (i) is the correct form which was used to solve part (b).

Also note that this equation gives the displacement of the particle in the last 1 second and not necessarily the distance covered in that second.

Freely Falling Bodies

A common example of motion in a straight line with constant acceleration is free fall of a body near the earth's surface. If air resistance is neglected and a body is dropped near the surface of the earth, it falls along a vertical straight line. The acceleration is in the vertically downward direction and its magnitude is almost constant if the height is small as compared with the radius of the earth (6400 km). This magnitude is approximately equal to $9 \cdot 8 \text{ m/s}^2$ or 32 ft/s^2 and is denoted by the letter g.

If we take vertically upward as the positive Y-axis, acceleration is along the negative Y-axis and we write $a = -g$. The equation (3.12) to (3.14) may be written in this case as

$$v = u - gt$$

$$y = ut - \frac{1}{2} gt^2$$

$$v^2 = u^2 - 2gy.$$

Here y is the y-coordinate (that is the height above the origin) at time t, u is the velocity in y direction at $t = 0$ and v is the velocity in y direction at time t. The position of the particle at $t = 0$ is $y = 0$.

Sometimes it is convenient to choose vertically downward as the positive Y-axis. Then $a = g$ and the equations (3.12) to (3.14) become

$$v = u + gt$$

$$y = ut + \frac{1}{2} gt^2$$

$$v^2 = u^2 + 2gy.$$

Example 3.7

A ball is thrown up at a speed of 4·0 m/s. Find the maximum height reached by the ball. Take g = 10 m/s².

Solution : Let us take vertically upward direction as the positive Y-axis. We have $u = 4 \cdot 0 \text{ m/s}$ and $a = -10 \text{ m/s}^2$. At the highest point the velocity becomes zero. Using the formula.

$$v^2 = u^2 + 2ay,$$
$$0 = (4.0 \text{ m/s})^2 + 2(-10 \text{ m/s}^2)y$$
or, $$y = \frac{16 \text{ m}^2/\text{s}^2}{20 \text{ m/s}^2} = 0.80 \text{ m}.$$

3.7 MOTION IN A PLANE

If a particle is free to move in a plane, its position can be located with two coordinates. We choose the plane of motion as the X-Y plane. We choose a suitable instant as $t = 0$ and choose the origin at the place where the particle is situated at $t = 0$. Any two convenient mutually perpendicular directions in the X-Y plane are chosen as the X and Y-axes.

The position of the particle at a time t is completely specified by its coordinates (x, y). The coordinates at time $t + \Delta t$ are $(x + \Delta x, y + \Delta y)$. Figure (3.8) shows the positions at t and $t + \Delta t$ as A and B respectively. The displacement during the time interval t to $t + \Delta t$ is

$$\vec{\Delta r} = \vec{AB} = \vec{AC} + \vec{CB}$$
$$= \Delta x \, \vec{i} + \Delta y \, \vec{j}$$
or, $$\frac{\vec{\Delta r}}{\Delta t} = \frac{\Delta x}{\Delta t} \vec{i} + \frac{\Delta y}{\Delta t} \vec{j}.$$

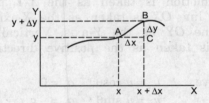

Figure 3.8

Taking limits as $\Delta t \to 0$

$$\vec{v} = \frac{dx}{dt} \vec{i} + \frac{dy}{dt} \vec{j}. \qquad \ldots (3.15)$$

Thus, we see that the x-component of the velocity is

$$v_x = \frac{dx}{dt} \qquad \ldots (3.16)$$

and the y-component is

$$v_y = \frac{dy}{dt}. \qquad \ldots (3.17)$$

Differentiating (3.15) with respect to time,

$$\vec{a} = \frac{d\vec{v}}{dt} = \frac{dv_x}{dt} \vec{i} + \frac{dv_y}{dt} \vec{j}$$

Thus, the acceleration has components

$$a_x = \frac{dv_x}{dt} \qquad \ldots (3.18)$$

and $$a_y = \frac{dv_y}{dt}. \qquad \ldots (3.19)$$

We see that the x-coordinate, the x-component of velocity v_x and the x-component of acceleration a_x are related by

$$v_x = \frac{dx}{dt} \quad \text{and} \quad a_x = \frac{dv_x}{dt}.$$

These equations are identical to equations (3.9) and (3.10). Thus, if a_x is constant, integrating these equations we get

$$v_x = u_x + a_x t$$
$$x = u_x t + \frac{1}{2} a_x t^2 \qquad \ldots (3.20)$$
$$v_x^2 = u_x^2 + 2a_x x$$

where u_x is the x-component of the velocity at $t = 0$. Similarly we have

$$v_y = \frac{dy}{dt} \quad \text{and} \quad a_y = \frac{dv_y}{dt}$$

and if a_y is constant,

$$v_y = u_y + a_y t$$
$$y = u_y t + \frac{1}{2} a_y t^2 \qquad \ldots (3.21)$$
$$v_y^2 = u_y^2 + 2a_y y$$

The general scheme for the discussion of motion in a plane is therefore simple. The x-coordinate, the x-component of velocity and the x-component of acceleration are related by equations of straight line motion along the X-axis. Similarly the y-coordinate, the y-component of velocity and the y-component of acceleration are related by the equations of straight line motion along the Y-axis. The problem of motion in a plane is thus, broken up into two independent problems of straight line motion, one along the X-axis and the other along the Y-axis.

Example 3.8

A particle moves in the X-Y plane with a constant acceleration of 1.5 m/s^2 in the direction making an angle of 37° with the X-axis. At $t = 0$ the particle is at the origin and its velocity is 8.0 m/s along the X-axis. Find the velocity and the position of the particle at $t = 4.0$ s.

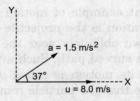

Figure 3.9

Solution : $a_x = (1.5 \text{ m/s}^2)(\cos 37°)$

$$= (1.5 \text{ m/s}^2) \times \frac{4}{5} = 1.2 \text{ m/s}^2$$

and $a_y = (1.5 \text{ m/s}^2)(\sin 37°)$

$$= (1.5 \text{ m/s}^2) \times \frac{3}{5} = 0.90 \text{ m/s}^2.$$

The initial velocity has components

$$u_x = 8.0 \text{ m/s}$$

and $u_y = 0$

At $t = 0$, $x = 0$ and $y = 0$.

The x-component of the velocity at time $t = 4.0$ s is given by

$$v_x = u_x + a_x t$$

$$= 8.0 \text{ m/s} + (1.2 \text{ m/s}^2)(4.0 \text{ s})$$

$$= 8.0 \text{ m/s} + 4.8 \text{ m/s} = 12.8 \text{ m/s}.$$

The y-component of velocity at $t = 4.0$ s is given by

$$v_y = u_y + a_y t$$

$$= 0 + (0.90 \text{ m/s}^2)(4.0 \text{ s}) = 3.6 \text{ m/s}.$$

The velocity of the particle at $t = 4.0$ s is

$$v = \sqrt{v_x^2 + v_y^2} = \sqrt{(12.8 \text{ m/s})^2 + (3.6 \text{ m/s})^2}$$

$$= 13.3 \text{ m/s}.$$

The velocity makes an angle θ with the X-axis where

$$\tan\theta = \frac{v_y}{v_x} = \frac{3.6 \text{ m/s}}{12.8 \text{ m/s}} = \frac{9}{32}.$$

The x-coordinate at $t = 4.0$ s is

$$x = u_x t + \frac{1}{2} a_x t^2$$

$$= (8.0 \text{ m/s})(4.0 \text{ s}) + \frac{1}{2}(1.2 \text{ m/s}^2)(4.0 \text{ s})^2$$

$$= 32 \text{ m} + 9.6 \text{ m} = 41.6 \text{ m}.$$

The y-coordinate at $t = 4.0$ s is

$$y = u_y t + \frac{1}{2} a_y t^2$$

$$= \frac{1}{2}(0.90 \text{ m/s}^2)(4.0 \text{ s})^2$$

$$= 7.2 \text{ m}.$$

Thus, the particle is at (41.6 m, 7.2 m) at 4.0 s.

3.8 PROJECTILE MOTION

An important example of motion in a plane with constant acceleration is the projectile motion. When a particle is thrown obliquely near the earth's surface, it moves along a curved path. Such a particle is called a *projectile* and its motion is called *projectile motion*. We shall assume that the particle remains close to the surface of the earth and the air resistance is negligible. The acceleration of the particle is then almost

constant. It is in the vertically downward direction and its magnitude is g which is about 9.8 m/s^2.

Let us first make ourselves familiar with certain terms used in discussing projectile motion. Figure (3.10) shows a particle projected from the point O with an initial velocity u at an angle θ with the horizontal. It goes through the highest point A and falls at B on the horizontal surface through O. The point O is called the *point of projection*, the angle θ is called the *angle of projection* and the distance OB is called the *horizontal range* or simply *range*. The total time taken by the particle in describing the path OAB is called the *time of flight*.

The motion of the projectile can be discussed separately for the horizontal and vertical parts. We take the origin at the point of projection. The instant

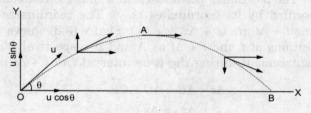

Figure 3.10

when the particle is projected is taken as $t = 0$. The plane of motion is taken as the X-Y plane. The horizontal line OX is taken as the X-axis and the vertical line OY as the Y-axis. Vertically upward direction is taken as the positive direction of the Y-axis.

We have $u_x = u\cos\theta$; $a_x = 0$

$u_y = u\sin\theta$; $a_y = -g$.

Horizontal Motion

As $a_x = 0$, we have

$$v_x = u_x + a_x t = u_x = u\cos\theta$$

and $x = u_x t + \frac{1}{2} a_x t^2 = u_x t = ut\cos\theta$.

As indicated in figure (3.10), the x-component of the velocity remains constant as the particle moves.

Vertical Motion

The acceleration of the particle is g in the downward direction. Thus, $a_y = -g$. The y-component of the initial velocity is u_y. Thus,

$$v_y = u_y - gt$$

and $y = u_y t - \frac{1}{2} gt^2$.

Also we have,

$$v_y^2 = u_y^2 - 2gy.$$

The vertical motion is identical to the motion of a particle projected vertically upward with speed $u \sin\theta$. The horizontal motion of the particle is identical to a particle moving horizontally with uniform velocity $u \cos\theta$.

Time of Flight

Consider the situation shown in figure (3.10). The particle is projected from the point O and reaches the same horizontal plane at the point B. The total time taken to reach B is the time of flight.

Suppose the particle is at B at a time t. The equation for horizontal motion gives

$$OB = x = ut \cos\theta$$

The y-coordinate at the point B is zero. Thus, from the equation of vertical motion,

$$y = ut \sin\theta - \frac{1}{2} gt^2$$

or, $$0 = ut \sin\theta - \frac{1}{2} gt^2$$

or, $$t(u \sin\theta - \frac{1}{2} gt) = 0.$$

Thus, either $t = 0$ or, $t = \dfrac{2u \sin\theta}{g}$.

Now $t = 0$ corresponds to the position O of the particle. The time at which it reaches B is thus,

$$T = \frac{2u \sin\theta}{g}.   \qquad \ldots \text{(3.22)}$$

This is the time of flight.

Range

The distance OB is the horizontal range. It is the distance travelled by the particle in time $T = \dfrac{2u \sin\theta}{g}$. By the equation of horizontal motion,

$$x = (u\cos\theta)t$$

or, $$OB = (u \cos\theta)\left(\frac{2u \sin\theta}{g}\right)$$

$$= \frac{2u^2 \sin\theta \cos\theta}{g}$$

$$= \frac{u^2 \sin 2\theta}{g}.   \qquad \ldots \text{(3.23)}$$

Maximum Height Reached

At the maximum height (A in figure 3.10) the velocity of the particle is horizontal. The vertical component of velocity is thus, zero at the highest point. The maximum height is the y-coordinate of the particle when the vertical component of velocity becomes zero.

We have,

$$v_y = u_y - gt$$

$$= u \sin\theta - gt.$$

At the maximum height

$$0 = u \sin\theta - gt$$

or, $$t = \frac{u \sin\theta}{g}.   \qquad \ldots \text{(3.24)}$$

The maximum height is

$$H = u_y t - \frac{1}{2} gt^2$$

$$= (u \sin\theta)\left(\frac{u \sin\theta}{g}\right) - \frac{1}{2} g\left(\frac{u \sin\theta}{g}\right)^2$$

$$= \frac{u^2 \sin^2\theta}{g} - \frac{1}{2}\frac{u^2 \sin^2\theta}{g}$$

$$= \frac{u^2 \sin^2\theta}{2g}.   \qquad \ldots \text{(3.25)}$$

Equation (3.24) gives the time taken in reaching the maximum height. Comparison with equation (3.22) shows that it is exactly half the time of the flight. Thus, the time taken in ascending the maximum height equals the time taken in descending back to the same horizontal plane.

Example 3.9

A ball is thrown from a field with a speed of 12·0 m/s at an angle of 45° with the horizontal. At what distance will it hit the field again ? Take g = 10·0 m/s².

Solution : The horizontal range $= \dfrac{u^2 \sin 2\theta}{g}$

$$= \frac{(12 \text{ m/s})^2 \times \sin(2 \times 45°)}{10 \text{ m/s}^2}$$

$$= \frac{144 \text{ m}^2/\text{s}^2}{10 \cdot 0 \text{ m/s}^2} = 14 \cdot 4 \text{ m}.$$

Thus, the ball hits the field at 14·4 m from the point of projection.

3.9 CHANGE OF FRAME

So far we have discussed the motion of a particle with respect to a given frame of reference. The frame can be chosen according to the convenience of the problem. The position $\vec{r}$, the velocity $\vec{v}$ and the acceleration $\vec{a}$ of a particle depend on the frame chosen. Let us see how can we relate the position, velocity and acceleration of a particle measured in two different frames.

Consider two frames of reference S and S' and suppose a particle P is observed from both the frames. The frames may be moving with respect to each other. Figure (3.11) shows the situation.

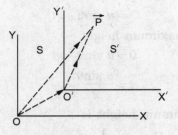

Figure 3.11

The position vector of the particle P with respect to the frame S is $\overrightarrow{r_{P,S}} = \overrightarrow{OP}$. The position vector of the particle with respect to the frame S' is $\overrightarrow{r_{P,S'}} = \overrightarrow{O'P}$. The position of the frame S' (the origin of frame S' in fact) with respect to the frame S is OO'.

It is clear that

$$\overrightarrow{OP} = \overrightarrow{OO'} + \overrightarrow{O'P} = \overrightarrow{O'P} + \overrightarrow{OO'}$$

or, $\overrightarrow{r_{P,S}} = \overrightarrow{r_{P,S'}} + \overrightarrow{r_{S',S}}.$ ... (3.26)

The position of the particle with respect to S is equal to the position of the particle with respect to S' plus the position of S' with respect to S.

If we differentiate equation (3.26) with respect to time, we get

$$\frac{d}{dt}(\overrightarrow{r_{P,S}}) = \frac{d}{dt}(\overrightarrow{r_{P,S'}}) + \frac{d}{dt}(\overrightarrow{r_{S',S}})$$

or, $\overrightarrow{v_{P,S}} = \overrightarrow{v_{P,S'}} + \overrightarrow{v_{S',S}}$ ... (3.27)

where $\overrightarrow{v_{P,S}}$ is the velocity of the particle with respect to S, $\overrightarrow{v_{P,S'}}$ is the velocity of the particle with respect to S' and $\overrightarrow{v_{S',S}}$ is the velocity of the frame S' with respect to S. The velocity of the particle with respect to S is equal to the velocity of the particle with respect to S' plus the velocity of S' with respect to S.

It is assumed that the meaning of time is same in both the frames. Similarly it is assumed that $\frac{d}{dt}$ has same meaning in both the frames. These assumptions are not correct if the velocity of one frame with respect to the other is so large that it is comparable to 3×10^8 m/s, or if one frame rotates with respect to the other. If the frames only translate with respect to each other with small velocity, the above assumptions are correct.

Equation (3.27) may be rewritten as

$$\overrightarrow{v_{P,S'}} = \overrightarrow{v_{P,S}} - \overrightarrow{v_{S',S}}.$$ ... (3.28)

Thus, if the velocities of two bodies (here the particle and the frame S') are known with respect to a common frame (here S) we can find the velocity of one body with respect to the other body. The velocity of body 1 with respect to the body 2 is obtained by subtracting the velocity of body 2 from the velocity of body 1.

When we say that the muzzle velocity of a bullet is 60 m/s we mean the velocity of the bullet with respect to the gun. If the gun is mounted in a train moving with a speed of 20 m/s with respect to the ground and the bullet is fired in the direction of the train's motion, its velocity with respect to the ground will be 80 m/s. Similarly, when we say that a swimmer can swim at a speed of 5 km/h we mean the velocity of the swimmer with respect to the water. If the water itself is flowing at 3 km/h with respect to the ground and the swimmer swims in the direction of the current, he or she will move at the speed of 8 km/h with respect to the ground.

Example 3.10

A swimmer can swim in still water at a rate 4·0 km/h. If he swims in a river flowing at 3·0 km/h and keeps his direction (with respect to water) perpendicular to the current, find his velocity with respect to the ground.

Solution : The velocity of the swimmer with respect to water is $\overrightarrow{v_{S,R}} = 4\cdot0$ km/h in the direction perpendicular to the river. The velocity of river with respect to the ground is $\overrightarrow{v_{R,G}} = 3\cdot0$ km/h along the length of the river. The velocity of the swimmer with respect to the ground is $\overrightarrow{v_{S,G}}$ where

$$\overrightarrow{v_{S,G}} = \overrightarrow{v_{S,R}} + \overrightarrow{v_{R,G}}.$$

Figure (3.12) shows the velocities. It is clear that,

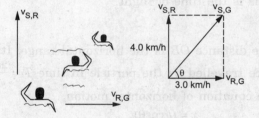

Figure 3.12

$$v_{S,G} = \sqrt{(4\cdot0 \text{ km/h})^2 + (3\cdot0 \text{ km/h})^2}$$

$$= 5\cdot0 \text{ km/h}$$

The angle θ made with the direction of flow is

$$\tan\theta = \frac{4\cdot0 \text{ km/h}}{3\cdot0 \text{ km/h}} = \frac{4}{3}.$$

Example 3.11

A man is walking on a level road at a speed of 3·0 km/h. Rain drops fall vertically with a speed of 4·0 km/h. Find the velocity of the raindrops with respect to the man.

Solution : We have to find the velocity of raindrops with respect to the man. The velocity of the rain as well as the velocity of the man are given with respect to the street. We have

$$\vec{v}_{rain,\,man} = \vec{v}_{rain,\,street} - \vec{v}_{man,\,street}.$$

Figure (3.13) shows the velocities.

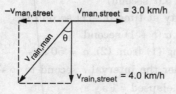

Figure 3.13

It is clear from the figure that

$$v_{rain,\,man} = \sqrt{(4.0\ \text{km/h})^2 + (3.0\ \text{km/h})^2}$$

$$= 5.0\ \text{km/h}.$$

The angle with the vertical is θ, where

$$\tan\theta = \frac{3.0\ \text{km/h}}{4.0\ \text{km/h}} = \frac{3}{4}.$$

Thus, the rain appears to fall at an angle $\tan^{-1}$ (3/4) with the speed 5·0 km/h as viewed by the man.

The relation between the accelerations measured from two frames can be obtained by differentiating equation (3.27) with respect to time.

We have,

$$\frac{d}{dt}(\vec{v}_{P,\,S}) = \frac{d}{dt}(\vec{v}_{P,\,S'}) + \frac{d}{dt}(\vec{v}_{S',\,S})$$

or, $$\vec{a}_{P,\,S} = \vec{a}_{P,\,S'} + \vec{a}_{S',\,S}. \qquad \ldots (3.29)$$

If S' moves with respect to S at a uniform velocity, $\vec{a}_{S',\,S} = 0$ and so

$$\vec{a}_{P,\,S} = \vec{a}_{P,\,S'}.$$

If two frames are moving with respect to each other with uniform velocity, acceleration of a body is same in both the frames.

Worked Out Examples

1. *A man walks at a speed of 6 km/hr for 1 km and 8 km/hr for the next 1 km. What is his average speed for the walk of 2 km ?*

Solution : Distance travelled is 2 km.

Time taken $$= \frac{1\ \text{km}}{6\ \text{km/hr}} + \frac{1\ \text{km}}{8\ \text{km/hr}}$$

$$= \left(\frac{1}{6} + \frac{1}{8}\right) \text{hr} = \frac{7}{24}\ \text{hr}.$$

Average speed $$= \frac{2\ \text{km} \times 24}{7\ \text{hr}} = \frac{48}{7}\ \text{km/hr}$$

$$\approx 7\ \text{km/hr}.$$

2. *The I.Sc. lecture theatre of a college is 40 ft wide and has a door at a corner. A teacher enters at 12·00 noon through the door and makes 10 rounds along the 40 ft wall back and forth during the period and finally leaves the class-room at 12·50 p.m. through the same door. Compute his average speed and average velocity.*

Solution : Total distance travelled in 50 minutes = 800 ft.

Average speed $$= \frac{800}{50}\ \text{ft/min} = 16\ \text{ft/min}.$$

At 12·00 noon he is at the door and at 12·50 pm he is again at the same door.

The displacement during the 50 min interval is zero.

Average velocity = zero.

3. *The position of a particle moving on X-axis is given by*

$$x = At^3 + Bt^2 + Ct + D.$$

The numerical values of A, B, C, D are 1, 4, −2 and 5

respectively and SI units are used. Find (a) the dimensions of A, B, C and D, (b) the velocity of the particle at t = 4 s, (c) the acceleration of the particle at t = 4 s, (d) the average velocity during the interval t = 0 to t = 4 s, (e) the average acceleration during the interval t = 0 to t = 4 s.

Solution : (a) Dimensions of x, At^3, Bt^2, Ct and D must be identical and in this case each is length. Thus,

$$[At^3] = \text{L, or, } [A] = \text{LT}^{-3}$$

$$[Bt^2] = \text{L, or, } [B] = \text{LT}^{-2}$$

$$[Ct] = \text{L, or, } [C] = \text{LT}^{-1}$$

and $$[D] = \text{L}.$$

(b) $x = At^3 + Bt^2 + Ct + D$

or, $v = \dfrac{dx}{dt} = 3At^2 + 2Bt + C.$

Thus, at $t = 4$ s, the velocity

$$= 3(1\ \text{m/s}^3)\,(16\ \text{s}^2) + 2(4\ \text{m/s}^2)\,(4\ \text{s}) + (-2\ \text{m/s})$$

$$= (48 + 32 - 2)\ \text{m/s} = 78\ \text{m/s}.$$

(c) $v = 3At^2 + 2Bt + C$

or, $a = \dfrac{dv}{dt} = 6At + 2B.$

At $t = 4$ s, $a = 6(1\ \text{m/s}^3)\,(4\ \text{s}) + 2(4\ \text{m/s}^2) = 32\ \text{m/s}^2.$

(d) $x = At^3 + Bt^2 + Ct + D.$

Position at $t = 0$ is $x = D = 5$ m.

Position at $t = 4$ s is

$$(1\ \text{m/s}^3)\,(64\ \text{s}^3) + (4\ \text{m/s}^2)\,(16\ \text{s}^2) - (2\ \text{m/s})\,(4\ \text{s}) + 5\ \text{m}$$

$$= (64 + 64 - 8 + 5)\ \text{m} = 125\ \text{m}.$$

Thus, the displacement during 0 to 4 s is
125 m − 5 m = 120 m.

Average velocity $= \dfrac{120 \text{ m}}{4 \text{ s}} = 30$ m/s.

(e) $v = 3At^2 + 2Bt + C$.

Velocity at $t = 0$ is $C = -2$ m/s.

Velocity at $t = 4$ s is $= 78$ m/s.

Average acceleration $= \dfrac{v_2 - v_1}{t_2 - t_1} = 20$ m/s^2.

4. *From the velocity-time graph of a particle given in figure (3-W1), describe the motion of the particle qualitatively in the interval 0 to 4 s. Find (a) the distance travelled during first two seconds, (b) during the time 2 s to 4 s, (c) during the time 0 to 4 s, (d) displacement during 0 to 4 s, (e) acceleration at t = 1/2 s and (f) acceleration at t = 2 s.*

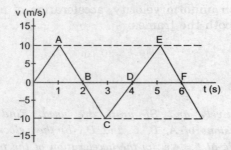

Figure 3-W1

Solution : At $t = 0$, the particle is at rest, say at the origin. After that the velocity is positive, so that the particle moves in the positive x direction. Its speed increases till 1 second when it starts decreasing. The particle continues to move further in positive x direction. At $t = 2$ s, its velocity is reduced to zero, it has moved through a maximum positive x distance. Then it changes its direction, velocity being negative, but increasing in magnitude. At $t = 3$ s velocity is maximum in the negative x direction and then the magnitude starts decreasing. It comes to rest at $t = 4$ s.

(a) Distance during 0 to 2 s = Area of OAB

$$= \frac{1}{2} \times 2 \text{ s} \times 10 \text{ m/s} = 10 \text{ m}.$$

(b) Distance during 2 to 4 s = Area of BCD = 10 m. The particle has moved in negative x direction during this period.

(c) The distance travelled during 0 to 4s = 10 m + 10 m
= 20 m.

(d) displacement during 0 to 4 s = 10 m + (− 10 m) = 0.

(e) at $t = 1/2$ s acceleration = slope of line OA = 10 m/s^2.

(f) at $t = 2$ s acceleration = slope of line ABC = − 10 m/s^2.

5. *A particle starts from rest with a constant acceleration. At a time t second, the speed is found to be 100 m/s and one second later the speed becomes 150 m/s. Find (a) the acceleration and (b) the distance travelled during the $(t+1)^{th}$ second.*

Solution : (a) Velocity at time t second is

100 m/s $= a.(t$ second)   ... (1)

and velocity at time $(t + 1)$ second is

150 m/s $= a.(t + 1)$ second.   ... (2)

Subtracting (1) from (2), $a = 50$ m/s^2

(b) Consider the interval t second to $(t + 1)$ second,

time elapsed = 1 s

initial velocity = 100 m/s

final velocity = 150 m/s.

Thus, $(150 \text{ m/s})^2 = (100 \text{ m/s})^2 + 2(50 \text{ m/s}^2) x$

or, $x = 125$ m.

6. *A boy stretches a stone against the rubber tape of a catapult or 'gulel' (a device used to detach mangoes from the tree by boys in Indian villages) through a distance of 24 cm before leaving it. The tape returns to its normal position accelerating the stone over the stretched length. The stone leaves the gulel with a speed 2·2 m/s. Assuming that the acceleration is constant while the stone was being pushed by the tape, find its magnitude.*

Solution : Consider the accelerated 24 cm motion of the stone.

Initial velocity = 0

Final velocity = 2·2 m/s

Distance travelled = 24 cm = 0·24 m

Using $v^2 = u^2 + 2ax$,

$$a = \frac{4·84 \text{ m}^2/\text{s}^2}{2 \times 0·24 \text{ m}} = 10·1 \text{ m/s}^2.$$

7. *A police inspector in a jeep is chasing a pickpocket on a straight road. The jeep is going at its maximum speed v (assumed uniform). The pickpocket rides on the motorcycle of a waiting friend when the jeep is at a distance d away, and the motorcycle starts with a constant acceleration a. Show that the pickpocket will be caught if $v \geq \sqrt{2ad}$.*

Solution : Suppose the pickpocket is caught at a time t after the motorcycle starts. The distance travelled by the motorcycle during this interval is

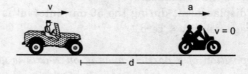

Figure 3-W2

$$s = \frac{1}{2} at^2. \qquad \qquad \qquad \text{... (i)}$$

During this interval the jeep travels a distance

$$s + d = vt. \qquad \qquad \qquad \text{... (ii)}$$

By (i) and (ii),

$$\frac{1}{2} at^2 - vt + d = 0$$

or,

$$t = \frac{v \pm \sqrt{v^2 - 2ad}}{a}.$$

The pickpocket will be caught if t is real and positive. This will be possible if

$$v^2 \geq 2ad \quad \text{or, } v \geq \sqrt{2ad}.$$

8. *A car is moving at a constant speed of 40 km/h along a straight road which heads towards a large vertical wall and makes a sharp 90° turn by the side of the wall. A fly flying at a constant speed of 100 km/h, starts from the wall towards the car at an instant when the car is 20 km away, flies until it reaches the glasspane of the car and returns to the wall at the same speed. It continues to fly between the car and the wall till the car makes the 90° turn. (a) What is the total distance the fly has travelled during this period ? (b) How many trips has it made between the car and the wall ?*

Solution : (a) The time taken by the car to cover 20 km before the turn is $\frac{20 \text{ km}}{40 \text{ km/h}} = \frac{1}{2}$ h. The fly moves at a constant speed of 100 km/h during this time. Hence the total distance coverd by it is $100 \frac{\text{km}}{\text{h}} \times \frac{1}{2}$ h $= 50$ km.

(b) Suppose the car is at a distance x away (at A) when the fly is at the wall (at O). The fly hits the glasspane at B, taking a time t. Then

$$AB = (40 \text{ km/h})t,$$

and

$$OB = (100 \text{ km/h})t.$$

Thus,

$$x = AB + OB$$

$$= (140 \text{ km/h})t$$

or,

$$t = \frac{x}{140 \text{ km/h}}, \text{ or } OB = \frac{5}{7}x.$$

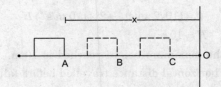

Figure 3-W3

The fly returns to the wall and during this period the car moves the distance BC. The time taken by the fly in this return path is

$$\left(\frac{5x/7}{100 \text{ km/h}} \right) = \frac{x}{140 \text{ km/h}}.$$

Thus,

$$BC = \frac{40x}{140} = \frac{2}{7}x$$

or,

$$OC = OB - BC = \frac{3}{7}x.$$

If at the beginning of the round trip (wall to the car and back) the car is at a distance x away, it is $\frac{3}{7}x$ away when the next trip again starts.

Distance of the car at the beginning of the 1st trip $= 20$ km.

Distance of the car at the beginning of the 2nd trip

$$= \frac{3}{7} \times 20 \text{ km}.$$

Distance of the car at the beginning of the 3rd trip

$$= \left(\frac{3}{7} \right)^2 \times 20 \text{ km}.$$

Distance of the car at the beginning of the 4th trip

$$= \left(\frac{3}{7} \right)^3 \times 20 \text{ km}.$$

Distance of the car at the beginning of the nth trip

$$= \left(\frac{3}{7} \right)^{n-1} \times 20 \text{ km}.$$

Trips will go on till the car reaches the turn that is the distance reduces to zero. This will be the case when n becomes infinity. Hence the fly makes an infinite number of trips before the car takes the turn.

9. *A ball is dropped from a height of 19·6 m above the ground. It rebounds from the ground and raises itself up to the same height. Take the starting point as the origin and vertically downward as the positive X-axis. Draw approximate plots of x versus t, v versus t and a versus t. Neglect the small interval during which the ball was in contact with the ground.*

Solution : Since the acceleration of the ball during the contact is different from 'g', we have to treat the downward motion and the upward motion separately.

For the downward motion : $a = g = 9\cdot8$ m/s^2,

$$x = ut + \frac{1}{2} at^2 = (4\cdot9 \text{ m/s}^2)t^2.$$

The ball reaches the ground when $x = 19\cdot6$ m. This gives $t = 2$ s. After that it moves up, x decreases and at $t = 4$ s, x becomes zero, the ball reaching the initial point. We have at $t = 0$, $\qquad x = 0$

$$t = 1 \text{ s}, \qquad x = 4\cdot9 \text{ m}$$
$$t = 2 \text{ s}, \qquad x = 19\cdot6 \text{ m}$$
$$t = 3 \text{ s}, \qquad x = 4\cdot9 \text{ m}$$
$$t = 4 \text{ s}, \qquad x = 0.$$

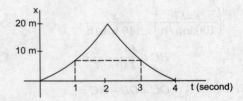

Figure 3-W4

Velocity : During the first two seconds,

$$v = u + at = (9.8 \text{ m/s}^2)t$$

at $t = 0$ $v = 0$

at $t = 1$ s, $v = 9.8$ m/s

at $t = 2$ s, $v = 19.6$ m/s.

During the next two seconds the ball goes upward, velocity is negative, magnitude decreasing and at $t = 4$ s, $v = 0$. Thus,

at $t = 2$ s, $v = -19.6$ m/s

at $t = 3$ s, $v = -9.8$ m/s

at $t = 4$ s, $v = 0$.

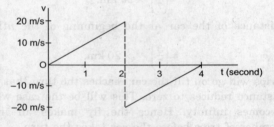

Figure 3-W5

At $t = 2$ s there is an abrupt change in velocity from 19.6 m/s to -19.6 m/s. In fact this change in velocity takes place over a small interval during which the ball remains in contact with the ground.

Acceleration : The acceleration is constant 9.8 m/s^2 throughout the motion (except at $t = 2$ s).

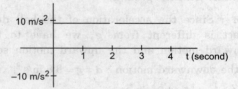

Figure 3-W6

10. *A stone is dropped from a balloon going up with a uniform velocity of 5.0 m/s. If the balloon was 50 m high when the stone was dropped, find its height when the stone hits the ground. Take $g = 10 \text{ m/s}^2$.*

Solution : At $t = 0$, the stone was going up with a velocity of 5.0 m/s. After that it moved as a freely falling particle with downward acceleration g. Take vertically upward

as the positive X-axis. If it reaches the ground at time t,

$$x = -50 \text{ m}, \quad u = 5 \text{ m/s}, \quad a = -10 \text{ m/s}^2.$$

We have $x = ut + \dfrac{1}{2} at^2$

or, $-50 \text{ m} = (5 \text{ m/s}).t + \dfrac{1}{2} \times (-10 \text{ m/s}^2)t^2$

or, $t = \dfrac{1 \pm \sqrt{41}}{2}$ s.

or, $t = -2.7$ s   or, 3.7 s.

Negative t has no significance in this problem. The stone reaches the ground at $t = 3.7$ s. During this time the balloon has moved uniformly up. The distance covered by it is

$$5 \text{ m/s} \times 3.7 \text{ s} = 18.5 \text{ m}.$$

Hence, the height of the balloon when the stone reaches the ground is 50 m + 18.5 m = 68.5 m.

11. *A football is kicked with a velocity of 20 m/s at an angle of 45° with the horizontal. (a) Find the time taken by the ball to strike the ground. (b) Find the maximum height it reaches. (c) How far away from the kick does it hit the ground ? Take $g = 10 \text{ m/s}^2$.*

Solution : (a) Take the origin at the point where the ball is kicked, vertically upward as the Y-axis and the horizontal in the plane of motion as the X-axis. The initial velocity has the components

$$u_x = (20 \text{ m/s}) \cos 45° = 10 \sqrt{2} \text{ m/s}$$

and $u_y = (20 \text{ m/s}) \sin 45° = 10 \sqrt{2}$ m/s.

When the ball reaches the ground, $y = 0$.

Using $y = u_y t - \dfrac{1}{2} gt^2$,

$$0 = (10\sqrt{2} \text{ m/s})\, t - \dfrac{1}{2} \times (10 \text{ m/s}^2) \times t^2$$

or, $t = 2\sqrt{2}$ s = 2.8 s.

Thus, it takes 2.8 s for the football to fall on the ground.

(b) At the highest point $v_y = 0$. Using the equation

$$v_y^2 = u_y^2 - 2gy,$$

$$0 = (10\sqrt{2} \text{ m/s})^2 - 2 \times (10 \text{ m/s}^2) H$$

or, $H = 10$ m.

Thus, the maximum height reached is 10 m.

(c) The horizontal distance travelled before falling to the ground is $x = u_x t$

$$= (10\sqrt{2} \text{ m/s}) (2\sqrt{2} \text{ s}) = 40 \text{ m}.$$

12. *A helicopter on flood relief mission, flying horizontally with a speed u at an altitude H, has to drop a food packet for a victim standing on the ground. At what distance from the victim should the packet be dropped ? The victim stands in the vertical plane of the helicopter's motion.*

Solution : The velocity of the food packet at the time of release is u and is horizontal. The vertical velocity at the time of release is zero.

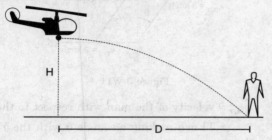

Figure 3-W7

Vertical motion : If t be the time taken by the packet to reach the victim, we have for vertical motion,

$$H = \frac{1}{2} g t^2 \quad \text{or,} \quad t = \sqrt{\frac{2H}{g}}. \quad \ldots \text{ (i)}$$

Horizontal motion : If D be the horizontal distance travelled by the packet, we have $D = ut$. Putting t from (i),

$$D = u \sqrt{\frac{2H}{g}}.$$

The distance between the victim and the packet at the time of release is

$$\sqrt{D^2 + H^2} = \sqrt{\frac{2u^2 H}{g} + H^2}.$$

13. *A particle is projected horizontally with a speed u from the top of a plane inclined at an angle θ with the horizontal. How far from the point of projection will the particle strike the plane ?*

Solution : Take X, Y-axes as shown in figure (3-W8). Suppose that the particle strikes the plane at a point P with coordinates (x, y). Consider the motion between A and P.

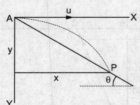

Figure 3-W8

Motion in x-direction :

    Initial velocity $= u$

    Acceleration $= 0$

$$x = ut. \quad \ldots \text{ (i)}$$

Motion in y-direction :

    Initial velocity $= 0$

    Acceleration $= g$

$$y = \frac{1}{2} g t^2. \quad \ldots \text{ (ii)}$$

Eliminating t from (i) and (ii)

$$y = \frac{1}{2} g \frac{x^2}{u^2}.$$

Also

$$y = x \tan\theta.$$

Thus, $\dfrac{gx^2}{2u^2} = x \tan\theta$ giving $x = 0$, or, $\dfrac{2u^2 \tan\theta}{g}$.

Clearly the point P corresponds to $x = \dfrac{2u^2 \tan\theta}{g}$,

then $y = x \tan\theta = \dfrac{2u^2 \tan^2\theta}{g}$.

The distance $AP = l = \sqrt{x^2 + y^2}$

$$= \frac{2u^2}{g} \tan\theta \sqrt{1 + \tan^2\theta}$$

$$= \frac{2u^2}{g} \tan\theta \sec\theta.$$

Alternatively : Take the axes as shown in figure 3-W9. Consider the motion between A and P.

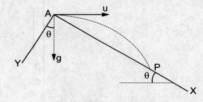

Figure 3-W9

Motion along the X-axis :

    Initial velocity $= u \cos\theta$

    Acceleration $= g \sin\theta$

    Displacement $= AP$.

Thus, $AP = (u \cos\theta) t + \dfrac{1}{2} (g \sin\theta) t^2$.   ... (i)

Motion along the Y-axis :

    Initial velocity $= - u \sin\theta$

    Acceleration $= g \cos\theta$

    Displacement $= 0$.

Thus, $\quad 0 = - ut \sin\theta + \dfrac{1}{2} g t^2 \cos\theta$

or, $\quad t = 0, \quad \dfrac{2u \sin\theta}{g \cos\theta}$.

Clearly, the point P corresponds to $t = \dfrac{2u \sin\theta}{g \cos\theta}$.

Putting this value of t in (i),

$$AP = (u \cos\theta) \left(\frac{2u \sin\theta}{g \cos\theta} \right) + \frac{g \sin\theta}{2} \left(\frac{2u \sin\theta}{g \cos\theta} \right)^2$$

$$= \frac{2u^2 \sin\theta}{g} + \frac{2u^2 \sin\theta \tan^2\theta}{g}$$

$$= \frac{2u^2}{g} \sin\theta \sec^2\theta = \frac{2u^2}{g} \tan\theta \sec\theta.$$

14. *A projectile is fired with a speed u at an angle θ with the horizontal. Find its speed when its direction of motion makes an angle α with the horizontal.*

Solution : Let the speed be v when it makes an angle α with the horizontal. As the horizontal component of velocity remains constant,

$$v \cos\alpha = u \cos\theta$$

or, $v = u \cos\theta \sec\alpha.$

15. *A bullet is fired horizontally aiming at an object which starts falling at the instant the bullet is fired. Show that the bullet will hit the object.*

Solution : The situation is shown in figure (3-W10). The object starts falling from the point B. Draw a vertical line BC through B. Suppose the bullet reaches the line BC at a point D and it takes a time t in doing so.

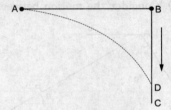

Figure 3-W10

Consider the vertical motion of the bullet. The initial vertical velocity = 0. The distance travelled vertically $= BD = \frac{1}{2}gt^{2}.$ In time t the object also travels a distance $\frac{1}{2}gt^{2} = BD$. Hence at time t, the object will also be at the same point D. Thus, the bullet hits the object at point D.

16. *A man can swim in still water at a speed of 3 km/h. He wants to cross a river that flows at 2 km/h and reach the point directly opposite to his starting point. (a) In which direction should he try to swim (that is, find the angle his body makes with the river flow) ? (b) How much time will he take to cross the river if the river is 500 m wide ?*

Solution : (a) The situation is shown in figure (3-W11). The X-axis is chosen along the river flow and the origin at the starting position of the man. The direction of the velocity of man with respect to ground is along the Y-axis (perpendicular to the river). We have to find the direction of velocity of the man with respect to water.

Let $\vec{v}_{r,g}$ = velocity of the river with respect to the ground

= 2 km/h along the X-axis

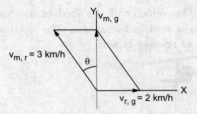

Figure 3-W11

$\vec{v}_{m,r}$ = velocity of the man with respect to the river
= 3 km/h making an angle θ with the Y-axis

and $\vec{v}_{m,g}$ = velocity of the man with respect to the ground along the Y-axis.

We have

$$\vec{v}_{m,g} = \vec{v}_{m,r} + \vec{v}_{r,g}. \qquad \ldots \text{(i)}$$

Taking components along the X-axis

$$0 = -(3 \text{ km/h})\sin\theta + 2 \text{ km/h}$$

or, $\sin\theta = \dfrac{2}{3}.$

(b) Taking components in equation (i) along the Y-axis,

$$v_{m,g} = (3 \text{ km/h}) \cos\theta + 0$$

or, $v_{m,g} = \sqrt{5} \text{ km/h}.$

$$\text{Time} = \frac{\text{Displacement in } y \text{ direction}}{\text{Velocity in } y \text{ direction}}$$

$$= \frac{0.5 \text{ km}}{\sqrt{5} \text{ km/h}} = \frac{\sqrt{5}}{10} \text{ h}.$$

17. *A man can swim at a speed of 3 km/h in still water. He wants to cross a 500 m wide river flowing at 2 km/h. He keeps himself always at an angle of 120° with the river flow while swimming.*

(a) Find the time he takes to cross the river. (b) At what point on the opposite bank will he arrive ?

Solution : The situation is shown in figure (3-W12).

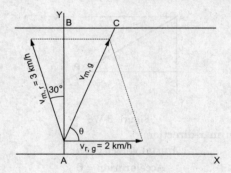

Figure 3-W12

Here $\vec{v}_{r,g}$ = velocity of the river with respect to the ground

$\vec{v}_{m,r}$ = velocity of the man with respect to the river

$\vec{v}_{m,g}$ = velocity of the man with respect to the ground.

(a) We have,

$$\vec{v}_{m,g} = \vec{v}_{m,r} + \vec{v}_{r,g} \qquad \dots \text{ (i)}$$

Hence, the velocity with respect to the ground is along AC. Taking y-components in equation (i),

$$\vec{v}_{m,g} \sin\theta = 3 \text{ km/h} \cos30° + 2 \text{ km/h} \cos90° = \frac{3\sqrt{3}}{2} \text{ km/h.}$$

Time taken to cross the river

$$= \frac{\text{displacement along the } Y\text{-axis}}{\text{velocity along the } Y\text{-axis}}$$

$$= \frac{1/2 \text{ km}}{3\sqrt{3}/2 \text{ km/h}} = \frac{1}{3/3} \text{ h.}$$

(b) Taking x-components in equation (i),

$$\vec{v}_{m,g} \cos\theta = -3 \text{ km/h} \sin30° + 2 \text{ km/h}$$

$$= \frac{1}{2} \text{ km/h.}$$

Displacement along the X-axis as the man crosses the river

$$= (\text{velocity along the } X\text{-axis}) \cdot (\text{time})$$

$$= \left(\frac{1 \text{ km}}{2 \text{ h}}\right) \times \left(\frac{1}{3\sqrt{3}} \text{ h}\right) = \frac{1}{6\sqrt{3}} \text{ km.}$$

18. *A man standing on a road has to hold his umbrella at 30° with the vertical to keep the rain away. He throws the umbrella and starts running at 10 km/h. He finds that raindrops are hitting his head vertically. Find the speed of raindrops with respect to (a) the road, (b) the moving man.*

   Solution : When the man is at rest with respect to the ground, the rain comes to him at an angle 30° with the vertical. This is the direction of the velocity of raindrops with respect to the ground. The situation when the man runs is shown in the figure (3-W13b).

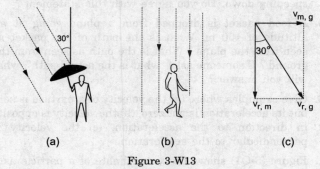

   (a)   (b)   (c)

   Figure 3-W13

   Here $\vec{v}_{r,g}$ = velocity of the rain with respect to the ground
   $\vec{v}_{m,g}$ = velocity of the man with respect to the ground
   and $\vec{v}_{r,m}$ = velocity of the rain with respect to the man.
   We have, $\qquad \vec{v}_{r,g} = \vec{v}_{r,m} + \vec{v}_{m,g}.$ ... (i)
   Taking horizontal components, equation (i) gives
   $$v_{r,g} \sin30° = v_{m,g} = 10 \text{ km/h}$$
   or, $v_{r,g} = \dfrac{10 \text{ km/h}}{\sin30°} = 20 \text{ km/h,}$

Taking vertical components, equation (i) gives

$$v_{r,g} \cos30° = v_{r,m}$$

or, $\qquad v_{r,m} = (20 \text{ km/h}) \dfrac{\sqrt{3}}{2}$

$$= 10\sqrt{3} \text{ km/h.}$$

19. *A man running on a horizontal road at 8 km/h finds the rain falling vertically. He increases his speed to 12 km/h and finds that the drops make angle 30° with the vertical. Find the speed and direction of the rain with respect to the road.*

   Solution :

   We have $\qquad \vec{v}_{rain, road} = \vec{v}_{rain, man} + \vec{v}_{man, road}$ ... (i)
   The two situations given in the problem may be represented by the following figure.

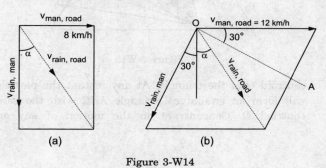

   Figure 3-W14

   $v_{rain, road}$ is same in magnitude and direction in both the figures.
   Taking horizontal components in equation (i) for figure (3-W14a),
   $$v_{rain, road} \sin\alpha = 8 \text{ km/h.} \qquad \dots \text{ (ii)}$$
   Now consider figure (3-W14b). Draw a line $OA \perp v_{rain, man}$ as shown.
   Taking components in equation (i) along the line OA.
   $$v_{rain, road} \sin(30° + \alpha) = 12 \text{ km/h} \cos30°. \qquad \dots \text{ (iii)}$$
   From (ii) and (iii),
   $$\frac{\sin(30° + \alpha)}{\sin\alpha} = \frac{12 \times \sqrt{3}}{8 \times 2}$$
   or, $\qquad \dfrac{\sin30°\cos\alpha + \cos30°\sin\alpha}{\sin\alpha} = \dfrac{3\sqrt{3}}{4}$
   or, $\qquad \dfrac{1}{2} \cot\alpha + \dfrac{\sqrt{3}}{2} = \dfrac{3\sqrt{3}}{4}$
   or, $\qquad \cot\alpha = \dfrac{\sqrt{3}}{2}$
   or, $\qquad \alpha = \cot^{-1} \dfrac{\sqrt{3}}{2}.$

   From (ii), $\qquad v_{rain, road} = \dfrac{8 \text{ km/h}}{\sin\alpha} = 4\sqrt{7} \text{ km/h.}$

20. *Three particles A, B and C are situated at the vertices of an equilateral triangle ABC of side d at t = 0. Each*

of the particles moves with constant speed v. A always has its velocity along AB, B along BC and C along CA. At what time will the particles meet each other?

Solution : The motion of the particles is roughly sketched in figure (3-W15). By symmetry they will meet at the

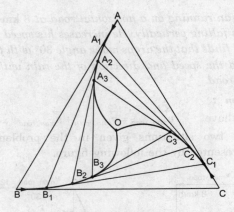

Figure 3-W15

centroid O of the triangle. At any instant the particles will form an equilateral triangle ABC with the same centriod O. Concentrate on the motion of any one

particle, say A. At any instant its velocity makes angle 30° with AO.

The component of this velocity along AO is $v \cos 30°$. This component is the rate of decrease of the distance AO. Initially,

$$AO = \frac{2}{3}\sqrt{d^2 - \left(\frac{d}{2}\right)^2} = \frac{d}{\sqrt{3}}$$

Therefore, the time taken for AO to become zero

$$= \frac{d/\sqrt{3}}{v \cos 30°} = \frac{2d}{\sqrt{3}\, v \times \sqrt{3}} = \frac{2d}{3v}.$$

Alternative : Velocity of A is v along AB. The velocity of B is along BC. Its component along BA is $v \cos 60° = v/2$. Thus, the separation AB decreases at the rate

$$v + \frac{v}{2} = \frac{3v}{2}.$$

Since this rate is constant, the time taken in reducing the separation AB from d to zero is

$$t = \frac{d}{\dfrac{3v}{2}} = \frac{2d}{3v}.$$

□

QUESTIONS FOR SHORT ANSWER

1. Galileo was punished by the Church for teaching that the sun is stationary and the earth moves around it. His opponents held the view that the earth is stationary and the sun moves around it. If the absolute motion has no meaning, are the two viewpoints not equally correct or equally wrong?

2. When a particle moves with constant velocity, its average velocity, its instantaneous velocity and its speed are all equal. Comment on this statement.

3. A car travels at a speed of 60 km/hr due north and the other at a speed of 60 km/hr due east. Are the velocities equal? If no, which one is greater? If you find any of the questions irrelevant, explain.

4. A ball is thrown vertically upward with a speed of 20 m/s. Draw a graph showing the velocity of the ball as a function of time as it goes up and then comes back.

5. The velocity of a particle is towards west at an instant. Its acceleration is not towards west, not towards east, not towards north and not towards south. Give an example of this type of motion.

6. At which point on its path a projectile has the smallest speed?

7. Two particles A and B start from rest and move for equal time on a straight line. The particle A has an acceleration a for the first half of the total time and $2a$ for the second half. The particle B has an acceleration

$2a$ for the first half and a for the second half. Which particle has covered larger distance?

8. If a particle is accelerating, it is either speeding up or speeding down. Do you agree with this statement?

9. A food packet is dropped from a plane going at an altitude of 100 m. What is the path of the packet as seen from the plane? What is the path as seen from the ground? If someone asks "what is the actual path", what will you answer?

10. Give examples where (a) the velocity of a particle is zero but its acceleration is not zero, (b) the velocity is opposite in direction to the acceleration, (c) the velocity is perpendicular to the acceleration.

11. Figure (3-Q1) shows the x coordinate of a particle as a function of time. Find the signs of v_x and a_x at $t = t_1$, $t = t_2$ and $t = t_3$.

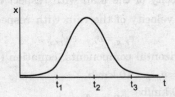

Figure 3-Q1

12. A player hits a baseball at some angle. The ball goes high up in space. The player runs and catches the ball before it hits the ground. Which of the two (the player or the ball) has greater displacement ?

13. The increase in the speed of a car is proportional to the additional petrol put into the engine. Is it possible to

14. accelerate a car without putting more petrol or less petrol into the engine ?

14. Rain is falling vertically. A man running on the road keeps his umbrella tilted but a man standing on the street keeps his umbrella vertical to protect himself from the rain. But both of them keep their umbrella vertical to avoid the vertical sun-rays. Explain.

OBJECTIVE I

1. A motor car is going due north at a speed of 50 km/h. It makes a 90° left turn without changing the speed. The change in the velocity of the car is about
   (a) 50 km/h towards west
   (b) 70 km/h towards south-west
   (c) 70 km/h towards north-west
   (d) zero.

2. Figure (3-Q2) shows the displacement-time graph of a particle moving on the X-axis.

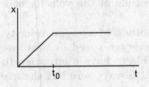

Figure 3-Q2

   (a) the particle is continuously going in positive x direction
   (b) the particle is at rest
   (c) the velocity increases up to a time t_0, and then becomes constant
   (d) the particle moves at a constant velocity up to a time t_0, and then stops.

3. A particle has a velocity u towards east at $t = 0$. Its acceleration is towards west and is constant. Let x_A and x_B be the magnitude of displacements in the first 10 seconds and the next 10 seconds
   (a) $x_A < x_B$ (b) $x_A = x_B$ (c) $x_A > x_B$
   (d) the information is insufficient to decide the relation of x_A with x_B.

4. A person travelling on a straight line moves with a uniform velocity v_1 for some time and with uniform velocity v_2 for the next equal time. The average velocity v is given by
   (a) $v = \dfrac{v_1 + v_2}{2}$ (b) $v = \sqrt{v_1 v_2}$
   (c) $\dfrac{2}{v} = \dfrac{1}{v_1} + \dfrac{1}{v_2}$ (d) $\dfrac{1}{v} = \dfrac{1}{v_1} + \dfrac{1}{v_2}$.

5. A person travelling on a straight line moves with a uniform velocity v_1 for a distance x and with a uniform velocity v_2 for the next equal distance. The average velocity v is given by

   (a) $v = \dfrac{v_1 + v_2}{2}$ (b) $v = \sqrt{v_1 v_2}$
   (c) $\dfrac{2}{v} = \dfrac{1}{v_1} + \dfrac{1}{v_2}$ (d) $\dfrac{1}{v} = \dfrac{1}{v_1} + \dfrac{1}{v_2}$.

6. A stone is released from an elevator going up with an acceleration a. The acceleration of the stone after the release is
   (a) a upward   (b) $(g - a)$ upward
   (c) $(g - a)$ downward   (d) g downward.

7. A person standing near the edge of the top of a building throws two balls A and B. The ball A is thrown vertically upward and B is thrown vertically downward with the same speed. The ball A hits the ground with a speed v_A and the ball B hits the ground with a speed v_B. We have
   (a) $v_A > v_B$, (b) $v_A < v_B$ (c) $v_A = v_B$
   (d) the relation between v_A and v_B depends on height of the building above the ground.

8. In a projectile motion the velocity
   (a) is always perpendicular to the acceleration
   (b) is never perpendicular to the acceleration
   (c) is perpendicular to the acceleration for one instant only
   (d) is perpendicular to the acceleration for two instants.

9. Two bullets are fired simultaneously, horizontally and with different speeds from the same place. Which bullet will hit the ground first ?
   (a) the faster one   (b) the slower one
   (c) both will reach simultaneously
   (d) depends on the masses.

10. The range of a projectile fired at an angle of 15° is 50 m. If it is fired with the same speed at an angle of 45°, its range will be
    (a) 25 m   (b) 37 m   (c) 50 m   (d) 100 m.

11. Two projectiles A and B are projected with angle of projection 15° for the projectile A and 45° for the projectile B. If R_A and R_B be the horizontal range for the two projectiles, then
    (a) $R_A < R_B$ (b) $R_A = R_B$ (c) $R_A > R_B$
    (d) the information is insufficient to decide the relation of R_A with R_B.

12. A river is flowing from west to east at a speed of 5 metres per minute. A man on the south bank of the river, capable of swimming at 10 metres per minute in still water, wants to swim across the river in the shortest time. He should swim in a direction

(a) due north   (b) 30° east of north
(c) 30° north of west   (d) 60° east of north.

13. In the arrangement shown in figure (3-Q3), the ends P and Q of an inextensible string move downwards with uniform speed u. Pulleys A and B are fixed. The mass M moves upwards with a speed
    (a) $2u \cos\theta$ (b) $u/\cos\theta$ (c) $2u/\cos\theta$ (d) $u\cos\theta$.

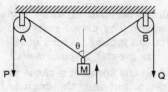

Figure 3-Q3

OBJECTIVE II

1. Consider the motion of the tip of the minute hand of a clock. In one hour
   (a) the displacement is zero
   (b) the distance covered is zero
   (c) the average speed is zero
   (d) the average velocity is zero

2. A particle moves along the X-axis as
   $$x = u(t - 2 \text{ s}) + a(t - 2 \text{ s})^2.$$
   (a) the initial velocity of the particle is u
   (b) the acceleration of the particle is a
   (c) the acceleration of the particle is $2a$
   (d) at $t = 2$ s particle is at the origin.

3. Pick the correct statements :
   (a) Average speed of a particle in a given time is never less than the magnitude of the average velocity.

   (b) It is possible to have a situation in which $\left|\dfrac{d\vec{v}}{dt}\right| \neq 0$ but $\dfrac{d}{dt}\left|\vec{v}\right| = 0$.

   (c) The average velocity of a particle is zero in a time interval. It is possible that the instantaneous velocity is never zero in the interval.

   (d) The average velocity of a particle moving on a straight line is zero in a time interval. It is possible that the instantaneous velocity is never zero in the interval. (Infinite accelerations are not allowed.)

4. An object may have
   (a) varying speed without having varying velocity
   (b) varying velocity without having varying speed
   (c) nonzero acceleration without having varying velocity
   (d) nonzero acceleration without having varying speed.

5. Mark the correct statements for a particle going on a straight line :
   (a) If the velocity and acceleration have opposite sign, the object is slowing down.
   (b) If the position and velocity have opposite sign, the particle is moving towards the origin.
   (c) If the velocity is zero at an instant, the acceleration should also be zero at that instant.
   (d) If the velocity is zero for a time interval, the acceleration is zero at any instant within the time interval.

6. The velocity of a particle is zero at $t = 0$.
   (a) The acceleration at $t = 0$ must be zero.
   (b) The acceleration at $t = 0$ may be zero.
   (c) If the acceleration is zero from $t = 0$ to $t = 10$ s, the speed is also zero in this interval.
   (d) If the speed is zero from $t = 0$ to $t = 10$ s the acceleration is also zero in this interval.

7. Mark the correct statements :
   (a) The magnitude of the velocity of a particle is equal to its speed.
   (b) The magnitude of average velocity in an interval is equal to its average speed in that interval.
   (c) It is possible to have a situation in which the speed of a particle is always zero but the average speed is not zero.
   (d) It is possible to have a situation in which the speed of the particle is never zero but the average speed in an interval is zero.

8. The velocity-time plot for a particle moving on a straight line is shown in the figure (3-Q4).

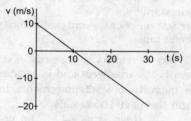

Figure 3-Q4

   (a) The particle has a constant acceleration.
   (b) The particle has never turned around.
   (c) The particle has zero displacement.
   (d) The average speed in the interval 0 to 10 s is the same as the average speed in the interval 10 s to 20 s.

9. Figure (3-Q5) shows the position of a particle moving on the X-axis as a function of time.
   (a) The particle has come to rest 6 times.
   (b) The maximum speed is at $t = 6$ s.
   (c) The velocity remains positive for $t = 0$ to $t = 6$ s.
   (d) The average velocity for the total period shown is negative.

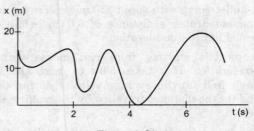

Figure 3-Q5

10. The accelerations of a particle as seen from two frames S_1 and S_2 have equal magnitude 4 m/s^2.
(a) The frames must be at rest with respect to each other.
(b) The frames may be moving with respect to each other but neither should be accelerated with respect to the other.
(c) The acceleration of S_2 with respect to S_1 may either be zero or 8 m/s^2.
(d) The acceleration of S_2 with respect to S_1 may be anything between zero and 8 m/s^2.

EXERCISES

1. A man has to go 50 m due north, 40 m due east and 20 m due south to reach a field. (a) What distance he has to walk to reach the field? (b) What is his displacement from his house to the field?

2. A particle starts from the origin, goes along the X-axis to the point (20 m, 0) and then returns along the same line to the point (−20 m, 0). Find the distance and displacement of the particle during the trip.

3. It is 260 km from Patna to Ranchi by air and 320 km by road. An aeroplane takes 30 minutes to go from Patna to Ranchi whereas a delux bus takes 8 hours. (a) Find the average speed of the plane. (b) Find the average speed of the bus. (c) Find the average velocity of the plane. (d) Find the average velocity of the bus.

4. When a person leaves his home for sightseeing by his car, the meter reads 12352 km. When he returns home after two hours the reading is 12416 km. (a) What is the average speed of the car during this period? (b) What is the average velocity?

5. An athelete takes 2·0 s to reach his maximum speed of 18·0 km/h. What is the magnitude of his average acceleration?

6. The speed of a car as a function of time is shown in figure (3-E1). Find the distance travelled by the car in 8 seconds and its acceleration.

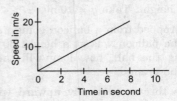

Figure 3-E1

7. The acceleration of a cart started at $t = 0$, varies with time as shown in figure (3-E2). Find the distance travelled in 30 seconds and draw the position-time graph.

8. Figure (3-E3) shows the graph of velocity versus time for a particle going along the X-axis. Find (a) the

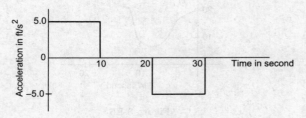

Figure 3-E2

acceleration, (b) the distance travelled in 0 to 10 s and (c) the displacement in 0 to 10 s.

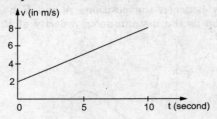

Figure 3-E3

9. Figure (3-E4) shows the graph of the x-coordinate of a particle going along the X-axis as a function of time. Find (a) the average velocity during 0 to 10 s, (b) instantaneous velocity at 2, 5, 8 and 12s.

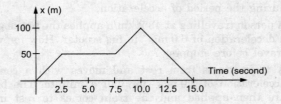

Figure 3-E4

10. From the velocity–time plot shown in figure (3-E5), find the distance travelled by the particle during the first 40

seconds. Also find the average velocity during this period.

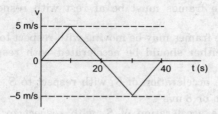

Figure 3-E5

11. Figure (3-E6) shows x-t graph of a particle. Find the time t such that the average velocity of the particle during the period 0 to t is zero.

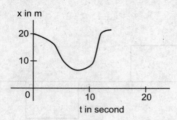

Figure 3-E6

12. A particle starts from a point A and travels along the solid curve shown in figure (3-E7). Find approximately the position B of the particle such that the average velocity between the positions A and B has the same direction as the instantaneous velocity at B.

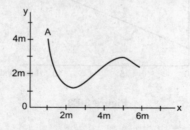

Figure 3-E7

13. An object having a velocity 4.0 m/s is accelerated at the rate of 1.2 m/s^2 for 5.0 s. Find the distance travelled during the period of acceleration.

14. A person travelling at 43.2 km/h applies the brake giving a deceleration of 6.0 m/s^2 to his scooter. How far will it travel before stopping ?

15. A train starts from rest and moves with a constant acceleration of 2.0 m/s^2 for half a minute. The brakes are then applied and the train comes to rest in one minute. Find (a) the total distance moved by the train, (b) the maximum speed attained by the train and (c) the position(s) of the train at half the maximum speed.

16. A bullet travelling with a velocity of 16 m/s penetrates a tree trunk and comes to rest in 0.4 m. Find the time taken during the retardation.

17. A bullet going with speed 350 m/s enters a concrete wall and penetrates a distance of 5.0 cm before coming to rest. Find the deceleration.

18. A particle starting from rest moves with constant acceleration. If it takes 5.0 s to reach the speed 18.0 km/h find (a) the average velocity during this period, and (b) the distance travelled by the particle during this period.

19. A driver takes 0.20 s to apply the brakes after he sees a need for it. This is called the reaction time of the driver. If he is driving a car at a speed of 54 km/h and the brakes cause a deceleration of 6.0 m/s^2, find the distance travelled by the car after he sees the need to put the brakes on.

20. Complete the following table :

Car Model	Driver X Reaction time 0.20 s	Driver Y Reaction time 0.30 s
A (deceleration on hard braking = 6.0 m/s^2)	Speed = 54 km/h Braking distance $a = $ .... Total stopping distance $b = $	Speed = 72 km/h Braking distance $c = $ .... Total stopping distance $d = $ ....
B (deceleration on hard braking = 7.5 m/s^2)	Speed = 54 km/h Braking distance $e = $ .... Total stopping distance $f = $	Speed = 72km/h Braking distance $g = $ .... Total stopping distance $h = $ ....

21. A police jeep is chasing a culprit going on a motorbike. The motorbike crosses a turning at a speed of 72 km/h. The jeep follows it at a speed of 90 km/h, crossing the turning ten seconds later than the bike. Assuming that they travel at constant speeds, how far from the turning will the jeep catch up with the bike ?

22. A car travelling at 60 km/h overtakes another car travelling at 42 km/h. Assuming each car to be 5.0 m long, find the time taken during the overtake and the total road distance used for the overtake.

23. A ball is projected vertically upward with a speed of 50 m/s. Find (a) the maximum height, (b) the time to reach the maximum height, (c) the speed at half the maximum height. Take $g = 10$ m/s^2.

24. A ball is dropped from a balloon going up at a speed of 7 m/s. If the balloon was at a height 60 m at the time of dropping the ball, how long will the ball take in reaching the ground ?

25. A stone is thrown vertically upward with a speed of 28 m/s. (a) Find the maximum height reached by the stone. (b) Find its velocity one second before it reaches the maximum height. (c) Does the answer of part (b) change if the initial speed is more than 28 m/s such as 40 m/s or 80 m/s ?

26. A person sitting on the top of a tall building is dropping balls at regular intervals of one second. Find the positions of the 3rd, 4th and 5th ball when the 6th ball is being dropped.

27. A healthy youngman standing at a distance of 7 m from a 11·8 m high building sees a kid slipping from the top floor. With what speed (assumed uniform) should he run to catch the kid at the arms height (1·8 m) ?

28. An NCC parade is going at a uniform speed of 6 km/h through a place under a berry tree on which a bird is sitting at a height of 12·1 m. At a particular instant the bird drops a berry. Which cadet (give the distance from the tree at the instant) will receive the berry on his uniform ?

29. A ball is dropped from a height. If it takes 0·200 s to cross the last 6·00 m before hitting the ground, find the height from which it was dropped. Take $g = 10$ m/s^2.

30. A ball is dropped from a height of 5 m onto a sandy floor and penetrates the sand up to 10 cm before coming to rest. Find the retardation of the ball in sand assuming it to be uniform.

31. An elevator is descending with uniform acceleration. To measure the acceleration, a person in the elevator drops a coin at the moment the elevator starts. The coin is 6 ft above the floor of the elevator at the time it is dropped. The person observes that the coin strikes the floor in 1 second. Calculate from these data the acceleration of the elevator.

32. A ball is thrown horizontally from a point 100 m above the ground with a speed of 20 m/s. Find (a) the time it takes to reach the ground, (b) the horizontal distance it travels before reaching the ground, (c) the velocity (direction and magnitude) with which it strikes the ground.

33. A ball is thrown at a speed of 40 m/s at an angle of 60° with the horizontal. Find (a) the maximum height reached and (b) the range of the ball. Take $g = 10$ m/s^2.

34. In a soccer practice session the football is kept at the centre of the field 40 yards from the 10 ft high goalposts. A goal is attempted by kicking the football at a speed of 64 ft/s at an angle of 45° to the horizontal. Will the ball reach the goal post ?

35. A popular game in Indian villages is *goli* which is played with small glass balls called golis. The goli of one player is situated at a distance of 2·0 m from the goli of the second player. This second player has to project his goli by keeping the thumb of the left hand at the place of his goli, holding the goli between his two middle fingers and making the throw. If the projected goli hits the goli of the first player, the second player wins. If the height from which the goli is projected is 19·6 cm from the ground and the goli is to be projected horizontally, with what speed should it be projected so that it directly hits the stationary goli without falling on the ground earlier ?

36. Figure (3-E8) shows a 11·7 ft wide ditch with the approach roads at an angle of 15° with the horizontal. With what minimum speed should a motorbike be moving on the road so that it safely crosses the ditch ?

Figure 3-E8

Assume that the length of the bike is 5 ft, and it leaves the road when the front part runs out of the approach road.

37. A person standing on the top of a cliff 171 ft high has to throw a packet to his friend standing on the ground 228 ft horizontally away. If he throws the packet directly aiming at the friend with a speed of 15·0 ft/s, how short will the packet fall ?

38. A ball is projected from a point on the floor with a speed of 15 m/s at an angle of 60° with the horizontal. Will it hit a vertical wall 5 m away from the point of projection and perpendicular to the plane of projection without hitting the floor ? Will the answer differ if the wall is 22 m away ?

39. Find the average velocity of a projectile between the instants it crosses half the maximum height. It is projected with a speed u at an angle θ with the horizontal.

40. A bomb is dropped from a plane flying horizontally with uniform speed. Show that the bomb will explode vertically below the plane. Is the statement true if the plane flies with uniform speed but not horizontally ?

41. A boy standing on a long railroad car throws a ball straight upwards. The car is moving on the horizontal road with an acceleration of 1 m/s^2 and the projection velocity in the vertical direction is 9·8 m/s. How far behind the boy will the ball fall on the car ?

42. A staircase contains three steps each 10 cm high and 20 cm wide (figure 3-E9). What should be the minimum horizontal velocity of a ball rolling off the uppermost plane so as to hit directly the lowest plane ?

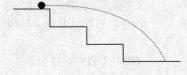

Figure 3-E9

43. A person is standing on a truck moving with a constant velocity of 14·7 m/s on a horizontal road. The man throws a ball in such a way that it returns to the truck after the truck has moved 58·8 m. Find the speed and the angle of projection (a) as seen from the truck, (b) as seen from the road.

44. The benches of a gallery in a cricket stadium are 1 m wide and 1 m high. A batsman strikes the ball at a level one metre above the ground and hits a mammoth sixer. The ball starts at 35 m/s at an angle of 53° with the horizontal. The benches are perpendicular to the plane of motion and the first bench is 110 m from the batsman. On which bench will the ball hit ?

45. A man is sitting on the shore of a river. He is in the line of a 1·0 m long boat and is 5·5 m away from the centre of the boat. He wishes to throw an apple into the boat. If he can throw the apple only with a speed of 10 m/s, find the minimum and maximum angles of projection for successful shot. Assume that the point of

projection and the edge of the boat are in the same horizontal level.

46. A river 400 m wide is flowing at a rate of 2·0 m/s. A boat is sailing at a velocity of 10 m/s with respect to the water, in a direction perpendicular to the river. (a) Find the time taken by the boat to reach the opposite bank. (b) How far from the point directly opposite to the starting point does the boat reach the opposite bank ?

47. A swimmer wishes to cross a 500 m wide river flowing at 5 km/h. His speed with respect to water is 3 km/h. (a) If he heads in a direction making an angle θ with the flow, find the time he takes to cross the river. (b) Find the shortest possible time to cross the river.

48. Consider the situation of the previous problem. The man has to reach the other shore at the point directly opposite to his starting point. If he reaches the other shore somewhere else, he has to walk down to this point. Find the minimum distance that he has to walk.

49. An aeroplane has to go from a point A to another point B, 500 km away due 30° east of north. A wind is blowing due north at a speed of 20 m/s. The air-speed of the plane is 150 m/s. (a) Find the direction in which the pilot should head the plane to reach the point B. (b) Find the time taken by the plane to go from A to B.

50. Two friends A and B are standing a distance x apart in an open field and wind is blowing from A to B. A beats a drum and B hears the sound t_1 time after he sees the event. A and B interchange their positions and the experiment is repeated. This time B hears the drum t_2 time after he sees the event. Calculate the velocity of sound in still air v and the velocity of wind u. Neglect the time light takes in travelling between the friends.

51. Suppose A and B in the previous problem change their positions in such a way that the line joining them becomes perpendicular to the direction of wind while maintaining the separation x. What will be the time lag B finds between seeing and hearing the drum beating by A ?

52. Six particles situated at the corners of a regular hexagon of side a move at a constant speed v. Each particle maintains a direction towards the particle at the next corner. Calculate the time the particles will take to meet each other.

□

ANSWERS

OBJECTIVE I

1. (b) 2. (d) 3. (d) 4. (a) 5. (c) 6. (d)
7. (c) 8. (c) 9. (c) 10. (d) 11. (d) 12. (a)
13. (b)

OBJECTIVE II

1. (a), (d)   2. (c), (d)   3. (a), (b), (c)
4. (b), (d)   5. (a), (b), (d)   6. (b), (c), (d)
7. (a)   8. (a), (d)   9. (a), (d)
10. (d)

EXERCISES

1. (a) 110 m   (b) 50 m, $\tan^{-1} 3/4$ north to east
2. 60 m, 20 m in the negative direction
3. (a) 520 km/h   (b) 40 km/h
   (c) 520 km/h Patna to Ranchi
   (d) 32·5 km/h Patna to Ranchi
4. 32 km/h   (b) zero
5. 2·5 m/s²
6. 80 m, 2·5 m/s²
7. 1000 ft
8. (a) 0·6 m/s²   (b) 50 m   (c) 50 m
9. (a) 10 m/s   (b) 20 m/s, zero, 20 m/s, −20 m/s
10. 100 m, zero
11. 12 s
12. x = 5 m, y = 3 m
13. 35 m
14. 12 m
15. (a) 2·7 km   (b) 60 m/s   (c) 225 m and 2·25 km
16. 0·05 s
17. $12·2 \times 10^5$ m/s²
18. (a) 2·5 m/s   (b) 12·5 m
19. 22 m
20. (a) 19 m   (b) 22 m   (c) 33 m   (d) 39 m
    (e) 15 m   (f) 18 m   (g) 27 m   (h) 33 m
21. 1·0 km
22. 2 s, 38 m
23. (a) 125 m   (b) 5 s   (c) 35 m/s
24. 4·3 s
25. (a) 40 m   (b) 9·8 m/s   (c) No
26. 44·1 m, 19·6 m and 4·9 m below the top
27. 4·9 m/s
28. 2·62 m
29. 48 m
30. 490 m/s²
31. 20 ft/s²
32. (a) 4·5 s   (b) 90 m   (c) 49 m/s, θ = 66° with horizontal
33. (a) 60 m   (b) 80√3 m
34. Yes
35. 10 m/s
36. 32 ft/s

37. 192 ft

38. Yes, Yes

39. $u\cos\theta$, horizontal in the plane of projection

41. 2 m

42. 2 m/s

43. (a) 19·6 m/s upward
    (b) 24·5 m/s at 53° with horizontal

44. Sixth

45. Minimum angle 15°, maximum angle 75° but there is an interval of 53° between 15° and 75°, which is not allowed for successful shot

46. (a) 40 s   (b) 80 m

47. (a) $\dfrac{10\ \text{minutes}}{\sin\theta}$ (b) 10 minutes

48. 2/3 km

49. (a) $\sin^{-1}(1/15)$ east of the line AB (b) 50 min

50. $\dfrac{x}{2}\left(\dfrac{1}{t_1}+\dfrac{1}{t_2}\right),\ \dfrac{x}{2}\left(\dfrac{1}{t_1}-\dfrac{1}{t_2}\right)$

51. $\dfrac{x}{\sqrt{v^2-u^2}}$

52. $2\,a/v$.

□

CHAPTER 4

THE FORCES

4.1 INTRODUCTION

Force is a word which we have all heard about. When you push or pull some object you exert a force on it. If you push a body you exert a force away from yourself; when you pull, you exert a force toward yourself. When you hold a heavy block in your hand you exert a large force; when you hold a light block, you exert a small force.

Can nonliving bodies exert a force ? Yes, they can. If we stand in a great storm, we feel that the wind is exerting a force on us. When we suspend a heavy block from a rope, the rope holds the block just as a man can hold it in air. When we comb our dry hair and bring the comb close to small pieces of paper, the pieces jump to the comb. The comb has attracted the paper pieces i.e. the comb has exerted force on the pieces. When a cork is dipped in water it comes to the surface; if we want to keep it inside water, we have to push it downward. We say that water exerts a force on the cork in the upward direction.

The SI unit for measuring the force is called a *newton*. Approximately, it is the force needed to hold a body of mass 102 g near the earth's surface. An accurate quantitative definition can be framed using Newton's laws of motion to be studied in the next chapter.

Force is an interaction between two objects. Force is exerted by an object A on another object B. For any force you may ask two questions, (i) who exerted this force and (ii) on which object was this force exerted ? Thus, when a block is kept on a table, the table exerts a force on the block to hold it.

Force is a vector quantity and if more than one forces act on a particle we can find the resultant force using the laws of vector addition. Note that in all the examples quoted above, if a body A exerts a force on B, the body B also exerts a force on A. Thus, the table exerts a force on the block to hold it and the block exerts a force on the table to press it down. When a heavy block is suspended by a rope, the rope exerts a force on the block to hold it and the block exerts a force on the rope to make it tight and stretched. In fact these are a few examples of Newton's third law of motion which may be stated as follows.

Newton's Third Law of Motion

If a body A exerts a force $\vec{F}$ on another body B, then B exerts a force $-\vec{F}$ on A, the two forces acting along the line joining the bodies.

The two forces $\vec{F}$ and $-\vec{F}$ connected by Newton's third law are called *action-reaction pair*. Any one may be called 'action' and the other 'reaction'.

We shall discuss this law in greater detail in the next chapter.

The various types of forces in nature can be grouped in four categories :

    (a) Gravitational,   (b) Electromagnetic,

    (c) Nuclear   and (d) Weak.

4.2 GRAVITATIONAL FORCE

Any two bodies attract each other by virtue of their masses. The force of attraction between two point masses is $F = G\dfrac{m_1 m_2}{r^2}$, where m_1 and m_2 are the masses of the particles and r is the distance between them. G is a universal constant having the value $6{\cdot}67 \times 10^{-11}$ N-m^2/kg^2. To find the gravitational force on an extended body by another such body, we have to write the force on each particle of the 1st body by all the particles of the second body and then we have to sum up vectorially all the forces acting on the first body. For example, suppose each body contains just three particles, and let $\vec{F}_{ij}$ denote the force on the i th particle of the first body due to the j th particle of the second body. To find the resultant force on the first body (figure 4.1), we have to add the following 9 forces :

$$\vec{F}_{11},\ \vec{F}_{12},\ \vec{F}_{13},\ \vec{F}_{21},\ \vec{F}_{22},\ \vec{F}_{23},\ \vec{F}_{31},\ \vec{F}_{32},\ \vec{F}_{33}.$$

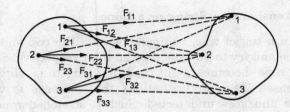

Figure 4.1

For large bodies having a large number of particles, we have to add quite a large number of forces. If the bodies are assumed continuous (a good approximation in our course), one has to go through the integration process for the infinite summation involved. However, the integration yields a particularly simple result for a special case which is of great practical importance and we quote it below. The proof of this result will be given in a later chapter.

The gravitational force exerted by a spherically symmetric body of mass m_1 on another such body of mass m_2 kept outside the first body is $G\frac{m_1m_2}{r^2}$, where r is the distance between the centres of the two bodies. Thus, for the calculation of gravitational force between two spherically symmetric bodies, they can be treated as point masses placed at their centres.

Gravitational Force on Small Bodies by the Earth

The force of attraction exerted by the earth on other objects is called *gravity*. Consider the earth to be a homogeneous sphere of radius R and mass M. The values of R and M are roughly 6400 km and 6×10^{24} kg respectively. Assuming that the earth is spherically symmetric, the force it exerts on a particle of mass m kept near its surface is by the previous result, $F = G\frac{Mm}{R^2}$. The direction of this force is towards the centre of the earth which is called the *vertically downward* direction.

The same formula is valid to a good approximation even if we have a body of some other shape instead of a particle, provided the body is very small in size as compared to the earth. The quantity $G\frac{M}{R^2}$ is a constant and has the dimensions of acceleration. It is called the *acceleration due to gravity*, and is denoted by the letter g (a quantity much different from G). Its value is approximately 9.8 m/s^2. For simplicity of calculations we shall often use $g = 10$ m/s^2. We shall find in the next chapter that all bodies falling towards earth (remaining all the time close to the earth's surface) have this particular value of acceleration and hence the name acceleration due to gravity. Thus, the force exerted by the earth on a small body of mass m, kept near the earth's surface is mg in the vertically downward direction.

The gravitational constant G is so small that the gravitational force becomes appreciable only if at least one of the two bodies has a large mass. To have an idea of the magnitude of gravitational forces in practical life, consider two small bodies of mass 10 kg each, separated by 0.5 m. The gravitational force is

$$F = \frac{6.7 \times 10^{-11}\ \text{N--m}^2/\text{kg}^2 \times 10^2\ \text{kg}^2}{0.25\ \text{m}^2}$$

$$= 2.7 \times 10^{-8}\ \text{N}$$

a force needed to hold about 3 microgram. In many of the situations we encounter, it is a good approximation to neglect all the gravitational forces other than that exerted by the earth.

4.3 ELECTROMAGNETIC (EM) FORCE

Over and above the gravitational force $G\frac{m_1m_2}{r^2}$, the particles may exert upon each other electromagnetic forces. If two particles having charges q_1 and q_2 are at rest with respect to the observer, the force between them has a magnitude

$$F = \frac{1}{4\pi\varepsilon_0}\frac{q_1q_2}{r^2}$$

where $\varepsilon = 8.85419 \times 10^{-12}$ C^2/N--m^2 is a constant. The quantity $\frac{1}{4\pi\varepsilon_0}$ is $9.0 \times 10^9\ \frac{\text{N--m}^2}{\text{C}^2}$.

This is called *Coulomb force* and it acts along the line joining the particles. If q_1 and q_2 are of same nature (both positive or both negative), the force is repulsive otherwise it is attractive. It is this force which is responsible for the attraction of small paper pieces when brought near a recently used comb. The electromagnetic force between moving charged paritcles is comparatively more complicated and contains terms other than the Coulomb force.

Ordinary matter is composed of electrons, protons and neutrons. Each electron has 1.6×10^{-19} coulomb of negative charge and each proton has an equal amount of positive charge. In atoms, the electrons are bound by the electromagnetic force acting on them due to the protons. The atoms combine to form molecules due to the electromagnetic forces. A lot of atomic and molecular phenomena result from electromagnetic forces between the subatomic particles (electrons, protons, charged mesons, etc.).

Apart from the atomic and molecular phenomena, the electromagnetic forces show up in many forms in daily experience. Some examples having practical importance given below.

(a) Forces between Two Surfaces in Contact

When we put two bodies in contact with each other, the atoms at the two surfaces come close to each other. The charged constituents of the atoms of the two bodies exert great forces on each other and a measurable force results out of it. We say that the two bodies in contact exert forces on each other. When you place a book on a table, the table exerts an upward force on the book to hold it. This force comes from the electromagnetic forces acting between the atoms and molecules of the surface of the book and of the table.

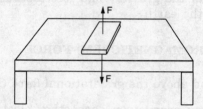

Figure 4.2

Generally, the forces between the two objects in contact are along the common normal (perpendicular) to the surfaces of contact and is that of a push or repulsion. Thus, the table pushes the book away from it (i.e., upward) and the book pushes the table downward (again away from it).

However, the forces between the two bodies in contact may have a component parallel to the surface of contact. This component is known as *friction*. We assume existence of frictionless surfaces which can exert forces only along the direction perpendicular to them. The bodies with smooth surfaces can exert only small amount of forces parallel to the surface and hence are close to frictionless surface. Thus, it is difficult to stay on a smooth metallic lamp-post, because it cannot exert enough vertical force and so it will not hold you there. The same is not true if you try to stay on the trunk of a tree which is quite rough. We shall often use the word smooth to mean frictionless.

The contact forces obey Newton's third law. Thus the book in figure (4.2) exerts a downward force F on the table to press it down and the table exerts an equal upward force F on the book to hold it there. When you stay on the trunk of a tree, it exerts a frictional upward force (frictional force because it is parallel to the surface of the tree) on you to hold you there, and you exert an equal frictional downward force on the tree.

(b) Tension in a String or a Rope

In a tug of war, two persons hold the two ends of a rope and try to pull the rope on their respective sides. The rope becomes tight and its length is slightly increased. In many situations this increase is very small and goes undetected. Such a stretched rope is said to be in a state of tension.

Similarly, if a heavy block hangs from a ceiling by a string, the string is in a state of tension. The electrons and protons of the string near the lower end exert forces on the electrons and protons of the block and the resultant of these forces is the force exerted by the string on the block. It is the resultant of these electromagnetic forces which supports the block and prevents it from falling. A string or rope under tension exerts electromagnetic forces on the bodies attached at the two ends to *pull* them.

(c) Force due to a Spring

When a metallic wire is coiled it becomes a spring. The straight line distance between the ends of a spring is called its length. If a spring is placed on a horizontal surface with no horizontal force on it, its length is called the *natural length*. Every spring has its own natural length. The spring can be stretched to increase its length and it can be compressed to decrease its length. When a spring is stretched, it pulls the bodies attached to its ends and when compressed, it pushes the bodies attached to its ends. If the extension or the compression is not too large, the force exerted by the spring is proportional to the change in its length. Thus, if the spring has a length x and its natural length is x_0 the magnitude of the force exerted by it will be

$$F = k|x - x_0| = k|\Delta x|.$$

If the spring is extended, the force will be directed towards its centre and if compressed, it will be directed away from the centre. The proportionality constant k, which is the force per unit extension or compression, is called the *spring constant* of the spring. This force again comes into picture due to the electromagnetic forces between the atoms of the material.

The macroscopic bodies which we have to generally deal with are electrically neutral. Hence two bodies not in contact do not exert appreciable electromagnetic forces. The forces between the charged particles of the first body and those of the second body have both attractive and repulsive nature and hence they largely cancel each other. This is not the case with gravitational forces. The gravitational forces between the particles of one body and those of the other body are all attractive and hence they add to give an appreciable gravitational force in many cases. Thus, the gravitational force between the earth and a 1 kg block kept 100 m above the earth's surface is about 9·8 N whereas the electromagnetic force between the earth and this block is almost zero even though both these bodies contain a very large number of charged particles, the electrons and the protons.

Example 4.1

Suppose the exact charge neutrality does not hold in a world and the electron has a charge 1% less in magnitude than the proton. Calculate the Coulomb force acting between two blocks of iron each of mass 1 kg separated by a distance of 1 m. Number of protons in an iron atom = 26 and 58 kg of iron contains 6×10^{26} atoms.

Solution : Each atom of iron will have a net positive charge $26 \times 0.01 \times 1.6 \times 10^{-19}$ C on it in the assumed world. The total positive charge on a 1 kg block would be

$$\frac{6 \times 10^{26}}{58} \times 26 \times 1.6 \times 10^{-21} \text{ C}$$

$$= 4.3 \times 10^{5} \text{ C}.$$

The Coulomb force between the two blocks is

$$= \frac{1}{4\pi\varepsilon_0} \frac{q_1 q_2}{r^2} = \frac{9.0 \times 10^{9} \text{ N–m}^2/\text{C}^2 \times (4.3 \times 10^{5} \text{ C})^2}{(1 \text{ m})^2}$$

$$= 9 \times 10^{9} \times 18.49 \times 10^{10} \text{ N}$$

$$= 1.7 \times 10^{21} \text{ N}.$$

A tremendous force indeed !

4.4 NUCLEAR FORCES

Each atom contains a certain number of protons and neutrons in its nucleus. The nucleus occupies a volume of about 10^{-44} m^3 whereas the atom itself has a volume of about 10^{-23} m^3. Thus, the nucleus occupies only $1/10^{21}$ of the volume of the atom. Yet it contains about 99·98% of the mass of the atom. The atomic nucleus of a non-radioactive element is a stable particle. For example, if both the electrons are removed from a helium atom, we get the bare nucleus of helium which is called an *alpha particle*. The alpha particle is a stable object and once created it can remain intact until it is not made to interact with other objects.

An alpha particle contains two protons and two neutrons. The protons will repel each other due to the Coulomb force and will try to break the nucleus. Neutrons will be silent spectators in this electromagnetic drama (Remember, neutron is an uncharged particle). Then, why does the Coulomb force fail to break the nucleus ? Can it be the gravitational attractive force which keeps the nucleus bound ? All the protons and the neutrons will take part in this attraction, but if calculated, the gravitational attraction will turn out to be totally negligible as compared to the Coulomb repulsion.

In fact, a third kind of force, altogether different and over and above the gravitational and electromagnetic force, is operating here. These forces are called *Nuclear forces* and are exerted only if the interacting particles are protons or neutrons or both. (There are some more cases where this force operates but we shall not deal with them.) These forces are largely attractive, but are short ranged. The forces are much weaker than the Coulomb force if the separation between the particles is more than say 10^{-14} m. But for smaller separation ($\approx 10^{-15}$ m) the nuclear force is much stronger than the Coulomb force and being attractive it holds the nucleus stable.

Being short ranged, these forces come into picture only if the changes within the nucleus are discussed. As bare nuclei are less frequently encountered in daily life, one is generally unaware of these forces. Radioactivity, nuclear energy (fission, fusion) etc. result from nuclear forces.

4.5 WEAK FORCES

Yet another kind of forces is encountered when reactions involving protons, electrons and neutrons take place. A neutron can change itself into a proton and simultaneously emit an electron and a particle called *antinutrino*. This is called β^- decay. Never think that a neutron is made up of a proton, an electron and an antineutrino. A proton can also change into neutron and simultaneously emit a positron (and a neutrino). This is called β^+ decay. The forces responsible for these changes are different from gravitational, electromagnetic or nuclear forces. Such forces are called weak forces. The range of weak forces is very small, in fact much smaller than the size of a proton or a neutron. Thus, its effect is experienced inside such particles only.

4.6 SCOPE OF CLASSICAL PHYSICS

The behaviour of all the bodies of linear sizes greater than 10^{-6} m are adequately described on the basis of relatively a small number of very simple laws of nature. These laws are the Newton's laws of motion, Newton's law of gravitation, Maxwell's electromagnetism, Laws of thermodynamics and the Lorentz force. The principles of physics based on them is called the *classical physics*. The formulation of classical physics is quite accurate for heavenly bodies like the sun, the earth, the moon etc. and is equally good for the behaviour of grains of sand and the raindrops. However, for the subatomic particles much smaller than 10^{-6} m (such as atoms, nuclei etc.) these rules do not work well. The behaviour of such particles is governed by *quantum physics*. In fact, at such short dimensions the very concept of "particle" breaks down. The perception of the nature is altogether different at this scale. The validity of classical physics also depends on the velocities involved. The classical mechanics as formulated by Newton has to be considerably changed when velocities comparable to 3×10^8 m/s are involved. This is the speed of light in vacuum and is the upper limit of speed which material particle can ever reach. No matter how great and how long you apply a force, you can never get a particle going with a speed greater than 3×10^8 m/s. The mechanics of particles moving with these large velocities is known as *relativistic mechanics* and was formulated by Einstein in 1905.

Thus, classical physics is a good description of the nature if we are concerned with the particles of linear size $> 10^{-6}$ m moving with velocities $< 10^8$ m/s. In a major part of this book, we shall work within these restrictions and hence learn the techniques of classical physics. The size restriction automatically excludes any appreciable effects of nuclear or weak forces and we need to consider only the gravitational and electro-magnetic forces. We might consider the subatomic particles here and there but shall assume the existence of gravitational and electromagnetic forces only and that classical physics is valid for these particles. The results arrived at by our analysis may only be approximately true because we shall be applying the laws which are not correct in that domain. But even that may play an important role in the understanding of nature. We shall also assume that the Newton's third law is valid for the forces which we shall be dealing with. In the final chapters we shall briefly discuss quantum physics and some of its important consequences.

Worked Out Examples

1. *Figure (4-W1) shows two hydrogen atoms. Show on a separate diagram all the electric forces acting on different particles of the system.*

Figure 4-W1

Solution : Each particle exerts electric forces on the remaining three particles. Thus there exist $4 \times 3 = 12$ forces in all. Figure (4-W2) shows them.

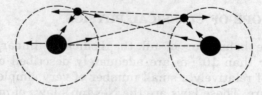

Figure 4-W2

2. *Figure (4-W3) shows two rods each of length l placed side by side, with their facing ends separated by a distance a. Charges + q, – q reside on the rods as shown. Calculate the electric force on the rod A due to the rod B. Discuss the cases when l>>a, a>>l.*

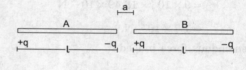

Figure 4-W3

Solution : The force on the rod A due to the charge $+q$ of the rod B

$$= -\frac{q^2}{4 \pi \varepsilon_0 (l+a)^2} + \frac{q^2}{4 \pi \varepsilon_0 a^2}$$

towards right. The force on this rod due to the charge $-q$

$$= \frac{q^2}{4 \pi \varepsilon_0 (2l+a)^2} - \frac{q^2}{4 \pi \varepsilon_0 (l+a)^2}$$

towards right.

The resultant force on the rod is

$$F = \frac{q^2}{4 \pi \varepsilon_0} \left[\frac{1}{a^2} - \frac{2}{(l+a)^2} + \frac{1}{(2l+a)^2} \right] \text{ towards right.}$$

If $l >> a$, the last two terms in the square bracket are negligible as compared to the first term. Then,

$$F \approx \frac{q^2}{4 \pi \varepsilon_0 a^2}.$$

If $a >> l$,

$$F \approx \frac{q^2}{4 \pi \varepsilon_0} \left[\frac{1}{a^2} - \frac{2}{a^2} + \frac{1}{a^2} \right] \approx 0.$$

Two neutral objects placed far away exert only negligible force on each other but when they are placed closer they may exert appreciable force.

3. *Calculate the ratio of electric to gravitational force between two electrons.*

Solution : The electric force $= \dfrac{e^2}{4 \pi \varepsilon_0 r^2}$

and the gravitational force $= \dfrac{G(m_e)^2}{r^2}$.

The ratio is $\dfrac{e^2}{4 \pi \varepsilon_0 G (m_e)^2}$

$$= \dfrac{9 \times 10^9 \, \dfrac{\text{N--m}^2}{\text{C}^2} \times (1 \cdot 6 \times 10^{-19} \, \text{C})^2}{6 \cdot 67 \times 10^{-11} \, \dfrac{\text{N--m}^2}{\text{kg}^2} \times (9 \cdot 1 \times 10^{-31} \, \text{kg})^2} = 4 \cdot 17 \times 10^{42} .$$

□

QUESTIONS FOR SHORT ANSWER

1. A body of mass m is placed on a table. The earth is pulling the body with a force mg. Taking this force to be the action what is the reaction ?

2. A boy is sitting on a chair placed on the floor of a room. Write as many action-reaction pairs of forces as you can.

3. A lawyer alleges in court that the police has forced his client to issue a statement of confession. What kind of force is this ?

4. When you hold a pen and write on your notebook, what kind of force is exerted by you on the pen ? By the pen on the notebook ? By you on the notebook ?

5. Is it true that the reaction of a gravitational force is always gravitational, of an electromagnetic force is always electromagnetic and so on ?

6. Suppose the magnitude of Nuclear force between two protons varies with the distance between them as shown in figure (4-Q1). Estimate the ratio "Nuclear force/Coulomb force" for (a) $x = 8$ fm (b) $x = 4$ fm, (c) $x = 2$ fm and (d) $x = 1$ fm (1 fm $= 10^{-15}$ m).

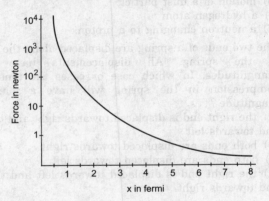

Figure 4-Q1

7. List all the forces acting on the block B in figure (4-Q2).

8. List all the forces acting on (a) the pulley A, (b) the boy and (c) the block C in figure (4-Q3).

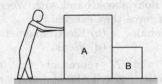

Figure 4-Q2

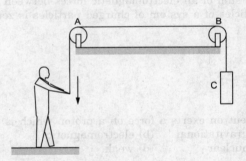

Figure 4-Q3

9. Figure (4-Q4) shows a boy pulling a wagon on a road. List as many forces as you can which are relevant with this figure. Find the pairs of forces connected by Newton's third law of motion.

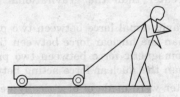

Figure 4-Q4

10. Figure (4-Q5) shows a cart. Complete the table shown below.

Force on	Force by	Nature of the force	Direction
Cart	1 2 3 :		
Horse	1 2 3 :		
Driver	1 2 3 :		

Figure 4-Q5

OBJECTIVE I

1. When Neils Bohr shook hand with Werner Heisenberg, what kind of force they exerted ?
   (a) Gravitational   (b) Electromagnetic
   (c) Nuclear   (d) Weak.

2. Let E, G and N represent the magnitudes of electromagnetic, gravitational and nuclear forces between two electrons at a given separation. Then
   (a) $N>E>G$ (b) $E>N>G$ (c) $G>N>E$ (d) $E>G>N$.

3. The sum of all electromagnetic forces between different particles of a system of charged particles is zero

(a) only if all the particles are positively charged
(b) only if all the particles are negatively charged
(c) only if half the particles are positively charged and half are negatively charged
(d) irrespective of the signs of the charges.

4. A 60 kg man pushes a 40 kg man by a force of 60 N. The 40 kg man has pushed the other man with a force of
   (a) 40 N   (b) 0   (c) 60 N   (d) 20 N.

OBJECTIVE II

1. A neutron exerts a force on a proton which is
   (a) gravitational   (b) electromagnetic
   (c) nuclear   (d) weak.

2. A proton exerts a force on a proton which is
   (a) gravitational   (b) electromagnetic
   (c) nuclear   (d) weak.

3. Mark the correct statements :
   (a) The nuclear force between two protons is always greater than the electromagnetic force between them.
   (b) The electromagnetic force between two protons is always greater than the gravitational force between them.
   (c) The gravitational force between two protons may be greater than the nuclear force between them.
   (d) Electromagnetic force between two protons may be greater than the nuclear force acting between them.

4. If all matter were made of electrically neutral particles such as neutrons,
   (a) there would be no force of friction
   (b) there would be no tension in the string
   (c) it would not be possible to sit on a chair
   (d) the earth could not move around the sun.

5. Which of the following systems may be adequately described by classical physics ?
   (a) motion of a cricket ball
   (b) motion of a dust particle
   (c) a hydrogen atom
   (d) a neutron changing to a proton.

6. The two ends of a spring are displaced along the length of the spring. All displacements have equal mangnitudes. In which case or cases the tension or compression in the spring will have a maximum magnitude ?
   (a) the right end is displaced towards right and the left end towards left
   (b) both ends are displaced towards right
   (c) both ends are displaced towards left
   (d) the right end is displaced towards left and the left end towards right.

7. Action and reaction
   (a) act on two different objects
   (b) have equal magnitude
   (c) have opposite directions
   (d) have resultant zero.

EXERCISES

1. The gravitational force acting on a particle of 1 g due to a similar particle is equal to 6.67×10^{-17} N. Calculate the separation between the particles.

2. Calculate the force with which you attract the earth.

3. At what distance should two charges, each equal to 1 C, be placed so that the force between them equals your weight ?

4. Two spherical bodies, each of mass 50 kg, are placed at a separation of 20 cm. Equal charges are placed on the bodies and it is found that the force of Coulomb repulsion equals the gravitational attraction in magnitude. Find the magnitude of the charge placed on either body.

5. A monkey is sitting on a tree limb. The limb exerts a normal force of 48 N and a frictional force of 20 N. Find the magnitude of the total force exerted by the limb on the monkey.

6. A body builder exerts a force of 150 N against a bullworker and compresses it by 20 cm. Calculate the spring constant of the spring in the bullworker.

7. A satellite is projected vertically upwards from an earth station. At what height above the earth's surface will the force on the satellite due to the earth be reduced to half its value at the earth station ? (Radius of the earth is 6400 km.)

8. Two charged particles placed at a separation of 20 cm exert 20 N of Coulomb force on each other. What will be the force if the separation is increased to 25 cm ?

9. The force with which the earth attracts an object is called the weight of the object. Calculate the weight of the moon from the following data : The universal constant of gravitation $G = 6.67 \times 10^{-11}$ N–m^2/kg^2, mass of the moon $= 7.36 \times 10^{22}$ kg, mass of the earth $= 6 \times 10^{24}$ kg and the distance between the earth and the moon $= 3.8 \times 10^5$ km.

10. Find the ratio of the magnitude of the electric force to the gravitational force acting between two protons.

11. The average separation between the proton and the electron in a hydrogen atom in ground state is 5.3×10^{-11} m. (a) Calculate the Coulomb force between them at this separation. (b) When the atom goes into its first excited state the average separation between the proton and the electron increases to four times its value in the ground state. What is the Coulomb force in this state ?

12. The geostationary orbit of the earth is at a distance of about 36000 km from the earth's surface. Find the weight of a 120-kg equipment placed in a geostationary satellite. The radius of the earth is 6400 km.

□

ANSWERS

OBJECTIVE I

1. (b)   2. (d)   3. (d)   4. (c)

OBJECTIVE II

1. (a), (c)   2. (a), (b), (c)   3. (b), (c), (d)

4. (a), (b), (c)   5. (a), (b)   6. (a), (d)

7. (a), (b), (c), (d)

EXERCISES

1. 1 m

4. 4.3×10^{-9} C

5. 52 N

6. 750 N/m

7. 2650 km

8. 13 N

9. 2×10^{20} N

10. 1.24×10^{36}

11. (a) 8.2×10^{-8} N,(b) 5.1×10^{-9} N

12. 27 N

□

CHAPTER 5

NEWTON'S LAWS OF MOTION

Newton's laws of motion are of central importance in classical physics. A large number of principles and results may be derived from Newton's laws. The first two laws relate to the type of motion of a system that results from a given set of forces. These laws may be interpreted in a variety of ways and it is slightly uninteresting and annoying at the outset to go into the technical details of the interpretation. The precise definitions of mass, force and acceleration should be given before we relate them. And these definitions themselves need use of Newton's laws. Thus, these laws turn out to be definitions to some extent. We shall assume that we know how to assign mass to a body, how to assign the magnitude and direction to a force and how to measure the acceleration with respect to a given frame of reference. Some discussions of these aspects were given in the previous chapters. The development here does not follow the historical track these laws have gone through, but are explained to make them simple to apply.

5.1 FIRST LAW OF MOTION

If the (vector) sum of all the forces acting on a particle is zero then and only then the particle remains unaccelerated (i.e., remains at rest or moves with constant velocity).

If the sum of all the forces on a given particle is $\vec{F}$ and its acceleration is $\vec{a}$, the above statement may also be written as

"$\vec{a} = 0$ *if and only if* $\vec{F} = 0$".

Thus, if the sum of the forces acting on a particle is known to be zero, we can be sure that the particle is unaccelerated, or if we know that a particle is unaccelerated, we can be sure that the sum of the forces acting on the particle is zero.

However, the concept of rest, motion or acceleration is meaningful only when a frame of reference is specified. Also the acceleration of the

particle is, in general, different when measured from different frames. Is it possible then, that the first law is valid in all frames of reference ?

Let us consider the situation shown in figure (5.1). An elevator cabin falls down after the cable breaks. The cabin and all the bodies fixed in the cabin are accelerated with respect to the earth and the acceleration is about 9.8 m/s^2 in the downward direction.

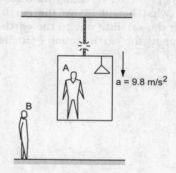

Figure 5.1

Consider the lamp in the cabin. The forces acting on the lamp are (a) the gravitational force W by the earth and (b) the electromagnetic force T (tension) by the rope. The direction of W is downward and the directon of T is upward. The sum is $(W - T)$ downward.

Measure the acceleration of the lamp from the frame of reference of the cabin. The lamp is at rest. The acceleration of the lamp is zero. The person A who measured this acceleration is a learned one and uses Newton's first law to conclude that the sum of the forces acting on the particle is zero, i.e.,

$$W - T = 0 \text{ or, } W = T.$$

Instead, if we measure the acceleration from the ground, the lamp has an acceleration of 9.8 m/s^2. Thus, $a \neq 0$ and hence the person B who measured this acceleration, concludes from Newton's first law that the sum of the forces is not zero. Thus, $W - T \neq 0$ or $W \neq T$. If A measures acceleration and applies the first law he gets $W = T$. If B measures acceleration and applies the same first law, he gets $W \neq T$. Both of them cannot be correct simultaneously as W and T can be either equal or unequal. At least one of the two frames is a bad frame and one should not apply the first law in that frame.

There are some frames of reference in which Newton's first law is valid. Measure acceleration from such a frame and you are allowed to say that "$\vec{a} = 0$ if and only if $\vec{F} = 0$". But there are frames in which Newton's first law is not valid. You may find that even if the sum of the forces is not zero, the acceleration is still zero. Or you may find that the sum of the forces is zero, yet the particle is accelerated. So the validity of Newton's first law depends on the frame of reference from which the observer measures the state of rest, motion and acceleration of the particle.

A frame of reference in which Newton's first law is valid is called an *inertial frame of reference*. A frame in which Newton's first law is not valid is called a *noninertial frame of reference*.

Newton's first law, thus, reduces to a definition of inertial frame. Why do we call it a law then? Suppose after going through this lesson, you keep the book on your table fixed rigidly with the earth (figure 5.2).

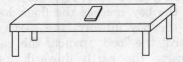

Figure 5.2

The book is at rest with respect to the earth. The acceleration of the book with respect to the earth is zero. The forces on the book are (a) the gravitational force $\vec{W}$ exerted by the earth and (b) the contact force $\vec{\mathcal{N}}$ by the table. Is the sum of $\vec{W}$ and $\vec{\mathcal{N}}$ zero? A very accurate measurement will give the answer "No". The sum of the forces is not zero although the book is at rest. The earth is not strictly an inertial frame. However, the sum is not too different from zero and we can say that the earth is an inertial frame of reference to a good approximation. Thus, for routine affairs, "$\vec{a} = 0$ if and only if $\vec{F} = 0$" is true in the earth frame of reference. This fact was identified and formulated by Newton and is known as Newton's *first law*. If we restrict that all measurements will be made from the earth frame, indeed it becomes a law. If we try to universalise this to different frames, it becomes a definition. We shall assume that unless stated otherwise, we are working from an inertial frame of reference.

Example 5.1

A heavy particle of mass 0·50 kg is hanging from a string fixed with the roof. Find the force exerted by the string on the particle (Figure 5.3). Take $g = 9\cdot8$ m/s^2.

Figure 5.3

Solution : The forces acting on the particle are

(a) pull of the earth, $0\cdot50$ kg $\times 9\cdot8$ m/s$^2 = 4\cdot9$ N, vertically downward

(b) pull of the string, T vertically upward.

The particle is at rest with respect to the earth (which we assume to be an inertial frame). Hence, the sum of the forces should be zero. Therefore, T is $4\cdot9$ N acting vertically upward.

Inertial Frames other than Earth

Suppose S is an inertial frame and S' a frame moving uniformly with respect to S. Consider a particle P having acceleration $\vec{a}_{P,S}$ with respect to S and $\vec{a}_{P,S'}$ with respect to S'.

We know that,

$$\vec{a}_{P,S} = \vec{a}_{P,S'} + \vec{a}_{S',S}.$$

As S' moves uniformly with respect to S,

$$\vec{a}_{S',S} = 0.$$

Thus, $\qquad\qquad \vec{a}_{P,S} = \vec{a}_{P,S'}$ ... (i)

Now S is an inertial frame. So from definition, $\vec{a}_{P,S} = 0$, if and only if $\vec{F} = 0$ and hence, from (i), $\vec{a}_{P,S'} = 0$ if and only if $\vec{F} = 0$.

Thus, S' is also an inertial frame. We arrive at an important result : *All frames moving uniformly with respect to an inertial frame are themselves inertial.* Thus, a train moving with uniform velocity with respect to the ground, a plane flying with uniform velocity with respect to a highway, etc., are examples of inertial frames. The sum of the forces acting on a suitcase kept on the shelf of a ship sailing smoothly and uniformly on a calm sea is zero.

5.2 SECOND LAW OF MOTION

The acceleration of a particle as measured from an inertial frame is given by the (vector) sum of all the forces acting on the particle divided by its mass.

In symbols : $\vec{a} = \vec{F}/m$ or, $\vec{F} = m\,\vec{a}$.   ... (5.2)

The inertial frame is already defined by the first law of motion. A force $\vec{F}$ acting on a particle of mass m produces an acceleration $\vec{F}/m$ in it with respect to an inertial frame. This is a law of nature. If the force ceases to act at some instant, the acceleration becomes zero at the same instant. In equation (5.2) $\vec{a}$ and $\vec{F}$ are measured at the same instant of time.

5.3 WORKING WITH NEWTON'S FIRST AND SECOND LAW

Newton's laws refer to a particle and relate the forces acting on the particle with its acceleration and its mass. Before attempting to write an equation from Newton's law, we should very clearly understand which particle we are considering. In any practical situation, we deal with extended bodies which are collection of a large number of particles. The laws as stated above may be used even if the object under consideration is an extended body, provided each part of this body has the same acceleration (in magnitude and direction). A systematic algorithm for writing equations from Newton's laws is as follows :

Step 1 : Decide the System

The first step is to decide the system on which the laws of motion are to be applied. The system may be a single particle, a block, a combination of two blocks one kept over the other, two blocks connected by a string, a piece of string etc. The only restriction is that all parts of the system should have identical acceleration.

Consider the situation shown in figure (5.4). The block B does not slip over A, the disc D slides over the string and all parts of the string are tight.

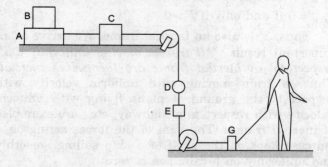

Figure 5.4

A and B move together. C is not in contact with A or B. But as the length of the string between A and C does not change, the distance moved by C in any

time interval is same as that by A. The same is true for G. The distance moved by G in any time interval is same as that by A, B or C. The direction of motion is also the same for A, B, C and G. They have identical accelerations. We can take any of these blocks as a system or any combination of the blocks from these as a system. Some of the examples are (A), (B), $(A + B)$, $(B + C)$, $(A + B + C)$, $(C + G)$, $(A + C + G)$, $(A + B + C + G)$ etc. The distance covered by E is also the same as the distance covered by G but their directions are different. E moves in a vertical line whereas G in a horizontal line. $(E + G)$ should not be taken as a system. At least at this stage we are unable to apply Newton's law treating $E + G$ as a single particle. As the disc D slides over the string the distance covered by D is not equal to that by E in the same time interval. We should not treat $D + E$ as a system. *Think carefully.*

Step 2 : Identify the Forces

Once the system is decided, make a list of the forces acting *on* the system due to all the objects other than the system. Any force applied *by* the system should not be included in the list of the forces.

Consider the situation shown in figure (5.5). The boy stands on the floor balancing a heavy load on his head. The load presses the boy, the boy pushes the load upward the boy presses the floor downward, the floor pushes the boy upward, the earth attracts the load downward, the load attracts the earth upward, the boy attracts the earth upward and the earth attracts the boy downward. There are many forces operating in this world. Which of these forces should we include in the list of forces ?

Figure 5.5

We cannot answer this question. Not because we do not know, but because we have not yet specified the system. Which is the body under consideration ? Do not try to identify forces before you have decided the system. Suppose we concentrate on the state of motion of the boy. We should then concentrate on the forces acting *on* the boy. The forces are listed in the upper half of table (5.1). Instead, if we take the load as the system and discuss the equilibrium of the load, the list of the forces will be different. These forces appear in the lower half of table (5.1).

Table 5.1

System	Force exerted by	Magnitude of the force	Direction of the force	Nature of the force
	Earth	W	Downward	Gravitational
Boy	Floor	$\mathcal{N}$	Upward	Electro-magnetic
	Load	$\mathcal{N}_1$	Downward	,,
	Earth	W'	Downward	Gravitational
Load	Boy	$\mathcal{N}_1$	Upward	Electro-magnetic

One may furnish as much information as one has about the magnitude and direction of the forces. The contact forces may have directions other than normal to the contact surface if the surfaces are rough. We shall discuss more about it under the heading of friction.

Step 3 : Make a Free Body Diagram

Now, represent the system by a point in a separate diagram and draw vectors representing the forces acting on the system with this point as the common origin. The forces may lie along a line, may be distributed in a plane (coplanar) or may be distributed in the space (non-planar). We shall rarely encounter situations dealing with non-planar forces. For coplanar forces the plane of diagram represents the plane of the forces acting on the system. Indicate the magnitudes and directions of the forces in this diagram. This is called a *free body diagram*. The free body diagram for the example discussed above with the boy as the system and with the load as the system are shown in figure (5.6).

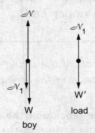

Figure 5.6

Step 4 : Choose Axes and Write Equations

Any three mutually perpendicular directions may be chosen as the X-Y-Z axes. We give below some suggestions for choosing the axes to solve problems.

If the forces are coplanar, only two axes, say X and Y, taken in the plane of forces are needed. Choose the X-axis along the direction in which the system is known to have or is likely to have the acceleration. A direction perpendicular to it may be chosen as the Y-axis. If the system is in equilibrium, any mutually perpendicular directions in the plane of the diagram may be chosen as the axes. Write the components of all the forces along the X-axis and equate their sum to the product of the mass of the system and its acceleration. This gives you one equation. Write the components of the forces along the Y-axis and equate the sum to zero. This gives you another equation. If the forces are collinear, this second equation is not needed.

If necessary you can go to step 1, choose another object as the system, repeat steps 2, 3 and 4 to get more equations. These are called equations of motion. Use mathematical techniques to get the unknown quantities out of these equations. This completes the algorithm.

The magnitudes of acceleration of different objects in a given situation are often related through kinematics. This should be properly foreseen and used together with the equations of motion. For example in figure (5.4) the accelerations of C and E have same magnitudes. Equations of motion for C and for E should use the same variable a for acceleration.

Example 5.2

A block of mass M is pulled on a smooth horizontal table by a string making an angle θ with the horizontal as shown in figure (5.7). If the acceleration of the block is a, find the force applied by the string and by the table on the block.

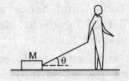

Figure 5.7

Solution : Let us consider the block as the system.
The forces on the block are
(a) pull of the earth, Mg, vertically downward,
(b) contact force by the table, $\mathcal{N}$, vertically upward,
(c) pull of the string, T, along the string.
The free body diagram for the block is shown in figure (5.8).
The acceleration of the block is horizontal and towards the right. Take this direction as the X-axis and vertically upward direction as the Y-axis. We have,

Figure 5.8

component of Mg along the X-axis $= 0$
component of $\mathcal{N}$ along the X-axis $= 0$
component of T along the X-axis $= T\cos\theta$.
Hence the total force along the X-axis $= T\cos\theta$.
Using Newton's law, $T\cos\theta = Ma$.   ... (i)
    Component of Mg along the Y-axis $= -Mg$
    component of $\mathcal{N}$ along the Y-axis $= \mathcal{N}$
    component of T along the Y-axis $= T\sin\theta$.
    Total force along the Y-axis $= \mathcal{N} + T\sin\theta - Mg$.
Using Newton's law, $\mathcal{N} + T\sin\theta - Mg = 0$.   ... (ii)

From equation (i), $T = \dfrac{Ma}{\cos\theta}$. Putting this in equation (ii)

$\mathcal{N} = Mg - Ma\tan\theta$.

5.4 NEWTON'S THIRD LAW OF MOTION

Newton's third law has already been introduced in chapter 4. *"If a body A exerts a force $\vec{F}$ on another body B, then B exerts a force $-\vec{F}$ on A."*

Thus, the force exerted by A on B and that by B on A are equal in magnitude but opposite in direction. This law connects the forces exerted by two bodies on one another. The forces connected by the third law act on two different bodies and hence will never appear together in the list of forces at step 2 of applying Newton's first or second law.

For example, suppose a table exerts an upward force $\mathcal{N}$ on a block placed on it. This force should be accounted if we consider the block as the system. The block pushes the table down with an equal force $\mathcal{N}$. But this force acts on the table and should be considered only if we take the table as the system. Thus, only one of the two forces connected by the third law may appear in the equation of motion depending on the system chosen. The force exerted by the earth on a particle of mass M is Mg downward and therefore, by the particle on the earth is Mg upward. These two forces will not cancel each other. The downward force on the particle will cause acceleration of the particle and that on the earth will cause acceleration (how large ?) of the earth.

Newton's third law of motion is not strictly correct when interaction between two bodies separated by a large distance is considered. We come across such deviations when we study electric and magnetic forces.

Working with the Tension in a String

The idea of tension was qualitatively introduced in chapter 4. Suppose a block of mass M is hanging through a string from the ceiling (figure 5.9).

Figure 5.9

Consider a cross-section of the string at A. The cross-section divides the string in two parts, lower part and the upper part. The two parts are in physical contact at the cross-section at A. The lower part of the string will exert an electromagnetic force on the upper part and the upper part will exert an electromagnetic force on the lower part. According to the third law, these two forces will have equal magnitude. The lower part pulls down the upper part with a force T and the upper part pulls up the lower part with equal force T. The common magnitude of the forces exerted by the two parts of the string on each other is called the tension in the string at A. What is the tension in the string at the lower end ? The block and the string are in contact at this end and exert electromagnetic forces on each other. The common magnitude of these forces is the tension in the string at the lower end. What is the tension in the string at the upper end ? At this end, the string and the ceiling meet. The string pulls the ceiling down and the ceiling pulls the string up. The common magnitude of these forces is the tension in the string at the upper end.

Example 5.3

The mass of the part of the string below A in figure (5.9) is m. Find the tension of the string at the lower end and at A.

Solution : To get the tension at the lower end we need the force exerted by the string on the block.

Take the block as the system. The forces on it are

(a) pull of the string, T, upward,

(b) pull of the earth, Mg, downward,

The free body diagram for the block is shown in figure (5.10a). As the acceleration of the block is zero, these forces should add to zero. Hence the tension at the lower end is $T = Mg$.

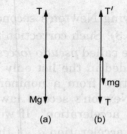

Figure 5.10

To get the tension T at A we need the force exerted by the upper part of the string on the lower part of the string. For this we may write the equation of motion for the lower part of the string. So take the string below A as the system. The forces acting on this part are

(a) T', upward, by the upper part of the string

(b) mg, downward, by the earth

(c) T, downward, by the block.

Note that in (c) we have written T for the force by the block on the string. We have already used the symbol T for the force by the string on the block. We have used Newton's third law here. The force exerted by the block on the string is equal in magnitude to the force exerted by the string on the block.

The free body diagram for this part is shown in figure (5.10b). As the system under consideration (the lower part of the string) is in equilibrium, Newton's first law gives

$$T' = T + mg$$

But $T = Mg$ hence, $T' = (M + m)g$.

Example 5.4 _____

The block shown in figure (5.11) has a mass M and descends with an acceleration a. The mass of the string below the point A is m. Find the tension of the string at the point A and at the lower end.

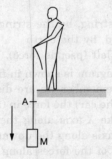

Figure 5.11

Solution : Consider "the block + the part of the string below A" as the system. Let the tension at A be T. The forces acting on this system are

(a) $(M + m)g$, downward, by the earth.

(b) T, upward, by the upper part of the string.

The first is gravitational and the second is electromagnetic. We do not have to write the force by the string on the block. This electromagnetic force is by one part of the system on the other part. Only the forces acting on the system by the objects other than the system are to be included.

The system is descending with an acceleration a. Taking the downward direction as the X-axis, the total force along the X-axis is $(M + m)g - T$. Using Newton's law

$$(M + m)g - T = (M + m)a.$$

or, $$T = (M + m)(g - a). \qquad \ldots \text{(i)}$$

We have omitted the free body diagram. This you can do if you can draw the free body diagram in your mind and write the equations correctly.

To get the tension T' at the lower end we can put $m = 0$ in (i).

Effectively, we take the point A at the lower end. Thus, we get $T' = M(g - a)$.

Suppose the string in *Example 5.3* or *5.4* is very light so that we can neglect the mass of the string. Then $T' = T$. The tension is then the same throughout the string. This result is of general nature. The tension at all the points in a string or a spring is the same provided it is assumed massless and no massive particle or body is connected in between.

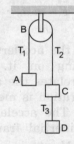

Figure 5.12

If the string in figure (5.12) is light, the tension T_1 of the string is same at all the points between the block A and the pulley B. The tension T_2 is same at all the points between the pulley B and the block C. The tension T_3 is same at all the points between the block C and the block D. The three tensions T_1, T_2 and T_3 may be different from each other. If the pulley B is also light, then $T_1 = T_2$.

5.5 PSEUDO FORCES

In this section we discuss the techniques of solving the motion of a body with respect to a noninertial frame of reference.

Consider the situation shown in figure (5.13). Suppose the frame of reference S' moves with a constant acceleration $\vec{a_0}$ with respect to an inertial frame S. The acceleration of a particle P measured with respect to S' is $\vec{a}_{P,S'} = \vec{a}$ and that with respect to S is $\vec{a}_{P,S}$. The acceleration of S' with respect to S is $\vec{a}_{S',S} = \vec{a_0}$.

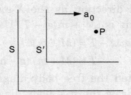

Figure 5.13

Since S' is translating with respect to S we have,

$$\vec{a}_{P,S'} = \vec{a}_{P,S} + \vec{a}_{S,S'} = \vec{a}_{P,S} - \vec{a}_{S',S}$$

or, $$\vec{a} = \vec{a}_{P,S} - \vec{a_0}$$

or, $$m\,\vec{a} = m\,\vec{a}_{P,S} - m\,\vec{a_0}$$

where m is the mass of the particle P. Since S is an inertial frame $m\,\vec{a}_{P,S}$ is equal to the sum of all the forces acting on P. Writing this sum as $\vec{F}$, we get

$$m\,\vec{a} = \vec{F} - m\,\vec{a_0}$$

or, $$\vec{a} = \frac{\vec{F} - m\,\vec{a_0}}{m}.$$ ... (5.3)

This equation relates the acceleration of the particle and the forces acting on it. Compare it with equation (5.2) which relates the acceleration and the force when the acceleration is measured with respect to an inertial frame. The acceleration of the frame (with respect to an inertial frame) comes into the equation of a particle. Newton's second law $\vec{a} = \vec{F}/m$ is not valid in such a noninertial frame. An extra term $-m\,\vec{a_0}$ has to be added to the sum of all the forces acting on the particle before writing the equation $\vec{a} = \vec{F}/m$. Note that in this extra term, m is the mass of the particle under consideration and $\vec{a_0}$ is the acceleration of the working frame of reference with respect to some inertial frame.

However, we people spend most of our lifetime on the earth which is an (approximate) inertial frame. We are so familiar with the Newton's laws that we would still like to use the terminology of Newton's laws even when we use a noninertial frame. This can be done if we agree to call $(-m\,\vec{a_0})$ a *force* acting on the particle. Then while preparing the list of the forces acting on the particle P, we include all the (real) forces acting on P by all other objects and also include an imaginary

force $-m\,\vec{a_0}$. Applying Newton's second law will then lead to equation (5.3). Such correction terms $-m\,a_0$ in the list of forces are called *pseudo forces*. This so-called force is to be included in the list only because we are discussing the motion from a noninertial frame and still want to use Newton's second law as "total force equals mass times acceleration". If we work from an inertial frame, the acceleration $\vec{a_0}$ of the frame is zero and no pseudo force is needed. The pseudo forces are also called *inertial forces* although their need arises because of the use of noninertial frames.

Example 5.5

A pendulum is hanging from the ceiling of a car having an acceleration a_0 with respect to the road. Find the angle made by the string with the vertical.

Solution : The situation is shown in figure (5.14a). Suppose the mass of the bob is m and the string makes an angle θ with the vertical. We shall work from the car frame. This frame is noninertial as it has an acceleration $\vec{a_0}$ with respect to an inertial frame (the road). Hence, if we use Newton's second law we shall have to include a pseudo force.

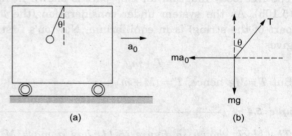

Figure 5.14

Take the bob as the system.

The forces are :

(a) T along the string, by the string
(b) mg downward, by the earth
(c) ma_0 towards left (pseudo force).

The free body diagram is shown in figure (5.14b). As the bob is at rest (remember we are discussing the motion with respect to the car) the force in (a), (b) and (c) should add to zero. Take X-axis along the forward horizontal direction and Y-axis along the upward vertical direction. The components of the forces along the X-axis give

$$T\sin\theta - m\,a_0 = 0 \quad \text{or,} \quad T\sin\theta = m\,a_0 \qquad \text{... (i)}$$

and the components along the Y-axis give

$$T\cos\theta - mg = 0 \quad \text{or,} \quad T\cos\theta = mg. \qquad \text{... (ii)}$$

Dividing (i) by (ii) $\tan\theta = a_0/g$.

Thus, the string makes an angle $\tan^{-1}(a_0/g)$ with the vertical.

5.6 THE HORSE AND THE CART

A good example which illustrates the ideas discussed in this chapter is the motion of a cart pulled by a horse. Suppose the cart is at rest when the driver whips the horse. The horse pulls the cart and the cart accelerates forward. The question posed is as follows. The horse pulls the cart by a force F_1 in the forward direction. From the third law of motion the cart pulls the horse by an equal force $F_2 = F_1$ in the backward direction. The sum of these forces is, therefore, zero (figure 5.15). Why should then the cart accelerate forward ?

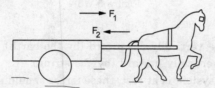

F$_1$: Force on the cart by the horse

F$_2$: Force on the horse by the cart

$$F_1 = F_2 = F$$

Figure 5.15

Try to locate the mistake in the argument. According to our scheme, we should first decide the system. We can take the horse as the system or the cart as the system or the cart and the horse taken together as the system. Suppose you take the cart as the system. Then the forces on the cart should be listed and the forces on the horse should not enter the discussion. The force on the cart is F_1 in the forward direction and the acceleration of the cart is also in the forward direction. How much is this acceleration ? Take the mass of the cart to be M_C. Is the acceleration of the cart $a = F_1/M_C$ in forward direction ? Think carefully. We shall return to this question.

Let us now try to understand the motion of the horse. This time we have to consider the forces on the horse. The forward force F_1 by the horse acts on the cart and it should not be taken into account when we discuss the motion of the horse. The force on the horse by the cart is F_2 in the backward direction. Why does the horse go in the forward direction when whipped ? The horse exerts a force on the cart in the forward direction and hence the cart is accelerated forward. But the cart exerts an equal force on the horse in the backward direction. Why is the horse not accelerated in backward direction ? (Imagine this situation. If the cart is accelerated forward and the horse backward, the horse will sit on the cart kicking out the driver and the passengers.) Where are we wrong ? We have not considered *all* the forces acting on the horse. The

road pushes the horse by a force P which has a forward component. This force acts on the horse and we must add this force when we discuss the motion of the horse. The horse accelerates forward if the forward component f of the force P exceeds F_2 (Figure 5.16). The acceleration of the horse is $(f - F_2)/M_h$. We should make sure that *all* the forces acting on the system are added. Note that the force of gravity acting on the horse has no forward component.

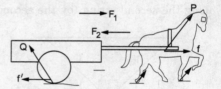

Figure 5.16

Going back to the previous paragraph the acceleration of the cart may not be F_1/M_C. The road exerts a force Q on the cart which may have a backward component f'. The total force on the cart is $F_1 - f'$. The acceleration of the cart is then $a = \dfrac{F_1 - f'}{M_C}$ in the forward direction.

The forces f and f' are self adjustable and they so adjust their values that $\dfrac{F_1 - f'}{M_C} = \dfrac{f - F_2}{M_h}$. The acceleration of the horse and that of the cart are equal in magnitude and direction and hence they move together.

So, once again we remind you that only the forces on the system are to be considered to discuss the motion of the system and all the forces acting on the system are to be considered. Only then apply $\vec{F} = m\vec{a}$.

5.7 INERTIA

A particle is accelerated (in an inertial frame) if and only if a resultant force acts on it. Loosely speaking, the particle does not change its state of rest or of uniform motion along a straight line unless it is forced to do this. This unwillingness of a particle to change its state of rest or of uniform motion along a straight line is called as *inertia*. We can understand the property of inertia in more precise terms as follows. If equal forces are applied on two particles, in general, the acceleration of the particles will be different. The property of a particle to allow a smaller acceleration is called *inertia*. It is clear that larger the mass of the particle, smaller will be the acceleration and hence larger will be the inertia.

Worked Out Examples

1. *A body of mass m is suspended by two strings making angles α and β with the horizontal. Find the tensions in the strings.*

Solution : Take the body of mass m as the system. The forces acting on the system are

(i) mg downwards (by the earth),

(ii) T_1 along the first string (by the first string) and

(iii) T_2 along the second string (by the second string).

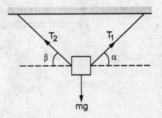

Figure 5-W1

These forces are shown in figure (5-W1). As the body is in equilibrium, these forces must add to zero. Taking horizontal components,

$$T_1 \cos\alpha - T_2 \cos\beta + mg \cos\frac{\pi}{2} = 0$$

or, $T_1 \cos\alpha = T_2 \cos\beta.$ ... (i)

Taking vertical components,

$$T_1 \sin\alpha + T_2 \sin\beta - mg = 0.$$ ... (ii)

Eliminating T_2 from (i) and (ii),

$$T_1 \sin\alpha + T_1 \frac{\cos\alpha}{\cos\beta} \sin\beta = mg$$

or, $T_1 = \dfrac{mg}{\sin\alpha + \dfrac{\cos\alpha}{\cos\beta}\sin\beta} = \dfrac{mg\cos\beta}{\sin(\alpha+\beta)}.$

From (i), $T_2 = \dfrac{mg\cos\alpha}{\sin(\alpha+\beta)}.$

2. *Two bodies of masses m_1 and m_2 are connected by a light string going over a smooth light pulley at the end of an incline. The mass m_1 lies on the incline and m_2 hangs vertically. The system is at rest. Find the angle of the incline and the force exerted by the incline on the body of mass m_1 (figure 5-W2).*

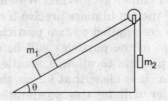

Figure 5-W2

Solution : Figure (5-W3) shows the situation with the forces on m_1 and m_2 shown. Take the body of mass m_2 as the system. The forces acting on it are

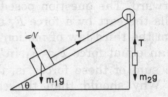

Figure 5-W3

(i) $m_2 g$ vertically downward (by the earth),

(ii) T vertically upward (by the string).

As the system is at rest, these forces should add to zero. This gives $T = m_2 g.$ ... (i)

Next, consider the body of mass m_1 as the system. The forces acting on this system are

(i) $m_1 g$ vertically downward (by the earth),

(ii) T along the string up the incline (by the string),

(iii) $\mathscr{N}$ normal to the incline (by the incline).

As the string and the pulley are all light and smooth, the tension in the string is uniform everywhere. Hence, same T is used for the equations of m_1 and m_2. As the system is in equilibrium, these forces should add to zero.

Taking components parallel to the incline,

$$T = m_1 g \cos\left(\frac{\pi}{2} - \theta\right) = m_1 g \sin\theta.$$ ... (ii)

Taking components along the normal to the incline,

$$\mathscr{N} = m_1 g \cos\theta.$$ ... (iii)

Eliminating T from (i) and (ii),

$$m_2 g = m_1 g \sin\theta$$

or, $\sin\theta = m_2 / m_1$

giving $\theta = \sin^{-1}(m_2/m_1).$

From (iii) $\mathscr{N} = m_1 g \sqrt{1 - (m_2/m_1)^2}.$

3. *A bullet moving at 250 m/s penetrates 5 cm into a tree limb before coming to rest. Assuming that the force exerted by the tree limb is uniform, find its magnitude. Mass of the bullet is 10 g.*

Solution : The tree limb exerts a force on the bullet in the direction opposite to its velocity. This force causes deceleration and hence the velocity decreases from 250 m/s to zero in 5 cm. We have to find the force exerted by the tree limb on the bullet. If a be the deceleration of the bullet, we have,

$$u = 250 \text{ m/s} , \ v = 0 , \ x = 5 \text{ cm} = 0.05 \text{ m}$$

giving, $a = \dfrac{(250 \text{ m/s})^2 - 0^2}{2 \times 0{\cdot}05 \text{ m}} = 625000 \text{ m/s}^2$.

The force on the bullet is $F = ma = 6250 \text{ N}$.

4. *The force on a particle of mass 10 g is $(\vec{i}\,10 + \vec{j}\,5)$ N. If it starts from rest what would be its position at time $t = 5$ s ?*

Solution : We have $F_x = 10$ N giving

$$a_x = \dfrac{F_x}{m} = \dfrac{10 \text{ N}}{0{\cdot}01 \text{ kg}} = 1000 \text{ m/s}^2.$$

As this is a case of constant acceleration in x-direction,

$$x = u_x t + \tfrac{1}{2} a_x t^2 = \tfrac{1}{2} \times 1000 \text{ m/s}^2 \times (5 \text{ s})^2$$

$$= 12500 \text{ m}$$

Similarly, $a_y = \dfrac{F_y}{m} = \dfrac{5 \text{ N}}{0{\cdot}01 \text{ kg}} = 500 \text{ m/s}^2$

and $\qquad y = 6250 \text{ m}.$

Thus, the position of the particle at $t = 5$ s is,

$$\vec{r} = (\vec{i}\,12500 + \vec{j}\,6250) \text{ m}.$$

5. *With what acceleration 'a' should the box of figure (5-W4) descend so that the block of mass M exerts a force $Mg/4$ on the floor of the box ?*

Figure 5-W4

Solution : The block is at rest with respect to the box which is accelerated with respect to the ground. Hence, the acceleration of the block with respect to the ground is 'a' downward. The forces on the block are

(i) Mg downward (by the earth) and

(ii) $\mathcal{N}$ upward (by the floor).

The equation of motion of the block is, therefore

$$Mg - \mathcal{N} = Ma.$$

If $\mathcal{N} = Mg/4$, the above equation gives $a = 3g/4$. The block and hence the box should descend with an acceleration $3g/4$.

6. *A block 'A' of mass m is tied to a fixed point C on a horizontal table through a string passing round a massless smooth pulley B (figure 5-W5). A force F is applied by the experimenter to the pulley. Show that if the pulley is displaced by a distance x, the block will be displaced by 2x. Find the acceleration of the block and the pulley.*

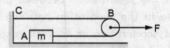

Figure 5-W5

Solution : Suppose the pulley is displaced to B' and the block to A' (figure 5-W6). The length of the string is $CB + BA$ and is also equal to $CB + BB' + B'B + BA'$. Hence, $CB + BA' + A'A = CB + BB' + B'B + BA'$

or, $A'A = 2 \, BB'$.

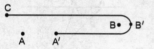

Figure 5-W6

The displacement of A is, therefore, twice the displacement of B in any given time interval. Diffrentiating twice, we find that the acceleration of A is twice the acceleration of B.

To find the acceleration of the block we will need the tension in the string. That can be obtained by considering the pulley as the system.

The forces acting on the pulley are

(i) F towards right by the experimenter,

(ii) T towards left by the portion BC of the string and

(iii) T towards left by the portion BA of the string.

The vertical forces, if any, add to zero as there is no vertical motion.

As the mass of the pulley is zero, the equation of motion is

$F - 2T = 0$ giving $T = F/2$.

Now consider the block as the system. The only horizontal force acting on the block is the tension T towards right. The acceleration of the block is, therefore,

$a = T/m = \dfrac{F}{2\,m}$. The acceleration of the pulley is

$a/2 = \dfrac{F}{4\,m}$.

7. *A smooth ring A of mass m can slide on a fixed horizontal rod. A string tied to the ring passes over a fixed pulley B and carries a block C of mass M ($= 2\,m$) as shown in figure (5-W7). At an instant the string between the ring and the pulley makes an angle θ with the rod. (a) Show that, if the ring slides with a speed v, the block descends with speed v cos θ. (b) With what acceleration will the ring start moving if the system is released from rest with $\theta = 30°$?*

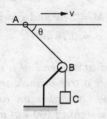

Figure 5-W7

Solution : (a) Suppose in a small time interval Δt the ring is displaced from A to A' (figure 5-W8) and the block from C to C'. Drop a perpendicular $A'P$ from A' to AB. For small displacement $A'B \approx PB$. Since the length of the string is constant, we have

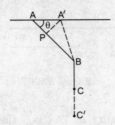

Figure 5-W8

$$AB + BC = A'B + BC'$$
or,$$\quad AP + PB + BC = A'B + BC'$$
or,$$\quad AP = BC' - BC = CC' \quad \text{(as } A'B \approx PB)$$
or,$$\quad AA' \cos\theta = CC'$$
or,$$\quad \frac{AA' \cos\theta}{\Delta t} = \frac{CC'}{\Delta t}$$

or, (velocity of the ring) $\cos\theta$ = (velocity of the block).

(b) If the initial acceleration of the ring is a, that of the block will be $a \cos\theta$. Let T be the tension in the string at this instant. Consider the block as the system. The forces acting on the block are

(i) Mg downward due to the earth, and

(ii) T upward due to the string.

The equation of motion of the block is

$$Mg - T = Ma \cos\theta. \qquad \ldots \text{ (i)}$$

Now consider the ring as the system. The forces on the ring are

(i) Mg downward due to gravity,

(ii) $\mathcal{N}$ upward due to the rod,

(iii) T along the string due to the string.

Taking components along the rod, the equation of motion of the ring is

$$T \cos\theta = ma. \qquad \ldots \text{ (ii)}$$

From (i) and (ii)

$$Mg - \frac{ma}{\cos\theta} = M a \cos\theta$$

or,$$\qquad a = \frac{M g \cos\theta}{m + M \cos^2\theta}.$$

Putting $\theta = 30°$, $M = 2\,m$ and $g = 9.8$ m/s^2; therefore

$$a = 6.78 \text{ m/s}^2.$$

8. *A light rope fixed at one end of a wooden clamp on the ground passes over a tree branch and hangs on the other side (figure 5-W9). It makes an angle of 30° with the ground. A man weighing (60 kg) wants to climb up the rope. The wooden clamp can come out of the ground if*

an upward force greater than 360 N is applied to it. Find the maximum acceleration in the upward direction with which the man can climb safely. Neglect friction at the tree branch. Take $g = 10$ m/s^2.

Figure 5-W9

Solution : Let T be the tension in the rope. The upward force on the clamp is $T \sin 30° = T/2$. The maximum tension that will not detach the clamp from the ground is, therefore, given by

$$\frac{T}{2} = 360 \text{ N}$$

or,$$\qquad T = 720 \text{ N}.$$

If the acceleration of the man in the upward direction is a, the equation of motion of the man is

$$T - 600 \text{ N} = (60 \text{ kg})\, a$$

The maximum acceleration of the man for safe climbing is, therefore

$$a = \frac{720 \text{ N} - 600 \text{ N}}{60 \text{ kg}} = 2 \text{ m/s}^2.$$

9. *Three blocks of masses m_1, m_2 and m_3 are connected as shown in the figure (5-W10). All the surfaces are frictionless and the string and the pulleys are light. Find the acceleration of m_1.*

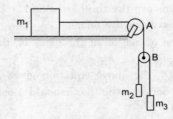

Figure 5-W10

Solution : Suppose the acceleration of m_1 is a_0 towards right. That will also be the downward acceleration of the pulley B because the string connecting m_1 and B is constant in length. Also the string connecting m_2 and m_3 has a constant length. This implies that the decrease in the separation between m_2 and B equals the increase in the separation between m_3 and B. So, the upward acceleration of m_2 with respect to B equals the downward acceleration of m_3 with respect to B. Let this acceleration be a.

The acceleration of m_2 with respect to the ground $= a_0 - a$ (downward) and the acceleration of m_3 with respect to the ground $= a_0 + a$ (downward).

These accelerations will be used in Newton's laws. Let the tension be T in the upper string and T' in the lower string. Consider the motion of the pulley B.

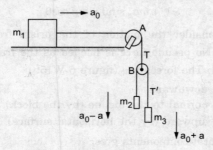

Figure 5-W11

The forces on this light pulley are
(a) T upwards by the upper string and
(b) $2T'$ downwards by the lower string.
As the mass of the pulley is negligible,
$$2T' - T = 0$$
giving
$$T' = T/2. \qquad \dots \text{(i)}$$

Motion of m_1 :

The acceleration is a_0 in the horizontal direction. The forces on m_1 are
(a) T by the string (horizontal).
(b) $m_1 g$ by the earth (vertically downwards) and
(c) $\mathcal{N}$ by the table (vertically upwards).
In the horizontal direction, the equation is
$$T = m_1 a_0. \qquad \dots \text{(ii)}$$

Motion of m_2 : acceleration is $a_0 - a$ in the downward direction. The forces on m_2 are
(a) $m_2 g$ downward by the earth and
(b) $T' = T/2$ upward by the string.
Thus, $\qquad m_2 g - \dfrac{T}{2} = m_2(a_0 - a) \qquad \dots \text{(iii)}$

Motion of m_3 : The acceleration is $(a_0 + a)$ downward. The forces on m_3 are
(a) $m_3 g$ downward by the earth and
(b) $T' = T/2$ upward by the string. Thus,
$$m_3 g - \dfrac{T}{2} = m_3(a_0 + a). \qquad \dots \text{(iv)}$$

We want to calculate a_0, so we shall eliminate T and a from (ii), (iii) and (iv).

Putting T from (ii) in (iii) and (iv),
$$a_0 - a = \frac{m_2 g - m_1 a_0 / 2}{m_2} = g - \frac{m_1 a_0}{2 m_2}$$

and $\qquad a_0 + a = \dfrac{m_3 g - m_1 a_0 / 2}{m_3} = g - \dfrac{m_1 a_0}{2 m_3}.$

Adding, $\qquad 2a_0 = 2g - \dfrac{m_1 a_0}{2}\left(\dfrac{1}{m_2} + \dfrac{1}{m_3}\right)$

or, $\qquad a_0 = g - \dfrac{m_1 a_0}{4}\left(\dfrac{1}{m_2} + \dfrac{1}{m_3}\right)$

or, $\qquad a_0\left[1 + \dfrac{m_1}{4}\left(\dfrac{1}{m_2} + \dfrac{1}{m_3}\right)\right] = g$

or, $\qquad a_0 = \dfrac{g}{1 + \dfrac{m_1}{4}\left(\dfrac{1}{m_2} + \dfrac{1}{m_3}\right)}.$

10. *A particle slides down a smooth inclined plane of elevation* θ, *fixed in an elevator going up with an acceleration* a_0 *(figure 5-W12). The base of the incline has a length* L. *Find the time taken by the particle to reach the bottom.*

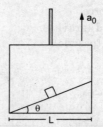

Figure 5-W12

Solution : Let us work in the elevator frame. A pseudo force ma_0 in the downward direction is to be applied on the particle of mass m together with the real forces. Thus, the forces on m are (figure 5-W13)
(i) $\mathcal{N}$ normal force,
(ii) mg downward (by the earth),
(iii) ma_0 downward (pseudo).

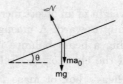

Figure 5-W13

Let a be the acceleration of the particle with respect to the incline. Taking components of the forces parallel to the incline and applying Newton's law,
$$m g \sin\theta + m a_0 \sin\theta = m a$$
or, $\qquad a = (g + a_0)\sin\theta.$
This is the acceleration with respect to the elevator. In this frame, the distance travelled by the particle is $L/\cos\theta$. Hence,
$$\frac{L}{\cos\theta} = \frac{1}{2}(g + a_0)\sin\theta . t^2$$

or, $\qquad t = \left[\dfrac{2L}{(g + a_0)\sin\theta \cos\theta}\right]^{1/2}.$

11. *All the surfaces shown in figure (5-W14) are assumed to be frictionless. The block of mass m slides on the prism which in turn slides backward on the horizontal surface. Find the acceleration of the smaller block with respect to the prism.*

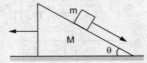

Figure 5-W14

Solution : Let the acceleration of the prism be a_0 in the backward direction. Consider the motion of the smaller block from the frame of the prism.

The forces on the block are (figure 5-W15a)

(i) $\mathcal{N}$ normal force,

(ii) mg downward (gravity),

(iii) ma_0 forward (pseudo).

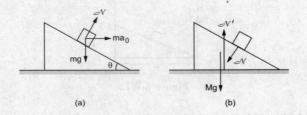

(a)   (b)

Figure 5-W15

The block slides down the plane. Components of the forces parallel to the incline give

$$ma_0 \cos\theta + mg \sin\theta = ma$$

or, $$a = a_0 \cos\theta + g \sin\theta. \qquad \dots \text{(i)}$$

Components of the force perpendicular to the incline give

$$\mathcal{N} + ma_0 \sin\theta = mg \cos\theta. \qquad \dots \text{(ii)}$$

Now consider the motion of the prism from the lab frame. No pseudo force is needed as the frame used is inertial. The forces are (figure 5-W15b)

(i) Mg downward,

(ii) $\mathcal{N}$ normal to the incline (by the block),

(iii) $\mathcal{N}'$ upward (by the horizontal surface).

Horizontal components give,

$$\mathcal{N} \sin\theta = Ma_0 \quad \text{or,} \quad \mathcal{N} = Ma_0/\sin\theta. \qquad \dots \text{(iii)}$$

Putting in (ii)

$$\frac{Ma_0}{\sin\theta} + ma_0 \sin\theta = mg \cos\theta$$

or, $$a_0 = \frac{m g \sin\theta \cos\theta}{M + m \sin^2\theta}.$$

From (i), $$a = \frac{m g \sin\theta \cos^2\theta}{M + m \sin^2\theta} + g \sin\theta$$

$$= \frac{(M + m) g \sin\theta}{M + m \sin^2\theta}.$$

□

QUESTIONS FOR SHORT ANSWER

1. The apparent weight of an object increases in an elevator while accelerating upward. A moongphaliwala sells his moongphali using a beam balance in an elevator. Will he gain more if the elevator is accelerating up ?

2. A boy puts a heavy box of mass M on his head and jumps down from the top of a multistoried building to the ground. How much is the force exerted by the box on his head during his free fall ? Does the force greatly increase during the period he balances himself after striking the ground ?

3. A person drops a coin. Describe the path of the coin as seen by the person if he is in (a) a car moving at constant velocity and (b) in a freely falling elevator.

4. Is it possible for a particle to describe a curved path if no force acts on it ? Does your answer depend on the frame of reference chosen to view the particle ?

5. You are riding in a car. The driver suddenly applies the brakes and you are pushed forward. Who pushed you forward ?

6. It is sometimes heard that inertial frame of reference is only an ideal concept and no such inertial frame actually exists. Comment.

7. An object is placed far away from all the objects that can exert force on it. A frame of reference is constructed by taking the origin and axes fixed in this object. Will the frame be necessarily inertial ?

8. Figure (5-Q1) shows a light spring balance connected to two blocks of mass 20 kg each. The graduations in the balance measure the tension in the spring. (a) What is the reading of the balance? (b) Will the reading change if the balance is heavy, say 2·0 kg ? (c) What will happen if the spring is light but the blocks have unequal masses ?

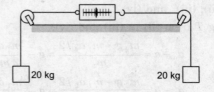

Figure 5-Q1

9. The acceleration of a particle is zero as measured from an inertial frame of reference. Can we conclude that no force acts on the particle ?

10. Suppose you are running fast in a field when you suddenly find a snake in front of you. You stop quickly. Which force is responsible for your deceleration ?

11. If you jump barefooted on a hard surface, your legs get injured. But they are not injured if you jump on a soft surface like sand or pillow. Explain.

12. According to Newton's third law each team pulls the opposite team with equal force in a tug of war. Why then one team wins and the other loses ?

13. A spy jumps from an airplane with his parachute. The spy accelerates downward for some time when the parachute opens. The acceleration is suddenly checked and the spy slowly falls on the ground. Explain the action of parachute in checking the acceleration.

14. Consider a book lying on a table. The weight of the book and the normal force by the table on the book are equal in magnitude and opposite in direction. Is this an example of Newton's third law ?

15. Two blocks of unequal masses are tied by a spring. The blocks are pulled stretching the spring slightly and the system is released on a frictionless horizontal platform. Are the forces due to the spring on the two blocks equal and opposite ? If yes, is it an example of Newton's third law ?

16. When a train starts, the head of a standing passenger seems to be pushed backward. Analyse the situation from the ground frame. Does it really go backward ? Coming back to the train frame, how do you explain the backward movement of the head on the basis of Newton's laws ?

17. A plumb bob is hung from the ceiling of a train compartment. If the train moves with an acceleration 'a' along a straight horizontal track, the string supporting the bob makes an angle $\tan^{-1}(a/g)$ with the normal to the ceiling. Suppose the train moves on an inclined straight track with uniform velocity. If the angle of incline is $\tan^{-1}(a/g)$, the string again makes the same angle with the normal to the ceiling. Can a person sitting inside the compartment tell by looking at the plumb line whether the train is accelerated on a horizontal straight track or it is going on an incline ? If yes, how ? If no, suggest a method to do so.

OBJECTIVE I

1. A body of weight w_1 is suspended from the ceiling of a room through a chain of weight w_2. The ceiling pulls the chain by a force
   (a) w_1 (b) w_2 (c) $w_1 + w_2$ (d) $\dfrac{w_1 + w_2}{2}$.

2. When a horse pulls a cart, the force that helps the horse to move forward is the force exerted by
   (a) the cart on the horse   (b) the ground on the horse
   (c) the ground on the cart   (d) the horse on the ground.

3. A car accelerates on a horizontal road due to the force exerted by
   (a) the engine of the car   (b) the driver of the car
   (c) the earth   (d) the road.

4. A block of mass 10 kg is suspended through two light spring balances as shown in figure (5-Q2).

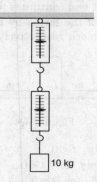

Figure 5-Q2

   (a) Both the scales will read 10 kg.
   (b) Both the scales will read 5 kg.
   (c) The upper scale will read 10 kg and the lower zero.
   (d) The readings may be anything but their sum will be 10 kg.

5. A block of mass m is placed on a smooth inclined plane of inclination θ with the horizontal. The force exerted by the plane on the block has a magnitude
   (a) mg (b) $mg/\cos\theta$ (c) $mg\cos\theta$ (d) $mg\tan\theta$.

6. A block of mass m is placed on a smooth wedge of inclination θ. The whole system is accelerated horizontally so that the block does not slip on the wedge. The force exerted by the wedge on the block has a magnitude
   (a) mg (b) $mg/\cos\theta$ (c) $mg\cos\theta$ (d) $mg\tan\theta$.

7. Neglect the effect of rotation of the earth. Suppose the earth suddenly stops attracting objects placed near its surface. A person standing on the surface of the earth will
   (a) fly up   (b) slip along the surface
   (c) fly along a tangent to the earth's surface
   (d) remain standing.

8. Three rigid rods are joined to form an equilateral triangle ABC of side 1 m. Three particles carrying charges 20 μC each are attached to the vertices of the triangle. The whole system is at rest in an inertial frame. The resultant force on the charged particle at A has the magnitude
   (a) zero   (b) 3·6 N   (c) 3·6√3 N   (d) 7·2 N.

9. A force F_1 acts on a particle so as to accelerate it from rest to a velocity v. The force F_1 is then replaced by F_2 which decelerates it to rest.
   (a) F_1 must be equal to F_2 (b) F_1 may be equal to F_2
   (c) F_1 must be unequal to F_2 (d) none of these.

10. Two objects A and B are thrown upward simultaneously with the same speed. The mass of A is greater than the mass of B. Suppose the air exerts a constant and equal force of resistance on the two bodies.
    (a) The two bodies will reach the same height.
    (b) A will go higher than B.
    (c) B will go higher than A.
    (d) Any of the above three may happen depending on the speed with which the objects are thrown.

11. A smooth wedge A is fitted in a chamber hanging from a fixed ceiling near the earth's surface. A block B placed at the top of the wedge takes a time T to slide down the length of the wedge. If the block is placed at the top of the wedge and the cable supporting the chamber is broken at the same instant, the block will
    (a) take a time longer than T to slide down the wedge
    (b) take a time shorter than T to slide down the wedge
    (c) remain at the top of the wedge
    (d) jump off the wedge.

12. In an imaginary atmosphere, the air exerts a small force F on any particle in the direction of the particle's motion. A particle of mass m projected upward takes a time t_1 in reaching the maximum height and t_2 in the return journey to the original point. Then
    (a) $t_1 < t_2$ (b) $t_1 > t_2$ (c) $t_1 = t_2$ (d) the relation between t_1 and t_2 depends on the mass of the particle.

13. A person standing on the floor of an elevator drops a coin. The coin reaches the floor of the elevator in a time t_1 if the elevator is stationary and in time t_2 if it is moving uniformly. Then
    (a) $t_1 = t_2$ (b) $t_1 < t_2$ (c) $t_1 > t_2$ (d) $t_1 < t_2$ or $t_1 > t_2$ depending on whether the lift is going up or down.

14. A free ^{238}U nucleus kept in a train emits an alpha particle. When the train is stationary, a nucleus decays and a passenger measures that the separation between the alpha particle and the recoiling nucleus becomes x at time t after the decay. If the decay takes place while the train is moving at a uniform velocity v, the distance between the alpha particle and the recoiling nucleus at a time t after the decay as measured by the passenger is
    (a) $x + v t$ (b) $x - v t$ (c) x
    (d) depends on the direction of the train.

OBJECTIVE II

1. A reference frame attached to the earth
   (a) is an inertial frame by definition
   (b) cannot be an inertial frame because the earth is revolving around the sun
   (c) is an inertial frame because Newton's laws are applicable in this frame
   (d) cannot be an inertial frame because the earth is rotating about its axis.

2. A particle stays at rest as seen in a frame. We can conclude that
   (a) the frame is inertial
   (b) resultant force on the particle is zero
   (c) the frame may be inertial but the resultant force on the particle is zero
   (d) the frame may be noninertial but there is a nonzero resultant force.

3. A particle is found to be at rest when seen from a frame S_1 and moving with a constant velocity when seen from another frame S_2. Mark out the possible options.
   (a) Both the frames are inertial.
   (b) Both the frames are noninertial.
   (c) S_1 is inertial and S_2 is noninertial.
   (d) S_1 is noninertial and S_2 is inertial.

4. Figure (5-Q3) shows the displacement of a particle going along the X-axis as a function of time. The force acting on the particle is zero in the region
   (a) AB (b) BC (c) CD (d) DE.

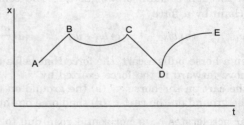

Figure 5-Q3

5. Figure (5-Q4) shows a heavy block kept on a frictionless surface and being pulled by two ropes of equal mass m. At $t = 0$, the force on the left rope is withdrawn but the force on the right end continues to act. Let F_1 and F_2 be the magnitudes of the forces by the right rope and the left rope on the block respectively.

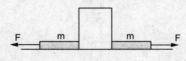

Figure 5-Q4

   (a) $F_1 = F_2 = F$ for $t < 0$
   (b) $F_1 = F_2 = F + mg$ for $t < 0$
   (c) $F_1 = F$, $F_2 = F$ for $t > 0$
   (d) $F_1 < F$, $F_2 = F$ for $t > 0$.

6. The force exerted by the floor of an elevator on the foot of a person standing there is more than the weight of the person if the elevator is
(a) going up and slowing down
(b) going up and speeding up
(c) going down and slowing down
(d) going down and speeding up.

7. If the tension in the cable supporting an elevator is equal to the weight of the elevator, the elevator may be
(a) going up with increasing speed
(b) going down with increasing speed
(c) going up with uniform speed
(d) going down with uniform speed.

8. A particle is observed from two frames S_1 and S_2. The frame S_2 moves with respect to S_1 with an acceleration a. Let F_1 and F_2 be the pseudo forces on the particle when seen from S_1 and S_2 respectively. Which of the following are not possible ?
(a) $F_1 = 0$, $F_2 \neq 0$ (b) $F_1 \neq 0$, $F_2 = 0$
(c) $F_1 \neq 0$, $F_2 \neq 0$ (d) $F_1 = 0$, $F_2 = 0$.

9. A person says that he measured the acceleration of a particle to be nonzero while no force was acting on the particle.
(a) He is a liar.
(b) His clock might have run slow.
(c) His meter scale might have been longer than the standard.
(d) He might have used noninertial frame.

EXERCISES

1. A block of mass 2 kg placed on a long frictionless horizontal table is pulled horizontally by a constant force F. It is found to move 10 m in the first two seconds. Find the magnitude of F.

2. A car moving at 40 km/h is to be stopped by applying brakes in the next 4·0 m. If the car weighs 2000 kg, what average force must be applied on it ?

3. In a TV picture tube electrons are ejected from the cathode with negligible speed and reach a velocity of 5×10^6 m/s in travelling one centimeter. Assuming straight line motion, find the constant force exerted on the electron. The mass of the electron is $9 \cdot 1 \times 10^{-31}$ kg.

4. A block of mass 0·2 kg is suspended from the ceiling by a light string. A second block of mass 0·3 kg is suspended from the first block through another string. Find the tensions in the two strings. Take $g = 10$ m/s^2.

5. Two blocks of equal mass m are tied to each other through a light string and placed on a smooth horizontal table. One of the blocks is pulled along the line joining them with a constant force F. Find the tension in the string joining the blocks.

6. A particle of mass 50 g moves on a straight line. The variation of speed with time is shown in figure (5-E1). Find the force acting on the particle at $t = 2$, 4 and 6 seconds.

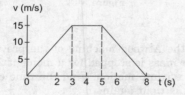

Figure 5-E1

7. Two blocks A and B of mass m_A and m_B respectively are kept in contact on a frictionless table. The experimenter pushes the block A from behind so that the blocks accelerate. If the block A exerts a force F on the block B, what is the force exerted by the experimenter on A ?

8. Raindrops of radius 1 mm and mass 4 mg are falling with a speed of 30 m/s on the head of a bald person. The drops splash on the head and come to rest. Assuming equivalently that the drops cover a distance equal to their radii on the head, estimate the force exerted by each drop on the head.

9. A particle of mass 0·3 kg is subjected to a force $F = -kx$ with $k = 15$ N/m. What will be its initial acceleration if it is released from a point $x = 20$ cm ?

10. Both the springs shown in figure (5-E2) are unstretched. If the block is displaced by a distance x and released, what will be the initial acceleration?

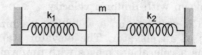

Figure 5-E2

11. A small block B is placed on another block A of mass 5 kg and length 20 cm. Initially the block B is near the right end of block A (figure 5-E3). A constant horizontal force of 10 N is applied to the block A. All the surfaces are assumed frictionless. Find the time elapsed before the block B separates from A.

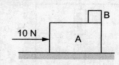

Figure 5-E3

12. A man has fallen into a ditch of width d and two of his friends are slowly pulling him out using a light rope and two fixed pulleys as shown in figure (5-E4). Show that the force (assumed equal for both the friends) exerted by each friend on the rope increases as the man moves up. Find the force when the man is at a depth h.

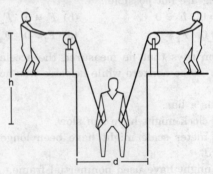

Figure 5-E4

13. The elevator shown in figure (5-E5) is descending with an acceleration of 2 m/s^2. The mass of the block A is 0·5 kg. What force is exerted by the block A on the block B ?

Figure 5-E5

14. A pendulum bob of mass 50 g is suspended from the ceiling of an elevator. Find the tension in the string if the elevator (a) goes up with acceleration 1·2 m/s^2, (b) goes up with deceleration 1·2 m/s^2, (c) goes up with uniform velocity, (d) goes down with acceleration 1·2 m/s^2, (e) goes down with deceleration 1·2 m/s^2 and (f) goes down with uniform velocity.

15. A person is standing on a weighing machine placed on the floor of an elevator. The elevator starts going up with some acceleration, moves with uniform velocity for a while and finally decelerates to stop. The maximum and the minimum weights recorded are 72 kg and 60 kg. Assuming that the magnitudes of the acceleration and the deceleration are the same, find (a) the true weight of the person and (b) the magnitude of the acceleration. Take $g = 9·9$ m/s^2.

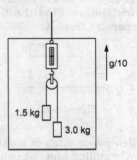

Figure 5-E6

16. Find the reading of the spring balance shown in figure (5-E6). The elevator is going up with an acceleration of $g/10$, the pulley and the string are light and the pulley is smooth.

17. A block of 2 kg is suspended from the ceiling through a massless spring of spring constant $k = 100$ N/m. What is the elongation of the spring ? If another 1 kg is added to the block, what would be the further elongation ?

18. Suppose the ceiling in the previous problem is that of an elevator which is going up with an acceleration of 2·0 m/s^2. Find the elongations.

19. The force of buoyancy exerted by the atmosphere on a balloon is B in the upward direction and remains constant. The force of air resistance on the balloon acts opposite to the direction of velocity and is proportional to it. The balloon carries a mass M and is found to fall down near the earth's surface with a constant velocity v. How much mass should be removed from the balloon so that it may rise with a constant velocity v ?

20. An empty plastic box of mass m is found to accelerate up at the rate of $g/6$ when placed deep inside water. How much sand should be put inside the box so that it may accelerate down at the rate of $g/6$?

21. A force $\vec{F} = \vec{v} \times \vec{A}$ is exerted on a particle in addition to the force of gravity, where $\vec{v}$ is the velocity of the particle and $\vec{A}$ is a constant vector in the horizontal direction. With what minimum speed a particle of mass m be projected so that it continues to move undeflected with a constant velocity ?

22. In a simple Atwood machine, two unequal masses m_1 and m_2 are connected by a string going over a clamped light smooth pulley. In a typical arrangement (figure 5-E7) $m_1 = 300$ g and $m_2 = 600$ g. The system is released from rest. (a) Find the distance travelled by the first block in the first two seconds. (b) Find the tension in the string. (c) Find the force exerted by the clamp on the pulley.

Figure 5-E7

23. Consider the Atwood machine of the previous problem. The larger mass is stopped for a moment 2·0 s after the system is set into motion. Find the time elapsed before the string is tight again.

24. Figure (5-E8) shows a uniform rod of length 30 cm having a mass of 3·0 kg. The strings shown in the figure are pulled by constant forces of 20 N and 32 N. Find the force exerted by the 20 cm part of the rod on the 10 cm part. All the surfaces are smooth and the strings and the pulleys are light.

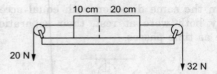

Figure 5-E8

25. Consider the situation shown in figure (5-E9). All the surfaces are frictionless and the string and the pulley are light. Find the magnitude of the acceleration of the two blocks.

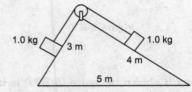

Figure 5-E9

26. A constant force $F = m_2 g / 2$ is applied on the block of mass m_1 as shown in figure (5-E10). The string and the pulley are light and the surface of the table is smooth. Find the acceleration of m_1.

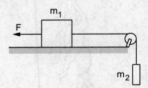

Figure 5-E10

27. In figure (5-E11) $m_1 = 5$ kg, $m_2 = 2$ kg and $F = 1$ N. Find the acceleration of either block. Describe the motion of m_1 if the string breaks but F continues to act.

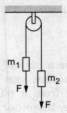

Figure 5-E11

28. Let $m_1 = 1$ kg, $m_2 = 2$ kg and $m_3 = 3$ kg in figure (5-E12). Find the accelerations of m_1, m_2 and m_3. The string from the upper pulley to m_1 is 20 cm when the system is released from rest. How long will it take before m_1 strikes the pulley?

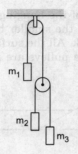

Figure 5-E12

29. In the previous problem, suppose $m_2 = 2 \cdot 0$ kg and $m_3 = 3 \cdot 0$ kg. What should be the mass m so that it remains at rest?

30. Calculate the tension in the string shown in figure (5-E13). The pulley and the string are light and all surfaces are frictionless. Take $g = 10$ m/s^2.

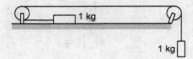

Figure 5-E13

31. Consider the situation shown in figure (5-E14). Both the pulleys and the string are light and all the surfaces are frictionless. (a) Find the acceleration of the mass M. (b) Find the tension in the string. (c) Calculate the force exerted by the clamp on the pulley A in the figure.

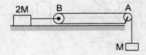

Figure 5-E14

32. Find the acceleration of the block of mass M in the situation shown in figure (5-E15). All the surfaces are frictionless and the pulleys and the string are light.

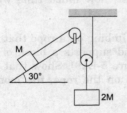

Figure 5-E15

33. Find the mass M of the hanging block in figure (5-E16) which will prevent the smaller block from slipping over the triangular block. All the surfaces are frictionless and the strings and the pulleys are light.

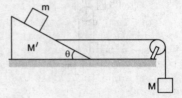

Figure 5-E16

34. Find the acceleration of the blocks A and B in the three situations shown in figure (5-E17).

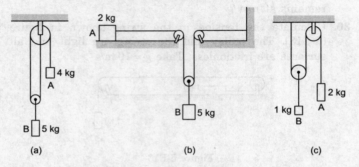

(a)   (b)   (c)

Figure 5-E17

35. Find the acceleration of the 500 g block in figure (5-E18).

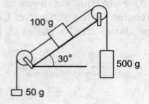

Figure 5-E18

36. A monkey of mass 15 kg is climbing on a rope with one end fixed to the ceiling. If it wishes to go up with an acceleration of 1 m/s^2, how much force should it apply to the rope? If the rope is 5 m long and the monkey starts from rest, how much time will it take to reach the ceiling?

37. A monkey is climbing on a rope that goes over a smooth light pulley and supports a block of equal mass at the other end (figure 5-E19). Show that whatever force the monkey exerts on the rope, the monkey and the block

move in the same direction with equal acceleration. If initially both were at rest, their separation will not change as time passes.

Figure 5-E19

38. The monkey B shown in figure (5-E20) is holding on to the tail of the monkey A which is climbing up a rope. The masses of the monkeys A and B are 5 kg and 2 kg respectively. If A can tolerate a tension of 30 N in its tail, what force should it apply on the rope in order to carry the monkey B with it? Take $g = 10$ m/s^2.

Figure 5-E20

39. Figure (5-E21) shows a man of mass 60 kg standing on a light weighing machine kept in a box of mass 30 kg. The box is hanging from a pulley fixed to the ceiling through a light rope, the other end of which is held by the man himself. If the man manages to keep the box at rest, what is the weight shown by the machine? What force should he exert on the rope to get his correct weight on the machine?

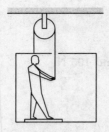

Figure 5-E21

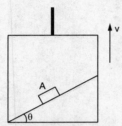

Figure 5-E22

40. A block A can slide on a frictionless incline of angle θ and length l, kept inside an elevator going up with uniform velocity v (figure 5-E22). Find the time taken by the block to slide down the length of the incline if it is released from the top of the incline.

41. A car is speeding up on a horizontal road with an acceleration a. Consider the following situations in the car. (i) A ball is suspended from the ceiling through a string and is maintaining a constant angle with the vertical. Find this angle. (ii) A block is kept on a smooth incline and does not slip on the incline. Find the angle of the incline with the horizontal.

42. A block is kept on the floor of an elevator at rest. The elevator starts descending with an acceleration of 12 m/s^2. Find the displacement of the block during the first 0.2 s after the start. Take $g = 10 \text{ m/s}^2$.

□

ANSWERS

OBJECTIVE I

1. (c)	2. (b)	3. (d)	4. (a)	5. (c)	6. (b)
7. (d)	8. (a)	9. (b)	10. (b)	11. (c)	12. (b)
13. (a)	14. (c)				

OBJECTIVE II

1. (b), (d)	2. (c), (d)	3. (a), (b)
4. (a), (c)	5. (a)	6. (b), (c)
7. (c), (d)	8. (d)	9. (d)

EXERCISES

1. 10 N

2. 3.1×10^4 N

3. 1.1×10^{-15} N

4. 5 N and 3 N

5. $F/2$

6. 0.25 N along the motion, zero and 0.25 N opposite to the motion.

7. $F\left(1 + \dfrac{m_A}{m_B}\right)$

8. 1.8 N

9. 10 m/s^2

10. $(k_1 + k_2)\dfrac{x}{m}$ opposite to the displacement.

11. 0.45 s.

12. $\dfrac{mg}{4h}\sqrt{d^2 + 4h^2}$

13. 4 N

14. (a) 0.55 N   (b) 0.43 N   (c) 0.49 N
    (d) 0.43 N   (e) 0.55 N   (f) 0.49 N

15. 66 kg and 0.9 m/s^2

16. 4.4 kg

17. 0.2 m, 0.1 m

18. 0.24 m, 0.12 m

19. $2\left(M - \dfrac{B}{g}\right)$

20. $2m/5$

21. mg/A

22. (a) 6.5 m   (b) 3.9 N   (c) 7.8 N

23. $2/3$ s

24. 24 N

25. $g/10$

26. $\dfrac{m_2 g}{2(m_1 + m_2)}$ towards right

27. 4.3 m/s^2, moves downward with acceleration $g + 0.2 \text{ m/s}^2$

28. $\frac{19}{29} g \ (up)$, $\frac{17}{29} g \ (down)$, $\frac{21}{29} g \ (down)$, $0·25$ s

29. 4·8 kg

30. 5 N

31. (a) $2 g/3$ (b) $Mg/3$

 (c) $\sqrt{2} \, Mg/3$ at an angle of 45° with the horizontal

32. $g/3$ up the plane

33. $\dfrac{M' + m}{\cot\theta - 1}$

34. (a) $\dfrac{2}{7} g$ downward, $\dfrac{g}{7}$ upward

 (b) $\dfrac{10}{13} g$ forward, $\dfrac{5}{13} g$ downward

 (c) $\dfrac{2}{3} g$ downward, $\dfrac{g}{3}$ upward

35. $\dfrac{8}{13} g$ downward

36. 165 N, $\sqrt{10}$ s

38. between 70 N and 105 N

39. 15 kg, 1800 N

40. $\sqrt{\dfrac{2\,l}{g \sin\theta}}$

41. $\tan^{-1}(a/g)$ in each case

42. 20 cm

□

CHAPTER 6

FRICTION

6.1 FRICTION AS THE COMPONENT OF CONTACT FORCE

When two bodies are kept in contact, electro-magnetic forces act between the charged particles at the surfaces of the bodies. As a result, each body exerts a contact force on the other. The magnitudes of the contact forces acting on the two bodies are equal but their directions are opposite and hence the contact forces obey Newton's third law.

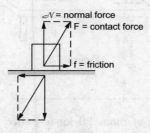

Figure 6.1

The direction of the contact force acting on a particular body is not necessarily perpendicular to the contact surface. We can resolve this contact force into two components, one perpendicular to the contact surface and the other parallel to it (Figure 6.1). The perpendicular component is called the *normal contact force* or *normal force* and the parallel component is called *friction*.

Example 6.1

A body of mass 400 g *slides on a rough horizontal surface. If the frictional force is* 3·0 N, *find (a) the angle made by the contact force on the body with the vertical and (b) the magnitude of the contact force. Take* $g = 10 \text{ m/s}^2$.

Solution : Let the contact force on the block by the surface be F which makes an angle θ with the vertical (figure 6.2).

Figure 6.2

The component of F perpendicular to the contact surface is the normal force $\mathcal{N}$ and the component of F parallel to the surface is the friction f. As the surface is horizontal, $\mathcal{N}$ is vertically upward. For vertical equilibrium,

$$\mathcal{N} = Mg = (0·400 \text{ kg}) (10 \text{ m/s}^2) = 4·0 \text{ N}.$$

The frictional force is $f = 3·0$ N.

(a) $$\tan \theta = \frac{f}{\mathcal{N}} = \frac{3}{4}$$

or, $$\theta = \tan^{-1}(3/4) = 37°.$$

(b) The magnitude of the contact force is

$$F = \sqrt{\mathcal{N}^2 + f^2}$$

$$= \sqrt{(4·0 \text{ N})^2 + (3·0 \text{ N})^2} = 5·0 \text{ N}.$$

Friction can operate between a given pair of solids, between a solid and a fluid or between a pair of fluids. Frictional force exerted by fluids is called *viscous force* and we shall study it in a later chapter. Here we shall study about the frictional forces operating between a pair of solid surfaces.

When two solid bodies slip over each other, the force of friction is called *kinetic friction*. When two bodies do not slip on each other, the force of friction is called *static friction*.

It is difficult to work out a reliable theory of friction starting from the electromagnetic interaction between the particles at the surface. However, a wide range of observations can be summarized in a small number of *laws of friction* which we shall discuss.

6.2 KINETIC FRICTION

When two bodies in contact move with respect to each other, rubbing the surfaces in contact, the friction between them is called kinetic friction. The directions of the frictional forces are such that the relative slipping is opposed by the friction.

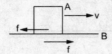

Figure 6.3

Suppose a body A placed in contact with B is moved with respect to it as shown in figure (6.3). The force of friction acting on A due to B will be opposite to the velocity of A with respect to B. In figure (6.3) this force is shown towards left. The force of friction on B due to A is opposite to the velocity of B with respect to A. In figure (6.3) this force is shown towards right. The force of kinetic friction opposes the relative motion. We can formulate the rules for finding the direction and magnitude of kinetic friction as follows :

(a) Direction of Kinetic Friction

The kinetic friction on a body A slipping against another body B is opposite to the velocity of A with respect to B.

It should be carefully noted that the velocity coming into picture is with respect to the body applying the force of friction.

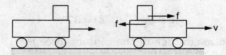

Figure 6.4

As another example, suppose we have a long box having wheels and moving on a horizontal road (figure 6.4). A small block is placed on the box which slips on the box to fall from the rear end. As seen from the road, both the box and the block are moving towards right, of course the velocity of the block is smaller than that of the box. What is the direction of the kinetic friction acting on the block due to the box ? The velocity of the block as seen from the box is towards left. Thus, the friction on the block is towards right. The friction acting on the box due to the block is towards left.

(b) Magnitude of the Kinetic Friction

The magnitude of the kinetic friction is proportional to the normal force acting between the two bodies. We can write

$$f_k = \mu_k \mathcal{N} \qquad \ldots \ (6.1)$$

where $\mathcal{N}$ is the normal force. The proportionality constant μ_k is called the *coefficient of kinetic friction* and its value depends on the nature of the two surfaces in contact. If the surfaces are smooth μ_k will be small, if the surfaces are rough μ_k will be large. It also depends on the materials of the two bodies in contact.

According to equation (6.1) the coefficient of kinetic friction does not depend on the speed of the sliding bodies. Once the bodies slip on each other the frictional force is $\mu_k \mathcal{N}$, whatever be the speed. This is approximately true for relative speeds not too large (say for speeds < 10 m/s).

We also see from equation (6.1) that as long as the normal force $\mathcal{N}$ is same, the frictional force is independent of the area of the surface in contact. For example, if a rectangular slab is slid over a table, the frictional force is same whether the slab lies flat on the table or it stands on its face of smaller area (figure 6.5)

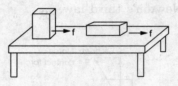

Figure 6.5

Example 6.2

A heavy box of mass 20 kg is pulled on a horizontal surface by applying a horizontal force. If the coefficient of kinetic friction between the box and the horizontal surface is 0·25, find the force of friction exerted by the horizontal surface on the box.

Solution : The situation is shown in figure (6.6). In the vertical direction there is no acceleration, so

$$\mathcal{N} = Mg.$$

As the box slides on the horizontal surface, the surface exerts kinetic friction on the box. The magnitude of the kinetic friction is

$$f_k = \mu_k \mathcal{N} = \mu_k Mg$$

$$= 0·25 \times (20 \text{ kg}) \times (9·8 \text{ m/s}^2) = 49 \text{ N}.$$

This force acts in the direction opposite to the pull.

6.3 STATIC FRICTION

Frictional forces can also act between two bodies which are in contact but are not sliding with respect to each other. The friction in such cases is called *static friction*. For example, suppose several labourers are trying to push a heavy almirah on the floor to take it out of a room (figure 6.7).

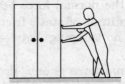

Figure 6.7

The almirah is heavy and even the most sincere effort by them is not able to slide it on the floor even by a millimeter. As the almirah is at rest the resultant force on the almirah should be zero. Thus, something is exerting a force on the almirah in the opposite direction. In this case, it is the floor which exerts a frictional force on the almirah. The labourers push the almirah towards left in figure (6.7) and the floor exerts a frictional force on the almirah towards right. This is an example of static friction.

How strong is this frictional force ? Suppose the almirah is pushed with a small force in the beginning and the force is gradually increased. It does not slide until the force applied is greater than a minimum value say F. The force of static friction is equal and opposite to the force exerted by the labourers as long as the almirah is at rest. This means that the magnitude of static friction adjusts its value according to the applied force. As the applied force increases, the frictional force also increases. The static friction is thus, self adjustable. It adjusts its magnitude (and direction) in such a way that together with other forces applied on the body, it maintains 'relative rest' between the two surfaces. However, the frictional force cannot go beyond a maximum. When the applied force exceeds this maximum, friction fails to increase its value and slipping starts. The maximum static friction that a body can exert on the other body in contact with it, is called *limiting friction*. This limiting friction is proportional to the normal contact force between the two bodies. We can write

$$f_{max} = \mu_s \mathcal{N} \qquad \dots (6.2)$$

where f_{max} is the maximum possible force of static friction and $\mathcal{N}$ is the normal force. The constant of proportionality is called the *coefficient of static friction* and its value again depends on the material and roughness of the two surfaces in contact. In general, μ_s is slightly greater than μ_k. As long as the normal force is constant, the maximum possible friction does not depend on the area of the surfaces in contact.

Once again we emphasise that $\mu_s \mathcal{N}$ is the **maximum** possible force of static friction that **can** act between the bodies. The actual force of static friction may be smaller than $\mu_s \mathcal{N}$ and its value depends on other forces acting on the body. The magnitude of frictional force is equal to that required to keep the body at relative rest. Thus,

$$f_s \le f_{max} = \mu_s \mathcal{N}. \qquad \dots (6.3)$$

Example 6.3

A boy (30 kg) sitting on his horse whips it. The horse speeds up at an average acceleration of $2 \cdot 0$ m/s^2. (a) If the boy does not slide back, what is the force of friction exerted by the horse on the boy ? (b) If the boy slides back during the acceleration, what can be said about the coefficient of static friction between the horse and the boy. Take $g = 10$ m/s^2.

Solution : (a) The forces acting on the boy are
(i) the weight Mg.
(ii) the normal contact force $\mathcal{N}$ and
(iii) the static friction f_s.

Figure 6.8

As the boy does not slide back, its acceleration a is equal to the acceleration of the horse. As friction is the only horizontal force, it must act along the acceleration and its magnitude is given by Newton's second law

$$f_s = Ma = (30 \text{ kg}) (2 \cdot 0 \text{ m/s}^2) = 60 \text{ N}.$$

(b) If the boy slides back, the horse could not exert a friction of 60 N on the boy. The maximum force of static friction that the horse may exert on the boy is

$$f_s = \mu_s \mathcal{N} = \mu_s Mg$$

$$= \mu_s (30 \text{ kg}) (10 \text{ m/s}^2) = \mu_s 300 \text{ N}$$

where μ_s is the coefficient of static friction. Thus,

$$\mu_s (300 \text{ N}) < 60 \text{ N}$$

or, $$\mu_s < \frac{60}{300} = 0 \cdot 20.$$

Finding the Direction of Static Friction

The direction of static friction on a body is such that the total force acting on it keeps it at rest with respect to the body in contact. Newton's first or second law can often be used to find the direction of static friction. Figure (6.9) shows a block A placed on another block B which is placed on a horizontal table.

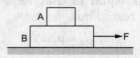

Figure 6.9

The block B is pulled by a force F towards right. Suppose the force is small and the blocks do not move. Let us focus our attention on the upper block. The upper block is at rest with respect to the ground which is assumed to be inertial. Thus, the resultant force on the upper block is zero (Newton's first law). As no other external force acts on the upper block the friction acting on the upper block due to the lower block, must be zero. If the force F is increased, the two blocks move together towards right, with some acceleration. As the upper block accelerates towards right the resultant force on it must be towards right. As friction is the only horizontal force on the upper block it must be towards right.

Notice that it is the friction on the upper block which accelerates it towards right. It is a general misconception that friction always opposes the motion. It is not really true. In many cases friction causes the motion. A vehicle accelerates on the road only because the frictional force on the vehicle due to the road drives it. It is not possible to accelerate a vehicle on a frictionless road. Friction opposes the relative motion between the bodies in contact.

Another way to find the direction of static friction is as follows. For a moment consider the surfaces to be frictionless. In absence of friction the bodies will start slipping against each other. One should then find the direction of friction as opposite to the velocity with respect to the body applying the friction.

6.4 LAWS OF FRICTION

We can summarise the laws of friction between two bodies in contact as follows :

(1) If the bodies slip over each other, the force of friction is given by

$$f_k = \mu_k \mathcal{N}$$

where $\mathcal{N}$ is the normal contact force and μ_k is the coefficient of kinetic friction between the surfaces.

(2) The direction of kinetic friction on a body is opposite to the velocity of this body with respect to the body applying the force of friction.

(3) If the bodies do not slip over each other, the force of friction is given by

$$f_s \leq \mu_s \mathcal{N}$$

where μ_s is the coefficient of static friction between the bodies and $\mathcal{N}$ is the normal force between them. The direction and magnitude of static friction are such that the condition of no slipping between the bodies is ensured.

(4) The frictional force f_k or f_s does not depend on the area of contact as long as the normal force $\mathcal{N}$ is same.

Table (6.1) gives a rough estimate of the values of coefficient of static friction between certain pairs of materials. The actual value depends on the degree of smoothness and other environmental factors. For example, wood may be prepared at various degrees of smoothness and the friction coefficient will varry.

Table 6.1 : *The Friction Coefficients*

Material	μ_s	Material	μ_s
Steel and steel	0·58	Copper and copper	1·60
Steel and brass	0·35	Teflon and teflon	0·04
Glass and glass	1·00	Rubber tyre on dry concrete road	1·0
Wood and wood	0·35		
Wood and metal	0·40	Rubber tyre on wet concrete road	0·7
Ice and ice	0·10		

Dust, impurities, surface oxidation etc. have a great role in determining the friction coefficient. Suppose we take two blocks of pure copper, clean them carefully to remove any oxide or dust layer at the surfaces, heat them to push out any dissolved gases and keep them in contact with each other in an evacuated chamber at a very low pressure of air. The blocks stick to each other and a large force is needed to slide one over the other. The friction coefficient as defined above, becomes much larger than one. If a small amount of air is allowed to go into the chamber so that some oxidation takes place at the surface, the friction coefficient reduces to usual values.

6.5 UNDERSTANDING FRICTION AT ATOMIC LEVEL

It has already been pointed out that friction appears because of the interaction between the charged particles of the two bodies near the surfaces of contact. Any macroscopic object like a steel plate or a wood piece has irregular surface at atomic scale. A polished steel surface may look plane to naked eyes but if seen under a powerful microscope, its surface is found to be quite irregular. Figure (6.10) shows qualitatively how an apparently plane surface may be at the atomic scale.

Figure 6.10

When two bodies are kept one over the other, the real area in contact is much smaller than the total surface area of the bodies (figure 6.11) The distance between the particles of the two bodies becomes very small at these actual points of contact and the molecular forces start operating across the surface. Molecular bonds are formed at these contact points. When one of the two bodies is pulled over the other, these bonds are broken, the materials under the bond is deformed and new bonds are formed. The local deformation of the bodies send vibration waves into the bodies. These vibrations finally damp out and the energy appears as the increased random motion of the particles of the bodies. The bodies thus, become heated. A force is, therefore, needed to start the motion or to maintain the motion.

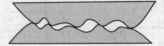

Figure 6.11

6.6 A LABORATORY METHOD TO MEASURE FRICTION COEFFICIENT

(a) Horizontal Table Method

Figure (6.12) shows the apparatus. A wooden plank A is fixed on a wooden frame kept on a table. A frictionless pulley is fixed to one end of the plank. A block B is kept on the plank and is attached to a hanger H by a string which passes over the pulley.

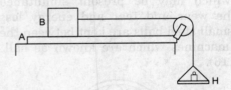

Figure 6.12

The plank is kept in a horizontal position. The friction coefficient between the block B and the plank A can be obtained by using this apparatus.

The weights of the block B and the hanger H are measured. Standard weights are kept on the hanger. The weights are gradually increased and the minimum weight needed to just slide the block is noted.

Suppose the weight of the block is W_1 and the weight of the hanger together with the standard weights is W_2 when the block just starts to slide. The tension in the string is W_2 and same is the force of friction on the block by the plank. Thus, the maximum force of static friction on the block is $f_{max} = W_2$. The normal force on the block by the plank is equal to the weight of the block itself as the block is in vertical equilibrium. Thus, the normal force is $\mathcal{N} = W_1$.

The coefficient of static friction is

$$\mu_s = \frac{f_{max}}{\mathcal{N}} = \frac{W_2}{W_1}.$$

To obtain the coefficient of kinetic friction, the weight on the hanger is slightly reduced and the block is gently pushed with a finger to move it on the plank. The weight on the hanger is so adjusted that once pushed, the block continues to move on the plank with uniform speed. In this case, the tension in the string equals the force of kinetic friction. As the hanger also moves with uniform velocity, the tension equals the weight of the hanger plus the standard weights kept in it. For vertical equilibrium of the block, the normal force on the block equals the weight of the block. Thus, if W_1 is the weight of the block and W_2' is the weight of the hanger plus the standard weights, the coefficient of kinetic friction is

$$\mu_k = \frac{f_k}{\mathcal{N}} = \frac{W_2'}{W_1}.$$

One can put certain standard weights on the block to increase the normal force and repeat the experiment. It can be verified that the force of friction also increases and $f_k / \mathcal{N}$ comes out to be the same as it should be because the nature of the surfaces is same. If the block is kept on the plank on some other face, the area of contact is changed. It can be verified by repeating the above experiment that the force of friction does not depend on the area of contact for a given value of normal contact force.

(b) Inclined Table Method

In this method no pulley is needed. A wooden plank A is fixed on a wooden frame. One end of the plank is fixed to the frame on a hinge and the other end can be moved vertically and can be fixed at the desired position. Thus, the plank can be fixed in an inclined position and the angle of incline can be adjusted. A schematic diagram is shown in figure (6.13).

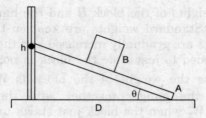

Figure 6.13

Block B is placed on the incline and the angle of the incline is gradually increased. The angle of the incline is so adjusted that the block just starts to slide. The height h and the horizontal distance D between the two ends of the plank are measured. The angle of incline θ satisfies

$$\tan\theta = h/D.$$

Let m be the mass of the block. The forces on the block in case of limiting equilibrium are (figure 6.14)

(i) weight of the block mg,

(ii) the normal contact force $\mathcal{N}$, and

(iii) the force of static friction f_s.

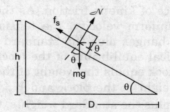

Figure 6.14

Taking components along the incline and applying Newton's first law,

$$f_s = mg\sin\theta.$$

Taking components along the normal to the incline,

$$\mathcal{N} = mg\cos\theta.$$

Thus, the coefficient of static friction between the block and the plank is

$$\mu_s = \frac{f_s}{\mathcal{N}} = \frac{mg\sin\theta}{mg\cos\theta} = \tan\theta = \frac{h}{D}.$$

To obtain the kinetic friction, the inclination is reduced slightly and the block is made to move on the plank by gently pushing it with a finger. The inclination is so adjusted that once started, the block continues with uniform velocity on the plank. The height h' and the distance D' are noted. An identical analysis shows that the force of kinetic friction is

$$f_k = mg\sin\theta$$

and the normal contact force is

$$\mathcal{N} = mg\cos\theta$$

so that the coefficient of kinetic friction between the block and the plank is

$$\mu_k = \frac{f_k}{\mathcal{N}} = \tan\theta = h'/D'.$$

Example 6.4

A wooden block is kept on a polished wooden plank and the inclination of the plank is gradually increased. It is found that the block starts slipping when the plank makes an angle of 18° with the horizontal. However, once started the block can continue with uniform speed if the inclination is reduced to 15°. Find the coefficients of static and kinetic friction between the block and the plank.

Solution : The coefficient of static friction is

$$\mu_s = \tan 18°$$

and the coefficient of kinetic friction is

$$\mu_k = \tan 15°$$

Rolling Friction

It is quite difficult to pull a heavy iron box on a rough floor. However, if the box is provided with four wheels, also made of iron, it becomes easier to move the box on the same floor.

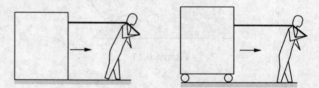

Figure 6.15

The wheel does not slide on the floor rather it rolls on the floor. The surfaces at contact do not rub each other. The velocity of the point of contact of the wheel with respect to the floor remains zero all the time although the centre of the wheel moves forward. The friction in the case of rolling is quite small as compared to kinetic friction. Quite often the rolling friction is negligible in comparison to the static or kinetic friction which may be present simultaneously. To reduce the wear and tear and energy loss against friction, small steel balls are kept between the rotating parts of machines which are known as ball bearings (figure 6.16).

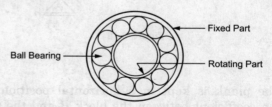

Figure 6.16

As one part moves with respect to the other, the balls roll on the two parts. No kinetic friction is involed

and rolling friction being very small causes much less energy loss.

Worked Out Examples

1. *The coefficient of static friction between a block of mass m and an incline is* $\mu_s = 0.3$. *(a) What can be the maximum angle* θ *of the incline with the horizontal so that the block does not slip on the plane ? (b) If the incline makes an angle* $\theta/2$ *with the horizontal, find the frictional force on the block.*

Solution : The situation is shown in figure (6-W1).

(a) the forces on the block are

(i) the weight mg downward by the earth,

(ii) the normal contact force $\mathcal{N}$ by the incline, and

(iii) the friction f parallel to the incline up the plane, by the incline.

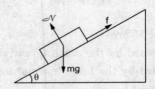

Figure 6-W1

As the block is at rest, these forces should add up to zero. Also, since θ is the maximum angle to prevent slipping, this is a case of limiting equilibrium and so $f = \mu_s \mathcal{N}$.

Taking components prependicular to the incline,

$$\mathcal{N} - mg \cos\theta = 0$$

or, $\mathcal{N} = mg \cos\theta.$ ... (i)

Taking components parallel to the incline,

$$f - mg \sin\theta = 0$$

or, $f = mg \sin\theta$

or, $\mu_s \mathcal{N} = mg \sin\theta.$ ... (ii)

Dividing (ii) by (i) $\mu_s = \tan\theta$

or, $\theta = \tan^{-1} \mu_s = \tan^{-1} (0.3).$

(b) If the angle of incline is reduced to $\theta/2$, the equilibrium is not limiting, and hence the force of static friction f is less than $\mu_s \mathcal{N}$. To know the value of f, we proceed as in part (a) and get the equations

$$\mathcal{N} = mg \cos(\theta/2)$$

and $f = mg \sin(\theta/2).$

Thus, the force of friction is $mg \sin(\theta/2).$

2. *A horizontal force of* 20 N *is applied to a block of mass* 4 kg *resting on a rough horizontal table. If the block does*

not move on the table, how much frictional force the table is applying on the block ? What can be said about the coefficient of static friction between the block and the table ? Take $g = 10$ m/s^2.

Solution : The situation is shown in figure (6-W2). The forces on the block are

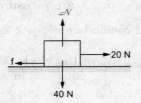

Figure 6-W2

(a) 4 kg $\times$ 10 m/s^2 = 40 N downward by the earth,

(b) $\mathcal{N}$ upward by the table,

(c) 20 N towards right by the experimenter and

(d) f towards left by the table (friction).

As the block is at rest, these forces should add up to zero. Taking horizontal and vertical components,

$$f = 20 \text{ N} \quad \text{and} \quad \mathcal{N} = 40 \text{ N}.$$

Thus, the table exerts a frictional (static) force of 20 N on the block in the direction opposite to the applied force. Since it is a case of static friction,

$$f \le \mu_s \mathcal{N}, \quad \text{or,} \quad \mu_s \ge f/\mathcal{N} \quad \text{or,} \quad \mu_s \ge 0.5.$$

3. *The coefficient of static friction between the block of* 2 kg *and the table shown in figure (6-W3) is* $\mu_s = 0.2$. *What should be the maximum value of m so that the blocks do not move ? Take* $g = 10$ m/s^2. *The string and the pulley are light and smooth.*

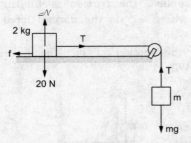

Figure 6-W3

Solution : Consider the equilibrium of the block of mass m. The forces on this block are

(a) *mg* downward by the earth and

(b) *T* upward by the string.

Hence, $T - mg = 0$ or, $T = mg$.   ... (i)

Now consider the equilibrium of the 2 kg block. The forces on this block are

(a) *T* towards right by the string,

(b) *f* towards left (friction) by the table,

(c) 20 N downward (weight) by the earth and

(d) $\mathcal{N}$ upward (normal force) by the table.

For vertical equilibrium of this block,

$$\mathcal{N} = 20 \text{ N}. \qquad \text{... (ii)}$$

As *m* is the largest mass which can be used without moving the system, the friction is limiting.

Thus, $f = \mu_s \mathcal{N}$.   ... (iii)

For horizontal equilibrium of the 2 kg block,

$$f = T. \qquad \text{... (iv)}$$

Using equations (i), (iii) and (iv)

$$\mu_s \mathcal{N} = mg$$

or, $0.2 \times 20 \text{ N} = mg$

or, $m = \dfrac{0.2 \times 20}{10} \text{ kg} = 0.4 \text{ kg}.$

4. *The coefficient of static friction between the two blocks shown in figure (6-W4) is μ and the table is smooth. What maximum horizontal force F can be applied to the block of mass M so that the blocks move together ?*

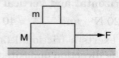

Figure 6-W4

Solution : When the maximum force *F* is applied, both the blocks move together towards right. The only horizontal force on the upper block of mass *m* is that due to the friction by the lower block of mass *M*. Hence this force on *m* should be towards right. The force of friction on *M* by *m* should be towards left by Newton's third law. As we are talking of the maximum possible force *F* that can be applied, the friction is limiting and hence $f = \mu \mathcal{N}$, where $\mathcal{N}$ is the normal force between the blocks.

Consider the motion of *m*. The forces on *m* are (figure 6-W5),

Figure 6-W5

(a) *mg* downward by the earth (gravity),

(b) $\mathcal{N}$ upward by the block *M* (normal force) and

(c) $f = \mu \mathcal{N}$ (friction) towards right by the block *M*.

In the vertical direction, there is no acceleration. This gives

$$\mathcal{N} = mg. \qquad \text{... (i)}$$

In the horizontal direction, let the acceleration be *a*, then

$$\mu \mathcal{N} = m a$$

or, $\mu mg = ma$

or, $a = \mu g.$ ... (ii)

Next, consider the motion of *M* (figure 6-W6).

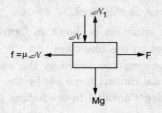

Figure 6-W6

The forces on *M* are

(a) *Mg* downward by the earth (gravity),

(b) $\mathcal{N}_1$ upward by the table (normal force),

(c) $\mathcal{N}$ downward by *m* (normal force),

(d) $f = \mu \mathcal{N}$ (friction) towards left by *m* and

(e) *F* (applied force) by the experimenter.

The equation of motion is

$$F - \mu \mathcal{N} = M a$$

or, $F - \mu mg = M \mu g$ [Using (i) and (ii)]

or, $F = \mu g (M + m).$

5. *A block slides down an incline of angle 30° with an acceleration g/4. Find the kinetic friction coeffcient.*

Solution : Let the mass of the block be *m*. The forces on the block are (Figure 6-W7),

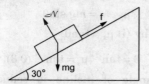

Figure 6-W7

(a) *mg* downward by the earth (gravity),

(b) $\mathcal{N}$ normal force by the incline and

(c) *f* up the plane, (friction) by the incline.

Taking components parallel to the incline and writing Newton's second law,

$$mg \sin 30° - f = mg/4$$

or, $f = mg/4.$

There is no acceleration perpendicular to the incline. Hence,

$$\mathcal{N} = mg \cos 30° = mg \cdot \frac{\sqrt{3}}{2}.$$

As the block is slipping on the incline, friction is $f = \mu_k \mathcal{N}$.

So,

$$\mu_k = \frac{f}{\mathcal{N}} = \frac{mg}{4\,mg\,\sqrt{3}/2} = \frac{1}{2\sqrt{3}}.$$

6. *A block of mass 2·5 kg is kept on a rough horizontal surface. It is found that the block does not slide if a horizontal force less than 15 N is applied to it. Also it is found that it takes 5 seconds to slide through the first 10 m if a horizontal force of 15 N is applied and the block is gently pushed to start the motion. Taking $g = 10$ m/s^2, calculate the coefficients of static and kinetic friction between the block and the surface.*

Solution : The forces acting on the block are shown in figure (6-W8). Here $M = 2·5$ kg and $F = 15$ N.

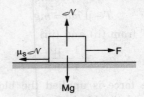

Figure 6-W8

When $F = 15$ N is applied to the block, the block remains in limiting equilibrium. The force of friction is thus $f = \mu_s \mathcal{N}$. Applying Newton's first law,

$$f = \mu_s \mathcal{N} \quad \text{and} \quad \mathcal{N} = mg$$

so that $\quad F = \mu_s Mg$

or, $\qquad \mu_s = \dfrac{F}{mg} = \dfrac{15\ \text{N}}{(2·5\ \text{kg})\,(10\ \text{m/s}^2)} = 0·60.$

When the block is gently pushed to start the motion, kinetic friction acts between the block and the surface. Since the block takes 5 second to slide through the first 10 m, the acceleration a is given by

$$10\ \text{m} = \frac{1}{2}\,a\,(5\ \text{s})^2$$

or, $\qquad a = \dfrac{20}{25}\ \text{m/s}^2 = 0·8\ \text{m/s}^2.$

The frictional force is

$$f = \mu_k \mathcal{N} = \mu_k Mg.$$

Applying Newton's second law

$$F - \mu_k Mg = Ma$$

or, $\qquad \mu_k = \dfrac{F - Ma}{Mg}$

$$= \frac{15\ \text{N} - (2·5\ \text{kg})\,(0·8\ \text{m/s}^2)}{(2·5\ \text{kg})\,(10\ \text{m/s}^2)} = 0·52.$$

7. *A block placed on a horizontal surface is being pushed by a force F making an angle θ with the vertical. If the friction coefficient is μ, how much force is needed to get the block just started. Discuss the situation when $\tan\theta < \mu$.*

Solution : The situation is shown in figure (6-W9). In the limiting equilibrium the frictional force f will be equal to $\mu \mathcal{N}$. For horizontal equilibrium

$$F \sin\theta = \mu \mathcal{N}$$

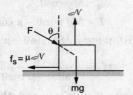

Figure 6-W9

For vertical equilibrium

$$F \cos\theta + mg = \mathcal{N}.$$

Eliminating $\mathcal{N}$ from these equations,

$$F \sin\theta = \mu F \cos\theta + \mu\,mg$$

or, $\qquad F = \dfrac{\mu\,mg}{\sin\theta - \mu\cos\theta}.$

If $\tan\theta < \mu$ we have $(\sin\theta - \mu\cos\theta) < 0$ and then F is negative. So for angles less than $\tan^{-1}\mu$, one cannot push the block ahead, however large the force may be.

8. *Find the maximum value of M/m in the situation shown in figure (6-W10) so that the system remains at rest. Friction coefficient at both the contacts is μ. Discuss the situation when $\tan\theta < \mu$.*

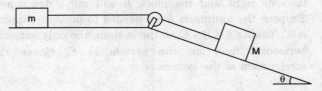

Figure 6-W10

Solution : Figure (6-W11) shows the forces acting on the two blocks. As we are looking for the maximum value of M/m, the equilibrium is limiting. Hence, the frictional forces are equal to μ times the corresponding normal forces.

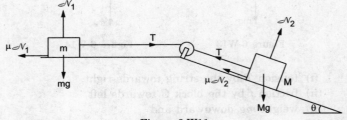

Figure 6-W11

Equilibrium of the block m gives

$T = \mu \mathcal{N}_1$ and $\mathcal{N}_1 = mg$

which gives

$$T = \mu \, mg. \qquad \ldots \text{(i)}$$

Next, consider the equilibrium of the block M. Taking components parallel to the incline

$$T + \mu \, \mathcal{N}_2 = Mg \sin\theta.$$

Taking components normal to the incline

$$\mathcal{N}_2 = Mg \cos\theta.$$

These give $T = Mg \, (\sin\theta - \mu \cos\theta).$ ... (ii)

From (i) and (ii), $\mu \, mg = Mg \, (\sin\theta - \mu \cos\theta)$

or, $$M/m = \frac{\mu}{\sin\theta - \mu \cos\theta}$$

If $\tan\theta < \mu$, $(\sin\theta - \mu \cos\theta) < 0$ and the system will not slide for any value of M/m.

9. *Consider the situation shown in figure (6-W12). The horizontal surface below the bigger block is smooth. The coefficient of friction between the blocks is* μ. *Find the minimum and the maximum force F that can be applied in order to keep the smaller block at rest with respect to the bigger block.*

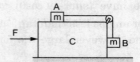

Figure 6-W12

Solution : If no force is applied, the block A will slip on C towards right and the block B will move downward. Suppose the minimum force needed to prevent slipping is F. Taking $A + B + C$ as the system, the only external horizontal force on the system is F. Hence the acceleration of the system is

$$a = \frac{F}{M + 2m}. \qquad \ldots \text{(i)}$$

Now take the block A as the system. The forces on A are (figure 6-W13),

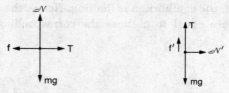

Figure 6-W13   Figure 6-W14

  (i) tension T by the string towards right,
 (ii) friction f by the block C towards left,
(iii) weight mg downward and
 (iv) normal force $\mathcal{N}$ upward.

For vertical equilibrium $\mathcal{N} = mg$.

As the minimum force needed to prevent slipping is applied, the friction is limiting. Thus,

$$f = \mu \, \mathcal{N} = \mu \, mg.$$

As the block moves towards right with an acceleration a,

$$T - f = ma$$

or, $$T - \mu \, mg = ma. \qquad \ldots \text{(ii)}$$

Now take the block B as the system. The forces are (figure 6-W14),

  (i) tension T upward,
 (ii) weight mg downward,
(iii) normal force $\mathcal{N}'$ towards right, and
 (iv) friction f' upward.

As the block moves towards right with an acceleration a,

$$\mathcal{N}' = ma.$$

As the friction is limiting, $f' = \mu \, \mathcal{N}' = \mu \, ma.$

For vertical equilibrium

$$T + f' = mg$$

or, $$T + \mu \, ma = mg. \qquad \ldots \text{(iii)}$$

Eliminating T from (ii) and (iii)

$$a_{\min} = \frac{1 - \mu}{1 + \mu} g .$$

When a large force is applied the block A slips on C towards left and the block B slips on C in the upward direction. The friction on A is towards right and that on B is downwards. Solving as above, the acceleration in this case is

$$a_{\max} = \frac{1 + \mu}{1 - \mu} g .$$

Thus, a lies between $\dfrac{1 - \mu}{1 + \mu} g$ and $\dfrac{1 + \mu}{1 - \mu} g$.

From (i) the force F should be between

$$\frac{1 - \mu}{1 + \mu} (M + 2m) g \text{ and } \frac{1 + \mu}{1 - \mu} (M + 2m) g.$$

10. *Figure (6-W15) shows two blocks connected by a light string placed on the two inclined parts of a triangular structure. The coefficients of static and kinetic friction are* 0·28 *and* 0·25 *respectively at each of the surfaces. (a) Find the minimum and maximum values of m for which the system remains at rest. (b) Find the acceleration of either block if m is given the minimum value calculated in the first part and is gently pushed up the incline for a short while.*

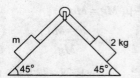

Figure 6-W15

Solution : (a) Take the 2 kg block as the system. The forces on this block are shown in figure (6-W16) with $M = 2$ kg. It is assumed that m has its minimum value so that the 2 kg block has a tendency to slip down. As the block is in equilibrium, the resultant force should be zero.

Figure 6-W16   Figure 6-W17

Taking components $\perp$ to the incline
$$\mathcal{N} = Mg \cos 45° = Mg / \sqrt{2}.$$
Taking components $\parallel$ to the incline
$$T + f = Mg \sin 45° = Mg / \sqrt{2}$$
or, $T = Mg / \sqrt{2} - f.$

As it is a case of limiting equilibrium,
$$f = \mu_s \mathcal{N}$$
or, $T = \dfrac{Mg}{\sqrt{2}} - \mu_s \dfrac{Mg}{\sqrt{2}} = \dfrac{Mg}{\sqrt{2}} (1 - \mu_s).$ ... (i)

Now consider the other block as the system. The forces acting on this block are shown in figure (6-W17).

Taking components $\perp$ to the incline,
$$\mathcal{N}' = mg \cos 45° = mg / \sqrt{2}.$$
Taking components $\parallel$ to the incline
$$T = mg \sin 45° + f' = \dfrac{mg}{\sqrt{2}} + f'.$$

As it is the case of limiting equilibrium
$$f' = \mu_s \mathcal{N}' = \mu_s \dfrac{mg}{\sqrt{2}}.$$

Thus, $T = \dfrac{mg}{\sqrt{2}} (1 + \mu_s).$ ... (ii)

From (i) and (ii)
$$m(1 + \mu_s) = M (1 - \mu_s)$$ ... (iii)

or, $m = \dfrac{(1 - \mu_s)}{(1 + \mu_s)} M = \dfrac{1 - 0.28}{1 + 0.28} \times 2$ kg
$$= \dfrac{9}{8} \text{ kg}.$$

When maximum possible value of m is supplied, the directions of friction are reversed because m has the tendency to slip down and 2 kg block to slip up. Thus, the maximum value of m can be obtained from (iii) by putting $\mu = -0.28$. Thus, the maximum value of m is
$$m = \dfrac{1 + 0.28}{1 - 0.28} \times 2 \text{ kg}$$
$$= \dfrac{32}{9} \text{ kg}.$$

(b) If $m = 9/8$ kg and the system is gently pushed, kinetic friction will operate. Thus,
$$f = \mu_k \cdot \dfrac{Mg}{\sqrt{2}} \qquad \text{and} \qquad f' = \dfrac{\mu_k \, mg}{\sqrt{2}},$$
where $\mu_k = 0.25$. If the acceleration is a, Newton's second law for M gives (figure 6-W16).
$$Mg \sin 45° - T - f = Ma$$
or, $\dfrac{Mg}{\sqrt{2}} - T - \dfrac{\mu_k Mg}{\sqrt{2}} = Ma.$ ... (iv)

Applying Newton's second law m (figure 6-W17),
$$T - mg \sin 45° - f' = ma$$
or, $T - \dfrac{mg}{\sqrt{2}} - \dfrac{\mu_k \, mg}{\sqrt{2}} = ma.$ ... (v)

Adding (iv) and (v)
$$\dfrac{Mg}{\sqrt{2}} (1 - \mu_k) - \dfrac{mg}{\sqrt{2}} (1 + \mu_k) = (M + m) a$$
or, $a = \dfrac{M(1 - \mu_k) - m (1 + \mu_k)}{\sqrt{2} \, (M + m)} g$
$$= \dfrac{2 \times 0.75 - 9/8 \times 1.25}{\sqrt{2} \, (2 + 9/8)} g$$
$$= 0.21 \text{ m/s}^2.$$

□

QUESTIONS FOR SHORT ANSWER

1. For most of the surfaces used in daily life, the friction coefficient is less than 1. Is it always necessary that the friction coefficient is less than 1 ?

2. Why is it easier to push a heavy block from behind than to press it on the top and push ?

3. What is the average friction force when a person has a usual 1 km walk ?

4. Why is it difficult to walk on solid ice ?

5. Can you accelerate a car on a frictionless horizontal road by putting more petrol in the engine ? Can you stop a car going on a frictionless horizontal road by applying brakes ?

6. Spring fitted doors close by themselves when released. You want to keep the door open for a long time, say for an hour. If you put a half kg stone in front of the open door, it does not help. The stone slides with the door and the door gets closed. However, if you sandwitch a

20 g piece of wood in the small gap between the door and the floor, the door stays open. Explain why a much lighter piece of wood is able to keep the door open while the heavy stone fails.

7. A classroom demonstration of Newton's first law is as follows : A glass is covered with a plastic card and a coin is placed on the card. The card is given a quick strike and the coin falls in the glass. (a) Should the friction coefficient between the card and the coin be small or large ? (b) Should the coin be light or heavy ? (c) Why does the experiment fail if the card is gently pushed ?

8. Can a tug of war be ever won on a frictionless surface ?

9. Why do tyres have a better grip of the road while going on a level road than while going on an incline ?

10. You are standing with your bag in your hands, on the ice in the middle of a pond. The ice is so slippery that it can offer no friction. How can you come out of the ice ?

11. When two surfaces are polished, the friction coefficient between them decreases. But the friction coefficient increases and becomes very large if the surfaces are made highly smooth. Explain.

OBJECTIVE I

1. In a situation the contact force by a rough horizontal surface on a body placed on it has constant magnitude. If the angle between this force and the vertical is decreased, the frictional force between the surface and the body will
(a) increase
(b) decrease
(c) remain the same
(d) may increase or decrease.

2. While walking on ice, one should take small steps to avoid slipping. This is because smaller steps ensure
(a) larger friction
(b) smaller friction
(c) larger normal force
(d) smaller normal force.

3. A body of mass M is kept on a rough horizontal surface (friction coefficient = μ). A person is trying to pull the body by applying a horizontal force but the body is not moving. The force by the surface on A is F, where
(a) $F = Mg$
(b) $F = \mu Mg$
(c) $Mg \le F \le Mg \sqrt{1 + \mu^2}$
(d) $Mg \ge F \ge Mg \sqrt{1 - \mu^2}$.

4. A scooter starting from rest moves with a constant acceleration for a time Δt_1, then with a constant velocity for the next Δt_2 and finally with a constant deceleration for the next Δt_3 to come to rest. A 500 N man sitting on the scooter behind the driver manages to stay at rest with respect to the scooter without touching any other part. The force exerted by the seat on the man is
(a) 500 N throughout the journey
(b) less than 500 N throughout the journey
(c) more than 500 N throughout the journey
(d) > 500 N for time Δt_1 and Δt_3 and 500 N for Δt_2.

5. Consider the situation shown in figure (6-Q1). The wall is smooth but the surfaces of A and B in contact are rough. The friction on B due to A in equilibrium

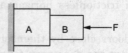

Figure 6-Q1

(a) is upward
(b) is downward
(c) is zero
(d) the system cannot remain in equilibrium.

6. Suppose all the surfaces in the previous problem are rough. The direction of friction on B due to A
(a) is upward
(b) is downward
(c) is zero
(d) depends on the masses of A and B.

7. Two cars of unequal masses use similar tyres. If they are moving at the same initial speed, the minimum stopping distance
(a) is smaller for the heavier car
(b) is smaller for the lighter car
(c) is same for both cars
(d) depends on the volume of the car.

8. In order to stop a car in shortest distance on a horizontal road, one should
(a) apply the brakes very hard so that the wheels stop rotating
(b) apply the brakes hard enough to just prevent slipping
(c) pump the brakes (press and release)
(d) shut the engine off and not apply brakes.

9. A block A kept on an inclined surface just begins to slide if the inclination is 30°. The block is replaced by another block B and it is found that it just begins to slide if the inclination is 40°.
(a) mass of A > mass of B
(b) mass of A < mass of B
(c) mass of A = mass of B
(d) all the three are possible.

10. A boy of mass M is applying a horizontal force to slide a box of mass M' on a rough horizontal surface. The coefficient of friction between the shoes of the boy and the floor is μ and that between the box and the floor is μ'. In which of the following cases it is certainly not possible to slide the box ?
(a) $\mu < \mu'$, $M < M'$
(b) $\mu > \mu'$, $M < M'$
(c) $\mu < \mu'$, $M > M'$
(d) $\mu > \mu'$, $M > M'$.

OBJECTIVE II

1. Let F, F_N and f denote the magnitudes of the contact force, normal force and the friction exerted by one surface on the other kept in contact. If none of these is zero,
   (a) $F > F_N$ (b) $F > f$ (c) $F_N > f$ (d) $F_N - f < F < F_N + f$.

2. The contact force exerted by a body A on another body B is equal to the normal force between the bodies. We conclude that
   (a) the surfaces must be frictionless
   (b) the force of friction between the bodies is zero
   (c) the magnitude of normal force equals that of friction
   (d) the bodies may be rough but they don't slip on each other.

3. Mark the correct statements about the friction between two bodies.
   (a) Static friction is always greater than the kinetic friction.
   (b) Coefficient of static friction is always greater than the coefficient of kinetic friction.

   (c) Limiting friction is always greater than the kinetic friction.
   (d) Limiting friction is never less than static friction.

4. A block is placed on a rough floor and a horizontal force F is applied on it. The force of friction f by the floor on the block is measured for different values of F and a graph is plotted between them.
   (a) The graph is a straight line of slope 45°.
   (b) The graph is a straight line parallel to the F-axis.
   (c) The graph is a straight line of slope 45° for small F and a straight line parallel to the F-axis for large F.
   (d) There is a small kink on the graph.

5. Consider a vehicle going on a horizontal road towards east. Neglect any force by the air. The frictional forces on the vehicle by the road
   (a) is towards east if the vehicle is accelerating
   (b) is zero if the vehicle is moving with a uniform velocity
   (c) must be towards east
   (d) must be towards west.

EXERCISES

1. A body slipping on a rough horizontal plane moves with a deceleration of 4.0 m/s^2. What is the coefficient of kinetic friction between the block and the plane ?

2. A block is projected along a rough horizontal road with a speed of 10 m/s. If the coefficient of kinetic friction is 0.10, how far will it travel before coming to rest ?

3. A block of mass m is kept on a horizontal table. If the static friction coefficient is μ, find the frictional force acting on the block.

4. A block slides down an inclined surface of inclination 30° with the horizontal. Starting from rest it covers 8 m in the first two seconds. Find the coefficient of kinetic friction between the two.

5. Suppose the block of the previous problem is pushed down the incline with a force of 4 N. How far will the block move in the first two seconds after starting from rest ? The mass of the block is 4 kg.

6. A body of mass 2 kg is lying on a rough inclined plane of inclination 30°. Find the magnitude of the force parallel to the incline needed to make the block move
   (a) up the incline (b) down the incline. Coefficient of static friction = 0.2.

7. Repeat part (a) of problem 6 if the push is applied horizontally and not parallel to the incline.

8. In a children-park an inclined plane is constructed with an angle of incline 45° in the middle part (figure 6-E1). Find the acceleration of a boy sliding on it if the friction coefficient between the cloth of the boy and the incline is 0.6 and $g = 10$ m/s^2.

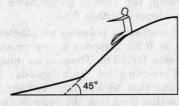

Figure 6-E1

9. A body starts slipping down an incline and moves half meter in half second. How long will it take to move the next half meter ?

10. The angle between the resultant contact force and the normal force exerted by a body on the other is called the *angle of friction*. Show that, if λ be the angle of friction and μ the coefficient of static friction, $\lambda \le \tan^{-1} \mu$.

11. Consider the situation shown in figure (6-E2). Calculate (a) the acceleration of the 1.0 kg blocks, (b) the tension in the string connecting the 1.0 kg blocks and (c) the tension in the string attached to 0.50 kg.

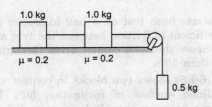

Figure 6-E2

12. If the tension in the string in figure (6-E3) is 16 N and the acceleration of each block is 0.5 m/s^2, find the friction coefficients at the two contacts with the blocks.

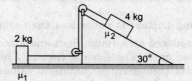

Figure 6-E3

13. The friction coefficient between the table and the block shown in figure (6-E4) is 0.2. Find the tensions in the two strings.

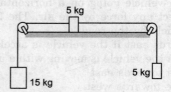

Figure 6-E4

14. The friction coefficient between a road and the tyre of a vehicle is 4/3. Find the maximum incline the road may have so that once hard brakes are applied and the wheel starts skidding, the vehicle going down at a speed of 36 km/hr is stopped within 5 m.

15. The friction coefficient between an athelete's shoes and the ground is 0.90. Suppose a superman wears these shoes and races for 50 m. There is no upper limit on his capacity of running at high speeds. (a) Find the minimum time that he will have to take in completing the 50 m starting from rest. (b) Suppose he takes exactly this minimum time to complete the 50 m, what minimum time will he take to stop ?

16. A car is going at a speed of 21.6 km/hr when it encounters a 12.8 m long slope of angle $30°$ (figure 6-E5). The friction coefficient between the road and the tyre is $1/2\sqrt{3}$. Show that no matter how hard the driver applies the brakes, the car will reach the bottom with a speed greater than 36 km/hr. Take $g = 10$ m/s^2.

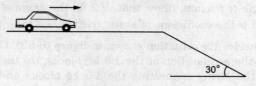

Figure 6-E5

17. A car starts from rest on a half kilometer long bridge. The coefficient of friction between the tyre and the road is 1.0. Show that one cannot drive through the bridge in less than 10 s.

18. Figure (6-E6) shows two blocks in contact sliding down an inclined surface of inclination $30°$. The friction coefficient between the block of mass 2.0 kg and the incline is μ_1, and that between the block of mass 4.0 kg

and the incline is μ_2. Calculate the acceleration of the 2.0 kg block if (a) $\mu_1 = 0.20$ and $\mu_2 = 0.30$, (b) $\mu_1 = 0.30$ and $\mu_2 = 0.20$. Take $g = 10$ m/s^2.

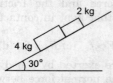

Figure 6-E6

19. Two masses M_1 and M_2 are connected by a light rod and the system is slipping down a rough incline of angle θ with the horizontal. The friction coefficient at both the contacts is μ. Find the acceleration of the system and the force by the rod on one of the blocks.

20. A block of mass M is kept on a rough horizontal surface. The coefficient of static friction between the block and the surface is μ. The block is to be pulled by applying a force to it. What minimum force is needed to slide the block ? In which direction should this force act ?

21. The friction coefficient between the board and the floor shown in figure (6-E7) is μ. Find the maximum force that the man can exert on the rope so that the board does not slip on the floor.

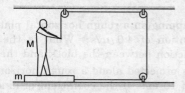

Figure 6-E7

22. A 2 kg block is placed over a 4 kg block and both are placed on a smooth horizontal surface. The coefficient of friction between the blocks is 0.20. Find the acceleration of the two blocks if a horizontal force of 12 N is applied to (a) the upper block, (b) the lower block. Take $g = 10$ m/s^2.

23. Find the accelerations a_1, a_2, a_3 of the three blocks shown in figure (6-E8) if a horizontal force of 10 N is applied on (a) 2 kg block, (b) 3 kg block, (c) 7 kg block. Take $g = 10$ m/s^2.

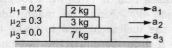

Figure 6-E8

24. The friction coefficient between the two blocks shown in figure (6-E9) is μ but the floor is smooth. (a) What maximum horizontal force F can be applied without disturbing the equilibrium of the system ? (b) Suppose the horizontal force applied is double of that found in part (a). Find the accelerations of the two masses.

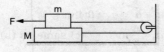

Figure 6-E9

25. Suppose the entire system of the previous question is kept inside an elevator which is coming down with an acceleration $a < g$. Repeat parts (a) and (b).

26. Consider the situation shown in figure (6-E9). Suppose a small electric field E exists in the space in the vertically upward direction and the upper block carries a positive charge Q on its top surface. The friction coefficient between the two blocks is μ but the floor is smooth. What maximum horizontal force F can be applied without disturbing the equilibrium?
[Hint : The force on a charge Q by the electric field E is $F = QE$ in the direction of E.]

27. A block of mass m slips on a rough horizontal table under the action of a horizontal force applied to it. The coefficient of friction between the block and the table is μ. The table does not move on the floor. Find the total frictional force applied by the floor on the legs of the table. Do you need the friction coefficient between the table and the floor or the mass of the table?

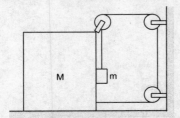

Figure 6-E10

28. Find the acceleration of the block of mass M in the situation of figure (6-E10). The coefficient of friction between the two blocks is $μ_1$ and that between the bigger block and the ground is $μ_2$.

29. A block of mass 2 kg is pushed against a rough vertical wall with a force of 40 N, coefficient of static friction being 0·5. Another horizontal force of 15 N, is applied on the block in a direction parallel to the wall. Will the block move? If yes, in which direction? If no, find the frictional force exerted by the wall on the block.

30. A person (40 kg) is managing to be at rest between two vertical walls by pressing one wall A by his hands and feet and the other wall B by his back (figure 6-E11). Assume that the friction coefficient between his body and the walls is 0·8 and that limiting friction acts at all the contacts. (a) Show that the person pushes the two walls with equal force. (b) Find the normal force exerted by either wall on the person. Take $g = 10$ m/s^2.

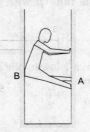

Figure 6-E11

31. Figure (6-E12) shows a small block of mass m kept at the left end of a larger block of mass M and length l. The system can slide on a horizontal road. The system is started towards right with an initial velocity v. The friction coefficient between the road and the bigger block is μ and that between the block is μ/2. Find the time elapsed before the smaller blocks separates from the bigger block.

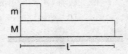

Figure 6-E12

□

ANSWERS

OBJECTIVE I

1. (b) 2. (b) 3. (c) 4. (d) 5. (d) 6. (a)
7. (c) 8. (b) 9. (d) 10. (a)

OBJECTIVE II

1. (a), (b), (d) 2. (b), (d) 3. (b), (c), (d)
4. (c), (d) 5. (a), (b)

EXERCISES

1. 0·4
2. 50 m
3. zero
4. 0·11
5. 10 m
6. (a) 13 N (b) zero

7. 17·5 N

8. $2\sqrt{2}$ m/s^2

9. 0·21 s

11. (a) 0·4 m/s^2 (b) 2·4 N   (c) 4·8 N

12. $\mu_1 = 0.75$, $\mu_2 = 0.06$

13. 96 N in the left string and 68 N in the right

14. 16°

15. (a) $\dfrac{10}{3}$ s (b) $\dfrac{10}{3}$ s

18. 2·7 m/s^2, 2·4 m/s^2

19. $a = g (\sin\theta - \mu\cos\theta)$, zero

20. $\dfrac{\mu\, mg}{\sqrt{1 + \mu^2}}$ at an angle $\tan^{-1}\mu$ with the horizontal

21. $\dfrac{\mu\,(M + m)\, g}{1 + \mu}$

22. (a) upper block 4 m/s^2, lower block 1 m/s^2
    (b) both blocks 2 m/s^2

23. (a) $a_1 = 3$ m/s^2, $a_2 = a_3 = 0.4$ m/s^2
    (b) $a_1 = a_2 = a_3 = \dfrac{5}{6}$ m/s^2 (c) same as (b)

24. (a) $2\mu\, mg$ (b) $\dfrac{2\mu\, mg}{M + m}$ in opposite directions

25. (a) $2\mu\, m\,(g - a)$ (b) $\dfrac{2\mu\, m\,(g - a)}{m + M}$

26. $2\mu\,(mg - QE)$

27. $\mu\, mg$

28. $\dfrac{[2\,m - \mu_2\,(M + m)]\, g}{M + m\,[5 + 2\,(\mu_1 - \mu_2)]}$

29. it will move at an angle of 53° with the 15 N force

30. (b) 250 N

31. $\sqrt{\dfrac{4\,M\,l}{(M + m)\,\mu\, g}}$

CHAPTER 7

CIRCULAR MOTION

7.1 ANGULAR VARIABLES

Suppose a particle P is moving in a circle of radius r (figure 7.1). Let O be the centre of the circle. Let O be the origin and OX the X-axis. The position of the particle P at a given instant may be described by the angle θ between OP and OX. We call θ the *angular position* of the particle. As the particle moves on the circle, its angular position θ changes. Suppose the particle goes to a nearby point P' in time Δt so that θ increases to $\theta + \Delta\theta$. The rate of change of angular position is called *angular velocity*. Thus, the angular velocity is

$$\omega = \lim_{\Delta t \to 0} \frac{\Delta\theta}{\Delta t} = \frac{d\theta}{dt}.$$

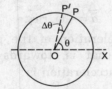

Figure 7.1

The rate of change of angular velocity is called *angular acceleration*. Thus, the angular acceleration is

$$\alpha = \frac{d\omega}{dt} = \frac{d^2\theta}{dt^2}.$$

If the angular acceleration α is constant, we have

$$\theta = \omega_0 t + \frac{1}{2}\alpha t^2 \qquad \ldots (7.1)$$

$$\omega = \omega_0 + \alpha t \qquad \ldots (7.2)$$

and $$\omega^2 = \omega_0^2 + 2\alpha\theta \qquad \ldots (7.3)$$

where ω_0 and ω are the angular velocities at $t = 0$ and at time t and θ is the angular position at time t. The linear distance PP' travelled by the particle in time Δt is

$$\Delta s = r\,\Delta\theta$$

or, $$\frac{\Delta s}{\Delta t} = r\frac{\Delta\theta}{\Delta t}$$

or, $$v = r\,\omega \qquad \ldots (7.4)$$

where v is the linear speed of the particle. Differentiating equation (7.4) with respect to time, the rate of change of speed is

$$a_t = \frac{dv}{dt} = r\frac{d\omega}{dt}$$

or, $$a_t = r\,\alpha. \qquad \ldots (7.5)$$

Remember that $a_t = \frac{dv}{dt}$ is the rate of change of speed and is not the rate of the change of velocity. It is, therefore, not equal to the net acceleration.

We shall show that a_t is the component of acceleration along the tangent and hence we have used the suffix t. It is called the *tangential acceleration*.

Example 7.1

A particle moves in a circle of radius 20 cm *with a linear speed of* 10 m/s. *Find the angular velocity.*

Solution : The angular velocity is

$$\omega = \frac{v}{r} = \frac{10 \text{ m/s}}{20 \text{ cm}} = 50 \text{ rad/s}.$$

Example 7.2

A particle travels in a circle of radius 20 cm *at a speed that uniformly increases. If the speed changes from* 5·0 m/s *to* 6·0 m/s *in* 2·0 s, *find the angular acceleration.*

Solution : The tangential acceleration is given by

$$a_t = \frac{dv}{dt} = \frac{v_2 - v_1}{t_2 - t_1}$$

$$= \frac{6·0 - 5·0}{2·0} \text{ m/s}^2 = 0·5 \text{ m/s}^2.$$

The angular acceleration is $\alpha = a_t / r$

$$= \frac{0·5 \text{ m/s}^2}{20 \text{ cm}} = 2·5 \text{ rad/s}^2.$$

7.2 UNIT VECTORS ALONG THE RADIUS AND THE TANGENT

Consider a particle moving in a circle. Suppose the particle is at a point P in the circle at a given instant (figure 7.2). Take the centre of the circle to be the origin, a line OX as the X-axis and a perpendicular radius OY as the Y-axis. The angular position of the particle at this instant is θ.

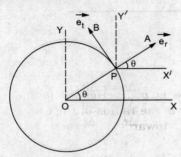

Figure 7.2

Draw a unit vector $\vec{PA} = \vec{e_r}$ along the outward radius and a unit vector $\vec{PB} = \vec{e_t}$ along the tangent in the direction of increasing θ. We call $\vec{e_r}$ the *radial unit vector* and $\vec{e_t}$ the *tangential unit vector*. Draw PX' parallel to the X-axis and PY' parallel to the Y-axis. From the figure,

$$\vec{PA} = \vec{i}\, PA \cos\theta + \vec{j}\, PA \sin\theta$$

or, $\vec{e_r} = \vec{i} \cos\theta + \vec{j} \sin\theta,$ ... (7.6)

where $\vec{i}$ and $\vec{j}$ are the unit vectors along the X and Y axes respectively. Similarly,

$$\vec{PB} = -\vec{i}\, PB \sin\theta + \vec{j}\, PB \cos\theta$$

or, $\vec{e_t} = -\vec{i} \sin\theta + \vec{j} \cos\theta.$ ... (7.7)

7.3 ACCELERATION IN CIRCULAR MOTION

Consider the situation shown in figure (7.2). It is clear from the figure that the position vector of the particle at time t is

$$\vec{r} = \vec{OP} = OP\, \vec{e_r}$$
$$= r\, (\vec{i} \cos\theta + \vec{j} \sin\theta). \qquad \text{... (i)}$$

Differentiating equation (i) with respect to time, the velocity of the particle at time t is

$$\vec{v} = \frac{d\vec{r}}{dt} = \frac{d}{dt}\,[r\,(\vec{i} \cos\theta + \vec{j} \sin\theta)]$$
$$= r\left[\vec{i}\left(-\sin\theta\,\frac{d\theta}{dt}\right) + \vec{j}\left(\cos\theta\,\frac{d\theta}{dt}\right)\right]$$
$$= r\,\omega[-\vec{i} \sin\theta + \vec{j} \cos\theta]. \qquad \text{... (ii)}$$

The term $r\omega$ is the speed of the particle at time t (equation 7.4) and the vector in the square bracket is the unit vector $\vec{e_t}$ along the tangent. Thus, the velocity of the particle at any instant is along the tangent to the circle and its magnitude is $v = r\omega$.

The acceleration of the particle at time t is $\vec{a} = \dfrac{d\vec{v}}{dt}$. From (ii),

$$\vec{a} = r\left[\omega\,\frac{d}{dt}\,[-\vec{i} \sin\theta + \vec{j} \cos\theta] + \frac{d\omega}{dt}\,[-\vec{i} \sin\theta + \vec{j} \cos\theta]\right]$$

$$= \omega r\left[-\vec{i} \cos\theta\,\frac{d\theta}{dt} - \vec{j} \sin\theta\,\frac{d\theta}{dt}\right] + r\,\frac{d\omega}{dt}\,\vec{e_t}$$

$$= -\omega^2 r\,[\vec{i} \cos\theta + \vec{j} \sin\theta] + r\,\frac{d\omega}{dt}\,\vec{e_t}$$

$$= -\omega^2 r\,\vec{e_r} + \frac{dv}{dt}\,\vec{e_t}, \qquad \text{... (7.8)}$$

where $\vec{e_r}$ and $\vec{e_t}$ are the unit vectors along the radial and tangential directions respectively and v is the speed of the particle at time t. We have used

$$r\,\frac{d\omega}{dt} = \frac{d}{dt}\,(r\omega) = \frac{dv}{dt}.$$

Uniform Circular Motion

If the particle moves in the circle with a uniform speed, we call it a *uniform circular motion*. In this case, $\dfrac{dv}{dt} = 0$ and equation (7.8) gives

$$\vec{a} = -\omega^2 r\,\vec{e_r}.$$

Thus, the acceleration of the particle is in the direction of $-\vec{e_r}$, that is, towards the centre. The magnitude of the acceleration is

$$a_r = \omega^2 r$$

$$= \frac{v^2}{r^2}\, r = \frac{v^2}{r}. \qquad \text{... (7.9)}$$

Thus, if a particle moves in a circle of radius r with a constant speed v, its acceleration is v^2/r directed towards the centre. This acceleration is called *centripetal acceleration*. Note that the speed remains constant, the direction continuously changes and hence the "velocity" changes and there is an acceleration during the motion.

Example 7.3

Find the magnitude of the linear acceleration of a particle moving in a circle of radius 10 cm with uniform speed completing the circle in 4 s.

Solution : The distance covered in completing the circle is $2\pi r = 2\pi \times 10$ cm. The linear speed is

$$v = 2\pi r/t$$

$$= \frac{2\pi \times 10 \text{ cm}}{4 \text{ s}} = 5\pi \text{ cm/s}.$$

The linear acceleration is

$$a = \frac{v^2}{r} = \frac{(5\pi \text{ cm/s})^2}{10 \text{ cm}} = 2\cdot5\, \pi^2 \text{ cm/s}^2.$$

This acceleration is directed towards the centre of the circle.

Nonuniform Circular Motion

If the speed of the particle moving in a circle is not constant, the acceleration has both the radial and the tangential components. According to equation (7.8), the radial and the tangential accelerations are

$$a_r = -\omega^2 r = -v^2/r$$
$$\text{and} \quad a_t = \frac{dv}{dt} \qquad\qquad \dots \text{ (7.10)}$$

Thus, the component of the acceleration towards the centre is $\omega^2 r = v^2/r$ and the component along the tangent (along the direction of motion) is dv/dt. The magnitude of the acceleration is

$$a = \sqrt{a_r^2 + a_t^2} = \sqrt{\left(\frac{v^2}{r}\right)^2 + \left(\frac{dv}{dt}\right)^2}.$$

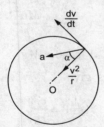

Figure 7.3

The direction of this resultant acceleration makes an angle α with the radius (figure 7.3) where

$$\tan\alpha = \left(\frac{dv}{dt}\right) \Big/ \left(\frac{v^2}{r}\right).$$

Example 7.4

A particle moves in a circle of radius 20 cm. Its linear speed is given by $v = 2\,t$, where t is in second and v in metre/second. Find the radial and tangential acceleration at $t = 3$ s.

Solution : The linear speed at $t = 3$ s is

$$v = 2\,t = 6 \text{ m/s}.$$

The radial acceleration at $t = 3$ s is

$$a_r = v^2/r = \frac{36 \text{ m}^2/\text{s}^2}{0\cdot20 \text{ m}} = 180 \text{ m/s}^2.$$

The tangential acceleration is

$$a_t = \frac{dv}{dt} = \frac{d\,(2t)}{dt} = 2 \text{ m/s}^2.$$

7.4 DYNAMICS OF CIRCULAR MOTION

If a particle moves in a circle as seen from an inertial frame, a resultant nonzero force must act on the particle. That is because a particle moving in a circle is accelerated and acceleration can be produced in an inertial frame only if a resultant force acts on it. If the speed of the particle remains constant, the acceleration of the particle is towards the centre and its magnitude is v^2/r. Here v is the speed of the particle and r is the radius of the circle. The resultant force must act towards the centre and its magnitude F must satisfy

$$a = \frac{F}{m}$$
$$\text{or,} \qquad \frac{v^2}{r} = \frac{F}{m}$$
$$\text{or,} \qquad F = \frac{mv^2}{r}. \qquad\qquad \dots \text{ (7.11)}$$

Since this resultant force is directed towards the centre, it is called *centripetal force*. Thus, a centripetal force of magnitude mv^2/r is needed to keep the particle in uniform circular motion.

It should be clearly understood that "centripetal force" is another word for "force towards the centre". This force must originate from some external source such as gravitation, tension, friction, coulomb force, etc. Centripetal force is not a new kind of force, just as an "upward force" or a "downward force" is not a new kind of force.

Example 7.5

A small block of mass 100 g moves with uniform speed in a horizontal circular groove, with vertical side walls, of radius 25 cm. If the block takes 2·0 s to complete one round, find the normal contact force by the side wall of the groove.

Solution : The speed of the block is

$$v = \frac{2\pi \times (25 \text{ cm})}{2\cdot0 \text{ s}} = 0\cdot785 \text{ m/s}.$$

The acceleration of the block is

$$a = \frac{v^2}{r} = \frac{(0\cdot785 \text{ m/s})^2}{0\cdot25 \text{ m}} = 2\cdot5 \text{ m/s}^2$$

towards the centre. The only force in this direction is the normal contact force due to the side walls. Thus, from Newton's second law, this force is

$$\mathcal{N} = ma = (0\cdot100 \text{ kg})(2\cdot5 \text{ m/s}^2) = 0\cdot25 \text{ N}.$$

7.5 CIRCULAR TURNINGS AND BANKING OF ROADS

When vehicles go through turnings, they travel along a nearly circular arc. There must be some force which will produce the required acceleration. If the vehicle goes in a horizontal circular path, this resultant force is also horizontal. Consider the situation as shown in figure (7.4). A vehicle of mass M moving at a speed v is making a turn on the circular path of radius r. The external forces acting on the vehicle are

(i) weight Mg

(ii) Normal contact force $\mathcal{N}$ and

(iii) friction f_s.

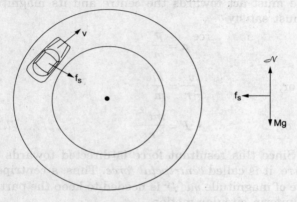

Figure 7.4

If the road is horizontal, the normal force $\mathcal{N}$ is vertically upward. The only horizontal force that can act towards the centre is the friction f_s. This is static friction and is self adjustable. The tyres get a tendency to skid outward and the frictional force which opposes this skidding acts towards the centre. Thus, for a safe turn we must have

$$\frac{v^2}{r} = \frac{f_s}{M}$$

or,

$$f_s = \frac{Mv^2}{r}.$$

However, there is a limit to the magnitude of the frictional force. If μ_s is the coefficient of static friction between the tyres and the road, the magnitude of friction f_s cannot exceed $\mu_s \mathcal{N}$. For vertical equilibrium $\mathcal{N} = Mg$, so that

$$f_s \leq \mu_s Mg.$$

Thus, for a safe turn

$$\frac{Mv^2}{r} \leq \mu_s Mg.$$

or,

$$\mu_s \geq \frac{v^2}{rg}. \qquad \ldots (7.12)$$

Friction is not always reliable at circular turns if high speeds and sharp turns are involved. To avoid dependence on friction, the roads are banked at the turn so that the outer part of the road is somewhat lifted up as compared to the inner part (figure 7.5).

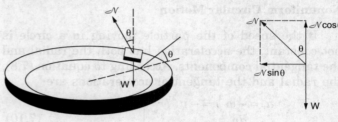

Figure 7.5

The surface of the road makes an angle θ with the horizontal throughout the turn. The normal force $\mathcal{N}$ makes an angle θ with the vertical. At the correct speed, the horizontal component of $\mathcal{N}$ is sufficient to produce the acceleration towards the centre and the self adjustable frictional force keeps its value zero. Applying Newton's second law along the radius and the first law in the vertical direction,

$$\mathcal{N} \sin\theta = \frac{Mv^2}{r}$$

and

$$\mathcal{N} \cos\theta = Mg.$$

These equations give

$$\tan\theta = \frac{v^2}{rg}. \qquad \ldots (7.13)$$

The angle θ depends on the speed of the vehicle as well as on the radius of the turn. Roads are banked for the average expected speed of the vehicles. If the speed of a particular vehicle is a little less or a little more than the correct speed, the self adjustable static friction operates between the tyres and the road and the vehicle does not skid or slip. If the speed is too different from that given by equation (7.13), even the maximum friction cannot prevent a skid or a slip.

Example 7.6

The road at a circular turn of radius 10 m is banked by an angle of 10°. With what speed should a vehicle move on the turn so that the normal contact force is able to provide the necessary centripetal force?

Solution : If v is the correct speed,

$$\tan\theta = \frac{v^2}{rg}$$

or, $v = \sqrt{rg \tan \theta}$

$= \sqrt{(10 \text{ m}) (9 \cdot 8 \text{ m/s}^2) (\tan 10°)} = 4 \cdot 2 \text{ m/s}.$

7.6 CENTRIFUGAL FORCE

We discussed in chapter 5 that Newton's laws of motion are not valid if one is working from a noninertial frame. If the frame translates with respect to an inertial frame with an acceleration $\vec{a_0}$, one must assume the existence of a pseudo force $- m\vec{a_0}$, acting on a particle of mass m. Once this pseudo force is included, one can use Newton's laws in their usual form. What pseudo force is needed if the frame of reference rotates at a constant angular velocity ω with respect to an inertial frame ?

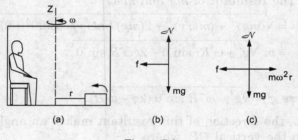

Figure 7.6

Suppose the observer is sitting in a closed cabin which is made to rotate about the vertical Z-axis at a uniform angular velocity ω (figure 7.6). The X and Y axes are fixed in the cabin. Consider a heavy box of mass m kept on the floor at a distance r from the Z-axis. Suppose the floor and the box are rough and the box does not slip on the floor as the cabin rotates. The box is at rest with respect to the cabin and hence is rotating with respect to the ground at an angular velocity ω. Let us first analyse the motion of the box from the ground frame. In this frame (which is inertial) the box is moving in a circle of radius r. It, therefore, has an acceleration $v^2/r = \omega^2 r$ towards the centre. The resultant force on the box must be towards the centre and its magnitude must be $m\omega^2 r$. The forces on the box are

(a) weight mg

(b) normal force $\mathscr{N}$ by the floor

(c) friction f by the floor.

Figure (7.6b) shows the free body diagram for the box. Since the resultant is towards the centre and its magnitude is $m\omega^2 r$, we should have

$$f = m\omega^2 r.$$

The floor exerts a force of static friction $f = m\omega^2 r$ towards the origin.

Now consider the same box when observed from the frame of the rotating cabin. The observer there finds that the box is at rest. If he or she applies Newton's laws, the resultant force on the box should be zero. The weight and the normal contact force balance each other but the frictional force $f = m\omega^2 r$ acts on the box towards the origin. To make the resultant zero, a pseudo force must be assumed which acts on the box away from the centre (radially outward) and has a magnitude $m\omega^2 r$. This pseudo force is called the *centrifugal force*. The analysis from the rotating frame is as follows :

The forces on the box are

(a) weight mg

(b) normal force $\mathscr{N}$

(c) friction f

(d) centrifugal force $m\omega^2 r$.

The free body diagram is shown in figure (7.6c). As the box is at rest, Newton's first law gives

$$f = m\omega^2 r.$$

Note that we get the same equation for friction as we got from the ground frame. But we had to apply Newton's second law from the ground frame and Newton's first law from the rotating frame. Let us now summarise our discussion.

Suppose we are working from a frame of reference that is rotating at a constant angular velocity ω with respect to an inertial frame. If we analyse the dynamics of a particle of mass m kept at a distance r from the axis of rotation, we have to assume that a force $m\omega^2 r$ acts radially outward on the particle. Only then we can apply Newton's laws of motion in the rotating frame. This radially outward pseudo force is called the centrifugal force.

In fact, centrifugal force is a sufficient pseudo force, only if we are analysing the particles at rest in a uniformly rotating frame. If we analyse the motion of a particle that moves in the rotating frame, we may have to assume other pseudo forces, together with the centrifugal force. Such forces are called the *coriolis forces*. The coriolis force is perpendicular to the velocity of the particle and also perpendicular to the axis of rotation of the frame. Once again, we emphasise that all these pseudo forces, centrifugal or coriolis, are needed only if the working frame is rotating. If we work from an inertial frame, there is no need to apply any pseudo force.

It is a common misconception among the beginners that centrifugal force acts on a particle because the particle goes on a circle. Centrifugal force acts (or is assumed to act) because we describe the particle from a rotating frame which is noninertial and still use Newton's laws.

7.7 EFFECT OF EARTH'S ROTATION ON APPARENT WEIGHT

The earth rotates about its axis at an angular speed of one revolution per 24 hours. The line joining the north and the south poles is the axis of rotation. Every point on the earth moves in a circle. A point at equator moves in a circle of radius equal to the radius of the earth and the centre of the circle is same as the centre of the earth. For any other point on the earth, the circle of rotation is smaller than this. Consider a place P on the earth (figure 7.7).

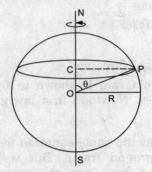

Figure 7.7

Drop a perpendicular PC from P to the axis SN. The place P rotates in a circle with the centre at C. The radius of this circle is CP. The angle between the axis SN and the radius OP through P is called the *colatitude* of the place P. We have

$$CP = OP \sin\theta$$

or, $r = R \sin\theta$

where R is the radius of the earth.

If we work from the frame of reference of the earth, we shall have to assume the existence of the pseudo forces. In particular, a centrifugal force $m\omega^2 r$ has to be assumed on any particle of mass m placed at P. Here ω is the angular speed of the earth. If we discuss the equilibrium of bodies at rest in the earth's frame, no other pseudo force is needed.

Consider a heavy particle of mass m suspended through a string from the ceiling of a laboratory at colatitude θ (figure 7.8). Looking from the earth's frame the particle is in equilibrium and the forces on it are

(a) gravitational attraction mg towards the centre of the earth, i.e., vertically downward,

(b) centrifugal force $m\omega^2 r$ towards CP and

(c) the tension in the string T along the string.

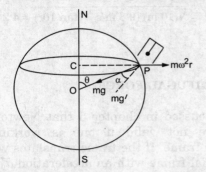

Figure 7.8

As the particle is in equilibrium (in the frame of earth), the three forces on the particle should add up to zero.

The resultant of mg and $m\omega^2 r$

$$= \sqrt{(mg)^2 + (m\omega^2 r)^2 + 2(mg)(m\omega^2 r)\cos(90° + \theta)}$$

$$= m\sqrt{g^2 + \omega^4 R^2 \sin^2\theta - 2g\omega^2 R \sin^2\theta}$$

$$= mg'$$

where $g' = \sqrt{g^2 - \omega^2 R \sin^2\theta\,(2g - \omega^2 R)}.$ ... (7.14)

Also, the direction of this resultant makes an angle α with the vertical OP, where

$$\tan\alpha = \frac{m\omega^2 r \sin(90° + \theta)}{mg + m\omega^2 r \cos(90° + \theta)}$$

$$= \frac{\omega^2 R \sin\theta \cos\theta}{g - \omega^2 R \sin^2\theta}.$$ ... (7.15)

As the three forces acting on the particle must add up to zero, the force of tension must be equal and opposite to the resultant of the rest two. Thus, the magnitude of the tension in the string must be mg' and the direction of the string should make an angle α with the true vertical.

The direction of g' is the apparent vertical direction, because a plumb line stays in this direction only. The walls of the buildings are constructed by making them parallel to g' and not to g. The water surface placed at rest is perpendicular to g'.

The magnitude of g' is also different from g. As $2g > \omega^2 R$, it is clear from equation (7.14) that $g' < g$. One way of measuring the weight of a body is to suspend it by a string and find the tension in the string. The tension itself is taken as a measure of the weight. As $T = mg'$, the weight so observed is less than the true weight mg. This is known as the *apparent weight*. Similarly, if a person stands on the platform of a weighing machine, the platform exerts a normal force $\mathcal{N}$ which is equal to mg'. The reading of the machine responds to the force exerted on it and hence the weight recorded is the apparent weight mg'.

At equator, $\theta = 90°$ and equation (7.14) gives

$$g' = \sqrt{g^2 - 2g\omega^2 R + \omega^4 R^2}$$

$$= g - \omega^2 R$$

or, $mg' = mg - m\omega^2 R.$ ... (7.16)

This can be obtained in a more straightforward way. At the equator, $m\omega^2 R$ is directly opposite to mg and the resultant is simply $mg - m\omega^2 R$. Also, this resultant is towards the centre of the earth so that at the equator the plumb line stands along the true vertical.

At poles, $\theta = 0$ and equation (7.14) gives $g' = g$ and equation (7.15) shows that $\alpha = 0$. Thus, there is no apparent change in g at the poles. This is because the poles themselves do not rotate and hence the effect of earth's rotation is not felt there.

Example 7.7 _____

A body weighs 98 N on a spring balance at the north pole. What will be its weight recorded on the same scale if it is shifted to the equator ? Use $g = GM/R^2 = 9.8$ m/s^2 and the radius of the earth $R = 6400$ km.

Solution : At poles, the apparent weight is same as the true weight.
Thus,

$$98 \text{ N} = mg = m(9.8 \text{ m/s}^2)$$

or, $m = 10$ kg.
At the equator, the apparent weight is

$$mg' = mg - m\omega^2 R.$$

The radius of the earth is 6400 km and the angular speed is

$$\omega = \frac{2\pi \text{ rad}}{24 \times 60 \times 60 \text{ s}} = 7.27 \times 10^{-5} \text{ rad/s}.$$

Thus,

$$mg' = 98 \text{ N} - (10 \text{ kg}) (7.27 \times 10^{-5} \text{ s}^{-1})^2 (6400 \text{ km})$$

$$= 97.66 \text{ N}.$$

Worked Out Examples

1. *A car has to move on a level turn of radius 45 m. If the coefficient of static friction between the tyre and the road is $\mu_s = 2.0$, find the maximum speed the car can take without skidding.*

Solution : Let the mass of the car be M. The forces on the car are

(a) weight Mg downward
(b) normal force $\mathcal{N}$ by the road upward
(c) friction f_s by the road towards the centre.

The car is going on a horizontal circle of radius R, so it is accelerating. The acceleration is towards the centre and its magnitude is v^2/R, where v is the speed. For vertical direction, acceleration = 0. Resolving the forces in vertical and horizontal directions and applying Newton's laws, we have

$$\mathcal{N} = mg$$

and $f_s = Mv^2/R.$

As we are looking for the maximum speed for no skidding, it is a case of limiting friction and hence $f_s = \mu_s \mathcal{N} = \mu_s Mg$.
So, we have

$$\mu_s Mg = Mv^2/R$$

or, $v^2 = \mu_s gR.$

Putting the values, $v = \sqrt{2 \times 10 \text{ m/s}^2 \times 45 \text{ m}}$
$$= 30 \text{ m/s} = 108 \text{ km/hr}.$$

2. *A circular track of radius 600 m is to be designed for cars at an average speed of 180 km/hr. What should be the angle of banking of the track ?*

Solution : Let the angle of banking be θ. The forces on the car are (figure 7-W1)

(a) weight of the car Mg downward and
(b) normal force $\mathcal{N}$.

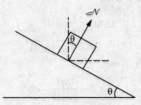

Figure 7-W1

For proper banking, static frictional force is not needed. For vertical direction the acceleration is zero. So,

$$\mathcal{N} \cos\theta = Mg.$$ ... (i)

For horizontal direction, the acceleration is v^2/r towards the centre, so that

$$\mathcal{N} \sin\theta = Mv^2/r.$$ ... (ii)

From (i) and (ii),
$$\tan\theta = v^2/rg.$$

Putting the values, $\tan\theta = \dfrac{(180 \text{ km/hr})^2}{(600 \text{ m})(10 \text{ m/s}^2)} = 0.4167$

or, $\theta = 22.6°$.

3. *A particle of mass m is suspended from a ceiling through a string of length L. The particle moves in a horizontal circle of radius r. Find (a) the speed of the particle and (b) the tension in the string. Such a system is called a conical pendulum.*

Solution : The situation is shown in figure (7-W2). The angle θ made by the string with the vertical is given by
$$\sin\theta = r/L. \qquad \ldots \text{ (i)}$$

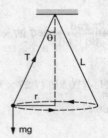

Figure 7-W2

The forces on the particle are

(a) the tension T along the string and

(b) the weight mg vertically downward.

The particle is moving in a circle with a constant speed v. Thus, the radial acceleration towards the centre has magnitude v^2/r. Resolving the forces along the radial direction and applying Newton's second law,
$$T\sin\theta = m(v^2/r). \qquad \ldots \text{ (ii)}$$

As there is no acceleration in vertical direction, we have from Newton's first law,
$$T\cos\theta = mg. \qquad \ldots \text{ (iii)}$$

Dividing (ii) by (iii),
$$\tan\theta = \frac{v^2}{rg}$$
or, $v = \sqrt{rg \tan\theta}$.

And from (iii),
$$T = \frac{mg}{\cos\theta}.$$

Using (i),
$$v = \frac{r\sqrt{g}}{(L^2 - r^2)^{1/4}} \text{ and } T = \frac{mgL}{(L^2 - r^2)^{1/2}}.$$

4. *One end of a massless spring of spring constant 100 N/m and natural length 0.5 m is fixed and the other end is connected to a particle of mass 0.5 kg lying on a frictionless horizontal table. The spring remains*

horizontal. If the mass is made to rotate at an angular velocity of 2 rad/s, find the elongation of the spring.

Solution : The particle is moving in a horizontal circle, so it is accelerated towards the centre with magnitude v^2/r. The horizontal force on the particle is due to the spring and equals kl, where l is the elongation and k is the spring constant. Thus,
$$kl = mv^2/r = m\omega^2 r = m\omega^2(l_0 + l).$$

Here ω is the angular velocity, l_0 is the natural length (0.5 m) and $l_0 + l$ is the total length of the spring which is also the radius of the circle along which the particle moves.

Thus, $(k - m\omega^2)l = m\omega^2 l_0$

or, $l = \dfrac{m\omega^2 l_0}{k - m\omega^2}$.

Putting the values,
$$l = \frac{0.5 \times 4 \times 0.5}{100 - 0.5 \times 4} \text{ m} \approx \frac{1}{100} \text{ m} = 1 \text{ cm}.$$

5. *A simple pendulum is constructed by attaching a bob of mass m to a string of length L fixed at its upper end. The bob oscillates in a vertical circle. It is found that the speed of the bob is v when the string makes an angle θ with the vertical. Find the tension in the string at this instant.*

Solution : The forces acting on the bob are (figure 7-W3)

(a) the tension T

(b) the weight mg.

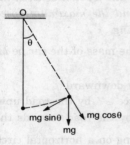

Figure 7-W3

As the bob moves in a vertical circle with centre at O, the radial acceleration is v^2/L towards O. Taking the components along this radius and applying Newton's second law, we get,
$$T - mg\cos\theta = mv^2/L$$
or, $T = m(g\cos\theta + v^2/L)$.

6. *A cylindrical bucket filled with water is whirled around in a vertical circle of radius r. What can be the minimum speed at the top of the path if water does not fall out from the bucket? If it continues with this speed, what normal contact force the bucket exerts on water at the lowest point of the path?*

Solution : Consider water as the system. At the top of the circle its acceleration towards the centre is vertically downward with magnitude v^2/r. The forces on water are (figure 7-W4)

(a) weight Mg downward and

(b) normal force by the bucket, also downward.

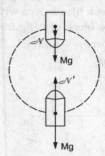

Figure 7-W4

So, from Newton's second law

$$Mg + \mathcal{N} = Mv^2/r.$$

For water not to fall out from the bucket, $\mathcal{N} \geq 0$.

Hence, $Mv^2/r \geq Mg$ or, $v^2 \geq rg$.

The minimum speed at the top must be $\sqrt{rg}$.

If the bucket continues on the circle with this minimum speed $\sqrt{rg}$, the forces at the bottom of the path are

(a) weight Mg downward and

(b) normal contact force $\mathcal{N}'$ by the bucket upward.

The acceleration is towards the centre which is vertically upward, so

$$\mathcal{N}' - Mg = Mv^2/r$$

or, $$\mathcal{N}' = M(g + v^2/r) = 2\,Mg.$$

7. *A fighter plane is pulling out for a dive at a speed of 900 km/hr. Assuming its path to be a vertical circle of radius 2000 m and its mass to be 16000 kg, find the force exerted by the air on it at the lowest point. Take $g = 9.8$ m/s^2.*

Solution : At the lowest point in the path the acceleration is vertically upward (towards the centre) and its magnitude is v^2/r.

The forces on the plane are

(a) weight Mg downward and

(b) force F by the air upward.

Hence, Newton's second law of motion gives

$$F - Mg = Mv^2/r$$

or, $$F = M(g + v^2/r).$$

Here $v = 900$ km/hr $= \dfrac{9 \times 10^5}{3600}$ m/s $= 250$ m/s

or, $F = 16000\left(9.8 + \dfrac{62500}{2000}\right)$ N $= 6.56 \times 10^5$ N (upward).

8. *Figure (7-W5) shows a rod of length 20 cm pivoted near an end and which is made to rotate in a horizontal plane with a constant angular speed. A ball of mass m is suspended by a string also of length 20 cm from the other end of the rod. If the angle θ made by the string with the vertical is 30°, find the angular speed of the rotation. Take $g = 10$ m/s^2.*

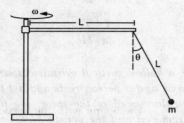

Figure 7-W5

Solution : Let the angular speed be ω. As is clear from the figure, the ball moves in a horizontal circle of radius $L + L\sin\theta$, where $L = 20$ cm. Its acceleration is, therefore, $\omega^2(L + L\sin\theta)$ towards the centre. The forces on the bob are (figure 7-W5)

(a) the tension T along the string and

(b) the weight mg.

Resolving the forces along the radius and applying Newton's second law,

$$T\sin\theta = m\omega^2 L\,(1 + \sin\theta). \qquad \text{... (i)}$$

Applying Newton's first law in the vertical direction,

$$T\cos\theta = mg. \qquad \text{... (ii)}$$

Dividing (i) by (ii),

$$\tan\theta = \frac{\omega^2 L(1 + \sin\theta)}{g}$$

or, $$\omega^2 = \frac{g\tan\theta}{L(1 + \sin\theta)} = \frac{(10\text{ m/s}^2)\,(1/\sqrt3)}{(0.20\text{ m})\,(1 + 1/2)}$$

or, $$\omega = 4.4 \text{ rad/s}.$$

9. *Two blocks each of mass M are connected to the ends of a light frame as shown in figure (7-W6). The frame is rotated about the vertical line of symmetry. The rod breaks if the tension in it exceeds T_0. Find the maximum frequency with which the frame may be rotated without breaking the rod.*

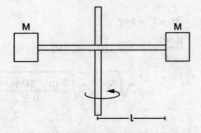

Figure 7-W6

Solution : Consider one of the blocks. If the frequency of revolution is f, the angular velocity is $\omega = 2\pi f$. The acceleration towards the centre is $v^2/l = \omega^2 l = 4\pi^2 f^2 l$. The only horizontal force on the block is the tension of the rod. At the point of breaking, this force is T_0. So from Newton's second law,

$$T_0 = M \cdot 4\pi^2 f^2 l$$

or,
$$f = \frac{1}{2\pi}\left[\frac{T_0}{Ml}\right]^{1/2}.$$

10. *In a rotor, a hollow vertical cylindrical structure rotates about its axis and a person rests against the inner wall. At a particular speed of the rotor, the floor below the person is removed and the person hangs resting against the wall without any floor. If the radius of the rotor is 2 m and the coefficient of static friction between the wall and the person is 0·2, find the minimum speed at which the floor may be removed. Take $g = 10$ m/s^2.*

Solution : The situation is shown in figure (7-W7).

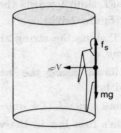

Figure 7-W7

When the floor is removed, the forces on the person are
(a) weight mg downward
(b) normal force $\mathcal{N}$ due to the wall, towards the centre
(c) frictional force f_s, parallel to the wall, upward.

The person is moving in a circle with a uniform speed, so its acceleration is v^2/r towards the centre.
Newton's law for the horizontal direction (2nd law) and for the vertical direction (1st law) give

$$\mathcal{N} = mv^2/r \qquad \dots \text{(i)}$$

and
$$f_s = mg. \qquad \dots \text{(ii)}$$

For the minimum speed when the floor may be removed, the friction is limiting one and so equals $\mu_s \mathcal{N}$. This gives

$$\mu_s \mathcal{N} = mg$$

or,
$$\frac{\mu_s m v^2}{r} = mg \quad [\text{using (i)}]$$

or,
$$v = \sqrt{\frac{rg}{\mu_s}} = \sqrt{\frac{2 \text{ m} \times 10 \text{ m/s}^2}{0\cdot 2}} = 10 \text{ m/s}.$$

11. *A hemispherical bowl of radius R is set rotating about its axis of symmetry which is kept vertical. A small block*

kept in the bowl rotates with the bowl without slipping on its surface. If the surface of the bowl is smooth, and the angle made by the radius through the block with the vertical is θ, *find the angular speed at which the bowl is rotating.*

Solution : Suppose the angular speed of rotation of the bowl is ω. The block also moves with this angular speed. The forces on the block are (figure 7-W8)
(a) the normal force $\mathcal{N}$ and
(b) the weight mg.

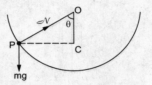

Figure 7-W8

The block moves in a horizontal circle with the centre at C, so that the radius is $PC = OP \sin\theta = R \sin\theta$. Its acceleration is, therefore, $\omega^2 R \sin\theta$. Resolving the forces along PC and applying Newton's second law,

$$\mathcal{N} \sin\theta = m\omega^2 R \sin\theta$$

or,
$$\mathcal{N} = m\omega^2 R. \qquad \dots \text{(i)}$$

As there is no vertical acceleration,

$$\mathcal{N} \cos\theta = mg. \qquad \dots \text{(ii)}$$

Dividing (i) by (ii),

$$\frac{1}{\cos\theta} = \frac{\omega^2 R}{g}.$$

or,
$$\omega = \sqrt{\frac{g}{R \cos\theta}}.$$

12. *A metal ring of mass m and radius R is placed on a smooth horizontal table and is set rotating about its own axis in such a way that each part of the ring moves with a speed v. Find the tension in the ring.*

Solution : Consider a small part ACB of the ring that subtends an angle $\Delta\theta$ at the centre as shown in figure (7-W9). Let the tension in the ring be T.

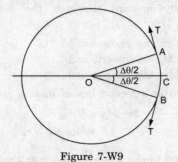

Figure 7-W9

The forces on this small part ACB are
(a) tension T by the part of the ring left to A,
(b) tension T by the part of the ring right to B,

(c) weight $(\Delta m)g$ and

(d) normal force $\mathcal{N}$ by the table.

The tension at A acts along the tangent at A and the tension at B acts along the tangent at B. As the small part ACB moves in a circle of radius R at a constant speed v, its acceleration is towards the centre (along CO) and has a magnitude $(\Delta m)v^2/R$.

Resolving the forces along the radius CO,

$$T \cos\left(90° - \frac{\Delta\theta}{2}\right) + T \cos\left(90° - \frac{\Delta\theta}{2}\right) = (\Delta m)\left(\frac{v^2}{R}\right)$$

or, $$2T \sin\frac{\Delta\theta}{2} = (\Delta m)\left(\frac{v^2}{R}\right). \qquad \dots \text{ (i)}$$

The length of the part ACB is $R\Delta\theta$. As the total mass of the ring is m, the mass of the part ACB will be

$$\Delta m = \frac{m}{2\pi R}R\Delta\theta = \frac{m\Delta\theta}{2\pi}.$$

Putting Δm in (i),

$$2T \sin\frac{\Delta\theta}{2} = \frac{m}{2\pi}\Delta\theta\left(\frac{v^2}{R}\right)$$

or, $$T = \frac{mv^2}{2\pi R}\frac{\Delta\theta/2}{\sin(\Delta\theta/2)}$$

As $\Delta\theta$ is very small, $\dfrac{\Delta\theta/2}{\sin(\Delta\theta/2)} \approx 1$ and $T = \dfrac{mv^2}{2\pi R}$.

13. *A table with smooth horizontal surface is turning at an angular speed ω about its axis. A groove is made on the surface along a radius and a particle is gently placed inside the groove at a distance a from the centre. Find the speed of the particle as its distance from the centre becomes L.*

Solution : The situation is shown in figure (7-W10).

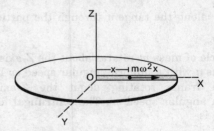

Figure 7-W10

Let us work from the frame of reference of the table. Let us take the origin at the centre of rotation O and the X-axis along the groove (figure 7-W10). The Y-axis is along the line perpendicular to OX coplanar with the surface of the table and the Z-axis is along the vertical. Suppose at time t the particle in the groove is at a distance x from the origin and is moving along the X-axis with a speed v. The forces acting on the particle (including the pseudo forces that we must assume because we have taken our frame on the table which is rotating and is noninertial) are

(a) weight mg vertically downward,

(b) normal contact force $\mathcal{N}_1$ vertically upward by the bottom surface of the groove,

(c) normal contact force $\mathcal{N}_2$ parallel to the Y-axis by the side walls of the groove,

(d) centrifugal force $m\omega^2 x$ along the X-axis, and

(e) coriolis force along Y-axis (coriolis force is perpendicular to the velocity of the particle and the axis of rotation.)

As the particle can only move in the groove, its acceleration is along the X-axis. The only force along the X-axis is the centrifugal force $m\omega^2 x$. All the other forces are perpendicular to the X-axis and have no components along the X-axis.

Thus, the acceleration along the X-axis is

$$a = \frac{F}{m} = \frac{m\omega^2 x}{m} = \omega^2 x$$

or, $$\frac{dv}{dt} = \omega^2 x$$

or, $$\frac{dv}{dx} \cdot \frac{dx}{dt} = \omega^2 x$$

or, $$\frac{dv}{dx} \cdot v = \omega^2 x$$

or, $$v\, dv = \omega^2 x\, dx$$

or, $$\int_0^v v\, dv = \int_a^L \omega^2 x\, dx$$

or, $$\left[\frac{1}{2}v^2\right]_0^v = \left[\frac{1}{2}\omega^2 x^2\right]_a^L$$

or, $$\frac{v^2}{2} = \frac{1}{2}\omega^2(L^2 - a^2)$$

or, $$v = \omega\sqrt{L^2 - a^2}.$$

□

QUESTIONS FOR SHORT ANSWER

1. You are driving a motorcycle on a horizontal road. It is moving with a uniform velocity. Is it possible to accelerate the motorcyle without putting higher petrol input rate into the engine ?

2. Some washing machines have cloth driers. It contains a drum in which wet clothes are kept. As the drum rotates, the water particles get separated from the cloth. The general description of this action is that "the centrifugal force throws the water particles away from the drum". Comment on this statement from the viewpoint of an observer rotating with the drum and the observer who is washing the clothes.

3. A small coin is placed on a record rotating at $33\frac{1}{3}$ rev/minute. The coin does not slip on the record. Where does it get the required centripetal force from ?

4. A bird while flying takes a left turn, where does it get the centripetal force from ?

5. Is it necessary to express all angles in radian while using the equation $\omega = \omega_0 + \alpha t$?

6. After a good meal at a party you wash your hands and find that you have forgotten to bring your handkerchief. You shake your hands vigorously to remove the water as much as you can. Why is water removed in this process ?

7. A smooth block loosely fits in a circular tube placed on a horizontal surface. The block moves in a uniform circular motion along the tube (figure 7-Q1). Which wall (inner or outer) will exert a nonzero normal contact force on the block ?

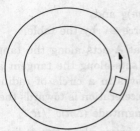

Figure 7-Q1

8. Consider the circular motion of the earth around the sun. Which of the following statements is more appropriate ?
(a) Gravitational attraction of the sun on the earth is equal to the centripetal force.
(b) Gravitational attraction of the sun on the earth is the centripetal force.

9. A car driver going at some speed v suddenly finds a wide wall at a distance r. Should he apply brakes or turn the car in a circle of radius r to avoid hitting the wall ?

10. A heavy mass m is hanging from a string in equilibrium without breaking it. When this same mass is set into oscillation, the string breaks. Explain.

OBJECTIVE I

1. When a particle moves in a circle with a uniform speed
(a) its velocity and acceleration are both constant
(b) its velocity is constant but the acceleration changes
(c) its acceleration is constant but the velocity changes
(d) its velocity and acceleration both change.

2. Two cars having masses m_1 and m_2 move in circles of radii r_1 and r_2 respectively. If they complete the circle in equal time, the ratio of their angular speeds ω_1/ω_2 is
(a) m_1/m_2 (b) r_1/r_2 (c) $m_1 r_1/m_2 r_2$ (d) 1.

3. A car moves at a constant speed on a road as shown in figure (7-Q2). The normal force by the road on the car is N_A and N_B when it is at the points A and B respectively.
(a) $N_A = N_B$ (b) $N_A > N_B$ (c) $N_A < N_B$ (d) insufficient information to decide the relation of N_A and N_B.

Figure 7-Q2

4. A particle of mass m is observed from an inertial frame of reference and is found to move in a circle of radius r with a uniform speed v. The centrifugal force on it is

(a) $\dfrac{mv^2}{r}$ towards the centre

(b) $\dfrac{mv^2}{r}$ away from the centre

(c) $\dfrac{mv^2}{r}$ along the tangent through the particle

(d) zero.

5. A particle of mass m rotates about the Z-axis in a circle of radius a with a uniform angular speed ω. It is viewed from a frame rotating about the Z-axis with a uniform angular speed ω_0. The centrifugal force on the particle is
(a) $m\omega^2 a$ (b) $m\omega_0^2 a$ (c) $m\left(\dfrac{\omega + \omega_0}{2}\right)^2 a$ (d) $m\omega\omega_0 a$.

6. A particle is kept fixed on a turntable rotating uniformly. As seen from the ground the particle goes in a circle, its speed is 20 cm/s and acceleration is 20 cm/s². The particle is now shifted to a new position to make the radius half of the original value. The new values of the speed and acceleration will be
(a) 10 cm/s, 10 cm/s²   (b) 10 cm/s, 80 cm/s²
(c) 40 cm/s, 10 cm/s²   (d) 40 cm/s, 40 cm/s².

7. Water in a bucket is whirled in a vertical circle with a string attached to it. The water does not fall down even when the bucket is inverted at the top of its path. We conclude that in this position

(a) $mg = \dfrac{mv^2}{r}$

(b) mg is greater than $\dfrac{mv^2}{r}$

(c) mg is not greater than $\dfrac{mv^2}{r}$

(d) mg is not less than $\dfrac{mv^2}{r}$.

8. A stone of mass m tied to a string of length l is rotated in a circle with the other end of the string as the centre. The speed of the stone is v. If the string breaks, the stone will move
   (a) towards the centre
   (b) away from the centre
   (c) along a tangent
   (d) will stop.

9. A coin placed on a rotating turntable just slips if it is placed at a distance of 4 cm from the centre. If the angular velocity of the turntable is doubled, it will just slip at a distance of
   (a) 1 cm
   (b) 2 cm
   (c) 4 cm
   (d) 8 cm.

10. A motorcyle is going on an overbridge of radius R. The driver maintains a constant speed. As the motorcycle is ascending on the overbridge, the normal force on it
    (a) increases
    (b) decreases
    (c) remains the same
    (d) fluctuates.

11. Three identical cars A, B and C are moving at the same speed on three bridges. The car A goes on a plane bridge, B on a bridge convex upward and C goes on a bridge concave upward. Let F_A, F_B and F_C be the normal forces exerted by the cars on the bridges when they are at the middle of bridges.
    (a) F_A is maximum of the three forces.
    (b) F_B is maximum of the three forces.
    (c) F_C is maximum of the three forces.
    (d) $F_A = F_B = F_C$.

12. A train A runs from east to west and another train B of the same mass runs from west to east at the same speed along the equator. A presses the track with a force F_1 and B presses the track with a force F_2.
    (a) $F_1 > F_2$.
    (b) $F_1 < F_2$.
    (c) $F_1 = F_2$.
    (d) the information is insufficient to find the relation between F_1 and F_2.

13. If the earth stops rotating, the apparent value of g on its surface will
    (a) increase everywhere
    (b) decrease everywhere
    (c) remain the same everywhere
    (d) increase at some places and remain the same at some other places.

14. A rod of length L is pivoted at one end and is rotated with a uniform angular velocity in a horizontal plane. Let T_1 and T_2 be the tensions at the points $L/4$ and $3L/4$ away from the pivoted ends.
    (a) $T_1 > T_2$. (b) $T_2 > T_1$. (c) $T_1 = T_2$. (d) The relation between T_1 and T_2 depends on whether the rod rotates clockwise or anticlockwise.

15. A simple pendulum having a bob of mass m is suspended from the ceiling of a car used in a stunt film shooting. The car moves up along an inclined cliff at a speed v and makes a jump to leave the cliff and lands at some distance. Let R be the maximum height of the car from the top of the cliff. The tension in the string when the car is in air is
    (a) mg (b) $mg - \dfrac{mv^2}{R}$ (c) $mg + \dfrac{mv^2}{R}$ (d) zero.

16. Let θ denote the angular displacement of a simple pendulum oscillating in a vertical plane. If the mass of the bob is m, the tension in the string is $mg\cos\theta$
    (a) always
    (b) never
    (c) at the extreme positions
    (d) at the mean position.

OBJECTIVE II

1. An object follows a curved path. The following quantities may remain constant during the motion
   (a) speed
   (b) velocity
   (c) acceleration
   (d) magnitude of acceleration.

2. Assume that the earth goes round the sun in a circular orbit with a constant speed of 30 km/s.
   (a) The average velocity of the earth from 1st Jan, 90 to 30th June, 90 is zero.
   (b) The average acceleration during the above period is 60 km/s^2.
   (c) The average speed from 1st Jan, 90 to 31st Dec, 90 is zero.
   (d) The instantaneous acceleration of the earth points towards the sun.

3. The position vector of a particle in a circular motion about the origin sweeps out equal area in equal time. Its
   (a) velocity remains constant
   (b) speed remains constant
   (c) acceleration remains constant
   (d) tangential acceleration remains constant.

4. A particle is going in a spiral path as shown in figure (7-Q3) with constant speed.

Figure 7-Q3

   (a) The velocity of the particle is constant.
   (b) The acceleration of the particle is constant.

(c) The magnitude of acceleration is constant.

(d) The magnitude of acceleration is decreasing continuously.

5. A car of mass M is moving on a horizontal circular path of radius r. At an instant its speed is v and is increasing at a rate a.

(a) The acceleration of the car is towards the centre of the path.

(b) The magnitude of the frictional force on the car is greater than $\dfrac{mv^2}{r}$.

(c) The friction coefficient between the ground and the car is not less than a/g.

(d) The friction coefficient between the ground and the car is $\mu = \tan^{-1}\dfrac{v^2}{rg}$.

6. A circular road of radius r is banked for a speed $v = 40$ km/hr. A car of mass m attempts to go on the circular road. The friction coefficient between the tyre and the road is negligible.

(a) The car cannot make a turn without skidding.

(b) If the car turns at a speed less than 40 km/hr, it will slip down.

(c) If the car turns at the correct speed of 40 km/hr, the force by the road on the car is equal to $\dfrac{mv^2}{r}$.

(d) If the car turns at the correct speed of 40 km/hr, the force by the road on the car is greater than mg as well as greater than $\dfrac{mv^2}{r}$.

7. A person applies a constant force $\vec{F}$ on a particle of mass m and finds that the particle moves in a circle of radius r with a uniform speed v as seen from an inertial frame of reference.

(a) This is not possible.

(b) There are other forces on the particle.

(c) The resultant of the other forces is $\dfrac{mv^2}{r}$ towards the centre.

(d) The resultant of the other forces varies in magnitude as well as in direction.

EXERCISES

1. Find the acceleration of the moon with respect to the earth from the following data : Distance between the earth and the moon $= 3\cdot85 \times 10^5$ km and the time taken by the moon to complete one revolution around the earth $= 27\cdot3$ days.

2. Find the acceleration of a particle placed on the surface of the earth at the equator due to earth's rotation. The diameter of earth $= 12800$ km and it takes 24 hours for the earth to complete one revolution about its axis.

3. A particle moves in a circle of radius $1\cdot0$ cm at a speed given by $v = 2\cdot0\,t$ where v is in cm/s and t in seconds.
(a) Find the radial acceleration of the particle at $t = 1$ s.
(b) Find the tangential acceleration at $t = 1$ s. (c) Find the magnitude of the acceleration at $t = 1$ s.

4. A scooter weighing 150 kg together with its rider moving at 36 km/hr is to take a turn of radius 30 m. What horizontal force on the scooter is needed to make the turn possible ?

5. If the horizontal force needed for the turn in the previous problem is to be supplied by the normal force by the road, what should be the proper angle of banking ?

6. A park has a radius of 10 m. If a vehicle goes round it at an average speed of 18 km/hr, what should be the proper angle of banking ?

7. If the road of the previous problem is horizontal (no banking), what should be the minimum friction coefficient so that a scooter going at 18 km/hr does not skid ?

8. A circular road of radius 50 m has the angle of banking equal to 30°. At what speed should a vehicle go on this road so that the friction is not used ?

9. In the Bohr model of hydrogen atom, the electron is treated as a particle going in a circle with the centre at the proton. The proton itself is assumed to be fixed in an inertial frame. The centripetal force is provided by the Coloumb attraction. In the ground state, the electron goes round the proton in a circle of radius $5\cdot3 \times 10^{-11}$ m. Find the speed of the electron in the ground state. Mass of the electron $= 9\cdot1 \times 10^{-31}$ kg and charge of the electron $= 1\cdot6 \times 10^{-19}$ C.

10. A stone is fastened to one end of a string and is whirled in a vertical circle of radius R. Find the minimum speed the stone can have at the highest point of the circle.

11. A ceiling fan has a diameter (of the circle through the outer edges of the three blades) of 120 cm and rpm 1500 at full speed. Consider a particle of mass 1 g sticking at the outer end of a blade. How much force does it experience when the fan runs at full speed ? Who exerts this force on the particle ? How much force does the particle exert on the blade along its surface ?

12. A mosquito is sitting on an L.P. record disc rotating on a turn table at $33\frac{1}{3}$ revolutions per minute. The distance of the mosquito from the centre of the turn table is 10 cm. Show that the friction coefficient between the record and the mosquito is greater than $\pi^2/81$. Take $g = 10$ m/s^2.

13. A simple pendulum is suspended from the ceiling of a car taking a turn of radius 10 m at a speed of 36 km/h. Find the angle made by the string of the pendulum with the vertical if this angle does not change during the turn. Take $g = 10$ m/s^2.

14. The bob of a simple pendulum of length 1 m has mass 100 g and a speed of 1·4 m/s at the lowest point in its path. Find the tension in the string at this instant.

15. Suppose the bob of the previous problem has a speed of 1·4 m/s when the string makes an angle of 0·20 radian with the vertical. Find the tension at this instant. You can use $\cos\theta \approx 1 - \theta^2/2$ and $\sin\theta \approx \theta$ for small θ.

16. Suppose the amplitude of a simple pendulum having a bob of mass m is θ_0. Find the tension in the string when the bob is at its extreme position.

17. A person stands on a spring balance at the equator. (a) By what fraction is the balance reading less than his true weight? (b) If the speed of earth's rotation is increased by such an amount that the balance reading is half the true weight, what will be the length of the day in this case?

18. A turn of radius 20 m is banked for the vehicles going at a speed of 36 km/h. If the coefficient of static friction between the road and the tyre is 0·4, what are the possible speeds of a vehicle so that it neither slips down nor skids up?

19. A motorcycle has to move with a constant speed on an overbridge which is in the form of a circular arc of radius R and has a total length L. Suppose the motorcycle starts from the highest point. (a) What can its maximum velocity be for which the contact with the road is not broken at the highest point? (b) If the motorcycle goes at speed $1/\sqrt{2}$ times the maximum found in part (a), where will it lose the contact with the road? (c) What maximum uniform speed can it maintain on the bridge if it does not lose contact anywhere on the bridge?

20. A car goes on a horizontal circular road of radius R, the speed increasing at a constant rate $\dfrac{dv}{dt} = a$. The friction coefficient between the road and the tyre is μ. Find the speed at which the car will skid.

21. A block of mass m is kept on a horizontal ruler. The friction coefficient between the ruler and the block is μ. The ruler is fixed at one end and the block is at a distance L from the fixed end. The ruler is rotated about the fixed end in the horizontal plane through the fixed end. (a) What can the maximum angular speed be for which the block does not slip? (b) If the angular speed of the ruler is uniformly increased from zero at an angular acceleration α, at what angular speed will the block slip?

22. A track consists of two circular parts ABC and CDE of equal radius 100 m and joined smoothly as shown in figure (7-E1). Each part subtends a right angle at its centre. A cycle weighing 100 kg together with the rider travels at a constant speed of 18 km/h on the track. (a) Find the normal contact force by the road on the cycle when it is at B and at D. (b) Find the force of friction exerted by the track on the tyres when the cycle is at B, C and D. (c) Find the normal force between the road and the cycle just before and just after the cycle crosses C. (d) What should be the minimum friction coefficient between the road and the tyre, which will

ensure that the cyclist can move with constant speed? Take $g = 10 \text{ m/s}^2$.

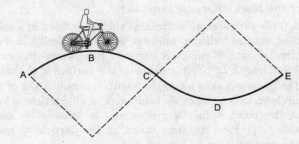

Figure 7-E1

23. In a children's park a heavy rod is pivoted at the centre and is made to rotate about the pivot so that the rod always remains horizontal. Two kids hold the rod near the ends and thus rotate with the rod (figure 7-E2). Let the mass of each kid be 15 kg, the distance between the points of the rod where the two kids hold it be 3·0 m and suppose that the rod rotates at the rate of 20 revolutions per minute. Find the force of friction exerted by the rod on one of the kids.

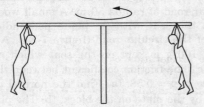

Figure 7-E2

24. A hemispherical bowl of radius R is rotated about its axis of symmetry which is kept vertical. A small block is kept in the bowl at a position where the radius makes an angle θ with the vertical. The block rotates with the bowl without any slipping. The friction coefficient between the block and the bowl surface is μ. Find the range of the angular speed for which the block will not slip.

25. A particle is projected with a speed u at an angle θ with the horizontal. Consider a small part of its path near the highest position and take it approximately to be a circular arc. What is the radius of this circle? This radius is called the radius of curvature of the curve at the point.

26. What is the radius of curvature of the parabola traced out by the projectile in the previous problem at a point where the particle velocity makes an angle $\theta/2$ with the horizontal?

27. A block of mass m moves on a horizontal circle against the wall of a cylindrical room of radius R. The floor of the room on which the block moves is smooth but the friction coefficient between the wall and the block is μ. The block is given an initial speed v_0. As a function of the speed v write (a) the normal force by the wall on the block, (b) the frictional force by the wall and (c) the tangential acceleration of the block. (d) Integrate the tangential acceleration $\left(\dfrac{dv}{dt}=v\,\dfrac{dv}{ds}\right)$ to obtain the speed of the block after one revolution.

28. A table with smooth horizontal surface is fixed in a cabin that rotates with a uniform angular velocity ω in a circular path of radius R (figure 7-E3). A smooth groove AB of length $L(\ll R)$ is made on the surface of the table. The groove makes an angle θ with the radius OA of the circle in which the cabin rotates. A small particle is kept at the point A in the groove and is released to move along AB. Find the time taken by the particle to reach the point B.

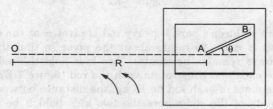

Figure 7-E3

29. A car moving at a speed of 36 km/hr is taking a turn on a circular road of radius 50 m. A small wooden plate is kept on the seat with its plane perpendicular to the radius of the circular road (figure 7-E4). A small block of mass 100 g is kept on the seat which rests against the plate. The friction coefficient between the block and the plate is $\mu = 0.58$. (a) Find the normal contact force exerted by the plate on the block. (b) The plate is slowly turned so that the angle between the normal to the plate and the radius of the road slowly increases. Find the angle at which the block will just start sliding on the plate.

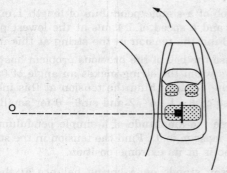

Figure 7-E4

30. A table with smooth horizontal surface is placed in a cabin which moves in a circle of a large radius R (figure 7-E5). A smooth pulley of small radius is fastened to the table. Two masses m and $2m$ placed on the table are connected through a string going over the pulley. Initially the masses are held by a person with the strings along the outward radius and then the system is released from rest (with respect to the cabin). Find the magnitude of the initial acceleration of the masses as seen from the cabin and the tension in the string.

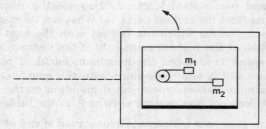

Figure 7-E5

□

ANSWERS

OBJECTIVE I

1. (d)   2. (d)   3. (c)   4. (d)   5. (b)   6. (a)
7. (c)   8. (c)   9. (a)   10. (a)   11. (c)   12. (a)
13. (d)   14. (a)   15. (d)   16. (c)

OBJECTIVE II

1. (a), (d)   2. (d)   3. (b), (d)
4. (c)   5. (b), (c)   6. (b), (d)
7. (b), (d)

EXERCISES

1. 2.73×10^{-3} m/s^2

2. 0.0336 m/s^2
3. (a) 4.0 cm/s^2 (b) 2.0 cm/s^2 (c) $\sqrt{20}$ cm/s^2
4. 500 N
5. $\tan^{-1}(1/3)$
6. $\tan^{-1}(1/4)$
7. 0.25
8. 17 m/s
9. 2.2×10^6 m/s
10. $\sqrt{Rg}$
11. 14.8 N, 14.8 N
13. 45°
14. 1.2 N

15. 1·16 N

16. $mg\cos\theta_0$

17. (a) $3·5\times10^{-3}$ (b) 2·0 hour

18. Between 14·7 km/h and 54 km/hr

19. (a) $\sqrt{Rg}$,
    (b) a distance $\pi R/3$ along the bridge from the highest point,
    (c) $\sqrt{gR\cos(L/2R)}$

20. $\left[(\mu^2 g^2-a^2)R^2\right]^{1/4}$

21. (a) $\sqrt{\mu g/L}$ (b) $\left[\left(\dfrac{\mu g}{L}\right)^2-\alpha^2\right]^{1/4}$

22. (a) 975 N, 1025 N   (b) 0, 707 N, 0
    (c) 682 N, 732 N   (d) 1·037

23. $10\pi^2$ N

24. $\left[\dfrac{g(\sin\theta-\mu\cos\theta)}{R\sin\theta(\cos\theta+\mu\sin\theta)}\right]^{1/2}$ to $\left[\dfrac{g(\sin\theta+\mu\cos\theta)}{R\sin\theta(\cos\theta-\mu\sin\theta)}\right]^{1/2}$

25. $\dfrac{u^2\cos^2\theta}{g}$

26. $\dfrac{u^2\cos^2\theta}{g\cos^3(\theta/2)}$

27. (a) $\dfrac{mv^2}{R}$ (b) $\dfrac{\mu mv^2}{R}$ (c) $-\dfrac{\mu v^2}{R}$ (d) $v_0 e^{-2\pi\mu}$

28. $\sqrt{\dfrac{2L}{\omega^2 R\cos\theta}}$

29. (a) 0·2 N   (b) 30°

30. $\dfrac{\omega^2 R}{3},\dfrac{4}{3}m\omega^2 R$

CHAPTER 8

WORK AND ENERGY

8.1 KINETIC ENERGY

A dancing, running man is said to be more energetic compared to a sleeping snoring man. In physics, a moving particle is said to have more energy than an identical particle at rest. Quantitatively the energy of the moving particle (over and above its energy at rest) is defined by

$$K(v) = \frac{1}{2} m v^2 = \frac{1}{2} m \vec{v} \cdot \vec{v} \qquad \dots (8.1)$$

and is called the *kinetic energy* of the particle. The kinetic energy of a system of particles is the sum of the kinetic energies of all its constituent particles, i.e.,

$$K = \sum_i \frac{1}{2} m_i v_i^2 .$$

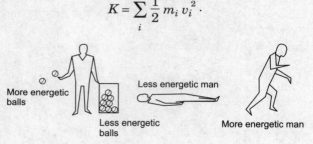

More energetic balls

Less energetic balls

Less energetic man

More energetic man

Figure 8.1

The kinetic energy of a particle or a system of particles can increase or decrease or remain constant as time passes.

If no force is applied on the particle, its velocity v remains constant and hence the kinetic energy remains the same. A force is necessary to change the kinetic energy of a particle. If the resultant force acting on a particle is perpendicular to its velocity, the speed of the particle does not change and hence the kinetic energy does not change. Kinetic energy changes only when the speed changes and that happens only when the resultant force has a tangential component. When a particle falls near the earth's surface, the force of gravity is parallel to its velocity. Its kinetic energy increases as time passes. On the other hand, a particle projected upward has the force opposite to the velocity and its kinetic energy decreases.

From the definition of kinetic energy

$$\frac{dK}{dt} = \frac{d}{dt}\left(\frac{1}{2} m v^2\right) = m v \frac{dv}{dt} = F_t\, v,$$

where F_t is the resultant tangential force. If the resultant force $\vec{F}$ makes an angle θ with the velocity,

$$F_t = F \cos\theta \text{ and } \frac{dK}{dt} = Fv \cos\theta = \vec{F} \cdot \vec{v} = \vec{F} \cdot \frac{\vec{dr}}{dt}$$

or, $\qquad dK = \vec{F} \cdot \vec{dr}. \qquad \dots (8.2)$

8.2 WORK AND WORK-ENERGY THEOREM

The quantity $\vec{F} \cdot \vec{dr} = F\, dr \cos\theta$ is called the *work done* by the force $\vec{F}$ on the particle during the small displacement dr.

The work done on the particle by a force $\vec{F}$ acting on it during a finite displacement is obtained by

$$W = \int \vec{F} \cdot \vec{dr} = \int F \cos\theta\, dr, \qquad \dots (8.3)$$

where the integration is to be performed along the path of the particle. If $\vec{F}$ is the resultant force on the particle we can use equation (8.2) to get

$$W = \int \vec{F} \cdot \vec{dr} = \int dK = K_2 - K_1.$$

Thus, *the work done on a particle by the resultant force is equal to the change in its kinetic energy.* This is called the *work-energy theorem.*

Let $\vec{F}_1, \vec{F}_2, \vec{F}_3, \dots$ be the individual forces acting on a particle. The resultant force is $\vec{F} = \vec{F}_1 + \vec{F}_2 + \vec{F}_3 \dots$, and the work done by the resultant force on the particle is

$$W = \int \vec{F} \cdot \vec{dr}$$

$$= (\vec{F}_1 + \vec{F}_2 + \vec{F}_3 \dots\dots) \cdot \vec{dr}$$

$$= \int \vec{F}_1 \cdot \vec{dr} + \int \vec{F}_2 \cdot \vec{dr} + \int \vec{F}_3 \cdot \vec{dr} \dots,$$

where $= \int \vec{F}_1 \cdot \vec{dr}$ is the work done on the particle by $\vec{F}_1$ and so on. Thus, *the work done by the resultant force is equal to the sum of the work done by the individual forces.* Note that the work done on a particle by an individual force is not equal to the change in its kinetic energy; the sum of the work done by all the forces acting on the particle (which is equal to the work done by the resultant force) is equal to the change in its kinetic energy.

The rate of doing work is called the *power* delivered. The work done by a force $\vec{F}$ in a small displacement $\vec{dr}$ is $dW = \vec{F} \cdot \vec{dr}$.

Thus, the power delivered by the force is

$$P = \frac{dW}{dt} = \vec{F} \cdot \frac{\vec{dr}}{dt} = \vec{F} \cdot \vec{v}.$$

The SI unit of power is joule/second and is written as "watt". A commonly used unit of power is *horsepower* which is equal to 746 W.

8.3 CALCULATION OF WORK DONE

The work done by a force on a particle during a displacement has been defined as

$$W = \int \vec{F} \cdot \vec{dr}.$$

Constant Force

Suppose, the force is constant (in direction and magnitude) during the displacement. Then $W = \int \vec{F} \cdot \vec{dr} = \vec{F} \cdot \int \vec{dr} = \vec{F} \cdot \vec{r}$, where $\vec{r}$ is the total displacement of the particle during which the work is calculated. If θ be the angle between the constant force $\vec{F}$ and the displacement $\vec{r}$, the work is

$$W = Fr \cos\theta. \qquad \ldots (8.4)$$

In particular, if the displacement is along the force, as is the case with a freely and vertically falling particle, $\theta = 0$ and $W = Fr$.

The force of gravity ($\vec{mg}$) is constant in magnitude and direction if the particle moves near the surface of the earth. Suppose a particle moves from A to B along some curve and that $\vec{AB}$ makes an angle θ with the vertical as shown in figure (8.2). The work done by the force of gravity during the transit from A to B is

$$W = mg\,(AB)\cos\theta = mgh,$$

where h is the height descended by the particle. If a particle ascends a height h, the work done by the force of gravity is $-mgh$.

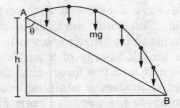

Figure 8.2

If the particle goes from the point A to the point B along some other curve, the work done by the force of gravity is again mgh. We see that the work done by a constant force in going from A to B depends only on the positions of A and B and not on the actual path taken. In case of gravity, the work is weight mg times the height descended. If a particle starts from A and reaches to the same point A after some time, the work done by gravity during this round trip is zero, as the height descended is zero. We shall encounter other forces having this property.

Spring Force

Consider the situation shown in figure (8.3). One end of a spring is attached to a fixed vertical support and the other end to a block which can move on a horizontal table. Let $x = 0$ denote the position of the block when the spring is in its natural length. We shall calculate the work done on the block by the spring-force as the block moves from $x = 0$ to $x = x_1$.

Figure 8.3

The force on the block is k times the elongation of the spring. But the elongation changes as the block moves and so does the force. We cannot take $\vec{F}$ out of the integration $\int \vec{F} \cdot \vec{dr}$. We have to write the work done during a small interval in which the block moves from x to $x + dx$. The force in this interval is kx and the displacement is dx. The force and the displacement are opposite in direction.

So, $$\vec{F} \cdot \vec{dr} = -F\,dx = -kx\,dx$$

during this interval. The total work done as the block is displaced from $x = 0$ to $x = x_1$ is

$$W = \int_0^{x_1} -kx\,dx = \left[-\frac{1}{2}kx^2\right]_0^{x_1} = -\frac{1}{2}kx_1^2.$$

If the block moves from $x = x_1$ to $x = x_2$, the limits of integration are x_1 and x_2 and the work done is

$$W = \left(\frac{1}{2}kx_1^2 - \frac{1}{2}kx_2^2\right). \qquad \ldots (8.5)$$

Note that if the block is displaced from x_1 to x_2 and brought back to $x = x_1$, the work done by the spring-force is zero. The work done during the return journey is negative of the work during the onward journey. The net work done by the spring-force in a round trip is zero.

Three positions of a spring are shown in figure (8.4). In (i) the spring is in its natural length, in (ii) it is compressed by an amount x and in (iii) it is elongated by an amount x. Work done by the spring-force on the block in various situations is shown in the following table.

Table 8.1

Initial state of the spring	Final state of the spring	x_1	x_2	W
Natural	Compressed	0	$-x$	$-\frac{1}{2}kx^2$
Natural	Elongated	0	x	$-\frac{1}{2}kx^2$
Elongated	Natural	x	0	$\frac{1}{2}kx^2$
Compressed	Natural	$-x$	0	$\frac{1}{2}kx^2$
Elongated	Compressed	x	$-x$	0
Compressed	Elongated	$-x$	x	0

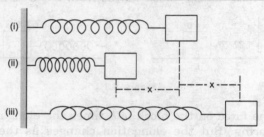

Figure 8.4

Force Perpendicular to Velocity

Suppose $\vec{F} \perp \vec{v}$ for all the time. Then $\vec{F} \cdot \vec{dr} = \vec{F} \cdot \vec{v}\, dt$ is zero in any small interval and the work done by this force is zero.

For example, if a particle is fastened to the end of a string and is whirled in a circular path, the tension is always perpendicular to the velocity of the particle and hence the work done by the tension is zero in circular motion.

Example 8.1

A spring of spring constant 50 N/m is compressed from its natural position through 1 cm. Find the work done by the spring-force on the agency compressing the spring.

Solution : The magnitude of the work is

$$\frac{1}{2}kx^2 = \frac{1}{2} \times (50 \text{ N/m}) \times (1 \text{ cm})^2$$

$$= (25 \text{ N/m}) \times (1 \times 10^{-2}\text{m})^2 = 2 \cdot 5 \times 10^{-3} \text{ J}.$$

As the compressed spring will push the agency, the force will be opposite to the displacement of the point of

application and the work will be negative. Thus, the work done by the spring-force is –2·5 mJ.

The following three cases occur quite frequently :

(a) The force is perpendicular to the velocity at all the instants. The work done by the force is then zero.

(b) The force is constant (both in magnitude and direction). The work done by the force is $W = Fd\cos\theta$, where F and d are magnitudes of the force and the displacement and θ is the angle between them. The amount of work done depends only on the end positions and not on the intermediate path. The work in a round trip is zero. Force of gravity on the bodies near the earth's surface is an example.

The work done due to the force of gravity on a particle of mass m is mgh, where h is the vertical height 'descended' by the particle.

(c) The force is $F = -kx$ as is the case with an elastic spring. The magnitude of the work done by the force during a displacement x from or to its natural position ($x = 0$) is $\frac{1}{2}kx^2$. The work may be $+\frac{1}{2}kx^2$ or $-\frac{1}{2}kx^2$ depending on whether the force and the displacement are along the same or opposite directions.

Example 8.2

A particle of mass 20 g is thrown vertically upwards with a speed of 10 m/s. Find the work done by the force of gravity during the time the particle goes up.

Solution : Suppose the particle reaches a maximum height h. As the velocity at the highest point is zero, we have

$$0 = u^2 - 2gh$$

or,

$$h = \frac{u^2}{2g}.$$

The work done by the force of gravity is

$$-mgh = -mg\frac{u^2}{2g} = -\frac{1}{2}mu^2$$

$$= -\frac{1}{2}(0\cdot02 \text{ kg}) \times (10 \text{ m/s})^2 = -1\cdot0 \text{ J}.$$

8.4 WORK-ENERGY THEOREM FOR A SYSTEM OF PARTICLES

So far we have considered the work done on a single particle. The total work done on a particle equals the change in its kinetic energy. In other words, to change the kinetic energy of a particle we have to apply a force on it and the force must do work on it. Next, consider a system containing more than one particle and suppose the particles exert forces on each other. As a simple example, take a system of two charged particles as shown in figure (8.5) attracting each other (such as a positive and a negative charge).

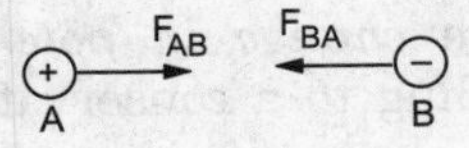

$$F_{AB} \qquad F_{BA}$$
$$(+) \qquad (-)$$
$$A \qquad B$$

Figure 8.5

Because of mutual attraction, the particles are accelerated towards each other and the kinetic energy of the system increases. We have not applied any external force on the system, yet the kinetic energy has changed. Let us examine this in more detail. The particle B exerts a force $\vec{F}_{AB}$ on A. As A moves towards B, this force does work. The work done by this force is equal to the increase in the kinetic energy of A.

Similarly, A exerts a force $\vec{F}_{BA}$ on B. This force does work on B and this work is equal to the increase in the kinetic energy of B. The work by $\vec{F}_{AB}$ + the work by $\vec{F}_{BA}$ is equal to the increase in the total kinetic energy of the two particles. Note that $\vec{F}_{AB} = -\vec{F}_{BA}$, so that $\vec{F}_{AB} + \vec{F}_{BA} = 0$. But the work by $\vec{F}_{AB}$ + the work by $\vec{F}_{BA} \neq 0$. The two forces are opposite in direction but the displacements are also opposite. Thus, the work done by both the forces are positive and are added. The total work done on different particles of the system by the internal forces may not be zero. The change in the kinetic energy of a system is equal to the work done on the system by the external as well as the internal forces.

8.5 POTENTIAL ENERGY

Consider the example of the two charged particles A and B taken in the previous section. Suppose at some instant t_1 the particles are at positions A, B and are going away from each other with speeds v_1 and v_2 (figure 8.6).

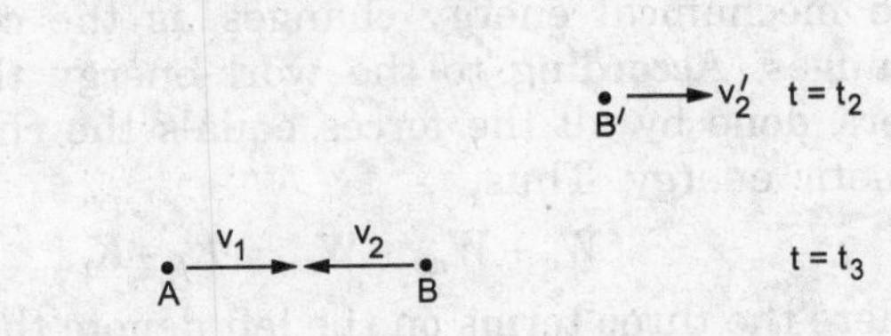

$$v_1 \leftarrow A \qquad B \rightarrow v_2 \qquad t = t_1$$
$$v_1' \leftarrow A' \qquad B' \rightarrow v_2' \quad t = t_2$$
$$A \xrightarrow{v_1} \quad \xleftarrow{v_2} B \qquad t = t_3$$

Figure 8.6

The kinetic energy of the system is K_1. We call the positions of the particles at time t_1 as configuration-1. The particle B attracts A and hence the speed v_1 decreases as time passes. Similarly, the speed v_2 of B

decreases. Thus, the kinetic energy of the two-particle system decreases as time passes. Suppose at a time t_2, the particles are at A' and B', the speeds have changed to v_1' and v_2' and the kinetic energy becomes K_2. We call the positions of the particles at time t_2 as configuration-2. The kinetic energy of the system is decreased by $K_1 - K_2$.

However, if you wait for some more time, the particles return to the original positions A and B, i.e., in configuration-1. At this time, say t_3, the particles move towards each other with speeds v_1 and v_2. Their kinetic energy is again K_1.

When the particles were in configuration-1 the kinetic energy was K_1. When they reached configuration-2 it decreased to K_2. The kinetic energy has decreased but is not lost for ever. We just have to wait. When the particles return to configuration-1 at time t_3, the kinetic energy again becomes K_1. It seems meaningful and reasonable if we think of yet another kind of energy which depends on the configuration. We call this as the *potential energy* of the system. Some kinetic energy was converted into potential energy when the system passed from configuration-1 to configuration-2. As the system returns to configuration-1, this potential energy is converted back into kinetic energy. The sum of the kinetic energy and the potential energy remains constant.

How do we precisely define the potential energy of a system ? Before defining potential energy, let us discuss the idea of conservative and nonconservative forces.

8.6 CONSERVATIVE AND NONCONSERVATIVE FORCES

Let us consider the following two examples.

(1) Suppose a block of mass m rests on a rough horizontal table (figure 8.7). It is dragged horizontally towards right through a distance l and then back to its initial position. Let μ be the friction coefficient between the block and the table. Let us calculate the work done by friction during the round trip.

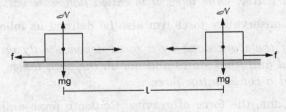

Figure 8.7

The normal force between the table and the block is $\mathcal{N} = mg$ and hence the force of friction is μmg. When the block moves towards right, friction on it is towards left and the work by friction is $(-\mu mgl)$. When the block moves towards left, friction on it is towards right and the work is again $(-\mu mgl)$.

Hence, the total work done by the force of friction in the round trip is $(-2\mu mgl)$.

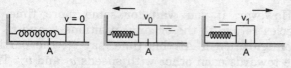

Figure 8.8

(2) Suppose a block connected by a spring is kept on a rough table as shown in figure (8.8). The block is pulled aside and then released. It moves towards the centre A and has some velocity v_0 as it passes through the centre. It goes to the other side of A and then comes back. This time it passes through the centre with somewhat smaller velocity v_1. Compare these two cases in which the block is at A, once going towards left and then towards right. In both the cases the system (table + block + spring) has the same configuration. The spring has the same length. The block is at the same point on the table and the table of course is fixed to the ground. The kinetic energy in the second case is less than the kinetic energy in the first case. This loss in the kinetic energy is a real loss. Every time the block passes through the mean position A, the kinetic energy of the system is smaller and in due course, the block stops on the table. We hold friction as the culprit, because in absence of friction the system regains its kinetic energy as it returns to its original configuration. Remember, work done by friction in a round trip is negative and not zero [example (1) above].

We divide the forces in two categories (a) conservative forces and (b) nonconservative forces. If the work done by a force during a round trip of a system is always zero, the force is said to be conservative. Otherwise, it is called nonconservative.

Conservative force can also be defined as follows :

If the work done by a force depends only on the initial and final states and not on the path taken, it is called a conservative force.

Thus, the force of gravity, Coulomb force and the force of spring are conservative forces, as the work done by these forces are zero in a round trip. The force of friction is nonconservative because the work done by the friction is not zero in a round trip.

8.7 DEFINITION OF POTENTIAL ENERGY AND CONSERVATION OF MECHANICAL ENERGY

We define the change in potential energy of a system corresponding to a conservative internal force as

$$U_f - U_i = -W = -\int_i^f \vec{F} \cdot d\vec{r}$$

where W is the work done by the internal force on the system as the system passes from the initial configuration i to the final configuration f.

We don't (or can't) define potential energy corresponding to a nonconservative internal force.

Suppose only conservative internal forces operate between the parts of the system and the potential energy U is defined corresponding to these forces. There are either no external forces or the work done by them is zero. We have

$$U_f - U_i = -W = -(K_f - K_i)$$

or, $\qquad U_f + K_f = U_i + K_i.$ $\qquad$ ... (8.6)

The sum of the kinetic energy and the potential energy is called the total mechanical energy. We see from equation (8.6) that the total mechanical energy of a system remains constant if the internal forces are conservative and the external forces do no work. This is called the principle of conservation of energy.

The total mechanical energy $K + U$ is not constant if nonconservative forces, such as friction, act between the parts of the system. We can't apply the principle of conservation of energy in presence of nonconservative forces. The work-energy theorem is still valid even in the presence of nonconservative forces.

Note that only a change in potential energy is defined above. We are free to choose the zero potential energy in any configuration just as we are free to choose the origin in space anywhere we like.

If nonconservative internal forces operate within the system, or external forces do work on the system, the mechanical energy changes as the configuration changes. According to the work-energy theorem, the work done by all the forces equals the change in kinetic energy. Thus,

$$W_c + W_{nc} + W_{ext} = K_f - K_i$$

where the three terms on the left denote the work done by the conservative internal forces, nonconservative internal forces and the external forces.

As $\qquad W_c = -(U_f - U_i),$

we get

$$W_{nc} + W_{ext} = (K_f + U_f) - (K_i + U_i)$$

$$= E_f - E_i \qquad\qquad ... (8.7)$$

where $E = K + U$ is the total mechanical energy.

If the internal forces are conservative but external forces also act on the system and they do work, $W_{nc} = 0$ and from (8.7),

$$W_{ext} = E_f - E_i . \qquad \ldots (8.8)$$

The work done by the external forces equals the change in the mechanical energy of the system.

Let us summarise the concepts developed so far in this chapter.

(1) Work done on a particle is equal to the change in its kinetic energy.

(2) Work done on a system by all the (external and internal) forces is equal to the change in its kinetic energy.

(3) A force is called conservative if the work done by it during a round trip of a system is always zero. The force of gravitation, Coulomb force, force by a spring etc. are conservative. If the work done by it during a round trip is not zero, the force is nonconservative. Friction is an example of nonconservative force.

(4) The change in the potential energy of a system corresponding to conservative internal forces is equal to negative of the work done by these forces.

(5) If no external forces act (or the work done by them is zero) and the internal forces are conservative, the mechanical energy of the system remains constant. This is known as the principle of conservation of mechanical energy.

(6) If some of the internal forces are nonconservative, the mechanical energy of the system is not constant.

(7) If the internal forces are conservative, the work done by the external forces is equal to the change in mechanical energy.

Example 8.3

Two charged particles A and B repel each other by a force k/r^2, where k is a constant and r is the separation between them. The particle A is clamped to a fixed point in the lab and the particle B which has a mass m, is released from rest with an initial separation r_0 from A. Find the change in the potential energy of the two-particle system as the separation increases to a large value. What will be the speed of the particle B in this situation?

Solution : The situation is shown in figure (8.9). Take $A + B$ as the system. The only external force acting on the system is that needed to hold A fixed. (You can imagine the experiment being conducted in a gravity free region or the particles may be kept and allowed to move on a smooth horizontal surface, so that the normal force balances the force of gravity). This force does no work

on the system because it acts on the charge A which does not move. Thus, the external forces do no work and internal forces are conservative. The total mechanical energy must, therefore, remain constant. There are two internal forces; F_{AB} acting on A and F_{BA} acting on B. The force F_{AB} does no work because it acts on A which does not move. The work done by F_{BA} as the particle B is taken away is,

$$W = \int \vec{F} \cdot d\vec{r} = \int_{r_0}^{\infty} \frac{k}{r^2} dr = \frac{k}{r_0} . \qquad \ldots (i)$$

External force

$F_{AB} = k/r^2 \leftarrow$ A $\longrightarrow$ B $\rightarrow F_{BA} = k/r^2$

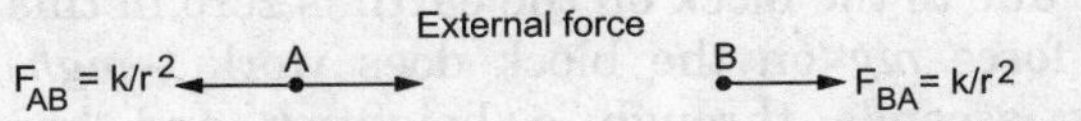

Figure 8.9

The change in the potential energy of the system is

$$U_f - U_i = -W = -\frac{k}{r_0} .$$

As the total mechanical energy is conserved,

$$K_f + U_f = K_i + U_i$$
or, $$K_f = K_i - (U_f - U_i)$$
or, $$\frac{1}{2} mv^2 = \frac{k}{r_0}$$
or, $$v = \sqrt{\frac{2k}{mr_0}} .$$

8.8 CHANGE IN THE POTENTIAL ENERGY IN A RIGID-BODY-MOTION

If the separation between the particles do not change during motion, such as in the case of the motion of a rigid body, the internal forces do no work. This is a consequence of Newton's third law. As an example, consider a system of two particles A and B. Suppose, the particles move in such a way that the line AB translates parallel to itself. The displacement $d\vec{r_A}$ of the particle A is equal to the displacement $d\vec{r_B}$ of the particle B in any short time interval. The net work done by the internal forces $\vec{F}_{AB}$ and $\vec{F}_{BA}$ is

$$W = \int (\vec{F}_{AB} \cdot d\vec{r_A} + \vec{F}_{BA} \cdot d\vec{r_B})$$
$$= \int (\vec{F}_{AB} + \vec{F}_{BA}) \cdot d\vec{r_A} = 0.$$

Thus, the work done by $\vec{F}_{AB}$ and $\vec{F}_{BA}$ add up to zero. Even if AB does not translate parallel to itself but rotates, the result is true. The internal forces acting between the particles of a rigid body do no work in its motion and we need not consider the potential energy corresponding to these forces.

The potential energy of a system changes only when the separations between the parts of the system change. In other words, *the potential energy depends only on the separation between the interacting particles.*

8.9 GRAVITATIONAL POTENTIAL ENERGY

Consider a block of mass m kept near the surface of the earth and suppose it is raised through a height h. Consider "the earth + the block" as the system. The gravitational force between the earth and the block is conservative and we can define a potential energy corresponding to this force. The earth is very heavy as compared to the block and so one can neglect its acceleration. Thus, we take our reference frame attached to the earth, it will still be very nearly an inertial frame. The work done by the gravitational force due to the block on the earth is zero in this frame. The force mg on the block does work $(-mgh)$ if the block ascends through a height h and hence the potential energy is increased by mgh. Thus, *if a block of mass m ascends a height h above the earth's surface (h << radius of earth), the potential energy of the "earth + block" system increases by mgh.* If the block descends by a height h, the potential energy decreases by mgh. Since the earth almost remains fixed, it is customary to call the potential energy of the earth-block system as the potential energy of the block only. We then say that the gravitational potential energy of the "block" is increased by an amount mgh when it is raised through a hieght h above the earth's surface.

We have been talking in terms of the changes in gravitational potential energy. We can choose any position of the block and call the gravitational potential energy to be zero in this position. The potential energy at a height h above this position is mgh. The position of the zero potential energy is chosen according to the convenience of the problem.

Example 8.4

A block of mass m slides along a frictionless surface as shown in the figure (8.10). If it is released from rest at A, what is its speed at B?

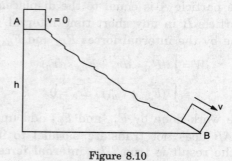

Figure 8.10

Solution : Take the block + the earth as the system. Only the block moves, so only the work done on the block will contribute to the gravitational potential energy. As it descends through a height h between A and B, the potential energy decreases by mgh. The normal contact force $\mathcal{N}$ on the block by the surface does no work as it

is perpendicular to its velocity. No external force does any work on the system. Hence,

increase in kinetic energy = decrease in potential energy

or, $\frac{1}{2}mv^2 = mgh$ or, $v = \sqrt{2gh}$.

Example 8.5

A pendulum bob has a speed 3 m/s while passing through its lowest position. What is its speed when it makes an angle of 60° with the vertical? The length of the pendulum is 0·5 m. Take g = 10 m/s².

Solution : Take the bob + earth as the system. The external force acting on the system is that due to the string. But this force is always perpendicular to the velocity of the bob and so the work done by this force is zero. Hence, the total mechanical energy will remain constant. As is clear from figure (8.11), the height ascended by the bob at an angular displacement θ is $l - l\cos\theta = l(1 - \cos\theta)$. The increase in the potential energy is $mgl(1 - \cos\theta)$. This should be equal to the decrease in the kinetic energy of the system. Again, as the earth does not move in the lab frame, this is the decrease in the kinetic energy of the bob. If the speed at an angular displacement θ is v_1, the decrease in kinetic energy is

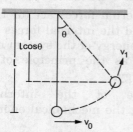

Figure 8.11

$$\frac{1}{2}mv_0^2 - \frac{1}{2}mv_1^2,$$

where v_0 is the speed of the block at the lowest position.

Thus, $\frac{1}{2}mv_0^2 - \frac{1}{2}mv_1^2 = mgl(1 - \cos\theta)$

or, $v_1 = \sqrt{v_0^2 - 2gl(1 - \cos\theta)}$

$$= \sqrt{(9 \text{ m}^2/\text{s}^2) - 2 \times (10 \text{ m/s}^2) \times (0{\cdot}5 \text{ m})\left(1 - \frac{1}{2}\right)}$$

$$= 2 \text{ m/s}.$$

8.10 POTENTIAL ENERGY OF A COMPRESSED OR EXTENDED SPRING

Consider a massless spring of natural length l, one end of which is fastened to a wall (figure 8.12). The other end is attached to a block which is slowly pulled on a smooth horizontal surface to extend the spring. Take the spring as the system. When it is elongated by a distance x, the tension in it is kx, where k is its spring constant. It pulls the wall towards right and the block towards left by forces of magnitude kx. The forces exerted on the spring are (i) kx towards left by the wall and (ii) kx towards right by the block.

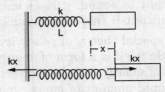

Figure 8.12

How much work has been done on the spring by these two external forces ? The force by the wall does no work as the point of application is fixed. The force by the block does work $\int_{0}^{x} kx\,dx = \frac{1}{2}kx^2$. The work is positive as the force is towards right and the particles of the spring, on which this force is acting, also move towards right. Thus, the total external work done on the spring is $\frac{1}{2}kx^2$, when the spring is elongated by an amount x from its natural length. The same is the external work done on the spring if it is compressed by a distance x.

We have seen (equation 8.8) that the external work done on a system is equal to the change in its total mechanical energy. The spring is assumed to be massless and hence its kinetic energy remains zero all the time. Thus, its potential energy has increased by $\frac{1}{2}kx^2$.

We conclude that a stretched or compressed spring has a potential energy $\frac{1}{2}kx^2$ larger than its potential energy at its natural length. The potential energy of the spring corresponds to the internal forces between the particles of the spring when it is stretched or compressed. It is called *elastic potential energy* or the *strain energy* of the spring. Again, the calculation gives only the change in the elastic potential energy of the spring and we are free to choose any length of the spring and call the potential energy zero at that length. It is customary to choose the potential energy of a spring in its natural length to be zero. With this choice *the potential energy of a spring is $\frac{1}{2}kx^2$, where x is the elongation or the compression of the spring.*

Example 8.6

A block of mass m, attached to a spring of spring constant k, oscillates on a smooth horizontal table. The

other end of the spring is fixed to a wall. If it has a speed v when the spring is at its natural length, how far will it move on the table before coming to an instantaneous rest ?

Solution : Consider the block + the spring as the system. The external forces acting on the system are (a) the force of gravity, (b) the normal force by the table and (c) the force by the wall. None of these do any work on this system and hence the total mechanical energy is conserved. If the block moves a distance x before comming to rest, we have,

$$\frac{1}{2}mv^2 = \frac{1}{2}kx^2$$

or, $$x = v\sqrt{m/k}.$$

Example 8.7

A block of mass m is suspended through a spring of spring constant k and is in equilibrium. A sharp blow gives the block an initial downward velocity v. How far below the equilibrium position, the block comes to an instantaneous rest ?

Solution : Let us consider the block + the spring + the earth as the system. The system has gravitational potential energy corresponding to the force between the block and the earth as well as the elastic potential energy corresponding to the spring-force. The total mechanical energy includes kinetic energy, gravitational potential energy and elastic potential energy.

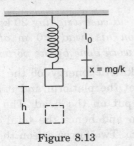

Figure 8.13

When the block is in equilibrium, it is acted upon by two forces, (a) the force of gravity mg and (b) the tension in the spring $T = kx$, where x is the elongation. For equilibrium, $mg = kx$, so that the spring is stretched by a length $x = mg/k$. The potential energy of the spring in this position is

$$\frac{1}{2}k\,(mg/k)^2 = \frac{m^2g^2}{2k}.$$

Take the gravitational potential energy to be zero in this position. The total mechanical energy of the system just after the blow is

$$\frac{1}{2}mv^2 + \frac{m^2g^2}{2k}.$$

The only external force on this system is that due to the ceiling which does no work. Hence, the mechanical energy of this system remains constant. If the block descends through a height h before coming to an instantaneous rest, the elastic potential energy becomes $\frac{1}{2} k (mg/k + h)^2$ and the gravitational potential energy $- mgh$. The kinetic energy is zero in this state. Thus, we have

$$\frac{1}{2} mv^2 + \frac{m^2 g^2}{2k} = \frac{1}{2} k (mg/k + h)^2 - mgh.$$

Solving this we get,

$$h = v \sqrt{m/k}.$$

Compare this with the result obtained in Example (8.6). If we neglect gravity and consider the length of the spring in equilibrium position as the natural length, the answer is same. This simplification is often used while dealing with vertical springs.

8.11 DIFFERENT FORMS OF ENERGY : MASS ENERGY EQUIVALENCE

The kinetic energy and the potential energy of a system, taken together, form mechanical energy. Energy can exist in many other forms. In measuring kinetic energy of an extended body, we use the speed of the body as a whole. Even if we keep the body at rest, the particles in it are continuously moving inside the body. These particles also exert forces on each other and there is a potential energy corresponding to these forces. The total energy corresponding to the internal motion of molecules and their interaction, is called *internal energy* or *thermal energy* of the body. Light and sound are other forms of energy. When a source emits light or sound, it loses energy. Chemical energy is significant if there are chemical reactions.

Einstein's special theory of relativity shows that a material particle itself is a form of energy. Thus, about 8.18×10^{-14} J of energy may be converted to form an electron and equal amount of energy may be obtained by destroying an electron. The ralation between the mass of a particle m and its equivalent energy E is given as

$$E = mc^2,$$

where $c = 3 \times 10^8$ m/s is the speed of light in vacuum.

When all forms of energy are taken into account, we arrive at the generalised law of conservation of energy.

Energy can never be created or destroyed, it can only be changed from one form into another.

Worked Out Examples

1. *A porter lifts a suitcase weighing 20 kg from the platform and puts it on his head 2·0 m above the platform. Calculate the work done by the porter on the suitcase.*

Solution : The kinetic energy of the suitcase was zero when it was at the platform and it again became zero when it was put on the head. The change in kinetic energy is zero and hence the total work done on the suitcase is zero. Two forces act on the suitcase, one due to gravity and the other due to the porter. Thus, the work done by the porter is negative of the work done by gravity. As the suitcase is lifted up, the work done by gravity is

$$W = - mgh$$

$$= - (20 \text{ kg}) (9·8 \text{ m/s}^2) (2 \text{ m}) = - 392 \text{ J}.$$

The work done by the porter is 392 J $\approx$ 390 J.

2. *An elevator weighing 500 kg is to be lifted up at a constant velocity of 0·20 m/s. What would be the minimum horsepower of the motor to be used ?*

Solution : As the elevator is going up with a uniform velocity, the total work done on it is zero in any time interval. The work done by the motor is, therefore, equal to the work done by the force of gravity in that interval (in magnitude). The rate of doing work, i.e., the power delivered is

$$P = F v = mgv$$

$$= (500 \text{ kg}) (9·8 \text{ m/s}^2) (0·2 \text{ m/s}) = 980 \text{ W}$$

Assuming no loss against friction etc., in the motor, the minimum horsepower of the motor is

$$P = 980 \text{ W} = \frac{980}{746} \text{ hp} = 1·3 \text{ hp}.$$

3. *A block of mass 2·0 kg is pulled up on a smooth incline of angle 30° with the horizontal. If the block moves with an acceleration of 1·0 m/s², find the power delivered by the pulling force at a time 4·0 s after the motion starts. What is the average power delivered during the 4·0 s after the motion starts ?*

Solution : The forces acting on the block are shown in figure (8-W1). Resolving the forces parallel to the incline, we get

$$F - mg \sin\theta = ma$$

or, $$F = mg \sin\theta + ma$$

$$= (2·0 \text{ kg}) [(9·8 \text{ m/s}^2) (1/2) + 1·0 \text{ m/s}^2] = 11·8 \text{ N}.$$

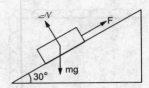

Figure 8-W1

The velocity at $t = 4.0$ s is

$$v = at = (1.0 \text{ m/s}^2) (4.0 \text{ s}) = 4.0 \text{ m/s}.$$

The power delivered by the force at $t = 4.0$ s is

$$P = \vec{F} \cdot \vec{v} = (11.8 \text{ N}) (4.0 \text{ m/s}) \approx 47 \text{ W}.$$

The displacement during the first four seconds is

$$x = \frac{1}{2} at^2 = \frac{1}{2} (1.0 \text{ m/s}^2) (16 \text{ s}^2) = 8.0 \text{ m}.$$

The work done in these four seconds is, therefore,

$$W = \vec{F} \cdot \vec{d} = (11.8 \text{ N}) (8.0 \text{ m}) = 94.4 \text{ J}.$$

The average power delivered $= \dfrac{94.4 \text{ J}}{4.0 \text{ s}}$

$$= 23.6 \text{ W} \approx 24 \text{ W}.$$

4. A force $F = (10 + 0.50 x)$ acts on a particle in the x direction, where F is in newton and x in meter. Find the work done by this force during a displacement from $x = 0$ to $x = 2.0$ m.

Solution : As the force is variable, we shall find the work done in a small displacement x to $x + dx$ and then integrate it to find the total work. The work done in this small displacement is

$$dW = \vec{F} \cdot \vec{dx} = (10 + 0.5 x) \, dx.$$

Thus, $W = \displaystyle\int_0^{2.0} (10 + 0.50 x) \, dx$

$$= \left[10 x + 0.50 \frac{x^2}{2} \right]_0^{2.0} = 21 \text{ J}.$$

5. A body dropped from a height H reaches the ground with a speed of $1.2 \sqrt{gH}$. Calculate the work done by air-friction.

Solution : The forces acting on the body are the force of gravity and the air-friction. By work-energy theorem, the total work done on the body is

$$W = \frac{1}{2} m (1.2 \sqrt{gH})^2 - 0 = 0.72 \, mgH.$$

The work done by the force of gravity is mgH. Hence, the work done by the air-friction is

$$0.72 \, mgH - mgH = -0.28 \, mgH.$$

6. A block of mass M is pulled along a horizontal surface by applying a force at an angle θ with the horizontal.

The friction coefficient between the block and the surface is μ. If the block travels at a uniform velocity, find the work done by this applied force during a displacement d of the block.

Solution : Forces on the block are

(i) its weight Mg,
(ii) the normal force $\mathcal{N}$,
(iii) the applied force F and
(iv) the kinetic friction $\mu \mathcal{N}$.

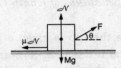

Figure 8-W2

The forces are shown in figure (8-W2). As the block moves with a uniform velocity, the forces add up to zero. Taking horizontal and vertical components,

$$F \cos\theta = \mu \mathcal{N}$$

and $\qquad F \sin\theta + \mathcal{N} = Mg.$

Eliminating $\mathcal{N}$ from these equations,

$$F \cos\theta = \mu (Mg - F \sin\theta)$$

or, $\qquad F = \dfrac{\mu \, Mg}{\cos\theta + \mu \sin\theta}.$

The work done by this force during a displacement d is

$$W = F d \cos\theta = \frac{\mu \, Mgd \cos\theta}{\cos\theta + \mu \sin\theta}.$$

7. Two cylindrical vessels of equal cross-sectional area A contain water upto heights h_1 and h_2. The vessels are interconnected so that the levels in them become equal. Calculate the work done by the force of gravity during the process. The density of water is ρ.

Solution : Since the total volume of the water is constant, the height in each vessel after interconnection will be $(h_1 + h_2)/2$. The level in the left vessel shown in the figure, drops from A to C and that in the right vessel rises from B to D. Effectively, the water in the part AC has dropped down to DB.

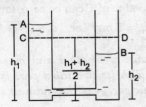

Figure 8-W3

The mass of this volume of water is

$$m = \rho A \left(h_1 - \frac{h_1 + h_2}{2} \right)$$

$$= \rho A \left(\frac{h_1 - h_2}{2}\right).$$

The height descended by this water is $AC = (h_1 - h_2)/2$. The work done by the force of gravity during this process is, therefore,

$$= \rho A \left(\frac{h_1 - h_2}{2}\right)^2 g.$$

8. *What minimum horizontal speed should be given to the bob of a simple pendulum of length l so that it describes a complete circle ?*

Solution : Suppose the bob is given a horizontal speed v_0 at the bottom and it describes a complete vertical circle. Let its speed at the highest point be v. Taking the gravitational potential energy to be zero at the bottom, the conservation of energy gives,

$$\frac{1}{2} mv_0^2 = \frac{1}{2} mv^2 + 2mgl$$

or, $mv^2 = mv_0^2 - 4\, mgl.$ ... (i)

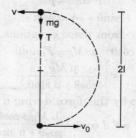

Figure 8-W4

The forces acting on the bob at the highest point are mg due to the gravity and T due to the tension in the string. The resultant force towards the centre is, therefore, $mg + T$. As the bob is moving in a circle, its acceleration towards the centre is v^2/l. Applying Newton's second law and using (i),

$$mg + T = m\frac{v^2}{l} = \frac{1}{l}\,(mv_0^2 - 4mgl)$$

or, $mv_0^2 = 5\, mgl + T\, l.$

Now, for v_0 to be minimum, T should be minimum. As the minimum value of T can be zero, for minimum speed,

$$mv_0^2 = 5\, mgl \quad \text{or,} \quad v_0 = \sqrt{5\, gl}.$$

9. *A uniform chain of length l and mass m overhangs a smooth table with its two third part lying on the table. Find the kinetic energy of the chain as it completely slips off the table.*

Solution : Let us take the zero of potential energy at the table. Consider a part dx of the chain at a depth x below the surface of the table. The mass of this part is $dm = m/l\ dx$ and hence its potential energy is $- (m/l\ dx)gx$.

Figure 8-W5

The potential energy of the $l/3$ of the chain that overhangs is $U_1 = \int_0^{l/3} -\frac{m}{l}\, gx\, dx$

$$= -\left[\frac{m}{l}\, g \left(\frac{x^2}{2}\right)\right]_0^{l/3} = -\frac{1}{18}\, mgl.$$

This is also the potential energy of the full chain in the initial position because the part lying on the table has zero potential energy. The potential energy of the chain when it completely slips off the table is

$$U_2 = \int_0^{l} -\frac{m}{l}\, gx\, dx = -\frac{1}{2}\, mgl.$$

The loss in potential energy $= \left(-\frac{1}{18}\, mgl\right) - \left(-\frac{1}{2}\, mgl\right)$

$$= \frac{4}{9}\, mgl.$$

This should be equal to the gain in the kinetic energy. But the initial kinetic enegry is zero. Hence, the kinetic energy of the chain as it completely slips off the table is $\frac{4}{9}\, mgl$.

10. *A block of mass m is pushed against a spring of spring constant k fixed at one end to a wall. The block can slide on a frictionless table as shown in figure (8-W6). The natural length of the spring is L_0 and it is compressed to half its natural length when the block is released. Find the velocity of the block as a function of its distance x from the wall.*

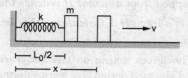

Figure 8-W6

Solution : When the block is released, the spring pushes it towards right. The velocity of the block increases till the spring acquires its natural length. Thereafter, the block loses contact with the spring and moves with constant velocity.

Initially, the compression of the spring is $L_0/2$. When the distance of the block from the wall becomes x, where

$x < L_0$, the compression is $(L_0 - x)$. Using the principle of conservation of energy,

$$\frac{1}{2} k \left(\frac{L_0}{2}\right)^2 = \frac{1}{2} k (L_0 - x)^2 + \frac{1}{2} mv^2.$$

Solving this,

$$v = \sqrt{\frac{k}{m}} \left[\frac{L_0^2}{4} - (L_0 - x)^2\right]^{1/2}.$$

When the spring acquires its natural length, $x = L_0$ and $v = \sqrt{\frac{k}{m}} \frac{L_0}{2}$. Thereafter, the block continues with this velocity.

11. *A particle is placed at the point A of a frictionless track ABC as shown in figure (8-W7). It is pushed slightly towards right. Find its speed when it reaches the point B. Take $g = 10$ m/s^2.*

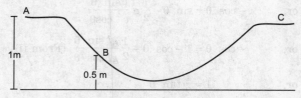

Figure 8-W7

Solution : Let us take the gravitational potential energy to be zero at the horizontal surface shown in the figure. The potential energies of the particle at A and B are

$$U_A = Mg \,(1 \text{ m})$$

and

$$U_B = Mg \,(0\cdot5 \text{ m}).$$

The kinetic energy at the point A is zero. As the track is frictionless, no energy is lost. The normal force on the particle does no work. Applying the principle of conservation of energy,

$$U_A + K_A = U_B + K_B$$

or,

$$Mg(1 \text{ m}) = Mg(0\cdot5 \text{ m}) + \frac{1}{2} Mv_B^2$$

or,

$$\frac{1}{2} v_B^2 = g(1 \text{ m} - 0\cdot5 \text{ m})$$

$$= (10 \text{ m/s}^2) \times 0\cdot5 \text{ m}$$

$$= 5 \text{ m}^2/\text{s}^2$$

or,

$$v_B = \sqrt{10} \text{ m/s}.$$

12. *Figure (8-W8) shows a smooth curved track terminating in a smooth horizontal part. A spring of spring constant 400 N/m is attached at one end to a wedge fixed rigidly with the horizontal part. A 40 g mass is released from rest at a height of 4·9 m on the curved track. Find the maximum compression of the spring.*

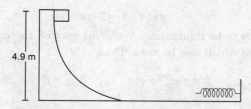

Figure 8-W8

Solution : At the instant of maximum compression the speed of the 40 g mass reduces to zero. Taking the gravitational potential energy to be zero at the horizontal part, the conservation of energy shows,

$$mgh = \frac{1}{2} kx^2$$

where $m = 0\cdot04$ kg, $h = 4\cdot9$ m, $k = 400$ N/m and x is the maximum compression.

Thus, $x = \sqrt{\dfrac{2mgh}{k}}$

$$= \sqrt{\frac{2 \times (0\cdot04 \text{ kg}) \times (9\cdot8 \text{ m/s}^2) \times (4\cdot9 \text{ m})}{(400 \text{ N/m})}}$$

$$= 9\cdot8 \text{ cm}.$$

13. *Figure (8-W9) shows a loop-the-loop track of radius R. A car (without engine) starts from a platform at a distance h above the top of the loop and goes around the loop without falling off the track. Find the minimum value of h for a successful looping. Neglect friction.*

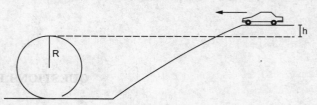

Figure 8-W9

Solution : Suppose the speed of the car at the topmost point of the loop is v. Taking the gravitational potential energy to be zero at the platform and assuming that the car starts with a negligible speed, the conservation of energy shows,

$$0 = -mgh + \frac{1}{2} mv^2$$

or,

$$mv^2 = 2 mgh, \qquad \ldots \text{ (i)}$$

where m is the mass of the car. The car moving in a circle must have radial acceleration v^2/R at this instant. The forces on the car are, mg due to gravity and $\mathscr{N}$ due to the contact with the track. Both these forces are in radial direction at the top of the loop. Thus, from Newton's Law

$$mg + \mathscr{N} = \frac{mv^2}{R}$$

or, $mg + \mathcal{N} = 2\,mgh/R.$

For h to be minimum, $\mathcal{N}$ should assume the minimum value which can be zero. Thus,

$$2\,mg\,\frac{h_{min}}{R} = mg \quad \text{or,} \quad h_{min} = R/2.$$

14. *A heavy particle is suspended by a string of length l. The particle is given a horizontal velocity v_0. The string becomes slack at some angle and the particle proceeds on a parabola. Find the value of v_0 if the particle passes through the point of suspension.*

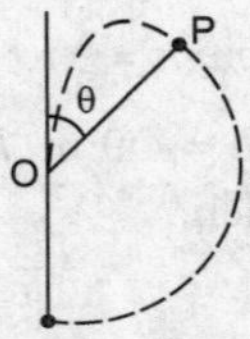

Figure 8-W10

Solution : Suppose the string becomes slack when the particle reaches the point P (figure 8-W10). Suppose the string OP makes an angle θ with the upward vertical. The only force acting on the particle at P is its weight mg. The radial component of the force is $mg\cos\theta$. As the particle moves on the circle upto P,

$$mg\cos\theta = m\left(\frac{v^2}{l}\right)$$

or, $v^2 = gl\cos\theta$ ... (i)

where v is its speed at P. Using conservation of energy,

$$\frac{1}{2}mv_0^2 = \frac{1}{2}mv^2 + mgl\,(1 + \cos\theta)$$

or, $v^2 = v_0^2 - 2gl(1 + \cos\theta).$ ... (ii)

From (i) and (ii), $v_0^2 - 2\,g\,l\,(1 + \cos\theta) = g\,l\cos\theta$

or, $v_0^2 = gl\,(2 + 3\cos\theta).$ ... (iii)

Now onwards the particle goes in a parabola under the action of gravity. As it passes through the point of suspension O, the equations for horizontal and vertical motions give,

$$l\sin\theta = (v\cos\theta)\,t$$

and $-l\cos\theta = (v\sin\theta)\,t - \dfrac{1}{2}gt^2$

or, $-l\cos\theta = (v\sin\theta)\left(\dfrac{l\sin\theta}{v\cos\theta}\right) - \dfrac{1}{2}g\left(\dfrac{l\sin\theta}{v\cos\theta}\right)^2$

or, $-\cos^2\theta = \sin^2\theta - \dfrac{1}{2}g\,\dfrac{l\sin^2\theta}{v^2\cos\theta}$

or, $-\cos^2\theta = 1 - \cos^2\theta - \dfrac{1}{2}\dfrac{gl\sin^2\theta}{gl\cos^2\theta}$ [From (i)]

or, $1 = \dfrac{1}{2}\tan^2\theta$

or, $\tan\theta = \sqrt{2}.$

From (iii), $v_0 = [gl\,(2 + \sqrt{3})]^{1/2}.$

□

QUESTIONS FOR SHORT ANSWER

1. When you lift a box from the floor and put it on an almirah the potential energy of the box increases, but there is no change in its kinetic energy. Is it a violation of conservation of energy ?

2. A particle is released from the top of an incline of height h. Does the kinetic energy of the particle at the bottom of the incline depend on the angle of incline ? Do you need any more information to answer this question in Yes or No ?

3. Can the work by kinetic friction on an object be positive ? Zero ?

4. Can static friction do nonzero work on an object ? If yes, give an example. If no, give reason.

5. Can normal force do a nonzero work on an object. If yes, give an example. If no, give reason.

6. Can kinetic energy of a system be increased without applying any external force on the system ?

7. Is work-energy theorem valid in noninertial frames ?

8. A heavy box is kept on a smooth inclined plane and is pushed up by a force F acting parallel to the plane. Does the work done by the force F as the box goes from A to B depend on how fast the box was moving at A and B ? Does the work by the force of gravity depend on this ?

9. One person says that the potential energy of a particular book kept in an almirah is 20 J and the other says it is 30 J. Is one of them necessarily wrong ?

10. A book is lifted from the floor and is kept in an almirah. One person says that the potential energy of the book is increased by 20 J and the other says it is increased by 30 J. Is one of them necessarily wrong ?

11. In one of the exercises to strengthen the wrist and fingers, a person squeezes and releases a soft rubber ball. Is the work done on the ball positive, negative or zero during compression ? During expansion ?

12. In tug of war, the team that exerts a larger tangential force on the ground wins. Consider the period in which a team is dragging the opposite team by applying a larger tangential force on the ground. List which of the

following works are positive, which are negative and which are zero ?
(a) work by the winning team on the losing team
(b) work by the losing team on the winning team
(c) work by the ground on the winning team
(d) work by the ground on the losing team
(e) total external work on the two teams.

13. When an apple falls from a tree what happens to its gravitational potential energy just as it reaches the ground ? After it strikes the ground ?

14. When you push your bicycle up on an incline the potential energy of the bicycle and yourself increases. Where does this energy come from ?

15. The magnetic force on a charged particle is always perpendicular to its velocity. Can the magnetic force change the velocity of the particle ? Speed of the particle ?

16. A ball is given a speed v on a rough horizontal surface. The ball travels through a distance l on the surface and stops. (a) What are the initial and final kinetic energies of the ball ? (b) What is the work done by the kinetic friction ?

17. Consider the situation of the previous question from a frame moving with a speed v_0 parallel to the initial velocity of the block. (a) What are the initial and final kinetic energies ? (b) What is the work done by the kinetic friction ?

OBJECTIVE I

1. A heavy stone is thrown from a cliff of height h with a speed v. The stone will hit the ground with maximum speed if it is thrown
(a) vertically downward   (b) vertically upward
(c) horizontally
(d) the speed does not depend on the initial direction.

2. Two springs A and $B(k_A = 2k_B)$ are stretched by applying forces of equal magnitudes at the four ends. If the energy stored in A is E, that in B is
(a) $E/2$ (b) $2E$ (c) E (d) $E/4$.

3. Two equal masses are attached to the two ends of a spring of spring constant k. The masses are pulled out symmetrically to stretch the spring by a length x over its natural length. The work done by the spring on each mass is
(a) $\frac{1}{2} kx^2$ (b) $-\frac{1}{2} kx^2$ (c) $\frac{1}{4} kx^2$ (d) $-\frac{1}{4} kx^2$.

4. The negative of the work done by the conservative internal forces on a system equals the change in
(a) total energy   (b) kinetic energy
(c) potential energy   (d) none of these.

5. The work done by the external forces on a system equals the change in
(a) total energy   (b) kinetic energy
(c) potential energy   (d) none of these.

6. The work done by all the forces (external and internal) on a system equals the change in

(a) total energy   (b) kinetic energy
(c) potential energy   (d) none of these.

7. _____ of a two particle system depends only on the separation between the two particles. The most appropriate choice for the blank space in the above sentence is
(a) Kinetic energy   (b) Total mechanical energy
(c) Potential energy   (d) Total energy.

8. A small block of mass m is kept on a rough inclined surface of inclination θ fixed in an elevator. The elevator goes up with a uniform velocity v and the block does not slide on the wedge. The work done by the force of friction on the block in time t will be
(a) zero   (b) $mgvt \cos^2\theta$
(c) $mgvt \sin^2\theta$ (d) $mgvt \sin 2\theta$.

9. A block of mass m slides down a smooth vertical circular track. During the motion, the block is in
(a) vertical equilibrium   (b) horizontal equilibrium
(c) radial equilibrium   (d) none of these.

10. A particle is rotated in a vertical circle by connecting it to a string of length l and keeping the other end of the string fixed. The minimum speed of the particle when the string is horizontal for which the particle will complete the circle is
(a) $\sqrt{gl}$ (b) $\sqrt{2gl}$ (c) $\sqrt{3gl}$ (d) $\sqrt{5gl}$.

OBJECTIVE II

1. A heavy stone is thrown from a cliff of height h in a given direction. The speed with which it hits the ground
(a) must depend on the speed of projection
(b) must be larger than the speed of projection

(c) must be independent of the speed of projection
(d) may be smaller than the speed of projection.

2. The total work done on a particle is equal to the change in its kinetic energy
(a) always

(b) only if the forces acting on it are conservative

(c) only if gravitational force alone acts on it

(d) only if elastic force alone acts on it.

3. A particle is acted upon by a force of constant magnitude which is always perpendicular to the velocity of the particle. The motion of the particle takes place in a plane. It follows that
   (a) its velocity is constant
   (b) its acceleration is constant
   (c) its kinetic energy is constant
   (d) it moves in a circular path.

4. Consider two observers moving with respect to each other at a speed v along a straight line. They observe a block of mass m moving a distance l on a rough surface. The following quantities will be same as observed by the two observers
   (a) kinetic energy of the block at time t
   (b) work done by friction
   (c) total work done on the block
   (d) acceleration of the block.

5. You lift a suitcase from the floor and keep it on a table. The work done by you on the suitcase does not depend on
   (a) the path taken by the suitcase
   (b) the time taken by you in doing so
   (c) the weight of the suitcase
   (d) your weight.

6. No work is done by a force on an object if
   (a) the force is always perpendicular to its velocity
   (b) the force is always perpendicular to its acceleration
   (c) the force is constant
   (d) the object moves in such a way that the point of application of the force remains fixed.

7. A particle of mass m is attached to a light string of length l, the other end of which is fixed. Initially the string is kept horizontal and the particle is given an upward velocity v. The particle is just able to complete a circle.
   (a) The string becomes slack when the particle reaches

its highest point.

(b) The velocity of the particle becomes zero at the highest point.

(c) The kinetic energy of the ball in initial position was $\frac{1}{2} mv^2 = mgl$.

(d) The particle again passes through the initial position.

8. The kinetic energy of a particle continuously increases with time.
   (a) The resultant force on the particle must be parallel to the velocity at all instants.
   (b) The resultant force on the particle must be at an angle less than 90° all the time.
   (c) Its height above the ground level must continuously decrease.
   (d) The magnitude of its linear momentum is increasing continuously.

9. One end of a light spring of spring constant k is fixed to a wall and the other end is tied to a block placed on a smooth horizontal surface. In a displacement, the work done by the spring is $\frac{1}{2} kx^2$. The possible cases are
   (a) the spring was initially compressed by a distance x and was finally in its natural length
   (b) it was initially stretched by a distance x and finally was in its natural length
   (c) it was initially in its natural length and finally in a compressed position
   (d) it was initially in its natural length and finally in a stretched position.

10. A block of mass M is hanging over a smooth and light pulley through a light string. The other end of the string is pulled by a constant force F. The kinetic energy of the block increases by 20 J in 1 s.
    (a) The tension in the string is Mg.
    (b) The tension in the string is F.
    (c) The work done by the tension on the block is 20 J in the above 1 s.
    (d) The work done by the force of gravity is −20 J in the above 1 s.

EXERCISES

1. The mass of cyclist together with the bike is 90 kg. Calculate the increase in kinetic energy if the speed increases from 6·0 km/h to 12 km/h.

2. A block of mass 2·00 kg moving at a speed of 10·0 m/s accelerates at 3·00 m/s^2 for 5·00 s. Compute its final kinetic energy.

3. A box is pushed through 4·0 m across a floor offering 100 N resistance. How much work is done by the resisting force ?

4. A block of mass 5·0 kg slides down an incline of inclination 30° and length 10 m. Find the work done by the force of gravity.

5. A constant force of 2·50 N accelerates a stationary particle of mass 15 g through a displacement of 2·50 m. Find the work done and the average power delivered.

6. A particle moves from a point $\vec{r_1} = (2 \text{ m}) \vec{i} + (3 \text{ m}) \vec{j}$ to another point $\vec{r_2} = (3 \text{ m}) \vec{i} + (2 \text{ m}) \vec{j}$ during which a certain force $\vec{F} = (5 \text{ N}) \vec{i} + (5 \text{ N}) \vec{j}$ acts on it. Find the work done by the force on the particle during the displacement.

7. A man moves on a straight horizontal road with a block of mass 2 kg in his hand. If he covers a distance of 40 m with an acceleration of 0·5 m/s^2, find the work done by the man on the block during the motion.

8. A force $F = a + bx$ acts on a particle in the x-direction, where a and b are constants. Find the work done by this force during a displacement from $x = 0$ to $x = d$.

9. A block of mass 250 g slides down an incline of inclination 37° with a uniform speed. Find the work done against the friction as the block slides through 1·0 m.

10. A block of mass m is kept over another block of mass M and the system rests on a horizontal surface (figure 8-E1). A constant horizontal force F acting on the lower block produces an acceleration $\dfrac{F}{2(m+M)}$ in the system, the two blocks always move together. (a) Find the coefficient of kinetic friction between the bigger block and the horizontal surface. (b) Find the frictional force acting on the smaller block. (c) Find the work done by the force of friction on the smaller block by the bigger block during a displacement d of the system.

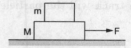

Figure 8-E1

11. A box weighing 2000 N is to be slowly slid through 20 m on a straight track having friction coefficient 0·2 with the box. (a) Find the work done by the person pulling the box with a chain at an angle θ with the horizontal. (b) Find the work when the person has chosen a value of θ which ensures him the minimum magnitude of the force.

12. A block of weight 100 N is slowly slid up on a smooth incline of inclination 37° by a person. Calculate the work done by the person in moving the block through a distance of 2·0 m, if the driving force is (a) parallel to the incline and (b) in the horizontal direction.

13. Find the average frictional force needed to stop a car weighing 500 kg in a distance of 25 m if the initial speed is 72 km/h.

14. Find the average force needed to accelerate a car weighing 500 kg from rest to 72 km/h in a distance of 25 m.

15. A particle of mass m moves on a straight line with its velocity varying with the distance travelled according to the equation $v = a\sqrt{x}$, where a is a constant. Find the total work done by all the forces during a displacement from $x = 0$ to $x = d$.

16. A block of mass 2·0 kg kept at rest on an inclined plane of inclination 37° is pulled up the plane by applying a constant force of 20 N parallel to the incline. The force acts for one second. (a) Show that the work done by the applied force does not exceed 40 J. (b) Find the work done by the force of gravity in that one second if the work done by the applied force is 40 J. (c) Find the kinetic energy of the block at the instant the force ceases to act. Take $g = 10$ m/s^2.

17. A block of mass 2·0 kg is pushed down an inclined plane of inclination 37° with a force of 20 N acting parallel to the incline. It is found that the block moves on the incline with an acceleration of 10 m/s^2. If the block

started from rest, find the work done (a) by the applied force in the first second, (b) by the weight of the block in the first second and (c) by the frictional force acting on the block in the first second. Take $g = 10$ m/s^2.

18. A 250 g block slides on a rough horizontal table. Find the work done by the frictional force in bringing the block to rest if it is initially moving at a speed of 40 cm/s. If the friction coefficient between the table and the block is 0·1, how far does the block move before coming to rest ?

19. Water falling from a 50 m high fall is to be used for generating electric energy. If $1·8 \times 10^5$ kg of water falls per hour and half the gravitational potential energy can be converted into electric energy, how many 100 W lamps can be lit ?

20. A person is painting his house walls. He stands on a ladder with a bucket containing paint in one hand and a brush in other. Suddenly the bucket slips from his hand and falls down on the floor. If the bucket with the paint had a mass of 6·0 kg and was at a height of 2·0 m at the time it slipped, how much gravitational potential energy is lost together with the paint ?

21. A projectile is fired from the top of a 40 m high cliff with an initial speed of 50 m/s at an unknown angle. Find its speed when it hits the ground.

22. The 200 m free style women's swimming gold medal at Seol Olympic 1988 went to Heike Friendrich of East Germany when she set a new Olympic record of 1 minute and 57·56 seconds. Assume that she covered most of the distance with a uniform speed and had to exert 460 W to maintain her speed. Calculate the average force of resistance offered by the water during the swim.

23. The US athlete Florence Griffith-Joyner won the 100 m sprint gold medal at Seol Olympic 1988 setting a new Olympic record of 10·54 s. Assume that she achieved her maximum speed in a very short-time and then ran the race with that speed till she crossed the line. Take her mass to be 50 kg. (a) Calculate the kinetic energy of Griffith-Joyner at her full speed. (b) Assuming that the track, the wind etc. offered an average resistance of one tenth of her weight, calculate the work done by the resistance during the run. (c) What power Griffith-Joyner had to exert to maintain uniform speed ?

24. A water pump lifts water from a level 10 m below the ground. Water is pumped at a rate of 30 kg/minute with negligible velocity. Calculate the minimum horsepower the engine should have to do this.

25. An unruly demonstrator lifts a stone of mass 200 g from the ground and throws it at his opponent. At the time of projection, the stone is 150 cm above the ground and has a speed of 3·00 m/s. Calculate the work done by the demonstrator during the process. If it takes one second for the demonstrator to lift the stone and throw, what horsepower does he use ?

26. In a factory it is desired to lift 2000 kg of metal through a distance of 12 m in 1 minute. Find the minimum horsepower of the engine to be used.

27. A scooter company gives the following specifications about its product.

Weight of the scooter — 95 kg
Maximum speed — 60 km/h
Maximum engine power — 3·5 hp
Pick up time to get the maximum speed — 5 s
Check the validity of these specifications.

28. A block of mass 30·0 kg is being brought down by a chain. If the block acquires a speed of 40·0 cm/s in dropping down 2·00 m, find the work done by the chain during the process.

29. The heavier block in an Atwood machine has a mass twice that of the lighter one. The tension in the string is 16·0 N when the system is set into motion. Find the decrease in the gravitational potential energy during the first second after the system is released from rest.

30. The two blocks in an Atwood machine have masses 2·0 kg and 3·0 kg. Find the work done by gravity during the fourth second after the system is released from rest.

31. Consider the situation shown in figure (8-E2). The system is released from rest and the block of mass 1·0 kg is found to have a speed 0·3 m/s after it has descended through a distance of 1 m. Find the coefficient of kinetic friction between the block and the table.

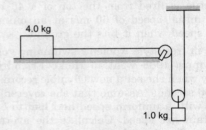

4.0 kg

1.0 kg

Figure 8-E2

32. A block of mass 100 g is moved with a speed of 5·0 m/s at the highest point in a closed circular tube of radius 10 cm kept in a vertical plane. The cross-section of the tube is such that the block just fits in it. The block makes several oscillations inside the tube and finally stops at the lowest point. Find the work done by the tube on the block during the process.

33. A car weighing 1400 kg is moving at a speed of 54 km/h up a hill when the motor stops. If it is just able to reach the destination which is at a height of 10 m above the point, calculate the work done against friction (negative of the work done by the friction).

34. A small block of mass 200 g is kept at the top of a frictionless incline which is 10 m long and 3·2 m high. How much work was required (a) to lift the block from the ground and put it at the top, (b) to slide the block up the incline ? What will be the speed of the block when it reaches the ground, if (c) it falls off the incline and drops vertically on the ground (d) it slides down the incline ? Take $g = 10$ m/s^2.

35. In a children's park, there is a slide which has a total length of 10 m and a height of 8·0 m (figure 8-E3). Vertical ladder are provided to reach the top. A boy weighing 200 N climbs up the ladder to the top of the slide and slides down to the ground. The average friction

offered by the slide is three tenth of his weight. Find (a) the work done by the boy on the ladder as he goes up, (b) the work done by the slide on the boy as he comes down, (c) the work done by the ladder on the boy as he goes up. Neglect any work done by forces inside the body of the boy.

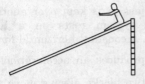

Figure 8-E3

36. Figure (8-E4) shows a particle sliding on a frictionless track which terminates in a straight horizontal section. If the particle starts slipping from the point A, how far away from the track will the particle hit the ground ?

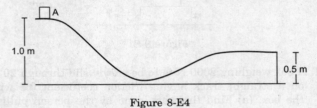

1.0 m

0.5 m

Figure 8-E4

37. A block weighing 10 N travels down a smooth curved track AB joined to a rough horizontal surface (figure 8-E5). The rough surface has a friction coefficient of 0·20 with the block. If the block starts slipping on the track from a point 1·0 m above the horizontal surface, how far will it move on the rough surface ?

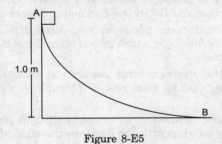

A

1.0 m

B

Figure 8-E5

38. A uniform chain of mass m and length l overhangs a table with its two third part on the table. Find the work to be done by a person to put the hanging part back on the table.

39. A uniform chain of length L and mass M overhangs a horizontal table with its two third part on the table. The friction coefficient between the table and the chain is μ. Find the work done by the friction during the period the chain slips off the table.

40. A block of mass 1 kg is placed at the point A of a rough track shown in figure (8-E6). If slightly pushed towards right, it stops at the point B of the track. Calculate the work done by the frictional force on the block during its transit from A to B.

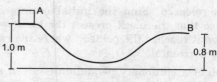

Figure 8-E6

41. A block of mass 5·0 kg is suspended from the end of a vertical spring which is stretched by 10 cm under the load of the block. The block is given a sharp impulse from below so that it acquires an upward speed of 2·0 m/s. How high will it rise ? Take $g = 10$ m/s^2.

42. A block of mass 250 g is kept on a vertical spring of spring constant 100 N/m fixed from below. The spring is now compressed to have a length 10 cm shorter than its natural length and the system is released from this position. How high does the block rise ? Take $g = 10$ m/s^2.

43. Figure (8-E7) shows a spring fixed at the bottom end of an incline of inclination 37°. A small block of mass 2 kg starts slipping down the incline from a point 4·8 m away from the spring. The block compresses the spring by 20 cm, stops momentarily and then rebounds through a distance of 1 m up the incline. Find (a) the friction coefficient between the plane and the block and (b) the spring constant of the spring. Take $g = 10$ m/s^2.

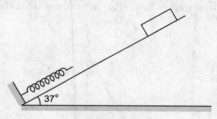

Figure 8-E7

44. A block of mass m moving at a speed v compresses a spring through a distance x before its speed is halved. Find the spring constant of the spring.

45. Consider the situation shown in figure (8-E8). Initially the spring is unstretched when the system is released from rest. Assuming no friction in the pulley, find the maximum elongation of the spring.

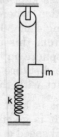

Figure 8-E8

46. A block of mass m is attached to two unstretched springs of spring constants k_1 and k_2 as shown in figure (8-E9). The block is displaced towards right through a distance

x and is released. Find the speed of the block as it passes through the mean position shown.

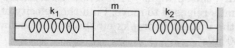

Figure 8-E9

47. A block of mass m sliding on a smooth horizontal surface with a velocity $\vec{v}$ meets a long horizontal spring fixed at one end and having spring constant k as shown in figure (8-E10). Find the maximum compression of the spring. Will the velocity of the block be the same as $\vec{v}$ when it comes back to the original position shown ?

Figure 8-E10

48. A small block of mass 100 g is pressed against a horizontal spring fixed at one end to compress the spring through 5·0 cm (figure 8-E11). The spring constant is 100 N/m. When released, the block moves horizontally till it leaves the spring. Where will it hit the ground 2 m below the spring ?

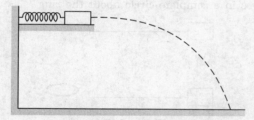

Figure 8-E11

49. A small heavy block is attached to the lower end of a light rod of length l which can be rotated about its clamped upper end. What minimum horizontal velocity should the block be given so that it moves in a complete vertical circle ?

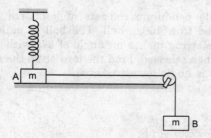

Figure 8-E12

50. Figure (8-E12) shows two blocks A and B, each having a mass of 320 g connected by a light string passing over a smooth light pulley. The horizontal surface on which the block A can slide is smooth. The block A is attached to a spring of spring constant 40 N/m whose other end is fixed to a support 40 cm above the horizontal surface. Initially, the spring is vertical and unstretched when the system is released to move. Find the velocity of the block A at the instant it breaks off the surface below it. Take $g = 10$ m/s^2.

51. One end of a spring of natural length h and spring constant k is fixed at the ground and the other is fitted with a smooth ring of mass m which is allowed to slide on a horizontal rod fixed at a height h (figure 8-E13). Initially, the spring makes an angle of 37° with the vertical when the system is released from rest. Find the speed of the ring when the spring becomes vertical.

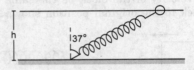

Figure 8-E13

52. Figure (8-E14) shows a light rod of length l rigidly attached to a small heavy block at one end and a hook at the other end. The system is released from rest with the rod in a horizontal position. There is a fixed smooth ring at a depth h below the initial position of the hook and the hook gets into the ring as it reaches there. What should be the minimum value of h so that the block moves in a complete circle about the ring ?

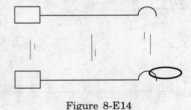

Figure 8-E14

53. The bob of a pendulum at rest is given a sharp hit to impart a horizontal velocity $\sqrt{10\,gl}$, where l is the length of the pendulum. Find the tension in the string when (a) the string is horizontal, (b) the bob is at its highest point and (c) the string makes an angle of 60° with the upward vertical.

54. A simple pendulum consists of a 50 cm long string connected to a 100 g ball. The ball is pulled aside so that the string makes an angle of 37° with the vertical and is then released. Find the tension in the string when the bob is at its lowest position.

Figure 8-E15

55. Figure (8-E15) shows a smooth track, a part of which is a circle of radius R. A block of mass m is pushed against a spring of spring constant k fixed at the left end and

is then released. Find the initial compression of the spring so that the block presses the track with a force mg when it reaches the point P, where the radius of the track is horizontal.

56. The bob of a stationary pendulum is given a sharp hit to impart it a horizontal speed of $\sqrt{3\,gl}$. Find the angle rotated by the string before it becomes slack.

57. A heavy particle is suspended by a 1·5 m long string. It is given a horizontal velocity of $\sqrt{57}$ m/s. (a) Find the angle made by the string with the upward vertical, when it becomes slack. (b) Find the speed of the particle at this instant. (c) Find the maximum height reached by the particle over the point of suspension. Take $g = 10$ m/s^2.

58. A simple pendulum of length L having a bob of mass m is deflected from its rest position by an angle θ and released (figure 8-E16). The string hits a peg which is fixed at a distance x below the point of suspension and the bob starts going in a circle centred at the peg. (a) Assuming that initially the bob has a height less than the peg, show that the maximum height reached by the bob equals its initial height. (b) If the pendulum is released with $\theta = 90°$ and $x = L/2$ find the maximum height reached by the bob above its lowest position before the string becomes slack. (c) Find the minimum value of x/L for which the bob goes in a complete circle about the peg when the pendulum is released from $\theta = 90°$.

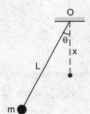

Figure 8-E16

59. A particle slides on the surface of a fixed smooth sphere starting from the topmost point. Find the angle rotated by the radius through the particle, when it leaves contact with the sphere.

60. A particle of mass m is kept on a fixed, smooth sphere of radius R at a position, where the radius through the particle makes an angle of 30° with the vertical. The particle is released from this position. (a) What is the force exerted by the sphere on the particle just after the release ? (b) Find the distance travelled by the particle before it leaves contact with the sphere.

61. A particle of mass m is kept on the top of a smooth sphere of radius R. It is given a sharp impulse which imparts it a horizontal speed v. (a) Find the normal force between the sphere and the particle just after the impulse. (b) What should be the minimum value of v for which the particle does not slip on the sphere ? (c) Assuming the velocity v to be half the minimum calculated in part (b) find the angle made by the radius

through the particle with the vertical when it leaves the sphere.

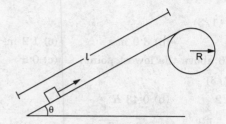

Figure 8-E17

62. Figure (8-E17) shows a smooth track which consists of a straight inclined part of length l joining smoothly with the circular part. A particle of mass m is projected up the incline from its bottom. (a) Find the minimum projection-speed v_0 for which the particle reaches the top of the track. (b) Assuming that the projection-speed is $2v_0$ and that the block does not lose contact with the track before reaching its top, find the force acting on it when it reaches the top. (c) Assuming that the projection-speed is only slightly greater than v_0, where will the block lose contact with the track ?

63. A chain of length l and mass m lies on the surface of a smooth sphere of radius $R > l$ with one end tied to the top of the sphere. (a) Find the gravitational potential energy of the chain with reference level at the centre of the sphere. (b) Suppose the chain is released and slides down the sphere. Find the kinetic energy of the chain, when it has slid through an angle θ. (c) Find the tangential acceleration $\dfrac{dv}{dt}$ of the chain when the chain starts sliding down.

64. A smooth sphere of radius R is made to translate in a straight line with a constant acceleration a. A particle kept on the top of the sphere is released from there at zero velocity with respect to the sphere. Find the speed of the particle with respect to the sphere as a function of the angle θ it slides.

□

ANSWERS

OBJECTIVE I

1. (d)   2. (b)   3. (d)   4. (c)   5. (a)   6. (b)
7. (c)   8. (c)   9. (d)   10. (c)

OBJECTIVE II

1. (a), (b)   2. (a)   3. (c), (d)
4. (d)   5. (a), (b), (d)   6. (a), (d)
7. (a), (d)   8. (b), (d)   9. (a), (b)
10. (b)

EXERCISES

1. 375 J
2. 625 J
3. − 400 J
4. 245 J
5. 6·25 J, 36·1 W
6. zero
7. 40 J
8. $\left(a + \dfrac{1}{2} bd\right) d$
9. 1·5 J
10. (a) $\dfrac{F}{2(M+m)g}$ (b) $\dfrac{mF}{2(M+m)}$ (c) $\dfrac{mFd}{2(M+m)}$
11. (a) $\dfrac{40000 \text{ J}}{5 + \tan\theta}$ (b) 7690 J

12. (a) 120 J   (b) 120 J
13. 4000 N
14. 4000 N
15. $ma^2 d/2$
16. (b) − 24 J   (c) 16 J
17. (a) 100 J   (b) 60 J   (c) − 60 J
18. − 0·02 J, 8·2 cm
19. 122
20. 118 J
21. 58 m/s
22. 270 N
23. (a) 2250 J   (b) − 4900 J   (c) 465 W
24. $6·6 \times 10^{-2}$ hp
25. 3·84 J, $5·14 \times 10^{-3}$ hp
26. 5·3 hp
27. Seems to be somewhat overclaimed.
28. − 586 J
29. 19·6 J
30. 67 J
31. 0·12
32. − 1·45 J
33. 20300 J
34. (a) 6·4 J   (b) 6·4 J   (c) 8·0 m/s   (d) 8·0 m/s
35. (a) zero   (b) − 600 J   (c) 1600 J
36. At a horizontal distance of 1 m from the end of the track.
37. 5·0 m

38. $mgl/18$

39. $-2\mu MgL/9$

40. -2 J

41. 20 cm

42. 20 cm

43. (a) 0·5   (b) 1000 N/m

44. $\dfrac{3\,mv^2}{4\,x^2}$

45. $2\,mg/k$

46. $\sqrt{\dfrac{k_1+k_2}{m}}\,x$

47. $v\sqrt{m/k}$, No

48. At a horizontal distance of 1 m from the free end of the spring.

49. $2\sqrt{gl}$

50. 1·5 m/s

51. $\dfrac{h}{4}\sqrt{k/m}$

52. l

53. (a) $8\,mg$ (b) $5\,mg$ (c) $6·5\,mg$

54. 1·4 N

55. $\sqrt{\dfrac{3\,mg\,R}{k}}$

56. $\cos^{-1}(-1/3)$

57. (a) 53°   (b) 3·0 m/s   (c) 1·2 m

58. (b) $5L/6$ above the lowest point   (c) 0·6

59. $\cos^{-1}(2/3)$

60. $\sqrt{3}\,mg/2$ (b) $0·43\,R$

61. (a) $mg-\dfrac{mv^2}{R}$ (b) $\sqrt{Rg}$ (c) $\cos^{-1}(3/4)$

62. (a) $\sqrt{2g\,[R(1-\cos\theta)+l\,\sin\theta]}$ (b) $6\,mg\left(1-\cos\theta+\dfrac{l}{R}\sin\theta\right)$

(c) The radius through the particle makes an angle $\cos^{-1}(2/3)$ with the vertical.

63. (a) $\dfrac{mR^2g}{l}\sin(l/R)$

(b) $\dfrac{mR^2g}{l}\left[\sin\left(\dfrac{l}{R}\right)+\sin\theta-\sin\left(\theta+\dfrac{l}{R}\right)\right]$

(c) $\dfrac{Rg}{l}[1-\cos(l/R)]$

64. $[2R(a\,\sin\theta+g-g\,\cos\theta)]^{1/2}$

□

CHAPTER 9

CENTRE OF MASS, LINEAR MOMENTUM, COLLISION

9.1 CENTRE OF MASS

Suppose a spin bowler throws a cricket ball vertically upward. Being a spinner, his fingers turn while throwing the ball and the ball goes up spinning rapidly. Focus your attention to a particular point on the surface of the ball. How does it move in the space ? Because the ball is spinning as well as rising up, in general, the path of a particle at the surface is complicated, not confined to a straight line or to a plane. The centre of the ball, however, still goes on the vertical straight line and the spinner's fingers could not make its path complicated. If he does not throw the ball vertically up, rather passes it to his fellow fielder, the centre of the ball goes in a parabola.

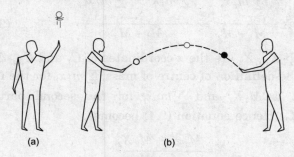

(a)   (b)

Figure 9.1

All the points of the ball do not go in parabolic paths. If the ball is spinning, the paths of most of the particles of the ball are complicated. But the centre of the ball always goes in a parabola irrespective of how the ball is thrown. (In fact the presence of air makes the path of the centre slightly different from a parabola and bowlers utilise this deviation. This effect will be discussed in a later chapter. At present we neglect it.)

The centre of the ball is a very special point which is called the *centre of mass* of the ball. Its motion is just like the motion of a single particle thrown.

Definition of Centre of Mass

Let us consider a collection of N particles (Figure 9.2). Let the mass of the ith particle be m_i and its coordinates with reference to the chosen axes be x_i, y_i, z_i. Write the product $m_i x_i$ for each of the particles and add them to get $\sum m_i x_i$. Similarly get $\sum_i m_i y_i$ and $\sum_i m_i z_i$. Then find

$$X = \frac{1}{M} \sum_i m_i x_i, \quad Y = \frac{1}{M} \sum_i m_i y_i \text{ and } Z = \frac{1}{M} \sum_i m_i z_i$$

where $M = \sum_i m_i$ is the total mass of the system.

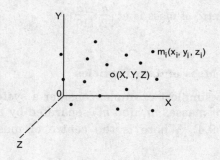

Figure 9.2

Locate the point with coordinates (X, Y, Z). This point is called the *centre of mass* of the given collection of the particles. If the position vector of the i th particle is $\vec{r_i}$, the centre of mass is defined to have the position vector

$$\vec{R}_{CM} = \frac{1}{M} \sum_i m_i \vec{r_i}. \qquad \dots (9.1)$$

Taking x, y, z components of this equation, we get the coordinates of centre of mass as defined above

$$X = \frac{1}{M} \sum_i m_i x_i, \quad Y = \frac{1}{M} \sum_i m_i y_i, \quad Z = \frac{1}{M} \sum_i m_i z_i \quad \dots (9.2)$$

Example 9.1

Four particles A, B, C and D having masses m, 2m, 3m and 4m respectively are placed in order at the corners of a square of side a. Locate the centre of mass.

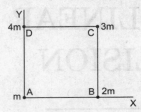

Figure 9.3

Solution : Take the axes as shown in figure (9.3). The coordinates of the four particles are as follows :

Particle	mass	x-coordinate	y-coordinate
A	m	0	0
B	$2m$	a	0
C	$3m$	a	a
D	$4m$	0	a

Hence, the coordinates of the centre of mass of the four-particle system are

$$X = \frac{m \cdot 0 + 2\,m\,a + 3\,m\,a + 4\,m \cdot 0}{m + 2\,m + 3\,m + 4\,m} = \frac{a}{2}$$

$$Y = \frac{m \cdot 0 + 2\,m \cdot 0 + 3\,m\,a + 4\,m\,a}{m + 2\,m + 3\,m + 4\,m} = \frac{7a}{10}$$

The centre of mass is at $\left(\dfrac{a}{2}, \dfrac{7a}{10}\right)$.

Centre of Mass of Two Particles

As the simplest example, consider a system of two particles of masses m_1 and m_2 separated by a distance d (figure 9.4). Where is the centre of mass of this system ?

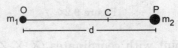

Figure 9.4

Take the origin at m_1 and the X-axis along the line joining m_1 and m_2. The coordinates of m_1 are $(0, 0, 0)$ and of m_2 are $(d, 0, 0)$. So,

$$\sum_i m_i x_i = m_1 0 + m_2 d = m_2 d, \quad \sum_i m_i y_i = 0, \quad \sum_i m_i z_i = 0.$$

The total mass is $M = m_1 + m_2$. By definition, the centre of mass will be at $\left(\dfrac{m_2 d}{m_1 + m_2}, 0, 0\right)$. We find that the centre of mass of a system of two particles is

situated on the line joining the particles. If O, C, P be the positions of m_1, the centre of mass and m_2 respectively, we have

$$OC = \frac{m_2 d}{m_1 + m_2} \quad \text{and} \quad CP = \frac{m_1 d}{m_1 + m_2}$$

so that $m_1(OC) = m_2(CP)$ ... (9.3)

The centre of mass divides internally the line joining the two particles in inverse ratio of their masses.

Centre of Mass of Several Groups of Particles

Consider a collection of $N_1 + N_2$ particles. We call the group of N_1 particles as the first part and the other group of N_2 particles as the second part. Suppose the first part has its centre of mass at C_1 and the total mass M_1 (figure 9.5). Similarly the second part has its centre of mass at C_2 and the total mass M_2. Where is the centre of mass of the system of $N_1 + N_2$ particles ?

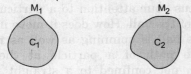

Figure 9.5

The x-coordinate of the centre of mass is

$$X = \frac{\sum_{i=1}^{N_1+N_2} m_i x_i}{M_1 + M_2} = \frac{\sum_{i=1}^{N_1} m_i x_i + \sum_{i=N_1+1}^{N_1+N_2} m_i x_i}{M_1 + M_2}. \quad \text{... (9.4)}$$

If X_1, X_2 are the x-coordinates of C_1 and C_2, then by the definition of centre of mass, $\sum m_i x_i$ for the first part is $M_1 X_1$ and $\sum m_i x_i$ for the second part is $M_2 X_2$. Hence equation (9.4) becomes,

$$X = \frac{M_1 X_1 + M_2 X_2}{M_1 + M_2}$$

Similarly, $Y = \dfrac{M_1 Y_1 + M_2 Y_2}{M_1 + M_2}$

and $Z = \dfrac{M_1 Z_1 + M_2 Z_2}{M_1 + M_2}$.

But this is also the centre of mass of two point particles of masses M_1 and M_2 placed at C_1 and C_2 respectively. Thus, we obtain a very useful result. *If we know the centres of mass of parts of the system and their masses, we can get the combined centre of mass by treating the parts as point particles placed at their respective centres of mass.*

Example 9.2

Two identical uniform rods AB and CD, each of length L are jointed to form a T-shaped frame as shown in figure (9.6). Locate the centre of mass of the frame. The centre of mass of a uniform rod is at the middle point of the rod.

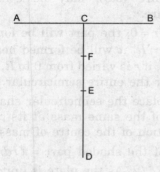

Figure 9.6

Solution : Let the mass of each rod be m. Take the centre C of the rod AB as the origin and CD as the Y-axis. The rod AB has mass m and its centre of mass is at C. For the calculation of the centre of mass of the combined system, AB may be replaced by a point particle of mass m placed at the point C. Similarly the rod CD may be replaced by a point particle of mass m placed at the centre E of the rod CD. Thus, the frame is equivalent to a system of two particles of equal masses m each, placed at C and E. The centre of mass of this pair of particles will be at the middle point F of CE.

The centre of mass of the frame is, therefore, on the rod CD at a distance $L/4$ from C.

9.2 CENTRE OF MASS OF CONTINUOUS BODIES

If we consider the body to have continuous distribution of matter, the summation in the formula of centre of mass should be replaced by integration. So, we do not talk of the ith particle, rather we talk of a small element of the body having a mass dm. If x, y, z are the coordinates of this small mass dm, we write the coordinates of the centre of mass as

$$X = \frac{1}{M} \int x\, dm, \quad Y = \frac{1}{M} \int y\, dm, \quad Z = \frac{1}{M} \int z\, dm. \quad \dots \ (9.5)$$

The integration is to be performed under proper limits so that as the integration variable goes through the limits, the elements cover the entire body. We illustrate the method with three examples.

(a) Centre of Mass of a Uniform Straight Rod

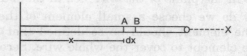

Figure 9.7

Let M and L be the mass and the length of the rod respectively. Take the left end of the rod as the origin and the X-axis along the rod (figure 9.7). Consider an element of the rod between the positions x and $x + dx$. If $x = 0$, the element is at the left end of the rod. If $x = L$, the element is at its right end. So as x varies from 0 through L, the elements cover the entire rod. As the rod is uniform, the mass per unit length is M/L and hence the mass of the element is $dm = (M/L)\, dx$. The coordinates of the element are $(x, 0, 0)$. (The coordinates of different points of the element differ, but the difference is less than dx and that much is harmless as integration will automatically correct it. So x-coordinate of the left end of the element may be called the "x-coordinate of the element.")

The x-coordinate of the centre of mass of the rod is

$$X = \frac{1}{M} \int x\, dm = \frac{1}{M} \int_0^L x \left(\frac{M}{L}\, dx\right)$$

$$= \frac{1}{L}\left[\frac{x^2}{2}\right]_0^L = \frac{L}{2}.$$

The y-coordinate is

$$Y = \frac{1}{M} \int y\, dm = 0$$

and similarly $Z = 0$. The centre of mass is at $\left(\frac{L}{2}, 0, 0\right)$, i.e., at the middle point of the rod.

(b) Centre of Mass of a Uniform Semicircular Wire

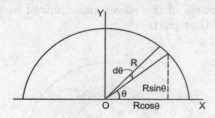

Figure 9.8

Let M be the mass and R the radius of a uniform semicircular wire. Take its centre as the origin, the line joining the ends as the X-axis, and the Y-axis in the plane of the wire (figure 9.8). The centre of mass must be in the plane of the wire i.e., in the X-Y plane.

How do we choose a small element of the wire? First, the element should be so defined that we can vary the element to cover the whole wire. Secondly, if we are interested in $\int x \, dm$, the x-coordinates of different parts of the element should only infinitesimally differ in range. We select the element as follows. Take a radius making an angle θ with the X-axis and rotate it further by an angle $d\theta$. Note the points of intersection of the radius with the wire during this rotation. This gives an element of length $R \, d\theta$. When we take $\theta = 0$, the element is situated near the right edge of the wire. As θ is gradually increased to π, the element takes all positions on the wire i.e., the whole wire is covered. The "coordinates of the element" are $(R \cos\theta, R \sin\theta)$. Note that the coordinates of different parts of the element differ only by an infinitesimal amount.

As the wire is uniform, the mass per unit length of the wire is $\dfrac{M}{\pi R}$. The mass of the element is, therefore,

$$dm = \left(\frac{M}{\pi R} \right)(R \, d\theta) = \frac{M}{\pi} \, d\theta.$$

The coordinates of the centre of mass are

$$X = \frac{1}{M} \int x \, dm = \frac{1}{M} \int_0^\pi (R \cos\theta) \left(\frac{M}{\pi} \right) d\theta = 0$$

and

$$Y = \frac{1}{M} \int y \, dm = \frac{1}{M} \int_0^\pi (R \sin\theta) \left(\frac{M}{\pi} \right) d\theta = \frac{2R}{\pi}$$

The centre of mass is at $\left(0, \dfrac{2R}{\pi} \right)$.

(c) Centre of Mass of a Uniform Semicircular Plate

This problem can be worked out using the result obtained for the semicircular wire and that any part of the system (semicircular plate) may be replaced by a point particle of the same mass placed at the centre of mass of that part.

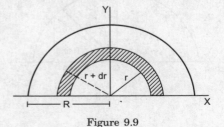

Figure 9.9

Figure (9.9) shows the semicircular plate. We take the origin at the centre of the semicircular plate, the X-axis along the straight edge and the Y-axis in the plane of the plate. Let M be the mass and R be its radius. Let us draw a semicircle of radius r on the plate with the centre at the origin. We increase r to $r + dr$ and draw another semicircle with the same centre. Consider the part of the plate between the two semicircles of radii r and $r + dr$. This part, shown shaded in figure (9.9), may be considered as a semicircular wire.

If we take $r = 0$, the part will be formed near the centre and if $r = R$, it will be formed near the edge of the plate. Thus, if r is varied from 0 to R, the elemental parts will cover the entire semicircular plate.

We can replace the semicircular shaded part by a point particle of the same mass at its centre of mass for the calculation of the centre of mass of the plate.

The area of the shaded part $= \pi r \, dr$. The area of the plate is $\pi R^2 / 2$. As the plate is uniform, the mass per unit area is $\dfrac{M}{\pi R^2 / 2}$. Hence the mass of the semicircular element

$$\frac{M}{\pi R^2 / 2} (\pi r \, dr) = \frac{2 M r \, dr}{R^2}.$$

The y-coordinate of the centre of mass of this wire is $2r/\pi$. The y-coordinate of the centre of mass of the plate is, therefore,

$$Y = \frac{1}{M} \int_0^R \left(\frac{2r}{\pi} \right) \left(\frac{2 M r}{R^2} \, dr \right) = \frac{1}{M} \cdot \frac{4 M}{\pi R^2} \frac{R^3}{3} = \frac{4 R}{3 \pi}.$$

The x-coordinate of the centre of mass is zero by symmetry.

9.3 MOTION OF THE CENTRE OF MASS

Consider two particles A and B of masses m_1 and m_2 respectively. Take the line joining A and B as the X-axis. Let the coordinates of the particles at time t be x_1 and x_2. Suppose no external force acts on the two-particle-system. The particles A and B, however, exert forces on each other and the particles accelerate along the line joining them. Suppose the particles are initially at rest and the force between them is attractive. The particles will then move along the line AB as shown in figure (9.10).

Figure 9.10

The centre of mass at time t is situated at

$$X = \frac{m_1 x_1 + m_2 x_2}{m_1 + m_2}.$$

As time passes, x_1, x_2 change and hence X changes and the centre of mass moves along the X-axis. Velocity of the centre of mass at time t is

$$V_{CM} = \frac{dx}{dt} = \frac{m_1 v_1 + m_2 v_2}{m_1 + m_2}. \qquad \ldots (9.6)$$

The acceleration of the centre of mass is

$$a_{CM} = \frac{dV_{CM}}{dt} = \frac{m_1 a_1 + m_2 a_2}{m_1 + m_2}. \qquad \ldots (9.7)$$

Suppose the magnitude of the forces between the particles is F. As the only force acting on A is F towards B, its acceleration is $a_1 = F/m_1$. The force on B is $(-F)$ and hence $a_2 = -F/m_2$

Putting in (9.7),

$$a_{CM} = \frac{m_1(F/m_1) + m_2(-F/m_2)}{m_1 + m_2} = 0.$$

That means, the velocity of the centre of mass does not change with time. But as we assumed, initially the particles are at rest. Thus, at this instant, $v_1 = v_2 = 0$ and from (9.5) $V_{CM} = 0$. Hence the centre of mass remains fixed and does not change with time.

Thus, *if no external force acts on a two-particle-system and its centre of mass is at rest (say in the inertial frame A) initially, it remains fixed (in the inertial frame A) even when the particles individually move and accelerate.* Let us now generalise this result.

Consider a system of N particles, the ith particle having a mass m_i and the position vector $\vec{r_i}$ with respect to an inertial frame. Each particle is acted upon by forces due to all other $(N-1)$ particles and forces due to the sources outside the system. The acceleration of the ith particle is

$$\vec{a_i} = \frac{1}{m_i} \left(\sum_{j \neq i} \vec{F_{ij}} + \vec{F_i}^{\,ext} \right) \text{(Newton's second law)}$$

or, $$m_i \vec{a_i} = \left(\sum_{j \neq i} \vec{F_{ij}} + \vec{F_i}^{\,ext} \right).$$

Here $\vec{F_{ij}}$ is the force on the ith particle due to the jth particle and $\vec{F_i}^{\,ext}$ is the vector sum of the forces acting on the ith particle by the external sources. Summing over all the particles

$$\sum_i m_i \vec{a_i} = \sum_{i \neq j} \sum_j \vec{F_{ij}} + \sum_i \vec{F_i}^{\,ext} = \vec{F}^{\,ext}. \qquad \ldots (9.8)$$

The internal forces $\vec{F_{ij}}$ add up to zero as they cancel in pairs ($\vec{F_{ij}} + \vec{F_{ji}} = 0$) by Newton's third law. $\vec{F}^{\,ext}$ is the sum of all the forces acting on all the particles by the external sources.

Now $\sum_i m_i \vec{r_i} = M \vec{R_{CM}}$ giving $\sum_i m_i \vec{a_i} = M \vec{a_{CM}}$

Putting in (9.8),

$$M \vec{a_{CM}} = \vec{F}^{\,ext}. \qquad \ldots (9.9)$$

If the external forces acting on the system add to zero, $\vec{a_{CM}} = 0$ and hence the velocity of the centre of mass is constant. If initially the centre of mass was at rest with respect to an inertial frame, it will continue to be at rest with respect to that frame. The individual particles may go on complicated paths changing their positions, but the centre of mass will be obtained at the same position.

If the centre of mass was moving with respect to the inertial frame at a speed v along a particular direction, it will continue its motion along the same straight line with the same speed. Thus, *the motion of the centre of mass of the system is not affected by the internal forces. If the external forces add up to zero, the centre of mass has no acceleration.*

Example 9.3

Two charged particles of masses m and 2m are placed a distance d apart on a smooth horizontal table. Because of their mutual attraction, they move towards each other and collide. Where will the collision occur with respect to the initial positions ?

Solution : As the table is smooth, there is no friction. The weight of the particles and the normal force balance each other as there is no motion in the vertical direction. Thus, taking the two particles as constituting the system, the sum of the external forces acting on the system is zero. The forces of attraction between the particles are the internal forces as we have included both the particles in the system. Therefore, the centre of mass of the system will have no acceleration.

Initially, the two particles are placed on the table and their velocities are zero. The velocity of the centre of mass is, therefore, zero. As time passes, the particles move, but the centre of mass will continue to be at the same place. At the time of collision, the two particles are at one place and the centre of mass will also be at that place. As the centre of mass does not move, the collision will take place at the centre of mass.

The centre of mass will be at a distance $2d/3$ from the initial position of the particle of mass m towards the other particle and the collision will take place there.

When the external forces do not add up to zero, the centre of mass is accelerated and the acceleration is given by equation (9.9)

$$\vec{a_{CM}} = \frac{\vec{F}^{\,ext}}{M}.$$

If we have a single particle of mass M on which a force $\vec{F}^{\,ext}$ acts, its acceleration would be the same as

$\dfrac{\vec{F}^{\,ext}}{M}$. Thus *the motion of the centre of mass of a system is identical to the motion of a single particle of mass equal to the mass of the given system, acted upon by the same external forces that act on the system.*

To explain this statement, once again consider the spinning ball of figure (9.1b). The ball is spinning and at the same time moving under gravity. To find the motion of the centre of mass of the ball, which is actually the centre of the ball, we imagine a particle of mass equal to that of the ball. We throw this particle with the velocity v, which the centre of mass had at the time of projection. What is the motion of this single particle of mass M subjected to the force Mg downward, thrown initially with velocity v? It is a parabolic motion, given by,

$$x = v_x\, t, \quad y = v_y\, t - \tfrac{1}{2} g t^{\,2}. \qquad \ldots (9.10)$$

The centre of the ball exactly traces this curve with coordinates given by this equation only.

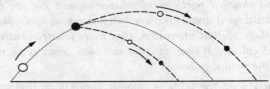

Figure 9.11

Next, suppose the ball breaks up into two parts (figure 9.11) because of some internal stress, while moving along the parabola. The two parts go on two different parabolae because the velocities of the parts change at the instant of breaking. Locate the two parts at some instant t and calculate the position of the centre of mass of the combination at that instant. It will be found at the same point on the original parabola where the centre would have been at the instant t according to equation (9.10).

9.4 LINEAR MOMENTUM AND ITS CONSERVATION PRINCIPLE

The (linear) momentum of a particle is defined as $\vec{p} = m\vec{v}$. The momentum of an N-particle system is the (vector) sum of the momenta of the N particles i.e.,

$$\vec{P} = \sum_i \vec{p}_i = \sum_i m_i \vec{v}_i.$$

But $\displaystyle\sum_i m_i \vec{v}_i = \frac{d}{dt}\sum_i m_i \vec{r}_i = \frac{d}{dt} M \vec{R}_{CM} = M \vec{V}_{CM}.$

Thus, $\qquad\qquad \vec{P} = M \vec{V}_{CM}. \qquad \ldots (9.11)$

As we have seen, if the external forces acting on the system add up to zero, the centre of mass moves with constant velocity, which means $\vec{P}$ = constant. Thus the

linear momentum of a system remains constant (in magnitude and direction) if the external forces acting on the system add up to zero. This is known as *the principle of conservation of linear momentum.*

Consider a trivial example of a single particle on which no force acts (imagine a practical situation where this can be achieved). Looking from an inertial frame, the particle is moving with uniform velocity and so its momentum remains constant as time passes.

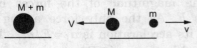

Figure 9.12

As a different example, consider a radioactive nucleus at rest which emits an alpha particle along the X-axis. Let m and M be the masses of the alpha particle and the residual nucleus respectively. Take the entire nucleus as the system. The alpha particle is ejected from the nucleus because of the forces between the neutrons and protons of the nucleus (this is the nuclear force and not gravitational or electromagnetic). There is no external force acting on the system and hence its linear momentum should not change. The linear momentum before the emission was zero as the nucleus was at rest. After the emission, the system is broken up into two parts, the alpha particle and the residual nucleus. If the alpha particle is emitted with a speed v, the residual nucleus must recoil in the opposite direction with a speed V, so that

$$M \vec{V} + m \vec{v} = 0 \quad \text{or,} \quad \vec{V} = -\frac{m}{M} \vec{v}.$$

9.5 ROCKET PROPULSION

In a rocket, the fuel burns and produces gases at high temperatures. These gases are ejected out of the rocket from a nozzle at the backside of the rocket. The ejecting gas exerts a forward force on the rocket which helps it in accelerating.

Suppose, a rocket together with its fuel has a mass M_0 at $t = 0$. Let the gas be ejected at a constant rate $r = -\dfrac{dM}{dt}$. Also suppose, the gas is ejected at a constant velocity u with respect to the rocket.

At time t, the mass of the rocket together with the remaining fuel is

$$M = M_0 - rt.$$

If the velocity of the rocket at time t is v, the linear momemtum of this mass M is

$$P = Mv = (M_0 - rt)v. \qquad \ldots (i)$$

Consider a small time interval Δt. A mass $\Delta M = r\Delta t$ of the gas is ejected in this time and the velocity of the rocket becomes $v + \Delta v$. The velocity of the gas with respect to ground is

$$\vec{v}_{\text{gas, ground}} = \vec{v}_{\text{gas, rocket}} + \vec{v}_{\text{rocket, ground}}$$

$$= -u + v$$

in the forward direction.

The linear momentum of the mass M at $t + \Delta t$ is,

$$(M - \Delta M)(v + \Delta v) + \Delta M(v - u). \qquad \text{... (ii)}$$

Assuming no external force on the rocket-fuel system, from (i) and (ii),

$$(M - \Delta M)(v + \Delta v) + \Delta M(v - u) = Mv$$

or, $$(M - \Delta M)(\Delta v) = (\Delta M)u$$

or, $$\Delta v = \frac{(\Delta M)u}{M - \Delta M}$$

or, $$\frac{\Delta v}{\Delta t} = \frac{\Delta M}{\Delta t} \frac{u}{M - \Delta M} = \frac{ru}{M - r\Delta t}$$

Taking the limit as $\Delta t \to 0$,

$$\frac{dv}{dt} = \frac{ru}{M} = \frac{ru}{M_0 - rt}.$$

This gives the acceleration of the rocket. We see that the acceleration keeps on increasing as time passes. If the rocket starts at $t = 0$ and we neglect any external force such as gravity,

$$\int_0^v dv = ru \int_0^t \frac{dt}{M_0 - rt}$$

or, $$v = ru\left(-\frac{1}{r}\right)\ln\frac{M_0 - rt}{M_0}$$

or, $$v = u\ln\frac{M_0}{M_0 - rt}.$$

9.6 COLLISION

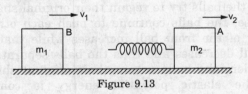

Figure 9.13

Consider the situation shown in figure (9.13). Two blocks of masses m_1 and m_2 are moving on the same straight line on a frictionless horizontal table. The block m_2, which is ahead of m_1, is going with a speed v_2 smaller than the speed v_1 of m_1. A spring is attached to the rear end of m_2. Since $v_1 > v_2$, the block m_1 will touch the rear of the spring at some instant, say t_1. Then onwards, the velocity of the left end of the spring will be equal to the velocity of m_1 (as they are in contact). The velocity of the right end of the spring will be same as that of m_2 (as they are in contact). Since m_1 moves faster than m_2, the length of the

spring will decrease. The spring will be compressed. As it is compressed, it pushes back both the blocks with forces kx where x is the compression and k, the spring constant. This force is in the direction of the velocity of m_2, hence m_2 will accelerate. However, this is opposite to the velocity of m_1 and so m_1 will decelerate. The velocity of the front block A (which was slower initially) will gradually increase, and the velocity of the rear block B (which was faster initially) will gradually decrease. The spring will continue to become more and more compressed as long as the rear block B is faster than the front block A. There will be an instant $t_1 + \Delta t_1$, when the two blocks will have equal velocities. At this instant, both the ends of the spring will move with the same velocity and no further compression will take place. This corresponds to the maximum compression of the spring. Thus, "the spring-compression is maximum when the two blocks attain equal velocities".

Now, the spring being already compressed, it continues to push back the two blocks. Thus, the front block A will still be accelerated and the rear block B will still be decelerated. At $t_1 + \Delta t_1$ the velocities were equal and hence, after $t_1 + \Delta t_1$ the front block will move faster than the rear block. And so do the ends of the spring as they are in contact with the blocks. The spring will thus increase its length. This process will continue till the spring acquires its natural length, say at a time $t_1 + \Delta t_1 + \Delta t_2$. Once the spring regains its natural length, it stops exerting any force on the blocks. As the two blocks are moving with different velocities by this time, the rear one slower, the rear block will leave contact with the spring and the blocks will move with constant velocities. Their separation will go on increasing.

During the whole process, the momentum of the two-blocks system remains constant. The momentum before the instant t_1 was $m_1v_1 + m_2v_2 = P$. At time $t_1 + \Delta t_1$, the two blocks have equal velocities say V and we have $m_1V + m_2V = P$. After the contact is broken, the blocks finally attain constant velocities v_1' and $v_2'(v_2' > v_1')$ and the momentum will be $m_1v_1' + m_2v_2' = P$. In fact, take the velocities of the blocks at any instant, before the collision, during the collision or after the collision; the momentum will be equal to P. This is because there is no resultant external force acting on the system. Note that the spring being massless, exerts equal and opposite forces on the blocks.

Next, consider the energy of the system. As there is no friction anywhere, the sum of the kinetic energy and the elastic potential energy remains constant. The gravitational potential energy does not come into the picture, as the motion is horizontal. The elastic potential energy is $\frac{1}{2} k x^2$ when the spring is compressed by x. If u_1 and u_2 are the speeds at this time, we have,

$$\frac{1}{2} m_1 u_1^2 + \frac{1}{2} m_2 u_2^2 + \frac{1}{2} k x^2 = E$$

where E is the total energy of the system.

At and before $t = t_1$, the spring is at its natural length so that,

$$\frac{1}{2} m_1 v_1^2 + \frac{1}{2} m_2 v_2^2 = E. \qquad \dots \text{(i)}$$

At time $t = t_1 + \Delta t_1$, $u_1 = u_2 = V$ and the compression of the spring is maximum. Thus,

$$\frac{1}{2} (m_1 + m_2) V^2 + \frac{1}{2} k x_{\max}^2 = E.$$

At and after $t = t_1 + \Delta t_1 + \Delta t_2$, the spring acquires its natural length, so that,

$$\frac{1}{2} m_1 v_1'^2 + \frac{1}{2} m_2 v_2'^2 = E. \qquad \dots \text{(ii)}$$

From (i) and (ii),

$$\frac{1}{2} m_1 v_1^2 + \frac{1}{2} m_2 v_2^2 = \frac{1}{2} m_1 v_1'^2 + \frac{1}{2} m_2 v_2'^2.$$

The kinetic energy before the collision is the same as the kinetic energy after the collision. However, we can not say that the kinetic energy remains constant because it changes as a function of time, during the interval t_1 to $t_1 + \Delta t_1 + \Delta t_2$.

Example 9.4

Each of the blocks shown in figure (9.14) has mass 1 kg. The rear block moves with a speed of 2 m/s towards the front block kept at rest. The spring attached to the front block is light and has a spring constant 50 N/m. Find the maximum compression of the spring.

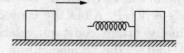

Figure 9.14

Solution : Maximum compression will take place when the blocks move with equal velocity. As no net external force acts on the system of the two blocks, the total linear momentum will remain constant. If V is the common speed at maximum compression, we have,

$$(1 \text{ kg}) (2 \text{ m/s}) = (1 \text{ kg}) V + (1 \text{ kg}) V$$

or, $\qquad\qquad V = 1 \text{ m/s}.$

Initial kinetic energy $= \frac{1}{2} (1 \text{ kg}) (2 \text{ m/s})^2 = 2 \text{ J}$

Final kinetic energy

$$= \frac{1}{2} (1 \text{ kg}) (1 \text{ m/s})^2 + \frac{1}{2} (1 \text{ kg}) (1 \text{ m/s})^2$$

$$= 1 \text{ J}.$$

The kinetic energy lost is stored as the elastic energy in the spring.

Hence, $\frac{1}{2} (50 \text{ N/m}) x^2 = 2 \text{ J} - 1 \text{ J} = 1 \text{ J}$

or, $\qquad\qquad x = 0\cdot2 \text{ m}.$

Almost similar is the situation when two balls collide with each other and no spring is put between them (figure 9.15). At the instant they come into contact, the rear ball has a larger velocity v_1 and the front ball has a smaller velocity v_2. But the surfaces in contact must move equal distance in any time interval as long as they remain in contact. The balls have to be deformed at the contact.

Figure 9.15

The deformed balls push each other and the velocities of the two balls change. The total kinetic energy of the two balls decreases as some energy is converted into the elastic potential energy of the deformed balls. The deformation is maximum (and the kinetic energy minimum) when the two balls attain equal velocities. Total momentum of the balls remains constant. The behaviour of the balls after this depends on the nature of the materials of the balls. If the balls are perfectly elastic, forces may develop inside them so that the balls try to regain their original shapes. In this case, the balls continue to push each other, the velocity of the front ball increases while that of the rear ball decreases and thus the balls separate. After separation, the balls regain their original shapes so that the elastic potential energy is completely converted back into kinetic energy. Thus, although the kinetic energy is not constant, the initial kinetic energy is equal to the final kinetic energy. Such a collision is called an *elastic collision*.

On the contrary, if the materials of the balls are *perfectly inelastic*, the balls have no tendency to regain their original shapes after maximum deformation. As a result, they do not push each other and continue to move with the common velocity with their deformed shapes. The kinetic energy decreases at the time of deformation and thereafter remains constant at this decreased value. Such a collision is called an *inelastic collision*.

If the material is *partially elastic,* the balls try to regain their original shapes, they push each other, even after maximum deformation. The velocities further change, the balls separate but the shapes are not completely recovered. Some energy remains inside the deformed ball. The final kinetic energy is, therefore, less than the initial kinetic energy. But the loss of kinetic energy is not as large as that in the case of a perfectly inelastic collision.

Thus, for an elastic collision,

$$m_1\vec{v_1} + m_2\vec{v_2} = m_1\vec{v_1}' + m_2\vec{v_2}' \left.\vphantom{\frac{1}{2}}\right| $$
$$\text{and } \frac{1}{2}m_1v_1^{\,2} + \frac{1}{2}m_2v_2^{\,2} = \frac{1}{2}m_1v_1'^{\,2} + \frac{1}{2}m_2v_2'^{\,2} \quad \dots \ (9.12)$$

i.e., $\qquad K_f = K_i$.

For an inelastic collision, $\vec{v_1}' = \vec{v_2}' = \vec{V}$,

$$m_1\vec{v_1} + m_2\vec{v_2} = m_1\vec{V} + m_2\vec{V} \qquad \dots \ (9.13)$$

and $\qquad K_f < K_i$.

For a partially elastic collision,

$$m_1\vec{v_1} + m_2\vec{v_2} = m_1\vec{v_1}' + m_2\vec{v_2}'$$
$$K_f < K_i, \quad \Delta K = K_i - K_f$$

is the loss of kinetic energy. It is less than that in the case of a perfectly inelastic collision. For one dimensional collision (head-on collision) the vector sign may be removed.

9.7 ELASTIC COLLISION IN ONE DIMENSION

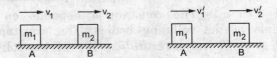

Figure 9.16

Consider two elastic bodies A and B moving along the same line (figure 9.16). The body A has a mass m_1 and moves with a velocity v_1 towards right and the body B has a mass m_2 and moves with a velocity v_2 in the same direction. We assume $v_1 > v_2$ so that the two bodies may collide. Let v_1' and v_2' be the final velocities of the bodies after the collision. The total linear momentum of the two bodies remains constant, so that,

$$m_1v_1 + m_2v_2 = m_1v_1' + m_2v_2' \qquad \dots \ (i)$$

or, $\quad m_1v_1 - m_1v_1' = m_2v_2' - m_2v_2$

or, $\quad m_1(v_1 - v_1') = m_2(v_2' - v_2). \qquad \dots \ (ii)$

Also, since the collision is elastic, the kinetic energy before the collision is equal to the kinetic energy after the collision. Hence,

$$\frac{1}{2}m_1v_1^{\,2} + \frac{1}{2}m_2v_2^{\,2} = \frac{1}{2}m_1v_1'^{\,2} + \frac{1}{2}m_2v_2'^{\,2}$$

or, $\quad m_1v_1^{\,2} - m_1v_1'^{\,2} = m_2v_2'^{\,2} - m_2v_2^{\,2}$

or, $\qquad m_1(v_1^{\,2} - v_1'^{\,2}) = m_2(v_2'^{\,2} - v_2^{\,2}). \qquad \dots \ (iii)$

Dividing (iii) by (ii),

$$v_1 + v_1' = v_2' + v_2$$

or, $\qquad v_1 - v_2 = v_2' - v_1'. \qquad \dots \ (iv)$

Now, $(v_1 - v_2)$ is the rate at which the separation between the bodies decreases before the collision. Similarly, $(v_2' - v_1')$ is the rate of increase of separation after the collision. So the equation (iv) may be written as

Velocity of separation (after collision)

= *Velocity of approach (before collision).* ... (9.14)

This result is very useful in solving problems involving elastic collision. The final velocities v_1' and v_2' may be obtained from equation (i) and (iv). Multiply equation (iv) by m_2 and subtract from equation (i).

$$2m_2v_2 + (m_1 - m_2)v_1 = (m_1 + m_2)v_1'$$

or, $\quad v_1' = \dfrac{(m_1 - m_2)}{m_1 + m_2}v_1 + \dfrac{2m_2}{m_1 + m_2}v_2. \qquad \dots \ (9.15)$

Now multiply equation (iv) by m_1 and add to equation (i),

$$2m_1v_1 - (m_1 - m_2)v_2 = (m_2 + m_1)v_2'$$

or, $\quad v_2' = \dfrac{2m_1v_1}{m_1 + m_2} - \dfrac{(m_1 - m_2)v_2}{m_1 + m_2}. \qquad \dots \ (9.16)$

Equations (9.15) and (9.16) give the final velocities in terms of the initial velocities and the masses.

Special cases :

(a) Elastic collision between a heavy body and a light body :

Let $m_1 \gg m_2$. A heavy body hits a light body from behind.

We have,

$$\frac{m_1 - m_2}{m_1 + m_2} \approx 1, \quad \frac{2m_2}{m_1 + m_2} \approx 0$$

and $\qquad \dfrac{2m_1}{m_1 + m_2} \approx 2$.

With these approximations the final velocities of the bodies are, from (9.15) and (9.16),

$$v_1' \approx v_1 \text{ and } v_2' \approx 2v_1 - v_2.$$

The heavier body continues to move with almost the same velocity. If the lighter body were kept at rest $v_2 = 0$, $v_2' = 2v_1$ which means the lighter body, after getting a push from the heavier body will fly away with a velocity double the velocity of the heavier body.

Next suppose $m_2 \gg m_1$. A light body hits a heavy body from behind.

We have,

$$\frac{m_1 - m_2}{m_1 + m_2} \approx -1$$

$$\frac{2m_2}{m_1 + m_2} \approx 2$$

and

$$\frac{2m_1}{m_1 + m_2} \approx 0$$

The final velocities of the bodies are, from (9.15) and (9.16),

$$v_1' \approx -v_1 + 2v_2 \quad \text{and} \quad v_2' \approx v_2.$$

The heavier body continues to move with almost the same velocity, the velocity of the lighter body changes. If the heavier body were at rest, $v_2 = 0$ then $v_1' = -v_1$, the lighter body returns after collision with almost the same speed. This is the case when a ball collides elastically with a fixed wall and returns with the same speed.

(b) Elastic collision of two bodies of equal mass :

Putting $m_1 = m_2$ in equation (9.15) and (9.16)

$$v_1' = v_2 \quad \text{and} \quad v_2' = v_1.$$

When two bodies of equal mass collide elastically, their velocities are mutually interchanged.

9.8 PERFECTLY INELASTIC COLLISION IN ONE DIMENSION

Final Velocity

When perfectly inelastic bodies moving along the same line collide, they stick to each other. Let m_1 and m_2 be the masses, v_1 and v_2 be their velocities before the collision and V be the common velocity of the bodies after the collision. By the conservation of linear momentum,

$$m_1 v_1 + m_2 v_2 = m_1 V + m_2 V$$

or,

$$V = \frac{m_1 v_1 + m_2 v_2}{m_1 + m_2}. \qquad \ldots \text{ (i)}$$

Loss in Kinetic Energy

The kinetic energy before the collision is

$$\frac{1}{2} m_1 v_1^2 + \frac{1}{2} m_2 v_2^2$$

and that after the collision is $\frac{1}{2}(m_1 + m_2)V^2$. Using equation (i), the loss in kinetic energy due to the collision is

$$\frac{1}{2} m_1 v_1^2 + \frac{1}{2} m_2 v_2^2 - \frac{1}{2}(m_1 + m_2)V^2$$

$$= \frac{1}{2}\left[m_1 v_1^2 + m_2 v_2^2 - \frac{(m_1 v_1 + m_2 v_2)^2}{m_1 + m_2} \right]$$

$$= \frac{1}{2}\left[\frac{m_1 m_2 (v_1^2 + v_2^2 - 2v_1 v_2)}{m_1 + m_2} \right]$$

$$= \frac{m_1 m_2 (v_1 - v_2)^2}{2(m_1 + m_2)}.$$

We see that the loss in kinetic energy is positive.

Example 9.5

A cart A of mass 50 kg moving at a speed of 20 km/h hits a lighter cart B of mass 20 kg moving towards it at a speed of 10 km/h. The two carts cling to each other. Find the speed of the combined mass after the collision.

Solution : This is an example of inelastic collision. As the carts move towards each other, their momenta have opposite sign. If the common speed after the collision is V, momentum conservation gives

$$(50 \text{ kg})(20 \text{ km/h}) - (20 \text{ kg})(10 \text{ km/h}) = (70 \text{ kg})V$$

or

$$V = \frac{80}{7} \text{ km/h}.$$

9.9 COEFFICIENT OF RESTITUTION

We have seen that for a perfectly elastic collision

velocity of separation = velocity of approach

and for a perfectly inelastic collision

velocity of separation = 0.

In general, the bodies are neither perfectly elastic nor perfectly inelastic. In that case we can write

velocity of separation = e (velocity of approach),

where $0 < e < 1$. The constant e depends on the materials of the colliding bodies. This constant is known as *coefficient of restitution*. If $e = 1$, the collision is perfectly elastic and if $e = 0$, the collision is perfectly inelastic.

Example 9.6

A block of mass m moving at speed v collides with another block of mass 2 m at rest. The lighter block comes to rest after the collision. Find the coefficient of restitution.

Solution : Suppose the second block moves at speed v' towards right after the collision. From the principle of conservation of momentum,

$$mv = 2mv' \quad \text{or} \quad v' = v/2.$$

Hence, the velocity of separation $= v/2$ and the velocity of approach $= v$. By definition,

$$e = \frac{\text{velocity of the separation}}{\text{velocity of approach}} = \frac{v/2}{v} = \frac{1}{2}.$$

9.10 ELASTIC COLLISION IN TWO DIMENSIONS

Consider two objects A and B of mass m_1 and m_2 kept on the X-axis (figure 9.17). Initially, the object

B is at rest and A moves towards B with a speed u_1. If the collision is not *head-on* (the force during the collision is not along the initial velocity), the objects move along different lines. Suppose the object A moves with a velocity $\vec{v_1}$ making an angle θ with the X-axis and the object B moves with a velocity $\vec{v_2}$ making an angle Φ with the same axis. Also, suppose $\vec{v_1}$ and $\vec{v_2}$ lie in X-Y plane. Using conservation of momentum in X and Y directions, we get

$$m_1u_1 = m_1v_1\cos\theta + m_2v_2\cos\Phi \qquad ... (i)$$

$$\text{and} \qquad 0 = m_1v_1\sin\theta - m_2v_2\sin\Phi. \qquad ... (ii)$$

If the collision is elastic, the final kinetic energy is equal to the initial kinetic energy. Thus,

$$\frac{1}{2}m_1u_1^2 = \frac{1}{2}m_1v_1^2 + \frac{1}{2}m_2v_2^2. \qquad ... (iii)$$

We have four unknowns v_1, v_2, θ and Φ to describe the final motion whereas there are only three relations. Thus, the final motion cannot be uniquely determined with this information.

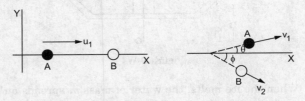

Figure 9.17

In fact, the final motion depends on the angle between the line of force during the collision and the direction of initial velocity. The momentum of each object must be individually conserved in the direction perpendicular to the force. The motion along the line of force may be treated as a one-dimensional collision.

9.11 IMPULSE AND IMPULSIVE FORCE

When two bodies collide, they exert forces on each other while in contact. The momentum of each body is changed due to the force on it exerted by the other. On an ordinary scale, the time duration of this contact is very small and yet the change in momentum is sizeable. This means that the magnitude of the force must be large on an ordinary scale. Such large forces acting for a very short duration are called *impulsive forces*. The force may not be uniform while the contact lasts.

The change in momentum produced by such an impulsive force is

$$\vec{P_f} - \vec{P_i} = \int_{P_i}^{P_f} d\vec{P} = \int_{t_i}^{t_f}\frac{d\vec{P}}{dt}dt = \int_{t_i}^{t_f}\vec{F}\,dt. \qquad ... (9.17)$$

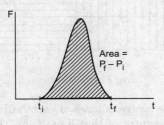

Figure 9.18

This quantity $\int_{t_i}^{t_f}\vec{F}\,dt$ is known as the impulse of the force $\vec{F}$ during the time interval t_i to t_f and is equal to the change in the momentum of the body on which it acts. Obviously, it is the area under the $F-t$ curve for one-dimensional motion (figure 9.18).

Worked Out Examples

1. *Three particles of masses 0·50 kg, 1·0 kg and 1·5 kg are placed at the three corners of a right-angled triangle of sides 3·0 cm, 4·0 cm and 5·0 cm as shown in figure (9-W1). Locate the centre of mass of the system.*

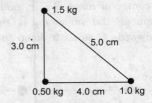

Figure 9-W1.

Solution : Let us take the 4·0 cm line as the X-axis and the 3·0 cm line as the Y-axis. The coordinates of the three particles are as follows :

m	x	y
0·50 kg	0	0
1·0 kg	4·0 cm	0
1·5 kg	0	3·0 cm

The x-coordinate of the centre of mass is

$$X = \frac{m_1x_1 + m_2x_2 + m_3x_3}{m_1 + m_2 + m_3}$$

$$= \frac{(0·50\text{ kg})\cdot 0 + (1·0\text{ kg})\cdot(4·0\text{ cm}) + (1·5\text{ kg})\cdot 0}{0·50\text{ kg} + 1·0\text{ kg} + 1·5\text{ kg}}$$

$$= \frac{4 \text{ kg-cm}}{3 \text{ kg}} = 1 \cdot 3 \text{ cm}.$$

The y-coordinate of the centre of mass is

$$Y = \frac{m_1 y_1 + m_2 y_2 + m_3 y_3}{m_1 + m_2 + m_3}$$

$$= \frac{(0 \cdot 50 \text{ kg}) \cdot 0 + (1 \cdot 0 \text{ kg}) \cdot 0 + (1 \cdot 5 \text{ kg}) (3 \cdot 0 \text{ cm})}{0 \cdot 50 \text{ kg} + 1 \cdot 0 \text{ kg} + 1 \cdot 5 \text{ kg}}$$

$$= \frac{4 \cdot 5 \text{ kg-cm}}{3 \text{ kg}} = 1 \cdot 5 \text{ cm}.$$

Thus, the centre of mass is $1 \cdot 3$ cm right and $1 \cdot 5$ cm above the $0 \cdot 5$ kg particle.

2. *Half of the rectangular plate shown in figure (9-W2) is made of a material of density ρ_1 and the other half of density ρ_2. The length of the plate is L. Locate the centre of mass of the plate.*

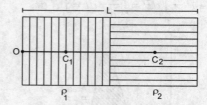

Figure 9-W2

Solution : The centre of mass of each half is located at the geometrical centre of that half. Thus, the left half may be replaced by a point particle of mass $K\rho_1$ placed at C_1 and the right half may be replaced by a point particle of mass $K\rho_2$ placed at C_2. This replacement is for the specific purpose of locating the combined centre of mass. Take the middle point of the left edge to be the origin. The x-coordinate of C_1 is $L/4$ and that of C_2 is $3L/4$. Hence, the x-coordinate of the centre of mass is

$$X = \frac{(K\rho_1)\dfrac{L}{4} + (K\rho_2)\dfrac{3L}{4}}{K\rho_1 + K\rho_2}$$

$$= \frac{(\rho_1 + 3\rho_2)}{4(\rho_1 + \rho_2)} L.$$

The combined centre of mass is this much to the right of the assumed origin.

3. *The density of a linear rod of length L varies as $\rho = A + Bx$ where x is the distance from the left end. Locate the centre of mass.*

Figure 9-W3

Solution : Let the cross-sectional area be α. The mass of an element of length dx located at a distance x away from the left end is $(A + Bx)\,\alpha\,dx$. The x-coordinate of the centre of mass is given by

$$X_{CM} = \frac{\int x\, dm}{\int dm} = \frac{\displaystyle\int_0^L x\,(A + Bx)\,\alpha\,dx}{\displaystyle\int_0^L (A + Bx)\,\alpha\,dx}$$

$$= \frac{A\dfrac{L^2}{2} + B\dfrac{L^3}{3}}{AL + B\dfrac{L^2}{2}} = \frac{3AL + 2BL^2}{3(2A + BL)}.$$

4. *A cubical block of ice of mass m and edge L is placed in a large tray of mass M. If the ice melts, how far does the centre of mass of the system "ice plus tray" come down ?*

Solution : Consider figure (9-W4). Suppose the centre of mass of the tray is a distance x_1 above the origin and that of the ice is a distance x_2 above the origin. The height of the centre of mass of the ice-tray system is

$$x = \frac{m x_2 + M x_1}{m + M}.$$

Figure 9-W4

When the ice melts, the water of mass m spreads on the surface of the tray. As the tray is large, the height of water is negligible. The centre of mass of the water is then on the surface of the tray and is at a distance $x_2 - L/2$ above the origin. The new centre of mass of the ice-tray system will be at the height

$$x' = \frac{m\left(x_2 - \dfrac{L}{2}\right) + M x_1}{m + M}.$$

The shift in the centre of mass $= x - x' = \dfrac{mL}{2(m + M)}.$

5. *Consider a two-particle system with the particles having masses m_1 and m_2. If the first particle is pushed towards the centre of mass through a distance d, by what distance should the second particle be moved so as to keep the centre of mass at the same position ?*

Solution : Consider figure (9-W5). Suppose the distance of m_1 from the centre of mass C is x_1 and that of m_2 from C is x_2. Suppose the mass m_2 is moved through a distance d' towards C so as to keep the centre of mass at C.

Figure 9-W5

Then,
$$m_1 x_1 = m_2 x_2 \qquad \text{... (i)}$$
and
$$m_1 (x_1 - d) = m_2 (x_2 - d'). \qquad \text{... (ii)}$$
Subtracting (ii) from (i)
$$m_1 d = m_2 d'$$
or,
$$d' = \frac{m_1}{m_2} d.$$

6. *A body of mass 2·5 kg is subjected to the forces shown in figure (9-W6). Find the acceleration of the centre of mass.*

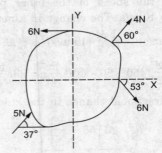

Figure 9-W6

Solution : Take the X and Y axes as shown in the figure. The x-component of the resultant force is
$$F_x = -6 \text{ N} + (5 \text{ N}) \cos 37° + (6 \text{ N}) \cos 53° + (4 \text{ N}) \cos 60°$$
$$= -6 \text{ N} + (5 \text{ N}) \cdot (4/5) + (6 \text{ N}) \cdot (3/5) + (4 \text{ N}) \cdot (1/2) = 3·6 \text{ N}.$$
Similarly, the y-component of the resultant force is
$$F_y = 5 \text{ N} \sin 37° - (6 \text{ N}) \sin 53° + 4 \text{ N} \sin 60°$$
$$= (5 \text{ N}) \cdot (3/5) - (6 \text{ N}) \cdot (4/5) + (4 \text{ N}) \cdot (\sqrt{3}/2) = 1·7 \text{ N} \cdot$$
The magnitude of the resultant force is
$$F = \sqrt{F_x^2 + F_y^2} = \sqrt{(3·6 \text{ N})^2 + (1·7 \text{ N})^2} \approx 4·0 \text{ N}.$$
The direction of the resultant force makes an angle θ with the X-axis where
$$\tan\theta = \frac{F_y}{F_x} = \frac{1·7}{3·6} = 0·47.$$
The acceleration of the centre of mass is
$$a_{CM} = \frac{F}{M} = \frac{4·0 \text{ N}}{2·5 \text{ kg}} = 1·6 \text{ m/s}^2$$
in the direction of the resultant force.

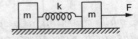

Figure 9-W7

7. *Two blocks of equal mass m are connected by an unstretched spring and the system is kept at rest on a frictionless horizontal surface. A constant force F is applied on one of the blocks pulling it away from the other as shown in figure (9-W7). (a) Find the position of the centre of mass at time t. (b) If the extension of the*

spring is x_0 at time t, find the displacement of the two blocks at this instant.

Solution : (a) The acceleration of the centre of mass is given by
$$a_{CM} = \frac{F}{M} = \frac{F}{2m}.$$
The position of the centre of mass at time t is
$$x = \frac{1}{2} a_{CM} t^2 = \frac{F t^2}{4m}.$$
(b) Suppose the displacement of the first block is x_1 and that of the second is x_2. As the centre of mass is at x, we should have
$$x = \frac{m x_1 + m x_2}{2m}$$
or,
$$\frac{F t^2}{4m} = \frac{x_1 + x_2}{2}$$
or,
$$x_1 + x_2 = \frac{F t^2}{2m}. \qquad \text{... (i)}$$
The extension of the spring is $x_2 - x_1$. Therefore,
$$x_2 - x_1 = x_0. \qquad \text{... (ii)}$$
from (i) and (ii), $x_1 = \frac{1}{2}\left(\frac{F t^2}{2m} - x_0\right)$
and
$$x_2 = \frac{1}{2}\left(\frac{F t^2}{2m} + x_0\right).$$

8. *A projectile is fired at a speed of 100 m/s at an angle of 37° above the horizontal. At the highest point, the projectile breaks into two parts of mass ratio 1 : 3, the smaller coming to rest. Find the distance from the launching point to the point where the heavier piece lands.*

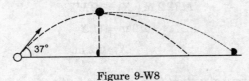

Figure 9-W8

Solution : See figure (9-W8). At the highest point, the projectile has horizontal velocity. The lighter part comes to rest. Hence the heavier part will move with increased horizontal velocity. In vertical direction, both parts have zero velocity and undergo same acceleration, hence they will cover equal vertical displacements in a given time. Thus, both will hit the ground together. As internal forces do not affect the motion of the centre of mass, the centre of mass hits the ground at the position where the original projectile would have landed. The range of the original projectile is
$$x_{CM} = \frac{2 u^2 \sin\theta \cos\theta}{g} = \frac{2 \times 10^4 \times \frac{3}{5} \times \frac{4}{5}}{10} \text{ m}$$
$$= 960 \text{ m}.$$

The centre of mass will hit the ground at this position. As the smaller block comes to rest after breaking, it falls down vertically and hits the ground at half of the range i.e., at $x = 480$ m. If the heavier block hits the ground at x_2, then

$$x_{CM} = \frac{m_1 x_1 + m_2 x_2}{m_1 + m_2}$$

or, $960 \text{ m} = \dfrac{\dfrac{M}{4} \times 480 \text{ m} + \dfrac{3\,M}{4} \times x_2}{M}$

or, $x_2 = 1120$ m.

9. *A block of mass M is placed on the top of a bigger block of mass 10 M as shown in figure (9-W9). All the surfaces are frictionless. The system is released from rest. Find the distance moved by the bigger block at the instant the smaller block reaches the ground.*

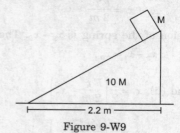

M

10 M

2.2 m

Figure 9-W9

Solution : If the bigger block moves towards right by a distance X, the smaller block will move towards left by a distance $(2\cdot2 \text{ m} - X)$. Taking the two blocks together as the system, there is no horizontal external force on it. The centre of mass, which was at rest initially, will remain at the same horizontal position.
Thus,

$$M (2\cdot2 \text{ m} - X) = 10\,MX$$

or, $2\cdot2 \text{ m} = 11\,X$

or, $X = 0\cdot2$ m.

10. *The hero of a stunt film fires 50 g bullets from a machine gun, each at a speed of 1·0 km/s. If he fires 20 bullets in 4 seconds, what average force does he exert against the machine gun during this period?*

Solution : The momentum of each bullet

$$= (0\cdot050 \text{ kg}) (1000 \text{ m/s}) = 50 \text{ kg-m/s}.$$

The gun is imparted this much of momentum by each bullet fired. Thus, the rate of change of momentum of the gun

$$= \frac{(50 \text{ kg-m/s}) \times 20}{4 \text{ s}} = 250 \text{ N}$$

In order to hold the gun, the hero must exert a force of 250 N against the gun.

11. *A block moving horizontally on a smooth surface with a speed of 20 m/s bursts into two equal parts continuing in the same direction. If one of the parts moves at 30 m/s, with what speed does the second part move and what is the fractional change in the kinetic energy?*

Solution : There is no external force on the block. Internal forces break the block in two parts. The linear momentum of the block before the break should, therefore, be equal to the linear momentum of the two parts after the break. As all the velocities are in same direction, we get,

$$M (20 \text{ m/s}) = \frac{M}{2} (30 \text{ m/s}) + \frac{M}{2} v$$

where v is the speed of the other part. From this equation $v = 10$ m/s. The change in kinetic energy is

$$\frac{1}{2} \frac{M}{2} (30 \text{ m/s})^2 + \frac{1}{2} \frac{M}{2} (10 \text{ m/s})^2 - \frac{1}{2} M (20 \text{ m/s})^2$$

$$= \frac{M}{2} (450 + 50 - 400) \frac{\text{m}^2}{\text{s}^2} = \left(50 \frac{\text{m}^2}{\text{s}^2}\right) M.$$

Hence, the fractional change in the kinetic energy

$$= \frac{M \left(50 \dfrac{\text{m}^2}{\text{s}^2}\right)}{\dfrac{1}{2} M (20 \text{ m/s})^2} = \frac{1}{4}.$$

12. *A car of mass M is moving with a uniform velocity v on a horizontal road when the hero of a Hindi film drops himself on it from above. Taking the mass of the hero to be m, what will be the velocity of the car after the event?*

Solution : Consider the car plus the hero as the system. In the horizontal direction, there is no external force. Since the hero has fallen vertically, so his initial horizontal momentum = 0.

Initial horizontal momemtum of the system $= Mv$ towards right.

Finally the hero sticks to the roof of the car, so they move with equal horizontal velocity say V. Final horizontal momentum of the system

$$= (M + m) V$$

Hence, $M v = (M + m) V$

or, $V = \dfrac{M v}{M + m}.$

13. *A space shuttle, while travelling at a speed of 4000 km/h with respect to the earth, disconnects and ejects a module backward, weighing one fifth of the residual part. If the shuttle ejects the disconnected module at a speed of 100 km/h with respect to the state of the shuttle before the ejection, find the final velocity of the shuttle.*

Solution : Suppose the mass of the shuttle including the module is M. The mass of the module will be $M/6$. The total linear momentum before disconnection

$$= M (4000 \text{ km/h}).$$

The velocity of the ejected module with respect to the earth
= its velocity with respect to the shuttle + the velocity of the shuttle with respect to the earth

$$= -100 \text{ km/h} + 4000 \text{ km/h} = 3900 \text{ km/h} .$$

If the final velocity of the shuttle is V then the total final linear momentum

$$= \frac{5M}{6} V + \frac{M}{6} \times 3900 \text{ km/h}.$$

By the principle of conservation of linear momentum,

$$M (4000 \text{ km/h}) = \frac{5M}{6} V + \frac{M}{6} \times 3900 \text{ km/h}$$

or, $V = 4020 \text{ km/h} .$

14. *A boy of mass 25 kg stands on a board of mass 10 kg which in turn is kept on a frictionless horizontal ice surface. The boy makes a jump with a velocity component 5 m/s in a horizontal direction with respect to the ice. With what velocity does the board recoil? With what rate are the boy and the board separating from each other?*

Solution : Consider the "board + boy" as a system. The external forces on this system are (a) weight of the system and (b) normal contact force by the ice surface. Both these forces are vertical and there is no external force in horizontal direction. The horizontal component of linear momentum of the "board + boy" system is, therefore, constant.

If the board recoils at a speed v,

$$0 = (25 \text{ kg}) \times (5 \text{ m/s}) - (10 \text{ kg})v$$

or, $v = 12 \cdot 5 \text{ m/s}.$

The boy and the board are separating with a rate

$$5 \text{ m/s} + 12 \cdot 5 \text{ m/s} = 17 \cdot 5 \text{ m/s}.$$

15. *A man of mass m is standing on a platform of mass M kept on smooth ice. If the man starts moving on the platform with a speed v relative to the platform, with what velocity relative to the ice does the platform recoil?*

Solution : Consider the situation shown in figure (9-W10). Suppose the man moves at a speed w towards right and the platform recoils at a speed V towards left, both relative to the ice. Hence, the speed of the man relative to the platform is $V + w$. By the question,

$$V + w = v, \text{ or } w = v - V. \qquad \dots \text{ (i)}$$

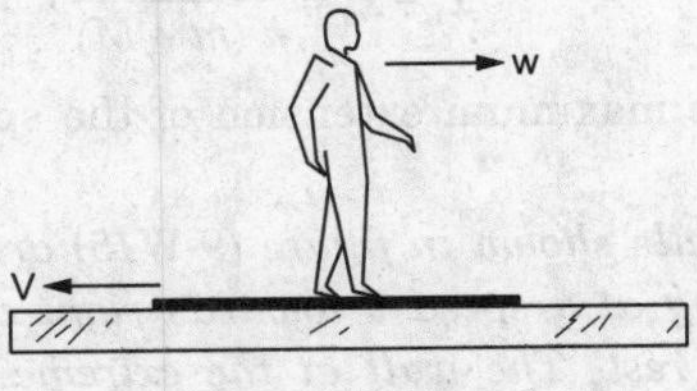

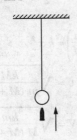

Figure 9-W10

Taking the platform and the man to be the system, there is no external horizontal force on the system. The linear

momentum of the system remains constant. Initially, both the man and the platform were at rest. Thus,

$$0 = MV - mw$$

or, $MV = m (v - V)$ [Using (i)]

or, $V = \dfrac{m v}{M + m} .$

16. *A ball of mass m, moving with a velocity v along X-axis, strikes another ball of mass 2m kept at rest. The first ball comes to rest after collision and the other breaks into two equal pieces. One of the pieces starts moving along Y-axis with a speed v_1. What will be the velocity of the other piece?*

Solution : The total linear momentum of the balls before the collision is mv along the X-axis. After the collision, momentum of the first ball = 0, momentum of the first piece $= m v_1$ along the Y-axis and momentum of the second piece $= m v_2$ along its direction of motion where v_2 is the speed of the second piece. These three should add to mv along the X-axis, which is the initial momentum of the system.

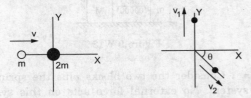

Figure 9-W11

Taking components along the X-axis,

$$m v_2 \cos\theta = m v \qquad \dots \text{ (i)}$$

and taking components along the Y-axis,

$$m v_2 \sin\theta = m v_1. \qquad \dots \text{ (ii)}$$

From (i) and (ii),

$$v_2 = \sqrt{v^2 + v_1^2} \text{ and } \tan\theta = v_1 / v.$$

17. *A bullet of mass 50 g is fired from below into the bob of mass 450 g of a long simple pendulum as shown in figure (9-W12). The bullet remains inside the bob and the bob rises through a height of 1·8 m. Find the speed of the bullet. Take g = 10 m/s².*

Figure 9-W12

Solution : Let the speed of the bullet be v. Let the common velocity of the bullet and the bob, after the bullet is embedded into the bob, is V. By the principle of conservation of linear momentum,

$$V = \frac{(0.05 \text{ kg})v}{0.45 \text{ kg} + 0.05 \text{ kg}} = \frac{v}{10}.$$

The string becomes loose and the bob will go up with a deceleration of $g = 10 \text{ m/s}^2$. As it comes to rest at a height of 1.8 m, using the equation $v^2 = u^2 + 2ax$,

$$1.8 \text{ m} = \frac{(v/10)^2}{2 \times 10 \text{ m/s}^2}$$

or, $v = 60$ m/s.

18. *A light spring of spring constant k is kept compressed between two blocks of masses m and M on a smooth horizontal surface (figure 9-W13). When released, the blocks acquire velocities in opposite directions. The spring loses contact with the blocks when it acquires natural length. If the spring was initially compressed through a distance x, find the final speeds of the two blocks.*

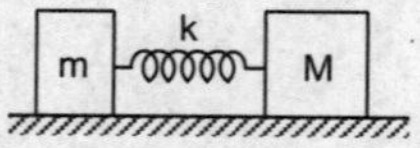

Figure 9-W13

Solution : Consider the two blocks plus the spring to be the system. No external force acts on this system in horizontal direction. Hence, the linear momentum will remain constant. As the spring is light, it has no linear momentum. Suppose the block of mass M moves with a speed V and the other block with a speed v after losing contact with the spring. As the blocks are released from rest, the initial momentum is zero. The final momentum is $MV - mv$ towards right. Thus,

$$MV - mv = 0 \quad \text{or,} \quad V = \frac{m}{M} v. \qquad \dots \text{(i)}$$

Initially, the energy of the system $= \frac{1}{2} kx^2$.

Finally, the energy of the system $= \frac{1}{2} mv^2 + \frac{1}{2} MV^2$.

As there is no friction,

$$\frac{1}{2} mv^2 + \frac{1}{2} MV^2 = \frac{1}{2} kx^2. \qquad \dots \text{(ii)}$$

Using (i) and (ii),

$$mv^2 \left(1 + \frac{m}{M}\right) = kx^2$$

or, $$v = \sqrt{\frac{kM}{m(M+m)}} x$$

and $$V = \sqrt{\frac{km}{M(M+m)}} x.$$

19. *A block of mass m is connected to another block of mass M by a massless spring of spring constant k. The blocks are kept on a smooth horizontal plane. Initially, the blocks are at rest and the spring is unstretched when a constant force F starts acting on the block of mass M to pull it. Find the maximum extension of the spring.*

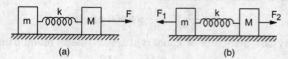

(a)   (b)

Figure 9-W14

Solution : Let us take the two blocks plus the spring as the system. The centre of mass of the system moves with an acceleration $a = \frac{F}{m+M}$. Let us work from a reference frame with its origin at the centre of mass. As this frame is accelerated with respect to the ground we have to apply a pseudo force ma towards left on the block of mass m and Ma towards left on the block of mass M. The net external force on m is

$$F_1 = ma = \frac{mF}{m+M} \text{ towards left}$$

and the net external force on M is

$$F_2 = F - Ma = F - \frac{MF}{m+M} = \frac{mF}{m+M} \text{ towards right.}$$

The situation from this frame is shown in figure (9-W14b). As the centre of mass is at rest in this frame, the blocks move in opposite directions and come to instantaneous rest at some instant. The extension of the spring will be maximum at this instant. Suppose the left block is displaced through a distance x_1 and the right block through a distance x_2 from the initial positions. The total work done by the external forces F_1 and F_2 in this period are

$$W = F_1 x_1 + F_2 x_2 = \frac{mF}{m+M}(x_1 + x_2).$$

This should be equal to the increase in the potential energy of the spring as there is no change in the kinetic energy. Thus,

$$\frac{mF}{m+M}(x_1 + x_2) = \frac{1}{2} k (x_1 + x_2)^2$$

or, $$x_1 + x_2 = \frac{2mF}{k(m+M)}.$$

This is the maximum extension of the spring.

20. *The two balls shown in figure (9-W15) are identical, the first moving at a speed v towards right and the second staying at rest. The wall at the extreme right is fixed. Assume all collisions to be elastic. Show that the speeds of the balls remain unchanged after all the collisions have taken place.*

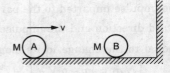

Figure 9-W15

Solution : 1st collision : As the balls have equal mass and make elastic collision, the velocities are interchanged. Hence, after the first collision, the ball A comes to rest and the ball B moves towards right at a speed v.

2nd collision : The ball B moving with a speed v, collides with the wall and rebounds. As the wall is rigid and may be taken to be of infinite mass, momentum conservation gives no useful result. Velocity of separation should be equal to the velocity of approach. Hence, the ball rebounds at the same speed v towards left.

3rd collision : The ball B moving towards left at the speed v again collides with the ball A kept at rest. As the masses are equal and the collision is elastic, the velocities are interchanged. Thus, the ball B comes to rest and the ball A moves towards left at a speed v. No further collision takes place. Thus, the speeds of the balls remain the same as their initial values.

21. *A block of mass m moving at a velocity v collides head on with another block of mass 2m at rest. If the coefficient of restitution is 1/2, find the velocities of the blocks after the collision.*

Solution : Suppose after the collision the block of mass m moves at a velocity u_1 and the block of mass $2m$ moves at a velocity u_2. By conservation of momentum,

$$mv = mu_1 + 2mu_2. \qquad \ldots \text{(i)}$$

The velocity of separation is $u_2 - u_1$ and the velocity of approach is v.

So, $\qquad u_2 - u_1 = v/2. \qquad \ldots \text{(ii)}$

From (i) and (ii), $u_1 = 0$ and $u_2 = v/2$.

22. *A block of mass 1·2 kg moving at a speed of 20 cm/s collides head-on with a similar block kept at rest. The coefficient of restitution is 3/5. Find the loss of kinetic energy during the collision.*

Solution : Suppose the first block moves at a speed v_1 and the second at v_2 after the collision. Since the collision is head-on, the two blocks move along the original direction of motion of the first block.

By conservation of linear momentum,

$$(1\text{·}2 \text{ kg}) (20 \text{ cm/s}) = (1\text{·}2 \text{ kg}) v_1 + (1\text{·}2 \text{ kg}) v_2$$

or, $\qquad v_1 + v_2 = 20 \text{ cm/s}. \qquad \ldots \text{(i)}$

The velocity of separation is $v_2 - v_1$ and the velocity of approach is 20 cm/s. As the coefficient of restitution is 3/5, we have,

$$v_2 - v_1 = (3/5) \times 20 \text{ cm/s} = 12 \text{ cm/s}. \qquad \ldots \text{(ii)}$$

By (i) and (ii),

$$v_1 = 4 \text{ cm/s} \quad \text{and} \quad v_2 = 16 \text{ cm/s}.$$

The loss in kinetic energy is

$$\frac{1}{2} (1\text{·}2 \text{ kg})[(20 \text{ cm/s})^2 - (4 \text{ cm/s})^2 - (16 \text{ cm/s})^2]$$

$$= (0\text{·}6 \text{ kg}) [0\text{·}04 \text{ m}^2/\text{s}^2 - 0\text{·}0016 \text{ m}^2/\text{s}^2 - 0\text{·}0256 \text{ m}^2/\text{s}^2]$$

$$= (0\text{·}6 \text{ kg}) (0\text{·}0128 \text{ m}^2/\text{s}^2) = 7\text{·}7 \times 10^{-3} \text{ J}.$$

23. *A ball of mass m hits the floor with a speed v making an angle of incidence θ with the normal. The coefficient of restitution is e. Find the speed of the reflected ball and the angle of reflection of the ball.*

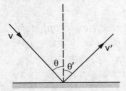

Figure 9-W16

Solution : See figure (9-W16). Suppose the angle of reflection is θ' and the speed after the collision is v'. The floor exerts a force on the ball along the normal during the collision. There is no force parallel to the surface. Thus, the parallel component of the velocity of the ball remains unchanged. This gives

$$v' \sin\theta' = v \sin\theta. \qquad \ldots \text{(i)}$$

For the components normal to the floor,

the velocity of separation $= v' \cos\theta'$

and the velocity of approach $= v \cos\theta$.

Hence, $\qquad v' \cos\theta' = e \, v \cos\theta. \qquad \ldots \text{(ii)}$

From (i) and (ii),

$$v' = v \sqrt{\sin^2\theta + e^2 \cos^2\theta}$$

and $\qquad \tan\theta' = \dfrac{\tan\theta}{e}.$

For elastic collision, $e = 1$ so that $\theta' = \theta$ and $v' = v$.

24. *A block of mass m and a pan of equal mass are connected by a string going over a smooth light pulley as shown in figure (9-W17). Initially the system is at rest when a particle of mass m falls on the pan and sticks to it. If the particle strikes the pan with a speed v find the speed with which the system moves just after the collision.*

Solution : Let the required speed be V.

As there is a sudden change in the speed of the block, the tension must change by a large amount during the collision.

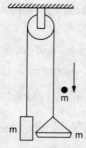

Figure 9-W17

Let N = magnitude of the contact force between the particle and the pan

T = tension in the string

Consider the impulse imparted to the particle. The force is N in upward direction and the impulse is $\int N \, dt$. This should be equal to the change in its momentum.

Thus, $$\int N \, dt = mv - mV. \qquad \text{... (i)}$$

Similarly considering the impulse imparted to the pan,

$$\int (N - T) dt = mV \qquad \text{... (ii)}$$

and that to the block,

$$\int T \, dt = mV. \qquad \text{... (iii)}$$

Adding (ii) and (iii),

$$\int N \, dt = 2 \, mV.$$

Comparing with (i),

$$mv - mV = 2mV$$

or, $$V = v/3.$$

□

QUESTIONS FOR SHORT ANSWER

1. Can the centre of mass of a body be at a point outside the body ?

2. If all the particles of a system lie in X-Y plane, is it necessary that the centre of mass be in X-Y plane ?

3. If all the particle of a system lie in a cube, is it neccesary that the centre of mass be in the cube ?

4. The centre of mass is defined as $\vec{R} = \dfrac{1}{M} \sum_i m_i \vec{r_i}$. Suppose we define "centre of charge" as $\vec{R_c} = \dfrac{1}{Q} \sum_i q_i \vec{r_i}$ where q_i represents the ith charge placed at $\vec{r_i}$ and Q is the total charge of the system.
(a) Can the centre of charge of a two-charge system be outside the line segment joining the charges ?
(b) If all the charges of a system are in X-Y plane, is it necessary that the centre of charge be in X-Y plane ?
(c) If all the charges of a system lie in a cube, is it necessary that the centre of charge be in the cube ?

5. The weight Mg of an extended body is generally shown in a diagram to act through the centre of mass. Does it mean that the earth does not attract other particles ?

6. A bob suspended from the ceiling of a car which is accelerating on a horizontal road. The bob stays at rest with respect to the car with the string making an angle θ with the vertical. The linear momentum of the bob as seen from the road is increasing with time. Is it a violation of conservation of linear momentum ? If not, where is the external force which changes the linear momentum ?

7. You are waiting for a train on a railway platform. Your three-year-old niece is standing on your iron trunk containing the luggage. Why does the trunk not recoil as she jumps off as she jumps off on the platform ?

8. In a head-on collision between two particles, is it necessary that the particles will acquire a common velocity at least for one instant ?

9. A collision experiment is done on a horizontal table kept in an elevator. Do you expect a change in the results if the elevator is accelerated up or down because of the noninertial character of the frame ?

10. Two bodies make an elastic head-on collision on a smooth horizontal table kept in a car. Do you expect a change in the result if the car is accelerated on a horizontal road because of the noninertial character of the frame ? Does the equation "Velocity of separation = Velocity of approach" remain valid in an accelerating car ? Does the equation "final momentum = initial momentum" remain valid in the accelerating car ?

11. If the total mechanical energy of a particle is zero, is its linear momentum necessarily zero ? Is it necessarily nonzero ?

12. If the linear momentum of a particle is known, can you find its kinetic energy ? If the kinetic energy of a particle is known can you find its linear momentum ?

13. What can be said about the centre of mass of a uniform hemisphere without making any calculation ? Will its distance from the centre be more than $r/2$ or less than $r/2$?

14. You are holding a cage containing a bird. Do you have to make less effort if the bird flies from its position in the cage and manages to stay in the middle without touching the walls of the cage ? Does it make a difference whether the cage is completely closed or it has rods to let air pass ?

15. A fat person is standing on a light plank floating on a calm lake. The person walks from one end to the other on the plank. His friend sitting on the shore watches him and finds that the person hardly moves any distance because the plank moves backward about the same distance as the person moves on the plank. Explain.

16. A high-jumper successfully clears the bar. Is it possible that his centre of mass crossed the bar from below it ? Try it with appropriate figures.

17. Which of the two persons shown in figure (9-Q1) is more likely to fall down ? Which external force is responsible for his falling down ?

Figure 9-Q1

18. Suppose we define a quantity 'Linear Momentum' as
        linear momentum = mass × speed.
The linear momentum of a system of particles is the sum of linear momenta of the individual particles. Can we state a principle of conservation of linear momentum as "linear momentum of a system remains constant if no external force acts on it" ?

19. Use the definition of linear momentum from the previous question. Can we state the principle of conservation of linear momentum for a single particle ?

20. To accelerate a car we ignite petrol in the engine of the car. Since only an external force can accelerate the centre of mass, is it proper to say that "the force generated by the engine accelerates the car" ?

21. A ball is moved on a horizontal table with some velocity. The ball stops after moving some distance. Which external force is responsible for the change in the momentum of the ball ?

22. Consider the situation of the previous problem. Take "the table plus the ball" as the system. Friction between the table and the ball is then an internal force. As the ball slows down, the momentum of the system decreases. Which external force is responsible for this change in the momentum ?

23. When a nucleus at rest emits a beta particle, it is found that the velocities of the recoiling nucleus and the beta particle are not along the same straight line. How can this be possible in view of the principle of conservation of momentum ?

24. A van is standing on a frictionless portion of a horizontal road. To start the engine, the vehicle must be set in motion in the forward direction. How can the persons sitting inside the van do it without coming out and pushing from behind ?

25. In one-dimensional elastic collision of equal masses, the velocities are interchanged. Can velocities in a one-dimensional collision be interchanged if the masses are not equal ?

OBJECTIVE I

1. Consider the following two equations :
$$\text{(A)} \quad \vec{R} = \frac{1}{M} \sum_i m_i \vec{r_i}$$
and
$$\text{(B)} \quad \vec{a}_{CM} = \frac{\vec{F}}{M}.$$
In a noninertial frame
(a) both are correct   (b) both are wrong
(c) A is correct but B is wrong
(d) B is correct but A is wrong.

2. Consider the following two statements :
(A) Linear momentum of the system remains constant.
(B) Centre of mass of the system remains at rest.
  (a) A implies B and B implies A.
  (b) A does not imply B and B does not imply A.
  (c) A implies B but B does not imply A.
  (d) B implies A but A does not imply B.

3. Consider the following two statements :
(A) Linear momentum of a system of particles is zero.
(B) Kinetic energy of a system of particles is zero.
  (a) A implies B and B implies A.
  (b) A does not imply B and B does not imply A.

(c) A implies B but B does not imply A.
(d) B implies A but A does not imply B.

4. Consider the following two statements :
(A) The linear momentum of a particle is independent of the frame of reference.
(B) The kinetic energy of a particle is independent of the frame of reference.
(a) Both A and B are true.   (b) A is true but B is false.
(c) A is false but B is true.   (d) both A and B are false.

5. All the particles of a body are situated at a distance R from the origin. The distance of the centre of mass of the body from the origin is
(a) $= R$ (b) $\le R$ (c) $> R$ (d) $\ge R$.

6. A circular plate of diameter d is kept in contact with a square plate of edge d as shown in figure (9-Q2). The density of the material and the thickness are same

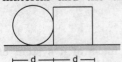

Figure 9-Q2

everywhere. The centre of mass of the composite system will be

(a) inside the circular plate (b) inside the square plate
(c) at the point of contact   (d) outside the system.

7. Consider a system of two identical particles. One of the particles is at rest and the other has an acceleration $\vec{a}$. The centre of mass has an acceleration

(a) zero   (b) $\frac{1}{2}\vec{a}$ (c) $\vec{a}$ (d) $2\vec{a}$.

8. Internal forces can change
(a) the linear momentum but not the kinetic energy
(b) the kinetic energy but not the linear momentum
(c) linear momentum as well as kinetic energy
(d) neither the linear momentum nor the kinetic energy.

9. A bullet hits a block kept at rest on a smooth horizontal surface and gets embedded into it. Which of the following does not change ?
(a) linear momentum of the block
(b) kinetic energy of the block
(c) gravitational potential energy of the block
(d) temperature of the block.

10. A uniform sphere is placed on a smooth horizontal surface and a horizontal force F is applied on it at a distance h above the surface. The acceleration of the centre
(a) is maximum when $h = 0$
(b) is maximum when $h = R$
(c) is maximum when $h = 2R$
(d) is independent of h.

11. A body falling vertically downwards under gravity breaks in two parts of unequal masses. The centre of mass of the two parts taken together shifts horizontally towards
(a) heavier piece   (b) lighter piece
(c) does not shift horizontally
(d) depends on the vertical velocity at the time of breaking.

12. A ball kept in a closed box moves in the box making collisions with the walls. The box is kept on a smooth surface. The velocity of the centre of mass
(a) of the box remains constant
(b) of the box plus the ball system remains constant
(c) of the ball remains constant
(d) of the ball relative to the box remains constant.

13. A body at rest breaks into two pieces of equal masses. The parts will move
(a) in same direction   (b) along different lines
(c) in opposite directions with equal speeds
(d) in opposite directions with unequal speeds.

14. A heavy ring of mass m is clamped on the periphery of a light circular disc. A small particle having equal mass is clamped at the centre of the disc. The system is rotated in such a way that the centre moves in a circle of radius r with a uniform speed v. We conclude that an external force

(a) $\frac{mv^2}{r}$ must be acting on the central particle

(b) $\frac{2mv^2}{r}$ must be acting on the central particle

(c) $\frac{2mv^2}{r}$ must be acting on the system

(d) $\frac{2mv^2}{r}$ must be acting on the ring.

15. The quantities remaining constant in a collision are
(a) momentum, kinetic energy and temperature
(b) momentum and kinetic energy but not temperature
(c) momentum and temperature but not kinetic energy
(d) momentum, but neither kinetic energy nor temperature.

16. A nucleus moving with a velocity $\vec{v}$ emits an α-particle. Let the velocities of the α-particle and the remaining nucleus be $\vec{v}_1$ and $\vec{v}_2$ and their masses be m_1 and m_2.
(a) $\vec{v}$, $\vec{v}_1$ and $\vec{v}_2$ must be parallel to each other.
(b) None of the two of $\vec{v}$, $\vec{v}_1$ and $\vec{v}_2$ should be parallel to each other.
(c) $\vec{v}_1 + \vec{v}_2$ must be parallel to $\vec{v}$.
(d) $m_1\vec{v}_1 + m_2\vec{v}_2$ must be parallel to $\vec{v}$.

17. A shell is fired from a cannon with a velocity V at an angle θ with the horizontal direction. At the highest point in its path, it explodes into two pieces of equal masses. One of the pieces retraces its path to the cannon. The speed of the other piece immediately after the explosion is

(a) $3V\cos\theta$ (b) $2V\cos\theta$ (c) $\frac{3}{2}V\cos\theta$ (d) $V\cos\theta$.

18. In an elastic collision
(a) the initial kinetic energy is equal to the final kinetic energy
(b) the final kinetic energy is less than the initial kinetic energy
(c) the kinetic energy remains constant
(d) the kinetic energy first increases then decreases.

19. In an inelastic collsion
(a) the initial kinetic energy is equal to the final kinetic energy
(b) the final kinetic energy is less than the initial kinetic energy
(c) the kinetic energy remains the constant
(d) the kinetic energy first increases then decreases.

OBJECTIVE II

1. The centre of mass of a system of particles is at the origin. It follows that
(a) the number of particles to the right of the origin is equal to the number of particles to the left
(b) the total mass of the particles to the right of the origin is same as the total mass to the left of the origin

(c) the number of particles on X-axis should be equal to the number of particles on Y-axis

(d) if there is a particle on the positive X-axis, there must be at least one particle on the negative X-axis.

2. A body has its centre of mass at the origin. The x-coordinates of the particles
(a) may be all positive   (b) may be all negative
(c) may be all non-negative
(d) may be positive for some case and negative in other cases.

3. In which of the following cases the centre of mass of a rod is certainly not at its centre ?
(a) the density continuously increases from left to right
(b) the density continuously decreases from left to right
(c) the density decreases from left to right upto the centre and then increases
(d) the density increases from left to right upto the centre and then decreases.

4. If the external forces acting on a system have zero resultant, the centre of mass
(a) must not move   (b) must not accelerate
(c) may move   (d) may accelerate.

5. A nonzero external force acts on a system of particles. The velocity and the acceleration of the centre of mass are found to be v_0 and a_0 at an instant t. It is possible that
(a) $v_0 = 0, a_0 = 0$ (b) $v_0 = 0, a_0 \neq 0$,
(c) $v_0 \neq 0, a_0 = 0$ (d) $v_0 \neq 0, a_0 \neq 0$.

6. Two balls are thrown simultaneously in air. The acceleration of the centre of mass of the two balls while in air
(a) depends on the direction of the motion of the balls
(b) depends on the masses of the two balls
(c) depends on the speeds of the two balls
(d) is equal to g.

7. A block moving in air breaks in two parts and the parts separate
(a) the total momentum must be conserved

(b) the total kinetic energy must be conserved
(c) the total momentum must change
(d) the total kinetic energy must change.

8. In an elastic collision
(a) the kinetic energy remains constant
(b) the linear momentum remains constant
(c) the final kinetic energy is equal to the initial kinetic energy
(d) the final linear momentum is equal to the initial linear momentum.

9. A ball hits a floor and rebounds after an inelastic collision. In this case
(a) the momentum of the ball just after the collision is same as that just before the collision
(b) the mechanical energy of the ball remains the same during the collision
(c) the total momentum of the ball and the earth is conserved
(d) the total energy of the ball and the earth remains the same.

10. A body moving towards a finite body at rest collides with it. It is possible that
(a) both the bodies come to rest
(b) both the bodies move after collision
(c) the moving body comes to rest and the stationary body starts moving
(d) the stationary body remains stationary, the moving body changes its velocity.

11. In a head-on elastic collision of two bodies of equal masses
(a) the velocities are interchanged
(b) the speeds are interchanged
(c) the momenta are interchanged
(d) the faster body slows down and the slower body speeds up.

EXERCISES

1. Three particles of masses 1·0 kg, 2·0 kg and 3·0 kg are placed at the corners A, B and C respectively of an equilateral triangle ABC of edge 1 m. Locate the centre of mass of the system.

2. The structure of a water molecule is shown in figure (9-E1). Find the distance of the centre of mass of the molecule from the centre of the oxygen atom.

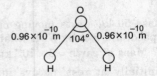

Figure 9-E1

3. Seven homogeneous bricks, each of length L, are arranged as shown in figure (9-E2). Each brick is displaced with respect to the one in contact by $L/10$. Find the x-coordinate of the centre of mass relative to the origin shown.

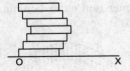

Figure 9-E2

4. A uniform disc of radius R is put over another uniform disc of radius 2R of the same thickness and density. The

peripheries of the two discs touch each other. Locate the centre of mass of the system.

5. A disc of radius R is cut out from a larger disc of radius $2R$ in such a way that the edge of the hole touches the edge of the disc. Locate the centre of mass of the residual disc.

6. A square plate of edge d and a circular disc of diameter d are placed touching each other at the midpoint of an edge of the plate as shown in figure (9-Q2). Locate the centre of mass of the combination, assuming same mass per unit area for the two plates.

7. Calculate the velocity of the centre of mass of the system of particles shown in figure (9-E3).

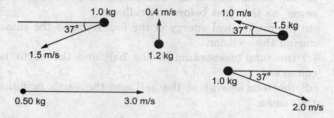

Figure 9-E3

8. Two blocks of masses 10 kg and 20 kg are placed on the X-axis. The first mass is moved on the axis by a distance of 2 cm. By what distance should the second mass be moved to keep the position of the centre of mass unchanged ?

9. Two blocks of masses 10 kg and 30 kg are placed along a vertical line. The first block is raised through a height of 7 cm. By what distance should the second mass be moved to raise the centre of mass by 1 cm ?

10. Consider a gravity-free hall in which a tray of mass M, carrying a cubical block of ice of mass m and edge L, is at rest in the middle (figure 9-E4). If the ice melts, by what distance does the centre of mass of "the tray plus the ice" system descend ?

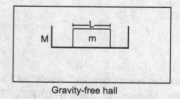

Gravity-free hall

Figure 9-E4

11. Find the centre of mass of a uniform plate having semicircular inner and outer boundaries of radii R_1 and R_2 (figure 9-E5).

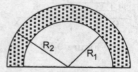

Figure 9-E5

12. Mr. Verma (50 kg) and Mr. Mathur (60 kg) are sitting at the two extremes of a 4 m long boat (40 kg) standing still in water. To discuss a mechanics problem, they come to the middle of the boat. Neglecting friction with water, how far does the boat move on the water during the process ?

13. A cart of mass M is at rest on a frictionless horizontal surface and a pendulum bob of mass m hangs from the roof of the cart (figure 9-E6). The string breaks, the bob falls on the floor, makes several collisions on the floor and finally lands up in a small slot made in the floor. The horizontal distance between the string and the slot is L. Find the displacement of the cart during this process.

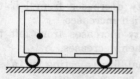

Figure 9-E6

14. The balloon, the light rope and the monkey shown in figure (9-E7) are at rest in the air. If the monkey reaches the top of the rope, by what distance does the balloon descend ? Mass of the balloon = M, mass of the monkey = m and the length of the rope ascended by the monkey = L.

Figure 9-E7

15. Find the ratio of the linear momenta of two particles of masses 1·0 kg and 4·0 kg if their kinetic energies are equal.

16. A uranium-238 nucleus, initially at rest, emits an alpha particle with a speed of $1·4 \times 10^7$ m/s. Calculate the recoil speed of the residual nucleus thorium-234. Assume that the mass of a nucleus is proportional to the mass number.

17. A man of mass 50 kg starts moving on the earth and acquires a speed of 1·8 m/s. With what speed does the earth recoil ? Mass of earth = 6×10^{24} kg.

18. A neutron initially at rest, decays into a proton, an electron and an antineutrino. The ejected electron has a momentum of $1·4 \times 10^{-26}$ kg-m/s and the antineutrino

6.4×10^{-27} kg-m/s. Find the recoil speed of the proton (a) if the electron and the antineutrino are ejected along the same direction and (b) if they are ejected along perpendicular directions. Mass of the proton $= 1.67 \times 10^{-27}$ kg.

19. A man of mass M having a bag of mass m slips from the roof of a tall building of height H and starts falling vertically (figure 9-E8). When at a height h from the ground, he notices that the ground below him is pretty hard, but there is a pond at a horizontal distance x from the line of fall. In order to save himself he throws the bag horizontally (with respect to himself) in the direction opposite to the pond. Calculate the minimum horizontal velocity imparted to the bag so that the man lands in the water. If the man just succeeds to avoid the hard ground, where will the bag land ?

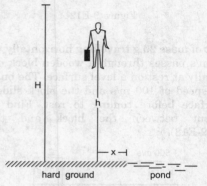

Figure 9-E8

20. A ball of mass 50 g moving at a speed of 2·0 m/s strikes a plane surface at an angle of incidence 45°. The ball is reflected by the plane at equal angle of reflection with the same speed. Calculate (a) the magnitude of the change in momentum of the ball (b) the change in the magnitude of the momentum of the ball.

21. Light in certain cases may be considered as a stream of particles called photons. Each photon has a linear momentum h/λ where h is the Planck's constant and λ is the wavelength of the light. A beam of light of wavelength λ is incident on a plane mirror at an angle of incidence θ. Calculate the change in the linear momentum of a photon as the beam is reflected by the mirror.

22. A block at rest explodes into three equal parts. Two parts start moving along X and Y axes respectively with equal speeds of 10 m/s. Find the initial velocity of the third part.

Figure 9-E9

23. Two fat astronauts each of mass 120 kg are travelling in a closed spaceship moving at a speed of 15 km/s in the outer space far removed from all other material objects. The total mass of the spaceship and its contents including the astronauts is 660 kg. If the astronauts do slimming exercise and thereby reduce their masses to 90 kg each, with what velocity will the spaceship move ?

24. During a heavy rain, hailstones of average size 1·0 cm in diameter fall with an average speed of 20 m/s. Suppose 2000 hailstones strike every square meter of a 10 m × 10 m roof perpendicularly in one second and assume that the hailstones do not rebound. Calculate the average force exerted by the falling hailstones on the roof. Density of a hailstone is 900 kg/m^3.

25. A ball of mass m is dropped onto a floor from a certain height. The collision is perfectly elastic and the ball rebounds to the same height and again falls. Find the average force exerted by the ball on the floor during a long time interval.

26. A railroad car of mass M is at rest on frictionless rails when a man of mass m starts moving on the car towards the engine. If the car recoils with a speed v backward on the rails, with what velocity is the man approaching the engine ?

27. A gun is mounted on a railroad car. The mass of the car, the gun, the shells and the operator is $50\,m$ where m is the mass of one shell. If the velocity of the shell with respect to the gun (in its state before firing) is 200 m/s, what is the recoil speed of the car after the second shot ? Neglect friction.

28. Two persons each of mass m are standing at the two extremes of a railroad car of mass M resting on a smooth track (figure 9-E10). The person on left jumps to the left with a horizontal speed u with respect to the state of the car before the jump. Thereafter, the other person jumps to the right, again with the same horizontal speed u with respect to the state of the car before his jump. Find the velocity of the car after both the persons have jumped off.

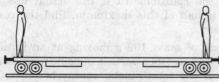

Figure 9-E10

29. Figure (9-E11) shows a small block of mass m which is started with a speed v on the horizontal part of the bigger block of mass M placed on a horizontal floor. The curved part of the surface shown is semicircular. All the surfaces are frictionless. Find the speed of the bigger block when the smaller block reaches the point A of the surface.

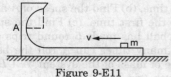

Figure 9-E11

30. In a typical Indian *Bugghi* (a luxury cart drawn by horses), a wooden plate is fixed on the rear on which one person can sit. A bugghi of mass 200 kg is moving at a speed of 10 km/h. As it overtakes a school boy walking at a speed of 4 km/h, the boy sits on the wooden plate. If the mass of the boy is 25 kg, what will be the new velocity of the bugghi ?

31. A ball of mass 0·50 kg moving at a speed of 5·0 m/s collides with another ball of mass 1·0 kg. After the collision the balls stick together and remain motionless. What was the velocity of the 1·0 kg block before the collision ?

32. A 60 kg man skating with a speed of 10 m/s collides with a 40 kg skater at rest and they cling to each other. Find the loss of kinetic energy during the collision.

33. Consider a head-on collision between two particles of masses m_1 and m_2. The initial speeds of the particles are u_1 and u_2 in the same direction. The collision starts at $t = 0$ and the particles interact for a time interval Δt. During the collision, the speed of the first particle varies as

$$v(t) = u_1 + \frac{t}{\Delta t}(v_1 - u_1).$$

Find the speed of the second particle as a function of time during the collision.

34. A bullet of mass m moving at a speed v hits a ball of mass M kept at rest. A small part having mass m' breaks from the ball and sticks to the bullet. The remaining ball is found to move at a speed v_1 in the direction of the bullet. Find the velocity of the bullet after the collision.

35. A ball of mass m moving at a speed v makes a head-on collision with an identical ball at rest. The kinetic energy of the balls after the collision is three fourths of the original. Find the coefficient of restitution.

36. A block of mass 2·0 kg moving at 2·0 m/s collides head on with another block of equal mass kept at rest. (a) Find the maximum possible loss in kinetic energy due to the collision. (b) If the actual loss in kinetic energy is half of this maximum, find the coefficient of restitution.

37. A particle of mass 100 g moving at an initial speed u collides with another particle of same mass kept initially at rest. If the total kinetic energy becomes 0·2 J after the collision, what could be the minimum and the maximum value of u.

38. Two friends A and B (each weighing 40 kg) are sitting on a frictionless platform some distance d apart. A rolls a ball of mass 4 kg on the platform towards B which B catches. Then B rolls the ball towards A and A catches it. The ball keeps on moving back and forth between A and B. The ball has a fixed speed of 5 m/s on the platform. (a) Find the speed of A after he rolls the ball for the first time. (b) Find the speed of A after he catches the ball for the first time. (c) Find the speeds of A and B after the ball has made 5 round trips and is held by A. (d) How many times can A roll the ball ? (e) Where is the centre of mass of the system "A + B + ball" at the end of the nth trip ?

39. A ball falls on the ground from a height of 2·0 m and rebounds up to a height of 1·5 m. Find the coefficient of restitution.

40. In a gamma decay process, the internal energy of a nucleus of mass M decreases, a gamma photon of energy E and linear momentum E/c is emitted and the nucleus recoils. Find the decrease in internal energy.

41. A block of mass 2·0 kg is moving on a frictionless horizontal surface with a velocity of 1·0 m/s (figure 9-E12) towards another block of equal mass kept at rest. The spring constant of the spring fixed at one end is 100 N/m. Find the maximum compression of the spring.

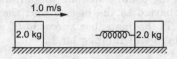

Figure 9-E12

42. A bullet of mass 20 g travelling horizontally with a speed of 500 m/s passes through a wooden block of mass 10·0 kg initially at rest on a level surface. The bullet emerges with a speed of 100 m/s and the block slides 20 cm on the surface before coming to rest. Find the friction coefficient between the block and the surface (figure 9-E13).

Figure 9-E13

43. A projectile is fired with a speed u at an angle θ above a horizontal field. The coefficient of restitution of collision between the projectile and the field is e. How far from the starting point, does the projectile makes its second collision with the field ?

44. A ball falls on an inclined plane of inclination θ from a height h above the point of impact and makes a perfectly elastic collision. Where will it hit the plane again ?

45. Solve the previous problem if the coefficient of restitution is e. Use $\theta = 45°$, $e = \frac{3}{4}$ and $h = 5$ m.

46. A block of mass 200 g is suspended through a vertical spring. The spring is stretched by 1·0 cm when the block is in equilibrium. A particle of mass 120 g is dropped on the block from a height of 45 cm. The particle sticks to the block after the impact. Find the maximum extension of the spring. Take $g = 10$ m/s^2.

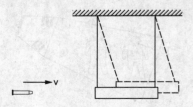

Figure 9-E14

47. A bullet of mass 25 g is fired horizontally into a ballistic pendulum of mass 5·0 kg and gets embedded in it (figure 9-E14). If the centre of the pendulum rises by a distance of 10 cm, find the speed of the bullet.

48. A bullet of mass 20 g moving horizontally at a speed of 300 m/s is fired into a wooden block of mass 500 g suspended by a long string. The bullet crosses the block and emerges on the other side. If the centre of mass of the block rises through a height of 20·0 cm, find the speed of the bullet as it emerges from the block.

49. Two masses m_1 and m_2 are connected by a spring of spring constant k and are placed on a frictionless horizontal surface. Initially the spring is stretched through a distance x_0 when the system is released from rest. Find the distance moved by the two masses before they again come to rest.

50. Two blocks of masses m_1 and m_2 are connected by a spring of spring constant k (figure 9-E15). The block of mass m_2 is given a sharp impulse so that it acquires a velocity v_0 towards right. Find (a) the velocity of the centre of mass, (b) the maximum elongation that the spring will suffer.

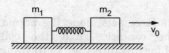

Figure 9-E15

51. Consider the situation of the previous problem. Suppose each of the blocks is pulled by a constant force F instead of any impulse. Find the maximum elongation that the spring will suffer and the distances moved by the two blocks in the process.

52. Consider the situation of the previous problem. Suppose the block of mass m_1 is pulled by a constant force F_1 and the other block is pulled by a constant force F_2. Find the maximum elongation that the spring will suffer.

53. Consider a gravity-free hall in which an experimenter of mass 50 kg is resting on a 5 kg pillow, 8 ft above the floor of the hall. He pushes the pillow down so that it starts falling at a speed of 8 ft/s. The pillow makes a perfectly elastic collision with the floor, rebounds and reaches the experimenter's head. Find the time elapsed in the process.

54. The track shown in figure (9-E16) is frictionless. The block B of mass $2m$ is lying at rest and the block A of mass m is pushed along the track with some speed. The collision between A and B is perfectly elastic. With what velocity should the block A be started to get the sleeping man awakened ?

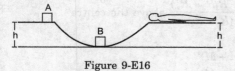

Figure 9-E16

55. A bullet of mass 10 g moving horizontally at a speed of $50\sqrt{7}$ m/s strikes a block of mass 490 g kept on a

frictionless track as shown in figure (9-E17). The bullet remains inside the block and the system proceeds towards the semicircular track of radius 0·2 m. Where will the block strike the horizontal part after leaving the semicircular track ?

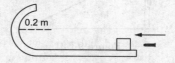

Figure 9-E17

56. Two balls having masses m and $2m$ are fastened to two light strings of same length l (figure 9-E18). The other ends of the strings are fixed at O. The strings are kept in the same horizontal line and the system is released from rest. The collision between the balls is elastic. (a) Find the velocities of the balls just after their collision. (b) How high will the balls rise after the collision ?

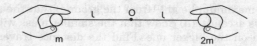

Figure 9-E18

57. A uniform chain of mass M and length L is held vertically in such a way that its lower end just touches the horizontal floor. The chain is released from rest in this position. Any portion that strikes the floor comes to rest. Assuming that the chain does not form a heap on the floor, calculate the force exerted by it on the floor when a length x has reached the floor.

58. The blocks shown in figure (9-E19) have equal masses. The surface of A is smooth but that of B has a friction coefficient of 0·10 with the floor. Block A is moving at a speed of 10 m/s towards B which is kept at rest. Find the distance travelled by B if (a) the collision is perfectly elastic and (b) the collision is perfectly inelastic. Take $g = 10$ m/s^2.

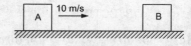

Figure 9-E19

59. The friction coefficient between the horizontal surface and each of the blocks shown in figure (9-E20) is 0·20. The collision between the blocks is perfectly elastic. Find the separation between the two blocks when they come to rest. Take $g = 10$ m/s^2.

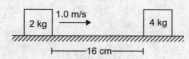

Figure 9-E20

60. A block of mass m is placed on a triangular block of mass M, which in turn is placed on a horizontal surface as shown in figure (9-E21). Assuming frictionless surfaces find the velocity of the triangular block when the smaller block reaches the bottom end.

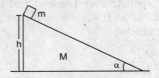

Figure 9-E21

61. Figure (9-E22) shows a small body of mass m placed over a larger mass M whose surface is horizontal near the smaller mass and gradually curves to become vertical. The smaller mass is pushed on the longer one at a speed v and the system is left to itself. Assume that all the surfaces are frictionless. (a) Find the speed of the larger block when the smaller block is sliding on the vertical part. (b) Find the speed of the smaller mass when it breaks off the larger mass at height h. (c) Find the maximum height (from the ground) that the smaller mass ascends. (d) Show that the smaller mass will again land on the bigger one. Find the distance traversed by the bigger block during the time when the smaller block was in its flight under gravity.

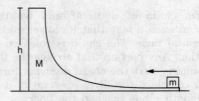

Figure 9-E22

□

62. A small block of superdense material has a mass of 3×10^{24} kg. It is situated at a height h (much smaller than the earth's radius) from where it falls on the earth's surface. Find its speed when its height from the earth's surface has reduced to $h/2$. The mass of the earth is 6×10^{24} kg.

63. A body of mass m makes an elastic collision with another identical body at rest. Show that if the collision is not head-on, the bodies go at right angle to each other after the collision.

64. A small particle travelling with a velocity v collides elastically with a spherical body of equal mass and of radius r initially kept at rest. The centre of this spherical body is located a distance $\rho(< r)$ away from the direction of motion of the particle (figure 9-E23). Find the final velocities of the two particles.

Figure 9-E23

[**Hint** : The force acts along the normal to the sphere through the contact. Treat the collision as one-dimensional for this direction. In the tangential direction no force acts and the velocities do not change].

ANSWERS

OBJECTIVE I

1. (c)	2. (d)	3. (d)	4. (d)	5. (b)	6. (b)
7. (b)	8. (b)	9. (c)	10. (d)	11. (c)	12. (b)
13. (c)	14. (c)	15. (d)	16. (d)	17. (a)	18. (a)
19. (b)					

OBJECTIVE II

1. none	2. (c), (d)	3. (a), (b)
4. (b), (c)	5. (b), (d)	6. (d)
7. (a), (d)	8. (b), (c), (d)	9. (c), (d)
10. (b), (c)	11. all	

EXERCISES

1. Taking AB as the x-axis and A as the origin, the centre of mass is at $(7/12$ m, $\sqrt{3}/4$ m$)$

2. 6.6×10^{-12} m

3. $22\,L/35$

4. At $R/5$ from the centre of the bigger disc towards the centre of the smaller disc

5. At $R/3$ from the centre of the original disc away from the centre of the hole

6. $\dfrac{4d}{4+\pi}$ right to the centre of the disc

7. 0·20 m/s at 45° below the direction towards right

8. 1 cm

9. 1 cm downward

10. zero

11. $\dfrac{4(R_1^2 + R_1 R_2 + R_2^2)}{3\pi (R_1 + R_2)}$ above the centre

12. 13 cm

13. $mL/(m + M)$

14. $mL/(m + M)$

15. 1 : 2

16. $2·4 \times 10^5$ m/s

17. 1.5×10^{-23} m/s

18. (a) 12·2 m/s   (b) 9·2 m/s

19. $\dfrac{Mx\sqrt{g}}{m\left[\sqrt{2H}-\sqrt{2(H-h)}\right]}$, Mx/m left to the line of fall

20. (a) 0·14 kg-m/s (b) zero

21. $2h\cos\theta/\lambda$

22. $10\sqrt{2}$ m/s 135° below the X-axis

23. 15 km/s

24. 1900 N

25. mg

26. $\left(1+\dfrac{M}{m}\right)v$

27. $200\left(\dfrac{1}{49}+\dfrac{1}{48}\right)$ m/s

28. $\dfrac{m^2 u}{M(M+m)}$ towards left

29. $\dfrac{mv}{M+m}$

30. $\dfrac{28}{3}$ km/h

31. 2·5 m/s opposite to the direction of motion of the first ball

32. 1200 J

33. $u_2 - \dfrac{m_1}{m_2}\dfrac{t}{\Delta t}(v_1-u_1)$

34. $\dfrac{mv-(M-m')v_1}{m+m'}$ in the initial direction

35. $1/\sqrt{2}$ 36. 2 J, $1/\sqrt{2}$

37. 2 m/s, $2\sqrt{2}$ m/s

38. (a) 0·5 m/s (b) $\dfrac{10}{11}$ m/s (c) $\dfrac{50}{11}$ m/s, 5 m/s (d) 6 (e) $\dfrac{10}{21}d$
    away from the initial position of A towards B

39. $\sqrt{3}/2$

40. $E+\dfrac{E^2}{2Mc^2}$

41. 10 cm

42. 0·16

43. $\dfrac{(1+e)u^2\sin 2\theta}{g}$

44. $8h\sin\theta$ along the incline

45. 18·5 m along the incline

46. 6·1 cm

47. 280 m/s

48. 250 m/s

49. $\dfrac{2m_2 x_0}{m_1+m_2}$, $\dfrac{2m_1 x_0}{m_1+m_2}$

50. (a) $\dfrac{m_2 v_0}{m_1+m_2}$ (b) $v_0\left[\dfrac{m_1 m_2}{(m_1+m_2)k}\right]^{1/2}$

51. $2F/k$, $\dfrac{2Fm_2}{k(m_1+m_2)}$, $\dfrac{2Fm_1}{k(m_1+m_2)}$

52. $\dfrac{2(m_1 F_2+m_2 F_1)}{k(m_1+m_2)}$

53. 2·22 s

54. Greater than $\sqrt{2.5gh}$

55. At the junction of the straight and the curved parts

56. (a) Light ball $\dfrac{\sqrt{50gl}}{3}$ towards left, heavy ball $\dfrac{\sqrt{2gl}}{3}$
    towards right (b) Light ball $2l$ and heavy ball $\dfrac{l}{9}$

57. $3Mgx/L$

58. (a) 50 m (b) 25 m

59. 5 cm

60. $\left[\dfrac{2m^2 gh\cos^2\alpha}{(M+m)(M+m\sin^2\alpha)}\right]^{1/2}$

61. (a) $\dfrac{mv}{M+m}$ (b) $\left[\dfrac{(M^2+Mm+m^2)}{(M+m)^2}v^2-2gh\right]^{1/2}$
    (c) $\dfrac{Mv^2}{2g(M+m)}$ (d) $\dfrac{2mv[Mv^2-2(M+m)gh]^{1/2}}{g(M+m)^{3/2}}$

62. $\sqrt{\dfrac{2gh}{3}}$

64. The small particle goes along the tangent with a speed of $v\rho/r$ and the spherical body goes perpendicular to the smaller particle with a speed of $\dfrac{v}{r}\sqrt{r^2-\rho^2}$

□

CHAPTER 10

ROTATIONAL MECHANICS

Consider a pulley fixed at a typical Indian well on which a rope is wound with one end attached to a bucket. When the bucket is released, the pulley starts rotating. As the bucket goes down, the pulley rotates more rapidly till the bucket goes into the water.

Take the pulley as the system. The centre of mass of the pulley is at its geometrical centre which remains at rest. However, the other particles of the pulley move and are accelerated. The pulley is said to be executing rotational motion. Also, the rotational motion is not uniform. Since $\vec{a}_{CM} = 0$, the resultant external force $\vec{F}$ acting on the pulley must be zero. Even then the pulley is not in rotational equilibrium. We shall now study this type of motion.

10.1 ROTATION OF A RIGID BODY ABOUT A GIVEN FIXED LINE

Take a rigid body like a plate or a ball or your tennis racket or anything else present nearby and hold it between your fingers at two points. Now keep these two points fixed and then displace the body (try it with any rigid body at hand).

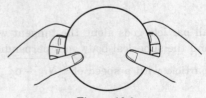

Figure 10.1

Notice the kind of displacement you can produce. In particular, notice that each particle of the rigid body goes in a circle, the centre being on the line joining the two fixed points between your finger tips. Let us call this line the axis of rotation. In fact, the centre of the circular path of a particle is at the foot of the perpendicular from the particle to this axis. Different particles move in different circles, the planes of all these circles are parallel to each other, and the radii depend on the distances of the particles from this axis. The particles on the axis remain stationary, those close

to this line move on smaller circles and those far away from this line move in larger circles. However, each particle takes equal time to complete its circle.

Such a displacement of a rigid body in which a given line is held fixed, is called *rotation of the rigid body about the given line*. The line itself is called the *axis of rotation*.

Examples : (1) Consider the door of your almirah. When you open the door, the vertical line passing through the hinges is held fixed and that is the axis of rotation. Each point of the door describes a circle with the centre at the foot of the perpendicular from the particle on the axis. All these circles are horizontal and thus perpendicular to the axis.

(2) Consider the ceiling fan in your room. When it is on, each point on its body goes in a circle. Locate the centres of the circles traced by different particles on the three blades of the fan and the body covering the motor. All these centres lie on a vertical line through the centre of the body. The fan rotates about this vertical line.

(3) Look at the on–off switch on the front panel of your gas stove in the kitchen. To put the gas on, you push the switch a little, and then you rotate it. While rotating, each particle of the switch moves on a circle. Think about the centres of all such circles. They lie on a straight line (generally horizontal, towards the operator). This is the axis of rotation and the switch rotates about this axis.

Sometimes the axis may not pass through the body. Consider a record rotating on the turntable of a record player. Suppose a fly is sitting on the record near the rim. Look at the path of any particle of the fly. It is a circle with the centre on the vertical line through the centre of the record. The fly is "rotating about this vertical line" (can you consider the fly as a rigid body ?). The axis of rotation is lying completely outside the fly.

If each particle of a rigid body moves in a circle, with centres of all the circles on a straight line and with planes of the circles perpendicular to this line, we say that the body is rotating about this line. The straight line itself is called the *axis of rotation*.

10.2 KINEMATICS

Consider a rigid body rotating about a given fixed line. Take this line as the Z-axis. Consider a particle P of the body (figure 10.2). Look at its position P_0 at $t = 0$. Draw a perpendicular P_0Q to the axis of rotation. At time t, the particle moves to P. Let $\angle PQP_0 = \theta$. We say that the particle P has rotated through an angle θ. In fact, all the particles of the body have also rotated through the same angle θ and so we say that the whole rigid body has rotated through an angle θ. The "angular position" of the body at time t is said to be θ. If P has made a complete revolution on its circle, every particle has done so and we say that the body has rotated through an angle of 2π. So the rotation of a rigid body is measured by the rotation of the line QP from its initial position.

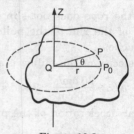

Figure 10.2

Now, suppose the angular position of the body at time t is θ. During a time Δt, it further rotates through $\Delta\theta$, so that its angular position becomes $\theta + \Delta\theta$. The average angular velocity during the time interval Δt is

$$\omega = \frac{\Delta\theta}{\Delta t}.$$

The instantaneous angular velocity at time t is

$$\omega = \frac{d\theta}{dt}.$$

We associate the direction of the axis of rotation with the angular velocity. If the body rotates anticlockwise as seen through the axis, the angular velocity is towards the viewer. If it rotates clockwise, the angular velocity is away from the reader. It turns out that the angular velocity adds like a vector and hence it becomes a vector quantity. The magnitude of angular velocity is called *angular speed*. However, we shall continue to use the word angular velocity if the direction of the axis is clear from the context. The SI unit for angular velocity is radian/sec (rad/s). Quite often the angular velocity is given in revolutions per second (rev/s). The conversion in radian per second may be made using $1\ \text{rev} = 2\pi$ radian.

If the body rotates through equal angles in equal time intervals (irrespective of the smallness of the intervals), we say that it rotates with uniform angular velocity. In this case $\omega = d\theta/dt =$ constant and thus $\theta = \omega t$. If it is not the case, the body is said to be rotationally "accelerated". The angular acceleration is defined as

$$\alpha = \frac{d\omega}{dt} = \frac{d}{dt}\left(\frac{d\theta}{dt}\right) = \frac{d^2\theta}{dt^2}.$$

If the angular acceleration α is constant, we have

$$\omega = \omega_0 + \alpha t \qquad \qquad \dots (10.1)$$

$$\theta = \omega_0 t + \frac{1}{2}\alpha t^2 \qquad \qquad \dots (10.2)$$

and $\qquad\qquad \omega^2 = \omega_0^2 + 2\alpha\theta \qquad\qquad \dots (10.3)$

where ω_0 is the angular velocity of the body at $t = 0$.

As an example, think of your ceiling fan. Switch on the fan. The fan rotates about a vertical line (axis). The angle rotated by the fan in the first second is small, that in the second second is larger, that in the third second is still larger and so on. The fan, thus, has an angular acceleration. The angular velocity $\omega = d\theta/dt$ increases with time. Wait for about a couple of minutes. The fan has now attained full speed. The angle rotated in any time interval is now equal to the angle rotated in the successive equal time interval. The fan is rotating uniformly about the vertical axis. Now switch off the fan. The angle rotated in any second is smaller than the angle rotated in the previous second. The angular velocity $d\omega/dt$ decreases as time passes, and finally it becomes zero when the fan stops. The fan has an angular deceleration.

Given the axis of rotation, the body can rotate in two directions. Looking through the axis, it may be clockwise or anticlockwise. One has to define the "positive" rotation. This may be defined according to the convenience of the problem, but once decided, one has to stick to the choice. The angular displacement, angular velocity and the angular acceleration may accordingly be positive or negative.

Notice the similarity between the motion of a particle on a straight line and the rotation of a rigid body about a fixed axis. The position of the particle was decided by a single variable x, which could be positive or negative according to the choice of the positive direction of the X-axis. The rate of change of position gave the velocity and the rate of change of velocity gave the acceleration.

Example 10.1 ———————————————————

The motor of an engine is rotating about its axis with an angular velocity of 100 *rev/minute. It comes to rest in* 15 s, *after being switched off. Assuming constant angular deceleration, calculate the number of revolutions made by it before coming to rest.*

Solution : The initial angular velocity = 100 rev/minute

$$= (10\,\pi/3)\ \text{rad/s}.$$

Final angular velocity = 0.

Time interval = 15 s.

Let the angular acceleration be α. Using the equation $\omega = \omega_0 + \alpha t$, we obtain $\alpha = (-2\pi/9)\ \text{rad/s}^2$.

The angle rotated by the motor during this motion is

$$\theta = \omega_0 t + \frac{1}{2}\,\alpha t^2$$

$$= \left(\frac{10\pi}{3}\,\frac{\text{rad}}{\text{s}}\right)(15\ \text{s}) - \frac{1}{2}\left(\frac{2\pi}{9}\,\frac{\text{rad}}{\text{s}^2}\right)(15\ \text{s})^2$$

$$= 25\pi\ \text{rad} = 12{\cdot}5\ \text{revolutions}.$$

Hence the motor rotates through 12·5 revolutions before coming to rest.

Example 10.2 ─────────────

Starting from rest, a fan takes five seconds to attain the maximum speed of 400 rpm(revolutions per minute). Assuming constant acceleration, find the time taken by the fan in attaining half the maximum speed.

Solution : Let the angular acceleration be α. According to the question,

$$400\ \text{rev/min} = 0 + \alpha\ 5\ \text{s} \qquad \dots\ (i)$$

Let t be the time taken in attaining the speed of 200 rev/min which is half the maximum.

Then, $200\ \text{rev/min} = 0 + \alpha t$ $\dots$ (ii)

Dividing (i) by (ii), we get,

$$2 = 5\ \text{s}/t \quad \text{or,} \quad t = 2{\cdot}5\ \text{s}.$$

Relation between the Linear Motion of a Particle of a Rigid Body and its Rotation

Consider a point P of the rigid body rotating about a fixed axis as shown in figure (10.2). As the body rotates, this point moves on a circle. The radius of this circle is the perpendicular distance of the particle from the axis of rotation. Let it be r. If the body rotates through an angle θ, so does the radius joining the particle with the centre of its circle. The linear distance moved by the particle is $s = r\theta$ along the circle.

The linear speed along the tangent is

$$v = \frac{ds}{dt} = r \cdot \frac{d\theta}{dt} = r\omega \qquad \dots\ (10.4)$$

and the linear acceleration along the tangent, i.e., the tangential acceleration, is

$$a = \frac{dv}{dt} = r \cdot \frac{d\omega}{dt} = r\alpha. \qquad \dots\ (10.5)$$

The relations $v = r\omega$ and $a = r\alpha$ are very useful and their meanings should be clearly understood. For different particles of the rigid body, the radius r of their circles has different values, but ω and α are same for all the particles. Thus, the linear speed and the tangential acceleration of different particles are different. For $r = 0$, i.e., for the particles on the axis, $v = r\omega = 0$ and $a = r\alpha = 0$, consistent with the fact that the particles on the axis do not move at all.

Example 10.3 ─────────────

A bucket is being lowered down into a well through a rope passing over a fixed pulley of radius 10 cm. *Assume that the rope does not slip on the pulley. Find the angular velocity and angular acceleration of the pulley at an instant when the bucket is going down at a speed of* 20 cm/s *and has an acceleration of* 4·0 m/s^2.

Solution : Since the rope does not slip on the pulley, the linear speed v of the rim of the pulley is same as the speed of the bucket.

The angular velocity of the pulley is then

$$\omega = v/r = \frac{20\ \text{cm/s}}{10\ \text{cm}} = 2\ \text{rad/s}$$

and the angular acceleration of the pulley is

$$\alpha = a/r = \frac{4{\cdot}0\ \text{m/s}^2}{10\ \text{cm}} = 40\ \text{rad/s}^2.$$

10.3 ROTATIONAL DYNAMICS

When one switches a fan on, the centre of the fan remains unmoved while the fan rotates with an angular acceleration. As the centre of mass remains at rest, the external forces acting on the fan must add to zero. This means that one can have angular acceleration even if the resultant external force is zero. But then why do we need to switch on the fan in order to start it ? If an angular acceleration may be achieved with zero total external force, why does not a wheel chair start rotating on the floor as soon as one wishes it to do so. Why are we compelled to use our muscles to set it into rotation ? In fact, one cannot have angular acceleration without external forces.

What is then the relation between the force and the angular acceleration ? We find that even if the resultant external force is zero, we may have angular acceleration. We also find that without applying an external force we cannot have an angular acceleration. What is responsible for producing angular acceleration ? The answer is *torque* which we define below.

10.4 TORQUE OF A FORCE ABOUT THE AXIS OF ROTATION

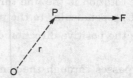

Figure 10.3

Consider a force $\vec{F}$ acting on a particle P. Choose an origin O and let $\vec{r}$ be the position vector of the particle experiencing the force. We define *the torque of the force F about O* as

$$\vec{\Gamma} = \vec{r} \times \vec{F} \qquad \dots \text{(10.6)}$$

This is a vector quantity having its direction perpendicular to $\vec{r}$ and $\vec{F}$ according to the rule of cross product. Now consider a rigid body rotating about a given axis of rotation AB (figure 10.4). Let F be a force acting on the particle P of the body. F may not be in the plane ABP. Take the origin O somewhere on the axis of rotation.

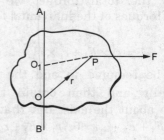

Figure 10.4

The torque of F about O is $\vec{\Gamma} = \vec{r} \times \vec{F}$. Its component along OA is called the torque of $\vec{F}$ *about OA*. To calculate it, we should find the vector $\vec{r} \times \vec{F}$ and then find out the angle θ it makes with OA. The torque about OA is then $|\vec{r} \times \vec{F}| \cos\theta$. The torque of a force about a line is independent of the choice of the origin as long as it is chosen on the line. This can be shown as given below. Let O_1 be any point on the line AB (figure 10.4). The torque of F about O_1 is

$$\vec{O_1P} \times \vec{F} = (\vec{O_1O} + \vec{OP}) \times \vec{F} = \vec{O_1O} \times \vec{F} + \vec{OP} \times \vec{F}.$$

As $\vec{O_1O} \times \vec{F} \perp \vec{O_1O}$, this term will have no component along AB.

Thus, the component of $\vec{O_1P} \times \vec{F}$ is equal to that of $\vec{OP} \times \vec{F}$.

There are some special cases which occur frequently.

Case I

$$\vec{F} \parallel \vec{AB}.$$

$\vec{r} \times \vec{F}$ is perpendicular to $\vec{F}$, but $\vec{F} \parallel \vec{AB}$, hence $\vec{r} \times \vec{F}$ is perpendicular to $\vec{AB}$. The component of $\vec{r} \times \vec{F}$ along $\vec{AB}$ is, therefore, zero.

Case II

F intersects AB (say at O)

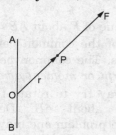

Figure 10.5

Taking the point of intersection as the origin, we see that $\vec{r}(= \vec{OP})$ and $\vec{F}$ are in the same line. The torque about O is $\vec{r} \times \vec{F} = 0$. Hence the component along OA is zero.

Case III

$\vec{F} \perp \vec{AB}$ but $\vec{F}$ and AB do not intersect.

In three dimensions, two lines may be perpendicular without intersecting each other. For example, a vertical line on the surface of a wall of your room and a horizontal line on the opposite wall are mutually perpendicular but they never intersect. Two nonparallel and nonintersecting lines are called *skew* lines.

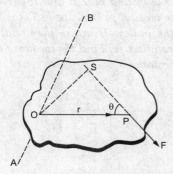

Figure 10.6

Figure (10.6) shows the plane through the particle P that is perpendicular to the axis of rotation AB. Suppose the plane intersects the axis at the point O. The force F is in this plane. Taking the origin at O,

$$\vec{\Gamma} = \vec{r} \times \vec{F} = \vec{OP} \times \vec{F}.$$

Thus, $\qquad \Gamma = rF \sin\theta = F . (OS)$

where OS is the perpendicular from O to the line of action of the force $\vec{F}$. The line OS is also perpendicular to the axis of rotation. It is thus the length of the common perpendicular to the force and the axis of rotation.

The direction of $\vec{\Gamma} = \overrightarrow{OP} \times \vec{F}$ is along the axis AB because $\overrightarrow{AB} \perp \overrightarrow{OP}$ and $\overrightarrow{AB} \perp \vec{F}$. The torque about AB is, therefore, equal to the magnitude of $\vec{\Gamma}$ that is $F.(OS)$.

Thus, the torque of F about AB = magnitude of the force $F \times$ length of the common perpendicular to the force and the axis. The common perpendicular OS is called the *lever arm or moment arm* of this torque.

The torque may try to rotate the body clockwise or anticlockwise about AB. Depending on the convenience of the problem one may be called positive and the other negative. It is conventional to take the torque positive if the body rotates anticlockwise as viewed through the axis.

Case IV

$\vec{F}$ and $\overrightarrow{OA}$ are skew but not perpendicular.

Take components of $\vec{F}$ parallel and perpendicular to the axis.

The torque of the parallel part is zero from case I and that of the perpendicular part may be found as in case III.

In most of the applications that we shall see, cases I, II or III will apply.

Example 10.4

Consider a pulley fixed at its centre of mass by a clamp. A light rope is wound over it and the free end is tied to a block. The tension in the rope is T. (a) Write the forces acting on the pulley. How are they related? (b) Locate the axis of rotation. (c) Find the torque of the forces about the axis of rotation.

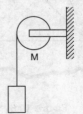

Figure 10.7

Solution : (a) The forces on the pulley are (figure 10.7)
   (i) attraction by the earth, Mg vertically downward,
   (ii) tension T by the rope, along the rope,
   (iii) contact force $\mathscr{N}$ by the support at the centre.

$\mathscr{N} = T + Mg$ (centre of mass of the pulley is at rest, so Newton's 1st law applies).

(b) The axis of rotation is the line through the centre of the pulley and perpendicular to the plane of the pulley.

(c) Let us take the positive direction of the axis towards the reader.

The force Mg passes through the centre of mass and it intersects the axis of rotation. Hence the torque of Mg about the axis is zero (Case II). Similarly, the torque of the contact force $\mathscr{N}$ is also zero.

The tension T is along the tangent of the rim in the vertically downward direction. The tension and the axis of rotation are perpendicular but never intersect. Case III applies. Join the point where the rope leaves the rim to the centre. This line is the common perpendicular to the tension and the axis. Hence the torque is $T.r$ (positive, since it will try to rotate the pulley anticlockwise).

If there are more than one forces $\vec{F}_1, \vec{F}_2, \vec{F}_3, \ldots$ acting on a body, one can define the *total torque* acting on the body about a given line.

To obtain the total torque, we have to get separately the torques of the individual forces and then add them.

$$\vec{\Gamma} = \vec{r_1} \times \vec{F}_1 + \vec{r_2} \times \vec{F}_2 + \ldots$$

You may be tempted to add the forces $\vec{F}_1, \vec{F}_2, \vec{F}_3, \ldots$ vectorially and then obtain the torque of resultant force about the axis. But that won't always work. Even if $\vec{F}_1 + \vec{F}_2 + \ldots = 0$, $\vec{r_1} \times \vec{F}_1 + \vec{r_2} \times \vec{F}_2 + \ldots$ may not. However, if the forces act on the same particle, one can add the forces and then take the torque of the resultant.

10.5 $\Gamma = I\alpha$

We are now in a position to tell how the angular acceleration is produced when the resultant force on the body is zero. It is the total torque that decides the angular acceleration. Although the resultant force on the fan in our example is zero, the total torque is not. Whereas, if one does not apply any force, the torque is also zero and no angular acceleration is produced. For angular acceleration, there must be a torque.

To have linear acceleration of a particle, the total force on the particle should be nonzero. The acceleration of the particle is proportional to the force applied on it. To have angular acceleration about an axis you must have a nonzero torque on the body about the axis of rotation. Do we also have the relation that the angular acceleration is proportional to the total torque on the body? Let us hope so.

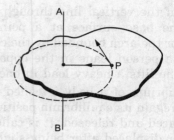

Figure 10.8

Consider a rigid body rotating about a fixed axis AB (figure 10.8). Consider a particle P of mass m rotating in a circle of radius r.

The radial acceleration of the particle $= \dfrac{v^2}{r} = \omega^2 r$.

Thus, the radial force on it $= m\omega^2 r$.

The tangential acceleration of the particle $= \dfrac{dv}{dt}$.

Thus, the tangential force on it

$$= m\frac{dv}{dt} = mr\frac{d\omega}{dt} = m\,r\,\alpha .$$

The torque of $m\omega^2 r$ about AB is zero as it intersects the axis and that of $mr\alpha$ is $mr^2\alpha$ as the force and the axis are skew and perpendicular. Thus, the torque of the resultant force acting on P is $mr^2\alpha$. Summing over all the particles, the total torque of all the forces acting on all the particles of the body is

$$\Gamma^{total} = \sum_i m_i r_i^2 \,\alpha = I\alpha \qquad \ldots \text{(i)}$$

where

$$I = \sum_i m_i r_i^2 . \qquad \ldots \text{(10.7)}$$

The quantity I is called the *moment of inertia* of the body about the axis of rotation. Note that m_i is the mass of the ith particle and r_i is its perpendicular distance from the axis.

We have $\Gamma^{total} = \sum_i (\vec{r_i} \times \vec{F_i})$ where $\vec{F_i}$ is the resultant force on the ith particle. This resultant force consists of forces by all the other particles as well as other external forces applied on the ith particle. Thus,

$$\Gamma^{total} = \sum_i \vec{r_i} \times \left(\sum_{j \neq i} \vec{F_{ij}} + \vec{F_i}^{\,ext} \right)$$

where $\vec{F_{ij}}$ is the force on the ith particle by the jth particle and $\vec{F_i}^{\,ext}$ is the external force applied on the ith particle. When summation is made on both i and j, the first summation contains pairs like $\vec{r_i} \times \vec{F_{ij}} + \vec{r_j} \times \vec{F_{ji}}$. Newton's third law tells us that $\vec{F_{ij}} = -\vec{F_{ji}}$ so that such pairs become $(\vec{r_i} - \vec{r_j}) \times \vec{F_{ij}}$. Also

the force $\vec{F_{ij}}$ is along the line joining the particles so that $(\vec{r_i} - \vec{r_j}) \parallel \vec{F_{ij}}$ and the cross product is zero. Thus, it is necessary to consider only the torques of the external forces applied on the rigid body and (i) becomes

$$\Gamma^{ext} = I\alpha \qquad \ldots \text{(10.8)}$$

where the torque and the moment of inertia are both evaluated about the axis of rotation.

Note the similarity between $\Gamma = I\alpha$ and $F = Ma$. Also, note the dissimilarity between the behaviour of M and I. The mass M is a property of the body and does not depend on the choice of the origin or the axes or the kind of motion it undergoes (as long as we are dealing with velocities much less than 3×10^8 m/s). But the moment of inertia $I = \sum_i m_i r_i^2$ depends on the choice of the axis about which it is calculated. The quantity r_i is the perpendicular distance of the ith particle from the "axis". Changing the axis changes r_i and hence I.

Moment of inertia of bodies of simple geometrical shapes may be calculated using the techniques of integration. We shall discuss the calculation for bodies of different shapes in somewhat greater detail in a later section.

Note that $\Gamma = I\alpha$ is not an independent rule of nature. It is derived from the more basic Newton's laws of motion.

Example 10.5

A wheel of radius 10 cm can rotate freely about its centre as shown in figure (10.9). A string is wrapped over its rim and is pulled by a force of 5·0 N. It is found that the torque produces an angular acceleration 2·0 rad/s² in the wheel. Calculate the moment of inertia of the wheel.

5.0 N

Figure 10.9

Solution : The forces acting on the wheel are (i) W due to gravity, (ii) $\mathcal{N}$ due to the support at the centre and (iii) F due to tension. The torque of W and $\mathcal{N}$ are separately zero and that of F is $F.r$. The net torque is

$$\Gamma = (5·0\ \text{N}).(10\ \text{cm}) = 0·50\ \text{N-m}.$$

The moment of inertia is

$$I = \frac{\Gamma}{\alpha} = \frac{0·50\ \text{N-m}}{2\ \text{rad/s}^2} = 0·25\ \text{kg-m}^2.$$

10.6 BODIES IN EQUILIBRIUM

The centre of mass of a body remains in equilibrium if the total external force acting on the body is zero. This follows from the equation $F = Ma$. Similarly, a body remains in rotational equilibrium if the total external torque acting on the body is zero. This follows from the equation $\Gamma = I\alpha$. Thus, if a body remains at rest in an inertial frame, the total external force acting on the body should be zero in any direction and the total external torque should be zero about any line.

We shall often find situations in which all the forces acting on a body lie in a single plane as shown in figure (10.10).

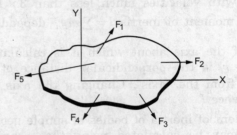

Figure 10.10

Let us take this plane as the X-Y plane. For translational equilibrium

$$\sum F_x = 0 \qquad \dots \text{(i)}$$

and

$$\sum F_y = 0. \qquad \dots \text{(ii)}$$

As all the forces are in the X-Y plane, F_z is identically zero for each force and so $\sum F_z = 0$ is automatically satisfied. Now consider rotational equilibrium. The torque of each force about the X-axis is identically zero because either the force intersects the axis or it is parallel to it. Similarly, the torque of each force about the Y-axis is identically zero. In fact, the torque about any line in the X-Y plane is zero.

Thus, the condition of rotational equilibrium is

$$\sum \Gamma_z = 0. \qquad \dots \text{(iii)}$$

While taking torque about the Z-axis, the origin can be chosen at any point in the plane of the forces. That is, the torque can be taken about any line perpendicular to the plane of the forces. In general, the torque is different about different lines but it can be shown that if the resultant force is zero, the total torque about any line perpendicular to the plane of the forces is equal. If it is zero about one such line, it will be zero about all such lines.

If a body is placed on a horizontal surface, the torque of the contact forces about the centre of mass should be zero to maintain the equilibrium. This may

happen only if the vertical line through the centre of mass cuts the base surface at a point within the contact area or the area bounded by the contact points. That is why a person leans in the opposite direction when he or she lifts a heavy load in one hand.

The equilibrium of a body is called *stable* if the body tries to regain its equilibrium position after being slightly displaced and released. It is called *unstable* if it gets further displaced after being slightly displaced and released. If it can stay in equilibrium even after being slightly displaced and released, it is said to be in *neutral equilibrium*.

In the case of stable equilibrium, the centre of mass goes higher on being slightly displaced. For unstable equilibrium it goes lower and for neutral equilibrium it stays at the same height.

10.7 BENDING OF A CYCLIST ON A HORIZONTAL TURN

Suppose a cyclist is going at a speed v on a circular horizontal road of radius r which is not banked. Consider the cycle and the rider together as the system. The centre of mass C (figure 10.11a) of the system is going in a circle with the centre at O and radius r.

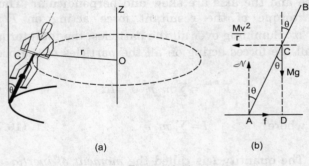

Figure 10.11

Let us choose O as the origin, OC as the X-axis and vertically upward as the Z-axis. This frame is rotating at an angular speed $\omega = v/r$ about the Z-axis. In this frame the system is at rest. Since we are working from a rotating frame of reference, we will have to apply a centrifugal force on each particle. The net centrifugal force on the system will be $M\omega^2 r = Mv^2/r$, where M is the total mass of the system. This force will act through the centre of mass. Since the system is at rest in this frame, no other pseudo force is needed.

Figure (10.11b) shows the forces. The cycle is bent at an angle θ with the vertical. The forces are

 (i) weight Mg,

 (ii) normal force $\mathcal{N}$,

(iii) friction f and,

(iv) centrifugal force Mv^2/r.

In the frame considered, the system is at rest. Thus, the total external force and the total external torque must be zero. Let us consider the torques of all the forces about the point A. The torques of $\mathcal{N}$ and f about A are zero because these forces pass through A. The torque of Mg about A is $Mg(AD)$ in the clockwise direction and that of $\dfrac{Mv^2}{r}$ is $\dfrac{Mv^2}{r}(CD)$ in the anti-clockwise direction. For rotational equilibrium,

$$Mg\,(AD) = \frac{Mv^2}{r}(CD)$$

or,
$$\frac{AD}{CD} = \frac{v^2}{rg}$$

or,
$$\tan\theta = \frac{v^2}{rg} \qquad \ldots (10.9)$$

Thus the cyclist bends at an angle $\tan^{-1}\left(\dfrac{v^2}{rg}\right)$ with the vertical.

10.8 ANGULAR MOMENTUM

Angular momentum of a particle about a point O is defined as

$$\vec{l} = \vec{r} \times \vec{p} \qquad \ldots (10.10)$$

where $\vec{p}$ is the linear momentum and $\vec{r}$ is the position vector of the particle from the given point O. The angular momentum of a system of particles is the vector sum of the angular momenta of the particles of the system. Thus,

$$\vec{L} = \sum_i \vec{l_i} = \sum (\vec{r_i} \times \vec{p_i}).$$

Suppose a particle P of mass m moves at a velocity $\vec{v}$ (figure 10.12). Its angular momentum about a point O is,

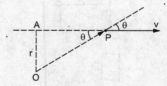

Figure 10.12

$$\vec{l} = \vec{OP} \times (m\vec{v})$$

or,
$$l = mv\, OP \sin\theta = mvr \qquad \ldots (10.11)$$

where $r = OA = OP \sin\theta$ is the perpendicular distance of the line of motion from O.

As in the case of torque, we define the angular momentum of a particle "about a line" say AB. Take any point O on the line AB and obtain the angular momentum $\vec{r} \times \vec{p}$ of the particle about O. The

component of $\vec{r} \times \vec{p}$ along the line AB is called the angular momentum of the particle "about AB". The point O may be chosen anywhere on the line AB.

10.9 $L = I\omega$

Suppose a particle is going in a circle of radius r and at some instant the speed of the particle is v (figure 10.13a). What is the angular momentum of the particle about the axis of the circle?

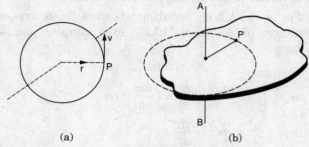

(a)   (b)

Figure 10.13

As the origin may be chosen anywhere on the axis, we choose it at the centre of the circle. Then $\vec{r}$ is along a radius and $\vec{v}$ is along the tangent so that $\vec{r}$ is perpendicular to $\vec{v}$ and $l = |\vec{r} \times \vec{p}| = mvr$. Also $\vec{r} \times \vec{p}$ is perpendicular to $\vec{r}$ and $\vec{p}$ and hence is along the axis. Thus, the component of $\vec{r} \times \vec{p}$ along the axis is mvr itself.

Next consider a rigid body rotating about an axis AB (figure 10.13b). Let the angular velocity of the body be ω. Consider the ith particle going in a circle of radius r_i with its plane perpendicular to AB. The linear velocity of this particle at this instant is $v_i = r_i\omega$. The angular momentum of this particle about $AB = m_i v_i r_i = m_i r_i^2 \omega$. The angular momentum of the whole body about AB is the sum of these components, i.e.,

$$L = \sum m_i r_i^2\, \omega = I\omega \qquad \ldots (10.12)$$

where I is the moment of inertia of the body about AB.

10.10 CONSERVATION OF ANGULAR MOMENTUM

We have defined the angular momentum of a body as $\vec{L} = \sum (\vec{r_i} \times \vec{p_i})$. Differentiating with respect to time,

$$\frac{d\vec{L}}{dt} = \frac{d}{dt}\sum (\vec{r_i} \times \vec{p_i})$$

$$= \sum_i \left[\frac{d\vec{r_i}}{dt} \times \vec{p_i} + \vec{r_i} \times \frac{d\vec{p_i}}{dt}\right]$$

$$= \sum_i \left[\vec{v_i} \times m\vec{v_i} + \vec{r_i} \times \vec{F_i}\right]$$

$$= \sum_i (\vec{r_i} \times \vec{F_i}) = \vec{\Gamma}^{\,total} \qquad \ldots (i)$$

where $\vec{F_i}$ is the total force acting on the ith particle. This includes any external force as well as the forces on the ith particle by all the other particles. When summation is taken over all the particles, the internal torques add to zero. Thus, (i) becomes

$$\frac{d\vec{L}}{dt} = \vec{\Gamma}^{ext} \qquad \dots (10.13)$$

where $\vec{\Gamma}^{ext}$ is the total torque on the system due to all the external forces acting on the system.

For a rigid body rotating about a fixed axis, we can arrive at equation (10.13) in a simpler manner. We have

$$L = I\omega$$

or,

$$\frac{dL}{dt} = I\frac{d\omega}{dt} = I\alpha$$

or,

$$\frac{dL}{dt} = \Gamma^{ext}.$$

Equation (10.13) shows that

If the total external torque on a system is zero, its angular momentum remains constant.

This is known as the *principle of conservation of angular momentum.*

Example 10.6

A wheel is rotating at an angular speed ω about its axis which is kept vertical. An identical wheel initially at rest is gently dropped into the same axle and the two wheels start rotating with a common angular speed. Find this common angular speed.

Solution : Let the moment of inertia of the wheel about the axis be I. Initially the first wheel is rotating at the angular speed ω about the axle and the second wheel is at rest. Take both the wheels together as the system. The total angular momentum of the system before the coupling is $I\omega + 0 = I\omega$. When the second wheel is dropped into the axle, the two wheels slip on each other and exert forces of friction. The forces of friction have torques about the axis of rotation but these are torques of internal forces. No external torque is applied on the two-wheel system and hence the angular momentum of the system remains unchanged. If the common angular speed is ω', the total angular momentum of the two-wheel system is $2I\omega'$ after the coupling. Thus,

$$I\omega = 2I\omega'$$

or,

$$\omega' = \omega/2.$$

10.11 ANGULAR IMPULSE

The angular impulse of a torque in a given time interval is defined as

$$J = \int_{t_1}^{t_2} \Gamma \, dt.$$

If Γ be the resultant torque acting on a body

$$\Gamma = \frac{dL}{dt}, \text{ or, } \Gamma dt = dL.$$

Integrating this

$$J = L_2 - L_1.$$

Thus, the change in angular momentum is equal to the angular impulse of the resultant torque.

10.12 KINETIC ENERGY OF A RIGID BODY ROTATING ABOUT A GIVEN AXIS

Consider a rigid body rotating about a line AB with an angular speed ω. The ith particle is going in a circle of radius r_i with a linear speed $v_i = \omega r_i$. The kinetic energy of this particle is $\frac{1}{2} m_i(\omega r_i)^2$. The kinetic energy of the whole body is

$$\sum \frac{1}{2} m_i \omega^2 r_i^2 = \frac{1}{2} \sum (m_i r_i^2)\omega^2 = \frac{1}{2} I\omega^2.$$

Sometimes it is called rotational kinetic energy. It is not a new kind of kinetic energy as is clear from the derivation. It is the sum of $\frac{1}{2} mv^2$ of all the particles.

Example 10.7

A wheel of moment of inertia I and radius r is free to rotate about its centre as shown in figure (10.14). A string is wrapped over its rim and a block of mass m is attached to the free end of the string. The system is released from rest. Find the speed of the block as it descends through a height h.

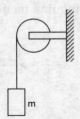

Figure 10.14

Solution : Let the speed of the block be v when it descends through a height h. So is the speed of the string and hence of a particle at the rim of the wheel. The angular velocity of the wheel is v/r and its kinetic energy at this instant is $\frac{1}{2} I(v/r)^2$. Using the principle of conservation of energy, the gravitational potential energy lost by the block must be equal to the kinetic energy gained by the block and the wheel. Thus,

$$mgh = \frac{1}{2}mv^2 + \frac{1}{2}I\frac{v^2}{r^2}$$

or, $$v = \left[\frac{2\,mgh}{m + I/r^2}\right]^{1/2}.$$

10.13 POWER DELIVERED AND WORK DONE BY A TORQUE

Consider a rigid body rotating about a fixed axis on which a torque acts. The torque produces angular acceleration and the kinetic energy increases. The rate of increase of the kinetic energy equals the rate of doing work on it, i.e., the power delivered by the torque.

$$P = \frac{dW}{dt} = \frac{dK}{dt}$$

$$= \frac{d}{dt}\left(\frac{1}{2}I\omega^2\right) = I\omega\frac{d\omega}{dt} = I\alpha\omega = \Gamma\omega.$$

The work done in an infinitesimal angular displacement $d\theta$ is

$$dW = Pdt = \Gamma\omega\,dt = \Gamma\,d\theta.$$

The work done in a finite angular displacement θ_1 to θ_2 is

$$W = \int_{\theta_1}^{\theta_2} \Gamma\,d\theta. \qquad \ldots \ (10.14)$$

10.14 CALCULATION OF MOMENT OF INERTIA

We have defined the moment of inertia of a system about a given line as

$$I = \sum_i m_i r_i^2$$

where m_i is the mass of the ith particle and r_i is its perpendicular distance from the given line. If the system is considered to be a collection of discrete particles, this definition may directly be used to calculate the moment of inertia.

Example 10.8

Consider a light rod with two heavy mass particles at its ends. Let AB be a line perpendicular to the rod as shown in figure (10.15). What is the moment of inertia of the system about AB ?

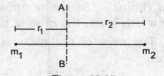

Figure 10.15

Solution : Moment of inertia of the particle on the left is $m_1 r_1^2$.

Moment of inertia of the particle on the right is $m_2 r_2^2$.

Moment of inertia of the rod is negligible as the rod is light.

Thus, the moment of inertia of the system about AB is

$$m_1 r_1^2 + m_2 r_2^2.$$

Example 10.9

Three particles, each of mass m, are situated at the vertices of an equilateral triangle ABC of side L (figure 10.16). Find the moment of inertia of the system about the line AX perpendicular to AB in the plane of ABC.

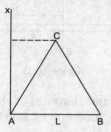

Figure 10.16

Solution : Perpendicular distance of A from $AX = 0$

"   " B "   " $= L$

"   " C "   " $= L/2$.

Thus, the moment of inertia of the particle at $A = 0$, of the particle at $B = mL^2$, and of the particle at $C = m(L/2)^2$. The moment of inertia of the three-particle system about AX is

$$0 + mL^2 + m(L/2)^2 = \frac{5\,mL^2}{4}.$$

Note that the particles on the axis do not contribute to the moment of inertia.

Moment of Inertia of Continuous Mass Distributions

If the body is assumed to be continuous, one can use the technique of integration to obtain its moment of inertia about a given line. Consider a small element of the body. The element should be so chosen that the perpendiculars from different points of the element to the given line differ only by infinitesimal amounts. Let its mass be dm and its perpendicular distance from the given line be r. Evaluate the product $r^2 dm$ and integrate it over the appropriate limits to cover the whole body. Thus,

$$I = \int r^2 dm$$

under proper limits.

We can call $r^2 dm$ the moment of inertia of the small element. Moment of inertia of the body about the given line is the sum of the moments of inertia of its constituent elements about the same line.

(A) Uniform rod about a perpendicular bisector

Consider a uniform rod of mass M and length l (figure 10.17) and suppose the moment of inertia is to be calculated about the bisector AB. Take the origin at the middle point O of the rod. Consider the element of the rod between a distance x and $x + dx$ from the origin. As the rod is uniform,

Mass per unit length of the rod $= M/l$

so that the mass of the element $= (M/l)dx$.

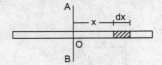

Figure 10.17

The perpendicular distance of the element from the line AB is x. The moment of inertia of this element about AB is

$$dI = \frac{M}{l} dx\, x^2.$$

When $x = -l/2$, the element is at the left end of the rod. As x is changed from $-l/2$ to $l/2$, the elements cover the whole rod.

Thus, the moment of inertia of the entire rod about AB is

$$I = \int_{-l/2}^{l/2} \frac{M}{l} x^2\, dx = \left[\frac{M}{l}\frac{x^3}{3} \right]_{-l/2}^{l/2} = \frac{Ml^2}{12}.$$

(B) Moment of inertia of a rectangular plate about a line parallel to an edge and passing through the centre

The situation is shown in figure (10.18). Draw a line parallel to AB at a distance x from it and another at a distance $x + dx$. We can take the strip enclosed between the two lines as the small element.

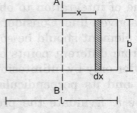

Figure 10.18

It is "small" because the perpendiculars from different points of the strip to AB differ by not more than dx. As the plate is uniform,

its mass per unit area $= \dfrac{M}{bl}$.

Mass of the strip $= \dfrac{M}{bl} b\, dx = \dfrac{M}{l} dx$.

The perpendicular distance of the strip from $AB = x$. The moment of inertia of the strip about $AB = dI = \dfrac{M}{l} dx\, x^2$. The moment of inertia of the given plate is, therefore,

$$I = \int_{-l/2}^{l/2} \frac{M}{l} x^2\, dx = \frac{Ml^2}{12}.$$

The moment of inertia of the plate about the line parallel to the other edge and passing through the centre may be obtained from the above formula by replacing l by b and thus,

$$I = \frac{Mb^2}{12}.$$

(C) Moment of inertia of a circular ring about its axis (the line perpendicular to the plane of the ring through its centre)

Suppose the radius of the ring is R and its mass is M. As all the elements of the ring are at the same perpendicular distance R from the axis, the moment of inertia of the ring is

$$I = \int r^2 dm = \int R^2 dm = R^2 \int dm = MR^2.$$

(D) Moment of inertia of a uniform circular plate about its axis

Let the mass of the plate be M and its radius R (figure 10.19). The centre is at O and the axis OX is perpendicular to the plane of the plate.

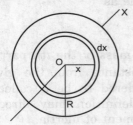

Figure 10.19

Draw two concentric circles of radii x and $x + dx$, both centred at O and consider the area of the plate in between the two circles.

This part of the plate may be considered to be a circular ring of radius x. As the periphery of the ring is $2\pi x$ and its width is dx, the area of this elementary ring is $2\pi x dx$. The area of the plate is πR^2. As the plate is uniform,

its mass per unit area $= \dfrac{M}{\pi R^2}$.

Mass of the ring $= \dfrac{M}{\pi R^2} 2\pi x\, dx = \dfrac{2Mx\,dx}{R^2}$.

Using the result obtained above for a circular ring, the moment of inertia of the elementary ring about OX is

$$dI = \left[\frac{2\,Mxdx}{R^2}\right] x^2.$$

The moment of inertia of the plate about OX is

$$I = \int_0^R \frac{2\,M}{R^2} x^3 \, dx = \frac{MR^2}{2}.$$

(E) Moment of inertia of a hollow cylinder about its axis

Suppose the radius of the cylinder is R and its mass is M. As every element of this cylinder is at the same perpendicular distance R from the axis, the moment of inertia of the hollow cylinder about its axis is

$$I = \int R^2 dm = R^2 \int dm = MR^2.$$

(F) Moment of inertia of a uniform solid cylinder about its axis

Let the mass of the cylinder be M and its radius R. Draw two cylindrical surfaces of radii x and $x + dx$ coaxial with the given cylinder. Consider the part of the cylinder in between the two surfaces (figure 10.20). This part of the cylinder may be considered to be a hollow cylinder of radius x. The area of cross-section of the wall of this hollow cylinder is $2\pi\,x\,dx$. If the length of the cylinder is l, the volume of the material of this elementary hollow cylinder is $2\pi\,x\,dx\,l$.

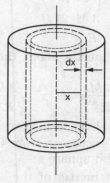

Figure 10.20

The volume of the solid cylinder is $\pi R^2 l$ and it is uniform, hence its mass per unit volume is

$$\rho = \frac{M}{\pi R^2 l}.$$

The mass of the hollow cylinder considered is

$$\frac{M}{\pi R^2 l} 2\pi x\, dx\, l = \frac{2\,M}{R^2} x dx.$$

As its radius is x, its moment of inertia about the given axis is

$$dI = \left[\frac{2\,M}{R^2} x\, dx\right] x^2.$$

The moment of inertia of the solid cylinder is, therefore,

$$I = \int_0^R \frac{2\,M}{R^2} x^3 dx = \frac{MR^2}{2}.$$

Note that the formula does not depend on the length of the cylinder.

(G) Moment of inertia of a uniform hollow sphere about a diameter

Let M and R be the mass and the radius of the sphere, O its centre and OX the given axis (figure 10.21). The mass is spread over the surface of the sphere and the inside is hollow.

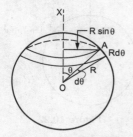

Figure 10.21

Let us consider a radius OA of the sphere at an angle θ with the axis OX and rotate this radius about OX. The point A traces a circle on the sphere. Now change θ to $\theta + d\theta$ and get another circle of somewhat larger radius on the sphere. The part of the sphere between these two circles, shown in the figure, forms a ring of radius $R \sin\theta$. The width of this ring is $Rd\theta$ and its periphery is $2\pi R \sin\theta$. Hence,

the area of the ring $= (2\pi R \sin\theta)\,(Rd\theta)$.

Mass per unit area of the sphere $= \dfrac{M}{4\pi R^2}$.

The mass of the ring

$$= \frac{M}{4\pi R^2} (2\pi R \sin\theta)\,(Rd\theta) = \frac{M}{2} \sin\theta\, d\theta.$$

The moment of inertia of this elemental ring about OX is

$$dI = \left(\frac{M}{2} \sin\theta\, d\theta\right) (R \sin\theta)^2.$$
$$= \frac{M}{2} R^2 \sin^3\theta\, d\theta$$

As θ increases from 0 to π, the elemental rings cover the whole spherical surface. The moment of inertia of the hollow sphere is, therefore,

$$I = \int_0^\pi \frac{M}{2} R^2 \sin^3\theta \, d\theta = \frac{MR^2}{2}\left[\int_0^\pi (1 - \cos^2\theta)\sin\theta \, d\theta\right]$$

$$= \frac{MR^2}{2}\left[\int_{\theta=0}^\pi -(1 - \cos^2\theta) \, d(\cos\theta)\right]$$

$$= \frac{-MR^2}{2}\left[\cos\theta - \frac{\cos^3\theta}{3}\right]_0^\pi = \frac{2}{3} MR^2.$$

Alternative method

Consider any particle P of the surface, having coordinates (x_i, y_i, z_i) with respect to the centre O as the origin (figure 10.22) and OX as the X-axis. Let PQ be the perpendicular to OX. Then $OQ = x_i$. That is the definition of x-coordinate.

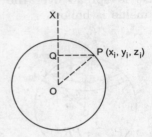

Figure 10.22

Thus, $PQ^2 = OP^2 - OQ^2$

$$= \left(x_i^2 + y_i^2 + z_i^2\right) - x_i^2 = y_i^2 + z_i^2.$$

The moment of inertia of the particle P about the X-axis

$$= m_i (y_i^2 + z_i^2).$$

The moment of inertia of the hollow sphere about the X-axis is, therefore,

$$I_x = \sum_i m_i \left(y_i^2 + z_i^2\right).$$

Similarly, the moment of inertia of the hollow sphere about the Y-axis is

$$I_y = \sum_i m_i \left(z_i^2 + x_i^2\right)$$

and about the Z-axis it is

$$I_z = \sum_i m_i \left(x_i^2 + y_i^2\right)$$

Adding these three equations we get

$$I_x + I_y + I_z = \sum_i 2 m_i \left(x_i^2 + y_i^2 + z_i^2\right)$$

$$= \sum_i 2 m_i R^2 = 2 MR^2.$$

As the mass is uniformly distributed over the entire surface of the sphere, all diameters are equivalent. Hence I_x, I_y and I_z must be equal.

Thus, $$I = \frac{I_x + I_y + I_z}{3} = \frac{2}{3} MR^2.$$

(H) Moment of inertia of a uniform solid sphere about a diameter

Let M and R be the mass and radius of the given solid sphere. Let O be the centre and OX the given axis. Draw two spheres of radii x and $x + dx$ concentric with the given solid sphere. The thin spherical shell trapped between these spheres may be treated as a hollow sphere of radius x.

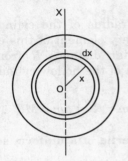

Figure 10.23

The mass per unit volume of the solid sphere

$$= \frac{M}{\frac{4}{3}\pi R^3} = \frac{3 M}{4 \pi R^3}.$$

The thin hollow sphere considered above has a surface area $4\pi x^2$ and thickness dx. Its volume is $4\pi x^2 dx$ and hence its mass is

$$= \left(\frac{3 M}{4 \pi R^3}\right)(4\pi x^2 dx)$$

$$= \frac{3 M}{R^3} x^2 dx.$$

Its moment of inertia about the diameter OX is, therefore,

$$dI = \frac{2}{3}\left[\frac{3 M}{R^3} x^2 dx\right] x^2 = \frac{2 M}{R^3} x^4 dx.$$

If $x = 0$, the shell is formed at the centre of the solid sphere. As x increases from 0 to R, the shells cover the whole solid sphere.

The moment of inertia of the solid sphere about OX is, therefore,

$$I = \int_0^R \frac{2 M}{R^3} x^4 dx = \frac{2}{5} MR^2.$$

10.15 TWO IMPORTANT THEOREMS ON MOMENT OF INERTIA

Theorem of Parallel Axes

Suppose we have to obtain the moment of inertia of a body about a given line AB (figure 10.24). Let C

be the centre of mass of the body and let CZ be the line parallel to AB through C. Let I and I_0 be the moments of inertia of the body about AB and CZ respectively. The parallel axes theorem states that

$$I = I_0 + Md^2$$

where d is the perpendicular distance between the parallel lines AB and CZ and M is the mass of the body.

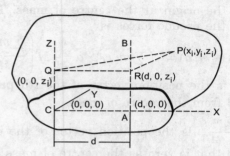

Figure 10.24

Take C to be the origin and CZ the Z-axis. Let CA be the perpendicular from C to AB. Take CA to be the X-axis. As $CA = d$, the coordinates of A are $(d, 0, 0)$.

Let P be an arbitrary particle of the body with the coordinates (x_i, y_i, z_i). Let PQ and PR be the perpendiculars from P to CZ and AB respectively. Note that P may not be in the plane containing CZ and AB. We have $CQ = z_i$. Also $AR = CQ = z_i$. Thus, the point Q has coordinates $(0, 0, z_i)$ and the point R has coordinates $(d, 0, z_i)$.

$$I = \sum_i m_i (PR)^2$$

$$= \sum_i m_i \left[(x_i - d)^2 + (y_i - 0)^2 + (z_i - z_i)^2 \right]$$

$$= \sum_i m_i (x_i^2 + y_i^2 + d^2 - 2 x_i d)$$

$$= \sum_i m_i (x_i^2 + y_i^2) + \sum_i m_i d^2 - 2d \sum_i m_i x_i \quad \ldots \text{(i)}$$

We have

$$\sum_i m_i x_i = MX_{CM} = 0.$$

The moment of inertia about CZ is,

$$I_0 = \sum_i m_i (PQ)^2$$

$$= \sum_i m_i [(x_i - 0)^2 + (y_i - 0)^2 + (z_i - z_i)^2]$$

$$= \sum_i m_i (x_i^2 + y_i^2)$$

From (i),

$$I = I_0 + \sum_i m_i d^2 = I_0 + Md^2.$$

Theorem of Perpendicular Axes

This theorem is applicable only to the plane bodies. Let X and Y-axes be chosen in the plane of the body and Z-axis perpendicular to this plane, three axes being mutually perpendicular. Then the theorem states that

$$I_z = I_x + I_y.$$

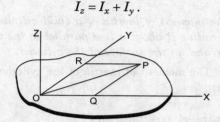

Figure 10.25

Consider an arbitrary particle P of the body (figure 10.25). Let PQ and PR be the perpendiculars from P on the X and the Y-axes respectively. Also PO is the perpendicular from P to the Z-axis. Thus, the moment of inertia of the body about the Z-axis is

$$I_z = \sum_i m_i (PO)^2 = \sum_i m_i (PQ^2 + OQ^2)$$

$$= \sum_i m_i (PQ^2 + PR^2)$$

$$= \sum_i m_i (PQ)^2 + \sum_i m_i (PR)^2$$

$$= I_x + I_y.$$

Example 10.10

Find the moment of inertia of a uniform ring of mass M and radius R about a diameter.

Solution :

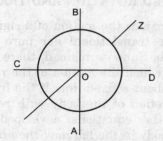

Figure 10.26

Let AB and CD be two mutually perpendicular diameters of the ring. Take them as X and Y-axes and the line perpendicular to the plane of the ring through the centre as the Z-axis. The moment of inertia of the ring about the Z-axis is $I = MR^2$. As the ring is uniform, all of its diameters are equivalent and so $I_x = I_y$. From perpendicular axes theorem,

$$I_z = I_x + I_y. \quad \text{Hence } I_x = \frac{I_z}{2} = \frac{MR^2}{2}.$$

Similarly, the moment of inertia of a uniform disc about a diameter is $MR^2/4$.

Example 10.11

Find the moment of inertia of a solid cylinder of mass M and radius R about a line parallel to the axis of the cylinder and on the surface of the cylinder.

Solution : The moment of inertia of the cylinder about its axis $= \frac{MR^2}{2}$.

Using parallel axes theorem

$$I = I_0 + MR^2 = \frac{MR^2}{2} + MR^2 = \frac{3}{2}MR^2.$$

Similarly, the moment of inertia of a solid sphere about a tangent is

$$\frac{2}{5}MR^2 + MR^2 = \frac{7}{5}MR^2.$$

Radius of Gyration

The radius of gyration k of a body about a given line is defined by the equation

$$I = Mk^2$$

where I is its moment of inertia about the given line and M is its total mass. It is the radius of a ring with the given line as the axis such that if the total mass of the body is distributed on the ring, it will have the same moment of inertia I. For example, the radius of gyration of a uniform disc of radius r about its axis is $r/\sqrt{2}$.

10.16 COMBINED ROTATION AND TRANSLATION

We now consider the motion of a rigid body which is neither pure translational nor pure rotational as seen from a lab. Suppose instead, there is a frame of reference A in which the motion of the rigid body is a pure rotation about a fixed line. If the frame A is also inertial, the motion of the body with respect to A is governed by the equations developed above. The motion of the body in the lab may then be obtained by adding the motion of A with respect to the lab to the motion of the body in A.

If the frame A is noninertial, we do not hope $\Gamma^{ext} = I\alpha$ to hold. In the derivation of this equation we used $F = ma$ for each particle and this holds good only if a is measured from an inertial frame. If the frame A has an acceleration $\vec{a}$ in a fixed direction with respect to an inertial frame, we have to apply a pseudo

force $-m\vec{a}$ to each particle. These pseudo forces produce a pseudo torque about the axis.

Pleasantly, there exists a very special and very useful case where $\Gamma^{ext} = I\alpha$ does hold even if the angular acceleration α is measured from a noninertial frame A. And that special case is, when the axis of rotation in the frame A passes through the centre of mass.

Take the origin at the centre of mass. The total torque of the pseudo forces is

$$\sum \vec{r_i} \times (-m_i \vec{a}) = -\left(\sum m_i \vec{r_i}\right) \times \vec{a} = -M\left(\frac{\sum m_i \vec{r_i}}{M}\right) \times \vec{a}$$

where $\vec{r_i}$ is the position vector of the ith particle as measured from the centre of mass.

But $\frac{\sum m_i \vec{r_i}}{M}$ is the position vector of the centre of mass and that is zero as the centre of mass is at the origin. Hence the pseudo torque is zero and we get $\Gamma^{ext} = I\alpha$. To make the point more explicit, we write $\Gamma_{cm} = I_{cm}\alpha$, reminding us that the equation is valid in a noninertial frame, only if the axis of rotation passes through the centre of mass and the torques and the moment of inertia are evaluated about the axis through the centre of mass.

So, the working rule for discussing combined rotation and translation is as follows. List the external forces acting on the body. The vector sum divided by the mass of the body gives the acceleration of the centre of mass. Then find the torque of the external forces and the moment of inertia of the body about a line through the centre of mass and perpendicular to the plane of motion of the particles. Note that this line may not be the axis of rotation in the lab frame. Still calculate Γ and I about this line. The angular acceleration α about the centre of mass will be obtained by $\alpha = \Gamma/I$.

Thus $\quad \vec{a}_{cm} = \vec{F}^{ext}/M$

and $\quad \alpha = \Gamma_{cm}^{ext}/I_{cm}$ ... (10.15)

These equations together with the initial conditions completely determine the motion.

10.17 ROLLING

When you go on a bicycle on a straight road what distance on the road is covered during one full pedal? Suppose a particular spoke of the bicycle is painted black and is vertical at some instant pointing downward. After one full pedal the spoke is again vertical in the similar position. We say that the wheel has made one full rotation. During this period the bicycle has moved through a distance $2\pi R$ in normal cycling on a good, free road. Here R is the radius of the wheel. The wheels are said to be 'rolling' on the road.

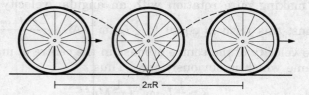

Figure 10.27

Looking from the road frame, the wheel is not making pure rotation about a fixed line. The particles of the wheel do not go on circles. The path of a particle at the rim will be something like that shown in figure (10.27), whereas the centre of the wheel goes in a straight line. But we still say that during one pedal the wheel has made one rotation, i.e., it has rotated through an angle of 2π. By this we mean that the spoke that was vertical (pointing downward from the centre) again became vertical in the similar position. In this period the centre of the wheel has moved through a distance $2\pi R$. In half of this period, the wheel has moved through a distance πR and the spoke makes an angle of π with its original direction. During a short time-interval Δt, the wheel moves through a distance Δx and the spoke rotates by $\Delta\theta$. Thus the wheel rotates and at the same time moves forward. The relation between the displacement of (the centre of) the wheel and the angle rotated by (a spoke of) the wheel is $\Delta x = R\Delta\theta$. Dividing by Δt and taking limits, we get

$$v = R\omega,$$

where v is the linear speed of the centre of mass and ω is the angular velocity of the wheel.

This type of motion of a wheel (or any other object with circular boundary) in which the centre of the wheel moves in a straight line and the wheel rotates in its plane about its centre with $v = R\omega$, is called *pure rolling*.

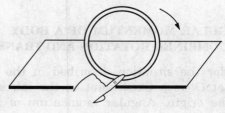

Figure 10.28

Place a ring on a horizontal surface as shown in figure (10.28) and put your finger on the lowest part. Use other hand to rotate the ring a little while the finger is kept on the lowest point. This is approximately a small part of rolling motion. Note the displacements of different particles of the ring. The centre has moved forward a little, say Δx. The topmost point has moved approximately double of this distance. The part in contact with the horizontal surface below the finger has almost been in the same position.

In pure rolling, the velocity of the contact point is zero. The velocity of the centre of mass is $v_{cm} = R\omega$ and that of the topmost point is $v_{top} = 2R\omega = 2v_{cm}$.

Next, consider another type of combination of rotation and translation, in which the wheel moves through a distance greater than $2\pi R$ in one full rotation. Hold the ring of figure (10.28) between three fingers, apply a forward force to move it fast on the table and rotate it slowly through the fingers. Its angular velocity $\omega = d\theta/dt$ is small and $v_{cm} > R\omega$. This is a case of rolling with forward slipping. This type of motion occurs when you apply sudden brakes to the bicycle on a road which is fairly smooth after rain. The cycle stops after a long distance and the wheel rotates only little during this period. If you look at the particles in contact, these will be found rubbing the road in the forward direction. The particles in contact have a velocity in the forward direction. In this case $v_{cm} > R\omega$. An extreme example of this type occurs when the wheel does not rotate at all and translates with linear velocity v. Then $v_{cm} = v$ and $\omega = 0$.

Yet another type of rolling with slipping occurs when the wheel moves a distance shorter than $2\pi R$ while making one rotation. In this case, the velocity $v_{cm} < R\omega$. Hold the ring of figure (10.28) between three fingers, rotate it fast and translate it slowly. It will move a small distance on the table and rotate fast. If you drive a bicycle on a road on which a lot of mud is present, sometimes the wheel rotates fast but moves a little. If you look at the particles in contact, they rub the road in the backward direction. The centre moves less than $2\pi R$ during one full rotation and $v_{cm} < R\omega$.

These situations may be visualised in a different manner which gives another interpretation of rolling. Consider a wheel of radius r with its axis fixed in a second-hand car. The wheel may rotate freely about this axis. Suppose the floor of the second-hand car has a hole in it and the wheel just touches the road through the hole. Suppose the person sitting on the back seat rotates the wheel at a uniform angular velocity ω and the driver drives the car at a uniform velocity v on the road which is parallel to the plane of the wheel as shown in figure (10.29). The two motions are independent. The backseater is rotating the wheel at an angular velocity according to his will and the driver is driving the car at a velocity according to his will.

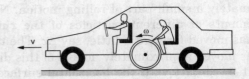

Figure 10.29

Look at the wheel from the road. If the persons inside the car agree to choose v and ω in such a way that $v = \omega r$, the wheel is in pure rolling on the road. Looking from the road, the centre of the wheel is moving forward at a speed v and the wheel is rotating at an angular velocity ω with $v = \omega r$. The velocity of the lowest particle with respect to the road = its velocity with respect to the car + velocity of the car with respect to the road. So,

$$v_{contact,\,road} = v_{contact,\,car} + v_{car,\,road} = -\omega r + v = 0.$$

If the driver drives the car at a higher speed, $v > \omega r$, the wheel rubs the road and we have rolling with forward slipping. In this case

$$v_{contact,\,road} = v_{contact,\,car} + v_{car,\,road} = -\omega r + v > 0$$

Similarly, if $v < \omega r$, we have rolling with backward slipping,

$$v_{contact,\,road} = -\omega r + v < 0,$$

the particles at contact rub the road backward.

10.18 KINETIC ENERGY OF A BODY IN COMBINED ROTATION AND TRANSLATION

Consider a body in combined translational and rotational motion in the lab frame. Suppose in the frame of the centre of mass, the body is making a pure rotation with an angular velocity ω. The centre of mass itself is moving in the lab frame at a velocity $\vec{v}_0$. The velocity of a particle of mass m_i is $\vec{v}_{i,\,cm}$ with respect to the centre-of-mass frame and $\vec{v}_i$ with respect to the lab frame. We have,

$$\vec{v}_i = \vec{v}_{i,\,cm} + \vec{v}_0$$

The kinetic energy of the particle in the lab frame is

$$\frac{1}{2} m_i v_i^2 = \frac{1}{2} m_i \, (\vec{v}_{i,\,cm} + \vec{v}_0) \cdot (\vec{v}_{i,\,cm} + \vec{v}_0)$$

$$= \frac{1}{2} m_i v_{i,\,cm}^2 + \frac{1}{2} m_i v_0^2 + \frac{1}{2} m_i \, (2\vec{v}_{i,\,cm} \cdot \vec{v}_0).$$

Summing over all the particles, the total kinetic energy of the body in the lab frame is

$$K = \sum_i \frac{1}{2} m_i v_i^2 = \sum_i \frac{1}{2} m_i v_{i,\,cm}^2 + \frac{1}{2} \sum_i m_i v_0^2 + \left(\sum_i m_i \vec{v}_{i,\,cm} \right) \cdot \vec{v}_0.$$

Now $\sum_i \frac{1}{2} m_i v_{i,\,cm}^2$ is the kinetic energy of the body in the centre of mass frame. In this frame, the body is making pure rotation with an angular velocity ω. Thus, this term is equal to $\frac{1}{2} I_{cm} \omega^2$. Also $\dfrac{\sum m_i \vec{v}_{i,\,cm}}{M}$ is the velocity of the centre of mass in the centre of mass frame which is obviously zero. Thus,

$$K = \frac{1}{2} I_{cm} \omega^2 + \frac{1}{2} M v_0^2.$$

In the case of pure rolling, $v_0 = R\omega$ so that

$$K = \frac{1}{2}(I_{cm} + MR^2)\omega^2.$$

Using the parallel axes theorem, $I_{cm} + MR^2 = I$, which is the moment of inertia of the wheel about the line through the point of contact and parallel to the axis. Thus, $K = \frac{1}{2} I \omega^2$.

This gives another interpretation of rolling. At any instant a rolling body may be considered to be in pure rotation about an axis through the point of contact. This axis translates forward with a speed v_0.

Example 10.12

A uniform sphere of mass 200 g rolls without slipping on a plane surface so that its centre moves at a speed of 2·00 cm/s. Find its kinetic energy.

Solution : As the sphere rolls without slipping on the plane surface, its angular speed about the center is $\omega = \dfrac{v_{cm}}{r}$. The kinetic energy is

$$K = \frac{1}{2} I_{cm} \omega^2 + \frac{1}{2} M v_{cm}^2$$

$$= \frac{1}{2} \cdot \frac{2}{5} Mr^2 \omega^2 + \frac{1}{2} M v_{cm}^2$$

$$= \frac{1}{5} M v_{cm}^2 + \frac{1}{2} M v_{cm}^2 = \frac{7}{10} M v_{cm}^2$$

$$= \frac{7}{10} (0 \cdot 200 \text{ kg}) (0 \cdot 02 \text{ m/s})^2 = 5 \cdot 6 \times 10^{-5} \text{ J}.$$

10.19 ANGULAR MOMENTUM OF A BODY IN COMBINED ROTATION AND TRANSLATION

Consider the situation described in the previous section. Let O be a fixed point in the lab which we take as the origin. Angular momentum of the body about O is

$$\vec{L} = \sum_i m_i \vec{r}_i \times \vec{v}_i$$

$$= \sum_i m_i \, (\vec{r}_{i,\,cm} + \vec{r}_0) \times (\vec{v}_{i,\,cm} + \vec{v}_0).$$

Here, $\vec{r}_0$ is the position vector of the centre of mass. Thus,

$$\vec{L} = \sum_i m_i \,(\vec{r}_{i,\,cm} \times \vec{v}_{i,\,cm}) + \left(\sum_i m_i \,\vec{r}_{i,\,cm}\right) \times \vec{v}_0$$
$$+ \vec{r}_0 \times \left(\sum_i m_i \,\vec{v}_{i,\,cm}\right) + \left(\sum_i m_i\right) \vec{r}_0 \times \vec{v}_0.$$

Now, $\sum_i m_i \vec{r}_{i,\,cm} = M\,\vec{R}_{cm,\,cm} = 0$

and $\sum_i m_i \vec{v}_{i,\,cm} = M\,\vec{V}_{cm,\,cm} = 0.$

Thus, $\vec{L} = \sum_i m_i \,(\vec{r}_{i,\,cm} \times \vec{v}_{i,\,cm}) + M\,\vec{r}_0 \times \vec{v}_0$

$$= \vec{L}_{cm} + M\,\vec{r}_0 \times \vec{v}_0.$$

The first term $\vec{L}_{cm}$ represents the angular momentum of the body as seen from the centre-of-mass frame. The second term $M\,\vec{r}_0 \times \vec{v}_0$ equals the angular momentum of the body if it is assumed to be concentrated at the centre of mass translating with the velocity $\vec{v}_0$.

10.20 WHY DOES A ROLLING SPHERE SLOW DOWN ?

When a sphere is rolled on a horizontal table it slows down and eventually stops. Figure (10.30) shows the situation. The forces acting on the sphere are (a) weight mg, (b) friction at the contact and (c) the normal force. As the centre of the sphere decelerates, the friction should be opposite to its velocity, that is towards left in figure (10.30). But this friction will have a clockwise torque that should increase the angular velocity of the sphere. There must be an anticlockwise torque that causes the decrease in the angular velocity.

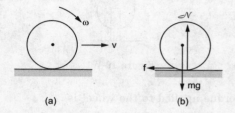

Figure 10.30

In fact, when the sphere rolls on the table, both the sphere and the surface deform near the contact. The contact is not at a single point as we normally assume, rather there is an area of contact. The front part pushes the table a bit more strongly than the back part. As a result, the normal force does not pass through the centre, it is shifted towards the right. This force, then, has an anticlockwise torque. The net torque causes an angular deceleration.

Worked Out Examples

1. *A wheel rotates with a constant acceleration of* 2·0 rad/s². *If the wheel starts from rest, how many revolutions will it make in the first* 10 *seconds ?*

Solution : The angular displacement in the first 10 seconds is given by

$$\theta = \omega_0 t + \frac{1}{2}\alpha t^2 = \frac{1}{2}(2 \cdot 0 \text{ rad/s}^2)(10 \text{ s})^2 = 100 \text{ rad}.$$

As the wheel turns by 2π radian in each revolution, the number of revolutions in 10 s is

$$n = \frac{100}{2\pi} = 16.$$

2. *The wheel of a motor, accelerated uniformly from rest, rotates through* 2·5 *radian during the first second. Find the angle rotated during the next second.*

Solution : As the angular acceleration is constant, we have

$$\theta = \omega_0 t + \frac{1}{2}\alpha t^2 = \frac{1}{2}\alpha t^2.$$

Thus, $2 \cdot 5 \text{ rad} = \frac{1}{2}\alpha(1 \text{ s})^2$

$$\alpha = 5 \text{ rad/s}^2$$

or, $\alpha = 5 \text{ rad/s}^2.$

The angle rotated during the first two seconds is

$$= \frac{1}{2} \times (5 \text{ rad/s}^2)(2 \text{ s})^2 = 10 \text{ rad}.$$

Thus, the angle rotated during the 2nd second is

$$10 \text{ rad} - 2 \cdot 5 \text{ rad} = 7 \cdot 5 \text{ rad}.$$

3. *A wheel having moment of inertia* 2 kg-m² *about its axis, rotates at* 50 rpm *about this axis. Find the torque that can stop the wheel in one minute.*

Solution : The initial angular velocity

$$= 50 \text{ rpm} = \frac{5\pi}{3} \text{ rad/s}.$$

Using $\omega = \omega_0 + \alpha t$,

$$\alpha = \frac{\omega - \omega_0}{t} = \frac{0 - \dfrac{5\pi}{3}}{60} \text{ rad/s}^2 = -\frac{\pi}{36} \text{ rad/s}^2.$$

The torque that can produce this deceleration is

$$\Gamma = I\,|\,\alpha\,| = (2 \text{ kg-m}^2)\left(\frac{\pi}{36} \text{ rad/s}^2\right) = \frac{\pi}{18} \text{ N-m}.$$

4. *A string is wrapped around the rim of a wheel of moment of inertia* 0·20 kg-m² *and radius* 20 cm. *The wheel is free to rotate about its axis. Initially, the wheel is at rest. The string is now pulled by a force of* 20 N. *Find the angular velocity of the wheel after* 5·0 *seconds.*

Solution :

Figure 10-W1

The torque applied to the wheel is

$$\Gamma = F . r = (20 \text{ N}) (0·20 \text{ m}) = 4·0 \text{ N-m}.$$

The angular acceleration produced is

$$\alpha = \frac{\Gamma}{I} = \frac{4·0 \text{ N-m}}{0·20 \text{ kg-m}^2} = 20 \text{ rad/s}^2.$$

The angular velocity after 5·0 seconds is

$$\omega = \omega_0 + \alpha t = (20 \text{ rad/s}^2) (5·0 \text{ s}) = 100 \text{ rad/s}.$$

5. *A wheel of radius r and moment of inertia I about its axis is fixed at the top of an inclined plane of inclination* θ *as shown in figure (10-W2). A string is wrapped round the wheel and its free end supports a block of mass M which can slide on the plane. Initially, the wheel is rotating at a speed* ω *in a direction such that the block slides up the plane. How far will the block move before stopping ?*

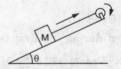

Figure 10-W2

Solution : Suppose the deceleration of the block is a. The linear deceleration of the rim of the wheel is also a. The angular deceleration of the wheel is $\alpha = a/r$. If the tension in the string is T, the equations of motion are as follows:

$$Mg \sin\theta - T = Ma$$

and $$Tr = I\alpha = I a/r.$$

Eliminating T from these equations,

$$Mg \sin\theta - I \frac{a}{r^2} = Ma$$

giving, $$a = \frac{Mg r^2 \sin\theta}{I + Mr^2}.$$

The initial velocity of the block up the incline is $v = \omega r$. Thus, the distance moved by the block before stopping is

$$x = \frac{v^2}{2a} = \frac{\omega^2 r^2 (I + Mr^2)}{2 Mg r^2 \sin\theta} = \frac{(I + Mr^2)\omega^2}{2 Mg \sin\theta}.$$

6. *The pulley shown in figure (10-W3) has a moment of inertia I about its axis and its radius is R. Find the magnitude of the acceleration of the two blocks. Assume that the string is light and does not slip on the pulley.*

Figure 10-W3

Solution : Suppose the tension in the left string is T_1 and that in the right string is T_2. Suppose the block of mass M goes down with an acceleration a and the other block moves up with the same acceleration. This is also the tangential acceleration of the rim of the wheel as the string does not slip over the rim. The angular acceleration of the wheel is, therefore, $\alpha = a/R$. The equations of motion for the mass M, the mass m and the pulley are as follows :

$$Mg - T_1 = Ma \qquad \ldots \text{ (i)}$$
$$T_2 - mg = ma \qquad \ldots \text{ (ii)}$$
$$T_1 R - T_2 R = I\alpha = Ia/R. \qquad \ldots \text{ (iii)}$$

Putting T_1 and T_2 from (i) and (ii) into (iii),

$$[M(g - a) - m(g + a)] R = I \frac{a}{R}$$

which gives $$a = \frac{(M - m)gR^2}{I + (M + m) R^2}.$$

7. *Two small kids weighing* 10 kg *and* 15 kg *respectively are trying to balance a seesaw of total length* 5·0 m, *with the fulcrum at the centre. If one of the kids is sitting at an end, where should the other sit ?*

Solution :

Figure 10-W4

It is clear that the 10 kg kid should sit at the end and the 15 kg kid should sit closer to the centre. Suppose his distance from the centre is x. As the kids are in equilibrium, the normal force between a kid and the seesaw equals the weight of that kid. Considering the rotational equilibrium of the seesaw, the torques of the forces acting on it should add to zero. The forces are (a) (15 kg)g downward by the 15 kg kid,

(b) (10 kg)g downward by the 10 kg kid,

(c) weight of the seesaw and

(d) the normal force by the fulcrum.

Taking torques about the fulcrum,

$$(15 \text{ kg})g\, x = (10 \text{ kg})g\,(2 \cdot 5 \text{ m})$$

or, $x = 1 \cdot 7$ m.

8. *A uniform ladder of mass* 10 kg *leans against a smooth vertical wall making an angle of* 53° *with it. The other end rests on a rough horizontal floor. Find the normal force and the frictional force that the floor exerts on the ladder.*

Solution :

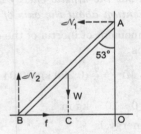

Figure 10-W5

The forces acting on the ladder are shown in figure (10-W5). They are

(a) its weight W,

(b) normal force $\mathcal{N}_1$ by the vertical wall,

(c) normal force $\mathcal{N}_2$ by the floor and

(d) frictional force f by the floor.

Taking horizontal and vertical components

$$\mathcal{N}_1 = f \qquad\qquad\qquad \text{... (i)}$$

and $\mathcal{N}_2 = W.$ ... (ii)

Taking torque about B,

$$\mathcal{N}_1 (AO) = W(CB)$$

or, $\mathcal{N}_1 (AB) \cos 53° = W \dfrac{AB}{2} \sin 53°$

or, $\mathcal{N}_1 \dfrac{3}{5} = \dfrac{W}{2}\dfrac{4}{5}$

or, $\mathcal{N}_1 = \dfrac{2}{3} W.$ ... (iii)

The normal force by the floor is

$$\mathcal{N}_2 = W = (10 \text{ kg}) (9 \cdot 8 \text{ m/s}^2) = 98 \text{ N}.$$

The frictional force is

$$f = \mathcal{N}_1 = \dfrac{2}{3} W = 65 \text{ N}.$$

9. *The ladder shown in figure (10-W6) has negligible mass and rests on a frictionless floor. The crossbar connects the two legs of the ladder at the middle. The angle between the two legs is* 60°. *The fat person sitting on the*

ladder has a mass of 80 kg. *Find the contact force exerted by the floor on each leg and the tension in the crossbar.*

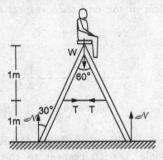

Figure 10-W6

Solution : The forces acting on different parts are shown in figure (10-W6). Consider the vertical equilibrium of "the ladder plus the person" system. The forces acting on this system are its weight (80 kg)g and the contact force $\mathcal{N} + \mathcal{N} = 2\,\mathcal{N}$ due to the floor. Thus,

$$2\,\mathcal{N} = (80 \text{ kg})\, g$$

or, $\mathcal{N} = (40 \text{ kg}) (9 \cdot 8 \text{ m/s}^2) = 392 \text{ N}.$

Next consider the equilibrium of the left leg of the ladder. Taking torques of the forces acting on it about the upper end,

$$\mathcal{N}\,(2 \text{ m})\tan 30° = T(1 \text{ m})$$

or, $T = \mathcal{N}\,\dfrac{2}{\sqrt{3}} = (392 \text{ N}) \times \dfrac{2}{\sqrt{3}} \approx 450 \text{ N}.$

10. *Two small balls A and B, each of mass m, are attached rigidly to the ends of a light rod of length d. The structure rotates about the perpendicular bisector of the rod at an angular speed* ω. *Calculate the angular momentum of the individual balls and of the system about the axis of rotation.*

Solution :

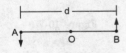

Figure 10-W7

Consider the situation shown in figure (10-W7). The velocity of the ball A with respect to the centre O is $v = \dfrac{\omega d}{2}$. The angular momentum of the ball with respect to the axis is $L_1 = mvr = m\left(\dfrac{\omega d}{2}\right)\left(\dfrac{d}{2}\right) = \dfrac{1}{4} m\omega d^2.$

The same is the angular momentum L_2 of the second ball. The angular momentum of the system is equal to sum of these two angular momenta i.e., $L = \dfrac{1}{2} m\omega d^2.$

11. *Two particles of mass m each are attached to a light rod of length d, one at its centre and the other at a free end.*

The rod is fixed at the other end and is rotated in a plane at an angular speed ω. Calculate the angular momentum of the particle at the end with respect to the particle at the centre.

Solution :

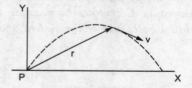

Figure 10-W8

The situation is shown in figure (10-W8). The velocity of the particle A with respect to the fixed end O is $v_A = \omega\left(\dfrac{d}{2}\right)$ and that of B with respect to O is $v_B = \omega d$. Hence the velocity of B with respect to A is $v_B - v_A = \omega\left(\dfrac{d}{2}\right)$. The angular momentum of B with respect to A is, therefore,

$$L = mvr = m\omega\left(\frac{d}{2}\right)\frac{d}{2} = \frac{1}{4}\,m\omega d^{\,2}$$

along the direction perpendicular to the plane of rotation.

12. *A particle is projected at time t = 0 from a point P with a speed v_0 at an angle of 45° to the horizontal. Find the magnitude and the direction of the angular momentum of the particle about the point P at time t = v_0/g.*

Solution : Let us take the origin at P, X-axis along the horizontal and Y-axis along the vertically upward direction as shown in figure (10-W9). For horizontal motion during the time 0 to t,

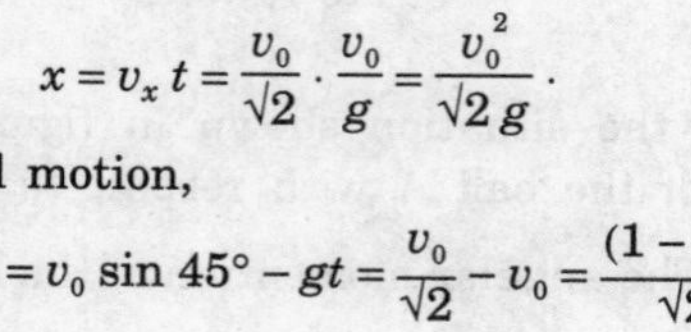

Figure 10-W9

$$v_x = v_0 \cos 45° = v_0/\sqrt{2}$$

and

$$x = v_x\,t = \frac{v_0}{\sqrt{2}} \cdot \frac{v_0}{g} = \frac{v_0^{\,2}}{\sqrt{2}\,g}\,.$$

For vertical motion,

$$v_y = v_0 \sin 45° - gt = \frac{v_0}{\sqrt{2}} - v_0 = \frac{(1 - \sqrt{2})}{\sqrt{2}}\,v_0$$

and

$$y = (v_0 \sin 45°)\,t - \frac{1}{2}\,gt^{\,2}$$

$$= \frac{v_0^{\,2}}{\sqrt{2}\,g} - \frac{v_0^{\,2}}{2\,g} = \frac{v_0^{\,2}}{2\,g}\,(\sqrt{2} - 1)\,.$$

The angular momentum of the particle at time t about the origin is

$$\vec{L} = \vec{r} \times \vec{p} = m\,\vec{r} \times \vec{v}$$

$$= m\,(\vec{i}\,x + \vec{j}\,y) \times (\vec{i}\,v_x + \vec{j}\,v_y)$$

$$= m\,(\vec{k}\,x\,v_y - \vec{k}\,y\,v_x)$$

$$= m\,\vec{k}\left[\left(\frac{v_0^{\,2}}{\sqrt{2}\,g}\right)\frac{v_0}{\sqrt{2}}\,(1 - \sqrt{2}) - \frac{v_0^{\,2}}{2\,g}\,(\sqrt{2} - 1)\,\frac{v_0}{\sqrt{2}}\right]$$

$$= -\,\vec{k}\,\frac{m v_0^{\,3}}{2\sqrt{2}\,g}\,.$$

Thus, the angular momentum of the particle is $\dfrac{m v_0^{\,3}}{2\sqrt{2}\,g}$ in the negative Z-direction, i.e., perpendicular to the plane of motion, going into the plane.

13. *A uniform circular disc of mass 200 g and radius 4·0 cm is rotated about one of its diameter at an angular speed of 10 rad/s. Find the kinetic energy of the disc and its angular momentum about the axis of rotation.*

Solution : The moment of inertia of the circular disc about its diameter is

$$I = \frac{1}{4}\,Mr^{\,2} = \frac{1}{4}\,(0{\cdot}200\ \text{kg})\,(0{\cdot}04\ \text{m})^{\,2}$$

$$= 8{\cdot}0 \times 10^{\,-5}\ \text{kg-m}^{\,2}.$$

The kinetic energy is

$$K = \frac{1}{2}\,I\omega^{\,2} = \frac{1}{2}\,(8{\cdot}0 \times 10^{\,-5}\ \text{kg-m}^{\,2})\,(100\ \text{rad}^{\,2}/\text{s}^{\,2})$$

$$= 4{\cdot}0 \times 10^{\,-3}\ \text{J}$$

and the angular momentum about the axis of rotation is

$$L = I\omega = (8{\cdot}0 \times 10^{\,-5}\ \text{kg-m}^{\,2})\,(10\ \text{rad/s})$$

$$= 8{\cdot}0 \times 10^{\,-4}\ \text{kg-m}^{\,2}/\text{s} = 8{\cdot}0 \times 10^{\,-4}\ \text{J-s}.$$

14. *A wheel rotating at an angular speed of 20 rad/s is brought to rest by a constant torque in 4·0 seconds. If the moment of inertia of the wheel about the axis of rotation is 0·20 kg-m^2, find the work done by the torque in the first two seconds.*

Solution : The angular deceleration of the wheel during the 4·0 seconds may be obtained by the equation

$$\omega = \omega_0 - \alpha t$$

or,

$$\alpha = \frac{\omega_0 - \omega}{t} = \frac{20\ \text{rad/s}}{4{\cdot}0\ \text{s}} = 5{\cdot}0\ \text{rad/s}^{\,2}.$$

The torque applied to produce this deceleration is

$$\Gamma = I\alpha = (0{\cdot}20\ \text{kg-m}^{\,2})\,(5{\cdot}0\ \text{rad/s}^{\,2}) = 1{\cdot}0\ \text{N-m}.$$

The angle rotated in the first two seconds is

$$\theta = \omega_0 t - \frac{1}{2}\,\alpha t^{\,2}$$

$$= (20\ \text{rad/s})\,(2\ \text{s}) - \frac{1}{2}\,(5{\cdot}0\ \text{rad/s}^{\,2})\,(4{\cdot}0\ \text{s}^{\,2})$$

$$= 40\ \text{rad} - 10\ \text{rad} = 30\ \text{rad}.$$

The work done by the torque in the first 2 seconds is, therefore,

$$W = \Gamma\theta = (1{\cdot}0\ \text{N-m})\,(30\ \text{rad}) = 30\ \text{J}.$$

15. *Two masses M and m are connected by a light string going over a pulley of radius r. The pulley is free to rotate about its axis which is kept horizontal. The moment of inertia of the pulley about the axis is I. The system is released from rest. Find the angular momentum of the system when the mass M has descended through a height h. The string does not slip over the pulley.*

Solution :

Figure 10-W10

The situation is shown in figure (10-W10). Let the speed of the masses be v at time t. This will also be the speed of a point on the rim of the wheel and hence the angular velocity of the wheel at time t will be v/r. If the height descended by the mass M is h, the loss in the potential energy of the "masses plus the pulley" system is $Mgh - mgh$. The gain in kinetic energy is $\frac{1}{2}Mv^2 + \frac{1}{2}mv^2 + \frac{1}{2}I\left(\frac{v}{r}\right)^2$. As no energy is lost,

$$\frac{1}{2}\left(M + m + \frac{I}{r^2}\right)v^2 = (M - m)gh$$

or,

$$v^2 = \frac{2(M - m)gh}{M + m + \dfrac{I}{r^2}}.$$

The angular momentum of the mass M is Mvr and that of the mass m is mvr in the same direction. The angular momentum of the pulley is $I\omega = Iv/r$. The total angular momentum is

$$\left[(M + m)r + \frac{I}{r}\right]v = \left[\left(M + m + \frac{I}{r^2}\right)r\right]\sqrt{\frac{2(M - m)gh}{M + m + \dfrac{I}{r^2}}}.$$

$$= \sqrt{2(M - m)\left(M + m + \frac{I}{r^2}\right)r^2gh}.$$

Figure 10-W11

16. *Figure (10-W11) shows a mass m placed on a frictionless horizontal table and attached to a string passing through a small hole in the surface. Initially, the mass moves in a circle of radius r_0 with a speed v_0 and the free end of*

the string is held by a person. The person pulls on the string slowly to decrease the radius of the circle to r. (a) Find the tension in the string when the mass moves in the circle of radius r. (b) Calculate the change in the kinetic energy of the mass.

Solution : The torque acting on the mass m about the vertical axis through the hole is zero. The angular momentum about this axis, therefore, remains constant. If the speed of the mass is v when it moves in the circle of radius r, we have

$$mv_0 r_0 = mvr$$

or,

$$v = \frac{r_0}{r}v_0. \qquad \ldots \text{(i)}$$

(a) The tension $T = \dfrac{mv^2}{r} = \dfrac{mr_0^2 v_0^2}{r^3}$.

(b) The change in kinetic energy $= \dfrac{1}{2}mv^2 - \dfrac{1}{2}mv_0^2$.

By (i), it is $\dfrac{1}{2}mv_0^2\left[\dfrac{r_0^2}{r^2} - 1\right]$.

17. *A uniform rod of mass m and length l is kept vertical with the lower end clamped. It is slightly pushed to let it fall down under gravity. Find its angular speed when the rod is passing through its lowest position. Neglect any friction at the clamp. What will be the linear speed of the free end at this instant ?*

Solution :

Figure 10-W12

As the rod reaches its lowest position, the centre of mass is lowered by a distance l. Its gravitational potential energy is decreased by mgl. As no energy is lost against friction, this should be equal to the increase in the kinetic energy. As the rotation occurs about the horizontal axis through the clamped end, the moment of inertia is $I = ml^2/3$. Thus,

$$\frac{1}{2}I\omega^2 = mgl$$

$$\frac{1}{2}\left(\frac{ml^2}{3}\right)\omega^2 = mgl$$

or,

$$\omega = \sqrt{\frac{6g}{l}}.$$

The linear speed of the free end is

$$v = l\omega = \sqrt{6\,gl}.$$

18. *Four particles each of mass m are kept at the four corners of a square of edge a. Find the moment of inertia of the system about a line perpendicular to the plane of the square and passing through the centre of the square.*

Solution :

Figure 10-W13

The perpendicular distance of every particle from the given line is $a/\sqrt{2}$. The moment of inertia of one particle is, therefore, $m(a/\sqrt{2})^2 = \frac{1}{2} ma^2$. The moment of inertia of the system is, therefore, $4 \times \frac{1}{2} ma^2 = 2 ma^2$.

19. *Two identical spheres each of mass 1·20 kg and radius 10·0 cm are fixed at the ends of a light rod so that the separation between the centres is 50·0 cm. Find the moment of inertia of the system about an axis perpendicular to the rod passing through its middle point.*

Solution :

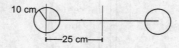

Figure 10-W14

Consider the diameter of one of the spheres parallel to the given axis. The moment of inertia of this sphere about the diameter is

$$I = \frac{2}{5} mR^2 = \frac{2}{5} (1\cdot 20 \text{ kg}) (0\cdot 1 \text{ m})^2$$

$$= 4\cdot 8 \times 10^{-3} \text{ kg-m}^2.$$

Its moment of inertia about the given axis is obtained by using the parallel axes theorem. Thus,

$$I = I_{cm} + md^2$$

$$= 4\cdot 8 \times 10^{-3} \text{ kg-m}^2 + (1\cdot 20 \text{ kg}) (0\cdot 25 \text{ m})^2$$

$$= 4\cdot 8 \times 10^{-3} \text{ kg-m}^2 + 0\cdot 075 \text{ kg-m}^2$$

$$= 79\cdot 8 \times 10^{-3} \text{ kg-m}^2.$$

The moment of inertia of the second sphere is also the same so that the moment of inertia of the system is

$$2 \times 79\cdot 8 \times 10^{-3} \text{ kg-m}^2 \approx 0\cdot 160 \text{ kg-m}^2.$$

20. *Two uniform identical rods each of mass M and length l are joined to form a cross as shown in figure (10-W15). Find the moment of inertia of the cross about a bisector as shown dotted in the figure.*

Figure 10-W15

Solution : Consider the line perpendicular to the plane of the figure through the centre of the cross. The moment of inertia of each rod about this line is $\frac{Ml^2}{12}$ and hence the moment of inertia of the cross is $\frac{Ml^2}{6}$. The moment of inertia of the cross about the two bisectors are equal by symmetry and according to the theorem of perpendicular axes, the moment of inertia of the cross about the bisector is $\frac{Ml^2}{12}$.

21. *A uniform rod of mass M and length a lies on a smooth horizontal plane. A particle of mass m moving at a speed v perpendicular to the length of the rod strikes it at a distance a/4 from the centre and stops after the collision. Find (a) the velocity of the centre of the rod and (b) the angular velocity of the rod about its centre just after the collision.*

Solution :

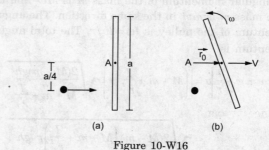

(a)   (b)

Figure 10-W16

The situation is shown in figure (10-W16a). Consider the rod and the particle together as the system. As there is no external resultant force, the linear momentum of the system will remain constant. Also there is no resultant external torque on the system and so the angular momentum of the system about any line will remain constant.

Suppose the velocity of the centre of the rod is V and the angular velocity about the centre is ω.

(a) The linear momentum before the collision is mv and that after the collision is MV. Thus,

$$mv = MV, \text{ or } V = \frac{m}{M} v.$$

(b) Let A be the centre of the rod when it is at rest. Let AB be the line perpendicular to the plane of the figure. Consider the angular momentum of "the rod plus the particle" system about AB. Initially the rod is at rest. The angular momentum of the particle about AB is

$$L = mv(a/4).$$

After the collision, the particle comes to rest. The angular momentum of the rod about A is

$$\vec{L} = \vec{L}_{cm} + M\,\vec{r}_0 \times \vec{V}.$$

As $\vec{r}_0 \parallel \vec{V},$ $\vec{r}_0 \times \vec{V} = 0.$

Thus, $\vec{L} = \vec{L}_{cm}.$

Hence the angular momentum of the rod about AB is

$$L = I\omega = \frac{Ma^2}{12}\,\omega.$$

Thus, $\dfrac{mva}{4} = \dfrac{Ma^2}{12}\,\omega$ or, $\omega = \dfrac{3\,mv}{Ma}.$

22. *A wheel of perimeter 220 cm rolls on a level road at a speed of 9 km/h. How many revolutions does the wheel make per second ?*

Solution : As the wheel rolls on the road, its angular speed ω about the centre and the linear speed v of the centre are related as $v = \omega\, r.$

$$\therefore\ \omega = \frac{v}{r} = \frac{9\ \text{km/h}}{220\ \text{cm}/2\pi} = \frac{2\pi \times 9 \times 10^5}{220 \times 3600}\ \text{rad/s}.$$

$$= \frac{900}{22 \times 36}\ \text{rev/s} = \frac{25}{22}\ \text{rev/s}.$$

23. *A cylinder is released from rest from the top of an incline of inclination θ and length l. If the cylinder rolls without slipping, what will be its speed when it reaches the bottom ?*

Solution : Let the mass of the cylinder be m and its radius r. Suppose the linear speed of the cylinder when it reaches the bottom is v. As the cylinder rolls without slipping, its angular speed about its axis is $\omega = v/r.$ The kinetic energy at the bottom will be

$$K = \frac{1}{2}I\omega^2 + \frac{1}{2}mv^2$$

$$= \frac{1}{2}\left(\frac{1}{2}mr^2\right)\omega^2 + \frac{1}{2}mv^2 = \frac{1}{4}mv^2 + \frac{1}{2}mv^2 = \frac{3}{4}mv^2.$$

This should be equal to the loss of potential energy $mgl\sin\theta$. Thus, $\dfrac{3}{4}mv^2 = mgl\sin\theta$

or, $v = \sqrt{\dfrac{4}{3}gl\sin\theta}.$

24. *A sphere of mass m rolls without slipping on an inclined plane of inclination θ. Find the linear acceleration of the sphere and the force of friction acting on it. What should be the minimum coefficient of static friction to support pure rolling ?*

Solution : Suppose the radius of the sphere is r. The forces acting on the sphere are shown in figure (10-W17). They are (a) weight mg, (b) normal force $\mathcal{N}$ and (c) friction f.

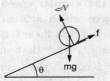

Figure 10-W17

Let the linear acceleration of the sphere down the plane be a. The equation for the linear motion of the centre of mass is

$$mg\sin\theta - f = ma. \qquad \ldots\ (i)$$

As the sphere rolls without slipping, its angular acceleration about the centre is a/r. The equation of rotational motion about the centre of mass is,

$$fr = \left(\frac{2}{5}mr^2\right)\left(\frac{a}{r}\right)$$

or, $f = \dfrac{2}{5}ma. \qquad \ldots\ (ii)$

From (i) and (ii),

$$a = \frac{5}{7}g\sin\theta$$

and $f = \dfrac{2}{7}mg\sin\theta.$

The normal force is equal to $mg\cos\theta$ as there is no acceleration perpendicular to the incline. The maximum friction that can act is, therefore, $\mu\,mg\cos\theta$, where μ is the coefficient of static friction. Thus, for pure rolling

$$\mu\,mg\cos\theta > \frac{2}{7}mg\sin\theta$$

or, $\mu > \dfrac{2}{7}\tan\theta.$

25. *Figure (10-W18) shows two cylinders of radii r_1 and r_2 having moments of inertia I_1 and I_2 about their respective axes. Initially, the cylinders rotate about their axes with angular speeds ω_1 and ω_2 as shown in the figure. The cylinders are moved closer to touch each other keeping the axes parallel. The cylinders first slip over each other at the contact but the slipping finally ceases due to the friction between them. Find the angular speeds of the cylinders after the slipping ceases.*

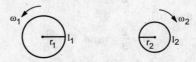

Figure 10-W18

Solution : When slipping ceases, the linear speeds of the points of contact of the two cylinders will be equal. If ω'_1 *and* ω'_2 be the respective angular speeds, we have

$$\omega'_1 r_1 = \omega'_2 r_2. \qquad \ldots \text{(i)}$$

The change in the angular speed is brought about by the frictional force which acts as long as the slipping exists. If this force f acts for a time t, the torque on the first cylinder is $f r_1$ and that on the second is $f r_2$. Assuming $\omega_1 r_1 > \omega_2 r_2$, the corresponding angular impulses are $-f r_1 t$ and $f r_2 t$. We, therefore, have

$$-f r_1 t = I_1(\omega'_1 - \omega_1)$$

and

$$f r_2 t = I_2(\omega'_2 - \omega_2)$$

or,

$$-\frac{I_1}{r_1}(\omega'_1 - \omega_1) = \frac{I_2}{r_2}(\omega'_2 - \omega_2). \qquad \ldots \text{(ii)}$$

Solving (i) and (ii),

$$\omega'_1 = \frac{I_1 \omega_1 r_2 + I_2 \omega_2 r_1}{I_2 r_1^2 + I_1 r_2^2} r_2 \text{ and } \omega'_2 = \frac{I_1 \omega_1 r_2 + I_2 \omega_2 r_1}{I_2 r_1^2 + I_1 r_2^2} r_1.$$

26. *A cylinder of mass m is suspended through two strings wrapped around it as shown in figure (10-W19). Find (a) the tension T in the string and (b) the speed of the cylinder as it falls through a distance h.*

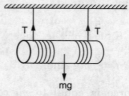

Figure 10-W19

Solution : The portion of the strings between the ceiling and the cylinder is at rest. Hence the points of the cylinder where the strings leave it are at rest. The cylinder is thus rolling without slipping on the strings. Suppose the centre of the cylinder falls with an acceleration a. The angular acceleration of the cylinder about its axis is $\alpha = a/R$, as the cylinder does not slip over the strings.

The equation of motion for the centre of mass of the cylinder is

$$mg - 2T = ma \qquad \ldots \text{(i)}$$

and for the motion about the centre of mass, it is

$$2Tr = \left(\frac{1}{2} mr^2 \alpha\right) = \frac{1}{2} mra$$

or,

$$2T = \frac{1}{2} ma. \qquad \ldots \text{(ii)}$$

From (i) and (ii),

$$a = \frac{2}{3} g \text{ and } T = \frac{mg}{6}.$$

As the centre of the cylinder starts moving from rest, the velocity after it has fallen through a distance h is

given by

$$v^2 = 2\left(\frac{2}{3} g\right) h$$

or,

$$v = \sqrt{\frac{4gh}{3}}.$$

27. *A force F acts tangentially at the highest point of a sphere of mass m kept on a rough horizontal plane. If the sphere rolls without slipping, find the acceleration of the centre of the sphere.*

Solution :

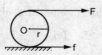

Figure 10-W20

The situation is shown in figure (10-W20). As the force F rotates the sphere, the point of contact has a tendency to slip towards left so that the static friction on the sphere will act towards right. Let r be the radius of the sphere and a be the linear acceleration of the centre of the sphere. The angular acceleration about the centre of the sphere is $\alpha = a/r$, as there is no slipping.

For the linear motion of the centre

$$F + f = ma \qquad \ldots \text{(i)}$$

and for the rotational motion about the centre,

$$Fr - fr = I\alpha = \left(\frac{2}{5} mr^2\right)\left(\frac{a}{r}\right)$$

or,

$$F - f = \frac{2}{5} ma. \qquad \ldots \text{(ii)}$$

From (i) and (ii),

$$2F = \frac{7}{5} ma \text{ or, } a = \frac{10 F}{7 m}.$$

28. *A sphere of mass M and radius r shown in figure (10-W21) slips on a rough horizontal plane. At some instant it has translational velocity v_0 and rotational velocity about the centre $\frac{v_0}{2r}$. Find the translational velocity after the sphere starts pure rolling.*

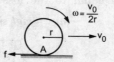

Figure 10-W21

Solution : Velocity of the centre $= v_0$ and the angular velocity about the centre $= \omega_0 = \frac{v_0}{2r}$. Thus, $v_0 > \omega_0 r$. The sphere slips forward and thus the friction by the plane on the sphere will act backward. As the friction is kinetic, its value is $\mu \mathcal{N} = \mu Mg$ and the sphere will be decelerated by $a_{cm} = f/M$. Hence,

$$v(t) = v_0 - \frac{f}{M} t \cdot \qquad \dots \text{(i)}$$

This friction will also have a torque $\Gamma = fr$ about the centre. This torque is clockwise and in the direction of ω_0. Hence the angular acceleration about the centre will be

$$\alpha = f \frac{r}{(2/5) Mr^2} = \frac{5f}{2Mr}$$

and the clockwise angular velocity at time t will be

$$\omega(t) = \omega_0 + \frac{5f}{2Mr} t = \frac{v_0}{2r} + \frac{5f}{2Mr} t$$

Pure rolling starts when $v(t) = r\omega(t)$

i.e., $$v(t) = \frac{v_0}{2} + \frac{5f}{2M} t \qquad \dots \text{(ii)}$$

Eliminating t from (i) and (ii),

$$\frac{5}{2} v(t) + v(t) = \frac{5}{2} v_0 + \frac{v_0}{2}$$

or, $$v(t) = \frac{2}{7} \times 3 v_0 = \frac{6}{7} v_0 .$$

Thus, the sphere rolls with translational velocity $6v_0/7$ in the forward direction.

Alternative : Let us consider the torque about the initial point of contact A. The force of friction passes through this point and hence its torque is zero. The normal force and the weight balance each other. The net torque about A is zero. Hence the angular momentum about A is conserved.
Initial angular momentum is,

$$L = L_{cm} + Mrv_0 = I_{cm} \omega_0 + Mrv_0$$
$$= \left(\frac{2}{5} Mr^2\right)\left(\frac{v_0}{2r}\right) + Mrv_0 = \frac{6}{5} Mrv_0 .$$

Suppose the translational velocity of the sphere, after it starts rolling, is v. The angular velocity is v/r. The angular momentum about A is,

$$L = L_{cm} + Mrv$$
$$= \left(\frac{2}{5} Mr^2\right)\left(\frac{v}{r}\right) + Mrv = \frac{7}{5} Mrv .$$

Thus, $$\frac{6}{5} Mrv_0 = \frac{7}{5} Mrv$$

or, $$v = \frac{6}{7} v_0 .$$

29. *The sphere shown in figure (10-W22) lies on a rough plane when a particle of mass m travelling at a speed v_0 collides and sticks with it. If the line of motion of the particle is at a distance h above the plane, find (a) the linear speed of the combined system just after the collision, (b) the angular speed of the system about the centre of the sphere just after the collision and (c) the value of h for which the sphere starts pure rolling on the plane. Assume that the mass M of the sphere is large compared to the mass of the particle so that the centre of mass of the combined system is not appreciably shifted from the centre of the sphere.*

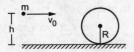

Figure 10-W22

Solution : Take the particle plus the sphere as the system.
(a) Using conservation of linear momentum, the linear speed of the combined system v is given by

$$mv_0 = (M + m)v \quad \text{or,} \quad v = \frac{mv_0}{M + m} . \qquad \dots \text{(i)}$$

(b) Next, we shall use conservation of angular momentum about the centre of mass, which is to be taken at the centre of the sphere $(M \gg m)$. Angular momentum of the particle before collision is $mv_0(h - R)$. If the system rotates with angular speed ω after collision, the angular momentum of the system becomes

$$\left(\frac{2}{5} MR^2 + mR^2\right)\omega.$$

Hence,

$$mv_0(h - R) = \left(\frac{2}{5} M + m\right) R^2 \omega$$

or, $$\omega = \frac{mv_0(h - R)}{\left(\frac{2}{5} M + m\right) R^2} .$$

(c) The sphere will start rolling just after the collision if

$$v = \omega R, \text{ i.e., } \frac{mv_0}{M + m} = \frac{mv_0(h - R)}{\left(\frac{2}{5} M + m\right) R}$$

giving, $$h = \left(\frac{\frac{7}{5} M + 2m}{M + m}\right) R \approx \frac{7}{5} R.$$

QUESTIONS FOR SHORT ANSWER

1. Can an object be in pure translation as well as in pure rotation ?

2. A simple pendulum is a point mass suspended by a light thread from a fixed point. The particle is displaced towards one side and then released. It makes small oscillations. Is the motion of such a simple pendulum a pure rotation ? If yes, where is the axis of rotation ?

3. In a rotating body, $a = \alpha r$ and $v = \omega r$. Thus $\dfrac{a}{\alpha} = \dfrac{v}{\omega}$. Can you use the theorems of ratio and proportion studied in algebra so as to write

$$\frac{a + \alpha}{a - \alpha} = \frac{v + \omega}{v - \omega}$$

4. A ball is whirled in a circle by attaching it to a fixed point with a string. Is there an angular rotation of the ball about its centre ? If yes, is this angular velocity equal to the angular velocity of the ball about the fixed point ?

5. The moon rotates about the earth in such a way that only one hemisphere of the moon faces the earth (figure 10-Q1). Can we ever see the "other face" of the moon from the earth ? Can a person on the moon ever see all the faces of the earth ?

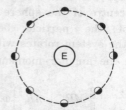

Figure 10-Q1

6. The torque of the weight of any body about any vertical axis is zero. Is it always correct ?

7. The torque of a force $\vec{F}$ about a point is defined as $\vec{\Gamma} = \vec{r} \times \vec{F}$. Suppose $\vec{r}, \vec{F}$ and $\vec{\Gamma}$ are all nonzero. Is $\vec{r} \times \vec{\Gamma} \parallel \vec{F}$ always true ? Is it ever true ?

8. A heavy particle of mass m falls freely near the earth's surface. What is the torque acting on this particle about a point 50 cm east to the line of motion ? Does this torque produce any angular acceleration in the particle ?

9. If several forces act on a particle, the total torque on the particle may be obtained by first finding the resultant force and then taking torque of this resultant. Prove this. Is this result valid for the forces acting on different particles of a body in such a way that their lines of action intersect at a common point ?

10. If the sum of all the forces acting on a body is zero, is it necessarily in equilibrium ? If the sum of all the forces on a particle is zero, is it necessarily in equilibrium ?

11. If the angular momentum of a body is found to be zero about a point, is it necessary that it will also be zero about a different point ?

12. If the resultant torque of all the forces acting on a body is zero about a point, is it necessary that it will be zero about any other point ?

13. A body is in translational equilibrium under the action of coplanar forces. If the torque of these forces is zero about a point, is it necessary that it will also be zero about any other point ?

14. A rectangular brick is kept on a table with a part of its length projecting out. It remains at rest if the length projected is slightly less than half the total length but it falls down if the length projected is slightly more than half the total length. Give reason.

15. When a fat person tries to touch his toes, keeping the legs straight, he generally falls. Explain with reference to figure (10-Q2).

Figure 10-Q2

16. A ladder is resting with one end on a vertical wall and the other end on a horizontal floor. Is it more likely to slip when a man stands near the bottom or near the top ?

17. When a body is weighed on an ordinary balance we demand that the arm should be horizontal if the weights on the two pans are equal. Suppose equal weights are put on the two pans, the arm is kept at an angle with the horizontal and released. Is the torque of the two weights about the middle point (point of support) zero ? Is the total torque zero ? If so, why does the arm rotate and finally become horizontal ?

18. The density of a rod AB continuously increases from A to B. Is it easier to set it in rotation by clamping it at A and applying a perpendicular force at B or by clamping it at B and applying the force at A ?

19. When tall buildings are constructed on earth, the duration of day–night slightly increases. Is it true ?

20. If the ice at the poles melts and flows towards the equator, how will it affect the duration of day–night ?

21. A hollow sphere, a solid sphere, a disc and a ring all having same mass and radius are rolled down on an inclined plane. If no slipping takes place, which one will take the smallest time to cover a given length ?

22. A sphere rolls on a horizontal surface. Is there any point of the sphere which has a vertical velocity ?

OBJECTIVE I

1. Let $\vec{A}$ be a unit vector along the axis of rotation of a purely rotating body and $\vec{B}$ be a unit vector along the velocity of a particle P of the body away from the axis. The value of $\vec{A} . \vec{B}$ is
   (a) 1   (b) −1   (c) 0   (d) None of these.

2. A body is uniformly rotating about an axis fixed in an inertial frame of reference. Let $\vec{A}$ be a unit vector along the axis of rotation and $\vec{B}$ be the unit vector along the resultant force on a particle P of the body away from the axis. The value of $\vec{A} . \vec{B}$ is
   (a) 1   (b) −1   (c) 0   (d) none of these.

3. A particle moves with a constant velocity parallel to the X-axis. Its angular momentum with respect to the origin
   (a) is zero   (b) remains constant
   (c) goes on increasing   (d) goes on decreasing.

4. A body is in pure rotation. The linear speed v of a particle, the distance r of the particle from the axis and the angular velocity ω of the body are related as $\omega = \dfrac{v}{r}$. Thus
   (a) $\omega \propto \dfrac{1}{r}$ (b) $\omega \propto r$
   (c) $\omega = 0$ (d) ω is independent of r.

5. Figure (10-Q3) shows a small wheel fixed coaxially on a bigger one of double the radius. The system rotates about the common axis. The strings supporting A and B do not slip on the wheels. If x and y be the distances travelled by A and B in the same time interval, then
   (a) $x = 2y$ (b) $x = y$ (c) $y = 2x$ (d) none of these.

Figure 10-Q3

6. A body is rotating uniformly about a vertical axis fixed in an inertial frame. The resultant force on a particle of the body not on the axis is
   (a) vertical   (b) horizontal and skew with the axis
   (c) horizontal and intersecting the axis
   (d) none of these.

7. A body is rotating nonuniformly about a vertical axis fixed in an inertial frame. The resultant force on a particle of the body not on the axis is
   (a) vertical   (b) horizontal and skew with the axis
   (c) horizontal and intersecting the axis
   (d) none of these.

8. Let $\vec{F}$ be a force acting on a particle having position vector $\vec{r}$. Let $\vec{\Gamma}$ be the torque of this force about the origin, then
   (a) $\vec{r} . \vec{\Gamma} = 0$ and $\vec{F} . \vec{\Gamma} = 0$ (b) $\vec{r} . \vec{\Gamma} = 0$ but $\vec{F} . \vec{\Gamma} \neq 0$
   (c) $\vec{r} . \vec{\Gamma} \neq 0$ but $\vec{F} . \vec{\Gamma} = 0$ (d) $\vec{r} . \vec{\Gamma} \neq 0$ and $\vec{F} . \vec{\Gamma} \neq 0$.

9. One end of a uniform rod of mass m and length l is clamped. The rod lies on a smooth horizontal surface and rotates on it about the clamped end at a uniform angular velocity ω. The force exerted by the clamp on the rod has a horizontal component
   (a) $m\omega^2 l$ (b) zero   (c) mg (d) $\dfrac{1}{2} m\omega^2 l$.

10. A uniform rod is kept vertically on a horizontal smooth surface at a point O. If it is rotated slightly and released, it falls down on the horizontal surface. The lower end will remain
    (a) at O (b) at a distance less than $l/2$ from O
    (c) at a distance $l/2$ from O
    (d) at a distance larger than $l/2$ from O.

11. A circular disc A of radius r is made from an iron plate of thickness t and another circular disc B of radius $4r$ is made from an iron plate of thickness $t/4$. The relation between the moments of inertia I_A and I_B is
    (a) $I_A > I_B$ (b) $I_A = I_B$ (c) $I_A < I_B$
    (d) depends on the actual values of t and r.

12. Equal torques act on the discs A and B of the previous problem, initially both being at rest. At a later instant, the linear speeds of a point on the rim of A and another point on the rim of B are v_A and v_B respectively. We have
    (a) $v_A > v_B$ (b) $v_A = v_B$ (c) $v_A < v_B$
    (d) the relation depends on the actual magnitude of the torques.

13. A closed cylindrical tube containing some water (not filling the entire tube) lies in a horizontal plane. If the tube is rotated about a perpendicular bisector, the moment of inertia of water about the axis
    (a) increases   (b) decreases   (c) remains constant
    (d) increases if the rotation is clockwise and decreases if it is anticlockwise.

14. The moment of inertia of a uniform semicircular wire of mass M and radius r about a line perpendicular to the plane of the wire through the centre is
    (a) Mr^2 (b) $\dfrac{1}{2} Mr^2$ (c) $\dfrac{1}{4} Mr^2$ (d) $\dfrac{2}{5} Mr^2$.

15. Let I_1 and I_2 be the moments of inertia of two bodies of identical geometrical shape, the first made of aluminium and the second of iron.
    (a) $I_1 < I_2$ (b) $I_1 = I_2$ (c) $I_1 > I_2$
    (d) relation between I_1 and I_2 depends on the actual shapes of the bodies.

16. A body having its centre of mass at the origin has three of its particles at $(a,0,0)$, $(0,a,0)$, $(0,0,a)$. The moments of inertia of the body about the X and Y axes are 0.20 kg-m^2 each. The moment of inertia about the Z-axis
    (a) is 0.20 kg-m^2 (b) is 0.40 kg-m^2
    (c) is $0.20\sqrt{2}$ kg-m^2
    (d) cannot be deduced with this information.

17. A cubical block of mass M and edge a slides down a rough inclined plane of inclination θ with a uniform

velocity. The torque of the normal force on the block about its centre has a magnitude

(a) zero   (b) Mga (c) $Mga \sin\theta$ (d) $\frac{1}{2} Mga \sin\theta$.

18. A thin circular ring of mass M and radius r is rotating about its axis with an angular speed ω. Two particles having mass m each are now attached at diametrically opposite points. The angular speed of the ring will become

(a) $\dfrac{\omega M}{M + m}$ (b) $\dfrac{\omega M}{M + 2\,m}$

(c) $\dfrac{\omega(M - 2\,m)}{M + 2\,m}$ (d) $\dfrac{\omega(M + 2\,m)}{M}$.

19. A person sitting firmly over a rotating stool has his arms stretched. If he folds his arms, his angular momentum about the axis of rotation

(a) increases   (b) decreases
(c) remains unchanged   (d) doubles.

20. The centre of a wheel rolling on a plane surface moves with a speed v_0. A particle on the rim of the wheel at the same level as the centre will be moving at speed

(a) zero   (b) v_0 (c) $\sqrt{2}v_0$ (d) $2v_0$.

21. A wheel of radius 20 cm is pushed to move it on a rough horizontal surface. It is found to move through a distance of 60 cm on the road during the time it completes one revolution about the centre. Assume that the linear and the angular accelerations are uniform. The frictional force acting on the wheel by the surface is
(a) along the velocity of the wheel
(b) opposite to the velocity of the wheel
(c) perpendicular to the velocity of the wheel
(d) zero.

22. The angular velocity of the engine (and hence of the wheel) of a scooter is proportional to the petrol input per second. The scooter is moving on a frictionless road with uniform velocity. If the petrol input is increased by 10%, the linear velocity of the scooter is increased by
(a) 50%   (b) 10%   (c) 20%   (d) 0%.

23. A solid sphere, a hollow sphere and a disc, all having same mass and radius, are placed at the top of a smooth incline and released. Least time will be taken in reaching the bottom by
(a) the solid sphere   (b) the hollow sphere
(c) the disc   (d) all will take same time.

24. A solid sphere, a hollow sphere and a disc, all having same mass and radius, are placed at the top of an incline and released. The friction coefficients between the objects and the incline are same and not sufficient to allow pure rolling. Least time will be taken in reaching the bottom by
(a) the solid sphere   (b) the hollow sphere
(c) the disc   (d) all will take same time.

25. In the previous question, the smallest kinetic energy at the bottom of the incline will be achieved by
(a) the solid sphere   (b) the hollow sphere
(c) the disc   (d) all will achieve same kinetic energy.

26. A string of negligible thickness is wrapped several times around a cylinder kept on a rough horizontal surface. A man standing at a distance l from the cylinder holds one end of the string and pulls the cylinder towards him (figure 10-Q4). There is no slipping anywhere. The length of the string passed through the hand of the man while the cylinder reaches his hands is
(a) l (b) $2l$ (c) $3l$ (d) $4l$.

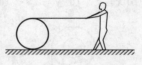

Figure 10-Q4

OBJECTIVE II

1. The axis of rotation of a purely rotating body
(a) must pass through the centre of mass
(b) may pass through the centre of mass
(c) must pass through a particle of the body
(d) may pass through a particle of the body.

2. Consider the following two equations

(A) $L = I\,\omega$ (B) $\dfrac{dL}{dt} = \Gamma$

In noninertial frames
(a) both A and B are true   (b) A is true but B is false
(c) B is true but A is false   (d) both A and B are false.

3. A particle moves on a straight line with a uniform velocity. Its angular momentum
(a) is always zero
(b) is zero about a point on the straight line
(c) is not zero about a point away from the straight line
(d) about any given point remains constant.

4. If there is no external force acting on a nonrigid body, which of the following quantities must remain constant ?
(a) angular momentum   (b) linear momentum
(c) kinetic energy   (d) moment of inertia.

5. Let I_A and I_B be moments of inertia of a body about two axes A and B respectively. The axis A passes through the centre of mass of the body but B does not.
(a) $I_A < I_B$ (b) If $I_A < I_B$, the axes are parallel
(c) If the axes are parallel, $I_A < I_B$
(d) If the axes are not parallel, $I_A \geq I_B$.

6. A sphere is rotating about a diameter.
(a) The particles on the surface of the sphere do not have any linear acceleration.
(b) The particles on the diameter mentioned above do not have any linear acceleration.
(c) Different particles on the surface have different

angular speeds.

(d) All the particles on the surface have same linear speed.

7. The density of a rod gradually decreases from one end to the other. It is pivoted at an end so that it can move about a vertical axis through the pivot. A horizontal force F is applied on the free end in a direction perpendicular to the rod. The quantities, that do not depend on which end of the rod is pivoted, are
(a) angular acceleration
(b) angular velocity when the rod completes one rotation
(c) angular momentum when the rod completes one rotation
(d) torque of the applied force.

8. Consider a wheel of a bicycle rolling on a level road at a linear speed v_0 (figure 10-Q5).
(a) the speed of the particle A is zero
(b) the speed of B, C and D are all equal to v_0
(c) the speed of C is $2v_0$
(d) the speed of B is greater than the speed of O.

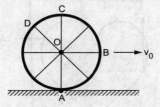

Figure 10-Q5

9. Two uniform solid spheres having unequal masses and unequal radii are released from rest from the same height on a rough incline. If the spheres roll without slipping,
(a) the heavier sphere reaches the bottom first
(b) the bigger sphere reaches the bottom first
(c) the two spheres reach the bottom together
(d) the information given is not sufficient to tell which sphere will reach the bottom first.

10. A hollow sphere and a solid sphere having same mass and same radii are rolled down a rough inclined plane.
(a) The hollow sphere reaches the bottom first.
(b) The solid sphere reaches the bottom with greater speed.
(c) The solid sphere reaches the bottom with greater kinetic energy.
(d) The two spheres will reach the bottom with same linear momentum.

11. A sphere cannot roll on
(a) a smooth horizontal surface
(b) a smooth inclined surface
(c) a rough horizontal surface
(d) a rough inclined surface.

12. In rear-wheel drive cars, the engine rotates the rear wheels and the front wheels rotate only because the car moves. If such a car accelerates on a horizontal road, the friction
(a) on the rear wheels is in the forward direction
(b) on the front wheels is in the backward direction
(c) on the rear wheels has larger magnitude than the friction on the front wheels
(d) on the car is in the backward direction.

13. A sphere can roll on a surface inclined at an angle θ if the friction coefficient is more than $\frac{2}{7}\tan\theta$. Suppose the friction coefficient is $\frac{1}{7}\tan\theta$. If a sphere is released from rest on the incline,
(a) it will stay at rest
(b) it will make pure translational motion
(c) it will translate and rotate about the centre
(d) the angular momentum of the sphere about its centre will remain constant.

14. A sphere is rolled on a rough horizontal surface. It gradually slows down and stops. The force of friction tries to
(a) decrease the linear velocity
(b) increase the angular velocity
(c) increase the linear momentum
(d) decrease the angular velocity.

15. Figure (10-Q6) shows a smooth inclined plane fixed in a car accelerating on a horizontal road. The angle of incline θ is related to the acceleration a of the car as $a = g\tan\theta$. If the sphere is set in pure rolling on the incline,
(a) it will continue pure rolling
(b) it will slip down the plane
(c) its linear velocity will increase
(d) its linear velocity will slowly decrease.

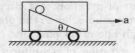

Figure 10-Q6

EXERCISES

1. A wheel is making revolutions about its axis with uniform angular acceleration. Starting from rest, it reaches 100 rev/sec in 4 seconds. Find the angular acceleration. Find the angle rotated during these four seconds.

2. A wheel rotating with uniform angular acceleration covers 50 revolutions in the first five seconds after the start. Find the angular acceleration and the angular velocity at the end of five seconds.

3. A wheel starting from rest is uniformly accelerated at 4 rad/s^2 for 10 seconds. It is allowed to rotate uniformly

for the next 10 seconds and is finally brought to rest in the next 10 seconds. Find the total angle rotated by the wheel.

4. A body rotates about a fixed axis with an angular acceleration of one radian/second/second. Through what angle does it rotate during the time in which its angular velocity increases from 5 rad/s to 15 rad/s.

5. Find the angular velocity of a body rotating with an acceleration of 2 rev/s^2 as it completes the 5th revolution after the start.

6. A disc of radius 10 cm is rotating about its axis at an angular speed of 20 rad/s. Find the linear speed of
(a) a point on the rim,
(b) the middle point of a radius.

7. A disc rotates about its axis with a constant angular acceleration of 4 rad/s^2. Find the radial and tangential accelerations of a particle at a distance of 1 cm from the axis at the end of the first second after the disc starts rotating.

8. A block hangs from a string wrapped on a disc of radius 20 cm free to rotate about its axis which is fixed in a horizontal position. If the angular speed of the disc is 10 rad/s at some instant, with what speed is the block going down at that instant ?

9. Three particles, each of mass 200 g, are kept at the corners of an equilateral triangle of side 10 cm. Find the moment of inertia of the system about an axis
(a) joining two of the particles and
(b) passing through one of the particles and perpendicular to the plane of the particles.

10. Particles of masses 1 g, 2 g, 3 g, ..., 100 g are kept at the marks 1 cm, 2 cm, 3 cm, ..., 100 cm respectively on a metre scale. Find the moment of inertia of the system of particles about a perpendicular bisector of the metre scale.

11. Find the moment of inertia of a pair of spheres, each having a mass m and radius r, kept in contact about the tangent passing through the point of contact.

12. The moment of inertia of a uniform rod of mass 0·50 kg and length 1 m is 0·10 kg-m^2 about a line perpendicular to the rod. Find the distance of this line from the middle point of the rod.

13. Find the radius of gyration of a circular ring of radius r about a line perpendicular to the plane of the ring and passing through one of its particles.

14. The radius of gyration of a uniform disc about a line perpendicular to the disc equals its radius. Find the distance of the line from the centre.

15. Find the moment of inertia of a uniform square plate of mass m and edge a about one of its diagonals.

16. The surface density (mass/area) of a circular disc of radius a depends on the distance from the centre as $\rho(r) = A + Br$. Find its moment of inertia about the line perpendicular to the plane of the disc through its centre.

17. A particle of mass m is projected with a speed u at an angle θ with the horizontal. Find the torque of the weight of the particle about the point of projection when the particle is at the highest point.

18. A simple pendulum of length l is pulled aside to make an angle θ with the vertical. Find the magnitude of the torque of the weight w of the bob about the point of suspension. When is the torque zero ?

19. When a force of 6·0 N is exerted at 30° to a wrench at a distance of 8 cm from the nut, it is just able to loosen the nut. What force F would be sufficient to loosen it if it acts perpendicularly to the wrench at 16 cm from the nut ?

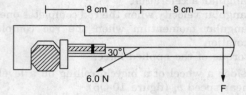

Figure 10-E1

20. Calculate the total torque acting on the body shown in figure (10-E2) about the point O.

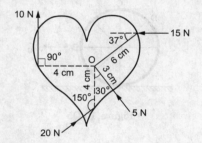

Figure 10-E2

21. A cubical block of mass m and edge a slides down a rough inclined plane of inclination θ with a uniform speed. Find the torque of the normal force acting on the block about its centre.

22. A rod of mass m and length L, lying horizontally, is free to rotate about a vertical axis through its centre. A horizontal force of constant magnitude F acts on the rod at a distance of $L/4$ from the centre. The force is always perpendicular to the rod. Find the angle rotated by the rod during the time t after the motion starts.

23. A square plate of mass 120 g and edge 5·0 cm rotates about one of the edges. If it has a uniform angular acceleration of 0·2 rad/s^2, what torque acts on the plate ?

24. Calculate the torque on the square plate of the previous problem if it rotates about a diagonal with the same angular acceleration.

25. A flywheel of moment of inertia 5·0 kg-m^2 is rotated at a speed of 60 rad/s. Because of the friction at the axle, it comes to rest in 5·0 minutes. Find (a) the average torque of the friction, (b) the total work done by the friction and (c) the angular momentum of the wheel 1 minute before it stops rotating.

26. Because of the friction between the water in oceans with the earth's surface, the rotational kinetic energy of the earth is continuously decreasing. If the earth's angular speed decreases by 0·0016 rad/day in 100 years, find the

average torque of the friction on the earth. Radius of the earth is 6400 km and its mass is $6 \cdot 0 \times 10^{24}$ kg.

27. A wheel rotating at a speed of 600 rpm (revolutions per minute) about its axis is brought to rest by applying a constant torque for 10 seconds. Find the angular deceleration and the angular velocity 5 seconds after the application of the torque.

28. A wheel of mass 10 kg and radius 20 cm is rotating at an angular speed of 100 rev/min when the motor is turned off. Neglecting the friction at the axle, calculate the force that must be applied tangentially to the wheel to bring it to rest in 10 revolutions.

29. A cylinder rotating at an angular speed of 50 rev/s is brought in contact with an identical stationary cylinder. Because of the kinetic friction, torques act on the two cylinders, accelerating the stationary one and decelerating the moving one. If the common magnitude of the acceleration and deceleration be one revolution per second square, how long will it take before the two cylinders have equal angular speed ?

30. A body rotating at 20 rad/s is acted upon by a constant torque providing it a deceleration of 2 rad/s^2. At what time will the body have kinetic energy same as the initial value if the torque continues to act ?

31. A light rod of length 1 m is pivoted at its centre and two masses of 5 kg and 2 kg are hung from the ends as shown in figure (10-E3). Find the initial angular acceleration of the rod assuming that it was horizontal in the beginning.

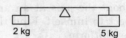

Figure 10-E3

32. Suppose the rod in the previous problem has a mass of 1 kg distributed uniformly over its length.
(a) Find the initial angular acceleration of the rod.
(b) Find the tension in the supports to the blocks of mass 2 kg and 5 kg.

33. Figure (10-E4) shows two blocks of masses m and M connected by a string passing over a pulley. The horizontal table over which the mass m slides is smooth. The pulley has a radius r and moment of inertia I about its axis and it can freely rotate about this axis. Find the acceleration of the mass M assuming that the string does not slip on the pulley.

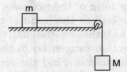

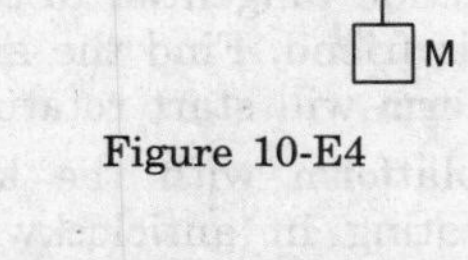

Figure 10-E4

34. A string is wrapped on a wheel of moment of inertia $0 \cdot 20$ kg-m^2 and radius 10 cm and goes through a light pulley to support a block of mass $2 \cdot 0$ kg as shown in figure (10-E5). Find the acceleration of the block.

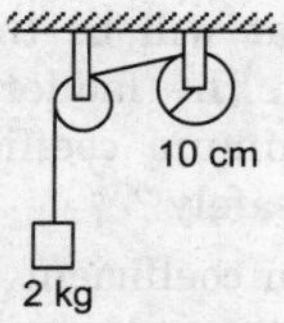

Figure 10-E5

35. Suppose the smaller pulley of the previous problem has its radius $5 \cdot 0$ cm and moment of inertia $0 \cdot 10$ kg-m^2. Find the tension in the part of the string joining the pulleys.

36. The pulleys in figure (10-E6) are identical, each having a radius R and moment of inertia I. Find the acceleration of the block M.

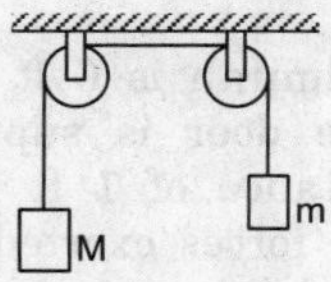

Figure 10-E6

37. The descending pulley shown in figure (10-E7) has a radius 20 cm and moment of inertia $0 \cdot 20$ kg-m^2. The fixed pulley is light and the horizontal plane frictionless. Find the acceleration of the block if its mass is $1 \cdot 0$ kg.

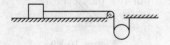

Figure 10-E7

38. The pulley shown in figure (10-E8) has a radius 10 cm and moment of inertia $0 \cdot 5$ kg-m^2 about its axis. Assuming the inclined planes to be frictionless, calculate the acceleration of the $4 \cdot 0$ kg block.

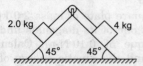

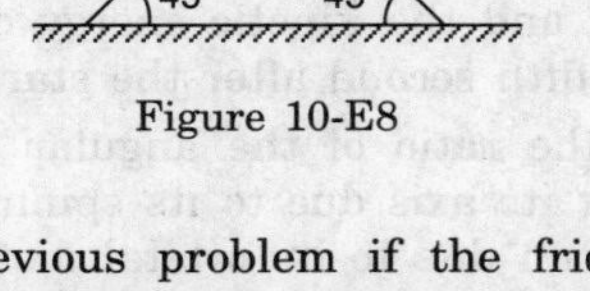

Figure 10-E8

39. Solve the previous problem if the friction coefficient between the $2 \cdot 0$ kg block and the plane below it is $0 \cdot 5$ and the plane below the $4 \cdot 0$ kg block is frictionless.

40. A uniform metre stick of mass 200 g is suspended from the ceiling through two vertical strings of equal lengths fixed at the ends. A small object of mass 20 g is placed on the stick at a distance of 70 cm from the left end. Find the tensions in the two strings.

41. A uniform ladder of length $10 \cdot 0$ m and mass $16 \cdot 0$ kg is resting against a vertical wall making an angle of 37° with it. The vertical wall is frictionless but the ground is rough. An electrician weighing $60 \cdot 0$ kg climbs up the ladder. If he stays on the ladder at a point $8 \cdot 00$ m from

the lower end, what will be the normal force and the force of friction on the ladder by the ground ? What should be the minimum coefficient of friction for the electrician to work safely ?

42. Suppose the friction coefficient between the ground and the ladder of the previous problem is 0·540. Find the maximum weight of a mechanic who could go up and do the work from the same position of the ladder.

43. A 6·5 m long ladder rests against a vertical wall reaching a height of 6·0 m. A 60 kg man stands half way up the ladder. (a) Find the torque of the force exerted by the man on the ladder about the upper end of the ladder. (b) Assuming the weight of the ladder to be negligible as compared to the man and assuming the wall to be smooth, find the force exerted by the ground on the ladder.

44. The door of an almirah is 6 ft high, 1·5 ft wide and weighs 8 kg. The door is supported by two hinges situated at a distance of 1 ft from the ends. If the magnitudes of the forces exerted by the hinges on the door are equal, find this magnitude.

45. A uniform rod of length L rests against a smooth roller as shown in figure (10-E9). Find the friction coefficient between the ground and the lower end if the minimum angle that the rod can make with the horizontal is θ.

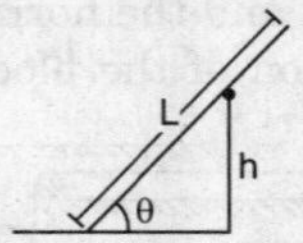

Figure 10-E9

46. A uniform rod of mass 300 g and length 50 cm rotates at a uniform angular speed of 2 rad/s about an axis perpendicular to the rod through an end. Calculate (a) the angular momentum of the rod about the axis of rotation, (b) the speed of the centre of the rod and (c) its kinetic energy.

47. A uniform square plate of mass 2·0 kg and edge 10 cm rotates about one of its diagonals under the action of a constant torque of 0·10 N-m. Calculate the angular momentum and the kinetic energy of the plate at the end of the fifth second after the start.

48. Calculate the ratio of the angular momentum of the earth about its axis due to its spinning motion to that about the sun due to its orbital motion. Radius of the earth = 6400 km and radius of the orbit of the earth about the sun = $1·5 \times 10^8$ km.

49. Two particles of masses m_1 and m_2 are joined by a light rigid rod of length r. The system rotates at an angular speed ω about an axis through the centre of mass of the system and perpendicular to the rod. Show that the angular momentum of the system is $L = \mu r^2 \omega$ where μ is the reduced mass of the system defined as $\mu = \dfrac{m_1 m_2}{m_1 + m_2}$.

50. A dumb-bell consists of two identical small balls of mass 1/2 kg each connected to the two ends of a 50 cm long

light rod. The dumb-bell is rotating about a fixed axis through the centre of the rod and perpendicular to it at an angular speed of 10 rad/s. An impulsive force of average magnitude 5·0 N acts on one of the masses in the direction of its velocity for 0·10 s. Find the new angular velocity of the system.

51. A wheel of moment of inertia 0·500 kg-m^2 and radius 20·0 cm is rotating about its axis at an angular speed of 20·0 rad/s. It picks up a stationary particle of mass 200 g at its edge. Find the new angular speed of the wheel.

52. A diver having a moment of inertia of 6·0 kg-m^2 about an axis through its centre of mass rotates at an angular speed of 2 rad/s about this axis. If he folds his hands and feet to decrease the moment of inertia to 5·0 kg-m^2, what will be the new angular speed ?

53. A boy is seated in a revolving chair revolving at an angular speed of 120 revolutions per minute. Two heavy balls form part of the revolving system and the boy can pull the balls closer to himself or may push them apart. If by pulling the balls closer, the boy decreases the moment of inertia of the system from 6 kg-m^2 to 2 kg-m^2, what will be the new angular speed ?

54. A boy is standing on a platform which is free to rotate about its axis. The boy holds an open umbrella in his hand. The axis of the umbrella coincides with that of the platform. The moment of inertia of "the platform plus the boy system" is $3·0 \times 10^{-3}$ kg-m^2 and that of the umbrella is $2·0 \times 10^{-3}$ kg-m^2. The boy starts spinning the umbrella about the axis at an angular speed of 2·0 rev/s with respect to himself. Find the angular velocity imparted to the platform.

55. A wheel of moment of inertia 0·10 kg-m^2 is rotating about a shaft at an angular speed of 160 rev/minute. A second wheel is set into rotation at 300 rev/minute and is coupled to the same shaft so that both the wheels finally rotate with a common angular speed of 200 rev/minute. Find the moment of inertia of the second wheel.

56. A kid of mass M stands at the edge of a platform of radius R which can be freely rotated about its axis. The moment of inertia of the platform is I. The system is at rest when a friend throws a ball of mass m and the kid catches it. If the velocity of the ball is v horizontally along the tangent to the edge of the platform when it was caught by the kid, find the angular speed of the platform after the event.

57. Suppose the platform of the previous problem is brought to rest with the ball in the hand of the kid standing on the rim. The kid throws the ball horizontally to his friend in a direction tangential to the rim with a speed v as seen by his friend. Find the angular velocity with which the platform will start rotating.

58. Suppose the platform with the kid in the previous problem is rotating in anticlockwise direction at an angular speed ω. The kid starts walking along the rim with a speed v relative to the platform also in the anticlockwise direction. Find the new angular speed of the platform.

59. A uniform rod of mass m and length l is struck at an end by a force F perpendicular to the rod for a short time interval t. Calculate
(a) the speed of the centre of mass, (b) the angular speed of the rod about the centre of mass, (c) the kinetic energy of the rod and (d) the angular momentum of the rod about the centre of mass after the force has stopped to act. Assume that t is so small that the rod does not appreciably change its direction while the force acts.

60. A uniform rod of length L lies on a smooth horizontal table. A particle moving on the table strikes the rod perpendicularly at an end and stops. Find the distance travelled by the centre of the rod by the time it turns through a right angle. Show that if the mass of the rod is four times that of the particle, the collision is elastic.

61. Suppose the particle of the previous problem has a mass m and a speed v before the collision and it sticks to the rod after the collision. The rod has a mass M. (a) Find the velocity of the centre of mass C of the system constituting "the rod plus the particle". (b) Find the velocity of the particle with respect to C before the collision. (c) Find the velocity of the rod with respect to C before the collision. (d) Find the angular momentum of the particle and of the rod about the centre of mass C before the collision. (e) Find the moment of inertia of the system about the vertical axis through the centre of mass C after the collision. (f) Find the velocity of the centre of mass C and the angular velocity of the system about the centre of mass after the collision.

62. Two small balls A and B, each of mass m, are joined rigidly by a light horizontal rod of length L. The rod is clamped at the centre in such a way that it can rotate freely about a vertical axis through its centre. The system is rotated with an angular speed ω about the axis. A particle P of mass m kept at rest sticks to the ball A as the ball collides with it. Find the new angular speed of the rod.

63. Two small balls A and B, each of mass m, are joined rigidly to the ends of a light rod of length L (figure 10-E10). The system translates on a frictionless horizontal surface with a velocity v_0 in a direction perpendicular to the rod. A particle P of mass m kept at rest on the surface sticks to the ball A as the ball collides with it. Find
(a) the linear speeds of the balls A and B after the collision, (b) the velocity of the centre of mass C of the system $A + B + P$ and (c) the angular speed of the system about C after the collision.

Figure 10-E10

[**Hint :** The light rod will exert a force on the ball B only along its length.]

64. Suppose the rod with the balls A and B of the previous problem is clamped at the centre in such a way that it can rotate freely about a horizontal axis through the clamp. The system is kept at rest in the horizontal position. A particle P of the same mass m is dropped from a height h on the ball B. The particle collides with B and sticks to it. (a) Find the angular momentum and the angular speed of the system just after the collision. (b) What should be the minimum value of h so that the system makes a full rotation after the collision.

65. Two blocks of masses 400 g and 200 g are connected through a light string going over a pulley which is free to rotate about its axis. The pulley has a moment of inertia $1{\cdot}6 \times 10^{-4}$ kg-m^2 and a radius $2{\cdot}0$ cm. Find (a) the kinetic energy of the system as the 400 g block falls through 50 cm, (b) the speed of the blocks at this instant.

66. The pulley shown in figure (10-E11) has a radius of 20 cm and moment of inertia $0{\cdot}2$ kg-m^2. The string going over it is attached at one end to a vertical spring of spring constant 50 N/m fixed from below, and supports a 1 kg mass at the other end. The system is released from rest with the spring at its natural length. Find the speed of the block when it has descended through 10 cm. Take $g = 10$ m/s^2.

Figure 10-E11

67. A metre stick is held vertically with one end on a rough horizontal floor. It is gently allowed to fall on the floor. Assuming that the end at the floor does not slip, find the angular speed of the rod when it hits the floor.

68. A metre stick weighing 240 g is pivoted at its upper end in such a way that it can freely rotate in a vertical plane through this end (figure 10-E12). A particle of mass 100 g is attached to the upper end of the stick through a light string of length l m. Initially, the rod is kept vertical and the string horizontal when the system is released from rest. The particle collides with the lower end of the stick and sticks there. Find the maximum angle through which the stick will rise.

Figure 10-E12

69. A uniform rod pivoted at its upper end hangs vertically. It is displaced through an angle of 60° and then released. Find the magnitude of the force acting on a particle of mass dm at the tip of the rod when the rod makes an angle of 37° with the vertical.

70. A cylinder rolls on a horizontal plane surface. If the speed of the centre is 25 m/s, what is the speed of the highest point ?

71. A sphere of mass m rolls on a plane surface. Find its kinetic energy at an instant when its centre moves with speed v.

72. A string is wrapped over the edge of a uniform disc and the free end is fixed with the ceiling. The disc moves down, unwinding the string. Find the downward acceleration of the disc.

73. A small spherical ball is released from a point at a height h on a rough track shown in figure (10-E13). Assuming that it does not slip anywhere, find its linear speed when it rolls on the horizontal part of the track.

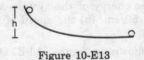

Figure 10-E13

74. A small disc is set rolling with a speed v on the horizontal part of the track of the previous problem from right to left. To what height will it climb up the curved part ?

75. A sphere starts rolling down an incline of inclination θ. Find the speed of its centre when it has covered a distance l.

76. A hollow sphere is released from the top of an inclined plane of inclination θ. (a) What should be the minimum coefficient of friction between the sphere and the plane to prevent sliding ? (b) Find the kinetic energy of the ball as it moves down a length l on the incline if the friction coefficient is half the value calculated in part (a).

77. A solid sphere of mass m is released from rest from the rim of a hemispherical cup so that it rolls along the surface. If the rim of the hemisphere is kept horizontal, find the normal force exerted by the cup on the ball when the ball reaches the bottom of the cup.

78. Figure (10-E14) shows a rough track, a portion of which is in the form of a cylinder of radius R. With what minimum linear speed should a sphere of radius r be set rolling on the horizontal part so that it completely goes round the circle on the cylindrical part.

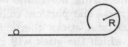

Figure 10-E14

79. Figure (10-E15) shows a small spherical ball of mass m rolling down the loop track. The ball is released on the linear portion at a vertical height H from the lowest point. The circular part shown has a radius R.
(a) Find the kinetic energy of the ball when it is at a point A where the radius makes an angle θ with the horizontal.
(b) Find the radial and the tangential accelerations of the centre when the ball is at A.

(c) Find the normal force and the frictional force acting on the ball if $H = 60$ cm, $R = 10$ cm, $\theta = 0$ and $m = 70$ g.

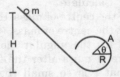

Figure 10-E15

80. A thin spherical shell of radius R lying on a rough horizontal surface is hit sharply and horizontally by a cue. Where should it be hit so that the shell does not slip on the surface ?

81. A uniform wheel of radius R is set into rotation about its axis at an angular speed ω. This rotating wheel is now placed on a rough horizontal surface with its axis horizontal. Because of friction at the contact, the wheel accelerates forward and its rotation decelerates till the wheel starts pure rolling on the surface. Find the linear speed of the wheel after it starts pure rolling.

82. A thin spherical shell lying on a rough horizontal surface is hit by a cue in such a way that the line of action passes through the centre of the shell. As a result, the shell starts moving with a linear speed v without any initial angular velocity. Find the linear speed of the shell after it starts pure rolling on the surface.

83. A hollow sphere of radius R lies on a smooth horizontal surface. It is pulled by a horizontal force acting tangentially from the highest point. Find the distance travelled by the sphere during the time it makes one full rotation.

84. A solid sphere of mass 0·50 kg is kept on a horizontal surface. The coefficient of static friction between the surfaces in contact is 2/7. What maximum force can be applied at the highest point in the horizontal direction so that the sphere does not slip on the surface ?

85. A solid sphere is set into motion on a rough horizontal surface with a linear speed v in the forward direction and an angular speed v/R in the anticlockwise direction as shown in figure (10-E16). Find the linear speed of the sphere (a) when it stops rotating and (b) when slipping finally ceases and pure rolling starts.

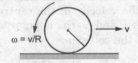

Figure 10-E16

86. A solid sphere rolling on a rough horizontal surface with a linear speed v collides elastically with a fixed, smooth, vertical wall. Find the speed of the sphere after it has started pure rolling in the backward direction.

□

ANSWERS

OBJECTIVE I

1. (c)   2. (c)   3. (b)   4. (d)   5. (c)   6. (c)
7. (b)   8. (a)   9. (d)   10. (c)   11. (c)   12. (a)
13. (a)   14. (a)   15. (a)   16. (d)   17. (d)   18. (b)
19. (b)   20. (c)   21. (a)   22. (d)   23. (d)   24. (d)
25. (b)   26. (b)

OBJECTIVE II

1. (b), (d)   2. (b)   3. (b), (c), (d)
4. (a), (b)   5. (c)   6. (b)
7. (d)   8. (a), (c), (d)   9. (c)
10. (b)   11. (b)   12. (a), (b), (c)
13. (c)   14. (a), (b)   15. (a)

EXERCISES

1. 25 rev/s^2, 400 π rad
2. 4 rev/s^2, 20 rev/s
3. 800 rad
4. 100 rad
5. 2 $\sqrt{5}$ rev/s
6. 2 m/s, 1 m/s
7. 16 cm/s^2, 4 cm/s^2
8. 2 m/s
9. 1.5×10^{-3} kg–m^2, 4.0×10^{-3} kg–m^2
10. 0·43 kg–m^2
11. $\dfrac{14\,mr^2}{5}$
12. 0·34 m
13. $\sqrt{2}\,r$
14. $r / \sqrt{2}$
15. $ma^2/12$
16. $2\pi\left(\dfrac{Aa^4}{4} + \dfrac{Ba^5}{5}\right)$
17. $mu^2 \sin\theta \cos\theta$ perpendicular to the plane of motion
18. $wl \sin\theta$, when the bob is at the lowest point
19. 1·5 N
20. 0·54 N-m
21. $\dfrac{1}{2}\,mg\,a\,\sin\theta$
22. $\dfrac{3\,Ft^2}{2\,ml}$
23. 2.0×10^{-5} N-m
24. 0.5×10^{-5} N-m
25. (a) 1·0 N-m   (b) 9·0 kJ   (c) 60 kg-m^2/s
26. 5.8×10^{20} N-m
27. 1 rev/s^2, 5 rev/s

28. 0·87 N
29. 25 s
30. 20 s
31. 8·4 rad/s^2
32. 8·0 rad/s^2, 27·6 N, 29 N
33. $\dfrac{Mg}{M + m + I/r^2}$
34. 0·89 m/s^2
35. 6·3 N
36. $\dfrac{(M - m)g}{M + m + 2\,I/R^2}$
37. 10 m/s^2
38. 0·25 m/s^2
39. 0·125 m/s^2
40. 1·04 N in the left string and 1·12 N in the right
41. 745 N, 412 N, 0·553
42. 44·0 kg
43. (a) 740 N-m
    (b) 590 N vertical and 120 N horizontal
44. 43 N
45. $\dfrac{L \cos\theta \sin^2\theta}{2\,h - L \cos^2\theta \sin\theta}$
46. (a) 0·05 kg-m^2/s   (b) 50 cm/s   (c) 0·05 J
47. 0·5 kg-m^2/s, 75 J
48. 2.66×10^{-7}
50. 12 rad/s
51. 19·7 rad/s
52. 2·4 rad/s
53. 360 rev/minute
54. 0·8 rev/s
55. 0·04 kg-m^2
56. $\dfrac{mvR}{I + (M + m)R^2}$
57. $\dfrac{mvR}{I + MR^2}$
58. $\omega - \dfrac{MvR}{I + MR^2}$
59. (a) $\dfrac{Ft}{m}$ (b) $\dfrac{6\,Ft}{ml}$ (c) $\dfrac{2\,F^2t^2}{m}$ (d) $\dfrac{Flt}{2}$
60. $\pi L / 12$
61. (a) $\dfrac{mv}{M + m}$ (b) $\dfrac{Mv}{M + m}$ (c) $-\dfrac{mv}{M + m}$
    (d) $\dfrac{M^2mvl}{2(M + m)^2}$, $\dfrac{Mm^2vl}{2(M + m)^2}$ (e) $\dfrac{M(M + 4\,m)L^2}{12(M + m)}$
    (f) $\dfrac{mv}{M + m}$, $\dfrac{6\,mv}{(M + 4\,m)L}$
62. $2\,\omega/3$

63. (a) $\dfrac{v_0}{2}, v_0$ (b) $\dfrac{2}{3} v_0$ along the initial motion of the rod

    (c) $\dfrac{v_0}{2L}$

64. (a) $\dfrac{mL\sqrt{gh}}{\sqrt{2}}, \dfrac{\sqrt{8gh}}{3L}$ (b) $\dfrac{3}{2}L$

65. (a) 0·98 J   (b) 1·4 m/s

66. 0·5 m/s

67. 5·4 rad/s

68. 41°

69. 0·9 $\sqrt{2} \, dm \, g$

70. 50 m/s

71. $\dfrac{7}{10} mv^2$

72. $\dfrac{2}{3} g$

73. $\sqrt{10 \, gh / 7}$

74. $\dfrac{3 v^2}{4g}$

75. $\sqrt{\dfrac{10}{7} g \, l \sin\theta}$

76. (a) $\dfrac{2}{5} \tan\theta$ (b) $\dfrac{7}{8} mgl \sin\theta$

77. 17 $mg/7$

78. $\sqrt{\dfrac{27}{7} g(R - r)}$

79. (a) $mg(H - R - R \sin\theta)$,

    (b) $\dfrac{10}{7} g \left(\dfrac{H}{R} - 1 - \sin\theta \right), -\dfrac{5}{7} g \cos\theta$

    (c) 4·9 N, 0·196 N upward

80. $2R/3$ above the centre

81. $\omega R / 3$

82. $3v/5$

83. $4 \pi R / 3$

84. 3·3 N

85. (a) $3v/5$ (b) $3v/7$

86. $3v/7$

□

CHAPTER 11

GRAVITATION

11.1 HISTORICAL INTRODUCTION

The motion of celestial bodies such as the moon, the earth, the planets, etc., has been a subject of great interest for a long time. Famous Indian astronomer and mathematician, Aryabhat, studied these motions in great detail, most likely in the 5th century A.D., and wrote his conclusions in his book *Aryabhatiya*. He established that the earth revolves about its own axis. He also gave description of motion of other celestial bodies as seen from the earth.

About a thousand years after Aryabhat, the brilliant combination of Tycho Brahe (1546–1601) and Johannes Kepler (1571–1630) studied the planetary motion in great detail. Kepler formulated his important findings in his three laws of planetary motion :

1. *All planets move in elliptical orbits with the sun at a focus.*
2. *The radius vector from the sun to the planet sweeps equal area in equal time.*
3. *The square of the time period of a planet is proportional to the cube of the semimajor axis of the ellipse.*

The year 1665 was very fruitful for Isaac Newton aged 23. He was forced to take rest at his home in Lincolnshire after his college at Cambridge was closed for an indefinite period due to plague. In this year, he performed brilliant theoretical and experimental tasks mainly in the field of mechanics and optics. In this same year he focussed his attention on the motion of the moon about the earth.

The moon makes a revolution about the earth in $T = 27.3$ days. The distance of the moon from the earth is $R = 3.85 \times 10^5$ km. The acceleration of the moon is, therefore,

$$a = \omega^2 R$$

$$= \frac{4\pi^2 \times (3.85 \times 10^5 \text{ km})}{(27.3 \text{ days})^2} = 0.0027 \text{ m s}^{-2}.$$

The first question before Newton was that what is the force that produces this acceleration. The acceleration is towards the centre of the orbit, that is towards the centre of the earth. Hence the force must act towards the centre of the earth. A natural guess was that the earth is attracting the moon. The saying goes that Newton was sitting under an apple tree when an apple fell down from the tree on the earth. This sparked the idea that the earth attracts all bodies towards its centre. The next question was what is the law governing this force.

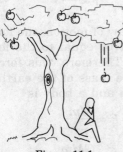

Figure 11.1

Newton had to make several daring assumptions which proved to be turning points in science and philosophy. He declared that the laws of nature are the same for earthly and celestial bodies. The force operating between the earth and an apple and that operating between the earth and the moon, must be governed by the same laws. This statement may look very obvious today but in the era before Newton, there was a general belief in the western countries that the earthly bodies are governed by certain rules and the heavenly bodies are governed by different rules. In particular, this heavenly structure was supposed to be so perfect that there could not be any change in the sky. This distinction was so sharp that when Tycho Brahe saw a new star in the sky, he did not believe his eyes as there could be no change in the sky. So the Newton's declaration was indeed revolutionary.

The acceleration of a body falling near the earth's surface is about $9·8 \text{ ms}^{-2}$. Thus,

$$\frac{a_{apple}}{a_{moon}} = \frac{9·8 \text{ m s}^{-2}}{0·0027 \text{ m s}^{-2}} = 3600.$$

Also,

$$\frac{\text{distance of the moon from the earth}}{\text{distance of the apple from the earth}}$$

$$= \frac{d_{moon}}{d_{apple}} = \frac{3·85 \times 10^5 \text{ km}}{6400 \text{ km}}$$

$$= 60$$

Thus, $\dfrac{a_{apple}}{a_{moon}} = \left(\dfrac{d_{moon}}{d_{apple}}\right)^2.$

Newton guessed that the acceleration of a body towards the earth is inversely proportional to the square of the distance of the body from the centre of the earth.

Thus, $a \propto \dfrac{1}{r^2}$.

Also, the force is mass times acceleration and so it is proportional to the mass of the body.

Hence,

$$F \propto \frac{m}{r^2}.$$

By the third law of motion, the force on a body due to the earth must be equal to the force on the earth due to the body. Therefore, this force should also be proportional to the mass of the earth. Thus, the force between the earth and a body is

$$F \propto \frac{Mm}{r^2}$$

or, $F = \dfrac{GMm}{r^2}.$ ... (11.1)

Newton further generalised the law by saying that not only the earth but all material bodies in the universe attract each other according to equation (11.1) with same value of G. The constant G is called *universal constant of gravitation* and its value is found to be $6·67 \times 10^{-11} \text{ N–m}^2/\text{kg}^2$. Equation (11.1) is known as the *universal law of gravitation*.

In this argument, the distance of the apple from the earth is taken to be equal to the radius of the earth. This means we have assumed that earth can be treated as a single particle placed at its centre. This is of course not obvious. Newton had spent several years to prove that indeed this can be done. A spherically symmetric body can be replaced by a point particle of equal mass placed at its centre for the

purpose of calculating gravitational force. In the process he discovered the methods of calculus that we have already learnt in Chapter 2. There is evidence that quite a bit of differential calculus was known to the ancient Indian mathematicians but this literature was almost certainly not known to Newton or other scientists of those days.

Example 11.1

Two particles of masses 1·0 kg and 2·0 kg are placed at a separation of 50 cm. Assuming that the only forces acting on the particles are their mutual gravitation, find the initial accelerations of the two particles.

Solution : The force of gravitation exerted by one particle on another is

$$F = \frac{G m_1 m_2}{r^2}$$

$$= \frac{6·67 \times 10^{-11} \dfrac{\text{N–m}^2}{\text{kg}^2} \times (1·0 \text{ kg}) \times (2·0 \text{ kg})}{(0·5 \text{ m})^2}$$

$$= 5·3 \times 10^{-10} \text{ N}.$$

The acceleration of 1·0 kg particle is

$$a_1 = \frac{F}{m_1} = \frac{5·3 \times 10^{-10} \text{ N}}{1·0 \text{ kg}}$$

$$= 5·3 \times 10^{-10} \text{ m s}^{-2}.$$

This acceleration is towards the 2·0 kg particle. The acceleration of the 2·0 kg particle is

$$a_2 = \frac{F}{m_2} = \frac{5·3 \times 10^{-10} \text{ N}}{2·0 \text{ kg}}$$

$$= 2·65 \times 10^{-10} \text{ m s}^{-2}.$$

This acceleration is towards the 1·0 kg particle.

11.2 MEASUREMENT OF GRAVITATIONAL CONSTANT G

The gravitational constant G is a small quantity and its measurement needs very sensitive arrangement. The first important successful measurement of this quantity was made by Cavendish in 1736 about 71 years after the law was formulated.

In this method, two small balls of equal mass are attached at the two ends of a light rod to form a dumb-bell. The rod is suspended vertically by a fine quartz wire. Two large spheres of equal mass are placed near the smaller spheres in such a way that all the four spheres are on a horizontal circle. The centre of the circle is at the middle point of the rod (figure 11.2).

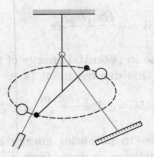

Figure 11.2

Two larger spheres lie on the opposite sides of the smaller balls at equal distance. A small plane mirror is attached to the vertical wire. A light beam, incident on the mirror, falls on a scale after reflection. If the wire rotates by an angle θ, the reflected beam rotates by 2θ and the spot on the scale moves. By measuring this movement of the spot on the scale and the distance between the mirror and the scale, the angle of deviation can be calculated. When the heavy balls are placed close to the small balls, a torque acts on the dumb-bell to rotate it. As the dumb-bell rotates, the suspension wire gets twisted and produces a torque on the dumb-bell in opposite direction. This torque is proportional to the angle rotated. The dumb-bell stays in equilibrium where the two torques have equal magnitude.

Let the mass of a heavy ball = M,

the mass of a small ball = m,

the distance between the centres of a heavy ball and the small ball placed close to it = r,

the deflection of the dumb-bell as it comes to equilibrium = θ,

the torsional constant of the suspension wire = k,

the length of the rod = l and

the distance between the scale and the mirror = D.

The force acting on each of the small balls is

$$F = G\,\frac{Mm}{r^2}.$$

Here we have used the fact that the gravitational force due to a uniform sphere is same as that due to a single particle of equal mass placed at the centre of the sphere. As the four balls are on the same horizontal circle and the heavy balls are placed close to the smaller balls, this force acts in a horizontal direction perpendicular to the length of the dumb-bell. The torque due to each of these gravitational forces about the suspension wire is $F(l/2)$.

The total gravitational torque on the dumb-bell is, therefore,

$$\Gamma = 2F(l/2)$$
$$= Fl\,.$$

The opposing torque produced by the suspension wire is $k\theta$. For rotational equilibrium,

$$Fl = k\theta$$

or,
$$\frac{GMml}{r^2} = k\theta$$

$$G = \frac{k\theta r^2}{Mml}. \qquad \ldots \text{ (i)}$$

In an experiment, the heavy balls are placed close to the smaller balls as shown in the figure and the dumb-bell is allowed to settle down. The light beam is adjusted so that the beam reflected by the plane mirror falls on the scale. Now the heavy balls are shifted in such a way that they are placed on the same horizontal circle at same distance from the smaller balls but on the opposite side. In figure (11.3), the original positions of the heavy balls are shown by A, B and the shifted positions by A', B'.

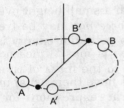

Figure 11.3

As the heavy balls are shifted to the new position, the dumb-bell rotates. If it was settled previously at an angle θ deviated from the mean position, it will now settle at the same angle θ on the other side. Thus, the total deflection of the dumb-bell due to the change in the positions of the heavy balls is 2θ. The reflected light beam deviates by an angle of 4θ.

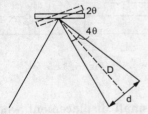

Figure 11.4

If the linear displacement of the light spot is d, we have (figure 11.4)

$$4\theta = \frac{d}{D}$$

or,
$$\theta = \frac{d}{4D}.$$

Substituting in (i),

$$G = \frac{kdr^2}{4MmlD}.$$

All the quantities on the right hand side are experimentally known and hence the value of G may be calculated.

11.3 GRAVITATIONAL POTENTIAL ENERGY

The concept of potential energy of a system was introduced in Chapter-8. The potential energy of a system corresponding to a conservative force was defined as

$$U_f - U_i = -\int_i^f \vec{F} \cdot d\vec{r}.$$

The change in potential energy is equal to the negative of the work done by the internal forces. We also calculated the change in gravitational potential energy of the earth–particle system when the particle was raised through a small height over earth's surface. In this case the force mg may be treated as constant and the change in potential energy is

$$U_f - U_i = mgh$$

where the symbols have their usual meanings. We now derive the general expression for the change in gravitational potential energy of a two-particle system.

Let a particle of mass m_1 be kept fixed at a point A (figure 11.5) and another particle of mass m_2 is taken from a point B to a point C. Initially, the distance between the particles is $AB = r_1$ and finally it becomes $AC = r_2$. We have to calculate the change in potential energy of the system of the two particles as the distance changes from r_1 to r_2.

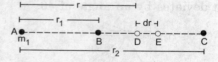

Figure 11.5

Consider a small displacement when the distance between the particles changes from r to $r + dr$. In the figure, this corresponds to the second particle going from D to E.

The force on the second particle is

$$F = \frac{Gm_1m_2}{r^2} \text{ along } \overrightarrow{DA}.$$

The work done by the gravitational force in the displacement is

$$dW = -\frac{Gm_1m_2}{r^2} dr.$$

The increase in potential energy of the two-particle system during this displacement is

$$dU = -dW = \frac{Gm_1m_2}{r^2} dr.$$

The increase in potential energy as the distance between the particles changes from r_1 to r_2 is

$$U(r_2) - U(r_1) = \int dU$$

$$= \int_{r_1}^{r_2} \frac{Gm_1m_2}{r^2} dr = Gm_1m_2 \int_{r_1}^{r_2} \frac{1}{r^2} dr$$

$$= Gm_1m_2 \left[-\frac{1}{r} \right]_{r_1}^{r_2}$$

$$= Gm_1m_2 \left(\frac{1}{r_1} - \frac{1}{r_2} \right). \qquad \ldots (11.2)$$

We choose the potential energy of the two-particle system to be zero when the distance between them is infinity. This means that we choose $U(\infty) = 0$. By (11.2) the potential energy $U(r)$, when the separation between the particles is r, is

$$U(r) = U(r) - U(\infty)$$

$$= Gm_1m_2 \left[\frac{1}{\infty} - \frac{1}{r} \right] = -\frac{Gm_1m_2}{r}.$$

The gravitational potential energy of a two-particle system is

$$U(r) = -\frac{Gm_1m_2}{r} \qquad \ldots (11.3)$$

where m_1 and m_2 are the masses of the particles, r is the separation between the particles and the potential energy is chosen to be zero when the separation is infinite.

We have proved this result by assuming that one of the particles is kept at rest and the other is displaced. However, as the potential energy depends only on the separation and not on the location of the particles, equation (11.3) is general.

Equation (11.3) gives the potential energy of a pair of particles. If there are three particles A, B and C, there are three pairs AB, AC and BC. The potential energy of the three-particle system is equal to the sum of the potential energies of the three pairs. For an N-particle system there are $N(N-1)/2$ pairs and the potential energy is calculated for each pair and added to get the total potential energy of the system.

Example 11.2

Find the work done in bringing three particles, each having a mass of 100 g, from large distances to the vertices of an equilateral triangle of side 20 cm.

Solution : When the separations are large, the gravitational potential energy is zero. When the particles are brought at the vertices of the triangle ABC, three pairs AB, BC and CA are formed. The potential energy of each pair is $-Gm_1m_2/r$ and hence the total potential energy becomes

$$U = 3 \times \left[-\frac{Gm_1m_2}{r} \right]$$

$$= 3 \times \left[-\frac{6 \cdot 67 \times 10^{-11} \, \text{N–m}^2/\text{kg}^2 \times (0 \cdot 1 \, \text{kg}) \times (0 \cdot 1 \, \text{kg})}{0 \cdot 20 \, \text{m}} \right]$$

$$= -1 \cdot 0 \times 10^{-11} \, \text{J} .$$

The work done by the gravitational forces is $W = -U = 1 \cdot 0 \times 10^{-11} \, \text{J}$. If the particles are brought by some external agency without changing the kinetic energy, the work done by the external agency is equal to the change in potential energy $= -1 \cdot 0 \times 10^{-11} \, \text{J}$.

11.4 GRAVITATIONAL POTENTIAL

Suppose a particle of mass m is taken from a point A to a point B while keeping all other masses fixed. Let U_A and U_B denote the gravitational potential energy when the mass m is at point A and point B respectively.

We define the "change in potential" $V_B - V_A$ between the two points as

$$V_B - V_A = \frac{U_B - U_A}{m} . \qquad \dots \text{(11.4)}$$

The equation defines only the change in potential. We can choose any point to have zero potential. Such a point is called a *reference point*. If A be the reference point, $V_A = 0$ and

$$V_B = \frac{U_B - U_A}{m} . \qquad \dots \text{(11.5)}$$

Thus, *gravitational potential at a point is equal to the change in potential energy per unit mass, as the mass is brought from the reference point to the given point.* If the particle is slowly brought without increasing the kinetic energy, the work done by the external agent equals the change in potential energy. Thus, the potential at a point may also be defined as *the work done per unit mass by an external agent in bringing a particle slowly from the reference point to the given point.* Generally the reference point is chosen at infinity so that the potential at infinity is zero.

The *SI* unit of gravitational potential is J kg^{-1}.

11.5 CALCULATION OF GRAVITATIONAL POTENTIAL

(A) Potential due to a Point Mass

Suppose a particle of mass M is kept at a point A (figure 11.6) and we have to calculate the potential at a point P at a distance r away from A. The reference point is at infinity.

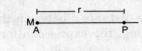

Figure 11.6

From equation (11.5), the potential at the point P is

$$V(r) = \frac{U(r) - U(\infty)}{m} .$$

But $\quad U(r) - U(\infty) = -\dfrac{GMm}{r} .$

so that,

$$V = -\frac{GM}{r} . \qquad \dots \text{(11.6)}$$

The gravitational potential due to a point mass M at a distance r is $-\dfrac{GM}{r}$.

(B) Potential due to a Uniform Ring at A Point on its Axis

Let the mass of the ring be M and its radius be a. We have to calculate the gravitational potential at a point P on the axis of the ring (figure 11.7). The centre is at O and $OP = r$.

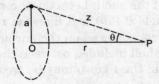

Figure 11.7

Consider any small part of the ring of mass dm. The point P is at a distance $z = \sqrt{a^2 + r^2}$ from dm.

The potential at P due to dm is

$$dV = -\frac{G \, dm}{z} = -\frac{G \, dm}{\sqrt{a^2 + r^2}} .$$

The potential V due to the whole ring is obtained by summing the contributions from all the parts. As the potential is a scalar quantity, we have

$$V = \int dV$$

$$= \int -\frac{G\,dm}{\sqrt{a^2 + r^2}}$$

$$= -\frac{G}{\sqrt{a^2 + r^2}} \int dm$$

$$= -\frac{GM}{\sqrt{a^2 + r^2}} . \qquad \ldots (11.7)$$

In terms of the distance z between the point P and any point of the ring, the expression for the potential is given by

$$V = -\frac{GM}{z} . \qquad \ldots (11.8)$$

(C) Potential due to a Uniform Thin Spherical Shell

Let the mass of the given spherical shell be M and the radius a. We have to calculate the potential due to this shell at a point P. The centre of the shell is at O and $OP = r$ (figure 11.8).

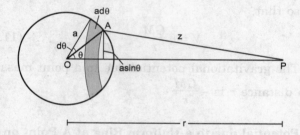

Figure 11.8

Let us draw a radius OA making an angle θ with OP. Let us rotate this radius about OP keeping the angle AOP fixed at value θ. The point A traces a circle on the surface of the shell. Let us now consider another radius at an angle $\theta + d\theta$ and likewise rotate it about OP. Another circle is traced on the surface of the shell. The part of the shell included between these two circles (shown shaded in the figure) may be treated as a ring.

The radius of this ring is $a \sin\theta$ and hence the perimeter is $2\pi a \sin\theta$. The width of the ring is $ad\theta$. The area of the ring is

$$(2\pi a \sin\theta)\,(ad\theta)$$

$$= 2\pi a^2 \sin\theta\,d\theta.$$

The total area of the shell is $4\pi a^2$. As the shell is uniform, the mass of the ring enclosed is

$$dm = \frac{M}{4\pi a^2} (2\pi a^2 \sin\theta\,d\theta)$$

$$= \frac{M}{2} \sin\theta\,d\theta .$$

Let the distance of any point of the ring from P be $AP = z$. From the triangle OAP

$$z^2 = a^2 + r^2 - 2ar \cos\theta$$

or, $$2z\,dz = 2ar \sin\theta\,d\theta$$

or, $$\sin\theta\,d\theta = \frac{z\,dz}{ar} .$$

Thus, the mass of the ring is

$$dm = \frac{M}{2} \sin\theta\,d\theta = \frac{M}{2ar} z\,dz.$$

As the distance of any point of the ring from P is z, the potential at P due to the ring is

$$dV = -\frac{G\,dm}{z}$$

$$= -\frac{GM}{2ar} dz .$$

As we vary θ from 0 to π, the rings formed on the shell cover up the whole shell. The potential due to the whole shell is obtained by integrating dV within the limits $\theta = 0$ to $\theta = \pi$.

Case I : P is outside the shell $(r > a)$

As figure (11.8) shows, when $\theta = 0$, the distance $z = AP = r - a$. When $\theta = \pi$, it is $z = r + a$. Thus, as θ varies from 0 to π, the distance z varies from $r - a$ to $r + a$. Thus,

$$V = \int dV = -\frac{GM}{2ar} \int_{r-a}^{r+a} dz$$

$$= -\frac{GM}{2ar} [z]_{r-a}^{r+a}$$

$$= -\frac{GM}{2ar} [(r + a) - (r - a)]$$

$$= -\frac{GM}{r} . \qquad \ldots (11.9)$$

To calculate the potential at an external point, a uniform spherical shell may be treated as a point particle of equal mass placed at its centre.

Case II : P is inside the shell $(r < a)$

In this case when $\theta = 0$, the distance $z = AP = a - r$ and when $\theta = \pi$ it is $z = a + r$ (figure 11.9). Thus, as θ varies from 0 to π, the distance z varies from $a - r$ to $a + r$. Thus, the potential due to the shell is

$$V = \int dV$$

$$= -\frac{GM}{2ar} [z]_{a-r}^{a+r}$$

$$= -\frac{GM}{2ar} [(a + r) - (a - r)]$$

$$= -\frac{GM}{a} . \qquad \ldots (11.10)$$

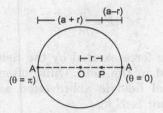

Figure 11.9

This does not depend on r. Thus, *the potential due to a uniform spherical shell is constant throughout the cavity of the shell.*

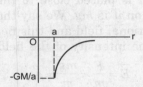

Figure 11.10

Figure (11.10) shows graphically the variation of potential with the distance from the centre of the shell.

Example 11.3

A particle of mass M is placed at the centre of a uniform spherical shell of equal mass and radius a. Find the gravitational potential at a point P at a distance $a/2$ from the centre.

Solution : The gravitational potential at the point P due to the particle at the centre is

$$V_1 = -\frac{GM}{a/2} = -\frac{2GM}{a}.$$

The potential at P due to the shell is

$$V_2 = -\frac{GM}{a}.$$

The net potential at P is $V_1 + V_2 = -\frac{3GM}{a}.$

(D) Potential due to a Uniform Solid Sphere

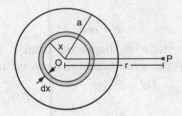

Figure 11.11

The situation is shown in figure (11.11). Let the mass of the sphere be M and its radius a. We have to

calculate the gravitational potential at a point P. Let $OP = r$.

Let us draw two spheres of radii x and $x + dx$ concentric with the given sphere. These two spheres enclose a thin spherical shell of volume $4\pi x^2 dx$. The volume of the given sphere is $\frac{4}{3}\pi a^3$. As the sphere is uniform, the mass of the shell is

$$dm = \frac{M}{\frac{4}{3}\pi a^3} 4\pi x^2\, dx = \frac{3M}{a^3} x^2\, dx.$$

The potential due to this shell at the point P is

$$dV = -\frac{G\,dm}{r} \text{ if } x < r \text{ and } dV = -\frac{G\,dm}{x} \text{ if } x > r.$$

Case I : Potential at an external point

Suppose the point P is outside the sphere (figure 11.11). The potential at P due to the shell considered is

$$dV = -\frac{G\,dm}{r}.$$

Thus, the potential due to the whole sphere is

$$V = \int dV = -\frac{G}{r} \int dm$$

$$= -\frac{GM}{r}. \qquad \ldots \ (11.11)$$

The gravitational potential due to a uniform sphere at an external point is same as that due to a single particle of equal mass placed at its centre.

Case II : Potential at an internal point

Let us divide the sphere in two parts by imagining a concentric spherical surface passing through P. The inner part has a mass

$$M' = \frac{M}{\frac{4}{3}\pi a^3} \times \frac{4}{3}\pi r^3 = \frac{Mr^3}{a^3}.$$

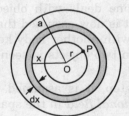

Figure 11.12

The potential at P due to this inner part is by equation (11.11)

$$V_1 = -\frac{GM'}{r}$$

$$= -\frac{GMr^2}{a^3}. \qquad \ldots \ (i)$$

To get the potential at P due to the outer part of the sphere, we divide this part in concentric shells. The mass of the shell between radii x and $x + dx$ is

$$dm = \frac{M}{\frac{4}{3}\pi a^3} 4\pi x^2 dx = \frac{3Mx^2 dx}{a^3}.$$

The potential at P due to this shell is,

$$\frac{-G\,dm}{x} = -3\frac{GM}{a^3} x\,dx.$$

The potential due to the outer part is

$$V_2 = \int_r^a -\frac{3GM}{a^3} x\,dx$$

$$= -\frac{3GM}{a^3}\left[\frac{x^2}{2}\right]_r^a$$

$$= \frac{-3GM}{2a^3}(a^2 - r^2). \qquad \dots \text{(ii)}$$

By (i) and (ii) the total potential at P is

$$V = V_1 + V_2$$

$$= -\frac{GMr^2}{a^3} - \frac{3GM}{2a^3}(a^2 - r^2)$$

$$= -\frac{GM}{2a^3}(3a^2 - r^2). \qquad \dots \text{(11.12)}$$

At the centre of the sphere the potential is

$$V = -\frac{3GM}{2a}.$$

11.6 GRAVITATIONAL FIELD

We have been saying all through that a body A exerts a force of gravitation on another body B kept at a distance. This is called *action at a distance* viewpoint. However, this viewpoint creates certain problems when one deals with objects separated by large distances. It is now assumed that a body can not directly interact with another body kept at a distance. The force between two objects is seen to be a two-step process.

In the first step, it is assumed that the body A creates a *gravitational field* in the space around it. The field has its own existence and has energy and momentum. This field has a definite direction at each point of the space and its intensity varies from point to point.

In the second step, it is assumed that when a body B is placed in a gravitational field, this field exerts a force on it. The direction and the intensity of the field is defined in terms of the force it exerts on a body placed in it. We define the *intensity of gravitational field* $\vec{E}$ at a point by the equation

$$\vec{E} = \frac{\vec{F}}{m} \qquad \dots \text{(11.13)}$$

where $\vec{F}$ is the force exerted by the field on a body of mass m placed in the field. Quite often the intensity of gravitational field is abbreviated as *gravitational field*. Its SI unit is N kg^{-1}.

Gravitational field adds according to the rules of vector addition. If $\vec{E}_1$ is the field due to a source S_1 and $\vec{E}_2$ is the field at the same point due to another source S_2, the resultant field when both the sources are present is $\vec{E}_1 + \vec{E}_2$.

If a mass m is placed close to the surface of the earth, the force on it is mg. We say that the earth has set up a gravitational field and this field exerts a force on the mass. The intensity of the field is

$$\vec{E} = \frac{\vec{F}}{m} = \frac{m\vec{g}}{m} = \vec{g}.$$

Thus, the intensity of the gravitational field near the surface of the earth is equal to the acceleration due to gravity. It should be clearly understood that the intensity of the gravitational field and the acceleration due to gravity are two separate physical quantities having equal magnitudes and directions.

Example 11.4

A particle of mass 50 g experiences a gravitational force of 2·0 N when placed at a particular point. Find the gravitational field at that point.

Solution : The gravitational field has a magnitude

$$E = \frac{F}{m} = \frac{2 \cdot 0 \text{ N}}{(50 \times 10^{-3} \text{ kg})} = 40 \text{ N kg}^{-1}.$$

This field is along the direction of the force.

11.7 RELATION BETWEEN GRAVITATIONAL FIELD AND POTENTIAL

Suppose the gravitational field at a point $\vec{r}$ due to a given mass distribution is $\vec{E}$. By definition (equation 11.13), the force on a particle of mass m when it is at $\vec{r}$ is

$$\vec{F} = m\vec{E}.$$

As the particle is displaced from $\vec{r}$ to $\vec{r} + d\vec{r}$ the work done by the gravitational force on it is

$$dW = \vec{F} \cdot d\vec{r}$$

$$= m\vec{E} \cdot d\vec{r}.$$

The change in potential energy during this displacement is

$$dU = -dW = -m\vec{E} \cdot d\vec{r}.$$

The change in potential is, by equation (11.4),

$$dV = \frac{dU}{m} = -\vec{E} \cdot \vec{dr}. \qquad \ldots (11.14)$$

Integrating between $\vec{r_1}$ and $\vec{r_2}$

$$V(\vec{r_2}) - V(\vec{r_1}) = -\int_{\vec{r_1}}^{\vec{r_2}} \vec{E} \cdot \vec{dr}. \qquad \ldots (11.15)$$

If $\vec{r_1}$ is taken at the reference point, $V(\vec{r_1}) = 0$. The potential $V(\vec{r})$ at any point $\vec{r}$ is, therefore,

$$V(\vec{r}) = -\int_{\vec{r_0}}^{\vec{r}} \vec{E} \cdot \vec{dr} \qquad \ldots (11.16)$$

where $\vec{r_0}$ denotes the reference point.

If we work in Cartesian coordinates, we can write

$$\vec{E} = \vec{i} E_x + \vec{j} E_y + \vec{k} E_z$$

and

$$\vec{dr} = \vec{i} dx + \vec{j} dy + \vec{k} dz$$

so that

$$\vec{E} \cdot \vec{dr} = E_x dx + E_y dy + E_z dz .$$

Equation (11.14) may be written as

$$dV = -E_x dx - E_y dy - E_z dz.$$

If y and z remain constant, $dy = dz = 0$.

Thus, $\qquad E_x = -\dfrac{\partial V}{\partial x} \qquad \ldots (11.17)$

Similarly, $\qquad E_y = -\dfrac{\partial V}{\partial y}$ and $E_z = -\dfrac{\partial V}{\partial z}$.

The symbol $\dfrac{\partial}{\partial x}$ means partial differentiation with respect to x treating y and z to be constants. Similarly for $\dfrac{\partial}{\partial y}$ and $\dfrac{\partial}{\partial z}$.

If the field is known, the potential may be obtained by integrating the field according to equation (11.16) and if the potential is known, the field may be obtained by differentiating the potential according to equation (11.17).

Example 11.5

The gravitational field due to a mass distribution is given by $E = K/x^3$ in X-direction. Taking the gravitational potential to be zero at infinity, find its value at a distance x.

Solution : The potential at a distance x is

$$V(x) = -\int_\infty^x E\, dx = -\int_\infty^x \frac{K}{x^3} dx$$

$$= \left[\frac{K}{2x^2}\right]_\infty^x = \frac{K}{2x^2} .$$

Example 11.6

The gravitational potential due to a mass distribution is

$$V = \frac{A}{\sqrt{x^2 + a^2}} \cdot \text{ Find the gravitational field.}$$

Solution : $\qquad V = \dfrac{A}{\sqrt{x^2 + a^2}} = A(x^2 + a^2)^{-1/2}.$

If the gravitational field is E,

$$E_x = -\frac{\partial V}{\partial x} = -A\left(-\frac{1}{2}\right)(x^2 + a^2)^{-3/2}(2x)$$

$$= \frac{Ax}{(x^2 + a^2)^{3/2}}$$

$$E_y = -\frac{\partial V}{\partial y} = 0 \text{ and } E_z = -\frac{\partial V}{\partial z} = 0.$$

The gravitational field is $\dfrac{Ax}{(x^2 + a^2)^{3/2}}$ in the x-direction.

11.8 CALCULATION OF GRAVITATIONAL FIELD

(A) Field due to a Point Mass

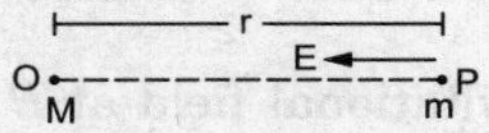

Figure 11.13

Suppose a particle of mass M is placed at a point O (figure 11.13) and a second particle of mass m is placed at a point P. Let $OP = r$. The mass M creates a field $\vec{E}$ at the site of mass m and this field exerts a force

$$\vec{F} = m\vec{E}$$

on the mass m. But the force $\vec{F}$ on the mass m due to the mass M is

$$F = \frac{GMm}{r^2}$$

acting along $\vec{PO}$. Thus, the gravitational field at P is

$$E = \frac{GM}{r^2} \qquad \ldots (11.18)$$

along $\vec{PO}$. If O is taken as the origin, the position vector of mass m is $\vec{r} = \vec{OP}$. Equation (11.18) may be rewritten in vector form as

$$= -\frac{GM}{r^2} \vec{e_r} \qquad \ldots (11.19)$$

where $\vec{e_r}$ is the unit vector along $\vec{r}$.

(B) Field due to a Uniform Circular Ring at a Point on its Axis

Figure (11.14) shows a uniform circular ring of radius a and mass M. Let P be a point on its axis at a distance r from the centre. We have to obtain the gravitational field at P due to the ring. By symmetry the field must be towards the centre that is along $\overrightarrow{PO}$.

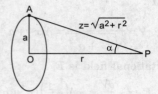

Figure 11.14

Consider any particle of mass dm on the ring, say at point A. The distance of this particle from P is $AP = z = \sqrt{a^2 + r^2}$. The gravitational field at P due to dm is along $\overrightarrow{PA}$ and its magnitude is

$$dE = \frac{G\,dm}{z^2}.$$

The component along PO is

$$dE\cos\alpha = \frac{G\,dm}{z^2}\cos\alpha.$$

The net gravitational field at P due to the ring is

$$E = \int \frac{G\,dm}{z^2}\cos\alpha = \frac{G\cos\alpha}{z^2}\int dm = \frac{GM\cos\alpha}{z^2}$$

$$= \frac{GMr}{(a^2 + r^2)^{3/2}}. \qquad \ldots (11.20)$$

The field is directed towards the centre of the ring.

(C) Field due to a Uniform Disc at a Point on its Axis

The situation is shown in figure (11.15). Let the mass of the disc be M and its radius be a. Let O be the centre of the disc and P be a point on its axis at a distance r from the centre. We have to find the gravitational field at P due to the disc.

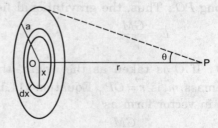

Figure 11.15

Let us draw a circle of radius x with the centre at O. We draw another concentric circle of radius $x + dx$. The part of the disc enclosed between these two circles can be treated as a uniform ring of radius x. The point P is on its axis at a distance r from the centre. The area of this ring is $2\pi x\,dx$. The area of the

whole disc is πa^2. As the disc is uniform, the mass of this ring is

$$dm = \frac{M}{\pi a^2} 2\pi x\,dx$$

$$= \frac{2M x\,dx}{a^2}.$$

The gravitational field at P due to the ring is, by equation (11.20),

$$dE = \frac{G\left(\dfrac{2M x\,dx}{a^2}\right)r}{(r^2 + x^2)^{3/2}}$$

$$= \frac{2GMr}{a^2}\frac{x\,dx}{(r^2 + x^2)^{3/2}}.$$

As x varies from 0 to a, the rings cover up the whole disc. The field due to each of these rings is in the same direction PO. Thus, the net field due to the whole disc is along PO and its magnitude is

$$E = \int_0^a \frac{2GMr}{a^2}\frac{x\,dx}{(r^2 + x^2)^{3/2}}$$

$$= \frac{2GMr}{a^2}\int_0^a \frac{x\,dx}{(r^2 + x^2)^{3/2}}. \qquad \ldots (i)$$

Let $r^2 + x^2 = z^2$.
Then $2x\,dx = 2z\,dz$ and

$$\int \frac{x\,dx}{(r^2 + x^2)^{3/2}} = \int \frac{z\,dz}{z^3}$$

$$= \int \frac{1}{z^2} dz = -\frac{1}{z} = -\frac{1}{\sqrt{r^2 + x^2}}.$$

From (i), $\quad E = \frac{2GMr}{a^2}\left[-\frac{1}{\sqrt{r^2 + x^2}}\right]_0^a$

$$= \frac{2GMr}{a^2}\left[\frac{1}{r} - \frac{1}{\sqrt{r^2 + a^2}}\right] \ldots (11.21)$$

Equation (11.21) may be expressed in terms of the angle θ subtended by a radius of the disc at P as,

$$E = \frac{2GM}{a^2}(1 - \cos\theta).$$

(D) Field due to a Uniform Thin Spherical Shell

We can use the construction of figure (11.8) to find the gravitational field at a point due to a uniform thin spherical shell. The figure is reproduced here (figure 11.16) with symbols having same meanings. The shaded ring has mass $dm = \frac{M}{2}\sin\theta\,d\theta$. The field at P due to this ring is

$$dE = \frac{G\,dm}{z^2}\cos\alpha = \frac{GM}{2}\frac{\sin\theta\,d\theta\cos\alpha}{z^2}. \qquad \ldots (i)$$

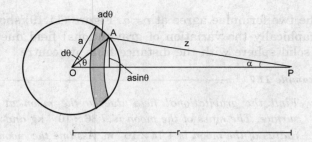

Figure 11.16

the sphere at a point outside the sphere at a distance r from the centre. Figure (11.17) shows the situation. The centre of the sphere is at O and the field is to be calculated at P.

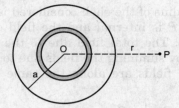

Figure 11.17

From the triangle OAP,

$$z^2 = a^2 + r^2 - 2ar\cos\theta$$

or,

$$2z\,dz = 2ar\sin\theta\,d\theta$$

or,

$$\sin\theta\,d\theta = \frac{z\,dz}{ar}. \qquad \dots \text{(ii)}$$

Also from the triangle OAP,

$$a^2 = z^2 + r^2 - 2zr\cos\alpha$$

or,

$$\cos\alpha = \frac{z^2 + r^2 - a^2}{2zr}. \qquad \dots \text{(iii)}$$

Putting from (ii) and (iii) in (i),

$$dE = \frac{GM}{4ar^2}\left(1 - \frac{a^2 - r^2}{z^2}\right)dz$$

or,

$$\int dE = \frac{GM}{4ar^2}\left[z + \frac{a^2 - r^2}{z}\right]$$

Case I : P is outside the shell ($r > a$)

In this case z varies from $r - a$ to $r + a$. The field due to the whole shell is

$$E = \frac{GM}{4ar^2}\left[z + \frac{a^2 - r^2}{z}\right]_{r-a}^{r+a} = \frac{GM}{r^2}.$$

We see that *the shell may be treated as a point particle of the same mass placed at its centre to calculate the gravitational field at an external point.*

Case II : P is inside the shell ($r < a$)

In this case z varies from $a - r$ to $a + r$ (figure 11.9). The field at P due to the whole shell is

$$E = \frac{GM}{4ar^2}\left[z + \frac{a^2 - r^2}{z}\right]_{a-r}^{a+r} = 0.$$

Hence *the field inside a uniform spherical shell is zero.*

(E) Gravitational Field due to a Uniform Solid Sphere

Case I : Field at an external point

Let the mass of the sphere be M and its radius be a. We have to calculate the gravitational field due to

Let us divide the sphere into thin spherical shells each centred at O. Let the mass of one such shell be dm. To calculate the gravitational field at P, we can replace the shell by a single particle of mass dm placed at the centre of the shell that is at O. The field at P due to this shell is then

$$dE = \frac{G\,dm}{r^2}$$

towards PO. The field due to the whole sphere may be obtained by summing the fields of all the shells making the solid sphere.

Thus,

$$E = \int dE$$

$$= \int \frac{G\,dm}{r^2} = \frac{G}{r^2}\int dm$$

$$= \frac{GM}{r^2}. \qquad \dots \text{(11.23)}$$

Thus, *a uniform sphere may be treated as a single particle of equal mass placed at its centre for calculating the gravitational field at an external point.*

This allows us to treat the earth as a point particle placed at its centre while calculating the force between the earth and an apple.

Case II : Field at an internal point

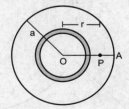

Figure 11.18

Suppose the point P is inside the solid sphere (figure 11.18). In this case $r < a$. The sphere may be divided into thin spherical shells all centered at O. Suppose the mass of such a shell is dm. If the radius of the shell is less than r, the point P is outside the shell and the field due to the shell is

$$dE = \frac{G\,dm}{r^2} \text{ along } PO.$$

If the radius of the shell considered is greater than r, the point P is internal and the field due to such a shell is zero. The total field due to the whole sphere is obtained by summing the fields due to all the shells. As all these fields are along the same direction, the net field is

$$E = \int dE$$

$$= \int \frac{G\,dm}{r^2} = \frac{G}{r^2} \int dm. \qquad \ldots \text{ (i)}$$

Only the masses of the shells with radii less than r should be added to get $\int dm$. These shells form a solid sphere of radius r. The volume of this sphere is $\frac{4}{3}\pi r^3$. The volume of the whole sphere is $\frac{4}{3}\pi a^3$. As the given sphere is uniform, the mass of the sphere of radius r is

$$\frac{M}{\frac{4}{3}\pi a^3} \cdot \left(\frac{4}{3}\pi r^3\right) = \frac{Mr^3}{a^3}.$$

Thus, $\int dm = \dfrac{Mr^3}{a^3}$

and by (i) $E = \dfrac{G}{r^2} \dfrac{Mr^3}{a^3}$

$$= \frac{GM}{a^3} r. \qquad \ldots \text{ (11.24)}$$

The gravitational field due to a uniform sphere at an internal point is proportional to the distance of the point from the centre of the sphere. At the centre itself, $r = 0$ and the field is zero. This is also expected from symmetry because any particle at the centre is equally pulled from all sides and the resultant must be zero. At the surface of the sphere, $r = a$ and

$$E = \frac{GM}{a^2}.$$

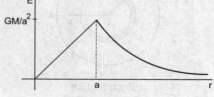

Figure 11.19

The formula (11.23) for the field at an external point also gives $E = \frac{GM}{a^2}$ at the surface of the sphere.

The two formulae agree at $r = a$. Figure (11.19) shows graphically the variation of gravitational field due to a solid sphere with the distance from its centre.

Example 11.7

Find the gravitational field due to the moon at its surface. The mass of the moon is $7{\cdot}36 \times 10^{22}$ kg and the radius of the moon is $1{\cdot}74 \times 10^6$ m. Assume the moon to be a spherically symmetric body.

Solution : To calculate the gravitational field at an external point, the moon may be replaced by a single particle of equal mass placed at its centre. Then the field at the surface is

$$E = \frac{GM}{a^2}$$

$$= \frac{6{\cdot}67 \times 10^{-11}\,\text{N--m}^2/\text{kg}^2 \times 7{\cdot}36 \times 10^{22}\,\text{kg}}{(1{\cdot}74 \times 10^6\,\text{m})^2}$$

$$= 1{\cdot}62 \text{ N kg}^{-1}.$$

This is about one sixth of the gravitational field due to the earth at its surface.

11.9 VARIATION IN THE VALUE OF g

The acceleration due to gravity is given by

$$g = \frac{F}{m}$$

where F is the force exerted by the earth on an object of mass m. This force is affected by a number of factors and hence g also depends on these factors.

(a) Height from the Surface of the Earth

If the object is placed at a distance h above the surface of the earth, the force of gravitation on it due to the earth is

$$F = \frac{GMm}{(R+h)^2}$$

where M is the mass of the earth and R is its radius.

Thus, $g = \dfrac{F}{m} = \dfrac{GM}{(R+h)^2}.$

We see that the value of g decreases as one goes up. We can write,

$$g = \frac{GM}{R^2\left(1+\dfrac{h}{R}\right)^2} = \frac{g_0}{\left(1+\dfrac{h}{R}\right)^2}$$

where $g_0 = \dfrac{GM}{R^2}$ is the value of g at the surface of the earth. If $h \ll R$,

$$g = g_0\left(1+\frac{h}{R}\right)^{-2} \approx g_0\left(1-\frac{2h}{R}\right).$$

If one goes a distance h inside the earth such as in mines, the value of g again decreases. The force by the earth is, by equation (11.24),

$$F = \frac{GMm}{R^3}(R-h)$$

or,

$$g = \frac{F}{m} = \frac{GM}{R^2}\left(\frac{R-h}{R}\right)$$

$$= g_0\left(1 - \frac{h}{R}\right).$$

The value of g is maximum at the surface of the earth and decreases with the increase in height as well as with depth similar to that shown in figure (11.19).

Example 11.8

Calculate the value of acceleration due to gravity at a point (a) 5·0 km above the earth's surface and (b) 5·0 km below the earth's surface. Radius of earth = 6400 km and the value of g at the surface of the earth is 9·80 m s^{-2}.

Solution :

(a) The value of g at a height h is (for $h \ll R$)

$$g = g_0\left(1 - \frac{2h}{R}\right)$$

$$= (9{\cdot}80 \text{ m s}^{-2})\left(1 - \frac{2 \times 5{\cdot}0 \text{ km}}{6400 \text{ km}}\right)$$

$$= 9{\cdot}78 \text{ m s}^{-2}.$$

(b) The value at a depth h is

$$g = g_0\left(1 - \frac{h}{R}\right)$$

$$= (9{\cdot}8 \text{ m s}^{-2})\left(1 - \frac{5{\cdot}0 \text{ km}}{6400 \text{ km}}\right)$$

$$= 9{\cdot}79 \text{ m s}^{-2}.$$

(b) Rotation of the Earth

As the earth rotates about its own axis the frame attached to the earth is noninertial. If we wish to use the familiar Newton's laws, we have to include pseudo forces. For an object at rest with respect to the earth, a centrifugal force $m\omega^2 r$ is to be added where m is the mass of the object, ω is the angular velocity of the earth and r is the radius of the circle in which the particle rotates.

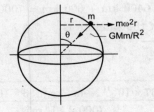

Figure 11.20

If the colatitude of the location of the particle is θ (figure 11.20), $r = R\sin\theta$ where R is the radius of the earth. Acceleration of an object falling near the earth's surface, as measured from the earth frame, is F/m where F is the vector sum of the gravitational force $\frac{GMm}{R^2} = mg$ and the centrifugal force $m\omega^2 r = m\omega^2 R\sin\theta$. The acceleration $F/m = g'$ is the apparent value of the acceleration due to gravity.

At the equator, $\theta = \pi/2$ and the centrifugal force is just opposite to the force of gravity. The resultant of these two is

$$F = mg - m\omega^2 R$$

or,

$$g' = g - \omega^2 R.$$

At the poles, $\theta = 0$ and the centrifugal force $m\omega^2 R\sin\theta = 0$. Thus, $F = mg$ and $g' = g$. Thus, the observed value of the acceleration due to gravity is minimum at the equator and is maximum at the poles. This effect had been discussed in the chapter on circular motion.

(c) Nonsphericity of the Earth

All formulae and equations have been derived by assuming that the earth is a uniform solid sphere. The shape of the earth slightly deviates from the perfect sphere. The radius in the equatorial plane is about 21 km larger than the radius along the poles. Due to this the force of gravity is more at the poles and less at the equator. The value of g is accordingly larger at the poles and less at the equator. Note that due to rotation of earth also, the value of g is smaller at the equator than that at the poles.

(d) Nonuniformity of the Earth

The earth is not a uniformly dense object. There are a variety of minerals, metals, water, oil, etc., inside the earth. Then at the surface there are mountains, seas, etc. Due to these nonuniformities in the mass distribution, the value of g is locally affected.

"Weighing" the Earth

The force exerted by the earth on a body is called the *weight* of the body. In this sense "weight of earth" is a meaningless concept. However, the mass of the earth can be determined by noting the acceleration due to gravity near the surface of the earth. We have,

$$g = \frac{GM}{R^2}$$

or,

$$M = gR^2/G$$

Putting $g = 9{\cdot}8$ m s^{-2}, $R = 6400$ km

and $G = 6 \cdot 67 \times 10^{-11} \dfrac{\text{N--m}^2}{\text{kg}^2}$

the mass of the earth comes out to be $5 \cdot 98 \times 10^{24}$ kg.

11.10 PLANETS AND SATELLITES

Planets

Planets move round the sun due to the gravitational attraction of the sun. The path of these planets are elliptical with the sun at a focus. However, the difference in major and minor axes is not large. The orbits can be treated as nearly circular for not too sophisticated calculations. Let us derive certain characteristics of the planetary motion in terms of the radius of the orbit assuming it to be perfectly circular.

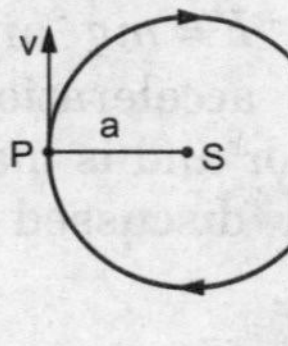

Figure 11.21

Let the mass of the sun be M and that of the planet under study be m. The mass of the sun is many times larger than the mass of the planet. The sun may, therefore, be treated as an inertial frame of reference.

Speed

Let the radius of the orbit be a and the speed of the planet in the orbit be v. By Newton's second law, the force on the planet equals its mass times the acceleration. Thus,

$$\frac{GMm}{a^2} = m\left(\frac{v^2}{a}\right)$$

or, $v = \sqrt{\dfrac{GM}{a}}$.   ... (11.25)

The speed of a planet is inversely proportional to the square root of the radius of its orbit.

Time period

The time taken by a planet in completing one revolution is its time period T. In one revolution it covers a linear distance of $2\pi a$ at speed v. Thus,

$$T = \frac{2\pi a}{v}$$

$$= \frac{2\pi a}{\sqrt{\dfrac{GM}{a}}} = \frac{2\pi}{\sqrt{GM}} a^{3/2}$$

or, $T^2 = \dfrac{4\pi^2}{GM} a^3$.   ... (11.26)

Energy

The kinetic energy of the planet is

$$K = \frac{1}{2} mv^2.$$

Using (11.25),

$$K = \frac{1}{2} m \, \frac{GM}{a} = \frac{GMm}{2a}.$$

The gravitational potential energy of the sun–planet system is

$$U = -\frac{GMm}{a}.$$

The total mechanical energy of the sun–planet system is

$$E = K + U = \frac{GMm}{2a} - \frac{GMm}{a} = -\frac{GMm}{2a}.$$

The total energy is negative. This is true for any bound system if the potential energy is taken to be zero at infinite separation.

Satellite

Satellites are launched from the earth so as to move round it. A number of rockets are fired from the satellite at proper time to establish the satellite in the desired orbit. Once the satellite is placed in the desired orbit with the correct speed for that orbit, it will continue to move in that orbit under gravitational attraction of the earth. All the equations derived above for planets are also true for satellites with M representing the mass of the earth and m representing the mass of the satellite.

Example 11.9

A satellite is revolving round the earth at a height of 600 km. Find (a) the speed of the satellite and (b) the time period of the satellite. Radius of the earth = 6400 km and mass of the earth = 6×10^{24} kg.

Solution : The distance of the satellite from the centre of the earth is 6400 km + 600 km = 7000 km.

The speed of the satellite is

$$v = \sqrt{\frac{GM}{a}}$$

$$= \sqrt{\frac{6 \cdot 67 \times 10^{-11} \, \text{N--m}^2/\text{kg}^2 \times 6 \times 10^{24} \, \text{kg}}{7000 \times 10^3 \, \text{m}}}$$

$$= 7 \cdot 6 \times 10^3 \, \text{m s}^{-1} = 7 \cdot 6 \, \text{km s}^{-1}.$$

The time period is

$$T = \frac{2\pi a}{v}$$

$$= \frac{2\pi \times 7000 \times 10^3 \, \text{m}}{7 \cdot 6 \times 10^3 \, \text{m s}^{-1}} = 5 \cdot 8 \times 10^3 \, \text{s}.$$

Geostationary Satellite

The earth rotates about its own axis (the line joining the north pole and the south pole) once in 24 hours. Suppose a satellite is established in an orbit in the plane of the equator. Suppose the height is such that the time period of the satellite is 24 hours and it moves in the same sense as the earth. The satellite will always be overhead a particular place on the equator. As seen from the earth, this satellite will appear to be stationary. Such a satellite is called *a geostationary satellite*. Such satellites are used for telecommunication, weather forecasting and other applications.

According to equation (11.26),

$$T^2 = \frac{4\pi^2}{GM} a^3$$

or,

$$a = \left(\frac{GMT^2}{4\pi^2} \right)^{1/3}.$$

Putting the values of G, $M = (6 \times 10^{24} \, \text{kg})$ and $T = (24 \, \text{hours})$; the radius of the geostationary orbit comes out to be $a = 4 \cdot 2 \times 10^4 \, \text{km}$. The height above the surface of the earth is about $3 \cdot 6 \times 10^4 \, \text{km}$.

11.11 KEPLER'S LAWS

From the observations of Tycho Brahe, Kepler formulated the laws of planetary motion which we have listed in the first section of this chapter. The first law states that the path of a planet is elliptical with the sun at a focus. Circular path is a special case of an ellipse when the major and minor axes are equal. For a circular path, the planet should have velocity perpendicular to the line joining it with the sun and the magnitude should satisfy equation (11.25), that is $v = \sqrt{\frac{GM}{a}}$. If these conditions are not satisfied, the planet moves in an ellipse.

The second law states that the radius vector from the sun to the planet sweeps out equal area in equal time. For a circular orbit, this is obvious because the speed of the particle remains constant.

The third law of Kepler states that the square of the time period of a planet is proportional to the cube of the semimajor axis. For a circular orbit semimajor axis is same as the radius. We have already proved this law for circular orbits in equation (11.26). As M

denotes mass of the sun, $\frac{4\pi^2}{GM}$ is fixed for all planets and $T^2 \propto a^3$.

11.12 WEIGHTLESSNESS IN A SATELLITE

A satellite moves round the earth in a circular orbit under the action of gravity. The acceleration of the satellite is $\frac{GM}{R^2}$ towards the centre of the earth, where M is the mass of the earth and R is the radius of the orbit of the satellite. Consider a body of mass m placed on a surface inside a satellite moving round the earth. The forces on the body are

(a) the gravitational pull of the earth $= \frac{GMm}{R^2}$,

(b) the contact force $\mathcal{N}$ by the surface.

By Newton's law,

$$G\frac{Mm}{R^2} - \mathcal{N} = m\left(\frac{GM}{R^2} \right) \text{ or, } \mathcal{N} = 0.$$

Thus, the surface does not exert any force on the body and hence its apparent weight is zero. No support is needed to hold a body in the satellite. All positions shown in figure (11.22) are equally comfortable.

Figure 11.22

One can analyse the situation from the frame of the satellite. Working in the satellite frame we have to add a centrifugal force on all bodies. If the mass of a body is m, the centrifugal force is $m\left(\frac{GM}{R^2} \right)$ away from the centre of the earth. This pseudo force exactly balances the weight of the body which is $\frac{GMm}{R^2}$ towards the centre of the earth. A body needs no support to stay at rest in the satellite and hence all positions are equally comfortable. Water will not fall down from the glass even if it is inverted. It will act like a "gravity-free hall". Such a state is called *weightlessness*.

It should be clear that the earth still attracts a body with the same force $\frac{GMm}{R^2}$. The feeling of weightlessness arises because one stays in a rotating frame.

11.13 ESCAPE VELOCITY

When a stone is thrown up it goes up to a maximum height and then returns. As the particle goes up, the gravitational potential energy increases and the kinetic energy of the particle decreases. The particle will continue to go up till its kinetic energy becomes zero and will return from there.

Let the initial velocity of the particle be u. The kinetic energy of the particle is $K = \frac{1}{2} mu^2$ and the gravitational potential energy of the earth–particle system is $U = -\frac{GMm}{R}$, where M is the mass of the earth, m is the mass of the particle and R is the radius of the earth. When it reaches a height h above the earth's surface, its speed becomes v. The kinetic energy there is $\frac{1}{2} mv^2$ and the gravitational potential energy is $-\frac{GMm}{R+h}$.

By conservation of energy

$$\frac{1}{2} mu^2 - \frac{GMm}{R} = \frac{1}{2} mv^2 - \frac{GMm}{R+h}$$

or, $$\frac{1}{2} mv^2 = \left[\frac{1}{2} mu^2 - \frac{GMm}{R}\right] + \frac{GMm}{R+h}. \quad \dots \text{(i)}$$

The particle will reach the maximum height when v becomes zero.

If $\frac{1}{2} mu^2 - \frac{GMm}{R} \geq 0$, the right-hand side of (i) is greater than zero for all values of h. Thus, $\frac{1}{2} mv^2$ never becomes zero. The particle's velocity never reaches zero and so the particle will continue to go farther and farther away from the earth. Thus, the particle will never return to the earth if

$$\frac{1}{2} mu^2 - \frac{GMm}{R} \geq 0$$

or, $$u \geq \sqrt{\frac{2GM}{R}}. \quad \dots \text{(11.27)}$$

This critical initial velocity is called the *escape velocity*. Putting the values of G, M and R, the escape velocity from the earth comes out to be 11.6 km s^{-1}. In this we have neglected the effect of other planets, stars and other objects in space. In fact, even if the initial velocity is somewhat less than the escape velocity, the particle may get attracted by some other celestial object and land up there.

Equation (11.27) is valid for any celestial object. For example, if something is thrown up from the surface of the moon, it will never return to the moon if the initial velocity is greater than $\sqrt{\frac{2GM}{R}}$, where M is the mass of the moon and R is the radius of the moon.

Example 11.10

Calculate the escape velocity from the moon. The mass of the moon $= 7.4 \times 10^{22}$ kg and radius of the moon $= 1740$ km.

Solution : The escape velocity is

$$v = \sqrt{\frac{2GM}{R}}$$

$$= \sqrt{\frac{2 \times 6.67 \times 10^{-11} \text{ N-m}^2/\text{kg}^2 \times 7.4 \times 10^{22} \text{ kg}}{1740 \times 10^3 \text{ m}}}$$

$$= 2.4 \text{ km s}^{-1}.$$

11.14 GRAVITATIONAL BINDING ENERGY

We have seen that if a particle of mass m placed on the earth is given an energy $\frac{1}{2} mu^2 = \frac{GMm}{R}$ or more, it finally escapes from earth. The minimum energy needed to take the particle infinitely away from the earth is called the *binding energy* of the earth–particle system. Thus, the binding energy of the earth–particle system is $\frac{GMm}{R}$.

11.15 BLACK HOLES

Consider a spherical body of mass M and radius R. Suppose, due to some reason the volume goes on decreasing while the mass remains the same. The escape velocity $\sqrt{\frac{2GM}{R}}$ from such a dense material will be very high. Suppose the radius is so small that

$$\sqrt{\frac{2GM}{R}} \geq c$$

where $c = 3 \times 10^8$ m s^{-1} is the speed of light. The escape velocity for such an object is equal to or greater than the speed of light. This means, anything starting from the object with a speed less than the speed of light will return to the object (neglecting the effect of other objects in space). According to the theory of relativity it is not possible to achieve a velocity greater than c for any material object. Thus, nothing can escape from such a dense material. Such objects are known as *black holes*. A number of such black holes exist in space. Even light cannot escape from a black hole.

11.16 INERTIAL AND GRAVITATIONAL MASS

Given two objects A and B, how can we determine the ratio of the mass of A to the mass of B. One way is to use Newton's second law of motion. If we apply equal forces F on each of the two objects,

$$F = m_A a_A \quad \text{and also} \quad F = m_B a_B.$$

Thus,
$$\frac{m_A}{m_B} = \frac{a_B}{a_A}$$

or,
$$m_A = \frac{a_B}{a_A} m_B. \qquad \ldots \text{(i)}$$

This equation may be used to "define the mass" of an object. Taking the object B to be the standard kilogram ($m_B = 1$ kg), mass of any object may be obtained by measuring their accelerations under equal force and using (i). The mass so defined is called *inertial mass*.

Another way to compare masses of two objects is based on the law of gravitation. The gravitational force exerted by a massive body on an object is proportional to the mass of the object. If F_A and F_B be the forces of attraction on the two objects due to the earth,

$$F_A = \frac{G m_A M}{R^2} \quad \text{and} \quad F_B = \frac{G m_B M}{R^2}.$$

Thus,
$$\frac{m_A}{m_B} = \frac{F_A}{F_B}$$

or,
$$m_A = \frac{F_A}{F_B} m_B. \qquad \ldots \text{(ii)}$$

We can use this equation to "define the mass" of an object. If B is a standard unit mass, by measuring the gravitational forces F_A and F_B we can obtain the mass of the object A. The mass so defined is called *gravitational mass*. When we measure the mass using a spring balance, we actually measure the gravitational mass.

Equivalence of Inertial and Gravitational Mass

The two definitions of mass, described above, are quite independent of each other. There is no obvious reason why the two should be identical. However, they happen to be identical. Several sophisticated experiments have been performed to test this equivalence and none of them has supplied any evidence against it. The general theory of relativity is based on the principle of equivalence of inertial and gravitational mass.

11.17 POSSIBLE CHANGES IN THE LAW OF GRAVITATION

There is some indication that the force between two masses is not as described in this chapter. The deviation from the simple law $F = \frac{GMm}{R^2}$ is being taken as an indication of the existence of a fifth interaction besides gravitational, electromagnetic, nuclear and weak. It has been reported (Phys. Rev. Lett. Jan 6, 1986) that the force between two masses may be better represented by

$$F = \frac{G_\infty m_1 m_2}{r^2} \left[1 + \left(1 + \frac{r}{\lambda} \right) \alpha \, e^{-\frac{r}{\lambda}} \right]$$

with $\alpha \approx -0.007$ and $\lambda \approx 200$ m. As α is negative, the second term in the square bracket represents a repulsive force. For $r \gg 200$ m

$$F = \frac{G_\infty m_1 m_2}{r^2}$$

which is the force operative between the earth and other objects. For $r \ll 200$ m

$$F = \frac{G_\infty m_1 m_2 (1 + \alpha)}{r^2} = \frac{G' m_1 m_2}{r^2}$$

where $G' = G_\infty (1 + \alpha)$.

This is the force we measure in a Cavendish-experiment. The value of G for small distances is about 1% less than the value of G for large distances.

Worked Out Examples

1. *Three particles A, B and C, each of mass m, are placed in a line with AB = BC = d. Find the gravitational force on a fourth particle P of same mass, placed at a distance d from the particle B on the perpendicular bisector of the line AC.*

Solution :

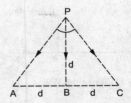

Figure 11-W1

The force at P due to A is
$$F_A = \frac{G m^2}{(AP)^2} = \frac{G m^2}{2 d^2}$$

along PA. The force at P due to C is
$$F_C = \frac{G m^2}{(CP)^2} = \frac{G m^2}{2 d^2}$$

along PC. The force at P due to B is
$$F_B = \frac{G m^2}{d^2} \quad \text{along } PB.$$

The resultant of F_A, F_B and F_C will be along PB. Clearly $\angle APB = \angle BPC = 45°$.

Component of F_A along $PB = F_A \cos 45° = \frac{G m^2}{2\sqrt{2} d^2}$.

Component of F_C along $PB = F_C \cos 45° = \dfrac{G\,m^2}{2\sqrt{2}\,d^2}$.

Component of F_B along $PB = \dfrac{G\,m^2}{d^2}$.

Hence, the resultant of the three forces is

$$\dfrac{G\,m^2}{d^2}\left(\dfrac{1}{2\sqrt{2}} + \dfrac{1}{2\sqrt{2}} + 1\right) = \dfrac{G\,m^2}{d^2}\left(1 + \dfrac{1}{\sqrt{2}}\right) \text{ along } PB.$$

2. *Find the distance of a point from the earth's centre where the resultant gravitational field due to the earth and the moon is zero. The mass of the earth is 6.0×10^{24} kg and that of the moon is 7.4×10^{22} kg. The distance between the earth and the moon is 4.0×10^5 km.*

Solution : The point must be on the line joining the centres of the earth and the moon and in between them. If the distance of the point from the earth is x, the distance from the moon is $(4.0 \times 10^5 \text{ km} - x)$. The magnitude of the gravitational field due to the earth is

$$E_1 = \dfrac{GM_e}{x^2} = \dfrac{G \times 6 \times 10^{24} \text{ kg}}{x^2}$$

and magnitude of the gravitational field due to the moon is

$$E_2 = \dfrac{GM_m}{(4.0 \times 10^5 \text{ km} - x)^2} = \dfrac{G \times 7.4 \times 10^{22} \text{ kg}}{(4.0 \times 10^5 \text{ km} - x)^2}.$$

These fields are in opposite directions. For the resultant field to be zero $E_1 = E_2$,

or, $\dfrac{6 \times 10^{24} \text{ kg}}{x^2} = \dfrac{7.4 \times 10^{22} \text{ kg}}{(4.0 \times 10^5 \text{ km} - x)^2}$

or, $\dfrac{x}{4.0 \times 10^5 \text{ km} - x} = \sqrt{\dfrac{6 \times 10^{24}}{7.4 \times 10^{22}}} = 9$

or, $x = 3.6 \times 10^5 \text{ km.}$

3. *Two particles of equal mass go round a circle of radius R under the action of their mutual gravitational attraction. Find the speed of each particle.*

Solution : The particles will always remain diametrically opposite so that the force on each particle will be directed along the radius. Consider the motion of one of the particles. The force on the particle is $F = \dfrac{G\,m^2}{4R^2}$. If the speed is v, its acceleration is v^2/R.

Thus, by Newton's law,

$$\dfrac{G\,m^2}{4R^2} = \dfrac{m\,v^2}{R}$$

or, $v = \sqrt{\dfrac{G\,m}{4R}}.$

4. *Two particles A and B of masses 1 kg and 2 kg respectively are kept 1 m apart and are released to move*

under mutual attraction. Find the speed of A when that of B is 3.6 cm/hour. What is the separation between the particles at this instant ?

Solution : The linear momentum of the pair $A + B$ is zero initially. As only mutual attraction is taken into account, which is internal when $A + B$ is taken as the system, the linear momentum will remain zero. The particles move in opposite directions. If the speed of A is v when the speed of B is 3.6 cm/hour $= 10^{-5}$ m s^{-1},

$$(1 \text{ kg})\,v = (2 \text{ kg})\,(10^{-5} \text{ m s}^{-1})$$

or, $v = 2 \times 10^{-5}$ m s^{-1}.

The potential energy of the pair is $-\dfrac{G\,m_A\,m_B}{R}$ with usual symbols. Initial potential energy

$$= -\dfrac{6.67 \times 10^{-11} \text{ N-m}^2/\text{kg}^2 \times 2 \text{ kg} \times 1 \text{ kg}}{1 \text{ m}}$$

$$= -13.34 \times 10^{-11} \text{ J.}$$

If the separation at the given instant is d, using conservation of energy,

$$-13.34 \times 10^{-11} \text{ J} + 0$$

$$= -\dfrac{13.34 \times 10^{-11} \text{ J-m}}{d} + \dfrac{1}{2}\,(2 \text{ kg})\,(10^{-5} \text{ m s}^{-1})^2$$

$$+ \dfrac{1}{2}\,(1 \text{ kg})\,(2 \times 10^{-5} \text{ m s}^{-1})^2$$

Solving this, $d = 0.31$ m.

5. *The gravitational field in a region is given by $\vec{E} = (10 \text{ N kg}^{-1})\,(\vec{i} + \vec{j})$. Find the work done by an external agent to slowly shift a particle of mass 2 kg from the point $(0,0)$ to a point $(5 \text{ m}, 4 \text{ m})$.*

Solution : As the particle is slowly shifted, its kinetic energy remains zero. The total work done on the particle is thus zero. The work done by the external agent should be negative of the work done by the gravitational field. The work done by the field is

$$\int_i^f \vec{F} \cdot d\vec{r}$$

Consider figure (11-W2). Suppose the particle is taken from O to A and then from A to B. The force on the particle is

$$\vec{F} = m\vec{E} = (2 \text{ kg})\,(10 \text{ N kg}^{-1})\,(\vec{i} + \vec{j}) = (20 \text{ N})\,(\vec{i} + \vec{j}).$$

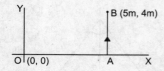

Figure 11-W2

The work done by the field during the displacement OA is

$$W_1 = \int_0^{5m} F_x \, dx$$

$$= \int_0^{5m} (20 \text{ N}) \, dx = 20 \text{ N} \times 5 \text{ m} = 100 \text{ J}.$$

Similarly, the work done in displacement AB is

$$W_2 = \int_0^{4m} F_y \, dy = \int_0^{4m} (20 \text{ N}) \, dy$$

$$= (20 \text{ N}) (4 \text{ m}) = 80 \text{ J}.$$

Thus, the total work done by the field, as the particle is shifted from O to B, is 180 J.

The work done by the external agent is −180 J.

Note that the work is independent of the path so that we can choose any path convenient to us from O to B.

6. *A uniform solid sphere of mass M and radius a is surrounded symmetrically by a uniform thin spherical shell of equal mass and radius $2\,a$. Find the gravitational field at a distance* (a) $\frac{3}{2} a$ *from the centre,* (b) $\frac{5}{2} a$ *from the centre.*

Solution :

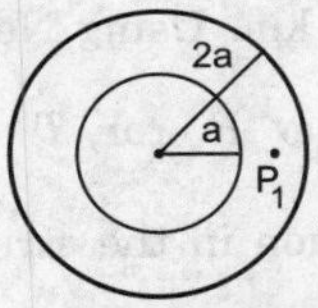

Figure 11-W3

Figure (11-W3) shows the situation. The point P_1 is at a distance $\frac{3}{2} a$ from the centre and P_2 is at a distance $\frac{5}{2} a$ from the centre. As P_1 is inside the cavity of the thin spherical shell, the field here due to the shell is zero. The field due to the solid sphere is

$$E = \frac{GM}{\left(\frac{3}{2} a\right)^2} = \frac{4\,GM}{9\,a^2}.$$

This is also the resultant field. The direction is towards the centre. The point P_2 is outside the sphere as well as the shell. Both may be replaced by single particles of the same mass at the centre. The field due to each of them is

$$E' = \frac{GM}{\left(\frac{5}{2} a\right)^2} = \frac{4\,GM}{25\,a^2}.$$

The resultant field is $E = 2\,E' = \dfrac{8\,GM}{25\,a^2}$ towards the centre.

7. *The density inside a solid sphere of radius a is given by $\rho = \rho_0\, a/r$, where ρ_0 is the density at the surface and r*

denotes the distance from the centre. Find the gravitational field due to this sphere at a distance $2\,a$ from its centre.

Solution : The field is required at a point outside the sphere. Dividing the sphere in concentric shells, each shell can be replaced by a point particle at its centre having mass equal to the mass of the shell. Thus, the whole sphere can be replaced by a point particle at its centre having mass equal to the mass of the given sphere. If the mass of the sphere is M, the gravitational field at the given point is

$$E = \frac{GM}{(2a)^2} = \frac{GM}{4a^2}. \qquad \ldots \text{(i)}$$

The mass M may be calculated as follows. Consider a concentric shell of radius r and thickness dr. Its volume is

$$dV = (4\pi r^2) \, dr$$

and its mass is

$$dM = \rho\, dV = \left(\rho_0 \frac{a}{r}\right)(4\pi r^2 dr)$$

$$= 4\pi \rho_0\, a r\, dr.$$

The mass of the whole sphere is

$$M = \int_0^a 4\pi \rho_0\, a r\, dr$$

$$= 2\pi \rho_0 a^3.$$

Thus, by (i) the gravitational field is

$$E = \frac{2\pi G \rho_0 a^3}{4a^2} = \frac{1}{2}\,\pi G \rho_0 a.$$

8. *A uniform ring of mass m and radius a is placed directly above a uniform sphere of mass M and of equal radius. The centre of the ring is at a distance $\sqrt{3}\,a$ from the centre of the sphere. Find the gravitational force exerted by the sphere on the ring.*

Solution : The gravitational field at any point on the ring due to the sphere is equal to the field due to a single particle of mass M placed at the centre of the sphere. Thus, the force on the ring due to the sphere is also equal to the force on it by a particle of mass M placed at this point. By Newton's third law it is equal to the force on the particle by the ring. Now the gravitational field due to the ring at a distance $d = \sqrt{3}\,a$ on its axis is

$$E = \frac{Gmd}{(a^2 + d^2)^{3/2}} = \frac{\sqrt{3}\, Gm}{8a^2}.$$

Figure 11-W4

The force on a particle of mass M placed here is

$$F = ME$$

$$= \frac{\sqrt{3}\,GMm}{8a^2}.$$

This is also the force due to the sphere on the ring.

9. *A particle is fired vertically upward with a speed of 9.8 km s^{-1}. Find the maximum height attained by the particle. Radius of earth $= 6400$ km and g at the surface $= 9.8$ m s^{-2}. Consider only earth's gravitation.*

Solution : At the surface of the earth, the potential energy of the earth–particle system is $-\dfrac{GMm}{R}$ with usual symbols. The kinetic energy is $\frac{1}{2}\,m v_0^2$ where $v_0 = 9.8$ km s^{-1}. At the maximum height the kinetic energy is zero. If the maximum height reached is H, the potential energy of the earth–particle system at this instant is $-\dfrac{GMm}{R+H}$. Using conservation of energy,

$$-\frac{GMm}{R} + \frac{1}{2}\,m v_0^2 = -\frac{GMm}{R+H}.$$

Writing $GM = gR^2$ and dividing by m,

$$-gR + \frac{v_0^2}{2} = \frac{-gR^2}{R+H}$$

or, $$\frac{R^2}{R+H} = R - \frac{v_0^2}{2g}$$

or, $$R+H = \frac{R^2}{R - \dfrac{v_0^2}{2g}}.$$

Putting the values of R, v_0 and g on the right side,

$$R+H = \frac{(6400 \text{ km})^2}{6400 \text{ km} - \dfrac{(9.8 \text{ km s}^{-1})^2}{2 \times 9.8 \text{ m s}^{-2}}}$$

$$= \frac{(6400 \text{ km})^2}{1500 \text{ km}} = 27300 \text{ km}$$

or, $$H = (27300 - 6400) \text{ km} = 20900 \text{ km}.$$

10. *A particle hanging from a spring stretches it by 1 cm at earth's surface. How much will the same particle stretch the spring at a place 800 km above the earth's surface ? Radius of the earth $= 6400$ km.*

Solution : Suppose the mass of the particle is m and the spring constant of the spring is k. The acceleration due to gravity at earth's surface is $g = \dfrac{GM}{R^2}$ with usual symbols. The extension in the spring is mg/k.

Hence, $$1 \text{ cm} = \frac{GMm}{kR^2}. \qquad \text{... (i)}$$

At a height $h = 800$ km, the extension is given by

$$x = \frac{GMm}{k(R+h)^2}. \qquad \text{... (ii)}$$

By (i) and (ii), $$\frac{x}{1 \text{ cm}} = \frac{R^2}{(R+h)^2}$$

$$\frac{(6400 \text{ km})^2}{(7200 \text{ km})^2} = 0.79.$$

Hence, $$x = 0.79 \text{ cm}.$$

11. *A simple pendulum has a time period exactly 2 s when used in a laboratory at north pole. What will be the time period if the same pendulum is used in a laboratory at equator ? Account for the earth's rotation only. Take $g = \dfrac{GM}{R^2} = 9.8$ m s^{-2} and radius of earth $= 6400$ km.*

Solution : Consider the pendulum in its mean position at the north pole. As the pole is on the axis of rotation, the bob is in equilibrium. Hence in the mean position, the tension T is balanced by earth's attraction. Thus, $T = \dfrac{GMm}{R^2} = mg$. The time period t is

$$t = 2\pi \sqrt{\frac{l}{T/m}} = 2\pi \sqrt{\frac{l}{g}}. \qquad \text{... (1)}$$

At equator, the lab and the pendulum rotate with the earth at angular velocity $\omega = \dfrac{2\pi \text{ radian}}{24 \text{ hour}}$ in a circle of radius equal to 6400 km. Using Newton's second law,

$$\frac{GMm}{R^2} - T' = m\omega^2 R \quad \text{or, } T' = m(g - \omega^2 R)$$

where T' is the tension in the string. The time period will be

$$t' = 2\pi \sqrt{\frac{l}{(T'/m)}} = 2\pi \sqrt{\frac{l}{g - \omega^2 R}}. \qquad \text{... (ii)}$$

By (i) and (ii)

$$\frac{t'}{t} = \sqrt{\frac{g}{g - \omega^2 R}} = \left(1 - \frac{\omega^2 R}{g}\right)^{-1/2}$$

or, $$t' \approx t\left(1 + \frac{\omega^2 R}{2g}\right).$$

Putting the values, $t' = 2.004$ seconds.

12. *A satellite is to revolve round the earth in a circle of radius 8000 km. With what speed should this satellite be projected into orbit ? What will be the time period ? Take g at the surface $= 9.8$ m s^{-2} and radius of the earth $= 6400$ km.*

Solution : Suppose, the speed of the satellite is v. The acceleration of the satellite is v^2/r, where r is the radius of the orbit. The force on the satellite is $\dfrac{GMm}{r^2}$ with usual symbols. Using Newton's second law,

$$\frac{GMm}{r^2} = m\frac{v^2}{r}$$

or, $v^2 = \dfrac{GM}{r} = \dfrac{g\,R^2}{r} = \dfrac{(9\cdot8\ \text{m s}^{-2})\,(6400\ \text{km})^2}{(8000\ \text{km})}$

giving $v = 7\cdot08\ \text{km s}^{-1}$.

The time period is $\dfrac{2\,\pi\,r}{v} = \dfrac{2\,\pi\,(8000\ \text{km})}{(7\cdot08\ \text{km s}^{-1})} \approx 118$ minutes.

13. *Two satellites S_1 and S_2 revolve round a planet in coplanar circular orbits in the same sense. Their periods of revolution are 1 h and 8 h respectively. The radius of the orbit of S_1 is 10^4 km. When S_2 is closest to S_1, find (a) the speed of S_2 relative to S_1 and (b) the angular speed of S_2 as observed by an astronaut in S_1.*

Solution : Let the mass of the planet be M, that of S_1 be m_1 and of S_2 be m_2. Let the radius of the orbit of S_1 be R_1 ($= 10^4$ km) and of S_2 be R_2.

Let v_1 and v_2 be the linear speeds of S_1 and S_2 with respect to the planet. Figure (11-W5) shows the situation.

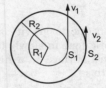

Figure 11-W5

As the square of the time period is proportional to the cube of the radius,

$$\left(\dfrac{R_2}{R_1}\right)^3 = \left(\dfrac{T_2}{T_1}\right)^2 = \left(\dfrac{8\ \text{h}}{1\ \text{h}}\right)^2 = 64$$

or, $\dfrac{R_2}{R_1} = 4$

or, $R_2 = 4R_1 = 4 \times 10^4$ km.

Now the time period of S_1 is 1 h. So,

$$\dfrac{2\,\pi\,R_1}{v_1} = 1\ \text{h}$$

or, $v_1 = \dfrac{2\,\pi\,R_1}{1\ \text{h}} = 2\,\pi \times 10^4\ \text{km h}^{-1}$

similarly, $v_2 = \dfrac{2\,\pi\,R_2}{8\,h} = \pi \times 10^4\ \text{km h}^{-1}$.

(a) At the closest separation, they are moving in the same direction. Hence the speed of S_2 with respect to S_1 is $|v_2 - v_1| = \pi \times 10^4\ \text{km h}^{-1}$.

(b) As seen from S_1, the satellite S_2 is at a distance $R_2 - R_1 = 3 \times 10^4$ km at the closest separation. Also, it is moving at $\pi \times 10^4\ \text{km h}^{-1}$ in a direction perpendicular to the line joining them. Thus, the angular speed of S_2 as observed by S_1 is

$$\omega = \dfrac{\pi \times 10^4\ \text{km h}^{-1}}{3 \times 10^4\ \text{km}} = \dfrac{\pi}{3}\ \text{rad h}^{-1}.$$

□

QUESTIONS FOR SHORT ANSWERS

1. Can two particles be in equilibrium under the action of their mutual gravitational force ? Can three particles be ? Can one of the three particles be ?

2. Is there any meaning of "Weight of the earth" ?

3. If heavier bodies are attracted more strongly by the earth, why don't they fall faster than the lighter bodies ?

4. Can you think of two particles which do not exert gravitational force on each other ?

5. The earth revolves round the sun because the sun attracts the earth. The sun also attracts the moon and this force is about twice as large as the attraction of the earth on the moon. Why does the moon not revolve round the sun ? Or does it ?

6. At noon, the sun and the earth pull the objects on the earth's surface in opposite directions. At midnight, the sun and the earth pull these objects in same direction. Is the weight of an object, as measured by a spring balance on the earth's surface, more at midnight as compared to its weight at noon ?

7. An apple falls from a tree. An insect in the apple finds that the earth is falling towards it with an acceleration g. Who exerts the force needed to accelerate the earth with this acceleration g ?

8. Suppose the gravitational potential due to a small system is k/r^2 at a distance r from it. What will be the gravitational field ? Can you think of any such system ? What happens if there were negative masses ?

9. The gravitational potential energy of a two-particle system is derived in this chapter as $U = -\dfrac{Gm_1m_2}{r}$. Does it follow from this equation that the potential energy for $r = \infty$ must be zero ? Can we choose the potential energy for $r = \infty$ to be 20 J and still use this formula ? If no, what formula should be used to calculate the gravitational potential energy at separation r ?

10. The weight of an object is more at the poles than at the equator. Is it beneficial to purchase goods at equator and sell them at the pole ? Does it matter whether a spring balance is used or an equal-beam balance is used ?

11. The weight of a body at the poles is greater than the weight at the equator. Is it the actual weight or the apparent weight we are talking about ? Does your answer depend on whether only the earth's rotation is taken into account or the flattening of the earth at the poles is also taken into account?

12. If the radius of the earth decreases by 1% without changing its mass, will the acceleration due to gravity at the surface of the earth increase or decrease? If so, by what per cent?

13. A nut becomes loose and gets detached from a satellite revolving around the earth. Will it land on the earth? If yes, where will it land? If no, how can an astronaut make it land on the earth?

14. Is it necessary for the plane of the orbit of a satellite to pass through the centre of the earth?

15. Consider earth satellites in circular orbits. A geostationary satellite must be at a height of about 36000 km from the earth's surface. Will any satellite moving at this height be a geostationary satellite? Will

any satellite moving at this height have a time period of 24 hours?

16. No part of India is situated on the equator. Is it possible to have a geostationary satellite which always remains over New Delhi?

17. As the earth rotates about its axis, a person living in his house at the equator goes in a circular orbit of radius equal to the radius of the earth. Why does he/she not feel weightless as a satellite passenger does?

18. Two satellites going in equatorial plane have almost same radii. As seen from the earth one moves from east to west and the other from west to east. Will they have the same time period as seen from the earth? If not, which one will have less time period?

19. A spacecraft consumes more fuel in going from the earth to the moon than it takes for a return trip. Comment on this statement.

OBJECTIVE I

1. The acceleration of moon with respect to earth is 0.0027 m s^{-2} and the acceleration of an apple falling on earth's surface is about 10 m s^{-2}. Assume that the radius of the moon is one fourth of the earth's radius. If the moon is stopped for an instant and then released, it will fall towards the earth. The initial acceleration of the moon towards the earth will be

(a) 10 m s^{-2} (b) 0.0027 m s^{-2} (c) 6.4 m s^{-2} (d) 5.0 m s^{-2}.

2. The acceleration of the moon just before it strikes the earth in the previous question is

(a) 10 m s^{-2} (b) 0.0027 m s^{-2} (c) 6.4 m s^{-2} (d) 5.0 m s^{-2}

3. Suppose, the acceleration due to gravity at the earth's surface is 10 m s^{-2} and at the surface of Mars it is 4.0 m s^{-2}. A 60 kg passenger goes from the earth to the Mars in a spaceship moving with a constant velocity. Neglect all other objects in the sky. Which part of figure (11-Q1) best represents the weight (net gravitational force) of the passenger as a function of time?

(a) A (b) B (c) C (d) D.

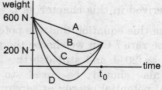

Figure 11-Q2

4. Consider a planet in some solar system which has a mass double the mass of the earth and density equal to the average density of the earth. An object weighing W on the earth will weigh

(a) W (b) $2 W$ (c) $W/2$ (d) $2^{1/3} W$ at the planet.

5. If the acceleration due to gravity at the surface of the earth is g, the work done in slowly lifting a body of mass m from the earth's surface to a height R equal to the radius of the earth is

(a) $\frac{1}{2} mgR$ (b) $2mgR$ (c) mgR (d) $\frac{1}{4} mgR$.

6. A person brings a mass of 1 kg from infinity to a point A. Initially the mass was at rest but it moves at a speed of 2 m s^{-1} as it reaches A. The work done by the person on the mass is -3 J. The potential at A is

(a) -3 J kg^{-1} (b) -2 J kg^{-1} (c) -5 J kg^{-1} (d) none of these.

7. Let V and E be the gravitational potential and gravitational field at a distance r from the centre of a uniform spherical shell. Consider the following two statements:
(A) The plot of V against r is discontinuous.
(B) The plot of E against r is discontinuous.
    (a) Both A and B are correct.
    (b) A is correct but B is wrong.
    (c) B is correct but A is wrong.
    (d) Both A and B are wrong.

8. Let V and E represent the gravitational potential and field at a distance r from the centre of a uniform solid sphere. Consider the two statements:
(A) the plot of V against r is discontinuous.
(B) The plot of E against r is discontinuous.
    (a) Both A and B are correct.
    (b) A is correct but B is wrong.
    (c) B is correct but A is wrong.
    (d) Both A and B are wrong.

9. Take the effect of bulging of earth and its rotation in account. Consider the following statements:
(A) There are points outside the earth where the value of g is equal to its value at the equator.
(B) There are points outside the earth where the value of g is equal to its value at the poles.

(a) Both A and B are correct.
(b) A is correct but B is wrong.
(c) B is correct but A is wrong.
(d) Both A and B are wrong.

10. The time period of an earth-satellite in circular orbit is independent of
(a) the mass of the satellite   (b) radius of the orbit
(c) none of them   (d) both of them.

11. The magnitude of gravitational potential energy of the moon–earth system is U with zero potential energy at infinite separation. The kinetic energy of the moon with respect to the earth is K.
(a) $U < K$ (b) $U > K$ (c) $U = K$.

12. Figure (11-Q2) shows the elliptical path of a planet about the sun. The two shaded parts have equal area. If t_1 and t_2 be the time taken by the planet to go from a to b and from c to d respectively,
(a) $t_1 < t_2$ (b) $t_1 = t_2$ (c) $t_1 > t_2$
(d) insufficient information to deduce the relation between t_1 and t_2.

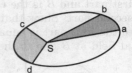

Figure 11-Q2

13. A person sitting in a chair in a satellite feels weightless because

(a) the earth does not attract the objects in a satellite
(b) the normal force by the chair on the person balances the earth's attraction
(c) the normal force is zero
(d) the person in satellite is not accelerated.

14. A body is suspended from a spring balance kept in a satellite. The reading of the balance is W_1 when the satellite goes in an orbit of radius R and is W_2 when it goes in an orbit of radius $2R$.
(a) $W_1 = W_2$ (b) $W_1 < W_2$ (c) $W_1 > W_2$ (d) $W_1 \neq W_2$.

15. The kinetic energy needed to project a body of mass m from the earth's surface to infinity is
(a) $\frac{1}{4} mgR$ (b) $\frac{1}{2} mgR$ (c) mgR (d) $2 mgR$.

16. A particle is kept at rest at a distance R (earth's radius) above the earth's surface. The minimum speed with which it should be projected so that it does not return is
(a) $\sqrt{\dfrac{GM}{4R}}$ (b) $\sqrt{\dfrac{GM}{2R}}$ (c) $\sqrt{\dfrac{GM}{R}}$ (d) $\sqrt{\dfrac{2GM}{R}}$.

17. A satellite is orbiting the earth close to its surface. A particle is to be projected from the satellite to just escape from the earth. The escape speed from the earth is v_e. Its speed with respect to the satellite
(a) will be less than v_e
(b) will be more than v_e
(c) will be equal to v_e
(d) will depend on direction of projection.

OBJECTIVE II

1. Let V and E denote the gravitational potential and gravitational field at a point. It is possible to have
(a) $V = 0$ and $E = 0$ (b) $V = 0$ and $E \neq 0$
(c) $V \neq 0$ and $E = 0$ (d) $V \neq 0$ and $E \neq 0$.

2. Inside a uniform spherical shell
(a) the gravitational potential is zero
(b) the gravitational field is zero
(c) the gravitational potential is same everywhere
(d) the gravitational field is same everywhere.

3. A uniform spherical shell gradually shrinks maintaining its shape. The gravitational potential at the centre
(a) increases   (b) decreases
(c) remains constant   (d) oscillates.

4. Consider a planet moving in an elliptical orbit round the sun. The work done on the planet by the gravitational force of the sun
(a) is zero in any small part of the orbit

(b) is zero in some parts of the orbit
(c) is zero in one complete revolution
(d) is zero in no part of the motion.

5. Two satellites A and B move round the earth in the same orbit. The mass of B is twice the mass of A.
(a) Speeds of A and B are equal.
(b) The potential energy of earth+A is same as that of earth+B.
(c) The kinetic energy of A and B are equal.
(d) The total energy of earth+A is same as that of earth+B.

6. Which of the following quantities remain constant in a planetary motion (consider elliptical orbits) as seen from the sun ?
(a) Speed   (b) Angular speed
(c) Kinetic Energy   (d) Angular momentum.

EXERCISES

1. Two spherical balls of mass 10 kg each are placed 10 cm apart. Find the gravitational force of attraction between them.

2. Four particles having masses m, $2m$, $3m$ and $4m$ are placed at the four corners of a square of edge a. Find

the gravitational force acting on a particle of mass m placed at the centre.

3. Three equal masses m are placed at the three corners of an equilateral triangle of side a. Find the force exerted by this system on another particle of mass m placed at (a) the mid-point of a side, (b) at the centre of the triangle.

4. Three uniform spheres each having a mass M and radius a are kept in such a way that each touches the other two. Find the magnitude of the gravitational force on any of the spheres due to the other two.

5. Four particles of equal masses M move along a circle of radius R under the action of their mutual gravitational attraction. Find the speed of each particle.

6. Find the acceleration due to gravity of the moon at a point 1000 km above the moon's surface. The mass of the moon is 7.4×10^{22} kg and its radius is 1740 km.

7. Two small bodies of masses 10 kg and 20 kg are kept a distance 1·0 m apart and released. Assuming that only mutual gravitational forces are acting, find the speeds of the particles when the separation decreases to 0·5 m.

8. A semicircular wire has a length L and mass M. A particle of mass m is placed at the centre of the circle. Find the gravitational attraction on the particle due to the wire.

9. Derive an expression for the gravitational field due to a uniform rod of length L and mass M at a point on its perpendicular bisector at a distance d from the centre.

10. Two concentric spherical shells have masses M_1, M_2 and radii R_1, R_2 $(R_1 < R_2)$. What is the force exerted by this system on a particle of mass m if it is placed at a distance $(R_1 + R_2)/2$ from the centre ?

11. A tunnel is dug along a diameter of the earth. Find the force on a particle of mass m placed in the tunnel at a distance x from the centre.

12. A tunnel is dug along a chord of the earth at a perpendicular distance $R/2$ from the earth's centre. The wall of the tunnel may be assumed to be frictionless. Find the force exerted by the wall on a particle of mass m when it is at a distance x from the centre of the tunnel.

13. A solid sphere of mass m and radius r is placed inside a hollow thin spherical shell of mass M and radius R as shown in figure (11-E1). A particle of mass m' is placed on the line joining the two centres at a distance x from the point of contact of the sphere and the shell. Find the magnitude of the resultant gravitational force on this particle due to the sphere and the shell if (a) $r < x < 2r$, (b) $2r < x < 2R$ and (c) $x > 2R$.

Figure 11-E1

14. A uniform metal sphere of radius a and mass M is surrounded by a thin uniform spherical shell of equal mass and radius $4a$ (figure 11-E2). The centre of the shell falls on the surface of the inner sphere. Find the gravitational field at the points P_1 and P_2 shown in the figure.

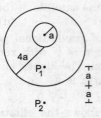

Figure 11-E2

15. A thin spherical shell having uniform density is cut in two parts by a plane and kept separated as shown in figure (11-E3). The point A is the centre of the plane section of the first part and B is the centre of the plane section of the second part. Show that the gravitational field at A due to the first part is equal in magnitude to the gravitational field at B due to the second part.

Figure 11-E3

16. Two small bodies of masses 2.00 kg and 4.00 kg are kept at rest at a separation of 2·0 m. Where should a particle of mass 0.10 kg be placed to experience no net gravitational force from these bodies ? The particle is placed at this point. What is the gravitational potential energy of the system of three particles with usual reference level ?

17. Three particles of mass m each are placed at the three corners of an equilateral triangle of side a. Find the work which should be done on this system to increase the sides of the triangle to $2a$.

18. A particle of mass 100 g is kept on the surface of a uniform sphere of mass 10 kg and radius 10 cm. Find the work to be done against the gravitational force between them to take the particle away from the sphere.

19. The gravitational field in a region is given by $\vec{E} = (5 \text{ N kg}^{-1})\,\vec{i} + (12 \text{ N kg}^{-1})\,\vec{j}$. (a) Find the magnitude of the gravitational force acting on a particle of mass 2 kg placed at the origin. (b) Find the potential at the points (12 m, 0) and (0, 5 m) if the potential at the origin is taken to be zero. (c) Find the change in gravitational potential energy if a particle of mass 2 kg is taken from the origin to the point (12 m, 5 m). (d) Find the change in potential energy if the particle is taken from (12 m, 0) to (0, 5 m).

20. The gravitational potential in a region is given by $V = 20 \text{ N kg}^{-1} (x + y)$. (a) Show that the equation is dimensionally correct. (b) Find the gravitational field at the point (x, y). Leave your answer in terms of the unit vectors $\vec{i}, \vec{j}, \vec{k}$. (c) Calculate the magnitude of the gravitational force on a particle of mass 500 g placed at the origin.

21. The gravitational field in a region is given by $\vec{E} = (2\vec{i} + 3\vec{j}) \text{ N kg}^{-1}$. Show that no work is done by the gravitational field when a particle is moved on the line $3y + 2x = 5$.

[**Hint :** If a line $y = mx + c$ makes angle θ with the X-axis, $m = \tan\theta$.]

22. Find the height over the earth's surface at which the weight of a body becomes half of its value at the surface.

23. What is the acceleration due to gravity on the top of Mount Everest ? Mount Everest is the highest mountain peak of the world at the height of 8848 m. The value at sea level is $9\cdot80 \text{ m s}^{-2}$.

24. Find the acceleration due to gravity in a mine of depth 640 m if the value at the surface is $9\cdot800 \text{ m s}^{-2}$. The radius of the earth is 6400 km.

25. A body is weighed by a spring balance to be $1\cdot000$ kg at the north pole. How much will it weigh at the equator ? Account for the earth's rotation only.

26. A body stretches a spring by a particular length at the earth's surface at equator. At what height above the south pole will it stretch the same spring by the same length ? Assume the earth to be spherical.

27. At what rate should the earth rotate so that the apparent g at the equator becomes zero ? What will be the length of the day in this situation ?

28. A pendulum having a bob of mass m is hanging in a ship sailing along the equator from east to west. When the ship is stationary with respect to water the tension in the string is T_0. (a) Find the speed of the ship due to rotation of the earth about its axis. (b) Find the difference between T_0 and the earth's attraction on the bob. (c) If the ship sails at speed v, what is the tension in the string ? Angular speed of earth's rotation is ω and radius of the earth is R.

29. The time taken by Mars to revolve round the sun is $1\cdot88$ years. Find the ratio of average distance between Mars and the sun to that between the earth and the sun.

30. The moon takes about $27\cdot3$ days to revolve round the earth in a nearly circular orbit of radius $3\cdot84 \times 10^5$ km. Calculate the mass of the earth from these data.

31. A Mars satellite moving in an orbit of radius $9\cdot4 \times 10^3$ km takes 27540 s to complete one revolution. Calculate the mass of Mars.

32. A satellite of mass 1000 kg is supposed to orbit the earth at a height of 2000 km above the earth's surface. Find (a) its speed in the orbit, (b) its kinetic energy, (c) the potential energy of the earth–satellite system and (d) its time period. Mass of the earth $= 6 \times 10^{24}$ kg.

33. (a) Find the radius of the circular orbit of a satellite moving with an angular speed equal to the angular speed of earth's rotation. (b) If the satellite is directly above the north pole at some instant, find the time it takes to come over the equatorial plane. Mass of the earth $= 6 \times 10^{24}$ kg.

34. What is the true weight of an object in a geostationary satellite that weighed exactly $10\cdot0$ N at the north pole ?

35. The radius of a planet is R_1 and a satellite revolves round it in a circle of radius R_2. The time period of revolution is T. Find the acceleration due to the gravitation of the planet at its surface.

36. Find the minimum colatitude which can directly receive a signal from a geostationary satellite.

37. A particle is fired vertically upward from earth's surface and it goes up to a maximum height of 6400 km. Find the initial speed of particle.

38. A particle is fired vertically upward with a speed of 15 km s^{-1}. With what speed will it move in intersteller space. Assume only earth's gravitational field.

39. A mass of 6×10^{24} kg (equal to the mass of the earth) is to be compressed in a sphere in such a way that the escape velocity from its surface is 3×10^8 m s^{-1}. What should be the radius of the sphere ?

□

ANSWERS

OBJECTIVE I

1. (b)	2. (c)	3. (c)	4. (d)	5. (a)	6. (c)
7. (c)	8. (d)	9. (b)	10. (a)	11. (b)	12. (b)
13. (c)	14. (a)	15. (c)	16. (c)	17. (d)	

OBJECTIVE II

1. all   2. (b), (c), (d)   3. (b)   4. (b), (c)   5. (a)   6. (d)

EXERCISES

1. $6\cdot67 \times 10^{-7}$ N

2. $\dfrac{4\sqrt{2}\, Gm^2}{a^2}$

3. (a) $\dfrac{4Gm^2}{3a^2}$, (b) zero

4. $\dfrac{\sqrt{3}\, GM^2}{4a^2}$

5. $\sqrt{\dfrac{GM}{R}\left(\dfrac{2\sqrt{2}+1}{4}\right)}$

6. 0.65 m s^{-2}

7. $4.2 \times 10^{-5} \text{ m s}^{-1}$ and $2.1 \times 10^{-5} \text{ m s}^{-1}$

8. $\dfrac{2\pi\,GMm}{L^2}$

9. $\dfrac{2\,Gm}{d\sqrt{L^2+4\,d^2}}$

10. $\dfrac{4GM_1m}{(R_1+R_2)^2}$

11. $\dfrac{GM_em}{R^3}\,x$

12. $\dfrac{GM_em}{2R^2}$

13. (a) $\dfrac{Gmm'(x-r)}{r^3}$ (b) $\dfrac{Gmm'}{(x-r)^2}$ (c) $\dfrac{GMm'}{(x-R)^2}+\dfrac{Gmm'}{(x-r)^2}$

14. $\dfrac{GM}{16a^2}$, $\dfrac{61\,GM}{900a^2}$

16. 0.83 m from the 2.00 kg body towards the other body, -3.06×10^{-10} J

17. $\dfrac{3Gm^2}{2a}$

18. 6.67×10^{-10} J

19. (a) 26 N   (b) -60 J kg^{-1}, -60 J kg^{-1} (c) -240 J (d) zero

20. (b) $-20(\vec{i}+\vec{j})\,\text{Nkg}^{-1}$ (c) $10\sqrt{2}$ N

22. $(\sqrt{2}-1)$ times the radius of the earth

23. 9.77 m s^{-2}

24. 9.799 m s^{-2}

25. 0.997 kg

26. 10 km approx.

27. $1.237 \times 10^{-3} \text{ rads}^{-1}$, 1.41 h

28. (a) ωR (b) $m\omega^2 R$ (c) $T_0 + 2\,m\omega v$ approx.

29. 1.52

30. 6.02×10^{24} kg

31. 6.5×10^{23} kg

32. (a) 6.90 kms^{-1} (b) 2.38×10^{10} J (c) -4.76×10^{10} J with usual reference (d) 2.12 hours

33. (a) 42300 km   (b) 6 hours

34. 0.23 N

35. $\dfrac{4\pi^2 R_2^3}{T^2 R_1^2}$

36. $\sin^{-1}(0.15)$

37. 7.9 km s^{-1}

38. 10.0 km s^{-1}

39. ≈ 9 mm

CHAPTER 12

SIMPLE HARMONIC MOTION

12.1 SIMPLE HARMONIC MOTION

When a body repeats its motion after regular time intervals we say that it is in *harmonic motion* or *periodic motion*. The time interval after which the motion is repeated is called the *time period*. If a body moves to and fro on the same path, it is said to perform *oscillations*. *Simple harmonic motion* (SHM) is a special type of oscillation in which the particle oscillates on a straight line, the acceleration of the particle is always directed towards a fixed point on the line and its magnitude is proportional to the displacement of the particle from this point. This fixed point is called the *centre of oscillation*. Taking this point as the origin and the line of motion as the X-axis, we can write the defining equation of a simple harmonic motion as

$$a = -\omega^2 x \qquad \ldots (12.1)$$

where ω^2 is a positive constant. If x is positive, a is negative and if x is negative, a is positive. This means that the acceleration is always directed towards the centre of oscillation.

If we are looking at the motion from an inertial frame,

$$a = F/m.$$

The defining equation (12.1) may thus be written as

$$F/m = -\omega^2 x$$
$$\text{or,} \qquad F = -m\omega^2 x$$
$$\text{or,} \qquad F = -kx. \qquad \ldots (12.2)$$

We can use equation (12.2) as the definition of SHM. A particle moving on a straight line executes simple harmonic motion if the resultant force acting on it is directed towards a fixed point on the line and is proportional to the displacement of the particle from this fixed point. The constant $k = m\omega^2$ is called the *force constant* or *spring constant*. The resultant force on the particle is zero when it is at the centre of oscillation. The centre of oscillation is, therefore, the

equilibrium position. A force which takes the particle back towards the equilibrium position is called a *restoring force*. Equation (12.2) represents a restoring force which is linear. Figure (12.1) shows the linear restoring force graphically.

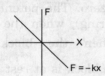

Figure 12.1

Example 12.1

The resultant force acting on a particle executing simple harmonic motion is 4 N *when it is* 5 cm *away from the centre of oscillation. Find the spring constant.*

Solution : The simple harmonic motion is defined as

$$F = -k\,x.$$

The spring constant is $k = \left| \dfrac{F}{x} \right|$

$$= \frac{4\,\text{N}}{5\,\text{cm}} = \frac{4\,\text{N}}{5 \times 10^{-2}\,\text{m}} = 80\,\text{N m}^{-1}.$$

12.2 QUALITATIVE NATURE OF SIMPLE HARMONIC MOTION

Let us consider a small block of mass m placed on a smooth horizontal surface and attached to a fixed wall through a spring as shown in figure (12.2). Let the spring constant of the spring be k.

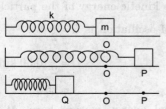

Figure 12.2

The block is at a position O when the spring is at its natural length. Suppose the block is taken to a point P stretching the spring by the distance $OP = A$ and is released from there.

At any point on its path the displacement x of the particle is equal to the extension of the spring from its natural length. The resultant force on the particle is given by $F = -kx$ and hence by definition the motion of the block is simple harmonic.

When the block is released from P, the force acts towards the centre O. The block is accelerated in that direction. The force continues to act towards O until the block reaches O. The speed thus increases all the time from P to O. When the block reaches O, its speed is maximum and it is going towards left. As it moves towards left from O, the spring becomes compressed. The spring pushes the block towards right and hence its speed decreases. The block moves to a point Q when its speed becomes zero. The potential energy of the system (block + spring), when the block is at P, is $\frac{1}{2} k (OP)^2$ and when the block is at Q it is $\frac{1}{2} k (OQ)^2$. Since the block is at rest at P as well as at Q, the kinetic energy is zero at both these positions. As we have assumed frictionless surface, principle of conservation of energy gives

$$\frac{1}{2} k (OP)^2 = \frac{1}{2} k (OQ)^2$$

or, $\qquad\qquad OP = OQ.$

The spring is now compressed and hence it pushes the block towards right. The block starts moving towards right, its speed increases upto O and then decreases to zero when it reaches P. Thus the particle oscillates between P and Q. As $OP = OQ$, it moves through equal distances on both sides of the centre of oscillation. The maximum displacement on either side from the centre of oscillation is called the *amplitude*.

Example 12.2

A particle of mass 0.50 kg executes a simple harmonic motion under a force $F = -(50 \text{ N m}^{-1})x$. If it crosses the centre of oscillation with a speed of 10 m s^{-1}, find the amplitude of the motion.

Solution : The kinetic energy of the particle when it is at the centre of oscillation is $E = \frac{1}{2} m v^2$

$$= \frac{1}{2} (0.50 \text{ kg}) (10 \text{ m s}^{-1})^2$$

$$= 25 \text{ J}.$$

The potential energy is zero here. At the maximum displacement $x = A$, the speed is zero and hence the

kinetic energy is zero. The potential energy here is $\frac{1}{2} k A^2$. As there is no loss of energy,

$$\frac{1}{2} k A^2 = 25 \text{ J}. \qquad\qquad \dots \text{ (i)}$$

The force on the particle is given by

$$F = -(50 \text{ N m}^{-1})x.$$

Thus, the spring constant is $k = 50 \text{ N m}^{-1}$.
Equation (i) gives

$$\frac{1}{2} (50 \text{ N m}^{-1}) A^2 = 25 \text{ J}$$

or, $\qquad\qquad A = 1 \text{ m}.$

12.3 EQUATION OF MOTION OF A SIMPLE HARMONIC MOTION

Consider a particle of mass m moving along the X-axis. Suppose, a force $F = -kx$ acts on the particle where k is a positive constant and x is the displacement of the particle from the assumed origin. The particle then executes a simple harmonic motion with the centre of oscillation at the origin. We shall calculate the displacement x and the velocity v as a function of time.

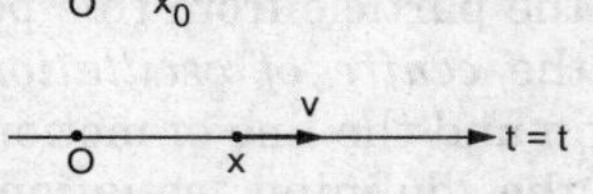

Figure 12.3

Suppose the position of the particle at $t = 0$ is x_0 and its velocity is v_0. Thus,

at $t = 0$, $x = x_0$ and $v = v_0$.

The acceleration of the particle at any instant is

$$a = \frac{F}{m} = -\frac{k}{m} x = -\omega^2 x$$

where $\quad \omega = \sqrt{km^{-1}}.$

Thus, $\qquad \dfrac{dv}{dt} = -\omega^2 x \qquad\qquad \dots \text{ (12.3)}$

or, $\qquad \dfrac{dv}{dx} \dfrac{dx}{dt} = -\omega^2 x$

or, $\qquad v \dfrac{dv}{dx} = -\omega^2 x$

or, $\qquad v\,dv = -\omega^2 x\,dx.$

The velocity of the particle is v_0 when the particle is at $x = x_0$. It becomes v when the displacement becomes x. We can integrate the above equation and write

$$\int_{v_0}^{v} v\,dv = \int_{x_0}^{x} -\omega^2 x\,dx$$

or, $\left[\dfrac{v^2}{2}\right]_{v_0}^{v} = -\omega^2 \left[\dfrac{x^2}{2}\right]_{x_0}^{x}$

or, $v^2 - v_0^2 = -\omega^2(x^2 - x_0^2)$

or, $v^2 = (v_0^2 + \omega^2 x_0^2 - \omega^2 x^2)$

or, $v = \sqrt{(v_0^2 + \omega^2 x_0^2) - \omega^2 x^2}$

or, $v = \omega \sqrt{\left(\dfrac{v_0^2}{\omega^2} + x_0^2\right) - x^2}$.

Writing $\left(\dfrac{v_0}{\omega}\right)^2 + x_0^2 = A^2$ ... (12.4)

the above equation becomes

$v = \omega \sqrt{A^2 - x^2}$. ... (12.5)

We can write this equation as

$\dfrac{dx}{dt} = \omega \sqrt{A^2 - x^2}$

or, $\dfrac{dx}{\sqrt{A^2 - x^2}} = \omega\, dt$.

At time $t = 0$ the displacement is $x = x_0$ and at time t the displacement becomes x. The above equation can be integrated as

$\int_{x_0}^{x} \dfrac{dx}{\sqrt{A^2 - x^2}} = \int_0^t \omega\, dt$

or, $\left[\sin^{-1}\dfrac{x}{A}\right]_{x_0}^{x} = [\omega t]_0^t$

or, $\sin^{-1}\dfrac{x}{A} - \sin^{-1}\dfrac{x_0}{A} = \omega t$.

Writing $\sin^{-1}\dfrac{x_0}{A} = \delta$, this becomes

$\sin^{-1}\dfrac{x}{A} = \omega t + \delta$

or, $x = A\sin(\omega t + \delta)$. ... (12.6)

The velocity at time t is

$v = \dfrac{dx}{dt} = A\omega\cos(\omega t + \delta)$. ... (12.7)

12.4 TERMS ASSOCIATED WITH SIMPLE HARMONIC MOTION

(a) Amplitude

Equation (12.6) gives the displacement of a particle in simple harmonic motion. As $\sin(\omega t + \delta)$ can take values between -1 and $+1$, the displacement x can take values between $-A$ and $+A$. This gives the physical significance of the constant A. It is the maximum displacement of the particle from the centre of oscillation, i.e, the amplitude of oscillation.

(b) Time Period

A particle in simple harmonic motion repeats its motion after a regular time interval. Suppose the particle is at a position x and its velocity is v at a certain time t. After some time the position of the particle will again be x and its velocity will again be v in the same direction. This part of the motion is called *one complete oscillation* and the time taken in one complete oscillation is called the *time period T*. Thus, in figure (12.4) Q to P and then back to Q is a complete oscillation, R to P to Q to R is a complete oscillation, O to P to Q to O is a complete oscillation, etc. Both the position and the velocity (magnitude as well as direction) repeat after each complete oscillation.

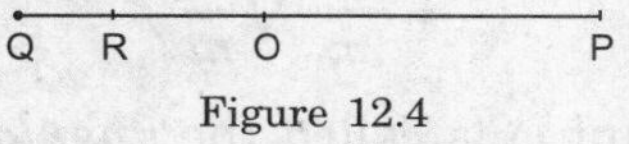

Figure 12.4

We have,

$x = A\sin(\omega t + \delta)$.

If T be the time period, x should have same value at t and $t + T$.

Thus, $\sin(\omega t + \delta) = \sin[\omega(t + T) + \delta]$.

Now the velocity is (equation 12.7)

$v = A\omega\cos(\omega t + \delta)$.

As the velocity also repeats its value after a time period, $\cos(\omega t + \delta) = \cos[\omega(t + T) + \delta]$.

Both $\sin(\omega t + \delta)$ and $\cos(\omega t + \delta)$ will repeat their values if the angle $(\omega t + \delta)$ increases by 2π or its multiple. As T is the smallest time for repetition,

$\omega(t + T) + \delta = (\omega t + \delta) + 2\pi$

or, $\omega T = 2\pi$

or, $T = \dfrac{2\pi}{\omega}$.

Remembering that $\omega = \sqrt{km^{-1}}$, we can write for the time period,

$T = \dfrac{2\pi}{\omega} = 2\pi\sqrt{\dfrac{m}{k}}$ ... (12.8)

where k is the force constant and m is the mass of the particle.

Example 12.3

A particle of mass 200 g executes a simple harmonic motion. The restoring force is provided by a spring of spring constant 80 N m^{-1}. Find the time period.

Solution : The time period is

$T = 2\pi\sqrt{\dfrac{m}{k}}$

$$= 2\pi \sqrt{\frac{200 \times 10^{-3}\,\text{kg}}{80\,\text{N m}^{-1}}}$$

$$= 2\pi \times 0.05\,\text{s} = 0.31\,\text{s}.$$

(c) Frequency and Angular Frequency

The reciprocal of time period is called the *frequency*. Physically, the frequency represents the number of oscillations per unit time. It is measured in cycles per second also known as *hertz* and written in symbols as Hz. Equation (12.8) shows that the frequency is

$$\nu = \frac{1}{T} = \frac{\omega}{2\pi} \qquad \ldots (12.9)$$

$$= \frac{1}{2\pi} \sqrt{\frac{k}{m}}. \qquad \ldots (12.10)$$

The constant ω is called the *angular frequency*.

(d) Phase

The quantity $\phi = \omega t + \delta$ is called the phase. It determines the status of the particle in simple harmonic motion. If the phase is zero at a certain instant, $x = A \sin(\omega t + \delta) = 0$ and $v = A\omega \cos(\omega t + \delta) = A\omega$. This means that the particle is crossing the mean position and is going towards the positive direction. If the phase is $\pi/2$, we get $x = A$, $v = 0$ so that the particle is at the positive extreme position. Figure (12.5) shows the status of the particle at different phases.

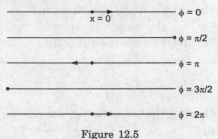

Figure 12.5

We see that as time increases the phase increases. An increase of 2π brings the particle to the same status in the motion. Thus, a phase $\omega t + \delta$ is equivalent to a phase $\omega t + \delta + 2\pi$. Similarly, a phase change of 4π, 6π, 8π, ..., etc., are equivalent to no phase change.

Figure (12.6) shows graphically the variation of position and velocity as a function of the phase.

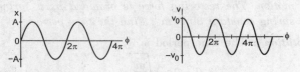

Figure 12.6

(e) Phase constant

The constant δ appearing in equation (12.6) is called the *phase constant*. This constant depends on the choice of the instant $t = 0$. To describe the motion quantitatively, a particular instant should be called $t = 0$ and measurement of time should be made from this instant. This instant may be chosen according to the convenience of the problem. Suppose we choose $t = 0$ at an instant when the particle is passing through its mean position and is going towards the positive direction. The phase $\omega t + \delta$ should then be zero. As $t = 0$ this means δ will be zero. The equation for displacement can then be written as

$$x = A \sin\omega t.$$

If we choose $t = 0$ at an instant when the particle is at its positive extreme position, the phase is $\pi/2$ at this instant. Thus $\omega t + \delta = \pi/2$ and hence $\delta = \pi/2$. The equation for the displacement is $x = A \sin(\omega t + \pi/2)$

or, $\qquad\qquad x = A \cos\omega t.$

Any instant can be chosen as $t = 0$ and hence the phase constant can be chosen arbitrarily. Quite often we shall choose $\delta = 0$ and write the equation for displacement as $x = A \sin\omega t$. Sometimes we may have to consider two or more simple harmonic motions together. The phase constant of any one can be chosen as $\delta = 0$. The phase constants of the rest will be determined by the actual situation. The general equation for displacement may be written as

$$x = A \sin(\omega t + \delta)$$
$$= A \sin\left(\omega t + \frac{\pi}{2} + \delta'\right)$$
$$= A \cos(\omega t + \delta')$$

where δ' is another arbitrary constant. The sine form and the cosine form are, therefore, equivalent. The value of phase constant, however, depends on the form chosen.

Example 12.4

A particle executes simple harmonic motion of amplitude A along the X-axis. At $t = 0$, the position of the particle is $x = A/2$ and it moves along the positive x-direction. Find the phase constant δ if the equation is written as $x = A \sin(\omega t + \delta)$.

Solution : We have $x = A \sin(\omega t + \delta)$. At $t = 0$, $x = A/2$.

Thus, $\qquad A/2 = A \sin\delta$

or, $\qquad \sin\delta = 1/2$

or, $\qquad \delta = \pi/6$ or $5\pi/6$.

The velocity is $v = \dfrac{dx}{dt} = A\omega \cos(\omega t + \delta)$.

At $\qquad t = 0$, $v = A\omega \cos\delta$.

Now, $\qquad \cos\dfrac{\pi}{6} = \dfrac{\sqrt{3}}{2}$ and $\cos\dfrac{5\pi}{6} = -\dfrac{\sqrt{3}}{2}$.

As v is positive at $t = 0$, δ must be equal to $\pi/6$.

12.5 SIMPLE HARMONIC MOTION AS A PROJECTION OF CIRCULAR MOTION

Consider a particle P moving on a circle of radius A with a constant angular speed ω (figure 12.7). Let us take the centre of the circle as the origin and two perpendicular diameters as the X and Y-axes. Suppose the particle P is on the X-axis at $t = 0$. The radius OP will make an angle $\theta = \omega t$ with the X-axis at time t. Drop perpendicular PQ on X-axis and PR on Y-axis. The x and y-coordinates of the particle at time t are

$$x = OQ = OP \cos \omega t$$

or,
$$x = A \cos \omega t \qquad \ldots (12.11)$$

and
$$y = OR = OP \sin \omega t$$

or,
$$y = A \sin \omega t. \qquad \ldots (12.12)$$

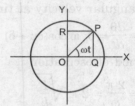

Figure 12.7

Equation (12.11) shows that the foot of perpendicular Q executes a simple harmonic motion on the X-axis. The amplitude is A and the angular frequency is ω. Similarly, equation (12.12) shows that the foot of perpendicular R executes a simple harmonic motion on the Y-axis. The amplitude is A and the angular frequency is ω. The phases of the two simple harmonic motions differ by $\pi/2$ [remember $\cos \omega t = \sin(\omega t + \pi/2)$].

Thus, the projection of a uniform circular motion on a diameter of the circle is a simple harmonic motion.

12.6 ENERGY CONSERVATION IN SIMPLE HARMONIC MOTION

Simple harmonic motion is defined by the equation
$$F = -kx.$$

The work done by the force F during a displacement from x to $x + dx$ is
$$dW = F \, dx$$
$$= -kx \, dx.$$

The work done in a displacement from $x = 0$ to x is
$$W = \int_0^x (-kx)dx = -\frac{1}{2}kx^2.$$

Let $U(x)$ be the potential energy of the system when the displacement is x. As the change in potential energy corresponding to a force is negative of the work done by this force,
$$U(x) - U(0) = -W = \frac{1}{2}kx^2.$$

Let us choose the potential energy to be zero when the particle is at the centre of oscillation $x = 0$.

Then
$$U(0) = 0 \text{ and } U(x) = \frac{1}{2}kx^2.$$

This expression for potential energy is same as that for a spring and has been used so far in this chapter.

As
$$\omega = \sqrt{\frac{k}{m}}, \quad k = m \omega^2$$

we can write $U(x) = \frac{1}{2} m \omega^2 x^2.$ $\qquad \ldots (12.13)$

The displacement and the velocity of a particle executing a simple harmonic motion are given by
$$x = A \sin(\omega t + \delta)$$
and
$$v = A \omega \cos(\omega t + \delta).$$

The potential energy at time t is, therefore,
$$U = \frac{1}{2} m \omega^2 x^2$$
$$= \frac{1}{2} m \omega^2 A^2 \sin^2(\omega t + \delta),$$

and the kinetic energy at time t is
$$K = \frac{1}{2} m v^2$$
$$= \frac{1}{2} m A^2 \omega^2 \cos^2(\omega t + \delta).$$

The total mechanical energy at time t is
$$E = U + K$$
$$= \frac{1}{2} m \omega^2 A^2 [\sin^2(\omega t + \delta) + (\cos^2(\omega t + \delta)]$$
$$= \frac{1}{2} m \omega^2 A^2. \qquad \ldots (12.14)$$

We see that the total mechanical energy at time t is independent of t. Thus, the mechanical energy remains constant as expected.

As an example, consider a small block of mass m placed on a smooth horizontal surface and attached to a fixed wall through a spring of spring constant k (figure 12.8).

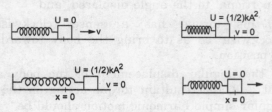

Figure 12.8

When displaced from the mean position (where the spring has its natural length), the block executes a simple harmonic motion. The spring is the agency exerting a force $F = -kx$ on the block. The potential energy of the system is the elastic potential energy stored in the spring.

At the mean position $x = 0$, the potential energy is zero. The kinetic energy is $\frac{1}{2} m v_0^2 = \frac{1}{2} m \omega^2 A^2$. All the mechanical energy is in the form of kinetic energy here. As the particle is displaced away from the mean position, the kinetic energy decreases and the potential energy increases. At the extreme positions $x = \pm A$, the speed v is zero and the kinetic energy decreases to zero. The potential energy is increased to its maximum value $\frac{1}{2} kA^2 = \frac{1}{2} m \omega^2 A^2$. All the mechanical energy is in the form of potential energy here.

Example 12.5

A particle of mass 40 g executes a simple harmonic motion of amplitude 2·0 cm. If the time period is 0·20 s, find the total mechanical energy of the system.

Solution : The total mechanical energy of the system is

$$E = \frac{1}{2} m \omega^2 A^2$$

$$= \frac{1}{2} m \left(\frac{2\pi}{T} \right)^2 A^2 = \frac{2\pi^2 m A^2}{T^2}$$

$$= \frac{2\pi^2 (40 \times 10^{-3} \text{ kg})(2 \cdot 0 \times 10^{-2} \text{ m})^2}{(0 \cdot 20 \text{ s})^2}$$

$$= 7 \cdot 9 \times 10^{-3} \text{ J}.$$

12.7 ANGULAR SIMPLE HARMONIC MOTION

A body free to rotate about a given axis can make angular oscillations. For example, a hanging umbrella makes angular oscillations when it is slightly pushed aside and released. The angular oscillations are called angular simple harmonic motion if

(a) there is a position of the body where the resultant torque on the body is zero, this position is the mean position $\theta = 0$,

(b) when the body is displaced through an angle from the mean position, a resultant torque acts which is proportional to the angle displaced, and

(c) this torque has a sense (clockwise or anticlockwise) so as to bring the body towards the mean position.

If the angular displacement of the body at an instant is θ, the resultant torque acting on the body in angular simple harmonic motion should be

$$\Gamma = -k\,\theta.$$

If the moment of inertia is I, the angular acceleration is

$$\alpha = \frac{\Gamma}{I} = -\frac{k}{I}\,\theta$$

or,

$$\frac{d^2\theta}{dt^2} = -\omega^2\,\theta \qquad \ldots \ (12.15)$$

where

$$\omega = \sqrt{kI^{-1}}.$$

Equation (12.15) is identical to equation (12.3) except for the symbols. The linear displacement x in (12.3) is replaced here by the angular displacement θ. Thus, equation (12.15) may be integrated in the similar manner and we shall get an equation similar to (12.6), i.e.,

$$\theta = \theta_0 \sin(\omega t + \delta) \qquad \ldots \ (12.16)$$

where θ_0 is the maximum angular displacement on either side. The angular velocity at time t is given by,

$$\Omega = \frac{d\theta}{dt} = \theta_0 \,\omega \cos(\omega t + \delta). \qquad \ldots \ (12.17)$$

The time period of oscillation is

$$T = \frac{2\pi}{\omega} = 2\pi \sqrt{\frac{I}{k}} \qquad \ldots \ (12.18)$$

and the frequency of oscillation is

$$\nu = \frac{1}{T} = \frac{1}{2\pi} \sqrt{\frac{k}{I}}. \qquad \ldots \ (12.19)$$

The quantity $\omega = \sqrt{kI^{-1}}$ is the angular frequency.

Example 12.6

A body makes angular simple harmonic motion of amplitude $\pi/10$ rad and time period 0·05 s. If the body is at a displacement $\theta = \pi/10$ rad at $t = 0$, write the equation giving the angular displacement as a function of time.

Solution : Let the required equation be
$$\theta = \theta_0 \sin(\omega t + \delta).$$

Here $\theta_0 = \text{amplitude} = \frac{\pi}{10} \text{ rad}$

$$\omega = \frac{2\pi}{T} = \frac{2\pi}{0 \cdot 05 \text{ s}} = 40\pi \text{ s}^{-1}$$

so that $\theta = \left(\frac{\pi}{10} \text{ rad} \right) \sin \left[\left(40\pi \text{ s}^{-1} \right) t + \delta \right].$ ... (i)

At $t = 0$, $\theta = \pi/10$ rad. Putting in (i),

$$\frac{\pi}{10} = \left(\frac{\pi}{10} \right) \sin \delta$$

or, $\sin \delta = 1$

or, $\delta = \pi/2.$

Thus by (i),

$$\theta = \left(\frac{\pi}{10} \text{ rad} \right) \sin \left[(40\pi \text{ s}^{-1}) t + \frac{\pi}{2} \right]$$

$$= \left(\frac{\pi}{10} \text{ rad} \right) \cos[(40\pi \text{ s}^{-1}) t].$$

Energy

The potential energy is

$$U = \frac{1}{2} k \theta^2 = \frac{1}{2} I \omega^2 \theta^2$$

and the kinetic energy is

$$K = \frac{1}{2} I \Omega^2.$$

The total energy is

$$E = U + K$$
$$= \frac{1}{2} I \omega^2 \theta^2 + \frac{1}{2} I \Omega^2.$$

Using $\quad \theta = \theta_0 \sin(\omega t + \delta)$

$$E = \frac{1}{2} I \omega^2 \theta_0^2 \sin^2(\omega t + \delta)$$
$$+ \frac{1}{2} I \theta_0^2 \omega^2 \cos^2(\omega t + \delta)$$
$$= \frac{1}{2} I \omega^2 \theta_0^2. \qquad \dots (12.20)$$

12.8 SIMPLE PENDULUM

A simple pendulum consists of a heavy particle suspended from a fixed support through a light inextensible string. Simple pendulum is an idealised model. In practice, one takes a small metallic sphere and suspends it through a string.

Figure (12.9) shows a simple pendulum in which a particle of mass m is suspended from the fixed support O through a light string of length l. The system can stay in equilibrium if the string is vertical. This is the mean or equilibrium position. If the particle is pulled aside and released, it oscillates in a circular arc with the centre at the point of suspension O.

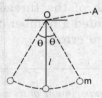

Figure 12.9

The position of the particle at any time can be described by the angle θ between the string and the vertical. The mean position or the equilibrium position corresponds to $\theta = 0$. The particle makes pure rotation about the horizontal line OA (figure 12.9) which is perpendicular to the plane of motion.

Let us see whether the motion of the particle is simple harmonic or not and find out its time period of oscillation.

Let the particle be at P at a time t when the string OP makes an angle θ with the vertical (figure 12.10).

Let OQ be the horizontal line in the plane of motion. Let PQ be the perpendicular to OQ.

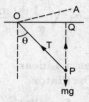

Figure 12.10

Forces acting on the particle are (a) the weight mg and (b) the tension T.

The torque of T about OA is zero as it intersects OA. The magnitude of the torque of mg about OA is

$$|\Gamma| = (mg)(OQ)$$
$$= mg (OP) \sin\theta$$
$$= mgl \sin\theta.$$

Also, the torque tries to bring the particle back towards $\theta = 0$. Thus, we can write

$$\Gamma = -mgl \sin\theta. \qquad \dots (12.21)$$

We see that the resultant torque is not proportional to the angular displacement and hence the motion is not angular simple harmonic. However, if the angular displacement is small, $\sin\theta$ is approximately equal to θ (expressed in radians) and equation (12.21) may be written as

$$\Gamma = -mgl\, \theta. \qquad \dots (12.22)$$

Thus, if the amplitude of oscillation is small, the motion of the particle is approximately angular simple harmonic. The moment of inertia of the particle about the axis of rotation OA is

$$I = m(OP)^2 = ml^2.$$

The angular acceleration is

$$\alpha = \frac{\Gamma}{I} = -\frac{mgl\,\theta}{ml^2} = -\frac{g}{l}\,\theta$$

or, $\qquad \alpha = -\omega^2 \theta$

where $\qquad \omega = \sqrt{gl^{-1}}.$

This is the equation of an angular simple harmonic motion. The constant $\omega = \sqrt{gl^{-1}}$ represents the angular frequency. The time period is

$$T = \frac{2\pi}{\omega} = 2\pi \sqrt{l/g}. \qquad \dots (12.23)$$

Example 12.7

Calculate the time period of a simple pendulum of length one meter. The acceleration due to gravity at the place is $\pi^2 \text{ m s}^{-2}$.

Solution : The time period is

$$T = 2\pi \sqrt{lg^{-1}}$$

$$= 2\pi \sqrt{\frac{1 \cdot 00 \text{ m}}{\pi^2 \text{ m s}^{-2}}} = 2 \cdot 0 \text{ s}.$$

Simple Pendulum as a Linear Simple Harmonic Oscillator

If the amplitude of oscillation is small, the path of the particle is approximately a straight line and the motion can be described as a linear simple harmonic motion. We rederive expression (12.23) for the time period using this approach.

Consider the situation shown in figure (12.11).

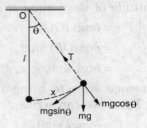

Figure 12.11

Suppose the string makes an angle θ with the vertical at time t. The distance of the particle from the equilibrium position along the arc is $x = l\theta$. The speed of the particle at time t is

$$v = \frac{dx}{dt}$$

and the tangential acceleration is

$$a_t = \frac{dv}{dt} = \frac{d^2x}{dt^2}. \qquad \ldots \text{(i)}$$

Forces acting on the particle are (a) the weight mg and (b) the tension T. The component of mg along the tangent to the path is $-mg\sin\theta$ and that of T is zero. Thus, the total tangential force on the particle is $-mg\sin\theta$. Using (i) we get

$$-mg\sin\theta = m\frac{d^2x}{dt^2}$$

or, $$\frac{d^2x}{dt^2} = -g\sin\theta. \qquad \ldots \text{(ii)}$$

If the amplitude of oscillation is small, $\sin\theta \approx \theta = xl^{-1}$. Equation (ii) above thus becomes (for small oscillations)

$$\frac{d^2x}{dt^2} = -\frac{g}{l}x$$

or, $$\frac{d^2x}{dt^2} = -\omega^2 x$$

where $$\omega = \sqrt{gl^{-1}}.$$

This equation represents a simple harmonic motion of the particle along the arc of the circle in which it moves. The angular frequency is $\omega = \sqrt{gl^{-1}}$ and the time period is

$$T = \frac{2\pi}{\omega} = 2\pi \sqrt{lg^{-1}}$$

which is same as in equation (12.23).

Determination of g in Laboratory

A simple pendulum provides an easy method to measure the value of 'g' in a laboratory. A small spherical ball with a hook is suspended from a clamp through a light thread as shown in figure (12.12).

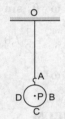

Figure 12.12

The lengths AC and BD are measured with slide callipers. The length OA of the thread is measured with a meter scale. The effective length is

$$OP = OA + AP = OA + AC - \frac{BD}{2}.$$

The bob is slightly pulled aside and gently released from rest. The pendulum starts making oscillations. The time for a number of oscillations (say 20 or 50) is measured with a stop watch and the time period is obtained. The value of g is calculated by equation (12.23). The length of the thread is varied and the experiment is repeated a number of times to minimise the effect of random errors.

Example 12.8

In a laboratory experiment with simple pendulum it was found that it took 36 s to complete 20 oscillations when the effective length was kept at 80 cm. Calculate the acceleration due to gravity from these data.

Solution : The time period of a simple pendulum is given by

$$T = 2\pi \sqrt{lg^{-1}}$$

or, $$g = \frac{4\pi^2 l}{T^2}. \qquad \ldots \text{(i)}$$

In the experiment described in the question, the time period is

$$T = \frac{36 \text{ s}}{20} = 1 \cdot 8 \text{ s}.$$

Thus, by (i),

$$g = \frac{4\pi^2 \times 0.80 \text{ m}}{(1.8 \text{ s})^2} = 9.75 \text{ m s}^{-2}.$$

12.9 PHYSICAL PENDULUM

Any rigid body suspended from a fixed support constitutes a physical pendulum. A circular ring suspended on a nail in a wall, a heavy metallic rod suspended through a hole in it, etc., are examples of physical pendulum. Figure (12.13) shows a physical pendulum. A rigid body is suspended through a hole at O. When the centre of mass C is vertically below O, the body may remain at rest. We call this position $\theta = 0$. When the body is pulled aside and released, it executes oscillations.

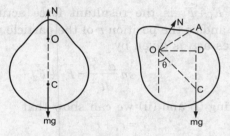

Figure 12.13

The body rotates about a horizontal axis through O and perpendicular to the plane of motion. Let this axis be OA. Suppose the angular displacement of the body is θ at time t. The line OC makes an angle θ with the vertical at this instant.

Forces on the body are (a) the weight mg and (b) the contact force $\mathcal{N}$ by the support at O.

The torque of $\mathcal{N}$ about OA is zero as the force $\mathcal{N}$ acts through the point O. The torque of mg has magnitude

$$|\Gamma| = mg \, (OD)$$
$$= mg \, (OC) \sin\theta = mgl \sin\theta$$

where $l = OC$ is the separation between the point of suspension and the centre of mass. This torque tries to bring the body back towards $\theta = 0$. Thus, we can write

$$\Gamma = -mgl\sin\theta.$$

If the moment of inertia of the body about OA is I, the angular acceleration becomes

$$\alpha = \frac{\Gamma}{I} = -\frac{mgl}{I} \sin\theta. \qquad \dots \text{(i)}$$

We see that the angular acceleration is not proportional to the angular displacement and the motion is not strictly simple harmonic. However, for small displacements $\sin\theta \approx \theta$ so that equation (i)

becomes

$$\alpha = -\omega^2 \theta$$

where $\omega^2 = mglI^{-1}$.

Thus, for small oscillations, the motion is **nearly simple harmonic**. The time period is

$$T = \frac{2\pi}{\omega} = 2\pi \sqrt{\frac{I}{mgl}}. \qquad \dots \text{(12.24)}$$

Example 12.9

A uniform rod of length 1.00 m is suspended through an end and is set into oscillation with small amplitude under gravity. Find the time period of oscillation.

Solution : For small amplitude the angular motion is nearly simple harmonic and the time period is given by

$$T = 2\pi \sqrt{\frac{I}{mgl}} = 2\pi \sqrt{\frac{(mL^2/3)}{mgL/2}}$$

$$= 2\pi \sqrt{\frac{2L}{3g}} = 2\pi \sqrt{\frac{2 \times 1.00 \text{ m}}{3 \times 9.80 \text{ m s}^{-2}}} = 1.64 \text{ s}.$$

12.10 TORSIONAL PENDULUM

In torsional pendulum, an extended body is suspended by a light thread or a wire. The body is rotated through an angle about the wire as the axis of rotation (figure 12.14).

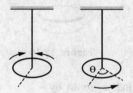

Figure 12.14

The wire remains vertical during this motion but a twist is produced in the wire. The lower end of the wire is rotated through an angle with the body but the upper end remains fixed with the support. Thus, a twist θ is produced. The twisted wire exerts a restoring torque on the body to bring it back to its original position in which the twist θ in the wire is zero. This torque has a magnitude proportional to the angle of twist which is equal to the angle rotated by the body. The proportionality constant is called the *torsional constant* of the wire. Thus, if the torsional constant of the wire is k and the body is rotated through an angle θ, the torque produced is $\Gamma = -k\theta$.

If I be the moment of inertia of the body about the vertical axis, the angular acceleration is

$$\alpha = \frac{\Gamma}{I} = -\frac{k}{I}\theta$$

$$= -\omega^2 \theta$$

where $\omega = \sqrt{\dfrac{k}{I}}$.

Thus, the motion of the body is simple harmonic and the time period is

$$T = \frac{2\pi}{\omega} = 2\pi \sqrt{\frac{I}{k}}. \qquad \ldots (12.25)$$

Example 12.10

A uniform disc of radius 5·0 cm and mass 200 g is fixed at its centre to a metal wire, the other end of which is fixed with a clamp. The hanging disc is rotated about the wire through an angle and is released. If the disc makes torsional oscillations with time period 0·20 s, find the torsional constant of the wire.

Solution : The situation is shown in figure (12.15). The moment of inertia of the disc about the wire is

$$I = \frac{mr^2}{2} = \frac{(0\cdot200 \text{ kg})(5\cdot0 \times 10^{-2} \text{ m})^2}{2}$$

$$= 2\cdot5 \times 10^{-4} \text{ kg-m}^2.$$

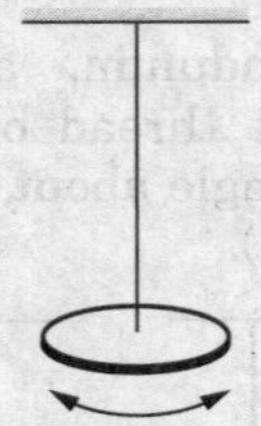

Figure 12.15

The time period is given by

$$T = 2\pi \sqrt{\frac{I}{k}}$$

or, $k = \dfrac{4\pi^2 I}{T^2}$

$$= \frac{4\pi^2(2\cdot5 \times 10^{-4} \text{ kg-m}^2)}{(0\cdot20 \text{ s})^2}$$

$$= 0\cdot25 \frac{\text{kg-m}^2}{\text{s}^2}.$$

12.11 COMPOSITION OF TWO SIMPLE HARMONIC MOTIONS

A simple harmonic motion is produced when a restoring force proportional to the displacement acts on a particle. If the particle is acted upon by two separate forces each of which can produce a simple harmonic motion, the resultant motion of the particle is a combination of two simple harmonic motions.

Let $\vec{r_1}$ denote the position of the particle at time t if the force $\vec{F_1}$ alone acts on it. Similarly, let $\vec{r_2}$ denote the position at time t if the force $\vec{F_2}$ alone acts on it. Newton's second law gives,

$$m\frac{d^2\vec{r_1}}{dt^2} = \vec{F_1}$$

and $m\dfrac{d^2\vec{r_2}}{dt^2} = \vec{F_2}.$

Adding them,

$$m\frac{d^2\vec{r_1}}{dt^2} + m\frac{d^2\vec{r_2}}{dt^2} = \vec{F_1} + \vec{F_2}$$

or, $m\dfrac{d^2}{dt^2}(\vec{r_1} + \vec{r_2}) = \vec{F_1} + \vec{F_2}. \qquad \ldots (i)$

But $\vec{F_1} + \vec{F_2}$ is the resultant force acting on the particle and so the position $\vec{r}$ of the particle when both the forces act, is given by

$$m\frac{d^2\vec{r}}{dt^2} = \vec{F_1} + \vec{F_2}. \qquad \ldots (ii)$$

Comparing (i) and (ii) we can show that

$$\vec{r} = \vec{r_1} + \vec{r_2}$$

and $\vec{u} = \vec{u_1} + \vec{u_2}$

if these conditions are met at $t = 0$.

Thus, if two forces $\vec{F_1}$ and $\vec{F_2}$ act together on a particle, its position at any instant can be obtained as follows. Assume that only the force $\vec{F_1}$ acts and find the position $\vec{r_1}$ at that instant. Then assume that only the force $\vec{F_2}$ acts and find the position $\vec{r_2}$ at that same instant. The actual position will be the vector sum of $\vec{r_1}$ and $\vec{r_2}$.

(A) Composition of two Simple Harmonic Motions in Same Direction

Suppose two forces act on a particle, the first alone would produce a simple harmonic motion given by

$$x_1 = A_1 \sin \omega t$$

and the second alone would produce a simple harmonic motion given by

$$x_2 = A_2 \sin(\omega t + \delta).$$

Both the motions are along the x-direction. The amplitudes may be different and their phases differ by δ. Their frequency is assumed to be same. The resultant position of the particle is then given by

$$x = x_1 + x_2$$

$$= A_1 \sin \omega t + A_2 \sin(\omega t + \delta)$$

$$= A_1 \sin \omega t + A_2 \sin \omega t \cos \delta + A_2 \cos \omega t \sin \delta$$

$$= (A_1 + A_2 \cos \delta) \sin \omega t + (A_2 \sin \delta) \cos \omega t$$

$= C \sin\omega t + D \cos\omega t$

$$= \sqrt{C^2 + D^2} \left[\frac{C}{\sqrt{C^2 + D^2}} \sin\omega t + \frac{D}{\sqrt{C^2 + D^2}} \cos\omega t \right] \quad \dots \text{ (i)}$$

where $C = A_1 + A_2 \cos\delta$ and $D = A_2 \sin\delta$.

Now $\dfrac{C}{\sqrt{C^2 + D^2}}$ and $\dfrac{D}{\sqrt{C^2 + D^2}}$ both have magnitudes less than 1 and the sum of their squares is 1. Thus, we can find an angle ε between 0 and 2π such that

$$\sin\varepsilon = \frac{D}{\sqrt{C^2 + D^2}} \quad \text{and} \quad \cos\varepsilon = \frac{C}{\sqrt{C^2 + D^2}}.$$

Equation (i) then becomes

$$x = \sqrt{C^2 + D^2} \, (\cos\varepsilon \, \sin\omega t + \sin\varepsilon \, \cos\omega t)$$

or, $x = A \sin(\omega t + \varepsilon)$ ... (12.26)

where

$$A = \sqrt{C^2 + D^2}$$

$$= \sqrt{(A_1 + A_2 \cos\delta)^2 + (A_2 \sin\delta)^2}$$

$$= \sqrt{A_1^2 + 2A_1 A_2 \cos\delta + A_2^2 \cos^2\delta + A_2^2 \sin^2\delta}$$

$$= \sqrt{A_1^2 + 2 A_1 A_2 \cos\delta + A_2^2} \quad \dots \text{ (12.27)}$$

and $\tan\varepsilon = \dfrac{D}{C} = \dfrac{A_2 \sin\delta}{A_1 + A_2 \cos\delta}.$ ... (12.28)

Equation (12.26) shows that the resultant of two simple harmonic motions along the same direction is itself a simple harmonic motion. The amplitude and phase of the resultant simple harmonic motion depend on the amplitudes of the two component simple harmonic motions as well as the phase difference between them.

Amplitude of The Resultant Simple Harmonic Motion

The amplitude of the resultant simple harmonic motion is given by equation (12.27),

$$A = \sqrt{A_1^2 + 2 A_1 A_2 \cos\delta + A_2^2}.$$

If $\delta = 0$, the two simple harmonic motions are in phase

$$A = \sqrt{A_1^2 + 2 A_1 A_2 + A_2^2} = A_1 + A_2.$$

The amplitude of the resultant motion is equal to the sum of amplitudes of the individual motions. This is the maximum possible amplitude.

If $\delta = \pi$, the two simple harmonic motions are out of phase and

$$A = \sqrt{A_1^2 - 2 A_1 A_2 + A_2^2} = A_1 - A_2 \text{ or } A_2 - A_1.$$

As the amplitude is always positive we can write $A = |A_1 - A_2|$. If $A_1 = A_2$ the resultant amplitude is zero and the particle does not oscillate at all.

For any value of δ other than 0 and π the resultant amplitude is between $|A_1 - A_2|$ and $A_1 + A_2$.

Example 12.11

Find the amplitude of the simple harmonic motion obtained by combining the motions

$$x_1 = (2 \cdot 0 \text{ cm}) \sin\omega t$$

and $x_2 = (2 \cdot 0 \text{ cm}) \sin(\omega t + \pi/3).$

Solution : The two equations given represent simple harmonic motions along X-axis with amplitudes $A_1 = 2 \cdot 0$ cm and $A_2 = 2 \cdot 0$ cm. The phase difference between the two simple harmonic motions is $\pi/3$. The resultant simple harmonic motion will have an amplitude A given by

$$A = \sqrt{A_1^2 + A_2^2 + 2 A_1 A_2 \cos\delta}$$

$$= \sqrt{(2 \cdot 0 \text{ cm})^2 + (2 \cdot 0 \text{ cm})^2 + 2 (2 \cdot 0 \text{ cm})^2 \cos\frac{\pi}{3}}$$

$$= 3 \cdot 5 \text{ cm}.$$

Vector Method of Combining Two Simple Harmonic Motions

There is a very useful method to remember the equations of resultant simple harmonic motion when two simple harmonic motions of same frequency and in same direction combine. Suppose the two individual motions are represented by

$$x_1 = A_1 \sin\omega t$$

and $x_2 = A_2 \sin(\omega t + \delta).$

Let us for a moment represent the first simple harmonic motion by a vector of magnitude A_1 and the second simple harmonic motion by another vector of magnitude A_2. We draw these vectors in figure (12.16). The vector A_2 is drawn at an angle δ with A_1 to represent that the second simple harmonic motion has a phase difference of δ with the first simple harmonic motion.

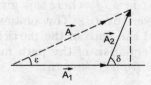

Figure 12.16

The resultant $\vec{A}$ of these two vectors will represent the resultant simple harmonic motion. As we know from vector algebra, the magnitude of the resultant vector is

$$A = \sqrt{A_1^2 + 2 A_1 A_2 \cos\delta + A_2^2}$$

which is same as equation (12.27). The resultant $\vec{A}$ makes an angle ε with $\vec{A_1}$, where

$$\tan\varepsilon = \frac{A_2 \sin\delta}{A_1 + A_2 \cos\delta}$$

which is same as equation (12.28).

This method can easily be extended to more than two vectors. Figure (12.17) shows the construction for adding three simple harmonic motions in the same direction.

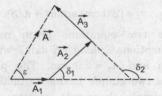

Figure 12.17

$$x_1 = A_1 \sin\omega t$$
$$x_2 = A_2 \sin(\omega t + \delta_1)$$
$$x_3 = A_3 \sin(\omega t + \delta_2).$$

The resultant motion is given by $x = A \sin(\omega t + \varepsilon)$.

(B) Composition of Two Simple Harmonic Motions in Perpendicular Directions

Suppose two forces act on a particle, the first alone would produce a simple harmonic motion in x-direction given by

$$x = A_1 \sin\omega t \qquad \ldots \text{ (i)}$$

and the second would produce a simple harmonic motion in y-direction given by

$$y = A_2 \sin(\omega t + \delta). \qquad \ldots \text{ (ii)}$$

The amplitudes A_1 and A_2 may be different and their phases differ by δ. The frequencies of the two simple harmonic motions are assumed to be equal. The resultant motion of the particle is a combination of the two simple harmonic motions. The position of the particle at time t is (x, y) where x is given by equation (i) and y is given by (ii). The motion is thus two-dimensional and the path of the particle is in general an ellipse. The equation of the path may be obtained by eliminating t from (i) and (ii).

By (i),

$$\sin\omega t = \frac{x}{A_1}.$$

Thus, $$\cos\omega t = \sqrt{1 - \frac{x^2}{A_1^2}}.$$

Putting in (ii)

$$y = A_2 [\sin\omega t \cos\delta + \cos\omega t \sin\delta]$$

$$= A_2 \left[\frac{x}{A_1} \cos\delta + \sqrt{1 - \frac{x^2}{A_1^2}} \sin\delta \right]$$

or, $$\left(\frac{y}{A_2} - \frac{x}{A_1} \cos\delta \right)^2 = \left(1 - \frac{x^2}{A_1^2} \right) \sin^2\delta$$

or, $$\frac{y^2}{A_2^2} - \frac{2xy}{A_1 A_2} \cos\delta + \frac{x^2}{A_1^2} \cos^2\delta$$

$$= \sin^2\delta - \frac{x^2}{A_1^2} \sin^2\delta$$

or, $$\frac{x^2}{A_1^2} + \frac{y^2}{A_2^2} - \frac{2xy \cos\delta}{A_1 A_2} = \sin^2\delta. \qquad \ldots \text{ (12.29)}$$

This is an equation of an ellipse and hence the particle moves in ellipse. Equation (i) shows that x remains between $-A_1$ and $+A_1$ and (ii) shows that y remains between A_2 and $-A_2$. Thus, the particle always remains inside the rectangle defined by

$$x = \pm A_1, \ y = \pm A_2.$$

The ellipse given by (12.29) is traced inside this rectangle and touches it on all the four sides (figure 12.18).

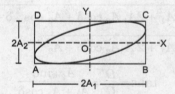

Figure 12.18

Special Cases

(a) $\delta = 0$

The two simple harmonic motions are in phase. When the x-coordinate of the particle crosses the value 0, the y-coordinate also crosses the value 0. When x-coordinate reaches its maximum value A_1, the y-coordinate also reaches its maximum value A_2. Similarly, when x-coordinate reaches its minimum value $-A_1$, the y-coordinate reaches its minimum value $-A_2$.

If we substitute $\delta = 0$ in equation (12.29) we get

$$\frac{x^2}{A_1^2} + \frac{y^2}{A_2^2} - \frac{2xy}{A_1 A_2} = 0$$

or, $$\left(\frac{x}{A_1} - \frac{y}{A_2} \right)^2 = 0$$

or, $$y = \frac{A_2}{A_1} x \qquad \ldots \text{ (iii)}$$

which is the equation of a straight line passing through the origin and having a slope $\tan^{-1}\dfrac{A_2}{A_1}$. Figure (12.19) shows the path. Equation (iii) represents the diagonal AC of the rectangle. The particle moves on this diagonal.

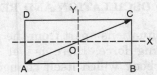

Figure 12.19

Equation (iii) can be directly obtained by dividing (i) by (ii) and putting $\delta = 0$. The displacement of the particle on this straight line at time t is

$$r = \sqrt{x^2 + y^2} = \sqrt{(A_1 \sin\omega t)^2 + (A_2 \sin\omega t)^2}$$
$$= \sqrt{(A_1^2 + A_2^2)}\, \sin\omega t.$$

Thus, the resultant motion is a simple harmonic motion with same frequency and phase as the component motions. The amplitude of the resultant simple harmonic motion is $\sqrt{A_1^2 + A_2^2}$ as is also clear from figure (12.19).

(b) $\delta = \pi$

The two simple harmonic motions are out of phase in this case. When the x-coordinate of the particle reaches its maximum value A_1, the y-coordinate reaches its minimum value $-A_2$. Similarly, when the x-coordinate reaches its minimum value $-A_1$, the y-coordinate takes its maximum value A_2.

Putting $\delta = \pi$ in equation (12.29) we get

$$\frac{x^2}{A_1^2} + \frac{y^2}{A_2^2} + \frac{2xy}{A_1 A_2} = 0$$

or, $$\left(\frac{x}{A_1} + \frac{y}{A_2}\right)^2 = 0$$

or, $$y = -\frac{A_2}{A_1} \cdot x$$

which is the equation of the line BD in figure (12.20).

Figure 12.20

Thus the particle oscillates on the diagonal BD of the rectangle as shown in figure (12.20).

The displacement on this line at time t may be obtained from equation (i) and (ii) (with $\delta = \pi$).

$$r = \sqrt{x^2 + y^2} = \sqrt{[A_1 \sin\omega t]^2 + [A_2 \sin(\omega t + \pi)]^2}$$
$$= \sqrt{A_1^2 \sin^2\omega t + A_2^2 \sin^2\omega t} = \sqrt{A_1^2 + A_2^2}\, \sin\omega t.$$

Thus the resultant motion is a simple harmonic motion with amplitude $\sqrt{A_1^2 + A_2^2}$.

(c) $\delta = \pi/2$

The two simple harmonic motions differ in phase by $\pi/2$. Equations (i) and (ii) may be written as

$$x = A_1 \sin\omega t$$
$$y = A_2 \sin(\omega t + \pi/2) = A_2 \cos\omega t.$$

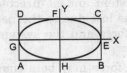

Figure 12.21

The x-coordinate takes its maximum value $x = A_1$ when $\sin\omega t = 1$. Then $\cos\omega t = 0$ and hence, the y-coordinate is zero. The particle is at the point E in figure (12.21). When x-coordinate reduces to 0, $\sin\omega t = 0$, and $\cos\omega t$ becomes 1. Then y-coordinate takes its maximum value A_2 so that the particle reaches the point F. Then x reduces to $-A_1$ and y becomes 0. This corresponds to the point G of figure (12.21). As x increases to 0 again, y takes its minimum value $-A_2$, the particle is at the point H. The motion of the particle is along an ellipse $EFGHE$ inscribed in the rectangle shown. The major and the minor axes of the ellipse are along the X and Y-axes.

Putting $\delta = \pi/2$ in equation (12.29) we get

$$\frac{x^2}{A_1^2} + \frac{y^2}{A_2^2} = 1$$

which is the standard equation of an ellipse with its axes along X and Y-axes and with its centre at the origin. The length of the major and minor axes are $2A_1$ and $2A_2$.

If $A_1 = A_2 = A$ together with $\delta = \pi/2$, the rectangle of figure (12.21) becomes a square and the ellipse becomes a circle. Equation (12.29) becomes

$$x^2 + y^2 = A^2$$

which represents a circle.

Thus, the combination of two simple harmonic motions of equal amplitude in perpendicular directions differing in phase by $\pi/2$ is a circular motion.

The circular motion may be clockwise or anticlockwise, depending on which component leads the other.

12.12 DAMPED HARMONIC MOTION

A particle will execute a simple harmonic motion with a constant amplitude if the resultant force on it is proportional to the displacement and is directed opposite to it. Nature provides a large number of situations in which such restoring force acts. The spring-mass system and the simple pendulum are examples. However, in many of the cases some kind of damping force is also present with the restoring force. The damping force may arise due to friction between the moving parts, air resistance or several other causes. The damping force is a function of speed of the moving system and is directed opposite to the velocity. Energy is lost due to the negative work done by the damping force and the system comes to a halt in due course.

The damping force may be a complicated function of speed. In several cases of practical interest the damping force is proportional to the speed. This force may then be written as

$$F = -bv.$$

The equation of motion is

$$m \frac{dv}{dt} = -kx - bv.$$

This equation can be solved using standard methods of calculus. For small damping the solution is of the form

$$x = A_0\, e^{-\frac{bt}{2m}} \sin(\omega' t + \delta) \qquad \ldots (12.30)$$

where $\omega' = \sqrt{(k/m) - (b/2m)^2} = \sqrt{\omega_0^2 - (b/2m)^2}$.

For small b, the angular frequency $\omega' \approx \sqrt{k/m} = \omega_0$. Thus, the system oscillates with almost the natural angular frequency $\sqrt{k/m}$ (with which the system will oscillate if there is no damping) and with amplitude decreasing with time according to the equation

$$A = A_0\, e^{-\frac{bt}{2m}}.$$

The amplitude decreases with time and finally becomes zero. Figure (12.22) shows qualitatively the displacement of the particle as a function of time.

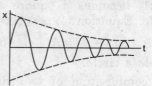

Figure 12.22

If the damping is large the system may not oscillate at all. If displaced, it will go towards the mean position and stay there without overshooting on the other side. The damping for which the oscillation just ceases is called *critical damping*.

12.13 FORCED OSCILLATION AND RESONANCE

In certain situations apart from the restoring force and the damping force, there is yet another force applied on the body which itself changes periodically with time. As a simplest case suppose a force $F = F_0 \sin\omega t$ is applied to a body of mass m on which a restoring force $-kx$ and a damping force $-bv$ is acting. The equation of motion for such a body is

$$m \frac{dv}{dt} = -kx - bv + F_0 \sin\omega t.$$

The motion is somewhat complicated for some time and after this the body oscillates with the frequency ω of the applied periodic force. The displacement is given by

$$x = A \sin(\omega t + \phi).$$

Such an oscillation is called *forced oscillation*. The amplitude of the oscillation is given by

$$A = \frac{F_0/m}{\sqrt{\left(\omega^2 - \omega_0^2\right)^2 + \left(b\omega/m\right)^2}} \qquad \ldots (12.31)$$

where $\omega_0 = \sqrt{k/m}$ is the natural angular frequency.

In forced oscillation the energy lost due to the damping force is compensated by the work done by the applied force. The oscillations with constant amplitude are, therefore, sustained.

If we vary the angular frequency ω of the applied force, this amplitude changes and becomes maximum when $\omega = \omega' = \sqrt{\omega_0^2 - b^2/(2m)^2}$. This condition is called *resonance*. For small damping $\omega' \approx \omega_0$ and the resonance occurs when the applied frequency is (almost) equal to the natural frequency.

Figure (12.23) shows the amplitude as a function of the applied frequency. We see that the amplitude is large if the damping is small. Also the resonance is sharp in this case, that is the amplitude rapidly falls if ω is different from ω_0.

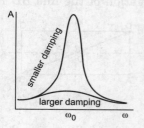

Figure 12.23

If the damping were ideally zero, the amplitude of the forced vibration at resonance would be infinity by equation (12.31). Some damping is always present in mechanical systems and the amplitude remains finite.

However, the amplitude may become very large if the damping is small and the applied frequency is close to the natural frequency. This effect is important in designing bridges and other civil constructions. On July 1, 1940, the newly constructed Tacoma Narrows Bridge (Washington) was opened for traffic. Only four months after this, a mild wind set up the bridge in resonant vibrations. In a few hours the amplitude became so large that the bridge could not stand the stress and a part broke off and went into the water below.

Worked Out Examples

1. *The equation of a particle executing simple harmonic motion is* $x = (5 \text{ m}) \sin\left[(\pi \text{ s}^{-1})t + \dfrac{\pi}{3}\right]$. *Write down the amplitude, time period and maximum speed. Also find the velocity at* $t = 1$ s.

Solution : Comparing with equation $x = A \sin(\omega t + \delta)$, we see that

the amplitude = 5 m,

and time period $= \dfrac{2\pi}{\omega} = \dfrac{2\pi}{\pi \text{ s}^{-1}} = 2$ s.

The maximum speed $= A\omega = 5 \text{ m} \times \pi \text{ s}^{-1} = 5\pi \text{ m s}^{-1}$.

The velocity at time $t = \dfrac{dx}{dt} = A\omega \cos(\omega t + \delta)$.

At $\quad t = 1$ s,

$$v = (5 \text{ m})(\pi \text{ s}^{-1})\cos\left(\pi + \dfrac{\pi}{3}\right) = -\dfrac{5\pi}{2} \text{ m s}^{-1}.$$

2. *A block of mass 5 kg executes simple harmonic motion under the restoring force of a spring. The amplitude and the time period of the motion are 0·1 m and 3·14 s respectively. Find the maximum force exerted by the spring on the block.*

Solution : The maximum force exerted on the block is kA when the block is at the extreme position.

The angular frequency $\omega = \dfrac{2\pi}{T} = 2 \text{ s}^{-1}$.

The spring constant $\quad = k = m\omega^2$

$$= (5 \text{ kg})(4 \text{ s}^{-2}) = 20 \text{ N m}^{-1}.$$

Maximum force $= kA = (20 \text{ N m}^{-1})(0·1 \text{ m}) = 2$ N.

3. *A particle executing simple harmonic motion has angular frequency* $6·28 \text{ s}^{-1}$ *and amplitude* 10 cm. *Find (a) the time period, (b) the maximum speed, (c) the maximum acceleration, (d) the speed when the displacement is 6 cm from the mean position, (e) the speed at* $t = 1/6$ s *assuming that the motion starts from rest at* $t = 0$.

Solution :

(a) Time period $= \dfrac{2\pi}{\omega} = \dfrac{2\pi}{6·28}$ s $= 1$ s.

(b) Maximum speed $= A\omega = (0·1 \text{ m})(6·28 \text{ s}^{-1})$

$$= 0·628 \text{ m s}^{-1}.$$

(c) Maximum acceleration $= A\omega^2$

$$= (0·1 \text{ m})(6·28 \text{ s}^{-1})^2$$

$$= 4 \text{ m s}^{-2}.$$

(d) $v = \omega \sqrt{A^2 - x^2} = (6·28 \text{ s}^{-1}) \sqrt{(10 \text{ cm})^2 - (6 \text{ cm})^2}$

$$= 50·2 \text{ cm s}^{-1}.$$

(e) At $t = 0$, the velocity is zero, i.e., the particle is at an extreme. The equation for displacement may be written as

$$x = A \cos\omega t.$$

The velocity is $v = -A \omega \sin \omega t$.

At $t = \dfrac{1}{6}$ s, $\quad v = -(0·1 \text{ m})(6·28 \text{ s}^{-1}) \sin\left(\dfrac{6·28}{6}\right)$

$$= (-0·628 \text{ m s}^{-1}) \sin\dfrac{\pi}{3}$$

$$= -54·4 \text{ cm s}^{-1}.$$

4. *A particle executes a simple harmonic motion of time period T. Find the time taken by the particle to go directly from its mean position to half the amplitude.*

Solution : Let the equation of motion be $x = A \sin\omega t$.

At $t = 0$, $x = 0$ and hence the particle is at its mean position. Its velocity is

$$v = A \omega \cos\omega t = A \omega$$

which is positive. So it is going towards $x = A/2$.

The particle will be at $x = A/2$, at a time t, where

$$\dfrac{A}{2} = A \sin\omega t$$

or, $\quad \sin\omega t = 1/2$

or, $\quad \omega t = \pi/6$.

Here minimum positive value of ωt is chosen because we are interested in finding the time taken by the particle to directly go from $x = 0$ to $x = A/2$.

Thus, $t = \dfrac{\pi}{6 \omega} = \dfrac{\pi}{6(2\pi/T)} = \dfrac{T}{12}$.

5. *A block of mass m hangs from a vertical spring of spring constant k. If it is displaced from its equilibrium position, find the time period of oscillations.*

Solution : Suppose the length of the spring is stretched by a length Δl. The tension in the spring is $k\,\Delta l$ and this is the force by the spring on the block. The other force on the block is mg due to gravity. For equilibrium, $mg = k\,\Delta l$ or $\Delta l = mg/k$. Take this position of the block as $x = 0$. If the block is further displaced by x, the resultant force is $k\left(\dfrac{mg}{k} + x\right) - mg = kx$.

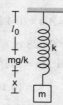

Figure 12-W1

Thus, the resultant force is proportional to the displacement. The motion is simple harmonic with a time period $T = 2\pi\sqrt{\dfrac{m}{k}}$.

We see that in vertical oscillations, gravity has no effect on time period. The only effect it has is to shift the equilibrium position by a distance mg/k as if the natural length is increased (or decreased if the lower end of the spring is fixed) by mg/k.

6. *A particle suspended from a vertical spring oscillates 10 times per second. At the highest point of oscillation the spring becomes unstretched. (a) Find the maximum speed of the block. (b) Find the speed when the spring is stretched by 0·20 cm. Take $g = \pi^2\ \text{m s}^{-2}$.*

Solution :

(a) The mean position of the particle during vertical oscillations is mg/k distance away from its position when the spring is unstretched. At the highest point, i.e., at an extreme position, the spring is unstretched.

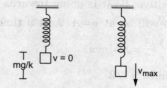

Figure 12-W2

Hence the amplitude is

$$A = \frac{mg}{k}. \qquad\qquad \dots \text{(i)}$$

The angular frequency is

$$\omega = \sqrt{\frac{k}{m}} = 2\pi\nu = (20\pi)\ \text{s}^{-1} \qquad \dots \text{(ii)}$$

or, $\qquad \dfrac{m}{k} = \dfrac{1}{400\,\pi^2}\ \text{s}^2.$

Putting in (i), the amplitude is

$$A = \left(\frac{1}{400\,\pi^2}\ \text{s}^2\right)\!\left(\pi^2\,\frac{\text{m}}{\text{s}^2}\right)$$

$$= \frac{1}{400}\ \text{m} = 0\cdot25\ \text{cm}.$$

The maximum speed $= A\,\omega$

$$= (0\cdot25\ \text{cm})\,(20\,\pi\ \text{s}^{-1}) = 5\,\pi\ \text{cm s}^{-1}.$$

(b) When the spring is stretched by 0·20 cm, the block is $0\cdot25\ \text{cm} - 0\cdot20\ \text{cm} = 0\cdot05\ \text{cm}$ above the mean position. The speed at this position will be

$$v = \omega\sqrt{A^2 - x^2}$$

$$= (20\,\pi\ \text{s}^{-1})\sqrt{(0\cdot25\ \text{cm})^2 - (0\cdot05\ \text{cm})^2}$$

$$\cong 15\cdot4\ \text{cm s}^{-1}.$$

7. *The pulley shown in figure (12-W3) has a moment of inertia I about its axis and mass m. Find the time period of vertical oscillation of its centre of mass. The spring has spring constant k and the string does not slip over the pulley.*

Figure 12-W3

Solution : Let us first find the equilibrium position. For rotational equilibrium of the pulley, the tensions in the two strings should be equal. Only then the torque on the pulley will be zero. Let this tension be T. The extension of the spring will be $y = T/k$, as the tension in the spring will be the same as the tension in the string. For translational equilibrium of the pulley,

$$2\,T = mg \quad\text{or,}\quad 2\,ky = mg \quad\text{or,}\quad y = \frac{mg}{2\,k}.$$

The spring is extended by a distance $\dfrac{mg}{2\,k}$ when the pulley is in equilibrium.

Now suppose, the centre of the pulley goes down further by a distance x. The total increase in the length of the string plus the spring is $2x$ (x on the left of the pulley and x on the right). As the string has a constant length, the extension of the spring is $2x$. The energy of the system is

$$U = \frac{1}{2}\,I\omega^2 + \frac{1}{2}\,mv^2 - mgx + \frac{1}{2}\,k\left(\frac{mg}{2\,k} + 2\,x\right)^2$$

$$= \frac{1}{2}\left(\frac{I}{r^2}+m\right)v^2 + \frac{m^2 g^2}{8\,k} + 2\,kx^2.$$

As the system is conservative, $\frac{dU}{dt}=0$,

giving $0=\left(\dfrac{I}{r^2}+m\right)v\,\dfrac{dv}{dt}+4\,kxv$

or, $\dfrac{dv}{dt}=-\dfrac{4\,kx}{\left(\dfrac{I}{r^2}+m\right)}$

or, $a=-\omega^2 x$, where $\omega^2=\dfrac{4\,k}{\left(\dfrac{I}{r^2}+m\right)}.$

Thus, the centre of mass of the pulley executes a simple harmonic motion with time period

$$T=2\pi \sqrt{\left(\frac{I}{r^2}+m\right)/(4\,k)}\;.$$

8. *The friction coefficient between the two blocks shown in figure (12-W4) is μ and the horizontal plane is smooth. (a) If the system is slightly displaced and released, find the time period. (b) Find the magnitude of the frictional force between the blocks when the displacement from the mean position is x. (c) What can be the maximum amplitude if the upper block does not slip relative to the lower block ?*

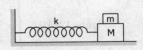

Figure 12-W4

Solution :

(a) For small amplitude, the two blocks oscillate together. The angular frequency is

$$\omega=\sqrt{\frac{k}{M+m}}$$

and so the time period $T=2\pi\sqrt{\dfrac{M+m}{k}}\;.$

(b) The acceleration of the blocks at displacement x from the mean position is

$$a=-\omega^2 x=\frac{-kx}{M+m}\;.$$

The resultant force on the upper block is, therefore,

$$ma=\frac{-mkx}{M+m}\;.$$

This force is provided by the friction of the lower block. Hence, the magnitude of the frictional force is $\dfrac{mk\,|x|}{M+m}\;.$

(c) Maximum force of friction required for simple harmonic motion of the upper block is $\dfrac{m\,k\,A}{M+m}$ at the

extreme positions. But the maximum frictional force can only be $\mu\,mg$. Hence

$$\frac{m\,k\,A}{M+m}=\mu\,mg \quad\text{or,}\quad A=\frac{\mu\,(M+m)\,g}{k}\;.$$

9. *The left block in figure (12-W5) collides inelastically with the right block and sticks to it. Find the amplitude of the resulting simple harmonic motion.*

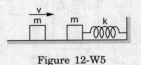

Figure 12-W5

Solution : Assuming the collision to last for a small interval only, we can apply the principle of conservation of momentum. The common velocity after the collision is $\dfrac{v}{2}$. The kinetic energy $=\dfrac{1}{2}(2m)\left(\dfrac{v}{2}\right)^2=\dfrac{1}{4}mv^2$. This is also the total energy of vibration as the spring is unstretched at this moment. If the amplitude is A, the total energy can also be written as $\dfrac{1}{2}kA^2$. Thus

$$\frac{1}{2}kA^2=\frac{1}{4}mv^2,\ \text{giving}\ A=\sqrt{\frac{m}{2\,k}}\,v.$$

10. *Describe the motion of the mass m shown in figure (12-W6). The walls and the block are elastic.*

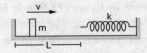

Figure 12-W6

Solution : The block reaches the spring with a speed v. It now compresses the spring. The block is decelerated due to the spring force, comes to rest when $\dfrac{1}{2}mv^2=\dfrac{1}{2}kx^2$ and returns back. It is accelerated due to the spring force till the spring acquires its natural length. The contact of the block with the spring is now broken. At this instant it has regained its speed v (towards left) as the spring is unstretched and no potential energy is stored. This process takes half the period of oscillation, i.e., $\pi\sqrt{m/k}$. The block strikes the left wall after a time L/v and as the collision is elastic, it rebounds with the same speed v. After a time L/v, it again reaches the spring and the process is repeated. The block thus undergoes periodic motion with time period $\pi\sqrt{m/k}+\dfrac{2L}{v}\;.$

11. *A block of mass m is suspended from the ceiling of a stationary standing elevator through a spring of spring constant k. Suddenly, the cable breaks and the elevator starts falling freely. Show that the block now executes a*

simple harmonic motion of amplitude mg/k in the elevator.

Solution : When the elevator is stationary, the spring is stretched to support the block. If the extension is x, the tension is kx which should balance the weight of the block.

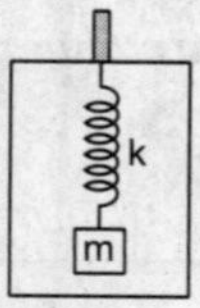

Figure 12-W7

Thus, $x = mg/k$. As the cable breaks, the elevator starts falling with acceleration 'g'. We shall work in the frame of reference of the elevator. Then we have to use a pseudo force mg upward on the block. This force will 'balance' the weight. Thus, the block is subjected to a net force kx by the spring when it is at a distance x from the position of unstretched spring. Hence, its motion in the elevator is simple harmonic with its mean position corresponding to the unstretched spring. Initially, the spring is stretched by $x = mg/k$, where the velocity of the block (with respect to the elevator) is zero. Thus, the amplitude of the resulting simple harmonic motion is mg/k.

12. *The spring shown in figure (12-W8) is kept in a stretched position with extension x_0 when the system is released. Assuming the horizontal surface to be frictionless, find the frequency of oscillation.*

Figure 12-W8

Solution : Considering "the two blocks plus the spring" as a system, there is no external resultant force on the system. Hence the centre of mass of the system will remain at rest. The mean positions of the two simple harmonic motions occur when the spring becomes unstretched. If the mass m moves towards right through a distance x and the mass M moves towards left through a distance X before the spring acquires natural length,

$$x + X = x_0. \qquad \dots \text{(i)}$$

x and X will be the amplitudes of the two blocks m and M respectively. As the centre of mass should not change during the motion, we should also have

$$mx = MX. \qquad \dots \text{(ii)}$$

From (i) and (ii), $x = \dfrac{Mx_0}{M + m}$ and $X = \dfrac{mx_0}{M + m}$.

Hence, the left block is $x = \dfrac{Mx_0}{M + m}$ distance away from its

mean position in the beginning of the motion. The force by the spring on this block at this instant is equal to the tension of spring, i.e., $T = kx_0$.

Now $x = \dfrac{Mx_0}{M + m}$ or, $x_0 = \dfrac{M + m}{M} x$

Thus, $T = \dfrac{k(M + m)}{M} x$ or, $a = \dfrac{T}{m} = \dfrac{k(M + m)}{Mm} x$.

The angular frequency is, therefore, $\omega = \sqrt{\dfrac{k(M + m)}{Mm}}$

and the frequency is $\nu = \dfrac{\omega}{2\pi} = \dfrac{1}{2\pi} \sqrt{\dfrac{k(M + m)}{Mm}}$.

13. *Assume that a narrow tunnel is dug between two diametrically opposite points of the earth. Treat the earth as a solid sphere of uniform density. Show that if a particle is released in this tunnel, it will execute a simple harmonic motion. Calculate the time period of this motion.*

Solution :

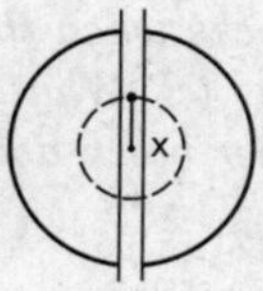

Figure 12-W9

Consider the situation shown in figure (12-W9). Suppose at an instant t the particle in the tunnel is at a distance x from the centre of the earth. Let us draw a sphere of radius x with its centre at the centre of the earth. Only the part of the earth within this sphere will exert a net attraction on the particle. Mass of this part is

$$M' = \frac{\frac{4}{3} \pi x^3}{\frac{4}{3} \pi R^3} M = \frac{x^3}{R^3} M.$$

The force of attraction is, therefore,

$$F = \frac{G(x^3/R^3) Mm}{x^2} = \frac{GMm}{R^3} x.$$

This force acts towards the centre of the earth. Thus, the resultant force on the particle is opposite to the displacement from the centre of the earth and is proportional to it. The particle, therefore, executes a simple harmonic motion in the tunnel with the centre of the earth as the mean position.

The force constant is $k = \dfrac{GMm}{R^3}$, so that the time period is

$$T = 2\pi \sqrt{\frac{m}{k}} = 2\pi \sqrt{\frac{R^3}{GM}} .$$

14. *A simple pendulum of length* 40 cm *oscillates with an angular amplitude of* 0·04 rad. *Find (a) the time period, (b) the linear amplitude of the bob, (c) the speed of the bob when the string makes* 0·02 rad *with the vertical and (d) the angular acceleration when the bob is in momentary rest. Take* $g = 10$ m s^{-2}.

Solution :

(a) The angular frequency is

$$\omega = \sqrt{g/l} = \sqrt{\frac{10 \text{ m s}^{-2}}{0·4 \text{ m}}} = 5 \text{ s}^{-1}.$$

The time period is

$$\frac{2\pi}{\omega} = \frac{2\pi}{5 \text{ s}^{-1}} = 1·26 \text{ s}.$$

(b) Linear amplitude $= 40$ cm $\times 0·04 = 1·6$ cm.

(c) Angular speed at displacement 0·02 rad is

$$\Omega = (5 \text{ s}^{-1}) \sqrt{(0·04)^2 - (0·02)^2} \text{ rad} = 0·17 \text{ rad s}^{-1}.$$

Linear speed of the bob at this instant

$$= (40 \text{ cm}) \times 0·17 \text{ s}^{-1} = 6·8 \text{ cm s}^{-1}.$$

(d) At momentary rest, the bob is in extreme position. Thus, the angular acceleration

$$\alpha = (0·04 \text{ rad})(25 \text{ s}^{-2}) = 1 \text{ rad s}^{-2}.$$

15. *A simple pendulum having a bob of mass m undergoes small oscillations with amplitude* θ_0. *Find the tension in the string as a function of the angle made by the string with the vertical. When is this tension maximum, and when is it minimum ?*

Solution : Suppose the speed of the bob at angle θ is v. Using conservation of energy between the extreme position and the position with angle θ,

$$\frac{1}{2} mv^2 = mgl \,(\cos\theta - \cos\theta_0). \qquad \dots \text{(i)}$$

Figure 12-W10

As the bob moves in a circular path, the force towards the centre should be equal to mv^2/l. Thus,

$$T - mg \cos\theta = mv^2/l.$$

Using (i),

$$T - mg\cos\theta = 2 mg \,(\cos\theta - \cos\theta_0)$$

or, $T = 3 mg \cos\theta - 2 mg \cos\theta_0.$

Now $\cos\theta$ is maximum at $\theta = 0$ and decreases as $|\theta|$ increases (for $|\theta| < 90°$).

Thus, the tension is maximum when $\theta = 0$, i.e., at the mean position and is minimum when $\theta = \pm \theta_0$, i.e., at extreme positions.

16. *A simple pendulum is taken at a place where its separation from the earth's surface is equal to the radius of the earth. Calculate the time period of small oscillations if the length of the string is* 1·0 m. *Take* $g = \pi^2$ m s^{-2} *at the surface of the earth.*

Solution : At a height R (radius of the earth) the acceleration due to gravity is

$$g' = \frac{GM}{(R+R)^2} = \frac{1}{4} \frac{GM}{R^2} = g/4.$$

The time period of small oscillations of the simple pendulum is

$$T = 2\pi \sqrt{l/g'} = 2\pi \sqrt{\frac{1·0 \text{ m}}{\frac{1}{4} \times \pi^2 \text{ m s}^{-2}}} = 2\pi \left(\frac{2}{\pi} \text{ s}\right) = 4 \text{ s}.$$

17. *A simple pendulum is suspended from the ceiling of a car accelerating uniformly on a horizontal road. If the acceleration is* a_0 *and the length of the pendulum is* l, *find the time period of small oscillations about the mean position.*

Solution : We shall work in the car frame. As it is accelerated with respect to the road, we shall have to apply a pseudo force ma_0 on the bob of mass m.

For mean position, the acceleration of the bob with respect to the car should be zero. If θ be the angle made by the string with the vertical, the tension, weight and the pseudo force will add to zero in this position.

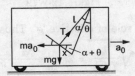

Figure 12-W11

Suppose, at some instant during oscillation, the string is further deflected by an angle α so that the displacement of the bob is x. Taking the components perpendicular to the string,

component of $T = 0$,

component of $mg = mg \sin(\alpha + \theta)$ and

component of $ma_0 = -ma_0 \cos(\alpha + \theta)$.

Thus, the resultant component F

$$= m[g \sin(\alpha + \theta) - a_0 \cos(\alpha + \theta)].$$

Expanding the sine and cosine and putting $\cos\alpha \approx 1$, $\sin\alpha \approx \alpha = x/l$, we get

$$F = m\left[g \sin\theta - a_0 \cos\theta + (g \cos\theta + a_0 \sin\theta)\frac{x}{l}\right]. \qquad \dots \text{(i)}$$

At $x = 0$, the force F on the bob should be zero, as this is the mean position. Thus by (i),

$$0 = m[g \sin\theta - a_0 \cos\theta] \qquad \text{... (ii)}$$

giving

$$\tan\theta = \frac{a_0}{g}$$

Thus,

$$\sin\theta = \frac{a_0}{\sqrt{a_0^2 + g^2}} \qquad \text{... (iii)}$$

$$\cos\theta = \frac{g}{\sqrt{a_0^2 + g^2}} . \qquad \text{... (iv)}$$

Putting (ii), (iii) and (iv) in (i), $F = m \sqrt{g^2 + a_0^2} \; \dfrac{x}{l}$

or, $\qquad F = m\,\omega^2 x$, where $\omega^2 = \dfrac{\sqrt{g^2 + a_0^2}}{l}$.

This is an equation of simple harmonic motion with time period

$$t = \frac{2\pi}{\omega} = 2\pi \frac{\sqrt{l}}{\left(g^2 + a_0^2\right)^{1/4}} .$$

An easy working rule may be found out as follows. In the mean position, the tension, the weight and the pseudo force balance.

From figure (12-W12), the tension is

$$T = \sqrt{(ma_0)^2 + (mg)^2}$$

or, $\qquad \dfrac{T}{m} = \sqrt{a_0^2 + g^2}$.

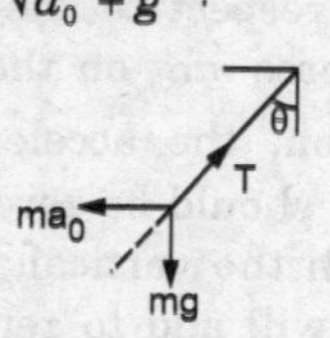

Figure 12-W12

This plays the role of effective 'g'. Thus the time period is

$$t = 2\pi \sqrt{\frac{l}{T/m}} = 2\pi \frac{\sqrt{l}}{[g^2 + a_0^2]^{1/4}} .$$

18. *A uniform meter stick is suspended through a small pin hole at the 10 cm mark. Find the time period of small oscillation about the point of suspension.*

Solution : Let the mass of the stick be m. The moment of inertia of the stick about the axis of rotation through the point of suspension is

$$I = \frac{ml^2}{12} + md^2,$$

where $l = 1$ m and $d = 40$ cm.

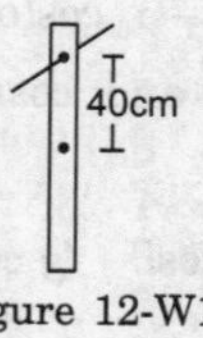

Figure 12-W13

The separation between the centre of mass of the stick and the point of suspension is $d = 40$ cm. The time period of this physical pendulum is

$$T = 2\pi \sqrt{\frac{I}{mgd}}$$

$$= 2\pi \sqrt{\left(\frac{ml^2}{12} + md^2\right) / (mgd)}$$

$$= 2\pi \left[\sqrt{\left(\frac{1}{12} + 0.16\right) / 4} \right] \text{s} = 1.55 \text{ s}.$$

19. *The moment of inertia of the disc used in a torsional pendulum about the suspension wire is 0.2 kg-m². It oscillates with a period of 2 s. Another disc is placed over the first one and the time period of the system becomes 2.5 s. Find the moment of inertia of the second disc about the wire.*

Figure 12-W14

Solution :

Let the torsional constant of the wire be k. The moment of inertia of the first disc about the wire is 0.2 kg-m². Hence, the time period is

$$2 \text{ s} = 2\pi \sqrt{\frac{I}{K}}$$

$$= 2\pi \sqrt{\frac{0.2 \text{ kg-m}^2}{k}} . \qquad \text{... (i)}$$

When the second disc having moment of inertia I_1 about the wire is added, the time period is

$$2.5 \text{ s} = 2\pi \sqrt{\frac{0.2 \text{ kg-m}^2 + I_1}{k}} \qquad \text{... (ii)}$$

From (i) and (ii), $\dfrac{6.25}{4} = \dfrac{0.2 \text{ kg-m}^2 + I_1}{0.2 \text{ kg-m}^2}$.

This gives $I_1 \approx 0.11$ kg-m².

20. *A uniform rod of mass m and length l is suspended through a light wire of length l and torsional constant k as shown in figure (12-W15). Find the time period if the system makes (a) small oscillations in the vertical plane about the suspension point and (b) angular oscillations in the horizontal plane about the centre of the rod.*

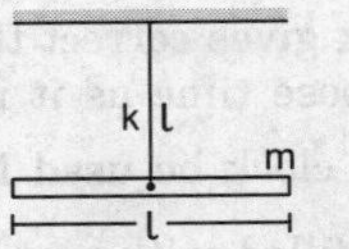

Figure 12-W15

Solution :

(a) The oscillations take place about the horizontal line through the point of suspension and perpendicular to the plane of the figure. The moment of inertia of the rod about this line is

$$\frac{ml^2}{12} + ml^2 = \frac{13}{12}ml^2.$$

The time period $= 2\pi \sqrt{\dfrac{I}{mgl}} = 2\pi \sqrt{\dfrac{13\,ml^2}{12\,mgl}}$

$$= 2\pi \sqrt{\frac{13\,l}{12\,g}}.$$

(b) The angular oscillations take place about the suspension wire. The moment of inertia about this line is $ml^2/12$. The time period is

$$2\pi \sqrt{\frac{I}{k}} = 2\pi \sqrt{\frac{ml^2}{12\,k}}.$$

21. *A particle is subjected to two simple harmonic motions*

$$x_1 = A_1 \sin\omega t$$

and $\qquad x_2 = A_2 \sin(\omega t + \pi/3).$

Find (a) the displacement at $t = 0$, (b) the maximum speed of the particle and (c) the maximum acceleration of the particle.

Solution :

(a) At $t = 0$, $\qquad x_1 = A_1 \sin\omega t = 0$

and $x_2 = A_2 \sin(\omega t + \pi/3)$

$$= A_2 \sin(\pi/3) = \frac{A_2 \sqrt{3}}{2}.$$

Thus, the resultant displacement at $t = 0$ is

$$x = x_1 + x_2 = \frac{A_2 \sqrt{3}}{2}.$$

(b) The resultant of the two motions is a simple harmonic motion of the same angular frequency ω. The amplitude of the resultant motion is

$$A = \sqrt{A_1^2 + A_2^2 + 2\,A_1 A_2 \cos(\pi/3)}$$

$$= \sqrt{A_1^2 + A_2^2 + A_1 A_2}.$$

The maximum speed is

$$v_{\max} = A\,\omega = \omega \sqrt{A_1^2 + A_2^2 + A_1 A_2}.$$

(c) The maximum acceleration is

$$a_{\max} = A\,\omega^2 = \omega^2 \sqrt{A_1^2 + A_2^2 + A_1 A_2}.$$

22. *A particle is subjected to two simple harmonic motions in the same direction having equal amplitudes and equal frequency. If the resultant amplitude is equal to the amplitude of the individual motions, find the phase difference between the individual motions.*

Solution : Let the amplitudes of the individual motions be A each. The resultant amplitude is also A. If the phase difference between the two motions is δ,

$$A = \sqrt{A^2 + A^2 + 2A \cdot A \cdot \cos\delta}$$

or, $\qquad = A\sqrt{2(1 + \cos\delta)} = 2A\cos\dfrac{\delta}{2}$

or, $\qquad \cos\dfrac{\delta}{2} = \dfrac{1}{2}$

or, $\qquad \delta = 2\pi/3.$

□

QUESTIONS FOR SHORT ANSWER

1. A person goes to bed at sharp 10·00 pm every day. Is it an example of periodic motion ? If yes, what is the time period ? If no, why ?

2. A particle executing simple harmonic motion comes to rest at the extreme positions. Is the resultant force on the particle zero at these positions according to Newton's first law ?

3. Can simple harmonic motion take place in a noninertial frame? If yes, should the ratio of the force applied with the displacement be constant ?

4. A particle executes simple harmonic motion. If you are told that its velocity at this instant is zero, can you say what is its displacement ? If you are told that its velocity

at this instant is maximum, can you say what is its displacement ?

5. A small creature moves with constant speed in a vertical circle on a bright day. Does its shadow formed by the sun on a horizontal plane move in a simple harmonic motion ?

6. A particle executes simple harmonic motion. Let P be a point near the mean position and Q be a point near an extreme. The speed of the particle at P is larger than the speed at Q. Still the particle crosses P and Q equal number of times in a given time interval. Does it make you unhappy ?

7. In measuring time period of a pendulum, it is advised to measure the time between consecutive passage through the mean position in the same direction. This is said to result in better accuracy than measuring time between consecutive passage through an extreme position. Explain.

8. It is proposed to move a particle in simple harmonic motion on a rough horizontal surface by applying an external force along the line of motion. Sketch the graph of the applied force against the position of the particle. Note that the applied force has two values for a given position depending on whether the particle is moving in positive or negative direction.

9. Can the potential energy in a simple harmonic motion be negative ? Will it be so if we choose zero potential energy at some point other than the mean position ?

10. The energy of a system in simple harmonic motion is given by $E = \frac{1}{2} m \omega^2 A^2$. Which of the following two statements is more appropriate ?
(A) The energy is increased because the amplitude is increased.
(B) The amplitude is increased because the energy is increased.

11. A pendulum clock gives correct time at the equator. Will it gain time or loose time as it is taken to the poles ?

12. Can a pendulum clock be used in an earth-satellite ?

13. A hollow sphere filled with water is used as the bob of a pendulum. Assume that the equation for simple pendulum is valid with the distance between the point of suspension and centre of mass of the bob acting as the effective length of the pendulum. If water slowly leaks out of the bob, how will the time period vary ?

14. A block of known mass is suspended from a fixed support through a light spring. Can you find the time period of vertical oscillation only by measuring the extension of the spring when the block is in equilibrium ?

15. A platoon of soldiers marches on a road in steps according to the sound of a marching band. The band is stopped and the soldiers are ordered to break the steps while crossing a bridge. Why ?

16. The force acting on a particle moving along X-axis is $F = - k(x - v_0 t)$ where k is a positive constant. An observer moving at a constant velocity v_0 along the X-axis looks at the particle. What kind of motion does he find for the particle ?

OBJECTIVE I

1. A student says that he had applied a force $F = - k\sqrt{x}$ on a particle and the particle moved in simple harmonic motion. He refuses to tell whether k is a constant or not. Assume that he has worked only with positive x and no other force acted on the particle.
(a) As x increases k increases.
(b) As x increases k decreases.
(c) As x increases k remains constant.
(d) The motion cannot be simple harmonic.

2. The time period of a particle in simple harmonic motion is equal to the time between consecutive appearances of the particle at a particular point in its motion. This point is
(a) the mean position   (b) an extreme position
(c) between the mean position and the positive extreme
(d) between the mean position and the negative extreme.

3. The time period of a particle in simple harmonic motion is equal to the smallest time between the particle acquiring a particular velocity $\vec{v}$. The value of v is
(a) v_{max} (b) 0
(c) between 0 and v_{max} (d) between 0 and $-v_{max}$.

4. The displacement of a particle in simple harmonic motion in one time period is
(a) A (b) $2A$ (c) $4A$ (d) zero.

5. The distance moved by a particle in simple harmonic motion in one time period is
(a) A (b) $2A$ (c) $4A$ (d) zero.

6. The average acceleration in one time period in a simple harmonic motion is
(a) $A \omega^2$ (b) $A \omega^2 / 2$ (c) $A \omega^2 / \sqrt{2}$ (d) zero.

7. The motion of a particle is given by $x = A \sin\omega t + B \cos\omega t$. The motion of the particle is
(a) not simple harmonic
(b) simple harmonic with amplitude $A + B$
(c) simple harmonic with amplitude $(A + B) / 2$
(d) simple harmonic with amplitude $\sqrt{A^2 + B^2}$.

8. The displacement of a particle is given by $\vec{r} = A(\vec{i} \cos\omega t + \vec{j} \sin\omega t)$. The motion of the particle is
(a) simple harmonic   (b) on a straight line
(c) on a circle   (d) with constant acceleration.

9. A particle moves on the X-axis according to the equation $x = A + B \sin\omega t$. The motion is simple harmonic with amplitude
(a) A (b) B (c) $A + B$ (d) $\sqrt{A^2 + B^2}$.

10. Figure (12-Q1) represents two simple harmonic motions.

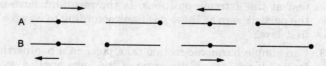

Figure 12-Q1

The parameter which has different values in the two motions is

(a) amplitude   (b) frequency

(c) phase   (d) maximum velocity.

11. The total mechanical energy of a spring-mass system in simple harmonic motion is $E = \frac{1}{2} m \omega^2 A^2$. Suppose the oscillating particle is replaced by another particle of double the mass while the amplitude A remains the same. The new mechanical energy will

(a) become $2E$ (b) become $E/2$

(c) become $\sqrt{2}E$ (d) remain E.

12. The average energy in one time period in simple harmonic motion is

(a) $\frac{1}{2} m \omega^2 A^2$ (b) $\frac{1}{4} m \omega^2 A^2$

(c) $m \omega^2 A^2$ (d) zero.

13. A particle executes simple harmonic motion with a frequency ν. The frequency with which the kinetic energy oscillates is

(a) $\nu/2$ (b) ν (c) 2ν (d) zero.

14. A particle executes simple harmonic motion under the restoring force provided by a spring. The time period is T. If the spring is divided in two equal parts and one part is used to continue the simple harmonic motion, the time period will

(a) remain T (b) become $2T$

(c) become $T/2$ (d) become $T/\sqrt{2}$.

15. Two bodies A and B of equal mass are suspended from two separate massless springs of spring constant k_1 and k_2 respectively. If the bodies oscillate vertically such that their maximum velocities are equal, the ratio of the amplitude of A to that of B is

(a) k_1/k_2 (b) $\sqrt{k_1/k_2}$

(c) k_2/k_1 (d) $\sqrt{k_2/k_1}$.

16. A spring-mass system oscillates with a frequency ν. If it is taken in an elevator slowly accelerating upward, the frequency will

(a) increase   (b) decrease

(c) remain same   (d) become zero.

17. A spring-mass system oscillates in a car. If the car accelerates on a horizontal road, the frequency of oscillation will

(a) increase   (b) decrease

(c) remain same   (d) become zero.

18. A pendulum clock that keeps correct time on the earth is taken to the moon. It will run

(a) at correct rate   (b) 6 times faster

(c) $\sqrt{6}$ times faster   (d) $\sqrt{6}$ times slower.

19. A wall clock uses a vertical spring-mass system to measure the time. Each time the mass reaches an extreme position, the clock advances by a second. The clock gives correct time at the equator. If the clock is taken to the poles it will

(a) run slow   (b) run fast

(c) stop working   (d) give correct time.

20. A pendulum clock keeping correct time is taken to high altitudes,

(a) it will keep correct time

(b) its length should be increased to keep correct time

(c) its length should be decreased to keep correct time

(d) it cannot keep correct time even if the length is changed.

21. The free end of a simple pendulum is attached to the ceiling of a box. The box is taken to a height and the pendulum is oscillated. When the bob is at its lowest point, the box is released to fall freely. As seen from the box during this period, the bob will

(a) continue its oscillation as before

(b) stop

(c) will go in a circular path

(d) move on a straight line.

OBJECTIVE II

1. Select the correct statements.

(a) A simple harmonic motion is necessarily periodic.

(b) A simple harmonic motion is necessarily oscillatory.

(c) An oscillatory motion is necessarily periodic.

(d) A periodic motion is necessarily oscillatory.

2. A particle moves in a circular path with a uniform speed. Its motion is

(a) periodic   (b) oscillatory

(c) simple harmonic   (d) angular simple harmonic.

3. A particle is fastened at the end of a string and is whirled in a vertical circle with the other end of the string being fixed. The motion of the particle is

(a) periodic   (b) oscillatory

(c) simple harmonic   (d) angular simple harmonic.

4. A particle moves in a circular path with a continuously increasing speed. Its motion is

(a) periodic   (b) oscillatory

(c) simple harmonic   (d) none of them.

5. The motion of a torsional pendulum is

(a) periodic   (b) oscillatory

(c) simple harmonic   (d) angular simple harmonic.

6. Which of the following quantities are always negative in a simple harmonic motion ?

(a) $\vec{F} . \vec{a}$.   (b) $\vec{v} . \vec{r}$.   (c) $\vec{a} . \vec{r}$.   (d) $\vec{F} . \vec{r}$.

7. Which of the following quantities are always positive in a simple harmonic motion ?

(a) $\vec{F} . \vec{a}$.   (b) $\vec{v} . \vec{r}$.   (c) $\vec{a} . \vec{r}$.   (d) $\vec{F} . \vec{r}$.

8. Which of the following quantities are always zero in a simple harmonic motion ?

(a) $\vec{F} \times \vec{a}$.   (b) $\vec{v} \times \vec{r}$.   (c) $\vec{a} \times \vec{r}$.   (d) $\vec{F} \times \vec{r}$.

9. Suppose a tunnel is dug along a diameter of the earth. A particle is dropped from a point, a distance h directly

above the tunnel. The motion of the particle as seen from the earth is
(a) simple harmonic   (b) parabolic
(c) on a straight line   (d) periodic.

10. For a particle executing simple harmonic motion, the acceleration is proportional to
(a) displacement from the mean position
(b) distance from the mean position
(c) distance travelled since $t = 0$
(d) speed.

11. A particle moves in the X-Y plane according to the equation
$$\vec{r} = (\vec{i} + 2\,\vec{j})\, A \cos\omega t.$$
The motion of the particle is
(a) on a straight line   (b) on an ellipse
(c) periodic   (d) simple harmonic.

12. A particle moves on the X-axis according to the equation $x = x_0 \sin^2 \omega t$. The motion is simple harmonic
(a) with amplitude x_0 (b) with amplitude $2x_0$
(c) with time period $\dfrac{2\pi}{\omega}$ (d) with time period $\dfrac{\pi}{\omega}$.

13. In a simple harmonic motion
(a) the potential energy is always equal to the kinetic energy
(b) the potential energy is never equal to the kinetic energy

(c) the average potential energy in any time interval is equal to the average kinetic energy in that time interval
(d) the average potential energy in one time period is equal to the average kinetic energy in this period.

14. In a simple harmonic motion
(a) the maximum potential energy equals the maximum kinetic energy
(b) the minimum potential energy equals the minimum kinetic energy
(c) the minimum potential energy equals the maximum kinetic energy
(d) the maximum potential energy equals the minimum kinetic energy.

15. An object is released from rest. The time it takes to fall through a distance h and the speed of the object as it falls through this distance are measured with a pendulum clock. The entire apparatus is taken on the moon and the experiment is repeated
(a) the measured times are same
(b) the measured speeds are same
(c) the actual times in the fall are equal
(d) the actual speeds are equal.

16. Which of the following will change the time period as they are taken to moon ?
(a) A simple pendulum   (b) A physical pendulum
(c) A torsional pendulum   (d) A spring-mass system

EXERCISES

1. A particle executes simple harmonic motion with an amplitude of 10 cm and time period 6 s. At $t = 0$ it is at position $x = 5$ cm going towards positive x-direction. Write the equation for the displacement x at time t. Find the magnitude of the acceleration of the particle at $t = 4$ s.

2. The position, velocity and acceleration of a particle executing simple harmonic motion are found to have magnitudes 2 cm, 1 m s^{-1} and 10 m s^{-2} at a certain instant. Find the amplitude and the time period of the motion.

3. A particle executes simple harmonic motion with an amplitude of 10 cm. At what distance from the mean position are the kinetic and potential energies equal ?

4. The maximum speed and acceleration of a particle executing simple harmonic motion are 10 cm s^{-1} and 50 cm s^{-2}. Find the position(s) of the particle when the speed is 8 cm s^{-1}.

5. A particle having mass 10 g oscillates according to the equation $x = (2{\cdot}0\ \text{cm}) \sin[(100\ \text{s}^{-1})t + \pi/6]$. Find (a) the amplitude, the time period and the spring constant (b) the position, the velocity and the acceleration at $t = 0$.

6. The equation of motion of a particle started at $t = 0$ is given by $x = 5 \sin (20\, t + \pi/3)$, where x is in centimetre and t in second. When does the particle
(a) first come to rest

(b) first have zero acceleration
(c) first have maximum speed ?

7. Consider a particle moving in simple harmonic motion according to the equation
$$x = 2{\cdot}0 \cos(50\,\pi\, t + \tan^{-1} 0{\cdot}75)$$
where x is in centimetre and t in second. The motion is started at $t = 0$. (a) When does the particle come to rest for the first time ? (b) When does the acceleration have its maximum magnitude for the first time ? (c) When does the particle come to rest for the second time ?

8. Consider a simple harmonic motion of time period T. Calculate the time taken for the displacement to change value from half the amplitude to the amplitude.

9. The pendulum of a clock is replaced by a spring-mass system with the spring having spring constant 0·1 N m^{-1}. What mass should be attached to the spring ?

10. A block suspended from a vertical spring is in equilibrium. Show that the extension of the spring equals the length of an equivalent simple pendulum, i.e., a pendulum having frequency same as that of the block.

11. A block of mass 0·5 kg hanging from a vertical spring executes simple harmonic motion of amplitude 0·1 m and time period 0·314 s. Find the maximum force exerted by the spring on the block.

12. A body of mass 2 kg suspended through a vertical spring executes simple harmonic motion of period 4 s. If the

oscillations are stopped and the body hangs in equilibrium, find the potential energy stored in the spring.

13. A spring stores 5 J of energy when stretched by 25 cm. It is kept vertical with the lower end fixed. A block fastened to its other end is made to undergo small oscillations. If the block makes 5 oscillations each second, what is the mass of the block ?

14. A small block of mass m is kept on a bigger block of mass M which is attached to a vertical spring of spring constant k as shown in the figure. The system oscillates vertically. (a) Find the resultant force on the smaller block when it is displaced through a distance x above its equilibrium position. (b) Find the normal force on the smaller block at this position. When is this force smallest in magnitude ? (c) What can be the maximum amplitude with which the two blocks may oscillate together ?

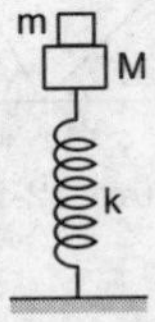

Figure 12-E1

15. The block of mass m_1 shown in figure (12-E2) is fastened to the spring and the block of mass m_2 is placed against it. (a) Find the compression of the spring in the equilibrium position. (b) The blocks are pushed a further distance $(2/k)$ $(m_1 + m_2)g \sin\theta$ against the spring and released. Find the position where the two blocks separate. (c) What is the common speed of blocks at the time of separation ?

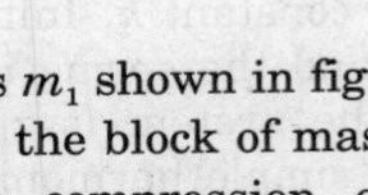

Figure 12-E2

16. In figure (12-E3) $k = 100$ N m^{-1}, $M = 1$ kg and $F = 10$ N. (a) Find the compression of the spring in the equilibrium position. (b) A sharp blow by some external agent imparts a speed of 2 m s^{-1} to the block towards left. Find the sum of the potential energy of the spring and the kinetic energy of the block at this instant. (c) Find the time period of the resulting simple harmonic motion. (d) Find the amplitude. (e) Write the potential energy of the spring when the block is at the left extreme. (f) Write the potential energy of the spring when the block is at the right extreme.
The answers of (b), (e) and (f) are different. Explain why this does not violate the principle of conservation of energy.

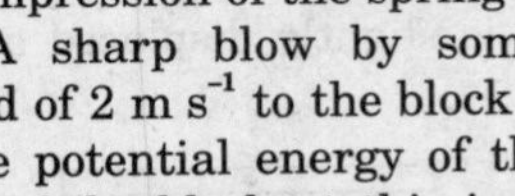

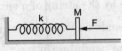

Figure 12-E3

17. Find the time period of the oscillation of mass m in figures 12-E4 a, b, c. What is the equivalent spring constant of the pair of springs in each case ?

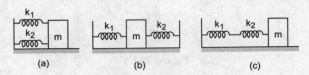

(a)   (b)   (c)

Figure 12-E4

18. The spring shown in figure (12-E5) is unstretched when a man starts pulling on the cord. The mass of the block is M. If the man exerts a constant force F, find (a) the amplitude and the time period of the motion of the block, (b) the energy stored in the spring when the block passes through the equilibrium position and (c) the kinetic energy of the block at this position.

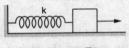

Figure 12-E5

19. A particle of mass m is attatched to three springs A, B and C of equal force constants k as shown in figure (12-E6). If the particle is pushed slightly against the spring C and released, find the time period of oscillation.

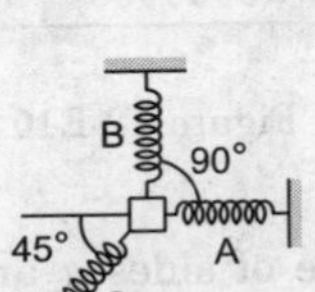

Figure 12-E6

20. Repeat the previous exercise if the angle between each pair of springs is 120° initially.

21. The springs shown in the figure (12-E7) are all unstretched in the beginning when a man starts pulling the block. The man exerts a constant force F on the block. Find the amplitude and the frequency of the motion of the block.

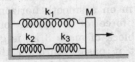

Figure 12-E7

22. Find the elastic potential energy stored in each spring shown in figure (12-E8), when the block is in equilibrium. Also find the time period of vertical oscillation of the block.

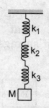

Figure 12-E8

23. The string, the spring and the pulley shown in figure (12-E9) are light. Find the time period of the mass m.

Figure 12-E9

24. Solve the previous problem if the pulley has a moment of inertia I about its axis and the string does not slip over it.

25. Consider the situation shown in figure (12-E10). Show that if the blocks are displaced slightly in opposite directions and released, they will execute simple harmonic motion. Calculate the time period.

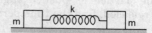

Figure 12-E10

26. A rectangular plate of sides a and b is suspended from a ceiling by two parallel strings of length L each (figure 12-E11). The separation between the strings is d. The plate is displaced slightly in its plane keeping the strings tight. Show that it will execute simple harmonic motion. Find the time period.

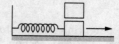

Figure 12-E11

27. A 1 kg block is executing simple harmonic motion of amplitude 0·1 m on a smooth horizontal surface under the restoring force of a spring of spring constant 100 N m^{-1}. A block of mass 3 kg is gently placed on it at the instant it passes through the mean position. Assuming that the two blocks move together, find the frequency and the amplitude of the motion.

Figure 12-E12

28. The left block in figure (12-E13) moves at a speed v towards the right block placed in equilibrium. All collisions to take place are elastic and the surfaces are frictionless. Show that the motions of the two blocks are periodic. Find the time period of these periodic motions. Neglect the widths of the blocks.

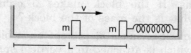

Figure 12-E13

29. Find the time period of the motion of the particle shown in figure (12-E14). Neglect the small effect of the bend near the bottom.

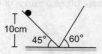

Figure 12-E14

30. All the surfaces shown in figure (12-E15) are frictionless. The mass of the car is M, that of the block is m and the spring has spring constant k. Initially, the car and the block are at rest and the spring is stretched through a length x_0 when the system is released. (a) Find the amplitudes of the simple harmonic motion of the block and of the car as seen from the road. (b) Find the time period(s) of the two simple harmonic motions.

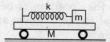

Figure 12-E15

31. A uniform plate of mass M stays horizontally and symmetrically on two wheels rotating in opposite directions (figure 12-E16). The separation between the wheels is L. The friction coefficient between each wheel and the plate is μ. Find the time period of oscillation of the plate if it is slightly displaced along its length and released.

Figure 12-E16

32. A pendulum having time period equal to two seconds is called a seconds pendulum. Those used in pendulum clocks are of this type. Find the length of a seconds pendulum at a place where $g = \pi^2$ m s^{-2}.

33. The angle made by the string of a simple pendulum with the vertical depends on time as $\theta = \dfrac{\pi}{90} \sin[(\pi \text{ s}^{-1}) t]$. Find the length of the pendulum if $g = \pi^2$ m s^{-2}.

34. The pendulum of a certain clock has time period 2·04 s. How fast or slow does the clock run during 24 hours ?

35. A pendulum clock giving correct time at a place where $g = 9\cdot800\text{ m s}^{-2}$ is taken to another place where it loses 24 seconds during 24 hours. Find the value of g at this new place.

36. A simple pendulum is constructed by hanging a heavy ball by a 5·0 m long string. It undergoes small oscillations. (a) How many oscillations does it make per second ? (b) What will be the frequency if the system is taken on the moon where acceleration due to gravitation of the moon is $1\cdot67\text{ m s}^{-2}$?

37. The maximum tension in the string of an oscillating pendulum is double of the minimum tension. Find the angular amplitude.

38. A small block oscillates back and forth on a smooth concave surface of radius R (figure 12-E17). Find the time period of small oscillation.

Figure 12-E17

39. A spherical ball of mass m and radius r rolls without slipping on a rough concave surface of large radius R. It makes small oscillations about the lowest point. Find the time period.

40. A simple pendulum of length 40 cm is taken inside a deep mine. Assume for the time being that the mine is 1600 km deep. Calculate the time period of the pendulum there. Radius of the earth = 6400 km.

41. Assume that a tunnel is dug across the earth (radius = R) passing through its centre. Find the time a particle takes to cover the length of the tunnel if (a) it is projected into the tunnel with a speed of $\sqrt{gR}$ (b) it is released from a height R above the tunnel (c) it is thrown vertically upward along the length of tunnel with a speed of $\sqrt{gR}$.

42. Assume that a tunnel is dug along a chord of the earth, at a perpendicular distance $R/2$ from the earth's centre where R is the radius of the earth. The wall of the tunnel is frictionless. (a) Find the gravitational force exerted by the earth on a particle of mass m placed in the tunnel at a distance x from the centre of the tunnel. (b) Find the component of this force along the tunnel and perpendicular to the tunnel. (c) Find the normal force exerted by the wall on the particle. (d) Find the resultant force on the particle. (e) Show that the motion of the particle in the tunnel is simple harmonic and find the time period.

43. A simple pendulum of length l is suspended through the ceiling of an elevator. Find the time period of small oscillations if the elevator (a) is going up with an acceleration a_0 (b) is going down with an acceleration a_0 and (c) is moving with a uniform velocity.

44. A simple pendulum of length 1 feet suspended from the ceiling of an elevator takes $\pi/3$ seconds to complete one oscillation. Find the acceleration of the elevator.

45. A simple pendulum fixed in a car has a time period of 4 seconds when the car is moving uniformly on a horizontal road. When the accelerator is pressed, the time period changes to 3·99 seconds. Making an approximate analysis, find the acceleration of the car.

46. A simple pendulum of length l is suspended from the ceiling of a car moving with a speed v on a circular horizontal road of radius r. (a) Find the tension in the string when it is at rest with respect to the car. (b) Find the time period of small oscillation.

47. The ear-ring of a lady shown in figure (12-E18) has a 3 cm long light suspension wire. (a) Find the time period of small oscillations if the lady is standing on the ground. (b) The lady now sits in a merry-go-round moving at 4 m s^{-1} in a circle of radius 2 m. Find the time period of small oscillations of the ear-ring.

Figure 12-E18

48. Find the time period of small oscillations of the following systems. (a) A metre stick suspended through the 20 cm mark. (b) A ring of mass m and radius r suspended through a point on its periphery. (c) A uniform square plate of edge a suspended through a corner. (d) A uniform disc of mass m and radius r suspended through a point $r/2$ away from the centre.

49. A uniform rod of length l is suspended by an end and is made to undergo small oscillations. Find the length of the simple pendulum having the time period equal to that of the rod.

50. A uniform disc of radius r is to be suspended through a small hole made in the disc. Find the minimum possible time period of the disc for small oscillations. What should be the distance of the hole from the centre for it to have minimum time period ?

51. A hollow sphere of radius 2 cm is attached to an 18 cm long thread to make a pendulum. Find the time period of oscillation of this pendulum. How does it differ from the time period calculated using the formula for a simple pendulum ?

52. A closed circular wire hung on a nail in a wall undergoes small oscillations of amplitude 2^0 and time period 2 s. Find (a) the radius of the circular wire, (b) the speed of the particle farthest away from the point of suspension as it goes through its mean position, (c) the acceleration of this particle as it goes through its mean position and (d) the acceleration of this particle when it is at an extreme position. Take $g = \pi^2\text{ m s}^{-2}$.

53. A uniform disc of mass m and radius r is suspended through a wire attached to its centre. If the time period of the torsional oscillations be T, what is the torsional constant of the wire?

54. Two small balls, each of mass m are connected by a light rigid rod of length L. The system is suspended from its centre by a thin wire of torsional constant k. The rod is rotated about the wire through an angle θ_0 and released. Find the force exerted by the rod on one of the balls as the system passes through the mean position.

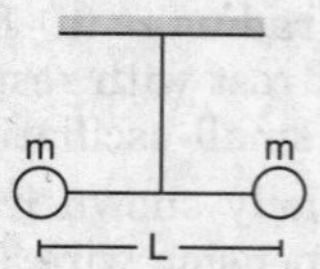

Figure 12-E19

55. A particle is subjected to two simple harmonic motions of same time period in the same direction. The amplitude of the first motion is 3·0 cm and that of second is 4·0 cm. Find the resultant amplitude if the phase difference between the motions is (a) 0°, (b) 60°, (c) 90°.

56. Three simple harmonic motions of equal amplitudes A and equal time periods in the same direction combine. The phase of the second motion is 60° ahead of the first and the phase of the third motion is 60° ahead of the second. Find the amplitude of the resultant motion.

57. A particle is subjected to two simple harmonic motions given by

$$x_1 = 2\cdot0 \sin(100\,\pi\,t) \text{ and } x_2 = 2\cdot0 \sin(120\,\pi\,t + \pi/3),$$

where x is in centimeter and t in second. Find the displacement of the particle at (a) $t = 0\cdot0125$, (b) $t = 0\cdot025$.

58. A particle is subjected to two simple harmonic motions, one along the X-axis and the other on a line making an angle of 45° with the X-axis. The two motions are given by

$$x = x_0 \sin\omega t \text{ and } s = s_0 \sin\omega t$$

Find the amplitude of the resultant motion.

□

ANSWERS

OBJECTIVE I

1. (a)	2. (b)	3. (a)	4. (d)	5. (c)	6. (d)
7. (d)	8. (c)	9. (b)	10. (c)	11. (d)	12. (a)
13. (c)	14. (d)	15. (d)	16. (c)	17. (c)	18. (d)
19. (d)	20. (c)	21. (c).			

OBJECTIVE II

1. (a), (b)	2. (a)	3. (a)
4. (d)	5. (a), (b), (d)	6. (c), (d)
7. (a)	8. all	9. (c), (d)
10. (a)	11. (a), (c), (d)	12. (d)
13. (d)	14. (a), (b)	15. (a), (b)
16. (a), (b).		

EXERCISES

1. $x = (10 \text{ cm}) \sin\left(\dfrac{2\pi}{6\text{ s}} t + \dfrac{\pi}{6}\right)$, $\approx 11 \text{ cm s}^{-2}$

2. 4·9 cm, 0·28 s

3. 5√2 cm

4. ± 1·2 cm from the mean position

5. (a) 2·0 cm, 0·063 s, 100 N m^{-1}

   (b) 1·0 cm, 1·73 m s^{-1}, 100 m s^{-2}

6. (a) $\dfrac{\pi}{120}$ s (b) $\dfrac{\pi}{30}$ s (c) $\dfrac{\pi}{30}$ s

7. (a) $1\cdot6 \times 10^{-2}$ s (b) $1\cdot6 \times 10^{-2}$ s (c) $3\cdot6 \times 10^{-2}$ s

8. $T/6$

9. ≈ 10 g

11. 25 N

12. 40 J

13. 0·16 kg

14. (a) $\dfrac{mkx}{M+m}$ (b) $mg - \dfrac{mkx}{M+m}$, at the highest point

   (c) $g\dfrac{(M+m)}{k}$

15. (a) $\dfrac{(m_1 + m_2)g \sin\theta}{k}$

   (b) When the spring acquires its natural length

   (c) $\sqrt{\dfrac{3}{k}(m_1 + m_2)}\ g \sin\theta$

16. (a) 10 cm (b) 2·5 J (c) $\pi/5$ s

   (d) 20 cm (e) 4·5 J (f) 0·5 J

17. (a) $2\pi\sqrt{\dfrac{m}{k_1 + k_2}}$ (b) $2\pi\sqrt{\dfrac{m}{k_1 + k_2}}$ (c) $2\pi\sqrt{\dfrac{m(k_1 + k_2)}{k_1 k_2}}$

18. (a) $\dfrac{F}{k}$, $2\pi\sqrt{\dfrac{M}{k}}$, (b) $\dfrac{F^2}{2k}$ (c) $\dfrac{F^2}{2k}$

19. $2\pi\sqrt{\dfrac{m}{2k}}$

20. $2\pi\sqrt{\dfrac{2m}{3k}}$

21. $\dfrac{F(k_2+k_3)}{k_1k_2+k_2k_3+k_3k_1}$, $\dfrac{1}{2\pi}\sqrt{\dfrac{k_1k_2+k_2k_3+k_3k_1}{M(k_2+k_3)}}$

22. $\dfrac{M^2g^2}{2k_1}$, $\dfrac{M^2g^2}{2k_2}$ and $\dfrac{M^2g^2}{2k_3}$ from above, time period

$= 2\pi\sqrt{M\left(\dfrac{1}{k_1}+\dfrac{1}{k_2}+\dfrac{1}{k_3}\right)}$

23. $2\pi\sqrt{\dfrac{m}{k}}$

24. $2\pi\sqrt{\dfrac{(m+I/r^2)}{k}}$

25. $2\pi\sqrt{\dfrac{m}{2k}}$

26. $2\pi\sqrt{\dfrac{L}{g}}$

27. $\dfrac{5}{2\pi}$ Hz, 5 cm

28. $\left(\pi\sqrt{\dfrac{m}{k}}+\dfrac{2L}{v}\right)$

29. ≈ 0.73 s

30. (a) $\dfrac{Mx_0}{M+m}$, $\dfrac{mx_0}{M+m}$ (b) $2\pi\sqrt{\dfrac{mM}{k(M+m)}}$

31. $2\pi\sqrt{\dfrac{L}{2\mu g}}$

32. 1 m

33. 1 m

34. 28·3 minutes slow

35. 9·795 m s^{-2}

36. (a) $0.70/\pi$ (b) $1/(2\pi\sqrt{3})$ Hz

37. $\cos^{-1}(3/4)$

38. $2\pi\sqrt{R/g}$

39. $2\pi\sqrt{\dfrac{7(R-r)}{5g}}$

40. 1·47 s

41. $\dfrac{\pi}{2}\sqrt{\dfrac{R}{g}}$ in each case

42. (a) $\dfrac{GMm}{R^3}\sqrt{x^2+R^2/4}$ (b) $\dfrac{GMm}{R^3}x$, $\dfrac{GMm}{2R^2}$

(c) $\dfrac{GMm}{2R^2}$, (d) $\dfrac{GMm}{R^3}x$ (e) $2\pi\sqrt{R^3/(GM)}$

43. (a) $2\pi\sqrt{\dfrac{l}{g+a_0}}$ (b) $2\pi\sqrt{\dfrac{l}{g-a_0}}$ (c) $2\pi\sqrt{\dfrac{l}{g}}$

44. 4 f s^{-2} upwards

45. $g/10$

46. (a) ma (b) $2\pi\sqrt{l/a}$, where $a=\left[g^2+\dfrac{v^4}{r^2}\right]^{1/2}$

47. (a) 0·34 s (b) 0·30 s

48. (a) 1·51 s (b) $2\pi\sqrt{\dfrac{2r}{g}}$ (c) $2\pi\sqrt{\dfrac{\sqrt8 a}{3g}}$ (d) $2\pi\sqrt{\dfrac{3r}{2g}}$

49. $2l/3$

50. $2\pi\sqrt{\dfrac{r\sqrt2}{g}}$, $r/\sqrt2$

51. 0·89 s, it is about 0·3% larger than the calculated value

52. (a) 50 cm (b) 11 cm s^{-1}
(c) 1·2 cm s^{-2} towards the point of suspension
(d) 34 cm s^{-2} towards the mean position

53. $\dfrac{2\pi^2mr^2}{T^2}$

54. $\left[\dfrac{k^2\theta_0^4}{L^2}+m^2g^2\right]^{1/2}$

55. (a) 7·0 cm (b) 6·1 cm (c) 5·0 cm

56. $2A$

57. (a) -2.41 cm (b) 0·27 cm

58. $\left[x_0^2+s_0^2+\sqrt2\,x_0s_0\right]^{1/2}$

CHAPTER 13

FLUID MECHANICS

13.1 FLUIDS

Matter is broadly divided into three categories, solid, liquid and gas. The intermolecular forces are strong in solids, so that the shape and size of solids do not easily change. This force is comparatively less in liquids and so the shape is easily changed. Although the shape of a liquid can be easily changed, the volume of a given mass of a liquid is not so easy to change. It needs quite a good effort to change the density of liquids. In gases, the intermolecular forces are very small and it is simple to change both the shape and the density of a gas. Liquids and gases together are called fluids, i.e., that which can flow.

In this chapter we shall largely deal with liquids. The equations derived may be applicable to gases in many cases with some modifications. We shall assume that the liquids we deal with are *incompressible and nonviscous*. The first condition means that the density of the liquid is independent of the variations in pressure and always remains constant. The second condition means that parts of the liquid in contact do not exert any tangential force on each other. The force by one part of the liquid on the other part is perpendicular to the surface of contact. Thus, there is no friction between the adjacent layers of a liquid.

13.2 PRESSURE IN A FLUID

Figure 13.1

Consider a point A in the fluid (figure 13.1). Imagine a small area ΔS containing the point A. The fluid on one side of the area presses the fluid on the other side and vice versa. Let the common magnitude of the forces be F. We define the pressure of the fluid at the point A as

$$P = \lim_{\Delta S \to 0} \frac{F}{\Delta S} \qquad \ldots \ (13.1)$$

For a homogeneous and nonviscous fluid, this quantity does not depend on the orientation of ΔS and hence we talk of pressure *at a point*. For such a fluid, pressure is a scalar quantity having only magnitude.

Unit of Pressure

The SI unit of pressure is N m^{-2} called *pascal* and abbreviated as Pa.

Variation of Pressure with Height

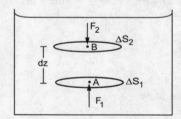

Figure 13.2

Let us consider two points A and B (figure 13.2) separated by a small vertical height dz. Imagine a horizontal area ΔS_1 containing A and an identical horizontal area ΔS_2 containing B. The area $\Delta S_1 = \Delta S_2 = \Delta S$. Consider the fluid enclosed between the two surfaces $\Delta S_1, \Delta S_2$ and the vertical boundary joining them. The vertical forces acting on this fluid are

(a) F_1, vertically upward by the fluid below it

(b) F_2, vertically downward by the fluid above it and

(c) weight W, vertically downward.

Let the pressure at the surface A be P and the pressure at B be $P + dP$. Then

$$F_1 = P \, \Delta S$$

and
$$F_2 = (P + dP)\Delta S.$$

The volume of the fluid considered is $(\Delta S)\,(dz)$. If the density of the fluid at A is ρ, the mass of the fluid considered is $\rho(\Delta S)\,(dz)$ and hence its weight W is

$$W = \rho\,(\Delta S)\,(dz)\,g.$$

For vertical equilibrium,

$$F_1 = F_2 + W$$

or,
$$P \, \Delta S = (P + dP)\,\Delta S + \rho\,g(dz)\,\Delta S$$

or,
$$dP = -\,\rho g \, dz \, . \qquad \dots \ (13.2)$$

As we move up through a height dz the pressure decreases by $\rho g \, dz$, where ρ is the density of the fluid at that point.

Now consider two points at $z = 0$ and $z = h$. If the pressure at $z = 0$ is P_1 and that at $z = h$ is P_2, then from equation (13.2)

$$\int_{P_1}^{P_2} dP = \int_0^z -\rho g \, dz$$

or,
$$P_2 - P_1 = \int_0^z -\rho g \, dz \, .$$

If the density is same everywhere

$$P_2 - P_1 = -\rho g z$$

or,
$$P_1 = P_2 + \rho g z \, . \qquad \dots \ (13.3)$$

Next consider two points A and B in the same horizontal line inside a fluid. Imagine a small vertical area ΔS_1 containing the point A and a similar vertical area ΔS_2 containing the point B.

Figure 13.3

The area $\Delta S_1 = \Delta S_2 = \Delta S$. Consider the liquid contained in the horizontal cylinder bounded by ΔS_1 and ΔS_2. If the pressures at A and B are P_1 and P_2 respectively, the forces in the direction AB are

(a) $P_1 \Delta S$ towards right and

(b) $P_2 \Delta S$ towards left.

If the fluid remains in equilibrium,

$$P_1 \Delta S = P_2 \Delta S \, .$$

or,
$$P_1 = P_2$$

Thus, the pressure is same at two points in the same horizontal level.

13.3 PASCAL'S LAW

We have seen in the previous section that the pressure difference between two points in a liquid at rest depends only on the difference in vertical height between the points. The difference is in fact $\rho g z$, where ρ is the density of the liquid (assumed constant) and z is the difference in vertical height. Suppose by some means the pressure at one point of the liquid is increased. The pressure at all other points of the liquid must also increase by the same amount because the pressure difference must be the same between two given points. This is the content of Pascal's law which may be stated as follows :

If the pressure in a liquid is changed at a particular point, the change is transmitted to the entire liquid without being diminished in magnitude.

Figure 13.4

As an example, suppose a flask fitted with a piston is filled with a liquid as shown in figure (13.4). Let an external force F be applied on the piston. If the cross-sectional area of the piston is A, the pressure just below the piston is increased by F/A. By Pascal's law, the pressure at any point B will also increase by the same amount F/A. This is because the pressure at B has to be $\rho g z$ more than the pressure at the piston, where z is the vertical distance *of* B below the piston. By applying the force we do not appreciably change z (as the liquid is supposed to be incompressible) and hence the pressure difference remains unchanged. As the pressure at the piston is increased by F/A, the pressure at B also increases by the same amount.

Pascal's law has several interesting applications. Figure (13.5) shows the principle of a *hydraulic lift* used to raise heavy loads such as a car.

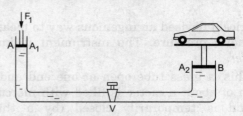

Figure 13.5

It consists of two vertical cylinders A and B of different cross-sectional areas A_1 and A_2 connected by a horizontal tube. Pistons are fitted in both the cylinder. The load is kept on a platform fixed with the piston of larger area. A liquid is filled in the equipment. A valve V is fitted in the horizontal tube which allows the liquid to go from A to B when pressed from the A-side. The piston A is pushed by a force F_1. The pressure in the liquid increases everywhere by an amount F_1/A_1. The valve V is open and the liquid flows into the cylinder B. It exerts an extra force $F_2 = A_2\left(\dfrac{F_1}{A_1}\right)$ on the larger piston in the upward direction which raises the load upward.

The advantage of this method is that if A_2 is much larger than A_1, even a small force F_1 is able to generate a large force F_2 which can raise the load. It may be noted that there is no gain in terms of work. The work done by F_1 is same as that by F_2. The piston A has to traverse a larger downward distance as compared to the height raised by B.

13.4 ATMOSPHERIC PRESSURE AND BAROMETER

The atmosphere of the earth is spread up to a height of about 200 km. This atmosphere presses the bodies on the surface of the earth. The force exerted by the air on any body is perpendicular to the surface of the body. We define *atmospheric pressure* as follows. Consider a small surface ΔS in contact with air. If the force exerted by the air on this part is F, the atmospheric pressure is

$$P_0 = \operatorname*{Lim}_{\Delta S \to 0} \frac{F}{\Delta S}.$$

Atmospheric pressure at the top of the atmosphere is zero as there is nothing above it to exert the force. The pressure at a distance z below the top will be $\int_0^z \rho g \, dz$. Remember, neither ρ nor g can be treated as constant over large variations in heights. However, the density of air is quite small and so the atmospheric pressure does not vary appreciably over small distances. Thus, we say that the atmospheric pressure at Patna is 76 cm of mercury without specifying whether it is at Gandhi Maidan or at the top of Golghar.

Torricelli devised an ingenious way to measure the atmospheric pressure. The instrument is known as *barometer*.

In this, a glass tube open at one end and having a length of about a meter is filled with mercury. The open end is temporarily closed (by a thumb or otherwise) and the tube is inverted in a cup of mercury. With the open end dipped into the cup, the

temporary closure is removed. The mercury column in the tube falls down a little and finally stays there.

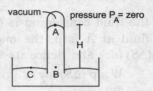

Figure 13.6

Figure (13.6) shows schematically the situation. The upper part of the tube contains vacuum as the mercury goes down and no air is allowed in. Thus, the pressure at the upper end A of the mercury column inside the tube is $P_A =$ zero. Let us consider a point C on the mercury surface in the cup and another point B in the tube at the same horizontal level. The pressure at C is equal to the atmospheric pressure. As B and C are in the same horizontal level, the pressures at B and C are equal. Thus, the pressure at B is equal to the atmospheric pressure P_0 in the lab.

Suppose the point B is at a depth H below A. If ρ be the density of mercury,

$$P_B = P_A + \rho g H$$

or, $P_0 = \rho g H$.   ... (13.4)

The height H of the mercury column in the tube above the surface in the cup is measured. Knowing the density of mercury and the acceleration due to gravity, the atmospheric pressure can be calculated using equation (13.4).

The atmospheric pressure is often given as the length of mercury column in a barometer. Thus, a pressure of 76 cm of mercury means

$$P_0 = (13{\cdot}6 \times 10^3 \text{ kg m}^{-3}) (9{\cdot}8 \text{ m s}^{-2}) (0{\cdot}76 \text{ m})$$

$$= 1{\cdot}01 \times 10^5 \text{ Pa}.$$

This pressure is written as 1 atm. If the tube is insufficient in length, the mercury column will not fall down and no vacuum will be created. The inner surface of the tube will be in contact with the mercury at the top and will exert a pressure P_A on it.

Example 13.1

Water is filled in a flask up to a height of 20 cm. *The bottom of the flask is circular with radius* 10 cm. *If the atmospheric pressure is* $1{\cdot}01 \times 10^5$ Pa, *find the force exerted by the water on the bottom. Take $g = 10$ m s^{-2} and density of water = 1000 kg m^{-3}.*

Solution : The pressure at the surface of the water is equal to the atmospheric pressure P_0. The pressure at the bottom is

$$P = P_0 + h\rho g$$
$$= 1{\cdot}01 \times 10^5 \, \text{Pa} + (0{\cdot}20 \, \text{m}) (1000 \, \text{kg m}^{-3}) (10 \, \text{m s}^{-2})$$
$$= 1{\cdot}01 \times 10^5 \, \text{Pa} + 0{\cdot}02 \times 10^5 \, \text{Pa}$$
$$= 1{\cdot}03 \times 10^5 \, \text{Pa}.$$

The area of the bottom $= \pi r^2 = 3{\cdot}14 \times (0{\cdot}1 \, \text{m})^2$
$$= 0{\cdot}0314 \, \text{m}^2 .$$

The force on the bottom is, therefore,
$$F = P \pi r^2$$
$$= (1{\cdot}03 \times 10^5 \, \text{Pa}) \times (0{\cdot}0314 \, \text{m}^2) = 3230 \, \text{N}.$$

Manometer

Manometer is a simple device to measure the pressure in a closed vessel containing a gas. It consists of a U-tube having some liquid. One end of the tube is open to the atmosphere and the other end is connected to the vessel (figure 13.7).

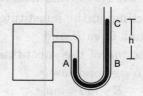

Figure 13.7

The pressure of the gas is equal to the pressure at A

$$= \text{pressure at } B$$
$$= \text{pressure at } C + h\rho g$$
$$= P_0 + h\rho g$$

when P_0 is the atmospheric pressure, $h = BC$ is the difference in levels of the liquid in the two arms and ρ is the density of the liquid.

The excess pressure $P - P_0$ is called the *quage pressure*.

13.5 ARCHIMEDES' PRINCIPLE

When a body is partially or fully dipped into a fluid, the fluid exerts forces on the body. At any small portion of the surface of the body, the force by the fluid is perpendicular to the surface and is equal to the pressure at that point multiplied by the area (figure 13.8). The resultant of all these contact forces is called the force of *buoyancy* or *buoyant force*.

Figure 13.8

Archimedes' principle states that *when a body is partially or fully dipped into a fluid at rest, the fluid exerts an upward force of buoyancy equal to the weight of the displaced fluid.*

Archimedes' principle is not an independent principle and may be deduced from Newton's laws of motion.

Consider the situation shown in figure (13.8) where a body is shown dipped into a fluid. Suppose the body dipped in the fluid is replaced by the same fluid of equal volume. As the entire fluid now becomes homogeneous, all parts will remain in equilibrium. The part of the fluid substituting the body also remains in equilibrium. Forces acting on this substituting fluid are

(a) the weight mg of this part of the fluid, and

(b) the resultant B of the contact forces by the remaining fluid.

As the substituting fluid is in equilibrium, these two should be equal and opposite. Thus,

$$B = mg \qquad \dots \ (13.5)$$

and it acts in the vertically upward direction.

Now the substituting fluid just occupies the space which was previously occupied by the body. Hence, the shape of the boundary of the substituting fluid is same as the boundary of the body. Thus, the magnitude and direction of the force due to the pressure on any small area of the boundary is same for the body as for the substituting fluid. The force of buoyancy on the body is, therefore, same as the force of buoyancy B on the substituting fluid.

From equation (13.5) the force of buoyancy on a dipped body is equal to the weight mg of the displaced fluid and acts along the vertically upward direction. This is Archimedes' principle.

Note that in this derivation we have assumed that the fluid is in equilibrium in an inertial frame. If it is not so, the force of buoyancy may be different from the weight of the displaced fluid.

Floatation

When a solid body is dipped into a fluid, the fluid exerts an upward force of buoyancy on the solid. If the force of buoyancy equals the weight of the solid, the solid will remain in equilibrium. This is called *floatation*. When the overall density of the solid is smaller than the density of the fluid, the solid floats with a part of it in the fluid. The fraction dipped is such that the weight of the displaced fluid equals the weight of the solid.

Example 13.2
_____

A 700 g *solid cube having an edge of length* 10 cm *floats in water. How much volume of the cube is outside the water* ? *Density of water* $= 1000$ kg m^{-3}.

Solution : The weight of the cube is balanced by the buoyant force. The buoyant force is equal to the weight of the water displaced. If a volume V of the cube is inside the water, the weight of the displaced water $= V\rho g$, where ρ is the density of water. Thus,

$$V\rho g = (0.7 \text{ kg}) g$$

or, $$V = \frac{0.7 \text{ kg}}{\rho} = \frac{0.7 \text{ kg}}{1000 \text{ kg m}^{-3}} = 7 \times 10^{-4} \text{ m}^3 = 700 \text{ cm}^3.$$

The total volume of the cube $= (10 \text{ cm})^3 = 1000 \text{ cm}^3$.

The volume outside the water is

$$1000 \text{ cm}^3 - 700 \text{ cm}^3 = 300 \text{ cm}^3.$$

13.6 PRESSURE DIFFERENCE AND BUOYANT FORCE IN ACCELERATING FLUIDS

Equations (13.3) and (13.5) were derived by assuming that the fluid under consideration is in equilibrium in an inertial frame. If this is not the case, the equations must be modified. We shall discuss some special cases of accelerating fluids.

A Liquid Placed in an Elevator

(a) Pressure Difference

Suppose a beaker contains some liquid and it is placed in an elevator which is going up with an acceleration a_0 (figure 13.9). Let A and B be two points in the liquid, B being at a vertical height z above A. Construct a small horizontal area ΔS around A and an equal horizontal area around B. Construct a vertical cylinder with the two areas as the faces. Consider the motion of the liquid contained within this cylinder. Let P_1 be the pressure at A and P_2 be the pressure at B.

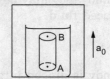

Figure 13.9

Forces acting on the liquid contained in the cylinder, in the vertical direction, are :

(a) $P_1 \Delta S$, upward due to the liquid below it

(b) $P_2 \Delta S$, downward due to the liquid above it and

(c) weight $mg = (\Delta S)z\rho g$ downward, where ρ is the density of the liquid.

Under the action of these three forces the liquid is accelerating upward with an acceleration a_0. From Newton's second law

$$P_1 \Delta S - P_2 \Delta S - mg = ma_0$$

or, $(P_1 - P_2)\Delta S = m(g + a_0) = (\Delta S)z\rho(g + a_0)$

or, $P_1 - P_2 = \rho(g + a_0)z$.   ... (13.6)

(b) Buoyant Force

Now suppose a body is dipped inside a liquid of density ρ placed in an elevator going up with an acceleration a_0. Let us calculate the force of buoyancy B on this body. As was done earlier, let us suppose that we substitute the body into the liquid by the same liquid of equal volume. The entire liquid becomes a homogenous mass and hence the substituted liquid is at rest with respect to the rest of the liquid. Thus, the substituted liquid is also going up with an acceleration a_0 together with the rest of the liquid.

The forces acting on the substituted liquid are

(a) the buoyant force B and

(b) the weight mg of the substituted liquid.

From Newton's second law

$$B - mg = ma_0$$

or, $B = m(g + a_0)$ ... (13.7)

Equation (13.6) and (13.7) are similar to the corresponding equations for unaccelerated liquid with the only difference that $g + a$ takes the role of g.

B Free Surface of a Liquid in Horizontal Acceleration

Consider a liquid placed in a beaker which is accelerating horizontally with an acceleration a_0 (figure 13.10). Let A and B be two points in the liquid at a separation l in the same horizontal line along the acceleration a_0. We shall first obtain the pressure difference between the points A and B.

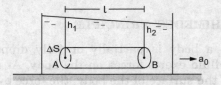

Figure 13.10

Construct a small vertical area ΔS around A and an equal area around B. Consider the liquid contained in the horizontal cylinder with the two areas as the flat faces. Let the pressure at A be P_1 and the pressure at B be P_2. The forces along the line AB are

(a) $P_1 \Delta S$ towards right due to the liquid on the left and

(b) $P_2 \Delta S$ towards left due to the liquid on the right.

Under the action of these forces, the liquid contained in the cylinder is accelerating towards right. From Newton's second law,

$$P_1 \Delta S - P_2 \Delta S = ma_0$$

or, $$(P_1 - P_2)\Delta S = (\Delta S)l\rho a_0$$

or, $$P_1 - P_2 = l\rho a_0 . \qquad \ldots (13.8)$$

The two points in the same horizontal line do not have equal pressure if the liquid is accelerated horizontally.

As there is no vertical acceleration, the equation (13.3) is valid. If the atmospheric pressure is P_0, the pressure at A is $P_1 = P_0 + h_1\rho g$ and the pressure at B is $P_2 = P_0 + h_2\rho g$, where h_1 and h_2 are the depths of A and B from the free surface. Substituting in (13.8)

$$h_1 \rho g - h_2 \rho g = l\rho a_0$$

or, $$\frac{h_1 - h_2}{l} = \frac{a_0}{g}$$

or, $$\tan\theta = \frac{a_0}{g}$$

where θ is the inclination of the free surface with the horizontal.

13.7 FLOW OF FLUIDS

The flow of fluid is in general a complex branch of mechanics. If you look at the motion of water in a fall (like Rallah fall near Manali or Kemti fall near Moussurie) the view is very pleasant. The water falls from a height and then proceeds on a flat bed or a slope with thumping, jumping and singing if you can appreciate the music. But if you try to analyse the motion of each particle on the basis of laws of mechanics, the task is tremendously difficult. Other examples of fluid flow are the sailing of clouds and the motion of smoke when a traditional Chulha using coal, wood or goitha (prepared from cowdung) in an Indian village is lit. The motion of each smoke particle is governed by the same Newton's laws but to predict the motion of a particular particle is not easy.

13.8 STEADY AND TURBULENT FLOW

Consider a liquid passing through a glass tube (figure 13.11). Concentrate on a particular point A in the tube and look at the particles arriving at A. If the velocity of the liquid is small, all the particles which come to A will have same speed and will move in same direction. As a particle goes from A to another point B, its speed and direction may change, but all the particles reaching A will have the same speed at A and all the particles reaching B will have the same speed at B. Also, if one particle passing through A has gone

through B, then all the particles passing through A go through B. Such a flow of fluid is called a *steady flow*.

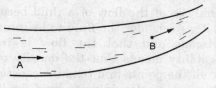

Figure 13.11

In steady flow the velocity of fluid particles reaching a particular point is the same at all time. Thus, each particle follows the same path as taken by a previous particle passing through that point.

If the liquid is pushed in the tube at a rapid rate, the flow may become turbulent. In this case, the velocities of different particles passing through the same point may be different and change erratically with time. The motion of water in a high fall or a fast flowing river is, in general, turbulent.

Steady flow is also called *streamline flow*.

Line of Flow : Streamline

The path taken by a particle in flowing fluid is called its *line of flow*. The tangent at any point on the line of flow gives the direction of motion of that particle at that point. In the case of steady flow, all the particles passing through a given point follow the same path and hence we have a unique line of flow passing through a given point. In this case, the line of flow is also called a *streamline*. Thus, the tangent to the streamline at any point gives the direction of all the particles passing through that point. It is clear that two streamlines cannot intersect, otherwise, the particle reaching at the intersection will have two different directions of motion.

Tube of Flow

Consider an area S in a fluid in steady flow. Draw streamlines from all the points of the periphery of S. These streamlines enclose a tube, of which S is a cross-section. Such a tube is called a *tube of flow*. As the streamlines do not cross each other, fluid flowing through differnt tubes of flow cannot intermix, although there is no physical partition between the tubes. When a liquid is passed slowly through a pipe, the pipe itself is one tube of flow.

Figure 13.12

13.9 IRROTATIONAL FLOW OF AN INCOMPRESSIBLE AND NONVISCOUS FLUID

The analysis of the flow of a fluid becomes much simplified if we consider the fluid to be incompressible and nonviscous and that the flow is irrotational. Incompressibility means that the density of the fluid is same at all the points and remains constant as time passes. This assumption is quite good for liquids and is valid in certain cases of flow of gases. Viscosity of a fluid is related to the internal friction when a layer of fluid slips over another layer. Mechanical energy is lost against such viscous forces. The assumption of a nonviscous fluid will mean that we are neglecting the effect of such internal friction. Irrotational flow means there is no net angular velocity of fluid particles. When you put some washing powder in a bucket containing water and mix it by rotating your hand in circular path along the wall of the bucket, the water comes into rotational motion. Quite often water flowing in rivers show small vortex formation where it goes in rotational motion about a centre. Now onwards we shall consider only the irrotational motion of an incompressible and nonviscous fluid.

13.10 EQUATION OF CONTINUITY

We have seen that the fluid going through a tube of flow does not intermix with fluid in other tubes. The total mass of fluid going into the tube through any cross section should, therefore, be equal to the total mass coming out of the same tube from any other cross section in the same time. This leads to the equation of continuity.

Let us consider two cross sections of a tube of flow at the points A and B (figure 13.13). Let the area of cross section at A be A_1 and that at B be A_2. Let the speed of the fluid be v_1 at A and v_2 at B.

Figure 13.13

How much fluid goes into the tube through the cross section at A in a time interval Δt? Let us construct a cylinder of length $v_1 \Delta t$ at A as shown in the figure. As the fluid at A has speed v_1, all the fluid included in this cylinder will cross through A_1 in the time interval Δt. Thus, the volume of the fluid going into the tube through the cross section at A is $A_1 v_1 \Delta t$. Similarly, the volume of the fluid going out of

the tube through the cross section at B is $A_2 v_2 \Delta t$. If the fluid is incompressible, we must have

$$A_1 v_1 \Delta t = A_2 v_2 \, \Delta t$$

or, $A_1 v_1 = A_2 v_2 .$ ... (13.9)

The product of the area of cross section and the speed remains the same at all points of a tube of flow. This is called the *equation of continuity* and expresses the law of conservation of mass in fluid dynamics.

Example 13.3

Figure (13.14) shows a liquid being pushed out of a tube by pressing a piston. The area of cross section of the piston is 1.0 cm^2 and that of the tube at the outlet is 20 mm^2. If the piston is pushed at a speed of 2 cm s^{-1}, what is the speed of the outgoing liquid?

Figure 13.14

Solution : From the equation of continuity

$$A_1 v_1 = A_2 v_2$$

or, $(1.0 \text{ cm}^2) (2 \text{ cm s}^{-1}) = (20 \text{ mm}^2) v_2$

or, $v_2 = \dfrac{1.0 \text{ cm}^2}{20 \text{ mm}^2} \times 2 \text{ cm s}^{-1}$

$$= \dfrac{100 \text{ mm}^2}{20 \text{ mm}^2} \times 2 \text{ cm s}^{-1} = 10 \text{ cm s}^{-1} .$$

13.11 BERNOULLI EQUATION

Bernoulli equation relates the speed of a fluid at a point, the pressure at that point and the height of that point above a reference level. It is just the application of work–energy theorem in the case of fluid flow.

We shall consider the case of irrotational and steady flow of an incompressible and nonviscous liquid. Figure (13.15) shows such a flow of a liquid in a tube of varying cross section and varying height. Consider the liquid contained between the cross sections A and B of the tube. The heights of A and B are h_1 and h_2 respectively from a reference level. This liquid advances into the tube and after a time Δt is contained between the cross sections A' and B' as shown in figure.

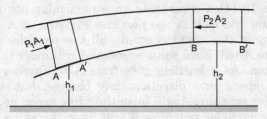

Figure 13.15

Suppose the area of cross section at $A = A_1$

the area of cross section at $B = A_2$

the speed of the liquid at $A = v_1$

the speed of the liquid at $B = v_2$

the pressure at $A = P_1$

the pressure at $B = P_2$

and the density of the liquid = ρ.

The distance $AA' = v_1 \Delta t$ and the distance $BB' = v_2 \Delta t$. The volume between A and A' is $A_1 v_1 \Delta t$ and the volume between B and B' is $A_2 v_2 \Delta t$. By the equation of continuity,

$$A_1 v_1 \Delta t = A_2 v_2 \Delta t .$$

The mass of this volume of liquid is

$$\Delta m = \rho A_1 v_1 \Delta t = \rho A_2 v_2 \Delta t. \qquad \dots \text{ (i)}$$

Let us calculate the total work done on the part of the liquid just considered.

The forces acting on this part of the liquid are

(a) $P_1 A_1$, by the liquid on the left

(b) $P_2 A_2$, by the liquid on the right

(c) $(\Delta m)g$, the weight of the liquid considered and

(d) $\mathcal{N}$, contact forces by the walls of the tube.

In time Δt, the point of application of $P_1 A_1$ is displaced by $AA' = v_1 \Delta t$. Thus, the work done by $P_1 A_1$ in time Δt is

$$W_1 = (P_1 A_1)\,(v_1 \Delta t) = P_1 \left(\frac{\Delta m}{\rho} \right).$$

Similarly, the work done by $P_2 A_2$ in time Δt is

$$W_2 = -(P_2 A_2)\,(v_2 \Delta t) = -P_2 \left(\frac{\Delta m}{\rho} \right).$$

The work done by the weight is equal to the negative of the change in gravitational potential energy.

The change in potential energy (P.E.) in time Δt is

P. E. of $A'BB'$ − P. E. of $AA'B$

= P. E. of $A'B$ + P. E. of BB'

  − P. E. of AA' − P. E. of $A'B$

= P. E. of BB' − P. E. of AA'

= $(\Delta m)gh_2 - (\Delta m)gh_1$.

Thus, the work done by the weight in time Δt is

$$W_3 = (\Delta m)gh_1 - (\Delta m)gh_2.$$

The contact force $\mathcal{N}$ does no work on the liquid because it is perpendicular to the velocity.

The total work done on the liquid considered, in the time interval Δt is

$$W = W_1 + W_2 + W_3$$

$$= P_1 \left(\frac{\Delta m}{\rho} \right) - P_2 \left(\frac{\Delta m}{\rho} \right) + (\Delta m)gh_1 - (\Delta m)gh_2 \quad \dots \text{ (ii)}$$

The change in kinetic energy (K.E.) of the same liquid in time Δt is

K.E. of $A'BB'$ − K.E. of $AA'B$

= K.E. of $A'B$ + K.E. of BB' − K.E. of AA' − K.E. of $A'B$

= K.E. of BB' − K.E. of AA'

$$= \frac{1}{2}\,(\Delta m)\,v_2^2 - \frac{1}{2}\,(\Delta m)v_1^2. \qquad \dots \text{ (iii)}$$

Since the flow is assumed to be steady, the speed at any point remains constant in time and hence the K.E. of the part $A'B$ is same at initial and final time and cancels out when change in kinetic energy of the system is considered.

By the work–energy theorem, the total work done on the system is equal to the change in its kinetic energy. Thus,

$$P_1 \left(\frac{\Delta m}{\rho} \right) - P_2 \left(\frac{\Delta m}{\rho} \right) + (\Delta m)gh_1 - (\Delta m)gh_2$$

$$= \frac{1}{2}\,(\Delta m)v_2^2 - \frac{1}{2}\,(\Delta m)v_1^2$$

or, $\quad \dfrac{P_1}{\rho} + gh_1 + \dfrac{1}{2}\,v_1^2 = \dfrac{P_2}{\rho} + gh_2 + \dfrac{1}{2}\,v_2^2$

or, $P_1 + \rho gh_1 + \dfrac{1}{2}\,\rho v_1^2 = P_2 + \rho gh_2 + \dfrac{1}{2}\,\rho v_2^2$ ... (13.10)

or, $\quad P + \rho gh + \dfrac{1}{2}\,\rho v^2 = \text{constant} \qquad \dots \text{ (13.11)}$

This is known as *Bernoulli equation.*

Example 13.4

Figure (13.16) shows a liquid of density $1200\ \text{kg m}^{-3}$ flowing steadily in a tube of varying cross section. The cross section at a point A is $1{\cdot}0\ \text{cm}^2$ and that at B is $20\ \text{mm}^2$, the points A and B are in the same horizontal plane. The speed of the liquid at A is $10\ \text{cm s}^{-1}$. Calculate the difference in pressures at A and B.

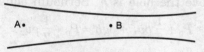

Figure 13.16

Solution : From equation of continuity, the speed v_2 at B is given by,

$$A_1 v_1 = A_2 v_2$$

or, $\quad (1{\cdot}0\ \text{cm}^2)\,(10\ \text{cm s}^{-1}) = (20\ \text{mm}^2)v_2$

or, $\quad v_2 = \dfrac{1{\cdot}0\ \text{cm}^2}{20\ \text{mm}^2} \times 10\ \text{cm s}^{-1} = 50\ \text{cm s}^{-1}.$

By Bernoulli equation,

$$P_1 + \rho gh_1 + \frac{1}{2}\,\rho v_1^2 = P_2 + \rho gh_2 + \frac{1}{2}\,\rho v_2^2.$$

Here $h_1 = h_2$. Thus,

$$P_1 - P_2 = \frac{1}{2}\rho v_2^2 - \frac{1}{2}\rho v_1^2$$

$$= \frac{1}{2} \times (1200 \text{ kg m}^{-3})\,(2500 \text{ cm}^2 \text{ s}^{-2} - 100 \text{ cm}^2 \text{ s}^{-2})$$

$$= 600 \text{ kg m}^{-3} \times 2400 \text{ cm}^2 \text{ s}^{-2} = 144 \text{ Pa.}$$

13.12 APPLICATIONS OF BERNOULLI EQUATION

(a) Hydrostatics

If the speed of the fluid is zero everywhere, we get the situation of hydrostatics. Putting $v_1 = v_2 = 0$ in the Bernoulli equation (13.10)

$$P_1 + \rho g h_1 = P_2 + \rho g h_2$$

or, $P_1 - P_2 = \rho g (h_2 - h_1)$

as expected from hydrostatics.

(b) Speed of Efflux

Consider a liquid of density ρ filled in a tank of large cross-sectional area A_1. There is a hole of cross-sectional area A_2 at the bottom and the liquid flows out of the tank through the hole. The situation is shown in figure (13.17). Suppose $A_2 \ll A_1$.

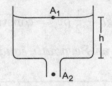

Figure 13.17

Let v_1 and v_2 be the speeds of the liquid at A_1 and A_2. As both the cross sections are open to the atmosphere, the pressures there equals the atmospheric pressure P_0. If the height of the free surface above the hole is h, Bernoulli equation gives

$$P_0 + \frac{1}{2}\rho v_1^2 + \rho g h = P_0 + \frac{1}{2}\rho v_2^2. \qquad \ldots \text{(i)}$$

By the equation of continuity

$$A_1 v_1 = A_2 v_2 \, .$$

Putting v_1 in terms of v_2 in (i),

$$\frac{1}{2}\rho \left(\frac{A_2}{A_1}\right)^2 v_2^2 + \rho g h = \frac{1}{2}\rho v_2^2$$

or, $\left[1 - \left(\dfrac{A_2}{A_1}\right)^2\right] v_2^2 = 2 gh.$

If $A_2 \ll A_1$, this equation reduces to $v_2^2 = 2 gh$

or, $v_2 = \sqrt{2 gh}$.

The speed of liquid coming out through a hole at a depth h below the free surface is the same as that of a particle fallen freely through the height h under gravity. This is known as Torricelli's theorem. The speed of the liquid coming out is called the speed of efflux.

Example 13.5

A water tank is constructed on the top of a building. With what speed will the water come out of a tap 6.0 m below the water level in the tank? Assume steady flow and that the pressure above the water level is equal to the atmospheric pressure.

Solution : The velocity is given by Torricelli's theorem

$$v = \sqrt{2 gh}$$

$$= \sqrt{2 \times (9.8 \text{ m s}^{-2}) \times (6.0 \text{ m})} \approx 11 \text{ m s}^{-1}.$$

(c) Ventury Tube

A ventury tube is used to measure the flow speed of a fluid in a tube. It consists of a constriction or a throat in the tube. As the fluid passes through the constriction, its speed increases in accordance with the equation of continuity. The pressure thus decreases as required by Bernoulli equation.

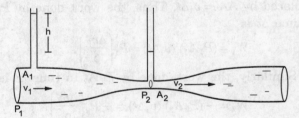

Figure 13.18

Figure (13.18) shows a ventury tube through which a liquid of density ρ is flowing. The area of cross section is A_1 at the wider part and A_2 at the constriction. Let the speeds of the liquid at A_1 and A_2 be v_1 and v_2 and the pressures at A_1 and A_2 be P_1 and P_2 respectively. By the equation of continuity

$$A_1 v_1 = A_2 v_2 \qquad \ldots \text{(i)}$$

and by Bernoulli equation,

$$P_1 + \frac{1}{2}\rho v_1^2 = P_2 + \frac{1}{2}\rho v_2^2$$

or, $(P_1 - P_2) = \dfrac{1}{2}\rho \left(v_2^2 - v_1^2\right). \qquad \ldots \text{(ii)}$

Figure (13.18) also shows two vertical tubes connected to the ventury tube at A_1 and A_2. If the difference in heights of the liquid levels in these tubes is h, we have

$$P_1 - P_2 = \rho g h.$$

Putting in (ii),

$$2gh = v_2^2 - v_1^2 \qquad \dots \text{(iii)}$$

Knowing A_1 and A_2, one can solve equations (i) and (iii) so as to get v_1 and v_2. This allows one to know the rate of flow of liquid past a cross section.

(d) Aspirator Pump

When a fluid passes through a region at a large speed, the pressure there decreases. This fact finds a number of useful applications. In an aspirator pump a barrel A terminates in a small constriction B (figure 13.19). A narrow tube C connects the constriction to a vessel containing the liquid to be sprayed. The air in the barrel A is pushed by the operator through a piston. As the air passes through the constriction B, its speed is considerably increased and consequently the pressure drops. Due to reduced pressure in the constriction B, the liquid is raised from the vessel and is sprayed with the expelled air.

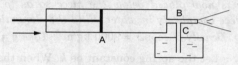

Figure 13.19

(e) Change of Plane of Motion of a Spinning Ball

Quite often when swing bowlers of cricket deliver the ball, the ball changes its plane of motion in air.

Such a deflection from the plane of projection may be explained on the basis of Bernoulli equation.

Suppose a ball spinning about the vertical direction is going ahead with some velocity in the horizontal direction in otherwise still air. Let us work in a frame in which the centre of the ball is at rest. In this frame the air moves past the ball at a speed v in the opposite direction. The situation is shown in (13.20).

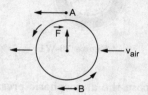

Figure 13.20

The plane of the figure represents horizontal plane. The air that goes from the A side of the ball in the figure is dragged by the spin of the ball and its speed increases. The air that goes from the B side of the ball in the figure suffers an opposite drag and its speed decreases. The pressure of air is reduced on the A side and is increased on the B side as required by the Bernoulli's theorem. As a result, a net force F acts on the ball from the B side to the A side due to this pressure difference. This force causes the deviation of the plane of motion.

Worked Out Examples

1. *A beaker of circular cross section of radius* 4 cm *is filled with mercury up to a height of* 10 cm. *Find the force exerted by the mercury on the bottom of the beaker. The atmospheric pressure* $= 10^5\,\text{N m}^{-2}$. *Density of mercury* $= 13600\,\text{kg m}^{-3}$. *Take* $g = 10\,\text{m s}^{-2}$.

Solution : The pressure at the surface

$$= \text{atmospheric pressure}$$

$$= 10^5\,\text{N m}^{-2}.$$

The pressure at the bottom

$$= 10^5\,\text{N m}^{-2} + h\rho g$$

$$= 10^5\,\text{N m}^{-2} + (0.1\,\text{m})\,(13600\,\text{kg m}^{-3})\,(10\,\text{m s}^{-2})$$

$$= 10^5\,\text{N m}^{-2} + 13600\,\text{N m}^{-2}$$

$$= 1.136 \times 10^5\,\text{N m}^{-2}.$$

The force exerted by the mercury on the bottom

$$= (1.136 \times 10^5\,\text{N m}^{-2}) \times (3.14 \times 0.04\,\text{m} \times 0.04\,\text{m})$$

$$= 571\,\text{N}.$$

2. *The density of air near earth's surface is* $1.3\,\text{kg m}^{-3}$ *and the atmospheric pressure is* $1.0 \times 10^5\,\text{N m}^{-2}$. *If the atmosphere had uniform density, same as that observed at the surface of the earth, what would be the height of the atmosphere to exert the same pressure ?*

Solution : Let the uniform density be ρ and atmospheric height be h. The pressure at the surface of the earth would be

$$p = \rho g h$$

or, $1.0 \times 10^5\,\text{N m}^{-2} = (1.3\,\text{kg m}^{-3})\,(9.8\,\text{m s}^{-2})\,h$

or, $$h = \frac{1.0 \times 10^5\,\text{N m}^{-2}}{(1.3\,\text{kg m}^{-3})\,(9.8\,\text{m s}^{-2})} = 7850\,\text{m}.$$

Even Mount Everest (8848 m) would have been outside the atmosphere.

3. *The liquids shown in figure (13-W1) in the two arms are mercury (specific gravity = 13·6) and water. If the difference of heights of the mercury columns is 2 cm, find the height h of the water column.*

Figure 13-W1

Solution : Suppose the atmospheric pressure = P_0.

Pressure at $A = P_0 + h$ (1000 kg m^{-3}) g.

Pressure at $B = P_0 + (0·02$ m$)(13600$ kg m^{-3}) g.

These pressures are equal as A and B are at the same horizontal level. Thus,

$$h = (0·02 \text{ m}) \ 13·6$$

$$\approx 0·27 \text{ m} = 27 \text{ cm}.$$

4. *A cylindrical vessel containing a liquid is closed by a smooth piston of mass m as shown in the figure. The area of cross section of the piston is A. If the atmospheric pressure is P_0, find the pressure of the liquid just below the piston.*

Figure 13-W2

Solution : Let the pressure of the liquid just below the piston be P. The forces acting on the piston are

(a) its weight, mg (downward)

(b) force due to the air above it, $P_0 A$ (downward)

(c) force due to the liquid below it, PA (upward).

If the piston is in equilibrium,

$$PA = P_0 A + mg$$

or,

$$P = P_0 + \frac{mg}{A}.$$

5. *The area of cross section of the two arms of a hydraulic press are 1 cm^2 and 10 cm^2 respectively (figure 13-W3). A force of 5 N is applied on the water in the thinner arm. What force should be applied on the water in the thicker arm so that the water may remain in equilibrium ?*

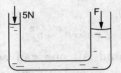

Figure 13-W3

Solution : In equilibrium, the pressures at the two surfaces should be equal as they lie in the same horizontal level. If the atmospheric pressure is P_0 and a force F is applied to maintain the equilibrium, the pressures are

$$P_0 + \frac{5 \text{ N}}{1 \text{ cm}^2} \text{ and } P_0 + \frac{F}{10 \text{ cm}^2} \text{ respectively.}$$

This gives $F = 50$ N.

6. *A copper piece of mass 10 g is suspended by a vertical spring. The spring elongates 1 cm over its natural length to keep the piece in equilibrium. A beaker containing water is now placed below the piece so as to immerse the piece completely in water. Find the elongation of the spring. Density of copper = 9000 kg m^{-3}. Take g = 10 m s^{-2}.*

Solution : Let the spring constant be k. When the piece is hanging in air, the equilibrium condition gives

$$k(1 \text{ cm}) = (0·01 \text{ kg}) (10 \text{ m s}^{-2})$$

or

$$k(1 \text{ cm}) = 0·1 \text{ N}. \qquad \ldots \text{ (i)}$$

The volume of the copper piece

$$= \frac{0·01 \text{ kg}}{9000 \text{ kg m}^{-3}} = \frac{1}{9} \times 10^{-5} \text{ m}^3.$$

This is also the volume of water displaced when the piece is immersed in water. The force of buoyancy

= weight of the liquid displaced

$$= \frac{1}{9} \times 10^{-5} \text{ m}^3 \times (1000 \text{ kg m}^{-3}) \times (10 \text{ m s}^{-2})$$

$$= 0·011 \text{ N}.$$

If the elongation of the spring is x when the piece is immersed in water, the equilibrium condition of the piece gives,

$$kx = 0·1 \text{ N} - 0·011 \text{ N} = 0·089 \text{ N}. \qquad \ldots \text{ (ii)}$$

By (i) and (ii),

$$x = \frac{0·089}{0·1} \text{ cm} = 0·89 \text{ cm}.$$

7. *A cubical block of wood of edge 3 cm floats in water. The lower surface of the cube just touches the free end of a vertical spring fixed at the bottom of the pot. Find the maximum weight that can be put on the block without wetting it. Density of wood = 800 kg m^{-3} and spring constant of the spring = 50 N m^{-1}. Take g = 10 m s^{-2}.*

Figure 13-W4

Solution : The specific gravity of the block = 0·8. Hence the height inside water = 3 cm × 0·8 = 2·4 cm. The height outside water = 3 cm − 2·4 = 0·6 cm. Suppose the maximum weight that can be put without wetting it is W. The block in this case is completely immersed in the water. The volume of the displaced water

= volume of the block = $27 \times 10^{-6} \, m^3$.

Hence, the force of buoyancy

$= (27 \times 10^{-6} \, m^3) \times (1000 \, kg \, m^{-3}) \times (10 \, m \, s^{-2})$

$= 0·27 \, N$.

The spring is compressed by 0·6 cm and hence the upward force exerted by the spring

$= 50 \, N \, m^{-1} \times 0·6 \, cm = 0·3 \, N$.

The force of buoyancy and the spring force taken together balance the weight of the block plus the weight w put on the block. The weight of the block is

$W = (27 \times 10^{-6} \, m) \times (800 \, kg \, m^{-3}) \times (10 \, m \, s^{-2})$

$= 0·22 \, N$.

Thus, $w = 0·27 \, N + 0·3 \, N - 0·22 \, N$

$= 0·35 \, N$.

8. *A wooden plank of length 1 m and uniform cross section is hinged at one end to the bottom of a tank as shown in figure (13-W5). The tank is filled with water up to a height of 0·5 m. The specific gravity of the plank is 0·5. Find the angle θ that the plank makes with the vertical in the equilibrium position. (Exclude the case θ = 0.)*

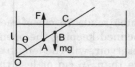

Figure 13-W5

Solution : The forces acting on the plank are shown in the figure. The height of water level is $l = 0·5$ m. The length of the plank is 1·0 m = $2l$. The weight of the plank acts through the centre B of the plank. We have $OB = l$. The buoyant force F acts through the point A which is the middle point of the dipped part OC of the plank.

We have $OA = \dfrac{OC}{2} = \dfrac{l}{2 \cos\theta}$.

Let the mass per unit length of the plank be ρ.

Its weight $mg = 2l\rho g$.

The mass of the part OC of the plank $= \left(\dfrac{l}{\cos\theta}\right)\rho$.

The mass of water displaced $= \dfrac{1}{0·5} \dfrac{l}{\cos\theta} \rho = \dfrac{2l\rho}{\cos\theta}$.

The buoyant force F is, therefore, $F = \dfrac{2l\rho g}{\cos\theta}$.

Now, for equilibrium, the torque of mg about O should balance the torque of F about O.

So, $mg(OB)\sin\theta = F(OA) \sin\theta$

or, $(2l\rho)l = \left(\dfrac{2l\rho}{\cos\theta}\right)\left(\dfrac{l}{2 \cos\theta}\right)$

or, $\cos^2\theta = \dfrac{1}{2}$

or, $\cos\theta = \dfrac{1}{\sqrt{2}}$, or, θ = 45°.

9. *A cylindrical block of wood of mass M is floating in water with its axis vertical. It is depressed a little and then released. Show that the motion of the block is simple harmonic and find its frequency.*

Solution : Suppose a height h of the block is dipped in the water in equilibrium position. If r be the radius of the cylindrical block, the volume of the water displaced $= \pi r^2 h$. For floating in equilibrium

$\pi r^2 h\rho g = W$ ... (i)

where ρ is the density of water and W the weight of the block.

Now suppose during the vertical motion, the block is further dipped through a distance x at some instant. The volume of the displaced water is $\pi r^2(h + x)$. The forces acting on the block are, the weight W vertically downward and the buoyancy $\pi r^2(h + x)\rho g$ vertically upward.

Net force on the block at displacement x from the equilibrium position is

$F = W - \pi r^2(h + x)\rho g$

$= W - \pi r^2 h\rho g - \pi r^2 \rho xg$

Using (i),

$F = -\pi r^2 \rho gx = -kx$, where $k = \pi r^2 \rho g$.

Thus, the block executes SHM with frequency

$\nu = \dfrac{1}{2\pi}\sqrt{\dfrac{k}{M}} = \dfrac{1}{2\pi}\sqrt{\dfrac{\pi r^2 \rho g}{M}}$.

10. *Water flows in a horizontal tube as shown in figure (13-W6). The pressure of water changes by 600 N m^{-2}*

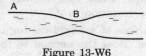

Figure 13-W6

between A and B where the areas of cross section are 30 cm^2 and 15 cm^2 respectively. Find the rate of flow of water through the tube.

Solution : Let the velocity at $A = v_A$ and that at $B = v_B$

By the equation of continuity, $\dfrac{v_B}{v_A} = \dfrac{30 \text{ cm}^2}{15 \text{ cm}^2} = 2$.

By Bernoulli equation,

$$P_A + \frac{1}{2}\rho v_A^2 = P_B + \frac{1}{2}\rho v_B^2$$

or, $$P_A - P_B = \frac{1}{2}\rho(2v_A)^2 - \frac{1}{2}\rho v_A^2 = \frac{3}{2}\rho v_A^2,$$

or, $$600 \text{ N m}^{-2} = \frac{3}{2}(1000 \text{ kg m}^{-3})\,v_A^2$$

or, $$v_A = \sqrt{0.4 \text{ m}^2\text{s}^{-2}} = 0.63 \text{ m s}^{-1}$$

The rate of flow $= (30 \text{ cm}^2)(0.63 \text{ m s}^{-1}) = 1890 \text{ cm}^3\text{s}^{-1}$.

11. *The area of cross section of a large tank is 0·5 m^2. It has an opening near the bottom having area of cross section 1 cm^2. A load of 20 kg is applied on the water at the top. Find the velocity of the water coming out of the opening at the time when the height of water level is 50 cm above the bottom. Take g = 10 m s^{-2}.*

Solution :

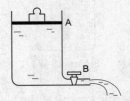

Figure 13-W7

As the area of cross section of the tank is large compared to that of the opening, the speed of water in the tank will be very small as compared to the speed at the opening. The pressure at the surface of water in the tank is that due to the atmosphere plus due to the load.

$$P_A = P_0 + \frac{(20 \text{ kg})(10 \text{ m s}^{-2})}{0.5 \text{ m}^2} = P_0 + 400 \text{ N m}^{-2}.$$

At the opening, the pressure is that due to the atmosphere.

Using Bernoulli equation

$$P_A + \rho g h + \frac{1}{2}\rho v_A^2 = P_B + \frac{1}{2}\rho v_B^2$$

or, $$P_0 + 400 \text{ N m}^{-2} + (1000 \text{ kg m}^{-3})(10 \text{ m s}^{-2})(0.5 \text{ m}) + 0$$
$$= P_0 + \frac{1}{2}(1000 \text{ kg m}^{-3})v_B^2$$

or, $$5400 \text{ N m}^{-2} = (500 \text{ kg m}^{-3})^3\,v_B^2$$

or, $$v_B \approx 3.3 \text{ m s}^{-1}.$$

□

QUESTIONS FOR SHORT ANSWER

1. Is it always true that the molecules of a dense liquid are heavier than the molecules of a lighter liquid ?

2. If someone presses a pointed needle against your skin, you are hurt. But if someone presses a rod against your skin with the same force, you easily tolerate. Explain.

3. In the derivation of $P_1 - P_2 = \rho g z$, it was assumed that the liquid is incompressible. Why will this equation not be strictly valid for a compressible liquid ?

4. Suppose the density of air at Madras is ρ_0 and atmospheric pressure is P_0. If we go up, the density and the pressure both decrease. Suppose we wish to calculate the pressure at a height 10 km above Madras. If we use the equation $P_0 - P = \rho_0 g z$, will we get a pressure more than the actual or less than the actual ? Neglect the variation in g. Does your answer change if you also consider the variation in g ?

5. The free surface of a liquid resting in an inertial frame is horizontal. Does the normal to the free surface pass through the centre of the earth ? Think separately if the liquid is (a) at the equator (b) at a pole (c) somewhere else.

6. A barometer tube reads 76 cm of mercury. If the tube is gradually inclined keeping the open end immersed in the mercury reservoir, will the length of mercury column be 76 cm, more than 76 cm or less than 76 cm ?

7. A one meter long glass tube is open at both ends. One end of the tube is dipped into a mercury cup, the tube is kept vertical and the air is pumped out of the tube by connecting the upper end to a suction pump. Can mercury be pulled up into the pump by this process ?

8. A satellite revolves round the earth. Air pressure inside the satellite is maintained at 76 cm of mercury. What will be the height of mercury column in a barometer tube 1 m long placed in the satellite ?

9. Consider the barometer shown in figure (13-Q1). If a small hole is made at a point P in the barometer tube, will the mercury come out from this hole ?

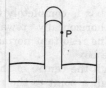

Figure 13-Q1

10. Is Archimedes' principle valid in an elevator accelerating up ? In a car accelerating on a level road ?

11. Why is it easier to swim in sea water than in fresh water ?

12. A glass of water has an ice cube floating in water. The water level just touches the rim of the glass. Will the water overflow when the ice melts ?

13. A ferry boat loaded with rocks has to pass under a bridge. The maximum height of the rocks is slightly more than the height of the bridge so that the boat just fails to pass under the bridge. Should some of the rocks be removed or some more rocks be added ?

14. Water is slowly coming out from a vertical pipe. As the water descends after coming out, its area of cross section reduces. Explain this on the basis of the equation of continuity.

15. While watering a distant plant, a gardener partially closes the exit hole of the pipe by putting his finger on it. Explain why this results in the water stream going to a larger distance.

16. A Gipsy car has a canvass top. When the car runs at high speed, the top bulges out. Explain.

OBJECTIVE I

1. A liquid can easily change its shape but a solid can not because
   (a) the density of a liquid is smaller than that of a solid
   (b) the forces between the molecules is stronger in solid than in liquids
   (c) the atoms combine to form bigger molecules in a solid
   (d) the average separation between the molecules is larger in solids.

2. Consider the equations
   $$P = \lim_{\Delta s \to 0} \frac{F}{\Delta S} \text{ and } P_1 - P_2 = \rho gz.$$
   In an elevator accelerating upward
   (a) both the equations are valid
   (b) the first is valid but not the second
   (c) the second is valid but not the first
   (d) both are invalid.

3. The three vessels shown in figure (13-Q2) have same base area. Equal volumes of a liquid are poured in the three vessels. The force on the base will be
   (a) maximum in vessel A (b) maximum in vessel B
   (c) maximum in vessel C (d) equal in all the vessels.

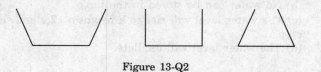

Figure 13-Q2

4. Equal mass of three liquids are kept in three identical cylindrical vessels A, B and C. The densities are ρ_A, ρ_B, ρ_C with $\rho_A < \rho_B < \rho_C$. The force on the base will be
   (a) maximum in vessel A (b) maximum in vessel B
   (c) maximum in vessel C (d) equal in all the vessels.

5. Figure (13-Q3) shows a siphon. The liquid shown is water. The pressure difference $P_B - P_A$ between the points A and B is

(a) 400 N m^{-2} (b) 3000 N m^{-2}
(c) 1000 N m^{-2} (d) zero.

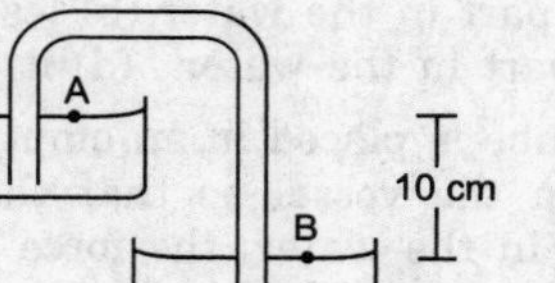

Figure 13-Q3

6. A beaker containing a liquid is kept inside a big closed jar. If the air inside the jar is continuously pumped out, the pressure in the liquid near the bottom of the liquid will
   (a) increase   (b) decrease   (c) remain constant
   (d) first decrease and then increase.

7. The pressure in a liquid at two points in the same horizontal plane are equal. Consider an elevator accelerating upward and a car accelerating on a horizontal road. The above statement is correct in
   (a) the car only
   (b) the elevator only
   (c) both of them
   (d) neither of them.

8. Suppose the pressure at the surface of mercury in a barometer tube is P_1 and the pressure at the surface of mercury in the cup is P_2.
   (a) $P_1 = 0, P_2 = $ atmospheric pressure
   (b) $P_1 = $ atmospheric pressure, $P_2 = 0$
   (c) $P_1 = P_2 = $ atmospheric pressure
   (d) $P_1 = P_2 = 0$.

9. A barometer kept in an elevator reads 76 cm when it is at rest. If the elevator goes up with increasing speed,

the reading will be

(a) zero   (b) 76 cm   (c) < 76 cm   (d) > 76 cm.

10. A barometer kept in an elevator accelerating upward reads 76 cm. The air pressure in the elevator is

(a) 76 cm   (b) < 76 cm   (c) > 76 cm   (d) zero.

11. To construct a barometer, a tube of length 1 m is filled completely with mercury and is inverted in a mercury cup. The barometer reading on a particular day is 76 cm. Suppose a 1 m tube is filled with mercury up to 76 cm and then closed by a cork. It is inverted in a mercury cup and the cork is removed. The height of mercury column in the tube over the surface in the cup will be

(a) zero   (b) 76 cm   (c) > 76 cm   (d) < 76 cm.

12. A 20 N metal block is suspended by a spring balance. A beaker containing some water is placed on a weighing machine which reads 40 N. The spring balance is now lowered so that the block gets immersed in the water. The spring balance now reads 16 N. The reading of the weighing machine will be

(a) 36 N   (b) 60 N   (c) 44 N   (d) 56 N.

13. A piece of wood is floating in water kept in a bottle. The bottle is connected to an air pump. Neglect the compressibility of water. When more air is pushed into the bottle from the pump, the piece of wood will float with

(a) larger part in the water   (b) lesser part in the water
(c) same part in the water   (d) it will sink.

14. A metal cube is placed in an empty vessel. When water is filled in the vessel so that the cube is completely immersed in the water, the force on the bottom of the vessel in contact with the cube

(a) will increase   (b) will decrease
(c) will remain the same   (d) will become zero.

15. A wooden object floats in water kept in a beaker. The object is near a side of the beaker (figure 13-Q4). Let P_1, P_2, P_3 be the pressures at the three points A, B and C of the bottom as shown in the figure.

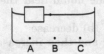

Figure 13-Q4

(a) $P_1 = P_2 = P_3$.
(b) $P_1 < P_2 < P_3$.
(c) $P_1 > P_2 > P_3$.
(d) $P_2 = P_3 \neq P_1$.

16. A closed cubical box is completely filled with water and is accelerated horizontally towards right with an acceleration a. The resultant normal force by the water on the top of the box

(a) passes through the centre of the top
(b) passes through a point to the right of the centre
(c) passes through a point to the left of the centre
(d) becomes zero.

17. Consider the situation of the previous problem. Let the water push the left wall by a force F_1 and the right wall by a force F_2.

(a) $F_1 = F_2$ (b) $F_1 > F_2$ (c) $F_1 < F_2$
(d) the information is insufficient to know the relation between F_1 and F_2.

18. Water enters through end A with a speed v_1 and leaves through end B with a speed v_2 of a cylindrical tube AB. The tube is always completely filled with water. In case I the tube is horizontal, in case II it is vertical with the end A upward and in case III it is vertical with the end B upward. We have $v_1 = v_2$ for

(a) case I (b) case II (c) case III (d) each case.

19. Bernoulli theorem is based on conservation of

(a) momentum   (b) mass
(c) energy   (d) angular momentum.

20. Water is flowing through a long horizontal tube. Let P_A and P_B be the pressures at two points A and B of the tube.

(a) P_A must be equal to P_B.
(b) P_A must be greater than P_B.
(c) P_A must be smaller than P_B.
(d) $P_A = P_B$ only if the cross-sectional area at A and B are equal.

21. Water and mercury are filled in two cylindrical vessels up to same height. Both vessels have a hole in the wall near the bottom. The velocity of water and mercury coming out of the holes are v_1 and v_2 respectively.

(a) $v_1 = v_2$.
(b) $v_1 = 13 \cdot 6 \, v_2$.
(c) $v_1 = v_2 / 13 \cdot 6$.
(d) $v_1 = \sqrt{13 \cdot 6} \, v_2$.

22. A large cylindrical tank has a hole of area A at its bottom. Water is poured in the tank by a tube of equal cross-sectional area A ejecting water at the speed v.

(a) The water level in the tank will keep on rising.
(b) No water can be stored in the tank
(c) The water level will rise to a height $v^2 / 2g$ and then stop.
(d) The water level will oscillate.

OBJECTIVE II

1. A solid floats in a liquid in a partially dipped position.

(a) The solid exerts a force equal to its weight on the liquid.
(b) The liquid exerts a force of buoyancy on the solid which is equal to the weight of the solid.
(c) The weight of the displaced liquid equals the weight of the solid.
(d) The weight of the dipped part of the solid is equal to the weight of the displaced liquid.

2. The weight of an empty balloon on a spring balance is W_1. The weight becomes W_2 when the balloon is filled with air. Let the weight of the air itself be w. Neglect the thickness of the balloon when it is filled with air. Also neglect the difference in the densities of air inside and outside the balloon.
   (a) $W_2 = W_1$.   (b) $W_2 = W_1 + w$.
   (c) $W_2 < W_1 + w$.   (d) $W_2 > W_1$.

3. A solid is completely immersed in a liquid. The force exerted by the liquid on the solid will
   (a) increase if it is pushed deeper inside the liquid
   (b) change if its orientation is changed
   (c) decrease if it is taken partially out of the liquid
   (d) be in the vertically upward direction.

4. A closed vessel is half filled with water. There is a hole near the top of the vessel and air is pumped out from this hole.
   (a) The water level will rise up in the vessel.
   (b) The pressure at the surface of the water will decrease.
   (c) The force by the water on the bottom of the vessel will decrease.
   (d) The density of the liquid will decrease.

5. In a streamline flow,
   (a) the speed of a particle always remains same
   (b) the velocity of a particle always remains same
   (c) the kinetic energies of all the particles arriving at a given point are the same
   (d) the momenta of all the particles arriving at a given point are the same.

6. Water flows through two identical tubes A and B. A volume V_0 of water passes through the tube A and $2V_0$ through B in a given time. Which of the following may be correct ?
   (a) Flow in both the tubes are steady.
   (b) Flow in both the tubes are turbulent.
   (c) Flow is steady in A but turbulent in B.
   (d) Flow is steady in B but turbulent in A.

7. Water is flowing in streamline motion through a tube with its axis horizontal. Consider two points A and B in the tube at the same horizontal level.
   (a) The pressures at A and B are equal for any shape of the tube.
   (b) The pressures are never equal.
   (c) The pressures are equal if the tube has a uniform cross section.
   (d) The pressures may be equal even if the tube has a nonuniform cross section.

8. There is a small hole near the bottom of an open tank filled with a liquid. The speed of the water ejected does not depend on
   (a) area of the hole   (b) density of the liquid
   (c) height of the liquid from the hole
   (d) acceleration due to gravity.

EXERCISES

1. The surface of water in a water tank on the top of a house is 4 m above the tap level. Find the pressure of water at the tap when the tap is closed. Is it necessary to specify that the tap is closed ? Take $g = 10 \text{ m s}^{-2}$.

2. The heights of mercury surfaces in the two arms of the manometer shown in figure (13-E1) are 2 cm and 8 cm. Atmospheric pressure $= 1 \cdot 01 \times 10^5 \text{ N m}^{-2}$. Find (a) the pressure of the gas in the cylinder and (b) the pressure of mercury at the bottom of the U tube.

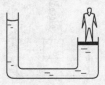

gas

Figure 13-E1

3. The area of cross section of the wider tube shown in figure (13-E2) is 900 cm^2. If the boy standing on the

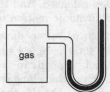

Figure 13-E2

piston weighs 45 kg, find the difference in the levels of water in the two tubes.

4. A glass full of water has a bottom of area 20 cm^2, top of area 20 cm^2, height 20 cm and volume half a litre.
   (a) Find the force exerted by the water on the bottom.
   (b) Considering the equilibrium of the water, find the resultant force exerted by the sides of the glass on the water. Atmospheric pressure $= 1 \cdot 0 \times 10^5 \text{ N m}^{-2}$. Density of water $= 1000 \text{ kg m}^{-3}$ and $g = 10 \text{ m s}^{-2}$. Take all numbers to be exact.

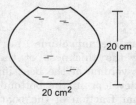

20 cm

20 cm^2

Figure 13-E3

5. Suppose the glass of the previous problem is covered by a jar and the air inside the jar is completely pumped out. (a) What will be the answers to the problem ? (b) Show that the answers do not change if a glass of different shape is used provided the height, the bottom area and the volume are unchanged.

6. If water be used to construct a barometer, what would be the height of water column at standard atmospheric pressure (76 cm of mercury) ?

7. Find the force exerted by the water on a $2 \, m^2$ plane surface of a large stone placed at the bottom of a sea 500 m deep. Does the force depend on the orientation of the surface ?

8. Water is filled in a rectangular tank of size $3 \, m \times 2 \, m \times 1 \, m$. (a) Find the total force exerted by the water on the bottom surface of the tank. (b) Consider a vertical side of area $2 \, m \times 1 \, m$. Take a horizontal strip of width δx metre in this side, situated at a depth of x metre from the surface of water. Find the force by the water on this strip. (c) Find the torque of the force calculated in part (b) about the bottom edge of this side. (d) Find the total force by the water on this side. (e) Find the total torque by the water on the side about the bottom edge. Neglect the atmospheric pressure and take $g = 10 \, m \, s^{-2}$.

9. An ornament weighing 36 g in air, weighs only 34 g in water. Assuming that some copper is mixed with gold to prepare the ornament, find the amount of copper in it. Specific gravity of gold is 19·3 and that of copper is 8·9.

10. Refer to the previous problem. Suppose, the goldsmith argues that he has not mixed copper or any other material with gold, rather some cavities might have been left inside the ornament. Calculate the volume of the cavities left that will allow the weights given in that problem.

11. A metal piece of mass 160 g lies in equilibrium inside a glass of water (figure 13-E4). The piece touches the bottom of the glass at a small number of points. If the density of the metal is $8000 \, kg \, m^{-3}$, find the normal force exerted by the bottom of the glass on the metal piece.

Figure 13-E4

12. A ferry boat has internal volume $1 \, m^3$ and weight 50 kg. (a) Neglecting the thickness of the wood, find the fraction of the volume of the boat immersed in water. (b) If a leak develops in the bottom and water starts coming in, what fraction of the boat's volume will be filled with water before water starts coming in from the sides ?

13. A cubical block of ice floating in water has to support a metal piece weighing 0·5 kg. What can be the minimum edge of the block so that it does not sink in water ? Specific gravity of ice = 0·9.

14. A cube of ice floats partly in water and partly in K.oil (figure 13-E5). Find the ratio of the volume of ice immersed in water to that in K.oil. Specific gravity of K.oil is 0·8 and that of ice is 0·9.

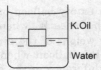

Figure 13-E5

15. A cubical box is to be constructed with iron sheets 1 mm in thickness. What can be the minimum value of the external edge so that the cube does not sink in water ? Density of iron $= 8000 \, kg \, m^{-3}$ and density of water $= 1000 \, kg \, m^{-3}$.

16. A cubical block of wood weighing 200 g has a lead piece fastened underneath. Find the mass of the lead piece which will just allow the block to float in water. Specific gravity of wood is 0·8 and that of lead is 11·3.

17. Solve the previous problem if the lead piece is fastened on the top surface of the block and the block is to float with its upper surface just dipping into water.

18. A cubical metal block of edge 12 cm floats in mercury with one fifth of the height inside the mercury. Water is poured till the surface of the block is just immersed in it. Find the height of the water column to be poured. Specific gravity of mercury = 13·6.

19. A hollow spherical body of inner and outer radii 6 cm and 8 cm respectively floats half-submerged in water. Find the density of the material of the sphere.

20. A solid sphere of radius 5 cm floats in water. If a maximum load of 0·1 kg can be put on it without wetting the load, find the specific gravity of the material of the sphere.

21. Find the ratio of the weights, as measured by a spring balance, of a 1 kg block of iron and a 1 kg block of wood. Density of iron $= 7800 \, kg \, m^{-3}$, density of wood $= 800 \, kg \, m^{-3}$ and density of air $= 1·293 \, kg \, m^{-3}$.

22. A cylindrical object of outer diameter 20 cm and mass 2 kg floats in water with its axis vertical. If it is slightly depressed and then released, find the time period of the resulting simple harmonic motion of the object.

23. A cylindrical object of outer diameter 10 cm, height 20 cm and density $8000 \, kg \, m^{-3}$ is supported by a vertical spring and is half dipped in water as shown in figure(13-E6). (a) Find the elongation of the spring in equilibrium condition. (b) If the object is slightly depressed and released, find the time period of resulting oscillations of the object. The spring constant $= 500 \, N \, m^{-1}$.

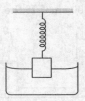

Figure 13-E6

24. A wooden block of mass 0·5 kg and density 800 kg m^{-3} is fastened to the free end of a vertical spring of spring constant 50 N m^{-1} fixed at the bottom. If the entire system is completely immersed in water, find (a) the elongation (or compression) of the spring in equilibrium and (b) the time-period of vertical oscillations of the block when it is slightly depressed and released.

25. A cube of ice of edge 4 cm is placed in an empty cylindrical glass of inner diameter 6 cm. Assume that the ice melts uniformly from each side so that it always retains its cubical shape. Remembering that ice is lighter than water, find the length of the edge of the ice cube at the instant it just leaves contact with the bottom of the glass.

26. A U-tube containing a liquid is accelerated horizontally with a constant acceleration a_0. If the separation between the vertical limbs is l, find the difference in the heights of the liquid in the two arms.

27. At Deoprayag (Garhwal) river Alaknanda mixes with the river Bhagirathi and becomes river Ganga. Suppose Alaknanda has a width of 12 m, Bhagirathi has a width of 8 m and Ganga has a width of 16 m. Assume that the depth of water is same in the three rivers. Let the average speed of water in Alaknanda be 20 km h^{-1} and in Bhagirathi be 16 km h^{-1}. Find the average speed of water in the river Ganga.

28. Water flows through a horizontal tube of variable cross section (figure 13-E7). The area of cross section at A and B are 4 mm^2 and 2 mm^2 respectively. If 1 cc of water enters per second through A, find (a) the speed of water at A, (b) the speed of water at B and (c) the pressure difference $P_A - P_B$.

Figure 13-E7

29. Suppose the tube in the previous problem is kept vertical with A upward but the other conditions remain the same. The separation between the cross sections at A and B is 15/16 cm. Repeat parts (a), (b) and (c) of the previous problem. Take $g = 10$ m s^{-2}.

30. Suppose the tube in the previous problem is kept vertical with B upward. Water enters through B at the rate of 1 cm^3 s^{-1}. Repeat parts (a), (b) and (c). Note that the speed decreases as the water falls down.

31. Water flows through a tube shown in figure (13-E8). The areas of cross section at A and B are 1 cm^2 and 0·5 cm^2 respectively. The height difference between A and B is 5 cm. If the speed of water at A is 10 cm s^{-1}, find (a) the speed at B and (b) the difference in pressures at A and B.

Figure 13-E8

32. Water flows through a horizontal tube as shown in figure (13-E9). If the difference of heights of water column in the vertical tubes is 2 cm, and the areas of cross section at A and B are 4 cm^2 and 2 cm^2 respectively, find the rate of flow of water across any section.

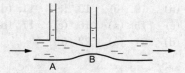

Figure 13-E9

33. Water flows through the tube shown in figure (13-E10). The areas of cross section of the wide and the narrow portions of the tube are 5 cm^2 and 2 cm^2 respectively. The rate of flow of water through the tube is 500 cm^3 s^{-1}. Find the difference of mercury levels in the U-tube.

Figure 13-E10

34. Water leaks out from an open tank through a hole of area 2 mm^2 in the bottom. Suppose water is filled up to a height of 80 cm and the area of cross section of the tank is 0·4 m^2. The pressure at the open surface and at the hole are equal to the atmospheric pressure. Neglect the small velocity of the water near the open surface in the tank. (a) Find the initial speed of water coming out of the hole. (b) Find the speed of water coming out when half of water has leaked out. (c) Find the volume of water leaked out during a time interval dt after the height remained is h. Thus find the decrease in height dh in terms of h and dt.
(d) From the result of part (c) find the time required for half of the water to leak out.

35. Water level is maintained in a cylindrical vessel up to a fixed height H. The vessel is kept on a horizontal plane. At what height above the bottom should a hole be made in the vessel so that the water stream coming out of the hole strikes the horizontal plane at the greatest distance from the vessel (figure 13-E11)?

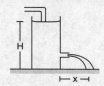

Figure 13.11

ANSWERS

OBJECTIVE I

1. (b)	2. (b)	3. (c)	4. (d)	5. (d)	6. (b)
7. (b)	8. (a)	9. (c)	10. (c)	11. (d)	12. (c)
13. (c)	14. (c)	15. (a)	16. (c)	17. (b)	18. (d)
19. (c)	20. (d)	21. (a)	22. (c)		

OBJECTIVE II

1. (a), (b), (c)	2. (a), (c)	3. (c), (d)
4. (b), (c)	5. (c), (d)	6. (a), (b), (c)
7. (c), (d)	8. (a), (b)	

EXERCISES

1. 40000 N/m^2, Yes

2. (a) $1 \cdot 09 \times 10^5 \text{ N/m}^2$ (b) $1 \cdot 12 \times 10^5 \text{ N/m}^2$

3. 50 cm

4. (a) 204 N   (b) 1 N upward

5. 4 N, 1 N upward

6. $1033 \cdot 6$ cm

7. 10^7 N, No

8. (a) 60000 N, (b) $20000 \, x \, \delta x$ N

    (c) $20000 \times (1-x) \delta x$ N–m (d) 10000 N,

    (e) $10000/3$ N–m

9. $2 \cdot 2$ g

10. $0 \cdot 112 \text{ cm}^3$

11. $1 \cdot 4$ N

12. (a) $\dfrac{1}{20}$ (b) $\dfrac{19}{20}$

13. 17 cm

14. 1 : 1

15. $4 \cdot 8$ cm

16. $54 \cdot 8$ g

17. 50 g

18. $10 \cdot 4$ cm

19. 865 kg m^{-3}

20. $0 \cdot 8$

21. $1 \cdot 0015$

22. $0 \cdot 5$ s

23. (a) $23 \cdot 5$ cm   (b) $0 \cdot 93$ s

24. (a) $2 \cdot 5$ cm   (b) $\pi / 5$ s

25. $2 \cdot 26$ cm

26. $a_0 l / g$

27. 23 km/h

28. (a) 25 cm/s,   (b) 50 cm/s   (c) 94 N/m^2

29. (a) 25 cm/s,   (b) 50 cm/s,   (d) zero

30. (a) 25 cm/s,   (b) 50 cm/s,   (c) 188 N/m^2

31. (a) 20 cm/s,   (b) 485 N/m^2

32. 146 cc/s

33. $2 \cdot 13$ cm

34. (a) 4 m/s,   (b) $\sqrt{8}$ m/s

    (c) $(2 \text{ mm}^2) \sqrt{2gh} \, dt$, $\sqrt{2gh} \times 5 \times 10^{-6} \, dt$

    (d) $6 \cdot 5$ hours

35. $H/2$.

□

CHAPTER 14

SOME MECHANICAL PROPERTIES
OF MATTER

14.1 MOLECULAR STRUCTURE OF A MATERIAL

Matter is made of molecules and atoms. An atom is made of a nucleus and electrons. The nucleus contains positively charged protons and neutrons, collectively called nucleons. Nuclear forces operating between different nucleons are responsible for the structure of the nucleus. Electromagnetic forces operate between a pair of electrons and between an electron and the nucleus. These forces are responsible for the structure of an atom. The forces between different atoms are responsible for the structure of a molecule and the forces between the molecules are responsible for the structure of the material as seen by us.

Interatomic and Intermolecular Forces

The force between two atoms can be typically represented by the potential energy curve shown in figure (14.1). The horizontal axis represents the separation between the atoms. The zero of potential energy is taken when the atoms are widely separated $(r = \infty)$.

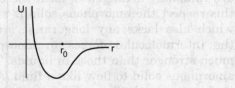

Figure 14.1

As the separation between the atoms is decreased from a large value, the potential energy also decreases, becoming negative. This shows that the force between the atoms is attractive in this range. As the separation is decreased to a particular value r_0, the potential energy is minimum. At this separation, the force is zero and the atoms can stay in equilibrium. If the

separation is further decreased, the potential energy increases. This means a repulsive force acts between the atoms at small separations.

A polyatomic molecule is formed when the atoms are arranged in such a fashion that the total potential energy of the system is minimum.

The force between two molecules has the same general nature as shown in figure (14.1). At large separation, the force between two molecules is weak and attractive. The force increases as the separation is decreased to a particular value and then decreases to zero at $r = r_0$. If the separation is further decreased, the force becomes repulsive.

Bonds

The atoms form molecules primarily due to the electrostatic interaction between the electrons and the nuclei. These interactions are described in terms of different kinds of *bonds*. We shall briefly discuss two important bonds that frequently occur in materials.

Ionic Bond

In an *ionic bond* two atoms come close to each other and an electron is completely transferred from one atom to the other. This leaves the first atom positively charged and the other one negatively charged. There is an electrostatic attraction between the ions which keeps them bound. For example, when a sodium atom comes close to a chlorine atom, an electron of the sodium atom is completely transferred to the chlorine atom. The positively charged sodium ion and the negatively charged chlorine ion attract each other to form an ionic bond resulting in sodium chloride molecule.

Covalent Bond

In many of the cases a complete transfer of electron from one atom to another does not take place to form a bond. Rather, electrons from neighbouring atoms are made available for sharing between the atoms. Such bonds are called *covalent bond*. When two hydrogen atoms come close to each other, both the electrons are available to both the nuclei. In other words, each electron moves through the total space occupied by the two atoms. Each electron is pulled by both the nuclei. Chlorine molecule is also formed by this mechanism. Two chlorine atoms share a pair of electrons to form the bond. Another example of covalent bond is hydrogen chloride (HCl) molecule.

Three States of Matter

If two molecules are kept at a separation $r = r_0$, they will stay in equilibrium. If they are slightly pulled apart so that $r > r_0$, an attractive force will operate between them. If they are slightly pushed so that $r < r_0$, a repulsive force will operate. Thus, if a molecule is slightly displaced from its equilibrium position, it will oscillate about its mean position. This is the situation in a solid. The molecules are close to each other, very nearly at the equilibrium separations. The amplitude of vibrations is very small and the molecules remain almost fixed at their positions. This explains why a solid has a fixed shape if no external forces act to deform it.

In liquids, the average separation between the molecules is somewhat larger. The attractive force is weak and the molecules are more free to move inside the whole mass of the liquid. In gases, the separation is much larger and the molecular force is very weak.

Solid State

In solids, the intermolecular forces are so strong that the molecules or ions remain almost fixed at their equilibrium positions. Quite often these equilibrium positions have a very regular three-dimensional arrangement which we call *crystal*. The positions occupied by the molecules or the ions are called *lattice points*. Because of this long range ordering, the molecules or ions combine to form large rigid solids.

The crystalline solids are divided into four categories depending on the nature of the bonding between the basic units.

Molecular Solid

In a molecular solid, the molecules are formed due to covalent bonds between the atoms. The bonding between the molecules depends on whether the molecules are *polar* or *nonpolar* as discussed below. If the centre of negative charge in a molecule coincides with the centre of the positive charge, the molecule is called *nonpolar*. Molecules of hydrogen, oxygen, chlorine, etc., are of this type. Otherwise, the molecule

is called a *polar* molecule. Water molecule is polar. The bond between polar molecules is called a *dipole–dipole bond*. The bond between nonpolar molecules is called a *van der Waals bond*. Molecular solids are usually soft and have low melting point. They are poor conductors of electricity.

Ionic Solid

In an ionic solid, the lattice points are occupied by positive and negative ions. The electrostatic attraction between these ions binds the solid. These attraction forces are quite strong so that the material is usually hard and has fairly high melting point. They are poor conductors of electricity.

Covalent Solid

In a covalent solid, atoms are arranged in the crystalline form. The neighbouring atoms are bound by shared electrons. Such covalent bonds extend in space so as to form a large solid structure. Diamond, silicon, etc., are examples of covalent solids. Each carbon atom is bonded to four neighbouring carbon atoms in a diamond structure. They are quite hard, have high melting point and are poor conductors of electricity.

Metallic Solid

In a metallic solid, positive ions are situated at the lattice points. These ions are formed by detaching one or more electrons from the constituent atoms. These electrons are highly mobile and move throughout the solid just like a gas. They are very good conductors of electricity.

Amorphous or Glassy State

There are several solids which do not exhibit a long range ordering. However, they still show a local ordering so that some molecules (say 4–5) are bonded together to form a structure. Such independent units are randomly arranged to form the extended solid. In this respect the amorphous solid is similar to a liquid which also lacks any long range ordering. However, the intermolecular forces in amorphous solids are much stronger than those in liquids. This prevents the amorphous solid to flow like a fluid. A typical example is glass made of silicon and oxygen together with some other elements like calcium and sodium. The structure contains strong Si–O–Si bonds, but the structure does not extend too far in space.

The amorphous solids do not have a well-defined melting point. Different bonds have different strengths and as the material is heated the weaker bonds break earlier starting the melting process. The stronger bonds break at higher temperatures to complete the melting process.

14.2 ELASTICITY

We have used the concept of a rigid solid body in which the distance between any two particles is always fixed. Real solid bodies do not exactly fulfil this condition. When external forces are applied, the body may get deformed. When deformed, internal forces develop which try to restore the body in its original shape. The extent to which the shape of a body is restored when the deforming forces are removed varies from material to material. The property to restore the natural shape or to oppose the deformation is called *elasticity*. If a body completely gains its natural shape after the removal of the deforming forces, it is called a perfectly *elastic* body. If a body remains in the deformed state and does not even partially regain its original shape after the removal of the deforming forces, it is called a perfectly *inelastic* or *plastic* body. Quite often, when the deforming forces are removed, the body partially regains the original shape. Such bodies are partially elastic.

Microscopic Reason of Elasticity

A solid body is composed of a great many molecules or atoms arranged in a particular fashion. Each molecule is acted upon by the forces due to the neighbouring molecules. The solid takes such a shape that each molecule finds itself in a position of stable equilibrium. When the body is deformed, the molecules are displaced from their original positions of stable equilibrium. The intermolecular distances change and restoring forces start acting on the molecules which drive them back to their original positions and the body takes its natural shape.

One can compare this situation to a spring-mass system. Consider a particle connected to several particles through springs. If this particle is displaced a little, the springs exert a resultant force which tries to bring the particle towards its natural position. In fact, the particle will oscillate about this position. In due course, the oscillations will be damped out and the particle will regain its original position.

14.3 STRESS

Longitudinal and Shearing Stress

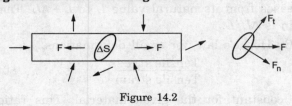

Figure 14.2

Consider a body (figure 14.2) on which several forces are acting. The resultant of these forces is zero

so that the centre of mass remains at rest. Due to the forces, the body gets deformed and internal forces appear. Consider any cross-sectional area ΔS of the body. The parts of the body on the two sides of ΔS exert forces $\vec{F}$, $-\vec{F}$ on each other. These internal forces $\vec{F}$, $-\vec{F}$ appear because of the deformation.

The force $\vec{F}$ may be resolved in two components, F_n normal to ΔS and F_t tangential to ΔS. We define the *normal stress* or *longitudinal stress* over the area as

$$\Gamma_n = \frac{F_n}{\Delta S} \qquad \dots (14.1)$$

and the *tangential stress* or *shearing stress* over the area as

$$\Gamma_t = \frac{F_t}{\Delta S} . \qquad \dots (14.2)$$

The longitudinal stress can be of two types. The two parts of the body on the two sides of ΔS may pull each other. The longitudinal stress is then called the *tensile stress*. This is the case when a rod or a wire is stretched by equal and opposite forces (figure 14.3). In case of tensile stress in a wire or a rod, the force F_n is just the tension.

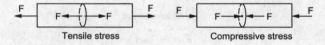

Tensile stress   Compressive stress

Figure 14.3

If the rod is pushed at the two ends with equal and opposite forces, it will be under compression. Taking any cross section ΔS of the rod the two parts on the two sides push each other. The longitudinal stress is then called *compressive stress*.

If the area is not specifically mentioned, a cross section perpendicular to the length is assumed.

Example 14.1

A load of 4·0 kg is suspended from a ceiling through a steel wire of radius 2·0 mm. Find the tensile stress developed in the wire when equilibrium is achieved. Take $g = 3\cdot1\pi$ m s^{-2}.

Solution : Tension in the wire is

$$F = 4\cdot0 \times 3\cdot1\pi \text{ N}.$$

The area of cross section is

$$A = \pi r^2 = \pi \times (2\cdot0 \times 10^{-3} \text{ m})^2$$
$$= 4\cdot0 \, \pi \times 10^{-6} \text{ m}^2.$$

Thus, the tensile stress developed

$$= \frac{F}{A} = \frac{4\cdot 0 \times 3\cdot 1\,\pi}{4\cdot 0\,\pi \times 10^{-6}}\ \mathrm{N\,m}^{-2}$$

$$= 3\cdot 1 \times 10^{6}\ \mathrm{N\,m}^{-2}.$$

Volume Stress

Another type of stress occurs when a body is acted upon by forces acting everywhere on the surface in such a way that (a) the force at any point is normal to the surface and (b) the magnitude of the force on any small surface area is proportional to the area. This is the case when a small solid body is immersed in a fluid. If the pressure at the location of the solid is P, the force on any area ΔS is $P\Delta S$ directed perpendicularly to the area. The force per unit area is then called *volume stress* (figure 14.4). It is

$$\Gamma_v = \frac{F}{A} \qquad \dots\ (14.3)$$

which is same as the pressure.

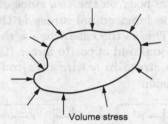

Volume stress

Figure 14.4

14.4 STRAIN

Associated with each type of stress defined above, there is a corresponding type of strain.

Longitudinal Strain

Consider a rod of length l being pulled by equal and opposite forces. The length of the rod increases from its natural value L to $L + \Delta L$. The fractional change $\Delta L / L$ is called the *longitudinal strain*.

$$\text{Longitudinal strain} = \Delta L / L. \qquad \dots\ (14.4)$$

If the length increases from its natural length, the longitudinal strain is called *tensile strain*. If the length decreases from its natural length, the longitudinal strain is called *compressive strain*.

Shearing Strain

This type of strain is produced when a shearing stress is present over a section. Consider a body with square cross section and suppose forces parallel to the surfaces are applied as shown in figure (14.5). Note that the resultant of the four forces shown is zero as well as the total torque of the four forces is zero.

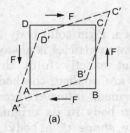 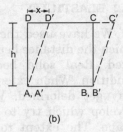

(a)   (b)

Figure 14.5

This ensures that the body remains in translational and rotational equilibrium after the deformation. Because of the tangential forces parallel to the faces, these faces are displaced. The shape of the cross section changes from a square to a parallelogram. In figure (14.5a) the dotted area represents the deformed cross section. To measure the deformation, we redraw the dotted area by rotating it a little so that one edge $A'B'$ coincides with its undeformed position AB. The drawing is presented in part (b) of figure (14.5).

We define the shearing strain as the displacement of a layer divided by its distance from the fixed layer. In the situation of figure (14.5),

$$\text{Shearing strain} = DD'/DA = x/h.$$

Shearing strain is also called *shear*.

Volume Strain

When a body is subjected to a volume stress, its volume changes. The *volume strain* is defined as the fractional change in volume. If V is the volume of unstressed body and $V + \Delta V$ is the volume when the volume stress exists, the volume strain is defined as

$$\text{Volume strain} = \Delta V / V.$$

14.5 HOOKE'S LAW AND THE MODULII OF ELASTICITY

If the deformation is small, the stress in a body is proportional to the corresponding strain.

This fact is known as Hooke's law. Thus, if a rod is stretched by equal and opposite forces F each, a tensile stress F/A is produced in the rod where A is the area of cross section. The length of the rod increases from its natural value L to $L + \Delta L$. Tensile strain is $\Delta L / L$.

By Hooke's law, for small deformations,

$$\frac{\text{Tensile stress}}{\text{Tensile strain}} = Y \qquad \dots\ (14.5)$$

is a constant for the given material. This ratio of tensile stress over tensile strain is called *Young modulus* for the material. In the situation described above, the Young modulus is

$$Y = \frac{F/A}{\Delta L/L} = \frac{FL}{A\Delta L}. \qquad \dots (14.6)$$

If the rod is compressed, compressive stress and compressive strain appear. Their ratio Y is same as that for the tensile case.

Example 14.2

A load of 4·0 kg is suspended from a ceiling through a steel wire of length 20 m and radius 2·0 mm. It is found that the length of the wire increases by 0·031 mm as equilibrium is achieved. Find Young modulus of steel. Take $g = 3·1\,\pi$ m s^{-2}.

Solution : The longitudinal stress $= \dfrac{(4\cdot0\text{ kg})(3\cdot1\,\pi\text{ m s}^{-2})}{\pi\,(2\cdot0\times10^{-3}\text{ m})^2}$

$$= 3\cdot1\times10^{6}\text{ N m}^{-2}.$$

The longitudinal strain $= \dfrac{0\cdot031\times10^{-3}\text{ m}}{2\cdot0\text{ m}}$

$$= 0\cdot0155\times10^{-3}$$

Thus $Y = \dfrac{3\cdot1\times10^{6}\text{ N m}^{-2}}{0\cdot0155\times10^{-3}} = 2\cdot0\times10^{11}\text{ N m}^{-2}.$

The ratio of shearing stress over shearing strain is called the *Shear modulus, Modulus of rigidity* or *Torsional modulus*. In the situation of figure (14.5) the shear modulus is

$$\eta = \frac{F/A}{x/h} = \frac{Fh}{Ax}. \qquad \dots (14.7)$$

The ratio of volume stress over volume strain is called *Bulk modulus*. If P be the volume stress (same as pressure) and ΔV be the increase in volume, the Bulk modulus is defined as

$$B = -\frac{P}{\Delta V/V}. \qquad \dots (14.8)$$

The minus sign makes B positive as volume actually decreases on applying pressure. Quite often, the change in volume is measured corresponding to a change in pressure. The bulk modulus is then defined as

$$B = -\frac{\Delta P}{\Delta V/V} = -V\frac{dP}{dV}.$$

Compressibility K is defined as the reciprocal of the bulk modulus.

$$K = \frac{1}{B} = -\frac{1}{V}\frac{dV}{dP}. \qquad \dots (14.9)$$

Yet another kind of modulus of elasticity is associated with the longitudinal stress and strain. When a rod or a wire is subjected to a tensile stress, its length increases in the direction of the tensile force. At the same time the length perpendicular to the

tensile force decreases. For a cylindrical rod, the length increases and the diameter decreases when the rod is stretched (Figure 14.6).

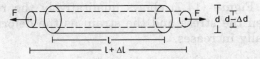

Figure 14.6

The fractional change in the transverse length is proportional to the fractional change in the longitudinal length. The constant of proportionality is called *Poisson ratio*. Thus, Poisson ratio is

$$\sigma = -\frac{\Delta d/d}{\Delta L/L}. \qquad \dots (14.10)$$

The minus sign ensures that σ is positive. Table (14.1) lists the elastic constants of some of the common materials. Table (14.2) lists compressibilities of some liquids.

Table 14.1 : *Elastic constants*

Material	Young Modulus Y 10^{11} N m^{-2}	Shear Modulus η 10^{11} N m^{-2}	Bulk Modulus B 10^{11} N m^{-2}	Poisson ratio σ
Aluminium	0·70	0·30	0·70	0·16
Brass	0·91	0·36	0·61	0·26
Copper	1·1	0·42	1·4	0·32
Iron	1·9	0·70	1·0	0·27
Steel	2·0	0·84	1·6	0·19
Tungsten	3·6	1·5	2·0	0·20

Table 14.2 : *Compressibilities of liquids*

Liquid	Compressibility K 10^{-11} m^2 N^{-1}
Carbon disulphide	64
Ethyl alcohol	110
Glycerine	21
Mercury	3·7
Water	49

14.6 RELATION BETWEEN LONGITUDINAL STRESS AND STRAIN

For a small deformation, the longitudinal stress is proportional to the longitudinal strain. What happens if the deformation is not small ? The relation of stress and strain is much more complicated in such a case and the nature depends on the material under study. We describe here the behaviour for two representative materials, a metal wire and a rubber piece.

Metal Wire

Suppose a metal wire is stretched by equal forces at the ends so that its length increases from its natural value. Figure (14.7) shows qualitatively the relation between the stress and the strain as the deformation gradually increases.

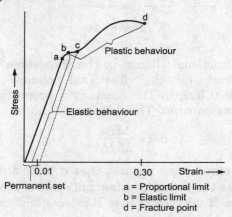

Figure 14.7

When the strain is small (say < 0·01), the stress is proportional to the strain. This is the region where Hooke's law is valid and where Young's modulus is defined. The point a on the curve represents the *proportional limit* up to which stress and strain are proportional.

If the strain is increased a little bit, the stress is not proportional to the strain. However, the wire still remains elastic. This means, if the stretching force is removed, the wire acquires its natural length. This behaviour is shown up to a point b on the curve known as the *elastic limit* or the *yield point*. If the wire is stretched beyond the elastic limit, the strain increases much more rapidly. If the stretching force is removed, the wire does not come back to its natural length. Some permanent increase in length takes place. In figure (14.7), we have shown this behaviour by the dashed line from c. The behaviour of the wire is now plastic. If the deformation is increased further, the wire breaks at a point d known as *fracture point*. The stress corresponding to this point is called *breaking stress*.

If large deformation takes place between the elastic limit and the fracture point, the material is called *ductile*. If it breaks soon after the elastic limit is crossed, it is called *brittle*.

Rubber

A distinctly different stress–strain relation exists for vulcanized rubber, the behaviour is qualitatively shown in figure (14.8). The material remains elastic even when it is stretched to over several times its original length. In the case shown in figure (14.8), the length is increased to 8 times its natural length, even then if the stretching forces are removed, it will come back to its original length.

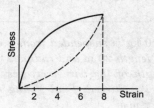

Figure 14.8

In this respect rubber is more elastic than a ductile metal like steel. However, the magnitude of stress for a given strain is much larger in steel than in rubber. This means large internal forces appear if the steel wire is deformed. In this sense, steel is more elastic than rubber. There are two important phenomena to note from figure (14.8). Firstly, in no part of this large deformation stress is proportional to strain. There is almost no region of proportionality. Secondly, when the deforming force is removed the original curve is not retraced although the sample finally acquires its natural length. The work done by the material in returning to its original shape is less than the work done by the deforming force when it was deformed. A particular amount of energy is, thus, absorbed by the material in the cycle which appears as heat. This phenomenon is called *elastic hysteresis*.

Elastic hysteresis has an important application in shock absorbers. If a padding of vulcanized rubber is given between a vibrating system and, say, a flat board, the rubber is compressed and released in every cycle of vibration. As energy is absorbed in the rubber in each cycle, only a part of the energy of vibrations is transmitted to the board.

14.7 ELASTIC POTENTIAL ENERGY OF A STRAINED BODY

When a body is in its natural shape, its potential energy corresponding to the molecular forces is minimum. We may take the potential energy in this state to be zero. When deformed, internal forces appear and work has to be done against these forces. Thus, the potential energy of the body is increased. This is called the *elastic potential energy*. We shall derive an expression for the increase in elastic potential energy when a wire is stretched from its natural length.

Suppose a wire having natural length L and cross-sectional area A is fixed at one end and is stretched

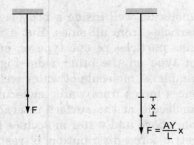

Figure 14.9

by an external force applied at the other end (figure 14.9). The force is so adjusted that the wire is only slowly stretched. This ensures that at any time during the extension the external force equals the tension in the wire. When the extension is x, the wire is under a longitudinal stress F/A, where F is the tension at this time. The strain is x/L.

If Young modulus is Y,

$$\frac{F/A}{x/L} = Y$$

or, $$F = \frac{AY}{L} x. \qquad \ldots \text{(i)}$$

The work done by the external force in a further extension dx is

$$dW = F\,dx.$$

Using (i),

$$dW = \frac{AY}{L} x\,dx.$$

The total work by the external force in an extension 0 to l is

$$W = \int_0^l \frac{AY}{L} x\,dx$$

$$= \frac{AY}{2L} l^2.$$

This work is stored into the wire as its elastic potential energy.

Thus, the elastic potential energy of the stretched wire is,

$$U = \frac{AY}{2L} l^2. \qquad \ldots \text{(14.11)}$$

This may be written as

$$U = \frac{1}{2}\left(AY\frac{l}{L}\right)l$$

$$= \frac{1}{2}\,(\text{maximum stretching force})\,(\text{extension}).$$

Equation (14.11) may also be written as

$$U = \frac{1}{2}\left(Y\frac{l}{L}\right)\frac{l}{L}(AL)$$

or, *Potential energy* $= \dfrac{1}{2} \times stress \times strain \times volume.$

$$\ldots \text{(14.12)}$$

Example 14.3

A steel wire of length $2 \cdot 0$ m is stretched through $2 \cdot 0$ mm. The cross-sectional area of the wire is $4 \cdot 0$ mm^2. Calculate the elastic potential energy stored in the wire in the stretched condition. Young modulus of steel $= 2 \cdot 0 \times 10^{11}$ N m^{-2}.

Solution : The strain in the wire $\dfrac{\Delta l}{l} = \dfrac{2 \cdot 0 \text{ mm}}{2 \cdot 0 \text{ m}} = 10^{-3}$.

The stress in the wire $= Y \times$ strain

$$= 2 \cdot 0 \times 10^{11} \text{ N m}^{-2} \times 10^{-3} = 2 \cdot 0 \times 10^8 \text{ N m}^{-2}.$$

The volume of the wire $= (4 \times 10^{-6} \text{ m}^2) \times (2 \cdot 0 \text{ m})$

$$= 8 \cdot 0 \times 10^{-6} \text{ m}^3.$$

The elastic potential energy stored

$$= \frac{1}{2} \times stress \times strain \times volume$$

$$= \frac{1}{2} \times 2 \cdot 0 \times 10^8 \text{ N m}^{-2} \times 10^{-3} \times 8 \cdot 0 \times 10^{-6} \text{ m}^3$$

$$= 0 \cdot 8 \text{ J}.$$

14.8 DETERMINATION OF YOUNG MODULUS IN LABORATORY

Figure (14.10) shows the experimental set up of a simple method to determine Young modulus in a laboratory. A long wire A (say 2–3 m) is suspended from a fixed support. It carries a fixed graduated scale and below it a heavy fixed load. This load keeps the wire straight and free from kinks. The wire itself serves as a reference. The experimental wire B of almost equal length is also suspended from the same support close to the reference wire. A vernier scale is attached at the free end of the experimental wire. This vernier scale can slide against the main scale attached to the reference wire.

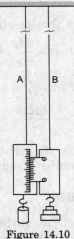

Figure 14.10

A hanger is attached at the lower end of the vernier scale. A number of slotted half kilogram or one kilogram weights may be slipped into the hanger.

First of all, the radius of the experimental wire is measured at several places with a screw gauge. From the average radius *r,* the breaking weight is determined using the standard value of the breaking stress for the material. Half of this breaking weight is the permissible weight.

Some initial load, say 1 kg or 2 kg, is kept on the hanger (this should be much smaller than the permissible weight). This keeps the experimental wire straight and kink-free. The reading of the main scale and vernier coincidence are noted. A known weight say 1/2 kg or 1 kg is slipped into the hanger. The set up is left for about a minute so that the elongation takes place fully. The reading on the scale are noted. The difference of the scale readings gives the extension due to the extra weight put. The weight is gradually increased up to the permissible weight and every time the extension is noted.

The experiment is repeated in reverse order decreasing the weight gradually in the same steps and everytime noting the extension.

From the data, extension versus load curve is plotted. This curve should be a straight line passing through the origin (figure 14.11). The slope of this line gives

$$\tan\theta = \frac{l}{Mg}.$$

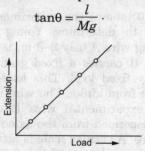

Figure 14.11

Now the stress due to the weight Mg at the end is

$$\text{stress} = \frac{Mg}{\pi r^2}$$

and

$$\text{strain} = \frac{l}{L}.$$

Thus,

$$Y = \frac{MgL}{\pi r^2 l} = \frac{L}{\pi r^2 \tan\theta}.$$

All the quantities on the right-hand side are known and hence Young modulus Y may be calculated.

14.9 SURFACE TENSION

The properties of a surface are quite often markedly different from the properties of the bulk material. A molecule well inside a body is surrounded by similar particles from all sides. But a molecule on the surface has particles of one type on one side and of a different type on the other side. Figure (14.12) shows an example. A molecule of water well inside the bulk experiences forces from water molecules from all sides but a molecule at the surface interacts with air molecules from above and water molecules from below. This asymmetric force distribution is responsible for surface tension.

Figure 14.12

By a surface we shall mean a layer approximately 10–15 molecular diameters. The force between two molecules decreases as the separation between them increases. The force becomes negligible if the separation exceeds 10–15 molecular diameters. Thus, if we go 10–15 molecular diameters deep, a molecule finds equal forces from all directions.

Figure 14.13

Imagine a line AB drawn on the surface of a liquid (figure 14.13). The line divides the surface in two parts, surface on one side and the surface on the other side of the line. Let us call them surface to the left of the line and surface to the right of the line. It is found that the two parts of the surface pull each other with a force proportional to the length of the line AB. These forces of pull are perpendicular to the line separating the two parts and are tangential to the surface. In this respect the surface of the liquid behaves like a stretched rubber sheet. The rubber sheet which is stretched from all sides is in the state of tension. Any part of the sheet pulls the adjacent part towards itself.

Let F be the common magnitude of the forces exerted on each other by the two parts of the surface across a line of length l. We define the surface tension S of the liquid as

$$S = F/l. \qquad \ldots (14.13)$$

The SI unit of surface tension is N m^{-1}.

Example 14.4

Water is kept in a beaker of radius 5·0 cm. Consider a diameter of the beaker on the surface of the water. Find the force by which the surface on one side of the diameter pulls the surface on the other side. Surface tension of water = 0·075 N m⁻¹.

Solution : The length of the diameter is

$$l = 2r = 10 \text{ cm}$$

$$= 0{\cdot}1 \text{ m}.$$

The surface tension is $S = F/l$. Thus,

$$F = Sl$$

$$= (0{\cdot}075 \text{ N m}^{-1}) \times (0{\cdot}1 \text{ m}) = 7{\cdot}5 \times 10^{-3} \text{ N}.$$

The fact that a liquid surface has the property of surface tension can be demonstrated by a number of simple experiments.

(a) Take a ring of wire and dip it in soap solution. When the ring is taken out, a soap film bounded by the ring is formed. Now take a loop of thread, wet it and place it gently on the soap film. The loop stays on the film in an irregular fashion as it is placed. Now prick a hole in the film inside the loop with a needle. The thread is radially pulled by the film surface outside and it takes a circular shape (figure 14.14).

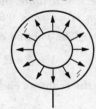

Figure 14.14

Before the pricking, there were surfaces both inside and outside the thread loop. Taking any small part of the thread, surfaces on both sides pulled it and the net force was zero. The thread could remain in any shape. Once the surface inside was punctured, the outside surface pulled the thread to take the circular shape.

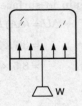

Figure 14.15

(b) Take a U-shaped frame of wire on which a light wire can slide (figure 14.15). Dip the frame in a soap solution and take it out. A soap film is formed between the frame and the sliding wire. If the frame is kept in a horizontal position and the friction is negligible, the sliding wire quickly slides towards the closing arm of the frame. This shows that the soap surface in contact with the wire pulls it parallel to the surface. If the frame is kept vertical with the sliding wire at the lower position, one can hang some weight from it to keep it in equilibrium. The force due to surface tension by the surface in contact with the sliding wire balances the weight.

Tendency to Decrease the Surface Area

The property of surface tension may also be described in terms of the tendency of a liquid to decrease its surface area. Because of the existence of forces across any line in the surface, the surface tends to shrink whenever it gets a chance to do so. The two demonstrations described above may help us in understanding the relation between the force of surface tension and the tendency to shrink the surface.

In the first example, the soap film is pricked in the middle. The remaining surface readjusts its shape so that a circular part bounded by the thread loop is excluded. The loop has a fixed length and the largest area that can be formed with a fixed periphery is a circle. This ensures that the surface of the soap solution takes the minimum possible area.

In the second example, the wire can slide on the frame. When kept in horizontal position, the wire slides to the closing arm of the U-shaped frame so that the surface shrinks.

There are numerous examples which illustrate that the surface of a liquid tries to make its area minimum. When a painting brush is inside a liquid, the bristles of the brush wave freely. When the brush is taken out of the liquid, surfaces are formed between the bristles. To minimise the area of these surfaces, they stick together.

A small drop of liquid takes a nearly spherical shape. This is because, for a given volume, the sphere assume the smallest surface area. Because of gravity there is some deviation from the spherical shape, but for small drops this may be neglected.

Table 14.3 gives the values of surface tension of some liquids.

Table 14.3 : *Surface tension*

Liquid	Surface tension N m⁻¹	Liquid	Surface Tension N m⁻¹
Mercury	0·465	Glycerine	0·063
Water	0·075	Carbon tetra chloride	0·027
Soap solution	0·030	Ethyl alcohol	0·022

14.10 SURFACE ENERGY

We have seen that a molecule well within the volume of a liquid is surrounded by the similar liquid molecules from all sides and hence there is no resultant force on it (figure 14.12). On the other hand, a molecule in the surface is surrounded by similar liquid molecules only on one side of the surface while on the other side it may be surrounded by air molecules or the molecules of the vapour of the liquid etc. These vapours having much less density exert only a small force. Thus, there is a resultant inward force on a molecule in the surface. This force tries to pull the molecule into the liquid. Thus, the surface layer remains in microscopic turbulence. Molecules are pulled back from the surface layer to the bulk and new molecules from the bulk go to the surface to fill the empty space.

When a molecule is taken from the inside to the surface layer, work is done against the inward resultant force while moving up in the layer. The potential energy is increased due to this work. A molecule in the surface has greater potential energy than a molecule well inside the liquid. The extra energy that a surface layer has is called the *surface energy*. The surface energy is related to the surface tension as discussed below.

Consider a U-shaped frame with a sliding wire on its arm. Suppose it is dipped in a soap solution, taken out and placed in a horizontal position (figure 14.16).

Figure 14.16

The soap film that is formed may look quite thin, but on the molecular scale its thickness is not small. It may have several hundred thousands molecular layers. So it has two surfaces enclosing a bulk of soap solution. Both the surfaces are in contact with the sliding wire and hence exert forces of surface tension on it. If S be the surface tension of the solution and l be the length of the sliding wire, each surface will pull the wire parallel to itself with a force Sl. The net force of pull F on the wire due to both the surfaces is

$$F = 2\,Sl\,.$$

One has to apply an external force equal and opposite to F so as to keep the wire in equilibrium.

Now suppose the wire is slowly pulled out by the external force through a distance x so that the area of the frame is increased by lx. As there are two surfaces

of the solution, a new surface area $2lx$ is created. The liquid from the inside is brought to create the new surface.

The work done by the external force in the displacement is

$$W = F\,x = 2Sl\,x = S\,(2lx)\,.$$

As there is no change in kinetic energy, the work done by the external force is stored as the potential energy of the new surface.

The increase in surface energy is

$$U = W = S\,(2lx)\,.$$

Thus, $\dfrac{U}{(2lx)} = S$

or, $\dfrac{U}{A} = S.$ ... (14.14)

We see that the surface tension of a liquid is equal to the surface energy per unit surface area.

In this interpretation, the SI unit of surface tension may be written as $J\,m^{-2}$. It may be verified that $N\,m^{-1}$ is equivalent to $J\,m^{-2}$.

Example 14.5

A water drop of radius 10^{-2} m is broken into 1000 equal droplets. Calculate the gain in surface energy. Surface tension of water is $0{\cdot}075\ N\,m^{-1}$.

Solution : The volume of the original drop is

$$V = \frac{4}{3}\,\pi R^{\,3},\ \text{where } R = 10^{-2}\,m.$$

If r is the radius of each broken droplet, the volume is also

$$V = 1000 \times \frac{4}{3}\,\pi r^{\,3}.$$

Thus, $1000\,r^{\,3} = R^{\,3}$

or, $r = R/10.$

The surface area of the original drop is $A_1 = 4\pi R^{\,2}$ and the surface area of the 1000 droplets is

$$A_2 = 1000 \times 4\,\pi\,r^{\,2} = 40\,\pi\,R^{\,2}.$$

The increase in area is

$$\Delta A = A_2 - A_1 = 40\,\pi R^{\,2} - 4\,\pi R^{\,2} = 36\,\pi R^{\,2}.$$

The gain in surface energy is

$$\Delta U = (\Delta A)\,S = 36\,\pi R^2 S$$

$$= 36 \times 3{\cdot}14 \times (10^{-4}\,m^{\,2}) \times (0{\cdot}075\ N\,m^{-1})$$

$$= 8{\cdot}5 \times 10^{-4}\,J.$$

14.11 EXCESS PRESSURE INSIDE A DROP

Let us consider a spherical drop of liquid of radius R (figure 14.17). If the drop is small, the effect of gravity may be neglected and the shape may be assumed to be spherical.

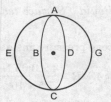

Figure 14.17

Imagine a diametric cross section *ABCD* of the drop which divides the drop in two hemispheres. The surfaces of the two hemispheres touch each other along the periphery *ABCDA*. Each hemispherical surface pulls the other hemispherical surface due to the surface tension.

Consider the equilibrium of the hemispherical surface *ABCDE*. Forces acting on this surface are

(i) F_1, due to the surface tension of the surface *ABCDG* in contact,

(ii) F_2, due to the air outside the surface *ABCDE* and

(iii) F_3, due to the liquid inside the surface *ABCDE*.

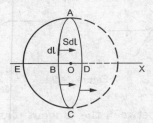

Figure 14.18

The force due to surface tension acts on the points of the periphery *ABCDA*. The force on any small part *dl* of this periphery is $S\,dl$ (figure 14.18) and acts parallel to the symmetry axis *OX*. The resultant of all these forces due to surface tension is

$$F_1 = 2\pi RS$$

along *OX*.

Now consider the forces due to the air outside the surface *ABCDE*. Consider a small part ΔS of the surface as shown in figure (14.19).

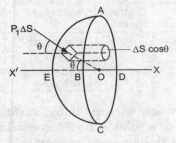

Figure 14.19

If the pressure just outside the surface is P_1, the force on this surface ΔS is $P_1\Delta S$ along the radial direction. By symmetry, the resultant of all such forces acting on different parts of the hemispherical surface must be along *OX*.

If the radius through ΔS makes an angle θ with *OX*, the component of $P_1\Delta S$ along *OX* will be $P_1\Delta S \cos\theta$. If we project the area ΔS on the diametric plane *ABCD*, the area of projection will be $\Delta S \cos\theta$. Thus, we can write,

component of $P_1\Delta S$ along *OX*

$= P_1$ (projection of ΔS on the plane *ABCD*).

When components of all the forces $P_1\Delta S$ on different ΔS are added, we get the resultant force due to the air outside the hemispherical surface. This resultant is then

$F_2 = P_1$ (Projection of the hemispherical surface *ABCDE* on the plane *ABCD*).

The projection of the hemispherical surface on the plane *ABCD* is the circular disc *ABCD* itself, having an area πR^2. Thus,

$$F_2 = P_1 \pi R^2.$$

Similarly, the resultant force on this surface due to the liquid inside is $F_3 = P_2 \cdot \pi R^2$, where P_2 is the pressure just inside the surface. This force will be in the direction *OX'*.

For equilibrium of the hemispherical surface *ABCDE* we should have,

$$F_1 + F_2 = F_3$$

or, $$2\pi RS + P_1\pi R^2 = P_2\pi R^2$$

or, $$P_2 - P_1 = 2S/R . \qquad \dots (14.15)$$

The pressure inside the surface is greater than the pressure outside the surface by an amount $2S/R$.

In the case of a drop, there is liquid on the concave side of the surface and air on the convex side. The pressure on the concave side is greater than the pressure on the convex side. This result is true in all cases. If we have an air bubble inside a liquid (figure 14.20), a single surface is formed. There is air on the concave side and liquid on the convex side. The pressure in the concave side (that is in the air) is greater than the pressure in the convex side (that is in the liquid) by an amount $2S/R$.

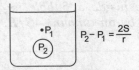

Figure 14.20

Find the excess pressure inside a mercury drop of radius 2·0 mm. The surface tension of mercury = 0·464 N m⁻¹.

Solution : The excess pressure inside the drop is

$$P_2 - P_1 = 2S/R$$

$$= \frac{2 \times 0.464 \text{ N m}^{-1}}{2.0 \times 10^{-3} \text{ m}} = 464 \text{ N m}^{-2}.$$

14.12 EXCESS PRESSURE IN A SOAP BUBBLE

Soap bubbles can be blown by dipping one end of a glass tube in a soap solution for a short time and then blowing air in it from the other end. Such a bubble has a small thickness and there is air both inside the bubble and outside the bubble. The thickness of the bubble may look small to eye but it still has hundreds of thousands of molecular layers. So it has two surface layers, one towards the outside air and the other towards the enclosed air. Between these two surface layers there is bulk soap solution.

Figure 14.21

Let the pressure of the air outside the bubble be P_1, that within the soap solution be P' and that of the air inside the bubble be P_2. Looking at the outer surface, the solution is on the concave side of the surface, hence

$$P' - P_1 = 2S/R$$

where R is the radius of the bubble. As the thickness of the bubble is small on a macroscopic scale, the difference in the radii of the two surfaces will be negligible.

Similarly, looking at the inner surface, the air is on the concave side of the surface, hence

$$P_2 - P' = 2S/R.$$

Adding the two equations

$$P_2 - P_1 = 4S/R. \qquad \ldots (14.16)$$

The pressure inside a bubble is greater than the pressure outside by an amount 4S/R.

A 0·02 cm *liquid column balances the excess pressure inside a soap bubble of radius 7·5 mm. Determine the*

density of the liquid. Surface tension of soap solution = 0·03 N m⁻¹.

Solution : The excess pressure inside a soap bubble is

$$\Delta P = 4S/R = \frac{4 \times 0.03 \text{ N m}^{-1}}{7.5 \times 10^{-3} \text{ m}} = 16 \text{ N m}^{-2}.$$

The pressure due to 0·02 cm of the liquid column is

$$\Delta P = h\rho g$$

$$= (0.02 \times 10^{-2} \text{ m}) \, \rho \, (9.8 \text{ m s}^{-2}).$$

Thus, $16 \text{ N m}^{-2} = (0.02 \times 10^{-2} \text{ m}) \, \rho \, (9.8 \text{ m s}^{-2})$

or, $\qquad \rho = 8.2 \times 10^{3} \text{ kg m}^{-3}.$

14.13 CONTACT ANGLE

When a liquid surface touches a solid surface, the shape of the liquid surface near the contact is generally curved. When a glass plate is immersed in water, the surface near the plate becomes concave as if the water is pulled up by the plate (figure 14.22). On the other hand, if a glass plate is immersed in mercury, the surface is depressed near the plate.

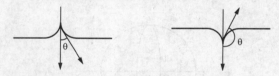

Figure 14.22

The angle between the tangent planes at the solid surface and the liquid surface at the contact is called the *contact angle*. In this the tangent plane to the solid surface is to be drawn towards the liquid and the tangent plane to the liquid is to be drawn away from the solid. Figure (14.22) shows the construction of contact angle. For the liquid that rises along the solid surface, the contact angle is smaller than 90°. For the liquid that is depressed along the solid surface, the contact angle is greater than 90°. Table (14.4) gives the contact angles for some of the pairs of solids and liquids.

Table 14.4 : *Contact angles*

Substance	Contact angle	Substance	Contact angle
Water with glass	0°	Water with paraffin	107°
Mercury with glass	140°	Methylene iodide with glass	29°

Let us now see why the liquid surface bends near the contact with a solid. A liquid in equilibrium cannot sustain tangential stress. The resultant force on any small part of the surface layer must be perpendicular to the surface there. Consider a small part of the liquid surface near its contact with the solid (figure 14.23).

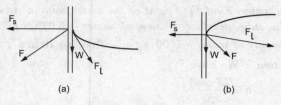

Figure 14.23

The forces acting on this part are

(a) F_s, attraction due to the molecules of the solid surface near it,

(b) F_l, the force due to the liquid molecules near this part, and

(c) W, the weight of the part considered.

The force between the molecules of the same material is known as *cohesive force* and the force between the molecules of different kinds of material is called *adhesive force*. Here F_s is adhesive force and F_l is cohesive force.

As is clear from the figure, the adhesive force F_s is perpendicular to the solid surface and is into the solid. The cohesive force F_l is in the liquid, its direction and magnitude depends on the shape of the liquid surface as this determines the distribution of the molecules attracting the part considered. Of course, F_s and F_l depend on the nature of the substances especially on their densities.

The direction of the resultant of F_s, F_l and W decides the shape of the surface near the contact. The liquid rests in such a way that the surface is perpendicular to this resultant. If the resultant passes through the solid (figure 14.23a), the surface is concave upward and the liquid rises along the solid. If the resultant passes through the liquid (figure 14.23b), the surface is convex upward and the liquid is depressed near the solid.

If a solid surface is just dipped in liquid (figure 14.24) so that it is not projected out, the force F_s will not be perpendicular to the solid. The actual angle between the solid surface and the liquid surface may be different from the standard contact angle for the pair.

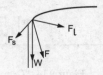

Figure 14.24

14.14 RISE OF LIQUID IN A CAPILLARY TUBE

When one end of a tube of small radius (known as a capillary tube) is dipped into a liquid, the liquid rises or is depressed in the tube. If the contact angle is less than 90°, the liquid rises. If it is greater than 90°, it is depressed.

Suppose a tube of radius r is dipped into a liquid of surface tension S and density ρ. Let the angle of contact between the solid and the liquid be θ. If the radius of the tube is small, the surface in the tube is nearly spherical. Figure (14.25) shows the situation.

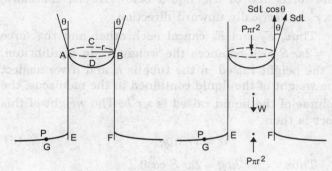

Figure 14.25

Consider the equilibrium of the part of liquid raised in the tube. In figure (14.25) this liquid is contained in the volume $ABEF$. Forces on this part of the liquid are

(a) F_1, by the surface of the tube on the surface $ABCD$ of the liquid,

(b) F_2, due to the pressure of the air above the surface $ABCD$,

(c) F_3, due to the pressure of the liquid below EF and

(d) the weight W of the liquid $ABEF$.

$ABCD$ is the surface of the liquid inside the capillary tube. It meets the wall of the tube along a circle of radius r. The angle made by the liquid surface with the surface of the tube is equal to the contact angle θ.

Consider a small part dl of the periphery $2\pi r$ along which the surface of the liquid and the tube meet. The liquid surface across this pulls the tube surface by a force $S\,dl$ tangentially along the liquid surface. From Newton's third law, the tube surface across this small part pulls the liquid surface by an equal force $S\,dl$ in opposite direction. The vertical component of this force is $S\,dl\cos\theta$. The total force exerted on the liquid surface by the tube surface across the contact circle is

$$F_1 = \int S\,dl\,\cos\theta$$

$$= S\cos\theta \int dl$$

$$= 2\pi r\, S\cos\theta. \qquad \ldots \text{(i)}$$

The horizontal component $Sdl \sin\theta$ adds to zero when summed over the entire periphery.

The force F_2 due to the pressure of the air outside the surface $ABCD$ is $P.\pi r^2$ where P is the atmospheric pressure. (This result was derived for hemispherical surface while deducing the excess pressure inside a drop. Same derivation works here.)

This force acts vertically downward. The pressure at EF is equal to the atmospheric pressure P. This is because EF is in the same horizontal plane as the free surface outside the tube and the pressure there is P. The force due to the liquid below EF is, therefore, $P\pi r^2$ in vertically upward direction.

Thus, F_2 and F_3 cancel each other and the force $F_1 = 2\pi r S \cos\theta$ balances the weight W in equilibrium. If the height raised in the tube is h and if we neglect the weight of the liquid contained in the meniscus, the volume of the liquid raised is $\pi r^2 h$. The weight of this part is then

$$W = \pi r^2 h \rho g. \qquad \qquad \text{... (ii)}$$

Thus, $\pi r^2 h \rho g = 2\pi r S \cos\theta$

so that $$h = \frac{2S \cos\theta}{r\rho g}. \qquad \qquad \text{... (14.17)}$$

We see that the height raised is inversely proportional to the radius of the capillary. If the contact angle θ is greater than 90°, the term $\cos\theta$ is negative and hence h is negative. The expression then gives the depression of the liquid in the tube.

The correction due to the weight of the liquid contained in the meniscus can be easily made if the contact angle is zero. This is the case with water rising in a glass capillary. The meniscus is then hemispherical (Figure 14.26).

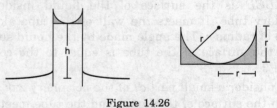

Figure 14.26

The volume of the shaded part is

$$(\pi r^2) r - \frac{1}{2}\left(\frac{4}{3}\pi r^3\right) = \frac{1}{3}\pi r^3.$$

The weight of the liquid contained in the meniscus is $\frac{1}{3}\pi r^3 \rho g$. Equation (ii) is then replaced by

$$\pi r^2 h \rho g + \frac{1}{3}\pi r^3 \rho g = 2\pi r S$$

or, $$h = \frac{2S}{r\rho g} - \frac{r}{3}. \qquad \qquad \text{... (14.18)}$$

Example 14.8
_____

A capillary tube of radius 0·20 mm is dipped vertically in water. Find the height of the water column raised in the tube. Surface tension of water = 0·075 N m⁻¹ and density of water = 1000 kg m⁻³. Take g = 10 m s⁻².

Solution : We have,

$$h = \frac{2S \cos\theta}{r\rho g}$$

$$= \frac{2 \times 0\cdot075 \text{ N m}^{-1} \times 1}{(0\cdot20 \times 10^{-3}\text{ m}) \times (1000 \text{ kg m}^{-3})\,(10 \text{ m s}^{-2})}$$

$$= 0\cdot075 \text{ m} = 7\cdot5 \text{ cm}.$$

Tube of Insufficient Length

Equation (14.17) or (14.18) gives the height raised in a capillary tube. If the tube is of a length less than h, the liquid does not overflow. The angle made by the liquid surface with the tube changes in such a way that the force $2\pi rS \cos\theta$ equals the weight of the liquid raised.

14.15 VISCOSITY

When a layer of a fluid slips or tends to slip on another layer in contact, the two layers exert tangential forces on each other. The directions are such that the relative motion between the layers is opposed. This property of a fluid to oppose relative motion between its layers is called *viscosity*. The forces between the layers opposing relative motion between them are known as the *forces of viscosity*. Thus, viscosity may be thought of as the internal friction of a fluid in motion.

If a solid surface is kept in contact with a fluid and is moved, forces of viscosity appear between the solid surface and the fluid layer in contact. The fluid in contact is dragged with the solid. If the viscosity is sufficient, the layer moves with the solid and there is no relative slipping. When a boat moves slowly on the water of a calm river, the water in contact with the boat is dragged with it, whereas the water in contact with the bed of the river remains at rest. Velocities of different layers are different. Let v be the velocity of the layer at a distance z from the bed and $v + dv$ be the velocity at a distance $z + dz$. (figure 14.27).

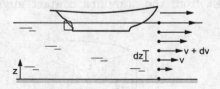

Figure 14.27

Thus, the velocity differs by dv in going through a distance dz perpendicular to it. The quantity dv/dz is called the *velocity gradient*.

The force of viscosity between two layers of a fluid is proportional to the velocity gradient in the direction perpendicular to the layers. Also, the force is proportional to the area of the layer.

Thus, if F is the force exerted by a layer of area A on a layer in contact,

$$F \propto A \text{ and } F \propto dv/dz$$

or, $F = -\eta A \, dv/dz.$ ... (14.19)

The negative sign is included as the force is frictional in nature and opposes relative motion. The constant of proportionality η is called the *coefficient of viscosity*.

The SI unit of viscosity can be easily worked out from equation (14.19). It is N–s m^{-2}. However, the corresponding CGS unit dyne–s cm^{-2} is in common use and is called a poise in honour of the French scientist Poiseuille. We have

$$1 \text{ poise} = 0{\cdot}1 \text{ N–s m}^{-2}.$$

Dimensions of the Coefficient of Viscosity

Writing dimensions of different variables in equation (14.19),

$$\text{MLT}^{-2} = [\eta] \, \text{L}^2 \cdot \frac{\text{L/T}}{\text{L}}$$

or, $[\eta] = \dfrac{\text{MLT}^{-2}}{\text{L}^2 \text{T}^{-1}}$

or, $[\eta] = \text{ML}^{-1}\text{T}^{-1}.$ ... (14.20)

The coefficient of viscosity strongly depends on temperature. Table (14.5) gives the values for some of the commom fluids.

Table 14.5 : *Coefficient of viscosity*

Temperature °C	Viscosity of castor oil, poise	Viscosity of water, centi- poise	Viscosity of air, micro- poise
0	53	1·792	171
20	9·86	1·005	181
40	2·31	0·656	190
60	0·80	0·469	200
80	0·30	0·357	209
100	0·17	0·284	218

14.16 FLOW THROUGH A NARROW TUBE : POISEUILLE'S EQUATION

Suppose a fluid flows through a narrow tube in steady flow. Because of viscosity, the layer in contact with the wall of the tube remains at rest and the layers away from the wall move fast. Poiseuille derived a formula for the rate of flow of viscous fluid through a cylindrical tube. We shall try to obtain the formula using dimensional analysis.

Suppose a fluid having coefficient of viscosity η and density ρ is flowing through a cylindrical tube of radius r and length l. Let P be the pressure difference in the liquid at the two ends. It is found that the volume of the liquid flowing per unit time through the tube depends on the pressure gradient P/l, the coefficient of viscosity η and the radius r. If V be the volume flowing in time t, we guess that

$$\frac{V}{t} = k \left(\frac{P}{l} \right)^a \eta^{\,b} r^{\,c}$$ ... (i)

where k is a dimensionless constant.

Taking dimensions,

$$\text{L}^3 \text{T}^{-1} = \left(\frac{\text{ML}^{-1}\text{T}^{-2}}{\text{L}} \right)^a (\text{ML}^{-1}\text{T}^{-1})^{\,b} \text{L}^c$$

or, $\text{L}^3\text{T}^{-1} = \text{M}^{a+b}\,\text{L}^{-2a-b+c}\,\text{T}^{-2a-b}$

Equating the exponents of M, L and T we get,

$$0 = a + b$$
$$3 = -2a - b + c$$
$$-1 = -2a - b.$$

Solving these equations,

$$a = 1, \quad b = -1 \quad \text{and} \quad c = 4.$$

Thus,

$$\frac{V}{t} = k \, \frac{Pr^4}{\eta l}.$$

The dimensionless constant k is equal to $\pi/8$ and hence the rate of flow is

$$\frac{V}{t} = \frac{\pi P r^4}{8 \eta l}.$$ ... (14.21)

This is *Poiseuille's formula*.

14.17 STOKES' LAW

When a solid body moves through a fluid, the fluid in contact with the solid is dragged with it. Relative velocities are established between the layers of the fluid near the solid so that the viscous forces start operating. The fluid exerts viscous force on the solid to oppose the motion of the solid. The magnitude of the viscous force depends on the shape and size of the solid body, its speed and the coefficient of viscosity of the fluid.

Suppose a spherical body of radius r moves at a speed v through a fluid of viscosity η. The viscous force F acting on the body depends on r, v and η. Assuming that the force is proportional to various powers of these quantities, we can obtain the dependence through dimensional analysis.

Let $\qquad F = k\, r^{a}\, v^{b}\, \eta^{c}$ $\qquad$ ... (i)

where k is a dimensionless constant. Taking dimensions on both sides,

$$M\,L\,T^{-2} = L^{a}\,(LT^{-1})^{b}\,(ML^{-1}T^{-1})^{c}.$$

Comparing the exponents of M, L and T,

$$1 = c$$
$$1 = a + b - c$$
$$-2 = -b - c$$

Solving these equations, $a = 1$, $b = 1$ and $c = 1$.

Thus, by (i), $F = k\, r\, v\, \eta$.

The dimensionless constant k equals 6π, so that the equation becomes

$$F = 6\,\pi\,\eta\, r\, v. \qquad ... (14.22)$$

This equation is known as *Stokes' law*.

Example 14.9 ────────────────────

An air bubble of diameter 2 mm rises steadily through a solution of density 1750 kg m^{-3} at the rate of 0·35 cm s^{-1}. Calculate the coefficient of viscosity of the solution. The density of air is negligible.

Solution : The force of buoyancy B is equal to the weight of the displaced liquid. Thus,

$$B = \frac{4}{3}\,\pi\, r^{3}\,\sigma g.$$

This force is upward. The viscous force acting downward is

$$F = 6\,\pi\,\eta r v.$$

The weight of the air bubble may be neglected as the density of air is small. For uniform velocity

$$F = B$$

or, $6\,\pi\,\eta r v = \dfrac{4}{3}\,\pi\, r^{3}\,\sigma g$

or, $\qquad \eta = \dfrac{2 r^{2}\sigma g}{9v}$

$$= \frac{2 \times (1 \times 10^{-3}\ \text{m})^{2} \times (1750\ \text{kg m}^{-3})\,(9 \cdot 8\ \text{m s}^{-2})}{9 \times (0 \cdot 35 \times 10^{-2}\ \text{m s}^{-1})}$$

$$\approx 11\ \text{poise}.$$

This appears to be a highly viscous liquid.

14.18 TERMINAL VELOCITY

The viscous force on a solid moving through a fluid is proportional to its velocity. When a solid is dropped in a fluid, the forces acting on it are

(a) weight W acting vertically downward,

(b) the viscous force F acting vertically upward and

(c) the buoyancy force B acting vertically upward.

The weight W and the buoyancy B are constant but the force F is proportional to the velocity v.

Initially, the velocity and hence the viscous force F is zero and the solid is accelerated due to the force $W-B$. Because of the acceleration the velocity increases. Accordingly, the viscous force also increases. At a certain instant the viscous force becomes equal to $W-B$. The net force then becomes zero and the solid falls with constant velocity. This constant velocity is known as the terminal velocity.

Consider a spherical body falling through a liquid. Suppose the density of the body $= \rho$, density of the liquid $= \sigma$, radius of the sphere $= r$ and the terminal velocity $= v_{0}$. The viscous force is

$$F = 6\pi\,\eta r v_{0}.$$

The weight $\qquad W = \dfrac{4}{3}\,\pi\, r^{3}\rho g$

and the buoyancy force $B = \dfrac{4}{3}\,\pi\, r^{3}\sigma g$.

We have

$$6\pi\,\eta r v_{0} = W - B = \frac{4}{3}\,\pi r^{3}\rho g - \frac{4}{3}\,\pi r^{3}\sigma g$$

or, $\qquad v_{0} = \dfrac{2\, r^{2}(\rho - \sigma)g}{9\,\eta}. \qquad ... (14.23)$

14.19 MEASURING COEFFICIENT OF VISCOSITY BY STOKES' METHOD

Viscosity of a liquid may be determined by measuring the terminal velocity of a solid sphere in it. Figure (14.28) shows the apparatus. A test tube A contains the experimental liquid and is fitted into a water bath B. A thermometer T measures the temperature of the bath. A tube C is fitted in the cork of the test tube A. There are three equidistant marks P, Q and R on the test tube well below the tube C.

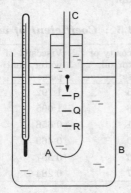

Figure 14.28

A spherical metal ball is dropped in the tube C. The time interval taken by the ball to pass through the length PQ and through the length QR are noted with the help of a stop watch. If these two are not equal, a smaller metal ball is tried. The process is repeated till the two time intervals are the same. In this case the ball has achieved its terminal velocity before passing through the mark P. The radius of the ball is determined by a screw guage. Its mass m is determined by weighing it. The length $PQ = QR$ is measured with a scale.

Let r = radius of the spherical ball
m = mass of the ball
t = time interval in passing through the length PQ or QR
d = length $PQ = QR$
η = coefficient of viscosity of the liquid
σ = density of the liquid.

The density of the solid is $\rho = \dfrac{m}{\frac{4}{3}\pi r^3}$ and the terminal velocity is $v_0 = d/t$. Using equation (14.23)

$$\eta = \frac{2}{9}\frac{(\rho - \sigma)gr^2}{d/t}.$$

This method is useful for a highly viscous liquid such as Castor oil.

14.20 CRITICAL VELOCITY AND REYNOLDS NUMBER

When a fluid flows in a tube with small velocity, the flow is steady. As the velocity is gradually increased, at one stage the flow becomes turbulent. The largest velocity which allows a steady flow is called the *critical velocity*.

Whether the flow will be steady or turbulent mainly depends on the density, velocity and the coefficient of viscosity of the fluid as well as the diameter of the tube through which the fluid is flowing. The quantity

$$N = \frac{\rho v D}{\eta} \qquad \dots \ (14.24)$$

is called the *Reynolds number* and plays a key role in determining the nature of flow. It is found that if the Reynolds number is less than 2000, the flow is steady. If it is greater than 3000, the flow is turbulent. If it is between 2000 and 3000, the flow is unstable. In this case it may be steady and may suddenly change to turbulent or it may be turbulent and may suddenly change to steady.

Worked Out Examples

1 *One end of a wire* 2 m *long and* 0·2 cm^2 *in cross section is fixed in a ceiling and a load of* 4·8 kg *is attached to the free end. Find the extension of the wire. Young modulus of steel* = $2·0 \times 10^{11}$ N m^{-2}. *Take* $g = 10$ m s^{-2}.

Solution : We have

$$Y = \frac{\text{stress}}{\text{strain}} = \frac{T/A}{l/L}$$

with symbols having their usual meanings. The extension is

$$l = \frac{TL}{AY}.$$

As the load is in equilibrium after the extension, the tension in the wire is equal to the weight of the load

$$= 4·8 \text{ kg} \times 10 \text{ m s}^{-2} = 48 \text{ N}$$

Thus, $l = \dfrac{(48 \text{ N}) (2 \text{ m})}{(0·2 \times 10^{-4} \text{ m}^2) \times (2·0 \times 10^{11} \text{ N m}^{-2})}$

$$= 2·4 \times 10^{-5} \text{ m}.$$

2. *One end of a nylon rope of length* 4·5 m *and diameter* 6 mm *is fixed to a tree-limb. A monkey weighing* 100 N *jumps to catch the free end and stays there. Find the elongation of the rope and the corresponding change in the diameter. Young modulus of nylon* = $4·8 \times 10^{11}$ N m^{-2} *and Poisson ratio of nylon* = 0·2.

Solution : As the monkey stays in equilibrium, the tension in the rope equals the weight of the monkey. Hence,

$$Y = \frac{\text{stress}}{\text{strain}} = \frac{T/A}{l/L}$$

or, $\quad l = \dfrac{TL}{AY}$

or, elongation = $l = \dfrac{(100 \text{ N}) \times (4·5 \text{ m})}{(\pi \times 9 \times 10^{-6} \text{ m}^2) \times (4·8 \times 10^{11} \text{ N m}^{-2})}$

$$= 3·32 \times 10^{-5} \text{ m}.$$

Again, Poisson ratio = $\dfrac{\Delta d/d}{l/L} = \dfrac{(\Delta d)L}{ld}$

or, $\quad 0·2 = \dfrac{\Delta d \times 4·5 \text{ m}}{(3·32 \times 10^{-5} \text{ m}) \times (6 \times 10^{-3} \text{ m})}$

or, $\quad \Delta d = \dfrac{0·2 \times 6 \times 3·32 \times 10^{-8} \text{ m}}{4·5}$

$$= 8·8 \times 10^{-9} \text{ m}.$$

3. *Two blocks of masses* 1 kg *and* 2 kg *are connected by a metal wire going over a smooth pulley as shown in figure (14-W1). The breaking stress of the metal is* 2×10^9 N m^{-2}. *What should be the minimum radius of the wire used if it is not to break ? Take* $g = 10$ m s^{-2}.

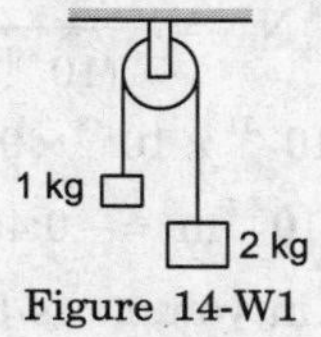

Figure 14-W1

Solution : The stress in the wire = $\dfrac{\text{Tension}}{\text{Area of cross section}}$.

To avoid breaking, this stress should not exceed the breaking stress.

Let the tension in the wire be T. The equations of motion of the two blocks are,

$$T - 10 \text{ N} = (1 \text{ kg}) \, a$$

and $$20 \text{ N} - T = (2 \text{ kg}) \, a.$$

Eliminating a from these equations,

$$T = (40/3) \text{ N}.$$

$$\text{The stress} = \frac{(40/3) \text{ N}}{\pi \, r^2}.$$

If the minimum radius needed to avoid breaking is r,

$$2 \times 10^9 \, \frac{\text{N}}{\text{m}^2} = \frac{(40/3) \text{ N}}{\pi \, r^2}.$$

Solving this,

$$r = 4 \cdot 6 \times 10^{-5} \text{ m}.$$

4. *Two wires of equal cross section but one made of steel and the other of copper, are joined end to end. When the combination is kept under tension, the elongations in the two wires are found to be equal. Find the ratio of the lengths of the two wires. Young modulus of steel = $2 \cdot 0 \times 10^{11}$ N m^{-2} and that of copper = $1 \cdot 1 \times 10^{11}$ N m^{-2}.*

Solution : As the cross sections of the wires are equal and same tension exists in both, the stresses developed are equal. Let the original lengths of the steel wire and the copper wire be L_s and L_c respectively and the elongation in each wire be l.

$$\frac{l}{L_s} = \frac{\text{stress}}{2 \cdot 0 \times 10^{11} \text{ N m}^{-2}} \qquad \dots \text{(i)}$$

and $$\frac{l}{L_c} = \frac{\text{stress}}{1 \cdot 1 \times 10^{11} \text{ N m}^{-2}}. \qquad \dots \text{(ii)}$$

Dividing (ii) by (i),

$$L_s / L_c = 2 \cdot 0 / 1 \cdot 1 = 20 : 11.$$

5. *Find the decrease in the volume of a sample of water from the following data. Initial volume = 1000 cm^3, initial pressure = 10^5 N m^{-2}, final pressure = 10^6 N m^{-2}, compressibility of water = 50×10^{-11} m^2 N^{-1}.*

Solution : The change in pressure

$$= \Delta P = 10^6 \text{ N m}^{-2} - 10^5 \text{ N m}^{-2}$$
$$= 9 \times 10^5 \text{ N m}^{-2}.$$

$$\text{Compressibility} = \frac{1}{\text{Bulk modulus}} = -\frac{\Delta V / V}{\Delta P}$$

or, $$50 \times 10^{-11} \text{ m}^2 \text{ N}^{-1} = -\frac{\Delta V}{(10^{-3} \text{ m}^3) \times (9 \times 10^5 \text{ N m}^{-2})}$$

or, $$\Delta V = -50 \times 10^{-11} \times 10^{-3} \times 9 \times 10^5 \text{ m}^3$$
$$= -4 \cdot 5 \times 10^{-7} \text{ m}^3 = -0 \cdot 45 \text{ cm}^3.$$

Thus the decrease in volume is $0 \cdot 45$ cm^3.

6. *One end of a metal wire is fixed to a ceiling and a load of 2 kg hangs from the other end. A similar wire is attached to the bottom of the load and another load of 1 kg hangs from this lower wire. Find the longitudinal strain in both the wires. Area of cross section of each wire is $0 \cdot 005$ cm^2 and Young modulus of the metal is $2 \cdot 0 \times 10^{11}$ N m^{-2}. Take $g = 10$ m s^{-2}.*

Solution : The situation is described in figure (14-W2). As the 1 kg mass is in equilibrium, the tension in the lower wire equals the weight of the load.

Figure 14-W2

Thus $$T_1 = 10 \text{ N}$$

$$\text{Stress} = 10 \text{ N}/0 \cdot 005 \text{ cm}^2$$
$$= 2 \times 10^7 \text{ N m}^{-2}.$$

$$\text{Longitudinal strain} = \frac{\text{stress}}{Y} = \frac{2 \times 10^7 \text{ N m}^{-2}}{2 \times 10^{11} \text{ N m}^{-2}} = 10^{-4}.$$

Considering the equilibrium of the upper block, we can write,

$$T_2 = 20 \text{ N} + T_1, \quad \text{or,} \quad T_2 = 30 \text{ N}.$$

$$\text{Stress} = 30 \text{ N}/0 \cdot 005 \text{ cm}^2$$
$$= 6 \times 10^7 \text{ N m}^{-2}.$$

$$\text{Longitudinal strain} = \frac{6 \times 10^7 \text{ N m}^{-2}}{2 \times 10^{11} \text{ N m}^{-2}} = 3 \times 10^{-4}.$$

7. *Each of the three blocks P, Q and R shown in figure (14-W3) has a mass of 3 kg. Each of the wires A and B has cross-sectional area $0 \cdot 005$ cm^2 and Young modulus 2×10^{11} N m^{-2}. Neglect friction. Find the longitudinal strain developed in each of the wires. Take $g = 10$ m s^{-2}.*

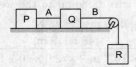

Figure 14-W3

Solution : The block R will descend vertically and the blocks P and Q will move on the frictionless horizontal table. Let the common magnitude of the acceleration be a. Let the tensions in the wires A and B be T_A and T_B respectively.

Writing the equations of motion of the blocks P, Q and R, we get,

$$T_A = (3 \text{ kg}) \, a \qquad \dots \text{(i)}$$

$$T_B - T_A = (3 \text{ kg}) a \qquad \ldots \text{(ii)}$$

and $(3 \text{ kg}) g - T_B = (3 \text{ kg}) a.$ $\ldots$ (iii)

By (i) and (ii),

$$T_B = 2 \, T_A.$$

By (i) and (iii),

$$T_A + T_B = (3 \text{ kg}) g = 30 \text{ N}$$

or, $3 \, T_A = 30 \text{ N}$

or, $T_A = 10 \text{ N}$ and $T_B = 20 \text{ N}.$

$$\text{Longitudinal strain} = \frac{\text{Longitudinal stress}}{\text{Young modulus}}$$

$$\text{Strain in wire } A = \frac{10 \text{ N}/0.005 \text{ cm}^2}{2 \times 10^{11} \text{ N m}^{-2}} = 10^{-4}$$

and strain in wire $B = \dfrac{20 \text{ N}/0.005 \text{ cm}^2}{2 \times 10^{11} \text{ N m}^{-2}} = 2 \times 10^{-4}.$

8. *A wire of area of cross section 3.0 mm^2 and natural length 50 cm is fixed at one end and a mass of 2.1 kg is hung from the other end. Find the elastic potential energy stored in the wire in steady state. Young modulus of the material of the wire $= 1.9 \times 10^{11} \text{ N m}^{-2}$. Take $g = 10 \text{ m s}^{-2}.$*

Solution : The volume of the wire is

$$V = (3.0 \text{ mm}^2) \, (50 \text{ cm})$$

$$= (3.0 \times 10^{-6} \text{ m}^2) \, (0.50 \text{ m}) = 1.5 \times 10^{-6} \text{ m}^3.$$

Tension in the wire is

$$T = mg$$

$$= (2.1 \text{ kg}) \, (10 \text{ m s}^{-2}) = 21 \text{ N}.$$

The stress $= T/A$

$$= \frac{21 \text{ N}}{3.0 \text{ mm}^2} = 7.0 \times 10^6 \text{ N m}^{-2}.$$

The strain $= \text{stress}/Y$

$$= \frac{7.0 \times 10^6 \text{ N m}^{-2}}{1.9 \times 10^{11} \text{ N m}^{-2}} = 3.7 \times 10^{-5}.$$

The elastic potential energy of the wire is

$$U = \frac{1}{2} \, (\text{stress}) \, (\text{strain}) \, (\text{volume})$$

$$= \frac{1}{2} \, (7.0 \times 10^6 \text{ N m}^{-2}) \, (3.7 \times 10^{-5}) \, (1.5 \times 10^{-6} \text{ m}^3)$$

$$= 1.9 \times 10^{-4} \text{ J}.$$

9. *A block of weight 10 N is fastened to one end of a wire of cross-sectional area 3 mm^2 and is rotated in a vertical circle of radius 20 cm. The speed of the block at the bottom of the circle is 2 m s^{-1}. Find the elongation of the wire when the block is at the bottom of the circle. Young modulus of the material of the wire $= 2 \times 10^{11} \text{ N m}^{-2}.$*

Solution : Forces acting on the block are (a) the tension T and (b) the weight W. At the lowest point, the resultant

force is $T - W$ towards the centre. As the block is going in a circle, the net force towards the centre should be mv^2/r with usual symbols. Thus,

$$T - W = mv^2/r$$

or, $T = W + mv^2/r$

$$= 10 \text{ N} + \frac{(1 \text{ kg}) \, (2 \text{ m s}^{-1})^2}{0.2 \text{ m}} = 30 \text{ N}$$

We have $Y = \dfrac{T/A}{l/L}$

or, $l = \dfrac{TL}{AY}$

$$= \frac{30 \text{ N} \times (20 \text{ cm})}{(3 \times 10^{-6} \text{ m}^2) \times (2 \times 10^{11} \text{ N m}^{-2})}$$

$$= 5 \times 10^{-5} \times 20 \text{ cm} = 10^{-3} \text{ cm}.$$

10. *A uniform heavy rod of weight W, cross-sectional area A and length L is hanging from a fixed support. Young modulus of the material of the rod is Y. Neglect the lateral contraction. Find the elongation of the rod.*

Solution : Consider a small length dx of the rod at a distance x from the fixed end. The part below this small element has length $L - x$. The tension T of the rod at the element equals the weight of the rod below it.

$$T = (L - x) \, \frac{W}{L}.$$

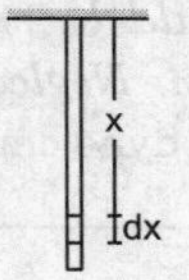

Figure 14-W4

Elongation in the element is given by

$$\text{elongation} = \text{original length} \times \text{stress}/Y$$

$$= \frac{T \, dx}{AY} = \frac{(L - x) \, W \, dx}{LAY}.$$

The total elongation $= \displaystyle\int_0^L \frac{(L - x) \, W \, dx}{LAY}$

$$= \frac{W}{LAY} \left(Lx - \frac{x^2}{2} \right)_0^L = \frac{WL}{2AY}.$$

11. *There is an air bubble of radius 1.0 mm in a liquid of surface tension 0.075 N m^{-1} and density 1000 kg m^{-3}. The bubble is at a depth of 10 cm below the free surface. By what amount is the pressure inside the bubble greater than the atmospheric pressure ? Take $g = 9.8 \text{ m s}^{-2}.$*

Solution :

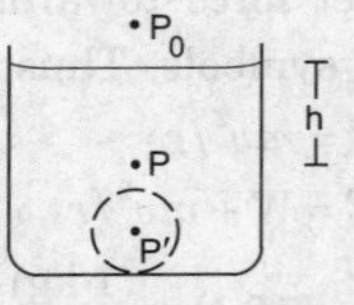

Figure 14-W5

Let the atmospheric pressure be P_0. The pressure of the liquid just outside the bubble is (figure 14-W5)

$$P = P_0 + h\rho g.$$

The pressure inside the bubble is

$$P' = P + \frac{2S}{r} = P_0 + h\rho g + \frac{2S}{r}$$

or, $P' - P_0$

$$= (10 \text{ cm}) (1000 \text{ kg m}^{-3}) (9 \cdot 8 \text{ m s}^{-2}) + \frac{2 \times 0 \cdot 075 \text{ N m}^{-1}}{1 \cdot 0 \times 10^{-3} \text{ m}}$$

$$= 980 \text{ N m}^{-2} + 150 \text{ N m}^{-2}$$

$$= 1130 \text{ Pa}.$$

12. *A light wire AB of length 10 cm can slide on a vertical frame as shown in figure (14-W6). There is a film of soap solution trapped between the frame and the wire. Find the load W that should be suspended from the wire to keep it in equilibrium. Neglect friction. Surface tension of soap solution = 25 dyne cm^{-1}. Take g = 10 m s^{-2}.*

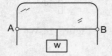

Figure 14-W6

Solution : Soap solution film will be formed on both sides of the frame. Each film is in contact with the wire along a distance of 10 cm. The force exerted by the film on the wire

$$= 2 \times (10 \text{ cm}) \times (25 \text{ dyne cm}^{-1})$$

$$= 500 \text{ dyne} = 5 \times 10^{-3} \text{ N}.$$

This force acts vertically upward and should be balanced by the load. Hence the load that should be suspended is 5×10^{-3} N. The mass of the load should be $\frac{5 \times 10^{-3} \text{ N}}{10 \text{ m s}^{-2}} = 5 \times 10^{-4} \text{ kg} = 0 \cdot 5 \text{ g}.$

13. *The lower end of a capillary tube is dipped into water and it is seen that the water rises through 7·5 cm in the capillary. Find the radius of the capillary. Surface tension of water = 7·5 × 10^{-2} N m^{-1}. Contact angle between water and glass = 0°. Take g = 10 m s^{-2}.*

Solution : We have,

$$h = \frac{2S \cos\theta}{r\rho g}$$

or,

$$r = \frac{2S \cos\theta}{h\rho g}$$

$$= \frac{2 \times (7 \cdot 5 \times 10^{-2} \text{ N m}^{-1}) \times 1}{(0 \cdot 075 \text{ m}) \times (1000 \text{ kg m}^{-3}) \times (10 \text{ m s}^{-2})}$$

$$= 2 \times 10^{-4} \text{ m} = 0 \cdot 2 \text{ mm}.$$

14. *Two mercury drops each of radius r merge to form a bigger drop. Calculate the surface energy released.*

Solution :

Surface area of one drop before merging $= 4\pi r^2$.

Total surface area of both the drops $= 8\pi r^2$.

Hence, the surface energy before merging $= 8\pi r^2 S$.

When the drops merge, the volume of the bigger drop

$$= 2 \times \frac{4}{3}\pi r^3 = \frac{8}{3}\pi r^3.$$

If the radius of this new drop is R,

$$\frac{4}{3}\pi R^3 = \frac{8}{3}\pi r^3$$

or, $R = 2^{1/3} r$

or, $4\pi R^2 = 4 \times 2^{2/3} \times \pi r^2$.

Hence, the surface energy $= 4 \times 2^{2/3} \times \pi r^2 S$.

The released surface energy $= 8\pi r^2 S - 4 \times 2^{2/3} \pi r^2 S$

$$\approx 1 \cdot 65 \pi r^2 S.$$

15. *A large wooden plate of area 10 m^2 floating on the surface of a river is made to move horizontally with a speed of 2 m s^{-1} by applying a tangential force. If the river is 1 m deep and the water in contact with the bed is stationary, find the tangential force needed to keep the plate moving. Coefficient of viscosity of water at the temperature of the river = 10^{-3} poise.*

Solution : The velocity decreases from 2 m s^{-1} to zero in 1 m of perpendicular length. Hence, velocity gradient

$$= dv/dx = 2 \text{ s}^{-1}.$$

Now, $\eta = \left| \dfrac{F/A}{dv/dx} \right|$

or, $10^{-3} \dfrac{\text{N–s}}{\text{m}^2} = \dfrac{F}{(10 \text{ m}^2)(2 \text{ s}^{-1})}$

or, $F = 0 \cdot 02 \text{ N}.$

16. *The velocity of water in a river is 18 km h^{-1} near the surface. If the river is 5 m deep, find the shearing stress between the horizontal layers of water. The coefficient of viscosity of water = 10^{-2} poise.*

Solution : The velocity gradient in vertical direction is

$$\frac{dv}{dx} = \frac{18 \text{ km h}^{-1}}{5 \text{ m}} = 1\cdot0 \text{ s}^{-1}.$$

The magnitude of the force of viscosity is

$$F = \eta A \frac{dv}{dx}$$

The shearing stress is

$$F/A = \eta \frac{dv}{dx} = (10^{-2} \text{ poise}) (1\cdot0 \text{ s}^{-1}) = 10^{-3} \text{ N m}^{-2}.$$

17. *Find the terminal velocity of a rain drop of radius 0·01 mm. The coefficient of viscosity of air is $1\cdot8 \times 10^{-5}$ N–s m^{-2} and its density is $1\cdot2$ kg m^{-3}. Density of water = 1000 kg m^{-3}. Take $g = 10$ m s^{-2}.*

Solution : The forces on the rain drop are

(a) the weight $\frac{4}{3} \pi r^3 \rho g$ downward,

(b) the force of buoyancy $\frac{4}{3} \pi r^3 \sigma g$ upward,

(c) the force of viscosity $6\pi\eta rv$ upward.

Here ρ is the density of water and σ is the density of air. At terminal velocity the net force is zero. As the density of air is much smaller than the density of water, the force of buoyance may be neglected.

Thus, at terminal velocity

$$6\pi\eta rv = \frac{4}{3} \pi r^3 \rho g$$

or,

$$v = \frac{2 r^2 \rho g}{9\eta}.$$

$$= \frac{2 \times (0\cdot01 \text{ mm})^2 \times (1000 \text{ kg m}^{-3}) (10 \text{ m s}^{-2})}{9 \times (1\cdot8 \times 10^{-5} \text{ N–s m}^{-2})}$$

$$\approx 1\cdot2 \text{ cm s}^{-2}.$$

□

QUESTIONS FOR SHORT ANSWER

1. The ratio stress/strain remains constant for small deformation of a metal wire. When the deformation is made larger, will this ratio increase or decrease ?

2. When a block of mass M is suspended by a long wire of length L, the elastic potential energy stored in the wire is $\frac{1}{2} \times$ stress $\times$ strain $\times$ volume. Show that it is equal to $\frac{1}{2} Mgl$, where l is the extension. The loss in gravitational potential energy of the mass earth system is Mgl. Where does the remaining $\frac{1}{2} Mgl$ energy go ?

3. When the skeleton of an elephant and the skeleton of a mouse are prepared in the same size, the bones of the elephant are shown thicker than those of the mouse. Explain why the bones of an elephant are thicker than proportionate. The bones are expected to withstand the stress due to the weight of the animal.

4. The yield point of a typical solid is about 1%. Suppose you are lying horizontally and two persons are pulling your hands and two persons are pulling your legs along your own length. How much will be the increase in your length if the strain is 1% ? Do you think your yield point is 1% or much less than that ?

5. When rubber sheets are used in a shock absorber, what happens to the energy of vibration ?

6. If a compressed spring is dissolved in acid, what happens to the elastic potential energy of the spring ?

7. A steel blade placed gently on the surface of water floats on it. If the same blade is kept well inside the water, it sinks. Explain.

8. When some wax is rubbed on a cloth, it becomes waterproof. Explain.

9. The contact angle between pure water and pure silver is 90°. If a capillary tube made of silver is dipped at one end in pure water, will the water rise in the capillary ?

10. It is said that a liquid rises or is depressed in a capillary due to the surface tension. If a liquid neither rises nor depresses in a capillary, can we conclude that the surface tension of the liquid is zero ?

11. The contact angle between water and glass is 0°. When water is poured in a glass to the maximum of its capacity, the water surface is convex upward. The angle of contact in such a situation is more than 90°. Explain.

12. A uniform vertical tube of circular cross section contains a liquid. The contact angle is 90°. Consider a diameter of the tube lying in the surface of the liquid. The surface to the right of this diameter pulls the surface on the left of it. What keeps the surface on the left in equilibrium ?

13. When a glass capillary tube is dipped at one end in water, water rises in the tube. The gravitational potential energy is thus increased. Is it a violation of conservation of energy ?

14. If a mosquito is dipped into water and released, it is not able to fly till it is dry again. Explain.

15. The force of surface tension acts tangentially to the surface whereas the force due to air pressure acts perpendicularly on the surface. How is then the force due to excess pressure inside a bubble balanced by the force due to the surface tension ?

16. When the size of a soap bubble is increased by pushing more air in it, the surface area increases. Does it mean that the average separation between the surface molecules is increased ?

17. Frictional force between solids operates even when they do not move with respect to each other. Do we have viscous force acting between two layers even if there is no relative motion ?

18. Water near the bed of a deep river is quiet while that near the surface flows. Give reasons.

19. If water in one flask and castor oil in other are violently shaken and kept on a table, which will come to rest earlier ?

OBJECTIVE I

1. A rope 1 cm in diameter breaks if the tension in it exceeds 500 N. The maximum tension that may be given to a similar rope of diameter 2 cm is
   (a) 500 N   (b) 250 N   (c) 1000 N   (d) 2000 N.

2. The breaking stress of a wire depends on
   (a) material of the wire (b) length of the wire
   (c) radius of the wire   (d) shape of the cross section.

3. A wire can sustain the weight of 20 kg before breaking. If the wire is cut into two equal parts, each part can sustain a weight of
   (a) 10 kg   (b) 20 kg   (c) 40 kg   (d) 80 kg.

4. Two wires A and B are made of same material. The wire A has a length l and diameter r while the wire B has a length $2l$ and diameter $r/2$. If the two wires are stretched by the same force, the elongation in A divided by the elongation in B is
   (a) 1/8   (b) 1/4   (c) 4   (d) 8.

5. A wire elongates by 1.0 mm when a load W is hung from it. If this wire goes over a pulley and two weights W each are hung at the two ends, the elongation of the wire will be
   (a) 0·5 m   (b) 1·0 mm   (c) 2·0 mm   (d) 4·0 mm.

6. A heavy uniform rod is hanging vertically from a fixed support. It is stretched by its own weight. The diameter of the rod is
   (a) smallest at the top and gradually increases down the rod
   (b) largest at the top and gradually decreases down the rod
   (c) uniform everywhere
   (d) maximum in the middle.

7. When a metal wire is stretched by a load, the fractional change in its volume $\Delta V/V$ is proportional to
   (a) $\dfrac{\Delta l}{l}$ (b) $\left(\dfrac{\Delta l}{l}\right)^2$ (c) $\sqrt{\Delta l/l}$ (d) none of these.

8. The length of a metal wire is l_1 when the tension in it is T_1 and is l_2 when the tension is T_2. The natural length of the wire is
   (a) $\dfrac{l_1 + l_2}{2}$ (b) $\sqrt{l_1 l_2}$ (c) $\dfrac{l_1 T_2 - l_2 T_1}{T_2 - T_1}$ (d) $\dfrac{l_1 T_2 + l_2 T_1}{T_2 + T_1}$.

9. A heavy mass is attached to a thin wire and is whirled in a vertical circle. The wire is most likely to break
   (a) when the mass is at the highest point
   (b) when the mass is at the lowest point
   (c) when the wire is horizontal
   (d) at an angle of $\cos^{-1}(1/3)$ from the upward vertical.

10. When a metal wire elongates by hanging a load on it, the gravitational potential energy is decreased.
    (a) This energy completely appears as the increased kinetic energy of the block.
    (b) This energy completely appears as the increased elastic potential energy of the wire.
    (c) This energy completely appears as heat.
    (d) None of these.

11. By a surface of a liquid we mean
    (a) a geometrical plane like $x = 0$
    (b) all molecules exposed to the atmosphere
    (c) a layer of thickness of the order of 10^{-8} m
    (d) a layer of thickness of the order of 10^{-4} m.

12 An ice cube is suspended in vacuum in a gravity free hall. As the ice melts it
    (a) will retain its cubical shape
    (b) will change its shape to spherical
    (c) will fall down on the floor of the hall
    (d) will fly up.

13. When water droplets merge to form a bigger drop
    (a) energy is liberated   (b) energy is absorbed
    (c) energy is neither liberated nor absobred
    (d) energy may either be liberated or absorbed depending on the nature of the liquid.

14. The dimension $ML^{-1}T^{-2}$ can correspond to
    (a) moment of a force   (b) surface tension
    (c) modulus of elasticity   (d) coefficient of viscosity.

15. Air is pushed into a soap bubble of radius r to double its radius. If the surface tension of the soap solution is S, the work done in the process is
    (a) $8\pi r^2 S$ (b) $12\pi r^2 S$ (c) $16\pi r^2 S$ (d) $24\pi r^2 S$.

16. If more air is pushed in a soap bubble, the pressure in it
    (a) decreases   (b) increases
    (c) remains same   (d) becomes zero.

17. If two soap bubbles of different radii are connected by a tube,
    (a) air flows from bigger bubble to the smaller bubble till the sizes become equal
    (b) air flows from bigger bubble to the smaller bubble till the sizes are interchanged
    (c) air flows from the smaller bubble to the bigger
    (d) there is no flow of air.

18. Figure (14-Q1) shows a capillary tube of radius r dipped into water. If the atmospheric pressure is P_0, the

pressure at point A is

(a) P_0 (b) $P_0 + \dfrac{2S}{r}$ (c) $P_0 - \dfrac{2S}{r}$ (d) $P_0 - \dfrac{4S}{r}$.

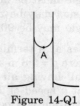

Figure 14-Q1

19. The excess pressure inside a soap bubble is twice the excess pressure inside a second soap bubble. The volume of the first bubble is n times the volume of the second where n is

(a) 4   (b) 2   (c) 1   (d) 0·125.

20. Which of the following graphs may represent the relation between the capillary rise h and the radius r of the capillary ?

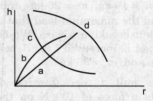

Figure 14-Q2

21. Water rises in a vertical capillary tube up to a length of 10 cm. If the tube is inclined at 45°, the length of water risen in the tube will be

(a) 10 cm   (b) $10\sqrt{2}$ cm
(c) $10/\sqrt{2}$ cm   (d) none of these.

22. A 20 cm long capillary tube is dipped in water. The water rises up to 8 cm. If the entire arrangement is put in a freely falling elevator, the length of water column in the capillary tube will be

(a) 8 cm   (b) 6 cm   (c) 10 cm   (d) 20 cm.

23. Viscosity is a property of
(a) liquids only   (b) solids only
(c) solids and liquids only   (d) liquids and gases only.

24. The force of viscosity is
(a) electromagnetic (b) gravitational (c) nuclear (d) weak.

25. The viscous force acting between two layers of a liquid is given by $\dfrac{F}{A} = -\eta \dfrac{dv}{dz}$. This F/A may be called

(a) pressure   (b) longitudinal stress
(c) tangential stress   (d) volume stress.

26. A raindrop falls near the surface of the earth with almost uniform velocity because
(a) its weight is negligible
(b) the force of surface tension balances its weight
(c) the force of viscosity of air balances its weight
(d) the drops are charged and atmospheric electric field balances its weight.

27. A piece of wood is taken deep inside a long column of water and released. It will move up
(a) with a constant upward acceleration
(b) with a decreasing upward acceleration
(c) with a deceleration
(d) with a uniform velocity.

28. A solid sphere falls with a terminal velocity of 20 m s^{-1} in air. If it is allowed to fall in vacuum,
(a) terminal velocity will be 20 m s^{-1}
(b) terminal velocity will be less than 20 m s^{-1}
(c) terminal velocity will be more than 20 m s^{-1}
(d) there will be no terminal velocity.

29. A spherical ball is dropped in a long column of a viscous liquid. The speed of the ball as a function of time may be best represented by the graph
(a) A (b) B (c) C (d) D.

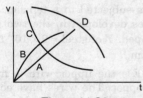

Figure 14-Q3

OBJECTIVE II

1. A student plots a graph from his readings on the determination of Young modulus of a metal wire but forgets to put the labels (figure 14-Q4). The quantities on X and Y-axes may be respectively
(a) weight hung and length increased
(b) stress applied and length increased
(c) stress applied and strain developed
(d) length increased and the weight hung.

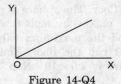

Figure 14-Q4

2. The properties of a surface are different from those of the bulk liquid because the surface molecules
(a) are smaller than other molelcules
(b) acquire charge due to collision from air molecules
(c) find different type of molecules in their range of influence
(d) feel a net force in one direction.

3. The rise of a liquid in a capillary tube depends on
(a) the material   (b) the length
(c) the outer radius   (d) the inner radius of the tube.

4. The contact angle between a solid and a liquid is a property of
(a) the material of the solid
(b) the material of the liquid

(c) the shape of the solid

(d) the mass of the solid.

5. A liquid is contained in a vertical tube of semicircular cross section (figure 14-Q5). The contact angle is zero. The force of surface tension on the curved part and on the flat part are in ratio

(a) 1 : 1   (b) 1 : 2   (c) π : 2   (d) 2 : π.

Figure 14-Q5

6. When a capillary tube is dipped into a liquid, the liquid neither rises nor falls in the capillary.

(a) The surface tension of the liquid must be zero.

(b) The contact angle must be 90°.

(c) The surface tension may be zero.

(d) The contact angle may be 90°.

7. A solid sphere moves at a terminal velocity of 20 m s^{-1} in air at a place where $g = 9.8$ m s^{-2}. The sphere is taken in a gravity-free hall having air at the same pressure and pushed down at a speed of 20 m s^{-1}.

(a) Its initial acceleration will be 9.8 m s^{-2} downward.

(b) Its initial acceleration will be 9.8 m s^{-2} upward.

(c) The magnitude of acceleration will decrease as the time passes.

(d) It will eventually stop.

EXERCISES

1. A load of 10 kg is suspended by a metal wire 3 m long and having a cross-sectional area 4 mm^2. Find (a) the stress (b) the strain and (c) the elongation. Young modulus of the metal is 2.0×10^{11} N m^{-2}.

2. A vertical metal cylinder of radius 2 cm and length 2 m is fixed at the lower end and a load of 100 kg is put on it. Find (a) the stress (b) the strain and (c) the compression of the cylinder. Young modulus of the metal $= 2 \times 10^{11}$ N m^{-2}.

3. The elastic limit of steel is 8×10^8 N m^{-2} and its Young modulus 2×10^{11} N m^{-2}. Find the maximum elongation of a half-metre steel wire that can be given without exceeding the elastic limit.

4. A steel wire and a copper wire of equal length and equal cross-sectional area are joined end to end and the combination is subjected to a tension. Find the ratio of (a) the stresses developed in the two wires and (b) the strains developed. Y of steel $= 2 \times 10^{11}$ N m^{-2}. Y of copper $= 1.3 \times 10^{11}$ N m^{-2}.

5. In figure (14-E1) the upper wire is made of steel and the lower of copper. The wires have equal cross section. Find the ratio of the longitudinal strains developed in the two wires.

Figure 14-E1

6. The two wires shown in figure (14-E2) are made of the

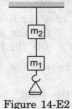

Figure 14-E2

same material which has a breaking stress of 8×10^8 N m^{-2}. The area of cross section of the upper wire is 0.006 cm^2 and that of the lower wire is 0.003 cm^2. The mass $m_1 = 10$ kg, $m_2 = 20$ kg and the hanger is light. (a) Find the maximum load that can be put on the hanger without breaking a wire. Which wire will break first if the load is increased ? (b) Repeat the above part if $m_1 = 10$ kg and $m_2 = 36$ kg.

7. Two persons pull a rope towards themselves. Each person exerts a force of 100 N on the rope. Find the Young modulus of the material of the rope if it extends in length by 1 cm. Original length of the rope = 2 m and the area of cross section = 2 cm^2.

8. A steel rod of cross-sectional area 4 cm^2 and length 2 m shrinks by 0.1 cm as the temperature decreases in night. If the rod is clamped at both ends during the day hours, find the tension developed in it during night hours. Young modulus of steel $= 1.9 \times 10^{11}$ N m^{-2}.

9. Consider the situation shown in figure (14-E3). The force F is equal to the $m_2 g / 2$. If the area of cross section of the string is A and its Young modulus Y, find the strain developed in it. The string is light and there is no friction anywhere.

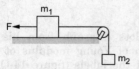

Figure 14-E3

10. A sphere of mass 20 kg is suspended by a metal wire of unstretched length 4 m and diameter 1 mm. When in equilibrium, there is a clear gap of 2 mm between the sphere and the floor. The sphere is gently pushed aside so that the wire makes an angle θ with the vertical and is released. Find the maximum value of θ so that the sphere does not rub the floor. Young modulus of the metal of the wire is 2.0×10^{11} N m^{-2}. Make appropriate approximations.

11. A steel wire of original length 1 m and cross-sectional area $4 \cdot 00$ mm^2 is clamped at the two ends so that it lies horizontally and without tension. If a load of $2 \cdot 16$ kg is suspended from the middle point of the wire, what would be its vertical depression ?

    Y of the steel = $2 \cdot 0 \times 10^{11}$ N m^{-2}. Take $g = 10$ m s^{-2}.

12. A copper wire of cross-sectional area $0 \cdot 01$ cm^2 is under a tension of 20 N. Find the decrease in the cross-sectional area. Young modulus of copper = $1 \cdot 1 \times 10^{11}$ N m^{-2} and Poisson ratio = $0 \cdot 32$.

    $$\left[\textbf{Hint :} \ \frac{\Delta A}{A} = 2 \ \frac{\Delta r}{r} \right]$$

13. Find the increase in pressure required to decrease the volume of a water sample by $0 \cdot 01\%$. Bulk modulus of water = $2 \cdot 1 \times 10^{9}$ N m^{-2}.

14. Estimate the change in the density of water in ocean at a depth of 400 m below the surface. The density of water at the surface = 1030 kg m^{-3} and the bulk modulus of water = 2×10^{9} N m^{-2}.

15. A steel plate of face area 4 cm^2 and thickness $0 \cdot 5$ cm is fixed rigidly at the lower surface. A tangential force of 10 N is applied on the upper surface. Find the lateral displacement of the upper surface with respect to the lower surface. Rigidity modulus of steel = $8 \cdot 4 \times 10^{10}$ N m^{-2}.

16. A $5 \cdot 0$ cm long straight piece of thread is kept on the surface of water. Find the force with which the surface on one side of the thread pulls it. Surface tension of water = $0 \cdot 076$ N m^{-1}.

17. Find the excess pressure inside (a) a drop of mercury of radius 2 mm (b) a soap bubble of radius 4 mm and (c) an air bubble of radius 4 mm formed inside a tank of water. Surface tension of mercury, soap solution and water are $0 \cdot 465$ N m^{-1}, $0 \cdot 03$ N m^{-1} and $0 \cdot 076$ N m^{-1} respectively.

18. Consider a small surface area of 1 mm^2 at the top of a mercury drop of radius $4 \cdot 0$ mm. Find the force exerted on this area (a) by the air above it (b) by the mercury below it and (c) by the mercury surface in contact with it. Atmospheric pressure = $1 \cdot 0 \times 10^{5}$ Pa and surface tension of mercury = $0 \cdot 465$ N m^{-1}. Neglect the effect of gravity. Assume all numbers to be exact.

19. The capillaries shown in figure (14-E4) have inner radii $0 \cdot 5$ mm, $1 \cdot 0$ mm and $1 \cdot 5$ mm respectively. The liquid in the beaker is water. Find the heights of water level in the capillaries. The surface tension of water is $7 \cdot 5 \times 10^{-2}$ N m^{-1}.

Figure 14-E4

20. The lower end of a capillary tube is immersed in mercury. The level of mercury in the tube is found to be 2 cm below the outer level. If the same tube is immersed in water, up to what height will the water rise in the capillary ?

21. A barometer is constructed with its tube having radius $1 \cdot 0$ mm. Assume that the surface of mercury in the tube is spherical in shape. If the atmospheric pressure is equal to 76 cm of mercury, what will be the height raised in the barometer tube? The contact angle of mercury with glass = 135° and surface tension of mercury = $0 \cdot 465$ N m^{-1}. Density of mercury = 13600 kg m^{-3}.

22. A capillary tube of radius $0 \cdot 50$ mm is dipped vertically in a pot of water. Find the difference between the pressure of the water in the tube $5 \cdot 0$ cm below the surface and the atmospheric pressure. Surface tension of water = $0 \cdot 075$ N m^{-1}.

23. Find the surface energy of water kept in a cylindrical vessel of radius $6 \cdot 0$ cm. Surface tension of water = $0 \cdot 075$ J m^{-2}.

24. A drop of mercury of radius 2 mm is split into 8 identical droplets. Find the increase in surface energy. Surface tension of mercury = $0 \cdot 465$ J m^{-2}.

25. A capillary tube of radius 1 mm is kept vertical with the lower end in water. (a) Find the height of water raised in the capillary. (b) If the length of the capillary tube is half the answer of part (a), find the angle θ made by the water surface in the capillary with the wall.

26. The lower end of a capillary tube of radius 1 mm is dipped vertically into mercury. (a) Find the depression of mercury column in the capillary. (b) If the length dipped inside is half the answer of part (a), find the angle made by the mercury surface at the end of the capillary with the vertical. Surface tension of mercury = $0 \cdot 465$ N m^{-1} and the contact angle of mercury with glass = 135°.

27. Two large glass plates are placed vertically and parallel to each other inside a tank of water with separation between the plates equal to 1 mm. Find the rise of water in the space between the plates. Surface tension of water = $0 \cdot 075$ N m^{-1}.

28. Consider an ice cube of edge $1 \cdot 0$ cm kept in a gravity-free hall. Find the surface area of the water when the ice melts. Neglect the difference in densities of ice and water.

29. A wire forming a loop is dipped into soap solution and taken out so that a film of soap solution is formed. A loop of $6 \cdot 28$ cm long thread is gently put on the film and the film is pricked with a needle inside the loop. The thread loop takes the shape of a circle. Find the tension in the thread. Surface tension of soap solution = $0 \cdot 030$ N m^{-1}.

30. A metal sphere of radius 1 mm and mass 50 mg falls vertically in glycerine. Find (a) the viscous force exerted by the glycerine on the sphere when the speed of the sphere is 1 cm s^{-1}, (b) the hydrostatic force exerted by the glycerine on the sphere and (c) the terminal velocity with which the sphere will move down without acceleration. Density of glycerine = 1260 kg m^{-3} and its coefficient of viscosity at room temperature = $8 \cdot 0$ poise.

31. Estimate the speed of vertically falling raindrops from the following data. Radius of the drops = $0 \cdot 02$ cm, viscosity of air = $1 \cdot 8 \times 10^{-4}$ poise, $g = 10$ m s^{-2} and density of water = 1000 kg m^{-3}.

32. Water flows at a speed of 6 cm s^{-1} through a tube of radius 1 cm. Coefficient of viscosity of water at room temperature is 0·01 poise. Calculate the Reynolds number. Is it a steady flow ?

□

ANSWERS

OBJECTIVE I

1. (d)	2. (a)	3. (b)	4. (a)	5. (b)	6. (a)
7. (a)	8. (c)	9. (b)	10. (d)	11. (c)	12. (b)
13. (a)	14. (c)	15. (d)	16. (a)	17. (c)	18. (c)
19. (d)	20. (c)	21. (b)	22. (d)	23. (d)	24. (a)
25. (c)	26. (c)	27. (b)	28. (d)	29. (b)	

OBJECTIVE II

1. all
2. (c), (d)
3. (a), (b), (d)
4. (a), (b)
5. (c)
6. (c), (d)
7. (b), (c), (d)

EXERCISES

1. (a) $2·5 \times 10^7$ N m^{-2} (b) $1·25 \times 10^{-4}$ (c) $3·75 \times 10^{-4}$ m

2. (a) $7·96 \times 10^5$ N m^{-2} (b) 4×10^{-6} (c) 8×10^{-6} m

3. 2 mm

4. (a) 1   (b) $\dfrac{\text{strain in copper wire}}{\text{strain in steel wire}} = \dfrac{20}{13}$

5. $\dfrac{\text{strain in copper wire}}{\text{strain in steel wire}} = 1·54$

6. (a) 14 kg, lower   (b) 2 kg, upper

7. 1×10^8 N m^{-2}

8. $3·8 \times 10^4$ N

9. $\dfrac{m_2 g(2m_1 + m_2)}{2 AY(m_1 + m_2)}$

10. 36·4°

11. 1·5 cm

12. $1·164 \times 10^{-6}$ cm^2

13. $2·1 \times 10^6$ N m^{-2}

14. 2 kg m^{-3}

15. $1·5 \times 10^{-9}$ m

16. $3·8 \times 10^{-3}$ N

17. (a) 465 N m^{-2} (b) 30 N m^{-2}
    (c) 38 N m^{-2}

18. (a) 0·1 N   (b) 0·10023 N
    (c) 0·00023 N

19. 3 cm in A, 1·5 cm in B, 1 cm in C

20. 5·73 cm

21. 75·5 cm

22. 190 N m^{-2}

23. $8·5 \times 10^{-4}$ J

24. 23·4 μ J

25. (a) 1·5 cm   (b) 60°

26. (a) 4·93 mm   (b) 111°

27. 1·5 cm

28. $(36\,\pi)^{1/3}$ cm^2

29. 6×10^{-4} N

30. (a) $1·5 \times 10^{-4}$ N   (b) $5·2 \times 10^{-5}$ N   (c) 2·9 cm s^{-1}

31. 5 m s^{-1}

32. 1200, yes.

□

CHAPTER 15

WAVE MOTION AND WAVES ON A STRING

15.1 WAVE MOTION

When a particle moves through space, it carries kinetic energy with itself. Wherever the particle goes, the energy goes with it. The energy is associated with the particle and is transported from one region of the space to the other together with the particle just like we ride a car and are taken from Lucknow to Varanasi with the car.

There is another way to transport energy from one part of space to the other without any bulk motion of material together with it. Sound is transmitted in air in this manner. When you say "Hello" to your friend, no material particle is ejected from your lips and falls on your friend's ear. You create some disturbance in the part of the air close to your lips. Energy is transferred to these air particles either by pushing them ahead or pulling them back. The density of the air in this part temporarily increases or decreases. These disturbed particles exert force on the next layer of air, transferring the disturbance to that layer. In this way, the disturbance proceeds in air and finally the air near the ear of the listener gets disturbed.

The disturbance produced in the air near the speaker travels in air, the air itself does not move. The air that is near the speaker at the time of uttering a word remains all the time near the speaker even when the message reaches the listener. This type of motion of energy is called a *wave motion*.

To give another example of propagation of energy without bulk motion of matter, suppose many persons are standing in a queue to buy cinema tickets from the ticket counter. It is not yet time, the counter is closed and the persons are getting annoyed. The last person in the queue is somewhat unruly, he leans forward pushing the man in front of him and then stands straight. The second last person, getting the jerk from behind, is forced to lean forward and push the man in front. This second last person manages to

stand straight again but the third last person temporarily loses balance and leans forward. The jerk thus travels down the queue and finally the person at the front of the queue feels it. With the jerk, travels the energy down the queue from one end to another though the last person and the first person are still in their previous positions.

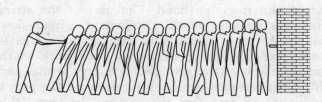

Figure 15.1

The world is full of examples of wave motion. When raindrops hit the surface of calm water, circular waves can be seen travelling on the surface. Any particle of water is only locally displaced for a short time but the disturbance spreads and the particles farther and farther get disturbed when the wave reaches them. Another common example of wave motion is the wave associated with light. One speciality about this wave is that it does not require any material medium for its propagation. The waves requiring a medium are called *mechanical waves* and those which do not require a medium are called *nonmechanical waves*.

In the present chapter, we shall study the waves on a stretched string, a mechanical wave in one dimension.

15.2 WAVE PULSE ON A STRING

Let us consider a long string with one end fixed to a wall and the other held by a person. The person pulls on the string keeping it tight. Suppose the person snaps his hand a little up and down producing a bump in the string near his hand (Figure 15.2). The operation takes a very small time, say, one-tenth of a second after which the person stands still holding the string tight in his hand. What happens as time passes ?

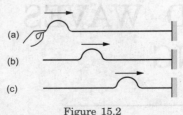

Figure 15.2

Experiments show that if the vertical displacement given is small, the disturbance travels down the string with constant speed. Figure (15.2) also shows the status of the string at successive instants. As time passes, the "bump" travels on the string towards right. For an elastic and homogeneous string, the bump moves with constant speed to cover equal distances in equal time. Also, the shape of the bump is not altered as it moves, provided the bump is small. Notice that no part of the string moves from left to right. The person is holding the left end tight and the string cannot slip from his hand. The part of the string, where the bump is present at an instant, is in up–down motion. As time passes, this part again regains its normal position. The person does some work on the part close to his hand giving some energy to that part. This disturbed part exerts elastic force on the part to the right and transfers the energy, the bump thus moves on to the right. In this way, different parts of the string are successively disturbed, transmitting the energy from left to right.

When a disturbance is localised only to a small part of the space at a time, we say that a *wave pulse* is passing through that part of the space. This happens when the source producing the disturbance (hand in this case) is active only for a short time. If the source is active for some extended time repeating its motion several times, we get a *wave train* or a *wave packet*. For example, if the person in figure (15.2) decides to vibrate his hand up and down 10 times and then stop, a wave train consisting of 10 loops will proceed on the string.

Equation of a Travelling Wave

Suppose, in the example of figure (15.2), the man starts snapping his hand at $t = 0$ and finishes his job at $t = \Delta t$. The vertical displacement y of the left end of the string is a function of time. It is zero for $t < 0$, has nonzero value for $0 < t < \Delta t$ and is again zero for $t > \Delta t$. Let us represent this function by $f(t)$. Take the left end of the string as the origin and take the X-axis

along the string towards right. The function $f(t)$ represents the displacement y of the particle at $x = 0$ as a function of time

$$y(x = 0, t) = f(t).$$

The disturbance travels on the string towards right with a constant speed v. Thus, the displacement, produced at the left end at time t, reaches the point x at time $t + x/v$. Similarly, the displacement of the particle at point x at time t was originated at the left end at the time $t - x/v$. But the displacement of the left end at time $t - x/v$ is $f(t - x/v)$. Hence,

$$y(x, t) = y(x = 0, t - x/v)$$
$$= f(t - x/v).$$

The displacement of the particle at x at time t, i.e., $y(x, t)$ is generally abbreviated as y and the wave equation is written as

$$y = f(t - x/v). \qquad \dots (15.1)$$

Equation (15.1) represents a wave travelling in the positive x-direction with a constant speed v. Such a wave is called a *travelling wave* or a *progressive wave*. The function f is arbitrary and depends on how the source moves. The time t and the position x must appear in the wave equation in the combination $t - x/v$ only. For example,

$$y = A \sin\frac{(t - x/v)}{T}, \ y = A\, e^{-\frac{(t - x/v)}{T}}$$

are valid wave equations. They represent waves travelling in positive x-direction with constant speed. The equation $y = A \sin\dfrac{(x^2 - v^2 t^2)}{L^2}$ does not represent a wave travelling in x-direction with a constant speed.

If a wave travels in negative x-direction with speed v, its general equation may be written as

$$y = f(t + x/v). \qquad \dots (15.2)$$

The wave travelling in positive x-direction (equation 15.1) can also be written as

$$y = f\!\left(\frac{vt - x}{v}\right)$$

or, $$y = g(x - vt), \qquad \dots (15.3)$$

where g is some other function having the following meaning. If we put $t = 0$ in equation (15.3), we get the displacement of various particles at $t = 0$, i.e.,

$$y(x, t = 0) = g(x).$$

Thus, $g(x)$ represents the shape of the string at $t = 0$. If the displacement of the different particles at $t = 0$ is represented by the function $g(x)$, the displacement of the particle at x at time t will be $y = g(x - vt)$. Similarly, if the wave is travelling along the negative x-direction and the displacement of different particles at $t = 0$ is $g(x)$, the displacement of the particle at x at time t will be

$$y = g(x + vt). \qquad \ldots (15.4)$$

Thus, the function f in equations (15.1) and (15.2) represents the displacement of the point $x = 0$ as time passes and g in (15.3) and (15.4) represents the displacement at $t = 0$ of different particles.

Example 15.1

A wave is propagating on a long stretched string along its length taken as the positive x-axis. The wave equation is given as

$$y = y_0 \, e^{-\left(\frac{t}{T} - \frac{x}{\lambda}\right)^2},$$

where $y_0 = 4$ mm, $T = 1.0$ s and $\lambda = 4$ cm. (a) Find the velocity of the wave. (b) Find the function $f(t)$ giving the displacement of the particle at $x = 0$. (c) Find the function $g(x)$ giving the shape of the string at $t = 0$. (d) Plot the shape $g(x)$ of the string at $t = 0$. (e) Plot the shape of the string at $t = 5$ s.

Solution : (a) The wave equation may be written as

$$y = y_0 \, e^{-\frac{1}{T^2}\left(t - \frac{x}{\lambda/T}\right)^2}.$$

Comparing with the general equation $y = f(t - x/v)$, we see that

$$v = \frac{\lambda}{T} = \frac{4 \text{ cm}}{1.0 \text{ s}} = 4 \text{ cm s}^{-1}.$$

(b) Putting $x = 0$ in the given equation,

$$f(t) = y_0 \, e^{-(t/T)^2}. \qquad \ldots \text{(i)}$$

(c) Putting $t = 0$ in the given equation

$$g(x) = y_0 \, e^{-(x/\lambda)^2}. \qquad \ldots \text{(ii)}$$

(d)

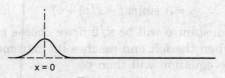

x = 0

Figure 15.3(a)

(e)

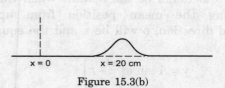

x = 0   x = 20 cm

Figure 15.3(b)

15.3 SINE WAVE TRAVELLING ON A STRING

What happens if the person holding the string in figure (15.2) keeps waving his hand up and down continuously. He keeps doing work on the string and

the energy is continuously supplied to the string. Any part of the string continues to vibrate up and down once the first disturbance has reached it. It receives energy from the left, transmits it to the right and the process continues till the person is not tired. The nature of vibration of any particle is similar to that of the left end, the only difference being that the motion is repeated after a time delay of x/v.

A very important special case arises when the person vibrates the left end $x = 0$ in a simple harmonic motion. The equation of motion of this end may then be written as

$$f(t) = A \sin \omega t, \qquad \ldots (15.5)$$

where A represents the amplitude and ω the angular frequency. The time period of oscillation is $T = 2\pi/\omega$ and the frequency of oscillation is $\nu = 1/T = \omega/2\pi$. The wave produced by such a vibrating source is called a *sine wave* or *sinusoidal wave*.

Since the displacement of the particle at $x = 0$ is given by (15.5), the displacement of the particle at x at time t will be

$$y = f(t - x/v)$$

or, $$y = A \sin \omega(t - x/v). \qquad \ldots (15.6)$$

This follows from the fact that the wave moves along the string with a constant speed v and the displacement of the particle at x at time t was originated at $x = 0$ at time $t - x/v$.

The velocity of the particle at x at time t is given by

$$\frac{\partial y}{\partial t} = A \, \omega \, \cos \omega(t - x/v). \qquad \ldots (15.7)$$

The symbol $\frac{\partial}{\partial t}$ is used in place of $\frac{d}{dt}$ to indicate that while differentiating with respect to t, we should treat x as constant. It is the same particle whose displacement should be considered as a function of time.

This velocity is totally different from the wave velocity v. The wave moves on the string at a constant velocity v along the x-axis, but the particle moves up and down with velocity $\frac{\partial y}{\partial t}$ which changes with x and t according to (15.7).

Figure (15.4) shows the shape of the string as time passes. Each particle of the string vibrates in simple harmonic motion with the same amplitude A and frequency ν. The phases of the vibrations are, however, different. When a particle P (figure 15.4) reaches its extreme position in upward direction, the particle Q little to its right, is still coming up and the particle R little to its left, has already crossed that phase and is going down. The phase difference is larger if the particles are separated farther.

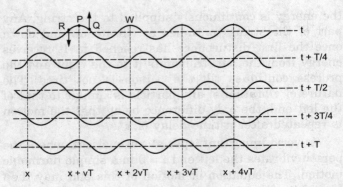

Figure 15.4

Each particle copies the motion of another particle at its left with a time delay of x/v, where x is the separation between the two particles. For the particles P and W, shown in figure (15.4), the separation is $\Delta x = vT$ and the particle W copies the motion of P after a time delay of $\Delta x/v = T$. But the motion of any particle at any instant is identical in all respects to its motion a time period T later. So, a delay of one time period is equivalent to no delay and hence, the particles P and W vibrate in the same phase. They reach their extreme positions together, they cross their mean positions together, their displacements are identical and their velocities are identical at any instant. Same is true for any pair of particles separated by a distance vT. This separation is called the *wavelength* of the wave and is denoted by the Greek letter λ. Thus, $\lambda = vT$.

The above relation can easily be derived mathematically. Suppose, the particles at x and $x + L$ vibrate in the same phase. By equation (15.6) and (15.7),

$$A \sin\left[\omega\left(t - \frac{x}{v}\right)\right] = A \sin\left[\omega\left(t - \frac{x+L}{v}\right)\right]$$

and $A\omega \cos\left[\omega\left(t - \frac{x}{v}\right)\right] = A\omega \cos\left[\omega\left(t - \frac{x+L}{v}\right)\right]$.

This gives

$$\omega\left(t - \frac{x}{v}\right) = \omega\left(t - \frac{x+L}{v}\right) + 2n\pi,$$

where n is an integer,

or, $\qquad 0 = -\dfrac{\omega L}{v} + 2n\pi$

or, $\qquad L = \dfrac{v}{\omega} 2n\pi.$

The minimum separation between the particles vibrating in same phase is obtained by putting $n = 1$ in the above equation. Thus, the wavelength is

$$\lambda = \frac{v}{\omega} 2\pi = vT. \qquad \ldots (15.8)$$

Also, $\qquad v = \lambda/T = \nu\lambda, \qquad \ldots (15.9)$

where $\nu = 1/T$ is the frequency of the wave.

This represents an important relation between the three characteristic parameters of a sine wave namely, the wave velocity, the frequency and the wavelength.

The quantity $2\pi/\lambda$ is called the *wave number* and is generally denoted by the letter k.

Thus, $\qquad k = \dfrac{2\pi}{\lambda} = \dfrac{2\pi\nu}{v} = \dfrac{\omega}{v}.$

The segment where the disturbance is positive is called a *crest* of the wave and the segment where the disturbance is negative is called a *trough*. The separation between consecutive crests or between consecutive troughs is equal to the wavelength.

Alternative Forms of Wave Equation

We have written the wave equation of a wave travelling in x-direction as

$$y = A \sin \omega(t - x/v).$$

This can also be written in several other forms such as,

$$y = A \sin(\omega t - kx) \qquad \ldots (15.10)$$

$$= A \sin 2\pi\left(\frac{t}{T} - \frac{x}{\lambda}\right) \qquad \ldots (15.11)$$

$$= A \sin k(vt - x). \qquad \ldots (15.12)$$

Also, it should be noted that we have made our particular choice of $t = 0$ in writing equation (15.5) from which the wave equation is deduced. The origin of time is chosen at an instant when the left end $x = 0$ is crossing its mean position $y = 0$ and is going up. For a general choice of the origin of time, we will have to add a phase constant so that the equation will be

$$y = A \sin[\omega(t - x/v) + \phi]. \qquad \ldots (15.13)$$

The constant ϕ will be $\pi/2$ if we choose $t = 0$ at an instant when the left end reaches its extreme position $y = A$. The equation will then be

$$y = A \cos \omega(t - x/v). \qquad \ldots (15.14)$$

If $t = 0$ is taken at the instant when the left end is crossing the mean position from upward to downward direction, ϕ will be π and the equation will be

$$y = A \sin \omega\left(\frac{x}{v} - t\right)$$

or, $\qquad y = A \sin(kx - \omega t). \qquad \ldots (15.15)$

Example 15.2

Consider the wave $y = (5 \text{ mm}) \sin[(1 \text{ cm}^{-1})x - (60 \text{ s}^{-1})t]$. Find (a) the amplitude, (b) the wave number, (c) the *wavelength, (d) the frequency, (e) the time period and (f) the wave velocity.*

Solution : Comparing the given equation with equation (15.15), we find

(a) amplitude $A = 5$ mm

(b) wave number $k = 1$ cm^{-1}

(c) wavelength $\lambda = \dfrac{2\pi}{k} = 2\pi$ cm

(d) frequency $\nu = \dfrac{\omega}{2\pi} = \dfrac{60}{2\pi}$ Hz

$$= \dfrac{30}{\pi} \text{ Hz}$$

(e) time period $T = \dfrac{1}{\nu} = \dfrac{\pi}{30}$ s

(f) wave velocity $v = \nu\,\lambda = 60$ cm s^{-1}.

15.4 VELOCITY OF A WAVE ON A STRING

The velocity of a wave travelling on a string depends on the elastic and the inertia properties of the string. When a part of the string gets disturbed, it exerts an extra force on the neighbouring part because of the elastic property. The neighbouring part responds to this force and the response depends on the inertia property. The elastic force in the string is measured by its tension F and the inertia by its mass per unit length. We have used the symbol F for tension and not T in order to avoid confusion with the time period.

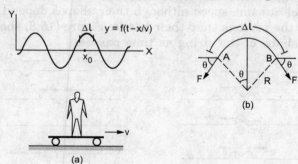

Figure 15.5

Suppose a wave $y = f\!\left(t - \dfrac{x}{v}\right)$ is travelling on the string in the positive x-direction with a speed v. Let us choose an observer who is riding on a car that moves along the x-direction with the same velocity v (figure 15.5). Looking from this frame, the pattern of the string is at rest but the entire string is moving towards the negative x-direction with a speed v. If a crest is opposite to the observer at any instant, it will always remain opposite to him with the same shape while the string will pass through this crest in opposite direction like a snake.

Consider a small element AB of the string of length Δl at the highest point of a crest. Any small curve may be approximated by a circular arc. Suppose the small element Δl forms an arc of radius R. The particles of the string in this element go in this circle with a speed v as the string slides through this part. The general situation is shown in figure (15.5a) and the expanded view of the part near Δl is shown in figure (15.5b).

We assume that the displacements are small so that the tension in the string does not appreciably change because of the disturbance. The element AB is pulled by the parts of the string to its right and to its left. Resultant force on this element is in the downward direction as shown in figure (15.5b) and its magnitude is

$$F_r = F\sin\theta + F\sin\theta = 2F\sin\theta.$$

As Δl is taken small, θ will be small and

$$\sin\theta \approx \dfrac{\Delta l/2}{R}$$

so that the resultant force on Δl is

$$F_r = 2F\left(\dfrac{\Delta l/2}{R}\right) = F\Delta l/R.$$

If μ be the mass per unit length of the string, the element AB has a mass $\Delta m = \Delta l\,\mu$. Its downward acceleration is

$$a = \dfrac{F_r}{\Delta m} = \dfrac{F\Delta l/R}{\mu\,\Delta l} = \dfrac{F}{\mu R}.$$

But the element is moving in a circle of radius R with a constant speed v. Its acceleration is, therefore, $a = \dfrac{v^2}{R}$. The above equation becomes

$$\dfrac{v^2}{R} = \dfrac{F}{\mu R}$$

or, $v = \sqrt{F/\mu}.$ ... (15.16)

The velocity of the wave on a string thus depends only on the tension F and the linear mass density μ. We have used the approximation that the tension F remains almost unchanged as the part of the string vibrates up and down. This approximation is valid only for small amplitudes because as the string vibrates, the lengths of its parts change during the course of vibration and hence, the tension changes.

Example 15.3

Figure (15.6) shows a string of linear mass density $1{\cdot}0$ g cm^{-1} on which a wave pulse is travelling. Find the

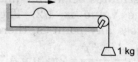

Figure 15.6

time taken by the pulse in travelling through a distance of 50 cm on the string. Take $g = 10 \text{ m s}^{-2}$.

Solution : The tension in the string is $F = mg = 10 \text{ N}$. The mass per unit length is $\mu = 1.0 \text{ g cm}^{-1} = 0.1 \text{ kg m}^{-1}$. The wave velocity is, therefore, $v = \sqrt{F/\mu} = \sqrt{\dfrac{10 \text{ N}}{0.1 \text{ kg m}^{-1}}}$

$= 10 \text{ m s}^{-1}$. The time taken by the pulse in travelling through 50 cm is, therefore, 0.05 s.

15.5 POWER TRANSMITTED ALONG THE STRING BY A SINE WAVE

When a travelling wave is established on a string, energy is transmitted along the direction of propagation of the wave. Consider again a sine wave travelling along a stretched string in x-direction. The equation for the displacement in y-direction is

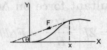

Figure 15.7

$$y = A \sin \omega(t - x/v). \qquad \dots \text{(i)}$$

Figure (15.7) shows a portion of the string at a time t to the right of position x. The string on the left of the point x exerts a force F on this part. The direction of this force is along the tangent to the string at position x. The component of the force along the Y-axis is

$$F_y = - F \sin\theta \approx - F \tan\theta = - F \frac{\partial y}{\partial x}.$$

The power delivered by the force F to the string on the right of position x is, therefore,

$$P = \left(- F \frac{\partial y}{\partial x}\right) \frac{\partial y}{\partial t}.$$

By (i), it is

$$- F \left[\left(- \frac{\omega}{v}\right) A \cos \omega(t - x/v)\right] [\omega A \cos \omega(t - x/v)]$$

$$= \frac{\omega^2 A^2 F}{v} \cos^2 \omega (t - x/v).$$

This is the rate at which energy is being transmitted from left to right across the point at x. The $\cos^2$ term oscillates between 0 and 1 during a cycle and its average value is 1/2. The average power transmitted across any point is, therefore,

$$P_{av} = \frac{1}{2} \frac{\omega^2 A^2 F}{v} = 2\pi^2 \mu v A^2 v^2. \qquad \dots \text{(15.17)}$$

The power transmitted along the string is proportional to the square of the amplitude and square of the frequency of the wave.

Example 15.4

The average power transmitted through a given point on a string supporting a sine wave is 0.20 W when the amplitude of the wave is 2.0 mm. What power will be transmitted through this point if the amplitude is increased to 3.0 mm.

Solution : Other things remaining the same, the power transmitted is proportional to the square of the amplitude.

Thus,

$$\frac{P_2}{P_1} = \frac{A_2^2}{A_1^2}$$

or,

$$\frac{P_2}{0.20 \text{ W}} = \frac{9}{4} = 2.25$$

or,

$$P_2 = 2.25 \times 0.20 \text{ W} = 0.45 \text{ W}.$$

15.6 INTERFERENCE AND THE PRINCIPLE OF SUPERPOSITION

So far we have considered a single wave passing on a string. Suppose two persons are holding the string at the two ends and snap their hands to start a wave pulse each. One pulse starts from the left end and travels on the string towards right, the other starts at the right end and travels towards left. The pulses travel at same speed although their shapes depend on how the persons snap their hands. Figure (15.8) shows the shape of the string as time passes.

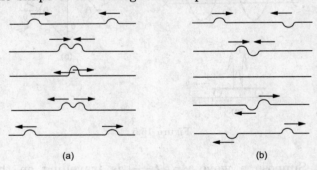

(a)   (b)

Figure 15.8

The pulses travel towards each other, overlap and recede from each other. The remarkable thing is that the shapes of the pulses, as they emerge after the overlap, are identical to their original shapes. Each pulse has passed the overlap region so smoothly as if the other pulse was not at all there. After the encounter, each pulse looks just as it looked before and each pulse travels just as it did before. The waves can pass through each other freely without being modified.

This is a unique property of the waves. The particles cannot pass through each other, they collide and their course of motion changes. How do we determine the shape of the string at the time when the pulses actually overlap ? The mechanism to know the resultant displacement of a particle which is acted upon by two or more waves simultaneously is very simple. The displacement of the particle is equal to the sum of the displacements the waves would have individually produced. If the first wave alone is travelling, let us say it displaces the particle by 0·2 cm upward and if the second wave alone is travelling, suppose the displacement of this same particle is 0·4 cm upward at that instant. The displacement of the particle at that instant will be 0·6 cm upward if both the waves pass through that particle simultaneously. The displacement of the particles, if the first wave alone were travelling, may be written as

$$y_1 = f_1(t - x/v)$$

and the displacement if the second wave alone were travelling may be written as

$$y_2 = f_2(t + x/v).$$

If both the waves are travelling on the string, the displacement of its different particles will be given by

$$y = y_1 + y_2 = f_1(t - x/v) + f_2(t + x/v).$$

The two individual displacements may be in opposite directions. The magnitude of the resulting displacement may be smaller than the magnitudes of the individual displacements.

If two wave pulses, approaching each other, are identical in shape except that one is inverted with respect to the other, at some instant the displacement of all the particles will be zero. However, the velocities of the particles will not be zero as the waves will emerge in the two directions shortly. Such a situation is shown in figure (15.8b). We see that there is an instant when the string is straight every where. But soon the wave pulses emerge which move away from each other.

Suppose one person snaps the end up and down whereas the other person snaps his end sideways. The displacements produced are at right angles to each other as indicated in figure (15.9). When the two waves overlap, the resultant displacement of any particle is the vector sum of the two individual displacements.

Figure 15.9

The above observations about the overlap of the waves may be summarised in the following statement which is known as the *principle of superposition*.

When two or more waves simultaneously pass through a point, the disturbance at the point is given by the sum of the disturbances each wave would produce in absence of the other wave(s).

In general, the principle of superposition is valid for small disturbances only. If the string is stretched too far, the individual displacements do not add to give the resultant displacement. Such waves are called *nonlinear waves*. In this course, we shall only be talking about linear waves which obey the superposition principle.

When two or more waves pass through the same region simultaneously we say that the waves interfere or the *interference of waves* takes place. The principle of superposition says that the phenomenon of wave interference is remarkably simple. Each wave makes its own contribution to the disturbance no matter what the other waves are doing.

15.7 INTERFERENCE OF WAVES GOING IN SAME DIRECTION

Suppose two identical sources send sinusoidal waves of same angular frequency ω in positive x-direction. Also, the wave velocity and hence, the wave number k is same for the two waves. One source may be started a little later than the other or the two sources may be situated at different points. The two waves arriving at a point then differ in phase. Let the amplitudes of the two waves be A_1 and A_2 and the two waves differ in phase by an angle δ. Their equations may be written as

$$y_1 = A_1 \sin(kx - \omega t)$$

and

$$y_2 = A_2 \sin(kx - \omega t + \delta).$$

According to the principle of superposition, the resultant wave is represented by

$$y = y_1 + y_2 = A_1 \sin(kx - \omega t) + A_2 \sin(kx - \omega t + \delta)$$

$$= A_1 \sin(kx - \omega t) + A_2 \sin(kx - \omega t) \cos\delta$$
$$+ A_2 \cos(kx - \omega t)\sin\delta$$

$$= \sin(kx - \omega t) (A_1 + A_2\cos\delta) + \cos(kx - \omega t) (A_2\sin\delta).$$

We can evaluate it using the method described in Chapter-12 to combine two simple harmonic motions. If we write

$$A_1 + A_2 \cos\delta = A \cos \varepsilon \qquad \ldots \text{ (i)}$$

and

$$A_2 \sin\delta = A \sin \varepsilon, \qquad \ldots \text{ (ii)}$$

we get

$$y = A [\sin(kx - \omega t) \cos \varepsilon + \cos(kx - \omega t) \sin \varepsilon]$$

$$= A \sin(kx - \omega t + \varepsilon).$$

Thus, the resultant is indeed a sine wave of amplitude A with a phase difference ε with the first wave. By (i) and (ii),

$$A^2 = A^2\cos^2\varepsilon + A^2\sin^2\varepsilon$$
$$= (A_1 + A_2\cos\delta)^2 + (A_2\sin\delta)^2$$
$$= A_1^2 + A_2^2 + 2A_1A_2\cos\delta$$

or, $\quad A = \sqrt{A_1^2 + A_2^2 + 2A_1A_2\cos\delta}.$ ... (15.18)

Also, $\tan\varepsilon = \dfrac{A\sin\varepsilon}{A\cos\varepsilon} = \dfrac{A_2\sin\delta}{A_1 + A_2\cos\delta}.$ ... (15.19)

As discussed in Chapter-12, these relations may be remembered by using a geometrical model. We draw a vector of length A_1 to represent $y_1 = A_1\sin(kx - \omega t)$ and another vector of length A_2 at an angle δ with the first one to represent $y_2 = A_2\sin(kx - \omega t + \delta)$. The resultant of the two vectors then represents the resultant wave $y = A\sin(kx - \omega t + \varepsilon)$. Figure (15.10) shows the construction.

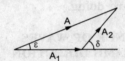

Figure 15.10

Constructive and Destructive Interference

We see from equation (15.18) that the resultant amplitude A is maximum when $\cos\delta = +1$, or $\delta = 2n\pi$ and is minimum when $\cos\delta = -1$, or $\delta = (2n+1)\pi$, where n is an integer. In the first case, the amplitude is $A_1 + A_2$ and in the second case, it is $|A_1 - A_2|$. The two cases are called *constructive* and *destructive* interferences respectively. The conditions may be written as,

constructive interference : $\delta = 2n\pi$
destructive interference : $\delta = (2n+1)\pi$ $\Big|$ ... (15.20)

Example 15.5

Two waves are simultaneously passing through a string. The equations of the waves are given by

$$y_1 = A_1\sin k(x - vt)$$
and $\qquad y_2 = A_2\sin k(x - vt + x_0),$

where the wave number $k = 6\cdot28$ cm^{-1} and $x_0 = 1\cdot50$ cm. The amplitudes are $A_1 = 5\cdot0$ mm and $A_2 = 4\cdot0$ mm. Find the phase difference between the waves and the amplitude of the resulting wave.

Solution : The phase of the first wave is $k(x - vt)$ and of the second is $k(x - vt + x_0)$.

The phase difference is, therefore,

$$\delta = k x_0 = (6\cdot28\text{ cm}^{-1})(1\cdot50\text{ cm}) = 2\pi \times 1\cdot5 = 3\pi.$$

The waves satisfy the condition of destructive interference. The amplitude of the resulting wave is given by

$$|A_1 - A_2| = 5\cdot0\text{ mm} - 4\cdot0\text{ mm} = 1\cdot0\text{ mm}.$$

15.8 REFLECTION AND TRANSMISSION OF WAVES

In figure (15.2), a wave pulse was generated at the left end which travelled on the string towards right. When the pulse reaches a particular element, the forces on the element from the left part of the string and from the right part act in such a way that the element is disturbed according to the shape of the pulse.

The situation is different when the pulse reaches the right end which is clamped at the wall. The element at the right end exerts a force on the clamp and the clamp exerts equal and opposite force on the element. The element at the right end is thus acted upon by the force from the string left to it and by the force from the clamp. As this end remains fixed, the two forces are opposite to each other. The force from the left part of the string transmits the forward wave pulse and hence, the force exerted by the clamp sends a return pulse on the string whose shape is similar to the original pulse but is inverted. The original pulse tries to pull the element at the fixed end up and the return pulse sent by the clamp tries to pull it down. The resultant displacement is zero. Thus, the wave is reflected from the fixed end and the reflected wave is inverted with respect to the original wave. The shape of the string at any time, while the pulse is being reflected, can be found by adding an inverted image pulse to the incident pulse (figure 15.11).

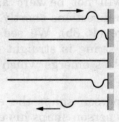

Figure 15.11

Let us now suppose that the right end of the string is attached to a light frictionless ring which can freely move on a vertical rod. A wave pulse is sent on the string from left (Figure 15.12). When the wave reaches the right end, the element at this end is acted on by the force from the left to go up. However, there is no corresponding restoring force from the right as the rod does not exert a vertical force on the ring. As a result, the right end is displaced in upward direction more than the height of the pulse, i.e., it overshoots the normal maximum displacement. The lack of restoring force from right can be equivalently described in the following way. An extra force acts from right which sends a wave from right to left with its shape identical to the original one. The element at the end is acted upon by both the incident and the reflected wave and the displacements add. Thus, a wave is reflected by the free end without inversion.

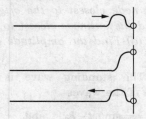

Figure 15.12

Quite often, the end point is neither completely fixed nor completely free to move. As an example, consider a light string attached to a heavier string as shown in figure (15.13). If a wave pulse is produced on the light string moving towards the junction, a part of the wave is reflected and a part is transmitted on the heavier string. The reflected wave is inverted with respect to the original one (figure 15.13a).

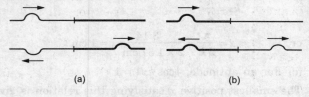

(a)   (b)

Figure 15.13

On the other hand, if the wave is produced on the heavier string, which moves towards the junction, a part will be reflected and a part transmitted, no inversion of wave shape will take place (figure 15.13b).

The rule about the inversion at reflection may be stated in terms of the wave velocity. The wave velocity is smaller for the heavier string ($v = \sqrt{F/\mu}$) and larger for the lighter string. The above observation may be stated as follows.

If a wave enters a region where the wave velocity is smaller, the reflected wave is inverted. If it enters a region where the wave velocity is larger, the reflected wave is not inverted. The transmitted wave is never inverted.

15.9 STANDING WAVES

Suppose two sine waves of equal amplitude and frequency propagate on a long string in opposite directions. The equations of the two waves are given by

$$y_1 = A \sin(\omega t - kx)$$

and

$$y_2 = A \sin(\omega t + kx + \delta).$$

These waves interfere to produce what we call *standing waves*. To understand these waves, let us discuss the special case when $\delta = 0$.

The resultant displacements of the particles of the string are given by the principle of superposition as

$$y = y_1 + y_2$$
$$= A \left[\sin(\omega t - kx) + \sin(\omega t + kx)\right]$$
$$= 2A \sin \omega t \cos kx$$

or,

$$y = (2A \cos kx) \sin \omega t. \qquad \ldots \text{(15.21)}$$

This equation can be interpreted as follows. Each particle of the string vibrates in a simple harmonic motion with an amplitude $|2A \cos kx|$. The amplitudes are not equal for all the particles. In particular, there are points where the amplitude $|2A \cos kx| = 0$. This will be the case when

$$\cos kx = 0$$

or,

$$kx = \left(n + \frac{1}{2}\right)\pi$$

or,

$$x = \left(n + \frac{1}{2}\right)\frac{\lambda}{2},$$

where n is an integer.

For these particles, $\cos kx = 0$ and by equation (15.21) the displacement y is zero all the time. Although these points are not physically clamped, they remain fixed as the two waves pass them simultaneously. Such points are known as *nodes*.

For the points where $|\cos kx| = 1$, the amplitude is maximum. Such points are known as *antinodes*.

We also see from equation (15.21) that at a time when $\sin \omega t = 1$, all the particles for which $\cos kx$ is positive reach their positive maximum displacement. At this particular instant, all the particles for which $\cos kx$ is negative, reach their negative maximum displacement. At a time when $\sin \omega t = 0$, all the particles cross their mean positions. Figure (15.14a) shows the change in the shape of the string as time passes. The time $t = 0$ in this figure corresponds to the instant when particles are at their maximum displacements. Figure (15.14b) shows the external appearance of the vibrating string. This type of wave is called a *standing wave* or a *stationary wave*. The particles at nodes do not move at all and the particles at the antinodes move with maximum amplitude.

It is clear that the separation between consecutive nodes or consecutive antinodes is $\lambda/2$. As the particles at the nodes do not move at all, energy cannot be transmitted across them. The main differences between a standing wave and a travelling wave are summarised below.

1. In a travelling wave, the disturbance produced in a region propagates with a definite velocity but in a standing wave, it is confined to the region where it is produced.

2. In a travelling wave, the motion of all the particles are similar in nature. In a standing wave, different particles move with different amplitudes.

3. In a standing wave, the particles at nodes always remain in rest. In travelling waves, there is no particle which always remains in rest.

4. In a standing wave, all the particles cross their mean positions together. In a travelling wave, there is no instant when all the particles are at the mean positions together.

5. In a standing wave, all the particles between two successive nodes reach their extreme positions together, thus moving in phase. In a travelling wave, the phases of nearby particles are always different.

6. In a travelling wave, energy is transmitted from one region of space to other but in a standing wave, the energy of one region is always confined in that region.

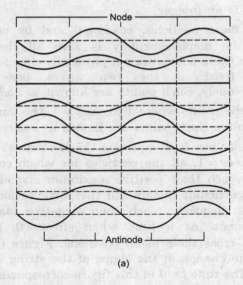

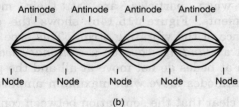

Figure 15.14

Example 15.6

Two travelling waves of equal amplitudes and equal frequencies move in opposite directions along a string. They interfere to produce a standing wave having the equation

$$y = A \cos kx \sin \omega t$$

in which $A = 1.0$ mm, $k = 1.57$ cm^{-1} and $\omega = 78.5$ s^{-1}. (a) Find the velocity of the component travelling waves. (b) Find the node closest to the origin in the region $x > 0$. (c) Find the antinode closest to the origin in the region $x > 0$. (d) Find the amplitude of the particle at $x = 2.33$ cm.

Solution : (a) The standing wave is formed by the superposition of the waves

$$y_1 = \frac{A}{2} \sin(\omega t - kx) \quad \text{and}$$

$$y_2 = \frac{A}{2} \sin(\omega t + kx).$$

The wave velocity (magnitude) of either of the waves is

$$v = \frac{\omega}{k} = \frac{78.5 \text{ s}^{-1}}{1.57 \text{ cm}^{-1}} = 50 \text{ cm s}^{-1}.$$

(b) For a node, $\cos kx = 0$.

The smallest positive x satisfying this relation is given by

$$kx = \frac{\pi}{2}$$

or, $$x = \frac{\pi}{2k} = \frac{3.14}{2 \times 1.57 \text{ cm}^{-1}} = 1 \text{ cm}.$$

(c) For an antinode, $|\cos kx| = 1$.

The smallest positive x satisfying this relation is given by

$$kx = \pi$$

or, $$x = \frac{\pi}{k} = 2 \text{ cm}.$$

(d) The amplitude of vibration of the particle at x is given by $|A \cos kx|$. For the given point,

$$kx = (1.57 \text{ cm}^{-1}) (2.33 \text{ cm}) = \frac{7}{6} \pi = \pi + \frac{\pi}{6}.$$

Thus, the amplitude will be

$$(1.0 \text{ mm}) \mid \cos(\pi + \pi/6) \mid = \frac{\sqrt{3}}{2} \text{ mm} = 0.86 \text{ mm}.$$

15.10 STANDING WAVES ON A STRING FIXED AT BOTH ENDS (QUALITATIVE DISCUSSION)

Consider a string of length L fixed at one end to a wall and the other end tied to a tuning fork which vibrates longitudinally with a small amplitude (figure 15.15). The fork produces sine waves of amplitude A which travel on the string towards the fixed end and get reflected from this end. The reflected waves which travel towards the fork are inverted in shape because they are reflected from a fixed end. These waves are again reflected from the fork. As the fork is heavy and vibrates longitudinally with a small amplitude, it acts like a fixed end and the waves reflected here are again inverted in shape. Therefore, the wave produced directly by the fork at this instant and the twice reflected wave have same shape, except that the twice reflected wave has already travelled a length $2L$.

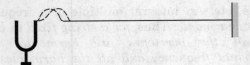

Figure 15.15

Suppose the length of the string is such that $2L = \lambda$. The two waves interfere constructively and the resultant wave that proceeds towards right has an amplitude $2A$. This wave of amplitude $2A$ is again reflected by the wall and then by the fork. This twice reflected wave again interferes constructively with the oncoming new wave and a wave of amplitude $3A$ is produced. Thus, as time passes, the amplitude keeps on increasing. The string gets energy from the vibrations of the fork and the amplitude builds up. Same arguments hold if $2L$ is any integral multiple of λ that is $L = n\lambda/2$, where n is an integer.

In the above discussion, we have neglected any loss of energy due to air viscosity or due to lack of flexibility of string. In actual practice, energy is lost by several processes and the loss increases as the amplitude of vibration increases. Ultimately, a balance is reached when the rate of energy received from the fork equals the rate of energy lost due to various damping processes. In the steady state, waves of constant amplitude are present on the string from left to right as well as from right to left. These waves, propagating in opposite directions, produce standing waves on the string. Nodes and antinodes are formed and the amplitudes of vibration are large at antinodes. We say that the string is in resonance with the fork. The condition, $L = n\lambda/2$, for such a resonance may be stated in a different way. We have from equation (15.9)

$$v = \nu\lambda$$
or, $$\lambda = v/\nu.$$

The condition for resonance is, therefore,

$$L = n\frac{\lambda}{2}$$

or, $$L = \frac{n\,v}{2\,\nu}$$

or, $$\nu = \frac{n\,v}{2\,L} = \frac{n}{2\,L}\sqrt{F/\mu}. \qquad \ldots (15.22)$$

The lowest frequency with which a standing wave can be set up in a string fixed at both the ends is thus

$$\nu_0 = \frac{1}{2\,L}\sqrt{F/\mu}. \qquad \ldots (15.23)$$

This is called the *fundamental frequency* of the string. The other possible frequencies of standing waves are integral multiples of the fundamental frequency. The frequencies given by equation (15.22) are called the *natural frequencies, normal frequencies or resonant frequencies*.

Example 15.7

A 50 cm *long wire of mass* 20 g *supports a mass of* 1·6 kg *as shown in figure (15.16). Find the fundamental frequency of the portion of the string between the wall and the pulley. Take* $g = 10$ m s^{-2}.

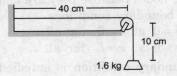

Figure 15.16

Solution : The tension in the string is $F = (1.6\ \text{kg})(10\ \text{m s}^{-2})$
$$= 16\ \text{N}.$$

The linear mass density is $\mu = \dfrac{20\ \text{g}}{50\ \text{cm}} = 0.04\ \text{kg m}^{-1}$.

The fundamental frequency is

$$\nu_0 = \frac{1}{2\,L}\sqrt{F/\mu}$$

$$= \frac{1}{2 \times (0.4\ \text{m})}\sqrt{\frac{16\ \text{N}}{0.04\ \text{kg m}^{-1}}} = 25\ \text{Hz}.$$

What happens if the resonance condition (15.23) is not met? The phase difference between the twice reflected wave and the new wave is not an integral multiple of 2π.

In fact, the phase difference with the new wave then depends on the number of reflections suffered by the original wave and hence, depends on time. At certain time instants, the amplitude is enhanced and at some other time instants, the amplitude is decreased. Thus, the average amplitude does not increase by interference and the vibrations are small. The string absorbs only a little amount of energy from the source.

15.11 ANALYTIC TREATMENT OF VIBRATION OF A STRING FIXED AT BOTH ENDS

Suppose a string of length L is kept fixed at the ends $x = 0$ and $x = L$ and sine waves are produced on it. For certain wave frequencies, standing waves are set up in the string. Due to the multiple reflection at the ends and damping effects, waves going in the positive x-direction interfere to give a resultant wave

$$y_1 = A \sin(kx - \omega t).$$

Similarly, the waves going in the negative x-direction interfere to give the resultant wave

$$y_2 = A \sin(kx + \omega t + \delta).$$

The resultant displacement of the particle of the string at position x and at time t is given by the principle of superposition as

$$y = y_1 + y_2 = A \sin(kx - \omega t) + A \sin(kx + \omega t + \delta)$$

$$= 2A \sin\left(kx + \frac{\delta}{2}\right) \cos\left(\omega t + \frac{\delta}{2}\right). \quad \dots \ (i)$$

If standing waves are formed, the ends $x = 0$ and $x = L$ must be nodes because they are kept fixed. Thus, we have the boundary conditions

$$y = 0 \text{ at } x = 0 \text{ for all } t$$

and $\qquad y = 0 \text{ at } x = L \text{ for all } t.$

The first boundary condition is satisfied by equation (i) if $\sin\frac{\delta}{2} = 0$,

or, $\qquad\qquad\qquad \delta = 0.$

Equation (i) then becomes

$$y = 2A \sin kx \cos \omega t. \qquad \dots \ (15.24)$$

The second boundary condition will be satisfied if

$$\sin kL = 0$$

or, $\qquad kL = n\,\pi, \qquad$ where $n = 1,2,3,4,5, \dots$

or, $\qquad \dfrac{2\pi L}{\lambda} = n\,\pi$

or, $\qquad L = \dfrac{n\lambda}{2}. \qquad\qquad \dots \ (15.25)$

If the length of the string is an integral multiple of $\lambda/2$, standing waves are produced. Again writing $\lambda = vT = \frac{v}{\nu}$, equation (15.25) becomes

$$\nu = \frac{n\,v}{2L} = \frac{n}{2L}\sqrt{F/\mu}$$

which is same as equation (15.22).

The lowest possible frequency is

$$\nu_0 = \frac{v}{2L} = \frac{1}{2L}\sqrt{F/\mu}. \qquad \dots \ (15.26)$$

This is the fundamental frequency of the string.

The other natural frequencies with which standing waves can be formed on the string are

$$\nu_1 = 2\,\nu_0 = \frac{2}{2L}\sqrt{F/\mu} \qquad \begin{array}{l}\text{1st overtone, or} \\ \text{2nd harmonic,}\end{array}$$

$$\nu_2 = 3\,\nu_0 = \frac{3}{2L}\sqrt{F/\mu} \qquad \begin{array}{l}\text{2nd overtone, or} \\ \text{3rd harmonic,}\end{array}$$

$$\nu_3 = 4\,\nu_0 = \frac{4}{2L}\sqrt{F/\mu} \qquad \begin{array}{l}\text{3rd overtone, or} \\ \text{4th harmonic,}\end{array}$$

etc. In general, any integral multiple of the fundamental frequency is an allowed frequency. These higher frequencies are called *overtones*. Thus, $\nu_1 = 2\,\nu_0$ is the first overtone, $\nu_2 = 3\,\nu_0$ is the second overtone, etc. An integral multiple of a frequency is called its *harmonic*. Thus, *for a string fixed at both the ends, all the overtones are harmonics of the fundamental frequency and all the harmonics of the fundamental frequency are overtones.*

This property is unique to the string and makes it so valuable in musical instruments such as violin, guitar, sitar, santoor, sarod.

Normal Modes of Vibration

When a string vibrates according to equation (15.24) with some natural frequency, it is said to vibrate in a *normal mode*. For the nth normal mode $k = \frac{n\pi}{L}$ and the equation for the displacement is, from equation (15.24),

$$y = 2A \sin\frac{n\pi x}{L} \cos 2\pi n\nu_0 t. \quad \dots \ (15.27)$$

For fundamental mode, $n = 1$ and the equation of the standing wave is, from (15.27),

$$y = 2A \sin\frac{\pi x}{L} \cos 2\pi\nu_0 t.$$

The amplitude of vibration of the particle at x is $2A \sin(\pi x/L)$ which is zero at $x = 0$ and at $x = L$. It is maximum at $x = L/2$ where $\sin(\pi x/L) = 1$. Thus, we have nodes at the ends and just one antinode at the middle point of the string.

In the first overtone, also known as the second harmonic, the constant n is equal to 2 and equation (15.27) becomes

$$y = 2A \sin\frac{2\pi x}{L} \cos 4\pi\nu_0 t.$$

The amplitude $2A \sin\frac{2\pi x}{L}$ is zero at $x = 0$, $L/2$ and L and is maximum at $L/4$ and $3L/4$. The middle point of the string is also a node and is not displaced during the vibration. The points $x = L/4$ and $x = 3L/4$ are the antinodes.

In the second overtone, $n = 3$ and equation (15.27) becomes

$$y = 2A \sin\frac{3\pi x}{L} \cos 6\pi\nu_0 t.$$

The nodes are at $x = 0$, $L/3$, $2L/3$ and L, where $\sin \frac{3\pi x}{L} = 0$. There are two nodes in between the ends. Antinodes occur midway between the nodes, i.e., at $x = L/6$, $L/2$ and $5L/6$.

Similarly, in the nth overtone, there are n nodes between the ends and $n+1$ antinodes midway between the nodes. The shape of the string as it vibrates in a normal mode is shown in figure (15.17) for some of the normal modes.

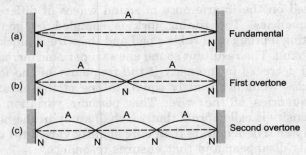

Figure 15.17

When the string of a musical instrument such as a sitar is plucked aside at some point, its shape does not correspond to any of the normal modes discussed above. In fact, the shape of the string is a combination of several normal modes and thus, a combination of frequencies are emitted.

15.12 VIBRATION OF A STRING FIXED AT ONE END

Standing waves can be produced on a string which is fixed at one end and whose other end is free to move in a transverse direction. Such a free end can be nearly achieved by connecting the string to a very light thread.

If the vibrations are produced by a source of "correct" frequency, standing waves are produced. If the end $x = 0$ is fixed and $x = L$ is free, the equation is again given by (15.24)

$$y = 2A \sin kx \cos \omega t$$

with the boundary condition that $x = L$ is an antinode. The boundary condition that $x = 0$ is a node is automatically satisfied by the above equation. For $x = L$ to be an antinode,

$$\sin kL = \pm 1$$

or, $$kL = \left(n + \frac{1}{2}\right)\pi$$

or, $$\frac{2\pi L}{\lambda} = \left(n + \frac{1}{2}\right)\pi$$

or, $$\frac{2L\nu}{v} = n + \frac{1}{2}$$

or, $$\nu = \left(n + \frac{1}{2}\right)\frac{v}{2L} = \frac{n + \frac{1}{2}}{2L}\sqrt{F/\mu}. \quad \ldots \ (15.28)$$

These are the normal frequencies of vibration. The fundamental frequency is obtained when $n = 0$, i.e.,

$$\nu_0 = v/4L.$$

The overtone frequencies are

$$\nu_1 = \frac{3v}{4L} = 3\nu_0,$$

$$\nu_2 = \frac{5v}{4L} = 5\nu_0,$$

$$\nu_3 = \frac{7v}{4L} = 7\nu_0, \ \text{etc.}$$

We see that all the harmonics of the fundamental are not the allowed frequencies for the standing waves. Only the odd harmonics are the overtones. Figure (15.18) shows shapes of the string for some of the normal modes.

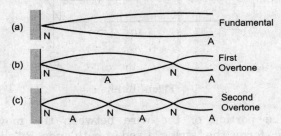

Figure 15.18

15.13 LAWS OF TRANSVERSE VIBRATIONS OF A STRING : SONOMETER

The fundamental frequency of vibration of a string fixed at both ends is given by equation (15.26). From this equation, one can immediately write the following statements known as "Laws of transverse vibrations of a string".

(a) **Law of length** – *The fundamental frequency of vibration of a string (fixed at both ends) is inversely proportional to the length of the string provided its tension and its mass per unit length remain the same.*

$$\nu \propto 1/L \ \text{if} \ F \ \text{and} \ \mu \ \text{are constants.}$$

(b) **Law of tension** – *The fundamental frequency of a string is proportional to the square root of its tension provided its length and the mass per unit length remain the same.*

$$\nu \propto \sqrt{F} \ \text{if} \ L \ \text{and} \ \mu \ \text{are constants.}$$

(c) **Law of mass** – *The fundamental frequency of a string is inversely proportional to the square root of the linear mass density, i.e., mass per unit length, provided the length and the tension remain the same.*

$\nu \propto \dfrac{1}{\sqrt{\mu}}$ if L and F are constants.

These laws may be experimentally studied with an apparatus called *sonometer*.

A typical design of a sonometer is shown in figure (15.19). One has a wooden box, also called the sound box, on which two bridges A and B are fixed at the ends. A metal wire C is welded with the bridges and is kept tight. This wire C is called the auxiliary wire. Another wire D, called the experimental wire is fixed at one end to the bridge A and passes over the second bridge B to hold a hanger H on which suitable weights can be put. Two small movable bridges C_1 and C_2 may slide under the auxiliary wire and another two movable bridges D_1 and D_2 may slide under the experimental wire.

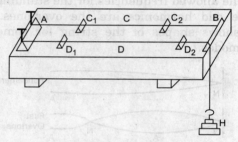

Figure 15.19

The portion of the wire between the movable bridges forms the "string" fixed at both ends. By sliding these bridges, the length of the wire may be changed. The tension of the experimental wire D may be changed by changing the weights on the hanger. One can remove the experimental wire itself and put another wire in its place thereby changing the mass per unit length.

The waves can be produced on the wire by vibrating a tuning fork (by holding its stem and gently hitting a prong on a rubber pad) and pressing its stem on the platform of the sound box of the sonometer. The simple harmonic disturbance is transmitted to the wire through the bridges. The frequency of vibration is same as that of the tuning fork. If this frequency happens to be equal to one of the natural frequencies of the wire, standing waves with large amplitudes are set up on it. The tuning fork is then said to be in "resonance" or in "unison" with the wire.

How can one identify whether the tuning fork is in resonance with the wire or not ? A simple method is to place a small piece of paper (called a paper rider) at the middle point of the wire between the movable bridges. When vibrations in the wire are induced by putting the tuning fork in contact with the board, the paper-piece also vibrates. If the tuning fork is in resonance with the fundamental mode of vibration of

the wire, the paper-piece is at the antinode. Because of the large amplitude of the wire there, it violently shakes and quite often jumps off the wire. Thus, the resonance can be detected just by visible inspection.

The paper-piece is also at an antinode if the wire is vibrating in its 3rd harmonic, although the amplitude will not be as large as it would be in the fundamental mode. The paper-piece may shake but not that violently.

Another good method to detect the resonance is based on the interference of sound waves of different frequencies. The tuning fork is sounded by gently hitting a prong on a rubber pad and the wire is plucked by hand. The resultant sound shows a periodic increase and decrease in intensity if the frequency of the fork is close (but not exactly equal) to one of the natural frequencies of the wire. This periodic variation in intensity is called *beats* that we shall study in the next chapter. The length is then only slightly varied till the beats disappear and that ensures resonance.

Law of Length

To study the law of length, only the experimental wire is needed. The wire is put under a tension by placing suitable weights (say 3 to 4 kg) on the hanger.

A tuning fork is vibrated and the length of the wire is adjusted by moving the movable bridges such that the fork is in resonance with the fundamental mode of vibration of the wire. The frequency ν of the tuning fork and the length l of the wire resonating with it are noted. The experiment is repeated with different tuning forks and the product νl is evaluated for each fork which should be a constant by the law of length.

Law of Tension

To study the law of tension, one may proceed as follows. A particular length of the experimental wire is selected by keeping the movable bridges D_1, D_2 fixed. The auxiliary wire is plucked. The vibration is transmitted to the experimental wire through the sound box. By adjusting the movable bridges C_1 and C_2, the fundamental frequency of the auxiliary wire is made equal to the fundamental frequency of the experimental wire by testing that the two wires resonate with each other. The tension in the experimental wire is changed and the length of the auxiliary wire is again adjusted to resonate with it. The experiment is repeated several times with different tensions and the corresponding lengths of the auxiliary wire are noted. Suppose l' represents the length of the auxiliary wire resonating with the fixed length of the experimental wire when the tension in it is T. Also suppose ν is the frequency of vibration of the wires in their fundamental modes in this situation. Then,

$$v \propto \frac{1}{l'} \text{ according to the law of length}$$

and $v \propto \sqrt{T}$ according to the law of tension.

Hence, $l' \propto 1/\sqrt{T}$.

The product $l'\sqrt{T}$ may be evaluated from the experiments which should be a constant.

Why do we have to use the auxiliary wire in the above scheme and not a tuning fork ? That is because, to adjust for the resonance, the variable quantity should be continuously changeable. As the length of the experimental wire is kept fixed and its frequency is to be compared as a function of tension, we need a source whose frequency can be continuously changed. Choosing different tuning forks to change the frequency will not work as the forks are available for discrete frequencies only.

Law of Mass

To study the law of mass, the length and the tension are to be kept constant and the mass per unit length is to be changed. Again, the auxiliary wire is used to resonate with the fixed length of the experimental wire as was suggested during the study of the law of tension. A fixed length of the experimental wire is chosen between the bridges D_1 and D_2 and a fixed tension is applied to it. The auxiliary wire is given a tension by hanging a certain load and its length is adjusted so that it resonates with the experimental wire. The experiment is repeated with different experimental wires keeping equal lengths between the movable bridges and applying equal tension. Each time the length l' of the auxiliary wire is adjusted to bring it in resonance with the experimental wire. The mass per unit length of each experimental wire is obtained by weighing a known length of the wire. We have

$$v \propto 1/l' \quad \text{according to the law of length}$$

and $v \propto 1/\sqrt{\mu}$ according to the law of mass.

Thus, $l' \propto \sqrt{\mu}$.

The law of mass is thus studied by obtaining $\frac{l'}{\sqrt{\mu}}$ each time which should be a constant.

Example 15.8

In a sonometer experiment, resonance is obtained when the experimental wire has a length of 21 cm between the bridges and the vibrations are excited by a tuning fork of frequency 256 Hz. If a tuning fork of frequency 384 Hz is used, what should be the length of the experimental wire to get the resonance.

Solution : By the law of length, $l_1 v_1 = l_2 v_2$

or, $$l_2 = \frac{v_1}{v_2} l_1 = \frac{256}{384} \times 21 \text{ cm} = 14 \text{ cm}.$$

15.14 TRANSVERSE AND LONGITUDINAL WAVES

The wave on a string is caused by the displacements of the particles of the string. These displacements are in a direction perpendicular to the direction of propagation of the wave. If the disturbance produced in a wave has a direction perpendicular to the direction of propagation of the wave, the wave is called a *transverse wave*. The wave on a string is a transverse wave. Another example of transverse wave is the light wave. It is the electric field which changes its value with space and time and the changes are propagated in space. The direction of the electric field is perpendicular to the direction of propagation of light when light travels in free space.

Sound waves are not transverse. The particles of the medium are pushed and pulled along the direction of propagation of sound. We shall study in some detail the mechanism of sound waves in the next chapter. If the disturbance produced as the wave passes is along the direction of the wave propagation, the wave is called a *longitudinal wave*. Sound waves are longitudinal.

All the waves cannot be characterised as either longitudinal or transverse. A very common example of a wave that is neither longitudinal nor transverse is a wave on the surface of water. When water in a steady lake is disturbed by shaking a finger in it, waves are produced on the water surface. The water particles move in elliptic or circular path as the wave passes through them. The elliptic motion has components both along and perpendicular to the direction of propagation of the wave.

15.15 POLARIZATION OF WAVES

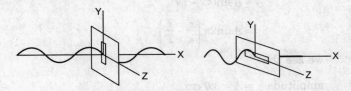

Figure 15.20

Suppose a stretched string goes through a slit made in a cardboard which is placed perpendicular to the string (figure 15.20). If we take the X-axis along the string, the cardboard will be in Y-Z plane. Suppose the particles of the string are displaced in y-direction as the wave passes. If the slit in the cardboard is also along the Y-axis, the part of the string in the slit can vibrate freely in the slit and the wave will pass through the slit. However, if the cardboard is rotated by 90° in its plane, the slit will point along the Z-axis. As the wave arrives at the slit, the part of the string in it tries to move along the Y-axis but the contact force by the cardboard does not allow it. The wave is not able to pass through the slit. If the slit is inclined to the Y-axis at some other angle, only a part of the wave is transmitted and in the transmitted wave the disturbance is produced parallel to the slit. Figure (15.21) suggests the same arrangement with two chairs.

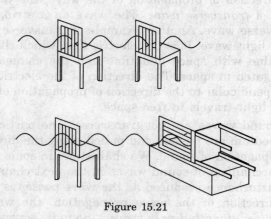

Figure 15.21

If the disturbance produced is always along a fixed direction, we say that the wave is linearly polarized in that direction. The waves considered in this chapter are linearly polarized in y-direction. Similarly, if a wave produces displacement along the z-direction, its equation is given by $z = A \sin \omega(t - x/v)$ and it is a linearly polarized wave, polarized in z-direction. Linearly polarized waves are also called *plane polarized*.

If each particle of the string moves in a small circle as the wave passes through it, the wave is called *circularly polarized*. If each particle goes in ellipse, the wave is called *elliptically polarized*.

Finally, if the particles are randomly displaced in the plane perpendicular to the direction of propagation, the wave is called *unpolarized*.

A circularly polarized or unpolarized wave passing through a slit does not show change in intensity as the slit is rotated in its plane. But the transmitted wave becomes linearly polarized in the direction parallel to the slit.

Worked Out Examples

1. *The displacement of a particle of a string carrying a travelling wave is given by*

$$y = (3.0 \text{ cm}) \sin 6.28(0.50x - 50\, t),$$

where x is in centimetre and t in second. Find (a) the amplitude, (b) the wavelength, (c) the frequency and (d) the speed of the wave.

Solution : Comparing with the standard wave equation

$$y = A \sin(kx - \omega t)$$

$$= A \sin 2\pi \left(\frac{x}{\lambda} - \frac{t}{T} \right)$$

we see that,

amplitude $= A = 3.0$ cm,

wavelength $= \lambda = \dfrac{1}{0.50}$ cm $= 2.0$ cm,

and the frequency $= \nu = \dfrac{1}{T} = 50$ Hz.

The speed of the wave is $v = \nu\lambda$

$$= (50 \text{ s}^{-1})(2.0 \text{ cm})$$

$$= 100 \text{ cm s}^{-1}.$$

2. *The equation for a wave travelling in x-direction on a string is*

$$y = (3.0 \text{ cm}) \sin[(3.14 \text{ cm}^{-1})\,x - (314 \text{ s}^{-1})t].$$

(a) Find the maximum velocity of a particle of the string.

(b) Find the acceleration of a particle at $x = 6.0$ cm at time $t = 0.11$ s.

Solution :

(a) The velocity of the particle at x at time t is

$$v = \frac{\partial y}{\partial t} = (3.0 \text{ cm})(-314 \text{ s}^{-1})\cos[(3.14 \text{ cm}^{-1})\,x - (314 \text{ s}^{-1})t]$$

$$= (-9.4 \text{ m s}^{-1})\cos[(3.14 \text{ cm}^{-1})\,x - (314 \text{ s}^{-1})t].$$

The maximum velocity of a particle will be

$$v = 9.4 \text{ m s}^{-1}.$$

(b) The acceleration of the particle at x at time t is

$$a = \frac{\partial v}{\partial t} = -(9.4 \text{ m s}^{-1})(314 \text{ s}^{-1})\sin[(3.14 \text{ cm}^{-1})\,x - (314 \text{ s}^{-1})t]$$

$$= -(2952 \text{ m s}^{-2})\sin[(3.14 \text{ cm}^{-1})\,x - (314 \text{ s}^{-1})t].$$

The acceleration of the particle at $x = 6.0$ cm at time $t = 0.11$ s is $a = -(2952 \text{ m s}^{-2})\sin[6\pi - 11\pi] = 0.$

3. *A long string having a cross-sectional area* 0.80 mm^2 *and density* 12.5 g cm^{-3}, *is subjected to a tension of* 64 N *along the X-axis. One end of this string is attached to a vibrator moving in transverse direction at a frequency of* 20 Hz. *At* $t = 0$, *the source is at a maximum displacement* $y = 1.0 \text{ cm}$. (a) *Find the speed of the wave travelling on the string.* (b) *Write the equation for the wave.* (c) *What is the displacement of the particle of the string at* $x = 50 \text{ cm}$ *at time* $t = 0.05 \text{ s}$? (d) *What is the velocity of this particle at this instant ?*

Solution :

(a) The mass of 1 m long part of the string is

$$m = (0.80 \text{ mm}^2) \times (1 \text{ m}) \times (12.5 \text{ g cm}^{-3})$$
$$= (0.80 \times 10^{-6} \text{ m}^3) \times (12.5 \times 10^3 \text{ kg m}^{-3})$$
$$= 0.01 \text{ kg}.$$

The linear mass density is $\mu = 0.01 \text{ kg m}^{-1}$. The wave speed is $v = \sqrt{F/\mu}$

$$= \sqrt{\frac{64 \text{ N}}{0.01 \text{ kg m}^{-1}}} = 80 \text{ m s}^{-1}.$$

(b) The amplitude of the source is $A = 1.0 \text{ cm}$ and the frequency is $\nu = 20 \text{ Hz}$. The angular frequency is $\omega = 2\pi\nu = 40\pi \text{ s}^{-1}$. Also at $t = 0$, the displacement is equal to its amplitude, i.e., at $t = 0, y = A$. The equation of motion of the source is, therefore,

$$y = (1.0 \text{ cm}) \cos[(40\pi \text{ s}^{-1}) t] \qquad \ldots \text{ (i)}$$

The equation of the wave travelling on the string along the positive X-axis is obtained by replacing t with $t - x/v$ in equation (i). It is, therefore,

$$y = (1.0 \text{ cm}) \cos\left[(40\pi \text{ s}^{-1})\left(t - \frac{x}{v}\right)\right]$$
$$= (1.0 \text{ cm}) \cos\left[(40\pi \text{ s}^{-1})t - \left(\frac{\pi}{2} \text{ m}^{-1}\right)x\right], \qquad \ldots \text{ (ii)}$$

where the value of v has been put from part (a).

(c) The displacement of the particle at $x = 50 \text{ cm}$ at time $t = 0.05 \text{ s}$ is by equation (ii),

$$y = (1.0 \text{ cm}) \cos\left[(40\pi \text{ s}^{-1}) (0.05 \text{ s}) - \left(\frac{\pi}{2} \text{ m}^{-1}\right)(0.5 \text{ m})\right]$$
$$= (1.0 \text{ cm}) \cos\left[2\pi - \frac{\pi}{4}\right]$$
$$= \frac{1.0 \text{ cm}}{\sqrt{2}} = 0.71 \text{ cm}.$$

(d) The velocity of the particle at position x at time t is, by equation (ii),

$$v = \frac{\partial y}{\partial t} = -(1.0 \text{ cm}) (40\pi \text{ s}^{-1}) \sin\left[(40\pi \text{ s}^{-1}) t - \left(\frac{\pi}{2} \text{ m}^{-1}\right)x\right].$$

Putting the values of x and t,

$$v = -(40\pi \text{ cm s}^{-1}) \sin\left(2\pi - \frac{\pi}{4}\right)$$
$$= \frac{40\pi}{\sqrt{2}} \text{ cm s}^{-1} \approx 89 \text{ cm s}^{-1}.$$

4. *The speed of a transverse wave, going on a wire having a length* 50 cm *and mass* 5.0 g, *is* 80 m s^{-1}. *The area of cross section of the wire is* 1.0 mm^2 *and its Young modulus is* $16 \times 10^{11} \text{ N m}^{-2}$. *Find the extension of the wire over its natural length.*

Solution : The linear mass density is

$$\mu = \frac{5 \times 10^{-3} \text{ kg}}{50 \times 10^{-2} \text{ m}} = 1.0 \times 10^{-2} \text{ kg m}^{-1}.$$

The wave speed is $v = \sqrt{F/\mu}$.

Thus, the tension is $F = \mu v^2$

$$= \left(1.0 \times 10^{-2} \text{ kg m}^{-1}\right) \times 6400 \text{ m}^2 \text{ s}^{-2} = 64 \text{ N}.$$

The Young modulus is given by

$$Y = \frac{F/A}{\Delta L / L}.$$

The extension is, therefore,

$$\Delta L = \frac{FL}{AY}$$

$$= \frac{(64 \text{ N}) (0.50 \text{ m})}{(1.0 \times 10^{-6} \text{ m}^2) \times (16 \times 10^{11} \text{ N m}^{-2})} = 0.02 \text{ mm}.$$

5. *A uniform rope of length* 12 m *and mass* 6 kg *hangs vertically from a rigid support. A block of mass* 2 kg *is attached to the free end of the rope. A transverse pulse of wavelength* 0.06 m *is produced at the lower end of the rope. What is the wavelength of the pulse when it reaches the top of the rope ?*

Solution : As the rope is heavy, its tension will be different at different points. The tension at the free end will be $(2 \text{ kg})g$ and that at the upper end it will be $(8 \text{ kg})g$.

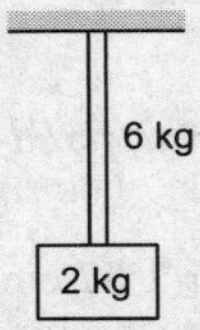

Figure 15-W1

We have, $\qquad\qquad v = \nu\lambda$

or, $\qquad\qquad \sqrt{F/\mu} = \nu\lambda$

or, $\qquad\qquad \sqrt{F/\lambda} = \nu \sqrt{\mu}. \qquad \ldots \text{ (i)}$

The frequency of the wave pulse will be the same everywhere on the rope as it depends only on the frequency of the source. The mass per unit length is also the same throughout the rope as it is uniform. Thus, by (i), $\frac{\sqrt{F}}{\lambda}$ is constant.

Hence, $\qquad\qquad \frac{\sqrt{(2 \text{ kg})g}}{0.06 \text{ m}} = \frac{\sqrt{(8 \text{ kg})g}}{\lambda_1}$,

where λ_1 is the wavelength at the top of the rope. This gives $\lambda_1 = 0.12 \text{ m}$.

6. *Two waves passing through a region are represented by*

$$y = (1 \cdot 0 \text{ cm}) \sin[(3 \cdot 14 \text{ cm}^{-1})x - (157 \text{ s}^{-1})t]$$

and $$y = (1 \cdot 5 \text{ cm}) \sin[(1 \cdot 57 \text{ cm}^{-1})x - (314 \text{ s}^{-1})t].$$

Find the displacement of the particle at $x = 4 \cdot 5$ cm at time $t = 5 \cdot 0$ ms.

Solution : According to the principle of superposition, each wave produces its disturbance independent of the other and the resultant disturbance is equal to the vector sum of the individual disturbances. The displacements of the particle at $x = 4 \cdot 5$ cm at time $t = 5 \cdot 0$ ms due to the two waves are,

$$y_1 = (1 \cdot 0 \text{ cm}) \sin[(3 \cdot 14 \text{ cm}^{-1}) (4 \cdot 5 \text{ cm})$$
$$- (157 \text{ s}^{-1}) (5 \cdot 0 \times 10^{-3} \text{ s})]$$

$$= (1 \cdot 0 \text{ cm}) \sin\left[4 \cdot 5\pi - \frac{\pi}{4}\right]$$

$$= (1 \cdot 0 \text{ cm}) \sin[4\pi + \pi/4] = \frac{1 \cdot 0 \text{ cm}}{\sqrt{2}}$$

and

$$y_2 = (1 \cdot 5 \text{ cm}) \sin[(1 \cdot 57 \text{ cm}^{-1}) (4 \cdot 5 \text{ cm})$$
$$- (314 \text{ s}^{-1}) (5 \cdot 0 \times 10^{-3} \text{ s})]$$

$$= (1 \cdot 5 \text{ cm}) \sin\left[2 \cdot 25\pi - \frac{\pi}{2}\right]$$

$$= (1 \cdot 5 \text{ cm}) \sin[2\pi - \pi/4]$$

$$= -(1 \cdot 5 \text{ cm}) \sin\frac{\pi}{4} = -\frac{1 \cdot 5 \text{ cm}}{\sqrt{2}}.$$

The net displacement is

$$y = y_1 + y_2 = \frac{-0 \cdot 5 \text{ cm}}{\sqrt{2}} = -0 \cdot 35 \text{ cm}.$$

7. *The vibrations of a string fixed at both ends are described by the equation*

$$y = (5 \cdot 00 \text{ mm}) \sin[(1 \cdot 57 \text{ cm}^{-1}) x] \sin[(314 \text{ s}^{-1}) t]$$

(a) What is the maximum displacement of the particle at $x = 5 \cdot 66$ cm ? (b) What are the wavelengths and the wave speeds of the two transverse waves that combine to give the above vibration ? (c) What is the velocity of the particle at $x = 5 \cdot 66$ cm at time $t = 2 \cdot 00$ s ? (d) If the length of the string is $10 \cdot 0$ cm, locate the nodes and the antinodes. How many loops are formed in the vibration ?

Solution :

(a) The amplitude of the vibration of the particle at position x is

$$A = |(5 \cdot 00 \text{ mm}) \sin[(1 \cdot 57 \text{ cm}^{-1}) x]|$$

For $x = 5 \cdot 66$ cm,

$$A = \left| (5 \cdot 00 \text{ mm}) \sin\left[\frac{\pi}{2} \times 5 \cdot 66\right] \right|$$

$$= \left| (5 \cdot 00 \text{ mm}) \sin\left(2 \cdot 5 \pi + \frac{\pi}{3}\right) \right|$$

$$= \left| (5 \cdot 00 \text{ mm}) \cos\frac{\pi}{3} \right| = 2 \cdot 50 \text{ mm}.$$

(b) From the given equation, the wave number $k = 1 \cdot 57 \text{ cm}^{-1}$ and the angular frequency $\omega = 314 \text{ s}^{-1}$. Thus, the wavelength is

$$\lambda = \frac{2\pi}{k} = \frac{2 \times 3 \cdot 14}{1 \cdot 57 \text{ cm}^{-1}} = 4 \cdot 00 \text{ cm}$$

and the frequency is $\nu = \dfrac{\omega}{2\pi} = \dfrac{314 \text{ s}^{-1}}{2 \times 3 \cdot 14} = 50 \text{ s}^{-1}$.

The wave speed is $v = \nu\lambda = (50 \text{ s}^{-1}) (4 \cdot 00 \text{ cm}) = 2 \cdot 00 \text{ m s}^{-1}$.

(c) The velocity of the particle at position x at time t is given by

$$v = \frac{\partial y}{\partial t} = (5 \cdot 00 \text{ mm}) \sin[(1 \cdot 57 \text{ cm}^{-1}) x]$$
$$[314 \text{ s}^{-1} \cos(314 \text{ s}^{-1}) t]$$

$$= (157 \text{ cm s}^{-1}) \sin(1 \cdot 57 \text{ cm}^{-1}) x \cos(314 \text{ s}^{-1})t.$$

Putting $x = 5 \cdot 66$ cm and $t = 2 \cdot 00$ s, the velocity of this particle at the given instant is

$$(157 \text{ cm s}^{-1}) \sin\left(\frac{5\pi}{2} + \frac{\pi}{3}\right) \cos(200 \pi)$$

$$= (157 \text{ cm s}^{-1}) \times \cos\frac{\pi}{3} \times 1 = 78 \cdot 5 \text{ cm s}^{-1}.$$

(d) The nodes occur where the amplitude is zero, i.e.,

$$\sin(1 \cdot 57 \text{ cm}^{-1}) x = 0.$$

or, $$\left(\frac{\pi}{2} \text{ cm}^{-1}\right)x = n\pi,$$

where n is an integer.

Thus, $x = 2 n$ cm.

The nodes, therefore, occur at $x = 0$, 2 cm, 4 cm, 6 cm, 8 cm and 10 cm. Antinodes occur in between them, i.e., at $x = 1$ cm, 3 cm, 5 cm, 7 cm and 9 cm. The string vibrates in 5 loops.

8. *A guitar string is 90 cm long and has a fundamental frequency of 124 Hz. Where should it be pressed to produce a fundamental frequency of 186 Hz ?*

Solution : The fundamental frequency of a string fixed at both ends is given by

$$\nu = \frac{1}{2 L} \sqrt{\frac{F}{\mu}}.$$

As F and μ are fixed, $\dfrac{\nu_1}{\nu_2} = \dfrac{L_2}{L_1}$

or, $$L_2 = \frac{\nu_1}{\nu_2} L_1 = \frac{124 \text{ Hz}}{186 \text{ Hz}} (90 \text{ cm}) = 60 \text{ cm}.$$

Thus, the string should be pressed at 60 cm from an end.

9. *A sonometer wire has a total length of* 1 m *between the fixed ends. Where should the two bridges be placed below the wire so that the three segments of the wire have their fundamental frequencies in the ratio* 1 : 2 : 3 ?

Solution : Suppose the lengths of the three segments are L_1, L_2 and L_3 respectively. The fundamental frequencies are

$$\nu_1 = \frac{1}{2 L_1} \sqrt{F/\mu}$$

$$\nu_2 = \frac{1}{2 L_2} \sqrt{F/\mu}$$

$$\nu_3 = \frac{1}{2 L_3} \sqrt{F/\mu}$$

so that $\nu_1 L_1 = \nu_2 L_2 = \nu_3 L_3.$ ... (i)

As $\nu_1 : \nu_2 : \nu_3 = 1 : 2 : 3$, we have

$$\nu_2 = 2\,\nu_1 \text{ and } \nu_3 = 3\,\nu_1 \text{ so that by (i)}$$

$$L_2 = \frac{\nu_1}{\nu_2} L_1 = \frac{L_1}{2}$$

and $L_3 = \dfrac{\nu_1}{\nu_3} L_1 = \dfrac{L_1}{3}.$

As $L_1 + L_2 + L_3 = 1$ m,

we get $L_1\left(1 + \dfrac{1}{2} + \dfrac{1}{3}\right) = 1$ m

or, $L_1 = \dfrac{6}{11}$ m.

Thus, $L_2 = \dfrac{L_1}{2} = \dfrac{3}{11}$ m

and $L_3 = \dfrac{L_1}{3} = \dfrac{2}{11}$ m.

One bridge should be placed at $\dfrac{6}{11}$ m from one end and the other should be placed at $\dfrac{2}{11}$ m from the other end.

10. *A wire having a linear mass density* $5{\cdot}0 \times 10^{-3}$ kg m^{-1} *is stretched between two rigid supports with a tension of* 450 N. *The wire resonates at a frequency of* 420 Hz. *The next higher frequency at which the same wire resonates is* 490 Hz. *Find the length of the wire.*

Solution : Suppose the wire vibrates at 420 Hz in its nth harmonic and at 490 Hz in its $(n + 1)$th harmonic.

$$420 \text{ s}^{-1} = \frac{n}{2 L} \sqrt{F/\mu} \qquad ... \text{ (i)}$$

and $490 \text{ s}^{-1} = \dfrac{(n + 1)}{2 L} \sqrt{F/\mu} \qquad ... \text{ (ii)}$

This gives $\dfrac{490}{420} = \dfrac{n + 1}{n}$

or, $n = 6.$

Putting the value in (i),

$$420 \text{ s}^{-1} = \frac{6}{2 L} \sqrt{\frac{450 \text{ N}}{5{\cdot}0 \times 10^{-3} \text{ kg m}^{-1}}} = \frac{900}{L} \text{ m s}^{-1}$$

or, $L = \dfrac{900}{420}$ m $= 2{\cdot}1$ m.

□

QUESTIONS FOR SHORT ANSWER

1. You are walking along a seashore and a mild wind is blowing. Is the motion of air a wave motion ?

2. The radio and TV programmes, telecast at the studio, reach our antenna by wave motion. Is it a mechanical wave or nonmechanical ?

3. A wave is represented by an equation $y = c_1 \sin (c_2 x + c_3 t)$. In which direction is the wave going ? Assume that c_1, c_2 and c_3 are all positive.

4. Show that the particle speed can never be equal to the wave speed in a sine wave if the amplitude is less than wavelength divided by 2π.

5. Two wave pulses identical in shape but inverted with respect to each other are produced at the two ends of a stretched string. At an instant when the pulses reach the middle, the string becomes completely straight. What happens to the energy of the two pulses ?

6. Show that for a wave travelling on a string

$$\frac{y_{\max}}{v_{\max}} = \frac{v_{\max}}{a_{\max}},$$

where the symbols have usual meanings. Can we use componendo and dividendo taught in algebra to write

$$\frac{y_{\max} + v_{\max}}{y_{\max} - v_{\max}} = \frac{v_{\max} + a_{\max}}{v_{\max} - a_{\max}} ?$$

7. What is the smallest positive phase constant which is equivalent to $7{\cdot}5\,\pi$?

8. A string clamped at both ends vibrates in its fundamental mode. Is there any position (except the ends) on the string which can be touched without disturbing the motion ? What if the string vibrates in its first overtone ?

OBJECTIVE I

1. A sine wave is travelling in a medium. The minimum distance between the two particles, always having same speed, is
   (a) $\lambda/4$ (b) $\lambda/3$ (c) $\lambda/2$ (d) λ.

2. A sine wave is travelling in a medium. A particular particle has zero displacement at a certain instant. The particle closest to it having zero displacement is at a distance
   (a) $\lambda/4$ (b) $\lambda/3$ (c) $\lambda/2$ (d) λ.

3. Which of the following equations represents a wave travelling along Y-axis ?
   (a) $x = A \sin (ky - \omega t)$ (b) $y = A \sin (kx - \omega t)$
   (c) $y = A \sin ky \cos \omega t$ (d) $y = A \cos ky \sin \omega t$.

4. The equation $y = A \sin^2 (kx - \omega t)$ represents a wave motion with
   (a) amplitude A, frequency $\omega/2\pi$
   (b) amplitude $A/2$, frequency ω/π
   (c) amplitude $2A$, frequency $\omega/4\pi$
   (d) does not represent a wave motion.

5. Which of the following is a mechanical wave ?
   (a) Radio waves   (b) X-rays
   (c) Light waves   (d) Sound waves.

6. A cork floating in a calm pond executes simple harmonic motion of frequency ν when a wave generated by a boat passes by it. The frequency of the wave is
   (a) ν (b) $\nu/2$ (c) 2ν (d) $\sqrt2\nu$.

7. Two strings A and B, made of same material, are stretched by same tension. The radius of string A is double of the radius of B. A transverse wave travels on A with speed v_A and on B with speed v_B. The ratio v_A/v_B is
   (a) $1/2$ (b) 2 (c) $1/4$ (d) 4.

8. Both the strings, shown in figure (15-Q1), are made of same material and have same cross section. The pulleys are light. The wave speed of a transverse wave in the string AB is v_1 and in CD it is v_2. Then v_1/v_2 is
   (a) 1 (b) 2 (c) $\sqrt2$ (d) $1/\sqrt2$.

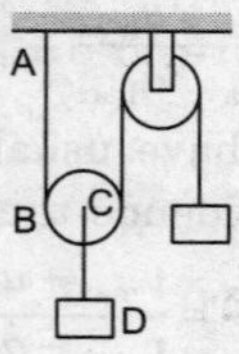

Figure 15-Q1

9. Velocity of sound in air is 332 m s^{-1}. Its velocity in vacuum will be
   (a) > 332 m s^{-1} (b) = 332 m s^{-1}
   (c) < 332 m s^{-1} (d) meaningless.

10. A wave pulse, travelling on a two-piece string, gets partially reflected and partially transmitted at the junction. The reflected wave is inverted in shape as compared to the incident one. If the incident wave has wavelength λ and the transmitted wave λ',

(a) $\lambda' > \lambda$ (b) $\lambda' = \lambda$ (c) $\lambda' < \lambda$
(d) nothing can be said about the relation of λ and λ'.

11. Two waves represented by $y = a \sin(\omega t - kx)$ and $y = a \cos(\omega t - kx)$ are superposed. The resultant wave will have an amplitude
    (a) a (b) $\sqrt2 a$ (c) $2a$ (d) 0.

12. Two wires A and B, having identical geometrical construction, are stretched from their natural length by small but equal amount. The Young modulus of the wires are Y_A and Y_B whereas the densities are ρ_A and ρ_B. It is given that $Y_A > Y_B$ and $\rho_A > \rho_B$. A transverse signal started at one end takes a time t_1 to reach the other end for A and t_2 for B.
    (a) $t_1 < t_2$ (b) $t_1 = t_2$ (c) $t_1 > t_2$
    (d) the information is insufficient to find the relation between t_1 and t_2.

13. Consider two waves passing through the same string. Principle of superposition for displacement says that the net displacement of a particle on the string is sum of the displacements produced by the two waves individually. Suppose we state similar principles for the net velocity of the particle and the net kinetic energy of the particle. Such a principle will be valid for
    (a) both the velocity and the kinetic energy
    (b) the velocity but not for the kinetic energy
    (c) the kinetic energy but not for the velocity
    (d) neither the velocity nor the kinetic energy.

14. Two wave pulses travel in opposite directions on a string and approach each other. The shape of one pulse is inverted with respect to the other.
    (a) The pulses will collide with each other and vanish after collision.
    (b) The pulses will reflect from each other, i.e., the pulse going towards right will finally move towards left and vice versa.
    (c) The pulses will pass through each other but their shapes will be modified.
    (d) The pulses will pass through each other without any change in their shapes.

15. Two periodic waves of amplitudes A_1 and A_2 pass through a region. If $A_1 > A_2$, the difference in the maximum and minimum resultant amplitude possible is
    (a) $2A_1$ (b) $2A_2$ (c) $A_1 + A_2$ (d) $A_1 - A_2$.

16. Two waves of equal amplitude A, and equal frequency travel in the same direction in a medium. The amplitude of the resultant wave is
    (a) 0 (b) A (c) $2A$ (d) between 0 and $2A$.

17. Two sine waves travel in the same direction in a medium. The amplitude of each wave is A and the phase difference between the two waves is 120°. The resultant amplitude will be
    (a) A (b) $2A$ (c) $4A$ (d) $\sqrt2 A$.

18. The fundamental frequency of a string is proportional to

(a) inverse of its length   (b) the diameter
(c) the tension   (d) the density.

19. A tuning fork of frequency 480 Hz is used to vibrate a sonometer wire having natural frequency 240 Hz. The wire will vibrate with a frequency of
(a) 240 Hz   (b) 480 Hz
(c) 720 Hz   (d) will not vibrate.

20. A tuning fork of frequency 480 Hz is used to vibrate a sonometer wire having natural frequency 410 Hz. The wire will vibrate with a frequency
(a) 410 Hz   (b) 480 Hz   (c) 820 Hz   (d) 960 Hz.

21. A sonometer wire of length l vibrates in fundamental mode when excited by a tuning fork of frequency 416 Hz.

If the length is doubled keeping other things same, the string will
(a) vibrate with a frequency of 416 Hz
(b) vibrate with a frequency of 208 Hz
(c) vibrate with a frequency of 832 Hz
(d) stop vibrating.

22. A sonometer wire supports a 4 kg load and vibrates in fundamental mode with a tuning fork of frequency 416 Hz. The length of the wire between the bridges is now doubled. In order to maintain fundamental mode, the load should be changed to
(a) 1 kg   (b) 2 kg   (c) 8 kg   (d) 16 kg.

OBJECTIVE II

1. A mechanical wave propagates in a medium along the X-axis. The particles of the medium
(a) must move on the X-axis
(b) must move on the Y-axis
(c) may move on the X-axis
(d) may move on the Y-axis.

2. A transverse wave travels along the Z-axis. The particles of the medium must move
(a) along the Z-axis   (b) along the X-axis
(c) along the Y-axis   (d) in the X-Y plane.

3. Longitudinal waves cannot
(a) have a unique wavelength   (b) transmit energy
(c) have a unique wave velocity (d) be polarized.

4. A wave going in a solid
(a) must be longitudinal   (b) may be longitudinal
(c) must be transverse   (d) may be transverse.

5. A wave moving in a gas
(a) must be longitudinal   (b) may be longitudinal
(c) must be transverse   (d) may be transverse.

6. Two particles A and B have a phase difference of π when a sine wave passes through the region.
(a) A oscillates at half the frequency of B.
(b) A and B move in opposite directions.
(c) A and B must be separated by half of the wavelength.
(d) The displacements at A and B have equal magnitudes.

7. A wave is represented by the equation
$$y = (0\cdot001 \text{ mm}) \sin[(50 \text{ s}^{-1})t + (2\cdot0 \text{ m}^{-1})x].$$
(a) The wave velocity $= 100 \text{ m s}^{-1}$.
(b) The wavelength $= 2\cdot0$ m.
(c) The frequency $= 25/\pi$ Hz.
(d) The amplitude $= 0\cdot001$ mm.

8. A standing wave is produced on a string clamped at one end and free at the other. The length of the string
(a) must be an integral multiple of $\lambda/4$
(b) must be an integral multiple of $\lambda/2$
(c) must be an integral multiple of λ
(d) may be an integral multiple of $\lambda/2$.

9. Mark out the correct options.
(a) The energy of any small part of a string remains constant in a travelling wave.
(b) The energy of any small part of a string remains constant in a standing wave.
(c) The energies of all the small parts of equal length are equal in a travelling wave.
(d) The energies of all the small parts of equal length are equal in a standing wave.

10. In a stationary wave,
(a) all the particles of the medium vibrate in phase
(b) all the antinodes vibrate in phase
(c) the alternate antinodes vibrate in phase
(d) all the particles between consecutive nodes vibrate in phase.

EXERCISES

1. A wave pulse passing on a string with a speed of 40 cm s^{-1} in the negative x-direction has its maximum at $x = 0$ at $t = 0$. Where will this maximum be located at $t = 5$ s ?

2. The equation of a wave travelling on a string stretched along the X-axis is given by
$$y = A\,e^{-\left(\frac{x}{a}+\frac{t}{T}\right)^2}.$$
   (a) Write the dimensions of A, a and T. (b) Find the wave speed. (c) In which direction is the wave

travelling ? (d) Where is the maximum of the pulse located at $t = T$? At $t = 2T$?

3. Figure (15-E1) shows a wave pulse at $t = 0$. The pulse moves to the right with a speed of 10 cm s^{-1}. Sketch the shape of the string at $t = 1$ s, 2 s and 3 s.

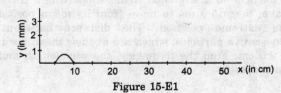

Figure 15-E1

4. A pulse travelling on a string is represented by the function

$$y = \frac{a^3}{(x - vt)^2 + a^2},$$

where $a = 5$ mm and $v = 20$ cm s^{-1}. Sketch the shape of the string at $t = 0, 1$ s and 2 s. Take $x = 0$ in the middle of the string.

5. The displacement of the particle at $x = 0$ of a stretched string carrying a wave in the positive x-direction is given by $f(t) = A \sin(t/T)$. The wave speed is v. Write the wave equation.

6. A wave pulse is travelling on a string with a speed v towards the positive X-axis. The shape of the string at $t = 0$ is given by $g(x) = A \sin(x/a)$, where A and a are constants.
(a) What are the dimensions of A and a ? (b) Write the equation of the wave for a general time t, if the wave speed is v.

7. A wave propagates on a string in the positive x-direction at a velocity v. The shape of the string at $t = t_0$ is given by $g(x, t_0) = A \sin(x/a)$. Write the wave equation for a general time t.

8. The equation of a wave travelling on a string is

$$y = (0.10 \text{ mm}) \sin[(31.4 \text{ m}^{-1})x + (314 \text{ s}^{-1})t].$$

(a) In which direction does the wave travel ? (b) Find the wave speed, the wavelength and the frequency of the wave. (c) What is the maximum displacement and the maximum speed of a portion of the string ?

9. A wave travels along the positive x-direction with a speed of 20 m s^{-1}. The amplitude of the wave is 0.20 cm and the wavelength 2.0 cm. (a) Write a suitable wave equation which describes this wave. (b) What is the displacement and velocity of the particle at $x = 2.0$ cm at time $t = 0$ according to the wave equation written ? Can you get different values of this quantity if the wave equation is written in a different fashion ?

10. A wave is described by the equation

$$y = (1.0 \text{ mm}) \sin \pi \left(\frac{x}{2.0 \text{ cm}} - \frac{t}{0.01 \text{ s}} \right).$$

(a) Find the time period and the wavelength ? (b) Write the equation for the velocity of the particles. Find the speed of the particle at $x = 1.0$ cm at time $t = 0.01$ s. (c) What are the speeds of the particles at $x = 3.0$ cm, 5.0 cm and 7.0 cm at $t = 0.01$ s ? (d) What are the speeds of the particles at $x = 1.0$ cm at $t = 0.011$, 0.012, and 0.013 s ?

11. A particle on a stretched string supporting a travelling wave, takes 5.0 ms to move from its mean position to the extreme position. The distance between two consecutive particles, which are at their mean positions, is 2.0 cm. Find the frequency, the wavelength and the wave speed.

12. Figure (15-E2) shows a plot of the transverse displacements of the particles of a string at $t = 0$ through which a travelling wave is passing in the positive x-direction. The wave speed is 20 cm s^{-1}. Find (a) the amplitude, (b) the wavelength, (c) the wave number and (d) the frequency of the wave.

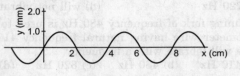

Figure 15-E2

13. A wave travelling on a string at a speed of 10 m s^{-1} causes each particle of the string to oscillate with a time period of 20 ms. (a) What is the wavelength of the wave ? (b) If the displacement of a particle is 1.5 mm at a certain instant, what will be the displacement of a particle 10 cm away from it at the same instant ?

14. A steel wire of length 64 cm weighs 5 g. If it is stretched by a force of 8 N, what would be the speed of a transverse wave passing on it ?

15. A string of length 20 cm and linear mass density 0.40 g cm^{-1} is fixed at both ends and is kept under a tension of 16 N. A wave pulse is produced at $t = 0$ near an end as shown in figure (15-E3), which travels towards the other end. (a) When will the string have the shape shown in the figure again ? (b) Sketch the shape of the string at a time half of that found in part (a).

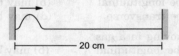

Figure 15-E3

16. A string of linear mass density 0.5 g cm^{-1} and a total length 30 cm is tied to a fixed wall at one end and to a frictionless ring at the other end (figure 15-E4). The ring can move on a vertical rod. A wave pulse is produced on the string which moves towards the ring at a speed of 20 cm s^{-1}. The pulse is symmetric about its maximum which is located at a distance of 20 cm from the end joined to the ring. (a) Assuming that the wave is reflected from the ends without loss of energy, find the time taken by the string to regain its shape. (b) The shape of the string changes periodically with time. Find this time period. (c) What is the tension in the string ?

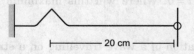

Figure 15-E4

17. Two wires of different densities but same area of cross section are soldered together at one end and are stretched to a tension T. The velocity of a transverse

wave in the first wire is double of that in the second wire. Find the ratio of the density of the first wire to that of the second wire.

18. A transverse wave described by

$$y = (0.02 \text{ m}) \sin[(1.0 \text{ m}^{-1}) x + (30 \text{ s}^{-1})t]$$

propagates on a stretched string having a linear mass density of $1.2 \times 10^{-4} \text{ kg m}^{-1}$. Find the tension in the string.

19. A travelling wave is produced on a long horizontal string by vibrating an end up and down sinusoidally. The amplitude of vibration is 1.0 cm and the displacement becomes zero 200 times per second. The linear mass density of the string is 0.10 kg m^{-1} and it is kept under a tension of 90 N. (a) Find the speed and the wavelength of the wave. (b) Assume that the wave moves in the positive x-direction and at $t = 0$, the end $x = 0$ is at its positive extreme position. Write the wave equation. (c) Find the velocity and acceleration of the particle at $x = 50$ cm at time $t = 10$ ms.

20. A string of length 40 cm and weighing 10 g is attached to a spring at one end and to a fixed wall at the other end. The spring has a spring constant of 160 N m^{-1} and is stretched by 1.0 cm. If a wave pulse is produced on the string near the wall, how much time will it take to reach the spring?

21. Two blocks each having a mass of 3.2 kg are connected by a wire CD and the system is suspended from the ceiling by another wire AB (figure 15-E5). The linear mass density of the wire AB is 10 g m^{-1} and that of CD is 8 g m^{-1}. Find the speed of a transverse wave pulse produced in AB and in CD.

Figure 15-E5

22. In the arrangement shown in figure (15-E6), the string has a mass of 4.5 g. How much time will it take for a transverse disturbance produced at the floor to reach the pulley? Take $g = 10$ m s^{-2}.

Figure 15-E6

23. A 4.0 kg block is suspended from the ceiling of an elevator through a string having a linear mass density of 19.2×10^{-3} kg m^{-1}. Find the speed (with respect to the string) with which a wave pulse can proceed on the string if the elevator accelerates up at the rate of 2.0 m s^{-2}. Take $g = 10$ m s^{-2}.

24. A heavy ball is suspended from the ceiling of a motor car through a light string. A transverse pulse travels at a speed of 60 cm s^{-1} on the string when the car is at rest and 62 cm s^{-1} when the car accelerates on a horizontal road. Find the acceleration of the car. Take $g = 10$ m s^{-2}.

25. A circular loop of string rotates about its axis on a frictionless horizontal plane at a uniform rate so that the tangential speed of any particle of the string is v. If a small transverse disturbance is produced at a point of the loop, with what speed (relative to the string) will this disturbance travel on the string?

26. A heavy but uniform rope of length L is suspended from a ceiling. (a) Write the velocity of a transverse wave travelling on the string as a function of the distance from the lower end. (b) If the rope is given a sudden sideways jerk at the bottom, how long will it take for the pulse to reach the ceiling? (c) A particle is dropped from the ceiling at the instant the bottom end is given the jerk. Where will the particle meet the pulse?

27. Two long strings A and B, each having linear mass density 1.2×10^{-2} kg m^{-1}, are stretched by different tensions 4.8 N and 7.5 N respectively and are kept parallel to each other with their left ends at $x = 0$. Wave pulses are produced on the strings at the left ends at $t = 0$ on string A and at $t = 20$ ms on string B. When and where will the pulse on B overtake that on A?

28. A transverse wave of amplitude 0.50 mm and frequency 100 Hz is produced on a wire stretched to a tension of 100 N. If the wave speed is 100 m s^{-1}, what average power is the source transmitting to the wire?

29. A 200 Hz wave with amplitude 1 mm travels on a long string of linear mass density 6 g m^{-1} kept under a tension of 60 N. (a) Find the average power transmitted across a given point on the string. (b) Find the total energy associated with the wave in a 2.0 m long portion of the sring.

30. A tuning fork of frequency 440 Hz is attached to a long string of linear mass density 0.01 kg m^{-1} kept under a tension of 49 N. The fork produces transverse waves of amplitude 0.50 mm on the string. (a) Find the wave speed and the wavelength of the waves. (b) Find the maximum speed and acceleration of a particle of the string. (c) At what average rate is the tuning fork transmitting energy to the string?

31. Two waves, travelling in the same direction through the same region, have equal frequencies, wavelengths and amplitudes. If the amplitude of each wave is 4 mm and the phase difference between the waves is 90°, what is the resultant amplitude?

32. Figure (15-E7) shows two wave pulses at $t = 0$ travelling on a string in opposite directions with the same wave

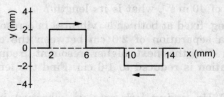

Figure 15-E7

speed 50 cm s^{-1}. Sketch the shape of the string at $t = 4$ ms, 6 ms, 8 ms, and 12 ms.

33. Two waves, each having a frequency of 100 Hz and a wavelength of 2·0 cm, are travelling in the same direction on a string. What is the phase difference between the waves (a) if the second wave was produced 0·015 s later than the first one at the same place, (b) if the two waves were produced at the same instant but the first one was produced a distance 4·0 cm behind the second one ? (c) If each of the waves has an amplitude of 2·0 mm, what would be the amplitudes of the resultant waves in part (a) and (b) ?

34. If the speed of a transverse wave on a stretched string of length 1 m is 60 m s^{-1}, what is the fundamental frequency of vibration ?

35. A wire of length 2·00 m is stretched to a tension of 160 N. If the fundamental frequency of vibration is 100 Hz, find its linear mass density.

36. A steel wire of mass 4·0 g and length 80 cm is fixed at the two ends. The tension in the wire is 50 N. Find the frequency and wavelength of the fourth harmonic of the fundamental.

37. A piano wire weighing 6·00 g and having a length of 90·0 cm emits a fundamental frequency corresponding to the "Middle C" ($v = 261·63$ Hz). Find the tension in the wire.

38. A sonometer wire having a length of 1·50 m between the bridges vibrates in its second harmonic in resonance with a tuning fork of frequency 256 Hz. What is the speed of the transverse wave on the wire ?

39. The length of the wire shown in figure (15-E8) between the pulley is 1·5 m and its mass is 12·0 g. Find the frequency of vibration with which the wire vibrates in two loops leaving the middle point of the wire between the pulleys at rest.

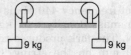

Figure 15-E8

40. A one-metre long stretched string having a mass of 40 g is attached to a tuning fork. The fork vibrates at 128 Hz in a direction perpendicular to the string. What should be the tension in the string if it is to vibrate in four loops ?

41. A wire, fixed at both ends is seen to vibrate at a resonant frequency of 240 Hz and also at 320 Hz. (a) What could be the maximum value of the fundamental frequency ? (b) If transverse waves can travel on this string at a speed of 40 m s^{-1}, what is its length ?

42. A string, fixed at both ends, vibrates in a resonant mode with a separation of 2·0 cm between the consecutive nodes. For the next higher resonant frequency, this separation is reduced to 1·6 cm. Find the length of the string.

43. A 660 Hz tuning fork sets up vibration in a string clamped at both ends. The wave speed for a transverse

wave on this string is 220 m s^{-1} and the string vibrates in three loops. (a) Find the length of the string. (b) If the maximum amplitude of a particle is 0·5 cm, write a suitable equation describing the motion.

44. A particular guitar wire is 30·0 cm long and vibrates at a frequency of 196 Hz when no finger is placed on it. The next higher notes on the scale are 220 Hz, 247 Hz, 262 Hz and 294 Hz. How far from the end of the string must the finger be placed to play these notes ?

45. A steel wire fixed at both ends has a fundamental frequency of 200 Hz. A person can hear sound of maximum frequency 14 kHz. What is the highest harmonic that can be played on this string which is audible to the person ?

46. Three resonant frequencies of a string are 90, 150 and 210 Hz. (a) Find the highest possible fundamental frequency of vibration of this string. (b) Which harmonics of the fundamental are the given frequencies ? (c) Which overtones are these frequencies ? (d) If the length of the string is 80 cm, what would be the speed of a transverse wave on this string ?

47. Two wires are kept tight between the same pair of supports. The tensions in the wires are in the ratio 2 : 1, the radii are in the ratio 3 : 1 and the densities are in the ratio 1 : 2. Find the ratio of their fundamental frequencies.

48. A uniform horizontal rod of length 40 cm and mass 1·2 kg is supported by two identical wires as shown in figure (15-E9). Where should a mass of 4·8 kg be placed on the rod so that the same tuning fork may excite the wire on left into its fundamental vibrations and that on right into its first overtone ? Take $g = 10$ m s^{-2}.

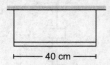

|← 40 cm →|

Figure 15-E9

49. Figure (15-E10) shows an aluminium wire of length 60 cm joined to a steel wire of length 80 cm and stretched between two fixed supports. The tension produced is 40 N. The cross-sectional area of the steel wire is 1·0 mm^2 and that of the aluminium wire is 3·0 mm^2. What could be the minimum frequency of a tuning fork which can produce standing waves in the system with the joint as a node ? The density of aluminium is 2·6 g cm^{-3} and that of steel is 7·8 g cm^{-3}.

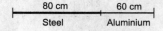

| 80 cm | 60 cm |
| Steel | Aluminium |

Figure 15-E10

50. A string of length L fixed at both ends vibrates in its fundamental mode at a frequency v and a maximum amplitude A. (a) Find the wavelength and the wave number k. (b) Take the origin at one end of the string and the X-axis along the string. Take the Y-axis along

the direction of the displacement. Take $t = 0$ at the instant when the middle point of the string passes through its mean position and is going towards the positive y-direction. Write the equation describing the standing wave.

51. A 2 m-long string fixed at both ends is set into vibrations in its first overtone. The wave speed on the string is 200 m s^{-1} and the amplitude is 0·5 cm. (a) Find the wavelength and the frequency. (b) Write the equation giving the displacement of different points as a function of time. Choose the X-axis along the string with the origin at one end and $t = 0$ at the instant when the point $x = 50$ cm has reached its maximum displacement.

52. The equation for the vibration of a string, fixed at both ends vibrating in its third harmonic, is given by

$$y = (0·4 \text{ cm}) \sin[(0·314 \text{ cm}^{-1}) x] \cos[(600\pi \text{ s}^{-1})t].$$

(a) What is the frequency of vibration ? (b) What are the positions of the nodes ? (c) What is the length of the string ? (d) What is the wavelength and the speed of two travelling waves that can interfere to give this vibration ?

53. The equation of a standing wave, produced on a string fixed at both ends, is

$$y = (0·4 \text{ cm}) \sin[(0·314 \text{ cm}^{-1}) x] \cos[(600\pi \text{ s}^{-1})t].$$

What could be the smallest length of the string ?

54. A 40 cm wire having a mass of 3·2 g is stretched between two fixed supports 40·05 cm apart. In its fundamental mode, the wire vibrates at 220 Hz. If the area of cross section of the wire is 1·0 mm^2, find its Young modulus.

55. Figure (15-E11) shows a string stretched by a block going over a pulley. The string vibrates in its tenth harmonic in unison with a particular tuning fork. When a beaker containing water is brought under the block so that the block is completely dipped into the beaker, the string vibrates in its eleventh harmonic. Find the density of the material of the block.

Figure 15-E11

56. A 2·00 m-long rope, having a mass of 80 g, is fixed at one end and is tied to a light string at the other end. The tension in the string is 256 N. (a) Find the frequencies of the fundamental and the first two overtones. (b) Find the wavelength in the fundamental and the first two overtones.

57. A heavy string is tied at one end to a movable support and to a light thread at the other end as shown in figure (15-E12). The thread goes over a fixed pulley and supports a weight to produce a tension. The lowest frequency with which the heavy string resonates is 120 Hz. If the movable support is pushed to the right by 10 cm so that the joint is placed on the pulley, what will be the minimum frequency at which the heavy string can resonate ?

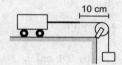

Figure 15-E12

□

ANSWERS

OBJECTIVE I

1. (c)	2. (c)	3. (a)	4. (b)	5. (d)	6. (a)
7. (a)	8. (d)	9. (d)	10. (c)	11. (b)	12. (d)
13. (b)	14. (d)	15. (b)	16. (d)	17. (a)	18. (a)
19. (b)	20. (b)	21. (a)	22. (d)		

OBJECTIVE II

1. (c), (d)	2. (d)	3. (d)
4. (b), (d)	5. (a)	6. (b), (c), (d)
7. (c), (d)	8. (a)	9. (b)
10. (c), (d)		

EXERCISES

1. At $x = -2$ m

2. (a) L, L, T (b) a/T
   (c) negative x-direction   (d) $x = -a$ and $x = -2a$

5. $f(x, t) = A \sin\left(\dfrac{t}{T} - \dfrac{x}{vT}\right)$

6. (a) L, L (b) $f(x, t) = A \sin\dfrac{x - vt}{a}$

7. $f(x, t) = A \sin\dfrac{x - v(t - t_0)}{a}$

8. (a) negative x-direction   (b) 10 m s^{-1}, 20 cm, 50 Hz
   (c) 0·10 mm, 3·14 cm s^{-1}

9. (a) $y = (0·20 \text{ cm}) \sin[(\pi \text{ cm}^{-1}) x - (2\pi \times 10^3 \text{ s}^{-1})t]$
   (b) zero, 4π m s^{-1}

10. (a) 20 ms, 4·0 cm   (b) zero
    (c) zero   (d) 9·7 cm s^{-1}, 18 cm s^{-1}, 25 cm s^{-1}
11. 50 Hz, 4·0 cm, 2·0 m s^{-1}
12. (a) 1·0 mm   (b) 4 cm   (c) 1·6 cm^{-1} (d) 5 Hz
13. (a) 20 cm   (b) − 1·5 mm
14. 32 m s^{-1}
15. (a) 0·02 s
16. (a) 2 s   (b) 3 s   (c) 2×10^{-3} N
17. 0·25
18. 0·108 N
19. (a) 30 m s^{-1}, 30 cm

    (b) $y = (1·0 \text{ cm}) \cos 2\pi \left[\dfrac{x}{30 \text{ cm}} - \dfrac{t}{0·01 \text{ s}} \right]$

    (c) − 5·4 m s^{-1}, 2·0 km s^{-2}
20. 0·05 s
21. 79 m s^{-1} and 63 m s^{-1}
22. 0·02 s
23. 50 m s^{-1}
24. 3·7 m s^{-2}
25. v
26. (a) $\sqrt{gx}$ (b) $\sqrt{4L/g}$

    (c) at a distance $\dfrac{L}{3}$ from the bottom

27. at $t = 100$ ms at $x = 2·0$ m
28. 49 mW
29. (a) 0·47 W   (b) 9·4 mJ
30. (a) 70 m s^{-1}, 16 cm (b) 1·4 m s^{-1}, 3·8 km s^{-2} (c) 0·67 W
31. 4√2 mm

33. (a) 3π   (b) 4π   (c) zero, 4·0 mm
34. 30 Hz
35. 1·00 g m^{-1}
36. 250 Hz, 40 cm
37. 1480 N
38. 384 m s^{-1}
39. 70 Hz
40. 164 N
41. (a) 80 Hz   (b) 25 cm
42. 8·0 cm
43. (a) 50 cm
    (b) (0·5 cm) sin[(0·06π cm^{-1})x] × cos[(1320π s^{-1})t]
44. 26·7 cm, 23·8 cm, 22·4 cm and 20·0 cm
45. 70
46. (a) 30 Hz   (b) 3rd, 5th and 7th
    (c) 2nd, 4th and 6th   (d) 48 m s^{-1}
47. 2 : 3
48. 5 cm from the left end
49. 180 Hz
50. (a) 2L, π/L   (b) $y = A \sin(\pi x/L) \sin(2\pi\nu t)$
51. (a) 2 m, 100 Hz
    (b) (0·5 cm) sin[(πm^{-1}) x] cos[(200π s^{-1})t]
52. (a) 300 Hz   (b) 0, 10 cm, 20 cm, 30 cm
    (c) 30 cm   (d) 20 cm, 60 m/s
53. 10 cm
54. 1·98 × 10^{11} N m^{-2}
55. 5·8 × 10^{3} kg m^{-3}
56. (a) 10 Hz, 30 Hz, 50 Hz   (b) 8·00 m, 2·67 m, 1·60 m
57. 240 Hz

□

CHAPTER 16

SOUND WAVES

16.1 THE NATURE AND PROPAGATION OF SOUND WAVES

Sound is produced in a material medium by a vibrating source. As the vibrating source moves forward, it compresses the medium past it, increasing the density locally. This part of the medium compresses the layer next to it by collisions. The compression travels in the medium at a speed which depends on the elastic and inertia properties of the medium. As the source moves back, it drags the medium and produces a rarefaction in the layer. The layer next to it is then dragged back and, thus, the rarefaction pulse passes forward. In this way, compression and rarefaction pulses are produced which travel in the medium.

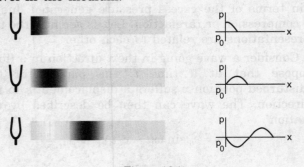

Figure 16.1

Figure (16.1) describes a typical case of propagation of sound waves. A tuning fork is vibrated in air. The prongs vibrate in simple harmonic motion. When the fork moves towards right, the layer next to it is compressed and consequently, the density is increased. The increase in density and hence, in pressure, is related to the velocity of the prong. The compression so produced travels in air towards right at the wave speed v. The velocity of the prong changes during the forward motion, being maximum at the mean position and zero at the extreme end. A compression wave pulse of length $vT/2$ is thus produced during the half period $T/2$ of forward motion. The prong now returns towards left and drags the air with it. The density and the

pressure of the layer close to it go below the normal level, a rarefaction pulse is thus produced. During this half period of backward motion of the prong, a rarefaction pulse of length $vT/2$ is produced. As the prong continues executing its simple harmonic motion, a series of alternate compression and rarefaction pulses are produced which travel down the air.

As the prong vibrates in simple harmonic motion, the pressure variations in the layer close to the prong also change in a simple harmonic fashion. The increase in pressure above its normal value may, therefore, be written as

$$\delta P = P - P_0 = \delta P_0 \sin \omega t,$$

where δP_0 is the maximum increase in pressure above its normal value. As this disturbance travels towards right with the speed v (the wave speed and not the particle speed), the equation for the excess pressure at any point x at any time t is given by

$$\delta P = \delta P_0 \sin \omega(t - x/v).$$

This is the equation of a wave travelling in x-direction with velocity v. The excess pressure oscillates between $+\delta P_0$ and $-\delta P_0$. The frequency of this wave is $\nu = \omega/(2\pi)$ and is equal to the frequency of vibration of the source. Henceforth, we shall use the symbol p for the excess pressure developed above the equilibrium pressure and p_0 for the maximum change in pressure. The wave equation is then

$$p = p_0 \sin \omega(t - x/v). \qquad \dots (16.1)$$

Sound waves constitute alternate compression and rarefaction pulses travelling in the medium. However, sound is audible only if the frequency of alteration of pressure is between 20 Hz to 20,000 Hz. These limits are subjective and may vary slightly from person to person. An average human ear is not able to detect disturbance in the medium if the frequency is outside this range. Electronic detectors can detect waves of lower and higher frequencies as well. A dog can hear sound of frequency up to about 50 kHz and a bat up to about 100 kHz. The waves with frequency below the audible range are called *infrasonic* waves and the waves with frequency above the audible range are called *ultrasonic*.

Example 16.1

A wave of wavelength 0·60 cm is produced in air and it travels at a speed of 300 m s^{-1}. Will it be audible ?

Solution : From the relation $v = \nu\,\lambda$, the frequency of the wave is

$$\nu = \frac{v}{\lambda} = \frac{300 \text{ m s}^{-1}}{0\cdot60 \times 10^{-2} \text{ m}} = 50000 \text{ Hz}.$$

This is much above the audible range. It is an ultrasonic wave and will not be audible.

The disturbance produced by a source of sound is not always a sine wave. A pure sine wave has a unique frequency but a disturbance of other waveform may have many frequency components in it. For example, when we clap our hands, a pulse of disturbance is created which travels in the air. This pulse does not have the shape of a sine wave. However, it can be obtained by superposition of a large number of sine waves of different frequencies and amplitudes. We then say that the clapping sound has all these frequency components in it.

The compression and rarefaction in a sound wave is caused due to the back and forth motion of the particles of the medium. This motion is along the direction of propagation of sound and hence the sound waves are longitudinal.

All directions, perpendicular to the direction of propagation, are equivalent and hence, a sound wave cannot be polarized. If we make a slit on a cardboard and place it in the path of the sound, rotating the cardboard in its plane will produce no effect on the intensity of sound on the other side.

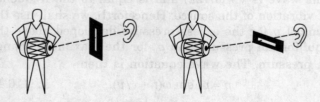

Figure 16.2

Wavefront

The sound produced at some point by a vibrating source travels in all directions in the medium if the medium is extended. The sound waves are, in general, three dimensional waves. For a small source, we have spherical layers of the medium on which the pressure at various elements have the same phase at a given instant. The compression, produced by the source at

say $t = 0$, reaches the spherical surface of radius $r = vt$ at time t and the pressure at all the points on this sphere is maximum at this instant. A half time-period later, the pressure at all the points on this sphere is reduced to minimum. The surface through the points, having the same phase of disturbance, is called a *wavefront*. For a homogeneous and isotropic medium, the wavefronts are normal to the direction of propagation.

For a point source placed in a homogeneous and isotropic medium, the wavefronts are spherical and the wave is called a *spherical wave*. If sound is produced by vibrating a large plane sheet, the disturbance produced in front of the sheet will have the same phase on a plane parallel to the sheet. The wavefronts are then planes (neglecting the end effects) and the direction of propagation is perpendicular to these planes. Such waves are called *plane waves*. The wavefront can have several other shapes. In this chapter, we shall mostly consider sound waves travelling in a fixed direction, i.e., plane waves. However, most of the results will be applicable to other waves also.

16.2 DISPLACEMENT WAVE AND PRESSURE WAVE

A longitudinal wave in a fluid (liquid or gas) can be described either in terms of the longitudinal displacement suffered by the particles of the medium or in terms of the excess pressure generated due to the compression or rarefaction. Let us see how the two representations are related to each other.

Consider a wave going in the x-direction in a fluid. Suppose that at a time t, the particle at the undisturbed position x suffers a displacement s in the x-direction. The wave can then be described by the equation

$$s = s_0 \sin \omega(t - x/v). \qquad \ldots \text{(i)}$$

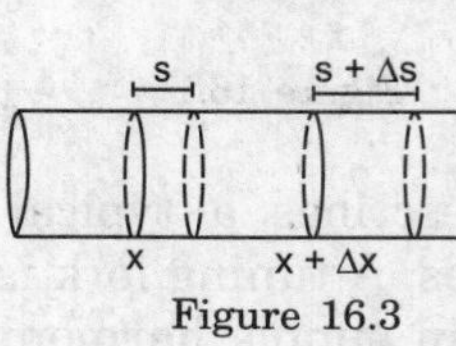

Figure 16.3

Consider the element of the material which is contained within x and $x + \Delta x$ (figure 16.3) in the undisturbed state. Considering a cross-sectional area A, the volume of the element in the undisturbed state is $A\,\Delta x$ and its mass is $\rho\,A\,\Delta x$. As the wave passes, the ends at x and $x + \Delta x$ are displaced by amounts s and $s + \Delta s$ according to equation (i) above. The increase in volume of this element at time t is

$$\Delta V = A\,\Delta s$$
$$= A\,s_0(-\omega/v)\cos\omega(t - x/v)\Delta x,$$

where Δs has been obtained by differentiating equation (i) with respect to x. The element is, therefore, under a volume strain.

$$\frac{\Delta V}{V} = \frac{-A s_0 \omega \cos \omega(t - x/v)\Delta x}{vA \, \Delta x}$$

$$= \frac{-s_0 \omega}{v} \cos \omega(t - x/v).$$

The corresponding stress, i.e., the excess pressure developed in the element at x at time t is,

$$p = B\left(\frac{-\Delta V}{V}\right),$$

where B is the bulk modulus of the material. Thus,

$$p = B \frac{s_0 \omega}{v} \cos \omega(t - x/v). \qquad \dots \text{ (ii)}$$

Comparing with (i), we see that the pressure amplitude p_0 and the displacement amplitude s_0 are related as

$$p_0 = \frac{B \omega}{v} s_0 = Bks_0, \qquad \dots \text{ (16.2)}$$

where k is the wave number. Also, we see from (i) and (ii) that the pressure wave differs in phase by $\pi/2$ from the displacement wave. The pressure maxima occur where the displacement is zero and displacement maxima occur where the pressure is at its normal level.

The fact that, displacement is zero where the pressure change is maximum and vice versa, puts the two descriptions on different footings. The human ear or an electronic detector responds to the change in pressure and not to the displacement in a straight forward way. Suppose two audio speakers are driven by the same amplifier and are placed facing each other (figure 16.4). A detector is placed midway between them.

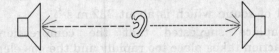

Figure 16.4

The displacement of the air particles near the detector will be zero as the two sources drive these particles in opposite directions. However, both send compression waves and rarefaction waves together. As a result, pressure increases at the detector simultaneously due to both sources. Accordingly, the pressure amplitude will be doubled, although the displacement remains zero here. A detector detects maximum intensity in such a condition. Thus, the description in terms of pressure wave is more appropriate than the description in terms of the displacement wave as far as sound properties are concerned.

Example 16.2

A sound wave of wavelength 40 cm travels in air. If the difference between the maximum and minimum pressures at a given point is $1.0 \times 10^{-3} \text{ N m}^{-2}$, find the amplitude of vibration of the particles of the medium. The bulk modulus of air is $1.4 \times 10^5 \text{ N m}^{-2}$.

Solution : The pressure amplitude is

$$p_0 = \frac{1.0 \times 10^{-3} \text{ N m}^{-2}}{2} = 0.5 \times 10^{-3} \text{ N m}^{-2}.$$

The displacement amplitude s_0 is given by

$$p_0 = B k s_0$$

or, $$s_0 = \frac{p_0}{B k} = \frac{p_0 \lambda}{2 \pi B}$$

$$= \frac{0.5 \times 10^{-3} \text{ N m}^{-2} \times (40 \times 10^{-2} \text{ m})}{2 \times 3.14 \times 1.4 \times 10^5 \text{ N m}^{-2}}$$

$$= 2.2 \times 10^{-10} \text{ m}.$$

16.3 SPEED OF A SOUND WAVE IN A MATERIAL MEDIUM

Consider again a sound wave going in x-direction in a fluid whose particles are displaced according to the equation

$$s = s_0 \sin \omega(t - x/v). \qquad \dots \text{ (i)}$$

The pressure varies according to the equation

$$p = \frac{B s_0 \omega}{v} \cos \omega(t - x/v). \qquad \dots \text{ (ii)}$$

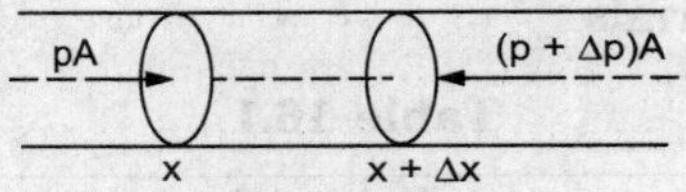

Figure 16.5

Consider the element of the fluid which is contained between the positions x and $x + \Delta x$ in the undisturbed state (figure 16.5). The excess pressure at time t at the end x is p and at $x + \Delta x$ it is $p + \Delta p$. Taking a cross-sectional area A, the force on the element from the left is pA and from the right it is $(p + \Delta p)A$. The resultant force on the element at time t is

$$\Delta F = Ap - A(p + \Delta p) = -A \, \Delta p$$

$$= -A \frac{B s_0 \omega}{v} (\omega/v) \Delta x \sin \omega(t - x/v)$$

$$= -A \frac{B s_0 \omega^2}{v^2} \sin \omega(t - x/v) \Delta x.$$

The change in pressure Δp between x and $x + \Delta x$ is obtained by differentiating equation (ii) with respect to x. If ρ is the normal density of the fluid, the mass of the element considered is $\rho\,A\,\Delta x$. Using Newton's second law of motion, the acceleration of the element is given by

$$a = \frac{\Delta F}{\rho\,A\,\Delta x} = -\frac{B\,s_0\,\omega^2}{\rho\,v^2}\sin\omega(t - x/v). \quad \text{... (iii)}$$

However, the acceleration can also be obtained from equation (i). It is

$$a = \frac{\partial^2 s}{\partial t^2}$$

or, $\qquad a = -\omega^2 s_0 \sin\omega(t - x/v). \quad \text{... (iv)}$

Comparing (iii) and (iv)

$$\frac{B\,s_0\,\omega^2}{\rho\,v^2} = \omega^2 s_0$$

or, $\qquad v = \sqrt{B/\rho}. \quad \text{... (16.3)}$

We see that the velocity of a longitudinal wave in a medium depends on its elastic properties and inertia properties as was the case with the waves on a string.

Sound Waves in Solids

Sound waves can travel in solids just like they can travel in fluids. The speed of longitudinal sound waves in a solid rod can be shown to be

$$v = \sqrt{Y/\rho} \quad \text{... (16.4)}$$

where Y is the Young modulus of the solid and ρ its density. For extended solids, the speed is a more complicated function of bulk modulus and shear modulus. Table (16.1) gives the speed of sound in some common materials.

Table 16.1

Medium	Speed m s^{-1}	Medium	Speed m s^{-1}
Air (dry 0°C)	332	Copper	3810
Hydrogen	1330	Aluminium	5000
Water	1486	Steel	5200

16.4 SPEED OF SOUND IN A GAS : NEWTON'S FORMULA AND LAPLACE'S CORRECTION

The speed of sound in a gas can be expressed in terms of its pressure and density. The derivation uses some of the properties of gases that we shall study in another chapter. We summarise these properties below.

(a) For a given mass of an ideal gas, the pressure, volume and the temperature are related as $\frac{PV}{T} = $ constant. If the temperature remains constant

(called an isothermal process), the pressure and the volume of a given mass of a gas satisfy $PV = $ constant.

Here T is the absolute temperature of the gas. This is known as *Boyle's law*.

(b) If no heat is supplied to a given mass of a gas (called an adiabatic process), its pressure and volume satisfy

$$PV^\gamma = \text{constant};$$

where γ is a constant for the given gas. It is, in fact, the ratio C_p/C_V of two specific heat capacities of the gas.

Newton suggested a theoretical expression for the velocity of sound wave in a gaseous medium. He assumed that when a sound wave propagates through a gas, the temperature variations in the layers of compression and rarefaction are negligible. The logic perhaps was that the layers are in contact with wider mass of the gas so that by exchanging heat with the surrounding the temperature of the layer will remain equal to that of the surrounding. Hence, the conditions are isothermal and Boyle's law will be applicable.

Thus, $\qquad PV = \text{constant}$

or, $\qquad P\Delta V + V\Delta P = 0$

or, $\qquad B = -\frac{\Delta P}{\Delta V/V} = P. \quad \text{... (i)}$

Using this result in equation (16.3), the speed of sound in the gas is given by

$$v = \sqrt{P/\rho}. \quad \text{... (16.5)}$$

The density of air at temperature 0°C and pressure 76 cm of mercury column is $\rho = 1{\cdot}293$ kg m^{-3}. This temperature and pressure is called standard temperature and pressure and is written as STP. According to equation (16.5), the speed of sound in air at this temperature and pressure should be 280 m s^{-1}. This value is somewhat smaller than the measured speed of sound which is about 332 m s^{-1}.

Laplace suggested that the compression or rarefaction takes place too rapidly and the gas element being compressed or rarefied does not get enough time to exchange heat with the surroundings. Thus, it is an adiabatic process and one should use the equation

$$PV^\gamma = \text{constant}.$$

Taking logarithms,

$$\ln P + \gamma \ln V = \text{constant}.$$

Taking differentials,

$$\frac{\Delta P}{P} + \gamma\frac{\Delta V}{V} = 0$$

or, $\qquad B = -\frac{\Delta P}{\Delta V/V} = \gamma P$

Thus, the speed of sound is $v = \sqrt{\dfrac{\gamma P}{\rho}}$ ... (16.6)

For air, $\gamma = 1\cdot4$ and putting values of P and ρ as before, equation (16.6) gives the speed of sound in air at STP to be 332 m s^{-1} which is quite close to the observed value.

16.5 EFFECT OF PRESSURE, TEMPERATURE AND HUMIDITY ON THE SPEED OF SOUND IN AIR

We have stated that for an ideal gas, the pressure, volume and temperature of a given mass satisfy

$$\frac{PV}{T} = \text{constant.}$$

As the density of a given mass is inversely proportional to its volume, the above equation may also be written as

$$\frac{P}{\rho} = cT,$$

where c is a constant. The speed of sound is

$$v = \sqrt{\frac{\gamma P}{\rho}} = \sqrt{\gamma cT}. \quad ... (16.7)$$

Thus, if pressure is changed but the temperature is kept constant, the density varies proportionally and P/ρ remains constant. The speed of sound is not affected by the change in pressure provided the temperature is kept constant.

If the temperature of air is changed then the speed of sound is also changed.

From equation (16.7),

$$v \propto \sqrt{T}.$$

At STP, the temperature is 0°C or 273 K. If the speed of sound at 0°C is v_0, its value at the room temperature T (in kelvin) will satisfy

$$\frac{v}{v_0} = \sqrt{\frac{T}{273}} = \sqrt{\frac{273 + t}{273}},$$

where t is the temperature in °C. This may be approximated as

$$\frac{v}{v_0} = \left(1 + \frac{t}{273}\right)^{\frac{1}{2}} \cong 1 + \frac{t}{546}$$

or, $\qquad v = v_0\left(1 + \dfrac{t}{546}\right).$

The density of water vapour is less than dry air at the same pressure. Thus, the density of moist air is less than that of dry air. As a result, the speed of sound increases with increasing humidity.

16.6 INTENSITY OF SOUND WAVES

As a wave travels in a medium, energy is transported from one part of the space to another part. The intensity of a sound wave is defined as the average energy crossing a unit cross-sectional area perpendicular to the direction of propagation of the wave in unit time. It may also be stated as the average power transmitted across a unit cross-sectional area perpendicular to the direction of propagation.

The loudness of sound that we feel is mainly related to the intensity of sound. It also depends on the frequency to some extent.

Consider again a sound wave travelling along the x-direction. Let the equations for the displacement of the particles and the excess pressure developed by the wave be given by

$$s = s_0 \sin \omega(t - x/v)$$

and $\qquad p = p_0 \cos \omega(t - x/v) \qquad$ ... (i)

where $\qquad p_0 = \dfrac{B\omega s_0}{v}.$

Consider a cross section of area A perpendicular to the x-direction. The medium to the left to it exerts a force pA on the medium to the right along the X-axis. The points of application of this force move longitudinally, that is along the force, with a speed $\dfrac{\partial s}{\partial t}$. Thus, the power W, transmitted by the wave from left to right across the cross section considered, is

$$W = (pA)\frac{\partial s}{\partial t}.$$

By (i),

$$W = A\, p_0 \cos \omega(t - x/v)\, \omega s_0 \cos \omega(t - x/v)$$

$$= \frac{A\,\omega^2 s_0^2 B}{v}\cos^2 \omega(t - x/v).$$

The average of $\cos^2 \omega(t - x/v)$ over a complete cycle or over a long time is 1/2. The intensity I, which is equal to the average power transmitted across unit cross-sectional area is thus,

$$I = \frac{1}{2}\frac{\omega^2 s_0^2 B}{v} = \frac{2\pi^2 B}{v}s_0^2\, v^2.$$

Using equation (16.2),

$$I = \frac{p_0^2\, v}{2B}. \qquad ... (16.8)$$

As $B = \rho v^2$, the intensity can also be written as

$$I = \frac{v}{2\rho v^2}p_0^2 = \frac{p_0^2}{2\rho v}. \qquad ... (16.9)$$

We see that the intensity is proportional to the square of the pressure amplitude p_0.

Example 16.3

The pressure amplitude in a sound wave from a radio receiver is $2 \cdot 0 \times 10^{-2} \, N \, m^{-2}$ and the intensity at a point is $5 \cdot 0 \times 10^{-7} \, W \, m^{-2}$. If by turning the "volume" knob the pressure amplitude is increased to $2 \cdot 5 \times 10^{-2} \, N \, m^{-2}$, evaluate the intensity.

Solution : The intensity is proportional to the square of the pressure amplitude.

Thus, $\dfrac{I'}{I} = \left(\dfrac{p'_0}{p_0}\right)^2$

or, $I' = \left(\dfrac{p'_0}{p_0}\right)^2 I = \left(\dfrac{2 \cdot 5}{2 \cdot 0}\right)^2 \times 5 \cdot 0 \times 10^{-7} \, W \, m^{-2}$

$= 7 \cdot 8 \times 10^{-7} \, W \, m^{-2}.$

16.7 APPEARANCE OF SOUND TO HUMAN EAR

The appearance of sound to a human ear is characterised by three parameters (a) *pitch* (b) *loudness* and (c) *quality*. All the three are subjective description of sound though they are related to objectively defined quantities. Pitch is related to frequency, loudness is related to intensity and quality is related to the waveform of the sound wave.

Pitch and Frequency

Pitch of a sound is that sensation by which we differentiate a buffallo voice, a male voice and a female voice. We say that a buffallo voice is of low pitch, a male voice has higher pitch and a female voice has (generally) still higher pitch. This sensation primarily depends on the dominant frequency present in the sound. Higher the frequency, higher will be the pitch and vice versa. The dominant frequency of a buffallo voice is smaller than that of a male voice which in turn is smaller than that of a female voice.

Loudness and Intensity

The loudness that we sense is related to the intensity of sound though it is not directly proportional to it. Our perception of loudness is better correlated with the *sound level* measured in decibels (abbreviated as dB) and defined as follows.

$$\beta = 10 \log_{10}\left(\dfrac{I}{I_0}\right), \qquad \dots \ (16.10)$$

where I is the intensity of the sound and I_0 is a constant reference intensity $10^{-12} \, W \, m^{-2}$. The reference intensity represents roughly the minimum intensity that is just audible at intermediate frequencies. For $I = I_0$, the sound level $\beta = 0$. Table (16.2) shows the approximate sound levels of some of the sounds commonly encountered.

Table 16.2 : *Sound Levels*

Minimum audible sound	≈ 0 dB
Whispering (at 1 m)	10 dB
Normal talk (at 1 m)	60 dB
Maximum tolerable sound	120 dB

Example 16.4

If the intensity is increased by a factor of 20, by how many decibels is the sound level increased ?

Solution : Let the initial intensity be I and the sound level be β_1. When the intensity is increased to $20\,I$, the level increases to β_2.

Then $\beta_1 = 10 \log (I/I_0)$

and $\beta_2 = 10 \log (20\,I/I_0)$.

Thus, $\beta_2 - \beta_1 = 10 \log (20\,I/I)$

$= 10 \log 20$

$= 13 \text{ dB}.$

Quality and Waveform

A sound generated by a source may contain a number of frequency components in it. Different frequency components have different amplitudes and superposition of them results in the actual waveform. The appearance of sound depends on this waveform apart from the dominant frequency and intensity. Figure (16.6) shows waveforms for a tuning fork, a clarinet and a cornet playing the same note (fundamental frequency = 440 Hz) with equal loudness.

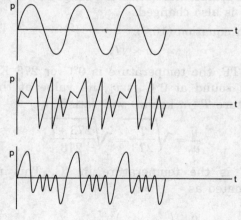

Figure 16.6

We differentiate between the sound from a tabla and that from a mridang by saying that they have different *quality*. A musical sound has certain well-defined frequencies which have considerable amplitude. These frequencies are generally harmonics of a fundamental frequency. Such a sound is particularly pleasant to the ear. On the other hand, a noise has frequencies that do not bear any well-defined relationship among themselves.

16.8 INTERFERENCE OF SOUND WAVES

The principle of superposition introduced in the previous chapter is valid for sound waves as well. If two or more waves pass through the same region of a medium, the resultant disturbance is equal to the sum of the disturbances produced by individual waves. Depending on the phase difference, the waves can interfere constructively or destructively leading to a corresponding increase or decrease in the resultant intensity. While discussing the interference of two sound waves, it is advised that the waves be expressed in terms of pressure change. The resultant change in pressure is the algebraic sum of the changes in pressure due to the individual waves. Thus, one should not add the displacement vectors so as to obtain the resultant displacement wave.

Figure (16.7) shows two tuning forks S_1 and S_2, placed side by side, which vibrate with equal frequency and equal amplitude. The point P is situated at a distance x from S_1 and $x + \Delta x$ from S_2.

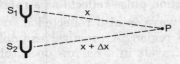

Figure 16.7

The forks may be set into vibration with a phase difference δ_0. In case of tuning forks, the phase difference δ_0 remains constant in time. Two sources whose phase difference remains constant in time are called *coherent sources*. If there were two drum beaters beating the drums independently, the sources would have been *incoherent*.

Suppose the two forks are vibrating in phase so that $\delta_0 = 0$. Also, let p_{01} and p_{02} be the amplitudes of the waves from S_1 and S_2 respectively. Let us examine the resultant change in pressure at a point P. The pressure change at P due to the two waves are described by

$$p_1 = p_{01} \sin(kx - \omega t)$$
$$p_2 = p_{02} \sin[k(x + \Delta x) - \omega t]$$
$$= p_{02} \sin[(kx - \omega t) + \delta],$$

where $\qquad \delta = k\, \Delta x = \dfrac{2\pi\, \Delta x}{\lambda} \qquad$ ... (16.11)

is the phase difference between the two waves reaching P. These equations are identical to those discussed in chapter 15, section 15.7. The resultant wave at P is given by

$$p = p_0 \sin[(kx - \omega t) + \varepsilon],$$

where $\qquad p_0^2 = p_{01}^2 + p_{02}^2 + 2\, p_{01}\, p_{02}\, \cos\delta,$

and $\qquad \tan\varepsilon = \dfrac{p_{02} \sin\delta}{p_{01} + p_{02} \cos\delta}.$

The resultant amplitude is maximum when $\delta = 2n\pi$ and is minimum when $\delta = (2n + 1)\,\pi$ where n is an integer. These are correspondingly the conditions for constructive and destructive interference

$$\left. \begin{array}{l} \delta = 2n\pi \qquad \text{constructive interference} \\ \delta = (2n + 1)\,\pi \;\; \text{destructive interference.} \end{array} \right\} \;\text{... (16.12)}$$

Using equation (16.11), i.e., $\delta = \dfrac{2\pi}{\lambda}\, \Delta x$, these conditions may be written in terms of the path difference as

$$\left. \begin{array}{l} \Delta x = n\lambda \qquad\qquad \text{(constructive)} \\ \Delta x = (n + 1/2)\,\lambda \qquad \text{(destructive).} \end{array} \right\} \;\text{... (16.13)}$$

At constructive interference,

$$p_0 = p_{01} + p_{02}$$

and at destructive interference,

$$p_0 = |\, p_{01} - p_{02}\,|.$$

Suppose $p_{01} = p_{02}$ and $\Delta x = \lambda/2$. The resultant pressure amplitude of the disturbance is zero and no sound is detected at such a point P. If $\Delta x = \lambda$, the amplitude is doubled. The intensity of a wave is proportional to the square of the amplitude and hence, at the points of constructive interference, the resultant intensity of sound is four times the intensity due to an individual source. This is a characteristic property of wave motion. Two sources can cancel the effects of each other or they can reinforce the effect.

If the sources have an initial phase difference δ_0 between them, the waves reaching P at time t are represented by

$$p = p_{01} \sin[kx - \omega t]$$

and $\qquad p = p_{02} \sin[k(x + \Delta x) - \omega t + \delta_0].$

The phase difference between these waves is

$$\delta = \delta_0 + k\, \Delta x = \delta_0 + \dfrac{2\pi\, \Delta x}{\lambda}.$$

The interference maxima and minima occur according to equation (16.12).

For incoherent sources, δ_0 is not constant and varies rapidly and randomly with time. At any point P, sometimes constructive and sometimes destructive interference takes place. If the intensity due to each source is I, the resultant intensity rapidly and randomly changes between zero and $4I$ so that the average observable intensity is $2I$. No interference effect is, therefore, observed. For observable interference, the sources must be coherent.

One way to obtain a pair of coherent sources is to obtain two sound waves from the same source by dividing the original wave along two different paths and then combining them. The two waves then differ in phase only because of different paths travelled.

A popular demonstration of interference of sound is given by the Quinke's apparatus figure (16.8).

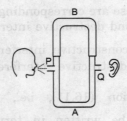

Figure 16.8

Sound produced near the end P travels down in P and is divided in two parts, one going through the tube A and the other through B. They recombine and the resultant sound moves along Q to reach the listener (which may be an electronic detector to do a quantitative analysis). The tube B can be slid in and out to change the path length of one of the waves. If the sound is produced at a unique frequency (a tuning fork may be used for it), the wavelength $\lambda\ (= v/\nu)$ has a single value. The intensity at Q will be a maximum or a minimum depending on whether the difference in path lengths is an integral multiple of λ or a half integral multiple. Thus, when the tube B is slowly pulled out the intensity at Q oscillates.

Phase Difference and Path Difference

From equation (16.11) we see that if a wave travels an extra distance Δx with respect to the other wave, a phase difference

$$\delta = \frac{\omega}{v}\,\Delta x = \frac{2\pi\,\Delta x}{\lambda}$$

is introduced between them.

Note carefully that this is the phase difference introduced due to the different path lengths covered by the waves from their origin. Any initial difference of phase that may exist between the sources must be added to it so as to get the actual phase difference.

Example 16.5 ─────────────────

Two sound waves, originating from the same source, travel along different paths in air and then meet at a point. If the source vibrates at a frequency of 1·0 kHz and one path is 83 cm longer than the other, what will be the nature of interference ? The speed of sound in air is 332 m s⁻¹.

Solution : The wavelength of sound wave is $\lambda = \dfrac{v}{\nu}$

$$= \frac{332 \text{ m s}^{-1}}{1\cdot 0 \times 10^{3} \text{ Hz}} = 0\cdot 332 \text{ m}.$$

The phase difference between the waves arriving at the point of observation is

$$\delta = \frac{2\pi}{\lambda}\,\Delta x = 2\pi \times \frac{0\cdot 83 \text{ m}}{0\cdot 332 \text{ m}} = 2\pi \times 2\cdot 5 = 5\pi.$$

As this is an odd multiple of π, the waves interfere destructively.

Reflection of Sound Waves

When there exists a discontinuity in the medium, the wave gets reflected. When a sound wave gets reflected from a rigid boundary, the particles at the boundary are unable to vibrate. Thus, a reflected wave is generated which interferes with the oncoming wave to produce zero displacement at the rigid boundary. At these points (zero displacement), the pressure variation is maximum. Thus, a reflected pressure wave has the same phase as the incident wave. That means, a compression pulse reflects as a compression pulse and a rarefaction pulse reflects as a rarefaction pulse.

A sound wave is also reflected if it encounters a low pressure region. A practical example is when a sound wave travels in a narrow open tube. When the wave reaches an open end, it gets reflected. The force on the particles there due to the outside air is quite small and hence, the particles vibrate with increased amplitude. As a result, the pressure there remains at the average value. Thus, the reflected pressure wave interferes destructively with the oncoming wave. There is a phase change of π in the pressure wave when it is reflected by an open end. That means, a compression pulse reflects as a rarefaction pulse and vice versa.

16.9 STANDING LONGITUDINAL WAVES AND VIBRATIONS OF AIR COLUMNS

If two longitudinal waves of the same frequency and amplitude travel through a medium in the opposite directions, standing waves are produced. If the equations of the two waves are written as

$$p_1 = p_0 \sin \omega(t - x/v)$$

and
$$p_2 = p_0 \sin \omega(t + x/v),$$

the resultant wave is by the principle of superposition,

$$\begin{aligned} p &= p_1 + p_2 \\ &= 2\,p_0 \cos(\omega x/v) \sin \omega t \\ &= 2\,p_0 \cos kx\, \sin \omega t. \end{aligned}$$

This equation is similar to the equation obtained in chapter 15 for standing waves on a string. Hence, all the characteristics of standing waves on a string are also present in longitudinal standing waves. At different points in the medium, the pressure amplitudes have different magnitudes. In particular, at certain points the pressure remains permanently at its average value, they are called the *pressure nodes* and midway between the nodes, there are *pressure antinodes* where the amplitude is maximum. The separation between two consecutive nodes or between two consecutive antinodes is $\lambda/2$. It may be noted that a pressure node is a displacement antinode and a pressure antinode is a displacement node.

Standing waves can be produced in air columns trapped in tubes of cylindrical shape. Organ pipes are such vibrating air columns.

(A) Closed Organ Pipe

A closed organ pipe is a cylindrical tube having an air column with one end closed. Sound waves are sent in by a source vibrating near the open end. An ingoing pressure wave gets reflected from the fixed end. This inverted wave is again reflected at the open end. After two reflections, it moves towards the fixed end and interferes with the new wave sent by the source in that direction. The twice reflected wave has travelled an extra distance of $2l$ causing a phase advance of $\frac{2\pi}{\lambda} \cdot 2l = \frac{4\pi l}{\lambda}$ with respect to the new wave sent in by the source. Also, the twice reflected wave suffered a phase change of π at the open end. The phase difference between the two waves is then $\delta = \frac{4\pi l}{\lambda} + \pi$. The waves interfere constructively if $\delta = 2n\pi$

or,
$$\frac{4\pi l}{\lambda} + \pi = 2n\pi$$

or,
$$l = (2n - 1)\frac{\lambda}{4}$$

where $n = 1, 2, 3, \ldots$. This may also be written as

$$l = (2n + 1)\frac{\lambda}{4}, \qquad \ldots (16.14)$$

where $n = 0, 1, 2, \ldots$.

In such a case, the amplitude goes on increasing until the energy dissipated through various damping effects equals the fresh input of energy from the source. Such waves exist in both the directions and they interfere to give standing waves of large amplitudes in the tube. The fixed end is always a pressure antinode (or displacement node) and the open end is a pressure node (or displacement antinode). In fact, the pressure node is not exactly at the open end because the air outside does exert some force on the air in the tube. We shall neglect this end correction for the time being.

The condition for having standing waves in a closed organ pipe is given by equation (16.14),

$$l = (2n + 1)\frac{\lambda}{4}.$$

The frequency ν is thus given by

$$\nu = \frac{v}{\lambda} = (2n + 1)\frac{v}{4l}. \qquad \ldots (16.15)$$

We see that there are certain discrete frequencies with which standing waves can be set up in a closed organ pipe. These frequencies are called *natural frequencies, normal frequencies or resonant frequencies.*

Figure (16.9) shows the variation of excess pressure and displacement of particles in a closed organ pipe for the first three resonant frequencies.

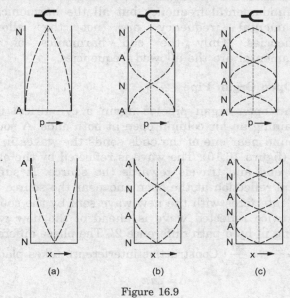

Figure 16.9

The minimum allowed frequency is obtained by putting $n = 0$ in equation (16.15). This is called the fundamental frequency ν_0 of the tube. We have

$$\nu_0 = \frac{v}{4l}. \qquad \ldots (16.16)$$

By equation (16.14), $l = \lambda/4$ in this case. A pressure antinode is formed at the closed end and a node is formed at the open end. There are no other nodes or antinodes in between. The air column is said to vibrate in its fundamental mode (figure 16.9a).

Putting $n = 1$ in equation (16.15), we get the first overtone frequency

$$\nu_1 = \frac{3v}{4l} = 3\,\nu_0.$$

By equation (16.14), the length of the tube in this mode is

$$l = 3\lambda/4.$$

In the first overtone mode of vibration (figure 16.9b), there is an antinode and a node in the air column apart from the ends.

In the second overtone, there are two nodes and two antinodes in the column apart from the ends (figure 16.10c). In this mode, $l = 5\lambda/4$ and the frequency is

$$\nu_2 = \frac{5v}{4l} = 5\nu_0.$$

The higher overtones can be described in a similar way.

Thus, an air column of length l fixed at one end can vibrate with frequencies $(2n+1)\nu_0$ where $\nu_0 = \frac{v}{4l}$ and n is an integer. We see that all the overtone frequencies are harmonics (i.e., integral multiple) of the fundamental frequency but all the harmonics of fundamental frequency are not the allowed frequencies. Only the odd harmonics of the fundamental are the allowed frequencies.

(B) Open Organ Pipe

An open organ pipe is again a cylindrical tube containing an air column open at both ends. A source of sound near one of the ends sends the waves in the pipe (figure 16.10). The wave is reflected by the other open end and travels towards the source. It suffers second reflection at the open end near the source and then interferes with the new wave sent by the source. The twice reflected wave is ahead of the new wave coming in by a path difference $2l$. The phase difference is $\delta = \frac{2\pi}{\lambda} 2l = \frac{4\pi l}{\lambda}$. Constructive interference takes place if

$$\delta = 2n\pi$$
$$l = n\lambda/2 \qquad\qquad \ldots \ (16.17)$$

where $n = 1, 2, 3, \ldots$.

The amplitude then keeps on growing. Waves moving in both the directions with large amplitudes are established and finally standing waves are set up. As already discussed, in this case the energy lost by various damping effects equals the energy input from the source. The frequencies with which a standing wave can be set up in an open organ pipe are

$$\nu = \frac{v}{\lambda} = \frac{nv}{2l}. \qquad\qquad \ldots \ (16.18)$$

Figure (16.10) shows the variation of excess pressure and displacement in the open organ pipe for the first three resonant frequencies. The minimum frequency ν_0 is obtained by putting $n = 1$ in equation (16.18). Thus,

$$\nu_0 = \frac{v}{2l}. \qquad\qquad \ldots \ (16.19)$$

This corresponds to the fundamental mode of vibration. By equation (16.18), $l = \lambda/2$ in the fundamental mode of vibration (figure 16.10a).

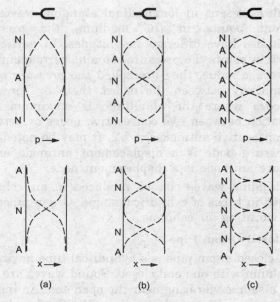

(a)   (b)   (c)

Figure 16.10

As the air at both ends is free to vibrate (neglecting the effect of the pressure of the air outside the pipe), pressure nodes are formed at these points. There is an antinode in between these nodes.

If the source vibrates at the frequency $\nu_0 = \frac{v}{2l}$, it will set up the column in the fundamental mode of vibration.

Putting $n = 2$ in equation (16.18), we get the frequency of the first overtone mode as

$$\nu_1 = 2\,\frac{v}{2l} = 2\nu_0.$$

The length of the tube is, by equation (16.17), $l = \lambda$. There are two pressure antinodes and one node apart from the nodes at the two ends. In the nth overtone, there are $(n+1)$ pressure antinodes. The frequency of the nth overtone is given by

$$\nu_n = \frac{nv}{2l} = n\nu_0.$$

The overtone frequencies are $\frac{2v}{2l}$, $\frac{3v}{2l}$, $\cdots$, etc. All the overtone frequencies are harmonics of the fundamental and all the harmonics of the fundamental are allowed overtone frequencies. There are no missing harmonics in an open organ pipe. The quality of sound from an open organ pipe is, therefore, richer than that from a closed organ pipe in which all the even harmonics of the fundamental are missing.

Example 16.6

An air column is constructed by fitting a movable piston in a long cylindrical tube. Longitudinal waves are sent in the tube by a tuning fork of frequency 416 Hz. How far from the open end should the piston be so that the air column in the tube may vibrate in its first overtone ? Speed of sound in air is 333 m s⁻¹.

Solution : The piston provides the closed end of the column and an antinode of pressure is formed there. At the open end, a pressure node is formed. In the first overtone there is one more node and an antinode in the column as shown in figure (16.11). The length of the tube should then be $3\lambda/4$.

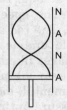

Figure 16.11

The wavelength is $\lambda = \dfrac{v}{\nu} = \dfrac{333 \text{ m s}^{-1}}{416 \text{ s}^{-1}} = 0{\cdot}800$ m

Thus, the length of the tube is

$$\frac{3\lambda}{4} = \frac{3 \times 0{\cdot}800 \text{ m}}{4} = 60{\cdot}0 \text{ cm}.$$

16.10 DETERMINATION OF SPEED OF SOUND IN AIR

(a) Resonance Column Method

Figure (16.12) shows schematically the diagram of a simple apparatus used in laboratories to measure the speed of sound in air. A long cylindrical glass tube (say about 1 m) is fixed on a vertical wooden frame. It is also called a resonance tube. A rubber tube connects the lower end of this glass tube to a vessel which can slide vertically on the same wooden frame. A meter scale is fitted parallel to and close to the glass tube.

Figure 16.12

The vessel contains water which also goes in the resonance tube through the rubber tube. The level of water in the resonance tube is same as that in the vessel. Thus, by sliding the vessel up and down, one can change the water level in the resonance tube.

A tuning fork (frequency 256 Hz if the tube is 1 m long) is vibrated by hitting it on a rubber pad and is held near the open end of the tube in such a way that the prongs vibrate parallel to the length of the tube. Longitudinal waves are then sent in the tube.

The water level in the tube is initially kept high. The tuning fork is vibrated and kept close to the open end, and the loudness of sound coming from the tube is estimated. The vessel is brought down a little to decrease the water level in the resonance tube. The tuning fork is again vibrated, kept close to the open end and the loudness of the sound coming from the tube is estimated. The process is repeated until the water level corresponding to the maximum loudness is located. Fine adjustments of water level are made to locate accurately the level corresponding to the maximum loudness. The length of the air column is read on the scale attached. In this case, the air column vibrates in resonance with the tuning fork. The minimum length of the air column for which the resonance takes place corresponds to the fundamental mode of vibration. A pressure antinode is formed at the water surface (which is the closed end of the air column) and a pressure node is formed near the open end. In fact, the node is formed slightly above the open end (end correction) because of the air-pressure from outside.

Thus, for the first resonance the length l_1 of the air column in the resonance tube is given by

$$l_1 + d = \frac{\lambda}{4}, \qquad \text{... (i)}$$

where d is the end correction.

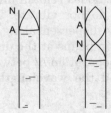

Figure 16.13

The length of the air column is increased to a little less than three times of l. The water level is adjusted so that the loudness of the sound coming from the tube becomes maximum again. The length of the air column is noted on the scale. In this second resonance the air column vibrates in the first overtone. There is one node and one antinode in between the ends of the column. The length l_2 of the column is given by

$$l_2 + d = 3\lambda/4. \qquad \text{... (ii)}$$

By (i) and (ii),

$$(l_2 - l_1) = \lambda/2, \quad \text{or,} \quad \lambda = 2(l_2 - l_1).$$

The frequency of the wave is same as the frequency of the tuning fork. Thus, the speed of sound in the air of the laboratory is

$$v = \nu\lambda = 2(l_2 - l_1)\,\nu. \qquad \ldots (16.20)$$

(b) Kundt's Tube Method of Determining the Speed of Sound in a Gas

The resonance column method described above can be used to find the speed of sound in air only, as the tube is open at the end to the atmosphere. In the Kundt's method, a gas is enclosed in a long cylindrical tube closed at both ends, one by a disc D and the other by a movable piston (figure 16.14). A metal rod is welded with the disc and is clamped exactly at the middle point. The length of the tube can be varied by moving the movable piston. Some powder is sprinkled inside the tube along its length.

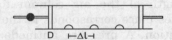

Figure 16.14

The rod is set into longitudinal vibrations electronically or by rubbing it with some rosined cloth or otherwise. If the length of the gas column is such that one of its resonant frequencies is equal to the frequency of the longitudinal vibration of the rod, standing waves are formed in the gas. The powder particles at the displacement antinodes fly apart due to the violent disturbance there, whereas the powder at the displacement nodes remain undisturbed because the particles here do not vibrate. Thus, the powder which was initially dispersed along the whole length of the tube collects in heaps at the displacement nodes. By measuring the separation Δl between the successive heaps, one can find the wavelength of sound in the enclosed gas

$$\lambda = 2\Delta l.$$

The length of the gas column is adjusted by moving the movable piston such that the gas resonates with the disc and the wavelength λ is obtained. If the frequency of the longitudinal vibration of the rod is ν, the speed of sound in the gas is given by

$$v = \nu\lambda = 2\,\Delta l\,\nu. \qquad \ldots (i)$$

If the frequency of the longitudinal vibrations in the rod is not known, the experiment is repeated with air filled in the tube. The length between the heaps of the powder, $\Delta l\,'$ is measured. The speed of sound in air is then

$$v' = 2\,\Delta l\,'\nu. \qquad \ldots (ii)$$

By (i) and (ii),

$$\frac{v}{v'} = \frac{\Delta l}{\Delta l\,'}$$

or,

$$v = v'\,\frac{\Delta l}{\Delta l\,'}.$$

Knowing the speed v' of sound in air, one can find the speed in the experimental gas.

Kundt's tube method can also be used to measure the speed of sound in a solid. Air at normal pressure is filled in the tube. The speed of sound in air is supposed to be known. The rod attached to the disc is clamped at the middle and is set into longitudinal vibration. The rod behaves like an open organ pipe as the two ends are free to vibrate. Assuming that it vibrates in its fundamental mode of vibration, the clamped point is a pressure antinode and the two ends of the rod are pressure nodes. Thus, the wavelength of sound in the rod is $\lambda = 2l$. If the powder piles up at successive distances Δl and the speed of sound in air is v_a, then $v_a = 2\,\Delta l\,\nu$. Also, if v be the speed of sound in the rod, $v = \nu\lambda = 2\,\nu l$.

Thus, $\qquad \dfrac{v}{v_a} = \dfrac{l}{\Delta l} \qquad$ or, $\qquad v = \dfrac{l}{\Delta l}\,v_a.$

As the speed v_a of sound in air is known, measurements of l and Δl give the speed of sound in the material of the rod.

16.11 BEATS

So far we have considered superposition of two sound waves of equal frequency. Let us now consider two sound waves having equal amplitudes and travelling in a medium in the same direction but having slightly different frequencies. The equations of the two waves are given by

$$p_1 = p_0 \sin \omega_1(t - x/v)$$
$$p_2 = p_0 \sin \omega_2(t - x/v),$$

where we have chosen the two waves to be in phase at $x = 0, t = 0$. The speed of sound wave does not depend on its frequency and hence, same wave speed v is used for both the equations. The angular frequencies ω_1 and ω_2 only slightly differ so that the difference $|\omega_1 - \omega_2|$ is small as compared to ω_1 or ω_2. By the principle of superposition, the resultant change in pressure is

$$p = p_1 + p_2$$
$$= p_0[\sin \omega_1(t - x/v) + \sin \omega_2(t - x/v)]$$
$$= 2\,p_0 \cos\left[\frac{\omega_1 - \omega_2}{2}\,(t - x/v)\right] \sin\left[\frac{\omega_1 + \omega_2}{2}\,(t - x/v)\right].$$

Writing $|\omega_1 - \omega_2| = \Delta\omega$, and $\dfrac{\omega_1 + \omega_2}{2} = \omega, \qquad \ldots (i)$

the resultant change in pressure is

$$p = 2 p_0 \cos \frac{\Delta\omega}{2} (t - x/v) \sin \omega(t - x/v) \quad \dots (16.21)$$

$$= A \sin \omega(t - x/v),$$

where $A = 2 p_0 \cos \frac{\Delta\omega}{2} (t - x/v).$ $\quad \dots (16.22)$

As $\omega \gg \frac{\Delta\omega}{2}$, the term A varies slowly with time as compared to $\sin \omega(t - x/v)$. Thus, we can interpret this equation by saying that the resultant disturbance is a wave of angular frequency $\omega = (\omega_1 + \omega_2)/2$ whose amplitude varies with time and is given by equation (16.22). As a negative value of amplitude has no meaning, the amplitude is, in fact, $| A |$.

Let us concentrate our attention to a particular position x and look for the pressure change there as a function of time. Equations (16.21) and (16.22) tell that the pressure oscillates back and forth with a frequency equal to the average frequency ω of the two waves but the amplitude of pressure variation itself changes periodically between $2p_0$ and zero.

Figure (16.15) shows the plots of

$$A = 2 p_0 \cos \frac{\Delta\omega}{2} (t - x/v), \quad B = \sin \omega(t - x/v)$$

and their product

$$p = 2 p_0 \cos \frac{\Delta\omega}{2} (t - x/v) \sin \omega(t - x/v)$$

as a function of time for a fixed x.

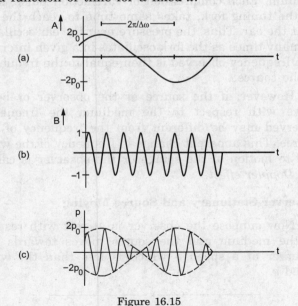

Figure 16.15

Variation of Intensity at a Point

The amplitude $| A |$ oscillates between 0 to $2 p_0$ with a frequency which is double of the frequency of A. This is because as A oscillates from $2 p_0$ to $-2 p_0$

(i.e., half the oscillation), the amplitude $| A |$ covers full oscillation from $2 p_0$ to zero to $2 p_0$ (figure 16.16).

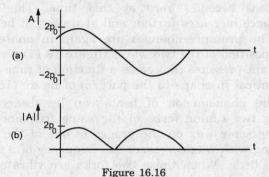

Figure 16.16

By equation (16.22), the frequency of variation of A is $\frac{\Delta\omega/2}{2\pi} = \frac{\Delta\omega}{4\pi}$. Thus, the frequency of amplitude variation is

$$\nu' = 2 \times \frac{\Delta\omega}{4\pi} = \frac{| \omega_1 - \omega_2 |}{2\pi} = | \nu_1 - \nu_2 |,$$

where ν_1 and ν_2 are the frequencies of the original waves. Notice that we have written this frequency as $| \nu_1 - \nu_2 |$. It is the difference between ν_1 and ν_2 with which the amplitude oscillates. The intensity is proportional to the square of the pressure amplitude and it also varies periodically with frequency $| \nu_1 - \nu_2 |$. This phenomenon of periodic variation of intensity of sound when two sound waves of slightly different frequencies interfere, is called *beats*. Specifically, one cycle of maximum intensity and minimum intensity is counted as one beat, so that the frequency of beats is $| \nu_1 - \nu_2 |$.

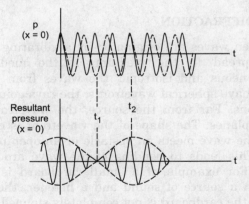

Figure 16.17

In figure (16.17), we explain the formation of beats graphically. The plots in part (a) show the pressure variation due to individual waves at a fixed position $x = 0$ as a function of time. At $t = 0$, the two waves produce pressure changes in phase. But as the frequencies and hence the time periods are slightly different, the phase difference grows and at a time t_1, the two pressure changes become out of phase. The resultant becomes zero at this time. The phase difference increases further and at time t_2, it becomes 2π. The pressure changes are again in phase. The superposition of the two waves (figure 16.17) gives the resultant pressure change as a function of time which is identical in shape to the part (c) of figure (16.15).

The phenomenon of beats can be observed by taking two tuning forks of the same frequency and putting some wax on the prongs of one of the forks. Loading with wax decreases the frequency of a tuning fork a little. When these two forks are vibrated and kept side by side, the listener can recognise the periodic variation of loudness of the resulting sound. The number of beats per second equals the difference in frequency.

For beats to be audible, the frequency $|\nu_1 - \nu_2|$ should not be very large. An average human ear cannot distinguish the variation of intensity if the variation is more than 16 times per second. Thus, the difference of the component frequencies should be less than 16 Hz for the beats to be heard.

Example 16.7

A tuning fork A of frequency 384 Hz *gives* 6 beats *in* 2 seconds *when sounded with another tuning fork B. What could be the frequency of B ?*

Solution : The frequency of beats is $|\nu_1 - \nu_2|$, which is 3 Hz according to the problem. The frequency of the tuning fork B is either 3 Hz more or 3 Hz less than the frequency of A. Thus, it could be either 381 Hz or 387 Hz.

16.12 DIFFRACTION

When waves are originated by a vibrating source, they spread in the medium. If the medium is homogeneous and isotropic, the waves from a point source have spherical wavefronts, the rays going in all directions. Far from the source, the wavefronts are nearly planes. The shape of the wavefront is changed when the wave meets an obstacle or an opening in its path. This leads to bending of the wave around the edges. For example, if a small cardboard is placed between a source of sound and a listener, the sound beyond the cardboard is not completely stopped, rather the waves bend at the edges of the cardboard to reach the listener. If a plane wave is passed through a small hole (an opening in a large obstacle), spherical waves are obtained on the other side as if the hole itself is a source sending waves in all directions (it is not a real source, no backward spherical waves are observed). Such bending of waves from an obstacle or an opening is called *diffraction*.

Diffraction is a characteristic property of wave motion and all kinds of waves exhibit diffraction.

The diffraction effects are appreciable when the dimensions of openings or the obstacles are comparable or smaller than the wavelength of the wave. If the opening or the obstacle is large compared to the wavelength, the diffraction effects are almost negligible.

The frequency of audible sound ranges from about 20 Hz to 20 kHz. Velocity of sound in air is around 332 m s^{-1}. The wavelength ($\lambda = v/\nu$) of audible sound in air thus ranges from 16 m to 1·6 cm. Quite often, the wavelength of sound is much larger than the obstacles or openings and diffraction is prominently displayed.

16.13 DOPPLER EFFECT

When a tuning fork is vibrated in air, sound waves travel from the fork. An observer stationed at some distance x from the fork receives the sound as the wave disturbs the air near his ear and the pressure varies between a maximum and a minimum. The pitch of the sound heard by the observer depends on how many times the pressure near the ear oscillates per unit time. Each time the fork moves forward it sends a compression pulse and each time it moves backward it sends a rarefaction pulse. Suppose the source and the observer are both at rest with respect to the medium. Each compression or rarefaction pulse, sent by the tuning fork, takes same time to reach the air near the ear. Thus, the pressure near the ear oscillates as many times as the fork oscillates in a given interval. The frequency observed is then equal to the frequency of the source.

However, if the source or the observer or both, move with respect to the medium, the frequency observed may be different from the frequency of the source. This apparent change in frequency of the wave due to motion of the source or the observer is called the *Doppler effect*.

Observer Stationary and Source Moving

Now suppose the observer is at rest with respect to the medium and the source moves towards the observer at a speed u which is less than the wave speed v.

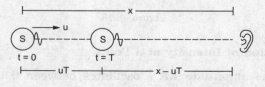

Figure 16.18

If the frequency of vibration of the source is ν_0, it sends compression pulses at a regular interval of $T = 1/\nu_0$. Suppose the separation between the source and the observer is x (figure 16.20) when a compression pulse is emitted at $t = 0$. The next compression pulse will be emitted after a time T. The source will travel a distance uT in this time and hence this second compression wave is emitted from a place which is at a distance $x - uT$ from the observer. The first pulse takes a time x/v to reach the observer whereas the next one takes $\frac{x - uT}{v}$.

Thus, the first compression wave reaches the observer at $t_1 = x/v$ and the next compression wave reaches at $t_2 = T + \frac{x - uT}{v}$. The time interval between the consecutive compression pulses detected by the observer is, therefore,

$$T' = t_2 - t_1$$
$$= T + \frac{x - uT}{v} - \frac{x}{v} = \left(1 - \frac{u}{v}\right)T = \frac{v - u}{v}\,T.$$

The apparent frequency of the sound as experienced by the observer is

$$\nu' = \frac{1}{T'},$$

or, $$\nu' = \frac{v}{v - u}\,\nu_0. \qquad \dots (16.23)$$

Similarly, if the source recedes from the observer at a speed u, the apparent frequency will be

$$\nu' = \frac{v}{v + u}\,\nu_0. \qquad \dots (16.24)$$

Source Stationary and Observer Moving

Next, consider the case when the source remains stationary with respect to the medium and the observer approaches the source with a speed u.

As the source remains stationary in the medium, compression pulses are emitted at regular interval T from the same point in the medium. These pulses travel down the medium with a speed v and at any instant the separation between two consecutive compression pulses is $\lambda = vT$ (figure 16.19)

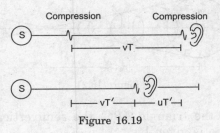

Figure 16.19

When the observer receives a compression pulse, the next compression pulse (towards the source) is a distance vT away from it. This second compression pulse moves towards the observer at a speed v and the observer moves towards it at a speed u. As a result, the observer will receive this second compression wave a time T' after receiving the first one where

$$T' = \frac{vT}{v + u}.$$

The apparent frequency of sound experienced by the observer is then $\nu' = \frac{1}{T'}$,

or, $$\nu' = \frac{v + u}{v}\,\nu_0. \qquad \dots (16.25)$$

Note that, in this case, it is not the same part of air that gives the sensation of pressure variation to the ear at frequency ν'. The pressure in any part of the air still oscillates with a frequency ν_0 but the observer moves in the medium to detect the pressure of some other part which reaches its maximum a little earlier. Similarly, if the source is stationary in the medium and the observer recedes from it at a speed u, the apparent frequency will be

$$\nu' = \frac{v - u}{v}\,\nu. \qquad \dots (16.26)$$

The equation (16.23) through (16.26) may be generalised as

$$\nu = \frac{v + u_o}{v - u_s}\,\nu_0 \qquad \dots (16.27)$$

where,

$v =$ speed of sound in the medium.

$u_o =$ speed of the observer with respect to the medium, considered positive when it moves towards the source and negative when it moves away from the source

and $u_s =$ speed of the source with respect to the medium, considered positive when it moves towards the observer and negative when it moves away from the observer.

It should be carefully noted that the speeds u_s and u_o are to be written with respect to the medium carrying the sound. If the medium itself is moving with respect to the given frame of reference, appropriate calculations must be made to obtain the speeds of the source and the observer with respect to the medium.

Example 16.8

A sound detector is placed on a railway platform. A train, approaching the platform at a speed of 36 km/h, sounds its whistle. The detector detects 12·0 kHz as the most dominant frequency in the whistle. If the train stops at the platform and sounds the whistle, what would be the most dominant frequency detected ? The speed of sound in air is 340 m s^{-1}.

Solution : Here the observer (detector) is at rest with respect to the medium (air). Suppose the dominant frequency as emitted by the train is v_0. When the train is at rest at the platform, the detector will detect the dominant frequency as v_0. When this same train was approaching the observer, the frequency detected was,

$$v' = \frac{v}{v - u_s} v_0$$

or, $$v_0 = \frac{v - u_s}{v} v' = \left(1 - \frac{u_s}{v}\right) v'.$$

The speed of the source is

$$u_s = 36 \text{ km h}^{-1} = \frac{36 \times 10^3 \text{ m}}{3600 \text{ s}} = 10 \text{ m s}^{-1}.$$

Thus, $$v_0 = \left(1 - \frac{10}{340}\right) \times 12 \cdot 0 \text{ kHz}$$

$$= 11 \cdot 6 \text{ kHz}.$$

We have derived the equations for Doppler shift in frequency assuming that the motion of the source or the observer is along the line joining the two. If the motion is along some other direction, the component of the velocity along the line joining the source and the observer should be used for u_s and u_o.

It is helpful to remember that the apparen frequency is larger than the actual, if the separation between the source and the observer is decreasing and is smaller if the separation is increasing. If you are standing on a platform and a whistling train passes by, you can easily notice the change in the pitch of the whistle. When the train is approaching you, the pitch is higher. As it passes through, there is a sudden fall in the pitch.

Change in Wavelength

If the source moves with respect to the medium, the wavelength becomes different from the wavelength observed when there is no relative motion between the source and the medium. The formula for apparent wavelength may be derived immediately from the relation $\lambda = v / v$ and equation (16.23). It is

$$\lambda' = \frac{v - u}{v} \lambda. \qquad \qquad \dots (16.28)$$

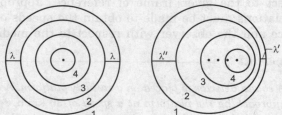

Figure 16.20

Figure 16.20 shows qualitatively the change in wavelength as the source moves through the medium. The circles represent the region of space where the pressure is maximum. They are wavefronts separated by a wavelength. We can say that these wavefronts representing the pressure maxima originate from the source and spread in all directions with a speed v.

Labels 1, 2, 3, 4 show wavefronts emitted successively at regular interval $T = 1/v$ from the source. Each wavefront will have its centre at the position where the source was situated while emitting the wavefront. The radius of a preceding wavefront will exceed the next one by an amount $\lambda = vT$.

When the source stays stationary, all the wavefronts are originated from the same position of the source and the separation between the successive wavefronts is equal to the difference in their radii. However, when the source moves, the centres of the wavefronts differ in position, so that the spacing between the successive wavefronts decreases along the direction of motion and increases on the opposite side. This separation being the new wavelength, the wavelength changes due to the motion of the source.

16.14 SONIC BOOMS

In the discussion of the Doppler effect, we considered only subsonic velocities for the source and the observer, that is, $u_s < v$ and $u_o < v$. What happens when the source moves through the medium at a speed u_s greater than the wave speed v ? A supersonic plane travels in air with a speed greater than the speed of sound in air. It sends a cracking sound called sonic boom which can break glass dishes, window panes and even cause damage to buildings. Let us extend figure (16.20) for the case where a tiny source moves through air with a speed $u_s > v$. The wavefronts are drawn for the pressure maxima. The spherical wavefronts intersect over the surface of a cone with the apex at the source. Because of constructive interference of a large number of waves arriving at the same instant on the surface of the cone, pressure waves of very large amplitude are sent with the conical wavefront. Such waves are one variety of shock waves.

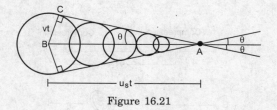

Figure 16.21

From the triangle *ABC*, the semivertical angle θ of the cone is given by

$$\sin\theta = \frac{vt}{u_s t} = \frac{v}{u_s}.$$

The ratio $\frac{u_s}{v}$ is called the "Mach Number".

As the tiny source moves, it drags the cone with it. When an observer on ground is intercepted by the cone surface, the boom is heard. There is a common misconception that the boom is produced at the instant the speed of the plane crosses the speed of sound and once it achieves the supersonic speed it sends no further shock wave. The sonic boom is not a one time affair that occurs when the speed just exceeds the speed of sound. As long as the plane moves with a supersonic speed, it continues to send the boom.

16.15 MUSICAL SCALE

A musical scale is a sequence of frequencies which have a particularly pleasing effect on the human ear. A widely used musical scale, called diatonic scale, has eight frequencies covering an octave. Each frequency is called a *note*. Table (16.3) gives these frequencies together with their Indian and Western names with the lowest of the octave at 256 Hz.

Table 16.3

Symbol	Indian name	Western name	Frequency Hz
C	Sa	Do	256
D	Re	Re	288
E	Ga	Mi	320
F	Ma	Fa	$341\frac{1}{3}$
G	Pa	Sol	384
A	Dha	La	$426\frac{2}{3}$
B	Ni	Ti	480
C_1	Sa	Do	512

16.16 ACOUSTICS OF BUILDINGS

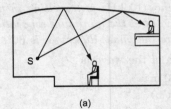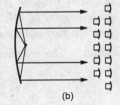

Figure 16.22

While designing an auditorium for speech or musical concerts, one has to take proper care for the absorption and reflection of sound. If these factors are poorly considered, a listener in the auditorium will not be able to clearly hear the sound. To have the intensity of sound almost uniform in the hall, the walls and the ceilings may be curved in proper fashion. Figure (16.22) shows a curved ceiling used to make sound audible uniformly at the balcony seats and the seats on the floor. Figure (16.22b) shows the use of a parabolic wall to make sound uniform across the width of the hall. Reflection of sound is helpful in maintaining a good loudness level throughout the hall. However, it also has several unwanted effects. Sound can reach a listener directly from the source as well as after reflection from a wall or the ceiling. This leads to *echo* which is heard after an interval of hearing the first sound. This echo interferes with the next sound signal affecting the clarity.

Another effect of multiple reflection is the *reverberation*. A listener hears the direct sound, sound coming after one reflection, after two reflections and so on. The time interval between the successive arrival of the same sound signal keeps on decreasing. Also, the intensity of the signal gradually decreases.

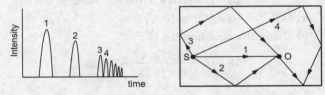

Figure 16.23

Figure (16.23) shows a typical situation. After sometime the signals coming from multiple reflections are so close that they form an almost continuous sound of decreasing intensity. This part of the sound is called *reverberant sound*. The time for which the reverberation persists is a major factor in the acoustics of halls. Quantitatively, the time taken by the reverberant sound to decrease its intensity by a factor of 10^6 is called the *reverberation time*. If the reverberation time is too large, it disturbs the listener. A sound signal from the source may not be clearly heard due to the presence of reverberation of the previous signal. There are certain materials which absorb sound very effectively. Reverberation may be decreased by fixing such materials on the walls, ceiling, floor, furnitures, etc. However, this process decreases the overall intensity level in the hall. Also in musical concerts, some amount of reverberation adds to the quality of music. An auditorium with a very small reverberation time is called *acoustically dead*. Thus, one has to make a compromise. The reverberation time should not be very large, otherwise unpleasant echos will seriously affect the clarity. On the other hand it should not be too small, otherwise intensity and quality will be seriously affected.

Electrical amplifying systems are often used in large auditorium. If a loudspeaker is kept near the back or at the side walls, a listener may hear the sound from the speaker earlier than the sound from the stage. Loudspeakers are, therefore, placed with proper inclinations and electronic delays are installed so that sound from the stage and from the loudspeaker reach a listener almost simultaneously. Another problem with electrical amplifying systems is *ringing*. The amplifying system may pick up sound from the loudspeaker to again amplify it. This gives a very unpleasant whistling sound.

One also has to avoid any noise coming from outside the auditorium or from different equipment inside the auditorium. Sound of fans, exhausts, airconditioners, etc., often create annoyance to the listener.

Worked Out Examples

1. *An ultrasound signal of frequency 50 kHz is sent vertically into sea water. The signal gets reflected from the ocean bed and returns to the surface 0·80 s after it was emitted. The speed of sound in sea water is 1500 m s⁻¹. (a) Find the depth of the sea. (b) What is the wavelength of this signal in water?*

Solution : (a) Let the depth of the sea be d. The total distance travelled by the signal is $2d$. By the question,

$$2d = (1500 \text{ m s}^{-1}) (0.8 \text{ s}) = 1200 \text{ m}$$

or, $d = 600$ m.

(b) Using the equation $v = \nu\lambda$,

$$\lambda = \frac{v}{\nu} = \frac{1500 \text{ m s}^{-1}}{50 \times 10^{3} \text{ s}^{-1}} = 3.0 \text{ cm.}$$

2. *An aeroplane is going towards east at a speed of 510 km h⁻¹ at a height of 2000 m. At a certain instant, the sound of the plane heard by a ground observer appears to come from a point vertically above him. Where is the plane at this instant? Speed of sound in air = 340 m s⁻¹.*

Solution :

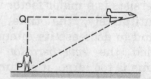

Figure 16-W1

The sound reaching the ground observer P, was emitted by the plane when it was at the point Q vertically above his head. The time taken by the sound to reach the observer is

$$t = \frac{2000 \text{ m}}{340 \text{ m s}^{-1}} = \frac{100}{17} \text{ s.}$$

The distance moved by the plane during this period is

$$d = (510 \text{ km h}^{-1}) \left(\frac{100}{17} \text{ s}\right)$$

$$= \frac{30 \times 10^{5}}{3600} \text{ m} = 833 \text{ m.}$$

Thus, the plane will be 833 m ahead of the observer on its line of motion when he hears the sound coming vertically to him.

3. *The equation of a sound wave in air is given by*

$$p = (0.01 \text{ N m}^{-2}) \sin[(1000 \text{ s}^{-1}) t - (3.0 \text{ m}^{-1}) x]$$

(a) Find the frequency, wavelength and the speed of sound wave in air. (b) If the equilibrium pressure of air is 1.0×10^{5} N m⁻², what are the maximum and minimum pressures at a point as the wave passes through that point.

Solution : (a) Comparing with the standard form of a travelling wave

$$p = p_0 \sin[\omega(t - x/v)]$$

we see that $\omega = 1000 \text{ s}^{-1}$. The frequency is

$$\nu = \frac{\omega}{2\pi} = \frac{1000}{2\pi} \text{ Hz} = 160 \text{ Hz.}$$

Also from the same comparison, $\omega/v = 3.0 \text{ m}^{-1}$

or, $$v = \frac{\omega}{3.0 \text{ m}^{-1}} = \frac{1000 \text{ s}^{-1}}{3.0 \text{ m}^{-1}}$$

$$\approx 330 \text{ m s}^{-1}.$$

The wavelength is $\lambda = \dfrac{v}{\nu} = \dfrac{330 \text{ m s}^{-1}}{160 \text{ Hz}} = 2.1 \text{ m.}$

(b) The pressure amplitude is $p_0 = 0.01 \text{ N m}^{-2}$. Hence, the maximum and minimum pressures at a point in the wave motion will be $(1.01 \times 10^{5} \pm 0.01) \text{ N m}^{-2}$.

4. *A sound wave of frequency 10 kHz is travelling in air with a speed of 340 m s⁻¹. Find the minimum separation between two points where the phase difference is 60°.*

Solution : The wavelength of the wave is

$$\lambda = \frac{v}{\nu} = \frac{340 \text{ m s}^{-1}}{10 \times 10^{3} \text{ s}^{-1}} = 3.4 \text{ cm.}$$

The wave number is $k = \dfrac{2\pi}{\lambda} = \dfrac{2\pi}{3.4} \text{ cm}^{-1}$.

The phase of the wave is $(kx - \omega t)$. At any given instant, the phase difference between two points at a separation d is kd. If this phase difference is 60°, i.e., $\pi/3$ radian;

$$\frac{\pi}{3} = \left(\frac{2\pi}{3.4} \text{ cm}^{-1}\right) d \text{ or } d = \frac{3.4}{6} \text{ cm} = 0.57 \text{ cm.}$$

5. *On a winter day sound travels* 336 *meters in one second. Find the atmospheric temperature. Speed of sound at* $0°C = 332$ *m* s^{-1}.

Solution : The speed of sound is proportional to the square root of the absolute temperature.

The speed of sound at $0°C$ or 273 K is 332 m s^{-1}. If the atmospheric temperature is T,

$$\frac{336 \text{ m s}^{-1}}{332 \text{ m s}^{-1}} = \sqrt{\frac{T}{273 \text{ K}}}$$

or, $T = \left(\frac{336}{332}\right)^2 \times 273 \text{ K} = 280 \text{ K}$

or, $t = 7°C$.

6. *The constant* γ *for oxygen as well as for hydrogen is* $1\cdot40$. *If the speed of sound in oxygen is* 470 *m* s^{-1}, *what will be the speed in hydrogen at the same temperature and pressure?*

Solution : The speed of sound in a gas is given by $v = \sqrt{\frac{\gamma P}{\rho}}$. At STP, $22\cdot4$ litres of oxygen has a mass of 32 g whereas the same volume of hydrogen has a mass of 2 g. Thus, the density of oxygen is 16 times the density of hydrogen at the same temperature and pressure. As γ is same for both the gases,

$$\frac{v \text{ (hydrogen)}}{v \text{ (oxygen)}} = \sqrt{\frac{\rho \text{(oxygen)}}{\rho \text{ (hydrogen)}}}$$

or, $v(\text{hydrogen}) = 4\, v \text{ (oxygen)}$
$$= 4 \times 470 \text{ m s}^{-1} = 1880 \text{ m s}^{-1}.$$

7. *A microphone of cross-sectional area* $0\cdot80$ cm^2 *is placed in front of a small speaker emitting* $3\cdot0$ W *of sound output. If the distance between the microphone and the speaker is* $2\cdot0$ m, *how much energy falls on the microphone in* $5\cdot0$ s?

Solution : The energy emitted by the speaker in one second is $3\cdot0$ J. Let us consider a sphere of radius $2\cdot0$ m centred at the speaker. The energy $3\cdot0$ J falls normally on the total surface of this sphere in one second. The energy falling on the area $0\cdot8$ cm^2 of the microphone in one second

$$= \frac{0\cdot8 \text{ cm}^2}{4 \pi (2\cdot0 \text{ m})^2} \times 3\cdot0 \text{ J} = 4\cdot8 \times 10^{-6} \text{ J}.$$

The energy falling on the microphone in $5\cdot0$ s is
$$4\cdot8 \times 10^{-6} \text{ J} \times 5 = 24 \text{ } \mu\text{J}.$$

8. *Find the amplitude of vibration of the particles of air through which a sound wave of intensity* $2\cdot0 \times 10^{-6}$ W m^{-2} *and frequency* $1\cdot0$ kHz *is passing. Density of air* $= 1\cdot2$ kg m^{-3} *and speed of sound in air* $= 330$ m s^{-1}.

Solution : The relation between the intensity of sound and the displacement amplitude is
$$I = 2 \pi^2 s_0^2 \nu^2 \rho_0 v$$

or, $s_0^2 = \dfrac{I}{2 \pi^2 \nu^2 \rho_0 v}$

$$= \frac{2\cdot0 \times 10^{-6} \text{ W m}^{-2}}{2 \pi^2 \times (1\cdot0 \times 10^6 \text{ s}^{-2}) \times (1\cdot2 \text{ kg m}^{-3}) \times (330 \text{ m s}^{-1})}$$

$$= 2\cdot53 \times 10^{-16} \text{ m}^2$$

or, $s_0 = 1\cdot6 \times 10^{-8}$ m.

9. *The sound level at a point is increased by* 30 dB. *By what factor is the pressure amplitude increased?*

Solution : The sound level in dB is
$$\beta = 10 \log_{10}\left(\frac{I}{I_0}\right).$$

If β_1 and β_2 are the sound levels and I_1 and I_2 are the intensities in the two cases,

$$\beta_2 - \beta_1 = 10\left[\log_{10}\left(\frac{I_2}{I_0}\right) - \log_{10}\left(\frac{I_1}{I_0}\right)\right]$$

or, $30 = 10 \log_{10}\left(\dfrac{I_2}{I_1}\right)$

or, $\dfrac{I_2}{I_1} = 10^3.$

As the intensity is proportional to the square of the pressure amplitude, we have $\dfrac{p_2}{p_1} = \sqrt{\dfrac{I_2}{I_1}} = \sqrt{1000} \approx 32.$

10. *Figure (16-W2) shows a tube structure in which a sound signal is sent from one end and is received at the other end. The semicircular part has a radius of* $20\cdot0$ cm. *The frequency of the sound source can be varied electronically between* 1000 *and* 4000 Hz. *Find the frequencies at which maxima of intensity are detected. The speed of sound in air* $= 340$ m s^{-1}.

Figure 16-W2

Solution : The sound wave bifurcates at the junction of the straight and the semicircular parts. The wave through the straight part travels a distance $l_1 = 2 \times 20$ cm and the wave through the curved part travels a distance $l_2 = \pi\, 20$ cm $= 62\cdot8$ cm before they meet again and travel to the receiver. The path difference between the two waves received is, therefore,

$$\Delta l = l_2 - l_1 = 62\cdot8 \text{ cm} - 40 \text{ cm} = 22\cdot8 \text{ cm} = 0\cdot228 \text{ m}.$$

The wavelength of either wave is $\frac{v}{\nu} = \frac{340 \text{ m s}^{-1}}{\nu}$. For constructive interference, $\Delta l = n \lambda$, where n is an integer.

or, $0.228 \text{ m} = n \frac{340 \text{ m s}^{-1}}{\nu}$

or, $\nu = n \frac{340 \text{ m s}^{-1}}{0.228 \text{ m}} = n \, 1491.2 \text{ Hz} \approx n \, 1490 \text{ Hz}.$

Thus, the frequencies within the specified range which cause maxima of intensity are 1490 Hz and 2980 Hz.

11. *A source emitting sound of frequency 180 Hz is placed in front of a wall at a distance of 2 m from it. A detector is also placed in front of the wall at the same distance from it. Find the minimum distance between the source and the detector for which the detector detects a maximum of sound. Speed of sound in air = 360 m s^{-1}.*

Solution :

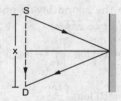

Figure 16-W3

The situation is shown in figure (16-W3). Suppose the detector is placed at a distance of x meter from the source. The direct wave received from the source travels a distance of x meter. The wave reaching the detector after reflection from the wall has travelled a distance of $2[(2)^2 + x^2/4]^{1/2}$ metre. The path difference between the two waves is

$$\Delta = \left\{ 2\left[(2)^2 + \frac{x^2}{4} \right]^{1/2} - x \right\} \text{ metre.}$$

Constructive interference will take place when $\Delta = \lambda, 2\lambda, \dots$. The minimum distance x for a maximum corresponds to

$$\Delta = \lambda. \qquad \dots \text{(i)}$$

The wavelength is $\lambda = \frac{v}{\nu} = \frac{360 \text{ m s}^{-1}}{180 \text{ s}^{-1}} = 2 \text{ m}.$

Thus, by (i), $2\left[(2)^2 + \frac{x^2}{4} \right]^{1/2} - x = 2$

or, $\left[4 + \frac{x^2}{4} \right]^{1/2} = 1 + \frac{x}{2}$

or, $4 + \frac{x^2}{4} = 1 + \frac{x^2}{4} + x$

or, $3 = x.$

Thus, the detector should be placed at a distance of 3 m from the source. Note that there is no abrupt phase change.

12. *A tuning fork vibrates at 264 Hz. Find the length of the shortest closed organ pipe that will resonate with the tuning fork. Speed of sound in air is 350 m s^{-1}.*

Solution : The resonant frequency of a closed organ pipe of length l is $\frac{nv}{4l}$, where n is a positive odd integer and v is the speed of sound in air. To resonate with the given tuning fork,

$$\frac{nv}{4l} = 264 \text{ s}^{-1}$$

or, $l = \frac{n \times 350 \text{ m s}^{-1}}{4 \times 264 \text{ s}^{-1}}.$

For l to be minimum, $n = 1$ so that

$$l_{min} = \frac{350}{4 \times 264} \text{ m} = 33 \text{ cm}.$$

13. *The fundamental frequency of a closed organ pipe is equal to the first overtone frequency of an open organ pipe. If the length of the open pipe is 60 cm, what is the length of the closed pipe ?*

Solution : The fundamental frequency of a closed organ pipe is $\frac{v}{4l_1}$. For an open pipe, the fundamental frequency is $\frac{v}{2l_2}$ and the first overtone is $\frac{2v}{2l_2} = \frac{v}{l_2}$. Here l_1 is the length of the closed pipe and $l_2 = 60$ cm is the length of the open pipe. We have,

$$\frac{v}{4l_1} = \frac{v}{60 \text{ cm}}$$

$$l_1 = \frac{1}{4} \times 60 \text{ cm} = 15 \text{ cm}.$$

14. *A tuning fork vibrating at frequency 800 Hz produces resonance in a resonance column tube. The upper end is open and the lower end is closed by the water surface which can be varied. Successive resonances are observed at lengths 9.75 cm, 31.25 cm and 52.75 cm. Calculate the speed of sound in air from these data.*

Solution : For the tube open at one end, the resonance frequencies are $\frac{nv}{4l}$, where n is a positive odd integer. If the tuning fork has a frequency ν and l_1, l_2, l_3 are the successive lengths of the tube in resonance with it, we have

$$\frac{nv}{4 \, l_1} = \nu$$

$$\frac{(n+2) v}{4 \, l_2} = \nu$$

$$\frac{(n+4) v}{4 \, l_3} = \nu$$

giving $l_3 - l_2 = l_2 - l_1 = \frac{2v}{4\nu} = \frac{v}{2\nu}.$

By the question, $l_3 - l_2 = (52 \cdot 75 - 31 \cdot 25)$ cm $= 21 \cdot 50$ cm
and $l_2 - l_1 = (31 \cdot 25 - 9 \cdot 75)$ cm $= 21 \cdot 50$ cm.

Thus, $\dfrac{v}{2v} = 21 \cdot 50$ cm

or, $v = 2v \times 21 \cdot 50$ cm $= 2 \times 800$ s$^{-1} \times 21 \cdot 50$ cm $= 344$ m s^{-1}.

15. *A certain organ pipe resonates in its fundamental mode at a frequency of 500 Hz in air. What will be the fundamental frequency if the air is replaced by hydrogen at the same temperature? The density of air is 1·20 kg m^{-3} and that of hydrogen is 0·089 kg m^{-3}.*

Solution : Suppose the speed of sound in hydrogen is v_h and that in air is v_a. The fundamental frequency of an organ pipe is proportional to the speed of sound in the gas contained in it. If the fundamental frequency with hydrogen in the tube is v, we have

$$\frac{v}{500 \text{ Hz}} = \frac{v_h}{v_a} = \sqrt{\frac{\rho_a}{\rho_h}} = \sqrt{\frac{1 \cdot 2}{0 \cdot 089}} = 3 \cdot 67$$

or, $v = 3 \cdot 67 \times 500$ Hz ≈ 1840 Hz.

16. *An aluminium rod having a length of 90·0 cm is clamped at its middle point and is set into longitudinal vibrations by stroking it with a rosined cloth. Assume that the rod vibrates in its fundamental mode of vibration. The density of aluminium is 2600 kg m^{-3} and its Young's modulus is 7·80 × 10^{10} N m^{-2}. Find (a) the speed of sound in aluminium, (b) the wavelength of sound waves produced in the rod, (c) the frequency of the sound produced and (d) the wavelength of the sound produced in air. Take the speed of sound in air to be 340 m s^{-1}.*

Solution : (a) The speed of sound in aluminium is

$$v = \sqrt{\frac{Y}{\rho}} = \sqrt{\frac{7 \cdot 80 \times 10^{10} \text{ N m}^{-2}}{2600 \text{ kg m}^{-3}}}$$
$$= 5480 \text{ m s}^{-1}.$$

(b) Since the rod is clamped at the middle, the middle point is a pressure antinode. The free ends of the rod are the nodes. As the rod vibrates in its fundamental mode, there are no other nodes or antinodes. The length of the rod, which is also the distance between the successive nodes, is, therefore, equal to half the wavelength. Thus, the wavelength of sound in the aluminium rod is
$$\lambda = 2\,l = 180 \text{ cm}.$$

(c) The frequency of the sound produced which is also equal to the frequency of vibration of the rod is

$$v = \frac{v}{\lambda} = \frac{5480 \text{ m s}^{-1}}{180 \text{ cm}} = 3050 \text{ Hz}.$$

(d) The wavelength of sound in air is
$$\lambda = \frac{v}{v} = \frac{340 \text{ m s}^{-1}}{3050 \text{ Hz}} = 11 \cdot 1 \text{ cm}.$$

17. *The string of a violin emits a note of 440 Hz at its correct tension. The string is bit taut and produces 4 beats per second with a tuning fork of frequency 440 Hz. Find the frequency of the note emitted by this taut string.*

Solution : The frequency of vibration of a string increases with increase in the tension. Thus, the note emitted by the string will be a little more than 440 Hz. As it produces 4 beats per second with the 440 Hz tuning fork, the frequency will be 444 Hz.

18. *A siren is fitted on a car going towards a vertical wall at a speed of 36 km/h. It produces sound of frequency 500 Hz. A person standing on the ground, behind the car, listens to the siren sound coming directly from the source as well as that coming after reflection from the wall. Calculate the apparent frequency of the wave (a) coming directly from the siren to the person and (b) coming after reflection. Take the speed of sound to be 340 m s^{-1}.*

Solution :

Figure 16-W4

The speed of the car is 36 km h^{-1} = 10 m s^{-1}.

(a) Here the observer is at rest with respect to the medium and the source is going away from the observer. The apparent frequency heard by the observer is, therefore,

$$v' = \frac{v}{v + u_s}\, v$$
$$= \frac{340}{340 + 10} \times 500 \text{ Hz} = 486 \text{ Hz}.$$

(b) The frequency received by the wall is
$$v'' = \frac{v}{v - u_s}\, v = \frac{340}{340 - 10} \times 500 \text{ Hz} = 515 \text{ Hz}.$$

The wall reflects this sound without changing the frequency. Thus, the frequency of the reflected wave as heard by the ground observer is 515 Hz.

19. *Two trains are moving towards each other at speeds of 72 km h^{-1} and 54 km h^{-1} relative to the ground. The first train sounds a whistle of frequency 600 Hz. Find the frequency of the whistle as heard by a passenger in the second train (a) before the trains meet and (b) after the trains have crossed each other. The speed of sound in air is 340 m s^{-1}.*

Solution : The speed of the first train = 72 km h^{-1} = 20 m s^{-1} and that of the second = 54 km h^{-1} = 15 m s^{-1}.

(a) Here both the source and the observer move with respect to the medium. Before the trains meet, the source is going towards the observer and the observer is also going towards the source. The apparent frequency heard by the observer will be

$$\nu' = \frac{v + u_o}{v - u_s}\nu$$

$$= \frac{340 + 15}{340 - 20} \times 600 \text{ Hz} = 666 \text{ Hz}.$$

(b) After the trains have crossed each other, the source goes away from the observer and the observer goes away from the source. The frequency heard by the observer is, therefore,

$$\nu'' = \frac{v - u_o}{v + u_s}\nu$$

$$= \frac{340 - 15}{340 + 20} \times 600 \text{ Hz} = 542 \text{ Hz}.$$

20. *A person going away from a factory on his scooter at a speed of 36 km h⁻¹ listens to the siren of the factory. If the main frequency of the siren is 600 Hz and a wind is blowing along the direction of the scooter at 36 km h⁻¹, find the main frequency as heard by the person.*

Solution : The speed of sound in still air is 340 m s⁻¹. Let us work from the frame of reference of the air. As both the observer and the wind are moving at the same speed along the same direction with respect to the ground, the observer is at rest with respect to the medium. The source (the siren) is moving with respect to the wind at a speed of 36 km h⁻¹, i.e., 10 m s⁻¹. As the source is going away from the observer who is at rest with respect to the medium, the frequency heard is

$$\nu' = \frac{v}{v + u_s}\nu = \frac{340}{340 + 10} \times 600 \text{ Hz} = 583 \text{ Hz}.$$

21. *A source and a detector move away from each other, each with a speed of 10 m s⁻¹ with respect to the ground with no wind. If the detector detects a frequency 1950 Hz of the sound coming from the source, what is the original frequency of the source ? Speed of sound in air = 340 m s⁻¹.*

Solution : If the original frequency of the source is ν, the apparent frequency heard by the observer is

$$\nu' = \frac{v - u_o}{v + u_s}\nu,$$

where u_o is the speed of the observer going away from the source and u_s is the speed of the source going away from the observer. By the question,

$$1950 \text{ Hz} = \frac{340 - 10}{340 + 10}\nu$$

or,

$$\nu = \frac{35}{33} \times 1950 \text{ Hz} = 2070 \text{ Hz}.$$

22. *The driver of a car approaching a vertical wall notices that the frequency of his car's horn changes from 440 Hz to 480 Hz when it gets reflected from the wall. Find the speed of the car if that of the sound is 330 m s⁻¹.*

Solution :

Figure 16-W5

Suppose the car is going towards the wall at a speed u. The wall is stationary with respect to the air and the horn is going towards it. If the frequency of the horn is ν, that received by the wall is

$$\nu' = \frac{v}{v - u}\nu.$$

The wall reflects this sound without changing the frequency. Thus, the wall becomes the source of frequency ν′ and the car-driver is the listener. The wall (which acts as the source now) is at rest with respect to the air and the car (which is the observer now) is going towards the wall at speed u. The frequency heard by the car-driver for this reflected wave is, therefore,

$$\nu'' = \frac{v + u}{v}\nu'$$

$$= \frac{v + u}{v} \cdot \frac{v}{v - u}\nu$$

$$= \frac{v + u}{v - u}\nu.$$

Putting the values,

$$480 = \frac{v + u}{v - u}440$$

or, $$\frac{v + u}{v - u} = \frac{48}{44}$$

or, $$\frac{u}{v} = \frac{4}{92}$$

or, $$u = \frac{4}{92} \times 330 \text{ m s}^{-1} = 14.3 \text{ m s}^{-1} \approx 52 \text{ km h}^{-1}.$$

23. *A train approaching a railway crossing at a speed of 120 km h⁻¹ sounds a short whistle at frequency 640 Hz when it is 300 m away from the crossing. The speed of sound in air is 340 m s⁻¹. What will be the frequency heard by a person standing on a road perpendicular to the track through the crossing at a distance of 400 m from the crossing ?*

Solution :

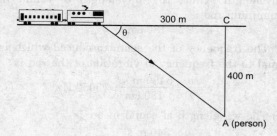

Figure 16-W6

The observer A is at rest with respect to the air and the source is travelling at a velocity of 120 km h^{-1} i.e., $\frac{100}{3}$ m s^{-1}. As is clear from the figure, the person receives the sound of the whistle in a direction BA making an angle θ with the track where $\cos\theta = 300/500 = 3/5$. The component of the velocity of the source (i.e., of the train) along this direction AB is $\frac{100}{3} \times \frac{3}{5}$ m s$^{-1} = 20$ m s^{-1}. As the source is approaching the person with this component, the frequency heard by the observer is

$$\nu' = \frac{v}{v - u\cos\theta}\nu = \frac{340}{340 - 20} \times 640 \text{ Hz} = 680 \text{ Hz.}$$

□

QUESTIONS FOR SHORT ANSWER

1. If you are walking on the moon, can you hear the sound of stones cracking behind you ? Can you hear the sound of your own footsteps ?

2. Can you hear your own words if you are standing in a perfect vacuum ? Can you hear your friend in the same conditions ?

3. A vertical rod is hit at one end. What kind of wave propagates in the rod if (a) the hit is made vertically (b) the hit is made horizontally ?

4. Two loudspeakers are arranged facing each other at some distance. Will a person standing behind one of the loudspeakers clearly hear the sound of the other loudspeaker or the clarity will be seriously damaged because of the 'collision' of the two sounds in between ?

5. The voice of a person, who has inhaled helium, has a remarkably high pitch. Explain on the basis of resonant vibration of vocal cord filled with air and with helium.

6. Draw a diagram to show the standing pressure wave and standing displacement wave for the 3rd overtone mode of vibration of an open organ pipe.

7. Two tuning forks vibrate with the same amplitude but the frequency of the first is double the frequency of the second. Which fork produces more intense sound in air ?

8. In discussing Doppler effect, we use the word "apparent frequency". Does it mean that the frequency of the sound is still that of the source and it is some physiological phenomenon in the listener's ear that gives rise to Doppler effect ? Think for the observer approaching the source and for the source approaching the observer.

OBJECTIVE I

1. Consider the following statements about sound passing through a gas.
   (A) The pressure of the gas at a point oscillates in time.
   (B) The position of a small layer of the gas oscillates in time.
   (a) Both A and B are correct.
   (b) A is correct but B is wrong.
   (c) B is correct but A is wrong.
   (d) Both A and B are wrong.

2. When we clap our hands, the sound produced is best described by
   (a) $p = p_0 \sin(kx - \omega t)$ (b) $p = p_0 \sin kx \cos \omega t$
   (c) $p = p_0 \cos kx \sin \omega t$ (d) $p = \Sigma p_{0n} \sin(k_n x - \omega_n t)$.
   Here p denotes the change in pressure from the equilibrium value.

3. The bulk modulus and the density of water are greater than those of air. With this much of information, we can say that velocity of sound in air
   (a) is larger than its value in water
   (b) is smaller than its value in water
   (c) is equal to its value in water
   (d) cannot be compared with its value in water.

4. A tuning fork sends sound waves in air. If the temperature of the air increases, which of the following parameters will change ?
   (a) Displacement amplitude   (b) Frequency
   (c) Wavelength   (d) Time period

5. When sound wave is refracted from air to water, which of the following will remain unchanged ?
   (a) Wave number   (b) Wavelength
   (c) Wave velocity   (d) Frequency

6. The speed of sound in a medium depends on
   (a) the elastic property but not on the inertia property
   (b) the inertia property but not on the elastic property
   (c) the elastic property as well as the inertia property
   (d) neither the elastic property nor the inertia property.

7. Two sound waves move in the same direction in the same medium. The pressure amplitudes of the waves are equal but the wavelength of the first wave is double the second. Let the average power transmitted across a cross section by the first wave be P_1 and that by the second wave be P_2. Then
   (a) $P_1 = P_2$ (b) $P_1 = 4P_2$
   (c) $P_2 = 2P_1$ (d) $P_2 = 4P_1$.

8. When two waves with same frequency and constant phase difference interfere,
   (a) there is a gain of energy
   (b) there is a loss of energy

(c) the energy is redistributed and the distribution changes with time

(d) the energy is redistributed and the distribution remains constant in time.

9. An open organ pipe of length L vibrates in its fundamental mode. The pressure variation is maximum
   (a) at the two ends
   (b) at the middle of the pipe
   (c) at distances $L/4$ inside the ends
   (d) at distances $L/8$ inside the ends.

10. An organ pipe, open at both ends, contains
    (a) longitudinal stationary waves
    (b) longitudinal travelling waves
    (c) transverse stationary waves
    (d) transverse travelling waves.

11. A cylindrical tube, open at both ends, has a fundamental frequency v. The tube is dipped vertically in water so that half of its length is inside the water. The new fundamental frequency is
    (a) $v/4$　　　　(b) $v/2$　　　　(c) v　　　　(d) $2v$.

12. The phenomenon of beats can take place
    (a) for longitudinal waves only
    (b) for transverse waves only
    (c) for both longitudinal and transverse waves
    (d) for sound waves only.

13. A tuning fork of frequency 512 Hz is vibrated with a sonometer wire and 6 beats per second are heard. The beat frequency reduces if the tension in the string is

slightly increased. The original frequency of vibration of the string is
(a) 506 Hz　　(b) 512 Hz　　(c) 518 Hz　　(d) 524 Hz.

14. The engine of a train sounds a whistle at frequency v. The frequency heard by a passenger is
    (a) $> v$　　　　(b) $< v$　　　　(c) $= \dfrac{1}{v}$　　　　(d) $= v$.

15. The change in frequency due to Doppler effect does not depend on
    (a) the speed of the source
    (b) the speed of the observer
    (c) the frequency of the source
    (d) separation between the source and the observer.

16. A small source of sound moves on a circle as shown in figure (16-Q1) and an observer is sitting at O. Let v_1, v_2, v_3 be the frequencies heard when the source is at A, B and C respectively.
    (a) $v_1 > v_2 > v_3$　　　　　　　　(b) $v_1 = v_2 > v_3$
    (c) $v_2 > v_3 > v_1$　　　　　　　　(d) $v_1 > v_3 > v_2$

Figure 16-Q1

OBJECTIVE II

1. When you speak to your friend, which of the following parameters have a unique value in the sound produced ?
   (a) Frequency　　　　　　　　(b) Wavelength
   (c) Amplitude　　　　　　　　(d) Wave velocity

2. An electrically maintained tuning fork vibrates with constant frequency and constant amplitude. If the temperature of the surrounding air increases but pressure remains constant, the sound produced will have
   (a) larger wavelength　　　　　(b) larger frequency
   (c) larger velocity　　　　　　(d) larger time period.

3. The fundamental frequency of a vibrating organ pipe is 200 Hz.
   (a) The first overtone is 400 Hz.
   (b) The first overtone may be 400 Hz.

(c) The first overtone may be 600 Hz.
(d) 600 Hz is an overtone.

4. A source of sound moves towards an observer.
   (a) The frequency of the source is increased.
   (b) The velocity of sound in the medium is increased.
   (c) The wavelength of sound in the medium towards the observer is decreased.
   (d) The amplitude of vibration of the particles is increased.

5. A listener is at rest with respect to the source of sound. A wind starts blowing along the line joining the source and the observer. Which of the following quantities do not change ?
   (a) Frequency　　　　　　　　(b) Velocity of sound
   (c) Wavelength　　　　　　　　(d) Time period

EXERCISES

1. A steel tube of length 1·00 m is struck at one end. A person with his ear close to the other end hears the sound of the blow twice, one travelling through the body of the tube and the other through the air in the tube.

Find the time gap between the two hearings. Use the table in the text for speeds of sound in various substances.

2. At a prayer meeting, the disciples sing *JAI-RAM JAI-RAM*. The sound amplified by a loudspeaker comes back after reflection from a building at a distance of 80 m from the meeting. What maximum time interval can be kept between one *JAI-RAM* and the next *JAI-RAM* so that the echo does not disturb a listener sitting in the meeting. Speed of sound in air is 320 m s^{-1}.

3. A man stands before a large wall at a distance of 50·0 m and claps his hands at regular intervals. Initially, the interval is large. He gradually reduces the interval and fixes it at a value when the echo of a clap merges with the next clap. If he has to clap 10 times during every 3 seconds, find the velocity of sound in air.

4. A person can hear sound waves in the frequency range 20 Hz to 20 kHz. Find the minimum and the maximum wavelengths of sound that is audible to the person. The speed of sound is 360 m s^{-1}.

5. Find the minimum and maximum wavelengths of sound in water that is in the audible range (20–20000 Hz) for an average human ear. Speed of sound in water = 1450 m s^{-1}.

6. Sound waves from a loudspeaker spread nearly uniformly in all directions if the wavelength of the sound is much larger than the diameter of the loudspeaker. (a) Calculate the frequency for which the wavelength of sound in air is ten times the diameter of the speaker if the diameter is 20 cm. (b) Sound is essentially transmitted in the forward direction if the wavelength is much shorter than the diameter of the speaker. Calculate the frequency at which the wavelength of the sound is one tenth of the diameter of the speaker described above. Take the speed of sound to be 340 m s^{-1}.

7. Ultrasonic waves of frequency 4·5 MHz are used to detect tumour in soft tissues. The speed of sound in tissue is 1·5 km s^{-1} and that in air is 340 m s^{-1}. Find the wavelength of this ultrasonic wave in air and in tissue.

8. The equation of a travelling sound wave is $y = 6·0 \sin (600 t - 1·8 x)$ where y is measured in 10^{-5} m, t in second and x in metre. (a) Find the ratio of the displacement amplitude of the particles to the wavelength of the wave. (b) Find the ratio of the velocity amplitude of the particles to the wave speed.

9. A sound wave of frequency 100 Hz is travelling in air. The speed of sound in air is 350 m s^{-1}. (a) By how much is the phase changed at a given point in 2·5 ms? (b) What is the phase difference at a given instant between two points separated by a distance of 10·0 cm along the direction of propagation?

10. Two point sources of sound are kept at a separation of 10 cm. They vibrate in phase to produce waves of wavelength 5·0 cm. What would be the phase difference between the two waves arriving at a point 20 cm from one source (a) on the line joining the sources and (b) on the perpendicular bisector of the line joining the sources?

11. Calculate the speed of sound in oxygen from the following data. The mass of 22·4 litre of oxygen at STP ($T = 273$ K and $p = 1·0 \times 10^5$ N m^{-2}) is 32 g, the molar heat capacity of oxygen at constant volume is $C_V = 2·5 R$ and that at constant pressure is $C_p = 3·5 R$.

12. The speed of sound as measured by a student in the laboratory on a winter day is 340 m s^{-1} when the room temperature is 17°C. What speed will be measured by another student repeating the experiment on a day when the room temperature is 32°C?

13. At what temperature will the speed of sound be double of its value at 0°C?

14. The absolute temperature of air in a region linearly increases from T_1 to T_2 in a space of width d. Find the time taken by a sound wave to go through the region in terms of T_1, T_2, d and the speed v of sound at 273 K. Evaluate this time for $T_1 = 280$ K, $T_2 = 310$ K, $d = 33$ m and $v = 330$ m s^{-1}.

15. Find the change in the volume of 1·0 litre kerosene when it is subjected to an extra pressure of $2·0 \times 10^5$ N m^{-2} from the following data. Density of kerosene = 800 kg m^{-3} and speed of sound in kerosene = 1330 m s^{-1}.

16. Calculate the bulk modulus of air from the following data about a sound wave of wavelength 35 cm travelling in air. The pressure at a point varies between $(1·0 \times 10^5 \pm 14)$ Pa and the particles of the air vibrate in simple harmonic motion of amplitude $5·5 \times 10^{-6}$ m.

17. A source of sound operates at 2·0 kHz, 20 W emitting sound uniformly in all directions. The speed of sound in air is 340 m s^{-1} and the density of air is 1·2 kg m^{-3}. (a) What is the intensity at a distance of 6·0 m from the source? (b) What will be the pressure amplitude at this point? (c) What will be the displacement amplitude at this point?

18. The intensity of sound from a point source is $1·0 \times 10^{-8}$ W m^{-2} at a distance of 5·0 m from the source. What will be the intensity at a distance of 25 m from the source?

19. The sound level at a point 5·0 m away from a point source is 40 dB. What will be the level at a point 50 m away from the source?

20. If the intensity of sound is doubled, by how many decibels does the sound level increase?

21. Sound with intensity larger than 120 dB appears painful to a person. A small speaker delivers 2·0 W of audio output. How close can the person get to the speaker without hurting his ears?

22. If the sound level in a room is increased from 50 dB to 60 dB, by what factor is the pressure amplitude increased?

23. The noise level in a classroom in absence of the teacher is 50 dB when 50 students are present. Assuming that on the average each student outputs same sound energy per second, what will be the noise level if the number of students is increased to 100?

24. In Quincke's experiment the sound detected is changed from a maximum to a minimum when the sliding tube is moved through a distance of 2·50 cm. Find the frequency of sound if the speed of sound in air is 340 m s^{-1}.

25. In Quincke's experiment, the sound intensity has a minimum value I at a particular position. As the sliding tube is pulled out by a distance of 16·5 mm, the intensity increases to a maximum of $9I$. Take the speed of sound in air to be 330 m s^{-1}. (a) Find the frequency of the sound source. (b) Find the ratio of the amplitudes of the two waves arriving at the detector assuming that it does not change much between the positions of minimum intensity and maximum intensity.

26. Two audio speakers are kept some distance apart and are driven by the same amplifier system. A person is sitting at a place 6·0 m from one of the speakers and 6·4 m from the other. If the sound signal is continuously varied from 500 Hz to 5000 Hz, what are the frequencies for which there is a destructive interference at the place of the listener? Speed of sound in air = 320 m s^{-1}.

27. A source of sound S and a detector D are placed at some distance from one another. A big cardboard is placed near the detector and perpendicular to the line SD as shown in figure (16-E1). It is gradually moved away and it is found that the intensity changes from a maximum to a minimum as the board is moved through a distance of 20 cm. Find the frequency of the sound emitted. Velocity of sound in air is 336 m s^{-1}.

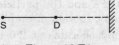

Figure 16-E1

28. A source S and a detector D are placed at a distance d apart. A big cardboard is placed at a distance $\sqrt{2}d$ from the source and the detector as shown in figure (16-E2). The source emits a wave of wavelength $= d/2$ which is received by the detector after reflection from the cardboard. It is found to be in phase with the direct wave received from the source. By what minimum distance should the cardboard be shifted away so that the reflected wave becomes out of phase with the direct wave ?

Figure 16-E2

29. Two stereo speakers are separated by a distance of 2·40 m. A person stands at a distance of 3·20 m directly in front of one of the speakers as shown in figure (16-E3). Find the frequencies in the audible range (20–20000 Hz) for which the listener will hear a minimum sound intensity. Speed of sound in air = 320 m s^{-1}.

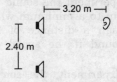

Figure 16-E3

30. Two sources of sound, S_1 and S_2, emitting waves of equal wavelength 20·0 cm, are placed with a separation of 20·0 cm between them. A detector can be moved on a line parallel to S_1S_2 and at a distance of 20·0 cm from it. Initially, the detector is equidistant from the two sources. Assuming that the waves emitted by the sources are in phase, find the minimum distance through which the detector should be shifted to detect a minimum of sound.

31. Two speakers S_1 and S_2, driven by the same amplifier, are placed at $y = 1·0$ m and $y = -1·0$ m (figure 16-E4). The speakers vibrate in phase at 600 Hz. A man stands at a point on the X-axis at a very large distance from the origin and starts moving parallel to the Y-axis. The speed of sound in air is 330 m s^{-1}. (a) At what angle θ will the intensity of sound drop to a minimum for the first time ? (b) At what angle will he hear a maximum of sound intensity for the first time ? (c) If he continues to walk along the line, how many more maxima can he hear ?

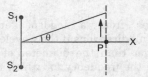

Figure 16-E4

32. Three sources of sound S_1, S_2 and S_3 of equal intensity are placed in a straight line with $S_1S_2 = S_2S_3$ (figure 16-E5). At a point P, far away from the sources, the wave coming from S_2 is 120° ahead in phase of that from S_1. Also, the wave coming from S_3 is 120° ahead of that from S_2. What would be the resultant intensity of sound at P ?

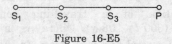

Figure 16-E5

33. Two coherent narrow slits emitting sound of wavelength λ in the same phase are placed parallel to each other at a small separation of 2λ. The sound is detected by moving a detector on the screen Σ at a distance $D(\gg \lambda)$ from the slit S_1 as shown in figure (16-E6). Find the distance x such that the intensity at P is equal to the intensity at O.

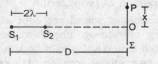

Figure 16-E6

34. Figure (16-E7) shows two coherent sources S_1 and S_2 which emit sound of wavelength λ in phase. The separation between the sources is 3λ. A circular wire of large radius is placed in such a way that S_1S_2 lies in its plane and the middle point of S_1S_2 is at the centre of

the wire. Find the angular positions θ on the wire for which constructive interference takes place.

Figure 16-E7

35. Two sources of sound S_1 and S_2 vibrate at same frequency and are in phase (figure 16-E8). The intensity of sound detected at a point P as shown in the figure is I_0 . (a) If θ equals 45°, what will be the intensity of sound detected at this point if one of the sources is switched off ? (b) What will be the answer of the previous part if θ = 60° ?

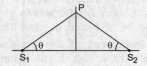

Figure 16-E8

36. Find the fundamental, first overtone and second overtone frequencies of an open organ pipe of length 20 cm. Speed of sound in air is 340 m s^{-1}.

37. A closed organ pipe can vibrate at a minimum frequency of 500 Hz. Find the length of the tube. Speed of sound in air = 340 m s^{-1}.

38. In a standing wave pattern in a vibrating air column, nodes are formed at a distance of 4·0 cm. If the speed of sound in air is 328 m s^{-1}, what is the frequency of the source ?

39. The separation between a node and the next antinode in a vibrating air column is 25 cm. If the speed of sound in air is 340 m s^{-1}, find the frequency of vibration of the air column.

40. A cylindrical metal tube has a length of 50 cm and is open at both ends. Find the frequencies between 1000 Hz and 2000 Hz at which the air column in the tube can resonate. Speed of sound in air is 340 m s^{-1}.

41. In a resonance column experiment, a tuning fork of frequency 400 Hz is used. The first resonance is observed when the air column has a length of 20·0 cm and the second resonance is observed when the air column has a length of 62·0 cm. (a) Find the speed of sound in air. (b) How much distance above the open end does the pressure node form ?

42. The first overtone frequency of a closed organ pipe P_1 is equal to the fundamental frequency of an open organ pipe P_2 . If the length of the pipe P_1 is 30 cm, what will be the length of P_2 ?

43. A copper rod of length 1·0 m is clamped at its middle point. Find the frequencies between 20 Hz and 20,000 Hz at which standing longitudinal waves can be set up in the rod. The speed of sound in copper is 3·8 km s^{-1}.

44. Find the greatest length of an organ pipe open at both ends that will have its fundamental frequency in the normal hearing range (20–20,000 Hz). Speed of sound in air = 340 m s^{-1}.

45. An open organ pipe has a length of 5 cm. (a) Find the fundamental frequency of vibration of this pipe. (b) What is the highest harmonic of such a tube that is in the audible range ? Speed of sound in air is 340 m s^{-1} and the audible range is 20–20,000 Hz.

46. An electronically driven loudspeaker is placed near the open end of a resonance column apparatus. The length of air column in the tube is 80 cm. The frequency of the loudspeaker can be varied between 20 Hz and 2 kHz. Find the frequencies at which the column will resonate. Speed of sound in air = 320 m s^{-1}.

47. Two successive resonance frequencies in an open organ pipe are 1620 Hz and 2268 Hz. Find the length of the tube. The speed of sound in air is 324 m s^{-1}.

48. A piston is fitted in a cylindrical tube of small cross section with the other end of the tube open. The tube resonates with a tuning fork of frequency 512 Hz. The piston is gradually pulled out of the tube and it is found that a second resonance occurs when the piston is pulled out through a distance of 32·0 cm. Calculate the speed of sound in the air of the tube.

49. A U-tube having unequal arm-lengths has water in it. A tuning fork of frequency 440 Hz can set up the air in the shorter arm in its fundamental mode of vibration and the same tuning fork can set up the air in the longer arm in its first overtone vibration. Find the length of the air columns. Neglect any end effect and assume that the speed of sound in air = 330 m s^{-1}.

50. Consider the situation shown in figure (16-E9). The wire which has a mass of 4·00 g oscillates in its second harmonic and sets the air column in the tube into vibrations in its fundamental mode. Assuming that the speed of sound in air is 340 m s^{-1}, find the tension in the wire.

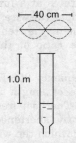

Figure 16-E9

51. A 30·0-cm-long wire having a mass of 10·0 g is fixed at the two ends and is vibrated in its fundamental mode. A 50·0-cm-long closed organ pipe, placed with its open end near the wire, is set up into resonance in its fundamental mode by the vibrating wire. Find the tension in the wire. Speed of sound in air = 340 m s^{-1}.

52. Show that if the room temperature changes by a small amount from T to $T + \Delta T$, the fundamental frequency of an organ pipe changes from ν to ν + Δν, where

$$\frac{\Delta v}{v} = \frac{1}{2} \frac{\Delta T}{T}.$$

53. The fundamental frequency of a closed pipe is 293 Hz when the air in it is at a temperature of 20°C. What will be its fundamental frequency when the temperature changes to 22°C ?

54. A Kundt's tube apparatus has a copper rod of length 1·0 m clamped at 25 cm from one of the ends. The tube contains air in which the speed of sound is 340 m/s. The powder collects in heaps separated by a distance of 5·0 cm. Find the speed of sound waves in copper.

55. A Kundt's tube apparatus has a steel rod of length 1·0 m clamped at the centre. It is vibrated in its fundamental mode at a frequency of 2600 Hz. The lycopodium powder dispersed in the tube collects into heaps separated by 6·5 cm. Calculate the speed of sound in steel and in air.

56. A source of sound with adjustable frequency produces 2 beats per second with a tuning fork when its frequency is either 476 Hz or 480 Hz. What is the frequency of the tuning fork ?

57. A tuning fork produces 4 beats per second with another tuning fork of frequency 256 Hz. The first one is now loaded with a little wax and the beat frequency is found to increase to 6 per second. What was the original frequency of the tuning fork ?

58. Calculate the frequency of beats produced in air when two sources of sound are activated, one emitting a wavelength of 32 cm and the other of 32·2 cm. The speed of sound in air is 350 m/s.

59. A tuning fork of unknown frequency makes 5 beats per second with another tuning fork which can cause a closed organ pipe of length 40 cm to vibrate in its fundamental mode. The beat frequency decreases when the first tuning fork is slightly loaded with wax. Find its original frequency. The speed of sound in air is 320 m/s.

60. A piano wire A vibrates at a fundamental frequency of 600 Hz. A second identical wire B produces 6 beats per second with it when the tension in A is slightly increased. Find the ratio of the tension in A to the tension in B.

61. A tuning fork of frequency 256 Hz produces 4 beats per second with a wire of length 25 cm vibrating in its fundamental mode. The beat frequency decreases when the length is slightly shortened. What could be the minimum length by which the wire be shortened so that it produces no beats with the tuning fork ?

62. A traffic policeman standing on a road sounds a whistle emitting the main frequency of 2·00 kHz. What could be the appparent frequency heard by a scooter-driver approaching the policeman at a speed of 36·0 km/h ? Speed of sound in air = 340 m/s.

63. The horn of a car emits sound with a dominant frequency of 2400 Hz. What will be the apparent dominant frequency heard by a person standing on the road in front of the car if the car is approaching at 18·0 km/h ? Speed of sound in air = 340 m/s.

64. A person riding a car moving at 72 km/h sounds a whistle emitting a wave of frequency 1250 Hz. What frequency will be heard by another person standing on the road (a) in front of the car (b) behind the car ? Speed of sound in air = 340 m/s.

65. A train approaching a platform at a speed of 54 km/h sounds a whistle. An observer on the platform finds its frequency to be 1620 Hz. The train passes the platform keeping the whistle on and without slowing down. What frequency will the observer hear after the train has crossed the platfrom ? The speed of sound in air = 332 m/s.

66. A bat emitting an ultrasonic wave of frequency 4.5×10^{4} Hz flies at a speed of 6 m/s between two parallel walls. Find the two frequencies heard by the bat and the beat frequency between the two. The speed of sound is 330 m/s.

67. A bullet passes past a person at a speed of 220 m/s. Find the fractional change in the frequency of the whistling sound heard by the person as the bullet crosses the person. Speed of sound in air = 330 m/s.

68. Two electric trains run at the same speed of 72 km/h along the same track and in the same direction with a separation of 2·4 km between them. The two trains simultaneously sound brief whistles. A person is situated at a perpendicular distance of 500 m from the track and is equidistant from the two trains at the instant of the whistling. If both the whistles were at 500 Hz and the speed of sound in air is 340 m/s, find the frequencies heard by the person.

69. A violin player riding on a slow train plays a 440 Hz note. Another violin player standing near the track plays the same note. When the two are close by and the train approaches the person on the ground, he hears 4·0 beats per second. The speed of sound in air = 340 m/s. (a) Calculate the speed of the train. (b) What beat frequency is heard by the player in the train ?

70. Two identical tuning forks vibrating at the same frequency 256 Hz are kept fixed at some distance apart. A listener runs between the forks at a speed of 3·0 m/s so that he approaches one tuning fork and recedes from the other (figure 16-E10). Find the beat frequency observed by the listener. Speed of sound in air = 332 m/s.

Figure 16-E10

71. Figure (16-E11) shows a person standing somewhere in between two identical tuning forks, each vibrating at

Figure 16-E11

512 Hz. If both the tuning forks move towards right at a speed of 5·5 m s^{-1}, find the number of beats heard by the listener. Speed of sound in air = 330 m s^{-1}.

72. A small source of sound vibrating at frequency 500 Hz is rotated in a circle of radius 100/π cm at a constant angular speed of 5·0 revolutions per second. A listener situates himself in the plane of the circle. Find the minimum and the maximum frequency of the sound observed. Speed of sound in air = 332 m s^{-1}.

73. Two trains are travelling towards each other both at a speed of 90 km h^{-1}. If one of the trains sounds a whistle at 500 Hz, what will be the apparent frequency heard in the other train ? Speed of sound in air = 350 m s^{-1}.

74. A traffic policeman sounds a whistle to stop a car-driver approaching towards him. The car-driver does not stop and takes the plea in court that because of the Doppler shift, the frequency of the whistle reaching him might have gone beyond the audible limit of 20 kHz and he did not hear it. Experiments showed that the whistle emits a sound with frequency close to 16 kHz. Assuming that the claim of the driver is true, how fast was he driving the car ? Take the speed of sound in air to be 330 m s^{-1}. Is this speed practical with today's technology ?

75. A car moving at 108 km h^{-1} finds another car in front of it going in the same direction at 72 km h^{-1}. The first car sounds a horn that has a dominant frequency of 800 Hz. What will be the apparent frequency heard by the driver in the front car ? Speed of sound in air = 330 m s^{-1}.

76. Two submarines are approaching each other in a calm sea. The first submarine travels at a speed of 36 km h^{-1} and the other at 54 km h^{-1} relative to the water. The first submarine sends a sound signal (sound waves in water are also called *sonar*) at a frequency of 2000 Hz. (a) At what frequency is this signal received by the second submarine ? (b) The signal is reflected from the second submarine. At what frequency is this signal received by the first submarine. Take the speed of the sound wave in water to be 1500 m s^{-1}.

77. A small source of sound oscillates in simple harmonic motion with an amplitude of 17 cm. A detector is placed along the line of motion of the source. The source emits a sound of frequency 800 Hz which travels at a speed of 340 m s^{-1}. If the width of the frequency band detected by the detector is 8 Hz, find the time period of the source.

78. A boy riding on his bike is going towards east at a speed of 4 $\sqrt{2}$ m s^{-1}. At a certain point he produces a sound pulse of frequency 1650 Hz that travels in air at a speed of 334 m s^{-1}. A second boy stands on the ground 45° south of east from him. Find the frequency of the pulse as received by the second boy.

79. A sound source, fixed at the origin, is continuously emitting sound at a frequency of 660 Hz. The sound travels in air at a speed of 330 m s^{-1}. A listener is moving along the line x = 336 m at a constant speed of 26 m s^{-1}. Find the frequency of the sound as observed by the listener when he is (a) at y = − 140 m, (b) at y = 0 and (c) at y = 140 m.

80. A train running at 108 km h^{-1} towards east whistles at a dominant frequency of 500 Hz. Speed of sound in air is 340 m/s. (a) What frequency will a passenger sitting near the open window hear ? (b) What frequency will a person standing near the track hear whom the train has just passed ? (c) A wind starts blowing towards east at a speed of 36 km h^{-1}. Calculate the frequencies heard by the passenger in the train and by the person standing near the track.

81. A boy riding on a bicycle going at 12 km h^{-1} towards a vertical wall whistles at his dog on the ground. If the frequency of the whistle is 1600 Hz and the speed of sound in air is 330 m s^{-1}, find (a) the frequency of the whistle as received by the wall (b) the frequency of the reflected whistle as received by the boy.

82. A person standing on a road sends a sound signal to the driver of a car going away from him at a speed of 72 km h^{-1}. The signal travelling at 330 m s^{-1} in air and having a frequency of 1600 Hz gets reflected from the body of the car and returns. Find the frequency of the reflected signal as heard by the person.

83. A car moves with a speed of 54 km h^{-1} towards a cliff. The horn of the car emits sound of frequency 400 Hz at a speed of 335 m s^{-1}. (a) Find the wavelength of the sound emitted by the horn in front of the car. (b) Find the wavelength of the wave reflected from the cliff. (c) What frequency does a person sitting in the car hear for the reflected sound wave ? (d) How many beats does he hear in 10 seconds between the sound coming directly from the horn and that coming after the reflection ?

84. An operator sitting in his base camp sends a sound signal of frequency 400 Hz. The signal is reflected back from a car moving towards him. The frequency of the reflected sound is found to be 410 Hz. Find the speed of the car. Speed of sound in air = 324 m s^{-1}.

85. Figure (16-E12) shows a source of sound moving along the X-axis at a speed of 22 m s^{-1} continuously emitting a sound of frequency 2·0 kHz which travels in air at a speed of 330 m s^{-1}. A listener Q stands on the Y-axis at a distance of 330 m from the origin. At t = 0, the source crosses the origin P. (a) When does the sound emitted from the source at P reach the listener Q ? (b) What will be the frequency heard by the listener at this instant ? (c) Where will the source be at this instant ?

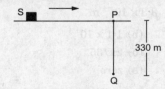

Figure 16-E12

86. A source emitting sound at frequency 4000 Hz, is moving along the Y-axis with a speed of 22 m s^{-1}. A listener is situated on the ground at the position (660 m, 0). Find the frequency of the sound received by the listener at the instant the source crosses the origin. Speed of sound in air = 330 m s^{-1}.

87. A source of sound emitting a 1200 Hz note travels along a straight line at a speed of 170 m s^{-1}. A detector is

placed at a distance of 200 m from the line of motion of the source. (a) Find the frequency of sound received by the detector at the instant when the source gets closest to it. (b) Find the distance between the source and the detector at the instant it detects the frequency 1200 Hz. Velocity of sound in air = 340 m s^{-1}.

88. A small source of sound S of frequency 500 Hz is attached to the end of a light string and is whirled in a vertical circle of radius 1·6 m. The string just remains tight when the source is at the highest point. (a) An observer is located in the same vertical plane at a large distance and at the same height as the centre of the circle (figure 16-E13). The speed of sound in air = 330 m s^{-1} and $g = 10$ m s^{-2}. Find the maximum frequency heard by the observer. (b) An observer is situated at a large distance vertically above the centre

of the circle. Find the frequencies heard by the observer corresponding to the sound emitted by the source when it is at the same height as the centre.

Figure 16-E13

89. A source emitting a sound of frequency ν is placed at a large distance from an observer. The source starts moving towards the observer with a uniform acceleration a. Find the frequency heard by the observer corresponding to the wave emitted just after the source starts. The speed of sound in the medium is v.

□

ANSWERS

OBJECTIVE I

1. (a)	2. (d)	3. (d)	4. (c)	5. (d)	6. (c)
7. (a)	8. (d)	9. (b)	10. (a)	11. (c)	12. (c)
13. (a)	14. (d)	15. (d)	16. (c)		

OBJECTIVE II

1. (d)   2. (a), (c)   3. (b), (c), (d)
4. (c)   5. (a), (d)

EXERCISES

1. 2·75 m s
2. 0·5 s
3. 333 m s^{-1}
4. 18 mm, 18 m
5. 7·25 cm, 72·5 m
6. (a) 170 Hz   (b) 17 kHz
7. $7·6 \times 10^{-5}$ m, $3·3 \times 10^{-4}$ m
8. (a) $1·7 \times 10^{-5}$ (b) $1·1 \times 10^{-4}$
9. (a) $\pi/2$ (b) $2\pi/35$
10. (a) zero   (b) zero
11. 310 m s^{-1}
12. 349 m s^{-1}
13. 819°C
14. $\dfrac{2d}{v} \cdot \dfrac{\sqrt{273}}{\sqrt{T_1} + \sqrt{T_2}}$, 96 m s^{-1}
15. 0·14 cm^3
16. $1·4 \times 10^5$ N m^{-2}
17. (a) 44 mW m^{-2} (b) 6·0 Pa   (c) $1·2 \times 10^{-6}$ m

18. $4·0 \times 10^{-10}$ W m^{-2}
19. 20 dB
20. 3 dB
21. 40 cm
22. $\sqrt{10}$
23. 53 dB
24. 3·4 kHz
25. (a) 5·0 kHz   (b) 2
26. 1200 Hz, 2000 Hz, 2800 Hz, 3600 Hz and 4400 Hz
27. 420 Hz
28. 0·13 d
29. $200 (2n + 1)$ Hz, where $n = 0, 1, 2, ..., 49$
30. 12·6 cm
31. (a) 7·9°   (b) 16°   (c) two
32. zero
33. $\sqrt{3} D$
34. 0°, 48·2°, 70·5°, 90° and similar points in other quadrants
35. (a) $I_0/4$ (b) $I_0/4$
36. 850 Hz, 1700 Hz and 2550 Hz
37. 17 cm
38. 4·1 kHz
39. 340 Hz
40. 1020 Hz, 1360 Hz and 1700 Hz
41. (a) 336 m s^{-1} (b) 1 cm
42. 20 cm
43. $1·9n$ kHz, where $n = 1, 2, 3, ..., 10$
44. 8·5 m
45. (a) 3·4 kHz   (b) 5
46. $100(2n + 1)$ Hz, where $n = 0, 1, 2, 3, ..., 9$
47. 25 cm

48. 328 m/s
49. 18.8 cm, 56.3 cm
50. 11.6 N
51. 347 N
53. 294 Hz
54. 3400 m/s
55. 5200 m/s, 338 m/s
56. 478 Hz
57. 252 Hz
58. 7 per second
59. 205 Hz
60. 1·02
61. 0·39 cm
62. 2·06 kHz
63. 2436 Hz
64. (a) 1328 Hz   (b) 1181 Hz
65. 1480 Hz
66. $4·67 \times 10^4$ Hz, $4·34 \times 10^4$ Hz, 3270 Hz
67. 0·8
68. 529 Hz, 474 Hz
69. (a) 11 km/h   (b) a little less than 4 beats/s
70. 4·6 Hz
71. 17·5 Hz, may not be able to distinguish

72. 485 Hz and 515 Hz
73. 577 Hz
74. 300 km/h
75. 827 Hz
76. (a) 2034 Hz   (b) 2068 Hz
77. 0·63 s
78. 1670 Hz
79. (a) 680 Hz   (b) 660 Hz   (c) 640 Hz
80. (a) 500 Hz   (b) 459 Hz
    (c) 500 Hz by the passenger and 458 by the person near the track
81. (a) 1616 Hz   (b) 1632 Hz
82. 1417 Hz
83. (a) 80 cm   (b) 80 cm   (c) 437 Hz
    (d) No beat may be heard
84. 4 m/s
85. (a) $t = 1$ second   (b) 2·0 kHz   (c) at $x = 22$ m
86. 4018 Hz
87. (a) 1600 Hz   (b) 224 m
88. (a) 514 Hz   (b) 490 Hz and 511 Hz
89. $\dfrac{2vv^2}{2vv - a}$

CHAPTER 17

LIGHT WAVES

17.1 WAVES OR PARTICLES

The question whether light is a wave or a particle has a very interesting and a long history. The investigations about the nature of light has unfolded a huge treasure of knowledge and understanding. This question has great contributions to the development of the theory of quantum mechanics which presents an altogether different picture of the world in which there are no particles, no positions, no momenta in an ordinary sense.

Newton, the greatest among the great, believed that light is a collection of particles. He believed that a light source emits tiny corpuscles of light and these corpuscles travel in straight lines when not acted upon by external forces. The fact that light seems to travel in straight lines and cast shadows behind the obstacles was perhaps the strongest evidence of the particle nature of light. Newton could explain the laws of reflection of light on the basis of elastic collisions of the particles of light with the surface it is incident upon. The laws of refraction were explained by assuming that the particles of denser medium, such as glass or water, strongly attract the particles of light causing a bending at the surface. Newton had performed a number of experiments to study the behaviour of light. The book *Optiks* written by him, gives a classic account of these experiments.

The Dutch physicist Christian Huygens (1629–1695), who was a contemporary of Newton, suggested that light may be a wave phenomenon. The apparent rectilinear propagation of light may be due to the fact that the wavelength of light may be much smaller than the dimensions of these openings and obstacles.

Huygens' proposal remained in a dump for almost about a century. The scientific community by and large had great faith in Newton's writings and the particle theory remained in chair for a long time when it was seriously challenged by the double-slit experiment of Thomas Young (1773–1829) in 1801. This experiment clearly established that light coming from two coherent sources interferes and produces maxima and minima depending on the path difference. A series of experiments on diffraction of light conducted by the French physicist Augustin Jean Fresnel (1788–1827), measurement of velocity of light in water by Foucault in 1850, development of theory of electromagnetic waves by Maxwell in 1860 which correctly predicted the speed of light, were parts of a long activity which put the corpuscle theory of light to an end and convincingly established that light is a wave phenomenon.

But the drama was not yet over. The climax came when the wave theory of light failed to explain Hallwachs and Lenard's observation in 1900 that when light falls on a metal surface, electrons are ejected and that the kinetic energy of the emitted electrons does not depend on the intensity of the light used. Hertz possibly had the first observation of this phenomenon in early 1880's. This observation is known as *photoelectric effect* and we shall study it in detail in a later chapter. Photoelectric effect was explained by another giant, Albert Einstein, in 1905 on a particle model of light only. The old question "waves or particles" was reopened and an amicable understanding was reached in accepting that light has dual character. It can behave as particles as well as waves depending on its interaction with the surrounding. Later, it was found that even the well-established particles such as electrons also have a dual character and can show interference and diffraction under suitable situations. We shall study the wave particle duality in a later chapter. In this chapter, we shall study the wave aspect of light.

17.2 THE NATURE OF LIGHT WAVES

In a wave motion, there is some quantity which changes its value with time and space. In the wave on a string, it is the transverse displacement of the particles that changes with time and is different for different particles at the same instant. In the case of sound waves, it is the pressure at a point in the medium that oscillates as time passes and has different values at different points at the same instant. We also know that it is the elastic properties of the medium that is responsible for the propagation of disturbance in a medium. The speed of a wave is determined by the elastic as well as the inertia properties of the medium.

The case with light waves is a bit different. The light waves need no material medium to travel. They can propagate in vacuum. Light is a nonmechanical wave. It was very difficult for the earlier physicists to conceive a wave propagating without a medium. Once the interference and diffraction experiments established the wave character of light, the search began for the medium responsible for the propagation of light waves. Light comes from the sun to the earth crossing millions of kilometers where apparently there is no material medium. What transmits the wave through this region ? Physicists assumed that a very dilute and highly elastic material medium is present everywhere in space and they named it "ether". Ether was never discovered and today we understand that light wave can propagate in vacuum.

The quantity that changes with space and time, in terms of which the wave equation should be written, is the electric field existing in space where light travels. We shall define and study electric field in later chapters, here we need only to know that (a) the electric field is a vector quantity and (b) the electric field is transverse to the direction of propagation of light (there are exceptions but we shall not discuss them).

Because light waves are transverse, they can be polarized. If a plane wave of light is travelling along the x-direction, the electric field may be along the y-direction or along the z-direction or in any other direction in the y-z plane. The equation of such a light wave may be written as

$$E = E_0 \sin \omega(t - x/v), \quad \ldots \quad (17.1)$$

where E_0 is the magnitude of the electric field at point x at time t. The speed of light is itself an interesting quantity. The speed of light in vacuum with respect to any observer is always the same and is very nearly equal to 3×10^8 m s^{-1}. This speed is a fixed universal constant irrespective of the state of motion of the observer. This needs a basic revision of our concepts about space and time and is the basis of special theory of relativity. The speed of light in vacuum is generally denoted by the letter c. When a light wave travels in a transparent material, the speed is decreased by a factor μ, called the refractive index of the material.

$$\mu = \frac{\text{speed of light in vacuum}}{\text{speed of light in the material}} \cdot \quad \ldots \quad (17.2)$$

For a spherical wave originating from a point source, the equation of the wave is of the form

$$E = \frac{aE_0}{r} \sin \omega(t - r/v),$$

where a is a constant.

The amplitude is proportional to the inverse of the distance and thus the intensity is proportional to the square of the inverse distance.

Example 17.1

The refractive index of glass is 1·5. Find the speed of light in glass.

Solution : We have

$$\mu = \frac{\text{speed of light in vacuum}}{\text{speed of light in the material}}$$

Thus, speed of light in glass

$$= \frac{\text{speed of light in vacuum}}{\mu}$$

$$= \frac{3 \cdot 0 \times 10^8 \text{ m s}^{-1}}{1 \cdot 5} = 2 \cdot 0 \times 10^8 \text{ m s}^{-1}.$$

The frequency of visible light varies from about 3800×10^{11} Hz to about 7800×10^{11} Hz. The corresponding wavelengths (obtained from $\lambda = c/\nu$) are 380 nm to 780 nm. The colour sensation to a human eye is related to the wavelength of the light. Light of wavelength close to 780 nm appears red, and that close to 380 nm appears violet. Table (17.1) shows a rough relationship between the colour sensed and the wavelength of light.

Table 17.1

Colour	Wavelength (order)
Red	620–780 nm
Orange	590–620 nm
Yellow	570–590 nm
Green	500–570 nm
Blue	450–500 nm
Violet	380–450 nm

Light of single wavelength is called *monochromatic light*. Equation (17.1) represents a monochromatic light wave. Often, the light emitted by a source is a mixture of light corresponding to different wavelengths. Depending on the composition of the mixture, a human eye senses a large number of colours. White light itself is a mixture of light of all wavelengths from about 380 nm to about 780 nm in appropriate proportion.

In fact, a strictly monochromatic light is not possible to obtain. There is always a spread in wavelength. The best monochromatic light are LASERs in which the spread in wavelength is very small but not zero. We shall use the word "monochromatic light" to mean that the light contains a dominant wavelength with only a little spread.

We discussed in the previous chapter that if a wave is obstructed during its propagation by an obstacle or an opening, it gets diffracted. A plane wave going through a small opening becomes more like a spherical wave on the other side. Thus, the wave bends at the edges. Also, if the dimensions of the obstacle or the opening is much larger than the wavelength, the diffraction is negligible and the rays go along straight lines.

In the case of light, the wavelength is around 380–780 nm. The obstacles or openings encountered in normal situations are generally of the order of millimeters or even larger. Thus, the wavelength is several thousands times smaller than the usual obstacles or openings. The diffraction is almost negligible and the light waves propagate in straight lines and cast shadows of the obstacles. The light can then be treated as light rays which are straight lines drawn from the source and which terminate at an opaque surface and which pass through an opening undeflected. This is known as the *Geometrical optics* approximation and majority of the phenomena in normal life may be discussed in this approximation. The three major rules governing geometrical optics are the following.

1. *Rectilinear propagation of light* : Light travels in straight lines unless it is reflected by a polished surface or the medium of propagation is changed.

2. *Reflection of light* : The angle of incidence and the angle of reflection (i.e., the angles made by the incident and the reflected rays with the normal to the surface) are equal. Also, the incident ray, the reflected ray and the normal to the reflecting surface are coplanar.

3. *Refraction of light* : When light travelling in one medium enters another medium, the angle of incidence i and the angle of refraction r (angle made by the refracted ray with the normal) satisfy

$$\frac{\sin i}{\sin r} = \frac{v_1}{v_2},$$

where v_1 and v_2 are the speeds of light in the first medium and the second medium respectively. Also, the incident ray, the refracted ray and the normal to the separating surface are coplanar.

The rectilinear propagation of light is explained on the basis of wave theory by observing that the wavelength of light is much smaller than the obstacles or openings usually encountered. The laws of reflection and refraction can also be explained by wave theory. The rigorous derivation involves somewhat complicated mathematics, but things can be fairly well-understood by a geometrical method proposed by Huygens. This method tells us how to construct the shape of a wavefront of light wave from the given shape at an earlier instant. We refer again from the previous chapters that (a) a surface on which the wave disturbance is in same phase at all points is called a wavefront, (b) the direction of propagation of a wave at a point is perpendicular to the wavefront through that point, (c) the wavefronts of a wave originating from a point source are spherical and (d) the wavefronts for a wave going along a fixed direction are planes perpendicular to that direction.

17.3 HUYGENS' PRINCIPLE

The first proposer of the wave theory of light, Huygens, considered light to be a mechanical wave moving in a hypothetical medium which was named as ether. If we consider a surface σ enclosing a light source S, the optical disturbance at any point beyond σ must reach after crossing σ. The particles of the surface σ vibrate as the wave from S reaches there and these vibrations cause the layer beyond to vibrate. We can thus assume that the particles on σ act as new sources of light waves emitting spherical waves and the disturbance at a point A (figure 17.1) beyond σ, is caused by the superposition of all these spherical waves coming from different points of σ. Huygens called the particles spreading the vibration beyond them as *secondary sources* and the spherical wavefronts emitted from these secondary sources as the *secondary wavelets*.

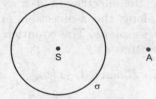

Figure 17.1

Huygens' principle may be stated in its most general form as follows :

Various points of an arbitrary surface, when reached by a wavefront, become secondary sources of light emitting secondary wavelets. The disturbance beyond the surface results from the superposition of these secondary wavelets.

Consider a spherical surface σ with its centre at a point source S emitting a pulse of light (figure 17.2).

The optical disturbance reaches the particles on σ at time $t = 0$ and lasts for a short interval in which the positive and negative disturbances are produced. These particles on σ then send spherical wavelets which spread beyond σ. At time t, each of these wavelets has a radius vt. In figure (17.2), the solid lines represent positive optical disturbance and the dashed lines represent negative optical disturbance. The sphere Σ is the geometrical envelope of all the secondary wavelets which were emitted at time $t = 0$ from the primary wavefront σ.

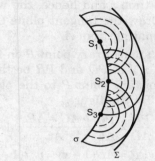

Figure 17.2

It is clear that at the points just inside Σ, only the positive disturbances of various secondary wavelets are meeting. The wavelets, therefore, interfere constructively at these points and produce finite disturbance. For points well inside Σ, some of the wavelets contribute positive disturbance and some others, centred at a nearby point of σ, produce negative disturbance. Thus, the resultant disturbance is zero at these points. The disturbance which was situated at σ at time $t = 0$ is, therefore, confined to a surface Σ at time t. Hence, the secondary wavelets from σ superpose in such a way that they produce a new wavefront at the geometrical envelope of the secondary wavelets.

This allows us to state the method of Huygens construction as follows :

Huygens Construction

Various points of an arbitrary surface, as they are reached by a wavefront, become the sources of secondary wavelets. The geometrical envelope of these wavelets at any given later instant represents the new position of the wavefront at that instant.

The method is quite general and although it was developed on the notion of mechanical waves it is valid for light waves. The surface used in the Huygens construction may have any arbitrary shape, not necessarily a wavefront itself. If the medium is homogeneous, (i.e., the optical properties of the medium are same everywhere) light moves forward

and does not reflect back. We assume, therefore, that the secondary wavelets are emitted only in the forward direction and the geometrical envelope of the wavelets is to be taken in the direction of advancement of the wave. If there is a change of medium, the wave may be reflected from the discontinuity just as a wave on a string is reflected from a fixed end or a free end. In that case, secondary wavelets on the backward side should also be considered.

Reflection of Light

Let us suppose that a parallel light beam is incident upon a reflecting plane surface σ such as a plane mirror. The wavefronts of the incident wave will be planes perpendicular to the direction of incidence. After reflection, the light returns in the same medium. Consider a particular wavefront AB of the incident light wave at $t = 0$ (figure 17.3). We shall construct the position of this wavefront at time t.

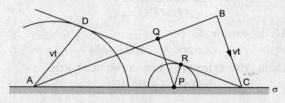

Figure 17.3

To apply Huygens construction, we use the reflecting surface σ for the sources of secondary wavelets. As the various points of σ are reached by the wavefront AB, they become sources of secondary wavelets. Because of the change of medium, the wavelets are emitted both in forward and backward directions. To study reflection, the wavelets emitted in the backward directions are to be considered.

Suppose, the point A of σ is reached by the wavefront AB at time $t = 0$. This point then emits a secondary wavelet. At time t, this wavelet becomes a hemispherical surface of radius vt centred at A. Here v is the speed of light. Let C be the point which is just reached by the wavefront at time t and hence the wavelet is a point at C itself. Draw the tangent plane CD from C to the hemispherical wavelet originated from A. Consider an arbitrary point P on the surface and let $AP/AC = x$. Let PQ be the perpendicular from P to AB and let PR be the perpendicular from P to CD. By the figure,

$$\frac{PR}{AD} = \frac{PC}{AC} = \frac{AC - AP}{AC} = 1 - x$$

or, $$PR = AD\,(1 - x) = vt(1 - x). \qquad \dots \ (i)$$

Also, $$\frac{QP}{BC} = \frac{AP}{AC} = x$$

or, $\qquad QP = x\, BC = xvt.$

The time taken by the wavefront to reach the point P is, therefore,

$$t_1 = \frac{QP}{v} = xt.$$

The point P becomes a source of secondary wavelets at time t_1. The radius of the wavelet at time t, originated from P is, therefore,

$$a = v(t - t_1) = v(t - xt) = vt(1 - x). \qquad \ldots \text{(ii)}$$

By (i) and (ii), we see that PR is the radius of the secondary wavelet at time t coming from P. As CD is perpendicular to PR, CD touches this wavelet. As P is an arbitrary point on σ, all the wavelets originated from different points of σ, touch CD at time t. Thus, CD is the envelope of all these wavelets at time t. It is, therefore, the new position of the wavefront AB. The reflected rays are perpendicular to this wavefront CD.

In triangles ABC and ADC :

$$AD = BC = vt,$$

AC is common,

and $\qquad \angle ADC = \angle ABC = 90°.$

Thus, the triangles are congruent and

$$\angle BAC = \angle DCA. \qquad \ldots \text{(iii)}$$

Now, the incident ray is perpendicular to AB and the normal is perpendicular to AC. The angle between the incident ray and the normal is, therefore, equal to the angle between AB and AC. Thus, $\angle BAC$ is equal to the angle of incidence.

Similarly, $\angle DCA$ represents the angle of reflection and we have proved in (iii) that the angle of incidence equals the angle of reflection. From the geometry, it is clear that the incident ray, the reflected ray and the normal to the surface AC lie in the plane of drawing and hence, are coplanar.

Refraction of Light

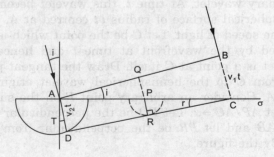

Figure 17.4

Suppose σ represents the surface separating two transparent media, medium 1 and medium 2 in which the speeds of light are v_1 and v_2 respectively. A parallel beam of light moving in medium 1 is incident

on the surface and enters medium 2. In figure (17.4), we show the incident wavefront AB in medium 1 at $t = 0$. The incident rays are perpendicular to this wavefront. To find the position of this wavefront after refraction, we apply the method of Huygens construction to the surface σ. The point A of the surface is reached by the wavefront AB at $t = 0$. This point becomes the source of secondary wavelet which expands in medium 2 at velocity v_2. At time t, this takes the shape of a hemisphere of radius $v_2\, t$ centred at A. The point C of the surface is just reached by the wavefront at time t and hence, the wavelet is a point at C itself. Draw the tangent plane CD from C to the wavelet originating from A.

Consider an arbitrary point P on the surface σ and let $AP/AC = x$. Let PQ and PR be the perpendiculars from this arbitrary point P to the planes AB and CD respectively. By the figure,

$$\frac{PR}{AD} = \frac{PC}{AC} = \frac{AC - AP}{AC} = 1 - x$$

or, $\qquad PR = AD(1 - x) = v_2\, t(1 - x). \qquad \ldots \text{(i)}$

Also, $\qquad \dfrac{QP}{BC} = \dfrac{AP}{AC} = x.$

Thus, $\qquad QP = x\, BC = xv_1\, t.$

The time, at which the wavefront arrives at P, is

$$t_1 = \frac{QP}{v_1} = xt.$$

The radius of the wavelet originated from P and going into the second medium is, therefore,

$$a = v_2(t - t_1) = v_2\, t(1 - x). \qquad \ldots \text{(ii)}$$

By (i) and (ii), we see that PR is the radius of the wavelet originating from P. As CD is perpendicular to PR, CD touches this wavelet. As P is an arbitrary point on σ, all the wavelets which originated from different points on σ touch CD at time t. The plane CD is, therefore, the geometrical envelope of all the secondary wavelets at time t. It is, therefore, the position of the wavefront AB at time t. The refracted rays are perpendicular to CD.

The angle BAC is also equal to the angle between the incident ray (which is perpendicular to AB) and the normal to the surface and hence, it is equal to the angle of incidence i. Similarly, $\angle ACD$ is equal to the angle of refraction r.

We have $\sin i = \dfrac{BC}{AC}$

and $\qquad \sin r = \dfrac{AD}{AC}$

so that

$$\frac{\sin i}{\sin r} = \frac{BC}{AD} = \frac{v_1\, t}{v_2\, t}$$

or,
$$\frac{\sin i}{\sin r} = \frac{v_1}{v_2}$$

which is called the *Snell's law*. The ratio v_1/v_2 is called the refractive index of medium 2 with respect to medium 1 and is denoted by μ_{21}. If the medium 1 is vacuum, μ_{21} is simply the refractive index of the medium 2 and is denoted by μ.

Also,
$$\mu_{21} = \frac{v_1}{v_2} = \frac{c/v_2}{c/v_1} = \frac{\mu_2}{\mu_1}.$$

From the figure, it is clear that the incident ray, the refracted ray and the normal to the surface σ are all in the plane of the drawing, i.e., they are coplanar.

Suppose light from air is incident on water. It bends towards the normal giving $i > r$. From Snell's law proved above, $v_1 > v_2$. Thus, according to the wave theory the speed of light should be greater in air than in water. This is opposite to the prediction of Newton's corpuscle theory. If light bends due to the attraction of the particles of a medium then speed of light should be greater in the medium. Later, experiments on measurement of speed of light confirmed wave theory.

Thus, the basic rules of geometrical optics could be understood in terms of the wave theory of light using Huygens' principle. In the rest of this chapter, we shall study the wave behaviour, such as the interference, diffraction and polarization of light.

17.4 YOUNG'S DOUBLE HOLE EXPERIMENT

Thomas Young in 1801 reported his experiment on the interference of light. He made a pinhole in a cardboard and allowed sunlight to pass through. This light was then allowed to fall upon another cardboard having two pinholes side by side placed symmetrically. The emergent light was received on a plane screen placed at some distance. At a given point on the screen, the waves from the two holes had different phases. These waves interfered to give a pattern of bright and dark areas. The variation of intensity on the screen demonstrated the interference taking place between the light waves reaching the screen from the two pinholes.

The pattern of bright and dark areas are sharply defined only if light of a single wavelength is used. Young's original experiments were performed with white light and he deduced from the experiments that the wavelength of extreme red light was around 1/36000 inch and that of the extreme violet was around 1/60000 inch. These results are quite close to their accurate measurements done with modern instruments.

17.5 YOUNG'S DOUBLE SLIT EXPERIMENT

In the double slit experiment, we use two long parallel slits as the sources of light in place of pin holes. The light coming out of the two slits is intercepted on a screen placed parallel to the plane of the slits. The slits are illuminated by a parallel beam of a monochromatic (of nearly a single wavelength) light. A series of dark and bright strips, called *fringes*, are observed on the screen. The arrangement of the experiment is schematically shown in figure (17.5a). Figure (17.5b) shows a cross section of the arrangement of the Young's double slit experiment.

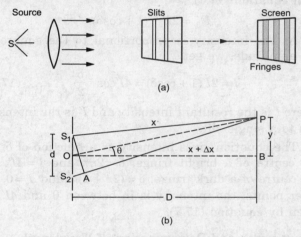

Figure 17.5

The two waves interfering at P have covered different distances $S_1P = x$ and $S_2P = x + \Delta x$. The electric fields at P due to the two waves may be written as
$$E_1 = E_{01} \sin(kx - \omega t)$$
and
$$E_2 = E_{02} \sin[k(x + \Delta x) - \omega t]$$
$$= E_{02} \sin[kx - \omega t + \delta],$$
where
$$\delta = \frac{\omega}{v} \Delta x = \frac{2\pi}{\lambda} \Delta x. \qquad \dots (17.3)$$

The situation is mathematically identical to that discussed in chapter 15, section 15.7. The resultant field at the point P is
$$E = E_0 \sin(kx - \omega t + \varepsilon),$$
where
$$E_0^2 = E_{01}^2 + E_{02}^2 + 2E_{01} E_{02} \cos\delta \qquad \dots (17.4)$$
and
$$\tan\varepsilon = \frac{E_{02} \sin\delta}{E_{01} + E_{02} \cos\delta}.$$

The conditions for constructive (bright fringe) and destructive (dark fringe) interferences are,
$$\left. \begin{array}{ll} \delta = 2n\pi & \text{for bright fringes} \\ \text{and} \quad \delta = (2n + 1)\pi & \text{for dark fringes} \end{array} \right\} \quad \dots (17.5)$$
where n is an integer.

Using, (17.3) these conditions may also be written as

$$\Delta x = n\lambda \qquad \text{for bright fringes}$$
$$\text{and} \quad \Delta x = \left(n + \frac{1}{2}\right)\lambda \quad \text{for dark fringes.} \quad \bigg| \quad \dots (17.6)$$

At the point B in figure (17.5b), $\Delta x = 0$ as $S_1 B = S_2 B$. This point is the centre of the bright fringe corresponding to $n = 0$.

Intensity Variation

If the two slits are identical, $E_{01} = E_{02} = E_0{}'$ and from equation (17.4),

$$E_0^{\,2} = 2E_0{}'^{\,2}(1 + \cos\delta).$$

As the intensity is proportional to the square of the amplitude, we get

$$I = 2I'(1 + \cos\delta) = 4I'\cos^2\frac{\delta}{2}, \qquad \dots (17.7)$$

where I is the resultant intensity and I' is the intensity due to a single slit.

The equation gives intensity as a function of δ. At the centre of a bright fringe, $\delta = 2n\pi$ and $I = 4I'$. At the centre of a dark fringe, $\delta = (2n+1)\pi$ and $I = 0$. At other points, the intensity is in between 0 and $4I'$ as given by equation (17.7).

Fringe-width and Determination of Wavelength

The separation on the screen between the centres of two consecutive bright fringes or two consecutive dark fringes is called the *fringe-width*. Suppose $S_1 A$ is the perpendicular from S_1 to $S_2 P$ (figure 17.5b). Suppose,

$D = OB$ = separation between the slits and the screen,

d = separation between the slits

and $D \gg d$.

Under the above approximation $(D \gg d)$, $S_1 P$ and $S_2 P$ are nearly parallel and hence $S_1 A$ is very nearly perpendicular to $S_1 P$, $S_2 P$ and OP. As $S_1 S_2$ is perpendicular to OB and $S_1 A$ is perpendicular (nearly) to OP, we have

$$\angle S_2 S_1 A = \angle POB = \theta.$$

This is a small angle as $D \gg d$.

The path difference is

$$\Delta x = PS_2 - PS_1 \approx PS_2 - PA$$
$$= S_2 A = d\sin\theta$$
$$\approx d\,\tan\theta = d\,\frac{y}{D}.$$

The centres of the bright fringes are obtained at distances y from the point B, where

$$\Delta x = d\,\frac{y}{D} = n\lambda \quad \text{(where } n \text{ is an integer)}$$

or,
$$y = \frac{nD\lambda}{d},$$

i.e., at $y = 0, \pm\dfrac{D\lambda}{d}, \pm\dfrac{2D\lambda}{d}, \pm\dfrac{3D\lambda}{d}, \dots,$ etc.

The centres of dark fringes will be obtained, where

$$\Delta x = d\,\frac{y}{D} = \left(n + \frac{1}{2}\right)\lambda$$

or,
$$y = \left(n + \frac{1}{2}\right)\frac{D\lambda}{d},$$

i.e., at $y = \pm\dfrac{D\lambda}{2d}, \pm\dfrac{3D\lambda}{2d}, \pm\dfrac{5D\lambda}{2d}, \dots$

The fringe-width is, therefore,

$$w = \frac{D\lambda}{d}. \qquad \dots (17.8)$$

By measuring D, d and W in an experiment, one can calculate the wavelength of the light used. We see from equation (17.8) that as the separation d between the slits is increased, the fringe-width is decreased. If d becomes much larger than λ, the fringe-width will be very small. The maxima and minima, in this case, will be so closely spaced that it will look like a uniform intensity pattern. This is an example of the general result that the wave effects are difficult to observe, if the wavelength is small compared to the dimensions of the obstructions or openings to the incident wavefront.

Example 17.2 ———————————————

In a Young's double slit experiment, the separation between the slits is 0.10 mm, the wavelength of light used is 600 nm and the interference pattern is observed on a screen 1.0 m away. Find the separation between the successive bright fringes.

Solution : The separation between the successive bright fringes is

$$w = \frac{D\lambda}{d} = \frac{1.0 \text{ m} \times 600 \times 10^{-9} \text{ m}}{0.10 \times 10^{-3} \text{ m}}$$
$$= 6.0 \times 10^{-3} \text{ m} = 6.0 \text{ mm.}$$

17.6 OPTICAL PATH

Consider a light wave travelling in a medium of refractive index μ. Its equation may be written as

$$E = E_0 \sin \omega(t - x/v) = E_0 \sin \omega(t - \mu x/c).$$

If the light wave travels a distance Δx, the phase changes by

$$\delta_1 = \mu\,\frac{\omega}{c}\,\Delta x. \qquad \dots (i)$$

Instead, if the light wave travels in vacuum, its equation will be

$$E = E_0 \sin \omega(t - x/c).$$

If the light travels through a distance $\mu \Delta x$, the phase changes by

$$\delta_2 = \frac{\omega}{c}(\mu \Delta x) = \mu \frac{\omega}{c} \Delta x. \qquad \ldots \text{(ii)}$$

By (i) and (ii), we see that a wave travelling through a distance Δx in a medium of refractive index μ suffers the same phase change as when it travels a distance $\mu \Delta x$ in vacuum. In other words, a path length of Δx in a medium of refractive index μ is equivalent to a path length of $\mu \Delta x$ in vacuum. The quantity $\mu \Delta x$ is called the *optical path* of the light. In dealing with interference of two waves, we need the difference between the optical paths travelled by the waves. The geometrical path and the optical path are equal only when light travels in vacuum or in air where the refractive index is close to 1.

The concept of optical path may also be introduced in terms of the change in wavelength as the wave changes its medium. The frequency of a wave is determined by the frequency of the source and is not changed when the wave enters a new medium. If the wavelength of light in vacuum is λ_0 and that in the medium is λ_n, then

$$\lambda_0 = \frac{c}{v}$$

and

$$\lambda_n = \frac{v}{v} = \frac{c}{\mu v}$$

so that

$$\lambda_n = \frac{\lambda_0}{\mu}.$$

At any given instant, the points differing by one wavelength have same phase of vibration. Thus, the points at separation λ_n in the medium have same phase of vibration. On the other hand, in vacuum, points at separation λ_0 will have same phase of vibration. Thus, a path λ_n in a medium is equivalent to a path $\lambda_0 = \mu \lambda_n$ in vacuum. In general, a path Δx, in a medium of refractive index μ, is equivalent to a path $\mu \Delta x$ in vacuum which is called the optical path.

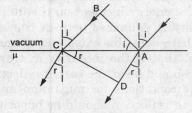

Figure 17.6

We can also understand the idea of optical path with the help of figure (17.6). Suppose a parallel beam

of light travelling in vacuum is incident on the surface AC of a medium of refractive index μ. AB is perpendicular to the incident rays and hence represents a wavefront of the incident light. Similarly CD is perpendicular to the refracted rays and represents a wavefront of the refracted light. Now phase of the wave has a constant value at different points of a wavefront. Thus phase at A = phase at B and phase at C = phase at D.

Thus, the phase difference between A and D = Phase difference between B and C. From the figure,

$$\mu = \frac{\sin i}{\sin r} = \frac{BC}{AC} \times \frac{AC}{AD} = \frac{BC}{AD}$$

or, $\qquad BC = \mu\,AD.$

The phase of light wave changes by equal amount whether it covers a distance $BC = \mu\,AD$ in vacuum or AD in the medium. Thus, a path AD in a medium of refractive index μ is equivalent to a path $\mu(AD)$ in vacuum which we call optical path.

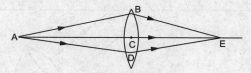

Figure 17.7

Consider the situation in figure (17.7). The geometrical paths ABE, ACE and ADE are different, but the optical paths are equal. This is because each path leads to the same phase difference, phase at E-phase at A. Note that the ray having longer geometrical path covers less distance in the lens as compared to the ray having shorter geometrical path.

Example 17.3

The wavelength of light coming from a sodium source is 589 nm. What will be its wavelength in water ? Refractive index of water = 1·33.

Solution : The wavelength in water is $\lambda = \lambda_0/\mu$, where λ_0 is the wavelength in vacuum and μ is the refractive index of water. Thus,

$$\lambda = \frac{589 \text{ nm}}{1·33} = 443 \text{ nm}.$$

17.7 INTERFERENCE FROM THIN FILMS

When oil floating on water is viewed in sunlight, beautiful colours appear. These colours appear because of interference between the light waves sent by the film as explained below.

Consider a thin film made of a transparent material with plane parallel faces separated by a distance d. Suppose a parallel beam of light is incident on the film at an angle i as shown in figure (17.8). The wave is divided into two parts at the upper surface, one is reflected and the other is refracted. The refracted part, which enters into the film, again gets divided at the lower surface into two parts; one is transmitted out of the film and the other is reflected back. Multiple reflections and refractions take place and a number of reflected waves as well as transmitted waves are sent by the film. The film may be viewed by the reflected light (more usual case) or by the transmitted light. We shall discuss the transmitted light first.

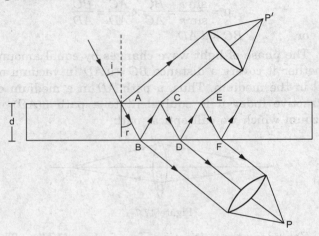

Figure 17.8

In figure (17.8), we have collected the parallel rays transmitted by the film by a converging lens at a point P. The amplitude of the individual transmitted waves is different for different waves; it gradually decreases as more reflections are involved. The wave BP, DP, FP, etc., interfere at P to produce a resultant intensity. Let us consider the phase difference between the two waves BP and DP. The two waves moved together and hence, remained in phase up to B where splitting occured and one wave followed the path BP and the other $BCDP$.

Let us discuss the special case for normal incidence when the angle of incidence $i = 0$. Then, the points B and D coincide. The path BP equals DP and the only extra distance travelled by the wave along DP is $BC + CD = 2d$. As this extra path is traversed in a medium of refractive index μ, the optical path difference between the waves BP and DP interfering at P is

$$\Delta x = 2\mu d.$$

The phase difference is

$$\delta = 2\pi \frac{\Delta x}{\lambda} = 2\pi \frac{2\mu d}{\lambda}.$$

This is also the phase difference between the waves DP and FP or in fact, between any consecutively transmitted waves. All these waves are in phase if

$$\delta = 2n\pi$$

or, $\qquad\qquad 2\mu d = n\lambda, \qquad\qquad \ldots \; (17.9)$

where n is an integer.

If this condition is satisfied, constructive interference takes place and the film is seen illuminated. On the other hand, if

$$2\mu d = \left(n + \frac{1}{2}\right)\lambda, \qquad\qquad \ldots \; (17.10)$$

$\delta = (2n + 1)\pi$ and the consecutive waves are out of phase. The waves cancel each other although complete cancellation does not take place because the interfering waves do not have equal amplitude. Still, the illumination will be comparatively less.

If white light is used, the film's thickness d will satisfy condition (17.9) for certain wavelengths and these colours will be strongly transmitted due to constructive interference. The colours corresponding to the wavelengths for which (17.10) is satisfied will be poorly transmitted due to destructive interference. This gives coloured appearance of the film.

Next, let us consider the case when the film is viewed by the light reflected by it. The reflected light consists of waves from A, C, E, ..., etc., (figure 17.8) which may be brought to a focus at a point P' by a converging lens. The optical path difference between the consecutively reflected waves reaching at P' is again $2\mu d$ in the limit of normal incidence $i = 0$. Experimental arrangement may be a bit difficult for an exact normal incidence and then collection of reflected light along the same direction. However, we can suppose that it is viewed by light falling very nearly normal to it. We may expect that the condition of maximum illumination and minimum illumination will be same as equations (17.9) and (17.10). But a simple argument conflicts the case. If for a given thickness and wavelength, destructive interference takes place both in reflection as well as in transmission; where does the light go then? What happens to the energy incident on the film? Similarly, if the intensity is enhanced both in transmission and reflection, where does this extra energy come from? It seems logical that if the intensity in transmission is increased, it should be at the cost of reflection and vice versa. So the conditions for maximum and minimum illumination in reflection should be opposite to that in transmission. We should have

$2\mu d = n\,\lambda$ for minimum illumination in reflection
$\qquad\qquad\qquad\qquad\qquad\qquad \ldots \; (17.11)$

and

$$2\mu d = \left(n + \frac{1}{2}\right)\lambda \quad \text{for maximum illumination in reflection.} \quad \ldots (17.12)$$

This comes out to be true experimentally. To explain why destructive interference takes place even when the optical path difference is an integral multiple of wavelength, let us recall our discussion of reflection and transmission of waves in chapter 15. If a composite string is prepared by joining a light string to a heavier one and if a wave pulse is sent from the lighter one towards the heavier one, a part is reflected from the junction and other is transmitted into the heavier string (figure 17.9a). The reflected pulse is inverted with respect to the incident pulse.

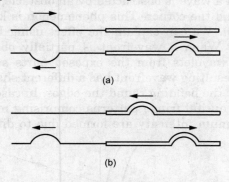

Figure 17.9

There is a sudden phase-change of π when a wave is reflected from a denser string. No such sudden phase change takes place if the wave is reflected from a rarer string (figure 17.9b). Same is true for light waves. The medium with higher refractive index is optically denser. When light is incident from air to a film, the reflected wave suffers a sudden phase change of π. The next wave, with which it interferes, suffers no such sudden phase change. If $2\mu d$ is equal to λ or its integral multiple, the second wave is out of phase with the first because the first has suffered a phase change of π. This explains the conditions (17.11) and (17.12).

Example 17.4

Find the minimum thickness of a film which will strongly reflect the light of wavelength 589 nm. The refractive index of the material of the film is 1·25.

Solution : For strong reflection, the least optical path difference introduced by the film should be $\lambda/2$. The optical path difference between the waves reflected from the two surfaces of the film is $2\mu d$. Thus, for strong reflection,

$$2\mu d = \lambda/2$$

or,

$$d = \frac{\lambda}{4\mu} = \frac{589 \text{ nm}}{4 \times 1·25} = 118 \text{ nm}.$$

17.8 FRESNEL BIPRISM

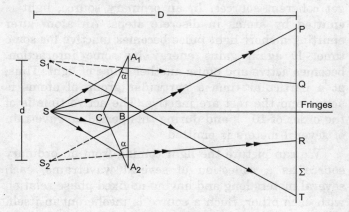

Figure 17.10

Figure (17.10) shows a schematic diagram of Fresnel biprism and interference of light using it. Two thin prisms A_1BC and A_2BC are joined at the bases to form a biprism. The refracting angles A_1 and A_2 (denoted by α in the figure) are of the order of half a degree each. In fact, it is a simple prism whose base angles are extremely small. A narrow slit S, allowing monochromatic light, is placed parallel to the refracting edge C. The light going through the prism A_1BC appears in a cone S_1QT and the light going through A_2BC appears in a cone S_2PR. Here S_1 and S_2 are the virtual images of S as formed by the prisms A_1BC and A_2BC. A screen Σ is placed to intercept the transmitted light. Interference fringes are formed on the portion QR of the screen where the two cones overlap.

One can treat the points S_1 and S_2 as two coherent sources sending light to the screen. The arrangement is then equivalent to a Young's double slit experiment with S_1 and S_2 acting as the two slits. Suppose the separation between S_1 and S_2 is d and the separation between the plane of S_1S_2 and Σ is D. The fringe-width obtained on the screen is

$$w = \frac{D\lambda}{d}.$$

17.9 COHERENT AND INCOHERENT SOURCES

Two sources of light waves are said to be *coherent* if the initial phase difference δ_0 between the waves emitted by the sources remains constant in time. If δ_0 changes randomly with time, the sources are called *incoherent*. Two waves produce interference pattern only if they originate from coherent sources. This condition is same as discussed for sound waves in the previous chapter. The process of light emission from ordinary sources such as the sun, a candle, an electric bulb, is such that one has to use special techniques to get coherent sources. In an ordinary source, light is emitted by atoms in discrete steps. An atom after emitting a short light pulse becomes inactive for some time. It again gains energy by some interaction, becomes active and emits another pulse of light. Thus, at a particular time a particular group of atoms is active and the rest are inactive. The active time is of the order of 10^{-8} s and during this period, a wavetrain of several meters is emitted.

We can picture the light coming from an ordinary source as a collection of several wavetrains, each several meters long and having no fixed phase relation with each other. Such a source is incoherent in itself. Different wavetrains are emitted by different groups of atoms and these groups act independently of each other, hence the phase varies randomly from train to train. If two lamps are substituted in place of the slits S_1 and S_2 in a Young's interference experiment, no fringe will be seen. This is because each source keeps on changing its phase randomly and hence, the phase difference between the two sources also changes randomly. That is why, a narrow aperture S_0 is used to select a particular wavetrain which is incident on the two slits together. This ensures that the initial phase difference of the wavelets originating from S_1 and S_2 does not change with time. When a new wavetrain is emitted by the lamp, the phase is randomly changed but that change is simultaneously communicated to both S_1 and S_2 and the phase difference remains unchanged. In order to obtain a fairly distinct interference pattern, the path difference between the two waves originating from coherent sources should be kept small. This is so because the wavetrains are finite in length and hence with large difference in path, the waves do not overlap at the same instant in the same region of space. The second wavetrain arrives well after the first train has already passed and hence, no interference takes place. In practice, the path difference should not exceed a few centimeters to observe a good interference pattern.

Because of the incoherent nature of the basic process of light emission in ordinary sources, these sources cannot emit highly monochromatic light. A strictly monochromatic light, having a well-defined single frequency or wavelength, must be a sine wave which has an infinite extension. A wavetrain of finite length may be described by the superposition of a number of sine waves of different wavelengths. Thus, the light emitted by an ordinary source always has a spread in wavelength. An ordinary sodium vapour lamp emits light of wavelength 589·0 nm and 589·6 nm with a spread of about ± 0·01 nm in each line. Shorter

the length of the wavetrain, larger is the spread in wavelength.

It has been made possible to produce light sources which emit very long wavetrains, of the order of several hundred metres. The spread in wavelength is accordingly very small. These sources are called *laser* sources. The atoms behave in a cooperative manner in such a source and hence the light is coherent. Two independent laser sources can produce interference fringes and the path difference may be several metres long.

17.10 DIFFRACTION OF LIGHT

When a wave is obstructed by an obstacle, the rays bend round the corner. This phenomenon is known as *diffraction*. We can explain the effect using Huygens' principle. When a wavefront is partially obstructed, only the wavelets from the exposed parts superpose and the resulting wavefront has a different shape. This allows for the bending round the edges. In case of light waves, beautiful fringe patterns comprising maximum and minimum intensity are formed due to diffraction.

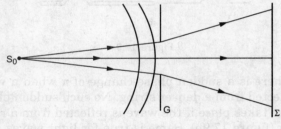

Figure 17.11

Figure (17.11) shows the basic arrangement for observing diffraction effects in light waves. It consists of a narrow source of light S_0, a diffracting element G (an obstacle or an opening) and a screen Σ. The wavefronts emitted by the source S_0 are partially obstructed by the element G. The secondary wavelets originating from different points of the unobstructed part interfere on the screen Σ and produce the diffraction pattern of varying intensity. A special case of diffraction, which is very important in practice and which is simpler to analyse mathematically, arises when the source S_0 and the screen Σ are far away from the diffracting element G. Plane waves are incident on G and the waves interfering at a particular point come parallel to each other. This special class of diffraction is called *Fraunhofer diffraction* after the physicist Joseph von Fraunhofer (1787–1826) who investigated such diffraction cases in great detail. Fraunhofer diffraction can be observed in a laboratory by placing converging lenses before and after G and keeping the source S_0 and the screen Σ in their focal planes respectively (figure 17.12). The source and the screen are effectively at infinite distance from the diffracting element.

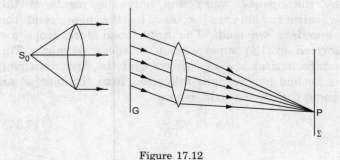

Figure 17.12

If the source or the screen is at a finite distance from the diffracting element G, it is called *Fresnel diffraction* after the physicist Augustin Jean Fresnel (1788–1827).

It is a coincidence that the two great physicists, Fraunhofer and Fresnel, investigating diffraction phenomenon lived a short life of equal number of years.

We shall now discuss some of the important cases of diffraction.

17.11 FRAUNHOFER DIFFRACTION BY A SINGLE SLIT

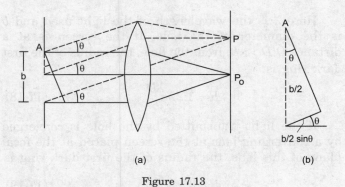

Figure 17.13

Suppose a parallel beam of light is incident normally on a slit of width b (figure 17.13). According to Huygens' principle, each and every point of the exposed part of the plane wavefront (i.e., every point of the slit) acts as a source of secondary wavelets spreading in all directions. The light is received by a screen placed at a large distance. In practice, this condition is achieved by placing the screen at the focal plane of a converging lens placed just after the slit. A particular point P on the screen receives waves from all the secondary sources. All these waves start parallel to each other from different points of the slit and interfere at P to give the resultant intensity.

At the point P_0 which is at the bisector plane of the slit, all the waves reach after travelling equal optical path and hence, are in phase. The waves, thus, interfere constructively with each other and maximum intensity is observed. As we move away from P_0, the waves arrive with different phases and the intensity is changed.

Let us consider a point P which collects the waves originating from different points of the slit at an angle θ. Figure (17.13) shows the perpendicular from the point A to the parallel rays. This perpendicular also represents the wavefront of the parallel beam diffracted at an angle θ. The optical paths from any point on this wavefront to the point P are equal. The optical path difference between the waves sent by the upper edge A of the slit and the wave sent by the centre of the slit is $\frac{b}{2}\sin\theta$. This is shown in expanded view in figure (17.13b). Consider the angle for which $\frac{b}{2}\sin\theta = \lambda/2$. The above mentioned two waves will have a phase difference

$$\delta = \frac{2\pi}{\lambda} \cdot \frac{\lambda}{2} = \pi.$$

The two waves will cancel each other. The wave from any point in the upper half of the slit is exactly cancelled by the wave from the point $b/2$ distance below it. The whole slit can be divided into such pairs and hence, the intensity at P will be zero. This is the condition of the first minimum, i.e., the first dark fringe.

So, $\dfrac{b}{2}\sin\theta = \dfrac{\lambda}{2}$

or, $b\sin\theta = \lambda$ (first minimum).

Similar arguments show that other minima (zero intensity) are located at points corresponding to $b\sin\theta = 2\lambda, 3\lambda, \ldots$

or, $b\sin\theta = n\lambda$ (dark fringe).   ... (17.13)

The points of the maximum intensity lie nearly midway between the successive minima. A detailed mathematical analysis shows that the amplitude $E_0{'}$ of the electric field at a general point P is,

$$E_0{'} = E_0\,\frac{\sin\beta}{\beta},\qquad \ldots (17.14)$$

where $\beta = \dfrac{1}{2}\dfrac{\omega}{v}\,b\sin\theta = \dfrac{\pi}{\lambda}\,b\sin\theta$ ... (17.15)

and E_0 is the amplitude at the point P_0 which corresponds at $\theta = 0$.

The intensity is proportional to the square of the amplitude. If I_0 represents the intensity at P_0, its value at P is

$$I = I_0 \frac{\sin^2\beta}{\beta^2}. \qquad \dots (17.16)$$

We draw, in figure (17.14), variation of the intensity as a function of $\sin\theta$.

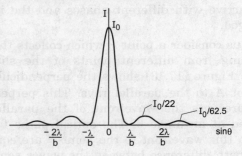

Figure 17.14

Most of the diffracted light is distributed between $\sin\theta = -\frac{\lambda}{b}$ and $+\frac{\lambda}{b}$. The intensity at the first maximum after the central one is only 1/22 of the intensity of the central maximum. This divergence in θ is inversely proportional to the width b of the slit. If the slit-width b is decreased, the divergence is increased and the light is diffracted in a wider cone. On the other hand, if the slit-width is large compared to the wavelength, $\lambda/b \approx 0$ and the light continues undiffracted in the direction $\theta = 0$. This clearly indicates that diffraction effects are observable only when the obstacle or the opening has dimensions comparable to the wavelength of the wave.

Example 17.5

A parallel beam of monochromatic light of wavelength 450 nm passes through a long slit of width 0·2 mm. Find the angular divergence in which most of the light is diffracted.

Solution : Most of the light is diffracted between the two first order minima. These minima occur at angles given by $b\sin\theta = \pm\lambda$

or, $\sin\theta = \pm\lambda/b$

$$= \pm\frac{450\times10^{-9}\,\text{m}}{0.2\times10^{-3}\,\text{m}} = \pm 2.25\times10^{-3}.$$

or, $\theta \approx \pm 2.25\times10^{-3}$ rad.

The angular divergence $= 4.5\times10^{-3}$ rad.

17.12 FRAUNHOFER DIFFRACTION BY A CIRCULAR APERTURE

When a parallel beam of light is passed through an opaque board with a circular hole in it, the light is diffracted by the hole. If received on a screen at a large distance, the pattern is a bright disc surrounded by alternate dark and bright rings of decreasing intensity as shown in figure (17.15). The wavefront is obstructed by the opaque board and only the points of the wavefront, that are exposed by the hole, send the secondary wavelets. The bright and dark rings are formed by the superposition of these wavelets. The mathematical analysis shows that the first dark ring is formed by the light diffracted from the hole at an angle θ with the axis, where

$$\sin\theta \approx 1.22\frac{\lambda}{b}. \qquad \dots (17.17)$$

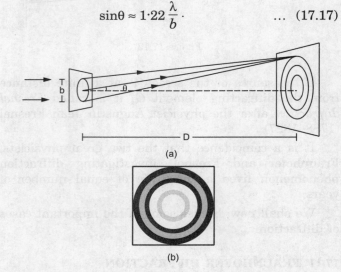

Figure 17.15

Here λ is the wavelength of the light used and b is the diameter of the hole. If the screen is at a distance $D(D \gg b)$ from the hole, the radius of the first dark ring is

$$R \approx 1.22\frac{\lambda D}{b}. \qquad \dots (17.18)$$

If the light transmitted by the hole is converged by a converging lens at the screen placed at the focal plane of this lens, the radius of the first dark ring is

$$R = 1.22\frac{\lambda f}{b}. \qquad \dots (17.19)$$

As most of the light coming from the hole is concentrated within the first dark ring, this radius is also called the *radius of the diffraction disc*.

Diffraction by a circular aperture is of great practical importance. In many of the optical instruments, lenses are used. When light passes through a lens, the wavefront is limited by its rim which is usually circular. If a parallel beam of light is incident on a converging lens, only the part intercepted by the lens gets transmitted into the converging beam. Thus, the light is diffracted by the lens. This lens itself works to converge the diffracted light in its focal plane and hence, we observe a bright disc, surrounded by alternate dark and bright rings, as the image. The radius of the diffraction disc is given by equation (17.19) where, *b* now stands for the diameter of the aperture of the lens.

The above discussion shows that a converging lens can never form a point image of a distant point source. In the best conditions, it produces a bright disc surrounded by dark and bright rings. If we assume that most of the light is concentrated within the central bright disc, we can say that the lens produces a disc image for a distant point source. This is not only true for a distant point source but also for any point source. The radius of the image disc is

$$R = 1.22 \frac{\lambda}{b} D,$$

where *D* is the distance from the lens at which the light is focussed.

Example 17.6

A beam of light of wavelength 590 nm *is focussed by a converging lens of diameter* 10.0 cm *at a distance of* 20 cm *from it. Find the diameter of the disc image formed.*

Solution : The angular radius of the central bright disc in a diffraction pattern from circular aperture is given by

$$\sin\theta \approx \frac{1.22\,\lambda}{b}$$

$$= \frac{1.22 \times 590 \times 10^{-9}\,\text{m}}{10.0 \times 10^{-2}\,\text{m}} = 0.7 \times 10^{-5}\,\text{rad}.$$

The radius of the bright disc is

$$0.7 \times 10^{-5} \times 20\,\text{cm} = 1.4 \times 10^{-4}\,\text{cm}.$$

The diameter of the disc image = 2.8×10^{-4} cm.

17.13 FRESNEL DIFFRACTION AT A STRAIGHT EDGE

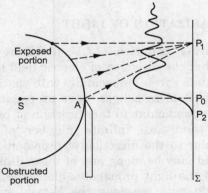

Figure 17.16

Consider the situation shown in figure (17.16). Let *S* be a narrow slit sending monochromatic light. The light is obstructed by an opaque obstacle having a sharp edge *A*. The light is collected on a screen Σ. The

portion of the screen below P_0 in the figure is the region of the geometrical shadow.

Cylindrical wavefronts emitted from the slit are obstructed by the obstacle. The points on the exposed portion of the wavefront emit secondary wavelets which interfere to produce varying intensity on the screen Σ.

The curve in the figure shows the variation of intensity of light on the screen. We see that the intensity gradually decreases as we go farther inside the region of geometrical shadow, i.e., below P_0. As we go above P_0, the intensity alternately increases and decreases. The difference of the maximum intensity and minimum intensity goes on decreasing as we go farther away from P_0 and finally we get uniform illumination.

17.14 LIMIT OF RESOLUTION

The fact that a lens forms a disc image of a point source, puts a limit on resolving two neighbouring points imaged by a lens.

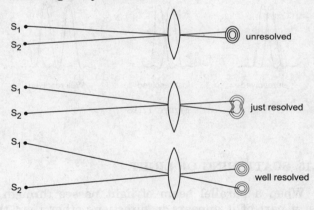

Figure 17.17

Suppose S_1 and S_2 are two point sources placed before a converging lens (figure 17.17). If the separation between the centres of the image-discs is small in comparison to the radii of the discs, the discs will largely overlap on one another and it will appear like a single disc. The two points are then not resolved. If S_1 and S_2 are moved apart, the centres of their image-discs also move apart. For a sufficient separation, one can distinguish the presence of two discs in the pattern. In this case, we say that the points are just resolved.

The angular radius θ of the diffraction disc is given by $\sin\theta = \frac{1.22\,\lambda}{b}$, where *b* is the radius of the lens. Thus, increasing the radius of the lens improves the resolution. This is the reason why objective lenses of powerful microscopes and telescopes are kept large in size.

The human eye is itself a converging lens which forms the image of the points (we see) on the retina. The above discussion then shows that two points very close to each other cannot be seen as two distinct points by the human eye.

Rayleigh Criterion

Whether two disc images of nearby points are resolved or not may depend on the person viewing the images. Rayleigh suggested a quantitative criterion for resolution. Two images are called just resolved in this criterion if the centre of one bright disc falls on the periphery of the second. This means, the radius of each bright disc should be equal to the separation between them. In this case, the resultant intensity has a minimum between the centres of the images. Figure (17.18) shows the variation of intensity when the two images are just resolved.

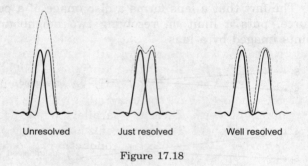

Unresolved   Just resolved   Well resolved

Figure 17.18

17.15 SCATTERING OF LIGHT

When a parallel beam of light passes through a gas, a part of it appears in directions other than the incident direction. This phenomenon is called *scattering of light*. The basic process in scattering is absorption of light by the molecules followed by its re-radiation in different directions. The strength of scattering can be measured by the loss of energy in the light beam as it passes through the gas. It should be distinguished from the absorption of light as it passes through a medium. In absorption, the light energy is converted into internal energy of the medium whereas in scattering, the light energy is radiated in other directions. The strength of scattering depends on the wavelength of the light beside the size of the particles which cause scattering. If these particles are smaller than the wavelength, the scattering is proportional to $1/\lambda^4$. This is known as *Rayleigh's law of scattering*. Thus, red light is scattered the least and violet is scattered the most. This is why, red signals are used to indicate dangers. Such a signal goes to large distances without an appreciable loss due to scattering.

The blue appearance of sky is due to scattering of sunlight from the atmosphere. When you look at the sky, it is the scattered light that enters the eyes. Among the shorter wavelengths, the colour blue is present in larger proportion in sunlight. Light of short wavelengths are strongly scattered by the air molecules and reach the observer. This explains the blue colour of sky. Another natural phenomenon related to the scattering of light is the red appearance of sun at the sunset and at the sunrise. At these times, the sunlight has to travel a large distance through the atmosphere. The blue and neighbouring colours are scattered away in the path and the light reaching the observer is predominantly red.

If the earth had no atmosphere, the sky would appear black and stars could be seen during day hours. In fact if you go about 20 km up, where the atmosphere becomes quite thin, the sky does appear black and stars are visible during day hours as astronauts have found.

Besides air molecules, water particles, dust, etc., also scatter light. The appearance of sky is affected by the presence of these scattering centres. On a humid day before rains, the sky appears light blue whereas, on a clear day it appears deep blue. The change in the quality of colour of sky results from the fact that the water droplets and the dust particles may have size greater than the wavelength of light. Rayleigh's law of scattering does not operate in this case and colours other than blue may be scattered in larger proportion. The appearance of sky in large industrial cities is also different from villages. An automobile engine typically ejects about 10^{11} particles per second, similarly for other machines. Such particles remain suspended in air for quite long time unless rain or wind clears them. Often the sky looks hazy with a greyish tinge in such areas.

17.16 POLARIZATION OF LIGHT

In writing equation (17.1) for light wave, we assumed that the direction of electric field is fixed and the magnitude varies sinusoidally with space and time. The electric field in a light wave propagating in free space is perpendicular to the direction of propagation. However, there are infinite number of directions perpendicular to the direction of propagation and the electric field may be along any of these directions. For example, if the light propagates along the X-axis, the electric field may be along the Y-axis, or along the Z-axis or along any direction in the Y-Z plane. If the electric field at a point always remains parallel to a fixed direction as the time passes, the light is called *linearly polarized* along that direction. For example, if the electric field at a point is always parallel to the

Y-axis, we say that the light is linearly polarized along the Y-axis. The same is also called *plane polarized* light. The plane containing the electric field and the direction of propagation is called the *plane of polarization*.

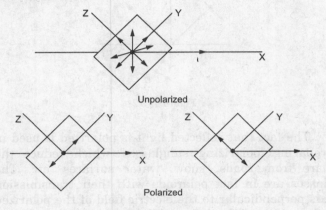

Figure 17.19

As we have mentioned earlier, light is emitted by atoms. The light pulse emitted by one atom in a single event has a fixed direction of electric field. However, the light pulses emitted by different atoms, in general, have electric fields in different directions. Hence, the resultant electric field at a point keeps on changing its direction randomly and rapidly. Such a light is called *unpolarized*. The light emitted by an ordinary source such as an electric lamp, a mercury tube, a candle, the sun, are unpolarized.

Suppose an unpolarized light wave travels along the X-axis. The electric field at any instant is in the Y-Z plane, we can break the field into its components E_y and E_z along the Y-axis and the Z-axis respectively. The fact that the resultant electric field changes its direction randomly may be mathematically expressed by saying that E_y and E_z have a phase difference δ that changes randomly with time. Thus,

$$E_y = E_1 \sin(\omega t - kx + \delta)$$
$$E_z = E_2 \sin(\omega t - kx).$$

The resultant electric field makes an angle θ with the Y-axis, where

$$\tan\theta = \frac{E_z}{E_y} = \frac{E_2 \sin(\omega t - kx)}{E_1 \sin(\omega t - kx + \delta)}.$$

Since δ changes randomly with time, so does θ and the light is unpolarized.

If δ is zero, $\tan\theta = E_2/E_1 = $ constant and the electric field is always parallel to a fixed direction. The light is linearly polarized.

If $\delta = \pi$, $\tan\theta = -E_2/E_1$ and again the electric field is parallel to a fixed direction and the light is linearly polarized.

If $\delta = \pi/2$ and $E_1 = E_2$, then

$$\tan\theta = \frac{E_z}{E_y} = \frac{E_2 \sin(\omega t - kx)}{E_1 \sin(\omega t - kx + \pi/2)}$$
$$= \tan(\omega t - kx)$$

or, $\theta = \omega t - kx.$

At any point x, the angle θ increases at a uniform rate ω. The electric field, therefore, rotates at a uniform angular speed ω. Also,

$$E^2 = E_y^2 + E_z^2 = E_1^2 \cos^2(\omega t - kx) + E_1^2 \sin^2(\omega t - kx) = E_1^2,$$

i.e., the magnitude of the field remains constant. The tip of the electric field, thus, goes in a circle at a uniform angular speed. Such a light is called a *circularly polarized light*.

If $\delta = \pi/2$ but $E_1 \neq E_2$, the tip of the electric field traces out an ellipse. Such a light wave is called an *elliptically polarized light*.

Polaroids

There are several methods to produce polarized light from the unpolarized light. An instrument used to produce polarized light from unpolarized light is called a *polarizer*. Plane sheets in the shape of circular discs called *polaroids* are commercially available which transmit light with *E*-vector parallel to a special direction in the sheet. These polaroids have long chains of hydrocarbons which become conducting at optical frequencies. When light falls perpendicularly on the sheet, the electric field parallel to the chains is absorbed in setting up electric currents in the chains but the field perpendicular to the chains gets transmitted. The direction perpendicular to the chains is called the *transmission axis* of the polaroid. When light passes through the polaroid, the transmitted light becomes linearly polarized with *E*-vector parallel to the transmission axis.

If linearly polarized light is incident on a polaroid with the *E*-vector parallel to the transmission axis, the light is completely transmitted by the polaroid. If the *E*-vector is perpendicular to the transmission axis, the light is completely stopped by the polaroid. If the *E*-vector is at an angle θ with the transmission axis, light is partially transmitted. The intensity of the transmitted light is

$$I = I_0 \cos^2 \theta, \qquad \qquad \dots (17.20)$$

where I_0 is the intensity when the incident *E*-vector is parallel to the transmission axis. This is known as the *law of Malus*.

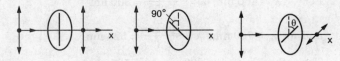

Figure 17.20

Polarization by Reflection and Refraction

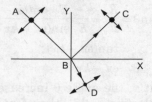

Figure 17.21

Consider a light beam from air incident on the surface of a transparent medium of refractive index μ. The incident ray, the reflected ray and the refracted ray are all in one plane. The plane is called the plane of incidence. In figure (17.21) we have shown this plane as the X-Y plane. Consider the incident light going along AB. The electric field $\vec{E}$ must be perpendicular to AB. If the incident light is unpolarized the electric field will randomly change its direction, remaining at all times in a plane perpendicular to AB. We can resolve the field in two components, one in the X-Y plane and the other along the Z-direction. In figure (17.21), the component in the X-Y plane is shown by the double-arrow perpendicular to AB and the component along the Z-direction by the solid dot.

Light with electric field along the Z-direction is more strongly reflected as compared to that in the X-Y plane. This is shown in the figure by reduced size of the double arrow. Similarly, the refracted light has a larger component of electric field in the X-Y plane shown in the figure by the reduced size of the solid dot.

If the light is incident on the surface with an angle of incidence i given by

$$\tan i = \mu, \qquad \qquad \ldots (17.21)$$

the reflected light is completely polarized with the electric field along the Z-direction as suggested by figure (17.22). The refracted ray is never completely polarized. The angle i given by equation (17.21) is called the *Brewster angle* and equation (17.21) itself is known as the *Brewster's law*.

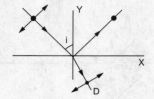

Figure 17.22

The fact that reflected light is polarized is used in preparing 'polarizing sunglasses' which reduce the glare from roads, snow, water surfaces, etc. The glasses are in fact polaroids with their transmission axis perpendicular to the electric field of the polarized reflected light. The reflected light, which is responsible for the glare, is thus largely absorbed. The direct light coming to the glasses is unpolarized and is less absorbed. In this respect the polarizing sunglasses are different from the ordinary dark-coloured sunglasses which absorb any light passing through them reducing the intensity to a large extent.

Polarization by Scattering

When unpolarized light is scattered by small particles, the scattered light is partially polarized. The blue light received from the sky is accordingly partially polarized. Though human eye does not distinguish between an unpolarized light and a polarized light, the eyes of a bee can detect the difference. Austrian Nobel Laureate Karl Von Frisch performed experiments for several years on bees and concluded that the bees cannot only distinguish unpolarized light from polarized light but can also determine the direction of polarization.

Worked Out Examples

1. *White light is a mixture of light of wavelengths between 400 nm and 700 nm. If this light goes through water (μ = 1·33) what are the limits of the wavelength there ?*

Solution : When a light having wavelength λ_0 in vacuum goes through a medium of refractive index μ, the wavelength in the medium becomes $\lambda = \lambda_0 / \mu$.

For $\lambda_0 = 400$ nm, $\lambda = \dfrac{400 \text{ nm}}{1·33} = 300$ nm

and for $\lambda_0 = 700$ nm, $\lambda = \dfrac{700 \text{ nm}}{1·33} = 525$ nm.

Thus, the limits are 300 nm and 525 nm.

2. *The optical path of a monochromatic light is the same if it goes through 2·00 cm of glass or 2·25 cm of water. If the refractive index of water is 1·33, what is the refractive index of glass ?*

Solution : When light travels through a distance x in a medium of refractive index μ, its optical path is μx. Thus, if μ is the refractive index of glass,

$$\mu(2·00 \text{ cm}) = 1·33 \times (2·25 \text{ cm})$$

or, $$\mu = 1·33 \times \frac{2·25}{2·00} = 1·50.$$

3. *White light is passed through a double slit and interference pattern is observed on a screen 2·5 m away. The separation between the slits is 0·5 mm. The first violet and red fringes are formed 2·0 mm and 3·5 mm away from the central white fringe. Calculate the wavelengths of the violet and the red light.*

Solution : For the first bright fringe, the distance from the centre is

$$y = \frac{D\lambda}{d}.$$

For violet light, $y = 2·0$ mm. Thus,

$$2·0 \text{ mm} = \frac{(2·5 \text{ m})\lambda}{0·5 \text{ mm}}$$

or,

$$\lambda = \frac{(0·5 \text{ mm})(2·0 \text{ mm})}{2·5 \text{ m}} = 400 \text{ nm}.$$

Similarly, for red light, $y = 3·5$ mm. Thus,

$$3·5 \text{ mm} = \frac{(2·5 \text{ m})\lambda}{0·5 \text{ mm}}$$

or,

$$\lambda = 700 \text{ nm}.$$

4. *A double slit experiment is performed with sodium (yellow) light of wavelength 589·3 nm and the interference pattern is observed on a screen 100 cm away. The tenth bright fringe has its centre at a distance of 12 mm from the central maximum. Find the separation between the slits.*

Solution : For the nth maximum fringe, the distance above the central line is

$$x = \frac{n\lambda D}{d}.$$

According to the data given,

$$x = 12 \text{ mm}, \ n = 10, \ \lambda = 589·3 \text{ nm}, \ D = 100 \text{ cm}.$$

Thus, the separation between the slits is

$$d = \frac{n\lambda D}{x} = \frac{10 \times 589·3 \times 10^{-9} \text{ m} \times 100 \times 10^{-2} \text{ m}}{12 \times 10^{-3} \text{ m}}$$

$$= 4·9 \times 10^{-4} \text{ m} = 0·49 \text{ mm}.$$

5. *The intensity of the light coming from one of the slits in a Young's double slit experiment is double the intensity from the other slit. Find the ratio of the maximum intensity to the minimum intensity in the interference fringe pattern observed.*

Solution : The intensity of the light originating from the first slit is double the intensity from the second slit. The amplitudes of the two interfering waves are in the ratio $\sqrt{2} : 1$, say $\sqrt{2}\,A$ and A.

At the point of constructive interference, the resultant amplitude becomes $(\sqrt{2}+1)A$. At the points of destructive interference, this amplitude is $(\sqrt{2}-1)A$. The ratio of the resultant intensities at the maxima to that

at the minima is

$$\frac{(\sqrt{2}+1)^2 A^2}{(\sqrt{2}-1)^2 A^2} = 34.$$

6. *The width of one of the two slits in a Young's double slit experiment is double of the other slit. Assuming that the amplitude of the light coming from a slit is proportional to the slit-width, find the ratio of the maximum to the minimum intensity in the interference pattern.*

Solution : Suppose the amplitude of the light wave coming from the narrower slit is A and that coming from the wider slit is $2A$. The maximum intensity occurs at a place where constructive interference takes place. Then the resultant amplitude is the sum of the individual amplitudes. Thus,

$$A_{max} = 2A + A = 3A.$$

The minimum intensity occurs at a place where destructive interference takes place. The resultant amplitude is then difference of the individual amplitudes. Thus,

$$A_{min} = 2A - A = A.$$

As the intensity is proportional to the square of the amplitude,

$$\frac{I_{max}}{I_{min}} = \frac{(A_{max})^2}{(A_{min})^2} = \frac{(3A)^2}{A^2} = 9.$$

7. *Two sources S_1 and S_2 emitting light of wavelength 600 nm are placed a distance $1·0 \times 10^{-2}$ cm apart. A detector can be moved on the line S_1P which is perpendicular to S_1S_2. (a) What would be the minimum and maximum path difference at the detector as it is moved along the line S_1P ? (b) Locate the position of the farthest minimum detected.*

Solution :

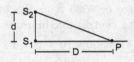

Figure 17-W1

(a) The situation is shown in figure (17-W1). The path difference is maximum when the detector is just at the position of S_1 and its value is equal to $d = 1·0 \times 10^{-2}$ cm. The path difference is minimum when the detector is at a large distance from S_1. The path difference is then close to zero.

(b) The farthest minimum occurs at a point P where the path difference is $\lambda/2$. If $S_1P = D$,

$$S_2P - S_1P = \frac{\lambda}{2}$$

or,

$$\sqrt{D^2 + d^2} - D = \frac{\lambda}{2}$$

or, $$D^2 + d^2 = \left(D + \frac{\lambda}{2}\right)^2$$

or, $$d^2 = D\lambda + \frac{\lambda^2}{4}$$

or, $$D = \frac{d^2}{\lambda} - \frac{\lambda}{4}$$

$$= \frac{(1 \cdot 0 \times 10^{-4}\ \text{m})^2}{600 \times 10^{-9}\ \text{m}} - 150 \times 10^{-9}\ \text{m} = 1 \cdot 7\ \text{cm}.$$

8. *A beam of light consisting of two wavelengths, 6500 Å and 5200 Å is used to obtain interference fringes in a Young's double slit experiment* $(1\ \text{Å} = 10^{-10}\ \text{m})$*. The distance between the slits is* 2·0 mm *and the distance between the plane of the slits and the screen is* 120 cm. *(a) Find the distance of the third bright fringe on the screen from the central maximum for the wavelength* 6500 Å. *(b) What is the least distance from the central maximum where the bright fringes due to both the wavelengths coincide ?*

Solution : (a) The centre of the nth bright fringe is at a distance $y = \dfrac{n\lambda D}{d}$ from the central maximum. For the 3rd bright fringe of 6500 Å,

$$y = \frac{3 \times 6500 \times 10^{-10}\ \text{m} \times 1 \cdot 2\ \text{m}}{2 \times 10^{-3}\ \text{m}}$$

$$= 0 \cdot 117\ \text{cm} \approx 0 \cdot 12\ \text{cm}.$$

(b) Suppose the mth bright fringe of 6500 Å coincides with the nth bright fringe of 5200 Å.

Then, $$\frac{m \times 6500\ \text{Å} \times D}{d} = \frac{n \times 5200\ \text{Å} \times D}{d}$$

or, $$\frac{m}{n} = \frac{5200}{6500} = \frac{4}{5}.$$

The minimum values of m and n that satisfy this equation are 4 and 5 respectively. The distance of the 4th bright fringe of 6500 Å or the 5th bright fringe of 5200 Å from the central maximum is

$$y = \frac{4 \times 6500 \times 10^{-10}\ \text{m} \times 1 \cdot 2\ \text{m}}{2 \times 10^{-3}\ \text{m}}$$

$$= 0 \cdot 156\ \text{cm} \approx 0 \cdot 16\ \text{cm}.$$

9. *Monochromatic light of wavelength* 600 nm *is used in a Young's double slit experiment. One of the slits is covered by a transparent sheet of thickness* $1 \cdot 8 \times 10^{-5}$ m *made of a material of refractive index* 1·6. *How many fringes will shift due to the introduction of the sheet ?*

Solution : When the light travels through a sheet of thickness t, the optical path travelled is μt, where μ is the refractive index. When one of the slits is covered by the sheet, air is replaced by the sheet and hence, the optical path changes by $(\mu - 1)t$. One fringe shifts when the optical path changes by one wavelength. Thus, the

number of fringes shifted due to the introduction of the sheet is

$$\frac{(\mu - 1)t}{\lambda} = \frac{(1 \cdot 6 - 1) \times 1 \cdot 8 \times 10^{-5}\ \text{m}}{600 \times 10^{-9}\ \text{m}} = 18.$$

10. *White light is incident normally on a glass plate of thickness* $0 \cdot 50 \times 10^{-6}$ *and index of refraction* 1·50. *Which wavelengths in the visible region* (400 nm–700 nm) *are strongly reflected by the plate ?*

Solution : The light of wavelength λ is strongly reflected if

$$2\mu d = \left(n + \frac{1}{2}\right)\lambda, \qquad \cdots\ \text{(i)}$$

where n is a nonnegative integer.

Here, $$2\mu d = 2 \times 1 \cdot 50 \times 0 \cdot 5 \times 10^{-6}\ \text{m}$$

$$= 1 \cdot 5 \times 10^{-6}\ \text{m}. \qquad \cdots\ \text{(ii)}$$

Putting $\lambda = 400$ nm in (i) and using (ii),

$$1 \cdot 5 \times 10^{-6}\ \text{m} = \left(n + \frac{1}{2}\right)(400 \times 10^{-9}\ \text{m})$$

or, $$n = 3 \cdot 25.$$

Putting $\lambda = 700$ nm in (i) and using (ii),

$$1 \cdot 5 \times 10^{-6}\ \text{m} = \left(n + \frac{1}{2}\right)(700 \times 10^{-9}\ \text{m})$$

or, $$n = 1 \cdot 66.$$

Thus, between 400 nm and 700 nm the integer n can take the values 2 and 3. Putting these values of n in (i), the wavelength become

$$\lambda = \frac{4\ \mu d}{2n + 1} = 600\ \text{nm and}\ \ 429\ \text{nm}.$$

Thus, light of wavelengths 429 nm and 600 nm are strongly reflected.

11. *A parallel beam of green light of wavelength* 546 nm *passes through a slit of width* 0·40 mm. *The transmitted light is collected on a screen* 40 cm *away. Find the distance between the two first order minima.*

Solution : The minima occur at an angular deviation θ given by $b \sin\theta = n\lambda$, where n is an integer. For the first order minima, $n = \pm 1$ so that $\sin\theta = \pm \dfrac{\lambda}{b}$. As the fringes are observed at a distance much larger than the width of the slit, the linear distances from the central maximum are given by

$$x = D\tan\theta$$

$$\approx D\sin\theta = \pm \frac{\lambda D}{b}.$$

Thus, the minima are formed at a distance $\dfrac{\lambda D}{b}$ from the central maximum on its two sides. The separation between the minima is

$$\frac{2\lambda D}{b} = \frac{2 \times 546 \times 10^{-9}\ \text{m} \times 40 \times 10^{-2}\ \text{m}}{0 \cdot 40 \times 10^{-3}\ \text{m}} = 1 \cdot 1\ \text{mm}.$$

QUESTIONS FOR SHORT ANSWER

1. Is the colour of 620 nm light and 780 nm light same ? Is the colour of 620 nm light and 621 nm light same ? How many colours are there in white light ?

2. The wavelength of light in a medium is $\lambda = \lambda_0 / \mu$, where λ is the wavelength in vacuum. A beam of red light ($\lambda_0 = 720$ nm) enters into water. The wavelength in water is $\lambda = \lambda_0 / \mu = 540$ nm. To a person under water does this light appear green ?

3. Whether the diffraction effects from a slit will be more clearly visible or less clearly, if the slit-width is increased ?

4. If we put a cardboard (say 20 cm × 20 cm) between a light source and our eyes, we can't see the light. But when we put the same cardboard between a sound source and our ear, we hear the sound almost clearly. Explain.

5. TV signals broadcast by Delhi studio cannot be directly received at Patna which is about 1000 km away. But the same signal goes some 36000 km away to a satellite, gets reflected and is then received at Patna. Explain.

6. Can we perform Young's double slit experiment with sound waves ? To get a reasonable "fringe pattern", what should be the order of separation between the slits ? How can the bright fringes and the dark fringes be detected in this case ?

7. Is it necessary to have two waves of equal intensity to study interference pattern ? Will there be an effect on clarity if the waves have unequal intenstity ?

8. Can we conclude from the interference phenomenon whether light is a transverse wave or a longitudinal wave ?

9. Why don't we have interference when two candles are placed close to each other and the intensity is seen at a distant screen ? What happens if the candles are replaced by laser sources ?

10. If the separation between the slits in a Young's double slit experiment is increased, what happens to the fringe-width ? If the separation is increased too much, will the fringe pattern remain detectable ?

11. Suppose white light falls on a double slit but one slit is covered by a violet filter (allowing $\lambda = 400$ nm). Describe the nature of the fringe pattern observed.

OBJECTIVE I

1. Light is
   (a) wave phenomenon   (b) particle phenomenon
   (c) both particle and wave phenomenon.

2. The speed of light depends
   (a) on elasticity of the medium only
   (b) on inertia of the medium only
   (c) on elasticity as well as inertia
   (d) neither on elasticity nor on inertia.

3. The equation of a light wave is written as $y = A \sin(kx - \omega t)$. Here, y represents
   (a) displacement of ether particles
   (b) pressure in the medium
   (c) density of the medium
   (d) electric field.

4. Which of the following properties show that light is a transverse wave ?
   (a) Reflection   (b) Interference
   (c) Diffraction   (d) Polarization

5. When light is refracted into a medium,
   (a) its wavelength and frequency both increase
   (b) its wavelength increases but frequency remains unchanged
   (c) its wavelength decreases but frequency remains unchanged
   (d) its wavelength and frequency both decrease.

6. When light is refracted, which of the following does not change ?
   (a) Wavelength   (b) Frequency
   (c) Velocity   (d) Amplitude

7. The amplitude modulated (AM) radio wave bends appreciably round the corners of a 1 m × 1 m board but the frequency modulated (FM) wave only negligibly bends. If the average wavelengths of AM and FM waves are λ_a and λ_f,
   (a) $\lambda_a > \lambda_f$ (b) $\lambda_a = \lambda_f$ (c) $\lambda_a < \lambda_f$
   (d) we don't have sufficient information to decide about the relation of λ_a and λ_f.

8. Which of the following sources gives best monochromatic light ?
   (a) A candle (b) A bulb (c) A mercury tube (d) A laser

9. The wavefronts of a light wave travelling in vacuum are given by $x + y + z = c$. The angle made by the direction of propagation of light with the X-axis is
   (a) 0°   (b) 45°   (c) 90°   (d) $\cos^{-1}(1/\sqrt{3})$.

10. The wavefronts of light coming from a distant source of unknown shape are nearly
   (a) plane   (b) elliptical   (c) cylindrical   (d) spherical.

11. The inverse square law of intensity (i.e., the intensity $\propto \dfrac{1}{r^2}$) is valid for a
   (a) point source   (b) line source
   (c) plane source   (d) cylindrical source.

12. Two sources are called coherent if they produce waves
   (a) of equal wavelength   (b) of equal velocity
   (c) having same shape of wavefront
   (d) having a constant phase difference.

13. When a drop of oil is spread on a water surface, it displays beautiful colours in daylight because of

(a) disperson of light   (b) reflection of light
(c) polarization of light   (d) interference of light.

14. Two coherent sources of different intensities send waves which interfere. The ratio of maximum intensity to the minimum intensity is 25. The intensities of the sources are in the ratio
(a) $25:1$ (b) $5:1$ (c) $9:4$ (d) $625:1$.

15. The slits in a Young's double slit experiment have equal width and the source is placed symmetrically with respect to the slits. The intensity at the central fringe is I_0. If one of the slits is closed, the intensity at this point will be
(a) I_0 (b) $I_0/4$ (c) $I_0/2$ (d) $4I_0$.

16. A thin transparent sheet is placed in front of a Young's double slit. The fringe-width will
(a) increase   (b) decrease
(c) remain same   (d) become nonuniform.

17. If Young's double slit experiment is performed in water,
(a) the fringe width will decrease
(b) the fringe width will increase
(c) the fringe width will remain unchanged
(d) there will be no fringe.

OBJECTIVE II

1. A light wave can travel
(a) in vacuum   (b) in vacuum only
(c) in a material medium   (d) in a material medium only.

2. Which of the following properties of light conclusively support wave theory of light ?
(a) Light obeys laws of reflection.
(b) Speed of light in water is smaller than the speed in vacuum.
(c) Light shows interference.
(d) Light shows photoelectric effect.

3. When light propagates in vacuum there is an electric field and a magnetic field. These fields
(a) are constant in time
(b) have zero average value
(c) are perpendicular to the direction of propagation of light.
(d) are mutually perpendicular.

4. Huygens' principle of secondary wavelets may be used to
(a) find the velocity of light in vacuum
(b) explain the particle behaviour of light
(c) find the new position of a wavefront
(d) explain Snell's law.

5. Three observers A, B and C measure the speed of light coming from a source to be v_A, v_B and v_C. The observer A moves towards the source and C moves away from the source at the same speed. The observer B stays stationary. The surrounding space is vacuum everywhere.

(a) $v_A > v_B > v_C$ (b) $v_A < v_B < v_C$
(c) $v_A = v_B = v_C$ (d) $v_B = \frac{1}{2}(v_A + v_C)$.

6. Suppose the medium in the previous question is water. Select the correct option(s) from the list given in that question.

7. Light waves travel in vacuum along the X-axis. Which of the following may represent the wavefronts ?
(a) $x = c$ (b) $y = c$ (c) $z = c$ (d) $x + y + z = c$.

8. If the source of light used in a Young's double slit experiment is changed from red to violet,
(a) the fringes will become brighter
(b) consecutive fringes will come closer
(c) the intensity of minima will increase
(d) the central bright fringe will become a dark fringe.

9. A Young's double slit experiment is performed with white light.
(a) The central fringe will be white.
(b) There will not be a completely dark fringe.
(c) The fringe next to the central will be red.
(d) The fringe next to the central will be violet.

10. Four light waves are represented by
   (i) $y = a_1 \sin \omega t$ (ii) $y = a_2 \sin(\omega t + \varepsilon)$
   (iii) $y = a_1 \sin 2\omega t$ (iv) $y = a_2 \sin 2(\omega t + \varepsilon)$.
Interference fringes may be observed due to superposition of
(a) (i) and (ii)   (b) (i) and (iii)
(c) (ii) and (iv)   (d) (iii) and (iv).

EXERCISES

1. Find the range of frequency of light that is visible to an average human being (400 nm $< \lambda < 700$ nm).

2. The wavelength of sodium light in air is 589 nm. (a) Find its frequency in air. (b) Find its wavelength in water (refractive index = 1.33). (c) Find its frequency in water. (d) Find its speed in water.

3. The index of refraction of fused quartz is 1.472 for light of wavelength 400 nm and is 1.452 for light of wavelength 760 nm. Find the speeds of light of these wavelengths in fused quartz.

4. The speed of the yellow light in a certain liquid is 2.4×10^8 m s^{-1}. Find the refractive index of the liquid.

5. Two narrow slits emitting light in phase are separated by a distance of 1.0 cm. The wavelength of the light is 5.0×10^{-7} m. The interference pattern is observed on a screen placed at a distance of 1.0 m. (a) Find the separation between the consecutive maxima. Can you expect to distinguish between these maxima ? (b) Find the separation between the sources which will give a separation of 1·0 mm between the consecutive maxima.

6. The separation between the consecutive dark fringes in a Young's double slit experiment is 1·0 mm. The screen is placed at a distance of 2·5 m from the slits and the separation between the slits is 1·0 mm. Calculate the wavelength of light used for the experiment.

7. In a double slit interference experiment, the separation between the slits is 1·0 mm, the wavelength of light used is $5·0 \times 10^{-7}$ m and the distance of the screen from the slits is 1·0 m. (a) Find the distance of the centre of the first minimum from the centre of the central maximum. (b) How many bright fringes are formed in one centimeter width on the screen ?

8. In a Young's double slit experiment, two narrow vertical slits placed 0·800 mm apart are illuminated by the same source of yellow light of wavelength 589 nm. How far are the adjacent bright bands in the interference pattern observed on a screen 2·00 m away ?

9. Find the angular separation between the consecutive bright fringes in a Young's double slit experiment with blue-green light of wavelength 500 nm. The separation between the slits is $2·0 \times 10^{-3}$ m.

10. A source emitting light of wavelengths 480 nm and 600 nm is used in a double slit interference experiment. The separation between the slits is 0·25 mm and the interference is observed on a screen placed at 150 cm from the slits. Find the linear separation between the first maximum (next to the central maximum) corresponding to the two wavelengths.

11. White light is used in a Young's double slit experiment. Find the minimum order of the violet fringe ($\lambda = 400$ nm) which overlaps with a red fringe ($\lambda = 700$ nm).

12. Find the thickness of a plate which will produce a change in optical path equal to half the wavelength λ of the light passing through it normally. The refractive index of the plate is μ.

13. A plate of thickness t made of a material of refractive index μ is placed in front of one of the slits in a double slit experiment. (a) Find the change in the optical path due to introduction of the plate. (b) What should be the minimum thickness t which will make the intensity at the centre of the fringe pattern zero ? Wavelength of the light used is λ. Neglect any absorption of light in the plate.

14. A transparent paper (refractive index = 1·45) of thickness 0·02 mm is pasted on one of the slits of a Young's double slit experiment which uses monochromatic light of wavelength 620 nm. How many fringes will cross through the centre if the paper is removed ?

15. In a Young's double slit experiment using mono-chromatic light, the fringe pattern shifts by a certain distance on the screen when a mica sheet of refractive index 1·6 and thickness 1·964 micron (1 micron = 10^{-6} m) is introduced in the path of one of the interfering waves. The mica sheet is then removed and the distance between the screen and the slits is doubled. It is found that the distance between the successive maxima now is the same as the observed fringe-shift upon the introduction of the mica sheet. Calculate the wavelength of the monochromatic light used in the experiment.

16. A mica strip and a polysterene strip are fitted on the two slits of a double slit apparatus. The thickness of the strips is 0·50 mm and the separation between the slits is 0·12 cm. The refractive index of mica and polysterene are 1·58 and 1·55 respectively for the light of wavelength 590 nm which is used in the experiment. The interference is observed on a screen a distance one meter away. (a) What would be the fringe-width ? (b) At what distance from the centre will the first maximum be located ?

17. Two transparent slabs having equal thickness but different refractive indices μ_1 and μ_2 are pasted side by side to form a composite slab. This slab is placed just after the double slit in a Young's experiment so that the light from one slit goes through one material and the light from the other slit goes through the other material. What should be the minimum thickness of the slab so that there is a minimum at the point P_0 which is equidistant from the slits ?

18. A thin paper of thickness 0·02 mm having a refractive index 1·45 is pasted across one of the slits in a Young's double slit experiment. The paper transmits 4/9 of the light energy falling on it. (a) Find the ratio of the maximum intensity to the minimum intensity in the fringe pattern. (b) How many fringes will cross through the centre if an identical paper piece is pasted on the other slit also ? The wavelength of the light used is 600 nm.

19. A Young's double slit apparatus has slits separated by 0·28 mm and a screen 48 cm away from the slits. The whole apparatus is immersed in water and the slits are illuminated by the red light ($\lambda = 700$ nm in vacuum). Find the fringe-width of the pattern formed on the screen.

20. A parallel beam of monochromatic light is used in a Young's double slit experiment. The slits are separated by a distance d and the screen is placed parallel to the plane of the slits. Show that if the incident beam makes an angle $\theta = \sin^{-1}\left(\dfrac{\lambda}{2d}\right)$ with the normal to the plane of the slits, there will be a dark fringe at the centre P_0 of the pattern.

21. A narrow slit S transmitting light of wavelength λ is placed a distance d above a large plane mirror as shown in figure (17-E1). The light coming directly from the slit

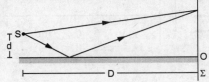

Figure 17-E1

and that coming after the reflection interfere at a screen Σ placed at a distance D from the slit. (a) What will be the intensity at a point just above the mirror, i.e., just above O ? (b) At what distance from O does the first maximum occur ?

22. A long narrow horizontal slit is placed 1 mm above a horizontal plane mirror. The interference between the light coming directly from the slit and that after reflection is seen on a screen 1·0 m away from the slit. Find the fringe-width if the light used has a wavelength of 700 nm.

23. Consider the situation of the previous problem. If the mirror reflects only 64% of the light energy falling on it, what will be the ratio of the maximum to the minimum intensity in the interference pattern observed on the screen ?

24. A double slit $S_1 - S_2$ is illuminated by a coherent light of wavelength λ. The slits are separated by a distance d. A plane mirror is placed in front of the double slit at a distance D_1 from it and a screen Σ is placed behind the double slit at a distance D_2 from it (figure 17-E2). The screen Σ receives only the light reflected by the mirror. Find the fringe-width of the interference pattern on the screen.

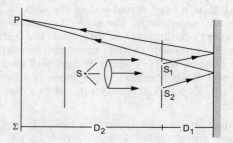

Figure 17-E2

25. White coherent light (400 nm–700 nm) is sent through the slits of a Young's double slit experiment (figure 17-E3). The separation between the slits is 0·5 mm and the screen is 50 cm away from the slits. There is a hole in the screen at a point 1·0 mm away (along the width of the fringes) from the central line. (a) Which wavelength(s) will be absent in the light coming from the hole ? (b) which wavelength(s) will have a strong intensity ?

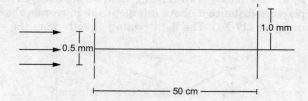

Figure 17-E3

26. Consider the arrangement shown in figure (17-E4). The distance D is large compared to the separation d between the slits. (a) Find the minimum value of d so that there is a dark fringe at O. (b) Suppose d has this value. Find the distance x at which the next bright fringe is formed. (c) Find the fringe-width.

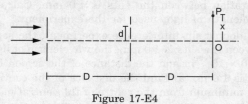

Figure 17-E4

27. Two coherent point sources S_1 and S_2 vibrating in phase emit light of wavelength λ. The separation between the sources is 2λ. Consider a line passing through S_2 and perpendicular to the line $S_1 S_2$. What is the smallest distance from S_2 where a minimum of intensity occurs ?

28. Figure (17-E5) shows three equidistant slits being illuminated by a monochromatic parallel beam of light. Let $BP_0 - AP_0 = \lambda/3$ and $D \gg \lambda$. (a) Show that in this case $d = \sqrt{2\lambda D/3}$. (b) Show that the intensity at P_0 is three times the intensity due to any of the three slits individually.

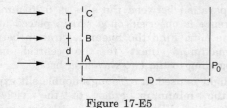

Figure 17-E5

29. In a Young's double slit experiment, the separation between the slits = 2·0 mm, the wavelength of the light = 600 nm and the distance of the screen from the slits = 2·0 m. If the intensity at the centre of the central maximum is 0·20 W m^{-2}, what will be the intensity at a point 0·5 cm away from this centre along the width of the fringes ?

30. In a Young's double slit interference experiment the fringe pattern is observed on a screen placed at a distance D from the slits. The slits are separated by a distance d and are illuminated by monochromatic light of wavelength λ. Find the distance from the central point where the intensity falls to (a) half the maximum, (b) one fourth of the maximum.

31. In a Young's double slit experiment $\lambda = 500$ nm, $d = 1·0$ mm and $D = 1·0$ m. Find the minimum distance from the central maximum for which the intensity is half of the maximum intensity.

32. The line-width of a bright fringe is sometimes defined as the separation between the points on the two sides of the central line where the intensity falls to half the maximum. Find the line-width of a bright fringe in a Young's double slit experiment in terms of λ, d and D where the symbols have their usual meanings.

33. Consider the situation shown in figure (17-E6). The two slits S_1 and S_2 placed symmetrically around the central line are illuminated by a monochromatic light of wavelength λ. The separation between the slits is d. The light transmitted by the slits falls on a screen Σ_1 placed at a distance D from the slits. The slit S_3 is at the central line and the slit S_4 is at a distance z from S_3. Another screen Σ_2 is placed a further distance D away from Σ_1. Find the ratio of the maximum to minimum intensity observed on Σ_2 if z is equal to

(a) $z = \dfrac{\lambda D}{2d}$,   (b) $\dfrac{\lambda D}{d}$,   (c) $\dfrac{\lambda D}{4d}$.

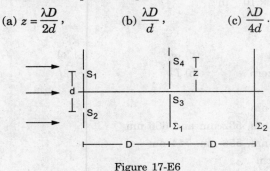

Figure 17-E6

34. Consider the arrangement shown in figure (17-E7). By some mechanism, the separation between the slits S_3 and S_4 can be changed. The intensity is measured at the

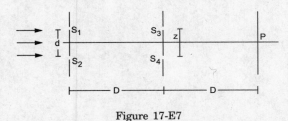

Figure 17-E7

point P which is at the common perpendicular bisector of S_1S_2 and S_3S_4. When $z = \dfrac{D\lambda}{2d}$, the intensity measured at P is I. Find this intensity when z is equal to

(a) $\dfrac{D\lambda}{d}$,   (b) $\dfrac{3D\lambda}{2d}$ and   (c) $\dfrac{2D\lambda}{d}$.

35. A soap film of thickness 0·0011 mm appears dark when seen by the reflected light of wavelength 580 nm. What is the index of refraction of the soap solution, if it is known to be between 1·2 and 1·5 ?

36. A parallel beam of light of wavelength 560 nm falls on a thin film of oil (refractive index = 1·4). What should be the minimum thickness of the film so that it strongly reflects the light ?

37. A parallel beam of white light is incident normally on a water film 1.0×10^{-4} cm thick. Find the wavelength in the visible range (400 nm–700 nm) which are strongly transmitted by the film. Refractive index of water = 1·33.

38. A glass surface is coated by an oil film of uniform thickness 1.00×10^{-4} cm. The index of refraction of the oil is 1·25 and that of the glass is 1·50. Find the wavelengths of light in the visible region (400 nm–750 nm) which are completely transmitted by the oil film under normal incidence.

39. Plane microwaves are incident on a long slit having a width of 5·0 cm. Calculate the wavelength of the microwaves if the first diffraction minimum is formed at $\theta = 30°$.

40. Light of wavelength 560 nm goes through a pinhole of diameter 0·20 mm and falls on a wall at a distance of 2·00 m. What will be the diameter of the central bright spot formed on the wall ?

41. A convex lens of diameter 8·0 cm is used to focus a parallel beam of light of wavelength 620 nm. If the light be focused at a distance of 20 cm from the lens, what would be the diameter of the central bright spot formed ?

□

ANSWERS

OBJECTIVE I

1. (c)	2. (d)	3. (d)	4. (d)	5. (c)	6. (b)
7. (a)	8. (d)	9. (d)	10. (a)	11. (a)	12. (d)
13. (d)	14. (c)	15. (b)	16. (c)	17. (a)	

OBJECTIVE II

1. (a), (c)	2. (b), (c)	3. (b), (c), (d)
4. (c), (d)	5. (c), (d)	6. (a), (d)
7. (a)	8. (b)	9. (a), (b), (d)
10. (a), (d)		

EXERCISES

1. 4.3×10^{14} Hz $- 7.5 \times 10^{14}$ Hz

2. (a) 5.09×10^{14} Hz   (b) 443 nm

    (c) 5.09×10^{14} Hz   (d) 2.25×10^{8} m s^{-1}

3. 2.04×10^{8} m s^{-1}, 2.07×10^{8} m s^{-1}

4. 1·25

5. (a) 0·05 mm   (b) 0·50 mm

6. 400 nm

7. (a) 0·25 mm   (b) 20

8. 1·47 mm

9. 0·014 degree

10. 0·72 mm

11. 7

12. $\dfrac{\lambda}{2(\mu - 1)}$

13. (a) $(\mu - 1)t$ (b) $\dfrac{\lambda}{2(\mu - 1)}$

14. 14·5

15. 590 nm

16. (a) $4·9 \times 10^{-4}$ m

   (b) 0·021 cm on one side and 0·028 cm on the other side

17. $\dfrac{\lambda}{2|\,\mu_1 - \mu_2\,|}$

18. (a) 25   (b) 15

19. 0·90 mm

21. (a) zero   (b) $\dfrac{D\lambda}{4d}$

22. 0·35 mm

23. 81 : 1

24. $\lambda(2D_1 + D_2)/d$

25. (a) 400 nm, 667 nm   (b) 500 nm

26. (a) $\sqrt{\dfrac{\lambda D}{2}}$ (b) d (c) $2d$

27. $7\lambda/12$

29. 0·05 W m^{-2}

30. (a) $\dfrac{D\lambda}{4d}$ (b) $\dfrac{D\lambda}{3d}$

31. $1·25 \times 10^{-4}$ m

32. $\dfrac{D\lambda}{2d}$

33. (a) 1   (b) ∞ (c) 34

34. (a) zero   (b) I (c) $2I$

35. 1·32

36. 100 nm

37. 443 nm, 532 nm and 666 nm

38. 455 nm, 556 nm, 714 nm

39. 2·5 cm

40. 6·85 mm

41. $1·9 \times 10^{-6}$ m

□

CHAPTER 18

GEOMETRICAL OPTICS

We have learnt that light in many cases behaves as a wave of short wavelength. A ray of light gives the direction of propagation of light. In absence of an obstacle, the rays advance in straight lines without changing directions. When light meets a surface separating two transparent media, reflection and refraction occur and the light rays bend. Light rays also bend round the edge of an obstacle limiting the wave front. But as the wavelength of light is usually much smaller than the size of the obstacles, this diffraction effect can usually be neglected. We then deal with *geometrical optics*.

18.1 REFLECTION AT SMOOTH SURFACES

A light ray is reflected by a smooth surface in accordance with the two laws of reflection :

(a) the angle of incidence is equal to the angle of reflection

(b) the incident ray, the reflected ray and the normal to the reflecting surface are coplanar.

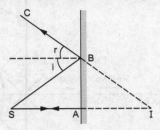

Figure 18.1

Figure (18.1) shows a point source S placed before a plane mirror. Consider a ray SA that falls normally on the mirror. This ray is reflected back along AS. Consider any other ray SB making an angle i with the normal. It is reflected along BC. Suppose AS and BC meet at a point I when produced behind the mirror. It is simple to show that the triangles SAB and ABI are congruent and $SA = AI$. Thus, all the reflected rays meet at I when produced behind the mirror. An eye receiving the reflected rays feels that the rays are diverging from the point I. The point I is called the *image* of the object S.

The basic laws of reflection are same for plane and curved surfaces. A normal can be drawn from any point of the curved surface by first drawing the tangent plane from that point and then drawing the line perpendicular to that plane. Angles of incidence and reflection are defined from this normal (figure 18.2). The angle of incidence is equal to the angle of reflection. The incident ray, the normal and the reflected ray are in the same plane.

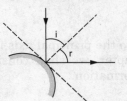

Figure 18.2

18.2 SPHERICAL MIRRORS

A spherical mirror is a part cut from a hollow sphere. Spherical mirrors are generally constructed from glass. One surface of the glass is silvered. The reflection takes place at the other surface. If reflection takes place at the convex surface, it is called a *convex mirror* and if reflection takes place at the concave surface, it is called a *concave mirror*.

Generally, a spherical mirror is constructed with a circular boundary. The centre of the sphere, of which the mirror is a part, is called the *centre of curvature* of the mirror. The radius of this sphere is called the *radius of curvature* of the mirror. The point on the mirror at the middle of the surface is called its *pole*. The line joining the pole and the centre of curvature is called the *principal axis*.

Focus

Suppose a light beam travelling in a direction parallel to the principal axis is incident on a concave mirror. If the aperture of the beam is small so that the light falls "near" the pole only, all the reflected rays cross the principal axis at nearly the same point (figure 18.3a). This point where the reflected rays converge is called the *focus* of the mirror.

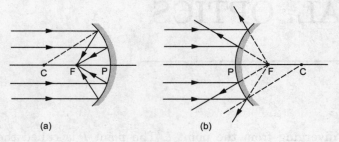

(a)   (b)

Figure 18.3

In case of a convex mirror, the reflected rays diverge after the reflection. Again, if the incident parallel beam has small aperture, the reflected rays appear to diverge from a point on the principal axis (figure 18.3b). This point is the focus of the convex mirror.

The plane through the focus and perpendicular to the principal axis is called the *focal plane*. The distance of the focus from the pole is called the *focal length* of the mirror.

Paraxial Rays

A ray close to the principal axis is called a paraxial ray. In this chapter, we shall consider only paraxial rays in image formation.

Image Tracing

When a point object is placed before a spherical mirror of small aperture, a point image is formed. To locate the position of the image, we draw two rays from the point object, make them incident on the mirror and trace the reflected rays. The line joining the point of incidence and the centre of curvature is the normal. A reflected ray is traced by applying the laws of reflection. If the reflected rays intersect, the point of intersection is the *real image*. If the rays diverge after reflection, a *virtual image* is formed at the point from where the rays seem to diverge. Figure (18.4) shows some examples.

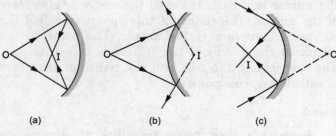

(a)   (b)   (c)

Figure 18.4

If the incident rays diverge from a point object, the object is called a *real object*. Sometimes the rays incident on the mirror do not diverge from a point, rather they converge towards the mirror (figure 18.4c). In this case, the point where these rays would meet if there were no mirror, is treated as the object. Such a point is called a *virtual object*.

Thus, the point of intersection of the incident rays is called the *object* and the point of intersection of the corresponding reflected rays is called its *image*.

Sign Convention

In image tracing, we come across the object distance, the image distance, the focal length and the radius of curvature. A system of signs for these quantities is necessary to derive relations connecting them which are consistent in all types of physical situations. We shall describe coordinate sign convention which is now widely used.

In this method, the pole is taken to be the origin and the principal axis as the X-axis. Usually, the positive of the axis is taken along the incident rays. The quantities u, v, R and f denote the x-coordinates of the object, the image, the centre of curvature and the focus respectively. Any of these quantities is positive if the corresponding point lies on the positive side of the origin and is negative if it is on the negative side. Figure (18.5) shows some typical situations. The signs of various quantities are tabulated below

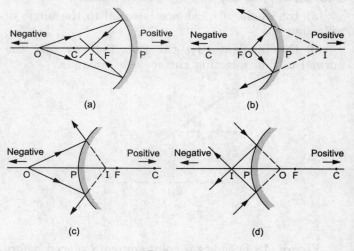

(a)   (b)

(c)   (d)

Figure 18.5

Figure	u	v	R	f
18.5a	−	−	−	−
18.5b	−	+	−	−
18.5c	−	+	+	+
18.5d	+	−	+	+

If the lengths perpendicular to the principal axis are needed, we should fix the positive direction of the Y-axis. Generally the upward is taken as positive of the Y-axis and downward as the negative of the Y-axis. Heights along the positive Y-axis are positive and heights along the negative Y-axis are negative. Quite often, we shall use the words "object-distance" and "image-distance" for u and v.

18.3 RELATION BETWEEN u, v AND R FOR SPHERICAL MIRRORS

Consider the situation shown in figure (18.6). A point object is placed at the point O of the principal axis of a concave mirror. A ray OA is incident on the mirror at A. It is reflected in the direction AI. Another ray OP travels along the principal axis. As PO is normal to the mirror at P, the ray is reflected back along PO. The reflected rays PO and AI intersect at I where the image is formed.

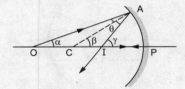

Figure 18.6

Let C be the centre of curvature. The line CA is the normal at A. Thus, by the laws of reflection, $\angle OAC = \angle CAI$. Let α, β, γ and θ denote the angles AOP, ACP, AIP and OAC respectively. As the exterior angle in a triangle equals the sum of the two opposite interior angles, we have,

from triangle OAC $\beta = \alpha + \theta$ ... (i)
and from triangle OAI $\gamma = \alpha + 2\theta$.   ... (ii)

Eliminating θ from (i) and (ii),
$$2\beta = \alpha + \gamma. \qquad ... (iii)$$

If the point A is close to P, the angles α, β and γ are small and we can write

$$\alpha \approx \frac{AP}{PO}, \quad \beta = \frac{AP}{PC} \quad \text{and} \quad \gamma \approx \frac{AP}{PI}.$$

As C is the centre of curvature, the equation for β is exact whereas the remaining two are approximate. Putting in (iii),

$$2\frac{AP}{PC} = \frac{AP}{PO} + \frac{AP}{PI}$$

or, $\dfrac{1}{PO} + \dfrac{1}{PI} = \dfrac{2}{PC}$.   ... (iv)

The pole P is taken as the origin and the principal axis as the X-axis. The rays are incident from left to right. We take the direction from left to right as the positive X-direction. The point O, I and C are situated to the left of the origin P in the figure. The quantities u, v and R are, therefore, negative. As the distances PO, PI and PC are positive, $PO = -u$, $PI = -v$ and $PC = -R$. Putting in (iv),

$$\frac{1}{-u} + \frac{1}{-v} = \frac{2}{-R}$$

or, $\dfrac{1}{u} + \dfrac{1}{v} = \dfrac{2}{R}$.   ... (18.1)

Although equation (18.1) is derived for a special situation shown in figure (18.6), it is also valid in all other situations with a spherical mirror. This is because we have taken proper care of the signs of u, v and R appearing in figure (18.6).

Example 18.1

A convex mirror has its radius of curvature 20 cm. Find the position of the image of an object placed at a distance of 12 cm from the mirror.

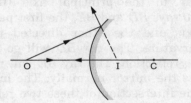

Figure 18.7

Solution : The situation is shown in figure (18.7). Here $u = -12$ cm and $R = +20$ cm. We have,

$$\frac{1}{u} + \frac{1}{v} = \frac{2}{R}$$

or, $\dfrac{1}{v} = \dfrac{2}{R} - \dfrac{1}{u}$

$$= \frac{2}{20 \text{ cm}} - \frac{1}{-12 \text{ cm}} = \frac{11}{60 \text{ cm}}$$

or, $v = \dfrac{60}{11}$ cm.

The positive sign of v shows that the image is formed on the right side of the mirror. It is a virtual image.

Relation between the Focal Length and the Radius of Curvature

If the object O in figure (18.6) is taken at a large distance, the rays coming from O and incident on the mirror become almost parallel. The image is then formed close to the focus. Thus, if $u = \infty$, $v = f$. Putting in (18.1),

$$\frac{1}{\infty} + \frac{1}{f} = \frac{2}{R}$$

or, $f = R/2$.   ... (18.2)

Equation (18.1) may also be written as

$$\frac{1}{u} + \frac{1}{v} = \frac{1}{f} \qquad \dots \text{(18.3)}$$

The focus is midway between the pole and the centre of curvature.

18.4 EXTENDED OBJECTS AND MAGNIFICATION

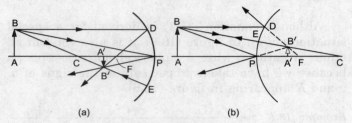

Figure 18.8

Suppose an object AB is placed on the principal axis of a spherical mirror with the length AB perpendicular to the principal axis (figure 18.8). Consider two rays BD and BE, the first parallel to the principal axis and the other directed towards the centre of curvature. The ray BD will go through the focus F after reflection. The ray BE will return along EB as it hits the mirror normally. The image of B is formed at the intersection of these two reflected rays. Thus, the image B' of the point B is traced. If we drop a perpendicular B'A' on the principal axis, it can be shown that A' is the image of A and A'B' is the image of AB. Figures (18.8a) and (18.8b) show the construction in two different situations.

Lateral Magnification

The ratio $\dfrac{\text{height of the image}}{\text{height of the objective}}$ is called *lateral* or *transverse magnification*. The height of the object (placed perpendicular to the principal axis) is taken to be positive. If the image is also on the same side of the principal axis, its height is also positive. The image is then erect. Figure (18.8b) shows an example. If the image is inverted, its height is taken as negative.

Consider the ray BP in figure (18.8) hitting the mirror at the pole P. The reflected ray passes through B' as B' is the image of B. The principal axis is the normal at P to the mirror. By the laws of reflection,

$$\angle BPA = \angle APB'.$$

Thus, the right-angled triangles ABP and A'B'P are similar. Thus,

$$\frac{A'B'}{AB} = \frac{PA'}{PA}. \qquad \dots \text{(i)}$$

In figure (18.8a); $A'B' = -h_2$, $AB = h_1$, $PA' = -v$ and $PA = -u$. Equation (i) gives

$$\frac{-h_2}{h_1} = \frac{-v}{-u}$$

or,

$$m = \frac{h_2}{h_1} = -\frac{v}{u}. \qquad \dots \text{(18.4)}$$

Since proper signs are used, this same relation is also valid in all other situations. For example, in figure 18.8(b), $A'B' = +h_2$, $AB = +h_1$, $PA' = +v$ and $PA = -u$. Equation (i) gives

$$\frac{h_2}{h_1} = \frac{v}{-u} \quad \text{or,} \quad m = -\frac{v}{u}.$$

Example 18.2

An object of length 2·5 cm is placed at a distance of 1·5 f from a concave mirror where f is the magnitude of the focal length of the mirror. The length of the object is perpendicular to the principal axis. Find the length of the image. Is the image erect or inverted?

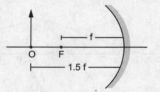

Figure 18.9

Solution : The given situation is shown in figure (18.9). The focal length $F = -f$, and $u = -1·5 f$. We have,

$$\frac{1}{u} + \frac{1}{v} = \frac{1}{F} \quad \text{or,} \quad \frac{1}{-1·5 f} + \frac{1}{v} = \frac{1}{-f}$$

or,

$$\frac{1}{v} = \frac{1}{1·5 f} - \frac{1}{f} = \frac{-1}{3 f}$$

or,

$$v = -3 f.$$

Now

$$m = -\frac{v}{u} = \frac{3 f}{-1·5 f} = -2$$

or,

$$\frac{h_2}{h_1} = -2 \quad \text{or,} \quad h_2 = -2 h_1 = -5·0 \text{ cm}.$$

The image is 5·0 cm long. The minus sign shows that it is inverted.

18.5 REFRACTION AT PLANE SURFACES

When a light ray is incident on a surface separating two transparent media, the ray bends at the time of changing the medium. The angle of incidence i and the angle of refraction r follow *Snell's law*

$$\frac{\sin i}{\sin r} = \frac{v_1}{v_2} = \frac{\mu_2}{\mu_1},$$

where v_1 and v_2 are the speeds of light in media 1 and 2 respectively and μ_1 and μ_2 are the refractive indices of media 1 and 2 respectively. For vacuum the refractive index μ equals 1. For air also, it is very close to 1.

Image due to Refraction at a Plane Surface

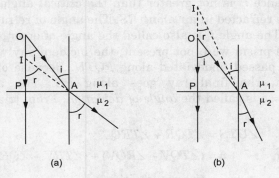

(a)   (b)

Figure 18.10

Consider the situation shown in figure (18.10). A point object O is placed in a medium of refractive index μ_1. Another medium of refractive index μ_2 has its boundary at PA. Consider two rays OP and OA originating from O. Let OP fall perpendicularly on PA and OA fall at PA at a small angle i with the normal. OP enters the second medium undeviated and OA enters making an angle r with the normal. When produced backward, these rays meet at I which is the virtual image of O. If i and r are small,

$$\sin i \approx \tan i = \frac{PA}{PO}$$

and

$$\sin r \approx \tan r = \frac{PA}{PI}.$$

Thus,

$$\frac{\mu_2}{\mu_1} = \frac{\sin i}{\sin r}$$

$$= \left(\frac{PA}{PO}\right) \cdot \left(\frac{PI}{PA}\right) = \frac{PI}{PO}. \qquad \dots \text{(i)}$$

Suppose medium 2 is air and an observer looks at the image from this medium (figure 18.10a). The real depth of the object inside medium 1 is PO whereas the depth as it appears to the observer is PI. Writing $\mu_2 = 1$ and $\mu_1 = \mu$, equation (i) gives

$$\frac{1}{\mu} = \frac{\text{apparent depth}}{\text{real depth}}$$

or,

$$\mu = \frac{\text{real depth}}{\text{apparent depth}}. \qquad \dots \text{(18.5)}$$

The image shifts closer to eye by an amount $OI = PO - PI$

$$= \left(\frac{PO - PI}{PO}\right) PO = \left(1 - \frac{PI}{PO}\right) PO$$

or,

$$\Delta t = \left(1 - \frac{1}{\mu}\right) t, \qquad \dots \text{(18.6)}$$

where t is the thickness of the medium over the object and Δt is the apparent shift in its position towards the observer. Note that Δt is positive in figure (18.10a) and negative in figure (18.10b).

Example 18.3

A printed page is kept pressed by a glass cube (μ = 1·5) of edge 6·0 cm. By what amount will the printed letters appear to be shifted when viewed from the top ?

Solution : The thickness of the cube $= t = 6\cdot0$ cm. The shift in the position of the printed letters is

$$\Delta t = \left(1 - \frac{1}{\mu}\right) t$$

$$= \left(1 - \frac{1}{1\cdot5}\right) \times 6\cdot0 \text{ cm} = 2\cdot0 \text{ cm}.$$

18.6 CRITICAL ANGLE

When a ray passes from an optically denser medium (larger μ) to an optically rarer medium (smaller μ), the angle of refraction r is greater than the corresponding angle of incidence i. We have,

$$\frac{\sin i}{\sin r} = \frac{\mu_2}{\mu_1} < 1.$$

If we gradually increase i, the corresponding r will also increase and at a certain stage r will become 90°. Let the angle of incidence for this case be θ_c. If i is increased further, there is no r which can satisfy Snell's law. Thus, the ray will not be refracted. Entire light is then reflected back into the first medium. This is called *total internal reflection*. The angle θ_c is called the *critical angle* for the given pair of media. Generally, critical angle of a medium is quoted for light going from the medium to the air. In this case, $\mu_2 = 1$. Writing $\mu_1 = \mu$, Snell's law gives

$$\frac{\sin\theta_c}{\sin 90°} = \frac{1}{\mu}$$

or,

$$\sin\theta_c = (1/\mu)$$

or,

$$\theta_c = \sin^{-1}(1/\mu). \qquad \dots \text{(18.7)}$$

Example 18.4

The critical angle for water is 48·2°. Find its refractive index.

Solution : $\mu = \dfrac{1}{\sin\theta_c} = \dfrac{1}{\sin 48\cdot2°} = 1\cdot34.$

18.7 OPTICAL FIBRE

Total internal reflection is the basic principle of a very useful branch of physics known as *fibre optics*. An *optical fibre* is a very thin fibre made of glass or plastic having a radius of the order of a micrometer (10^{-6} m). A bundle of such thin fibres forms a *light pipe*.

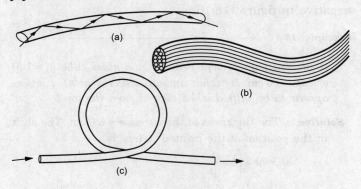

Figure 18.11

Figure (18.11a) shows the principle of light transmission by an optical fibre. Figure (18.11b) sketches a light pipe. Because of the small radius of the fibre, light going into it makes a nearly glancing incidence on the wall. The angle of incidence is greater than the critical angle and hence total internal reflection takes place. The light is thus transmitted along the fibre. Even if a light pipe is put in a complicated shape (figure 18.11c), the light is transmitted without any appreciable loss.

Light pipes using optical fibres may be used to see places which are difficult to reach such as inside of a human body. For example, a patient's stomach can be viewed by inserting one end of a light pipe into the stomach through the mouth. Light is sent down through one set of fibres in the pipe. This illuminates the inside of the stomach. The light from the inside travels back through another set of fibres in the pipe and the viewer gets the image at the outer end.

The other important application of fibre optics is to transmit communication signals through light pipes. For example, about 2000 telephone signals, appropriately mixed with light waves, may be simultaneously transmitted through a typical optical fibre. The clarity of the signals transmitted in this way is much better than other conventional methods.

The fibres in a light pipe must be optically insulated from each other. This is usually done by coating each fibre with a material having refractive index less than that of the fibre.

18.8 PRISM

Figure (18.12) shows the cross section of a prism. *AB* and *AC* represent the refracting surfaces. The angle *BAC* is the angle of the prism. Consider the prism to be placed in air. A ray *PQ*, incident on a refracting surface *AB*, gets refracted along *QR*. The angle of incidence and the angle of refraction are i and r respectively. The ray *QR* is incident on the surface *AC*. Here the light goes from an optically denser medium to an optically rarer medium. If the angle of incidence r' is not greater than the critical angle, the ray is refracted in air along *RS*. The angle of refraction is i'. The angle i' is also called the angle of emergence. If the prism were not present, the incident ray would have passed undeviated along *PQTU*. Because of the prism, the final ray goes along *RS*. The angle $UTS = \delta$ is called the *angle of deviation*. From triangle *TQR*,

$$\angle UTS = \angle TQR + \angle TRQ$$

or, $$\delta = (\angle TQV - \angle RQV) + (\angle TRV - \angle QRV)$$

$$= (i - r) + (i' - r')$$

$$= (i + i') - (r + r').   \qquad \dots \text{(i)}$$

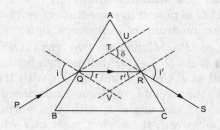

Figure 18.12

Now, the four angles of the quadrangle *AQVR* add to 360°. The angles *AQV* and *ARV* are 90° each. Thus,

$$A + \angle QVR = 180°.$$

Also, from the triangle *QRV*,

$$r + r' + \angle QVR = 180°.$$

So, $$r + r' = A. \qquad \dots \text{(18.8)}$$

Substituting in (i),

$$\delta = i + i' - A. \qquad \dots \text{(18.9)}$$

Angle of Minimum Deviation

The angle i' is determined by the angle of incidence i. Thus, the angle of deviation δ is also determined by i. For a particular value of angle of incidence, the angle of deviation is minimum. In this situation, the ray passes symmetrically through the prism, so that $i = i'$.

The above statement can be justified by assuming that there is a unique angle of minimum deviation. Suppose, when deviation is minimum, the angle of incidence is greater than the angle of emergence. Suppose, figure (18.13) shows the situation for minimum deviation. According to our assumption,

$$i > i'.$$

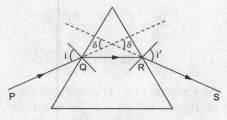

Figure 18.13

Now, if we send a ray along *SR*, it will retrace the path and will emerge along *QP*. Thus, the angle of deviation is same as before and hence, is minimum. According to our assumption, the angle of incidence is greater than the angle of emergence. Hence,

$$i' > i.$$

Thus, we get a contradiction. Similarly, if we assume that the angle of incidence is smaller than the angle of emergence for minimum deviation, we again get a contradiction. Hence, for minimum deviation, $i = i'$.

Relation between Refractive Index and the Angle of Minimum Deviation

Let the angle of minimum deviation be δ_m. For minimum deviation, $i = i'$ and $r = r'$. We have,

$$\delta_m = i + i' - A$$
$$= 2\,i - A$$

or,
$$i = \frac{A + \delta_m}{2}. \qquad \ldots \text{(i)}$$

Also,
$$r + r' = A$$

or,
$$r = A/2. \qquad \ldots \text{(ii)}$$

The refractive index is

$$\mu = \frac{\sin i}{\sin r}.$$

Using (i) and (ii),

$$\mu = \frac{\sin \dfrac{A + \delta_m}{2}}{\sin \dfrac{A}{2}}. \qquad \ldots \text{(18.10)}$$

If the angle of prism A is small, δ_m is also small. Equation (18.10) then becomes

$$\mu \approx \frac{\dfrac{A + \delta_m}{2}}{\dfrac{A}{2}}$$

or,
$$\delta_m = (\mu - 1)\,A. \qquad \ldots \text{(18.11)}$$

Example 18.5

The angle of minimum deviation from a prism is 37°. If the angle of prism is 53°, find the refractive index of the material of the prism.

Solution : $\mu = \dfrac{\sin \dfrac{A + \delta_m}{2}}{\sin \dfrac{A}{2}} = \dfrac{\sin \dfrac{53° + 37°}{2}}{\sin \dfrac{53°}{2}} = \dfrac{\sin 45°}{\sin 26\cdot5°}$

$$= 1\cdot58.$$

18.9 REFRACTION AT SPHERICAL SURFACES

When two transparent media are separated by a spherical surface, light incident on the surface gets refracted into the medium on other side. Suppose two transparent media having refractive indices μ_1 and μ_2 are separated by a spherical surface *AB* (figure 18.14). Let *C* be the centre of curvature of *AB*. Consider a point object *O* in the medium 1. Suppose the line *OC* cuts the spherical surface at *P*.

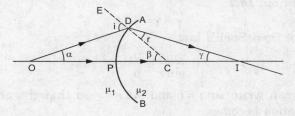

Figure 18.14

Several cases may arise. The surface may be concave towards the higher μ side or it may be convex. The object may be on the convex side or on the concave side. In figure (18.14), it is assumed that $\mu_2 > \mu_1$ and the object *O* is on the convex side of the surface.

Image Tracing

Consider two rays *OD* and *OP* originating from *O*. The ray *OP* falls normally on *AB*. It goes into medium 2 undeviated. Suppose the ray *OD* makes a small angle α with the line *OPC* and falls on the surface *AB* at a point *D*. The normal to *AB* at the point *D* is *DC*. The angle *ODE* = i is the angle of incidence. The ray is refracted along *DI*. The two refracted rays meet at the point *I* where the image is formed. The angle *CDI* = r is the angle of refraction. If the refracted rays actually meet, a real image is formed. If the refracted rays diverge after refraction, a virtual image is formed at the point from where these rays seem to diverge.

Sign Convention

The sign convention for refraction at spherical surface is quite similar to that used for spherical mirrors.

The line joining the object and the centre is taken as the X-axis. The positive direction of the axis is generally chosen along the direction of the incident rays. The point of intersection of the spherical surface with the axis is taken as the origin. The quantities u, v and R denote the x-coordinates of the object, the image and the centre of curvature respectively. Any of these quantities is positive if the corresponding point lies on the positive side of the origin and is negative if it is on the negative side. Similarly for the lengths perpendicular to the X-axis.

Relation between u, v and R

Refer to figure (18.14). Let $\angle DOP = \alpha$, $\angle DCP = \beta$ and $\angle DIC = \gamma$. For paraxial rays, D is close to P and α, i, r, β and γ are all small. From the triangle ODC,

$$\alpha + \beta = i \qquad \dots \text{(i)}$$

and from DCI,

$$r + \gamma = \beta. \qquad \dots \text{(ii)}$$

Also, from Snell's law,

$$\frac{\sin i}{\sin r} = \frac{\mu_2}{\mu_1}.$$

We can write $\sin i \approx i$ and $\sin r \approx r$ so that the above equation becomes

$$\mu_1 i = \mu_2 r. \qquad \dots \text{(iii)}$$

Putting i and r from (i) and (ii) into (iii),

$$\mu_1(\alpha + \beta) = \mu_2(\beta - \gamma)$$

or, $$\mu_1 \alpha + \mu_2 \gamma = (\mu_2 - \mu_1)\beta. \qquad \dots \text{(iv)}$$

As α, β and γ are small, from figure (18.14),

$$\alpha \approx \frac{DP}{PO}, \quad \beta = \frac{DP}{PC} \text{ and } \gamma \approx \frac{DP}{PI}.$$

The expression for β is exact as C is the centre of curvature. Putting in (iv),

$$\mu_1\left(\frac{DP}{PO}\right) + \mu_2\left(\frac{DP}{PI}\right) = (\mu_2 - \mu_1)\frac{DP}{PC}$$

or, $$\frac{\mu_1}{PO} + \frac{\mu_2}{PI} = \frac{\mu_2 - \mu_1}{PC}. \qquad \dots \text{(v)}$$

At this stage, proper sign convention must be used so that the formula derived is also valid for situations other than that shown in the figure.

In figure (18.14), the point P is the origin and OPC is the axis. As the incident ray comes from left to right, we choose this direction as the positive direction of the axis. We see that u is negative whereas v and R are positive. As the distances PO, PI and PC are positive, $PO = -u$, $PI = +v$ and $PC = +R$. From (v),

$$\frac{\mu_1}{-u} + \frac{\mu_2}{v} = \frac{\mu_2 - \mu_1}{R}$$

or, $$\frac{\mu_2}{v} - \frac{\mu_1}{u} = \frac{\mu_2 - \mu_1}{R}. \qquad \dots \text{(18.12)}$$

Although the formula (18.12) is derived for a particular situation of figure (18.14), it is valid for all other situations of refraction at a single spherical surface. This is because we have used the proper sign convention.

Example 18.6

Locate the image of the point object O in the situation shown in figure (18.15). The point C denotes the centre of curvature of the separating surface.

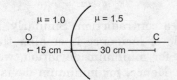

Figure 18.15

Solution : Here $u = -15$ cm, $R = 30$ cm, $\mu_1 = 1$ and $\mu_2 = 1 \cdot 5$. We have,

$$\frac{\mu_2}{v} - \frac{\mu_1}{u} = \frac{\mu_2 - \mu_1}{R}$$

or, $$\frac{1 \cdot 5}{v} - \frac{1 \cdot 0}{-15 \text{ cm}} = \frac{1 \cdot 5 - 1}{30 \text{ cm}}$$

or, $$\frac{1 \cdot 5}{v} = \frac{0 \cdot 5}{30 \text{ cm}} - \frac{1}{15 \text{ cm}}$$

or, $$v = -30 \text{ cm}.$$

The image is formed 30 cm left to the spherical surface and is virtual.

18.10 EXTENDED OBJECTS : LATERAL MAGNIFICATION

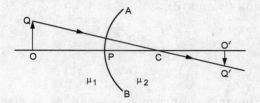

Figure 18.16

Consider the situation shown in figure (18.16). Let OQ be an extended object placed perpendicular to the line OPC. Consider the ray originating from Q and going towards QC. This ray is incident normally on the spherical surface AB. Thus, it goes undeviated in medium 2. The image of Q must be on the line QC.

The image of O will be formed on the line OPC. Let it be formed at O'. The position of O' may be located by using equation (18.12). If we drop a perpendicular from O' on OPC, the intersection Q' of this perpendicular with QC will be the image of Q. Thus, $O'Q'$ will be the image of OQ.

Lateral Magnification

The lateral or transverse magnification is defined as

$$m = \frac{h_2}{h_1},$$

where h_2 = height of the image and h_1 = height of the object. In figure (18.16), $OQ = + h_1$ and $O'Q' = - h_2$.

$$m = \frac{h_2}{h_1} = -\frac{O'Q'}{OQ}.$$

The triangle OCQ and $O'CQ'$ are similar. So,

$$m = -\frac{O'Q'}{OQ} = -\frac{O'C}{OC}$$

$$= -\frac{PO' - PC}{PO + PC}. \quad \ldots \text{(i)}$$

In figure (18.16), $PO = -u$, $PC = +R$ and $PO' = +v$. Equation (i) gives

$$m = -\frac{v - R}{-u + R}$$

$$= \frac{R - v}{R - u}. \quad \ldots \text{(ii)}$$

Also,

$$\frac{\mu_2}{v} - \frac{\mu_1}{u} = \frac{\mu_2 - \mu_1}{R}$$

or,

$$\frac{\mu_2 u - \mu_1 v}{uv} = \frac{\mu_2 - \mu_1}{R}$$

or,

$$R = \frac{(\mu_2 - \mu_1)uv}{\mu_2 u - \mu_1 v}.$$

This gives

$$R - v = \frac{\mu_1 v(v - u)}{\mu_2 u - \mu_1 v}$$

and

$$R - u = \frac{\mu_2 u(v - u)}{\mu_2 u - \mu_1 v}$$

Thus, by (ii),

$$m = \frac{\mu_1 v}{\mu_2 u}. \quad \ldots \text{(18.13)}$$

Example 18.7

Find the size of the image formed in the situation shown in figure (18.17).

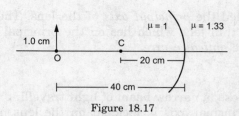

Figure 18.17

Solution : Here $u = -40$ cm, $R = -20$ cm, $\mu_1 = 1$, $\mu_2 = 1 \cdot 33$. We have,

$$\frac{\mu_2}{v} - \frac{\mu_1}{u} = \frac{\mu_2 - \mu_1}{R}$$

or,

$$\frac{1 \cdot 33}{v} - \frac{1}{-40 \text{ cm}} = \frac{1 \cdot 33 - 1}{-20 \text{ cm}}$$

or,

$$\frac{1 \cdot 33}{v} = -\frac{1}{40 \text{ cm}} - \frac{0 \cdot 33}{20 \text{ cm}}$$

or,

$$v = -32 \text{ cm}.$$

The magnification is

$$m = \frac{h_2}{h_1} = \frac{\mu_1 v}{\mu_2 u}$$

or,

$$\frac{h_2}{1 \cdot 0 \text{ cm}} = \frac{-32 \text{ cm}}{1 \cdot 33 \times (-40 \text{ cm})}$$

or,

$$h_2 = +0 \cdot 6 \text{ cm}.$$

The image is erect.

18.11 REFRACTION THROUGH THIN LENSES

A lens is one of the most familiar optical devices for a human being. We have lenses in our eyes and a good number of us supplement them with another set of lenses in our spectacles. A lens is made of a transparent material bounded by two spherical surfaces. The surfaces may be both convex, both concave or one convex and one concave. When the thickness of the lens is small compared to the other dimensions like object distance, we call it a *thin lens*. Figure (18.18) shows several lenses and paths of a number of rays going through them.

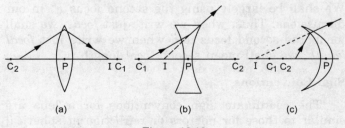

| (a) | (b) | (c) |

Figure 18.18

As there are two spherical surfaces, there are two centres of curvature C_1 and C_2 and correspondingly two radii of curvature R_1 and R_2. The line joining C_1 and

C_2 is called the *principal axis* of the lens. The centre P of the thin lens which lies on the principal axis, is called the *optical centre*.

Focus

Suppose, a narrow beam of light travelling parallel to the principal axis is incident on the lens near the optical centre (figure 18.19a).

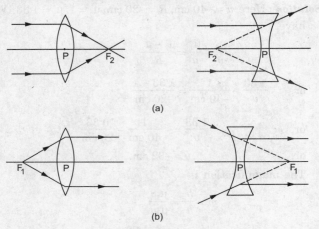

(a)

(b)

Figure 18.19

The rays are refracted twice and then come out of the lens. The emergent rays may converge at a point F_2 on the principal axis or they may seem to diverge from a point F_2 on the principal axis. In the first case, the lens is called a *convergent lens, converging lens or convex lens*. In the second case, it is called a *divergent lens, diverging lens* or *concave lens*. The point F_2 is called the *second focus* of the lens. The distance PF_2 from the optical centre is called the *second focal length*.

The *first focus* F_1 is defined as a point where an object should be placed to give emergent rays parallel to the principal axis (figure 18.19b). For a convergent lens, such an object is a real object and for a divergent lens, it is a virtual object. The distance PF_1 is the *first focal length*.

If the media on the two sides of a thin lens have same refractive index, the two focal lengths are equal. We shall be largely using the second focus F_2 in our discussions. Thus, when we write just *focus*, we shall mean the second focus and when we write just *focal length*, we shall mean second focal length.

Sign Conventions

The coordinate sign conventions for a lens are similar to those for mirrors or refraction at spherical surfaces. The optical centre is taken as the origin and the principal axis as the X-axis. The positive direction of the axis is generally taken along the incident rays. The quantities u, v, f, R_1 and R_2 represent the x-coordinates of the object, the image, the focus, first

centre of curvature and second centre of curvature respectively. The table below shows the signs of u, v, f, R_1 and R_2 in certain cases shown in figure (18.20).

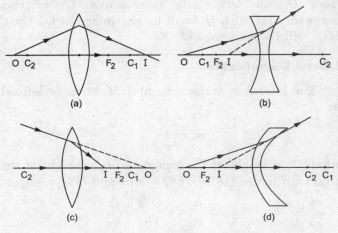

(a)   (b)

(c)   (d)

Figure 18.20

Figure	u	v	f	R_1	R_2
18.20a	−	+	+	+	−
18.20b	−	−	−	−	+
18.20c	+	+	+	+	−
18.20d	−	−	−	+	+

Generally, the incident rays and hence the positive direction of the axis is taken from left to right. Heights measured upwards are taken to be positive and the heights measured downward are taken to be negative.

With the usual choice of axes, f of a lens is positive for a converging lens and is negative for a diverging lens.

18.12 LENS MAKER'S FORMULA AND LENS FORMULA

Consider the situation shown in figure (18.21). $ADBE$ is a thin lens. An object O is placed on its principal axis. The two spherical surfaces of the lens have their centres at C_1 and C_2. The optical centre is at P and the principal axis cuts the two spherical surfaces at D and E.

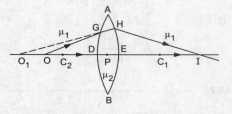

Figure 18.21

Let the refractive index of the material of the lens be μ_2 and suppose it is placed in a medium of refractive index μ_1. To trace the image of O, consider two rays OP and OG originating from O. The ray OP falls on the spherical surfaces perpendicularly and hence, it goes undeviated through the lens. The ray OG is refracted from a medium of refractive index μ_1 to another medium of refractive index μ_2. The centre of curvature of the surface ADB is at C_1. The ray is refracted along GH which meets the principal axis at O_1 (when produced backward in figure 18.21). Thus, due to this single refraction, the image of O is formed at O_1. The ray GH is incident on the spherical surface AEB. It is refracted from medium μ_2 to medium μ_1. The emergent ray HI intersects the principal axis at I where the final image is formed.

The general equation for refraction at a spherical surface is

$$\frac{\mu_2}{v} - \frac{\mu_1}{u} = \frac{\mu_2 - \mu_1}{R}. \qquad \dots \text{ (i)}$$

To use this equation for the first refraction at ADB, we should take the origin at D, whereas, for the second refraction at AEB, we should take the origin at E. As the lens is thin, the points D, P and E are all close to each other and we may take the origin at P for both these refractions.

For the first refraction, the object is at O, the image is at O_1 and the centre of curvature is at C_1. If u, v_1, and R_1, denote their x-coordinates,

$$\frac{\mu_2}{v_1} - \frac{\mu_1}{u} = \frac{\mu_2 - \mu_1}{R_1}. \qquad \dots \text{ (ii)}$$

For the second refraction at AEB, the incident rays GH and DE diverge from O_1. Thus, O_1 is the object for this refraction and its x-coordinate is v_1. The image is formed at I and the centre of curvature is at C_2. Their x-coordinates are v and R_2 respectively. The light goes from the medium μ_2 to medium μ_1. Applying equation (i),

$$\frac{\mu_1}{v} - \frac{\mu_2}{v_1} = \frac{\mu_1 - \mu_2}{R_2}. \qquad \dots \text{ (iii)}$$

Adding (ii) and (iii),

$$\mu_1\left(\frac{1}{v} - \frac{1}{u}\right) = (\mu_2 - \mu_1)\left(\frac{1}{R_1} - \frac{1}{R_2}\right)$$

or, $$\frac{1}{v} - \frac{1}{u} = \left(\frac{\mu_2}{\mu_1} - 1\right)\left(\frac{1}{R_1} - \frac{1}{R_2}\right). \qquad \dots \text{ (18.14)}$$

If the object O is taken far away from the lens, the image is formed close to the focus. Thus, for $u = \infty$, $v = f$. Putting in (18.14), we get,

$$\frac{1}{f} = \left(\frac{\mu_2}{\mu_1} - 1\right)\left(\frac{1}{R_1} - \frac{1}{R_2}\right). \qquad \dots \text{ (18.15)}$$

If the refractive index of the material of the lens is μ and it is placed in air, $\mu_2 = \mu$ and $\mu_1 = 1$ so that (18.15) becomes

$$\frac{1}{f} = (\mu - 1)\left(\frac{1}{R_1} - \frac{1}{R_2}\right). \qquad \dots \text{ (18.16)}$$

This is called *lens maker's formula* because it tells what curvatures will be needed to make a lens of desired focal length. Combining (18.14) and (18.15),

$$\frac{1}{v} - \frac{1}{u} = \frac{1}{f} \qquad \dots \text{ (18.17)}$$

which is known as the *lens formula*.

Example 18.8

A biconvex lens has radii of curvature 20 cm each. If the refractive index of the material of the lens is 1·5, what is its focal length ?

Solution : In a biconvex lens, centre of curvature of the first surface is on the positive side of the lens and that of the second surface is on the negative side. Thus, $R_1 = 20$ cm and $R_2 = -20$ cm.

We have,

$$\frac{1}{f} = (\mu - 1)\left(\frac{1}{R_1} - \frac{1}{R_2}\right)$$

or, $$\frac{1}{f} = (1\cdot5 - 1)\left(\frac{1}{20\text{ cm}} - \frac{1}{-20\text{ cm}}\right)$$

or, $$f = 20\text{ cm}.$$

18.13 EXTENDED OBJECTS : LATERAL MAGNIFICATION

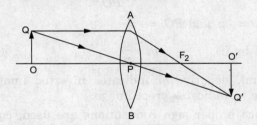

Figure 18.22

Consider the situation shown in figure (18.22). OQ is an extended object placed on the principal axis with its height perpendicular to the principal axis. To locate the image of Q, consider two rays QP and QA, the first one through the optical centre and the other parallel to the principal axis. The parts of the two surfaces at which the ray QP is refracted, are nearly parallel to each other. The lens near the optical centre, therefore, behaves like a rectangular slab. Thus, the ray passing through this region does not bend. Also, the lateral displacement produced is negligible as the thickness of the lens is small. Thus, a ray passing through the optical centre goes undeviated. The ray QP emerges in the same direction PQ'. The ray QA parallel to the principal axis must pass through the focus F_2. Thus, the emergent ray is along AF_2Q'. The image is formed where QPQ' and AF_2Q' intersect. Drop a perpendicular from Q' on the principal axis. This perpendicular $O'Q'$ is the image of OQ. Figure (18.23) shows image formation in some other cases.

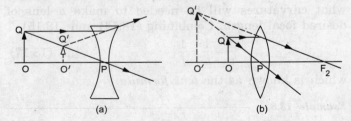

(a)   (b)

Figure 18.23

The lateral or transverse magnification is defined as

$$m = \frac{h_2}{h_1},$$

where h_2 = height of the image and h_1 = height of the object.

Referring to figure (18.22), the magnification is

$$m = \frac{h_2}{h_1} = \frac{-O'Q'}{OQ}.$$

From the similar triangles OQP and $O'Q'P$,

$$\frac{O'Q'}{OQ} = \frac{PO'}{PO}$$

so that $$m = -\frac{PO'}{PO}. \qquad \ldots \text{(i)}$$

But $PO = -u$ and $PO' = +v$

so that by (i), $$m = \frac{v}{u}. \qquad \ldots \text{(18.18)}$$

As usual, negative m indicates inverted image and positive m indicates erect image.

Since proper sign conventions are used, equation (18.18) is valid in all situations with a single thin lens, although it is derived for the particular situation of figure (18.22).

Example 18.9

An object of length 2·0 cm is placed perpendicular to the principal axis of a convex lens of focal length 12 cm. Find the size of the image if the object is at a distance of 8·0 cm from the lens.

Solution : We have $u = -8·0$ cm, and $f = +12$ cm

Using $$\frac{1}{v} - \frac{1}{u} = \frac{1}{f},$$

$$\frac{1}{v} = \frac{1}{12 \text{ cm}} + \frac{1}{-8·0 \text{ cm}}$$

or, $$v = -24 \text{ cm}.$$

Thus, $$m = \frac{v}{u} = \frac{-24 \text{ cm}}{-8·0 \text{ cm}} = 3.$$

Thus, $h_2 = 3 h_1 = 3 \times 2·0$ cm $= 6·0$ cm. The positive sign shows that the image is erect.

18.14 POWER OF A LENS

The power P of a lens is defined as $P = 1/f$, where f is the focal length. The SI unit of power of a lens is obviously m^{-1}. This is also known as *dioptre*. The focal length of a converging lens is positive and that of a diverging lens is negative. Thus, the power of a converging lens is positive and that of a diverging lens is negative.

18.15 THIN LENSES IN CONTACT

Figure (18.24) shows two lenses L_1 and L_2 placed in contact. The focal lengths of the lenses are f_1 and f_2 respectively.

Suppose, a point object is placed at a point O on the common principal axis. The first lens would form its image at O_1. This point O_1 works as the object for the second lens and the final image is formed at I.

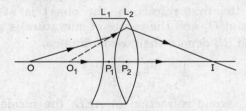

Figure 18.24

Let u = object-distance for the first lens,

v = final image-distance for the second lens,

v_1 = image-distance of the first image O_1 for the first lens. As the lenses are assumed to be thin, v_1 is also the object-distance for the second lens.

Then,

$$\frac{1}{v_1} - \frac{1}{u} = \frac{1}{f_1}$$

and $$\frac{1}{v} - \frac{1}{v_1} = \frac{1}{f_2}.$$

Adding these equations, we get

$$\frac{1}{v} - \frac{1}{u} = \frac{1}{f_1} + \frac{1}{f_2}. \qquad \ldots \text{(i)}$$

If the combination is replaced by a single lens of focal length F such that it forms the image of O at the same position I,

$$\frac{1}{v} - \frac{1}{u} = \frac{1}{F} \cdot \qquad \ldots \text{(ii)}$$

Such a lens is called the equivalent lens for the combination.

Comparing (i) and (ii),

$$\frac{1}{F} = \frac{1}{f_1} + \frac{1}{f_2} \cdot \qquad \ldots \text{(18.19)}$$

This F is the focal length of the equivalent lens for the combination. As the power of a lens is $P = 1/F$, equation (18.19) immediately gives

$$P = P_1 + P_2. \qquad \ldots \text{(18.20)}$$

Though equation (18.19) is derived for the situation shown in figure (18.24), it is true for any situation involving two thin lenses in contact.

18.16 TWO THIN LENSES SEPARATED BY A DISTANCE

When two thin lenses are separated by a distance, it is *not* equivalent to a single thin lens. In fact, such a combination can only be equivalent to a thick lens which has a more complicated theory.

In a special case when the object is placed at infinity, the combination may be replaced by a single thin lens. We shall now derive the position and focal length of the equivalent lens in this special case. To start with, let us derive an expression for the angle of deviation of a ray when it passes through a lens.

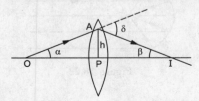

Figure 18.25

Let O be a point object on the principal axis of a lens (figure 18.25). Let OA be a ray incident on the lens at a point A, a height h above the optical centre. It is deviated through an angle δ and comes out along AI. It strikes the principal axis at I where the image is formed.

Let $\angle AOP = \alpha$ and $\angle AIP = \beta$. By triangle OAI,

$$\delta = \alpha + \beta.$$

If the height h is small as compared to PO and PI, the angles α, β are also small. Then,

$$\alpha \approx \tan\alpha = h/OP \text{ and } \beta \approx \tan\beta = h/PI.$$

Thus, $$\delta = \frac{h}{PO} + \frac{h}{PI} \qquad \ldots \text{(i)}$$

Now, $$PO = -u \text{ and } PI = +v.$$

so that by (i), $\delta = h\left(\dfrac{1}{v} - \dfrac{1}{u}\right)$

or, $$\delta = \frac{h}{f} \cdot \qquad \ldots \text{(18.21)}$$

Now, consider the situation shown in figure (18.26). Two thin lenses are placed coaxially at a separation d. The incident ray AB and the emergent ray CD intersect at E. The perpendicular from E to the principal axis falls at P. The equivalent lens should be placed at this position P. A ray ABE going parallel to the principal axis will go through the equivalent lens and emerge along ECD. The angle of deviation is $\delta = \delta_1 + \delta_2$ from triangle BEC. The focal length of the equivalent lens is $F = PD$.

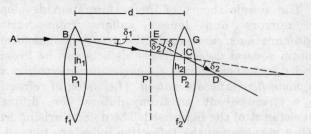

Figure 18.26

Using equation (18.21),

$$\delta_1 = \frac{h_1}{f_1}, \ \delta_2 = \frac{h_2}{f_2} \text{ and } \delta = \frac{h_1}{F} \cdot$$

As $$\delta = \delta_1 + \delta_2,$$

$$\frac{h_1}{F} = \frac{h_1}{f_1} + \frac{h_2}{f_2} \cdot \qquad \ldots \text{(ii)}$$

Now,

$$h_1 - h_2 = P_2 G - P_2 C = CG$$
$$= BG \tan\delta_1 \approx BG\,\delta_1$$

or, $$h_1 - h_2 = d\,\frac{h_1}{f_1} \qquad \ldots \text{(iii)}$$

or, $$h_2 = h_1 - d\,\frac{h_1}{f_1} \cdot \qquad \ldots \text{(iv)}$$

Thus, by (ii),

$$\frac{h_1}{F} = \frac{h_1}{f_1} + \frac{h_1}{f_2} - \frac{d\,(h_1/f_1)}{f_2} \cdot$$

or, $$\frac{1}{F} = \frac{1}{f_1} + \frac{1}{f_2} - \frac{d}{f_1 f_2} \cdot \qquad \ldots \text{(18.22)}$$

Position of the Equivalent Lens

We have, $$PP_2 = EG$$
$$= GC \cot\delta$$
$$= \frac{h_1 - h_2}{\tan\delta} \approx \frac{h_1 - h_2}{\delta}$$

By (iii), $h_1 - h_2 = \dfrac{d\,h_1}{f_1}$. Also, $\delta = \dfrac{h_1}{F}$ so that

$$PP_2 = \left(\frac{d\,h_1}{f_1}\right)\left(\frac{F}{h_1}\right) = \frac{d\,F}{f_1}. \qquad \ldots (18.23)$$

Thus, the equivalent lens is to be placed at a distance $d\,F/f_1$ behind the second lens.

Equation (18.22) and (18.23) are true only for the special case of parallel incident beam. If the object is at a finite distance, one should not use the above equations. The image position should be worked out using the lens equations for the two lenses separately.

18.17 DEFECTS OF IMAGES

The simple theory of image formation developed for mirrors and lenses suffers from various approximations. As a result, the actual images formed contain several defects. These defects can be broadly divided in two categories, (a) *chromatic aberration* and (b) *monochromatic aberration*. The index of refraction of a transparent medium differs for different wavelengths of the light used. The defects arising from such a variation of the refractive index are termed as chromatic aberrations. The other defects, which arise even if light of a single colour is used, are called monochromatic aberrations. We shall first discuss this type of defects.

A. Monochromatic Aberrations

(a) Spherical Aberration

All through the discussion of lenses and mirrors with spherical surfaces, it has been assumed that the aperture of the lens or the mirror is small and the light rays of interest make small angles with the principal axis. It is then possible to have a point image of a point object. However, this is only an approximation even if we neglect diffraction.

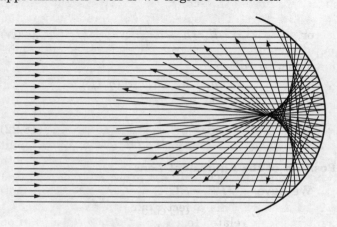

Figure 18.27

The rays reflect or refract from points at different distances from the principal axis. In general, they meet each other at different points. Thus, the image of a point object is a blurred surface. Such a defect is called *spherical aberration*. Figure (18.27) shows *spherical aberration* for a concave mirror for an object at infinity. The rays parallel to the principal axis are incident on the spherical surface of the concave mirror. The rays close to the principal axis (paraxial rays) are focused at the geometrical focus F of the mirror as given by the mirror formula. The rays farthest from the principal axis are called the marginal rays and are focused at a point F' somewhat closer to the mirror. The intermediate rays focus at different points between F and F'. Also, the rays reflected from a small portion away from the pole meet at a point off the axis. Thus, a three-dimensional blurred image is formed. The intersection of this image with the plane of figure is shown blackened in figure (18.27) and is called the *caustic curve*. If a screen is placed perpendicular to the principal axis, a disc image is formed on the screen. As the screen is moved parallel to itself, the disc becomes smallest at one position. This disc is closest to the ideal image and its periphery is called the *circle of least confusion*. The magnitude of spherical aberration may be measured from the distance FF' between the point where the paraxial rays converge and the point where the marginal rays converge.

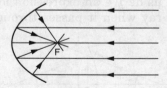

Figure 18.28

The parallel rays may be brought to focus at one point if a parabolic mirror is used. Also, if a point source is placed at the focus of a parabolic mirror, the reflected rays will be very nearly parallel. The reflectors in automobile headlights are made parabolic and the bulb is placed at the focus. The light beam is then nearly parallel and goes up to large distances.

Because of the finite aperture, a lens too produces a blurred disc type image of a point object. Figure (18.29) shows the situation for a convex and a concave

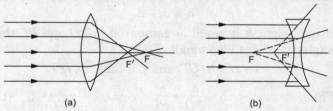

(a)   (b)

Figure 18.29

lens for the rays coming parallel to the principal axis. We see from the figure that the marginal rays are deviated a bit too strongly and hence, they meet at a point different from that given by geometrical optics formulae. Also, in the situation shown, the spherical aberration is opposite for convex and concave lens. The point F', where the marginal rays meet, is to the left of the focus for convex lens and is to the right of the focus for the concave lens.

The magnitude of spherical aberration for a lens depends on the radii of curvature and the object distance. The spherical aberration for a particular object distance can be reduced by properly choosing the radii of curvature. However, it cannot be reduced to zero for a single lens which forms a real image of a real object. A simple method to reduce spherical aberration is to use a stop before and in front of the lens. A stop is an opaque sheet with a small circular opening in it. It only allows a narrow pencil of rays to go through the lens hence reducing the aberration. However, this method reduces the intensity of the image as most of the light is cut off.

The spherical aberration is less if the total deviation of the rays is distributed over the two surfaces of the lens. A striking example is a planoconvex lens forming the image of a distant object. If the plane surface faces the incident rays, the spherical aberration is much larger than that in the case when the curved surface faces the incident rays (figure 18.30). In the former case, the total deviation occurs at a single surface whereas it is distributed at both the surfaces in the latter case.

Figure 18.30

The spherical aberration can also be reduced by using a combination of convex and concave lenses. A suitable combination can reduce the spherical aberration by compensation of positive and negative aberrations.

(b) Coma

We have seen that if a point object is placed on the principal axis of a lens and the image is received on a screen perpendicular to the principal axis, the image has a shape of a disc because of spherical aberration. The basic reason of this aberration is that the rays passing through different regions of the lens meet the principal axis at different points. If the point object is placed away from the principal axis and the image is received on a screen perpendicular to the axis, the shape of the image is like a comet. This defect is called *coma*. The basic reason is again the same. The lens fails to converge all the rays passing at different distances from the axis at a single point. Figure (18.31) explains the formation of coma. The paraxial rays form an image of P at P'. The rays passing through the shaded zone forms a circular image on the screen. The rays through outer zones of the lens form bigger circles with centres shifted. The image seen on the screen thus have a comet-like appearance.

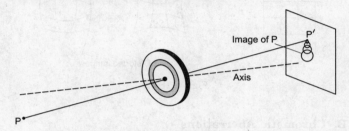

Figure 18.31

Coma can also be reduced by properly designing radii of curvature of the lens surfaces. It can also be reduced by appropriate stops placed at appropriate distances from the lens.

(c) Astigmatism

Spherical aberration and coma refer to the spreading of the image of a point object in a plane perpendicular to the principal axis. The image is also spread along the principal axis. Suppose, a point object is placed at a point off the axis of a converging lens. A screen is placed perpendicular to the axis and is moved along the axis. At a certain distance, an approximate line image is focussed. If the screen is moved further away, the shape of the image changes but it remains on the screen for quite a distance moved by the screen. The spreading of image along the principal axis is known as *astigmatism* (not to be confused with a defect of vision having the same name).

(d) Curvature

We have so far considered the image formed by a lens on a plane. However, it is not always true that the best image is formed along a plane. For a point object placed off the axis, the image is spread both along and perpendicular to the principal axis. The best image is, in general, obtained not on a plane but on a curved surface. This defect is known as *curvature*. It is intrinsically related to astigmatism. The astigmation or the curvature may be reduced by using proper stops placed at proper locations along the axis.

(e) Distortion

Distortion is the defect arising when extended objects are imaged. Different portions of the object are, in general, at different distances from the axis. The relation between the object distance and the image distance is not linear and hence, the magnification is not the same for all portions of the extended object. As a result, a line object is not imaged into a line but into a curve. Figure (18.32) shows some distorted images.

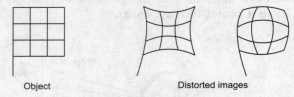

Object   Distorted images

Figure 18.32

B. Chromatic Aberrations

The refractive index of the material of a lens varies slightly with the wavelength and hence, the focal length is also different for different wavelengths. In the visible region, the focal length is maximum for red and minimum for violet. Thus, if white light is used, each colour forms a separate image of the object.

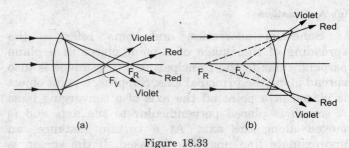

(a)   (b)

Figure 18.33

The violet rays are deviated more and hence, they form an image closer to the lens as compared to the image formed by the red rays. If light is incident on the lens from left to right, the violet image is to the left of the red image for convex lens and it is to the right of the red image for the concave lens. In the first case, the chromatic aberration is called positive and in the second case, it is negative. Thus, a proper combination of a convex and a concave lens may result in no chromatic aberration. Such a combination is called an *achromatic combination* for the pair of wavelengths. Also, the magnification v/u depends on the focal length and hence, on the wavelength. For an extended object, the images formed by light of different colours are of different sizes. A typical situation is shown in figure (18.33). Monochromatic aberration are assumed to be absent.

The separation between the images formed by extreme wavelengths of the visible range is called the *axial chromatic aberration* or *longitudinal chromatic aberration*. The difference in the size of the images (perpendicular to the principal axis) formed by the extreme wavelengths of the range is called the *lateral chromatic aberration* (figure 18.34).

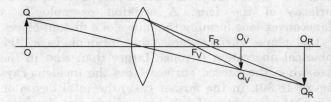

Figure 18.34

Worked Out Examples

1. *An object is placed on the principal axis of a concave mirror of focal length 10 cm at a distance of 8·0 cm from the pole. Find the position and the nature of the image.*

Solution : Here $u = -8·0$ cm and $f = -10$ cm.

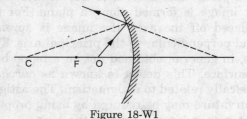

Figure 18-W1

We have,
$$\frac{1}{f} = \frac{1}{u} + \frac{1}{v}$$
or,
$$\frac{1}{v} = \frac{1}{f} - \frac{1}{u}$$
$$= \frac{1}{-10 \text{ cm}} - \frac{1}{-8·0 \text{ cm}}$$
$$= \frac{1}{40 \text{ cm}}$$
or, $v = 40$ cm.

The positive sign shows that the image is formed at 40 cm from the pole on the other side of the mirror (figure 18-W1). As the image is formed beyond the mirror, the reflected rays do not intersect, the image is thus virtual.

2. *A rod of length* 10 cm *lies along the principal axis of a concave mirror of focal length* 10 cm *in such a way that the end closer to the pole is* 20 cm *away from it. Find the length of the image.*

Solution :

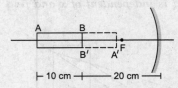

Figure 18-W2

The situation is shown in figure (18-W2). The radius of curvature of the mirror is $r = 2f = 20$ cm. Thus, the nearer end B of the rod AB is at the centre of the curvature and hence, its image will be formed at B itself. We shall now locate the image of A.

Here $u = -30$ cm and $f = -10$ cm. We have

$$\frac{1}{u} + \frac{1}{v} = \frac{1}{f}$$

or,

$$\frac{1}{v} = \frac{1}{f} - \frac{1}{u}$$

$$= \frac{1}{-10 \text{ cm}} - \frac{1}{-30 \text{ cm}}$$

or, $v = -15$ cm.

Thus, the image of A is formed at 15 cm from the pole. The length of the image is, therefore, 5·0 cm.

3. *At what distance from a convex mirror of focal length* 2·5 m *should a boy stand so that his image has a height equal to half the original height? The principal axis is perpendicular to the height.*

Solution : We have,

$$m = -\frac{v}{u} = \frac{1}{2}$$

or, $v = -\dfrac{u}{2}$.

Also,

$$\frac{1}{u} + \frac{1}{v} = \frac{1}{f}$$

or,

$$\frac{1}{u} + \frac{1}{-u/2} = \frac{1}{2·5 \text{ m}}$$

or,

$$-\frac{1}{u} = \frac{1}{2·5 \text{ m}}$$

or, $u = -2·5$ m.

Thus, he should stand at a distance of 2·5 m from the mirror.

4. *A* 2·0 cm *high object is placed on the principal axis of a concave mirror at a distance of* 12 cm *from the pole. If the image is inverted, real and* 5·0 cm *high, find the location of the image and the focal length of the mirror.*

Solution : The magnification is $m = -\dfrac{v}{u}$

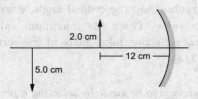

Figure 18-W3

or,

$$\frac{-5·0 \text{ cm}}{2·0 \text{ cm}} = \frac{-v}{-12 \text{ cm}}$$

or, $v = -30$ cm.

The image is formed at 30 cm from the pole on the side of the object. We have,

$$\frac{1}{f} = \frac{1}{v} + \frac{1}{u}$$

$$= \frac{1}{-30 \text{ cm}} + \frac{1}{-12 \text{ cm}} = -\frac{7}{60 \text{ cm}}$$

or, $f = -\dfrac{60 \text{ cm}}{7} = -8·6$ cm.

The focal length of the mirror is 8·6 cm.

5. *Consider the situation shown in figure (18-W4). Find the maximum angle* θ *for which the light suffers total internal reflection at the vertical surface.*

Solution :

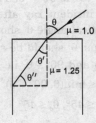

Figure 18-W4

The critical angle for this case is

$$\theta'' = \sin^{-1}\frac{1}{1·25} = \sin^{-1}\frac{4}{5}$$

or, $\sin\theta'' = \dfrac{4}{5}$.

Since $\theta'' = \dfrac{\pi}{2} - \theta'$, we have $\sin\theta' = \cos\theta'' = 3/5$. From Snell's law,

$$\frac{\sin\theta}{\sin\theta'} = 1·25$$

or, $\sin\theta = 1·25 \times \sin\theta'$

$$= 1·25 \times \frac{3}{5} = \frac{3}{4}$$

or, $\qquad \theta = \sin^{-1}\dfrac{3}{4}.$

If θ'' is greater than the critical angle, θ will be smaller than this value. Thus, the maximum value of θ, for which total reflection takes place at the vertical surface, is $\sin^{-1}(3/4)$.

6. *A right prism is to be made by selecting a proper material and the angles A and B (B ≤ A), as shown in figure (18-W5a). It is desired that a ray of light incident normally on AB emerges parallel to the incident direction after two total internal reflections. (a) What should be the minimum refractive index μ for this to be possible ? (b) For μ = 5/3, is it possible to achieve this with the angle A equal to 60 degrees ?*

Solution :

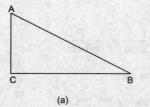 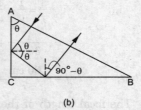

(a)   (b)

Figure 18-W5

(a) Consider the ray incident normally on *AB (figure 18-W5b)*. The angle of reflection at the surface *AC* is θ. It is clear from the figure that the angle of incidence at the second surface *CB* is $90° - \theta$. The emergent ray will be parallel to the incident ray after two total internal reflections. The critical angle θ_c should be less than θ as well as $90° - \theta$. Thus, θ_c should be smaller than or equal to the smaller of θ and $90° - \theta$, i.e.,

$$\theta_c \le \min(\theta, 90° - \theta).$$

As $\min (\theta, 90° - \theta) \le 45°$, $\theta_c \le 45°$

or, $\qquad \sin\theta_c \le \dfrac{1}{\sqrt 2} \qquad$ or, $\dfrac{1}{\mu} \le \dfrac{1}{\sqrt 2}$

or, $\qquad \mu \ge \sqrt 2.$

Thus, the refractive index of the material of the prism should be greater than or equal to $\sqrt 2$. In this case the given ray can undergo two internal reflections for a suitable θ.

(b) For $\mu = 5/3$, the critical angle θ_c is

$$\sin^{-1}(3/5) = 37°.$$

As the figure suggests, we consider the light incident normally on the face *AB*. The angle of incidence θ on the surface *AC* is equal to $\theta = 60°$. As this is larger than the critical angle $37°$, total internal reflection takes place here. The angle of incidence at the surface *CB* is $90° - \theta = 30°$. As this is less than the critical angle, total internal reflection does not take place at this surface.

7. *A point object O is placed in front of a transparent slab at a distance x from its closer surface. It is seen from the other side of the slab by light incident nearly normally to the slab. The thickness of the slab is t and its refractive index is μ. Show that the apparent shift in the position of the object is independent of x and find its value.*

Solution :

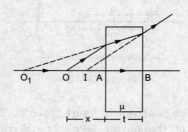

Figure 18-W6

The situation is shown in figure (18-W6). Because of the refraction at the first surface, the image of O is formed at O_1. For this refraction, the real depth is $AO = x$ and the apparent depth is AO_1. Also the first medium is air and the second is the slab. Thus,

$$\dfrac{x}{AO_1} = \dfrac{1}{\mu} \quad \text{or, } AO_1 = \mu x.$$

The point O_1 acts as the object for the refraction at the second surface. Due to this refraction the image of O_1 is formed at I. Thus,

$$\dfrac{BO_1}{BI} = \mu$$

or, $\qquad \dfrac{AB + AO_1}{BI} = \mu \quad$ or, $\dfrac{t + \mu x}{BI} = \mu$

or, $\qquad BI = x + \dfrac{t}{\mu}.$

The net shift in $OI = OB - BI = (x + t) - \left(x + \dfrac{t}{\mu}\right)$

$$= t\left(1 - \dfrac{1}{\mu}\right),$$

which is independent of x.

8. *Consider the situation shown in figure (18-W7). A plane mirror is fixed at a height h above the bottom of a beaker containing water (refractive index μ) up to a height d. Find the position of the image of the bottom formed by the mirror.*

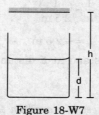

Figure 18-W7

Solution : The bottom of the beaker appears to be shifted up by a distance

$$\Delta t = \left(1 - \frac{1}{\mu}\right)d.$$

Thus, the apparent distance of the bottom from the mirror is $h - \Delta t = h - \left(1 - \frac{1}{\mu}\right)d = h - d + \frac{d}{\mu}$. The image is formed behind the mirror at a distance $h - d + \frac{d}{\mu}$.

9. *A beaker contains water up to a height h_1 and K.oil above water up to another height h_2. Find the apparent shift in the position of the bottom of the beaker when viewed from above. Refractive index of water is μ_1 and that of K.oil is μ_2.*

Solution : The apparent shift of the bottom due to the water is

$$\Delta t_1 = \left(1 - \frac{1}{\mu_1}\right)h_1$$

and due to the K.oil is

$$\Delta t_2 = \left(1 - \frac{1}{\mu_2}\right)h_2.$$

The total shift $= \Delta t_1 + \Delta t_2 = \left(1 - \frac{1}{\mu_1}\right)h_1 + \left(1 - \frac{1}{\mu_2}\right)h_2.$

10. *Monochromatic light is incident on the plane interface AB between two media of refractive indices μ_1 and μ_2 ($\mu_2 > \mu_1$) at an angle of incidence θ as shown in figure (18-W8). The angle θ is infinitesimally greater than the critical angle for the two media so that total internal reflection takes place. Now, if a transparent slab DEFG of uniform thickness and of refractive index μ_3 is introduced on the interface (as shown in the figure), show that for any value of μ_3 all light will ultimately be reflected back into medium II.*

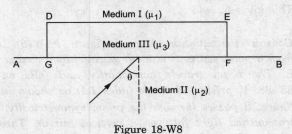

Figure 18-W8

Solution : We shall use the symbol $\gtrless$ to mean "infinitesimally greater than".

When the slab is not inserted, $\theta \gtrless \theta_c = \sin^{-1}(\mu_1/\mu_2)$

or, $\qquad\qquad \sin\theta \gtrless \mu_1/\mu_2.$

When the slab is inserted, we have two cases $\mu_3 \leq \mu_1$ and $\mu_3 > \mu_1$.

Case I : $\mu_3 \leq \mu_1$

We have $\sin\theta \gtrless \mu_1/\mu_2 \geq \mu_3/\mu_2.$

Thus, the light is incident on AB at an angle greater than the critical angle $\sin^{-1}(\mu_3/\mu_2)$. It suffers total internal reflection and goes back to medium II.

Case II : $\mu_3 > \mu_1$

$\sin\theta \gtrless \mu_1/\mu_2 < \mu_3/\mu_2$

Thus, the angle of incidence θ may be smaller than the critical angle $\sin^{-1}(\mu_3/\mu_2)$ and hence it may enter medium III. The angle of refraction θ' is given by (figure 18-W9)

$$\frac{\sin\theta}{\sin\theta'} = \frac{\mu_3}{\mu_2} \qquad\qquad \dots \text{(i)}$$

or, $\qquad\qquad \sin\theta' = \frac{\mu_2}{\mu_3}\sin\theta$

$$\gtrless \frac{\mu_2}{\mu_3} \cdot \frac{\mu_1}{\mu_2}.$$

Thus, $\qquad\qquad \sin\theta' \gtrless \frac{\mu_1}{\mu_3}$

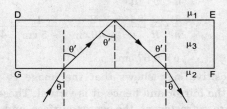

Figure 18-W9

or, $\qquad\qquad \theta' \gtrless \sin^{-1}\left(\frac{\mu_1}{\mu_3}\right). \qquad \dots \text{(ii)}$

As the slab has parallel faces, the angle of refraction at the face FG is equal to the angle of incidence at the face DE. Equation (ii) shows that this angle is infinitesimally greater than the critical angle here. Hence, the light suffers total internal reflection and falls at the surface FG at an angle of incidence θ'. At this face, it will refract into medium II and the angle of refraction will be θ as shown by equation (i). Thus, the total light energy is ultimately reflected back into medium II.

11. *A concave mirror of radius 40 cm lies on a horizontal table and water is filled in it up to a height of 5·00 cm (figure 18-W10). A small dust particle floats on the water surface at a point P vertically above the point of contact of the mirror with the table. Locate the image of the dust particle as seen from a point directly above it. The refractive index of water is 1·33.*

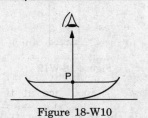

Figure 18-W10

Solution :

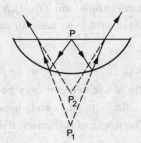

Figure 18-W11

The ray diagram is shown in figure (18-W11). Let us first locate the image formed by the concave mirror. Let us take vertically upward as the negative axis. Then $R = -40$ cm. The object distance is $u = -5$ cm. Using the mirror equation,

$$\frac{1}{u} + \frac{1}{v} = \frac{2}{R}$$

or,

$$\frac{1}{v} = \frac{2}{R} - \frac{1}{u} = \frac{2}{-40 \text{ cm}} - \frac{1}{-5 \text{ cm}} = \frac{6}{40 \text{ cm}}$$

or, $v = 6.67$ cm.

The positive sign shows that the image P_1 is formed below the mirror and hence, it is virtual. These reflected rays are refracted at the water surface and go to the observer. The depth of the point P_1 from the surface is 6.67 cm + 5.00 cm = 11.67 cm. Due to refraction at the water surface, the image P_1 will be shifted above by a distance

$$(11.67 \text{ cm}) \left(1 - \frac{1}{1.33}\right) = 2.92 \text{ cm}.$$

Thus, the final image is formed at a point (11.67 − 2.92) cm = 8.75 cm below the water surface.

12. *An object is placed 21 cm in front of a concave mirror of radius of curvature 20 cm. A glass slab of thickness 3 cm and refractive index 1.5 is placed close to the mirror in the space between the object and the mirror. Find the position of the final image formed. The distance of the nearer surface of the slab from the mirror is 10 cm.*

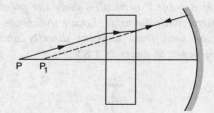

Figure 18-W12

Solution :
The situation is shown in figure (18-W12). Because of

the refraction at the two surfaces of the slab, the image of the object P is formed at P_1, shifted towards the mirror by a distance

$$t\left(1 - \frac{1}{\mu}\right) = (3 \text{ cm})\left(1 - \frac{1}{1.5}\right) = 1 \text{ cm}.$$

Thus, the rays falling on the concave mirror are diverging from P_1 which is at 21 cm − 1 cm = 20 cm from the mirror. But the radius of curvature is also 20 cm, hence P_1 is at the centre. The rays, therefore, fall normally on the mirror and hence, retrace their path. The final image is formed at P itself.

13. *The refractive indices of silicate flint glass for wavelengths 400 nm and 700 nm are 1.66 and 1.61 respectively. Find the minimum angles of deviation of an equilateral prism made of this glass for light of wavelength 400 nm and 700 nm.*

Solution : The minimum angle of deviation δ_m is given by

$$\mu = \frac{\sin\dfrac{A + \delta_m}{2}}{\sin\dfrac{A}{2}} = \frac{\sin\left(30° + \dfrac{\delta_m}{2}\right)}{\sin 30°}$$

$$= 2 \sin\left(30° + \frac{\delta_m}{2}\right).$$

For 400 nm light,

$$1.66 = 2 \sin(30° + \delta_m/2)$$

or, $\sin(30° + \delta_m/2) = 0.83$

or, $(30° + \delta_m/2) = 56°$

or, $\delta_m = 52°$.

For 700 nm light,

$$1.61 = 2 \sin(30° + \delta_m/2).$$

This gives $\delta_m = 48°$.

14. *Consider the situation shown in figure (18-W13). Light from a point source S is made parallel by a convex lens L. The beam travels horizontally and falls on an 88°-88°-4° prism (refractive index 1.5) as shown in the figure. It passes through the prism symmetrically. The transmitted light falls on a vertical mirror. Through what angle should the mirror be rotated so that an image of S is formed on S itself?*

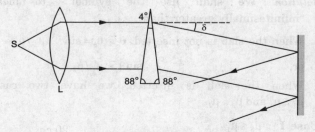

Figure 18-W13

Solution : The parallel beam after going through the prism will be deviated by an angle δ. If the mirror is also rotated by this angle δ, the rays will fall normally on it. The rays will be reflected back along the same path and form the image of S on itself.

As the prism is thin, the angle δ is given by

$$\delta = (\mu - 1) A$$

$$= (1.5 - 1) \times 4° = 2°.$$

Thus, the mirror should be rotated by 2°.

15. *Locate the image formed by refraction in the situation shown in figure (18-W14). The point C is the centre of curvature.*

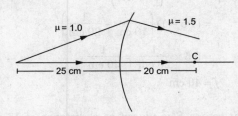

Figure 18-W14

Solution : We have,

$$\frac{\mu_2}{v} - \frac{\mu_1}{u} = \frac{\mu_2 - \mu_1}{R}. \qquad \dots \text{(i)}$$

Here $u = -25 \text{ cm}, R = 20 \text{ cm}, \mu_1 = 1.0$ and $\mu_2 = 1.5$.

Putting the values in (i),

$$\frac{1.5}{v} + \frac{1.0}{25 \text{ cm}} = \frac{1.5 - 1.0}{20 \text{ cm}}$$

or,

$$\frac{1.5}{v} = \frac{1}{40 \text{ cm}} - \frac{1}{25 \text{ cm}}$$

or,

$$v = -100 \text{ cm}.$$

As v is negative, the image is formed to the left of the separating surface at a distance of 100 cm from it.

16. *One end of a horizontal cylindrical glass rod (μ = 1·5) of radius 5·0 cm is rounded in the shape of a hemisphere. An object 0·5 mm high is placed perpendicular to the axis of the rod at a distance of 20·0 cm from the rounded edge. Locate the image of the object and find its height.*

Solution : Taking the origin at the vertex, $u = -20.0 \text{ cm}$ and $R = 5.0 \text{ cm}$.

We have,

$$\frac{\mu_2}{v} - \frac{\mu_1}{u} = \frac{\mu_2 - \mu_1}{R}$$

or,

$$\frac{1.5}{v} = \frac{1}{-20.0 \text{ cm}} + \frac{0.5}{5.0 \text{ cm}} = \frac{1}{20 \text{ cm}}$$

or,

$$v = 30 \text{ cm}.$$

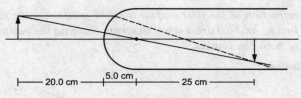

Figure 18-W15

The image is formed inside the rod at a distance of 30 cm from the vertex.

The magnification is $m = \frac{\mu_1 v}{\mu_2 u}$

$$= \frac{30 \text{ cm}}{-1.5 \times 20 \text{ cm}} = -1.$$

Thus, the image will be of same height (0·5 mm) as the object but it will be inverted.

17. *There is a small air bubble inside a glass sphere (μ = 1·5) of radius 10 cm. The bubble is 4·0 cm below the surface and is viewed normally from the outside (figure 18-W16). Find the apparent depth of the bubble.*

Solution :

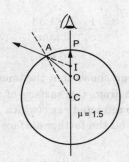

Figure 18-W16

The observer sees the image formed due to refraction at the spherical surface when the light from the bubble goes from the glass to the air.

Here $u = -4.0 \text{ cm}, R = -10 \text{ cm}, \mu_1 = 1.5$ and $\mu_2 = 1$.

We have,

$$\frac{\mu_2}{v} - \frac{\mu_1}{u} = \frac{\mu_2 - \mu_1}{R}$$

or,

$$\frac{1}{v} - \frac{1.5}{-4.0 \text{ cm}} = \frac{1 - 1.5}{-10 \text{ cm}}$$

or,

$$\frac{1}{v} = \frac{0.5}{10 \text{ cm}} - \frac{1.5}{4.0 \text{ cm}}$$

or,

$$v = -3.0 \text{ cm}.$$

Thus, the bubble will apear 3·0 cm below the surface.

18. *A parallel beam of light travelling in water (refractive index = 4/3) is refracted by a spherical air bubble of radius 2 mm situated in water. Assuming the light rays to be paraxial, (i) find the position of the image due to* refraction at the first surface and the position of the final image, and (ii) draw a ray diagram showing the positions of both the images.

Solution :

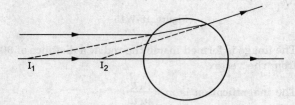

Figure 18-W17

The ray diagram is shown in figure 18-W17. The equation for refraction at a spherical surface is

$$\frac{\mu_2}{v} - \frac{\mu_1}{u} = \frac{\mu_2 - \mu_1}{R}. \qquad \dots \text{(i)}$$

For the first refraction (water to air); $\mu_1 = 1.33$, $\mu_2 = 1$, $u = \infty$, $R = +2$ mm.

Thus, $\dfrac{1}{v} = \dfrac{1 - 1.33}{2 \text{ mm}}$

or, $v = -6$ mm.

The negative sign shows that the image I_1 is virtual and forms at 6 mm from the surface of the bubble on the water side. The refracted rays (which seem to come from I_1) are incident on the farther surface of the bubble. For this refraction,

$$\mu_1 = 1, \ \mu_2 = 1.33, \ R = -2 \text{ mm}.$$

The object distance is $u = -(6 \text{ mm} + 4 \text{ mm}) = -10 \text{ mm}$. Using equation (i),

$$\frac{1.33}{v} + \frac{1}{10 \text{ mm}} = \frac{1.33 - 1}{-2 \text{ mm}}$$

or, $\dfrac{1.33}{v} = -\dfrac{0.33}{2 \text{ mm}} - \dfrac{1}{10 \text{ mm}}$

or, $v = -5$ mm.

The minus sign shows that the image is formed on the air side at 5 mm from the refracting surface.

Measuring from the centre of the bubble, the first image is formed at 8.0 mm from the centre and the second image is formed at 3.0 mm from the centre. Both images are formed on the side from which the incident rays are coming.

19. *Calculate the focal length of the thin lens shown in figure (18-W18). The points C_1 and C_2 denote the centres of curvature and the refractive index is 1.5.*

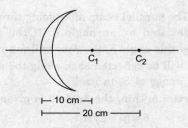

|— 10 cm —|
|——— 20 cm ———|

Figure 18-W18

Solution : As is clear from the figure, both the radii of curvature are positive. Thus, $R_1 = +10$ cm and $R_2 = +20$ cm. The focal length is given by

$$\frac{1}{f} = (\mu - 1)\left(\frac{1}{R_1} - \frac{1}{R_2}\right)$$

$$= (1.5 - 1)\left(\frac{1}{10 \text{ cm}} - \frac{1}{20 \text{ cm}}\right)$$

$$= 0.5 \times \frac{1}{20 \text{ cm}} = \frac{1}{40 \text{ cm}}$$

or, $f = 40$ cm.

20. *A point source S is placed at a distance of 15 cm from a converging lens of focal length 10 cm on its principal axis. Where should a diverging mirror of focal length 12 cm be placed so that a real image is formed on the source itself?*

Solution :

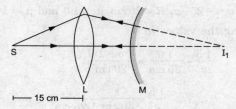

Figure 18-W19

The equation for the lens is

$$\frac{1}{v} - \frac{1}{u} = \frac{1}{f}. \qquad \dots \text{(i)}$$

Here $u = -15$ cm and $f = +10$ cm.

Using equation (i),

$$\frac{1}{v} + \frac{1}{15 \text{ cm}} = \frac{1}{10 \text{ cm}}$$

$$\frac{1}{v} = \frac{1}{10 \text{ cm}} - \frac{1}{15 \text{ cm}} = \frac{1}{30 \text{ cm}}$$

or, $v = 30$ cm.

The positive sign of v shows that the image I_1 is formed to the right of the lens in the figure. The diverging mirror is to be placed to the right in such a way that the light rays fall on the mirror perpendicularly. Then only the rays will retrace their path and form the final image on the object. Thus, the image I_1 formed by the lens should be at the centre of curvature of the mirror.

We have, $LI_1 = 30$ cm,

$$MI_1 = R = 2f = 24 \text{ cm},$$

Hence, $LM = LI_1 - MI_1 = 6$ cm.

Thus, the mirror should be placed 6 cm to the right of the lens.

21. *A converging lens of focal length* 15 cm *and a converging mirror of focal length* 20 cm *are placed with their principal axes coinciding. A point source S is placed on the principal axis at a distance of* 12 cm *from the lens as shown in figure (18-W20). It is found that the final beam comes out parallel to the principal axis. Find the separation between the mirror and the lens.*

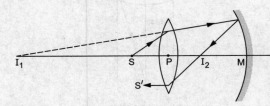

Figure 18-W20

Solution : Let us first locate the image of S formed by the lens. Here $u = -12$ cm and $f = 15$ cm. We have,

$$\frac{1}{v} - \frac{1}{u} = \frac{1}{f}$$

or,

$$\frac{1}{v} = \frac{1}{f} + \frac{1}{u}$$

$$= \frac{1}{15 \text{ cm}} - \frac{1}{12 \text{ cm}}$$

or, $v = -60$ cm.

The negative sign shows that the image is formed to the left of the lens as suggested in the figure. The image I_1 acts as the source for the mirror. The mirror forms an image I_2 of the source I_1. This image I_2 then acts as the source for the lens and the final beam comes out parallel to the principal axis. Clearly I_2 must be at the focus of the lens. We have,

$$I_1I_2 = I_1P + PI_2 = 60 \text{ cm} + 15 \text{ cm} = 75 \text{ cm}.$$

Suppose the distance of the mirror from I_2 is x cm. For the reflection from the mirror,

$$u = MI_1 = -(75 + x) \text{ cm}, \ v = -x \text{ cm and } f = -20 \text{ cm}.$$

Using

$$\frac{1}{v} + \frac{1}{u} = \frac{1}{f},$$

$$\frac{1}{x} + \frac{1}{75 + x} = \frac{1}{20}$$

or,

$$\frac{75 + 2x}{(75 + x) x} = \frac{1}{20}$$

or, $x^2 + 35x - 1500 = 0$

or,

$$x = \frac{-35 \pm \sqrt{35 \times 35 + 4 \times 1500}}{2}.$$

This gives $x = 25$ or -60.

As the negative sign has no physical meaning, only positive sign should be taken. Taking $x = 25$, the separation between the lens and the mirror is $(15 + 25)$ cm = 40 cm.

22. *A biconvex thin lens is prepared from glass* ($\mu = 1.5$), *the two bounding surfaces having equal radii of* 25 cm *each. One of the surfaces is silvered from outside to make it reflecting. Where should an object be placed before this lens so that the image is formed on the object itself?*

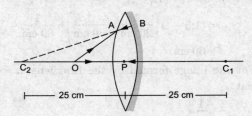

Figure 18-W21

Solution :
Refer to figure (18-W21). The object is placed at O. A ray OA starting from O gets refracted into the glass at the first surface and hits the silvered surface along AB. To get the image at the object, the rays should retrace their path after reflection from the silvered surface. This will happen only if AB falls normally on the silvered surface. Thus, AB should appear to come from the centre C_2 of the second surface. Thus, due to the refraction at the first surface, a virtual image of O is formed at C_2. For this case,

$$v = PC_2 = -25 \text{ cm}, \ R = PC_1 = +25 \text{ cm}, \ \mu_1 = 1, \ \mu_2 = 1.5.$$

We have,

$$\frac{\mu_2}{v} - \frac{\mu_1}{u} = \frac{\mu_2 - \mu_1}{R}$$

or,

$$\frac{1.5}{-25 \text{ cm}} - \frac{1}{u} = \frac{1.5 - 1}{25 \text{ cm}}$$

or,

$$\frac{1}{u} = -\frac{1.5}{25 \text{ cm}} - \frac{0.5}{25 \text{ cm}}$$

or, $u = -12.5$ cm.

Thus, the object should be placed at a distance of 12.5 cm from the lens.

23. *A concavo-convex (figure 18-W22) lens made of glass* ($\mu = 1.5$) *has surfaces of radii* 20 cm *and* 60 cm. *(a) Locate the image of an object placed* 80 cm *to the left of the lens along the principal axis. (b) A similar lens is placed coaxially at a distance of* 160 cm *right to it. Locate the position of the image.*

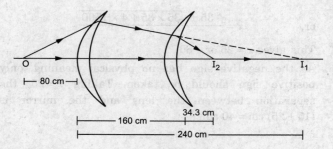

Figure 18-W22

Solution : The focal length of the lens is given by

$$\frac{1}{f} = (\mu - 1)\left(\frac{1}{R_1} - \frac{1}{R_2}\right)$$

$$= (1 \cdot 5 - 1)\left(\frac{1}{20 \text{ cm}} - \frac{1}{60 \text{ cm}}\right) = \frac{1}{60 \text{ cm}}$$

or, $f = 60$ cm.

(a) For the image formed by the first lens, $u = -80$ cm so that

$$\frac{1}{v} = \frac{1}{u} + \frac{1}{f}$$

$$= \frac{1}{-80 \text{ cm}} + \frac{1}{60 \text{ cm}} = \frac{1}{240 \text{ cm}}$$

or, $v = 240$ cm.

The first image I_1 would form 240 cm to the right of the first lens.

(b) The second lens intercepts the converging beam as suggested by the figure. The image I_1 acts as a virtual source for the second lens. For the image formed by this lens, $u = 240$ cm $- 160$ cm $= +80$ cm so that

$$\frac{1}{v} = \frac{1}{u} + \frac{1}{f}$$

$$= \frac{1}{80 \text{ cm}} + \frac{1}{60 \text{ cm}} = \frac{7}{240 \text{ cm}}$$

or, $v = 34 \cdot 3$ cm.

The final image is formed $34 \cdot 3$ cm to the right of the second lens.

24. *A thin lens* ($\mu = 1.5$) *of focal length* $+ 12$ *cm is immersed in water* ($\mu = 1 \cdot 33$). *What is its new focal length ?*

Solution : We have, $\dfrac{1}{f} = \left(\dfrac{\mu_2}{\mu_1} - 1\right)\left(\dfrac{1}{R_1} - \dfrac{1}{R_2}\right).$

When the lens is placed in air, $f = 12$ cm. Thus,

$$\frac{1}{12 \text{ cm}} = (1 \cdot 5 - 1)\left(\frac{1}{R_1} - \frac{1}{R_2}\right)$$

or, $\dfrac{1}{R_1} - \dfrac{1}{R_2} = \dfrac{1}{6 \text{ cm}}.$

If the focal length becomes f' when placed in water,

$$\frac{1}{f'} = \left(\frac{1 \cdot 5}{1 \cdot 33} - 1\right)\left(\frac{1}{R_1} - \frac{1}{R_2}\right)$$

$$= \frac{1}{8} \times \frac{1}{6 \text{ cm}} = \frac{1}{48 \text{ cm}} \qquad \text{or, } f' = 48 \text{ cm.}$$

25. *A long cylindrical tube containing water is closed by an equiconvex lens of focal length* 10 *cm in air. A point source is placed along the axis of the tube outside it at a distance of* 21 *cm from the lens. Locate the final image of the source. Refractive index of the material of the lens* $= 1 \cdot 5$ *and that of water* $= 1 \cdot 33$.

Solution :

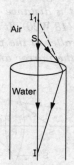

Figure 18-W23

The light from the source S gets refracted at the air–glass interface and then at the glass–water interface. Referring to the figure (18-W23), let us take vertically downward as the positive direction of the axis.

If the image due to the refraction at the first surface is formed at a distance v_1 from the surface, we have,

$$\frac{1 \cdot 5}{v_1} - \frac{1}{u} = \frac{1 \cdot 5 - 1}{R}, \qquad \qquad \dots \text{ (i)}$$

where R is the radius of curvature of the surface. As the lens is equiconvex, the radius of curvature of the second surface is $-R$. Also, the image formed by the first surface acts as the object for the second surface. Thus,

$$\frac{1 \cdot 33}{v} - \frac{1 \cdot 5}{v_1} = \frac{1 \cdot 33 - 1 \cdot 5}{-R}. \qquad \dots \text{ (ii)}$$

Adding (i) and (ii),

$$\frac{1 \cdot 33}{v} - \frac{1}{u} = \frac{1}{R}\,(0 \cdot 5 + 0 \cdot 17) = \frac{0 \cdot 67}{R}$$

or, $\dfrac{1 \cdot 33}{v} - \dfrac{1}{-21 \text{ cm}} = \dfrac{0 \cdot 67}{R}$

or, $\dfrac{4}{3v} + \dfrac{1}{21 \text{ cm}} = \dfrac{2}{3R}$

or, $\dfrac{1}{v} = \dfrac{1}{2R} - \dfrac{1}{28 \text{ cm}} \qquad \qquad \dots \text{ (iii)}$

The focal length of the lens in air is 10 cm. Using

$$\frac{1}{f} = (\mu - 1)\left(\frac{1}{R_1} - \frac{1}{R_2}\right),$$

$$\frac{1}{10 \text{ cm}} = (1 \cdot 5 - 1)\left(\frac{1}{R} + \frac{1}{R}\right)$$

or, $R = 10$ cm.

Thus, by (iii),

$$\frac{1}{v} = \frac{1}{20 \text{ cm}} - \frac{1}{28 \text{ cm}}$$

or, $v = 70$ cm.

The image is formed 70 cm inside the tube.

26. *A slide projector produces 500 times enlarged image of a slide on a screen 10 m away. Assume that the projector consists of a single convex lens used for magnification. If the screen is moved 2·0 m closer, by what distance should the slide be moved towards or away from the lens so that the image remains focussed on the screen?*

Solution : In the first case, $v = 10$ m and $\dfrac{v}{u} = -500$.

Thus, $u = -\dfrac{v}{500} = -\dfrac{1}{50}$ m $= -2·0$ cm. The focal length f is given by

$$\frac{1}{f} = \frac{1}{v} - \frac{1}{u} = \frac{1}{10 \text{ m}} + \frac{1}{2·0 \text{ cm}}.$$

If the screen is moved 2·0 m closer, $v = 8·0$ m. The object distance u' is given by

$$\frac{1}{v} - \frac{1}{u'} = \frac{1}{f}$$

or, $\dfrac{1}{u'} = \dfrac{1}{v} - \dfrac{1}{f} = \dfrac{1}{8·0 \text{ m}} - \dfrac{1}{10 \text{ m}} - \dfrac{1}{2·0 \text{ cm}}$

$$= \frac{1}{40 \text{ m}} - \frac{1}{2·0 \text{ cm}}$$

$$= -\frac{1}{2·0 \text{ cm}}\left(1 - \frac{1}{2000}\right)$$

or, $u' = -2·0 \text{ cm}\left(1 - \dfrac{1}{2000}\right)^{-1}$

$$\approx -2·0 \text{ cm}\left(1 + \frac{1}{2000}\right) = -2·0 \text{ cm} - \frac{1}{1000} \text{ cm}.$$

Thus, the slide should be taken $\dfrac{1}{1000}$ cm away from the lens.

27. *A convex lens focusses an object 10 cm from it on a screen placed 10 cm away from it. A glass plate ($\mu = 1·5$) of thickness 1·5 cm is inserted between the lens and the screen. Where should the object be placed so that its image is again focussed on the screen?*

Solution :

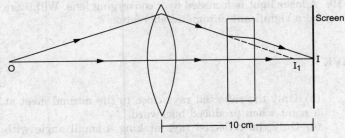

Figure 18-W24

$$\frac{1}{f} = \frac{1}{v} - \frac{1}{u} = \frac{1}{10 \text{ cm}} - \left(\frac{1}{-10 \text{ cm}}\right) = \frac{1}{5 \text{ cm}}.$$

So, the focal length of the lens is 5 cm. The situation with the glass plate inserted is shown in figure (18-W24). The object is placed at O. The lens would form the image at I_1 but the glass plate intercepts the rays and forms the image I on the screen.

The shift $I_1 I = t\left(1 - \dfrac{1}{\mu}\right)$

$$= (1·5 \text{ cm})\left(1 - \frac{1}{1·5}\right) = 0·5 \text{ cm}.$$

Thus, the lens forms the image at a distance 9·5 cm from itself. Using

$$\frac{1}{v} - \frac{1}{u} = \frac{1}{f},$$

$$\frac{1}{u} = \frac{1}{v} - \frac{1}{f} = \frac{1}{9·5 \text{ cm}} - \frac{1}{5 \text{ cm}}$$

or, $u = -10·6$ cm.

Thus, the object should be placed at a distance of 10·6 cm from the lens.

28. *Two convex lenses of focal length 20 cm each are placed coaxially with a separation of 60 cm between them. Find the image of a distant object formed by the combination by (a) using thin lens formula separately for the two lenses and (b) using the equivalent lens. Note that although the combination forms a real image of a distant object on the other side, it is equivalent to a diverging lens as far as the location of the final image is concerned.*

Solution :

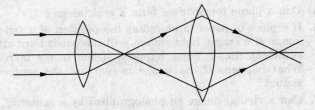

Figure 18-W25

(a) The first image is formed at the focus of the first lens. This is at 20 cm from the first lens and hence at $u = -40$ cm from the second. Using the lens formula for the second lens,

$$\frac{1}{v} = \frac{1}{u} + \frac{1}{f} = -\frac{1}{40 \text{ cm}} + \frac{1}{20 \text{ cm}}$$

or, $v = 40$ cm.

The final image is formed 40 cm to the right of the second lens.

(b) The equivalent focal length is

$$\frac{1}{F} = \frac{1}{f_1} + \frac{1}{f_2} - \frac{d}{f_1 f_2}$$

$$= \frac{1}{20 \text{ cm}} + \frac{1}{20 \text{ cm}} - \frac{60 \text{ cm}}{(20 \text{ cm})^2}$$

or, $F = -20$ cm.

It is a divergent lens. It should be kept at a distance

$$D = \frac{dF}{f_1} \text{ behind the second lens.}$$

Here, $D = \frac{(60 \text{ cm})(-20 \text{ cm})}{20 \text{ cm}} = -60 \text{ cm.}$

Thus, the equivalent divergent lens should be placed at a distance of 60 cm to the right of the second lens. The final image is formed at the focus of this divergent lens i.e., 20 cm to the left of it. It is, therefore, 40 cm to the right of the second lens.

□

QUESTIONS FOR SHORT ANSWER

1. Is the formula "Real depth/Apparent depth $= \mu$" valid if viewed from a position quite away from the normal ?

2. Can you ever have a situation in which a light ray goes undeviated through a prism ?

3. Why does a diamond shine more than a glass piece cut to the same shape ?

4. A narrow beam of light passes through a slab obliquely and is then received by an eye (figure 18-Q1). The index of refraction of the material in the slab fluctuates slowly with time. How will it appear to the eye? The twinkling of stars has a similar explanation.

Figure 18-Q1

5. Can a plane mirror ever form a real image ?

6. If a piece of paper is placed at the position of a virtual image of a strong light source, will the paper burn after sufficient time ? What happens if the image is real? What happens if the image is real but the source is virtual ?

7. Can a virtual image be photographed by a camera ?

8. In motor vehicles, a convex mirror is attached near the driver's seat to give him the view of the traffic behind. What is the special function of this convex mirror which a plane mirror can not do ?

9. If an object far away from a convex mirror moves towards the mirror, the image also moves. Does it move faster, slower or at the same speed as compared to the object ?

10. Suppose you are inside the water in a swimming pool near an edge. A friend is standing on the edge. Do you find your friend taller or shorter than his usual height ?

11. The equation of refraction at a spherical surface is

$$\frac{\mu_2}{v} - \frac{\mu_1}{u} = \frac{\mu_2 - \mu_1}{R}.$$

Taking $R = \infty$, show that this equation leads to the equation

$$\frac{\text{Real depth}}{\text{Apparent depth}} = \frac{\mu_2}{\mu_1}$$

for refraction at a plane surface.

12. A thin converging lens is formed with one surface convex and the other plane. Does the position of image depend on whether the convex surface or the plane surface faces the object ?

13. A single lens is mounted in a tube. A parallel beam enters the tube and emerges out of the tube as a divergent beam. Can you say with certainty that there is a diverging lens in the tube ?

14. An air bubble is formed inside water. Does it act as a converging lens or a diverging lens ?

15. Two converging lenses of unequal focal lengths can be used to reduce the aperture of a parallel beam of light without loosing the energy of the light. This increases the intensity. Describe how the converging lenses should be placed to do this.

16. If a spherical mirror is dipped in water, does its focal length change ?

17. If a thin lens is dipped in water, does its focal length change ?

18. Can mirrors give rise to chromatic aberration ?

19. A laser light is focussed by a converging lens. Will there be a significant chromatic aberration ?

OBJECTIVE I

1. A point source of light is placed in front of a plane mirror.

(a) All the reflected rays meet at a point when produced backward.

(b) Only the reflected rays close to the normal meet at a point when produced backward.

(c) Only the reflected rays making a small angle with

the mirror meet at a point when produced backward.

(d) Light of different colours make different images.

2. Total internal reflection can take place only if
(a) light goes from optically rarer medium (smaller refractive index) to optically denser medium
(b) light goes from optically denser medium to rarer medium
(c) the refractive indices of the two media are close to each other
(d) the refractive indices of the two media are widely different.

3. In image formation from spherical mirrors, only paraxial rays are considered because they
(a) are easy to handle geometrically
(b) contain most of the intensity of the incident light
(c) form nearly a point image of a point source
(d) show minimum dispersion effect.

4. A point object is placed at a distance of 30 cm from a convex mirror of focal length 30 cm. The image will form at
(a) infinity						(b) pole
(c) focus						(d) 15 cm behind the mirror.

5. Figure (18-Q2) shows two rays A and B being reflected by a mirror and going as A' and B'. The mirror
(a) is plane					(b) is convex
(c) is concave					(d) may be any spherical mirror.

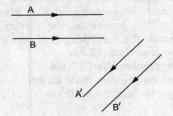

Figure 18-Q2

6. The image formed by a concave mirror
(a) is always real			(b) is always virtual
(c) is certainly real if the object is virtual
(d) is certainly virtual if the object is real.

7. Figure (18-Q3) shows three transparent media of refractive indices μ_1, μ_2 and μ_3. A point object O is placed in the medium μ_2. If the entire medium on the right of the spherical surface has refractive index μ_1, the image forms at O'. If this entire medium has refractive index μ_3, the image forms at O''. In the situation shown,
(a) the image forms between O' and O''
(b) the image forms to the left of O'
(c) the image forms to the right of O''
(d) two images form, one at O' and the other at O''.

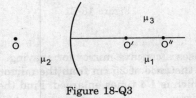

Figure 18-Q3

8. Four modifications are suggested in the lens formula to include the effect of the thickness t of the lens. Which one is likely to be correct ?
(a) $\dfrac{1}{v} - \dfrac{1}{u} = \dfrac{t}{uf}$ 				(b) $\dfrac{t}{v^2} - \dfrac{1}{u} = \dfrac{1}{f}$
(c) $\dfrac{1}{v-t} - \dfrac{1}{u+t} = \dfrac{1}{f}$ 			(d) $\dfrac{1}{v} - \dfrac{1}{u} + \dfrac{t}{uv} = \dfrac{t}{f}$.

9. A double convex lens has two surfaces of equal radii R and refractive index $m = 1.5$. We have,
(a) $f = R/2$		(b) $f = R$		(c) $f = -R$		(d) $f = 2R$.

10. A point source of light is placed at a distance of $2f$ from a converging lens of focal length f. The intensity on the other side of the lens is maximum at a distance
(a) f	(b) between f and $2f$	(c) $2f$	(d) more than $2f$.

11. A parallel beam of light is incident on a converging lens parallel to its principal axis. As one moves away from the lens on the other side on its principal axis, the intensity of light
(a) remains constant			(b) continuously increases
(c) continuously decreases
(d) first increases then decreases.

12. A symmetric double convex lens is cut in two equal parts by a plane perpendicular to the principal axis. If the power of the original lens was 4 D, the power of a cut-lens will be
(a) 2 D			(b) 3 D			(c) 4 D			(d) 5 D.

13. A symmetric double convex lens is cut in two equal parts by a plane containing the principal axis. If the power of the original lens was 4 D, the power of a divided lens will be
(a) 2 D			(b) 3 D			(c) 4 D			(d) 5 D.

14. Two concave lenses L_1 and L_2 are kept in contact with each other. If the space between the two lenses is filled with a material of smaller refractive index, the magnitude of the focal length of the combination
(a) becomes undefined			(b) remains unchanged
(c) increases					(d) decreases.

15. A thin lens is made with a material having refractive index $\mu = 1.5$. Both the sides are convex. It is dipped in water ($\mu = 1.33$). It will behave like
(a) a convergent lens			(b) a divergent lens
(c) a rectangular slab			(d) a prism.

16. A convex lens is made of a material having refractive index 1.2. Both the surfaces of the lens are convex. If it is dipped into water ($\mu = 1.33$), it will behave like
(a) a convergent lens			(b) a divergent lens
(c) a rectangular slab			(d) a prism.

17. A point object O is placed on the principal axis of a convex lens of focal length $f = 20$ cm at a distance of 40 cm to the left of it. The diameter of the lens is 10 cm. An eye is placed 60 cm to right of the lens and a distance h below the principal axis. The maximum value of h to see the image is
(a) 0		(b) 2.5 cm		(c) 5 cm		(d) 10 cm.

18. The rays of different colours fail to converge at a point after going through a converging lens. This defect is called
(a) spherical aberration		(b) distortion
(c) coma						(d) chromatic aberration.

OBJECTIVE II

1. If the light moving in a straight line bends by a small but fixed angle, it may be a case of
   (a) reflection   (b) refraction
   (c) diffraction   (d) dispersion.

2. Mark the correct options.
   (a) If the incident rays are converging, we have a real object.
   (b) If the final rays are converging, we have a real image.
   (c) The image of a virtual object is called a virtual image.
   (d) If the image is virtual, the corresponding object is called a virtual object.

3. Which of the following (referred to a spherical mirror) do (does) not depend on whether the rays are paraxial or not ?
   (a) Pole   (b) Focus
   (c) Radius of curvature (d) Principal axis

4. The image of an extended object, placed perpendicular to the principal axis of a mirror, will be erect if
   (a) the object and the image are both real
   (b) the object and the image are both virtual
   (c) the object is real but the image is virtual
   (d) the object is virtual but the image is real.

5. A convex lens forms a real image of a point object placed on its principal axis. If the upper half of the lens is painted black,
   (a) the image will be shifted downward
   (b) the image will be shifted upward
   (c) the image will not be shifted
   (d) the intensity of the image will decrease.

6. Consider three converging lenses L_1, L_2 and L_3 having identical geometrical construction. The index of refraction of L_1 and L_2 are μ_1 and μ_2 respectively. The upper half of the lens L_3 has a refractive index μ_1 and the lower half has μ_2 (figure 18-Q3). A point object O is imaged at O_1 by the lens L_1 and at O_2 by the lens L_2 placed in same position. If L_3 is placed at the same place,
   (a) there will be an image at O_1
   (b) there will be an image at O_2.
   (c) the only image will form somewhere between O_1 and O_2
   (d) the only image will form away from O_2.

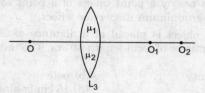

Figure 18-Q4

7. A screen is placed at a distance 40 cm away from an illuminated object. A converging lens is placed between the source and the screen and it is attempted to form the image of the source on the screen. If no position could be found, the focal length of the lens
   (a) must be less than 10 cm
   (b) must be greater than 10 cm
   (c) must not be greater than 20 cm
   (d) must not be less than 10 cm.

EXERCISES

1. A concave mirror having a radius of curvature 40 cm is placed in front of an illuminated point source at a distance of 30 cm from it. Find the location of the image.

2. A concave mirror forms an image of 20 cm high object on a screen placed 5·0 m away from the mirror. The height of the image is 50 cm. Find the focal length of the mirror and the distance between the mirror and the object.

3. A concave mirror has a focal length of 20 cm. Find the position or positions of an object for which the image-size is double of the object-size.

4. A 1 cm object is placed perpendicular to the principal axis of a convex mirror of focal length 7·5 cm. Find its distance from the mirror if the image formed is 0·6 cm in size.

5. A candle flame 1·6 cm high is imaged in a ball bearing of diameter 0·4 cm. If the ball bearing is 20 cm away from the flame, find the location and the height of the image.

6. A 3 cm tall object is placed at a distance of 7·5 cm from a convex mirror of focal length 6 cm. Find the location, size and nature of the image.

7. A U-shaped wire is placed before a concave mirror having radius of curvature 20 cm as shown in figure (18-E1). Find the total length of the image.

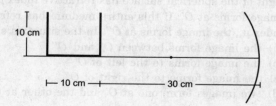

Figure 18-E1

8. A man uses a concave mirror for shaving. He keeps his face at a distance of 25 cm from the mirror and gets an image which is 1·4 times enlarged. Find the focal length of the mirror.

9. Find the diameter of the image of the moon formed by a spherical concave mirror of focal length 7·6 m. The diameter of the moon is 3450 km and the distance between the earth and the moon is $3·8 \times 10^{5}$ km.

10. A particle goes in a circle of radius 2·0 cm. A concave mirror of focal length 20 cm is placed with its principal axis passing through the centre of the circle and perpendicular to its plane. The distance between the pole of the mirror and the centre of the circle is 30 cm. Calculate the radius of the circle formed by the image.

11. A concave mirror of radius R is kept on a horizontal table (figure 18-E2). Water (refractive index = μ) is poured into it up to a height h. Where should an object be placed so that its image is formed on itself ?

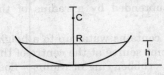

Figure 18-E2

12. A point source S is placed midway between two converging mirrors having equal focal length f as shown in figure (18-E3). Find the values of d for which only one image is formed.

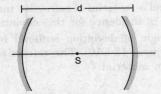

Figure 18-E3

13. A converging mirror M_1, a point source S and a diverging mirror M_2 are arranged as shown in figure (18-E4). The source is placed at a distance of 30 cm from M_1. The focal length of each of the mirrors is 20 cm. Consider only the images formed by a maximum of two reflections. It is found that one image is formed on the source itself. (a) Find the distance between the two mirrors. (b) Find the location of the image formed by the single reflection from M_2.

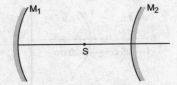

Figure 18-E4

14. A light ray falling at an angle of 45° with the surface of a clean slab of ice of thickness 1·00 m is refracted into it at an angle of 30°. Calculate the time taken by the light rays to cross the slab. Speed of light in vacuum $= 3 \times 10^{8}$ m s^{-1}.

15. A pole of length 1·00 m stands half dipped in a swimming pool with water level 50·0 cm higher than the bed. The refractive index of water is 1·33 and sunlight is coming at an angle of 45° with the vertical. Find the length of the shadow of the pole on the bed.

16. A small piece of wood is floating on the surface of a 2·5 m deep lake. Where does the shadow form on the bottom when the sun is just setting? Refractive index of water = 4/3.

17. An object P is focussed by a microscope M. A glass slab of thickness 2·1 cm is introduced between P and M. If the refractive index of the slab is 1·5, by what distance should the microscope be shifted to focus the object again ?

18. A vessel contains water up to a height of 20 cm and above it an oil up to another 20 cm. The refractive indices of the water and the oil are 1·33 and 1·30 respectively. Find the apparent depth of the vessel when viewed from above.

19. Locate the image of the point P as seen by the eye in the figure (18-E5).

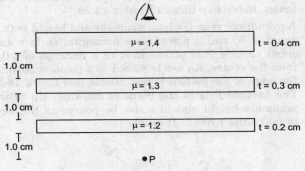

Figure 18-E5

20. k transparent slabs are arranged one over another. The refractive indices of the slabs are $\mu_1, \mu_2, \mu_3, \ldots \mu_k$ and the thicknesses are $t_1, t_2, t_3, \ldots t_k$. An object is seen through this combination with nearly perpendicular light. Find the equivalent refractive index of the system which will allow the image to be formed at the same place.

21. A cylindrical vessel of diameter 12 cm contains 800π cm^3 of water. A cylindrical glass piece of diameter 8·0 cm and height 8·0 cm is placed in the vessel. If the bottom of the vessel under the glass piece is seen by the paraxial rays (see figure 18-E6), locate its image. The index of refraction of glass is 1·50 and that of water is 1·33.

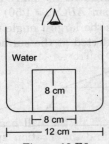

Figure 18-E6

22. Consider the situation in figure (18-E7). The bottom of the pot is a reflecting plane mirror, S is a small fish and T is a human eye. Refractive index of water is μ. (a) At what distance(s) from itself will the fish see the image(s) of the eye ? (b) At what distance(s) from itself will the eye see the image(s) of the fish.

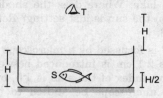

Figure 18-E7

23. A small object is placed at the centre of the bottom of a cylindrical vessel of radius 3 cm and height 4 cm filled completely with water. Consider the ray leaving the vessel through a corner. Suppose this ray and the ray along the axis of the vessel are used to trace the image. Find the apparent depth of the image and the ratio of real depth to the apparent depth under the assumptions taken. Refractive index of water = 1·33.

24. A cylindrical vessel, whose diameter and height both are equal to 30 cm, is placed on a horizontal surface and a small particle P is placed in it at a distance of 5·0 cm from the centre. An eye is placed at a position such that the edge of the bottom is just visible (see figure 18-E8). The particle P is in the plane of drawing. Up to what minimum height should water be poured in the vessel to make the particle P visible ?

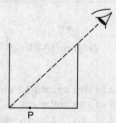

Figure 18-E8

25. A light ray is incident at an angle of 45° with the normal to a $\sqrt{2}$ cm thick plate ($\mu = 2·0$). Find the shift in the path of the light as it emerges out from the plate.

26. An optical fibre ($\mu = 1·72$) is surrounded by a glass coating ($\mu = 1·50$). Find the critical angle for total internal reflection at the fibre-glass interface.

27. A light ray is incident normally on the face AB of a right-angled prism ABC ($\mu = 1·50$) as shown in figure (18-E9). What is the largest angle ϕ for which the light ray is totally reflected at the surface AC ?

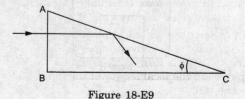

Figure 18-E9

28. Find the maximum angle of refraction when a light ray is refracted from glass ($\mu = 1·50$) to air.

29. Light is incident from glass ($\mu = 1·5$) to air. Sketch the variation of the angle of deviation δ with the angle of incident i for $0 < i < 90°$.

30. Light is incident from glass ($\mu = 1·50$) to water ($\mu = 1·33$). Find the range of the angle of deviation for which there are two angles of incidence.

31. Light falls from glass ($\mu = 1·5$) to air. Find the angle of incidence for which the angle of deviation is 90°.

32. A point source is placed at a depth h below the surface of water (refractive index = μ). (a) Show that light escapes through a circular area on the water surface with its centre directly above the point source. (b) Find the angle subtended by a radius of the area on the source.

33. A container contains water up to a height of 20 cm and there is a point source at the centre of the bottom of the container. A rubber ring of radius r floats centrally on the water. The ceiling of the room is 2·0 m above the water surface. (a) Find the radius of the shadow of the ring formed on the ceiling if $r = 15$ cm. (b) Find the maximum value of r for which the shadow of the ring is formed on the ceiling. Refractive index of water = 4/3.

34. Find the angle of minimum deviation for an equilateral prism made of a material of refractive index 1·732. What is the angle of incidence for this deviation ?

35. Find the angle of deviation suffered by the light ray shown in figure (18-E10). The refractive index $\mu = 1·5$ for the prism material.

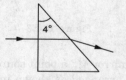

Figure 18-E10

36. A light ray, going through a prism with the angle of prism 60°, is found to deviate by 30°. What limit on the refractive index can be put from these data ?

37. Locate the image formed by refraction in the situation shown in figure (18-E11).

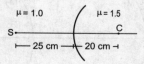

Figure 18-E11

38. A spherical surface of radius 30 cm separates two transparent media A and B with refractive indices 1·33 and 1·48 respectively. The medium A is on the convex side of the surface. Where should a point object be placed in medium A so that the paraxial rays become parallel after refraction at the surface ?

39. Figure (18-E12) shows a transparent hemisphere of radius 3·0 cm made of a material of refractive index 2·0. (a) A narrow beam of parallel rays is incident on the hemisphere as shown in the figure. Are the rays totally reflected at the plane surface? (b) Find the image formed by the refraction at the first surface. (c) Find the image formed by the reflection or by the refraction at the plane surface. (d) Trace qualitatively the final rays as they come out of the hemisphere.

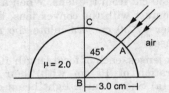

Figure 18-E12

40. A small object is embedded in a glass sphere (μ = 1·5) of radius 5·0 cm at a distance 1·5 cm left to the centre. Locate the image of the object as seen by an observer standing (a) to the left of the sphere and (b) to the right of the sphere.

41. A biconvex thick lens is constructed with glass (μ = 1·50). Each of the surfaces has a radius of 10 cm and the thickness at the middle is 5 cm. Locate the image of an object placed far away from the lens.

42. A narrow pencil of parallel light is incident normally on a solid transparent sphere of radius r. What should be the refractive index if the pencil is to be focussed (a) at the surface of the sphere, (b) at the centre of the sphere.

43. One end of a cylindrical glass rod (μ = 1·5) of radius 1·0 cm is rounded in the shape of a hemisphere. The rod is immersed in water (μ = 4/3) and an object is placed in the water along the axis of the rod at a distance of 8·0 cm from the rounded edge. Locate the image of the object.

44. A paperweight (μ = 1·5) in the form of a hemisphere of radius 3·0 cm is used to hold down a printed page. An observer looks at the page vertically through the paperweight. At what height above the page will the printed letters near the centre appear to the observer?

45. Solve the previous problem if the paperweight is inverted at its place so that the spherical surface touches the paper.

46. A hemispherical portion of the surface of a solid glass sphere (μ = 1·5) of radius r is silvered to make the inner side reflecting. An object is placed on the axis of the hemisphere at a distance 3r from the centre of the sphere. The light from the object is refracted at the unsilvered part, then reflected from the silvered part and again refracted at the unsilvered part. Locate the final image formed.

47. The convex surface of a thin concavo-convex lens of glass of refractive index 1·5 has a radius of curvature 20 cm.

The concave surface has a radius of curvature 60 cm. The convex side is silvered and placed on a horizontal surface as shown in figure (18-E13). (a) Where should a pin be placed on the axis so that its image is formed at the same place? (b) If the concave part is filled with water (μ = 4/3), find the distance through which the pin should be moved so that the image of the pin again coincides with the pin.

Figure 18-E13

48. A double convex lens has focal length 25 cm. The radius of curvature of one of the surfaces is double of the other. Find the radii, if the refractive index of the material of the lens is 1·5.

49. The radii of curvature of a lens are + 20 cm and + 30 cm. The material of the lens has a refracting index 1·6. Find the focal length of the lens (a) if it is placed in air, and (b) if it is placed in water (μ = 1·33).

50. Lenses are constructed by a material of refractive index 1·50. The magnitude of the radii of curvature are 20 cm and 30 cm. Find the focal lengths of the possible lenses with the above specifications.

51. A thin lens made of a material of refractive index μ_2 has a medium of refractive index μ_1 on one side and a medium of refractive index μ_3 on the other side. The lens is biconvex and the two radii of curvature have equal magnitude R. A beam of light travelling parallel to the principal axis is incident on the lens. Where will the image be formed if the beam is incident from (a) the medium μ_1 and (b) from the medium μ_3?

52. A convex lens has a focal length of 10 cm. Find the location and nature of the image if a point object is placed on the principal axis at a distance of (a) 9·8 cm, (b) 10·2 cm from the lens.

53. A slide projector has to project a 35 mm slide (35 mm × 23 mm) on a 2 m × 2 m screen at a distance of 10 m from the lens. What should be the focal length of the lens in the projector?

54. A particle executes a simple harmonic motion of amplitude 1·0 cm along the principal axis of a convex lens of focal length 12 cm. The mean position of oscillation is at 20 cm from the lens. Find the amplitude of oscillation of the image of the particle.

55. An extended object is placed at a distance of 5·0 cm from a convex lens of focal length 8·0 cm. (a) Draw the ray diagram (to the scale) to locate the image and from this, measure the distance of the image from the lens. (b) Find the position of the image from the lens formula and see how close the drawing is to the correct result.

56. A pin of length 2·00 cm is placed perpendicular to the principal axis of a converging lens. An inverted image of size 1·00 cm is formed at a distance of 40·0 cm from the pin. Find the focal length of the lens and its distance from the pin.

57. A convex lens produces a double size real image when an object is placed at a distance of 18 cm from it. Where should the object be placed to produce a triple size real image ?

58. A pin of length 2·0 cm lies along the principal axis of a converging lens, the centre being at a distance of 11 cm from the lens. The focal length of the lens is 6 cm. Find the size of the image.

59. The diameter of the sun is $1·4 \times 10^9$ m and its distance from the earth is $1·5 \times 10^{11}$ m. Find the radius of the image of the sun formed by a lens of focal length 20 cm.

60. A 5·0 diopter lens forms a virtual image which is 4 times the object placed perpendicularly on the principal axis of the lens. Find the distance of the object from the lens.

61. A diverging lens of focal length 20 cm and a converging mirror of focal length 10 cm are placed coaxially at a separation of 5 cm. Where should an object be placed so that a real image is formed at the object itself ?

62. A converging lens of focal length 12 cm and a diverging mirror of focal length 7·5 cm are placed 5·0 cm apart with their principal axes coinciding. Where should an object be placed so that its image falls on itself ?

63. A converging lens and a diverging mirror are placed at a separation of 15 cm. The focal length of the lens is 25 cm and that of the mirror is 40 cm. Where should a point source be placed between the lens and the mirror so that the light, after getting reflected by the mirror and then getting transmitted by the lens, comes out parallel to the principal axis ?

64. A converging lens of focal length 15 cm and a converging mirror of focal length 10 cm are placed 50 cm apart with common principal axis. A point source is placed in between the lens and the mirror at a distance of 40 cm from the lens. Find the locations of the two images formed.

65. Consider the situation described in the previous problem. Where should a point source be placed on the principal axis so that the two images form at the same place ?

66. A converging lens of focal length 15 cm and a converging mirror of focal length 10 cm are placed 50 cm apart. If a pin of length 2·0 cm is placed 30 cm from the lens farther away from the mirror, where will the final image form and what will be the size of the final image ?

67. A point object is placed on the principal axis of a convex lens ($f = 15$ cm) at a distance of 30 cm from it. A glass plate ($\mu = 1·50$) of thickness 1 cm is placed on the other side of the lens perpendicular to the axis. Locate the image of the point object.

68. A convex lens of focal length 20 cm and a concave lens of focal length 10 cm are placed 10 cm apart with their principal axes coinciding. A beam of light travelling parallel to the principal axis and having a beam diameter 5·0 mm, is incident on the combination. Show that the emergent beam is parallel to the incident one. Find the beam diameter of the emergent beam.

69. A diverging lens of focal length 20 cm and a converging lens of focal length 30 cm are placed 15 cm apart with their principal axes coinciding. Where should an object be placed on the principal axis so that its image is formed at infinity ?

70. A 5 mm high pin is placed at a distance of 15 cm from a convex lens of focal length 10 cm. A second lens of focal length 5 cm is placed 40 cm from the first lens and 55 cm from the pin. Find (a) the position of the final image, (b) its nature and (c) its size.

71. A point object is placed at a distance of 15 cm from a convex lens. The image is formed on the other side at a distance of 30 cm from the lens. When a concave lens is placed in contact with the convex lens, the image shifts away further by 30 cm. Calculate the focal lengths of the two lenses.

72. Two convex lenses, each of focal length 10 cm, are placed at a separation of 15 cm with their principal axes coinciding. (a) Show that a light beam coming parallel to the principal axis diverges as it comes out of the lens system. (b) Find the location of the virtual image formed by the lens system of an object placed far away. (c) Find the focal length of the equivalent lens. (Note that the sign of the focal length is positive although the lens system actually diverges a parallel beam incident on it.)

73. A ball is kept at a height h above the surface of a heavy transparent sphere made of a material of refractive index μ. The radius of the sphere is R. At $t = 0$, the ball is dropped to fall normally on the sphere. Find the speed of the image formed as a function of time for $t < \sqrt{\dfrac{2h}{g}}$. Consider only the image by a single refraction.

74. A particle is moving at a constant speed V from a large distance towards a concave mirror of radius R along its principal axis. Find the speed of the image formed by the mirror as a function of the distance x of the particle from the mirror.

75. A small block of mass m and a concave mirror of radius R fitted with a stand lie on a smooth horizontal table with a separation d between them. The mirror together with its stand has a mass m. The block is pushed at $t = 0$ towards the mirror so that it starts moving towards the mirror at a constant speed V and collides with it. The collision is perfectly elastic. Find the velocity of the image (a) at a time $t < d/V$, (b) at a time $t > d/V$.

76. A gun of mass M fires a bullet of mass m with a horizontal speed V. The gun is fitted with a concave mirror of focal length f facing towards the receding bullet. Find the speed of separation of the bullet and the image just after the gun was fired.

77. A mass $m = 50$ g is dropped on a vertical spring of spring constant 500 N m^{-1} from a height $h = 10$ cm as shown in figure (18-E14). The mass sticks to the spring and

Figure 18-E14

executes simple harmonic oscillations after that. A concave mirror of focal length 12 cm facing the mass is fixed with its principal axis coinciding with the line of motion of the mass, its pole being at a distance of 30 cm from the free end of the spring. Find the length in which the image of the mass oscillates.

78. Two concave mirrors of equal radii of curvature R are fixed on a stand facing opposite directions. The whole system has a mass m and is kept on a frictionless horizontal table (figure 18-E15).

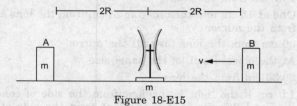

Figure 18-E15

Two blocks A and B, each of mass m, are placed on the two sides of the stand. At $t = 0$, the separation between A and the mirrors is $2R$ and also the separation between B and the mirrors is $2R$. The block B moves towards the mirror at a speed v. All collisions which take place

are elastic. Taking the original position of the mirrors–stand system to be $x = 0$ and X-axis along AB, find the position of the images of A and B at $t =$

(a) $\dfrac{R}{v}$ (b) $\dfrac{3R}{v}$ (c) $\dfrac{5R}{v}$.

79. Consider the situation shown in figure (18-E16). The elevator is going up with an acceleration of 2.00 m s^{-2} and the focal length of the mirror is 12.0 cm. All the surfaces are smooth and the pulley is light. The mass–pulley system is released from rest (with respect to the elevator) at $t = 0$ when the distance of B from the mirror is 42.0 cm. Find the distance between the image of the block B and the mirror at $t = 0.200$ s. Take $g = 10$ m s^{-2}.

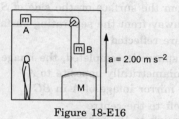

Figure 18-E16

□

ANSWERS

OBJECTIVE · I

1. (a)	2. (b)	3. (c)	4. (d)	5. (a)	6. (c)
7. (d)	8. (c)	9. (b)	10. (c)	11. (d)	12. (a)
13. (c)	14. (c)	15. (a)	16. (b)	17. (b)	18. (d)

OBJECTIVE II

1. (a), (b)	2. (b)	3. (a), (c), (d)
4. (c), (d)	5. (c), (d)	6. (a), (b)
7. (b)		

EXERCISES

1. 60 cm from the mirror on the side of the object
2. 1·43 m, 2·0 m
3. 10 cm or 30 cm from the mirror
4. 5 cm
5. 1·0 mm inside the ball bearing, 0·08 mm
6. $\dfrac{10}{3}$ cm from the mirror on the side opposite to the object, 1·33 cm, virtual and erect
7. 10 cm
8. 87·5 cm
9. 6·9 cm
10. 4·0 cm

11. $\dfrac{(R-h)}{\mu}$ above the water surface
12. $2f, 4f$
13. (a) 50 cm (b) 10 cm from the diverging mirror farther from the converging mirror
14. 5·44 ns
15. 81·5 cm
16. 2·83 m shifted from the position directly below the piece of the wood.
17. 0·70 cm
18. 30·4 cm
19. 0·2 cm above P
20. $\dfrac{\displaystyle\sum_{i=1}^{k} t_i}{\displaystyle\sum_{i=1}^{k} (t_i / \mu_i)}$
21. 7·1 cm above the bottom
22. (a) $H\left(\mu + \dfrac{1}{2}\right)$ above itself, $H\left(\mu + \dfrac{3}{2}\right)$ below itself

    (b) $H\left(1 + \dfrac{1}{2\mu}\right)$ below itself and $H\left(1 + \dfrac{3}{2\mu}\right)$ below itself

23. 2·25 cm, 1·78

24. 26·7 cm

25. 0·62 cm

26. $\sin^{-1}\dfrac{75}{86}$

27. $\cos^{-1}(2/3)$

28. 90°

30. 0 to $\cos^{-1}(8/9)$

31. 45°

32. (b) $\sin^{-1}(1/\mu)$

33. (a) 2·8 m   (b) 22·6 cm

34. 60°, 60°

35. 2°

36. $\mu \le \sqrt{2}$

37. 100 cm from the surface on the side of S

38. 266·0 cm away from the separating surface

39. (a) They are reflected

   (b) If the sphere is completed, the image forms at the point diametrically opposite to A

   (c) At the mirror image of A in BC

40. (a) 2 cm left to the centre
    (b) 2·65 cm left to the centre

41. 9·1 cm from the farther surface on the other side of the lens

42. (a) 2,

   (b) not possible, it will focus close to the centre if the refractive index is large.

43. At infinity

44. No shift is observed

45. 1 cm

46. At the reflecting surface of the sphere

47. (a) 15 cm from the lens on the axis
    (b) 1·14 cm towards the lens

48. 18·75 cm, 37·5 cm

49. (a) 100 cm   (b) 300 cm

50. ± 24 cm, ± 120 cm

51. (a) $\dfrac{\mu_3 R}{2\mu_2 - \mu_1 - \mu_3}$ (b) $\dfrac{\mu_1 R}{2\mu_2 - \mu_1 - \mu_3}$

52. (a) 490 cm on the side of the object, virtual
    (b) 510 cm on the other side, real

53. 17·2 cm

54. 2·3 cm

56. 8·89 cm, 26·7 cm

57. 16 cm

58. 3 cm

59. 0·93 mm

60. 15 cm

61. 60 cm from the lens further away from the mirror

62. 30 cm from the lens further away from the mirror

63. 1·67 cm from the lens

64. One at 15 cm and the other at 24 cm from the lens away from the mirror

65. 30 cm from the lens towards the mirror

66. At the object itself, of the same size

67. 30·33 cm from the lens

68. 1·0 cm if the light is incident from the side of concave lens and 2·5 mm if it is incident from the side of the convex lens

69. 60 cm from the diverging lens or 210 cm from the converging lens

70. (a) 10 cm from the second lens further away,
    (b) erect and real, (c) 10 mm

71. 10 cm for convex lens and 60 cm for concave lens

72. (b) 5 cm from the first lens towards the second lens
    (c) 20 cm

73. $\dfrac{\mu R^2 g t}{\left[(\mu-1)\left(h - \dfrac{1}{2}gt^2\right) - R\right]^2}$

74. $\dfrac{R^2 V}{(2x - R)^2}$

75. (a) $-\dfrac{R^2 V}{[2(d - Vt) - R]^2}$

   (b) $V\left[1 + \dfrac{R^2}{[2(Vt - d) - R]^2}\right]$

76. $2(1 + m/M)V$

77. 1·2 cm

78. (a) $x = -\dfrac{2R}{3}, R$ (b) $x = -2R, 0$ (c) $x = -3R, -\dfrac{4R}{3}$

79. 8·57 cm

□

CHAPTER 19

OPTICAL INSTRUMENTS

19.1 THE EYE

Optical instruments are used primarily to assist the eye in viewing an object. Let us first discuss in brief the construction of a human eye and the mechanism by which we see, the most common but most important experiment we do from the day we open our eyes.

Figure (19.1) shows schematically the basic components of an eye. The eye has a nearly spherical shape of diameter about an inch. The front portion is more sharply curved and is covered by a transparent protective membrane called the *cornea*. It is this portion which is visible from outside. Behind the cornea, we have a space filled with a liquid called the *aqueous humor* and behind that a *crystalline lens*.

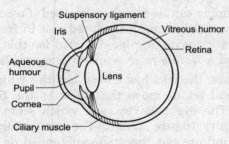

Figure 19.1

Between the aqueous humor and the lens, we have a muscular diaphragm called *iris*, which has a small hole in it called *pupil*. Iris is the coloured part that we see in an eye. The pupil appears black because any light falling on it goes into the eye and there is almost no chance of light coming back to the outside. The amount of light entering the eye, may be controlled by varying the aperture of the pupil with the help of the iris. In low-light condition, the iris expands the pupil to allow more light to go in. In good light conditions, it contracts the pupil.

The lens is hard in the middle and gradually becomes soft towards the outer edge. The curvature of the lens may be altered by the *ciliary muscles* to which

it is attached. The light entering the eye forms an image on the *retina* which covers the inside of the rear part of the eyeball. The retina contains about 125 million receptors called *rods* and *cones* which receive the light signal and about one million optic-nerve fibres which transmit the information to the brain. The space between the lens and the retina is filled with another liquid called the *vitreous humor*.

The aqueous humor and the vitreous humor have almost same refractive index 1·336. The refractive index of the material of the lens is different in different portions but on the average it is about 1·396. When light enters the eye from air, most of the bending occurs at the cornea itself because there is a sharp change in the refractive index. Some additional bending is done by the lens which is surrounded by a fluid of somewhat lower refractive index. In normal conditions, the light should be focussed on the retina.

The cornea–lens–fluid system is equivalent to a single converging lens whose focal length may be adjusted by the ciliary muscles. Now onwards, we shall use the word eye-lens to mean this equivalent lens.

When the eye is focussed on a distant object, the ciliary muscles are relaxed so that the focal length of the eye-lens has its maximum value which is equal to its distance from the retina. The parallel rays coming into the eye are then focussed on the retina and we see the object clearly.

When the eye is focussed on a closer object, the ciliary muscles are strained and the focal length of the eye-lens decreases. The ciliary muscles adjust the focal length in such a way that the image is again formed on the retina and we see the object clearly. This process of adjusting focal length is called *accommodation*. However, the muscles cannot be strained beyond a limit and hence, if the object is brought too close to the eye, the focal length cannot be adjusted to form the image on the retina. Thus, there is a minimum distance for the clear vision of an object.

The nearest point for which the image can be focussed on the retina, is called the *near point* of the eye. The distance of the near point from the eye is called the *least distance for clear vision*. This varies from person to person and with age. At a young age (say below 10 years), the muscles are strong and flexible and can bear more strain. The near point may be as close as 7–8 cm at this age. In old age, the muscles cannot sustain a large strain and the near point shifts to large values, say, 1 to 2 m or even more. We shall discuss about these defects of vision and use of glasses in a later section. The average value of the least distance for clear vision for a normal eye is generally taken to be 25 cm.

19.2 APPARENT SIZE

The size of an object as sensed by us is related to the size of the image formed on the retina. A larger image on the retina activates larger number of rods and cones attached to it and the object looks larger. As is clear from figure (19.2), if an object is taken away from the eye, the size of the image on the retina decreases and hence, the same object looks smaller. It is also clear from figure (19.2) that the size of the image on the retina is roughly proportional to the angle subtended by the object on the eye. This angle is known as the *visual angle* and optical instruments are used to increase this angle artificially in order to improve the clarity.

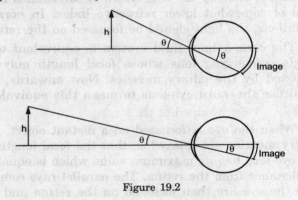

Figure 19.2

Example 19.1

Two boys, one 52 *inches tall and the other* 55 *inches tall, are standing at distances* 4·0 m *and* 5·0 m *respectively from an eye. Which boy will appear taller?*

Solution : The angle subtended by the first boy on the eye is

$$\alpha_1 = \frac{52 \text{ inch}}{4 \cdot 0 \text{ m}} = 13 \text{ inch/m}$$

and the angle subtended by the second boy is

$$\alpha_2 = \frac{55 \text{ inch}}{5 \cdot 0 \text{ m}} = 11 \text{ inch/m}.$$

As $\alpha_1 > \alpha_2$, the first boy will look taller to the eye.

19.3 SIMPLE MICROSCOPE

When we view an object with naked eyes, the object must be placed somewhere between infinity and the near point. The maximum angle is subtended on the eye when the object is placed at the near point. This angle is (figure 19.3a)

$$\theta_o = \frac{h}{D}, \qquad \qquad \dots \text{ (i)}$$

where h is the size of the object and D is the least distance for clear vision.

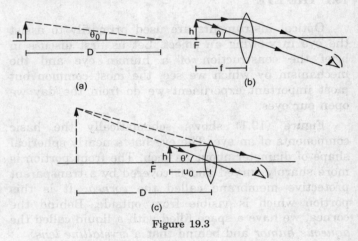

(a)

(b)

(c)

Figure 19.3

This angle can be further increased if a converging lens of short focal length is placed just in front of the eye. When a converging lens is used for this purpose, it is called a *simple microscope* or a *magnifier*.

Suppose, the lens has a focal length f which is less than D and let us move the object to the first focal point F. The eye receives rays which seem to come from infinity (figure 19.3b). The actual size of the image is infinite but the angle subtended on the lens (and hence on the eye) is

$$\theta = \frac{h}{f}. \qquad \qquad \dots \text{ (ii)}$$

As $f < D$, equations (i) and (ii) show that $\theta > \theta_o$. Hence, the eye perceives a larger image than it could have had without the microscope. As the image is situated at infinity, the ciliary muscles are least strained to focus the final image on the retina. This situation is known as *normal adjustment*. We define *magnifying power* of a microscope as θ/θ_o where θ is the angle subtended by the image on the eye when the microscope is used and θ_o is the angle subtended on the naked eye when the object is placed at the near point. This is also known as the *angular magnification*. Thus, *the magnifying power is the factor by which the image on the retina can be enlarged by using the microscope.*

In normal adjustment, the magnifying power of a simple microscope is, by (i) and (ii),

$$m = \frac{\theta}{\theta_o} = \frac{h/f}{h/D}$$

or, $$m = \frac{D}{f} \cdot \qquad \dots \text{(19.1)}$$

If $f < D$, the magnifying power is greater than 1.

The magnifying power can be further increased by moving the object still closer to the lens. Suppose, we move the object to a distance u_o from the lens such that the virtual erect image is formed at the near point (figure 19.3c). Though the eye is strained, it can still see the image clearly. The distance u_o can be calculated using the lens formula,

$$\frac{1}{u} = \frac{1}{v} - \frac{1}{f} .$$

Here $v = -D$ and $u = -u_o$, so that

$$\frac{1}{-u_o} = -\frac{1}{D} - \frac{1}{f}$$

or, $$\frac{D}{u_o} = 1 + \frac{D}{f} . \qquad \dots \text{(iii)}$$

The angle subtended by the image on the lens (and hence on the eye) is

$$\theta' = \frac{h}{u_o} .$$

The angular magnification or magnifying power in this case is

$$m = \frac{\theta'}{\theta_o} = \frac{h/u_o}{h/D}$$

$$= \frac{D}{u_o}$$

$$= 1 + \frac{D}{f} . \qquad \dots \text{(19.2)}$$

Equations (19.1) and (19.2) show that the magnification can be made large by choosing the focal length f small. However, due to several other aberrations the image becomes too defective at large magnification with a simple microscope. Roughly speaking, a magnification up to 4 is trouble-free.

The magnifying power is written with a unit X. Thus, if a magnifier produces an angular magnification of 10, it is called a 10 X magnifier.

19.4 COMPOUND MICROSCOPE

Figure (19.4) shows a simplified version of a compound microscope and the ray diagram for image formation. It consists of two converging lenses arranged coaxially. The one facing the object is called

the *objective* and the one close to the eye is called the *eyepiece* or *ocular*. The objective has a smaller aperture and smaller focal length than those of the eyepiece. The separation between the objective and the eyepiece can be varied by appropriate screws fixed on the panel of the microscope.

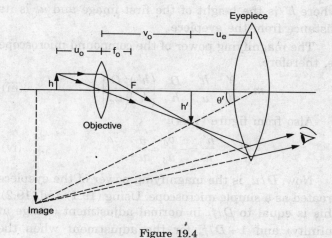

Figure 19.4

The object is placed at a distance u_o from the objective which is slightly greater than its focal length f_o. A real and inverted image is formed at a distance v_o on the other side of the objective. This image works as the object for the eyepiece. For normal adjustment, the position of the eyepiece is so adjusted that the image formed by the objective falls in the focal plane of the eyepiece. The final image is then formed at infinity. It is erect with respect to the first image and hence, inverted with respect to the object. The eye is least strained in this adjustment as it has to focus the parallel rays coming to it. The position of the eyepiece can also be adjusted in such a way that the final virtual image is formed at the near point. The angular magnification is increased in this case. The ray diagram in figure (19.4) refers to this case.

In effect, the eyepiece acts as a simple microscope used to view the first image. Thus, the magnification by a compound microscope is a two-step process. In the first step, the objective produces a magnified image of the given object. In the second step, the eyepiece produces an angular magnification. The overall angular magnification is the product of the two.

Magnifying power

Refer to figure (19.4). If an object of height h is seen by the naked eye, the largest image on the retina is formed when it is placed at the near point. The angle formed by the object on the eye in this situation is

$$\theta_o = \frac{h}{D} . \qquad \dots \text{(i)}$$

When a compound microscope is used, the final image subtends an angle θ' on the eyepiece (and hence on the eye) given by

$$\theta' = \frac{h'}{u_e}, \qquad \qquad \dots \text{(ii)}$$

where h' is the height of the first image and u_e is its distance from the eyepiece.

The magnifying power of the compound microscope is, therefore,

$$m = \frac{\theta'}{\theta_o} = \frac{h'}{u_e} \times \frac{D}{h} = \left(\frac{h'}{h}\right)\left(\frac{D}{u_e}\right). \qquad \dots \text{(iii)}$$

Also from figure (19.4),

$$\frac{h'}{h} = -\frac{v_o}{u_o} = \frac{v}{u}. \qquad \qquad \dots \text{(iv)}$$

Now, D/u_e is the magnifying power of the eyepiece treated as a simple microscope. Using (19.1) and (19.2), this is equal to D/f_e in normal adjustment (image at infinity) and $1 + D/f_e$ for the adjustment when the image is formed at the least distance for clear vision, i.e., at D. Thus, the magnifying power of the compound microscope is, by (iii),

$$m = \frac{v}{u}\left(\frac{D}{f_e}\right) \qquad \qquad \dots \text{(19.3)}$$

for normal adjustment and

$$m = \frac{v}{u}\left(1 + \frac{D}{f_e}\right) \qquad \dots \text{(19.4)}$$

for the adjustment when the final image is formed at the least distance for clear vision.

Using lens equation for the objective,

$$\frac{1}{v} - \frac{1}{u} = \frac{1}{f}$$

$$\text{or,} \qquad 1 - \frac{v}{u} = \frac{v}{f_o}$$

$$\text{or,} \qquad \frac{v}{u} = 1 - \frac{v}{f_o}.$$

In general, the focal length of the objective is very small so that $\frac{v}{f_o} \gg 1$. Also, the first image is close to the eyepiece so that $v \approx l$, where l is the tube-length (separation between the objective and the eyepiece).

Thus, $\qquad \dfrac{v}{u} = 1 - \dfrac{v}{f_o} \approx -\dfrac{v}{f_o} \approx -\dfrac{l}{f_o}.$

If these conditions are satisfied, the magnifying power of the compound microscope is, by (19.3) and (19.4),

$$m = -\frac{l}{f_o}\frac{D}{f_e}$$

for normal adjustment and

$$m = -\frac{l}{f_o}\left(1 + \frac{D}{f_e}\right)$$

for adjustment for the final image at the least distance for clear vision.

In an actual compound microscope each of the objective and the eyepiece consists of combination of several lenses instead of a single lens as assumed in the simplified version.

Example 19.2

A compound microscope has an objective of focal length 1 cm and an eyepiece of focal length 2·5 cm. An object has to be placed at a distance of 1·2 cm away from the objective for normal adjustment. (a) Find the angular magnification. (b) Find the length of the microscope tube.

Solution :

(a) If the first image is formed at a distance v from the objective, we have

$$\frac{1}{v} - \frac{1}{(-1·2 \text{ cm})} = \frac{1}{1 \text{ cm}}$$

or, $\qquad v = 6$ cm.

The angular magnification in normal adjustment is

$$m = \frac{v}{u}\frac{D}{f_e} = -\frac{6 \text{ cm}}{1·2 \text{ cm}}\cdot\frac{25 \text{ cm}}{2·5 \text{ cm}} = -50.$$

(b) For normal adjustment, the first image must be in the focal plane of the eyepiece.
The length of the tube is, therefore,

$$L = v + f_e = 6 \text{ cm} + 2·5 \text{ cm} = 8·5 \text{ cm}.$$

19.5 TELESCOPES

A microscope is used to view the objects placed close to it, say, within few centimeters. To look at distant objects such as a star, a planet or a distant tree, etc., we use another instrument called a *telescope*. We shall describe three types of telescopes which are in use.

(A) Astronomical Telescope

Figure (19.5) shows the construction and working of a simplified version of an astronomical telescope.

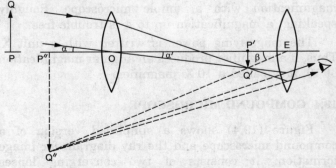

Figure 19.5

It consists of two converging lenses placed coaxially. The one facing the distant object is called the objective and has a large aperture and a large focal length. The other is called the eyepiece, as the eye is placed close to it. It has a smaller aperture and a smaller focal length. The lenses are fixed in tubes. The eyepiece tube can slide within the objective tube so that the separation between the objective and the eyepiece may be changed.

When the telescope is directed towards a distant object PQ, the objective forms a real image of the object in its focal plane. If the point P is on the principal axis, the image point P' is at the second focus of the objective. The rays coming from Q are focussed at Q'. The eyepiece forms a magnified virtual image $P''Q''$ of $P'Q'$. This image is finally seen by the eye. In normal adjustment, the position is so adjusted that the final image is formed at infinity. In such a case, the first image $P'Q'$ is formed in the first focal plane of the eyepiece. The eye is least strained to focus this final image. The image can be brought closer by pushing the eyepiece closer to the first image. Maximum angular magnification is produced when the final image is formed at the near point.

Magnifying Power

Suppose, the objective and the eyepiece have focal lengths f_o and f_e respectively and the object is situated at a large distance u_o from the objective. The object PQ in figure (19.5) subtends an angle α on the objective. Since the object is far away, the angle it would subtend on the eye, if there were no telescope, is also essentially α.

As u_o is very large, the first image $P'Q'$ is formed in the focal plane of the objective.

From the figure,

$$|\alpha| = |\alpha'| \approx |\tan\alpha'| = \frac{P'Q'}{OP'} = \frac{P'Q'}{f_o}. \qquad \dots \text{(i)}$$

The final image $P''Q''$ subtends an angle β on the eyepiece (and hence on the eye). We have from the triangle $P'Q'E$,

$$|\beta| \approx |\tan\beta| = \frac{P'Q'}{EP'}$$

or,

$$\left|\frac{\beta}{\alpha}\right| = \frac{f_o}{EP'}. \qquad \dots \text{(ii)}$$

If the telescope is set for normal adjustment so that the final image is formed at infinity, the first image $P'Q'$ must be in the focal plane of the eyepiece. Then $EP' = f_e$. Thus, equation (ii) becomes

$$\left|\frac{\beta}{\alpha}\right| = \frac{f_o}{f_e}. \qquad \dots \text{(iii)}$$

The angular magnification or the magnifying power of the telescope is defined as

$$m = \frac{\text{angle subtended by the final image on the eye}}{\text{angle subtended by the object on the unaided eye}}.$$

The angles β and α are formed on the opposite sides of the axis. Hence, their signs are opposite and β/α is negative. Thus,

$$m = \frac{\beta}{\alpha} = -\left|\frac{\beta}{\alpha}\right|.$$

Using equation (iii),

$$m = -\frac{f_o}{f_e}. \qquad \dots \text{(19.5)}$$

If the telescope is adjusted so that the final image is formed at the near point of the eye, the angular magnification is further increased. Let us apply the lens equation to the eyepiece in this case.

Here $u = -EP'$

and $v = -EP'' = -D$.

The lens equation is

$$\frac{1}{v} - \frac{1}{u} = \frac{1}{f}$$

or,

$$\frac{1}{-D} - \frac{1}{-EP'} = \frac{1}{f_e}$$

or,

$$\frac{1}{EP'} = \frac{1}{f_e} + \frac{1}{D} = \frac{f_e + D}{f_e D}. \qquad \dots \text{(iv)}$$

By (ii),

$$\left|\frac{\beta}{\alpha}\right| = \frac{f_o(f_e + D)}{f_e D}.$$

The magnification is

$$m = \frac{\beta}{\alpha} = -\left|\frac{\beta}{\alpha}\right|$$

$$= -\frac{f_o(f_e + D)}{f_e D}$$

$$= -\frac{f_o}{f_e}\left(1 + \frac{f_e}{D}\right). \qquad \dots \text{(19.6)}$$

Length of the Telescope

From figure (19.5), we see that the length of the telescope is

$$L = OP' + P'E = f_o + P'E.$$

For normal adjustment, $P'E = f_e$ so that $L = f_o + f_e$. For adjustment for near point vision, we have, by (iv) above,

$$P'E = \frac{f_e D}{f_e + D}$$

so that the length is $L = f_o + \dfrac{f_e D}{f_e + D}$.

(B) Terrestrial Telescope

In an astronomical telescope, the final image is inverted with respect to the object. This creates some practical difficulty if the telescope is used to see earthly objects.

Imagine, how would you feel if you are viewing a cricket match from the spectator's gallery using an astronomical telescope. You would clearly see the turns and breaks of the ball, but the players would look like hanging from the field and not standing on the field.

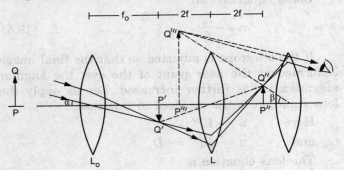

Figure 19.6

To remove this difficulty, a convex lens of focal length f is included between the objective and the eyepiece in such a way that the focal plane of the objective is a distance $2f$ away from this lens (figure 19.6). The objective forms the image $P'Q'$ of a distant object in its focal plane. The lens L forms an image $P''Q''$ which is inverted with respect to $P'Q'$. The eyepiece is adjusted in appropriate position to give the magnified view of $P''Q''$.

The role of the intermediate lens L is only to invert the image. The magnification produced by it is, therefore, -1. The magnifying power of a terrestrial telescope is, therefore, obtained from (19.5) for normal adjustment and from (19.6) for near point vision by multiplying by -1 on the right-hand side. Thus, for normal adjustment,

$$m = \frac{f_o}{f_e} \qquad \ldots (19.7)$$

and for final image at near point,

$$m = \frac{f_o}{f_e}\left(1 + \frac{f_e}{D}\right). \qquad \ldots (19.8)$$

To have an inverted image of same size, the object should be placed at a distance of $2f$ from a convex lens of focal length f. Thus, $P'P'' = 4f$ in figure (19.6) so that the length of a terrestrial telescope is $f_o + 4f + u_e$. For normal adjustment, u_e equals f_e so that the length is

$$L = f_o + 4f + f_e.$$

If the final image is formed at the near point,

$$u_e = \frac{f_e D}{f_e + D}$$

as derived for astronomical telescope. Thus,

$$L = f_o + 4f + \frac{f_e D}{f_e + D}.$$

(C) Galilean Telescope

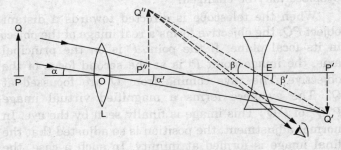

Figure 19.7

Figure (19.7) shows a simple model of Galilean telescope. A convergent lens is used as the objective and a divergent lens as the eyepiece. The objective L would form a real inverted image $P'Q'$ of a distant object in its focal plane. The eyepiece intercepts the converging rays in between. $P'Q'$ then acts as a virtual object for the eyepiece. The position of the eyepiece is so adjusted that the final image is formed at the desired position. For normal adjustment, the final image is formed at infinity producing least strain on the eyes. If the final image is formed at the least distance of clear vision, the angular magnification is maximum.

Magnifying Power

Suppose the objective and the eyepiece have focal lengths f_o and f_e respectively and the object is situated at a large distance u_o from the objective. The object PQ subtends an angle α on the objective. Since the object is far away, the angle it would subtend on an unaided eye is also essentially α.

As u_o is very large, the first image $P'Q'$ is formed in the focal plane of the objective. Thus, from figure (19.7),

$$|\alpha| = |\alpha'| \approx |\tan \alpha'| = \frac{P'Q'}{OP'} = \frac{P'Q'}{f_o}. \qquad \ldots (i)$$

The final image $P''Q''$ subtends an angle β on the eyepiece. If the eye is placed close to the eyepiece, this is also the angle formed by the final image on the eye. From the figure,

$$|\beta| = |\beta'| \approx |\tan \beta'| = \frac{P'Q'}{EP'}$$

or, $\quad\left|\dfrac{\beta}{\alpha}\right| = \dfrac{f_o}{EP'} \cdot$ ... (ii)

As β and α are formed on the same side of the axis, β and α have same sign. Thus,

$$\dfrac{\beta}{\alpha} = \left|\dfrac{\beta}{\alpha}\right|.$$

The angular magnification is, therefore,

$$m = \dfrac{\beta}{\alpha} = \left|\dfrac{\beta}{\alpha}\right| = \dfrac{f_o}{P'E} \cdot \qquad \text{... (iii)}$$

If the telescope is set for normal adjustment, the final image $P''Q''$ is formed at infinity. Then $P'E = -f_e$ and the angular magnification is

$$m = -\dfrac{f_o}{f_e} \cdot \qquad \text{... (19.9)}$$

Note that the focal length f_e is negative because the eyepiece is a diverging lens. Thus, m is positive as expected for an erect image. If the final image is formed at the near point, the magnification is increased.

The lens formula is

$$\dfrac{1}{v} - \dfrac{1}{u} = \dfrac{1}{f} \cdot$$

For the eyepiece,

$$v = -P''E = -D, \ u = P'E$$

and $\quad f = f_e$ (f_e is itself negative).

Thus,

$$\dfrac{1}{-D} - \dfrac{1}{P'E} = \dfrac{1}{f_e}$$

or, $\quad \dfrac{1}{P'E} = -\dfrac{1}{f_e} - \dfrac{1}{D}$

$$= -\dfrac{1}{f_e}\left(1 + \dfrac{f_e}{D}\right). \qquad \text{... (iv)}$$

By (iii), the angular magnification is

$$m = -\dfrac{f_o}{f_e}\left(1 + \dfrac{f_e}{D}\right).$$

Length of the Telescope

The length of a Galilean telescope is

$$L = OE = OP' - P'E$$
$$= f_o - P'E.$$

For normal adjustment, $P'E = -f_e$ and hence the length of the tube is

$$L = f_o + f_e = f_o - |f_e|.$$

For the adjustment for near point vision, by (iv),

$$P'E = \dfrac{-f_e D}{D + f_e} \ \text{and} \ L = f_o + \dfrac{f_e D}{D + f_e}$$

$$= f_o - \dfrac{|f_e|D}{D - |f_e|} \cdot$$

19.6 RESOLVING POWER OF A MICROSCOPE AND A TELESCOPE

The resolving power of a microscope is defined as the reciprocal of the distance between two objects which can be just resolved when seen through the microscope. It depends on the wavelength λ of the light, the refractive index μ of the medium between the object and the objective of the microscope, and the angle θ subtended by a radius of the objective on one of the object. It is given by

$$R = \dfrac{1}{\Delta d} = \dfrac{2\mu \sin\theta}{\lambda} \cdot$$

To increase the resolving power, the objective and the object are kept immersed in oil. This increases μ and hence R.

The resolving power of a telescope is defined as the reciprocal of the angular separation between two distant objects which are just resolved when viewed through a telescope. It is given by

$$R = \dfrac{1}{\Delta\theta} = \dfrac{a}{1\cdot22\,\lambda},$$

where a is the diameter of the objective of the telescope. That is why, the telescopes with larger objective aperture (1 m or more) are used in astronomical studies.

19.7 DEFECTS OF VISION

As described earlier, the ciliary muscles control the curvature of the lens in the eye and hence can alter the effective focal length of the system. When the muscles are fully relaxed, the focal length is maximum. When the muscles are strained, the curvature of the lens increases and the focal length decreases. For a clear vision, the image must be formed on the retina. The image-distance is, therefore, fixed for clear vision and it equals the distance of the retina from the eye-lens. It is about 2·5 cm for a grown-up person. If we apply the lens formula to eye, the magnitudes of the object-distance, the image-distance and the effective focal length satisfy

$$\dfrac{1}{v_o} + \dfrac{1}{u_o} = \dfrac{1}{f}$$

or, $\quad \dfrac{1}{u_o} = \dfrac{1}{f} - \dfrac{1}{v_o} \cdot \qquad \text{... (i)}$

Here v_o is fixed, hence by changing f, the eye can be focussed on objects placed at different values of u_o.

We see from (i) that as f increases, u_o increases and as f decreases, u_o decreases. The maximum distance one can see is given by

$$\dfrac{1}{u_{\max}} = \dfrac{1}{f_{\max}} - \dfrac{1}{v_o}, \qquad \text{... (ii)}$$

where f_{max} is the maximum focal length possible for the eye-lens.

The focal length is maximum when the ciliary muscles are fully relaxed. In a normal eye, this focal length equals the distance v_o from the lens to the retina. Thus,

$$v_o = f_{max} \quad \text{by (ii),} \quad u_{max} = \infty.$$

A person can theoretically have clear vision of objects situated at any large distance from the eye. For the closer objects, u is smaller and hence f should be smaller. The smallest distance at which a person can clearly see, is related to the minimum possible focal length f. The ciliary muscles are most strained in this position. By (ii), the closest distance for clear vision is given by

$$\frac{1}{u_{min}} = \frac{1}{f_{min}} - \frac{1}{v_o}. \qquad \text{... (iii)}$$

For an average grown-up person, u_{min} should be around 25 cm or less. This is a convenient distance at which one can hold an object in his/her hand and see. Thus, a normal eye can clearly see objects placed in the range starting from about 25 cm from the eye to a large distance, say, of the order of several kilometers. The nearest point where an eye can clearly see is called the *near point* and the farthest point up to which an eye can clearly see is called the *far point*. For a normal eye, the distance of the near point should be around 25 cm or less and the far point should be at infinity. We now describe some common defects of vision.

(A) Nearsightedness

A person suffering from this defect cannot see distant objects clearly. This is because f_{max} is less than the distance from the lens to the retina and the parallel rays coming from the distant object focus short of the retina. The ciliary muscles are fully relaxed in this case and any strain in it can only further decrease the focal length which is of no help to see distant objects.

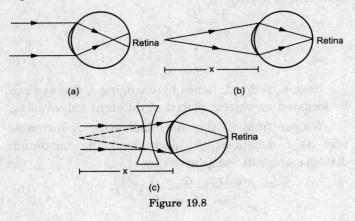

Figure 19.8

Nearsightedness is also called *myopia*. This may result because the lens is too thick or the diameter of the eyeball is larger than usual. The remedy of myopia is quite simple. The rays should be made a bit divergent before entering the eye so that they may focus a little later. Thus, a divergent lens should be given to a myopic person to enable him/her to see distant objects clearly.

Power of the Lens Needed

Suppose, a person can see an object at a maximum distance x. Thus, with fully relaxed muscles, rays coming from the distance x converge on the retina. Figure (19.8) shows the situation. As is clear from the figure, if the eye is to see a distant object clearly, the diverging lens should form the virtual image of this distant object at a distance x. Thus, the required focal length of the diverging lens is $f = -x$ and the power is

$$P = \frac{1}{f} = \frac{1}{-x}.$$

Example 19.3

A nearsighted man can clearly see objects up to a distance of 1·5 m. Calculate the power of the lens of the spectacles necessary for the remedy of this defect.

Solution : The lens should form a virtual image of a distant object at 1·5 m from the lens. Thus, it should be a divergent lens and its focal length should be −1·5 m. Hence,

$$f = -1·5 \text{ m}$$

or,

$$P = \frac{1}{f} = -\frac{1}{1·5} \text{ m}^{-1} = -0·67 \text{ D}.$$

(B) Farsightedness

A person suffering from farsightedness cannot clearly see objects close to the eye. The least distance for clear vision is appreciably larger than 25 cm and the person has to keep the object inconveniently away from the eye. Thus, reading a newspaper or viewing a small thing held in the hands is difficult for such a person.

Farsightedness is also known as *hyperopia*. Generally, it occurs when the eye-lens is too thin at the centre and/or the eyeball is shorter than normal. The ciliary muscles even in their most strained position are not able to reduce the focal length to appropriate value. The defect can also arise if the ciliary muscles become weak and are not able to strain enough to reduce the focal length to appropriate value. When farsightedness develops due to this reason, it is known as *presbyopia*.

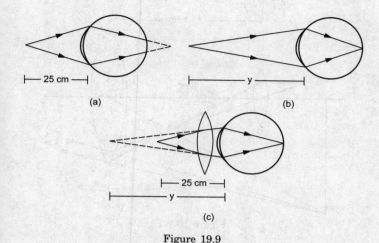

Figure 19.9

Figure (19.9) shows the situation and the remedy for farsightedness. The rays starting from the normal near point 25 cm would focus behind the retina. They should be made a bit less divergent before sending them to the eye so that they may focus on the retina. This can be achieved by putting a converging lens in front of the eye.

Suppose, the eye can clearly see an object at a minimum distance y. If the eye is to see clearly an object at 25 cm, the converging lens should form an image of this object at a distance y (figure 19.9c).

Here $u = -25$ cm and $v = -y$.

Using the lens formula

$$\frac{1}{v} - \frac{1}{u} = \frac{1}{f},$$

we get

$$\frac{1}{-y} - \frac{1}{-25 \text{ cm}} = \frac{1}{f}$$

or,

$$P = \frac{1}{f} = \frac{1}{25 \text{ cm}} - \frac{1}{y}.$$

(C) Astigmatism

Another kind of defect arises in the eye when the eye-lens develops different curvatures along different planes. Such a person cannot see all the directions equally well. A particular direction in the plane perpendicular to the line of sight is most visible. The direction perpendicular to this is least visible. Here is a 'do it yourself' test for astigmatism. Figure (19.10) shows four lines passing through a point. The lines are assumed to be drawn with equal intensity (you can draw such lines on a paper with equal intensity and do the test). If you can see all the lines equally distinct and intense, you are not astigmatic. If a particular line say (2)-(2) appears to be most intense and the perpendicular line (4)-(4) appears least intense, you are most likely astigmatic. If it is so, rotate the book through a right angle so that (2)-(2) takes the place of (4)-(4) and vice versa. If you are really astigmatic, you will find that now (4)-(4) appears most intense and (2)-(2) appears least intense.

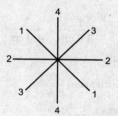

Figure 19.10

The remedy to astigmatism is also painless. Glasses with different curvatures in different planes are used to compensate for the deshaping of the eye-lens. Opticians call them cylindrical glasses.

A person may develop any of the above defects or a combination of more than one. Quite common in old age is the combination of nearsightedness and farsightedness. Such a person may need a converging glass for reading purpose and a diverging glass for seeing at a distance. Such persons either keep two sets of spectacles or a spectacle with upper portion divergent and lower portion convergent (bifocal).

Worked Out Examples

1. *An object is seen through a simple microscope of focal length 12 cm. Find the angular magnification produced if the image is formed at the near point of the eye which is 25 cm away from it.*

Solution : The angular magnification produced by a simple microscope when the image is formed at the near point of the eye is given by

$$m = 1 + \frac{D}{f}.$$

Here $f = 12$ cm, $D = 25$ cm. Hence,

$$m = 1 + \frac{25}{12} = 3 \cdot 08.$$

2. *A 10 D lens is used as a magnifier. Where should the object be placed to obtain maximum angular magnification for a normal eye (near point = 25 cm)?*

Solution : Maximum angular magnification is achieved when the final image is formed at the near point. Thus, $v = -25$ cm. The focal length is $f = \frac{1}{10}$ m = 10 cm.

We have,

$$\frac{1}{v} - \frac{1}{u} = \frac{1}{f}$$

or,

$$-\frac{1}{25 \text{ cm}} - \frac{1}{u} = \frac{1}{10 \text{ cm}}$$

or,

$$\frac{1}{u} = -\frac{1}{25 \text{ cm}} - \frac{1}{10 \text{ cm}}$$

or,

$$u = -\frac{50}{7} \text{ cm} = -7.1 \text{ cm}.$$

3. *A small object is placed at a distance of 3·6 cm from a magnifier of focal length 4·0 cm. (a) Find the position of the image. (b) Find the linear magnification. (c) Find the angular magnification.*

Solution :

(a) Using $\dfrac{1}{v} - \dfrac{1}{u} = \dfrac{1}{f}$,

$$\frac{1}{v} = \frac{1}{u} + \frac{1}{f} = \frac{1}{-3.6 \text{ cm}} + \frac{1}{4.0 \text{ cm}}.$$

or, $v = -36$ cm.

(b) Linear magnification $= \dfrac{v}{u}$

$$= \frac{-36 \text{ cm}}{-3.6 \text{ cm}} = 10.$$

(c) If the object is placed at a distance u_o from the lens, the angle subtended by the object on the lens is $\beta = \dfrac{h}{u_o}$ where h is the height of the object. The maximum angle subtended on the unaided eye is $\alpha = \dfrac{h}{D}$.

Thus, the angular magnification is

$$m = \frac{\beta}{\alpha} = \frac{D}{u_o} = \frac{25 \text{ cm}}{3.6 \text{ cm}} = 7.0.$$

4. *A compound microscope consists of an objective of focal length 1·0 cm and an eyepiece of focal length 5·0 cm separated by 12·2 cm. (a) At what distance from the objective should an object be placed to focus it properly so that the final image is formed at the least distance of clear vision (25 cm)? (b) Calculate the angular magnification in this case.*

Solution :

(a) For the eyepiece, $v_e = -25$ cm and $f_e = +5$ cm.

Using $\dfrac{1}{v_e} - \dfrac{1}{u_e} = \dfrac{1}{f_e}$,

$$\frac{1}{u_e} = \frac{1}{v_e} - \frac{1}{f_e}$$

$$= -\frac{1}{25 \text{ cm}} - \frac{1}{5 \text{ cm}}$$

or, $u_e = -\dfrac{25}{6}$ cm $= -4.17$ cm ≈ -4.2 cm.

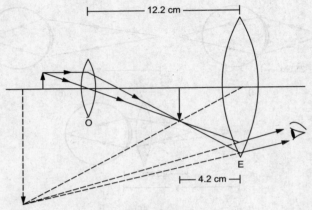

Figure 19-W1

As the objective is 12·2 cm away from the eyepiece, the image formed by the objective is $12.2 \text{ cm} - 4.2 \text{ cm} = 8.0 \text{ cm}$ away from it. For the objective,

$$v = +8.0 \text{ cm}, \quad f_o = +1.0 \text{ cm}.$$

Using

$$\frac{1}{v} - \frac{1}{u} = \frac{1}{f_o},$$

$$\frac{1}{u} = \frac{1}{v} - \frac{1}{f_o}$$

$$= \frac{1}{8.0 \text{ cm}} - \frac{1}{1.0 \text{ cm}}$$

or, $u = -\dfrac{8.0}{7.0}$ cm $= -1.1$ cm.

(b) The angular magnification is

$$m = \frac{v}{u}\left(1 + \frac{D}{f_e}\right)$$

$$= \frac{+8.0 \text{ cm}}{-1.1 \text{ cm}}\left(1 + \frac{25 \text{ cm}}{5 \text{ cm}}\right) \approx -44.$$

5. *The separation L between the objective ($f = 0.5$ cm) and the eyepiece ($f = 5$ cm) of a compound microscope is 7 cm. Where should a small object be placed so that the eye is least strained to see the image? Find the angular magnification produced by the microscope.*

Solution : The eye is least strained if the final image is formed at infinity. In such a case, the image formed by the objective should fall at the focus of the eyepiece. As $f_e = 5$ cm and $L = 7$ cm, this first image should be formed at $7 \text{ cm} - 5 \text{ cm} = 2 \text{ cm}$ from the objective. Thus, $v = +2$ cm. Also, $f_o = 0.5$ cm. For the objective, using

$$\frac{1}{v} - \frac{1}{u} = \frac{1}{f_o},$$

$$\frac{1}{u} = \frac{1}{v} - \frac{1}{f_o}$$

$$= \frac{1}{2 \text{ cm}} - \frac{1}{0.5 \text{ cm}}$$

or, $u = -\frac{2}{3}$ cm.

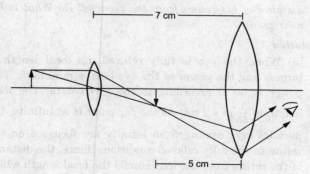

Figure 19-W2

The angular magnification in this case is

$$m = \frac{v}{u}\frac{D}{f_e}$$

$$= \frac{2 \text{ cm}}{-(2/3) \text{ cm}}\frac{25 \text{ cm}}{5 \text{ cm}} = -15.$$

6. *An astronomical telescope has an objective of focal length 200 cm and an eyepiece of focal length 4·0 cm. The telescope is focussed to see an object 10 km from the objective. The final image is formed at infinity. Find the length of the tube and the angular magnification produced by the telescope.*

Solution : As the object distance 10 km is much larger than the focal length 200 cm, the first image is formed almost at the focus of the objective. It is thus 200 cm from the objective. This image acts as the object for the eyepiece. To get the final image at infinity, this first image should be at the first focus of the eyepiece. The length of the tube is, therefore, 200 cm + 4 cm = 204 cm. The angular magnification in this case

$$m = -\frac{f_o}{f_e} = -\frac{200}{4} = -50.$$

7. *A Galilean telescope is constructed by an objective of focal length 50 cm and an eyepiece of focal length 5·0 cm. (a) Find the tube length and magnifying power when it is used to see an object at a large distance in normal adjustment. (b) If the telescope is to focus an object 2·0 m away from the objective, what should be the tube length and angular magnification, the image again forming at infinity?*

Solution :

$$f_o = 50 \text{ cm}, \quad f_e = -5 \text{ cm}.$$

(a) $L = f_o - |f_e| = (50 - 5)$ cm = 45 cm

and $m = -\frac{f_o}{f_e} = \frac{50}{5} = 10.$

(b) Using the equation $\frac{1}{v} - \frac{1}{u} = \frac{1}{f}$ for the objective,

$$\frac{1}{v} = \frac{1}{f_o} + \frac{1}{u}$$

$$= \frac{1}{50 \text{ cm}} + \frac{1}{-200 \text{ cm}}$$

or, $v = 66·67$ cm.

The tube length $L = v - |f_e| = (66·67 - 5)$ cm

or, $L = 61·67$ cm.

To calculate the angular magnification, we assume that the object remains at large distance from the eye. In this case, the angular magnification

$$m = \frac{v}{f_e} = \frac{66·67}{5} = 13·33.$$

v is the distance of the first image from the objective which is substituted for f_o.

8. *The image of the moon is focussed by a converging lens of focal length 50 cm on a plane screen. The image is seen by an unaided eye from a distance of 25 cm. Find the angular magnification achieved due to the converging lens.*

Solution :

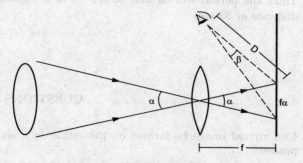

Figure 19-W3

Suppose the moon subtends an angle α on the lens. This will also be the angle subtended by the moon on the eye if the moon is directly viewed. The image is formed in the focal plane. The linear size of the image $\approx f\alpha = (50 \text{ cm})\alpha$.

If this image is seen from a distance of 25 cm, the angle formed by the image on the eye

$$|\beta| \approx \frac{(50 \text{ cm})|\alpha|}{25 \text{ cm}} = 2|\alpha|.$$

The angular magnification is

$$\frac{\beta}{\alpha} = -\left|\frac{\beta}{\alpha}\right| = -2.$$

9. *The near and far points of a person are at 40 cm and 250 cm respectively. Find the power of the lens he/she should use while reading at 25 cm. With this lens on the eye, what maximum distance is clearly visible?*

Solution : If an object is placed at 25 cm from the correcting lens, it should produce the virtual image at 40 cm. Thus, $u = -25$ cm, $v = -40$ cm.

$$\frac{1}{f} = \frac{1}{v} - \frac{1}{u}$$

$$= -\frac{1}{40 \text{ cm}} + \frac{1}{25 \text{ cm}}$$

or, $\qquad f = \frac{200}{3}$ cm $= +\frac{2}{3}$ m

or, $\qquad P = \frac{1}{f} = +1.5$ D.

The unaided eye can see a maximum distance of 250 cm. Suppose the maximum distance for clear vision is d when the lens is used. Then the object at a distance d is imaged by the lens at 250 cm. We have,

$$\frac{1}{v} - \frac{1}{u} = \frac{1}{f},$$

or, $\qquad -\frac{1}{250 \text{ cm}} - \frac{1}{d} = \frac{3}{200 \text{ cm}}$

or, $\qquad d = -53$ cm.

Thus, the person will be able to see up to a maximum distance of 53 cm.

---

10. *A young boy can adjust the power of his eye-lens between 50 D and 60 D. His far point is infinity. (a) What is the distance of his retina from the eye-lens? (b) What is his near point?*

Solution :

(a) When the eye is fully relaxed, its focal length is largest and the power of the eye-lens is minimum. This power is 50 D according to the given data. The focal length is $\frac{1}{50}$ m $= 2$ cm. As the far point is at infinity, the parallel rays coming from infinity are focussed on the retina in the fully relaxed condition. Hence, the distance of the retina from the lens equals the focal length which is 2 cm.

(b) When the eye is focussed at the near point, the power is maximum which is 60 D. The focal length in this case is $f = \frac{1}{60}$ m $= \frac{5}{3}$ cm. The image is formed on the retina and thus $v = 2$ cm. We have,

$$\frac{1}{v} - \frac{1}{u} = \frac{1}{f}$$

or, $\qquad \frac{1}{u} = \frac{1}{v} - \frac{1}{f} = \frac{1}{2 \text{ cm}} - \frac{3}{5 \text{ cm}}$

or, $\qquad u = -10$ cm.

The near point is at 10 cm.

□

QUESTIONS FOR SHORT ANSWER

1. Can virtual image be formed on the retina in a seeing process?

2. Can the image formed by a simple microscope be projected on a screen without using any additional lens or mirror?

3. The angular magnification of a system is less than one. Does it mean that the image formed is inverted?

4. A simple microscope using a single lens often shows coloured image of a white source. Why?

5. A magnifying glass is a converging lens placed close to the eye. A farsighted person uses spectacles having converging lenses. Compare the functions of a converging lens used as a magnifying glass and as spectacles.

6. A person is viewing an extended object. If a converging lens is placed in front of his eyes, will he feel that the size has increased?

7. The magnifying power of a converging lens used as a simple microscope is $\left(1 + \frac{D}{f}\right)$. A compound microscope is a combination of two such converging lenses. Why don't we have magnifying power $\left(1 + \frac{D}{f_o}\right)\left(1 + \frac{D}{f_e}\right)$? In other

words, why can the objective not be treated as a simple microscope but the eyepiece can?

8. By mistake, an eye surgeon puts a concave lens in place of the lens in the eye after a cataract operation. Will the patient be able to see clearly any object placed at any distance?

9. The magnifying power of a simple microscope is given by $1 + \frac{D}{f}$, where D is the least distance for clear vision. For farsighted persons, D is greater than the usual. Does it mean that the magnifying power of a simple microscope is greater for a farsighted person as compared to a normal person? Does it mean that a farsighted person can see an insect more clearly under a microscope than a normal person?

10. Why are the magnification properties of microscopes and telescopes defined in terms of the ratio of angles and not in terms of the ratio of sizes of objects and images?

11. An object is placed at a distance of 30 cm from a converging lens of focal length 15 cm. A normal eye (near point 25 cm, far point infinity) is placed close to the lens on the other side. (a) Can the eye see the object clearly? (b) What should be the minimum separation between the lens and the eye so that the eye can clearly see the

object? (c) Can a diverging lens, placed in contact with the converging lens, help in seeing the object clearly when the eye is close to the lens?

12. A compound microscope forms an inverted image of an object. In which of the following cases it is likely to

create difficulties? (a) Looking at small germs. (b) Looking at circular spots. (c) Looking at a vertical tube containing some water.

OBJECTIVE I

1. The size of an object as perceived by an eye depends primarily on
   (a) actual size of the object
   (b) distance of the object from the eye
   (c) aperture of the pupil
   (d) size of the image formed on the retina.

2. The muscles of a normal eye are least strained when the eye is focussed on an object
   (a) far away from the eye
   (b) very close to the eye
   (c) at about 25 cm from the eye
   (d) at about 1 m from the eye.

3. A normal eye is not able to see objects closer than 25 cm because
   (a) the focal length of the eye is 25 cm
   (b) the distance of the retina from the eye-lens is 25 cm
   (c) the eye is not able to decrease the distance between the eye-lens and the retina beyond a limit
   (d) the eye is not able to decrease the focal length beyond a limit.

4. When objects at different distances are seen by the eye, which of the following remain constant?
   (a) The focal length of the eye-lens.
   (b) The object-distance from the eye-lens.
   (c) The radii of curvature of the eye-lens.
   (d) The image-distance from the eye-lens.

5. A person A can clearly see objects between 25 cm and 200 cm. Which of the following may represent the range of clear vision for a person B having muscles stronger

than A, but all other parameters of eye identical to that of A?
   (a) 25 cm to 200 cm   (b) 18 cm to 200 cm
   (c) 25 cm to 300 cm   (d) 18 cm to 300 cm

6. The focal length of a normal eye-lens is about
   (a) 1 mm   (b) 2 cm   (c) 25 cm   (d) 1 m.

7. The distance of the eye-lens from the retina is x. For a normal eye, the maximum focal length of the eye-lens
   (a) $= x$ (b) $< x$ (c) $> x$ (d) $= 2x$.

8. A man wearing glasses of focal length $+1$ m cannot clearly see beyond 1 m
   (a) if he is farsighted   (b) if he is nearsighted
   (c) if his vision is normal   (d) in each of these cases

9. An object is placed at a distance u from a simple microscope of focal length f. The angular magnification obtained depends
   (a) on f but not on u (b) on u but not on f
   (c) on f as well as u (d) neither on f nor on u.

10. To increase the angular magnification of a simple microscope, one should increase
    (a) the focal length of the lens
    (b) the power of the lens
    (c) the aperture of the lens
    (d) the object size.

11. A man is looking at a small object placed at his near point. Without altering the position of his eye or the object, he puts a simple microscope of magnifying power 5 X before his eyes. The angular magnification achieved is
    (a) 5   (b) 2·5   (c) 1   (d) 0·2.

OBJECTIVE II

1. When we see an object, the image formed on the retina is
   (a) real   (b) virtual   (c) erect   (d) inverted.

2. In which of the following the final image is erect?
   (a) Simple microscope   (b) Compound microscope
   (c) Astronomical telescope   (d) Galilean telescope

3. The maximum focal length of the eye-lens of a person is greater than its distance from the retina. The eye is
   (a) always strained in looking at an object
   (b) strained for objects at large distances only
   (c) strained for objects at short distances only
   (d) unstrained for all distances.

4. Mark the correct options.
   (a) If the far point goes ahead, the power of the

divergent lens should be reduced.
   (b) If the near point goes ahead, the power of the convergent lens should be reduced.
   (c) If the far point is 1 m away from the eye, divergent lens should be used.
   (d) If the near point is 1 m away from the eye, divergent lens should be used.

5. The focal length of the objective of a compound microscope is f_o and its distance from the eyepiece is L. The object is placed at a distance u from the objective. For proper working of the instrument,
   (a) $L < u$ (b) $L > u$ (c) $f_o < L < 2f_o$ (d) $L > 2f_o$.

EXERCISES

1. A person looks at different trees in an open space with the following details. Arrange the trees in decreasing order of their apparent sizes.

Tree	Height(m)	Distance from the eye(m)
A	2·0	50
B	2·5	80
C	1·8	70
D	2·8	100

2. An object is to be seen through a simple microscope of focal length 12 cm. Where should the object be placed so as to produce maximum angular magnification? The least distance for clear vision is 25 cm.

3. A simple microscope has a magnifying power of 3·0 when the image is formed at the near point (25 cm) of a normal eye. (a) What is its focal length? (b) What will be its magnifying power if the image is formed at infinity?

4. A child has near point at 10 cm. What is the maximum angular magnification the child can have with a convex lens of focal length 10 cm?

5. A simple microscope is rated 5 X for a normal relaxed eye. What will be its magnifying power for a relaxed farsighted eye whose near point is 40 cm?

6. Find the maximum magnifying power of a compound microscope having a 25 diopter lens as the objective, a 5 diopter lens as the eyepiece and the separation 30 cm between the two lenses. The least distance for clear vision is 25 cm.

7. The separation between the objective and the eyepiece of a compound microscope can be adjusted between 9·8 cm to 11·8 cm. If the focal lengths of the objective and the eyepiece are 1·0 cm and 6 cm respectively, find the range of the magnifying power if the image is always needed at 24 cm from the eye.

8. An eye can distinguish between two points of an object if they are separated by more than 0·22 mm when the object is placed at 25 cm from the eye. The object is now seen by a compound microscope having a 20 D objective and 10 D eyepiece separated by a distance of 20 cm. The final image is formed at 25 cm from the eye. What is the minimum separation between two points of the object which can now be distinguished?

9. A compound microscope has a magnifying power of 100 when the image is formed at infinity. The objective has a focal length of 0·5 cm and the tube length is 6·5 cm. Find the focal length of the eyepiece.

10. A compound microscope consists of an objective of focal length 1 cm and an eyepiece of focal length 5 cm. An object is placed at a distance of 0·5 cm from the objective. What should be the separation between the lenses so that the microscope projects an inverted real image of the object on a screen 30 cm behind the eyepiece?

11. An optical instrument used for angular magnification has a 25 D objective and a 20 D eyepiece. The tube length is 25 cm when the eye is least strained.
(a) Whether it is a microscope or a telescope? (b) What is the angular magnification produced?

12. An astronomical telescope is to be designed to have a magnifying power of 50 in normal adjustment. If the length of the tube is 102 cm, find the powers of the objective and the eyepiece.

13. The eyepiece of an astronomical telescope has a focal length of 10 cm. The telescope is focussed for normal vision of distant objects when the tube length is 1·0 m. Find the focal length of the objective and the magnifying power of the telescope.

14. A Galilean telescope is 27 cm long when focussed to form an image at infinity. If the objective has a focal length of 30 cm, what is the focal length of the eyepiece?

15. A farsighted person cannot see objects placed closer to 50 cm. Find the power of the lens needed to see the objects at 20 cm.

16. A nearsighted person cannot clearly see beyond 200 cm. Find the power of the lens needed to see objects at large distances.

17. A person wears glasses of power – 2·5 D. Is the person farsighted or nearsighted? What is the far point of the person without the glasses?

18. A professor reads a greeting card received on his 50th birthday with + 2·5 D glasses keeping the card 25 cm away. Ten years later, he reads his farewell letter with the same glasses but he has to keep the letter 50 cm away. What power of lens should he now use?

19. A normal eye has retina 2 cm behind the eye-lens. What is the power of the eye-lens when the eye is (a) fully relaxed, (b) most strained?

20. The near point and the far point of a child are at 10 cm and 100 cm. If the retina is 2·0 cm behind the eye-lens, what is the range of the power of the eye-lens?

21. A nearsighted person cannot see beyond 25 cm. Assuming that the separation of the glass from the eye is 1 cm, find the power of lens needed to see distant objects.

22. A person has near point at 100 cm. What power of lens is needed to read at 20 cm if he/she uses (a) contact lens, (b) spectacles having glasses 2·0 cm separated from the eyes?

23. A lady uses + 1·5 D glasses to have normal vision from 25 cm onwards. She uses a 20 D lens as a simple microscope to see an object. Find the maximum magnifying power if she uses the microscope (a) together with her glass (b) without the glass. Do the answers suggest that an object can be more clearly seen through a microscope without using the correcting glasses?

24. A lady cannot see objects closer than 40 cm from the left eye and closer than 100 cm from the right eye. While on a mountaineering trip, she is lost from her team. She tries to make an astronomical telescope from her reading glasses to look for her teammates. (a) Which glass should she use as the eyepiece? (b) What magnification can she get with relaxed eye?

ANSWERS

OBJECTIVE I

1. (d)   2. (a)   3. (d)   4. (d)   5. (b)   6. (b)
7. (a)   8. (d)   9. (c)   10. (b)   11. (c)

OBJECTIVE II

1. (a), (d)   2. (a), (d)   3. (a)
4. (a), (c)   5. (b), (d)

EXERCISES

1. *A, B, D, C*
2. 8·1 cm from the lens
3. (a) 12·5 cm (b) 2·0
4. 2
5. 8 X
6. 8·4
7. 20 to 30
8. 0·04 mm
9. 2 cm
10. 5 cm
11. (a) microscope (b) 20
12. 1 D, 50 D
13. 90 cm, 9
14. 3 cm
15. 3 D
16. − 0·5 D
17. nearsighted, 40 cm
18. + 4·5 D
19. (a) 50 D (b) 54 D
20. +60 D to +51 D
21. − 4·2 D
22. (a) +4 D (b) +4·53 D
23. (a) 6 (b) 9
24. (a) right lens (b) 2

CHAPTER 20

DISPERSION AND SPECTRA

20.1 DISPERSION

As mentioned earlier, the refractive index of a material depends slightly on the wavelength of light. The relation between the two may be approximately described by the equation

$$\mu = \mu_0 + \frac{A}{\lambda^2},$$

where A is a small positive constant known as Cauchy's constant. The refractive index decreases as the wavelength increases. For visible light, it is maximum for the violet end and minimum for the red end. Figure (20.1) shows the variation of refractive index with wavelength for some transparent materials.

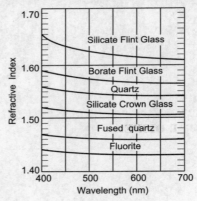

Figure 20.1

Because of the difference in refractive indices, light of different colours bend through different angles on refraction. If white light passes through a glass prism (figure 20.2), the violet rays deviate the most and the

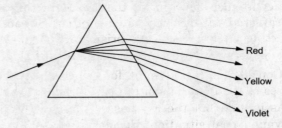

Figure 20.2

red rays deviate the least. Thus, white light is separated into its various component colours. This phenomenon of separation of different constituent colours of light while passing through a transparent medium is known as *dispersion of light*.

20.2 DISPERSIVE POWER

Consider a prism of a transparent material. When a beam of white light is passed through the prism, light of different wavelengths are deviated by different amounts. The overall deviation of the light beam is conventionally measured by the deviation of yellow light, as the wavelength of yellow light is roughly the average wavelength of the visible region. In figure (20.3), this deviation is shown by the symbol δ_y. It is clear that if δ_r and δ_v are the deviations for red and violet components, the angular divergence of the transmitted beam is $\delta_v - \delta_r$. This divergence is called *angular dispersion*.

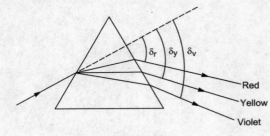

Figure 20.3

The mean deviation depends on the average refractive index μ and the angular dispersion depends on the difference $\mu_v - \mu_r$. It may be seen from figure (20.1) that if the average value of μ is small (fluorite), $\mu_v - \mu_r$ is also small and if the average value of μ is large (silicate flint glass), $\mu_v - \mu_r$ is also large. Thus, larger the mean deviation, larger will be the angular dispersion.

The *dispersive power* of a material is defined as the ratio of angular dispersion to the average deviation when a light beam is transmitted through a thin prism placed in a position so that the mean ray (ray having the mean wavelength) passes symmetrically through it.

When a light ray passes symmetrically through a prism of refracting angle A, it suffers minimum deviation δ given by

$$\mu = \frac{\sin\dfrac{A+\delta}{2}}{\sin\dfrac{A}{2}}.$$

If the refracting angle A is small, the deviation δ is also small. Then,

$$\mu \approx \frac{\dfrac{A+\delta}{2}}{\dfrac{A}{2}} = 1 + \frac{\delta}{A}$$

or, $\delta = (\mu - 1)A$.

This equation is also valid if the light ray does not pass symmetrically through the prism, but the angle A and the angle of incidence i are small.

Suppose, a beam of white light goes through such a prism. The deviation of violet, yellow and the red light are

$$\delta_v = (\mu_v - 1) A$$
$$\delta_y = (\mu_y - 1) A$$
and $$\delta_r = (\mu_r - 1) A.$$

The angular dispersion is $\delta_v - \delta_r = (\mu_v - \mu_r)A$. The average deviation is $\delta_y = (\mu_y - 1)A$. Thus, the dispersive power of the medium is

$$\omega = \frac{\mu_v - \mu_r}{\mu_y - 1}. \qquad \dots (20.1)$$

This equation itself may be taken as the definition of dispersive power.

Refractive index is a continuous function of wavelength. Usually three wavelengths are selected, one from violet, one from yellow and one from red region and dispersive power is defined as (20.1) for these wavelengths.

Example 20.1

Find the dispersive power of flint glass. The refractive indices of flint glass for red, yellow and violet light are 1·613, 1·620 and 1·632 respectively.

Solution : The dispersive power is $\omega = \dfrac{\mu_v - \mu_r}{\mu_y - 1}$

$$= \frac{1\cdot632 - 1\cdot613}{1\cdot620 - 1} = 0.0306.$$

Example 20.2

The focal lengths of a thin lens for red and violet light are 90·0 cm and 86·4 cm respectively. Find the dispersive

power of the material of the lens. Make appropriate assumptions.

Solution : We have

$$\frac{1}{f} = (\mu - 1)\left(\frac{1}{R_1} - \frac{1}{R_2}\right)$$

or, $$\mu - 1 = \frac{1}{f} \cdot \frac{1}{\dfrac{1}{R_1} - \dfrac{1}{R_2}} = \frac{K}{f}.$$

Thus, $$\mu_v - 1 = \frac{K}{f_v}$$

and, $$\mu_r - 1 = \frac{K}{f_r}$$

so that $$\mu_v - \mu_r = K\left(\frac{1}{f_v} - \frac{1}{f_r}\right)$$

$$= K\cdot\left[\frac{1}{86\cdot4 \text{ cm}} - \frac{1}{90 \text{ cm}}\right] = K \times 4\cdot6 \times 10^{-4}\text{ cm}^{-1}.$$

Also, we can assume that

$$\mu_y - 1 = \frac{\mu_v + \mu_r}{2} - 1 = \frac{\mu_v - 1}{2} + \frac{\mu_r - 1}{2}$$

$$= \frac{K}{2}\left(\frac{1}{f_v} + \frac{1}{f_r}\right)$$

$$= \frac{K}{2}\left[\frac{1}{86\cdot4 \text{ cm}} + \frac{1}{90 \text{ cm}}\right] = K \times 1\cdot1 \times 10^{-2}\text{ cm}^{-1}.$$

Thus, the dispersive power of the material of the lens is

$$\omega = \frac{\mu_v - \mu_r}{\mu_y - 1} = \frac{4\cdot6 \times 10^{-4}}{1\cdot1 \times 10^{-2}} = 0.042.$$

20.3 DISPERSION WITHOUT AVERAGE DEVIATION AND AVERAGE DEVIATION WITHOUT DISPERSION

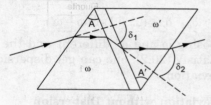

Figure 20.4

Figure (20.4) shows two thin prisms placed in contact in such a way that the two refracting angles are reversed with respect to each other. Suppose, the refracting angles of the two prisms are A and A' and their dispersive powers are ω and ω' respectively.

Consider a ray of light for which the refractive indices of the materials of the two prisms are μ and μ'. Assuming that the ray passes through the prisms in symmetrical situation, the deviations produced by the two prisms are

$$\delta_1 = (\mu - 1) A$$

and $$\delta_2 = (\mu' - 1) A'.$$

As the two deviations are opposite to each other, the net deviation is

$$\delta = \delta_1 - \delta_2$$
$$= (\mu - 1)A - (\mu' - 1)A'. \qquad \dots \text{ (i)}$$

If white light passes through the combination, the net deviation of the violet ray is

$$\delta_v = (\mu_v - 1)A - (\mu'_v - 1)A'$$

and that of the red ray is

$$\delta_r = (\mu_r - 1)A - (\mu'_r - 1)A'.$$

The angular dispersion produced by the combination is

$$\delta_v - \delta_r = (\mu_v - \mu_r)A - (\mu'_v - \mu'_r)A'. \qquad \dots \text{ (ii)}$$

The dispersive powers are given by

$$\omega = \frac{\mu_v - \mu_r}{\mu_y - 1}$$

and $$\omega' = \frac{\mu'_v - \mu'_r}{\mu'_y - 1}.$$

Thus, by (ii), the net angular dispersion is

$$\delta_v - \delta_r = (\mu_y - 1)\omega A - (\mu'_y - 1)\omega'A'. \qquad \dots \text{ (iii)}$$

The net deviation of the yellow ray, i.e., the average deviation, is, by (i),

$$\delta_y = (\mu_y - 1)A - (\mu'_y - 1)A'. \qquad \dots \text{ (iv)}$$

Dispersion without Average Deviation

If the combination is not to produce a net average deviation in the beam, δ_y should be 0. By (iv), the required condition is

$$(\mu_y - 1)A = (\mu'_y - 1)A' \qquad \dots \text{ (20.2)}$$

Using this in (iii), the net angular dispersion produced is

$$\delta_v - \delta_r = (\mu_y - 1)A (\omega - \omega'). \qquad \dots \text{ (20.3)}$$

By choosing ω and ω' different and the refracting angles to satisfy (20.2), one can get dispersion without average deviation.

Average Deviation without Dispersion

If the combination is not to produce a net dispersion, $\delta_v - \delta_r = 0$. By (iii),

$$(\mu_y - 1)\omega A = (\mu'_y - 1)\omega'A'. \qquad \dots \text{ (20.4)}$$

By (ii), this condition may also be written as

$$(\mu_v - \mu_r)A = (\mu'_v - \mu'_r)A'. \qquad \dots \text{ (20.5)}$$

The net average deviation produced is, by (i),

$$\delta = (\mu_y - 1)A - (\mu'_y - 1)A'$$
$$= (\mu_y - 1)A \left[1 - \frac{\mu'_y - 1}{\mu_y - 1} \frac{A'}{A} \right].$$

By (20.4),

$$\frac{(\mu'_y - 1)A'}{(\mu_y - 1)A} = \frac{\omega}{\omega'}$$

so that the net average deviation produced by the combination is

$$\delta = (\mu_y - 1) A \left(1 - \frac{\omega}{\omega'} \right). \qquad \dots \text{ (20.6)}$$

20.4 SPECTRUM

When light coming from a source is dispersed by a prism or by any other dispersing element, light of different wavelengths are deviated through different angles and get separated. Such a dispersed light may be received on a screen, on a photographic plate or it may be viewed directly by the eye. A collection of dispersed light giving its wavelength composition is called a *spectrum*. As a very simple demonstration, let white light fall on a prism and collect the transmitted light on a white wall or a white paper. A spectrum consisting of different colours from red to violet is obtained.

Pure and Impure Spectrum

The spectrum of visible light shows different colours. In an ideal situation, light of one wavelength should occupy one particular spatial position in the spectrum. In such a case, no two wavelengths overlap in the dispersed beam. Each colour then gives its sharp impression. Such a spectrum is called a *pure spectrum*. To get a pure spectrum,

(a) the light beam incident on the dispersing element (prism, grating, etc.) should be parallel, and

(b) the dispersed light should be focussed in such a way that all the rays of a particular wavelength are collected at one place.

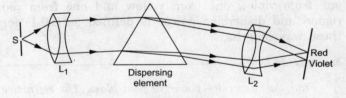

Figure 20.5

These conditions may be achieved to a good approximation using the arrangement shown in figure (20.5). A narrow slit S allows a thin pencil of light to be analyzed. The slit is placed in the focal plane of an achromatic lens combination L_1. The light is dispersed by the dispersing element such as a prism or a grating. The emergent rays for a particular wavelength are all parallel. Another achromatic lens combination L_2 is used to focus the emergent rays in its focal plane. Rays of one wavelength being parallel to each other are finally focussed at one place.

If the slit is wide, different points of the slit produce separate spectra which overlap each other. The colour impression gets diffused due to the overlap. Such a spectrum is called an *impure spectrum*.

20.5 KINDS OF SPECTRA

A. Emission Spectra

Light is emitted by an object when it is suitably excited by heating or by passing an electric discharge. When a light beam emitted by such a source is dispersed to get the spectrum, it is called an *emission spectrum*. An emission spectrum carries information about the source material. An emission spectrum can be of three types :

(a) Continuous Spectrum

Quite often, a source emits light which has continuously varying wavelengths in it. An electric bulb, a candle or a red hot iron piece emits light of this type. When such a light is dispersed, a bright spectrum continuously distributed on a dark background is obtained. The colours gradually change and there are no sharp boundaries in between. Such a spectrum is known as a *continuous emission spectrum*.

(b) Line Spectrum

All objects are made of atoms and molecules. The atoms and molecules can have certain fixed energies. An atom or a molecule having the lowest possible energy is said to be in its ground state, otherwise, in an excited state. An atom or molecule, in an excited state, can emit light to lower its energy. Light emitted in such a process has certain fixed wavelengths. The light emitted by one kind of atoms generally have widely separated wavelength components (figure 20.6a). When such a light is dispersed, we get certain sharp bright lines on a dark background. Such a spectrum is called *line emission spectrum*. It carries information about the atoms of the source. For example, when electric discharge is passed through sodium vapour, the vapour emits light of the wavelengths 589·0 nm and 589·6 nm. When dispersed by a high resolution grating, one obtains two bright yellow lines on a dark background.

(c) Band Spectrum

The molecular energy levels are generally grouped into several bunches, each bunch widely separated from the other, and the levels in a bunch being close to each other. Thus, the wavelengths emitted by such molecules are also grouped, each group being well-

separated from the other. The wavelengths in a group are close to one another and appear as continuous. The spectrum looks like separate bands of varying colours. Such a spectrum is called a *band emission spectrum*. Figure (20.6b) shows schematically the production and appearance of band spectra.

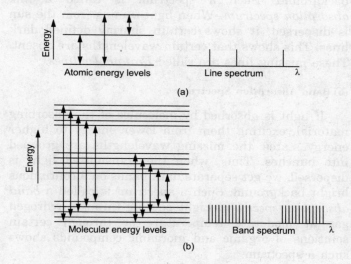

Figure 20.6

B. Absorption Spectrum

When white light having all wavelengths is passed through an absorbing material, the material may absorb certain wavelengths selectively. When the transmitted light is dispersed, we get dark lines or bands at the positions of the missing wavelengths superposed on an otherwise bright continuous coloured background (figure 20.7).

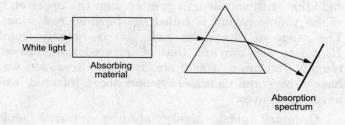

Figure 20.7

The missing wavelengths provide information about the absorbing material. Such a spectrum is called an *absorption spectrum*.

Absorption spectrum may be of two types depending on the absorbing material and the conditions, such as temperature, of the experiment.

(a) Line Absorption Spectrum

Light may be absorbed by atoms to take them from lower energy states to higher energy states. In this case, the missing wavelengths are widely separated and we get sharp dark lines on a continuous bright background. Such a spectrum is called a *line absorption spectrum*. When light coming from the sun is dispersed, it shows certain sharply defined dark lines. This shows that certain wavelengths are absent. These missing lines are called *Fraunhofer lines*.

(b) Band Absorption Spectrum

If light is absorbed by molecules of the absorbing material, exciting them from lower energy to higher energy states, the missing wavelengths are grouped into bunches. Thus, when the transmitted light is dispersed, we get separate dark bands on a continuous bright background. Such a spectrum is called a *band absorption spectrum*. Light passing through hydrogen gas at moderate temperature or through certain solutions of organic and inorganic compounds shows such a spectrum.

20.6 ULTRAVIOLET AND INFRARED SPECTRUM

When an object is suitably excited by heating or in some other way, it emits light. The light, that causes visual sensation to the eye, has a wavelength range from about 380 nm (violet) to about 780 nm (red). The light emitted by an excited object may have wavelengths beyond this visible region. We generally use the word light to mean visible light. That beyond the visible region is called by the general name *radiation*. The radiation with wavelength less than the lower end of the visible region (that is less than about 380 nm) is called *ultraviolet radiation* and the radiation with wavelength greater than the upper end of the visible region is called the *infrared radiation*. The range of ultraviolet radiation is roughly from 15 nm to 380 nm and that of infrared radiation is roughly 780 nm to 40000 nm. Beyond ultraviolet, we have X-rays and gamma-rays and above infrared, we have radiowaves.

Ordinary glass highly absorbs infrared and ultraviolet radiation. A prism made of quartz may be used for studying the spectrum in ultraviolet region. The dispersed radiation may be collected on a photographic plate. To study infrared spectrum, one can use a prism made of rocksalt. Infrared radiation considerably heats the object on which it falls. One way of detecting infrared radiation is from its heating effect. An instrument known as thermopile, which is sensitive to heat, is used to measure the dispersed infrared spectrum.

20.7 SPECTROMETER

Spectrometer is an instrument which is used to produce and study pure spectrum in visible region. It consists of basically three parts.

(a) Collimator

It consists of a long cylindrical tube fitted with an achromatic converging lens at one end. Another tube of slightly smaller diameter can slide into the first tube by a rack-and-pinion arrangement and has a linear slit at the outer end. The width of the slit may be adjusted by a screw. The distance between the slit and the lens may be changed by sliding the second tube into the first. The incident light is passed through the collimator to make it parallel before falling on the dispersing element.

(b) Prism Table

This is a horizontal platform which can be rotated about its axis and whose height may be adjusted. The dispersing element (prism, grating, etc.) is placed on the prism table. When the prism table rotates, a horizontal circular scale (graduated in degrees) rotates with it.

(c) Telescope

This is an astronomical telescope. The objective lens is fitted at one end of a long cylindrical tube. Another cylindrical tube can slide into it and contains the eyepiece. The dispersed light is passed through the telescope before falling to the eye which is placed just behind the eyepiece. A vernier scale is attached to the telescope which rotates on the horizontal circular scale when the telescope is rotated.

Levelling screws are provided under the main base, the collimator tube, the telescope tube and the prism table.

Adjustment and Working

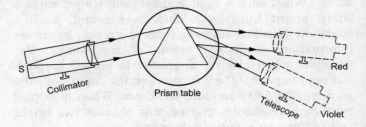

Figure 20.8

The collimator, the prism table and the telescope are fitted in one compact unit (figure 20.8). The prism table and the telescope can be independently rotated about the vertical axis of the prism table. The angle of rotation can be accurately measured by the vernier scale and the horizontal circular scale.

The axis of the collimator tube, of the telescope tube and the surface of the prism table are made horizontal with the help of levelling screws. The light source to be examined is placed behind the slit of the collimator. The distance between the slit and the collimating lens is so adjusted that the slit lies in the first focal plane of the lens and the rays coming from the collimator become parallel. This parallel beam is incident upon the dispersing element (prism, grating, etc.) placed on the prism table. The dispersed beam is received by the telescope which is focussed for parallel rays, that is, for normal adjustment. The telescope tube is rotated and light rays of different wavelengths are received at different angular positions of the telescope.

Application of Spectrometer

The spectrometer can be used in a wide variety of applications. We mention here a few simple ones. In all these applications, the spectrometer is adjusted as described above.

(a) Measuring the angle of a Prism

The spectrometer is levelled and adjusted for parallel rays. The prism is placed on the prism table with its refracting edge facing the collimator. The slit is illuminated by a sodium vapour lamp. The parallel beam coming from the collimator is divided into two parts falling on the two surfaces of the prism (figure 20.9).

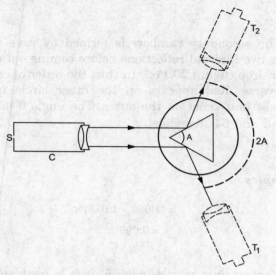

Figure 20.9

The telescope is rotated to a position T_1 where it receives the beam reflected by one surface. The image of the slit should coincide with the vertical crosswire of the telescope. The angular position is read on the base with the help of the vernier scale and the scale fixed in the base. The telescope is now rotated to position T_2 where it receives the beam reflected by the other surface. The image of the slit should again coincide with the vertical crosswire. The angular position is again read on the base. The difference of these two readings gives the angle rotated by the telescope. This angle is equal to $2A$ where A is the angle of prism. Sodium vapour lamp gives a nearly monochromatic light which makes the image identification easier.

(b) Measuring the Angle of Minimum Deviation for a Prism for a Given Wavelength

The spectrometer is adjusted as described before. The source emitting the light of the given wavelength is placed behind the slit.

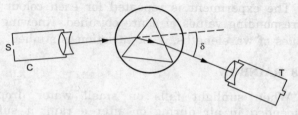

Figure 20.10

The telescope is rotated and placed at a position where the angle between the telescope axis and the collimator axis is large. The prism is placed on the prism table and the table is rotated to such a position that the refracted beam is received by the telescope (figure 20.10). The image of the slit is made to coincide with the crosswire. The angle between the axes of the collimator and the telescope is the angle of deviation δ. Now, the telescope is rotated slightly towards the collimator axis to decrease δ. The prism table is rotated to bring the image of the slit back at the crosswire. The process is repeated till a position comes where if the telescope is further rotated towards the collimator axis, it is not possible to bring the image at the crosswire for any position of the prism table. This position where the image can be last brought to the crosswire is the position of minimum deviation. The angle between the axes of the collimator and the telescope in this position is the angle of minimum deviation.

To measure this angle, the reading of vernier scale attached with the telescope is noted down. The prism is removed and the telescope is brought in line with the collimator so that the image of the slit forms at the crosswire. The reading of the vernier scale is again noted. The difference between the two readings gives the angle of minimum deviation.

(c) Variation of Refractive Index with Wavelength

To study the variation of refractive index μ with the wavelength λ, a source is chosen which emits light of sharply defined discrete wavelengths. Neon discharge tube is one such source.

The spectrometer is adjusted as before and a prism is placed on the prism table. A particular colour is chosen and the angle of minimum deviation for that colour is obtained by the method described above. This is done by always focusing the image of the slit formed by that colour. The refractive index of the material of the prism is calculated by the formula

$$\mu = \frac{\sin \dfrac{A + \delta_m}{2}}{\sin \dfrac{A}{2}} \cdot$$

The experiment is repeated for each colour and corresponding values of μ are obtained. Knowing the values of wavelengths, $\mu - \lambda$ variation is studied.

20.8 RAINBOW

When sunlight falls on small water droplets suspended in air during or after a rain, it suffers refraction, internal reflection and dispersion. If an observer has the sun at the back and the water droplets in front, he or she may see two rainbows, one inside the other. The inner one is called the *primary rainbow* and the outer one is called the *secondary rainbow*. Figure (20.11) shows the path of a typical ray forming the primary bow. It suffers a refraction followed by a internal reflection and then again a refraction. Dispersion takes place at both the refractions. It turns out that rays of a given colour are strongly returned by the droplet in a direction that corresponds to maximum deviation in its path. For light of red colour this maximum deviation is 137·8° so that the angle θ in figure (20.11a) is $180° - 137·8°$

= 42·2°. For violet this angle is 40·6° and for other colours it is in between 40·6° and 42·2°. Now consider an observer at P (figure 20.11b). Suppose sunrays are incident in a direction parallel to PX. Consider a cone with PX as its axis and semivertical angle 42·2°. All the droplets on the surface of this cone will return the light to P at an angle of 42·2°. This light will be predominantly red. Thus, the red rays coming to the observer will appear to come from a circle which subtends an angle of 42·2° on the eye. Similarly, the violet rays coming to the observer will appear to come from a circle which subtends an angle of 40·6° on the eye. The other colours form their respective circles of intermediate radii. From the ground level, only an arc of the rainbow is usually visible. A complete circular rainbow may be seen from an elevated position such as from an aeroplane.

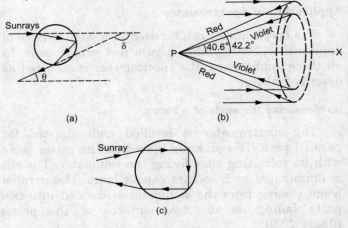

Figure 20.11

The secondary rainbow is formed by rays which suffer two internal reflections before coming out of the water drop (figure 20.11c). In this, the order of colours is reverse. Red appears on the inner circle in the rainbow and violet on the outer. The angle θ is 50·5° for red and 54° for violet.

Worked Out Examples

1. *The refractive indices of flint glass for red and violet light are 1·613 and 1·632 respectively. Find the angular dispersion produced by a thin prism of flint glass having refracting angle 5°.*

   Solution : Deviation of the red light is $\delta_r = (\mu_r - 1)A$ and deviation of the violet light is $\delta_v = (\mu_v - 1)A$.
   The dispersion $= \delta_v - \delta_r = (\mu_v - \mu_r)A$

   $$= (1·632 - 1·613) \times 5°$$
   $$= 0·095°.$$

2. *A crown glass prism of angle 5° is to be combined with a flint glass prism in such a way that the mean ray passes undeviated. Find (a) the angle of the flint glass prism needed and (b) the angular dispersion produced by the combination when white light goes through it.*

Refractive indices for red, yellow and violet light are 1·514, 1·517 and 1·523 respectively for crown glass and 1·613, 1·620 and 1·632 for flint glass.

Solution : The deviation produced by the crown prism is
$$\delta = (\mu - 1)A$$
and by the flint prism is
$$\delta' = (\mu' - 1)A'.$$

The prisms are placed with their angles inverted with respect to each other. The deviations are also in opposite directions. Thus, the net deviation is
$$D = \delta - \delta' = (\mu - 1)A - (\mu' - 1)A'. \qquad \dots \text{ (i)}$$

(a) If the net deviation for the mean ray is zero,
$$(\mu - 1)A = (\mu' - 1)A'.$$
or,
$$A' = \frac{(\mu - 1)}{(\mu' - 1)}A = \frac{1·517 - 1}{1·620 - 1} \times 5°$$
$$= 4·2°.$$

(b) The angular dispersion produced by the crown prism is
$$\delta_v - \delta_r = (\mu_v - \mu_r)A$$
and that by the flint prism is
$$\delta'_v - \delta'_r = (\mu'_v - \mu'_r)A'.$$
The net angular dispersion is,
$$\delta = (\mu_v - \mu_r)A - (\mu'_v - \mu'_r)A'$$
$$= (1·523 - 1·514) \times 5° - (1·632 - 1·613) \times 4·2°$$
$$= -0·0348°.$$
The angular dispersion has magnitude $0·0348°$.

3. *The dispersive powers of crown and flint glasses are 0·03 and 0·05 respectively. The refractive indices for yellow light for these glasses are 1·517 and 1·621 respectively. It is desired to form an achromatic combination of prisms of crown and flint glasses which can produce a deviation of 1° in the yellow ray. Find the refracting angles of the two prisms needed.*

Solution : Suppose, the angle of the crown prism needed is A and that of the flint prism is A'. We have
$$\omega = \frac{\mu_v - \mu_r}{\mu - 1}$$
or,
$$\mu_v - \mu_r = (\mu - 1)\omega.$$
The angular dispersion produced by the crown prism is
$$(\mu_v - \mu_r)A = (\mu - 1)\omega A.$$
Similarly, the angular dispersion produced by the flint prism is
$$(\mu' - 1)\omega'A'.$$
For achromatic combination, the net dispersion should be zero. Thus,
$$(\mu - 1)\omega A = (\mu' - 1)\omega'A'$$
or,
$$\frac{A'}{A} = \frac{(\mu - 1)\omega}{(\mu' - 1)\omega'} = \frac{0·517 \times 0·03}{0·621 \times 0·05} = 0·50. \qquad \dots \text{ (i)}$$
The deviation in the yellow ray produced by the crown prism is $\delta = (\mu - 1)A$ and by the flint prism is $\delta' = (\mu' - 1)A'$. The net deviation produced by the combination is
$$\delta - \delta' = (\mu - 1)A - (\mu' - 1)A'$$
or,
$$1° = 0·517\,A - 0·621\,A'. \qquad \dots \text{ (ii)}$$
Solving (i) and (ii), $A = 4·8°$ and $A' = 2·4°$. Thus, the crown prism should have its refracting angle $4·8°$ and that of the flint prism should be $2·4°$.

□

QUESTIONS FOR SHORT ANSWER

1. The equation $\omega = \dfrac{\mu_v - \mu_r}{\mu - 1}$ was derived for a prism having small refracting angle. Is it also valid for a prism of large refracting angle ? Is it also valid for a glass slab or a glass sphere ?

2. Can the dispersive power $\omega = \dfrac{\mu_v - \mu_r}{\mu - 1}$ be negative ? What is the sign of ω if a hollow prism is immersed into water ?

3. If three identical prisms are combined, is it possible to pass a beam that emerges undeviated ? Undispersed ?

4. "Monochromatic light should be used to produce pure spectrum". Comment on this statement.

5. Does focal length of a lens depend on the colour of the light used ? Does focal length of a mirror depend on the colour ?

6. Suggest a method to produce a rainbow in your house.

OBJECTIVE I

1. The angular dispersion produced by a prism
(a) increases if the average refractive index increases
(b) increases if the average refractive index decreases
(c) remains constant whether the average refractive index increases or decreases
(d) has no relation with average refractive index.

2. If a glass prism is dipped in water, its dispersive power
   (a) increases   (b) decreases   (c) does not change
   (d) may increase or decrease depending on whether the
   angle of the prism is less than or greater than 60°.

3. A prism can produce a minimum deviation δ in a light
   beam. If three such prisms are combined, the minimum
   deviation that can be produced in this beam is
   (a) 0   (b) δ   (c) 2δ   (d) 3δ.

4. Consider the following two statements :
   (A) Line spectra contain information about atoms.

(B) Band spectra contain information about molecules.
   (a) Both A and B are wrong.
   (b) A is correct but B is wrong.
   (c) B is correct but A is wrong.
   (d) Both A and B are correct.

5. The focal length of a converging lens are f_v and f_r for
   violet and red light respectively.
   (a) $f_v > f_r$.   (b) $f_v = f_r$.   (c) $f_v < f_r$.
   (d) Any of the three is possible depending on the value
   of the average refractive index μ.

OBJECTIVE II

1. A narrow beam of white light goes through a slab having
   parallel faces.
   (a) The light never splits in different colours.
   (b) The emergent beam is white.
   (c) The light inside the slab is split into different
   colours.
   (d) The light inside the slab is white.

2. By properly combining two prisms made of different
   materials, it is possible to
   (a) have dispersion without average deviation
   (b) have deviation without dispersion
   (c) have both dispersion and average deviation
   (d) have neither dispersion nor average deviation.

3. In producing a pure spectrum, the incident light is
   passed through a narrow slit placed in the focal plane
   of an achromatic lens because a narrow slit

(a) produces less diffraction
   (b) increases intensity
   (c) allows only one colour at a time
   (d) allows a more parallel beam when it passes through
   the lens.

4. Which of the following quantities related to a lens
   depend on the wavelength or wavelengths of the incident
   light ?
   (a) Power   (b) Focal length
   (c) Chromatic aberration   (d) Radii of curvature

5. Which of the following quantities increase when
   wavelength is increased ? Consider only the magnitudes.
   (a) The power of a converging lens.
   (b) The focal length of a converging lens.
   (c) The power of a diverging lens.
   (d) The focal length of a diverging lens.

EXERCISES

1. A flint glass prism and a crown glass prism are to be
   combined in such a way that the deviation of the mean
   ray is zero. The refractive index of flint and crown
   glasses for the mean ray are 1·620 and 1·518
   respectively. If the refracting angle of the flint prism is
   6·0°, what would be the refracting angle of the crown
   prism ?

2. A certain material has refractive indices 1·56, 1·60 and
   1·68 for red, yellow and violet light respectively.
   (a) Calculate the dispersive power. (b) Find the angular
   dispersion produced by a thin prism of angle 6° made
   of this material.

3. The focal lengths of a convex lens for red, yellow and
   violet rays are 100 cm, 98 cm and 96 cm respectively.
   Find the dispersive power of the material of the lens.

4. The refractive index of a material changes by 0·014 as
   the colour of the light changes from red to violet. A
   rectangular slab of height 2·00 cm made of this material
   is placed on a newspaper. When viewed normally in
   yellow light, the letters appear 1·32 cm below the top
   surface of the slab. Calculate the dispersive power of the
   material.

5. A thin prism is made of a material having refractive
   indices 1·61 and 1·65 for red and violet light. The

dispersive power of the material is 0·07. It is found that
   a beam of yellow light passing through the prism suffers
   a minimum deviation of 4·0° in favourable conditions.
   Calculate the angle of the prism.

6. The minimum deviations suffered by red, yellow and
   violet beams passing through an equilateral transparent
   prism are 38·4°, 38·7° and 39·2° respectively. Calculate
   the dispersive power of the medium.

7. Two prisms of identical geometrical shape are combined
   with their refracting angles oppositely directed. The
   materials of the prisms have refractive indices 1·52 and
   1·62 for violet light. A violet ray is deviated by 1·0° when
   passes symmetrically through this combination. What is
   the angle of the prisms ?

8. Three thin prisms are combined as shown in figure
   (20-E1). The refractive indices of the crown glass for red,
   yellow and violet rays are μ_r, μ_y and μ_v respectively and

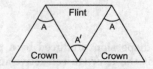

Figure 20-E1

those for the flint glass are μ'_r, μ'_y and μ'_v respectively. Find the ratio A'/A for which (a) there is no net angular dispersion, and (b) there is no net deviation in the yellow ray.

9. A thin prism of crown glass ($\mu_r = 1.515$, $\mu_v = 1.525$) and a thin prism of flint glass ($\mu_r = 1.612$, $\mu_v = 1.632$) are placed in contact with each other. Their refracting angles are $5.0°$ each and are similarly directed. Calculate the angular dispersion produced by the combination.

10. A thin prism of angle $6.0°$, $\omega = 0.07$ and $\mu_y = 1.50$ is combined with another thin prism having $\omega = 0.08$ and $\mu_y = 1.60$. The combination produces no deviation in the mean ray. (a) Find the angle of the second prism. (b) Find the net angular dispersion produced by the combination when a beam of white light passes through it. (c) If the prisms are similarly directed, what will be the deviation in the mean ray? (d) Find the angular dispersion in the situation described in (c).

11. The refractive index of a material M1 changes by 0.014 and that of another material M2 changes by 0.024 as the colour of the light is changed from red to violet. Two thin prisms, one made of M1($A = 5.3°$) and the other made of M2($A = 3.7°$) are combined with their refracting angles oppositely directed. (a) Find the angular dispersion produced by the combination. (b) The prisms are now combined with their refracting angles similarly directed. Find the angular dispersion produced by the combination.

ANSWERS

OBJECTIVE I

1. (a) 2. (b) 3. (b) 4. (d) 5. (c)

OBJECTIVE II

1. (b), (c) 2. (a), (b), (c) 3. (d) 4. (a), (b), (c)
5. (b), (d)

EXERCISES

1. $7.2°$
2. (a) 0.2 (b) $0.72°$

3. 0.041
4. 0.026
5. $7°$
6. 0.0206
7. $10°$
8. (a) $\dfrac{2(\mu_v - \mu_r)}{\mu'_v - \mu'_r}$ (b) $\dfrac{2(\mu_y - 1)}{\mu'_y - 1}$
9. $0.15°$
10. (a) $5°$ (b) $0.03°$ (c) $6°$ (d) $0.45°$
11. (a) $0.0146°$ (b) $0.163°$

CHAPTER 21

SPEED OF LIGHT

21.1 HISTORICAL INTRODUCTION

The speed of light in vacuum is a fundamental constant in physics. The most interesting fact about this speed is that if an object moves with this speed in one frame, it has the same speed in any other frame. This led to a major revision of our concept of space and time and is the key fact on which the special theory of relativity is based.

In 1983, the speed of light was defined to be exactly 299, 792, 458 m s^{-1}. In fact, the length of an object is now defined to be 299, 792, 458 m s^{-1} multiplied by the time taken by the light to cross it. Thus, when one sends light from one place to another place and measures the time taken by the light to do so, one is not measuring the speed of light, rather one is measuring the distance between the two places.

Prior to 1983, the length was defined independently and one had a separate metre. The speed of light could then be measured as the length divided by the time taken by the light to cross it.

Perhaps, the great Indian talents in the Vedic age had the knowledge of the speed of light. G. V. Raghavrao in his book quotes a verse from Rigveda (I, 50-4) *Yojananam Sahastra Dwe Dwe Shate Dwe Cha Yojane Aken Nimishardhena Krammana Namostute*. In this verse, the author pays respects to the one (the reference is to the sun light) who moves 2202 *yojans* in half *nimish*. Yojan is a quite common unit in India, it means 4 *kose*, each kose measuring 8000 British yards and each yard measuring 0·9144 m. The definition of the time unit nimish can be found in Shrimadbhagwat (III, 11-3 to 10) where it is mentioned that 15 nimishas make 1 *kashta*, 15 kashtas make one *laghu*, 30 laghus make 1 *muhurta* and 30 muhurtas make 1 *diva–ratri*. A diva–ratri is, of course, a day–night which is 24 hours in modern language. When you convert 2202 yojans per half nimish into SI units, it turns out to be $3·0 \times 10^{8}$ m s^{-1} up to two significant digits, a value quite accurate as we know it today.

In the modern era, perhaps the first attempt to measure the speed of light was made by Galileo. The design of the experiment was as follows. Two experimenters A and B, each having a lantern and a shutter, stand on two small hills. The shutter can cover or uncover the lantern. Initially, both the lanterns are covered. One of the persons A uncovers the lantern. The second person B uncovers his lantern when he sees the light from the lantern of A. The first person A covers his lantern when he sees the light from the lantern of B. The time elapsed between the uncovering and covering of the first lantern is measured. During this time, the light travels from the first person to the second person and then back. Knowing the distance and time, the speed of light may be calculated.

The proposed method failed because the speed of light is so large that a human being cannot respond with the required accuracy of timing. If the distance between the hills is as large as 15 km, the time taken by light in going back and forth is only one ten thousandth part of a second. The first recorded speed of light in modern era came through the astronomical observations by the Danish astronomer Olaf Roemer in 1676. The value obtained was about $2·1 \times 10^{8}$ m s^{-1}, somewhat smaller than the actual. In 1728, English astronomer Bradley measured the speed of light from his observations. The value was quite close to the correct one.

The first measurement of the speed of light from purely terrestrial experiments was reported by the French physicist Fizeau in 1849. The method was improved by another French physicist Foucault. Yet another method was proposed by American physicist Michelson. We now describe these three methods.

21.2 FIZEAU METHOD

Figure (21.1a) shows a schematic diagram of the arrangement used in this method. Light from a source S passes through a convex lens L_1. The transmitted beam is intercepted by a semi-transparent inclined

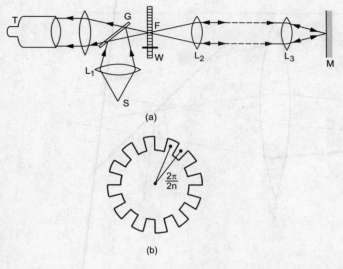

(a)

(b)

Figure 21.1

glass plate G. A part of the light is reflected and is converged near the rim of a toothed wheel W which can be set into rapid rotation. The light passing through the space between two consecutive teeth is made parallel by a convex lens L_2. This parallel beam travels for several kilometers (in the original Fizeau experiment it was 8·6 km) and is then converged by a convex lens L_3. A plane mirror M is placed in the focal plane of the lens L_3. The reflected light is again made parallel by the lens L_3 and it converges at the rim of the wheel. If it finds a gap, it falls on the glass plate G. The beam is partially transmitted and an observer receives these rays to see the image of S through a telescope.

When the wheel is rotated, it allows light to pass through in separate bursts. Light is passed when a gap comes at F and is stopped when a tooth comes there. The speed of rotation of the wheel is gradually increased while the observer keeps looking for the image. Initially, the image flickers but at a particular angular speed the image cannot be seen at all. This happens when the angular speed is such that by the time light passes through a gap, goes to the mirror M and comes back, the next tooth comes at F. Any light passing through the wheel does not return to the observer and the image cannot be seen. The angular speed of the wheel is carefully measured in this state.

Suppose, D = distance from the wheel W to the mirror M,

ω = angular speed of rotation of the wheel when the image is completely unseen for the first time,

n = number of teeth in the wheel.

The angle rotated by the wheel when a tooth comes in the place of its adjacent gap is $\theta = \frac{2\pi}{2n}$ (figure 21.1b). The time taken by the wheel in doing so is $\theta/\omega = \frac{\pi}{n\omega}$. In this time interval, the light travels a distance $2D$. The speed of light is, therefore,

$$c = \frac{2D}{\pi/n\omega} = \frac{2Dn\omega}{\pi}.$$

If the number of revolutions of the wheel per unit time is ν, we have $\omega = 2\pi\nu$ and the speed of light is

$$c = 4Dn\nu. \qquad \ldots (21.1)$$

One can use a concave mirror in place of the plane mirror. If the radius of curvature of this mirror be equal to its distance from the convex lens L_3 (i.e., equal to the focal length of L_3), a slight error in orientation of lens L_3 does not seriously affect the accuracy of the experiment.

There are two serious difficulties in this method. Since the light has to travel a large distance, the intensity decreases considerably and the final image becomes very dim. Secondly, the experiment cannot be done inside a laboratory. It needs an open space of several kilometers. These difficulties are removed in Foucault method.

21.3 FOUCAULT METHOD

The basic principle of Foucault's method can be understood with the help of figure (21.2). Light from a source S is partly transmitted by a glass plate G and is incident on a convex lens L. The distance of the lens from S is so adjusted that the beam transmitted through the lens is convergent. This beam is intercepted by a plane mirror M_1 which can be rotated about an axis perpendicular to the plane of the figure. The plane mirror reflects the light which converges on a concave mirror M_2. The distance between the two mirrors is equal to the radius of curvature of the concave mirror. The concave mirror reflects the light beam back to the plane mirror. The central ray is always incident on the concave mirror perpendicularly so that it retraces the path. If the plane mirror does not rotate, the rays retrace the path up to the glass plate G. A part of the beam is reflected by the glass plate and forms an image I of the source. Now, suppose the plane mirror M_1 rotates by an angle $\Delta\theta$ by the time light goes from M_1 to M_2 and comes back to it. The light reflected by M_1 then makes an angle $2\Delta\theta$ with the direction of the rays reflected earlier. Because of this deviation, the returning rays (shown dotted in figure 21.2) form an image I' of the source which is slightly shifted from the position I.

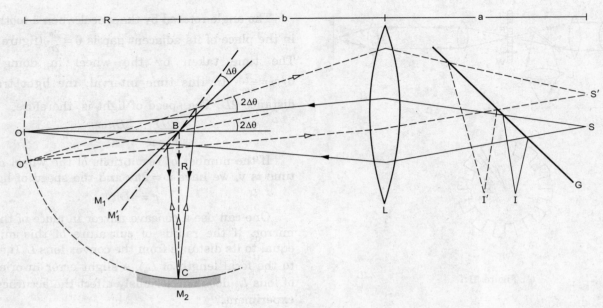

Figure 21.2

Suppose,

    R = radius of the concave mirror,

    ω = the angular speed of the plane mirror,

    s = the shift II',

    b = the distance from M_1 to L,

    a = the distance from L to S.

When the mirror is in position M_1, the rays reflected by it to the lens seem to come from a point O which is the image of the point C in M_1. When it has rotated by an angle $\Delta\theta$, the rays reflected by it to the lens seem to come from a point O' which is the image of C in the new position M'_1 of the mirror. The distance $BO = BC = R$. It is clear from the figure that

$$OO' = R.(2\Delta\theta). \qquad \qquad \text{... (i)}$$

Now, the rays reflected by the position M_1 of the mirror retrace the path and would converge at the source S itself. The glass plate partly reflects the beam to converge it at I. Thus, I is the image of S in the plate G acting as a plane mirror. Similarly, the rays reflected by the position M'_1 of the mirror are converged by the lens at a point S'. The glass plate G partly reflects the beam to converge it at I' which is the image of S' in G. It is clear that

$$SS' = II' = s. \qquad \qquad \text{... (ii)}$$

Thus, the lens L forms an image of O at S and of O' at S'. If we place an object of size OO' at O, its image will have the size SS' at S. Thus,

$$\frac{SS'}{OO'} = \text{magnification produced by } L$$

$$= \frac{\text{image-distance}}{\text{object-distance}}$$

$$= \frac{a}{R+b}.$$

Putting from (i) and (ii),

$$\frac{s}{2R\Delta\theta} = \frac{a}{R+b}. \qquad \qquad \text{... (iii)}$$

If the speed of light is c, it takes time $\Delta t = 2R/c$ to go from M_1 to M_2 and to come back. As the angular speed of M_1 is ω, the angle rotated by it in time Δt is

$$\Delta\theta = \omega\,\Delta t = \frac{2R\omega}{c}.$$

Putting in (iii),

$$\frac{s}{2R(2R\omega/c)} = \frac{a}{R+b}$$

or, $$c = \frac{4R^2\omega\,a}{s(R+b)}. \qquad \qquad \text{... (21.2)}$$

All the quantities on the right side may be measured in the experiment and hence, the speed of light may be calculated. Foucault obtained a value $2 \cdot 98 \times 10^8$ m s^{-1} from his measurement.

The space required in this experiment is quite small and hence, it may be performed inside a laboratory. Another advantage with this method is that one can put a tube of a transparent material between the two mirrors. The speed calculated by equation (21.2) then gives the speed of light in that material. It could be experimentally verified that light travels at a slower speed in a medium as compared to its speed in vacuum. This finding was contrary to the predictions of Newton's corpuscular theory.

21.4 MICHELSON METHOD

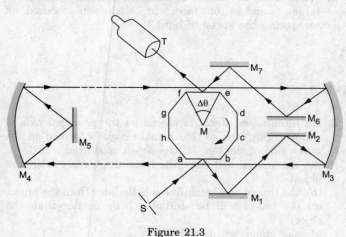

Figure 21.3

The scheme of Michelson method to measure the speed of light is shown in figure (21.3). Light from an intense source S is incident upon one face of a polygon-shaped mirror M. The light reflected from this surface is sent to the lower portion of a concave mirror M_3 after reflections from two plane mirrors M_1 and M_2. The geometry is set so that the light reflected from the concave mirror becomes parallel. This parallel beam of light is allowed to travel through a long distance (several kilometers) and falls on the lower portion of another concave mirror M_4. The parallel beam is converged at the focus of M_4 where a plane mirror M_5 is placed. M_5 reflects the beam back to the concave mirror M_4, this time at the upper portion. As M_5 is at the focus, the beam reflected by M_4 becomes parallel and travels back to the concave mirror M_3. After proper reflections from M_3 and the plane mirrors, it is sent to the polygonal mirror. A telescope is adjusted to receive the rays reflected by the polygonal mirror and hence, to form an image of the source.

Suppose the polygonal mirror M is stationary. Light from the source falls on the face ab of the mirror M and after reflections from all the mirrors, finally falls on the face ef of the mirror M. The image of S is seen in the telescope. If the polygonal mirror rotates, the face ef also turns a little while light travels between the two reflections from the polygonal mirror. The light thus fails to enter into the telescope and the image is not seen. If the rotational speed of the mirror is gradually increased, a stage comes when the adjacent face fg takes the place of ef by the time light comes there. Then, the light is again sent into the telescope.

In the experiment, one looks through the telescope and gradually increases the angular speed of the polygonal mirror. The image flickers initially and becomes steady at a particular angular speed of the mirror. This angular speed is measured.

Suppose,

N = the number of faces in the polygonal mirror,

ω = the angular speed of rotation of the mirror when the image becomes steady,

D = the distance travelled by the light between the reflections from the polygonal mirror.

If the speed of light is c, the time taken by the light to travel the distance D is $\Delta t = D/c$. The angle rotated by the mirror during this time is $\Delta \theta = 2\pi/N$.

The angular speed of the mirror is

$$\omega = \frac{\Delta \theta}{\Delta t} = \frac{2\pi/N}{D/c} = \frac{2\pi c}{DN}$$

or, $$c = \frac{D\omega N}{2\pi}.$$

If ν be the frequency of rotation, $\omega/2\pi = \nu$ and

$$c = D\nu N. \qquad \qquad \dots (21.3)$$

Michelson and his co-workers made a series of similar experiments. The first determination was made in 1879 with an octagonal rotating mirror. The latest in the series was underway at the time of the death of Michelson and was completed in 1935 by Pease and Pearson. This experiment used a rotating mirror with 32 faces.

□

QUESTIONS FOR SHORT ANSWER

1. The speed of sound in air is 332 m s^{-1}. Is it advisable to define the length 1 m as the distance travelled by sound in 1/332 s ?

2. Consider Galileo's method of measuring the speed of light using two lanterns. To get an accuracy of about 10%, the time taken by the experimenter in closing or opening the shutter should be about one tenth of the time taken by the light in going from one experimenter to the other. Assume that it takes 1/100 second for an experimenter to close or open the shutter. How far should the two experimenters be to get a 10% accuracy ? What are the difficulties in having this separation ?

3. In Fizeau method of measuring the speed of light, the toothed wheel is placed in the focal plane of a converging

lens. How would the experiment be affected if the wheel is slightly away from the focal plane ?

4. In the original Fizeau method, the light travelled 8·6 km and then returned. What could be the difficulty if this distance is taken as 8·6 m ?

5. What is the advantage of using a polygonal mirror with larger number of faces in Michelson method of measuring the speed of light ?

OBJECTIVE I

1. Light passes through a closed cylindrical tube containing a gas. If the gas is gradually pumped out, the speed of light inside the tube will
   (a) increase   (b) decrease   (c) remain constant
   (d) first increase and then decrease.

2. The speeds of red light and yellow light are exactly same
   (a) in vacuum but not in air
   (b) in air but not in vacuum
   (c) in vacuum as well as in air
   (d) neither in vacuum nor in air.

3. An illuminated object is placed on the principal axis of a converging lens so that a real image is formed on the other side of the lens. If the object is shifted a little,
   (a) the image will be shifted simultaneously with the object
   (b) the image will be shifted a little later than the object
   (c) the image will be shifted a little earlier than the object
   (d) the image will not shift.

OBJECTIVE II

1. The speed of light is 299,792,458 m s^{-1}
   (a) with respect to the earth
   (b) with respect to the sun
   (c) with respect to a train moving on the earth
   (d) with respect to a spaceship going in outer space.

2. Which of the following methods can be used to measure the speed of light in laboratory ?

   (a) Roemer method   (b) Fizeau method
   (c) Foucault method   (d) Michelson method

3. Which of the following methods can be used to measure the speed of light in water ?
   (a) Roemer method   (b) Fizeau method
   (c) Foucault method   (d) Michelson method

EXERCISES

1. In an experiment to measure the speed of light by Fizeau's apparatus, following data are used :
   Distance between the mirrors = 12·0 km,
   Number of teeth in the wheel = 180.
   Find the minimum angular speed of the wheel for which the image is not seen.

2. In an experiment with Foucault's apparatus, the various distances used are as follows :
   Distance between the rotating and the fixed mirror = 16 m
   Distance between the lens and the rotating mirror = 6 m,

   Distance between the source and the lens = 2 m.
   When the mirror is rotated at a speed of 356 revolutions per second, the image shifts by 0·7 mm. Calculate the speed of light from these data.

3. In a Michelson experiment for measuring speed of light, the distance travelled by light between two reflections from the rotating mirror is 4·8 km. The rotating mirror has a shape of a regular octagon. At what minimum angular speed of the mirror (other than zero) the image is formed at the position where a nonrotating mirror forms it ?

□

ANSWERS

OBJECTIVE I

1. (a)   2. (a)   3. (b)

OBJECTIVE II

1. (a), (b), (c), (d)   2. (c)   3. (c)

EXERCISES

1. $1 \cdot 25 \times 10^{4}$ deg s^{-1}

2. $2 \cdot 984 \times 10^{8}$ m s^{-1}

3. $7 \cdot 8 \times 10^{3}$ rev s^{-1}

□

CHAPTER 22

PHOTOMETRY

We see an object when light coming from the object enters our eyes and excites the sensation of vision. The brightness sensed by the eye depends on the amount of light energy entering into it and the wavelength distribution of this energy. In this chapter, we shall study the factors responsible for the sensation of brightness.

22.1 TOTAL RADIANT FLUX

The total energy of radiation emitted by a source per unit time is called its *total radiant flux*. This radiation contains components of various wavelengths extending even beyond the visible range. However, not all wavelengths have equal contribution in making up the total radiation. In calculating total radiant flux of a source, the total energy emitted per unit time in the whole range of wavelengths must be calculated.

The SI unit of total radiant flux of a source is *watt*.

22.2 LUMINOSITY OF RADIANT FLUX

The brightness produced by radiation depends on the wavelength of the radiation besides depending on the total radiant flux. For example, consider two 10 W sources of light, one emitting yellow light and the other red light. Though both emit equal energy per unit time, yellow will look brighter than the red. The *luminosity of radiant flux* measures the capacity to produce brightness sensation in eye. A relative comparison of luminosity of radiant flux of different wavelengths can be made by the curve in figure (22.1). The figure represents relative luminosity under normal light conditions for an average person. The scale on the vertical axis is chosen arbitrarily. We see that for normal light conditions, the luminosity is maximum for wavelength around 555 nm and falls off on both sides. Radiation is "visible" if its luminosity is not zero. As the luminosity falls off gradually, there are no sharp cut-offs of visible region.

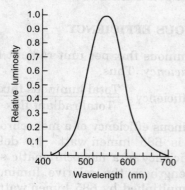

Figure 22.1

22.3 LUMINOUS FLUX : RELATIVE LUMINOSITY

In general, the radiation emitted by a source has components corresponding to a wide range of wavelengths. Different component wavelengths have different energies (in a given time) and different brightness producing capacities. The radiant flux is a quantity directly representing the total energy emitted per unit time. The *luminous flux* is a quantity directly representing the total brightness producing capacity of the source. Its unit is called *lumen*. The luminous flux of a source of 1/685 W emitting monochromatic light of wavelength 555 nm is called one lumen. In other words, a 1 W source emitting monochromatic light of wavelength 555 nm emits 685 lumen.

Relative luminosity of a wavelength refers to the fraction

$$\frac{\text{luminous flux of a source of given wavelength}}{\text{luminous flux of a 555 nm source of same power}}.$$

It is often represented as a percentage. Thus, figure (22.1) represents the relative luminosity as a function of wavelength.

It should be clear that the luminous flux depends on the radiant flux as well as on the wavelength distribution.

Example 22.1 ─────────────────────────

Find the luminous flux of a 10 W source of 600 nm. The relative luminosity at 600 nm is 0·6.

Solution : The luminous flux of a 1 W source of 555 nm = 685 lumen. Thus, the luminous flux of a 10 W source of 555 nm = 6850 lumen. The luminous flux of a 10 W source of 600 nm is, therefore, 0·6 × 6850 lumen = 4110 lumen.

For radiation having a range of wavelengths, the luminous flux gets contribution from each wavelength.

22.4 LUMINOUS EFFICIENCY

Total luminous flux per unit radiant flux is called *luminous efficiency.* Thus,

$$\text{Luminous efficiency} = \frac{\text{Total luminous flux}}{\text{Total radiant flux}} \quad \dots \ (22.1)$$

The luminous efficiency of a monochromatic source of 555 nm is 685 lumen watt^{-1} by definition. The luminous efficiency of a monochromatic source of any other wavelength is the relative luminosity of that wavelength multiplied by 685 lumen watt^{-1}.

An electric lamp glows when electric energy is given to it. However, not all the electric power given to it is converted into radiant flux. The term luminous efficiency is used in a slightly wider sense for such a light source. It is defined as the luminous flux divided by the power input to the source. Thus, it is the efficiency with which the power input to the source is used to produce brightness. We may call it *overall luminous efficiency.* Overall luminous efficiency

$$= \frac{\text{Luminous flux emitted}}{\text{Power input to the source}} . \quad \dots \ (22.2)$$

A good fraction of power given to a filament lamp is used to heat the filament to a certain temperature at which it glows. Also, a good fraction of the emitted radiation has a wavelength where the relative luminosity is small or zero. The overall luminous efficiency of a filament lamp is rarely more than 50 lumen watt^{-1}.

22.5 LUMINOUS INTENSITY OR ILLUMINATING POWER

In the chapter on Gauss's law, we shall describe in detail what is a solid angle. In brief, the solid angle measures the angular divergence of a cone and is defined as

$$\omega = \frac{A}{R^2} ,$$

where A is the area intercepted by the cone on a sphere of radius R centred at the apex of the cone (figure 22.2).

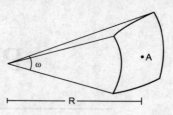

Figure 22.2

It is clear that the solid angle does not depend on the radius of the sphere. The SI unit of solid angle is called a *steradian* written in short as *sr*.

The *luminous intensity* of a source in a given direction is defined as

$$I = \frac{dF}{d\omega} , \quad \dots \ (22.3)$$

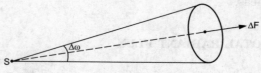

Figure 22.3

where dF is the luminous flux of the radiation emitted by the source in a small cone of solid angle $d\omega$ constructed around the given direction. The luminous intensity is also called just *intensity* in short. An ideal point source emits radiation uniformly in all directions. If the total luminous flux of the source is F, its intensity in any direction is

$$I = \frac{F}{(4\pi \ \text{sr})}$$

as the total solid angle at a point is 4π sr. For an extended source, the intensity is different in different directions.

The SI unit of luminous intensity is lumen/steradian. This is called a *candela* written in short as "cd". Luminous intensity is also called *illuminating power.*

Candela is one of the seven base units of SI. It is defined precisely as the luminous intensity of a blackbody of surface area $\frac{1}{60}$ cm^2 placed at the freezing temperature of platinum at a pressure of 101, 325 N m^{-2} in the direction perpendicular to the surface.

22.6 ILLUMINANCE

When radiation strikes a surface, the surface gets illuminated. We define the *illuminance* of a small area as follows. If dF be the luminous flux of the radiation striking a surface area dA, the illuminance of the area is defined as

$$E = \frac{dF}{dA} . \qquad \ldots (22.4)$$

The illuminance is, therefore, the luminous flux incident per unit area.

It is the illuminance which is directly related to the brightness of an illuminated area. The SI unit of illuminance is lumen m^{-2} and is called *lux*.

22.7 INVERSE SQUARE LAW

Consider a point source S and a small area ΔA around the point P at a distance r from the source (figure 22.4). Suppose, the angle between SP and the normal PN to the area is θ. Also suppose, the luminous intensity of the source in the direction SP is I.

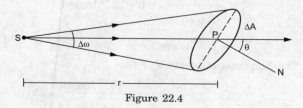

Figure 22.4

The solid angle subtended by the area ΔA at the source is

$$\Delta \omega = \frac{\Delta A \cos \theta}{r^2} .$$

The luminous flux going through this solid angle is

$$\Delta F = I \Delta \omega$$

$$= I \frac{\Delta A \cos \theta}{r^2} .$$

The illuminance at ΔA is

$$E = \frac{\Delta F}{\Delta A} \qquad \ldots (22.5)$$

or, $$E = \frac{I \cos \theta}{r^2} .$$

We note that

(a) the illuminance of a small area is inversely proportional to the square of the distance of the area from the source and

(b) the illuminance of a small area is proportional to $\cos \theta$ where θ is the angle made by the normal to the area with the direction of incident radiation.

The first observation is known as the *inverse square law*.

22.8 LAMBERT'S COSINE LAW

An ideal point source emits radiation uniformly in all directions. In general, sources are extended and such a source has different luminous intensity in different directions. If the source is in the form of a small plane surface, the radiation is emitted only in the forward half that is in a solid angle 2π around the forward normal. Even in this half, the intensity is different in different directions. The intensity is maximum along the normal to the surface and decreases as we consider directions away from this normal. For many surfaces, if the luminous intensity along the normal is I_0, it is

$$I = I_0 \cos \theta \qquad \ldots (22.6)$$

in a direction making an angle θ with the normal. Equation (22.6) is called *Lambert's cosine law*. The surfaces which radiate according to the Lambert's cosine law are called *perfectly diffused*.

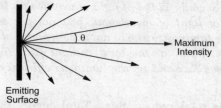

Figure 22.5

22.9 PHOTOMETERS

A photometer is used to compare the intensities of two point sources. The basic principle is as follows. Two screens are placed side by side. One screen is illuminated by the source S_1 only and the other screen by the source S_2 only. Light falls on the two screens at equal angles. The distances d_1 and d_2 of the sources from the screens are so adjusted that the two screens look equally bright. If I_1 and I_2 be the intensities of the sources, we must have for equal illuminance

$$\frac{I_1}{d_1^2} = \frac{I_2}{d_2^2}$$

or, $$\frac{I_1}{I_2} = \frac{d_1^2}{d_2^2} . \qquad \ldots (22.7)$$

A simple design proposed by Bunsen is now described (figure 22.6). It consists of an optical bench fitted with three vertical stands. The stands can slide along a straight rail on the bench.

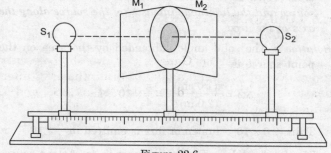

Figure 22.6

The distance between any two points on the rail may be read from a meter scale attached to the bench. The central stand contains a white paper with a grease spot. The other two stands carry the sources S_1 and S_2 to be compared. Two plane mirrors M_1 and M_2 are placed behind the central stand at proper inclination so that one side of the spot is imaged in one mirror and the other side of the spot is imaged in the other mirror. The two images can be seen simultaneously.

One of the sources is kept fixed at a distance from the spot and the position of the other is adjusted till the two spots seen in the mirrors appear equally bright. The distances d_1 and d_2 of the sources from the spot are measured in this condition. In this condition, the light falling on the spot from the two sources has equal intensity. If I_1 and I_2 be the intensity of the two sources, we have for equal illuminance,

$$\frac{I_1}{d_1^2} = \frac{I_2}{d_2^2} \quad \text{or,} \quad \frac{I_1}{I_2} = \frac{d_1^2}{d_2^2}.$$

Worked Out Examples

1. *A source emits* 12.0 J *of light of wavelength* 620 nm *and* 8.0 J *of light of wavelength* 580 nm *per second. The relative luminosity at 620 nm is 35% and that at 580 nm is 80%. Find (a) the total radiant flux, (b) the total luminous flux and (c) the luminous efficiency.*

Solution :

(a) The total radiant flux = Total energy radiated per unit time = 12 J/s + 8 J/s = 20 J/s = 20 W.

(b) The luminous flux corresponding to the 12 W of 620 nm radiation is

$$0.35 \times (12 \text{ W}) \times 685 \text{ lumen W}^{-1} = 2877 \text{ lumen}.$$

Similarly, the luminous flux corresponding to the 8 W of 580 nm radiation is

$$0.80 \times (8 \text{ W}) \times 685 \text{ lumen W}^{-1} = 4384 \text{ lumen}.$$

The luminous flux of the source is 2877 lumen + 4384 lumen

$$= 7261 \text{ lumen} \approx 7260 \text{ lumen}.$$

(c) The luminous efficiency $= \dfrac{\text{Total luminous flux}}{\text{Total radiant flux}}$

$$= \frac{7260 \text{ lumen}}{20 \text{ W}} = 363 \text{ lumen W}^{-1}.$$

2. *A circular area of radius* 1.0 cm *is placed at a distance of* 2.0 m *from a point source. The source emits light uniformly in all directions. The line joining the source to the centre of the area is normal to the area. It is found that* 2.0×10^{-3} lumen *of luminous flux is incident on the area. Calculate the total luminous flux emitted by the source and the luminous intensity of the source along the axis of the area.*

Solution : The solid angle subtended by the area on the point source is

$$\Delta\omega = \frac{\pi(1.0 \text{ cm})^2}{(2.0 \text{ m})^2} = \frac{\pi}{4} \times 10^{-4} \text{ sr}.$$

Thus, 2.0×10^{-3} lumen of flux is emitted in $\dfrac{\pi}{4} \times 10^{-4}$ sr.

The total solid angle at the source is 4π. As the source radiates uniformly in all directions, the total luminous flux is

$$F = \frac{4\pi}{\dfrac{\pi}{4} \times 10^{-4}} \times 2.0 \times 10^{-3} \text{ lumen}$$

$$= 320 \text{ lumen}.$$

The luminous intensity $= \Delta F / \Delta\omega$

$$= \frac{2.0 \times 10^{-3} \text{ lumen}}{\dfrac{\pi}{4} \times 10^{-4} \text{ sr}} = 25 \text{ cd}.$$

3. *The overall luminous efficiency of a 100 W electric lamp is 25 lumen W^{-1}. Assume that light is emitted by the lamp only in the forward half, and is uniformly distributed in all directions in this half. Calculate the luminous flux falling on a plane object of area 1 cm^2 placed at a distance of 50 cm from the lamp and perpendicular to the line joining the lamp and the object.*

Solution : The power input to the bulb = 100 W.

The luminous flux emitted by the bulb

$$= (25 \text{ lumen W}^{-1}) \times 100 \text{ W}$$

$$= 2500 \text{ lumen}.$$

Since light is emitted only in the forward half and is distributed uniformly in this half, the luminous intensity is

$$I = \Delta F / \Delta\omega$$

$$= \frac{2500 \text{ lumen}}{2\pi \text{ sr}}.$$

The solid angle subtended by the object on the lamp is

$$\Delta\omega = \frac{1 \text{ cm}^2}{(50 \text{ cm})^2} = \frac{1}{2500} \text{ sr}.$$

The luminous flux emitted in this solid angle is

$$\Delta F = I \, \Delta\omega$$

$$= \left(\frac{2500}{2\pi} \frac{\text{lumen}}{\text{sr}}\right)\left(\frac{1}{2500} \text{ sr}\right)$$

$$= \frac{1}{2\pi} \text{ lumen} = 0.16 \text{ lumen}.$$

4. *A point source emitting uniformly in all directions is placed above a table-top at a distance of 0·50 m from it. The luminous flux of the source is 1570 lumen. Find the illuminance at a small surface area of the table-top (a) directly below the source and (b) at a distance of 0·80 m from the source.*

Solution : Consider the situation shown in figure (22-W1). Let A be the point directly below the source S and B be the point at 0·80 m from the source.

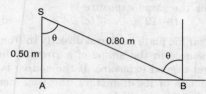

Figure 22-W1

The luminous flux of 1570 lumen is emitted uniformly in the solid angle 4π. The luminous intensity of the source in any direction is

$$I = \frac{1570 \text{ lumen}}{4\pi \text{ sr}}$$

$$= 125 \text{ cd}.$$

The illuminance is

$$E = \frac{I \cos\theta}{r^2}.$$

At the point A, $r = 0·50$ m and $\theta = 0$. Thus,

$$E_A = \frac{125 \text{ cd}}{0·25 \text{ m}^2} = 500 \text{ lux}.$$

At the point B, $r = 0·80$ m and $\cos\theta = \frac{SA}{SB} = \frac{0·50}{0·80} = \frac{5}{8}$.

Thus,

$$E_B = \frac{(125 \text{ cd}) \times \frac{5}{8}}{0·64 \text{ m}^2}$$

$$= 122 \text{ lux}.$$

5. *The luminous intensity of a small plane source of light along the forward normal is 160 candela. Assuming the source to be perfectly diffused, find the luminous flux emitted into a cone of solid angle 0·02 sr around a line making an angle of 60° with the forward normal.*

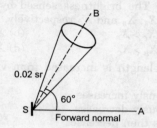

Figure 22-W2

Solution : The situation is shown in figure (22-W2). By Lambert's cosine law, the intensity in the direction SB is

$$I = I_0 \cos 60°,$$

where $I_0 = 160$ candela is the intensity along the forward normal.

Thus,

$$I = (160 \text{ candela})\left(\frac{1}{2}\right)$$

$$= 80 \text{ candela}.$$

The luminous flux emitted in the cone shown in the figure is

$$\Delta F = I \, \Delta\omega$$

$$= (80 \text{ candela}) (0·02 \text{ sr})$$

$$= 1·6 \text{ lumen}.$$

□

QUESTIONS FOR SHORT ANSWER

1. What is the luminous flux of a source emitting radio waves ?

2. The luminous flux of a 1 W sodium vapour lamp is more than that of a 10 kW source of ultraviolet radiation. Comment.

3. Light is incident normally on a small plane surface. If the surface is rotated by an angle of 30° about the incident light, does the illuminance of the surface increase, decrease or remain same ? Does your answer change if the light did not fall normally on the surface ?

4. A bulb is hanging over a table. At which portion of the table is the illuminance maximum ? If a plane mirror is placed above the bulb facing the table, will the illuminance on the table increase ?

5. The sun is less bright at morning and evening as compared to at noon although its distance from the observer is almost the same. Why ?

6. Why is the luminous efficiency small for a filament bulb as compared to a mercury vapour lamp ?

7. The yellow colour has a greater luminous efficiency as compared to the other colours. Can we increase the illuminating power of a white light source by putting a yellow plastic paper around this source ?

OBJECTIVE I

1. The one parameter that determines the brightness of a light source sensed by an eye is
(a) energy of light entering the eye per second
(b) wavelength of the light
(c) total radiant flux entering the eye
(d) total luminous flux entering the eye.

2. Three light sources A, B and C emit equal amount of radiant energy per unit time. The wavelengths emitted by the three sources are 450 nm, 555 nm and 700 nm respectively. The brightness sensed by an eye for the sources are X_A, X_B and X_C respectively. Then,
(a) $X_A > X_B$, $X_C > X_B$
(b) $X_A > X_B$, $X_B > X_C$
(c) $X_B > X_A$, $X_B > X_C$
(d) $X_B > X_A$, $X_C > X_B$.

3. As the wavelength is increased from violet to red, the luminosity
(a) continuously increases
(b) continuously decreases
(c) increases then decreases
(d) decreases then increases.

4. An electric bulb is hanging over a table at a height of 1 m above it. The illuminance on the table directly below the bulb is 40 lux. The illuminance at a point on the table 1 m away from the first point will be about
(a) 10 lux   (b) 14 lux   (c) 20 lux   (d) 28 lux.

5. Light from a point source falls on a screen. If the separation between the source and the screen is increased by 1%, the illuminance will decrease (nearly) by
(a) 0·5%   (b) 1%   (c) 2%   (d) 4%.

6. A battery-operated torch is adjusted to send an almost parallel beam of light. It produces an illuminance of 40 lux when the light falls on a wall 2 m away. The illuminance produced when it falls on a wall 4 m away is close to
(a) 40 lux   (b) 20 lux   (c) 10 lux   (d) 5 lux.

7. The intensity produced by a long cylindrical light source at a small distance r from the source is proportional to
(a) $\frac{1}{r^2}$ (b) $\frac{1}{r^3}$ (c) $\frac{1}{r}$ (d) none of these.

8. A photographic plate placed at a distance of 5 cm from a weak point source is exposed for 3 s. If the plate is kept at a distance of 10 cm from the source, the time needed for the same exposure is
(a) 3 s   (b) 12 s   (c) 24 s   (d) 48 s.

9. A photographic plate is placed directly in front of a small diffused source in the shape of a circular disc. It takes 12 s to get a good exposure. If the source is rotated by 60° about one of its diameters, the time needed to get the same exposure will be
(a) 6 s   (b) 12 s   (c) 24 s   (d) 48 s.

10. A point source of light moves in a straight line parallel to a plane table. Consider a small portion of the table directly below the line of movement of the source. The illuminance at this portion varies with its distance r from the source as
(a) $I \propto \frac{1}{r}$ (b) $I \propto \frac{1}{r^2}$ (c) $I \propto \frac{1}{r^3}$ (d) $I \propto \frac{1}{r^4}$.

11. Figure (22-Q1) shows a glowing mercury tube. The intensities at point A, B and C are related as
(a) $B > C > A$ (b) $A > C > B$
(c) $B = C > A$ (d) $B = C < A$.

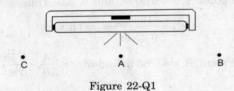

Figure 22-Q1

OBJECTIVE II

1. The brightness-producing capacity of a source
(a) does not depend on its power
(b) does not depend on the wavelength emitted
(c) depends on its power
(d) depends on the wavelength emitted.

2. A room is illuminated by an extended source. The illuminance at a particular portion of a wall can be increased by
(a) moving the source   (b) rotating the source
(c) bringing some mirrors in proper positions
(d) changing the colour of the source.

3. Mark the correct options.
(a) The luminous efficiency of a monochromatic source is always greater than that of a white light source of same power.
(b) The luminous efficiency of a monochromatic source of wavelength 555 nm is always greater than that of a white light source of same power.
(c) The illuminating power of a monochromatic source of wavelength 555 nm is always greater than that of a white light source of same power.
(d) The illuminating power of a monochromatic source is always greater than that of a white light source of same power.

4. Mark out the correct options.
(a) Luminous flux and radiant flux have same dimensions.
(b) Luminous flux and luminous intensity have same dimensions.
(c) Radiant flux and power have same dimensions.
(d) Relative luminosity is a dimensionless quantity.

EXERCISES

1. A source emits 45 joules of energy in 15 s. What is the radiant flux of the source ?

2. A photographic plate records sufficiently intense lines when it is exposed for 12 s to a source of 10 W. How long should it be exposed to a 12 W source radiating the light of same colour to get equally intense lines ?

3. Using figure (22.1), find the relative luminosity of wavelength (a) 480 nm, (b) 520 nm (c) 580 nm and (d) 600 nm.

4. The relative luminosity of wavelength 600 nm is 0·6. Find the radiant flux of 600 nm needed to produce the same brightness sensation as produced by 120 W of radiant flux at 555 nm.

5. The luminous flux of a monochromatic source of 1 W is 450 lumen. Find the relative luminosity at the wavelength emitted.

6. A source emits light of wavelengths 555 nm and 600 nm. The radiant flux of the 555 nm part is 40 W and of the 600 nm part is 30 W. The relative luminosity at 600 nm is 0·6. Find (a) the total radiant flux, (b) the total luminous flux, (c) the luminous efficiency.

7. A light source emits monochromatic light of wavelength 555 nm. The source consumes 100 W of electric power and emits 35 W of radiant flux. Calculate the overall luminous efficiency.

8. A source emits 31·4 W of radiant flux distributed uniformly in all directions. The luminous efficiency is 60 lumen watt^{-1}. What is the luminous intensity of the source ?

9. A point source emitting 628 lumen of luminous flux uniformly in all directions is placed at the origin. Calculate the illuminance on a small area placed at (1·0 m, 0, 0) in such a way that the normal to the area makes an angle of 37° with the X-axis.

10. The illuminance of a small area changes from 900 lumen m^{-2} to 400 lumen m^{-2} when it is shifted along its normal by 10 cm. Assuming that it is illuminated by a point source placed on the normal, find the distance between the source and the area in the original position.

11. A point source emitting light uniformly in all directions is placed 60 cm above a table-top. The illuminance at a point on the table-top, directly below the source, is 15 lux. Find the illuminance at a point on the table-top 80 cm away from the first point.

12. Light from a point source falls on a small area placed perpendicular to the incident light. If the area is rotated about the incident light by an angle of 60°, by what fraction will the illuminance change ?

13. A student is studying a book placed near the edge of a circular table of radius R. A point source of light is suspended directly above the centre of the table. What should be the height of the source above the table so as to produce maximum illuminance at the position of the book ?

14. Figure (22-E1) shows a small diffused plane source S placed over a horizontal table-top at a distance of 2·4 m with its plane parallel to the table-top. The illuminance at the point A directly below the source is 25 lux. Find the illuminance at a point B of the table at a distance of 1·8 m from A.

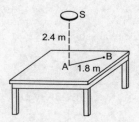

Figure 22-E1

15. An electric lamp and a candle produce equal illuminance at a photometer screen when they are placed at 80 cm and 20 cm from the screen respectively. The lamp is now covered with a thin paper which transmits 49% of the luminous flux. By what distance should the lamp be moved to balance the intensities at the screen again ?

16. Two light sources of intensities 8 cd and 12 cd are placed on the same side of a photometer screen at a distance of 40 cm from it. Where should a 80 cd source be placed to balance the illuminance ?

□

ANSWERS

OBJECTIVE I

1. (d) 2. (c) 3. (c) 4. (b) 5. (c) 6. (a)
7. (c) 8. (b) 9. (c) 10. (c) 11. (d)

OBJECTIVE II

1. (c), (d)   2. (a), (b), (c), (d)   3. (b), (c)
4. (b), (c), (d)

EXERCISES

1. 3 W

2. 10 s

3. (a) 0·14   (b) 0·68   (c) 0·92   (d) 0·66

4. 200 W

5. 66%

6. (a) 70 W   (b) 39730 lumen   (c) 568 lumen W^{-1}

7. 240 lumen W^{-1}
8. 150 cd
9. 40 lux
10. 20 cm
11. 3·24 lux

12. it will not change
13. $R/\sqrt{2}$
14. 10·2 lux
15. 24 cm
16. 80 cm

□

INDEX